THIS
OLD BOAT

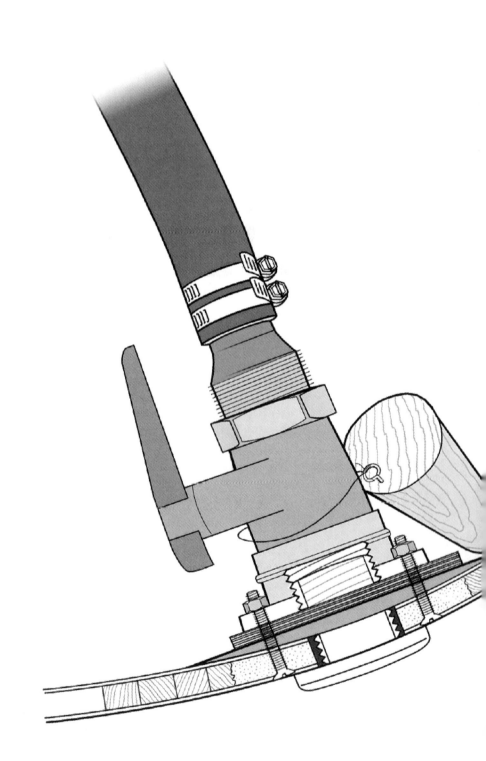

THIS
OLD BOAT

Second Edition

Don Casey

International Marine / McGraw-Hill
Camden, Maine | New York | Chicago | San Francisco | Lisbon | London | Madrid | Mexico City
| Milan | New Delhi | San Juan | Seoul | Singapore | Sydney | Toronto

The McGraw·Hill Companies

2 3 4 5 6 7 8 9   WCT WCT   2 1 0

© 1991, 2009 by International Marine

Library of Congress Cataloging-in-Publication Data
Casey, Don.
  This old boat / Don Casey.—2nd ed.
    p. cm.
  Includes index.
  ISBN 978-0-07-147794-9 (hbk. : alk. paper) 1.
Boats and boating—Maintenance and repair. 2.
Fiberglass boats—Maintenance and repair. I. Title.
  VM322.C37 2008
  623.822′30288—dc22

                              2008011541

ISBN 978-0-07-147794-9
MHID 0-07-147794-2

Questions regarding the content of this book should
be addressed to
www.internationalmarine.com

Questions regarding the ordering of this book
should be addressed to
The McGraw-Hill Companies
Customer Service Department
P.O. Box 547
Blacklick, OH 43004
Retail customers: 1-800-262-4729
Bookstores: 1-800-722-4726

Line illustrations by Fritz Seegers and Don Casey.

THIS BOOK IS DEDICATED TO

JUDY CASEY

WHO SHOWED ME HOW TO DO MORE WITH LESS, TO

EDWIN ARLINGTON ROBINSON

AND

ROBIN LEE GRAHAM

WHO POINTED ME DOWN THIS ROAD, AND TO

OLGA MORAN CASEY

WHO HAS TRAVELED IT WITH ME EVERY STEP.

Contents

"This book fills a much needed gap."
—MOSES HADA

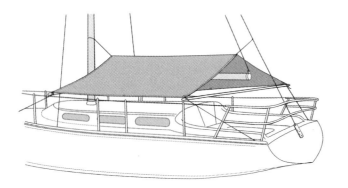

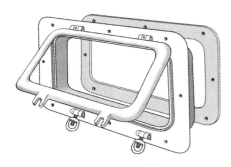

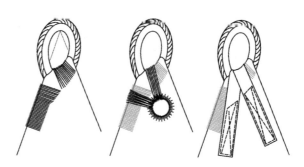

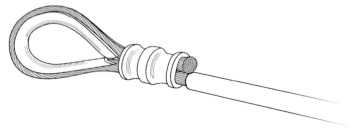

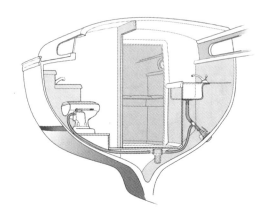

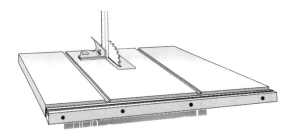

Acknowledgments

"I get by with a little help from my friends."
—JOHN LENNON

This book would not exist but for the number of fine boats built in the 1960s and 1970s by a handful of quality-conscious manufacturers. The contributions to boating of those pioneers in fiberglass boat construction cannot be overstated. When I began the first edition of this book almost 20 years ago I did not need to name those builders. Their boats occupied a significant number of slips in every marina, setting the standard against which newer or lesser boats were measured. Today the boats from those mostly defunct manufacturers are less familiar but no less deserving of veneration. Specifically, the genesis of the original edition of this book was the fact that then-20-year-old boats built by Allied, Bristol, C&C, Cape Dory, Jensen (Cal), Nicholson, Pearson, Sabre, and others offered far more boat for far less money than what was popping out of molds in 1990. New boats were carrying a new label—*coastal* cruiser—a not-so-subtle acknowledgment of lighter construction dictated by market realities. Brochures still showed Tahiti but the text did not claim that this particular boat would take you there.

Also at the time of the first edition, the cost of new boats was in a steep climb and manufacturers had all but abandoned smaller boats. So-called entry-level boats carried a six figure price tag. What was apparently invisible to boat company executives seemed obvious to me; namely that few would be willing to invest this kind of money to "try" a leisure activity, particularly when equal or superior used boats from the same manufacturer were available for a fraction of the price. This suggested to me the need for a kind of generic service manual for old boats.

As for the specific content, I started the original edition in the midst of a 15-year pile of sailing and boating magazines and a three-foot stack of boat books. My intent was just to collect the best ideas and techniques and put them into a single volume to provide a ready reference. My contribution would be to organize this body of borrowed knowledge and to make it both clearer and more fun. As it turned out, the project diverted my life. Since 1990 I have spent virtually every day on or around boats—sailing them, repairing them, and researching them. That means much of the information in this new edition is original or at least delivered with first-hand authority. Nevertheless at the core of this book and of my own expertise are the musings of a vast community of sailors and writers. So once again, I want to extend my genuine appreciation to all those who, knowingly or otherwise, taught me boatcraft.

For the book, the physical thing, credit goes entirely to the staff of International Marine, particularly to Molly Mulhern, who somehow reconciles deadlines with delays, words with art, and ink with white space to bind the content into an accessible and inviting package. Other IM associates whose influence is obvious to me if not to you are Margaret Cook, Janet Robbins, and Karen Steib. The longevity of this book leads me to also mention James R. Babb, Mary McCormick, and Pamela Benner whose first edition contributions live on in this one. I am also indebted to Jon Eaton who cajoled me into this fresh effort. Those of you familiar with the bar-napkin drawings in the first edition of this book will especially appreciate the wonderful art from Fritz Seegers, which hopefully clarifies where my words fail. Thanks, Fritz.

Finally, I want to acknowledge my wife, partner, and best friend, Olga. We all benefit from her questions and input as first reader, but more than that, my understanding of what makes a boat "work" has been immeasurably sharpened by observing what makes it work for Olga. It is a willing partner rather than perfectly cut sails that propels a cruising boat beyond the horizon. Ignore this truth at your own peril. To the extent that the boat can affect this equation, that the viewpoint of this book bears Olga's influence could be its most valuable feature.

Introduction

TO THE SECOND EDITION

*"Give a man a fish and you feed him for a day.
Teach a man to fish and you feed him for a lifetime."*
—**CHINESE PROVERB**

In Herman Wouk's wonderful Caribbean escape novel *Don't Stop the Carnival* there is a rogue character who describes himself as "just an old truth teller." I like that. It is a self-assessment worth living up to. The current truth about boating is that it gets harder to afford every year. In the nearly two decades since *This Old Boat* was originally published, shorelines and waterways have gotten markedly less boat friendly (unless you own a megayacht). Do-it-yourself boatyards continue to give way to condominium developments. Marinas have succumbed to the immediate return of converting to high-priced dockominiums. Both gasoline and diesel fuel have increased from less than $1 per gallon to more than $4. The price of a new offshore 35-foot sailboat has risen from an already astonishing $100,000 plus in 1991 to an astronomical $300,000 plus today and still rising. The cost of insurance is up. Storage costs are up. Haulout costs are up. What bought a gallon of bottom paint in the '90s buys a quart today. Hell, even the cost of this book has increased (but not so much).

Fortunately there are some other truths to tell. The first is that well-built fiberglass boats have proven to be nearly immortal. A cared-for or resuscitated 20-, 30-, or 40-year-old boat can deliver performance, comfort, and safety equal to or better than a new boat. That means that if you are looking at four-color brochures of a $400,000 boat, you can probably buy an equally capable boat in the used market for 20% of that amount, perhaps less. Old fiberglass boats remain one of the best bargains on the planet.

A second truth is that the less you spend on a boat, the more you can spend on boating. It is easy to lose sight of this essential truth when shopping for a boat, but if the purchase price is a stretch, you will be financially unable to comfortably maintain and operate this boat. This is a cascading problem because a big investment sits idle far less tolerably than a small one. Those with cruising dreams should additionally understand that where less money in the boat translates into more money in the bank, your cruise is likely to be enriched by inland excursions, rental cars, fine dining, and discretionary flights home.

A third truth is that fiberglass boats, older ones in particular, are not very complicated. A molded shell with molded or bonded accommodations and the machinery bolted in place, most boats have few critical tolerances, require almost no special tools, and do not need a computer to diagnose problems. From a do-it-yourself perspective, boats are more closely related to houses than to cars. There is almost nothing "professional" boatyard workers do that a motivated boatowner cannot do equally well—with a little guidance.

That's where I come in. With text as uncomplicated as I can make it and drawings focused on clarity, this book is a soup-to-nuts guide for just sprucing up or completely refurbishing your old boat. It is more than a repair manual, mechanical, electrical, or otherwise. The guiding premise is the proverb at the top of the page. You would starve if it was fishing I was teaching but you will find that you are in pretty good hands when the subject is boatwork. This book has the lofty aim of teaching you the handful of skills needed to effect virtually any renovation or improvement to an old boat. Mastering specific skills is the key to competence in any endeavor, and those required for working on boats are remarkably few and relatively easy. The full array is here for the taking.

If you own a copy of the original *This Old Boat*—honorably dog-eared, I hope—you might be wondering if there is enough fresh or additional material here to justify spending the money for the new edition. The answer is yes. The first five chapters will seem familiar to you, but those *you* likely don't need anyway. The stuff you do need has been completely rewritten. In this revised and expanded edition you will find a number of brand-new topics. All treatments of the original topics have been extensively updated to reflect changes in technology, in the boating environment, and in my knowledge. And then there are the illustrations.

For those of you just discovering *This Old Boat*, you should know that this book has already shown more than 100,000 sailors, boaters, and dreamers how to give substance to their boating aspirations. Don't take my word. An internet search will get you plenty of independent praise for *This Old Boat*. It is true that this is an entirely new book, but it remains faithful to the precepts that made the original so praiseworthy. I spent about 17 months writing the original while in a very real sense this edition is a 17-*year* effort. It

shows. So here you get the new-and-improved model, profusely illustrated, and you get five more new-to-you chapters than upgraders get. It is a bonus for you, one that might just refloat a foundering dream.

If you imagine yourself out on the water and you have been put off by the price of new boats, here is one more truth. Boats capable of doing whatever it is that fulfills your particular boating dream have been launched continuously for the last 50 years. Nearly all of those boats are still afloat, many lightly used. They sit idly, even forlornly, in marinas and creeks, in boatyards and backyards, ready to do exactly what they were designed to do. All they need is an owner with vision, determination, and a little knowledge. If you have the first two, this book will help you with the third.

So buy yourself a boat and make one improvement to it. Then another. And another. Whether you will give your old boat a new life or it will give you one is hard to say. Maybe *that* truth doesn't really matter.

Martinique, FWI
August 15, 2008

Introduction

TO THE FIRST EDITION

"The obvious is that which is never seen
until someone expresses it simply."
—KAHLIL GIBRAN

On the wall of my local marine chandlery, above a cash register that spits out bad news like a ticker tape on Black Monday, hangs a small plaque. It was placed there in an apparent effort to cheer the customers through commiseration, and it reads: "boat (bōt) *n*. A hole in the water, surrounded by wood, into which one pours money." As I part with all my cash and discover that my purchases will fit into my shirt pocket, *I* am not cheered.

It does cost money to own a boat. But there are ways to make it cost less—a lot less. Take *Nabila*, for example. Billionaire arms dealer Adrian Khashoggi reportedly spent about $90 million to build and equip his dream yacht. But other matters demanded Khashoggi's time and money. Enter Donald Trump. For a mere $29 million, he picked up Khashoggi's old boat. Of course she wasn't exactly the way The Donald wanted her, but with a million here and a million there, she was soon close enough. The cost to duplicate the boat at the time was estimated at more than $150 million!

Even for those of us who think of "a lot of money" in terms of hundreds rather than millions—perhaps especially for us—there is a lesson to be learned from this highly publicized transfer of ownership. When a boat loses the eye of her original owner, is she any less of a boat? Is she any less capable of satisfying the common dreams that dictate pleasure boat design?

In marinas, canals, and boatyards all across the country sit tens of thousands of boats in various stages of neglect. Many were designed with great vision, built with great care, delivered with great optimism. And perhaps once they did satisfy the dreams of their owners, but today their dull finish, graying wood, and tattered canvas fail to ignite excitement.

But you, smart person that you are, know better. You have asked yourself if the boats that manufacturers are turning out today satisfy dreams that much better than the boats they built 20 years ago. And you know that the answer is, in most cases, no. Or maybe you haven't considered this question at all; for you, the guiding factor is strictly economics. Either way, your boat is not new.

Owning a boat you can afford is no reason not to have a boat you are proud of. Starting with an old boat provides an almost unlimited opportunity to "do" the boat in a way that suits you. Changes can be made at one time in an extensive refit, or they can be made little by little over a period of years, as time, money, and motivation dictate. If you give the project sufficient thought and effort, you will end up with a boat that satisfies your specific tastes and requirements better than any new production boat could—and you will have poured a lot less money into that watery hole.

Transforming *your* boat from castoff to show-off is what this book is all about. In the pages that follow, you will find guidance for developing and executing a complete plan of improvement, repair, and modification. You will note an emphasis on sailboats; I am a sailor and these are the boats I know. But boats, all boats, are more similar than they are different, so most of the projects in this book, and *all* of the concepts and skills, are applicable to boats of any size, sailboats and powerboats alike.

This book will take you through a logical, orderly process of bringing your boat to progressively better condition. It will teach you to give your imagination a free rein; to look at your chalking and streaked hull and see instead the emerald light of some distant lagoon reflected in a mirror finish. It will help you to develop a list of all the changes necessary to give substance to your vision. You will learn how to plan the transformation and how to set priorities. You will find guidance for making intelligent choices among the myriad of possibilities. You will encounter practical solutions to common boat requirements, such as electrical power, and find fresh ideas for dealing effectively with such inherent limitations as scant stowage space.

But project management, consumer guidance, and a source of ideas, as important as these are, are only a small part of this book. Most of the text is devoted to showing how to make the desired changes, repairs, and enhancements. It tells you what tools and materials to use and how to use them.

Even if changing the bulb in a cabin light is the most complicated task you have previously attempted, that is no reason to assume that you cannot give substance to your vision. The skills required are not difficult and we begin most of the chapters with a simple project that allows you to learn and practice those skills. For example, in the chapter on working with fabrics, we begin by constructing a simple skirt to protect the hull from the fenders. If you can sew the seams and hems required for this simple item, you can also make a bimini top; the skills required are essentially the same. Likewise, if you can cut and

install a plywood shelf, you can build an entire cabinet. And if you can paint the inside of a locker, you can refinish a hull.

Clearly it is not possible to detail every imaginable enhancement project, but it is possible to address virtually all of the necessary skills. You need to master only the basic skills illuminated in the following pages to effect the transformation of a sound but tired older boat into a jewel that will turn heads in any anchorage, get you there in safety and comfort, and yield immeasurable pride—and measurable savings.

What more can you ask?

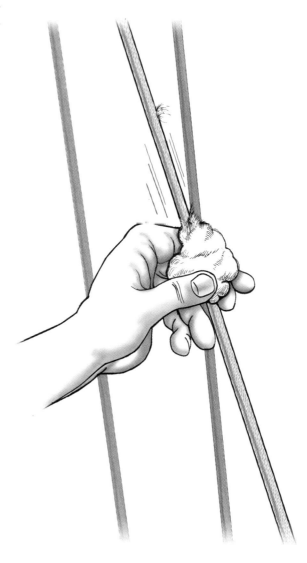

CHAPTER ONE

The Choice

"Men have learned to travel farther and faster,
though on errands not conspicuously improved.
This, I believe, is called progress."
—WILLIS FISHER

The mission of this book is to provide clear, easy-to-follow instructions for boat rehabilitations, repairs, and improvements that will save you money and add to your enjoyment of owning a boat. What boat is up to you. If you already own the apple of your eye, perfect in conception and flawed only with age or omission, this first chapter may not interest you. There is even the risk that my comments will reflect poorly on your judgment (or, from your point of view I suppose, on my judgment). Enraptured owners may skip this chapter.

You may also have come to this book not as a boater but as a dreamer. You watch the weekend parade of boats from shore, an observer only, prohibited from becoming a participant by the astronomical prices of new boats. Perhaps you have contemplated buying an old boat, but the affordable ones all seem so . . . tired. You are afraid of what you might be getting into.

Good news, Bunky. If you really want to join the parade, your only obstacle is you. Somewhere out there is a boat you can afford and that, with a little time and effort, can also be one you will take pride in.

Not so sure? Then this chapter comes too early for you. Come back to it later after you have had a chance to try your hand at some of the skills needed to refurbish an old boat. For the rest of you, those with that "you-just-show-me-what-to-do-and-I-can-do-it" attitude, I offer a few thoughts on choosing the *right* boat.

We had friends join us while we were cruising in the Bahamas some years ago. Richard, an avid fisherman and diver, had owned powerboats most of his life and spent almost every weekend on the water.

After a few days of exposure to the cruising life, he began to talk seriously about buying a sailboat. Like an evangelical preacher, I pointed out to him the "good" boats in the anchorage: an old Pearson Invicta with a powerful sheer; a Hinckley Bermuda 40 with the grace and beauty of a swan; a Morgan 34, related to the later Out Island series like Cinderella to her stepsisters; even a stout and capable Westsail. He umm-hmmed politely. Then late one afternoon a new boat came motoring in.

"What is that?"

It was a Coronado 41, to my eye one of the ugliest boats ever to go into production. But before I could voice that sentiment, Richard continued, "Now *that* is the kind of boat I want!"

The appeal of a specific boat is as individual as the person examining her. If you are prowling the docks and boatyards, trying to decide which boat is right for you and frustrated by the vast array of boats available, I suppose you would welcome a list of the "ten best" used boats to buy.

However, this is a *skills* book with the premise that if you master a skill, you can easily adapt it to your particular project. You will not find in these pages, for example, construction plans for *the* dish box. What good would that be? I don't know if you have Melamine for two or Wedgwood for twelve, if the box will be hidden away or a prominent feature of the galley, if it will be horizontal or vertical, or if it lies against a straight bulkhead or the compound curvature of your hull. What I do know is that if you can learn to visualize, plan, measure, cut, fit, glue, and finish, you can build the dish box that suits *your* needs.

1

Coronado 41: "She is not fair to outward view . . ."

In keeping with this premise I will not mislead you with a consensus of the so-called experts of the "best" old boats. Best for what? There are just too many variables for such lists to have any validity. Instead, I have compiled a list of ten specific considerations that may be applied against any boat to help you determine if she is the *right* boat for you. These are:

1. Beauty
2. Cost
3. Use
4. Quality
5. Size
6. Design
7. Accommodations
8. Rig
9. Power
10. Condition

BEAUTY

The boat you own should make your heart sing. As you dinghy away from her in the anchorage, she should hold your eye. She should stop you on the dock for one final gaze before you leave her, not to check but to admire. She should be the boat in your fantasy, the one anchored at the base of a verdant forest, tied stern-to in a tiny Mediterranean harbor, rolling off miles in the trades, carrying your family down the bay, leaving lesser sailors in your wake, or rafted with friends on the far side of the lake. In front of others she should make you feel inflated with a sense of pride. Alone you should feel humbled by a sense of privilege. If she does not affect you this way, keep looking.

Perhaps it seems odd to you that beauty leads my list of boat selection criteria. Assuming that most boat purchasers intend to sail away from shore farther than they can swim back, shouldn't something like seaworthiness lead the list?

Let's understand this list, shall we? The boat you select should satisfy all ten considerations, seaworthiness included. The purpose of the list is to provide an orderly sequence to the evaluation process, not unlike measure, cut, fit, and glue in the carpentry process. Similarly, every step is required.

I lead the list with beauty because, for most of us, boating—sailing in particular—fills some kind of aesthetic need. There is nothing pragmatic about pleasure boating. It is entirely a romantic endeavor. If the sight of the boat you are considering does not quicken your pulse, she will ultimately prove unsatisfactory no matter how seaworthy, commodious, or practical she is.

In recent years volume seems to have trumped sweet lines. For me a sailboat should be half fish, half bird, and no part condominium, but that has become

The boat that makes my heart sing.

a minority view. If a floating cottage is what you really want, then perhaps beauty for you is a walkaround bed, a walk-in shower, and a no-compromise galley. Who am I to say that these passions will prove any less enduring? The point is that you should select a boat that meets your definition of beauty. If you are going to devote the time, effort, and money to restoring an old boat, pick one that merits your devotion.

COST

If owning a boat puts too great a strain on your budget and prevents you from doing other things that were previously important and pleasurable parts of your life, discontent with boating cannot be far behind. Buying a boat that is too big, too fancy, or too complicated leads to disillusion far more quickly than buying too small, too plain, or too simple.

Because of statements similar to this one, I have often been called a minimalist. Not true. I see nothing whatsoever wrong with owning the largest boat you can *both afford and use*. But if paying for her keeps you from the enjoyment of using her, either in the physical sense for lack of time or in the mental sense from budget strain, what is the point?

Boating is a leisure time activity. It should require only discretionary income and not all of that. Maybe you think that if you only had the right boat, you would spend every free minute on the water. The odds are against you. Take a walk through any marina on a perfect Saturday and compare the number of empty slips to the number with boats still tied in them. I assure you that the owners of all those boats intended to use them every weekend, certainly every sunny weekend. What happened?

Reality. A sunny weekend is also perfect for tennis. Or golf. Or a cookout with friends. Or working on the lawn. Or a drive to Grandma's. There are also concerts and weddings, sporting events and sales. And there are weekends when it is rainy or cold or you just don't want to do anything.

Vacations aboard? Of course, but what about Yellowstone and Yosemite, Las Vegas and Disney World, the Rockies and the Alps, London and Paris, the Calgary Stampede and Mardi Gras, or Mom and Dad?

If living aboard is your objective, you can add housing costs into the equation. If you are preparing for an extended cruise you might also commit additional dollars, but you should never lose sight of the fact that every dollar you spend unnecessarily on the boat either postpones or shortens the cruise.

For the rest of us there is a number that represents the dollars that we can sensibly commit to boating. Aside from the cost of the boat, those dollars must also be sufficient to pay monthly dockage or storage fees, insurance, fuel, and upkeep, with some money left over to fund the cost of restoration and enhancement. You must be scrupulously honest in determining what that number is for you and equally vigilant in holding the line in the ensuing search for a boat that fits your budget constraints.

There is a tendency to let the ceiling creep up, to look at incrementally more expensive boats in the search for just the right boat. The most effective way to combat this is to avoid boats priced above your limit, but since there is often a big difference in the asking price of a used boat and her ultimate selling price, it may be unwise to restrict yourself too much. The risk is that the cost of the boat you choose will not be sufficiently negotiable to meet your budget requirements. If this happens to you, you may be able to lower the monthly cost with longer-term financing, electing a mooring rather than a dock, or some other creative action. If not, keep looking. There are a slew of old boats out there.

Typical marina scene on a perfect day for boating.

USE

The Miami-bound plane was still climbing through the clouds over Atlanta when the well-dressed guy in 11-E noticed the sailing magazine I was reading and struck up a conversation. In his second sentence, he told me that he had just bought a new sailboat. His breathless urgency to share that news with a total stranger marked the purchase as a Big Event.

I asked the obvious question, and from his briefcase he produced a color brochure for a Valiant 40. A bluewater boat. I reconsidered my accent-based assumption and asked if he lived in south Florida.

"No," he drawled. "Atlanta."

"And where," I inquired, "will you keep the boat?"

"Lake Lanier."

Lanier is a long, inland lake that is rarely more than 3 miles wide, hardly a challenging body for a

40-foot cruising boat. In a few years, he told me, he *hoped* to be able to go cruising and he wanted to have the boat to do it in. Meanwhile, he had saddled himself with a boat that was ill-suited for the kind of sailing that he *would* be doing.

An extreme example? Not really. We often make our selection more on the kind of boat we want instead of how we intend to use her. My frequent-flyer friend wanted a "real" cruising boat even though he knew his sailing would be limited to weekends on a lake. In my own marina is a dynamite little racer whose enamored owner cannot understand why his wife and daughters have lost interest in spending cramped weekends aboard. And there is a heavy, steel ketch, built to survive a navigational oversight in reef-strewn waters, that leaves her urban berth only once a year for the boatyard where her live-aboard owners wage a mechanical and chemical war against rust, corrosion, and electrolysis.

Before you begin looking at boats, you should know how you will use the one you select. Will you be racing, cruising, daysailing, or entertaining at the dock? Do you see yourself creaming along on sunny days or squinting into rain and spray with your feet planted on the coaming? Will you be sailing to St. Louis, St. Michaels, St. Thomas, or St. Helena?

Be wholly truthful with yourself, but—are you watching? here comes the sleight of hand—don't be too certain that you know the whole truth. Until you have eaten the meal, how can you know which course you prefer? A fast boat may arouse a competitiveness in you that you did not know existed. A capable boat may tempt you far beyond imagined horizons. A

Not the ideal boat for an after-work stress-relieving sail.

commodious boat may lead you to forsake shore life altogether.

Of course the boat you choose should be suitable for the use you anticipate, but utility is not a particularly good selection criterion. As quintessential yachtsman Arthur Beiser has sagely observed, you're not buying a truck. Allow your imagination into the equation. What kind of boating do you *want* to do? My traveling companion from Atlanta let this consideration dominate his decision. I would have counseled him to buy a boat more suitable for sailing on the lake, waiting to buy a heavy cruiser until he had a better grasp of how cruising might fit into his life, but if owning a bluewater boat keeps the dream alive for him, then I would be wrong.

The best approach, I think, is to give your imagination a free rein or, more accurately, a long rein, but not longer than 3 or 4 years. If you think there is even the slight possibility that you may sail for the South Seas within the next 3 years, by all means buy a boat capable of taking you there. But if the realities of work and mortgages and family have you thinking more in terms of a few weekends away, even though you may be dreaming of a voyage someday, the best boat to buy now is one that maximizes the enjoyment you will get from the boating you anticipate doing now. Maximizing enjoyment is, after all, what boating is about.

QUALITY

Determining the true quality of a boat is not always a simple matter. You can inspect the boat, looking for obvious clues like broken or replaced deck hardware, undersized rigging and attachments, rusting and corroding metal fittings, springy decks, gelcoat blisters, hull and deck separation, or evidence of water below. But the worst sins are often hidden behind attractive joinerwork or a glossy inner liner.

One of the benefits of buying an older boat, particularly a stock boat that has been produced a hundred, two hundred, or five hundred times is that a lot of inspection has already been done. Most of the chronic problems will have already surfaced. Consequently the boat will have a reputation. Talking with owners of the kind of boat you are considering will help you to ascertain that reputation. Locally you can find them by spending a few weekends prowling the docks. If you are using a broker, he or she may be able to come up with the names and telephone numbers of recent purchasers. For a broader cross section, spend some time on the Internet. Nearly all production boats have some kind of Web forum that can yield not only postings but direct contact opportunities.

Owners can provide valuable information about quality (and other things, such as speed), but their opinions are just that—opinions. The more owners you talk with, the more accurate will be the picture that emerges. Ask why they selected this particular boat, what other boats they considered, and why those were rejected. (Some of the other boats may be on your list of considerations.) Also seek out former owners who will not feel the same sense of loyalty that can color the opinions of current owners.

Magazine evaluations may also provide valuable information about the quality of a particular boat, but keep in mind that because magazines depend on advertising dollars, they almost never run a negative evaluation. There are some notable exceptions.

For more than 30 years *Practical Sailor* and ex-sister publication *Powerboat Reports* have conducted regular no-holds-barred reviews of older and new boats. Because these are consumer publications without advertising, their appraisals are candid, more complete, and typically supplemented by comments from a number of owners. However, since a particular boat is only reviewed once, the reviews you would be interested in might have been published decades ago. Fortunately *Practical Sailor* reprints all of its past reviews—more than 240 at last count—in a two-volume set titled *Practical Boat Buying*. At this writing the future of *Powerboat Reports* is uncertain, but its powerboat evaluation reprints are likely to remain available.

Following the publication of the first edition of *This Old Boat*, a new magazine titled *Good Old Boat* was launched. The similarity in titles is not a coincidence. *Good Old Boat* magazine is aimed squarely at affordable sailing. Every issue takes an in-depth look at one or more old boats. The featured evaluation includes a comparison to other boats of similar design. Because no boatbuilders advertise in *Good Old Boat*, the reviews are honest. Or because the reviews are honest, no boatbuilders advertise in *Good Old Boat*. Either way the budget-minded sailor wins. This magazine is currently hands-down the best topical resource for the old-boat owner.

In recent years, *Cruising World* magazine has also published "Classic Plastic" boat reviews. These short treatments are neither thorough nor very critical, but they are not candy-coated either. They do offer useful comparative data and clues of what to expect from a particular design. Similarly, *Sailing* magazine publishes a "Used Boat Notebook" column, written by John Kretschmer, a sailor with impressive credentials and a good eye. These columns are also available in a book collection called *Used Boat Notebook*.

Kretschmer's is not the only boat evaluation book available. John Vigor's *Twenty Small Sailboats to Take You Anywhere* will be an eye-opener if you think you are priced out of the cruising fraternity. Ferenc Máté's book *Best Boats to Build or Buy* is also useful.

It may be obvious that if you want to buy a boat to win races in a series, you will first determine what kind of boats are collecting the silver. Less obvious is the application of this same logic when your interest in boating is cruise oriented. Read as much as you can, both books and magazines, about the kind of cruising you want to do and pay attention to the kinds of boats that are out there doing it. Don't consider just the authors' boats; examine accompanying photos and try to identify the other boats in the harbor. Race results tell you about performance, but the repeated appearance of a particular type of boat in the text and photos of cruising literature is a fair barometer of quality.

Remember that we are not talking about condition. Quality has only to do with the materials and workmanship that went into the original construction of the boat, not with how she has been maintained.

The purchase of a boat of poor quality, regardless of how fast, spacious, or pretty she is or how well her cheap price fits into your limited budget, is *always* a mistake. In the first place, if the boat suffers a major failure, you cannot simply walk home. And even if your luck holds on that score, such a purchase is a bad financial decision. While improvements made to a quality boat typically add more value than their cost, the money you spend on a bum boat, no matter how well considered and beautifully executed your improvements are, does nothing to alter the boat's reputation and will have little, if any, impact on the resale value. You really will be throwing money into a hole in the water. When you have narrowed the field and start asking about a particular boat, if you don't consistently hear "great," or at least "good," pass her by no matter how attractive *you* find her. You cannot make a silk purse from a sow's ear.

SIZE

In America we like Big. We like big houses even if the mortgage puts our health at risk and the only time we go into some of the rooms is to clean them. We like big cars even if they cost us twice as much to get us from Point A to Point B, are difficult to wrestle through increasingly congested traffic or into compact parking spaces, and squander limited natural resources. We watch big heroes on our big-screen televisions. Even our elected officials wear lifts and stand on boxes to be big enough to get our votes. Big is good. Small is less.

Listen up. There are some very good reasons for buying a big boat. Space is one. If you have a family of six, you are not likely to find long-term contentment with a 19-foot Typhoon. Ditto if you want all your friends to join you in various ports around the world. Or if you want to have the board of directors aboard for cocktails.

Speed may be another reason. The bigger the boat, the faster she should be. The maximum hull speed of a displacement boat is generally calculated by multiplying the square root of the waterline length by 1.34. Using this formula we can determine that in ideal sailing conditions a 30-foot sailboat with a 24-foot waterline will have a hull speed of 6.6 knots, while a 40-footer with a 32-foot waterline will be almost exactly 1 knot faster. In a race the bigger boat will cross the finish line first, although on corrected time the smaller boat may be declared the winner. The big boat also will reach a cruising destination first, but my guess is that most weekend destinations are less than 20 miles away. That means that the crew of the 40-footer will still be setting the anchor when the smaller boat arrives. An extra knot may be very important for long passages, but if weekend cruising is your objective, fractionally higher hull speed is not going to be a very persuasive argument for selecting a larger boat.

A persuasive argument *can* be made on the basis of comfort. Greater interior volume allows for more shorelike accommodations—regular beds, real

This Crealock 37 is not only pretty but Pacific Seacraft–built boats enjoy a reputation for exceptional quality. (Janet Koch and Bob Conway)

chairs, a kitchen size galley The larger the boat, the more likely it is to have an auxiliary generator. This opens the door to air-conditioning, a microwave oven, a coffeemaker, and other AC appliances. For liveaboard comfort, there is no substitute for space.

Comfort offshore is another advantage of big boats. The bigger and heavier the boat, the slower and more comfortable will be her motion at sea. Do not confuse this *seakindliness* with *seaworthiness*. Seaworthiness is a function of design and construction, not size.

Often the consideration having the most sway is status. If you are buying a boat to impress your friends, particularly nonboating friends, buy the biggest boat you can afford. Period. Big impresses.

There are some equally compelling reasons to buy a small boat. The obvious one is cost. A quick comparison of listings will disclose that a 40-footer costs three times as much as a 30-footer of equivalent design and quality. And beyond the purchase price, the smaller boat will be cheaper to operate, cheaper to dock, cheaper to maintain, and cheaper to insure.

Ease of handling is another advantage of a small boat. Alain Colas single-handedly raced the 235-foot *Club Mediterranee* across the Atlantic, and a lot of cruising couples are competently plying the world's oceans in 50-footers and larger, but don't let anyone convince you that a "properly rigged" 50-footer is as easy to handle as a 25-foot boat. 'Tain't so, McGee, and you know it. Think about getting the main down and furled in a squall. Will it be easier to deal with 150 square feet of 5-ounce cloth or 600 feet of board-stiff 10-ounce? Right. Which boat would you prefer to sail to the dock? And if you blunder into shallow water, which one will be easier to get afloat?

Speaking of shallow water, smaller boats will take you a lot of places that a larger boat simply cannot reach. If your sailing area is shallow, draft will be a major consideration, and all things being equal, smaller boats have shallower draft. Smaller boats can also reach inland destinations denied boats with greater mast height.

Simplicity may be the biggest advantage of a small boat. Larger boats are, almost by definition, more complex, and every additional winch, pump, and head requires attention. Besides the smaller boat having fewer such complications, the maintenance and repair jobs that are necessary will be smaller, thus requiring less time. If your primary objective is spending the maximum time on the water, you should consider buying the smallest boat that will safely carry you and your crew to your intended destinations.

Who do you suppose spent the most money and expended the most energy to reach the identical destination? (Molly Mulhern)

DESIGN

If your objective is speed, you want a design that minimizes wetted-surface area. If you are going offshore, you want a hull that has plenty of reserve buoyancy in the ends. If you plan to live aboard, internal volume is a prime concern. *All* production designs are a compromise, an attempt to strike a balance between speed and comfort, between upwind and downwind abilities, between light-air performance and heavy-weather competence, between responsiveness and ease of handling, between function and beauty.

In the search for an appropriate old boat, some design considerations are fairly obvious. For example, the lack of directional stability inherent in most fin-keel designs will have the helmsman (or the autopilot) working constantly, which may not be a problem if you are racing on Wednesday nights but is a point to keep in mind if long passages are in your future. If your sailing will be in an area of typically light air, bypass heavy-displacement boats. Conversely, if you are planning a long cruise, the weight of the necessary equipment and supplies will severely compromise the performance of boats with light-displacement hulls, including small catamarans. But what about features with less obvious implications? Are full bilges better than slack ones? Are overhangs good or bad? Is a canoe stern more seaworthy than a transom? What about a reverse counter? Does a clipper bow offer advantages over a spoon bow? What about a plumb bow? What are the benefits and drawbacks of a centerboard? Of tumblehome? Of high freeboard? Of multiple hulls?

Volumes have been written about the science and subtleties of yacht design. I don't want to discourage you from doing your homework before you select the design that is right for you, but the fact is that even the most knowledgeable naval architects occasionally turn out a design that far exceeds their expectations. The whole exceeds the sum of the parts. And it is the whole you are interested in.

Beyond a sense of light versus heavy, fin keel versus full keel, and perhaps mono versus multi, you do not *need* to predetermine what other hull features you should be searching for in a stock boat. The designer has already considered all the trade-offs and made choices based on how he expected the boat to be used. If he designed the boat to win races and she does, his choices—whatever they were—were correct.

You are interested in how successful the *whole* boat is, not in individual design features. Just be sure to select a design that has a history of being successfully used the way you want to use her.

ACCOMMODATIONS

For many years I held on to a brochure for a 34-footer that proudly proclaimed "sleeps nine." It was not false advertising. The boat had two settees that each became a double berth, two pilot berths, a quarter berth, and a V-berth. But since there would be no place left to stand with both settees extended, I suppose everyone changed into their jammies in the cockpit. And with nine people sharing one head, God forbid that dinner disagreed with someone.

Ocean racers need large crews so designers loaded early "racer/cruisers" with bunks for that reason. But somehow potential first-time boat buyers equated this to the number of bedrooms in a house, making "how many does she sleep?" the question boat salesmen were asked more than any other. More was better. Evaluating a boat based on number of bunks is, of course, ridiculous. Most of us would have difficulty comfortably accommodating nine in our homes ashore, much less in a space smaller than a normal bedroom. (For Sale: Ranch-style 3 bedroom/2 bath, sleeps 128.) Family cruising does require a bunk for every member, but it can be difficult enough keeping everyone interested in the enterprise without subjecting them to sleeping accommodations that are little more than a padded version of a slave runner's hold.

How you evaluate accommodations will depend on what kind of alterations you are willing to undertake. It is possible to strip the interior of an old boat of all furniture and bulkheads and reconstruct the accommodations to your own design. If that is your intention, then your only interests will be the volume of the cabin space and the structural limitations of the existing bulkheads. But very few choose this course, and for good reason: it is difficult, time-consuming, and fraught with pitfalls. In addition, newer production boats may be built with an interior pan. Not only does this "mold" the furniture in place, it is generally integral to the boat's structural integrity, limiting if not what is possible, certainly what is practical.

More modest cabin modifications—remakes that require no bulkhead relocation and, to the extent possible, use the existing furniture—are easily undertaken by almost anyone. In nearly every case this makes better sense. When you are planning to limit major alterations, the interior requires closer evaluation. In later chapters we will consider specific features in more detail, but in a general overview of accommodations, there are six primary considerations:

- Berths
- Seats
- Galley
- Head
- Atmosphere
- Stowage

Fixed portholes: It is 94°F outside—how hot is the cabin?

The issue is not how many berths there are, but whether that number is sufficient for your needs and if they are long enough to be comfortable. Location and width also become considerations for all berths you expect to use while you are underway. Sea berths should be narrow and located in the center or after part of the boat.

Berths often do double duty as settees, with mixed success. Since you will likely spend as much time below sitting as reclining, comfortable seating is imperative. If the layout is workable, ergonomically shaped cushions can be added to improve seating comfort.

The longer you expect to be aboard, the more important the galley is. A good galley is compact but with adequate counter space. A deep sink, a quality stove, and a well-insulated cold box are all pluses, but these can be added. Galley space that is inadequate or poorly located is much more difficult to correct.

The head compartment must be either workable or of adequate size to allow the necessary modifications to make it workable. In all but the smallest boats that means the toilet must face forward or aft, not athwartship. The compartment should at least be large enough to allow pulling your pants up without opening the door. Away from the dock the value of a shower compartment is directly related to how much water the boat will carry or make.

Atmosphere is important too. By *atmosphere*, I mean light, air, and temperature. I have never been aboard a boat that was *too* bright below. The more portholes the better, and if they all open, that is better still. In warm weather the more opening hatches the boat has, the cooler the cabin will be, and if they are transparent or at least translucent, rainy days below will be far less gloomy. In cold weather, comfort will depend on a safe and efficient source of heat.

All of the equipment essential to the operation of the boat should have space allocated for stowage. You should not have to share bunk space with it. There should also be space for cookware, dishes, linens, towels, clothes, food, fishing and diving gear, tools, spares, and the myriad other items that you will take aboard. The longer you intend to be away from the dock, the more stowage space you will need. You can make numerous modifications to

make stowage more efficient but only if the space is there to work with.

I should not leave this subject without touching on safety. Adequate strong handholds, sturdy construction, and an absence of sharp corners will vastly reduce the likelihood of injury below. If these are not features of the boat you are considering, you will have to make the necessary modifications or look elsewhere.

Like hull design, the accommodation plan of a production boat is a series of compromises. There is almost nothing below that cannot be changed within the constraints of the volume of space available, but the more closely the existing layout matches your concept of the ideal layout, the less money and effort you will spend in achieving that ideal.

RIG

If you are looking at production fiberglass sailboats of any vintage, most will be sloop rigged unless they were originally marketed as passagemakers. Among

(Billy Black)

the latter group you will find ketches and cutters and a few older yawls.

Conventional wisdom is that the sloop goes to weather better than the other rigs and is the least complicated. The ketch offers the advantage of breaking the sail area up into smaller, more easily managed sails, but it is not quite as efficient on the wind. The cutter accomplishes the same thing but without the penalty in windward ability. No one is quite sure what the purpose of the yawl rig is. And schooners hang on because they make the heart go pitty-pat.

If you start your search with a driving partiality to a particular type of rig, unless it is a sloop you are severely restricting your possibilities. If you consider *only* sloops, you exclude some of the most capable sailboats. If your rig preference is firmly based in your own experience, I won't try to change your mind, but if it is based on what you have read or what your sailing friends tell you, listen up. Every type of rig has good points and bad points. When the architect matched a particular rig with his hull design, it was because he thought that rig was, on balance, the best for that boat. If you find a design that is right for your use, you will probably find the rig she carries satisfactory as well.

POWER

If you are looking for a powerboat, you probably know more about engines than I do. The vast majority of powerboats continue to be delivered with gasoline engines despite the inherent danger. The reasons are higher speeds and lower prices, both compelling arguments. But gasoline engines suffer in the marine environment. Behind loss of interest (or absence of time), tired motors are probably the second most common reason powerboats come up for sale. Failure to accurately evaluate the condition of the engine(s) can be a costly oversight.

In contrast to the preponderance of gasoline engines in powerboats, it is impossible to buy a new sailboat today with an inboard gasoline engine. That's good. A diesel is much better suited to the displacement speeds and infrequent use an engine gets aboard a sailboat, and it is less likely to send you to the next life.

As for old sailboats, the vast majority of auxiliary sailboats built in the 1960s and well into the '70s were delivered with gasoline engines because suitable small diesels were perceived as both prohibitively expensive and too heavy for the racer/cruisers of the day. Most of those old Grays and Atomic 4s have long since gone on to motor heaven, although there are still a few Atomics around and a company that supplies the parts to keep them going. But unless you are looking at very old sailboats, you are going to find a diesel in the engine compartment.

A well-maintained diesel engine should deliver 5,000 or more hours of service between overhauls. Given typical engine use of a locally sailed boat, that means every fiberglass sailboat outfitted with a diesel should still have a dependable engine. Get serious! That 5,000-hour number does not apply to engines with salt water rather than corrosion-inhibiting coolant running through them. It ignores some engines that were not all that dependable when they were brand-new. And far too few sailboat diesels are truly well maintained. You will do yourself a real service by assuming that the engine has been neglected and abused until a thorough mechanical survey determines otherwise.

A dependable engine will be a requirement in virtually any old boat refit. If the existing engine is not trustworthy, rebuilding should be the lower-cost option, but today that is rarely true for diesel auxiliaries. If parts are even available for a small diesel built 25 years ago, they will be shockingly expensive. Add to that the substantial labor cost of a rebuild, and you are approaching or exceeding the cost of a new engine. Then there is the fact that most of the engine remains 25 years old and the workmanship of the rebuild is of unpredictable quality. In most cases a new engine will turn out to be cheaper, and in all cases it will deliver a better result. In addition, while few of us can grind valves, hone cylinders, or resurface crankshaft journals, bolting a complete engine in place is easily within the capabilities of most determined boatowners. Guidance for repowering is provided in Chapter 9 of this book.

CONDITION

The previous nine considerations can be applied to all boats of a specific type. If one Morgan 34 meets your requirements, then all 347 built meet them (allowing for some differences in interior layout, rig, and power). Condition, on the other hand, must be evaluated boat by boat. Old boats vary widely in condition—from above improvement to above average to above water. The ones offered for sale will most often fall at the lower end of this spectrum.

There should be a direct relationship between condition and purchase price—the poorer the condition of the boat, the less she should cost. This is the relationship you are counting on when you choose to purchase an old boat rather than a new one. But the cheapest boat is not necessarily the best bargain. A great deal depends on exactly what is wrong with the boat. Before you purchase any boat, you should know every major deficiency she has and what each

Valuable help for you. A longer cruise for me.

will cost to correct. A boat-painting friend of mine is regularly asked to estimate the cost to refinish the hull and the deck of someone's just-purchased old boat. Too often when the painting estimate turns out to be higher than the purchase price, the new owner is dumbfounded. Of course, as you will see in Chapter 14, the cost of painting a boat does not have to be astronomical if you do it yourself, but you should know how you are going to deal with every *major* deficiency and the approximate cost *before* you buy the boat. Otherwise what appears to be a terrific bargain can turn into a very costly mistake.

A professional survey is nearly always money well spent. When you find a boat that captures your imagination, you may be inclined to overlook her flaws. There is nothing like a written survey report to drag you back down to earth. The survey can also be a good bargaining tool. The psychology of a "subject to survey" contract is such that the seller is often willing to pick up the repair tab on significant survey findings in order to keep the deal alive. And if you plan to insure the boat, most underwriters will require a recent survey anyway.

However, you only want to pay for one survey so you need to be fairly sure that the boat you hope to buy will pass a survey. That means evaluating her condition yourself. That process is not part of this book, but I have written a very thorough self-survey guide, *Inspecting the Aging Sailboat*, which I recommend to you. It is available through your bookseller.

With a big enough bank account, virtually any old boat can be reconditioned, but few of us have such deep pockets. Your objective here is to end up with the most boat for the smallest investment—in both money and time. An accurate assessment of the initial condition of any boat you are considering is essential if you are to meet that objective.

When you find the boat that best satisfies all ten selection criteria, buy her. Then give the left side of your brain a rest. It is time to close your eyes and contemplate the possibilities that your new boat will present to you.

(Charly and Dave Holmes)

CHAPTER TWO

The Dream

"Many men go fishing all their lives without knowing that it is not fish they are after."
—THOREAU

L et's get started. The concept of this book is the transformation of your old boat—but into what? That determination does *not* begin with assessing the condition of the gelcoat or choosing a color for new sail covers or buying new cabin lamps. You will eventually get to all of those things, but before you decide *what,* you need to know *why.* I realize that a dull finish, frayed canvas, and poor lighting answer the question for those items, but that's not the *why* I'm talking about.

THE INITIAL QUESTION: WHY?

Why did you decide on this boat? Broader, why buy *any* boat? Broader still, why do you want to be out on the water at all? Forget about the boat as an object. What does it represent? Exactly how do you expect your life to be enhanced by boating? You have spent

The early history of boating.

your money on a boat, perhaps a lot of money, and now you are about to reach even deeper into your pockets. Why?

Ancient man got involved in boating by some compelling need to get to the other side of some body of water. It is not difficult to imagine Og and his tribe starving on one side of a river while game drank along the opposite shore. When one of Og's lowbrow clan noticed a log floating across the water, the rest was, as they say, history.

We still use boats to get to the other side, but presumably the *why* for you is more than that. Most Americans buy boats for recreation, more specifically as a diversion for weekends. Boating is a counterpoint to the demands of the week, a way to "get away," a source of fun. You, no doubt, answered part of the *why* when you decided on the type of boat you would buy. If you imagined yourself out at daybreak, trailing enough fishing lines to keep the transom in shade, your choice of boat was different than it might have been had you pictured yourself driving the bow through a shower of diamonds on a fast close reach or cutting the dawn chill with a mug of steaming coffee in some distant fogbound cove.

Not that a single boat cannot be used in different ways, but if your primary interest was fishing, you bought a fishing boat; if it was sailing, you bought a sailboat; and if it was cruising, you bought a cruising boat. Those are pretty straightforward choices, but they still do not answer the total *why.* What is your underlying agenda? What is it that you want from your boat besides "fun"? Let's look at some of the possibilities and how they might affect your enhancement plan.

DIFFERING REQUIREMENTS

Boats are often purchased in the hope that boating will be an activity the entire family can enjoy together. It is an admirable objective. The concept of boating as a family activity, something more than a Sunday afternoon on the water, suggests more than just an adequate number of bunks. Does every member have some space of his or her own? Can meals be as good as (or better than) those at home? Is the boat a comfortable platform for *each* family member's favorite water activity—sailing, cruising, fishing, swimming, snorkeling, or scuba diving? Can a family member especially sensitive to the sun find shade? Can "best friends" be accommodated?

In contrast, maybe your boating is a solitary activity, an opportunity to spend time alone. Is the boat easily single-handed? Are the items important to your comfort close at hand? Is your personal safety adequately addressed when there is no assurance of assistance?

Perhaps you expect your boat to serve as your summer cottage. Small shortcomings, easily ignored on weekends, will have to be corrected. Is there adequate space for clothes? For food? Are you (and everyone else aboard) giving up television for the summer? What about videos? Your hair dryer? Your computer? Is refrigeration a requirement? Do you expect to have guests?

Forsaking brick and mortar to move aboard permanently raises requirements to another level. Is your "bed" better than adequate? Can the head accommodate daily ablutions for everyone aboard? Is there room for *all* of your clothes? Can you roast a Christmas turkey? Keep ice cream? Host a formal dinner? Stay warm in winter? Cool in summer? Are you an architect? A pianist?

Long-term cruising brings a different set of priorities. *Self-sufficiency* becomes the watchword. Can you carry ample water? Fuel? Tools and spare parts? Does generating capability exceed power consumption? Can you get the anchors up in adverse conditions? Can you stay dry underway? Do you have adequate ventilation?

If you imagine your boat anchored in the Papetoai Bay beneath the verdant peaks of Mooréa, new priorities emerge. Can the hull stand the rigors and uncertainty of the open ocean? What about the mast and rigging? Is the deck joint strong and watertight? Are there good sea berths? Is the galley serviceable at 30 degrees of heel? On both tacks? Can the dodger shed green water? Are the cockpit drains large enough?

It is essential that you understand your own motivation. The same old boat can be transformed into a weekender, a floating home, or a world cruiser, but the modifications necessary are substantially different in each case.

AROUND-THE-WORLD MISCONCEPTION

Too many boatowners, sailors in particular, believe that if the modifications they make are guided by the requirements for ocean voyaging, by virtue of such intense preparation the boat will handle the lesser demands of more modest use in a superior manner. Wrong!

Part of the reason for this fallacious belief probably has to do with boating literature. There are not a lot of books on library shelves about weekend cruising. Almost all are about voyaging, typically about circumnavigating, despite the fact that the overwhelming majority of sailors will never attempt anything more daring than an overnight passage in fair weather. But we *read* to go beyond what we *do*, and publishers know that a book titled *Between Hell and High Water: Rounding Cape Horn* is likely to sell better than *A Perfect Day on Biscayne Bay*.

The authors of all these voyaging books are anxious to share with the reader the lessons learned during their adventures. (If you are preparing to take off for the South Seas, you would be wise to study as many of these accounts as you can.) And while their opinions on specific issues vary, many of the lessons of voyaging are universal—the need for adequate rest; the need for tasty and nourishing meals; the need to stay dry; the need to keep the mast up; the need for hull, deck, hatch, and porthole integrity; the risk of a large cockpit; and so on. A kind of dogma has resulted that dictates much of what the sailing public sees as "proper."

As a result sea berths may occupy the best space aboard, even though the owner never intends to take the boat outside of the Chesapeake; a side galley may be rejected out of hand without considering how infrequently it may actually see use underway (or the fact that it may be ideal in every instance except one tack); or a doghouse may be added without regard to the detrimental effect it has on performance or on the exhilaration of the breeze in your hair during a brisk afternoon sail.

Books about ocean voyaging crowd the shelves. (Anna Shanstrom/ Armchair Sailor)

MATCHING FUNCTION AND FEATURE

The requirements of a yacht intended for more modest use are not just less; they are different. For long passages additional tankage for water and fuel may be a desirable modification. On a coastal cruise extra tanks will only forestall an occasional marina stop; additional tankage has no value at all for weekending. Meanwhile the tanks add weight if they are full and waste space if they aren't.

Converting drawers in the main cabin to easily accessible stowage for a broad array of tools is not a bad concept for the sailor heading off on an extended cruise. But for weekends aboard with children, convenient toy stowage will yield greater benefits.

Good sea berths do take on extreme importance if the boat will be underway for more than 36 hours. A "good" sea berth is always a single berth, however, and does little to contribute to connubial bliss aboard. On most boats, even cruising boats, a comfortable double berth will contribute far more than a sea berth toward making the time aboard pleasant.

Few voyagers headed for the remote atolls of the South Pacific would give the installation of a microwave oven a second thought—it occupies too much space, requires too much power, and what would you cook in it anyway? Yet aboard the same boat in Marina del Rey that serves as home to a professional couple, is there another galley enhancement with more benefit potential?

This same couple may lament limited space in the hanging lockers, perhaps finding a way to augment the boat's "closet" space. Aboard the voyaging

sister ship the effect on clothes left hanging for a 2,000-mile passage can be approximated by running them in a tumble dryer for about three weeks. The space occupied by the hanging locker is better utilized for some other purpose.

Even if your dream *is* running down your westing in the trades, resist modifications that are incompatible with the kind of boating you are doing now until you have a time frame in hand. Concentrate on projects that enhance your current activity. Besides offering a better short-term return, the quality of your later improvements will benefit from the delay both in concept and in execution. As your boating objectives evolve or solidify, deficiencies and weaknesses will surface in both the boat and your planned changes, siring new and better improvement ideas.

If shortcomings are serious enough, they may lead you back into the marketplace. If this is your first boat, keep in mind that almost no one finds long-term contentment with his or her initial selection. The first-boat ownership experience is on-the-job training. Some learn well and their second boat becomes a fixture of their lives for half a century. Others change boats like calendars. Whatever the case, embarking on too ambitious a program before you have spent sufficient time with your old boat risks wasting the effort.

Owning a boat that suits your current boating reality can provide the highest level of pleasure. (Greg Jones)

QUESTION NUMBER TWO: WHAT?

Once you have answered *why,* it is time to think about *what.* Reconditioning can be as simple as cleaning and painting, as complex as dismantling and reconstructing. The time required may be little more than a weekend, little less than a lifetime. You may choose to restore, modify, or completely redesign.

A restoration suggests that you have found a boat that fits your dream in virtually every detail. No design improvements are required, and you are only interested in bringing the boat back to new condition. A true restoration, one motivated by a sense of history, can be an arduous undertaking because of the difficulty of locating suppliers for replacement parts identical to the originals. Here I use *restoration* in a less restrictive sense to indicate that the design of the boat is unaltered and improvements are cosmetic or reparative in nature.

Modification is a more likely path. You have chosen a particular boat because you like most of her features, but there are a few things you would like to change. You find the standing rigging too light for your intended use. The existing engine is not powerful (or dependable) enough. You favor a wheel over a tiller. Lockers need shelves and dividers. You prefer additional galley space to a second quarter berth. You want refrigeration rather than an ice chest.

When the number and extent of your modifications become extreme, you have crossed the threshold from modification to redesign. A few features of the boat hold great attraction—hull shape and performance, perhaps—but you find much of the rest of the design ill-suited for your intended use. You might also be trying to make do with the boat you already own, a course shaped mostly by economics. In either case, you are willing to make extensive changes to the boat, restrained only by structural limitations and your own ability.

How you label your efforts is not that important. We are more concerned that you not limit yourself with some arbitrary restriction on your abilities. In the dream stage, assume that you can do anything. Can't make that leap yet? Then imagine yourself as a modest winner in the state lottery. (Not the top prize—that might have you jetting off to Finland to place your order for a new Swan.)

GENERATING A LIST

Time to get specific. With the picture of your "perfect day on the water" held clearly in your mind, write down every change that occurs to you to fit your old boat into that picture. Don't trust the fruit of this deliberation to your memory. You need a list, something you can physically look at, evaluate, manipulate, refer back to. I like a spiral-bound notebook for this purpose, but whatever you use, capture every want and idea permanently on paper.

Get all your senses involved. Do you *see* the wavering, luminous plaid of light reflecting from the hull? Write down "paint hull." Do you *hear* the reassuring diesel throb reflected off wooded banks? Write down "new engine." Do you *feel* the tendrils of a warm breeze probing the half sleep of an afternoon nap? Write down "cockpit cushions." Do you *smell* fresh bread baking in the galley? Write down "replace two-burner stove." Do you *taste* Greek table wine at a quayside café in Corfu? Write down "rubrails."

Give your mind free rein. Write down everything that occurs to you. Don't worry about getting your thoughts into any kind of order—we will deal with that in the next chapter. For now you just want to try to capture that picture in your mind.

It might help to spend a couple of hours aboard. Walk around the deck:

- Are the lifelines adequate and in good condition?
- What is the condition of the rigging?
- Are the anchors well stowed?
- Is there a good platform for handling ground tackle?
- Are the bow chocks adequate? What about the cleats?
- Are the running lights too small and ridiculously placed?
- Are there adequate strong handrails?
- Are the winches large enough and well placed?
- Is the cockpit comfortable?
- Is it protected from wind and spray? From too much sun?
- Is the nonskid really nonskid?
- Is the canvas crisp and bright?
- Is the gelcoat in good condition?
- Is this old boat the same color as the one in your vision?

Go below:

- Did you have to step on the galley counter?
- Was your footing secure?
- Does the cabin feel open or gloomy?
- Does the layout work?
- Are there ample secure handholds?
- Are fixtures substantial enough to arrest a lurch and rounded enough to do it gently?
- Is the head accommodating or disgusting?
- Are the settees comfortable?
- Are the bunks large enough?

- Is there adequate counter space in the galley?
- Can you heat the cabin and keep it cool?
- How is the lighting?
- Is there a great spot to sit and read? One for every crewmember?
- Can you bake lasagna? Chill beer? Make ice?
- Where do the charts go? The fishing rods? Extra sails? Wet rain gear? Tools? The wok?

Open everything:

- Are the lockers efficiently divided or open maws?
- Are there proper seacocks on every through-hull fitting? Can you close them? Are there any signs of leakage?
- Can the drawers open accidentally? The locker doors?
- Does the chain locker drain into the V-berth?
- Are there spaces behind the furniture that have no access?
- Where is the wiring?
- Is the electrical panel neat and accessible?
- Is there good access to the engine compartment?
- What is the condition of the engine?
- Is the bilge clean or coated with black "mayonnaise"?
- Are the bilge pumps adequate?

Look around:

- What about aesthetics? Does it feel warm below or as cold as a hospital room?
- Is there adequate brightwork? Too much?
- Did the builder substitute wood-grain plastic laminate for honest veneer?
- Is there a liner? Is it attractive?

Reality is rarely as good as the dream—but always better than the office. (Molly Mulhern)

- Does the countertop show years of wear? Is it ugly?
- What about the upholstery? Is it a good color? Good texture? Good quality? In good condition?
- Is the sole attractive and safe?
- Are the cabin lamps unobtrusive or as eye-catching as a wart?

What should emerge from this exercise is a long and undisciplined list of everything about your old boat that you would like to repair, replace, change, or improve. The list may get so long that it becomes paralyzing. Relax. This is not a contract. You are just trying to make sure that the changes you *do* make are the best ones. The more complete your list, the better.

THE THIRD QUESTION: HOW?

Knowing *what* you want to change is only half the process. Exactly *how* do you want to change it? This step is considerably more difficult. Let's select at random a few of the deficiencies that may have surfaced in the previous exercise and see how you might go about determining the best solution.

Take anchor handling, for example. Scratches and gouges in the hull at the bow are clear evidence that you need a better way to get the anchor back aboard. But how?

The molded-in nonskid on the deck wasn't all that great when it was new but now it's downright dangerous. How do you correct it?

There are seven bunks below but barely counter space for one pot and a salt shaker in the galley. Somehow the cabin space needs to be apportioned better. How?

Every seacock aboard is frozen or leaks or both. Can they be reconditioned or is replacement the only alternative? There are several types now. How do you determine which type to install?

Every bulkhead is surfaced with wood-grain plastic laminate and you hate it. (So do I.) How can you eliminate it?

It is time to reupholster below. Will your favorite color go with varnished mahogany? Should the pattern be large or small, or should you select a solid? How do you choose the type of fabric?

There are answers to all of these questions. In some instances the answer is clear-cut, black and white, the only appropriate conclusion. In others your course of action will hinge entirely on your own preference. Often past experience will provide the answer, particularly if you are not new to boating. For novice and old salt alike, common sense can point you in the right direction. But when you are not sure that you know the answer or that your answer is the best one, where do you find the answers you need? There are numbers of very good sources.

LOOKING AT OTHER BOATS

Try the docks. Walking out on the finger piers of a sizable marina can be an enlightening experience. Get a specific problem in mind and go for a stroll to see how others have solved it. Take your anchor-scarred bow, for example. As you walk along the dock, you will see a broad array of individual solutions to the very same problem. Will a bow roller work on your boat, or does an anchor davit seem like a better idea? Is a bowsprit a possibility, or perhaps an anchor platform? If these appurtenances seem likely to spoil the sweet lines of your classic, keep looking. You will probably see at least one boat with an anchor lining, a polished stainless sheathing at the bow to protect the hull from the anchor.

The docks don't offer much help for below-deck problems unless you can get invited aboard other boats—not that that's so difficult. Meeting as many other owners as you can will provide you with the opportunity to go aboard various boats to see how they are laid out, equipped, and adorned. And other owners are always willing to share their insight on a particular subject. One word of caution: sailors are notoriously opinionated, and sometimes the most opinionated are the least informed. Always get a second opinion, preferably from someone whose knowledge and judgment you trust.

Another way of going aboard a lot of boats is to attend a boat show. Go aboard every boat you can. Do not limit yourself to boats that "interest" you. You are only mining for ideas. Manufacturers and architects are constantly making design changes in response to owner complaints of shortcomings in their earlier models, perhaps some of the very deficiencies you are trying to correct in your older boat. If you pay attention, almost every boat you go aboard will exhibit some notable design feature or evolution that could be incorporated into your refit. The trick is not to just think, "Wow, what a great idea!" but rather, "How can I adapt this to my own boat?"

The best time to go to a boat show is when you already own a boat.

A stroll down the dock will provide a variety of anchor-handling ideas.

PEARLS IN PRINT

A third source of ideas is books, including this one. In later chapters, as we develop each skill, we will consider a number of ways to use that skill toward the enhancement of your boat. The number of potential projects I have included is considerable but by no means exhaustive. In bookstores, marine stores, and libraries you will find numerous other volumes, all with the potential to have just the right solution to a specific deficiency of your old boat.

Magazines are another excellent source of ideas. Since the first edition of this book, at least two magazines have been launched—*Good Old Boat* and *DIY Boat Owner*—that focus almost entirely on boat care and improvement. Most other boating magazines run some maintenance and enhancement articles, often providing step-by-step instructions. Even nontechnical articles provide an opportunity to examine a vast number of boats via the companion photographs, each potentially revealing features you might want to adapt. New-boat advertising often touts design enhancements. Product advertising is nearly all about a better solution. A few evenings perusing boating magazines can be very productive indeed.

Boating magazines full of fresh ideas abound.

The Internet offers a vast amount of useful guidance. There you will find active owners' associations; commercial boat and sail community sites with articles and sponsored "expert" pages; boat-specific chat rooms; product usage information posted by manufacturers and distributors; and individual blogs detailing refits, restorations, and product and gear performance. One problem with the Web, besides its sometimes numbing immensity, is that anyone can say anything, so the information you find there is not necessarily good information. Staying alert to potentially useful Web addresses mentioned in print articles can help you uncover the authoritative information that is available online.

If you are not yet familiar with catalog suppliers of marine equipment, take time out now to become familiar with them. They can provide you with a broad array of items that you may be unable to obtain locally, and often they can do so at discount prices. Just as important they are an endless source of ideas. The most common boat problems have almost all been addressed commercially, and those solutions are illustrated and offered for sale in the various catalogs—items such as solar-powered ventilators (for your mildew problem), attractive and efficient cabin lamps, teak bookshelves, nonskid deck covering, refrigeration conversions, and brushable urethane paints. Snap-apart hinges, Y-valves, and deck plugs may kindle your own original solutions.

MATERIAL ANSWERS

Materials can stimulate ideas. Wood is one of the most inspiring. Learning to shape, smooth, and finish wood has led many a person into woodworking as a lifelong leisure-time activity. With a few shop tools the possibilities are unlimited, but even with no more than common hand tools a block of wood can be shaped into a piece of furniture or a work of art. Plywood is less inspirational but no less useful. Bulkheads, fixtures, counters, and shelves are easily fabricated from a sheet of plywood. Wood veneer can change an unremarkable surface into a thing of beauty.

Plastics do not enjoy the same reverence as wood, but in many applications no other material works as well. Fiberglass boats are more appropriately called glass-reinforced plastic. With a can of polyester or epoxy resin and a piece of glass cloth you can repair a fiberglass hull, strengthen it, or attach virtually anything to it. Plastic laminates (Formica and others) are available in an incredible array of colors and patterns, providing an attractive and extremely durable covering for counters and other flat surfaces. Solid surface materials allow you to upgrade the countertops to the look of stone without the weight. Impact-resistant clear plastic is the only choice for portlights and the best choice for hatches because of the light it admits into the cabin. Dark acrylic doors can modernize a dated galley. Plastic mirrors can be used to expand a small space.

As incongruous as it may sound, a walk through a good scrap-metal yard can fire the imagination. Aluminum round stock might be just the thing to replace those rotten spreader tips. A bin of stainless tubing may suggest a custom-fabricated boarding ladder. A stack of sheet brass could prompt a solution to wear spots on the caprail.

Chemicals such as cleaners, paints, and varnishes suggest their own use, as do soft goods—leather, rubber, carpet, and fabric. Acrylic canvas, for example, is virtually the only material used to make sail covers and spray dodgers, and for good reason. It is strong; it resists rot, mildew, water, fading, and ultraviolet damage; it dries quickly; it is easy to sew; it comes in bright colors; and it looks damn nice. Considering these characteristics, it is not hard to imagine other uses for acrylic canvas. We will examine several possibilities in a later chapter.

SERENDIPITY

The ancient Romans recognized one more source of ideas with the proverb *mater artium necessitas*—"necessity is the mother of invention." A musician friend moved aboard a 27-footer with no fewer than three guitars. Tired of moving them every time he wanted to sit down, he was at a loss for a good solution—until one awakened him in the middle of the night. The next day he attached padded chocks to the underside of the foredeck, above the V-berth, and strapped the instruments in place. Easily accessible yet safe and completely out of the way, it was a harmonious solution in every way. Odd requirements

and unusual problems often suggest their own solutions if you keep your mind open to them.

Still keeping an open mind.

In this chapter I have tried to get you to unleash your imagination, to let your dream drive your actions. Your specific expectations from boating are unique, and the better you understand them, the easier it is to distinguish between boat features that contribute and those that detract.

Examining the specific features of your boat in the light of your own expectations should have led to a comprehensive list of deficiencies. The search for the best way to address each of those deficiencies does not end with the end of this chapter. Much of the remainder of this book offers ideas for your consideration. And new ideas appear every day—on other boats, in magazines, in books, in your daily routine.

Having determined *why, what,* and in at least some cases *how,* it is time to address the fourth question: *when?*

CHAPTER THREE

The Plan

*"You must know for which harbor you are headed
if you are to catch the right wind to take you there."*
—SENECA

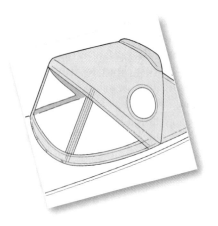

Examining your boat from stem to stern is not a bad plan, but reconditioning it in that order is, especially if the work will take place over a lengthy period of time. In this chapter we will develop a better plan.

The appeal of older boats is not limited to the economy-minded. An increasing number of classic wooden yachts have been rescued by well-heeled yachtsmen, with refit costs exceeding a million dollars not uncommon. Having any old boat reconditioned professionally, even one made of fiberglass, can be breathtakingly expensive. The plan we will be developing is based on the assumption that you do not intend to have your yard do all the work for you in a matter of a few weeks. This is not exactly clairvoyance. You surely did not come to this book just so you could make sure the yard was doing it right. Except

for the very wealthy, holding down the cost is almost always one of the attractions of buying an older boat. For a lot of us it can be the main attraction.

WHAT ORDER?

If you are among this last group (you have plenty of company), there can be a tendency to do projects in dollar order, getting what pop culture calls the most bang for the buck. This is a self-defeating course of action. When you first start the work you will be bubbling with enthusiasm and the frequent gratification of completing improvements keeps that enthusiasm stoked. As time drags on, however, the same high level of enthusiasm becomes more and more difficult to maintain. And just when you could most use the encouragement of moving closer to completion, the remaining items on the list will be those requiring more and more money, increasing the time between visible signs of progress. There is a very real risk of losing interest in the project altogether.

Limited time can lead to a parallel tendency to do the "easiest" tasks—those taking the least time—first. (The most kick for the tick?) For similar reasons this scheme will also make your project increasingly difficult to complete.

A BETTER PLAN

I am not suggesting that you forgo a quart of varnish, a brass barometer, or a new sail cover while you save up for a new engine. Nor am I saying that doing a 2-hour project when you have just 2 hours to devote is bad. Clearly both money and time will have an influence, but there are other considerations.

Safety is one. If the swaged end fittings on the shrouds are cracked, replacing them tops the list regardless of the cost or time required. The same applies to fragile lifelines, a faulty bilge pump, a loose rudder, or frozen seacocks. The first rule of boating is don't screw around with safety. We all have an inclination, especially when money is tight, to spend what is available on things we expect to add to our pleasure rather than on preventive measures or items we never expect to use. Giving in to that inclination risks your boat, your life, and the lives of those who sail with you.

The season is another consideration. I don't necessarily mean summer and winter, although on a day when even the mercury has better sense than to venture out of the bulb at the bottom of the thermometer, painting the hull is probably not a good idea. Weather aside, the season I am referring to is the boating season. Why deprive yourself of the opportunity to take advantage of those perfect weekends by decommissioning your boat in the heart of the season? Concentrate on items that allow you to work on the boat and use her too, saving disabling projects for the off-season. This is an especially strong consideration if your boat sits in a cradle half the year anyway, but even where the weather allows boating year-round, there will be months when it is typically too hot, too cold, too windy, or too something for boating. But not for boat work.

Special requirements are also a consideration. For example, a tricolor running light at the masthead can be installed from a two-blocked bosun's chair, but the anxiety factor is much lower if the mast is lying horizontally on horses. If re-rigging plans call for pulling the stick later, put off the light installation until then. Similarly, the day after you have completed your annual bottom job and relaunched is not the time to realize that the SSB transceiver you plan to install requires a dedicated underwater groundplate.

These last two examples really illustrate a specific aspect of the broader concept of appropriate

While the boat is decommissioned is a good time for disruptive renovations—some of which can be done at home on days like this. (Molly Mulhern)

order. The good building contractor makes sure that all plumbing lines are in place before pouring the concrete slab, that all wiring is complete before installing wallboard, that all painting is finished before laying carpet. We need to bring the same kind of order to reconditioning a boat. If oilcanning at the bow is a problem, strengthen the hull before you hide it behind some kind of ceiling. Water stains on interior joinerwork should lead to finding and stopping the leak before revarnishing is contemplated. The icebox should be adequately insulated on all sides before the refrigeration system is installed. After the new cushion covers have been fitted is a bad time to wish for thicker foam.

It is this need for order that necessitates a plan. You can take the helter-skelter list of desired changes from Chapter 2 and let time, money, and whim determine the order of completion. Or you can organize the list, taking into consideration, in addition to time and money, the safety imperative, conflicting boating objectives ("a time to work, a time to play"), how each change relates to others on the list, and the importance of each to your vision. A little time spent organizing the list now can save you a great deal of irritation and disappointment later on.

OTHER BENEFITS

Besides order, there are at least four other reasons to develop a master plan. The most obvious one is to allow you to generate a valid estimate of the money you'll need. This is the time to find out the price tag of your unrestrained vision, not when the money runs out. If you add up the dollars now and the total shocks you, you can moderate the project, plan to

Do this first!

Dream impaled on a financial reef?

Estimating time is more difficult than estimating cost. You can look in a catalog for the price of a refrigeration system, but how do you know how long it will take to install? Your problem is particularly knotty if you have never done anything similar before. Still, when you consider a job, some time estimate will come to mind. The best advice I can give you is to multiply that number by 2.5. Over the years I have found that most boatowners, novice and salt alike (including *moi*), are ridiculously optimistic in estimating how quickly they can accomplish a new task. Make your best guess, multiply that by 2.5, and you usually won't be very far off. Keep a written record of estimates and actual times if you want to fine-tune your estimating ability but don't expect stopwatch accuracy.

A third reason for a master plan is to provide continuity over the long haul. A comprehensive reconditioning can easily stretch over months or years. The plan insures that modifications made 18 months from now will be just as consistent with your vision as those made today.

The fourth reason is to enhance your sense of accomplishment. A few years ago I tried my hand at building a house. A unique design with no attic and no crawl space, it necessitated running all the wiring inside the walls. On the first day I installed the breaker panel and felt pretty good. On the second day I drilled dozens of holes in the wall studs and ran two circuits into the kitchen. On the third day there were three additional circuits, on the fourth a couple more. By the end of the week there were wires running all over the house and the results of my daily labor ceased to have any noticeable effect on the way the house looked. By the end of the second week there was no joy in Mudville. In the third week suicide seemed like the only way out. But while I was pondering whether the 14-gauge wire would take my weight or I would need to make the noose from 10-gauge, I was suddenly finished.

stretch it out over a longer period of time, or come to grips with the reality and ante up. Go blindly forward only to be stranded by insolvency in the middle of the project and you have committed the metaphorical equivalent of impaling your boat on a reef. It is a matter of navigation.

Time estimates are just as important. Most owners of old boats never really complete the transformation—there are always a few more things to be done. An estimate of the *total* time required is not that crucial, except as it relates to impending plans like a cruise next year or a growing or shrinking family. The time a specific enhancement will require *is* important. Can that new hatch be fitted and installed in a day, or will you have to devise some way to close the opening to weather and uninvited guests? If you start stripping and bleaching the brightwork will you get the new varnish on before the end of the weekend? Will one week in the yard be long enough to do all the bottom work you have planned?

Creating the boat you envision will require you to find ways to maintain that vision over the long haul. (Paul Ring)

When the things you are doing don't seem to move you any closer to achieving your vision, crossing out one more item on the master plan can provide much-needed positive reinforcement. I could have made my wiring job much more pleasant if I had listed all the circuits before I started and crossed off each as I completed it. This ploy works so well on my own need for direct gratification that before I start any job, I break it down into elementary components and list them. As I cross off each step, that little boost of a visible accomplishment keeps me involved in the job until every item has been lined through.

DEVELOPING YOUR PLAN

As important as these four additional functions of the master plan are, all could be accomplished almost as well with the random list of changes generated in Chapter 2. It is the need for bringing order to the project—for giving priority to safety concerns and emphasis to other significant changes, for accommodating interlocking relationships among the changes, and for reconciling time available with time required—that compels us to develop a more disciplined plan.

It is helpful at this point to think of your boat in terms of layers. The initial layer is the hull and deck, hatches and portholes, structural bulkheads, rigging, sails, and engine—those components central to the boat's integrity and essential for her to function. This is the basic *structure* of your boat.

The second layer is bonded, screwed, or bolted to the first. This layer includes built-in furniture and accommodations, appliances, lights, cleats, winches, handrails, electronics, and cushions. These *features* add comfort, versatility, and perhaps security.

The top layer is the *finish*—the gelcoat or paint on the hull and deck, the laminate on the bulkheads and counters, the oil or varnish on the teak, the fabric on the cushions. The finish layer has two functions—to preserve whatever is underneath and to improve its appearance.

Now with your list of desired repairs, modifications, and enhancements on one hand and a blank sheet with three columns labeled *Structure, Features,* and *Finish* on the other, you are going to place every item on the list into one of these categories.

If your boat has a problem with the hull-to-deck joint, the planned repair goes in the *Structure* column. If the porthole frames are badly corroded, their replacement is structural. The installation of a new hatch is structure. So is a new internal tank or repairing or strengthening the hull. Re-rigging, engine replacement, and new sails all go into the *Structure* column.

Structure.

Feature.

Finish.

Planning to add a new bow roller? Write it in the *Features* column. Adding or replacing winches? Installing refrigeration? Converting the starboard quarter berth to a chart table and stowage? Dividing lockers? Adding bookshelves? New stove? Additional handrails? A spray dodger? All of these should find their way into the *Features* column.

Painting the hull and varnishing the brightwork are obvious entries to the *Finish* column. Less obvious perhaps is the installation of nonskid material on the deck. Or reupholstering the cushions. Or polishing the stainless and brass. A new cover for the mainsail also goes into the *Finish* column.

Distinctions among each of these categories—structure, features, and finish—are not always clear. For example, because of the implications of their failure, I am inclined to think of repair or replacement of seacocks as structural—an essential part of the hull. But a valid argument could also be made for considering seacocks as a feature. Likewise, I would place the addition of a cockpit grating into the finish category, not unlike carpet on the cabin sole, but it might equally well be thought of as a feature.

For our purposes these distinctions among the three categories are of no real importance. We are merely trying to divide and conquer, to break a long list into more manageable pieces. This choice of categories is intended to give some order to that division. Clearly structural changes should happen first, refinishing last. If you consider the three columns, you should be able to conclude that, *generally*, the items in the first column should be addressed before those in the second column, those in the second column before those in the third. So if you think replacing a seacock belongs in column two, put it there. And if rearranging the layout seems more like a structural change than a change in features, by all means include it in the first column.

Although it is not apparent yet, we are on our way to developing a very simple matrix. Toward that objective, relabel the three columns *A, B,* and *C*. With your original list now divided into three groups, you already have a better handle on the project. Safety was one concern. Most items that represent a real risk to the boat should be in column *A*. Decommissioning was another concern. The items in columns *B* and *C* may involve significant inconvenience but typically they will not put the boat completely out of service for very long. And while all the issues of appropriate order are not resolved, categorizing your list this way does point out many of them.

ASSIGNING PRIORITY

OK, so you have brought some order to the list, but perhaps this is not the order you want to follow. Maybe you want to paint the hull before doing anything else. Maybe replacing the engine would be nice, but the old engine is running fine. Maybe you included a mizzen staysail on your list because the striped one in old photos of Irving Johnson's last *Yankee* looked so fabulous, but unless you come into unexpected money, you are not likely to actually spring for one. Fine. Taking your preferences into account is our next step.

For this step you need an oversize sheet of blank paper—something about 18 inches to a side. Four sheets of typing paper taped together will serve. An inch or so down from the top draw a line across the sheet. Do the same an inch in from the left edge. These two lines give you a small margin for labeling. Now, with two horizontal lines and two vertical lines, divide the remaining blank area into nine more or less equal rectangles. In the left margin, label the rows *A, B,* and *C*. (Look familiar?) In the top margin, label the columns *1, 2,* and *3*.

The letters are obvious, but what about the numbers? They simply represent the priority, from first to third, that you assign to each item regardless of category.

Specific improvements you want to make *now* will be listed in the first column. If painting the hull is a top priority for you, as you write it into the appropriate row—*C*—it goes in the first column.

Priority 2 items are somewhat less urgent. Still essential for satisfying your vision, their cost or the time required justifies a certain amount of delay. Or the reason for the change has not yet developed. A tired-but-still-running engine might incline you to place your plan to repower into this group. It would be listed in the second block in row *A*.

Priority 3 means "someday." This is where that mizzen staysail that you think "would be nice" belongs. If your budget is very limited, any number of changes that occurred to you in imagining the possibilities may, in the harsh light of reality, belong in the third priority. And if your dream has a "someday" aspect—someday you are going to take your boat from the English Channel to the Mediterranean Sea through the canals of Europe—changes specifically for that purpose can wait for more concrete plans.

Go through your entire list and place every item in the appropriate box. You should end up with a sheet that looks similar to the one illustrated. Every item on your original list now has a two-character designation. Replacing a stranded forestay is an *A1* matter. An urgent desire to refinish the hull is a *C1*. Strengthening

PRIORITY

		Immediate	Less Urgent	Someday
		1	**2**	**3**
Structure	**A**	New Forestay New Tiller Repair damaged Stern Replace spreader tips Replace chainplate - port upper New thru-hull fittings New Seacocks Restitch Mainsail • • •	New Mainsail Convert to roller furling Replace Cutless bearing Add Handrails • • •	Rub strake Water tank under V-berth • • •
Feature	**B**	Rebuild Head Larger bilge pump Service Winches Dish Rack Anchor Platform New Dodger • • •	Masthead Tricolor Remove Pilot berth Redesign Galley Install Refrigeration Closed cell cockpit cushions Anemometer Helm seat • • •	Cockpit Table Solar panels Wind Generator Chart Plotter Life raft • • •
Finish	**C**	Bottom paint Fix crazing in deck gelcoat Polish Hull Strip & Varnish teak • • •	Paint Hull Paint deck Headliner in Fwd cabin Reupholster V-berth New Settee cushion covers • • •	Refinish mast Formica bulkheads Cockpit Grating • • •

(Left vertical label: **TYPE OF ALTERATION**)

the bow for the rigors of Tierra del Fuego is probably an *A3*. For a San Diego–based boat, a refrigeration conversion might be a *B2*, radar a *B3*. A San Francisco skipper is likely to reverse these priorities.

FINE-TUNING

Converting the original list into a matrix like this serves two important functions. First, a picture of the most effective order for the project begins to emerge. *A1* items need to be done first, followed by *B1*, then *C1*, then *A2* and so on, ending with *C3*. Dependencies or direct relationships should always be vertical in the matrix, not diagonal. It makes no sense to have "redesign galley" in the *B2* block and "relaminate countertop" in *C1*. Either the new galley has to have a higher priority or the new countertop a lower one. The matrix also gives you a picture of how effectively you are planning this transformation. If everything seems to be in the first column, you have avoided the hard decisions. You must decide

which items are the most important, which are less important, and which are the least important. Assigning a rough estimate of the cost to every entry may help you make those decisions. You are trying to end up with a more or less even distribution among the columns.

The relationship among the three rows is also informative. If most of your planned changes fall into row *B*, you may be giving insufficient attention to your boat's structural integrity. If the *C* blocks are the fullest, your old boat must be exceptionally well designed and well maintained. If *A* and *C* have the lion's share of entries, you could be overlooking opportunities to make the boat better suited to your use. A sparsely inscribed row in the matrix, like an empty restaurant, does not necessarily indicate a problem, but it should make you wonder.

This matrix is an extremely useful planning tool, and we go through the step of creating it primarily for its visual impact. It displays, in the most conspicuous manner, an overview of the entire transformation you have envisioned and the anticipated order of its completion. Insufficient planning is immediately apparent, and the effect of corrective measures shows up instantly. However, as useful as it is, it does not provide the most convenient means of tracking your progress.

As you go from planning the project to administering it, you move from blueprint to ledger. The most convenient ledger in this case is your trusty spiral-bound notebook. By labeling nine pages *A1* through *C3* and copying the lists of items from the blocks of the matrix onto the appropriate pages of the notebook, you can transfer the information the matrix contains into a more usable format.

But wait! Before you do that, we need to re-address the issue of safety.

SAFETY REVISITED

Repairs and additions that are essential to safety need to be attended to first—period. The matrix accommodates that imperative to a degree by allowing you to assign safety initiatives a high priority, but even though you have labeled the replacement of a stranded forestay *A1*, your plan does not clearly show the importance of doing this particular *A1* job first. And a faulty bilge pump might be categorized *B1*, but its replacement cannot await the completion of all the other *A1* and *B1* items. The solution is to give deficiencies that represent a risk the VIP—Very Important Priority—treatment.

On a separate page, which I would label *S1*, list all the entries from the matrix that represent a response to an unacceptable safety risk. This does not necessarily include *all* the safety-motivated changes you may be contemplating. Installing handholds on either side of the companionway, a depth sounder, or an intermediate lifeline all represent safety enhancements, yet few would characterize sailing without them as an unacceptable risk. But a boat with questionable standing rigging, a cracked engine mount, weak or broken lifelines, or a loose rudder should not leave the dock. And corroded through-hull fittings, broken hose clamps, and sticky bilge-pump switches can sink your boat in the slip. Problems such as these *must* be corrected *first*.

BACK TO THE BOOK

After you have extracted the urgent safety concerns and grouped them first, you can copy the remaining entries from the matrix onto the appropriate pages of the notebook. When you finish, your notebook should contain ten separate lists in descending order of anticipated completion. You know that the most

urgent jobs are in the *S1* list, followed by *A1, B1,* and so on. If one weekend you have a sudden impulse to complete a *B3* job even though you have been working your way through the *B1* list, there is nothing to keep you from doing that. This is a plan, not a rule. Its purpose is to keep you on track but not to deprive you of spontaneity. Part of the attraction of upgrading an old boat is that the process itself is satisfying. If you restrict it too rigidly, it becomes too much like, God forbid, a job. It is called *pleasure* boating, remember.

KEEPING TABS

I mentioned the word *ledger* earlier, and that is exactly how you should use your notebook. With the entries down the left side of the page, the right side should be empty. With the help of a straightedge, divide this space into seven columns, each approximately as wide as the space between the page's lines. With the abbreviation *E$*, head the first column *Estimated Cost*. The second column is *Estimated Time*, and the third is the *Expected Start Date*. The next three columns are *Actual Cost, Actual Time,* and *Start Date*. The seventh column is to note that the item has been *Completed*.

I find the three estimate columns useful in planning the project. The *Actual Cost* lets me keep up with expenditures, and the *Actual Time* helps me with future estimates. The *Start Date* simply tells me at a glance that this item is underway. I usually write a date in the *Completed* column, but a check mark would serve.

You may think that seven columns represent entirely too much bookkeeping, but I encourage you to give it a try before you reject it. It isn't necessary to fill in every block. I rarely fill in a cost estimate for the small jobs unless I just happen to know the price. The same applies to time estimates. And I typically enter expected start dates only a month or two in advance, except for tasks that are related to some scheduled event—a haulout, for example. I am pretty good about keeping up with dollar expenditures and less diligent about time. My start column usually just has a *Y* (yes) in it.

You may be satisfied with less detail, or you may find that more is preferable. A blank for notations can be useful if you have space. If not, just add a *Notation* column. Notes about parts ordered or sudden flashes of genius or whatever can be written on another page, numbered, and each number entered in the column alongside the item to which it pertains.

The process of categorizing every change and repair, anticipating interdependencies, and assigning priorities does take some time, but once you have your

. . . and keeping it in order.

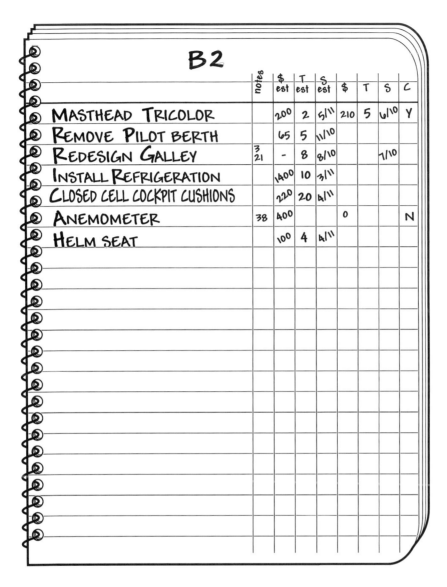

	notes	$ est	T est	S est	$	T	S	C
MASTHEAD TRICOLOR		200	2	5/11	210	5	6/10	Y
REMOVE PILOT BERTH		65	5	1/10				
REDESIGN GALLEY	3 21	-	8	8/10			7/10	
INSTALL REFRIGERATION		1400	10	3/11				
CLOSED CELL COCKPIT CUSHIONS		220	20	4/11				
ANEMOMETER	38	400			0			N
HELM SEAT		100	4	4/11				

(Pat and Walt Burgoyne)

notebook set up, very little time is required to keep a handle on the entire project. Checking off completions and noting expenditures (if you so choose) provides a thorough record of how the project is progressing. Referring to your notebook periodically has the added benefit of keeping you in touch with the entire project, not just the part in process.

As new changes and improvements occur to you (and they will), it is not necessary to go through the matrix process to get them into the notebook. You will know immediately what category they belong in and what priority you want to give them. Just add them to the appropriate list in the notebook, and they are immediately integrated into the plan.

Before you label me a Luddite, let me acknowledge that all of the project planning and monitoring can be done on computer with a spreadsheet program. If that is what you are comfortable with, by all means trade in your pencil for a keyboard and a mouse. However, the utility of a notebook that travels easily to and from the boat with you and is always available to capture unexpected inspiration should not be discounted.

KNOWING YOUR HAT SIZE

I keep two additional lists. The first is a shopping list. I am not talking about a list of paint or wood or screws that I need for the job I am about to start. Items on this shopping list are for changes scheduled sometime in the future. For example, if there is no real urgency but I know that I am going to re-rig using mechanical end fittings, I determine now what type, what size, and how many terminals I will need and put them on my shopping list. I also list the size and amount of wire I need. If I have already seen the cabin lamp that will be perfect over the new table I am constructing, I put the lamp on the list. If my mind is already made up for a specific radio, I write the manufacturer and model number on my list. (A word of caution about electronics: it is wise to postpone electronics decisions and purchases as long as possible to take full advantage of ever-changing technology.) Small items also make this list. If my prop shaft will require a 1-inch zinc collar at the next haulout, I put the collar on my list. If I plan to put some spare V-belts aboard, I note which ones and how many. The one requirement of my shopping list is that the entries are specific—not "compressor belts" but "3 Gates 41380 belts or equivalent."

My shopping list serves two functions. First, it lets me take advantage of opportunities. I had planned to add reading lights to my own boat and saw at a boat show some elegant ones fashioned entirely from teak that would be perfect—except that they were $49.95 each and I needed four. I wrote them on my shopping list to await their claim to two of the limited number of $100 bills that float into my hands. Two years later, browsing through a kind of marine trading post, I saw them again, this time for $15. Internet sites, bulletin boards, discounters, salvage outlets, flea markets, garage sales, other sailors, classifieds, sale flyers—all are potential sources of marine products at substantial savings, but only if you know exactly what you are looking for.

The list's second function is to juice my enthusiasm. When my zeal begins to wane a bit or nothing

seems to be getting done, I go online and order an item or two. I get a lift when I place the order and a second one when the item actually arrives. Blondie (Dagwood's wife, not the rock singer) was on to something all those times she lifted her spirits with a new hat.

LAST LIST (WHEW!)

One of my local marine suppliers gives away thin little notebooks about the size of a checkbook register, and I almost always have one of these with me. On a single page—a note card or a piece of paper can work just as well—I write down my plan of attack for my next visit to the boat. If I am going to the marina on Saturday and I plan to do several small jobs, I list them. If I have one project planned, I break it down into steps and list them. On the opposite page I list all the tools and supplies that I expect to need.

This daily list serves four functions. It keeps me focused all week on the jobs planned for the weekend. When I arrive at the boat, there is little wasted motion because I know exactly what I am there to accomplish. I have all the necessary tools and supplies with me (hopefully) when I get there. And as each job or step is completed and crossed out, I feel my vision getting closer.

A good plan will help you to achieve your vision with the least amount of wasted time. The least amount of wasted money is an equally important objective—perhaps more important. That issue is next.

When all the lists are crossed off. Still delivering dreams and turning heads at 40.

Dollars and Sense

"I'm living so far beyond my income that we may almost be said to be living apart."
—H. H. MUNRO

There is little value in talking here about expenses in absolute terms. With the dollars required just to replace the engine in an old Columbia 50, you could bring a neglected Cape Dory Typhoon back to new condition and beyond. Fitting out for an open-ended cruise to Polynesia will certainly cost more than a few comfort enhancements for weekends aboard. And when heiress Elizabeth Meyer decided to restore the 130-foot J-Boat *Endeavour*, you can bet your last buck she didn't start looking around for a do-it-yourself yard.

How much you are going to spend is a function of how big your boat is, her initial condition, the complexity of your vision, and the size of your bank account.

I don't know about your boat or your vision but I am going to make a wild guess about your net worth: the Bill & Melinda Gates Foundation does not have your number on its speed dial. How am I doing?

Thrift is a major element of the philosophy and the projects in this book. It is a good word, *thrift*. The dictionary defines it as "wise economy" in the management of money and other resources. It comes from the Old Norse word for prosperity.

Cheap is another thing altogether. *Cheap* means relatively low in cost; inexpensive. It can also mean of small value or poor quality. You need to be cautious about always taking the cheap route. You may be getting exactly what you pay for.

In the pages that follow, wise economy is our objective.

ECONOMY

A restrictive bank balance is usually a key element in the purchase of an old boat. It is also a key element in reconditioning her. Typical sentiment is that "a little money and a lot of TLC" will bring her back. TLC translates into substituting time for money. There are at least three reasons to do as much of the work required yourself as possible. Saving money is the one that comes to mind first.

If you *can* do the job, it will almost always cost you less than if you pay someone else to do it for you, often far less. When you hire someone to do something for you, boat-related or otherwise, you are paying for three distinct elements—time, materials, and knowledge or skill. Time and materials show up on the bill, but it is really the knowledge required (or the presumption of knowledge required) that determines the cost.

Refit costs increase with the size of the boat. (Molly Mulhern)

If your doctor tells you your health problem can only be corrected with delicate brain surgery, you don't pick up a couple of medical texts and a selection of surgical tools for your significant other, no matter how much the surgery is projected to cost. The risks are too high, the requirements too precise, the knowledge required too complex to offer any hope of success.

But boat repair is not brain surgery. Remember that. Hang around a boatyard for a day or two and you will discover that there is virtually nothing going on there that is beyond the capability of a reasonably handy boatowner.

That is not to say you should shun professional help. A true professional can do the job quicker, perhaps better, sometimes cheaper, and his or her depth of experience can provide a sense of assurance that may be lacking from your own first-time efforts. For example, if you start the job not knowing a pintle from a gudgeon, you will feel a lot less tentative about your rudder repair if you have a knowledgeable boatwright at least check it out. The absolute certainty required on a job that has safety implications may demand professional assistance.

When safety is not an issue or when you are confident that you can deal with the safety implications, doing the job yourself can have a startling effect on its cost. A few years back, in the middle of a wild and woolly winter night, I put the helm over and as the aged and overstressed genoa backwinded against the spreader tip, the sail ripped from head to foot. New sail time.

Conditioned to think of sailmaking as only marginally less difficult than brain surgery, I visited seven different professional sailmakers, providing each with exactly the same specifications. The results were instructive. There was no clear consensus among the sailmakers on any of the basic parameters—not on weight, not on weave, not on cut, and not on cost. The prices ranged from $800 to more than $1,900 and averaged around $1,300.

I knew nothing about building a sail, but apparently there was no "right" way. The more I looked into it, the less complicated it seemed. Knowing my way around a sewing machine from other canvas jobs, I decided to give it a go. Whether the sail I constructed is better or worse than the seven professional offerings is debatable, but it more than satisfied my requirements and my total cost was under $200!

I am not telling you that you should make your own suit of sails. The point here is that by doing it

myself I saved as much as $1,700 on a single sail with no compromise in quality (I used the same materials as the sailmakers), no disappointment in performance, and no safety risk. (If this particular economy interests you, you will find complete instructions for constructing and shaping sails in Chapter 16.)

A full suit of homemade sails. (Karen Larson)

KNOWLEDGE

My sailmaking experience also illustrates the second reason for doing a job yourself. I learned more about sail shape in one week than I had in a couple of decades of tweaking sheets. I had read a little about sail theory before this experience, but the responsibility of giving the sail the correct amount of draft in the right place converted all that hazy theory into working knowledge.

The more you do yourself, the more you will know about your boat. The knowledge you gain can be more important than the money you save. A sailing acquaintance, approaching the Bahamas in the dark after four days offshore from North Carolina, ran onto the reef east of Abaco. Bad weather was building and every effort to free the boat failed. Water below signaled the beginning of structural damage.

In a desperate effort to escape, the owner made a first-dawn decision to release the keel bolts.

Removing the necessary access panels, he and a crewmember began removing the nuts, releasing the last two simultaneously. The boat leaped from her ballast, and while the crewmember drove wooden plugs into the now-open holes, the owner piloted the lightened and frighteningly tender boat across the reef and into protected waters. Several days later, in calm weather, the ballast was retrieved, and the boat was made whole again on the ways at nearby Man-O-War Cay. The owner credited the fact that *he* had recently replaced the keel bolts with providing the knowledge required to take his boat-saving action.

You can never know too much about your own boat, and the farther you stray from boatyards, mechanics, and riggers, the more valuable that knowledge becomes. When you step off the companionway ladder into ankle-deep water, knowing exactly where every seacock is can make the difference between mopping up or swimming to shore.

QUALITY

The third reason you may find yourself doing your own work is that it may be the only way you can get a task done right. Because the truth in this statement typifies a worn spot in the fabric of our society, it saddens me to acknowledge. This is not a blanket indictment of everyone working in the marine trades. There are some fine craftsmen working on boats, some skilled workmen who take pride in their expertise, some boatyard supervisors who understand how unforgiving the ocean can be. But their numbers are diluted by those whose skill is marginal, whose pride in workmanship is nonexistent, and whose concern for your well-being lasts only as long as it takes your check to clear.

I have seen a mechanic forget to refill the engine with oil, a fiberglass "expert" patch a hole in a hull with a mixture of polyester resin and *beach sand*, a well-known canvas shop deliver an expensive "new" dodger with a patch in the top. For most of the items on your list, your own lack of expertise is a far less serious risk than such indifference. If you care enough, you can acquire the necessary skill.

NOT ALWAYS DO-IT-YOURSELF

This is not to say that you must do everything yourself. Indeed there may be a number of items on your list that you should *not* attempt. How many and which ones depend on you.

NO APTITUDE

You should not attempt repairs and enhancements for which you clearly have no aptitude. If every time you have tried to give your car a tune-up it had to be towed out of your driveway, attempting a major engine overhaul is probably not a good idea. If your last encounter with a band saw shortened two fingers on your left hand, a finishing sander may be the only power tool you should consider handling. If your efforts on a sewing machine always result in something that resembles the start of a loop-pile rug, you are not likely to be satisfied with a dodger of your own construction.

But be sure that your problem *is* aptitude, not simply that no one has ever gotten you off on the right foot. We will examine this distinction in much greater detail in the next chapter.

MATERIAL INTENSIVE

Some jobs on your list may be material intensive; that is, the cost of the materials required represents a significant portion of the cost of the job. Let's say that an engine-driven refrigeration system preengineered for your boat costs around $3,200. The dealer will give it to you in a carton for that price or installed for $3,500. For 10% more, the dealer assumes the aggravation and, more important, the responsibility of seeing that the system works. It could be $300 well spent, especially if you can persuade the mechanic to give you a running commentary while he does the job.

The proportional cost of the materials is not the only issue. When the materials have a high absolute cost, you might need knowledgeable assistance. It is one thing to feel your way through the installation of a $150 VHF radio, quite another to risk a $1,500 SSB unit. In some instances the materials are forgiving; if the seam in a new cushion cover is not quite right, pull it out and do it again. In others you can make a practice run; a scrap lumber mock-up will pinpoint problems *before* you cut that expensive piece of teak. But connections to your new SSB need to be right the first time. Likewise the hole you cut in the cabin top for the new hatch. And you cannot stop the chemical reaction once you mix the catalyst into expensive two-part paint. If you are tentative about a project in which an error will be costly, you may want to get help.

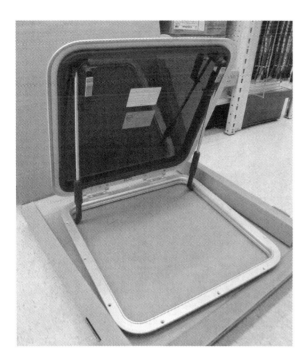

NO TIME

The time required to complete a job may indicate that you should pay someone else to do it. Keep in mind that we are talking strictly about the economics of your project.

Remember my story in the last chapter about wiring a new house. What took me almost a month to accomplish, a skilled electrician could have done in half that time, maybe less. What makes that significant is that I gave up a job that paid more than most electricians earn in order to do the wiring myself. In purely economic terms, it was not a good decision. The cost of materials aside, by doing the job myself, I neither earned nor spent any money. If instead of pulling wire I had stayed employed in my own specialty, I would have had to pay the electrician but would have earned enough in the four weeks to do that and still have more than half my earnings left over.

It is true that I got quicker with each circuit, but by the time I really got the hang of it, I was finished. And the value of acquiring the skill is questionable since I am never likely to use it again.

If you are tempted to give up gainful employment, take a leave of absence, or just turn down overtime in order to complete major modifications to your boat, take a hard look at the numbers. You may be financially wiser to do what you do and pay a specialist to do what he or she does.

This kind of reasoning has no application to the smaller tasks on your list. If you pay someone $300 to install your new anchor windlass, you cannot justify that expenditure based on your potential earnings unless doing the job yourself would actually result in the loss of those earnings. This is a job you could easily have done on the weekend instead of watching the Trojans take on the Fighting Irish. Your income for the week is unchanged either way, but it costs you $300 *not* to do the job yourself. If economy is important, *you* should have done it.

SPECIALIZATION

A number of items on your list may be so specialized as to preclude you from attempting them yourself. Electronics repairs come immediately to mind. If the autopilot corrects only to port, few of us are equipped to pinpoint the problem and correct it. A trained technician is required. With today's electronics, however, even a technician often makes no attempt to actually locate the problem. He or she simply replaces the entire circuit board. With the right board in hand, you could probably make the repair, but maintaining an inventory of spare circuit boards hardly makes economic sense.

Some jobs require special precautions. Safety or health risks may make doing it yourself a poor choice. While the two-part polyurethane paints that have revolutionized boat refinishing are relatively benign when applied with a brush or a roller, they are extremely dangerous when applied by spraying. If you decide to spray polyurethane on your hull, you should leave that job to someone who understands the nature of the risk and has the equipment necessary to deal with it.

Specialized tools (and the skill to use them) can be the issue. While much of the work necessary to complete an engine overhaul is within the capacity of many boatowners, reconditioning the cylinder head requires the services of a machine shop. If the engine is a diesel, repairs to the injection pump are even beyond the capacity of most machine shops. They will send the unit to a shop that specializes in the minimal tolerances the pump demands. A need for special tools and expensive equipment may eliminate doing it yourself as an option.

TOOLS

However, just because your toolbox does not include the needed tools is not always a good reason not to

attempt a job. If you need a special hand tool, a torque wrench for example, you can probably find someone in the marina or boatyard willing to loan you one. Expensive or very specialized tools can often be rented. If you will need the tool more than once, you should consider purchasing it.

Buying tools is a good place to learn the difference between *cheap* and *thrifty*. Quality tools are not cheap, but they are the definitive example of "wise economy." Most of my hand tools are more than 35 years old and still as good as the day they were purchased. The few cheap tools I ever owned broke or froze and were discarded years ago. I have usually selected Craftsman hand tools because of their availability and lifetime warranty, but there are others just as good. There is absolutely no need to pay a higher price for hand tools specifically marketed for the marine environment. If a standard Craftsman tool will last "forever," how do *marine* tools improve on that?

The extent of your tool inventory will depend on how extensive your planned modifications are. Typical refurbishing projects require amazingly few tools, and most of the necessary ones are not terribly expensive. We will examine specific tool requirements in later chapters, but a few comments about tools that represent a significant expense are appropriate here.

Before you hire work done because the job requires an expensive tool, you should evaluate that decision carefully. For my first quarter-century of maintaining and enhancing boats, I owned not a single shop tool—no lathe, no table saw, no band saw, no jigsaw, no drill press, no disk sander, no planer; nothing but hand power tools—yet my boat projects invariably turned out fine. However, when I eventually came up against the carpentry-intensive project of altering the interior layout of my old boat, I bought a table saw. It made every cut easier and more accurate. I could never go back to my circular saw and saber saw days. Small table saws have become relatively inexpensive, and if you have much woodwork planned, I strongly urge you to invest in one. A cost-saving ploy is to buy better-quality used tools, which can be sold at the end of the project for about what you paid for them—if you are willing to give them up.

Another specialty tool I recommend with equal vigor is a good sewing machine. One Christmas, about 25 years ago, Olga skipped the ties and socks and bought me a new commercial sewing machine. I am not supposed to know, but the cost was more than $600. It seemed like a lot of money at the time, but since then I have re-covered interior cushions several times; sewn three sets of cockpit cushions; and made bimini awnings, a couple of dodgers, rain-catching harbor awnings, a full boat cover, three sails, windscoops, rain hoods, sail covers (including roller-furling UV strips), hatch covers, winch covers, bug screens, fitted sheets, innumerable bags and pouches, and a fish-shaped wind

For interior carpentry, a table saw will save hours and deliver better results.

sock to bring luck to our little ship. The fish has never failed us, and I quit keeping tabs on the savings when they surpassed $10,000. Merry Christmas.

SHOPPING

You save on labor costs by doing some or all of the job yourself. You save on materials by shopping around. The assumption that a specific product will cost "about the same" regardless of where you buy it is wrong. As I write this, I have a note on my desk from calling five different local suppliers about a specific item. Incredibly the prices ranged from a high of $67 down to $16. Between two stores literally across the street from each other, one was *206% higher* than the other.

How can that be? Because prices are based not on how much an item costs the seller, but on how much the seller thinks a buyer will be willing to pay. I recently needed a bell bracket. This is a slightly wedge-shaped bit of sheet brass, half the size of a business card, with a rolled edge on the two converging sides. The price from my nearest supplier was $6. I passed, fabricating one from scrap in about 10 minutes, but that is not the point. I encountered the identical piece of hardware a few weeks later priced at less than $2.

I am not advocating driving all over town to save $4. What I am suggesting is comparison shopping. Remember the shopping list I described in the last chapter? With that in my pocket I am prepared to note prices whenever I visit a different supplier. Usually I find that a pattern emerges. It will come as no surprise that the purveyor of the $6 bell bracket is almost always the most expensive in my area on other items as well. How does the company stay in business? They are located next to a marina that caters to multimillion-dollar yachts, and their very complete inventory is more important than their prices to the professional captains they attract.

Be sure you are comparing oranges to oranges. Before leaving on a cruise I decided to buy a spare galley

foot pump to back up the two aging ones aboard. The Whale pumps had given excellent service, and a nationally known marine supply house sold a pump that was identical in appearance to a Whale pump except that it carried a house-brand sticker. Probably a way to discount Whale pumps, I thought, so I saved $10 and bought one. As it turned out, it was almost 2 years before I had occasion to install my "bargain" (further testament to the quality of my original Whales). When one of the old pumps eventually failed, the new one leaked so badly that I was forced to dismantle it, only to discover that it was not made by Whale and the quality was so poor that the leak could not be stopped. Significantly, I rebuilt the Whale pump using some salvaged parts from an even older pump, and it served for the rest of the trip. When considering costs, identical brand and model comparisons are the only valid ones.

SELECT QUALITY

My experience with the pump illustrates another tenet of thrift: select good quality. Instead of saving $10, my choice actually cost me $30 and a lot of aggravation. Had I examined the pump more carefully initially, I could have seen that it was a cheap knockoff. In the end I did what I should have done to start with—I bought the genuine article.

The consequences of selecting poor quality can be far more serious than a trickle of water across the cabin sole. A sailing friend, distressed at the prices of turnbuckle toggles, found some of unknown pedigree at a discount supplier. What could go wrong with a toggle? He found out 400 miles from Bermuda when one failed and the mast went over the side. How can you tell whether a toggle or a turnbuckle or an anchor shackle is strong enough? Not by looking at it! You are depending on the manufacturer's testing and quality controls. If a part is critical to the safety of the boat, be sure that it is backed by a reputable manufacturer.

(Courtesy Edson International)

A DISTANT DRUMMER

There is a footnote to the cheap toggle story. My friend went to this particular marine supplier for some other item, but when he ran across the toggles, he bought them because they were less than half the list price of the brand-name toggles he had intended to buy. Ironically those brand-name toggles were available at a significant discount from a major catalog supplier. A postmortem revealed that the cheap toggle that sent the mast over the side and sounded the death knell for his Atlantic crossing was only a couple of dollars less than the mail-order price for one of top quality.

When you are comparing prices, don't stop with the suppliers near your marina or in your hometown. A vast quantity of boating products is sold through catalog outlets and via the Internet, often at significant savings. Picking a selection of items at random, I just browsed the Internet and found Lewmar self-tailing winches that list for $1,660 offered online for $1,029. A Racor fuel filter with a $131 list can be had for $78. And a cartridge of polysulfide sealant that

Small companies without wide distribution can offer great products.

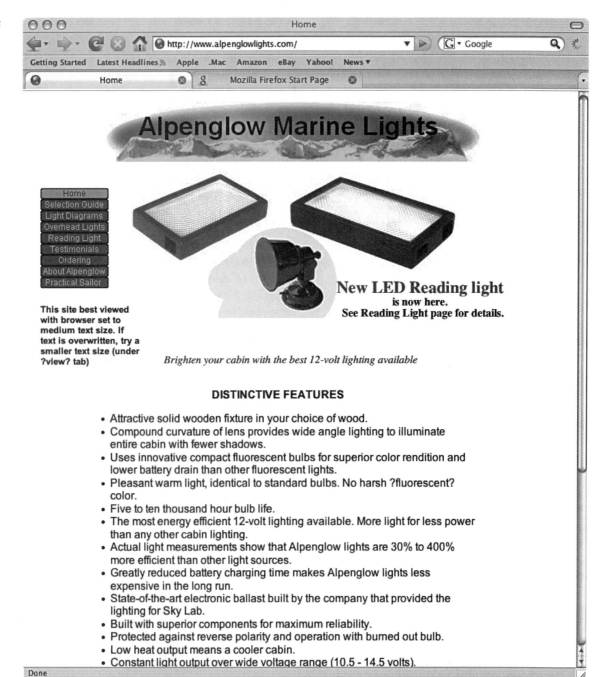

Brighten your cabin with the best 12-volt lighting available

DISTINCTIVE FEATURES

- Attractive solid wooden fixture in your choice of wood.
- Compound curvature of lens provides wide angle lighting to illuminate entire cabin with fewer shadows.
- Uses innovative compact fluorescent bulbs for superior color rendition and lower battery drain than other fluorescent lights.
- Pleasant warm light, identical to standard bulbs. No harsh ?fluorescent? color.
- Five to ten thousand hour bulb life.
- The most energy efficient 12-volt lighting available. More light for less power than any other cabin lighting.
- Actual light measurements show that Alpenglow lights are 30% to 400% more efficient than other light sources.
- Greatly reduced battery charging time makes Alpenglow lights less expensive in the long run.
- State-of-the-art electronic ballast built by the company that provided the lighting for Sky Lab.
- Built with superior components for maximum reliability.
- Protected against reverse polarity and operation with burned out bulb.
- Low heat output means a cooler cabin.
- Constant light output over wide voltage range (10.5 - 14.5 volts).

lists for $19.06 is sold by a catalog/Internet supplier for $11.48.

Remember my shopping list? Whenever I add an item to it, I typically consult two or three of the marine supply catalogs that I always have close at hand. Then I do an Internet search for online suppliers. Right away I have a good idea of what is available and at what price. If I already know exactly what I want, I note on my list the best price and who has it.

The Internet is particularly valuable for broadening your options. The products offered by West Marine or Defender Industries are rarely the only ones available, and they may not be the best. Retailing is imperfect, and buyers are charged with profit making rather than hard-nosed product comparison. The Internet allows a manufacturer to make its best case for its product directly to the consumer. Also on the Internet you may be able to find product reviews from individuals, which can help you sort out truth from hype.

Is mail order always less expensive? No. The shipping charges on heavy, oversize, or hazardous items can make the *delivered* price higher than the local price. Savings in state sales taxes might offset shipping charges, but if a mail-order supplier has a store in your state, most sales-tax states will require the merchandiser to collect sales tax. That can make an out-of-state-only merchandiser cheaper unless you live close to the competitor's store in your state. In that case you should be able to get catalog prices and save the shipping charges but not the taxes. To compete, local marine suppliers may also be willing to "meet" mail-order prices. Sales, boat-show specials, and the like can provide lower prices than the fixed ones in catalogs. The sealant I found for $11.48—plus shipping—by mail is often on sale for $10.95 at my local near-the-waterfront hardware store.

Specialty houses and wholesale suppliers are often a lower-cost alternative. When I need hose, I go to an industrial hose supplier and find the prices are about 50% lower than the best price from any marine source. When I need acrylic canvas, a local distributor invariably has the best price. When I was wishing for a sewing machine, I had my eye on one recommended by a sailmaker who also sold mail-order sailmaking supplies—including this particular machine. At the time the price of the sewing machine, "packaged" for the sailor, was $995. My resourceful wife bought the identical machine from a local commercial sewing machine company for 60% of that price.

WARRANTIES

A concern I have often heard expressed about mail-order shopping is "What if I have a problem with the item?" Deal with a reputable mail-order company and the answer to that question is "Pick up your telephone and call customer service." My experience has always been that Internet and catalog suppliers are just as eager for repeat business as the storefront variety.

Warranties are usually placed on items by their manufacturer, not the retailer, so warranty work should be more or less the same. For a time one popular mail-order outlet for marine electronics *doubled* the manufacturer's warranty as an incentive. If properly installed (which also means protected from the elements) modern marine electronics work when you initially turn them on, they are unlikely to develop a covered problem during the warranty period, but a longer warranty can't hurt—unless you have to pay more for it! The manufacturer either stands behind the product or it doesn't. "Extended" warranties are a way of increasing the profit from the sale, and I find them distasteful. Some powerboat manufacturers, for example, warranted their hulls for 1 year but for an additional charge of as much as several thousand dollars would *extend* the warranty to 3 years. I don't want a hull that is going to need warranty work. I want one that is going to be trouble free. If the manufacturer doesn't expect the hull to develop problems, then the company is ripping me off with a charge for nothing. If, on the other hand, the charge is intended to offset the warranty work they expect the hull to require during the 3-year period, this is probably not a boat I want to own.

The length of warranties is often *customary* rather than having any direct correlation with the expected life of the product. This means there is no reason to be particularly concerned about a 90-day warranty if that is what other manufacturers place on similar equipment. But if everyone else warrants for a year. . . . Conversely, if your item of choice has a significantly longer warranty, it could be a reflection of higher quality or nothing more than marketing strategy. In any case, a great warranty is no assurance that the item will perform when you need it. *Look for quality, not promises.*

ME, INC.

Early in our boating life Olga and I shared an anchorage with a beautifully finished Brown trimaran. We were soon invited aboard, and the nickel tour included a photo album of the boat under

construction, blanketed with heavy Michigan snow in some of the pictures. Mike told me that he had formed a boatbuilding company before starting the construction. That involved little more than having letterhead stationery and business cards printed and obtaining a tax number from the state—a total investment of less than $50. As a result he was usually able to obtain equipment and supplies at their true wholesale price.

Back home I decided to give Mike's method a try. This was before PCs and laser printers, so with a package of transfer letters, a copy machine, and a few sheets of linen paper, Don's Nautical Services was born. Commissioning was our business. I wrote on my new letterhead stationery to a major manufacturer of galley stoves, inquiring about a specific model, and they promptly responded with a wholesale price list. The shipping was FOB and COD, and a commercial address was necessary (I had the stove delivered to my employer's address), but the transaction presented no problems and I saved about $300 compared to the list price.

You will find that not all manufacturers, importers, and suppliers will deal with you. Someone may have a territorial exclusive in your area, and the manufacturer will simply refer you. A supplier may want to "qualify" you by sending a representative to determine how much business you are likely to represent. The manufacturer may require a minimum order, an established line of credit, or an occupational license number. I never advocate being anything less than *absolutely honest* with a potential supplier. If your transaction does not present a conflict or require special handling, most are happy to have the business. If you expect special service, you are out of line.

Should you find something inherently dishonest about this, reconsider. Mike was definitely in the boatbuilding business, and I was just as certainly commissioning. If the boats Mike and I were working on were not our own, the concept of a small business would be a natural, even as a weekend-only occupation. Do suppliers care who owns the boat you are working on? No. If you meet *their* qualifications—which often are as simple as walking through the door—they will do business with you. But remember that you are not buying a carload of their product. You have no reason to protest if they say "no."

RECYCLING

When you recondition an old boat, you will probably be trying to make use of all of the hardware and equipment that is still "good," so what could be more natural on an old boat than taking advantage of the savings available on used items? When I replaced my galley stove with one with an oven, I tried to sell the old stove. The new price was $425, and presumably there was some demand since the manufacturer was still making that model. My old one was polished and perfect, but I would have happily taken $40 for it had I found a buyer. And I would have thrown in a folding oven. I eventually gave the thing away to someone willing to store it until a buyer came along.

If a used item is not worn out, you might ask why the owner is getting rid of it. There could be a lot of reasons: Getting out of boating; changing boats; needing money; salvaging—bronze fittings outlast wooden planking; upgrading—my old stove was on the market because I wanted one with an oven; updating technology—when self-tailing winches hit the market, the used market was flooded with excellent standard winches; or reevaluating—a friend vacillated on the installation of an anchor windlass for several years before selling it (in the original carton) at a fraction of its cost. Even when it is not "new," used gear can be as good as new. Sometimes the quality of the old stuff is even better than that of today's goods. If you search actively, you may be surprised at what you will find.

The biggest problem with used marine equipment—with used items of any stripe—has long been getting the buyer and seller together. Newspaper classifieds used to be the most effective avenue, but declining readership and increasing ad rates have nearly eliminated this option except for big-ticket items. Weekly "shoppers" are cheap and effective in some communities. Yacht clubs and marinas typically provide bulletin boards to help sellers and buyers connect. Here potential buyers can take the initiative by posting a "wanted" card that may exhume the desired item from the bottom of some other boater's lazarette. Popular boating areas often have at least one used-gear outlet selling salvaged or consignment items or both. Pawnshops near the waterfront take in marine items. Garage sales and flea markets often include marine equipment, and in some boating areas, flea markets for marine equipment *only* are staged periodically.

The advantages of buying locally is that you can examine the item before you buy and there will be no shipping cost. The disadvantage is that your choices are likely to be limited. The Internet (eBay in particular) has revolutionized selling used items. Every old-boat owner should pick a couple of items he or she would like to put aboard and do an eBay search for these items. It will be a real eye-opener. The wealth of perfectly serviceable used equipment (and deeply discounted new gear) offered for sale on the Internet is astonishing. There is a caveat emptor aspect to shopping for used gear online, but with appropriate caution you are likely to be consistently satisfied with your purchases.

Another Internet resource every sailor should be aware of is sail brokers. A Google search for "used sails" will find you a dozen or more companies that deal in used sails. A sail that is a loser for the highly competitive sailor can be a definite winner for the

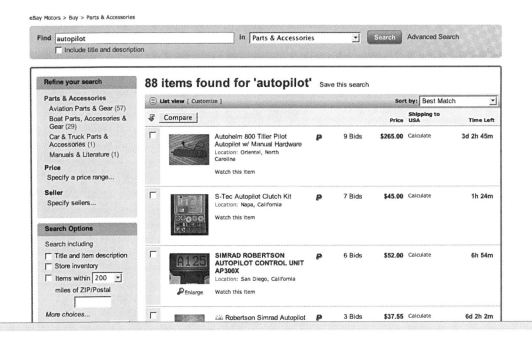

Exactly what you need, maybe at a bargain price, could be just a click away.

cruiser or casual sailor. Excellent used sails can be purchased for a fraction of their new cost, and my experiences with two different brokers are that their representations of the condition of the sails are pretty accurate. Here again, repeat business is their bread and butter, and you don't get return customers if you mislead them. Availability changes daily. Don't be in a hurry and you can spend hundreds rather than thousands to outfit your boat with professionally built sails capable of delivering years of good service.

But maybe the Gates Foundation does call you when facing a shortfall in their fundraising efforts so you aren't much interested in all this savings stuff. It is the satisfaction of working with your hands you are after, and you're starting to wonder when we're going to get to that part. How about now?

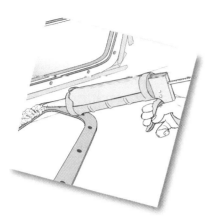

CHAPTER FIVE

Starting Small

"Eighty percent of success is showing up."
—WOODY ALLEN

Before we actually start cutting and painting and gluing and stuff, let's take one short detour. The purpose of this digression is illustrated by the old story of the burly mountain man who comes into town to replace his worn-out whipsaw. The salesman at the hardware store points out how much more efficient a chainsaw is and sells him one. A month later the mountain man returns to the store so wasted away that his shirt hangs on him like a plaid choir robe. He drops the new saw on the counter and demands his money back. "Don't cut half so good as my old one," he tells the salesman. Puzzled, the salesman gives the cord a pull, and over the rip of the exhaust he hears the mountain man yell, "What's that noise?"

The remainder of this book is a tool, and you will surely use it more efficiently if you know how to pull the cord. In the dozen or so chapters that follow, the objective is *not* to provide you with step-by-step instructions for a few generic enhancements to your old boat. The bookshelves are already full of such books, and while they are informative and useful, typically only a few of the projects they contain will be just right for your boat.

Not that there aren't any projects in this book. To the contrary, you will find detailed instructions for dozens of enhancements and improvements in the pages that follow, some of which are likely to fit your specific needs. I have tried to incorporate projects with broad applications. If you follow exactly the instructions provided, the physical result will be a specific item or improvement, but showing you how to build that specific item is not really the purpose of the instructions. I am focusing on the "big" project, the metamorphosis of your old boat

into the one in your vision. You are not likely to find every change on your list detailed here, but if I have succeeded in what I set out to do, you *will* find detailed illustrations of every skill necessary to make those changes. The projects included are a means to that end.

To be more specific, the purpose of the initial projects in the following chapters is to illustrate certain skills and to provide the opportunity to learn by doing. They represent a low level of difficulty, making success likely even for someone with no prior related experience. They are also low in cost, making failure, if not palatable, at least cheap and afford you the opportunity to give it another go. In most cases the project will result in legitimate enhancement, but even if you find the *thing* not especially useful, the exercise will be.

In the more advanced projects the dominant purpose becomes exemplifying what is possible. You can take a project whole, duplicating it and changing only the measurements to fit your boat. This is the probable approach to the installation of nonskid deck covering detailed in Chapter 14. Or you might use only the idea, changing the project entirely. If you build a galley-locker divider exactly like the one in Chapter 10, *my* pots will fit into *your* locker perfectly. You might also reject both the specific project and the general idea, extracting only the possibility. As an example, a thorough grasp of the techniques of canvaswork demonstrated in the various projects in Chapter 15 will enable you to effect many more fabric-incorporating enhancements than the few I have illustrated. I will often suggest other possibilities, but this book is about achieving your vision, not mine.

THE BASIC EIGHT

If the transformation of your old boat is to be at your own hands, you will need to be competent in eight basic skills:

1. Fiberglass work
2. Rigging
3. Mechanics
4. Carpentry
5. Electrics
6. Plumbing
7. Painting
8. Sewing

Some of these skills you undoubtedly bring with you. The others you will need to acquire. None of them are particularly difficult.

How difficult? If you can wet out a T-shirt with a paintbrush and a cup of water, you can do fiberglass work. If you can measure accurately, you can re-rig. If you can get the cap back on the toothpaste tube, you already have the skill to handle most of the mechanical jobs aboard. If you can trace a straight line along the edge of a ruler, boat carpentry will present you with few problems. If you connected the speaker

The cornerstone of mechanical skills.

wires to your stereo system, you can handle onboard electrical connections. If you have ever installed new end fittings on a garden hose, you are equipped to do boat plumbing. If you can drive a car, you can drive a sewing machine. And anyone can paint.

Am I oversimplifying? Perhaps, but not by much. Few if any of the skills required to refurbish an old boat will tax the abilities of the average sailor. I am not suggesting competence with the cap on the toothpaste qualifies you to rebuild a diesel engine. But recognize that the toothpaste cap threads onto the tube in exactly the same way as the bolts that attach the water pump, the nuts that hold the cylinder head to the block, and the cap screws that clamp the connecting rods around the crankshaft. If you have mastered removing and replacing that toothpaste cap, then you can learn to dismantle and reassemble virtually any mechanical item found aboard a boat.

STEP BY STEP

Notice that I said *learn*. I have already pointed out that in the chapters that follow, the emphasis is on teaching, on expanding basic skills to encompass a broader range of possibilities. Chapters usually begin with a project that illustrates the fundamental elements of the subject skill. Unless you already have experience in that skill, I recommend that you take the time to actually *do* the initial project. If it does not, in your particular case, lead to a useful enhancement, it is perfectly acceptable to alter the project to fit your needs. But even if your boat cannot directly benefit from the project in any form, you will. The most effective way to learn is by doing.

Following the initial project, each chapter typically provides detailed instructions for what I would call intermediate projects. Equipped with the knowledge and experience gained from the initial effort, you should find these more complex projects manageable. As the projects become more complex, instructions become less specific. By the time you are reconstructing the furniture below, it should no longer be necessary to tell you how deep to set the saw blade or to remind you to drill pilot holes for the screws.

You will probably not be surprised to discover that the last projects in each chapter (or occasionally in a supplementary chapter) are the most advanced. They require the most expertise in the subject skill, often in combination with one or more of the other skills. They also require the most ingenuity in adapting the illustrated concept to your specific requirements in the most effective way.

There is nothing particularly revolutionary about this crawl-before-you-walk approach. It is how you learned to read, to write, and to spell. It is also how you learned to run a computer, to cut hair, to cook *coq au vin à la Bourguignonne*, to pilot a 747, to close a deal, or whatever else it is that you do. With the same approach and the same dedication to learning boat enhancement skills, there is little reason not to expect an equal level of competence.

ME OR VERN?

We were on the hard for a fresh coat of bottom paint. To our starboard in the yard sat a not-so-old Endeavor 37. One afternoon a rusted-out VW bus arrived in a cloud of blue smoke, and the scruffy-looking driver pitched a power cord over the lifelines and went aboard. Fifteen minutes later he asked me to hold the outside part of a new through-hull fitting while he tightened the seacock from the inside. In another 10 minutes he was gone. When the owner popped by after work to check on the job, he came back down the ladder muttering obscenities.

"Problems?" I asked, wondering about my participation.

"That *@#@*! I told him exactly what I wanted and the stupid *@#@* still did it wrong."

If I had a dollar for every time I have heard an owner say something similar, I could pay to hire my own work done. He took me aboard to show me.

"Look at that! You can see the gap from here." Indeed, the installer had neglected to create a flat mounting surface. Only the top and bottom edges of the seacock flange touched the curved hull. "And

the damn thing is just threaded on. What does the *@#@* think those ears are for? And why right smack in the middle of the locker? The hole is there now, so I'm stuck with it, but I'll have to get somebody else out to reinstall the valve."

"Why don't you just do it yourself?"

"Me? No, no." His hands waved in the air in a crossing motion. "It would leak for sure if I did it."

Here was a guy who obviously knew everything he needed to know to install the new through-hull fitting. Yet he had hired some hard-core underachiever living in an old hulk out in the free anchorage to do the job for him. Why?

Lack of confidence. The psyche is a strange thing. It is often easier to have unfounded confidence in someone else than to have justifiable confidence in yourself. The guy you hire only has to say, "Sure, I can do that," and you turn your boat and perhaps your personal safety over to him. In Spock's words, "It is illogical, Captain."

Had I needed someone to install a through-hull fitting and been forced to choose either the owner or the guy he hired, it wouldn't have been close. The owner clearly knew more than the self-proclaimed "expert," but even if the owner did not know the first thing about through-hull fittings, he still would have been my choice. Why? Because of his character. He expected the work to be *good*, not just *good enough*.

I guessed this even before I talked to the owner. How? The way he dressed. The way his car looked. The condition of his boat. The shine on his shoes. The way he left those shoes at the ladder when he went aboard. Those things contrasted starkly with the filthy jeans and grimy, junk-laden van of the man he hired, with the way that person tossed the sharp-pronged cord into the cockpit, and with the way he carelessly walked through the blue mud of wet sanding on his way to boarding.

Of course boat work can be a dirty job. Sure a rusty old VW bus is perfect for hauling around boat parts. But I don't want someone who looks like he just played huggy-bear with a transmission working in the cabin of my boat. And if the inefficiency and poor aesthetics of years of accumulated junk don't bother him, how can I expect him to be sensitive to the efficiency and aesthetics of my boat? I certainly don't want someone who has so little concern for my boat that he chips my gelcoat and leaves blue footprints on the deck, companionway, and cabin sole.

Disclaimer time again. I am not saying that there are no competent people working on boats. *Au contraire*, in the same yard at the same time was another person whose skill and workmanship made my brown eyes green. (Significantly, he carried around a small album of photos of his own boat.) I am also not saying that you are somehow less worthy if you do not do your own work. What you hire to be done and what you do yourself are choices only you can make.

However, if you want to do your own work or if your financial situation is such that you *need* to do the work yourself but are deterred by a personal lack of confidence, you should reconsider. And if you turn the job over to someone on the strength of *his* confidence, you are deluding yourself. Give yourself a break. You didn't get to be vice president of Widgets International because you were unusually dense. And the typical Mr. Fixit isn't working on boats to fund his research into nuclear fusion.

LEARNING THE ROPES

The modest project that begins most chapters introduces you to a new skill. By doing that project you will discover that there is nothing mystical about the skill. With each subsequent project you become more knowledgeable in that skill area. By the time you complete the last project in the chapter, you will have advanced your knowledge to the point that the first project, no matter how difficult it may have seemed to you to start, now has a "see Spot run" quality to it.

If you already have experience in a specific skill, the first part of that chapter may seem too elementary. For that I apologize, but it is important to start with the basics for those boatowners who do not have the benefit of your experience. The tedium of the instructions should not prevent the initial project from having the same potential usefulness for your boat. And you may find the step-by-step instructions to be a useful review. In any case the subsequent projects build on the earlier ones, assuming an ever-broader understanding of the subject skill. The projects later in the chapter should challenge even the most experienced renovators.

DRESS REHEARSAL

Learning a skill in the least stressful manner is not the only benefit to starting small, but before we look at some others we need to take time out to clarify terms. Thus far I have been using the word *skill* to

Too loose.

Too tight

Perfect.

represent a specific type of endeavor. Carpentry is a skill. Painting is a different skill. Needlework is different from both. If we so choose, we can break needlework into canvas work, sailmaking, and upholstery; carpentry into rough carpentry, finish carpentry, and cabinetry; but regardless of how broad or narrow our definition, *the* skill refers to the endeavor. *Skill* used this way must not be confused with *skill* used to mean proficiency or expertise, referring to the quality of the work, not the type.

Proficiency comes with practice; the more you do something, the better you should become. So we start small to give you the opportunity to practice, to allow you to develop the necessary "feel." I cannot tell you how much to tighten a wood screw. I can say "tight" or "snug" or "until you feel significant resistance," but you won't really know what those terms mean until you have the screwdriver in your hand, until you give it that last twist, maybe not until you twist just a little too hard and the screw suddenly turns freely.

The more you practice, the more proficient you will become—but refurbishing your old boat is not a contest, not a championship. You are only trying to achieve competence, not renown. Once you have tightened a few screws, once you know what "tight" means, screws you install will be indistinguishable from those put in by a master carpenter. He may be faster than you, may know intuitively what size screw is appropriate and what size pilot hole to drill, but the end result will be the same—provided you have sufficient aptitude.

CRITICAL REVIEW

Determining aptitude is a third reason to begin our treatment of each skill with an elementary project. I have already stated unequivocally that *most* boatowners can learn to do everything required to make an old boat functionally new, a thing of beauty, and a source of pride. I did not say *every* boatowner. The reality of individual differences is that some of us will excel in some of the skills required and be less adept in others. Frustration can be avoided by the recognition and acceptance of low aptitude, but truly prohibitive deficiencies are rare.

Initial difficulty with a new concept does not necessarily signal a lack of aptitude. Learning is always a series of failures. Mastering the skills required for boat enhancement is no different. If you attempt the initial project and the results are less than stellar, try it again. Failure is far more likely to stem from unfamiliarity than from an innate aptitude deficiency. Yet we are too often like the child who takes one look at a new dish and says, "I don't like it." We claim to have a lack of aptitude without really having any idea whether we do or not. Put those prejudices aside and give the initial project your best effort. It may be that all you need is the right tools and clear instructions.

Of course, if you struggle to get the cap off the toothpaste tube and once you have, you throw it away to save further aggravation, enhancements that require wrenches and sockets and screwdrivers may be difficult for you no matter how clear the instructions. Or if you gave away your electric knife after your second trip to the emergency room, your confidence in your potential prowess with a saw and router may be misplaced—and dangerous. The initial projects in each chapter allow you to fail as well as succeed, to discover or confirm an inability to master a specific skill while failure is still more inconvenience than disaster.

BUILDING CONFIDENCE

Fortunately you are far more likely to discover a talent than an inability. Success in a small project will provide the boost in confidence you need to take on a larger project. As the projects become larger and more complex, confidence grows. Ultimately you should come to a point where no aspect of the rejuvenation seems beyond your abilities.

Confidence, if it is justified, is a wonderful thing. It opens up whole new vistas of possibilities. If you reach a point where you truly believe that you are capable of doing anything that you can imagine to your old boat, your project is then limited only by your imagination—and practical considerations such as time and money. Developing that kind of confidence is our objective.

CHAPTER ORGANIZATION

The first step in the restoration of a long-neglected old boat is to insure her seaworthiness. That means evaluating the hull and deck—including portholes and hatches—and correcting any deficiencies. Since we have already established that this old boat is fiberglass, the initial skill required is working with polyester resin and other plastics.

Once you know your old boat is not going to sink in the bay or at the dock, there is little reason why you cannot enjoy using her even while you are modifying and restoring her. The only requirement is that you establish the integrity of her rig if she is a sailboat or the dependability of her engine if she is a powerboat. Thus rigging and mechanics are the second and third skills covered.

Major modifications are the next likely step, requiring carpentry skills. Only after bulkheads and furniture are in place are you ready to tackle wiring, plumbing, or refrigeration. Painting and varnishing come next, followed by upholstery and canvas work.

This order should generally agree with the order of the jobs listed on your matrix. When it doesn't, simply skip to the chapter that you need.

In the pages to follow I can only share with you the knowledge required, push you to test your abilities, provide you with a program for honing your skills, and hope that these things nourish your confidence. If they do, I will accept some of the credit for the accompanying sense of satisfaction. But for the source of any sense of pride that may result, look to the person in the mirror.

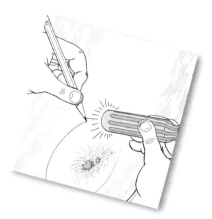

CHAPTER SIX

Scratch and Itch

*"Sometimes it is not good enough to do your best;
you have to do what's required."*
—WINSTON CHURCHILL

Giving substance to your vision for your old boat should begin with learning to work with the basic boatbuilding material. Wood held this distinction from hairy man through Harry Truman, but around 1947 boatbuilders began producing hulls molded with glass-reinforced plastic. Not only was this a more economical method of construction, but it produced a more durable boat. Within two decades virtually all of the production boats built in America featured molded fiberglass hulls and decks. Many fine old wooden boats are still around, and a handful of custom builders continue to build in wood, but for nearly half a century fiberglass has been the dominant material in boat construction.

WHY FIBERGLASS?

For me, at least, this is a good thing. I calculate that I have spent somewhere around 8 of the past 25 years aboard my old boat. That may sound like a lot, and it certainly means that my boat has seen more use than most boats in the marina, but if you look at that statement from the other side, you realize it also means that my boat was not in use about 70% of the time. When I am not using my boat, I like to be free of it.

I tend to give my boat about as much attention when I am not sailing as I give my tennis racquet when I am not playing tennis. Since molded composite racquets replaced wood, my aging Wilson is totally unaffected by my indifference as it rests patiently in my closet. My molded composite boat is not quite so immune to neglect, but when I do return to it, if I demonstrate my remorse with some extra attention, it tends to forgive. The souls of wooden-hulled boats, like wooden racquets, are more fragile, and if you ignore one for very long, it will commit suicide before

you have the chance to make up. That is exactly what most neglected old wooden boats have done.

This fact makes the purchase of a neglected wooden boat a much greater risk than rescuing a back-of-the-yard fiberglass boat. In fact the two concepts are opposites. The construction of a 35-year-old fiberglass boat is likely to be stronger than that of similar boats built today because early builders still had limited experience with the medium and tended to add a few extra laminates "just to be sure." Given just neglect and not severe mistreatment, there is little reason to expect an old fiberglass hull to be less sound than the day it left the builder's yard. With some cosmetic work and a few upgrades you should end up with a stronger boat at a fraction of new boat cost.

However, unless a wooden hull has been maintained impeccably, any assumption of seaworthiness is pure folly. And if it has been impeccably maintained, then it is not the kind of boat we are talking about in this book. Catch-22. Clearly you should survey any old boat you are considering investing your time and money in, regardless of the construction material, but a neglected wooden boat is far *more* likely to have serious structural deficiencies that require skilled repairs and far *less* likely to represent a financially sound investment. Owners of wooden boats find compensating spiritual rewards in their craft, and I am not trying to convert anyone. But for the rest of us the restoration of an old boat is viable *because of* the ability of fiberglass construction to shrug off years of neglect. It is a matter of practicality, not prejudice, that I am assuming hull and deck construction of fiberglass. Besides, the safest course for someone short on experience is to select a production boat with a great reputation, and for the last 45 years that means fiberglass.

Fiberglass boats are, of course, not without problems. The hull and deck of an older fiberglass boat are likely to suffer from one or more of eight possible conditions:

1. Dirty
2. Dull
3. Scratched
4. Cracked
5. Weak
6. Blistered
7. Delaminated
8. Structurally damaged

We are going to look at the resolution of each.

DIRTY

I know you don't need my help with this one but allow me to give you a bit of advice. Buy your cleaning supplies at your local version of a Piggly Wiggly. Marine supply shelves are loaded with dozens of overpriced proprietary "boat cleaners" promising miraculous results, but liquid laundry detergent such as Wisk, a spray bottle of Fantastik, and a nice fat sponge are probably all the cleaning supplies your lazarette needs to contain. A *soft* bristle brush works better on some types of nonskid, but stick with the sponge on the smooth stuff.

If you run up against a stain that shrugs off the Fantastik, squeeze a little lemon juice on it. Really. Next try kerosene or a cloth dampened with acetone. If that fails, trot down to your nearest hardware store for a quart of *brush cleaner*. This is a water-soluble, toluene-based product, not to be confused with the mineral spirits or paint thinner that you may have

The cleaning lineup.

used to actually clean brushes. If the stain persists, one proprietary product that does work is Marykate On & Off Hull & Bottom Cleaner. This is an unpleasant mix of acids that you have to handle with caution, but on some stains it works like magic.

If you get to this point and you still have a stain that you cannot remove, it is probably because the gelcoat has become porous from exposure and allowed the stain to penetrate. Try some of the other miracle cleaners if you like, but if they fail, your remaining option is to remove the offending layer of gelcoat and the stain with it.

DULL

Gelcoat is the paintlike surface layer of your hull and deck. New gelcoat gets its high gloss from the polished surface of the mold, but over time the gelcoat surface becomes rough from exposure. This roughness is microscopic, but it diffuses rather than reflects light, making the surface appear dull. To regain the shine, you must restore the smooth surface.

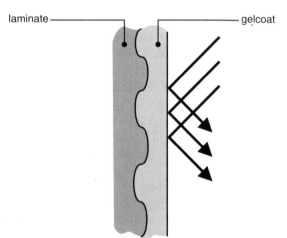

Parallel light reflection gives a mirrorlike shine.

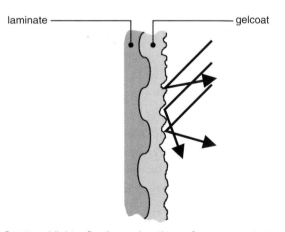

Scattered light reflection makes the surface appear dull.

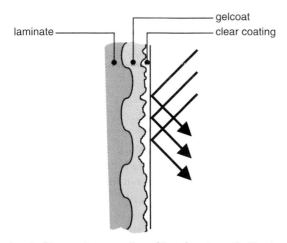

laminate — gelcoat
clear coating

Acrylic films and wax coatings fill surface irregularities to restore the gloss.

THE EASY WAY

Wet your dull gelcoat and it will have an admirable shine—until the water evaporates. A number of products have come on the market that "restore" the surface of the gelcoat by filling the microscopic pits and craters, similar to what water does momentarily. Results can be dramatic, but because restorers are an acrylic coating—similar to liquid floor wax—they have a similarly limited life. They also trap stains rather than removing them, although restorer kits often include a prep wash and sometimes a cleaner/polish in addition to the clear coating.

There are variations in the recommended application, but in general it is wash, polish, and coat. The acrylic sealer will be water-thin, so applying it to the hull is much easier than, say, applying paste wax, which restores the gloss in much the same way. Also, restorers dry to a hard film so no buffing is required. You do have to apply several coats—five is typical—to get a good shine, but drying times are short, so successive coats can be applied almost immediately. If the product you have selected doesn't include an applicator, use a sponge or a soft cloth to wipe the sealer onto the gelcoat. A multicoat application can restore the shine to dull gelcoat for up to a year in a moderate climate, but plan to remove the old coating with a special stripper when it is time for a fresh application.

THE SYSTEMIC WAY

Badly weathered gelcoat can challenge the capabilities of restorers, and embedded stains rule them out altogether. The appropriate treatment for stained and/or weathered gelcoat is the same because they stem from the same problem—a porous surface. If the gelcoat is thick enough and not porous all the way through, you can bring back the original gloss and color by removing the "dead" surface with polish, rubbing compound, or even sandpaper.

Gelcoat is sprayed into the polished mold before layup. It should be applied to a thickness of around 20 mils (0.020 inch), or about the thickness of 10 pages of this book, but the actual thickness and uniformity will have been determined by the skill and care of the person handling the spray gun the day the hull was started. In addition it is probable that a 20-year-old boat has already seen the business side of a polishing cloth a few times. Consequently you may have less to work with than you think, so it is prudent not to remove any more of the gelcoat than is absolutely necessary. If you are just trying to remove a stain, try a cleaner/polish first. This is the least abrasive, and polishes usually contain a mild solvent to assist in stain removal. Now rub until the stain is gone and the gelcoat looks new—or until your arm falls off into the dirt.

If the gelcoat is more than a dozen or so years old, polish is probably going to be too wimpy to restore a shine to the whole boat. Something a bit more abrasive is needed. In my adolescent years we used to shoehorn huge V-8 engines into Depression-era Ford coupes and paint these hot rods with 12 or 15 or 20 coats of lacquer. After the paint cured, we would rub most of it off with rubbing compound. The results were nothing short of spectacular—finishes that were as flawless and as deep as a mirror. Rubbing compound will do the same for gelcoat.

Using Rubbing Compound

Rubbing compound is more abrasive than polish and removes the old gelcoat much more quickly, so you first need to test your technique and the thickness of the gelcoat.

Dewax. Dewax. Dewax. In some inconspicuous spot, wipe the surface with the toluene-based brush cleaner mentioned earlier to remove wax and silicone, then rinse away the cleaner with water. Just because it is apparent that the boat has not been waxed in years, do not omit this step. Despite the fact that wax you apply to your car seems to evaporate before the swelling goes down in your elbow, 30-year-old gelcoat can still harbor traces of the original mold-release wax. Acetone will remove this wax, but if the boat was ever waxed with a silicone product, the silicone is very tenacious and requires a stronger solvent. An alternative to brush cleaner is lacquer thinner, which will be all or mostly toluene. Even better for removing silicone is *xylene.* You can also buy a quart of a proprietary dewaxing solvent such as Interlux 202 (Fiberglass Solvent Wash), which will be a mix of these solvents and others. Water sprayed on the gelcoat will "sheet" off when you have all the wax removed.

You use rubbing compound just like the polish, rubbing in a circular pattern with heavy pressure at first, then with progressively less pressure until the finish is glassy. The appropriate compound is one formulated specifically for gelcoat, typically labeled fiberglass compound. However, you can remove the surface of badly weathered gelcoat faster if you use automotive compound. Formulated for the enamel paint on cars, this will quickly cut the much softer gelcoat, but extra care is required.

Power-tool manufacturers market reasonably priced orbital polishers for the yuppie set to use on their BMWs, so if you are pleased with the results on the test spot and intend to use compound on the entire hull and deck, you might want to buy one or borrow your brother-in-law's. *Do not* chuck a sanding disk into your old drill and fit it with one of those drawstring polishing bonnets. It will eat right through the gelcoat, or you will burn out the drill running it slowly.

A couple of safety notes are in order. For any gelcoat restoration requiring more than hand polishing, the boat must be out of the water. I have seen boats machine polished in the water, but even if you are lucky enough not to be electrocuted, you will establish yourself as the marina idiot. Power tools around a boat in the water are risky enough without hanging head-down over the rail with one in your hands.

You *must* wipe down the entire hull with toluene or xylene (acetone will do only if you are *sure* that the hull has never been waxed with a silicone product) before you compound. You will save the risk of immediate skin irritation and who knows what future horrors if you put on rubber gloves before you use these or any other chemicals. Select gloves rated to resist chemicals, not dishwater.

The Last Hope

If the gelcoat is in bad shape, you could still be compounding this time next year. It's time to bring in the big guns. You are going to sand away the dead gelcoat. The exact schedule will depend on the condition of your gelcoat, but if compounding has failed, start with a sheet of 220-grit wet-or-dry sandpaper. The lower the number, the coarser the grit. You can keep this relationship straight if you think of the grit designation as the number of chunks of abrasive material it takes to fill the sheet.

Back at the inconspicuous spot, wipe the surface down again to remove the wax deposited by some rubbing compounds. Quarter the sheet of sandpaper. You can apply pressure with your fingers, but the paper will cut faster if you wrap it around a sanding block. Rubber sanding blocks, sold in all hardware stores, are better because they adapt somewhat to the contour of the hull, but a scrap of 1×2 will serve.

Keep a trickle of water running on your sanding area by holding the hose against the hull above where you are working. Use a piece of soft hose with the brass fitting removed to keep from marring the hull. Do I need to tell you not to cut off the end of a hose supplied by the boatyard?

Sand the test spot until the gelcoat has a uniform appearance. It will not be shiny, just smooth and evenly dull. For your first attempt at this, err on the side of sanding too little. You can sand more but you cannot unsand. Switch to 400-grit wet-or-dry until the surface is again uniform in appearance. You may have better results if you abandon the block at this point. Next switch to 600-grit wet-or-dry, then to 1000-grit. Finally, wipe the test spot dry and polish it to a high shine with the rubbing compound. If this fails to restore the surface before you cut all the way through to the underlying laminate, it is time to get out your old bugle and play taps. Your gelcoat is dead—period.

Power Assistance

If you do end up with a beautiful spot but it took you half a day—which doesn't bode well for the time it will take to do the entire hull—there is a way to do it faster. You will need a finishing sander. If you are buying one, buy a $1/4$-sheet palm sander and pay particular attention to how the paper is fastened. Some brands are much easier to load than others. If the clamp is configured with teeth to grip the paper, these eventually get sanded away enough to become ineffective.

Using 120-grit aluminum oxide sandpaper (it's brown), test this method of surface removal in another inconspicuous spot. Keep in mind that the sander is working at about 200 orbits per second, about a hundred times faster than your hand-powered sanding block, so be circumspect. Don't sand long—a few seconds will be sufficient for your test spot. And don't let the sander sit in one spot—keep it moving. Switch to 220-grit paper and run the sander quickly over the surface again. Follow this with wet sanding by hand in the same sequence as for hand sanding, first with 400-grit wet-or-dry paper, then with 600-grit, then with 1000-grit. *Never, never wet sand with a power sander.* Finish by compounding.

Where power sanding is the only timely way to restore the gloss, don't lose sight of the fact that if you are

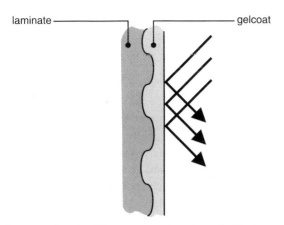

laminate ————————————— gelcoat

Compound and polish remove surface irregularities to restore shine.

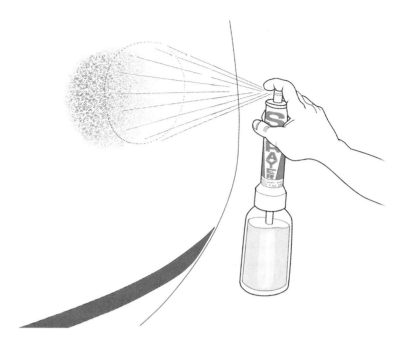

Spraying gelcoat with a Preval sprayer.

the least bit inattentive you will cut all the way through the gelcoat. Don't run the sander over any high spots in the hull or around any corners, such as the bow or where the quarter meets the transom. If you do, it will cut through the gelcoat to the underlying laminate in an instant. Even block sanding is not a good idea. Use finger pressure only to gently sand these areas.

Don't be too surprised if the results of your tests are disappointing. Gelcoat can hold its color and gloss forever if it is protected with a cover. Even regular waxing can give it a life span measured in decades. But too few boatowners wax regularly. Neglected gelcoat may be beyond redemption after as little as 10 years. When the gelcoat cannot be resuscitated, the only way to make the hull shine again is to apply a new finish.

It is possible to apply a new layer of gelcoat to the hull and deck, but this is rarely done except in countries where labor costs are very low. The original gelcoat was applied by spraying it onto the interior surface of a highly polished mold. The bottom surface of the gelcoat mirrored the mold's slick surface and became the glossy exterior of the hull when the hull was removed from the mold. The top surface of the gelcoat was not smooth, but this texture made for good adhesion to the fiberglass laminates that were applied over the sprayed coating. This inherent unevenness is not such a good thing when the gelcoat is being applied as an exterior coating. To obtain a mirror finish requires sanding the coating to remove the texture and other imperfections, then polishing the surface to produce the desired gloss. Paint, on the other hand, when applied with reasonable care, dries to a smooth, glossy finish. This makes paint the better alternative for do-it-yourself refinishing. We get to painting in Chapter 14.

It *can* be practical to spray a small area with gelcoat, but the gelcoat must be thinned to the consistency of milk to get it through the nozzle. Professionals use specialized reducers. You can use methylethyl ketone (MEK) for a small patch, but the flashing solvent is going to give the surface an orange-peel texture, with the film thickness varying as much as 8 or 10 mils. (Doubling the catalyst—up to 2%—helps, and you need additional catalyst for the thin application anyway.) As long as you let the solvent flash off completely between coats and apply sufficient thickness to allow sanding the cured surface smooth while retaining a gelcoat thickness of close to 20 mils, your end result should be OK. Rather than feeding polyester resin through a paint gun, for a small patch you will be better off using a disposable Preval sprayer, a canister and propellant combination that functions like a paint spray can loaded with your coating—thinned gelcoat in this case. Recoat within minutes and apply six or eight coats to insure adequate thickness to sand and buff to a smooth surface.

SCRATCHED

The vulnerability of the hulls of pleasure boats, especially sailboats, to disfiguring damage from even the lightest kiss of a piling or seawall is shameful. Pleasure boat manufacturers could learn from a visit to a commercial dock where robust rub strakes allow workboats to lie alongside the meanest wharf without damage. Meanwhile, the genteel yachtsman is expected to protect his boat's fine finish with ridiculous little inflatable fenders—8 inches of protection for 40 feet of hull. The result is usually a road map of scratches and gouges.

The appropriate method of scratch repair depends on the severity of the scratch and the overall condition of the gelcoat. Light scratches in the surface of a good gelcoat can be polished out with rubbing compound or, if they are somewhat deeper, sanded smooth and then polished. Deep gouges will require filling, then recoating with gelcoat. If the gelcoat is beyond redemption and you plan to paint the hull (or deck), you only need to fill and fair the scratch before painting.

For filling gelcoat hull and deck scratches, you have three choices of filler: polyester resin, gelcoat putty, and epoxy resin. Each is better in certain circumstances.

RESIN

Fiberglass is the marriage of glass fibers and a polymer resin. The liquid polymers used in fiberglass construction are called resins because of their visual similarity to the sticky amber liquid of the same name that drips from trees and ages into a hard, brittle, translucent substance. Fiberglass resins are not organic but chemical in nature. When cured they form a hard, brittle, translucent plastic, a most unlikely material for boat construction. But if this liquid resin is used to saturate a mat or weave of glass fibers, it binds the fibers together and cures into a tough, flexible material with more tensile strength than steel.

Chemists have concocted numerous polymer resins for different purposes but only three types are commonly used in boat construction—polyester, vinylester, and epoxy. Unless you *know* otherwise, it is safe to assume that your boat was laminated with polyester resin since vinylester is typically used mainly as a skin coat to improve blister resistance, and not 1 boat in 10,000 is epoxy laminated. Vinylester did not find its way into boat construction until the 1980s. Epoxy has been around longer. It is stronger and more adhesive than polyester or vinylester, resulting in a superior fiberglass, but it is difficult to work with, is a skin allergen, requires elevated temperatures to achieve full cure, and costs about three times as much as polyester. Until recently epoxy was used in hull lamination only when cost was secondary to maximum performance, but since 2003 epoxy hull construction has begun to appear in some production boats. These will likely be the desirable good old boats of the future.

Cost is less of a factor for repair work, and epoxy resins are often selected for their extra strength and superior adhesion. Although polyester resin in some form is also dominant in the market, it is less popular than epoxy for repair work. Gelcoat is a polyester resin with pigment added for color and UV resistance, as well as other additives to protect the cured surface from abrasion and water.

GELCOAT PUTTY

Back to the scratch repair. When the surface blemishes are minor and the rest of the gelcoat is in good condition, gelcoat putty is your best choice. Repair kits with putty, hardener, and a selection of tints are available. For more extensive repairs, make your own gelcoat putty by mixing a thixotropic (an egghead word for thickening) agent into white gelcoat. If you ask your supplier for a thickening agent and he gives you a bag of something that looks like talcum powder, don't be surprised—that's probably what it is.

Polyester resins, including gelcoat, are normally *air-inhibited*, meaning that the surface of the resin does not cure quickly and remains tacky if left exposed. The tacky surface provides an ideal base for subsequent laminates, thus air-inhibited resin may also be called *laminating* resin. Air-inhibited gelcoat is *not* what you want for surface repairs.

Non-air-inhibited resin, or *finishing* resin, will cure in free air. It is the same as laminating resin but with a wax added. This curing wax—variously known as tack-free additive (TFA), sanding aid, or air dry—floats to the surface and seals the resin from the air, allowing it to cure tack free. You can add curing wax to air-inhibited gelcoat to make it suitable for surface repairs, or you can seal it off from the air with plastic film, but it is easiest just to buy gelcoat that is non-air-inhibited. Gelcoat paste intended for scratch and gouge repair will not be air-inhibited.

If the hull is any color other than white, you will need to tint the gelcoat. Inorganic pigments in a resin base (color resins) specifically formulated for tinting polyester or epoxy resins are available individually in 1-ounce tubes or in six-color sets of $1/4$-ounce tubes. But before playing mad scientist, clean and compound the hull where the scratch is to reveal the true color of the old gelcoat. Wax a small spot on the hull away from the scratch. Now pour an exact amount of gelcoat or gelcoat paste into a small, unwaxed paper cup. I usually start with $1/2$ ounce. Add one drop of color resin. Stir. Too light? Add another drop. Stir. Repeat this process, keeping careful track of the number of drops, until the color matches the old gelcoat. Dabbing a little onto the hull will help you see tint differences.

When the color of the gelcoat calls for more than one tint, your task is more difficult, but the process is the same. Try to enjoy it and not let it frustrate

Mix in pigment one drop at a time.

you; resign yourself to the fact that a perfect match is unlikely. When you are satisfied with the color in the cup, write down the formula. For example, maybe your 1/2 ounce of gelcoat required seven drops of blue and two of black to achieve the right color.

It is easier to mix the tints into gelcoat than into gelcoat paste, so if you are working with gelcoat, tint first, then thicken. However, if the thickener alters the color, you may have to start over, thickening first. Thicken the gelcoat to a peanut butter consistency so it will stay in place when applied to a vertical surface.

Adding the Catalyst

It is time to add the hardener. The most common catalyst is methyl ethyl ketone peroxide (MEKP), not to be confused with the solvent MEK. The gelcoat manufacturer will supply the appropriate hardener and instructions regarding the amount to be added. Generally, polyester resin requires 1% to 2% of catalyst by volume—more to hasten the curing process, less to retard it. In hot weather the gelcoat (or resin) will require less hardener.

So what happens when the instructions say add the contents of the bottle of hardener to the can of gelcoat but you are only mixing 1/2 ounce? For larger amounts but less than a full can, you could use a proportional amount of catalyst; i.e., add 1/4 of the catalyst to 1/4 of the gelcoat, but when preparing small amounts, you should catalyze the resin by counting drops. If the hardener is not in a dropper bottle, you will need a small eyedropper. The number of drops in an ounce of catalyst will vary with its viscosity, but you will not be far off if you assume it to be about 400. That means to catalyze 1 ounce of gelcoat (at 1%) you would require about four drops of catalyst.

Back to our 1/2-ounce color test batch. Two drops of catalyst will kick off the curing process, but we want it to

go off more quickly, so let's double the catalyst amount to four drops. Stir it in thoroughly. It is more difficult to expose putty to the catalyst, so think purée and keep stirring until you are sure the two are evenly blended. The catalyst can darken the color but curing can lighten it, so dab a little of the colored and catalyzed gelcoat onto the waxed spot on the hull and let it harden.

Even if you are not color matching, you need to catalyze a measured test batch of gelcoat to "dial in" the amount of catalyst. Cure time is affected by temperature, light, and humidity. Watch the time and check your test dab every few minutes. You don't want it to go off—to begin to harden—in less than 30 minutes. If it does, you will need to reduce the amount of catalyst in your next mix. Hardening in about an hour is probably ideal, but a bit longer won't matter unless the waiting is holding you up. It is generally better to err on the side of too little hardener.

If the cured color of the test dab is not quite right, do it all again, making the necessary adjustment. A razor blade will take the test spot off the waxed hull. When you get the color match perfect (or run out of patience), write the final formula in your notebook. By now you should also know the best amount of catalyst for the current weather conditions.

A thin scratch will need to be opened with a rotary tool (Dremel) or simply by dragging the corner of a slotted screwdriver blade along its length. You only want to open it enough to allow you to get the putty into the bottom of the scratch and to bevel, or *chamfer*, the edges to give the putty a better surface for adhesion. If the gouge is already wide enough, just smooth and chamfer the edges. Clean the scratch thoroughly with a fresh rag dampened with acetone. Waxing the hull below the scratch will ease removing runs or drips.

Mix up enough putty to make all your repairs but no more than you can apply in 30 minutes. Be conscientious about stirring in the catalyst. Failing to fully distribute the catalyst will leave parts of your repair an uncured, sticky mess.

I tend to dab the putty into the scratch with a mixing stick to push it to the bottom and make sure I don't trap any air. Then I warp a small plastic spreader to make it slightly concave and drag it slowly over the scratch to smooth the surface, leaving a slight bulge. The putty is going to shrink when it cures and you want a little convexity to allow you to fair the surface. Clean up any putty that is not in the scratch.

If you are using air-inhibited gelcoat, this is when you seal it. Later we will coat a large repair with polyvinyl alcohol (PVA), a liquid that dries to a plastic film, but for small repairs a piece of plastic wrap

(Saran) or a section scissored from a ziptop freezer bag will do the job. Give the gelcoat time to begin to cure, then place the plastic over the repair. Tape the top edge to the hull, smooth the plastic onto the putty, then tape the bottom edge.

That's it. When the putty has cured, peel away the plastic (if you needed it) and sand the spot smooth as detailed previously. If your first repair attempt is a bit lumpy, you can cut it down with a finishing sander, but if you do this, you must keep the pressure very light or you will sand away the old gelcoat on either side of the repair. You will have better control block sanding with the narrow side of a 5-inch 1 × 2. Start with 120-grit dry paper and shave the repair flush. Switch to 220-grit wet-or dry wet, then 400-grit, 600-grit, and 1000-grit. Compound the area and polish it to a mirror finish. If you have done a reasonably good job of matching the color, the repair should be virtually undetectable.

REPAIRING DEEP GOUGES

Using gelcoat putty as the filler for deeper scratches can be less than satisfactory because the unreinforced resin is quite brittle. It is a better idea to do

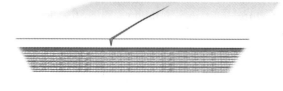
Gelcoat scratch.

Open into shallow V.
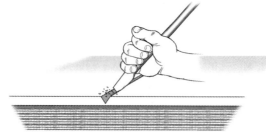

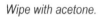
Wipe with acetone.
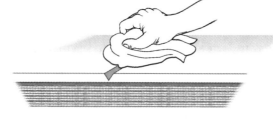

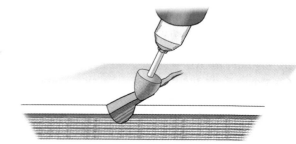
Gouge.

Fill, making the top slightly convex.

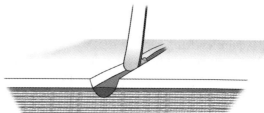
Chamfer the sides.

Seal with smooth plastic.
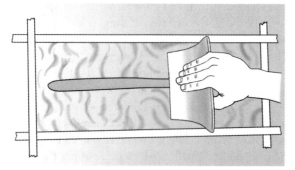

Fill to bottom of gelcoat.

Finish like scratch repair.

the repair in two steps. Strengthen a quantity of polyester resin by adding an equal amount, by volume, of chopped fiberglass. You can buy powder-like microfibers, or for a single small repair, you can make your own chopped glass by snipping the ends of a piece of glass cloth. Catalyze the resin, then mix in enough thickening agent to make a putty. Fill the gouge to the *bottom* of the old gelcoat. Do not cover with plastic. If you prefer, you can use polyester auto body putty (Bondo or the like) for this step.

When the filler reaches the gel state, tint a quantity of gelcoat paste or thickened gelcoat and fill the remaining depression, leaving a slight bulge. Seal with plastic if necessary. When it has cured, sand and polish to finish.

EPOXY

Despite its greater strength and better adhesion, epoxy is not a good choice when it will be coated with gelcoat. While epoxy adheres tenaciously to polyester resin, the reverse is not true. Gelcoat will not bond well to an underlayer of epoxy, and chemicals in the epoxy interfere with the cure of polyester. There are coupling agents that allow gelcoat to be applied over epoxy, but this is an unnecessary complication for the boatowner. If, however, your old gelcoat is beyond redemption, meaning that you intend to paint the surface after all blemishes are repaired, epoxy putty becomes the filler of choice.

A preprepared putty is the easiest to use, and you will be hard-pressed to find a proprietary product with a better reputation than Marine-Tex. This epoxy putty is not inexpensive but its versatility is legendary. I have been told that the gray is stronger than the white. It is also cheaper, but if you are on a "patch now, paint later" program, the white can be less obtrusive.

Buying epoxy resin rather than putty will likely be the wiser choice because of the resin's wider range of uses. You can thicken it into a putty by adding one or more available fillers; different fillers are used to give the epoxy various characteristics. Doing fiberglass layup with epoxy resin, whether as part of a repair or a new molding, delivers the strongest laminate. And epoxy is the adhesive you are likely to use for all gluing projects, including joinery.

You cannot adjust the cure time of epoxy by varying the amount of hardener as you can with polyester resin. Epoxy is a two-part mixture, and the parts must be combined in the specified ratio. You

For surfaces to be painted, repair deep gouges with a single application of thickened epoxy.

fill with epoxy putty

may have a choice of "slow" or "fast" hardeners to lengthen or shorten the cure time.

Almost everyone who maintains or refurbishes an old boat eventually buys epoxy by the gallon, along with dispensing pumps that measure out the resin and the hardener in the correct ratio. One pump of resin, one pump of hardener, stir vigorously for 60 seconds, and you are good to go. To make epoxy putty from epoxy resin you only need to mix in a filler. For gouge repair, the filler will be either milled fibers or colloidal silica. Stir the filler into the mixed epoxy a little at a time until the mix stiffens to peanut-butter-like consistency.

Filling a gouge with epoxy putty is not much different from filling it with polyester except that you will never need to seal the surface. The epoxy will cure in air. (Some epoxies will even cure underwater.) You also do not want the putty to bulge above the surface. There is no solvent evaporation with epoxy so it doesn't shrink in curing, and because it is harder than the surrounding gelcoat, any bulge will make it difficult to sand it flush. Draw your spreader over the repair a second time to make the repair as flush as possible.

A significant number of epoxy users become sensitized so that even the slightest future exposure results in skin rash. The inability to use epoxy is a major disadvantage for any old-boat owner, so always wear protective gloves. This and eye protection are the only real precautions for epoxy scratch repair, but when using epoxy in a confined space, ventilate well to avoid breathing the fumes.

CRACKED

You might think that repairing a crack is exactly the same as repairing a scratch. You might be wrong. It is important to understand what caused the crack before attempting any repair; otherwise the crack may return.

Cracks in the gelcoat are caused by movement. The flexible fiberglass laminates bend, but the unreinforced gelcoat is comparatively brittle, so it cracks. If the flexing is a one-time event—like the time our friend released the wrong halyard and his suspended wind generator crashed to the foredeck like a kamikaze helicopter—a surface repair is all that is required.

Often, however, cracks are not the result of a specific event but indicate some weakness in the construction. If cracks radiate out from beneath every stanchion base, there is an underlying problem. Parallel cracks along the corner where the foredeck turns up into the cabin trunk suggest flexing of the deck. Similar cracks around the perimeter of the cockpit sole point out another common problem area. A lasting repair can only be made by correcting the weakness. In the case of the stanchions, a larger backing plate might be an adequate solution, but in the other cases (actually in most cases), stress cracks can be repaired permanently only by stiffening the underlying laminate *before* executing cosmetic repair to the gelcoat. Once the cause has been eliminated, cracks *are* repaired like a scratch, by opening them and filling with thickened gelcoat.

CRAZING
Older boats may show *crazing*—tiny random cracks in the gelcoat—in the hull and the deck and from stem to stern. Often this condition is the result of good intentions gone wrong. The builder began the layup process with an extra-heavy layer of gelcoat and followed that with more laminates than were absolutely necessary. The extra laminates were a good thing (one of the attractions of older boats) but not so the thicker gelcoat, which just made the gelcoat less flexible. The unhappy result was a surface prone to crazing. Flexing was not strictly required; just the expansion and contraction of hot days and cool nights were sufficient, over time, to crack the gelcoat.

When the gelcoat is badly crazed, the only practical solution is painting. The preparation of a crazed surface for refinishing is detailed in Chapter 14. Less extensive crazing and cracking may be repaired like any other surface blemish, but the nature of a crack fosters the temptation to try to "paint" it out with gelcoat. Such a repair is unlikely to succeed because the gelcoat does not fill the crack, it just bridges it. You must open the crack to allow the gelcoat to penetrate and to provide more surface area for adequate adhesion. Beyond that, the permanence of the repair depends on correcting the weakness that caused the cracking.

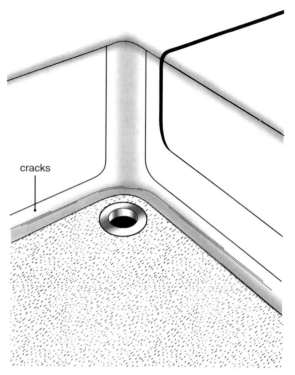

cracks

Parallel cracks where the cockpit sole turns up suggest hinging.

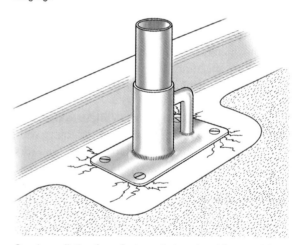

Cracks radiating from fastener holes signal the need for bigger backing plates.

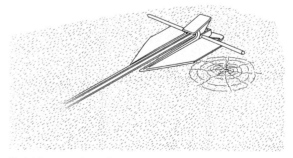

Point impact—here from the anchor stock—can crack the gelcoat in a starburst or bull's-eye pattern.

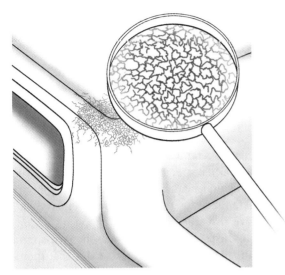

Crazing—also called alligatoring—typically stems from too-flexible laminate or too-thick gelcoat.

WEAK

In its most elementary form, strengthening involves adding laminates to the weak area. To do that, you need to be familiar with laying up fiberglass laminates. You could pick an inconspicuous spot inside the hull, someplace where you need extra laminates, and try your hand at fiberglass layup. But fiberglass work can be a sticky, gooey, messy proposition, prone to forgotten steps and incomplete preparation. If you stay away from the boat, you can practice layup technique virtually risk free until you master it.

FIBERGLASS MATERIALS

Fiberglass layup is layers of fiberglass material saturated with polyester (or epoxy) resin. Nothing more. The fiberglass material is exactly what it sounds like, a weave of glass fibers. For boat construction and repair, the glass comes in mat, roving, cloth, and stitched-together combinations of the three (see photos next page).

Chopped-Strand Mat

Chopped-strand mat looks like swept-up pieces of discarded thread. Irregular lengths of glass strands are combined randomly and glued together, not woven. Sometimes called CSM, the mat is sold from rolls like other fabrics. It comes in various weights, but always select $1^1/_2$-ounce mat unless you have a specific reason to do otherwise. Generally speaking, mat is the easiest fabric to shape, gives the best resin-to-glass ratio, yields the smoothest surface, is the most watertight, and is

the least subject to delamination. Unfortunately, the short fibers do not provide high tensile strength, which requires the continuous fibers of roving or cloth. Much standard CSM is incompatible with epoxy resin because of the binder that holds the strands together, but epoxy-compatible mat is available. If you will be using epoxy resin for your repair and you want to use mat, make sure it is the right type.

Roving

Rovings are loose bunches of parallel strands. Unwoven roving is a "fabric" made by laying flat rovings parallel and cross-stitching them together. The straight, continuous strands of unwoven roving add excellent strength but in only one direction; they add little strength perpendicular to the strands. This disadvantage is overcome through stitched-together "biaxial" or even "triaxial" composites or by simply laying alternating laminates crosswise.

The more common solution, the one used by most boatbuilders, is to use woven roving, in which the flat bundles of strands are loosely woven into a coarse, open weave fabric. Woven roving offers full strength in two directions and good strength in all directions.

Roving laminated to roving—whether woven or unwoven—is unacceptably easy to peel apart, but add a layer of chopped-strand mat between each layer of roving and the combination becomes highly resistant to separation. Do not miss the significance here. *In all fiberglass layup using polyester resin, at least every other layer should be chopped-strand mat.* I say "at least" because in some instances you may want to use more mat or just mat. Manufacturers have traditionally alternated the layers of mat with woven roving, and mat/roving composite fabrics are available to speed the process. However, for most of the fiberglass work an owner is likely to become involved in, fiberglass cloth will be a better material.

Fiberglass Cloth

Fiberglass cloth looks something like shiny canvas, but it's not as tightly woven and the thread is glass strands. Cloth is stronger for its weight than roving, yields a better glass-to-resin ratio, is less prone to pulling and unraveling in the laminating process, and looks nicer in the finished product. Epoxy laminations are often all cloth, the epoxy bond being strong enough to resist peeling.

Cloth is commonly available in weights from 2 to 20 ounces. That sounds heavy relative to $1^1/_2$-ounce mat, but don't be confused. Weight designations for

Mat.

Woven roving.

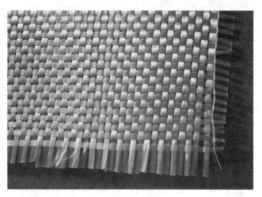

Cloth.

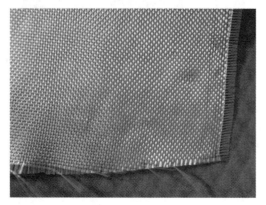

Fiberglass suppliers will carry only E-glass, with S glass being a special-order item. You are unlikely to have a need for S glass.

Other Materials

Unless you know what you're doing—and you won't learn it here—stay away from the "exotic" materials. These include polypropylene, xynole-polyester, Dynel, Kevlar, ceramic, carbon, and graphite. Each of these has specific strengths and weaknesses that you should fully understand before using them. None are essential to the restoration of an older fiberglass boat.

I have also failed to mention chopper-gun construction. Instead of wetting out chopped-strand mat, some manufacturers use a machine that sprays chopped-strand roving and polyester resin at the same time. Manufacturers usually claim that the gun gives them better control over the mix of glass and resin. Maybe so, but that is not the reason they are using a chopper gun. You get one gue$$. Chopper-gun layup goes very quickly, but unless the operator is very skillful and very attentive, the "perfect" mix will be thick in some places, not so thick in others. Chopper-gun construction does not enjoy an unsullied reputation.

LEARNING BY DOING

The best way to develop familiarity with hand layup is by doing it. Instead of working on the boat, we are going to lay up a small fiberglass part. Failures will not require any corrective action but may simply be tossed. The item illustrated is an instrument box. When instruments are installed in the aft end of the trunk, the rear of the instrument intrudes into the cabin. A fiberglass cover gives the installation a finished look.

I have selected a round instrument box because it provides an opportunity to deal with an array of difficulties that are likely to occur in other fiberglassing jobs. You may use the same technique to construct a square box or any shape that fits your need.

The list of materials you need is short:

- 1 quart polyester laminating (air-inhibited) resin
- 1 quart acetone
- 8 ounces PVA mold release
- Soft car wax
- 1 yard 1¹/₂-ounce chopped-strand mat
- 1 yard 10-ounce fiberglass cloth
- A few 1¹/₂-inch throwaway bristle brushes
- 1 Cool Whip tub or plastic refrigerator container (You'll also need a strawberry

mat are per *square foot*, while for cloth and roving they are per *square yard*. Leave the calculator in the drawer—1¹/₂-ounce mat weighs the same as 13¹/₂-ounce cloth. For any boat over 15 feet, there will be little if any fiberglass work that you cannot do with 1¹/₂-ounce mat and 10-ounce cloth. Be sure the cloth has been treated to remove manufacturing oils and waxes and that it is approved for the type of resin you are using. If you have a choice, buy it in 38-inch width.

E-Glass or S Glass

You may run across *E-glass* in the description of fiberglass fabrics. The "E" designation stands for *electrical grade*, and E-glass is the standard grade for boatbuilding and repair. S glass is *stronger* by about a third, but it costs up to nine times as much as E-glass.

shortcake; you can't just waste a whole tub full of Cool Whip!)
- 1 piece of thick cardboard (Foam-filled backer board is perfect.)
- A hot-glue gun or some adhesive caulk
- 1 canister of modeling clay
- A roll of waxed paper
- A package of throwaway plastic gloves

Note that this is far more resin and glass than you need but is probably the smallest practical amount you can purchase. Besides, if you do any other fiberglass work, these are the materials you will be using.

Building a Mold

First construct the mold. Cut the plastic tub to the appropriate depth, determined by the protrusion of the instrument being covered. Now cut two squares of the backer board 4 inches wider than the diameter of the tub. Invert the tub onto the center of each of the squares and trace around it. Carefully cut this circle from the center of one of the squares. On the other square, draw a second circle about $1/_8$ inch outside the first one and cut out this larger circle.

Place the tub top-down on a flat surface and drop the square with the smaller hole over it so that the square also lies on the flat surface. Join the two together with a bead of adhesive caulk and allow the adhesive to set. Hot-melt adhesive can speed the process.

Turn the mold over and center the square with the larger circle over the attached square and glue it in place. Now fill the step created by the two circles with modeling clay and shape it into a smooth radius. You should end up with a gentle curve between the vertical side of the tub and the horizontal surface of the cardboard. Some tubs have a radius at the bottom, but if you are using a container that has a sharp corner at the bottom, give it a radius with a fillet of clay. Run the edge of a coin around the fillet to get the radius uniform. We are relieving the corners because fiberglass cloth does not conform easily to sharp turns. (See illustrations pages 60–62.)

You now have a mold. Before you can use it, you need to coat it with wax to prevent the resin from adhering to it. Almost any soft wax will work, and four coats are not too many.

Cutting the Cloth

Next scissor the fiberglass to fit. A couple of layers of $1^1/_2$-ounce mat would be adequate for this particular part, but to learn more from the exercise, we are going to follow a four laminate schedule: two layers of mat, followed by a layer of 10-ounce cloth, and then another layer of mat. Now is a good time to get those gloves on.

Each layer will require three pieces of fabric: a circular piece 1 inch larger than the bottom diameter of the mold, a straight strip as wide as the mold is deep and $1/_2$ inch longer than the circumference, and a circular piece 2 inches wider in diameter than the top of the mold. Small notches around the edge of the bottom piece will allow the glass to turn up the sides more easily. Cut the center from the larger circular piece to form a ring $1^1/_2$ inches wide. Cut narrow, $1/_2$-inch notches into the inside edge of the ring at 1-inch intervals to allow the glass to turn down into the mold. Check the pieces for fit, then duplicate them twice from mat and once from cloth.

The Layup Process

Now paint the mold with the polyvinyl alcohol, a parting agent that will insure that the resin will not adhere to the mold. Let the PVA dry to a protective film. If you have gelcoat and want to use it, paint the inside of the mold and the flange with an even coat—not too heavily, about the thickness of six dollar bills. Let the gelcoat set before proceeding. It is not necessary to use gelcoat, and imperfections in the molded part will be easier to fair if the surface coat is paint.

Catalyze 2 or 3 ounces of resin in a paper or plastic cup and coat the surface of the mold or the solidified gelcoat with this resin. Lay the parts for the first two layers of mat on a piece of scrap cardboard and saturate them with catalyzed resin, using a brush to *gently* apply the resin. Scissoring the bristles of a throwaway brush to about half their original length gives you a better tool for applying resin to fiberglass. Properly saturated, the mat will be uniformly transparent. If you still see white strands, add more resin. When the pieces are wet through, pick up one of the strips and put it around the inside of the mold, overlapping the ends. Use the brush to smooth it into place. Next apply the circle to the bottom of the mold so that the notched perimeter turns up onto the strip already in place. Using the end of the brush, without adding any resin, stipple the mat into the corner and the two pieces together, working out any voids or bubbles. This is where you will really appreciate the shortened bristles.

Lay the saturated ring of mat on top of the mold and fold the inner edge down onto the strip. Smooth the ring and stipple the ring and the strip together. While the first layer is still wet, repeat the process with the second layer. If extra resin begins to puddle in the bottom of the mold, remove it with your brush.

Generally speaking it is a good idea to apply fiberglass two or three layers at a time. A single layer may generate insufficient exothermic heat to cure quickly, whereas too many layers may build up enough heat to "cook" the resin and weaken it. On a small part like this one, you could get away with doing all four laminates at once, but you are never wrong doing two at a time.

When the first two layers have gelled, mix up a new batch of resin. Paint the set surface with catalyzed resin, saturate the remaining pieces of cloth and mat, and repeat the steps just described. Apply the layer of cloth first. You will find that the cloth is a bit more difficult to work with, tending to wrinkle on anything but a flat surface, but a little patience will usually prevail.

After the last layer of mat, brushing on a small quantity of additional resin can give you a nicer finish. It is not important in this case, but it may be for modifications you may have in mind for your boat.

Because laminating resin is air-inhibited, the surface will remain tacky unless you seal it from the air. On a flat surface, a piece of plastic kitchen wrap will serve, but for a surface that is all curves and corners, a coat of PVA is a lot easier. Wait until the resin has started to kick (harden), then spritz or brush on a coat of PVA.

After the resin has hardened, simply pop it out of the mold. Now, while the laminate is still "green," is the best time to trim the flange to the size you want. You can snip off the excess without shattering the cut edge. Now drop the piece back into the mold and leave it for a couple of days to reach its full cure.

If the plastic tub had a dimple in its center, the instrument box will have the same feature. You can fill this and any other imperfections in the surface with polyester putty or thickened resin (or thickened gelcoat if the surface is gelcoat). First, though, wash the box with water to remove the PVA, then wipe it with toluene or acetone to remove wax residue. After the putty cures, sand the box and drill the mounting holes in the flange, along with any other holes required for the wires or cables that connect the instrument. Finish the cover with a couple of coats of paint.

That is all there is to laying up fiberglass. Don't try to make it more complicated than it is. If you had no problem with this exercise, you know all you need to know to handle 95% of the fiberglassing jobs you are likely to contemplate. With the additional step of constructing a mold, you can now also create, for example, a fiberglass dorade box, a taller lazarette hatch lid, or a seahood for the sliding companionway hatch.

If you don't know how the part might have looked because you can't get it out of the mold, if the brush is permanently attached because the resin kicked while you were still smoothing the glass, if the vertical pieces are bunched at the bottom like an old gym sock, if the "smooth" surface is more like a bad spike haircut, or if you had any other problems, try it again. Figure out what went wrong and correct it. The only expense will be the cost of a couple of brushes.

If you want to go for the advanced degree, hot-glue the bottom of the mold to the underside of a low table and wait until dark. Now crawl under the table and, by the light of a flashlight, lay up the instrument box in the inverted mold. (Hint: Let the saturated fiberglass get tacky before you put it into the mold.) This exercise will serve you well when you attempt to add laminates to a weak side deck or reinforce the cockpit sole.

1

Cut plastic tub to appropriate depth.

2

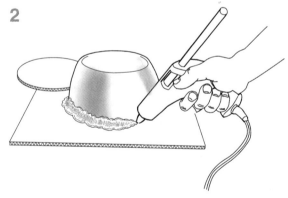

Make circular cutout in stiff cardboard, slip it over inverted tub, and glue in place.

3

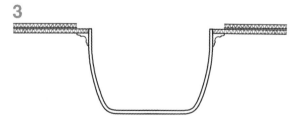

Glue second cardboard square with larger circular opening on top of first square.

4

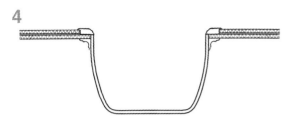

Fill step with modeling clay or other moldable substance to form a smooth radius.

5

Heavily coat mold with wax.

6

Coat waxed mold with PVA.

7

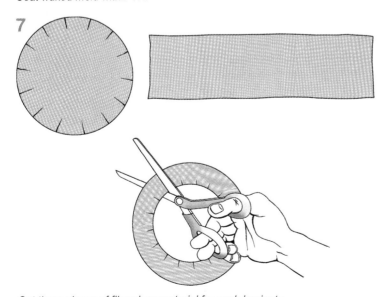

Cut three pieces of fiberglass material for each laminate.

8

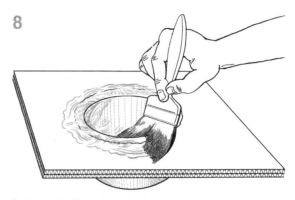

Paint mold with gelcoat (optional).

9

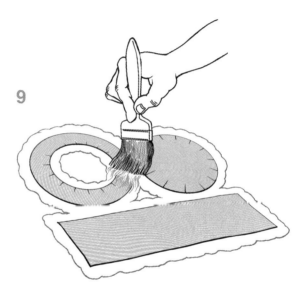

Saturate fiberglass pieces with resin.

10

Lay long strip around inside of mold, overlapping ends.

(Continued)

11

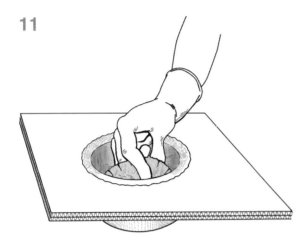

Put bottom piece in mold, overlapping strip.

12

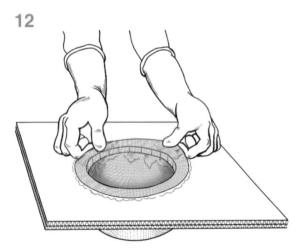

Put flange piece in place, overlapping strip.

13

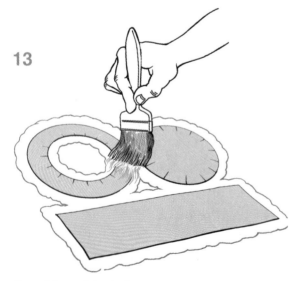

Repeat for each laminate.

14

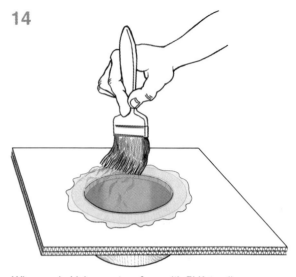

When resin kicks, coat surface with PVA to allow air-inhibited resin to cure tack free.

15

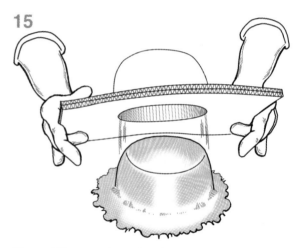

Flex mold to pop out cured part.

16

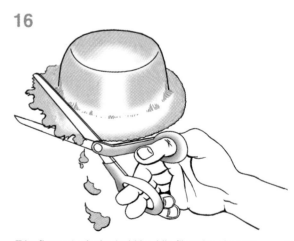

Trim flange to desired width while fiberglass is still "green."

ADDING STRENGTH

We started this exercise as a discussion of counteracting weakness. The truth is that a springy hull or deck may not be weak at all, but that bouncy feeling does not fill your heart with confidence. And even if you know that the laminate is plenty strong, flexing is murder on the gelcoat. More often than not it will be more stiffness you are after, not more strength. Stiffening comes next, but to increase strength, you add laminates. You should already be clear on laying up fiberglass, but there are some other considerations when you are adding laminates to a long-cured hull or deck.

First, resist the temptation to try to lay a single piece the size of a tablecloth. Anything bigger than a square yard will be more trouble than it's worth. If you are doing a big area, cut the fabric into several small pieces and overlap them a couple of inches.

You will probably be adding more than one layer and you want the edges to taper—and not just because it will look neater. An edge to your reinforcement will create a hard spot that can lead to a destructive flexing pattern. To achieve a taper, you will apply concentric layers, each an inch or so larger or smaller than the previous one.

Small First, Big First?

You may encounter conflicting guidance (including in the previous edition of this book) on whether to apply the largest piece first or the smallest piece first. Here is the definitive answer to that question: If you are using polyester or vinylester resin, put down the largest piece first. This will be mat, and it will give you the best bond to the underlying surface. If you put down the smallest piece first (also mat), the next layer (which will be cloth) will not have mat between it and the existing laminate beyond the perimeter of the underlying piece. This will make for a weaker bond.

If you are using epoxy resin, the order of the laminates does not actually make any difference in the strength of the repair for reinforcing or bonding. Small first tends to yield a neater appearance when the repair will not need to be faired, but when the larger layer drops over the edge of the one beneath, a void may be created, allowing the thinner epoxy resin to drain through. This can be avoided by laminating the large piece first. The relatively recent development of epoxy-compatible mat also makes a large-to-small schedule using mat between the cloth layers a possibility.

When filling a depression or doing reconstruction, the intuitive order is small to large, but the problem here is that we are trying to replace cutaway or ground-away fabric, and the new fabric, except for the bottom piece, will only attach to the original material at the perimeter—in effect, a butt joint. So the largest piece should go into the cavity first to maximize the surface area of the secondary bond. After that all subsequent laminates bond to this first piece and each other on a molecular level, but applying them in a large-to-small order still maximizes the mating surfaces.

What makes more difference than the size order of the laminates is the orientation of the fibers. With a patch or a reinforcement, you want to try to match the original laminates. In the hull of an old boat that generally means orienting woven fabrics with the strands horizontal and vertical, but you should verify this for the area of the hull you are repairing.

The first and alternating layers must be fiberglass mat when laminating with polyester resin.

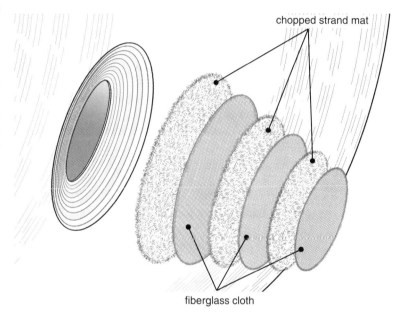

chopped strand mat

fiberglass cloth

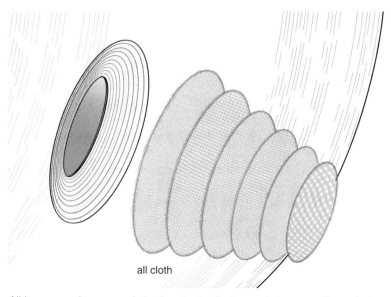

all cloth

All layers may be woven cloth when the laminating resin is epoxy. To maximize the area of the secondary bond apply the largest piece first.

Grinding Is Essential

Keep in mind that new laminates will not adhere to a fully cured surface unless you grind it. When you are using laminating resin you can add additional laminates without grinding because the resin *does not fully cure*. That is what air-inhibited means. But if the previous laminates were laid up with finishing resin, were sealed and allowed to cure, or are old, you must grind the surface before adding any laminates. To prevent a maddening itch, wear protective clothing (and don't wash it later with your BVDs). Protect your eyes with goggles and wear a dust mask—not one of the worthless throwaway kind, but a rubber one that seals against your face. Your lungs ought to be worth twenty bucks and change.

First wash the area to be reinforced with toluene or a proprietary dewaxing solvent. Next hold in place the largest of the laminates to be added and mark the outline. Chuck a sanding disk into your drill, stick on a 36-grit disk, and take the shine off everything inside that outline. Hold the grinder so that the dust is thrown away from you. A stiff wire wheel can do a better job on the bumpy surface of woven roving—often what you have on the inside of a hull—without removing as much material.

Wet Out in Place

With the surface ground and the precut pieces of glass laid out on scrap wood or cardboard, the process is exactly the one already described except that you don't need to wet out the fabric before you apply it unless you are working overhead. Rather, wet out the area inside the outline, then place the first layer of mat on the wet surface. This can be neater for big pieces if you roll the fabric around a tube or dowel, then unroll it onto the wet resin. You may need to use strips of tape at the top of the fabric to hold it in place on vertical surfaces until the resin becomes tacky.

If the area being reinforced is large, you will work faster if you pour your resin into a paint tray and use a foam roller instead of a brush to saturate the fiberglass. White fabric means you need more resin. Give the resin an opportunity to flow around the fibers before working it too much, then use the roller or a plastic spreader to compress the fabric and pick up excess resin. If you will be doing much laminating, buy a grooved roller. This does a better job of forcing trapped air out of the laminate. For small areas and for working the laminate into corners, stipple with a shortened throwaway brush.

If you are adding more than three laminates, apply them two at a time and allow the resin to kick before proceeding. Alternate materials, always starting with a layer of mat and finishing with a layer of cloth. If you are using epoxy resin, you can skip the mat, but you will need to start the layup with a base of thickened epoxy. A first and alternating layers of mat are essential with polyester. A combined layer of $1\frac{1}{2}$-ounce mat and 10-ounce cloth adds about $\frac{1}{10}$ inch to the thickness and about 10 ounces per square foot in weight. Remember that when using air-inhibited polyester you must seal the final laminate with a coat of PVA or with plastic film pressed in place and taped around the edges for the resin to cure tack free.

HAT-SHAPED STIFFENERS

When it is stiffness you're after, additional laminates are normally not the best way to achieve it. Reinforcing members—ribs and stringers—add more stiffness with less weight. The ease of flexing a wooden yardstick one way and the difficulty of flexing it the other illustrates the concept of stiffening members. If we put the edge of the yardstick against springy laminate and fiberglass it in place, we will make the laminate near the reinforcement rigid. We could then extract the yardstick because the fiberglass molded with a hollow in the middle—like a hat—would provide the stiffness alone. Because of this, hat-shaped reinforcements are often formed over foam or even cardboard instead of wood. To stiffen a larger area, attach more than one reinforcing member.

What you use as a form for the fiberglass hat you are going to construct is up to you. Possibilities include narrow strips of plywood, half-round molding, split cardboard tubing, V-folded corrugated pasteboard, split vinyl hose, plastic pipe, and strips of rigid foam.

I have come to prefer epoxy for laminating add-on stiffeners because of the resin's superior adhesion, which can be tested in an impact. However, let's at least make an effort to bring some truth to the issue of epoxy versus polyester. In honest-to-god, let's-glue-it-together-then-rip-it-apart lab tests, a polyester bond averaged around 70% of the strength of the original fiberglass laminate using the same resin. Epoxy failed at a little above 80%. That makes an epoxy bond *to fiberglass* about 15% stronger—not to be sneezed at but probably substantially less than you expected. The point of this is that polyester resin has been used to make successful boat repairs for half a century, and if for budget or comfort reasons, you want to use polyester, you will not be cheaping your way to a watery grave. For bonding to materials other than glass-reinforced polyester, however, polyester resin does not get such high marks.

Polyester requires a first layer and then alternating layers of chopped-strand mat, but if you use epoxy, use all cloth. It will be stronger, neater in appearance, and require less resin, but on a textured surface you must always put down a base of thickened resin to create a

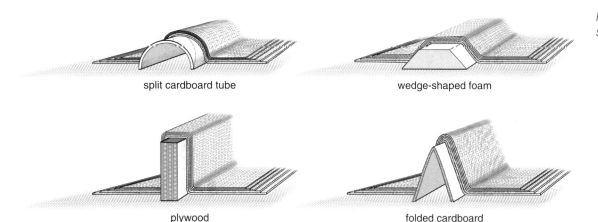

split cardboard tube   wedge-shaped foam

plywood   folded cardboard

solid bond. Cut the first strip of fabric as long as the reinforcement and wide enough to cover the form and extend out on both sides about 3½ inches. Cut three more strips, each about ¾ inch narrower and shorter than the one before. Four laminates will make a sturdy stiffener regardless of the composition of the form. If the form is wood or some other inflexible material, sand a taper on the bottom at the ends to avoid a hard spot.

Hold the form in place and mark the old fiberglass 4 inches from either side of the form. Wipe inside the lines with acetone or lacquer thinner (toluene) to remove the old sealing wax from the raw fiberglass, then grind the outlined area with a 36-grit disk or a stiff wire wheel. Put the form back in place and tack it there with hot glue or quick-setting epoxy. Paint both the form and the sanded surface with mixed epoxy resin, then let this kick. Thicken a fresh batch of epoxy with colloidal silica to a mayonnaise-like consistency; spread this over the still-tacky first coat, putting extra putty at the stiffener-laminate interface to form a fillet. Carefully center the largest strip of cloth over the form and push it down into the resin. The fabric should stay in place unless you are working overhead. Use a shortened paintbrush and a plastic spreader to embed the cloth in the thickened epoxy and smooth it against both the form and the laminate.

Mix a new batch of epoxy and saturate any areas of the first cloth layer that did not fully saturate from beneath. Center the next layer of cloth and smooth it into place. Because the span over the form increases with each laminate, the edges of subsequent layers should step back about ½ inch each. This avoids the hard spot a four-laminate-thick edge would cause. Wet out the cloth and use a plastic spreader to compress and smooth it. Apply the next two laminates in the same manner.

Doing four laminates in a single layup should not present any problem with overheating the resin, but if the stiffener is long, the open time may be inadequate, meaning that the epoxy will start to gel in the container before you have time to saturate all the laminates. The solution is to use small batches of epoxy, making up a new batch as you run out. Applied resin will be slower to cure because the generated heat is not as concentrated, so you will have no problem with a continuous layup using more than one batch of epoxy.

If the fabric fails to lie tightly against the underlying surface, epoxy resin can sometimes be too thin for the weave to retain, resulting in a condition known as *drain out*. The solution is to thicken the resin to a ketchup-like consistency using milled fibers or colloidal silica. The filler will not interfere with the resin wetting out the fabric but it will help hold the resin in place until it gels.

Finish the repair by painting on a couple of smoothing coats of resin, each applied after the previous application has stiffened.

ATTACHING MOUNTING BLOCKS

You use the same layup technique to attach other things to the hull. Say you want to install a deck-wash pump and the spot where you want to locate it is against the hull. In the age of wooden construction, boats had plenty of ribs and stringers that could be drilled for the mounting screws. But where do you drill the mounting holes when the hull is fiberglass? Where you *don't* drill them is directly into the hull. The correct way is to bond a wood block to the hull and mount the pump to the block.

You can use any kind of wood, but I like white oak because it holds a screw well and resists rot. Shape the block to fit the contour of the hull (see Chapter 10). You could simply grind the hull and stick the block down with thickened epoxy or 3M 5200 adhesive sealant, but aside from the glaring lack of elegance, the wood may eventually peel free. Laminating the block to the hull makes it part of the structure of the boat.

Because you are gluing the wood block to the hull and essentially sheathing it, epoxy resin is the better choice for this job. This is also a good project to give you additional practice at thickening epoxy resin to enable it to perform tasks plain resin cannot. The filler to use for bonding is colloidal silica. It is a good idea to keep a supply of this versatile powder next to your containers of epoxy. Also, because you are using epoxy, you will use cloth only in any weight between 6 and 10 ounces.

Dewax then grind an area 3 inches larger than the block in each direction. Also sand the block to enhance adhesion. If you did not round off the top edges when you shaped the block, do that now so the cloth will maintain contact with the wood when it drapes over the edge. Cut a piece of cloth large enough to contour over the block and extend 3 inches out onto the hull on all sides. Cut a square out of each corner so the material will, in effect, strap the block down in both directions. Cut a second piece of cloth to the same shape, but 1 inch narrower and shorter.

Half Pumps

Position the block and mark the perimeter with a pencil. Mix a small amount of epoxy. It is worth mentioning that a full pump of epoxy is often way too much for a single small glue job. At $100 a gallon, this is not a product you want to waste. I keep a supply of clear plastic, 1-ounce graduated measuring cups, which allows me to accurately mix as little as 6 cc of resin. More often, however, I use a half pump. To get the right mix, I first measure the amount of resin dispensed by a full pump. Then I begin a second pump into an empty measuring cup, stopping when dispensed resin is half the full pump amount and drawing a marker line around the pump tube where it enters the pump body. I make the same measurement for the hardener. With the pump tubes so marked, it is a simple matter to dispense a half measure of both components.

Seal the End Grain

Wet both the bottom of the block and the hull inside the penciled perimeter with the mixed resin. Saturating all sides to completely seal wood components you add to your old boat will give them immortality. This should become second nature when doing repairs and enhancements. End grain is particularly susceptible to damage from moisture, so give it a thorough resin coating. While you can hold the end-grain ends of the block horizontal is the best time to get maximum penetration.

Now thicken the epoxy still in the cup to a peanut-butter-like consistency with colloidal silica and spread this on the bottom of the block. Put the block

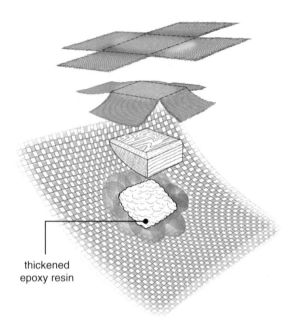

thickened epoxy resin

Capturing mounting blocks within encapsulating fiberglass assures permanence.

in place and twist it back and forth slightly to distribute the thickened resin as you apply pressure. Putty will squeeze out all around the perimeter. Holding the block in place, use the rounded end of a mixing stick to create a smooth fillet—or radius—between the edge of the block and the hull. You may have to move and add to the putty to get a smooth fillet all the way around the block. This fillet will support the fiberglass cloth, which you have already seen or will soon learn does not like sharp corners. Tape, brace, or hold the block in place long enough for the epoxy to grab.

Mix a second batch of epoxy, thickening it slightly to ketchup consistency. Wet out the surface of the block and the sanded area of the hull. Carefully position the smaller of the two pieces of cloth over the block and smooth it into position with a plastic spreader, pushing the cloth into the filleted corners where the block meets the hull. Saturate this layer, then apply and saturate the second layer. Note that because you are laminating with thickened epoxy, you are putting the largest piece on last for a more attractive finished look. To do this job with polyester resin, you would set the block on a saturated mat pad, with the first fabric layer also mat, followed by a slightly smaller cloth layer.

When the resin has cured, drill through the laminates into the block and mount the pump.

TABBING

In boats built with plywood interiors, bulkheads, furniture, dividers, and shelves are attached to a fiberglass hull in *almost* the same manner. Successive strips of mat and cloth are laid L-shaped along the joint, the widest extending out onto the hull several inches and up onto the part a similar distance. This is called *tabbing*. In boats manufactured with an interior pan or hull liner, the furniture is part of the mold and the bulkheads may bolt to molded flanges, but the liner itself and all components behind the liner will be tabbed to the hull.

For components you will tab or retab to the hull, fiberglass tapes with selvaged edges are available in a variety of widths specifically for this use, or you can cut cloth into strips of the width you need. The number of layers depends on the strength required. Two may be adequate to anchor a locker divider, but for a major bulkhead, six on each side will not be too many. A tabbed component can act like a pry bar to peel single-side tabbing. Tabbing both sides prevents this. To accommodate the curvature of the hull and make the strips lie smoothly, you may have to notch the fabric as you did for the instrument box.

Tabbing differs from the way we attached the mounting block in that the fiberglass does not encapsulate the member, but rather adheres to it. This is an important distinction. The bond between laminates of fiberglass is—for all practical purposes—permanent, but the bond between fiberglass and wood most assuredly is not. Wood shrinks and swells with changes in humidity, while the fiberglass is relatively unaffected. Release is inevitable. Nevertheless, tabbing is the standard way of mounting parts to a fiberglass hull. Done carefully a tabbed joint can last a long time, but before you offer your old boat as an example of just how long, take a flexible, thin-blade knife and see if you can run the blade between the fiberglass tabbing and the bulkheads. Don't blanch if you discover a bulkhead that is no longer attached.

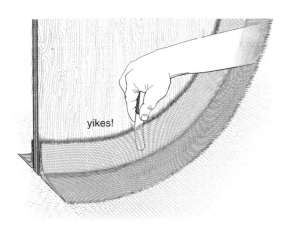

Tabbing done with polyester resin often separates from the wood surface of a bulkhead.

Reattaching Loose Tabbing

When the tabbing has released, there are two good ways to fix it. The most obvious is to grind away the old tabbing and lay up new fiberglass along the joint, as though you were tabbing the piece in place for the first time. The alternative is to reattach the bulkhead mechanically. Typically the tabbing has released from the plywood bulkhead but the leg on the hull is still firmly attached. In this case, an effective repair can be made by prying the gap open a bit and filling it with a polyurethane adhesive (3M 5200), then fastening the flap to the wood with a staggered row of screws. This is a strong, permanent repair.

If you want to retab the piece or tab a new part to the hull, proper technique will give the joint a longer life. Be sure you grind fiberglass surfaces well. If the part being attached is covered with plastic laminate, you must grind that completely away where the tabbing will attach. Paint or any other covering must likewise be removed. Even raw plywood needs to be coarsely sanded to clean and roughen the surface. Use only epoxy resin for tabbing. The bond between polyester and wood has a very short life, which is why you are retabbing. Even some boat manufacturers have finally abandoned polyester for this function.

Fillet corners where the surfaces intersect. For new attachments, a better solution than a putty fillet is a tent-shaped pad (with the top sliced off to the width of the bulkhead) of polyurethane foam *between* the part and the hull. Besides providing the desired fillet, the foam prevents the joint from causing a hard spot in the hull.

Permanent Tabbing

To make the attachment truly permanent, you need to take adhesion to wood out of the equation. For a new bulkhead, you can do this by *slotting*. Drill two $3/_8$-inch holes $3^1/_4$ inches apart and 1 inch from the edge of the bulkhead. With a saber saw, make two straight cuts between the two holes to create a $3/_8$-inch slot. Round the bottom edges of the slot with a router or sandpaper. Cut similar slots every 6 or 8 inches along the edge to be attached. Prepare all surfaces to be bonded. (See illustrations next page.)

Cut a series of 3-inch-wide fiberglass tape or cloth strips. With the slot 1 inch above the edge, the *shortest* tabbing strip should be 6 inches plus the width of the bulkhead. This allows the tabbing to extend out 2 inches. Prior layers should be 1 inch longer, giving a $1/_2$-inch stagger.

Wet out the bottom of the slot, the sides of the bulkhead beneath it, and the hull to a distance determined by how many laminates you intend to apply. Let this kick, then coat it with a bed of mayonnaise-consistency epoxy, creating a fillet in the process (if you have not incorporated a foam spacer). Feed your longest strip of cloth through the slot and press it into the thickened epoxy. Add and wet out the additional layers one at a time. A cardboard shield can make it easier to feed subsequent strips through the slot. When you are finished with the slots, tab the space between the slots in the usual manner, with the same number of laminates. Finish the joint neatly with a final laminate covering both the slotted and unslotted tabbing.

For existing bulkheads, you can achieve a similar result by drilling holes through the bulkhead along the tabbed edge and threading bundles of roving—loose fiberglass strands—through the holes. Spread and smooth these down onto the hull. When you capture them with your regular tabbing, they will mechanically fasten the bulkhead.

Tabbing through slots in the bulkhead provides a permanent attachment.

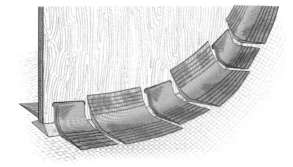

Tabbing normally between slots adds rigidity and provides a smooth base for the finish layer.

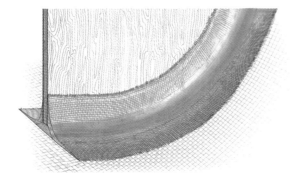

Covering tape gives a neat appearance.

Fiberglass strands passing through drilled holes, then captured beneath the regular tabbing, mechanically attach the bulkhead to the hull.

BLISTERED

By and large, boatowners suffer more from the discovery of gelcoat blisters than the boat does. Here is some advice: *GET OVER IT.* Surveys suggest that your old boat has about a 1 in 4 chance of developing gelcoat blisters. Unless the entire bottom takes on a goose-flesh appearance, gelcoat blisters are likely more of a cosmetic concern than a structural one.

Gelcoat, it turns out, is not waterproof. It is not as porous as, say, cardboard, but leave one side submerged for a long time and a few intrepid water molecules, attracted by a siren song from water-soluble chemicals on the other side, find their way through. This wouldn't be a problem if the water could drain back out, but it combines with the attracting chemicals into larger molecules that cannot pass through the exit. Meanwhile more water is crowding into the same space and pairing off. Pressure builds, pushing the gelcoat into a dome. Worse still, the dissolved chemicals are often acidic and, over time, attack the laminate.

The causes of blistering are legion, but the main ones are a variety of poor layup practices that result in a weak gelcoat or skin-coat bond and leave behind unbound chemicals. For an old boat this is only of academic interest anyway. If you have blisters, the real issue is what to do about them. Here is what you don't do. Don't immediately strip off all the old gelcoat no matter what your boatyard manager tells you.

If you discover blisters on your old boat, take a deep breath. Your boat is not in danger of sinking or dissolving. That doesn't mean you can ignore them, but blisters develop slowly, so you have lots of time to contemplate your alternatives. If they are *gelcoat* blisters, meaning they do not involve the laminate, just fill them. Even with the laminate involved, filling is still the first choice if you would characterize the number of blisters as "not too many." Only if you have "lots" of deep blisters or thousands of shallow ones does stripping become a consideration. Even then you should proceed with caution.

GELCOAT BLISTERS

The usual repair starts with cutting open the top of the blister with a chisel or a rotary tool. Blisters can be full of acidic liquid under champagne-bottle pressure, so wear goggles. Open the blister completely and flush out the liquid with a strong blast from a water hose. Take the time to look closely at each blister. The exposed laminate should look dark and translucent when it is wet. White fibers tell you the laminate is affected. While you wait for the hull and ground to dry, use a plastic mallet or the end of a screwdriver handle to tap the hull all around each blister. Sound laminate gives a sharp report. A dull or flat sound indicates additional delamination, meaning that the blister extends beyond the rotunda.

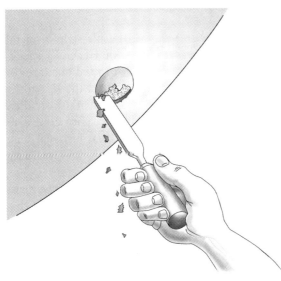

Open blisters with a sharp tool.

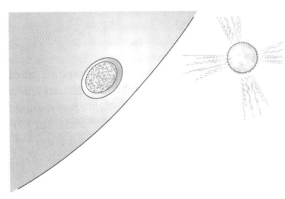

Grind each blister into a shallow dimple. Scrub and allow to dry.

When you can safely operate a power tool without risk of electrocution, run some kind of cutter around the perimeter of the blister to chamfer the edge. The best tool for this is a rotary tool with a grinding or sanding bit because you will grind away less of your boat and throw less dust into the air. On 20-mil gelcoat, the necessary 12-to-1 chamfer will be about $1/4$ inch wide. Grind the bottom of the blister as well, but only enough to clean it or remove damaged laminate. Also open any voids you found with your mallet.

A prepared blister will be a smooth dimple if small, a saucer if large. When you finish grinding, mix $1/4$ cup of trisodium phosphate (TSP, available from most hardware stores) into a gallon of water—hot, if you can manage it—and scrub the dimples and saucers squeaky clean using a stiff brush. Rinse thoroughly and let everything dry for at least two days; longer is better. If you dry-store your boat for the winter, grind and scrub blisters at haulout, but don't fill them until spring.

Filling

Because the primary factors in blister formation are permeability and poor bonding, filling blister cavities with polyester resin is just asking for more of the same. You need the much better secondary bond capability of epoxy, which fortunately also happens to be less permeable. So always do your blister repairs with epoxy.

If the boat has been sitting awhile, scrub the prepared cavities again to remove pollutants and any solutes that may have leached out. This will not affect the moisture content of the laminate. Wipe the blisters dry with clean paper towels. Mix a small quantity of epoxy, and using a shortened, narrow, throwaway paintbrush or an acid brush, wet out each cavity. If you follow immediately with your filler, it will have a tendency to skid out of the cavity, so allow this initial coating to begin to gel. If you have a lot of blisters, start with just 15 or 20 to get a feel for wait times and the pot life for your epoxy.

Thicken a small amount of fresh epoxy to a peanut-butter consistency. Although light fillers are easier to fair, I dislike hollow or absorbent fillers for underwater use. Thicken the epoxy with colloidal silica. Fill each cavity completely and fair it with a plastic spreader. Silica-thickened epoxy is difficult to sand, so take extra time to fair the filler as smoothly as possible while it is still wet. (See illustrations next page.)

If you have just a few large gelcoat blisters, you might want to try less destructive rebonding rather than filling. Essentially you drill a half dozen or so $3/16$-inch holes into the blister dome to

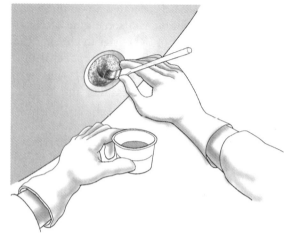

Wet each dry cavity with unthickened epoxy.

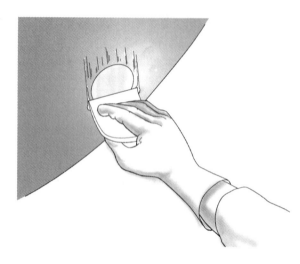

Fill with thickened epoxy.

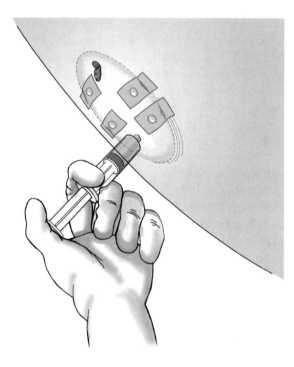

For an isolated large blister, rebonding can be a less destructive alternative.

drain and dry it. Fill an epoxy syringe with acetone or denatured alcohol and inject this into the lowest hole until it flows out of all the others. Let the acetone drain out; it will bring the remaining moisture and some contaminants with it. Wait a few days (or a winter) for the cavity to dry and the dome to collapse. Tape all the holes closed except the lowest and the highest. Inject epoxy resin slowly into the lowest hole until it runs out the highest, then tape both closed.

DEEP BLISTERS

Sometimes the weak bond is behind the first laminate and that is where the blister forms. Or the acidic solution in blisters left unattended begins to eat into the laminate. If you find damaged laminate when you open a blister, you have to grind back to sound material. In such cases, you need to replace the excavated fabric. The best material for this is cloth with a weight between 6 and 10 ounces. Do not use mat.

Span the cavity with a flexible strip of metal or plastic and measure its depth. Generally speaking, for every $1/64$ inch, you will need one layer of 9-ounce cloth. Cut the first piece to the size of the perimeter and the others incrementally smaller. For expediency we will fill the cavity almost to the top with laminate rather than just replacing the damaged laminate and filling the remaining depression with putty.

Wet the cavity with unthickened epoxy, making sure you saturate exposed fibers, then let this initial coat kick. Thicken a new batch of epoxy to a ketchup consistency with colloidal silica and coat the cavity with this mix. Push the largest piece of cloth into the epoxy, taking care to orient the threads vertically and horizontally. Wet out the cloth with the thickened epoxy. Apply the next piece, wet it out, and so on—wet-on-wet—until the cavity is almost full.

Release Fabric

Here you can make use of a really cool product called Peel Ply or release fabric, available from your epoxy supplier. Cut a piece an inch or two larger than the patch and press it against the top laminate. The fabric allows you to smooth and compress the laminate with a plastic spreader without shifting the fiberglass. A piece of plastic cut from a kitchen zipper bag will do the same job, but Peel Ply is better because it lets the air and the excess epoxy pass up through the fabric, where the air escapes and you can pick up the epoxy with your spreader. Leave the release fabric in place until the patch reaches full cure. The fabric does not bond to the epoxy and will lift off the waxy amine surface blush when you peel it away. Epoxy cured under release fabric will not need to be scrubbed with water.

If you expect to do a lot of epoxy repair work, here is a little money-saving tip. Peel Ply is nothing more than 100% Dacron cloth, sold at all fabric stores as lining or shower-curtain fabric. It must be 100% Dacron and have a smooth weave. Expect the cost to be one-fifth or less than the same fabric packaged for boat use.

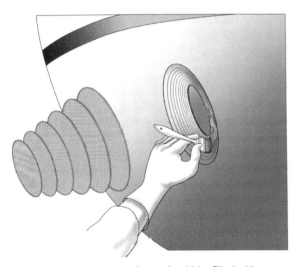

A blister involving the laminate should be filled with new fabric.

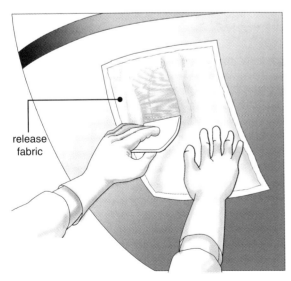

release fabric

Release fabric allows you to smooth and compress the repair laminates.

You will need to sand the repair, then fill and fair irregularities with epoxy thickened to a peanut-butter consistency with colloidal silica (for underwater fairing). Again, because the silica resists sanding, take extra time with your plastic spreader to level the putty. Finish with two coats of unthickened epoxy applied as the prior application kicks. Covering the final coat with release fabric will give you the smoothest finish and allow you to omit the scrubbing step. Otherwise wash the cured epoxy with water and a scrubber pad to remove the surface amine. Light block sanding should be all that is required to ready a repair for a barrier coat or bottom paint.

POX

Boat pox is a much more serious condition, related to the occasional blister like acne to the occasional pimple. If the bottom of your boat is covered with blisters, filling them probably won't cure the problem. Pox is a systemic condition probably indicating that the hull is saturated. Now you *are* looking at the need to strip the gelcoat because the laminate probably will not dry out otherwise.

"Probably"?

Here's the thing. Stripping the gelcoat and replacing it with something else is a big and difficult or big and expensive job, depending on whether you do it or have it done. And your new bottom is never going to have the perfect shape that came out of the mold. So what choice do you have?

Maybe none, but if 20% of the gelcoat is blistered, 80% isn't, which represents a solid base for maintaining the original shape of the boat if you don't strip it off. No yard is going to open and patch a thousand blisters, but you can. A day or two with a rotary tool can open a lot of blisters. Do this at the fall haulout, then in the spring, seal 6-inch squares of clear freezer bag over a few of the cavities with electrical tape all around and check them on sunny days. If the laminate is wet, moisture will condense on the inside of the plastic. If the plastic stays dry or almost dry, so is the laminate. In this case there is no reason to suspect that the laminate beneath the intact gelcoat will be wetter, but grind open a couple of spots and put plastic over them if it reassures you.

If the laminate is wet, leaving it wet risks hydrolysis which can destroy the integrity of the hull. Stripping the gelcoat (but never, ever by sandblasting!) and actively drying the laminate is ultimately your only option. But if the laminate is dry, you already know what to do; fill those thousand cavities with epoxy. In the case of a pox repair, an additional step is required.

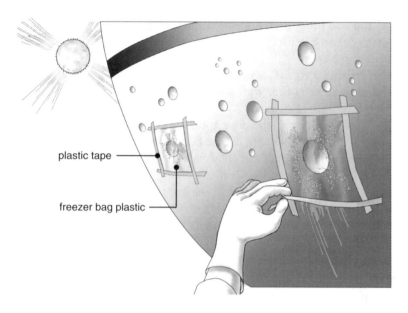

plastic tape

freezer bag plastic

Wet laminate will cause water condensation on the underside of the plastic on sunny days.

BARRIER COAT

At the time the previous edition of this book was written, the epoxy barrier coatings being routinely applied were no more effective at preventing osmosis than three coats of enamel, and they added to the problem when blisters eventually formed. Since then more effective protocols have emerged. Professionals often employ vinylester, either as a skin coat behind the gelcoat in new boat construction or as the laminating resin beneath an epoxy surface coat on a stripped boat. Vinylester needs to be at least 80 mils thick—about the thickness of 40 pages of this book—which is why it is used for laminating rather than as a surface coat. It also requires postcure, which means baking at some elevated temperature for up to four days. Amateur use of vinylester for barrier coating is a bad idea.

For the do-it-yourselfer, the only viable barrier coat is epoxy—either normal West System or System Three (or other) resin, or a proprietary epoxy barrier coat product such as Interprotect 2000E. The only two requirements to get good results are adequate surface preparation and adequate dry film thickness (DFT). Prep consists of scrubbing away surface amine from epoxy repairs, then dewaxing and sanding the entire hull and masking the waterline. Adequate DFT means six to eight coats depending on the product used.

If you choose a proprietary barrier coating, follow the manufacturer's instructions. To barrier coat with epoxy resin, you simply roll on coat after coat with a foam roller, applying the new one as soon as the prior one becomes tacky. An epoxy barrier coat should have a minimum DFT of 20 mils. As a rule you can apply around 8 ounces of epoxy at a time if

you pour the mix immediately into a paint tray. This spreads the epoxy, reducing exothermic heating and lengthening the pot life. All coats should be applied on the same day, which typically translates into coating just one side (maybe less) of the boat at a time. Check your starting point before each additional mix of epoxy. As soon as the initial application is firmly tacky, it is time to stop expanding the first coat and start the second coat.

Roll the epoxy out to a thin film. The enemy here is trapped bubbles, and the thinner the film, the easier it releases air. The first coat should be squeegeed firmly with a plastic spreader held nearly parallel to the surface to force the resin into the pores and pinholes of the sanded gelcoat. After that each coat should be rolled on, then "tipped" with a foam-roller-cover squeegee. This is a tool you make yourself by cutting a 7-inch foam roller in half, then slicing the half lengthwise into thirds. With a notched stick as a handle, a $1/3$ section of roller becomes the perfect tool to squeeze bubbles from epoxy. Having a second person tipping while you're applying the epoxy makes the application go faster. Tip each coat perpendicular to the way

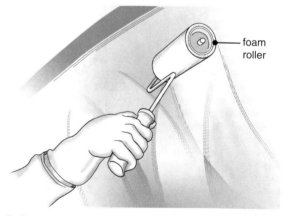

foam roller

Roll epoxy out to a thin film.

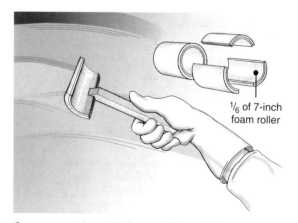

$1/6$ of 7-inch foam roller

Squeegee each coat to force out trapped air.

you tipped the previous one. You will need to change roller covers and tipping squeegees often as the epoxy in them begins to kick. Anticipate needing a fresh cover and squeegee at least every 15 linear feet of film application so be sure you have an adequate supply on hand.

There are barrier coat additives that can be mixed into the epoxy after the initial coat. I remain skeptical about whether these improve the performance of the coating but they do give the epoxy a tint, which makes it much easier to see what you're doing.

When you calculate that the coating is 20 mils thick, apply one more coat to make sure. If you plan to take this boat to the tropics, add two coats. Warm water will test a 10-coat application. Do not expect a barrier coat to last forever. Even epoxy is permeable, but if you apply the barrier adequately and carefully, you should be blister free for at least a decade.

Come back on day two and do the other side of the hull. Where the new application overlaps the previous one, wash and sand the overlap area first.

Should you barrier coat an old boat that does not have blisters? Not unless you plan to change the way you use it. It is simply a case of "if it ain't broke, don't fix it."

DELAMINATED

The separation of the layers of a fiberglass laminate generally stems from one of three conditions: overbending of the laminate, water penetration, or poor construction. Overbending, usually related to impact, requires the laminates to slide over one another (flex a paperback book sharply to get the idea), causing them to sheer apart. Water penetration is most destructive when the laminate includes an absorbent core—plywood or balsa, for example—but we have already seen that water also may combine with unbound chemicals in the laminate to form an acidic solution that attacks the resin. And if the laminates were not saturated thoroughly or compacted properly in the layup process, the bond between them may be fragile rather than robust.

How do you know you have internal delamination? The two places you are most likely to encounter it are in the deck and behind severe hull blisters. In the first case, you will often hear it as a crackle underfoot. In the second, you will see it when you open a blister. If you suspect delamination elsewhere—in a dent or soft spot or at the point of an impact—you can confirm or refute your suspicions by tapping the area with a light plastic mallet. Intact laminate sounds sharp; delamination sounds flat or dull.

RESIN INJECTION

Occasionally—maybe *rarely* is more accurate—you can repair delamination by just injecting resin into the void. This requires boring two holes into the void, one to let the resin in, the other to let the air out. If the void is in the hull, you may be able to drill the holes from the inside, leaving the gelcoat unmarred. For delamination in the deck, the holes must be bored from the top surface. Resin is squirted into one hole with an epoxy syringe (also available from your resin supplier) until it flows out of the other one. Simple.

Except that we already know that new resin does not adhere well to a cured surface, which is what we have inside the void, and grinding is obviously out of the question. Syrupy resin is also prone to trapping air rather than displacing it, particularly if the void has an irregular shape. These pockets will remain delaminated. Moisture inside the void will defeat injection entirely.

We can improve our chances of success by using epoxy resin instead of polyester. The epoxy will get a more tenacious grip on the unsanded surfaces inside the void and will be less affected by moisture. Injecting the resin from the lowest spot in the void, like filling an outboard gearbox, also helps. An irregular void will benefit from additional vent holes. Clamping with weights, bracing, or screws into the repair area will usually be necessary.

Where moisture has penetrated the void, it must be removed if the repair is to succeed. For delamination between layers of fiberglass, flushing the void with acetone can dry out the cavity sufficiently for the resin to adhere, but where wet core is involved, this is a losing proposition.

DELAMINATED CORE

Delamination of wood-cored decks is epidemic among old boats, which should not surprise anyone. Any bond between wood and polyester resin is conditional at best. If the core remains hermetically sealed, the bond can be amazingly durable, but allow moisture to reach the core and separation is sure to follow. How does water get into the core? Every cut or drilled hole in the deck is a potential spigot—mounting holes for cleats, stanchions, and tracks; openings for hatches, ventilators, chainplates, and deck pipes; screw holes for trim rings, anchor chocks, or teak decks.

A delaminated deck will usually snap and pop when you walk on it. A few test holes will tell you

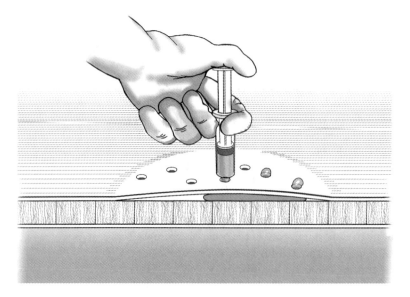

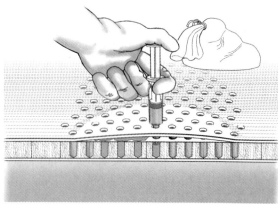

A pattern of holes left open to the air may allow core material to dry. Fill the drilled holes and void with injected epoxy. Use a weight to close the void between the skins and core.

Sometimes delamination can be repaired with resin injection.

if the core is wet or dry. If it is dry, go straight out and by a lottery ticket. When you get back, drill a few $^3/_{16}$-inch holes and glue the skin back to the core by injecting epoxy. Keep in mind that the core may have released on both sides, requiring resin to be injected below the core as well as above it. Feed and vent holes will need to pass through the core but not the bottom skin. This takes a bit of finesse, but don't worry—you're on a roll.

The rest of us are going to discover that the core is wet. Before any bonding can take place, you have to have a completely dry core. There are at least three approaches to achieving this, each with its own disadvantages.

Perforation

It is possible and occasionally even practical to perforate the delaminated area with a pegboardlike pattern of $^1/_8$-inch holes. These should penetrate the core but not the bottom skin. Venting the top skin and the core in this way allows moisture to escape. You can speed the process with heat or a vacuum, or you can just leave the deck open but protected for several months. To determine when the core is dry, periodically seal clear plastic over the perforated area on a sunny day. When little or no moisture condenses on the plastic, the exposed core is dry. Drill a few new holes between the old ones and do this test again to make sure all the wood is dry.

The remainder of the repair is simply injecting epoxy into each hole until it oozes from a neighboring hole. Seal oozing holes with a square of duct tape. Start at the lowest hole and work the entire area in a regular pattern, from low to high, until every hole has oozed and been taped closed. Place a piece of plastic over the repair area and put enough weight

on it to *compress* the skin but not *depress* it. When the epoxy is fully cured, remove the weight and plastic. Scrub, sand, fill, fair, and paint.

Top Skin Removal

Cored hulls are the exception in older boats, and hulls have few holes through the skins, so delaminated core most often has to do with the deck. In the vast majority of cases the best and easiest repair strategy is to remove the top skin, dry or replace the core, then bond the skin back in place. Depending on the extent of the delamination, this job can be range from easy to suicidal, but as a rule it is not as onerous as it sounds.

Map the delaminated area by sounding the deck with a plastic mallet. Outline the area with straight lines, giving the corners a radius. If after the repair you plan to apply a new paint-on or overlay nonskid surface, you can be guided just by the size and location of the delamination, but if you are trying to save the molded nonskid, try to place your outline in the center of the smooth areas of the deck. One caution: the damage generally extends farther than the sounding suggests, so be as generous as you dare with your perimeter. However, always leave at least 3 inches of the original deck beyond the cut line to provide a base for reattaching the skin.

Use a rotary tool with a cutoff wheel or a circular saw with a carbide blade (or a Fein reciprocating saw if you have one) and cut the outline *just through the top skin*. Use a sharpened, flexible putty knife as a chisel to cut the skin free from the core wherever it remains attached, taking care not to flex the skin any more than necessary. Peel the skin completely free and set it aside.

The core will almost certainly be either plywood or balsa. Wet plywood is rarely worth saving but balsa

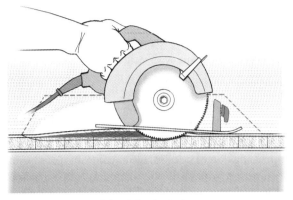

Cut the skin around the delaminated area.

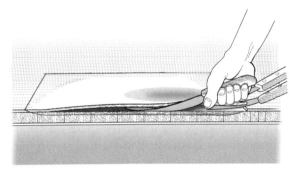

Pry the cut skin loose and set it aside.

in good condition can be allowed to dry, perhaps helped along with a vacuum, heat, or forced air. If it is completely saturated, drying could take months. Unless you are willing to wait that long, replacement is the appropriate course. Replacement is also required if the wood shows signs of deterioration.

Probe the core to identify the wet area. You can cut around the wet area in balsa with a utility knife but plywood will require a saw or router. Don't get too bold with the depth setting on the saw. You want to be sure that you do not cut the bottom skin. If the core is plywood, the repair will be stronger if the joints for the new core and the joints where the top skin is replaced are staggered. This is less of a concern with end-grain balsa. Use a sharp chisel to remove the old core and shave the bottom clean. Grind the bottom skin and the underside of the top skin with a 36-grit disk. Now is the time to push down on the middle of the bottom skin to get a sense of how stiff or flexible it is, so you will know how much pressure you can apply when bonding in the replacement core. It would be nice to support the bottom skin but typically you will not have ready access. If it is excessively flexible, you may need to glass in a stringer to stiffen it before going forward with the replacement.

Replacing the Core

On a heavily built old boat the choice of replacement core normally won't matter, but if the existing core is end-grain balsa, you avoid the potential for creating stress risers by putting balsa back. Balsa core material is not expensive, and if it's not available locally, it can be ordered from Defender Industries and other catalog suppliers as well as through the Internet. It comes in a range of thicknesses as small blocks on a fiberglass scrim. This block configuration allows the core to conform to the crown of the deck. For a small repair, end-grain cutoffs from a fir 2 × 4 will work equally well. Where hardware will be through-bolted, plywood or solid laminate should be substituted for the balsa.

If you intend to use plywood for the core replacement, you have two options. You can buy the thickness you need in marine-grade or void-free exterior-grade plywood—nothing less!—and cut it into 6-inch or 1-foot squares to allow it to follow the deck contour. Or you can laminate several layers of doorskin in place to create contoured plywood. If you make your own plywood, be sure you alternate the direction of the grain with each layer. Sand both sides of the plywood or doorskin to improve the bond.

Cut the core material to the size of the excavated area; put it in place dry to check the fit and to make sure it will not be higher than the old core. Set the top skin back in position to confirm that the new core does not interfere with its proper placement. Remove the skin and make orientation markings on top of the core—new and old—so there can be no confusion when you start the bond process. This step is essential, even if the core is a single piece.

Because we are bonding and not laminating, epoxy is the proper resin. There is nothing new from here on out. Mix up a batch of epoxy and thoroughly wet out the bottom skin, the sides of the remaining core, and the bottom and sides of the new core. If you are using plywood blocks, spend extra time saturating the edges. Let this wet-out application kick. Add colloidal silica to your next batch of epoxy until it has the consistency of mayonnaise, and spread it onto all wet-out surfaces. Put the new core piece or pieces in place according to your markings and compress each against the bottom skin, taking care not to deflect it. Epoxy should squeeze out all around the perimeter. Pick up all epoxy higher than the top, then weight the core and let the epoxy cure fully. A plastic garbage bag with a couple of inches of sand in it makes a good weight for core repair.

If you are forming plywood with doorskins, the process is the same, except you do not apply the thickened epoxy to the edge of the old core. After you wet out the bond surfaces between laminates, thicken the epoxy in the cup just slightly and paint this mix immediately onto one surface. Position the new laminate and weight it into shape. Make sure no squeeze-out curls over the perimeter where it will interfere with the next laminate. Give each bond long enough to solidly reach the initial cure before putting down the next laminate.

Reattaching the Outer Skin

With the new core bonded in, all that remains is to reattach the top skin. Start by putting it in place to check again for fit. Grind away any nibs of epoxy or high spots in the core that prevent the skin from sitting properly. Also grind the exposed surface of the old core if you have not done so already. If the skin sits too low or deflects when you press on it, whittle some thin shims to make it sit perfectly with your bag(s) of sand on it.

Mix a batch of unthickened epoxy and saturate the top of the old and new core. Keep applying epoxy until it completely fills the cuts between core blocks and all other voids in the core. You want the individual cells and the entire repair virtually encapsulated in resin. Wet the shims, taking care not to let them get out of position. Wet out the underside of the top skin.

Let the wet-out get tacky, then mix a new batch of epoxy and thicken it to mayonnaise consistency with colloidal silica. Spread this mixture on all the wet-out surfaces. Set the top skin in place so the cut line is uniform all around and push it firmly into the thickened resin. Epoxy should ooze out all around the perimeter. Run your hand over the surface to make sure it is sitting flush without any humps or dips. Pick up most of the squeeze-out with a spreader or a putty knife, then put a sandbag or two on the panel and let the epoxy reach full cure.

It would be nice if you could just putty the cut around the repair and gelcoat or paint it, but if you did, you would end up with a repair that was only marginally stronger than the bottom skin alone. This would become manifestly clear when you stepped off the cabin top and found yourself standing on the V-berth.

You have to *strongly* reattach the cut piece to the rest of the top skin. That means laminating it in place.

For a strong joint you need a scarf. I am not talking about laminating with strips of your paisley ascot. A *scarf* is a way of joining two pieces by cutting their ends at an angle and overlapping them. It is somewhere between a butt joint and a lamination, serving the purpose of the former with the strength of the latter.

Clearly the cutout piece is not going to overlap the remaining skin when reinstalled. Achieving a scarf joint requires a new piece of skin scarfed to *both parts*. You do this by grinding the joint into a shallow V. A joint as strong as the original laminate will require a 15-to-1 or even a 20-to-1 bevel, but a good compromise between width and strength is 12-to-1. On a $1/4$-inch skin the beveled surface will be 3 inches wide—the reason we left at least 3 inches of the original deck around the cutout. But we are scarfing the new piece of laminate to both pieces, so the width of the V will be 6 inches.

Use a grinder or disk sander to grind this 6-inch V around the perimeter of the replaced skin, with the cut line at the bottom of the V. If you want to complete the repair with a gelcoat finish, lay up the scarf with polyester resin and alternating layers of $1^1/_2$-ounce mat and 8- to 12-ounce cloth. If you are going to paint the repair, continue with your epoxy resin using just cloth. The first strip of fabric—mat if you're using polyester resin—should be the width of the V or slightly less if you plan to gelcoat. Each strip should be slightly narrower than the one before. For rounded corners, cut the fabric to match. When using polyester, apply four laminates, pause long enough for the resin to kick, then lay in additional laminates four at a time until the V is flush—or slightly indented if you are finishing with gelcoat. You do not need the cooling pause with epoxy unless the total thickness approaches $1/_2$ inch. You can estimate the number of laminates required by knowing that the finished thickness of *one* layer of compacted $1^1/_2$-ounce mat or *two* layers of 9-ounce cloth will be about 35 mils, close to $1/_{32}$ inch.

Encapsulate new core material in epoxy, then set the skin on a layer of thickened epoxy.

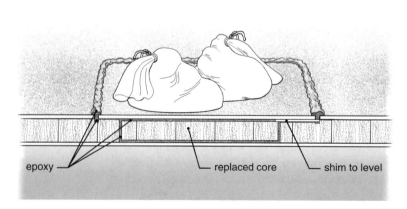

epoxy — | — replaced core | — shim to level

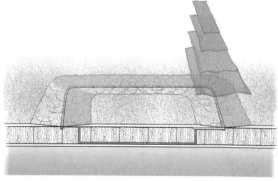

Reattach skin with a scarf joint on both sides of the cut line.

Concealing the Repair

After the laminates have cured, all that remains is to blend the repair into the deck. If the scars are all in smooth areas of the deck, you can treat them like any gelcoat gouge. Grind the repair if necessary to create a 20-mil-deep depression, then fill it with multiple coats of gelcoat or a single application of gelcoat paste. If the resin is air-inhibited, cover it with plastic or PVA as soon as it stiffens. When it is thoroughly cured, block sand, compound, and polish to a glassy finish.

Painting is easier than gelcoating. To prepare for painting, simply fill and fair the scarf joint. Painting is detailed in Chapter 14, but if you are not painting the entire deck, then mask a straight line where the paint will stop, usually across the narrow strip between nonskid panels, so the line will not be noticeable. If the repair cuts across a nonskid panel, symmetry can be reestablished by taping off a matching pattern on the opposite side of the deck, filling the molded nonskid pattern with epoxy putty, and painting this strip.

It is also possible to match the nonskid by taking a mold from the original. Clean and heavily wax a spot on deck that you select as the pattern for the mold, then give it three coats of PVA—you want to make absolutely sure that the resin will not adhere. Mask around a rectangular section of the waxed deck and paint this area with gelcoat. When the gelcoat has hardened, paint it with resin and add about three layers of saturated mat. Let the mold cure fully, then pry it from the deck. Now do almost the same thing again, except on the mold rather than the deck. This time tint the gelcoat to match the existing nonskid and back the gelcoat application with just two layers of mat. Remember to wax the mold and coat it with PVA. The new piece of laminate you pry from the mold will be an exact copy of the original surface, and it can be cut to the size required and bonded to the repair with epoxy putty. Handle it gently until it is in place to keep from cracking the gelcoat. The results of this process will generally be less detectable if you can allow a smooth margin around the new piece rather than butting it against existing nonskid.

For a deck that has required major surgery, the easiest way to hide the scars is to cover them with paint-on nonskid or rubber nonskid overlay (Treadmaster), and as a side benefit you get more secure footing. Both processes are detailed in Chapter 14. If you are going to overlay the deck, you might elect to lay up an entirely new top skin rather than graft the old piece in place and then grind off the texture in preparation for bonding the overlay. The perimeter of the cutout should still be beveled 12 to 1, and the new laminates laid in place in a large-to-small sequence.

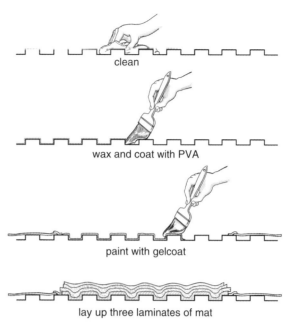

clean

wax and coat with PVA

paint with gelcoat

lay up three laminates of mat

peel up mold

Laying up laminate onto a heavily waxed molded nonskid section of the deck creates a mold that can be used to turn out laminate with a matching nonskid pattern.

The Bottom Skin Alternative

If you can get to the underside of the deck where the problem exists, you can do the repair without damaging the exterior finish of the boat by cutting away the bottom skin rather than the top skin. Unfortunately there is usually a molded headliner between you and the underside of the deck. Even then, it can sometimes make sense to cut away the headliner rather than scar a patterned and textured deck. This is a boat-by-boat decision but most of the time it is better to make the repair from the deck. Why? Aside from the headliner, there is likely to be furniture and/or bulkheads in the way below. You will be working in a confined area, grinding and doing layup overhead, corrupting the cabin with fiberglass dust and epoxy drips, and fighting gravity at every step. Successfully repairing core delamination from below requires a good supply of ingenuity, so I am going to detail the repair only in broad terms.

One benefit of working below is that you are not constrained by the deck pattern. Determine the approximate area of delamination by sounding, and mark a convenient perimeter on the bottom skin. Cut and peel away the skin, then cut and chisel out all damaged core material. Bond the replacement core to the underside of the sanded top skin, bracing it in place while the epoxy cures, then fill all voids with epoxy putty. When all of this is fully cured, sand the surface fair and grind a 12-to-1 bevel around the perimeter.

With careful alignment and good luck the bottom skin can be compressed into place in a single operation.

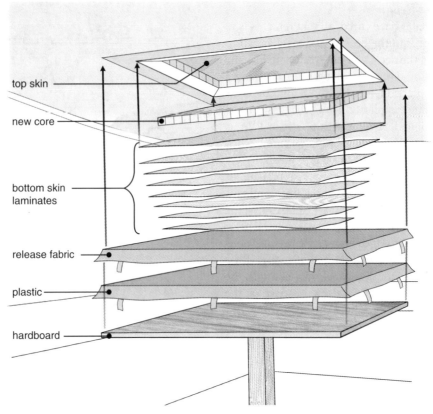

top skin

new core

bottom skin laminates

release fabric

plastic

hardboard

You can similarly bevel the edge of the removed skin and bond and scarf it back in place, but laying up the scarf upside down will be a challenge. It is usually better to lay up a new skin. This is where the rubber meets the road. You want to lay up the new bottom skin and apply it in one operation. To do this you will need a flexible panel a couple of inches larger than the cutout. Coated hardboard—Masonite—works well. Figure out a way to brace this panel tightly over the repair area. With the hardboard on a convenient flat work area, cover the entire top surface with plastic, taped on the bottom, then put down a layer of Peel Ply, which is also taped in place. Cut a paper pattern that perfectly matches the repair area to the outside of the bevel. Place this pattern on the Peel Ply, top side up, and trace around it with a marker. Remove the pattern, then measure near the corners from the outline to the perimeter of the hardboard panel. Transfer those measurements to the old skin. What you are trying to do is create alignment marks that will place the marked perimeter on the Peel Ply in perfect alignment with the outside of the bevel. When you are satisfied that they line up, trace a line on the old skin all the way around the hardboard to make repeating this alignment foolproof.

Determine how many laminates you will need to restore the skin to its full original thickness or *slightly* thicker. At 17 mils laminated thickness for

9-ounce cloth, a ¹/₈-inch skin—125 mils—would require eight laminates. Cut them in equally decreasing sizes, the largest matching the outside edge of the bevel and the smallest the cutout size. Use the paper pattern for cutting the cloth accurately.

Center the smallest piece of cloth in the marked perimeter on the Peel Ply and wet it out. Add the next piece and the next, pausing at four to let the epoxy release heat. Wet out the remaining layers, then coat the top layer with mayonnaise-consistency epoxy putty. Carefully lift the hardboard panel and position the patch in the depression, using the panel outline as your guide. The larger the patch, the more you need a second pair of hands. Brace the panel tightly against the overhead, clean up any squeeze-out, and pray. If you got the alignment right, when the epoxy has cured fully and you remove the Masonite, you will have a strong new bottom skin needing only minor cosmetic attention.

BELT AND SUSPENDERS
After you have gone to all of this trouble to replace a delaminated deck, you certainly do not want it to happen again. To insure against water penetration, for every mounting hole that passes through core material, drill it oversize through the top skin only, then use a bent nail chucked into a drill to pulverize the core around the hole as far back as possible. Vacuum out as much of the

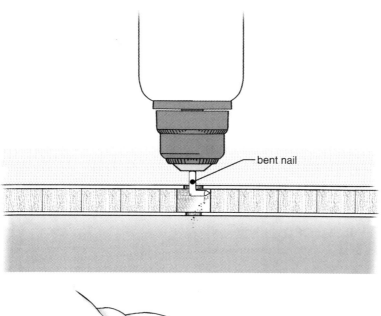

bent nail

To protect core from water intrusion, drill all fastener holes through top skin oversize, then pulverize and extract core material around the hole.

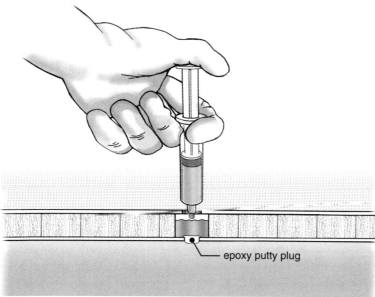

epoxy putty plug

Fill the created cavity with slightly thickened epoxy.

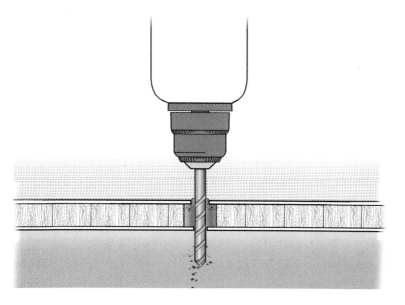

Redrill for fastener. Bed normally.

shredded core as you can. Tape across the bottom skin hole and inject epoxy thickened with colloidal silica to a ketchup consistency. Fill the cavity. If you cannot get to the bottom skin because of a molded liner, make up a small amount of very stiff putty and roll a ball just small enough to drop through the enlarged top hole. Tamp this gently into the bottom hole with a small dowel and let the plug cure. Now you should be able to fill the cavity. When the fastener hole is redrilled to the proper size, the core will be sealed away from the hole. Proper bedding is still essential to prevent water from entering the boat and as double protection against core penetration.

STRUCTURALLY DAMAGED

Thus far we have focused on internal delamination, either the release of the core or a modest void inside single-skin fiberglass. More severe damage to fiberglass construction almost always results in delamination as well, but it requires a different response. When the delamination is associated with some type of hull or deck trauma, there is little reason to attempt to rebond the damaged laminates. Instead you will need to cut away and discard the ruined laminate, reconstructing this section of your boat with new laminates.

IMPACT DAMAGE

There is a marker in Biscayne Bay that Olga invariably comments on as we sail by it, a not-so-subtle reminder that when she disagrees with me, it does not necessarily mean she is wrong. On a warm afternoon some summers ago we approached the same marker, and as it became apparent that we were not going to pass it on the correct side, I pinched up tighter on the light breeze. The gurgle at the bow faded. "Tack," my devoted mate counseled, but I had the bow pointed well clear of the marker and hung on. Unfortunately the current did not care where the bow was pointed, and we took the piling just abaft the starboard genoa winch. A stout rubstrake limited the damage to some splintered teak and a crushed ego, but in a different boat the consequences of my foolishness would have been far more serious.

Repairing damaged fiberglass is surprisingly easy. We have already seen how to repair damage that does not penetrate all of the laminates. When the area is broken or holed, the process is only slightly more complex.

Begin by cutting away the damaged glass. If the area is large, use a circular saw with a carbide blade or an abrasive cutoff wheel. For a smaller area, a saber saw is the tool of choice. Keep in mind that the impact that caused the hole undoubtedly caused some delamination. Sound the area with your mallet and outline the

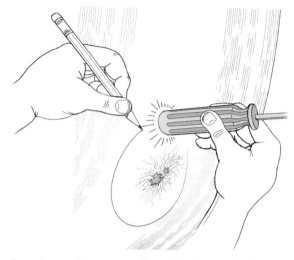

Sound around the damage for collateral delamination and draw a smooth cutout outline.

damage. Now go back and smooth that outline into a circular or oval shape. This is the piece you are going to cut away.

Before you begin cutting, go inside the boat and see if there is anything in the way of your repair. If, for example, a bulkhead or a cabinet is attached across the damaged area, you will have to decide how to deal with it. Usually the best way is to cut away part or all of the member that is interfering.

Now go back outside, take a deep breath, and cut around the circular outline. Fiberglass will eat up cheap saw blades, so buy rugged ones rated for cutting fiberglass, and cut slowly to keep from overheating the blade. Once the piece is removed, carefully examine the cut edge for any signs of delamination that your sounding may have missed. If you find any, enlarge the cutout until all edges are sound.

Working from the Inside

You repair blister damage from the outside because that is where the damage is, but damage that results in a hole all the way through the fiberglass gives you a choice. You want to make the repair from the inside if at all possible. There are two reasons for this. The first is that you are going to bevel the edge of the hole at least 12 to 1 to give adequate strength to the join between the old and new laminates. If the hull is $1/_2$ inch thick at the damaged spot, the bevel will measure 6 inches or more all the way around. Put a 6-inch bevel around a 3-inch hole, and you have a 15-inch patch to refinish if the bevel is on the outside, but only 3 inches if you work from the inside. The relative benefit of this diminishes as the size of the damaged area increases.

The second reason to make the repair from the inside is because you have to back the hole on one side or the other to provide a surface on which to lay up the laminates. This backing in effect provides a mold, and if the backing is smooth, the cured resin will mirror that surface. It is outside where you need that smooth surface, and backing the hole on the outside means doing the layup from inside.

Start the reconstruction process by dewaxing the interior surface at least a foot out from the hole in all directions. Next grind a 12-to-1 bevel around the hole. Make it 15-to-1 if you have space. While you have the grinder in hand, sand a rectangular area a few inches larger than the bevel. This is to allow a final laminate that carries out onto the hull to give the repair a finished appearance. Wipe down the ground surfaces, including the bevel, with a clean cloth dampened with acetone.

Backing the hole. After you have cut out the damage and beveled the hole from inside the boat, backing the hole is the next step. If you back the hole hastily and poorly, you will be filling and sanding, filling and sanding, and filling and sanding in a frustrating effort to get the surface fair. Do it carefully and well, and the repair will require a minimal amount of fairing and polishing.

Any hard, flexible material can be used as a backing. Glossy plastic laminate (Formica) or thin clear acrylic (Plexiglas) work especially well because they will readily take on the curve of the hull and can be held in place with duct tape. Stiffer backing, like coated hardboard, is better when the damaged area is large, but it will have to be screwed to the hull to hold it in position.

If you are fortunate enough that the damage is in a relatively flat spot or where the curvature is in only one direction, backing the hole will present no problem at all. Cut the backing material about 8 inches larger than the hole, hold it in place, and tape the edges down tightly. If you fail to cut the backing sufficiently oversize to carry out onto the hull several inches, it will lie flat across the hole rather than taking the hull's curvature, and the resulting repair will be flat.

With the backing temporarily in place, check the hole from the inside. The backing should rest tightly against the edge of the hole all the way around. If it does, you are good to go with the reconstruction. If it doesn't, then there is probably compound curvature (curving in two directions at the same time) in the hull in the damaged area. If you consider the distance between the hull and the backing as a crack rather than space, filling it with a bit of modeling clay will be all that is required, except for brushing in a second layer of gelcoat on either side of the hole near

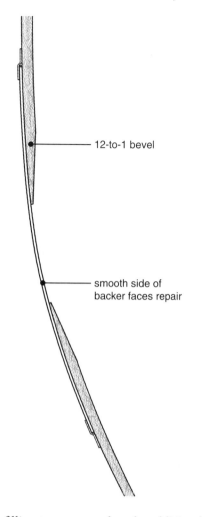

12-to-1 bevel

smooth side of backer faces repair

Glossy, waxed countertop laminate forms a perfect backing where the curvature is cylindrical rather than spherical.

the clay filling to accommodate the additional sanding that will be required to fair the raised sides.

If the compound curvature is more pronounced, thin acrylic screwed to the hull on all four sides can sometimes be induced to take the correct shape if warmed with a heat gun. Otherwise your easiest option is to wax a spot in the same location on the opposite side of the hull and paint it heavily with PVA. Coat the center portion of the waxed area with resin, then lay up two plies of mat. Let this cure, peel it, reverse it top to bottom, and it should provide the perfectly contoured backing/mold for your repair.

Apply a coat of wax to the gelcoat around the hole and paint it with PVA to prevent resin that finds its way between the hull and the backing from attaching. Also wax the backing and coat it with PVA. A strip of tape applied to the hull below the backing and turned out like a porch roof will kick resin trickles clear of the hull.

Making the repair. Allow the PVA to dry completely, then reattach the backing, sealing any cracks with modeling clay or other temporary filler. Coat the mold and the lower edge of the bevel with color-matched gelcoat to a uniform thickness of about 20 mils. You can check it using toothpicks as dipsticks. Compare the coated tip to the $1/_{32}$ markings on a scale ($1/_{32}$ inch is about 30 mils). This is where you want to use air-inhibited gelcoat. If what you are using is not air-inhibited, as soon as it gels, apply a coat of laminating resin.

Because we are gelcoating the repair, we are using polyester resin, which is detailed in this section. As an alternative you can do just the initial two mat laminates with polyester, let this cure, sand it, and finish the repair with epoxy.

Measure the thickness of the damaged cutout to estimate the number of laminates needed. The finished thickness of two layers of 9-ounce cloth or one layer of compacted $1^1/_2$-ounce mat is about $1/_{32}$ inch. Unless you are repairing a very large area, there is no compelling reason to be concerned about duplicating the original laminate schedule; this just adds an unnecessary complication. On a more modern hull the laminate schedule may be "engineered" to yield strength in a specific direction, but most older boats were simply laid up with mat and woven roving to a specified thickness. The manufacturer selected roving because it was cheaper and built up faster. You can do the same, but whether you use 18-ounce roving or 9-ounce cloth is not particularly important. It is far more important that you mix the resin properly, grind the old surface well, mate the old to the new with a generous scarf joint, work out all air bubbles, and compact the new laminates.

Cut the first piece of mat to the outside dimensions of the bevel and the second piece of mat only slightly smaller. The third smaller-still piece of fabric should be cloth. You start the patch with two layers of mat because they will make the laminate somewhat more waterproof and prevent the weave of the cloth from "printing through" the gelcoat. Cut the remaining layers of alternating mat and cloth, each smaller than the previous one so that it matches the decreasing diameter of the depression.

Begin the laminates by wetting the repair area out to the outside perimeter of the bevel with laminating resin, then pressing the largest piece of mat into the resin. If the damage is to a vertical part of the hull, you may need to hang the first layer of mat with masking tape strips at the top to keep it from sliding. Compress the dry mat into the resin with a plastic spreader, then saturate it using a roller or a shortened brush. Apply the next layer of mat in the same manner. The third layer will be cloth. You want to do three layers so that the top layer is cloth, which is less fragile than saturated mat. When the cloth is completely saturated, compress it with a spreader or a grooved roller to compact the laminate and force air bubbles out of the resin.

Allow these initial laminates to kick, then continue the process until you have rebuilt the damaged area to the original thickness. You can probably apply the laminates four at a time without a problem, but if this is your first major repair, take the safe route and apply only two, allowing them to harden and cool

Repairs made with polyester resin require the first two and every other laminate to be chopped-strand mat.

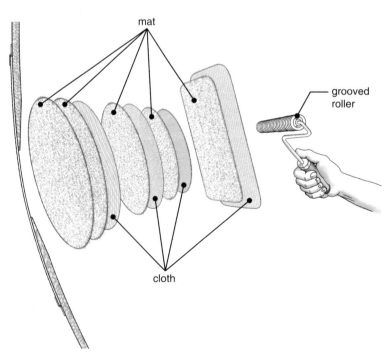

mat

grooved roller

cloth

before adding two more. Always do your compressing and smoothing on cloth layers, not on the fragile mat.

When the repair to the hole has been completed, grind the proud laminate ends and other irregularities off the interior surface of the patch, then apply a final rectangular layer of mat and cloth to hide the repair and give it a professionally finished look. Protect the final layer from the air to allow a tack-free cure.

Outside the hull, carefully peel the mold away. There may be a thin ridge of gelcoat around the perimeter of the hole, which a finishing sander will make short work of. Thickened gelcoat can be used to fill any screw holes and to correct other imperfections. Block sand the touch-up, compound if necessary, then polish the repair to match the surrounding area. Ta da!

Working from the Outside

You can make an equally sound repair working from the outside. This will be your choice if an inner liner, tankage, or complex cabinetry make working from the inside impractical. Even when you have inside access, working from the outside can be the better option for any repair that will be painted rather than finished with gelcoat. Working from the outside is typically more comfortable and perhaps easier. If you are not replacing the gelcoat, you should use epoxy resin for its superior adhesion and lower permeability. In this circumstance, the layup process is similar to a deep-blister repair—beveling the circumference and filling the depression with layers of cloth laid up wet on wet. There are two notable differences. Since the depth of the depression will be the thickness of the laminate, you may want to use a heavier cloth to build thickness more quickly. And of course, since the hole penetrates the hull, you will have to back the hole before you can make the repair.

When you cannot get to the back side of the hole, lay up two layers of 9-ounce cloth on a piece of waxed paper and allow them to cure. If the hull has significant curvature where you are making the repair, you can also lay up the backing piece on a waxed section of the hull near the damage to get the proper shape. Trim a disk or oval from this piece 1 inch larger than the hole in the hull. Reach into the hole with a toluene-saturated rag and dewax the perimeter back a couple of inches. Then reach inside with a piece of 36-grit sandpaper and sand the perimeter. Scrub the

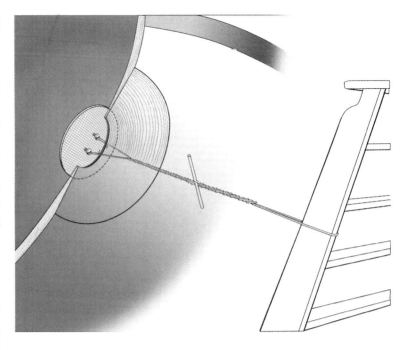

disk with water to remove the amine, then sand one side of the disk. Screw two sheet-metal screws into the sanded side of the disk about $1\frac{1}{2}$ inches from opposite edges. Wrap the ends of a short length of flexible wire under the heads of the screws. Bend the disk enough to insert it through the hole, holding on to the wire. Butter the perimeter with thickened epoxy, and centering the disk in the hole, pull it against the back side of the laminate with the wire handle. Pick up any epoxy that oozes out. Tie a string from the wire handle to some fixed object to hold the disk in place until the epoxy cures fully. Remove the two screws and fill the depression as detailed in the section on deep blisters.

Unless a freighter blows down on you, crushing your boat against the quay, this is likely all you'll ever need to know about fiberglass repair. Even then, bigger damage just means a bigger repair, not a different one. Spend time to get the backing really right and the repair will come out well every time.

Considering the advantages of glass-reinforced plastic in the construction of boats, it should not be surprising that a number of other plastics have found their way into marine use. These are the focus of the next chapter.

With the backing bonded in place, repairing damage from the outside is nearly identical to deep-blister repair.

CHAPTER SEVEN

Windows and Walls

"Let there be light."
—**GOD**

Plastic had already taken over boat construction when I first realized how much more world was open to you if you had a waterborne conveyance. I chose a sailboat because the sort of limitless horizon aspect of sailing appealed to me. A person of ordinary means could untie his sloop in San Diego, and by the time his credit card bills were past due, he could be lying on an ebony beach, engulfed by the sweet scent of frangipani, sipping from a coconut, and basking in the warm smile of a bronze-skinned South Seas maiden. We buy the sizzle, not the steak.

I was lucky with my first boat. I chose a 27-footer from the board of Carl Alberg, built by New England craftsmen who viewed this new material with a jaundiced eye. Their distrust made her heavy, but with her sweet lines, the weight affected her only in the lightest conditions. I bought her used of course, but there was an advertising brochure aboard that called her accommodations "light and airy." I had little quarrel with that characterization until the first rainy summer afternoon.

The airy part is self-explanatory; the rain necessitated closing all portholes and hatches. In south Florida that is approximately equivalent to putting the lid on a slow cooker. Except that the lid is glass, so at least a lamb chop has plenty of light when getting ready for dinner.

Not so with most older boats. The hatches, like the boat, are constructed of fiberglass. What happens to the light when the weather forces you to close the hatches? Consider this. The total area of the portholes in my old 27-footer—excluding those in the head and the hanging locker, which did not contribute to the illumination of the cabin—was about 3 square feet. The combined area of the forward hatch and companionway was about 13 square feet. So with the

hatches open, the total area admitting light below was about 16 square feet. Put in the boards and close the hatches, and the area admitting outside light dropped to 3 square feet—a reduction of *more than 80%!* And that does not take into account the poor light-gathering characteristics of openings in the side of the cabin compared to those in the overhead. The only thing light and airy about most old boats is the advertising copy.

Ventilation is not about hatches. It is about *openings,* a subject we will consider more closely in Chapters 10 and 15. But there is no reason for the daylight below to depend on open hatches. It carries the old fiberglass boat/refrigerator analogy a bit too far—close the door and the light goes out.

I recall wondering why the forward hatch in my boat was the color of toxic waste, in disgusting contrast to the pristine white of the cabin top and deck around it. It turned out to be an industry-wide response to the primal screams of sailing nyctophobes. And a pathetic response it was. Manufacturers simply omitted the gelcoat in laying up the hatches. After all, the hatch was already glass. Leave off the gelcoat and it becomes translucent, right? God made eyelids more translucent and their purpose is to shut light *out.*

Boat manufacturers eventually saw the light (pun intended), and newer boats are almost all delivered with transparent hatches, in effect bringing the light below. Part of the reason was the development of a water-clear polycarbonate resin called Lexan.

Clear plastics—Plexiglas, Lucite, Acrylite, and other acrylics—have been used in boat portlights for half a century. New acrylic has about twenty times the impact resistance of tempered glass but is not as stable. Acrylic hatches in particular, after a few years of horizontal exposure, become increasingly brittle. Given that a deck hatch's raison d'être is to keep the ocean out, more than a few early fiberglass boat manufacturers seem to have been unaware of this shortcoming. More attentive or responsible companies addressed it with hatches constructed of surprisingly thick plastic.

A related characteristic is acrylic's proclivity to develop a spiderweb of internal cracks as it is subjected to the stresses of age and movement. Besides weakening the plastic, these cracks cloud it, obscuring the view through hatch or portlight. A better material was needed.

That material was Lexan, the brand name for the polycarbonate resin manufactured by GE. Don't think of Lexan as just a more expensive Plexiglas. It is more expensive, but only by about 25% these days. However, Lexan is no more like acrylic than gin is like water. Roughly four times as break resistant as acrylic with better structural stability, Lexan was going to be the perfect material for boat hatches.

Where polycarbonates and acrylics *are* alike is in how you go about fabricating them into the item you want. They are deceptively easy to work with and great fun. Once you have made an item or two and discovered how easy it is, the biggest risk you run is getting carried away with the possibilities. In almost any boat, there are some excellent applications for clear plastic, but too much can look really tacky. I don't want to be a party to that, so if you can't exhibit some self-restraint, skip this section.

No, I haven't forgotten that I was discussing hatches and portlights. I will get back to that subject soon enough, but as I promised from the start, I first want to give you a chance to work with clear plastic on a low-cost, low-risk project. To keep the cost as low as possible we will be working with clear acrylic. The added expense of polycarbonate is only justified when strength is essential.

ACRYLIC ACCESSORIES

Acrylic is an inexpensive material. Sheet plastic comes in 4-by-8-foot sheets. At this writing the full sheet price of $1/_4$-inch clear is between $4 and $5 per square foot, but you don't have to buy a full sheet. Many suppliers will be happy to provide you with whatever size you need, although you should expect to pay a cutting charge, more per square foot than the full-sheet price, or both. Every cloud has its silver lining, however. Because suppliers provide cut sizes, many will have a scrap bin—the smaller pieces left over from filling an order. Often these scrap pieces can be purchased at giveaway prices. For cabin accessories small pieces are exactly what you need. Isn't it great how things work out?

A $1/_4$-inch thickness is about right for many cabin accessories but you can use thinner or thicker material where it seems appropriate. There are different types of acrylic. Plexiglas, for example, comes in about a dozen different varieties. For most onboard projects special characteristics are unnecessary. You just need standard clear acrylic with a film covering—or whatever you find in the scrap bin.

CREATING IN ACRYLIC

Mounted on the bulkhead above the head of my bunk is a clear acrylic bin. I did not make it or install it—it was an enhancement by the prior owner—but it is a shoo-in for my list of the ten most useful items aboard. At any given time it holds sunglasses, lip block, Blistex, keys, pens, a pad, rubber bands, change, an extra Croakies, a lighter, a penlight, gum, sunscreen, and a dozen other items. Ostensibly a teak bin would serve the same function, and we have such a bin right by the companionway—part of the original cabinetry. The teak bin is an equally convenient receptacle for small essentials but the difference comes in the effort required to locate and retrieve an item. The search for a loose key that *might* be in the teak bin usually leads to removing almost all the items and putting them on the settee while pressing my forehead against the bulkhead to peer down into the bin. I look directly into the acrylic bin, then reach in and pull out the item I want, regardless of whether it is on the top or the bottom. Acrylic is an especially good material for bins and racks because of its transparency.

To construct the acrylic bin described here, you will need a piece of $1/_4$-inch clear acrylic about 9 inches wide and 22 inches long. Cutting and drilling require no special tools. You can cut acrylic with almost any handsaw and most power saws, but for cutting irregular shapes a saber saw is the tool of choice. Use a blade intended for cutting plastics—a common item available from the plastic supplier or any hardware store. Drilling holes requires a drill, hand-powered or electric, and the appropriate bits. Special bits with a different chamfer angle at the tip are available for drilling plastic but any high-speed drill bit used carefully will do the job if it is a little dull. This is the time to use your oldest bits. To finish the sawn edges you will need an old hacksaw blade, some fine sandpaper, and a tube of toothpaste—any flavor.

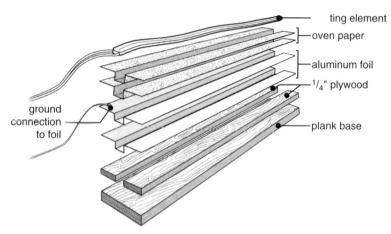

Strip heater.

Constructing a Strip Heater

Bending acrylic requires heating the plastic, which you can do with a heat gun, but a strip heater gives better results and is way easier to use. A strip heater is a special tool that you construct, but the central component is a heat strip that you must buy. A heat strip is a flexible heating element, sometimes with a plug already attached. When I was working on the first edition of this book, a 3-foot heat strip cost around $15 and every major sheet plastics supplier sold them. Now it may take an Internet search to find one, and you can expect the cost to be around $50. That is really too bad because it is a lot to spend on a first-time project, which too often means the versatility of bent acrylic goes undiscovered.

If you decide to spring for a heat strip, it will almost certainly come with instructions. But in case you find one in a garage sale or on eBay or you adapt a heating element intended for some other use, here are the basics. In addition to the heat strip you will need a plank or a piece of plywood about 40 inches long and 6 inches wide; a couple of strips of $^{1}/_{4}$-inch plywood, 3 feet long and $2^{1}/_{2}$ inches wide; some

heavy-duty aluminum foil; and some high-temperature paper—oven paper, available in supermarkets, will do. Nail the plywood strips to the plank with a gap in between just wide enough to accommodate the heat strip. The heating element must never touch the acrylic, so if you are adapting something and it is thicker than $^{1}/_{4}$ inch, you will need thicker plywood.

Cover the top of this construction with two layers of aluminum foil that follow the contour of the channel. For safety, you should attach a ground wire to the foil with a screw in the bottom of the channel. (This wire connects to the ground prong on the plug.) Dampen the oven paper so it will follow the channel contour and put two layers over the top of the foil. Fasten the paper in place, putting staples in the sides or bottom of the heater so they will not scratch the plastic. Position the heating element in the channel and pull it straight by tying it tightly between small nails driven into the plank ends.

A Versatile Design

With the heater assembled, you are ready to proceed. The detailed bin is around 12 inches wide (excluding the mounting flanges), but you can make yours as long or as short as you like, depending on how you want to use it and where it is to be mounted. If the bin will be a catchall, I would caution against making it more than 6 inches deep so you can easily retrieve items from the bottom. Making the bin wider at the mouth also makes access easier.

The first step is to construct a mock-up from stiff poster board. Use the illustration to duplicate the flat shape, adjusting it to any changes in dimension that may be appropriate in your case. Draw in the fold lines and the location of the mounting holes. Cut around the outline and fold it to shape. Try it for fit where you intend to mount it.

When you are satisfied with the mock-up, flatten it out again and use it for a pattern. The acrylic will

Generic pattern for the cut shape of sheet acrylic to be formed into a three-sided bin.

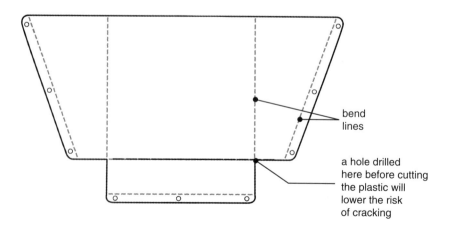

bend lines

a hole drilled here before cutting the plastic will lower the risk of cracking

have a protective paper or plastic film covering both sides. Leave that in place while you are cutting and drilling the plastic. Lay your pattern on the covering film and trace the outline. Puncture the pattern at the center of the marked mounting holes and use a pencil or marking pen to transfer their location to the film.

Cutting and Drilling

Acrylic can crack if mishandled but adequate caution avoids that. It is less brittle when it is warm so in the winter, work indoors. Inside corners will be less prone to crack if you drill them first, which is how we will start this bin. Laying the acrylic on a plank or a scrap of plywood, use a $1/4$-inch bit to drill a hole at the apex of both inside corners. If you let the bit get too big of a bite, it will crack the plastic, especially as it exits the hole at the bottom, so feed the drill slowly.

Feed slowly also applies to the saw. Cut around the marked outline with your saber saw, supporting the acrylic as close to the cut as possible by placing it on a flat surface, like the top of a workbench, and running the saw blade just beyond the edge of the bench. Reposition the piece as necessary. The acrylic will chip if you let it bounce or chatter when you are cutting it, so clamp it in place with a board on top if necessary. If the piece being cut off is large, support the cutoff as well. Use a moderate blade speed. If the blade gets too hot, it will begin to melt the plastic and bind. Lubricate the blade with beeswax or bar soap to reduce this tendency.

Lay the cutout piece on your scrap of wood and carefully drill the marked mounting holes. The edge of a hole should be no closer to the edge of the acrylic than 1.5 times the thickness of the plastic, making the minimum distance $3/8$ inch for this project. The bit should penetrate the wood beneath. It is in the process of drilling holes that you are most likely to crack the plastic, so go slowly and keep the pressure light. The plastic may also crack after it is mounted if it cannot expand and contract with temperature changes. For this reason always drill mounting holes in plastic a drill size or two larger than the screw or bolt that will pass through the hole.

After all the holes are drilled, clamp or hold the piece vertically and draw the *back* of a hacksaw blade (not the side with teeth) along the cut edge to remove the melted slag and most of the saw marks. An edge to be glued (in case you decide to build an aquarium) necessitates a special edge scraper to get the edge flat and square, but square is neither necessary nor even desirable on an exposed edge. Hand sand—or use a finishing sander if you have one—to put a smoother finish on the edges and round their corners slightly. Wet sand by hand with 600-grit paper, then use a buffing wheel

(*not* a disk) and a stick of buffing compound to finish the edges. The same thing can be accomplished less efficiently with a rag and a blob of white toothpaste.

Bending

That is the end of the difficult part. Bending the acrylic into the desired shape is all that is left and that's easy. Your pattern has six bend lines marked on it. Snip a $1/4$-inch notch in the pattern at both ends of each line. Peel away the adhesive covering from both sides of the acrylic and lay the notched pattern on one side. Using a grease pencil or felt-tip marker, transfer the notched locations to the acrylic. It is not necessary to connect the marks with a straight line since aligning a pair of notches over the straight heat strip will place the heater under the bend line. However, you can make all the marks and notes on the acrylic you want. Isopropyl alcohol will easily remove all traces of the marks.

Bending acrylic has three steps: heat, bend, and hold. You want to be sure you are making the bend in the right direction, and sometimes the sequence of the bends is important, but that is as complicated as it gets. I should comment here that polycarbonate up to around $3/16$ inch can also be bent the same way, but thicker polycarbonate may not heat all the way through unless you turn it over. We aren't going to bend polycarbonate, but in the event that you experience problems, your scrap-bin plastic might not be acrylic.

For this bin it makes sense to bend the bottom and sides first, then the flanges. Preheat the strip heater for 5 minutes. Place the acrylic flat on top of the heater and align the two marks that define the bend forming the bottom directly over the heating element (see illustration next page). To contain small, loose items, you want to minimize the space between the bottom and the sides so this bend should be as high as possible but must be below the inside corners to avoid interfering with the side bends. *Before* the plastic gets hot, dampen a tissue with isopropyl alcohol and clean away the two marks.

It will take the strip about 15 minutes to heat $1/4$-inch acrylic to the proper temperature. When the plastic is hot enough, it will be rubbery and soft, bending without any strain. A scrap of acrylic placed on the heater at the same time allows you to check without disturbing the position of the actual item. Keep track of how long heating takes. The other bends will all take a similar radius if you heat them for the same amount of time.

When the plastic is hot enough, leave the shortest side lying on the flat surface of the heater and quickly bend the rest of the piece up to a position about 5 degrees beyond the angle desired. Overbending counteracts the "memory" of the plastic, relieving some of the stresses in the bend. Now back the bend up to the desired angle. In this case it will be a little less than 90 degrees because the face of the bin slants away from the bulkhead. To get the angle correct, before you heat the plastic, refold the bottom and sides but not the flanges of your posterboard pattern and tape it in shape. Hold this against the face of the bin and match the bend angle. Move the piece off the heater and hold it in place until the plastic cools and the bend sets—typically about a minute.

Line up the heat strip with the marks for one of the sides. Remove the marks with alcohol. When the acrylic is hot enough, overbend by about 5 degrees, then back the bend up to vertical (90 degrees) and hold it there for about a minute. Repeat the process for the opposite side.

The next step is to bend the flanges. Note that these bends are in the opposite direction of the ones you have already made. For the smoothest bend you generally want to bend *away from* the heated side,

but that is not always possible. In this case it would require the inside of the bin to lie flat on the heater, but the bends you have already made prevent that. So you will have to bend toward the heated side.

Position the two marks for the bottom flange over the heat strip. Remove the marks. Check for readiness by picking up the test strip and bending it *down* 90 degrees. When the plastic is hot enough, lift the bin and quickly press the edge of the flange against your work table to make the bend, overbending by 5 degrees. Move the piece to the table edge, hold a wooden ruler or other straightedge flat on the flange, and back the bend up to an angle of 90 degrees with the bottom. Hold it in position until the plastic cools. Repeat this process for the other two flanges.

After the last bend, check the flanges on a level surface to see how flat they sit. If they are badly out of alignment, you can make adjustments by reheating the bends that seem to be wrong. You never need to reveal that it took you two tries.

Position the bend line directly over the heating element. At the same time place a scrap piece of the same material over the element.

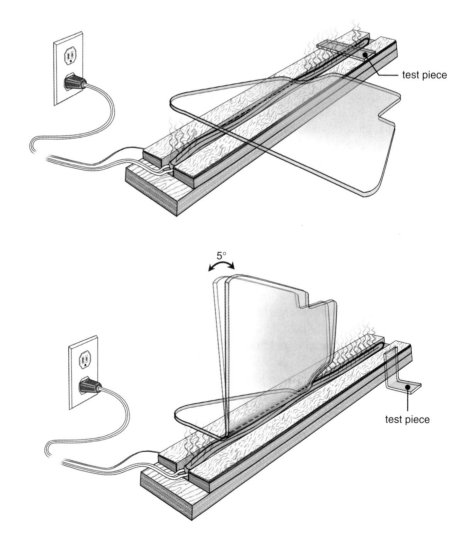

test piece

When the test material confirms that the plastic has heated sufficiently to bend like rubber, make the bend in the part, overbending by about 5 degrees, then reducing the bend to the desired angle. Hold until set.

5°

test piece

When you mount the bin, remember to use screws smaller than the mounting holes. *Never countersink acrylic or Lexan!* If you do, the screw will act like a wedge and crack the plastic—guaranteed. The best choice is oval-head screws used with finishing washers. The finishing washer spreads the compression out away from the hole and gives the mounting a professional look. If you don't want to spend the nickel for a finishing washer, then use round-head fasteners.

Other Acrylic Accessories

You can use this bin design with different dimensions to make a spice rack, a chart rack, a magazine bin, a kitchen wrap holder, or a shelf for CDs or DVDs or paperback books, or to provide utility space on the inside of cabinet doors. If your taste runs to acrylic toothbrush stands, paper towel holders, and wine racks, you can do those too. Cut large holes with a standard holesaw. Just keep the drill straight and cut slowly, and you should have no difficulty.

If an item requires joining two pieces of acrylic, buy a tube of acrylic cement from your plastics supplier. It is not really a glue but a solvent, softening the two pieces and actually fusing them together. The surfaces to be joined must mate well, but when they do, the solvent yields a very strong joint.

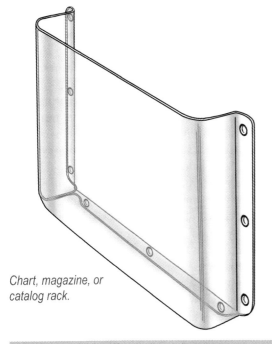

Utility bin.

Spice holder.

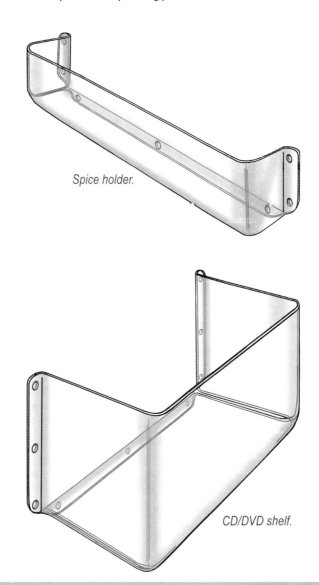

Chart, magazine, or catalog rack.

CD/DVD shelf.

The same bin with different dimensions can serve a variety of functions.

Once you are comfortable with sawing and drilling acrylic, you can move on to the more expensive polycarbonate. That takes us back to our discussion of hatches and portlights.

CLEAR HATCHES

Few changes—perhaps none for the cost—have as dramatic an effect on the living space in an old boat as replacing an opaque or a translucent hatch with a transparent one. The increase in cabin illumination cannot be overstated, but the virtues of a clear hatch extend beyond just that. You are, after all, out on the water to enjoy nature, not to be shut off from it. A transparent hatch will inevitably lead to the association of nights aboard with the wonder and beauty of a star-crowded sky. If corporate politics have dulled your romantic sensibilities, think of it as getting an office with windows.

MANUFACTURED HATCHES

In the case of a fiberglass deck hatch, one option that may be available is to replace it with a manufactured hatch. You will find a wide variety of designs and sizes on the Internet and in marine supply catalogs. Most are constructed of tinted acrylic in an extruded aluminum frame. Wait. Did I just say *acrylic*? What happened to Lexan?

As it turned out, Lexan suffered more than acrylic from UV degradation and its softer surface was more prone to scratches. Hatch manufacturers decided that longer life (for the hatch, not for you) and better scratch resistance were, on balance, more valuable than extra strength for the way most people use their boats. Plus, polycarbonate has some "give," which contributes to its strength, but this flexibility caused hatch manufacturers a great deal of trouble with the seal between the lens and the frame. Lexan is available with a hard coating that provides UV protection and makes the surface mar resistant, but it's twice the cost of acrylic. If I were headed to the Southern Ocean, I would want polycarbonate hatches, but if you buy a manufactured hatch, the lens will be acrylic. A thicker lens might be offered as an "offshore" option.

Manufactured hatches are ideal for installation as an *additional* hatch. A lot of older sailboats lack an overhead hatch in the main saloon, relying on the forward hatch to ventilate the whole boat. That might work in Rhode Island but it fails miserably in south Florida. A generous hatch in the main saloon provides light and ventilation, and in a hot climate it can transform the interior of a boat from miserable to comfortable. Similarly, a small overhead hatch in the head compartment can enhance comfort completely out of proportion to the size of the hatch or its cost. We will come back to adding a hatch, but when *replacing* an existing hatch, an irregular opening, molded coamings, excessive deck camber, or other complications may preclude the easy substitution of a manufactured hatch.

MODIFYING A FIBERGLASS HATCH

An easier and lower-cost course to a transparent forward hatch is to modify the existing hatch. The idea is to cut away the top of the hatch and replace it with a piece of clear plastic. If the hatch is flat or only slightly curved, this should not present any difficulty. If a square of hardboard can easily be made to assume the shape of the top of the hatch, you can proceed.

The first step is to select the material. Acrylic is the lower-cost alternative, and you will have a much easier time finding acrylic in the thickness and tint you want. However, if your hatch is not board-flat, you could be better served with plain polycarbonate. This is because forcing acrylic into a curve, even a modest curve, introduces stresses that sooner or later lead to cracking. The rule of thumb is that you can form sheet acrylic into a curve with a radius 200 times the thickness, but as the plastic ages, this ratio increases. You can heat the acrylic in your kitchen oven until it is soft, then drape it over your flannel-protected hatch to get a more radical curve. Or you can buy polycarbonate that will handle a camber with aplomb. Plus, polycarbonate is stronger, less susceptible to internal crazing, and more durable when latches and supports are bolted to it. The dual drawbacks of shorter life and lower scratch resistance cannot in this case be addressed with a mar-resistant polycarbonate because mar-resistant coatings will not tolerate *any* bend. The best solution for nearly flat hatches is probably thick acrylic. If you are offered a choice between extruded acrylic and cast acrylic, get the cast. For a hatch with some crown I would select uncoated polycarbonate, but all of this might become academic when you fold color into the mix.

The choice of clear or "smoked" is up to you. Most people find a bronze or gray tint more attractive than clear. A tint enhances daytime privacy and may actually protect your collection of Winslow Homer watercolors from UV fading when the boat is unoccupied. When you are aboard and the sun is out, the hatches are probably open. Smoked acrylic is readily available. You are likely to find smoked polycarbonate in less than full sheets harder to obtain.

Thickness will depend on the size of the hatch and what you expect it to resist. Thicker is better, but a piece of $1/2$-inch polycarbonate large enough to cover a typical forward hatch can easily cost more than $100—significantly cheaper than a manufactured hatch but still a lot of money for a little piece of plastic. If you are going offshore, pay the money. For coastal and inland boating, $3/8$-inch acrylic or $1/4$-inch polycarbonate will be plenty strong.

Remove the hatch from its hinges, lay it upside down on the masked piece of plastic, and trace around the outside perimeter. Cut the plastic to size, keeping the saber saw blade outside of the perimeter line. If the plastic is not from the scrap bin and *if the sides of the hatch are straight and parallel*, measure carefully and let the supplier cut the piece to size for you. Round the corners with your saber saw. Scrape the edges, then sand them, gently rounding the edge that will be on top but leaving the bottom edge square. If you have a router, you can put the radius on the top edge with a corner-round bit. Polish the edge.

Aligning the New Top

Now pay attention. You are eventually going to attach the plastic with machine screws but you want to be sure that the screws don't interfere with closing the hatch. Put the hatch back in place, then go below and trace the coaming onto the inside of the hatch. Remove the hatch and measure the width of the coaming. Using that measurement, draw a second outline on the inside of the hatch to approximate the outside of the coaming. Crosshatch the area between the two outlines. This is where the hatch rests on the coaming. Unless there is $3/4$ inch or more between the crosshatched area and the edge of the hatch—not very likely—fasteners for the new top will have to be countersunk into the bottom of the hatch.

To locate the mounting holes, draw a line on the underside of the hatch parallel to one side and about an inch inside. You can place the holes as close to the edge as 1.5 times the thickness of the new top—$3/8$ inch for $1/4$-inch plastic—but farther inboard is better. Measure from the adjoining side 2 inches along the line and mark the point. Do the same on the opposite end of the line. The rule of thumb for fastener spacing is 12 times the thickness of the plastic, so for $3/8$-inch acrylic, you want a fastener about every $4^1/_2$ inches. Measure the distance between the two marks and divide that into equal divisions of about $4^1/_2$ inches. For example, on an 18-inch hatch, the distance between the end marks is 14 inches, which can be divided into three equal divisions of $4^2/_3$ inches.

Close enough. Put cross marks on the fastener line every $4^2/_3$ inches. Repeat this process for the other three sides.

Using a $3/16$-inch bit and taking care to keep the drill perpendicular, drill the mounting holes through the old hatch. Three-sixteenths-inch machine screws are a good size for this application. Were there space to do so, you would use an oval head with a finishing washer on the top and a cap nut with a flat washer on the bottom, but this is not usually possible because the mounting holes are in the area where the hatch contacts the coaming. Instead you will be inserting flathead screws from the bottom. To allow them to sit flush, countersink the holes from the underside of the hatch.

With the stainless steel screws, regular hex nuts (for the original assembly), and flat washers at hand, place the piece of transparent plastic *exactly the way it goes* on top of the old hatch. Holding the two together, turn them over and lay the plastic on a wood surface. Using one of the holes in the hatch as a pilot, gently drill a $3/16$-inch hole through the plastic. Insert one of the screws through the hatch and into the plastic. Check again to make sure that the plastic is properly aligned. In the same side as the first hole, drill the next hole and insert a second screw. Check one more time for alignment. Now drill the remaining mounting holes in sequence along that side, inserting the screws as you go. Lift the assembly, push the screws through the plastic, put a washer and nut on each, and hand tighten.

Lay the assembly flat again with the line of nuts just beyond the edge of the support surface. Drill the nearest holes on the two adjacent sides. Insert the screws and tighten by hand. Drill and fasten the next two holes, repeating the sequence until the two sides are completely fastened. Drill the holes in the remaining side, inserting screws.

I don't want to make this task tedious, but perfect hole alignment is essential. If the holes don't quite match on a piece of wood, tightening the fastener crushes some of the wood fibers until all is in alignment. The plastic will not adjust—it will crack.

Now is the time to replace the hex nuts with cap nuts one at a time. If you have to shorten the screws, a high-speed rotary tool (Dremel) with a cutoff wheel makes short, neat work of this. Mark the length and remove the screw before cutting to prevent heating the plastic.

With all holes drilled and all screws sized, disassemble the two parts, taking care to mark the top so you can put it back in exactly the same way. Lay the plastic topside down on the wood surface, and put a small amount of beeswax in each of the holes. Run a ¹/₄-inch drill bit through each. With both acrylic and polycarbonate, you must always drill mounting holes oversize. The wax will leave the holes with a smoother finish.

Now you are going to cut away the fiberglass center of the old hatch. You do not want to disturb the way the hatch rests on the coaming, so the cutout will be the size of the hatch opening, which is the only place you need transparency anyway. You already marked the opening on the bottom of the hatch when you traced around the perimeter of the coaming. Drill a ³/₈-inch or larger hole in each corner of the outlined cutout, making the hole *tangent* to the two lines. The holes will give the corners an attractive radius and allow you to insert your saber-saw blade to make the cuts. With the center removed, smooth the edges of the cutout with coarse paper on a finishing sander or a sanding block.

Assembling the Hatch

Reattach the hatch to the top, pinning it in position by inserting at least three screws. Gingerly and with a light touch trace around the flange of the old hatch with a new single-edge razor blade to cut the protective film. This will allow you to peel the film from the sealant area but leave the rest of the lens protected. Separate the pieces.

Clean the top of the ring of original hatch that remains with acetone. Peel away the masking film from the perimeter of the bottom of the plastic and all of the film from the top, noting how the plastic aligns with the hatch *before* you tear away your notations. An extra step is possible here: scuff the seal surface of the new clear top with 80-grit paper and give it a couple of coats of topside enamel to match the color of the hatch. This will hide flaws in the bedding and, more important, protect the sealant from UV damage.

Mask the edge of the plastic top and the vertical rim of the old hatch with tape. Place the plastic topside down on a pad of newspaper. Heavily coat the remaining ring of the old hatch with silicone sealant. If you have not painted the rim of the top, white silicone gives a more attractive joint than clear on a white fiberglass hatch. Do not use polysulfide sealants on polycarbonate. You can use polyurethane (Sikaflex-295 UV), but it necessitates a special cleaner and an expensive primer. Follow the instructions here and you won't need the stronger bond of polyurethane.

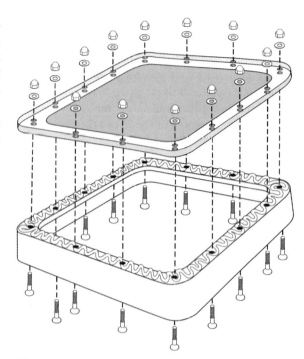

Giving a fiberglass hatch a clear lens.

Put a bit of sealant in each of the mounting holes in the plastic. Carefully place the hatch on the new top and insert several screws to hold the two in position. Following the same hole sequence you used for drilling, insert the screws and hand tighten the nuts. The idea with silicone sealant is to create a gasket, so you want some silicone to squeeze out all around both outside and inside to confirm that it is being compressed, but you do not want to squeeze out all

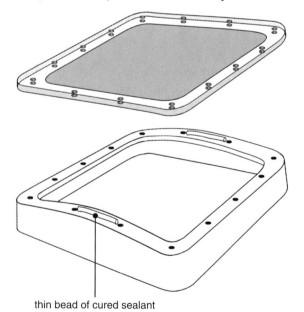

thin bead of cured sealant

For a hatch with a cambered top, cured silicone "standoffs" will prevent all sealant from being squeezed out at the apex.

of the sealant. After the sealant has cured for a day or two, hold the screws motionless and tighten the nuts about $^1/_4$ turn to put the gasket under compression.

A hatch with camber necessitates tightening the fasteners initially with a wrench to warp the lens. This squeezes the sealant out of the middle before the sides are sufficiently tight to seal. Counteract this situation before installing the plastic top by running a bead of silicone 3 or 4 inches long at the center of the front (curved) flange. Do the same on the rear flange. Flatten the beads to about $^1/_{16}$ inch with a strip of waxed paper and let them cure fully. Now install the plastic as outlined previously. The precured silicone will prevent the two pieces from squeezing together too tightly in the middle.

Do not try to wipe away the excess silicone sealant. It will just smear. After the silicone has cured fully, carefully trace the inside edge of the cutout with a razor knife or new single-edge razor blade. Cut all the way through the beaded silicone; it will pull away cleanly. Remove the remaining masking film at the same time. Use the blade to slice away the protruding bead of sealant around the outside of the hatch, then peel off the masking tape.

CLEAR TOPS ON WOOD FRAMES

Wooden hatches can be modified in almost the same manner. Instead of cutting an opening in the top, you will normally remove the existing top from the frame and replace it with clear plastic. If the original top is wood and screwed in place, the screws will be hidden beneath round wooden plugs called bungs. Drill a small hole in the center of the bung and thread a long screw into it. As the point of the screw encounters the screw head beneath the bung, it will lift the bung from the hole.

On a wood frame, attach the plastic top using oval-head #10 wood screws with finishing washers. The screws should penetrate the wood at least $^1/_2$ inch. Drill the plastic and the pilot holes in the frame at the same time, using a $^1/_8$-inch drill bit. Then turn the plastic over, put wax in the holes, and enlarge them to $^1/_4$ inch. Bed the joint with black silicone sealant.

A TRANSPARENT COMPANIONWAY

The benefits of transparency apply equally to the companionway hatch, and the modification is essentially the same as for the forward hatch. If the hatch slides into a seahood, be sure there is clearance for the probable extra height of the plastic top and the fasteners.

Clear dropboards for the companionway are excellent onboard applications for Lexan. If you want to replace the original wood boards, the plastic should be similar in thickness and cut to size using the original boards as patterns. You can bevel or rabbet the plastic just like the wood (see Chapter 10). If you just want a clear alternative for a rainy day at anchor, cut a single piece for the opening from $^1/_8$-inch acrylic or polycarbonate. It will store easily under a bunk. If you have difficulty cutting thin material, try clamping the piece between two pieces of scrap plywood and cutting all three layers together.

INSTALLING MANUFACTURED HATCHES

No enhancement to my own old boat improved livability more than a deck hatch over the main saloon, but it is not easy to bring yourself to cut a hole in the cabin top. There are good reasons to be cautious. A big hole in the cabin top weakens it, although if the near-universal installation of main saloon hatches in newer boats is any indication, this is not much of a concern. Just do not place the cutout near the mast if it is deck stepped or near other holes in the deck. There might also be wiring above the headliner, which your saw will surely cut.

The first requirement for installing a new hatch is to know what is on both sides of the surface. Decide on the size and location of your new hatch and tape the outline on the cabin headliner. Find two features that already pass through the deck—a mast, hardware mounting bolts, a ventilator, an existing hatch—and use distances to these features to create a second outline on deck directly above the one on the liner. Assess from both sides if the hatch will be well placed in this location.

Aside from a location that is clear of obstructions and away from other holes, there are at least three other issues to resolve. First, trace around the taped outline on deck with a bladeless saw to make sure you can saw around the entire outline without interference. If some deck feature intrudes, now is the time to determine how to work around it.

Second, span the outlined area athwartships with a straightedge to determine how much crown the deck has at your chosen spot. Deck hatches are designed to be mounted on a flat surface in spite of nearly all boat decks being curved. If your deck has excessive crown, is there a flatter alternative? Otherwise you must determine how you will create the required flat surface.

The third issue is wiring. On some boats with molded headliners, some of the wiring was routed over the top of the liner before the deck was installed. If that is a risk on your boat, use a hole-saw to remove a plug of the headliner from the center of the cutout, then peer and probe for wiring. If you find any, you may be able to push it aside. Otherwise take care to cut the wire near the middle of the cutout and not at the perimeter so you can splice in additional length to route the wire around the opening.

Now select a hatch that matches the quality of your boat and how you use it. It will come with detailed installation instructions, usually including a cutout template. Use the template (or the hatch) to outline the cutout on deck, making sure it is square with the centerline of the boat. Your outline should be thin, dark, and unambiguous.

It is tempting to load a fresh blade in the saber saw and simply follow the cutout outline. If you are skillful with a saber saw, this method might work for you. If not, you should first use a spade bit or a hole-saw to drill holes at each corner in such a way that one quarter of the circumference of each hole forms that corner of the cutout. Now you only have to make straight cuts from hole to hole.

If you have a fabric headliner, both the drill and the saw will snag and tear it. You need to cut it and move it out of the way first. Just inside the cutout outline at all four corners (this must be *inside* the corner hole circumference), drill a $1/_8$-inch hole through the deck, then use a sharp-pointed wire to poke through the holes and the headliner. Slice the headliner fabric in an X pattern between these four punched holes. Tape the flaps out of the way; you can trim them off later after you determine how to tighten and secure the liner around the new hatch. It is advisable to have a helper below to keep the headliner away from the drill (for the corners) and the saw when you are cutting. A circular saw can be better at cutting a straight line, and you can set the depth above the headliner, but because the saw cuts in an arc rather than vertically, you will need to complete the cutout with a saber saw.

The cutout will likely expose the core material. We already know the disastrous consequences of allowing water access to the core, so it is imperative to seal the raw edge. Bedding under the flange of the hatch is *not* adequate. Dig or grind out all the exposed core material around the cutout at least beyond where the fasteners will pass through the deck skin. Sand the interior surface of both skins. Saturate the cavity, particularly the exposed core, with unthickened epoxy. When this kicks, fill the cavity level with the cut edges with epoxy thickened to a peanut-butter consistency with fibers or silica. This not only seals the core, but it reinforces the cutout and provides a crush-resistant base for the flange.

In the likely event that the deck is not perfectly flat, you will need to fabricate a spacer that matches the deck curvature on the bottom and is flat on the

Drilled holes matching the radius of the corners of the cutout limit sawing to straight cuts.

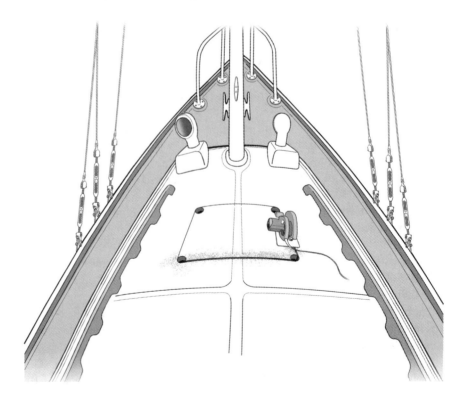

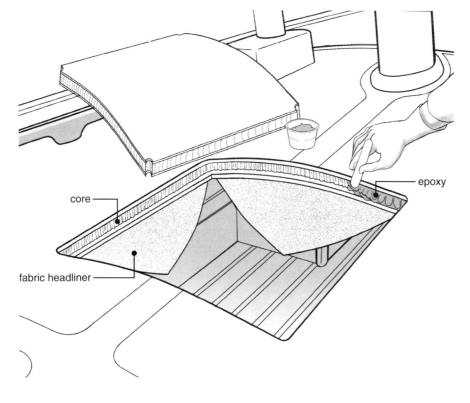

core

fabric headliner

epoxy

If there is exposed core around the perimeter of the cutout, excavate it beyond where the fastener holes will penetrate and fill the resulting cavity with silica-thickened epoxy.

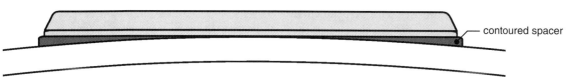

contoured spacer

A spacer or buildup is required if the deck is cambered where the hatch will be installed.

top, or you will need to build up the deck around the cutout with epoxy paste or fiberglass laminates. Grinding down the crown is almost never an option because it further weakens a deck that has already been insulted by a cutout.

Once you have the necessary board-flat base, dry-fit the hatch in the cutout and drill the holes for the mounting screws. The instructions that come with the hatch likely show screwing the hatch to the deck, possibly with the added security of through-bolting near the hinges, but this is not a particularly seaman-like mount. Screwed-to-the-deck hatches are fine on a coastal boat, but on any boat headed offshore, the hatch frame must be through-bolted all the way around. If you will be screwing the frame to the deck, take care that you use the correct bit for the screw size.

Mask the deck around the perimeter of the hatch and mask the edge of the flange. You can let the tape stand vertical; its purpose is to keep sealant squeeze-out off the frame.

Remove the hatch and completely coat the deck between the tape and the cutout with sealant. Use polysulfide if the hatch frame is metal, silicone or a silicone/polyurethane blend if it is plastic. Put the hatch back over the cutout and wiggle it gently to distribute the sealant. Insert the bolts or screws and snug them all. Now tighten them, following a pattern of each screw in sequence being as opposite as possible to the one before; i.e., right side, left side, front right, rear left, etc. Tighten just enough for some sealant to squeeze out around the full perimeter of the flange. Do not overtighten the screws or you will squeeze out all the sealant and the resulting metal-to-fiberglass joint will soon leak.

Allow polysulfide to cure a week, silicone a day, then tighten the nuts on through-bolts about half a turn to put the sealant under compression. Do not tighten screws or you will break the seal on them. Trace a razor knife around the perimeter of the hatch frame to separate the squeeze-out from the sealant under the frame. Peel the tape from the deck and the excess sealant will come with it. Remove the tape from the hatch and you're finished except for installing the trim ring below.

CRAZED AND CLOUDY HATCHES AND PORTS

If your fiberglass boat is more than 25 years old, you can be relatively certain that the fixed portlights are acrylic. You may find tempered glass in the opening ports, but the fixed ones will be plastic. Quarter-inch Plexiglas was pretty standard, sometimes replaced in later years by $\frac{1}{4}$-inch Lexan. If your boat has the original acrylic portlights, the view through them is almost certainly obscured by surface scratches and internal crazing.

Old acrylic hatches craze and crack, and polycarbonate hatches darken and erode from long exposure. For surface degradation both acrylic and polycarbonate will respond to polishing. For moderate degradation you could try Novus 3 Heavy Scratch Remover followed by Novus 2 Fine Scratch Remover. These products are widely available at motorcycle shops and auto parts stores. To get good results from Novus, you need a soft cotton cloth. Flannel is ideal.

If Novus isn't aggressive enough, you may still be able to remove surface damage from clear plastic in much the same way as you might restore badly weathered gelcoat—by wet sanding the plastic in one direction with very fine wet-or-dry paper, then using a finer grade of abrasive to wet sand perpendicular to the first sanding. The specific grits depend on the depth of the surface degradation and whether you are working on harder acrylic or softer polycarbonate. First determine which you are dealing with by dragging the sharp corner of a screwdriver blade across the plastic in an inconspicuous spot. If the blade makes a noise or chatters and cuts a scratch in the plastic, it is acrylic. If the blade drags across silently and dents rather than scratches, the plastic is polycarbonate.

With polycarbonate you will have a more difficult time polishing out surface scratches, and a grit any coarser than 1200 wet-or-dry (used wet) is likely to make the surface worse rather than better. Acrylic, on the other hand, can be attacked with something as coarse as 320-grit (wet), followed by progressively finer grades—always sanding perpendicular to the scratches made by the previous grade. At around 1000 grit you can switch to compound then polish, applied with the aid of a power buffer. This is a labor-intensive process but it can deliver excellent results. Make your initial effort in an inconspicuous spot.

If the degradation seems to be inside the plastic, replacement becomes the only option. Internal faults are more common with acrylic than with polycarbonate.

The lenses in manufactured hatches are bonded into the frame. When yours are scratched or crazed or cracked, some hatch manufacturers will sell you a replacement lens and the adhesive for installing it.

Others will tell you that you must send the hatch to them for lens replacement. Poppycock! As with most other repairs aboard, there is typically little reason why a determined boatowner cannot replace the lens in a manufactured hatch. What follows are generic instructions for doing just that.

HATCH LENS REPLACEMENT

Getting the old lens out is simply a matter of cutting it free. Use a razor knife with a new blade to cut the sealant completely around the perimeter of the lens on both the bottom and top. If the dogs are on the frame, I latch it and push the lens out from below. If the dogs (and/or support) are mounted to the lens, you must dismantle these, then push or *carefully* pry the old lens from the frame.

Nothing but Frame

The time-consuming part of this job is removing *all* of the old sealant. If you leave even the tiniest trace of it on the frame, the new sealant will not adhere and your hatch will leak between the frame and the lens. This is a certainty, so take the time to get all of the old sealant off the frame. Start by scraping; finish by sanding. A wire brush can be useful for the corner. Wipe everything with xylene or toluene.

If the frame is not anodized or you damaged the finish, corrosion can interfere with getting the best bond from the sealant. To prevent that problem, clean the metal surfaces the sealant will attach to with an acid cleaner such as Alumiprep, then coat them with a chromate conversion coating (Alodine).

Use a Router

While you are cleaning away old sealant, also clean up the edges of the old lens. The easiest way to get a perfect match is to give the old lens to your plastics supplier as a pattern. The second easiest way is for you to rout the new lens with a carbide flush-cut bit, using the old lens as a pattern. Either way, the edge of the old lens needs to be clean and nick free. If you cannot get the identical thickness of your old lens, choose one that is slightly thicker so water will not be trapped on the lens by a higher frame.

To do it yourself, saw a blank about $\frac{1}{4}$ inch larger all around than the old lens. You can rout-cut thin acrylic but you run a risk with thicker plastic, so it is better to just trim the edge with your router. Center the old lens on the blank and stick the two together solidly with double-sided tape. Turn the assembly over to put the old lens underneath, then set your router depth to run the flush-cut bearing against the edge (squeaky clean, right?) of the old lens.

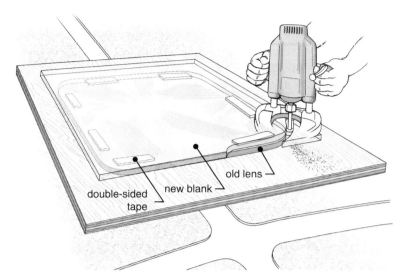

Duplicating the old lens is a snap with a router and a flush-cut bit. Protective film would still be in place but is omitted here for clarity.

double-sided tape

new blank

old lens

You want the bit to cut inside out, so feed the router in a counterclockwise direction when routing an outside perimeter (but clockwise when trimming an inside cutout). If you feed the wrong way, the bit tries to push away from the material, usually resulting in an uneven cut. It is a very good idea to practice your routing technique on some scrap material before attacking the lens blank.

Also drill hardware mounting holes while the two lenses are joined, using the old lens as a drill guide. Note the correct orientation on the masking film, then separate the two lenses.

The Right Goo

The right sealant for this job is GE SilPruf SCS2000 or Dow Corning 795 Silicone Building Sealant, both silicone-based adhesives formulated for structural glazing—bedding windows in commercial buildings. Start the process by making spacers to center the lens in the frame. With the lens correctly located, turn the assembly over and lightly trace around the inside perimeter of the frame with a new single-edge razor blade to cut the masking film. Take the lens out and peel the film outside the cut line. Mask the edges of the frame, inside and out.

Wipe the exposed surfaces (and edge) of the plastic with a rag saturated with isopropyl alcohol. While the alcohol is still wet, wipe dry with a clean paper towel to pick up all contaminants.

Apply a bead of sealant to the bottom lip of the frame and carefully position the lens, using your spacers to center it. Press down gently—enough to seat the lens on the sealant but not enough to squeeze all of the sealant out of the joint. Peek underneath to make sure you have *some* squeeze-out all around the frame. Remove the spacers if there is any chance of them touching the sealant. Wait about 30 minutes for the sealant to solidify so it holds the lens in position.

Press lens onto a bead of sealant on the frame lip and center with spacers.

Leave undisturbed for 30 minutes to allow sealant to solidify.

Fill gap between lens and frame with sealant, pushing the bead in front of the cartridge tip.

Hatch lens replacement is a two-step process.

Now, always pushing forward with the tip of the cartridge, fill the gap between the lens and the frame with sealant. Be sure you do not leave any air bubbles or voids. Fill the space to the top. Use a plastic spreader to dress the sealant flat. Pick up excess sealant beyond the joint.

Give the sealant 24 hours to cure, then trim it as necessary with a new razor blade and peel away all of the masking. These sealants reach full cure in about two weeks. The blue sky appears immediately.

FIXED-PORT REPLACEMENT

For fixed ports, sending them away is not an option. You are on your own. Portlight replacement can be a breeze or it can be a struggle every step of the way. The prime indicator of how it is going to go will be the condition of the portlight frames.

On most older boats the portlight frames are aluminum. Often the outside half of the frame is threaded for mounting bolts installed through the inside half. After a couple of decades either the mounting bolts are welded to the outside frame or the threads have turned into a white powder. Either way, when you take them apart, you cannot simply put them back together.

If the whole frame disintegrates, you are faced with chasing down the original supplier (you can send an inquiry to the boat manufacturer if they are still in business, but don't be surprised if they don't know who the supplier was), having new frames machined locally, finding similar frames and modifying the cabin-side openings to fit, or abandoning frames altogether and surface-mounting the replacement portlights.

Portlights with Frames

If the old frames are in reasonably good shape, replacing the plastic should present few problems. However, forget about rethreading stripped sockets in the outside frame. It was a bad idea to start with. Redrill the once-threaded holes through the frame and through-bolt both halves with oval-head machine screws and cap nuts. If the inner and outer frames are identical, reverse them to put the already countersunk frame outside.

Check the shape of the old portlights when you dismantle them. Some manufacturers did an exceedingly poor job of matching the radius of the plastic to the frame and/or the cutout on the cabin side. Rubber spacers were also used to "make up" the thickness difference between portlight and cabin side. If your portlights are too thin or poorly matched, make the necessary correction when you cut the replacements or have them cut. Quarter-inch or thicker acrylic has proven quite durable on normal-size portlights, but if your boat has oversize "windows" and/or you plan to sail well offshore, pay the premium for Lexan.

Be sure all the old bedding has been removed from the opening and the frames; wipe both with xylene. While the portlights are out, make sure there is no exposed core around the openings. If there is, dig it out and fill the cavity with epoxy putty.

Assemble the new window and modified frames to check for any fit problems. Trace around both frames with a new razor blade to cut the masking film. Mask the cabin side—outside and in—around the frames. Disassemble and remove the film on both sides from the perimeter of the portlight, leaving the center protected.

I like to bed the ports in two steps. Put the exterior frame in place dry and insert the bolts. Put the plastic in place and hold it there with a couple of strips of tape across the outside. Apply a generous layer of clear silicone sealant to the inside frame only, and while a helper pushes in on the bolts from outside as required, fit the frame over the bolts and seat it against the plastic and the inside cabin surface. Install the nuts and tighten them in steps in a "most-opposite" sequence (middle top, middle bottom, right top, left bottom, etc.) until some silicone squeezes out all around the inside and outside perimeter of the inside frame. *Stop.* When the silicone cures, both the portlight and the inside frame are bonded in place, and the outside of the portlight is perfectly flush with the cabin side.

When the silicone squeeze-out is solid to the touch, remove the nuts and *unscrew* the bolts to extract them. Coat the outside frame generously with silicone. Also fill in any space between the portlight and the cutout perimeter. Put the frame in place and insert the bolts, putting a necklace of silicone around each. Rethread the bolts through the inner frame, then hold each motionless while your helper installs and tightens the nuts evenly in a most-opposite sequence. Direct the tightening to achieve uniform squeeze-out all around the inside and outside perimeters of the outside frame. Again, *stop.* Wait a full day, then hold the bolts motionless and tighten each nut a half turn to put the silicone under compression. This should give you a permanently leak-free portlight installation.

Trace around the frames with your razor blade to cut the squeeze-out free from the silicone under the frame, then peel off all the masking. When you go below, try not to freak out at the difference clear portlights make. It's like having had cataract surgery.

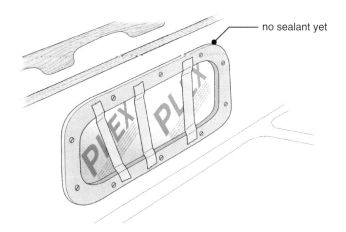

no sealant yet

Position the new lens and hold it against the "dry" outside frame with tape.

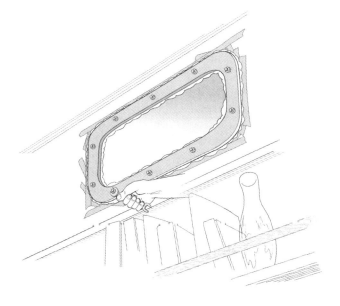

Assemble the inside frame on a generous bed of silicone sealant and snug fasteners to get squeeze-out all around. Allow to cure.

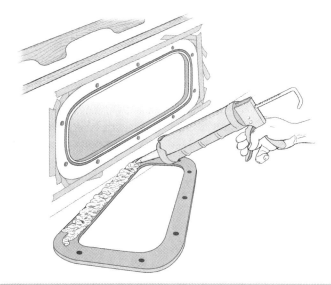

Remove fasteners, coat outside frame and fill void between lens and cabin side with sealant, then reassemble and snug fasteners for even perimeter squeeze-out.

Install framed portlight lenses in two steps.

Surface-Mounted Portlights

Lots of production boats have been delivered without frames around fixed portlights. The clear plastic is just bolted over the opening directly to the cabin side. This makes for a very strong installation, not unlike storm shutters.

Replacing surface-mounted portlights is straightforward. However, you may also consider replacing framed portlights with surface-mounted ones. Just discard the outer frame, fill the old fastener holes, and cut the new plastic to extend beyond the portlight opening at least three times the thickness of the plastic all around. Smoked plastic—acrylic or polycarbonate—is the universal choice for surface mounting because the tint hides the actual opening, allowing a great deal of latitude in shape and size. Dark surface-mounted ports will "update" the look of an older boat, and for stylistic reasons you may want to give the plastic a shape different from the opening. With some black poster board, a pair of scissors, and a roll of transparent tape, you can try a bit of rake at the forward end, for example, to see if it enhances or detracts.

Once you are happy with the shape and size, transfer the pattern to the plastic and cut out the blanks. Scrape, wet sand, and polish the edges. Draw a fastener location line 1.5 times the thickness of the plastic plus half the diameter of the mounting holes inside the edge of the perimeter. Mark fastener locations on this line spaced about twelve times the thickness of the plastic. For $3/8$-inch acrylic, for example, that makes fastener spacing about $4^1/_2$ inches. You can adjust this to achieve aesthetically pleasing spacing at the ends.

It seems unseamanlike to me to screw the portlights to the cabin side, but if this is how you choose to mount them, drill pilot-size holes at every fastener location marked on the protective film. Circle one hole at each end to serve as guide holes. Hold the portlight in the exact position you want it mounted and use one of the circled holes as a drill guide to drill a pilot hole in the cabin side. If you drill into core, stop. It will be easier and better to through-bolt the portlights than to bore all the fastener locations oversize from the outside and fill them with epoxy. This has to be done before drilling the final holes since perfect alignment is essential.

If the first hole is into or through solid fiberglass, insert a spare drill bit to pin the portlight in position. Check the alignment again and drill a second pilot hole using the circled hole at the opposite end as your drill guide. Remove the portlight, lay it exterior side down, and redrill the two circled holes to the exact outside diameter of the screws. Temporarily mount the portlight to the cabin side with screws through these two holes, and drill all of the other pilot holes using the portlight as your drill guide. While it is attached, mask the cabin side around the perimeter of the portlight, then go inside and trace around the opening with a new razor blade to cut the protective film.

Remove the portlight, place it exterior side down, and redrill all of the holes at least $1/_{16}$ inch larger than the screw diameter. Peel the masking film from the surface to be sealed. For longer sealant life, sand and paint the sealed surface of the portlight. Mask the edge of the plastic.

The ductile nature of fiberglass means the cabin side may not be perfectly fair. A trick to making sure you do not squeeze out all of the sealant in high spots, leaving a dry and leak-prone joint, is to put an O-ring or a small rubber washer around each screw on the interior side of the plastic. The mounted portlight will "float" on these washers, creating a gap for the sealant to fill. Put a finishing washer and a collar of sealant around each screw before inserting it to provide a seal between the screw and the plastic. Tighten the screws in a most-opposite sequence. Let the sealant cure, then trim away the squeeze-out and remove the masking.

Through-bolting delivers a more seaworthy installation and is the only sensible choice if the cabin side is cored. The process is similar to the one just described except that you drill holes the diameter of the bolts rather than pilot holes for screws. On solid fiberglass, you can secure the bolts inside with flat washers and cap nuts. If there is core in the cabin side, you will need to bore the holes oversize from the inside only and fill the cavities with epoxy putty, then using the portlight as a drill guide, redrill all the holes. Only after you have the final hole pattern drilled in the cabin side should you redrill the holes in the plastic $1/_{16}$ inch oversize.

If you have a molded liner, it is normally advisable to fill any space between the liner and the cabin side with epoxy putty all around the perimeter of the opening to provide a solid base for the mounting bolts. For a particularly neat and leak-free installation, counterbore the liner and/or the cored cabin side and through-bolt the portlights to the outer skin only using stainless steel tee-nuts. With the portlights finally mounted on a sealant gasket, tape the ends of the tee-nuts to avoid bonding the threads, then fill the counterbore with thickened epoxy. When the epoxy cures, the tee-nuts are cast in place, providing a robust attachment and eliminating any

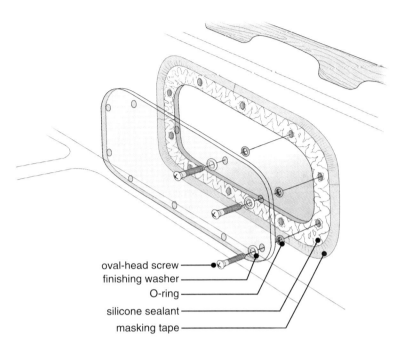

Thin O-rings installed on fasteners between the lens and the cabin side ensure an adequate gap for a leak-avoiding sealant "gasket."

oval-head screw
finishing washer
O-ring
silicone sealant
masking tape

possibility of a fastener leak. If the holes will not be hidden behind interior trim, make whatever cosmetic repairs are required.

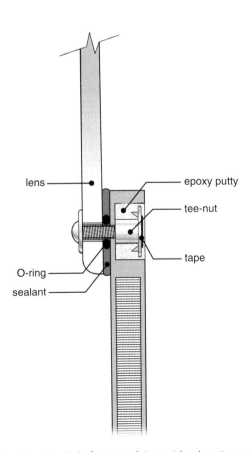

lens
O-ring
sealant
epoxy putty
tee-nut
tape

Threading deadlight fasteners into cast-in-place tee-nuts creates a strong and leak-free mount.

ACRYLIC MIRROR

A plastic product with underutilized application on boats is acrylic mirror. This is particularly true on older boats with smaller interior spaces. As any decorator will tell you, clever use of mirrors can expand a living space. Acrylic mirror has its best "gee whiz" application on an old boat as the back wall in the head compartment. The sensory effect of essentially doubling the size of this typically small space is astonishing. Acrylic mirror can similarly be used on a main saloon bulkhead to fool the senses. It can bring light into a dark galley as sliding cabinet doors. Or maybe you just want a full-length mirror on the back of the head door to check out your shore kit before heading out for the opera.

SEAL THE EDGES

Like other sheet plastic, acrylic mirror is sold by the sheet or cut to size. There are no special handling requirements other than to seal the edges. Acrylic is less stable than glass, and moisture will more quickly wick between the acrylic and the silvering, causing the mirror to turn black at the edges. You can prevent this by painting *all* edges with two or three coats of unthickened epoxy. Paint would probably work just as well but there could be compatibility issues between the solvents in the paint and the protective coating already on the mirror. Solventless epoxy does not have that risk.

Because acrylic is both light and essentially unbreakable, you can mount it with mirror tape—a strip or squares of foam with adhesive on both sides. This "floats" the mirror above the surface you are attaching it to, usually providing an undistorted

Covering a wall with acrylic mirror doubles the apparent size of a small space.

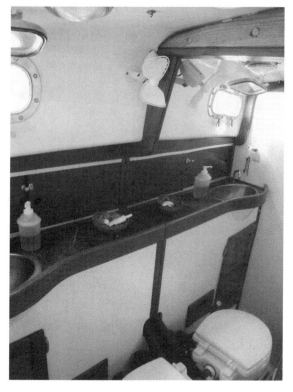

installation. Wipe the supporting surface with alcohol to remove grease and oils, then place squares of mirror tape at all corners and on 6- or 8-inch centers over the entire surface to be covered. Press the mirror in place. Trim with molding if you like. Done.

PLASTIC LAMINATES

Another plastic product that has found its way into boats is decorative laminate. For much of the last half of the 20th century, decorative laminate—often referred to as Formica, the best-known brand name—was the surface of choice for countertops and kitchen cabinets in most of the houses built in America. It is made of layers of kraft paper soaked in phenolic resin—reminiscent of fiberglass construction. The penultimate layer is colored or printed paper covered with a surface layer of tough, clear melamine. Decorative laminate is attractive, tough, incredibly versatile, and very easy to use.

Unlike acrylic, decorative laminate has to be bought in a full sheet, but the cost is usually reasonable. A standard sheet of plastic laminate is 4 feet by 8 feet. Most patterns will be available in both the standard horizontal grade ($^1/_{16}$ inch thick) and in a vertical grade ($^1/_{32}$ inch thick) intended for surfaces that will get little wear. The most likely uses of plastic laminate aboard an old boat are to resurface the counter in the galley and/or the head, which requires horizontal grade, and to cover bulkheads and cabinets, for which vertical grade is appropriate.

If your ultimate project is a countertop, select the color and pattern you want from among the scores of samples the supplier will show you. Be cautious about being too trendy. You could find yourself dissatisfied with your choice in a short time. A "butcher block" pattern, for example, was once all the rage. Now it just screams, "1976." Not that recovering is all that difficult, but removing and replacing the wood trim that typically accents galley counters can be. If your boat sees regular use, you will reupholster a couple of times before the laminate begins to show age. Buy a color and pattern that will allow you to change the cabin decor if you so choose.

PAPER PATTERN

The best way to get a perfect fit is with a paper pattern. Lay heavy kraft paper over the counter to be recovered and crease it into all of the intersections

Make a paper pattern for cutting new laminate to the correct size and shape.

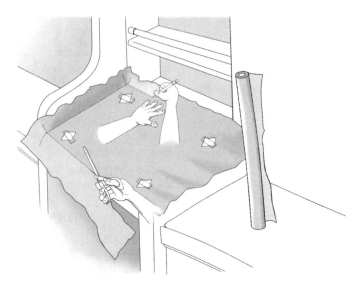

with vertical surfaces. If the paper wants to move around, "pin" it in place with double-sided tape, or cut a couple of holes in the middle and run regular tape across these. Cut the pattern on the crease lines and check it again to make sure the size and all the angles are exactly right. Write "top" on the pattern, then turn it over and write "bottom." You will be marking and cutting the laminate facedown, so when you are tracing the pattern onto the back side, you should see "bottom" written on the pattern.

Trace the outline of the piece or pieces you need on the bottom of the sheet of laminate. Again tape across holes on the pattern to hold it in place. If the back of the counter butts against a cabinet and is not covered with trim, lay out the piece to take advantage of the sheet's finished edge. For edges that you will cut, draw a second line about $1/4$ inch beyond the pattern to allow for trimming. Don't cut anything yet! You are just trying to "reserve" the laminate for its intended purpose.

A FIRST PROJECT

Now open the cabinet below the counter and remove one of the plywood shelves. If there aren't any, get one out of the cockpit lockers or the lazarette. If you don't have any shelves on the boat, read Chapter 10 and build one. Lay the shelf topside down on the back side of a section of the laminate not already designated for the counter. Hold your marker at an angle to trace an outline around the shelf about $1/4$ inch larger on all sides. Also outline a straight strip $1/2$ inch longer than the front edge of the shelf and $1/2$ inch wider than its thickness.

All decorative laminate has a tendency to chip when it is cut, which is why you always cut it slightly oversize. The thinner grade can be cut with tin snips or special scissors (a paper cutter does a nice job on smaller pieces) but it is prone to tearing. It can also be scored with a special tool and broken—like glass. Cut horizontal grade with a saber saw and a special plastic laminate blade, which will have no set to the teeth. Supporting *both sides* of the cut as close to the blade as possible, cut out the two pieces of laminate for the shelf. Do not cut out any of the other pieces.

Put a square of 60-grit sandpaper on your finishing sander and run it over the top and front edges of the shelf. If the shelf was previously painted, take the gloss off the paint or remove it altogether. If the shelf is already laminate covered, be sure there are no loose edges and heavily sand the old surface to give the glue a good bonding surface. Fill and fair any holes in the surface. When applying plastic laminate to any surface, that surface must be smooth (not slick), clean, and dry.

Contact Cement

Plastic laminate is glued in place with contact cement. I am not a fan of the water-based variety. Unfortunately the "right" contact cement—petroleum based—is also extremely volatile. You can take the shelf and the pieces of laminate out to the cockpit to coat them but you cannot do a counter or a bulkhead that way. When you are gluing below be sure that you have lots of ventilation and that everything that has a flame or might generate a spark is *off*. Don't even think about smoking; the Surgeon General is right. The cement is also toxic, so as soon as you have the parts coated, get out of there until it dries.

Use a throwaway bristle brush to coat the bottom of the laminate and the surface it will cover. One coat on both surfaces is usually enough, but new wood can sometimes absorb the cement, requiring a second coat. The coated surface should have a little sheen. Start the shelf by coating its front edge and the back of the cut strip. The edge of the shelf will probably require two coats. After the cement has dried tack free, line up the strip with the edge, overlapping on all sides. Do not let the glued surfaces touch or the shelf will grab the strip out of your hand like something from a Stephen King novel.

When you have the piece lined up, press it in place. It is a good idea to compress large areas with a rubber roller, but a roller tends to crack the overlap on a narrow surface, so compress the strip with your thumb.

Trim to Fit

Trimming away the overlap is next. The cheap way is with a mill file. Support the shelf vertically and file away the excess. You use the file much like a saw, holding it flat to the surface of the shelf and cutting the laminate with the edge of the file, always with downstrokes. If you will be doing all the trim with a file, you want to hold the overlap to no more than is absolutely necessary. Measure the width of the worst chip on the pieces you have already cut and reduce the overlap on future pieces (from the same material cut with the same saw) to that width plus $1/16$ inch.

If you have very much to cover with laminate, buy or borrow a router. It will change the task from drudgery to fun. A flush-trim blade makes short work of trimming the laminate. Run the router around the perimeter of the piece being trimmed and that's it. The roller guide gives a perfect edge every time. Inside corners or an inability to run the router around the *entire* perimeter of a fixed surface may necessitate some filing.

After the front piece is trimmed, evenly coat the top of the shelf and the bottom of the cut piece of laminate from edge to edge with contact cement, taking care not to leave any of either surface uncoated. To minimize the visibility of the seams, the usual sequence of installation is: sides (in this case, there is no point in covering the sides of an interior shelf), then the front, and finally the top. Let the glue dry tack free. If the can the cement comes in provides different instructions, follow them.

Preventing Premature Adhesion

Dry contact cement will stick only to other contact cement. To make positioning a large piece of laminate easy, lay waxed paper over the coated surface, covering every inch of it. Place the laminate on top of the paper and position it correctly. Without moving the laminate, carefully slide the paper partially from between the two and press the parts together. Now slide the paper out completely and compress the bond with a rubber roller or by hammering on a foot square of thick plywood that you move around the surface. Install the laminate on the shelf top in this manner, then run the router around the perimeter and the shelf is finished.

A NEW COUNTERTOP

The only difference in the shelf and a countertop or a bulkhead is the trim and molding that you may have to deal with. All of the wood trim will have to be removed. If it was installed with finishing nails, your task will not be difficult. Look at the trim carefully and you will see where the nail holes have been filled. Use a $1/16$-inch nail set to drive the nails completely through the molding. When all the nails have been located and driven through, the molding will come free.

Unfortunately (for the purpose of easy removal) trim is often glued in place as well. In this case, sharpen the edge of a stiff, 3-inch-wide putty knife and, after the nails have been driven through, drive the blade under the edge of the molding to release the glue bond. You may have to separate every inch of the trim but with patience you will be able to remove it without damaging it.

With the trim and all counter-mounted appliances or hardware removed, you should be ready to resurface the countertop. The first step is to make sure the existing laminate is well adhered. Tap the surface all over with the plastic handle of a screwdriver to sound for bond failure. Check the bond around exposed edges—the sink cutout, for example—with a sharp blade. If the old bond is failing, remove the laminate with a heat gun and a sharpened putty knife.

Normally the old laminate will be solidly attached. All that is required to prepare it for new laminate is heavily sanding the melamine surface

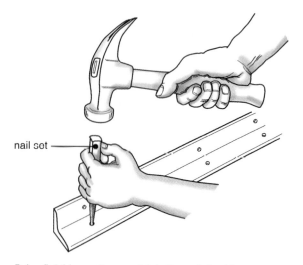

nail set

Drive finishing nails completely through the trim.

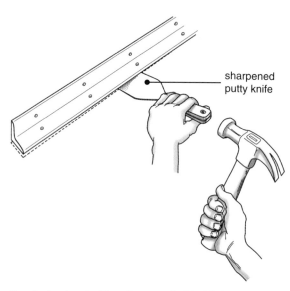

sharpened putty knife

Break glue bond with a sharpened wide-blade putty knife.

Removing interior wood trim.

with 60-grit paper. Using a finishing sander rather than a disk sander will make you less likely to create waves in the surface. Every square centimeter of the old laminate should be uniformly dull.

The rear of a countertop and sometimes the sides may not hide the edge of the laminate under any trim, necessitating a finished edge on the laminate *before* it is installed. If you cannot cut out the piece to take advantage of the edge of the sheet, double-stick the laminate to a straight plank, slightly overlapping, then dress the edge by running the flush-trim bit's roller guide against the plank edge.

It is not necessary to make the cutout holes in the laminate. After it is glued in place, you will drill a hole large enough to admit your flush-trim bit through the laminate in the cutout area, then just rout out the cutout piece using the actual edge of the cutout. This avoids all alignment concerns.

Laminated counter edges are common in kitchens but less so in galleys. If your counter has a laminated edge, as with the shelf, this is the piece you apply first. Press it in place with your thumbs, then trim it with a router and/or file. Only *after* it is trimmed can you roll it to tighten the bond without breaking the edges.

Coat the counter and the underside of the new laminate top with contact cement, then wait for it to dry tack free. Cover every inch of the counter with pieces of waxed paper, taking care not to let the paper turn up onto adjoining surfaces where it could get pinched by the new top. Position the new top, then slide one piece of paper out an inch or so and gently press the two surfaces together. Now slide all of the remaining paper out an inch or two to make sure none

3

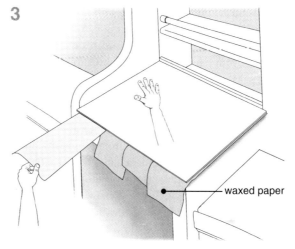

waxed paper

Position laminate, slide out separating paper, and press laminate in place.

1

Coat counter and laminate with contact cement. Coat transportable pieces in open air.

4

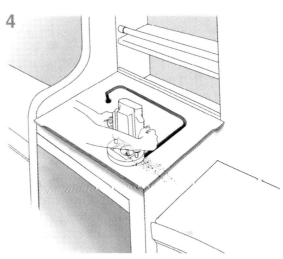

Rout cutouts and untrimmed edges.

2

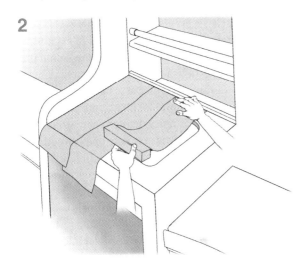

Cover dry cement on counter completely with waxed paper.

5

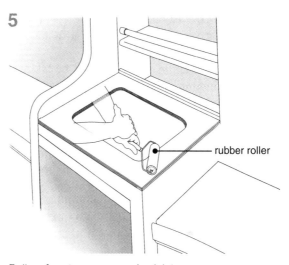

rubber roller

Roll surface to compress glue joint.

of it is pinched while you can still lift most of the top to free it. With all the paper separators free, slide them out one at a time, pressing the laminate down with the sweep of your hand. Work in one direction until all of the separators have been removed. Roll a rubber roller over the entire surface to flatten the laminate against the top, taking care not to roll over edges or cutout areas. Trim the perimeter with a router and/or a mill file. Drill a hole through the laminate in each cutout area large enough to admit a flush-trim router bit and rout out the cutouts. Now roll the entire surface including the edges with heavy pressure on the roller.

A seam is never a good idea on a countertop, and this caution would be almost pointless but for the emergence of the big cruising catamaran. If your counter is unusually large, check to see if your supplier can get you an oversize sheet of laminate—5 feet by 12 feet. If a seam is required, try to locate it in an inconspicuous spot and prerout the edges of the laminate to a precise fit. After both pieces are installed, cover the seam with a dishtowel and run a warm iron over it to soften the cement and embed the edges more securely. Heat from an iron or a heat gun is also useful in coaxing the laminate into sharper curves.

COVERING BULKHEADS

Vertical-grade laminate in some shade of white is the ideal covering for cabin bulkheads and cabinet faces. Laminate is an improvement over paint because it resists stains and marring, can be scrubbed repeatedly, and should last a couple of decades. White bulkheads are traditional in appearance, contrasting nicely with oiled or varnished wood trim. They make the cabin seem larger and brighter.

A lot of boat manufacturers recognized the benefits of plastic laminate, and your old boat probably has laminate-covered bulkheads. But many of those same manufacturers failed to see the advantages of white. Wood grain was their choice.

Wood-grain laminate is fabricated by taking a photograph of a real piece of wood, printing it on a 4 × 8 sheet of paper, and using that print as the penultimate layer in the laminate. When Olga and I had a Polaroid taken arm in arm with a cardboard cutout of Ronald Reagan, the Reagan Republican we sent the photo to was astonished, but no one on the sidewalk mistook the cutout for the real thing. No one will be fooled by wood-grain laminate either, except in a photograph. Sound snobbish? It is unintentional. I think decorative laminate is a great product. I just find "pretend wood" as appealing as plastic flowers. Maybe it's just a matter of taste.

When covering bulkheads, do not cut the laminate oversize where the edges will be covered by wood trim. Simply cut the piece to the size of your paper pattern and check it in place for fit. You will need a helper to hold the laminate in a curve away from the bulkhead, keeping the surfaces apart while you get the laminate aligned. It is usually possible to drape kraft paper from the top edge of the laminate as a separator, but you must be sure that the contact cement is totally dry and take care not to pinch the paper at an edge. A mistake here probably means doing it all again with a new piece of laminate, so carefully work out how you will make the perfect alignment *before* you apply cement to the surfaces. Rout cutouts for outlets and cabinet openings after the laminate is glued in place. A drilled hole admits the flush-trim router bit.

Whether bulkhead or countertop, when the laminate is installed and trimmed, reattach the molding with finishing nails. The plastic laminate is very hard, so drilled pilot holes may be necessary. Sink the nails below the surface of the trim with a nail set. Fill the new and old nail holes with matching wood putty. When the filler dries, sand away the excess, refinish the trim (Chapter 14), and move on to the next challenge.

CORIAN

Solid surface material has become exceedingly popular for kitchen countertops, with considerable justification. Unlike plastic laminate—which depends on a thin layer of melamine for its durability—Corian, Fountainhead, and similar solid surface materials are substantial and robust, and because the material is homogeneous, scratches and even burns can be polished out. However, the real reason for this material's popularity is even simpler—*it looks good*. Solid surface material is available in an ever-expanding selection of patterns and colors, including some that closely resemble polished stone. The latter delivers the look of a granite counter at a significantly lower cost. Of equal importance for boat applications, solid surface counters are much lighter than stone—but much heavier than plastic laminate on plywood.

Do not miss the significance of this last statement. In a light-displacement boat, exchanging a sizable laminated counter for solid surface is almost certain to give the boat a list. Half-inch solid surface weighs around $4\frac{1}{2}$ pounds per square foot, so proceed cautiously if you have considerable counter area. Also do not assume you will save the weight of the existing plywood counter. Solid surface material has good compressive strength but much less tensile strength, so it requires a solid underlay. You might be able to move to thinner plywood, but you will need to install the counter over a solid base.

You *can* buy a piece of solid surface material and cut it to fit yourself. It drills, saws, and routs almost identically to wood. And it sands and polishes like plastic. However, the industry is built around fabricating, so it may be nearly as economical to buy the top already cut and shaped to fit. It *will* be more economical if you have an unanticipated "oops" during your fabrication efforts. A word of caution, however: big countertop suppliers like Home Depot and Lowe's are generally unable to comprehend the sometimes unique requirements of a galley counter. You will do better to find a fabricator with whom you can have a direct conversation. The most foolproof method of getting exactly what you want is to cut and fit a plywood countertop, spending the time to get it exactly right, then take that to the fabricator as the pattern. Be sure you mark which side is the top.

Solid surface counter material is normally $1/2$ inch thick. Fabricators often double the thickness at the edges to give the illusion of mass, but a 1-inch edge can look wrong in a boat. A single thickness at the edge with an undermolding is likely to be more pleasing. This also allows for shorter overhang, an issue when space is at a premium.

Installation is no more complicated than gluing the counter to a plywood subcounter. You can reuse an existing surface-mounted sink and convert it into a cleaner and more functional undermount by

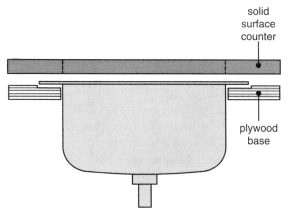

An undercounter mount avoids the detritus and moisture the rim of a surface-mount sink harbors.

relieving the plywood around the sink opening so the rim of the sink is flush with the top of the plywood. Solid surface kitchen counters are typically installed by sitting them on a bed of silicone, but for a boat counter you need a more secure attachment. Slightly thickened epoxy is the best choice because it will not prevent the top from seating against the underlay and delivers a bond stronger than either material. Run a bead of silicone around the sink rim just before putting the top in place to seal this joint from water penetration. Put bags of sand on the top to hold it in contact with the plywood. Be aware that if you ever need to replace a sink installed this way, you will have to cut it out from beneath. Also make sure the bottom of the sink will be higher than your waterline or the sink will not drain.

SEALANTS

When the various parts of a boat are assembled, we generally want the junctions to be watertight. Stockholm tar has been out of favor for a long time, but when some of our old boats were new boats, the most popular bedding compound was an oil-based guck that came in a can and looked exactly like peanut butter. Until it dried out.

Polymers and monomers changed all that. Today's sealants come in tubes and cartridges and "sausages" and can last 20 years or longer without drying out. In fact, they never really dry out. Like the rest of us, they just lose their grip.

There are scores of products from a couple of dozen manufacturers vying for your bucks. It all seems very confusing. Relax. Learn when to use just three types of sealants and you will be set.

POLYSULFIDE

The most versatile marine sealants are polysulfide based. Developed in the 1940s for the aircraft industry and originally called Thiokol, two-part polysulfide

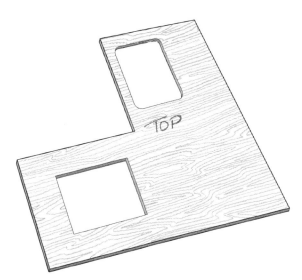

A perfect plywood pattern will get you a perfect solid surface top from the fabricator. It can also double as the counter underlay.

migrated to marine use to caulk teak decks more than half a century ago. Two-part polysulfide continues to be used for paying deck seams, although my (poor) teak-decked friends tell me that single-part polysulfide caulk formulations are equally long-lasting and infinitely easier to use.

One-part polysulfides have certainly changed the protocol for nearly all other sealing and bedding jobs. As durable as the two-part variety, although slower to cure, one-part polysulfide sealant is used right from the tube or cartridge. It bonds strongly to most surfaces, and the cured sealant is rubbery, allowing some give and flex. Polysulfide sealants typically cure tack free in about 48 hours and reach full cure in about a week. They are readily available in white, black, and brown (wood color). Popular brand names are 3M Marine Sealant 101 and BoatLife Life Calk.

Polysulfide can handle almost every caulking and sealant requirement aboard your old boat. Its versatility extends beyond bedding deck hardware. It can be used to seal items below the waterline as well—transducers and through-hull fittings, for example. It adheres well to wood, although in the case of oily woods such as teak, a primer is usually indicated. About the only times that polysulfide is not a good choice are as a bedding for plastic hardware and as a sealant for plastic portlights. The solvents in polysulfide sealants will leach the plasticizers from rigid thermoplastics—acrylic, polycarbonate, ABS, and PVC—causing the plastic to harden and crack. Polysulfide can be used to bed "plastic" fittings made from epoxy, nylon, Marelon (glass-reinforced nylon), or Delrin. *Polysulfide: for bedding everything except thermoplastic.*

POLYURETHANE

Polyurethane is really an adhesive more than a sealant. When you bed an item with polyurethane sealant, you have glued the item in place. For resealing a hull-to-deck joint or installing underwater through-hull fittings, it can be the best choice. But be cautious about using polyurethane on deck fittings and hardware. If you ever need to remove the fitting (ever hear of Murphy's Law?), it can be nearly impossible without destroying the part and perhaps damaging the deck. There is a spray solvent called DeBond Marine Formula that can break the polyurethane bond, but even this does not make removal easy, only less hopeless.

The ubiquitous 3M 5200 is not the only polyurethane sealant available. Sikaflex offers a number of

SEALANT SELECTION									
TO	*Fiberglass*	*Metal*	*Wood*	*Teak*	*Acrylic*	*Lexan*	*Marelon*	*Plastic*	*Rubber*
Fiberglass	U, M, P, S, E	X, P, E, U	P, X, E	P, E	G, S, E	G, S, E	U, P, X, S, E	S	P, X, S, E
Metal	X, P, E, U	S, U, E	P, X, E	P, E	G, S, E	G, S, E	U, P, X, S, E	S	P, X, S, E
Wood	P, X, E	P, X, E	P, S, X, E	P, S, E	S, E	S, E	P, X, E	S	P, E
Teak	P, E	P, E	P, S, E	P, S, E	S, E	S, E	P, S, E	S	P, E
Acrylic	G, S, E	G, S, E	S, E	S, E	S, E	S, E	S, E	S	S, E
Lexan	G, S, E	G, S, E	S, E	S, E	S, E	S, E	S, E	S	S, E
Marelon	U, P, X, S, E	U, P, X, S, E	P, X, E	P, S, E	S, E	S, E	U, P, X, S, E	S	P, E
Plastic	S	S	S	S	S	S	S	S	S
Rubber	P, X, S, E	P, X, S, E	P, E	P, E	S, E	S, E	P, E	S	P, E

Legend
E—Polyether (3M 4000UV, West Multi-Caulk)
G—Glazing silicone (Dow 795, GE SilPruf)
M—Methacrylate (Plexus MA)
P—Polysulfide (3M 101, BoatLife Life Calk)
S—Silicone (3M Marine Sealant Silicone, BoatLife Silicone Rubber)
U—Polyurethane (3M 5200, Sikaflex 291)
X—Polyurethane silicone mix (BoatLife Life Seal)
NOTE: The choice among recommended sealants will depend on the desired permanence of the joint and on whether it is above or below the waterline. Polyether sealant (E) is a relatively recent option with as yet unproven long-term performance.

highly regarded polyurethane sealants, some engineered to address specific sealant needs. Among the Sikaflex line is a reduced-strength polyurethane. Cure times for 3M 5200 sealant are similar to those of polysulfides, but 3M also offers fast-cure versions of both 5200 and the less-adherent 4200. Some Sikaflex polyurethane formulations skin in as little as half an hour and reach final cure in 72 hours. Polyurethanes come in colors similar to those of polysulfides, but unlike the sulfides, white polyurethane does not tend to yellow with age.

Polyurethanes will adhere tenaciously to teak without priming but it is not a good idea to use them on unvarnished teak because teak cleaners tend to soften the sealant. Polyurethanes, like polysulfides, should not be used to bed or seal plastics. Interestingly, it is the plastic that is the aggressor in this case. Both ABS and Lexan in particular outgas chemicals that compromise the polyurethane bond. Even when compatibility is not a problem, a plastic item bedded with polyurethane can probably never be removed in one piece. *Polyurethane: for a permanent bond.*

SILICONE

The third sealant is silicone. Many of us were first introduced to silicone when Dow put a candy kiss–shaped blob of it on the outside of all of their blister packages. We pulled and tugged on that little blob and were suitably impressed. We should have been. It is a terrific product. But many people have become disillusioned with silicone, mostly because their expectations were wrong.

Despite the grip that little blob had on the package, most silicone sealants are not very adhesive. As a caulk—where you run a bead around the edge of a joint and expect it to seal—silicone is rarely satisfactory. It soon releases, and if you pull on one corner, the entire bead will peel away as a single strand of cloudy rubber, like a giant rubber band.

It is this elasticity that defines the appropriate use for silicone sealant. When used properly, it forms wonderfully resilient gaskets that are impervious to almost any chemical assault. The gasket formed can even be used multiple times. Silicone makes an excellent insulating barrier between dissimilar metals. It is compatible with almost all marine materials, including plastics, but because of its poor adhesion, it should not be used below the waterline.

Silicone has such a wealth of other desirable characteristics that chemists continue to develop new formulations to improve adhesion. Silicone glazing compounds like SilPruf (mentioned earlier) have proven to be admirably tenacious. Another silicone-based sealant exhibiting better adhesion is BoatLife Life Seal, a silicone/polyurethane mix. Some silicone-based teak-deck sealants, specifically TDS and Maritime, have also begun to develop a dedicated following for their ease of use—no primer required—and their quicker cure times. But unless you buy a product specifically formulated for improved bond, you should think of silicone as a gasket material. *Silicone: to form a flexible gasket.*

BEYOND THE THREE

The search for a better mousetrap is ongoing, so some new sealant or caulk may replace one or all of those that boaters use today. One relatively new entrant to the field is polyether. Polyether-based caulks can be used most places where you might otherwise use polysulfide. Polyether is reputed to be extremely exposure tolerant, which might eventually make it a better choice than polysulfide, but for now there is not enough real-world familiarity to recommend abandoning polysulfide.

Methacrylate adhesive is another relatively recent import into marine use, but already this particular adhesive seems to be revolutionizing deck joint sealing. A number of boat manufacturers are now joining the deck to the hull with methacrylate adhesive, specifically Plexus MA—in some cases *without any mechanical fasteners*. The adhesive has so far proven to be stronger than the laminate, creating almost a monocoque construction. Whether methacrylate joints will be sound and leak free a decade or two after assembly is an open question, but so far this promises to be a most useful sealant for boats.

APPLICATION TECHNIQUE

None of these sealants will work well unless you give them a chance. If you crank down on the mounting bolts until you squeeze all of the product out, you might as well put the parts together without sealant. The correct technique is the same for all marine sealants, methacrylate excepted as it is really an adhesive.

Rule 1. Both surfaces must be clean and dry. That means peeling or scraping away every bit of old caulking and wiping the surfaces with toluene or acetone. If you try to caulk right over the old caulking, it will leak. I promise. The only exception is an intact silicone gasket where a thin coating of fresh silicone sealant on both sides will renew its grip.

Rule 2. Don't forget to check the mounting holes to see if they expose core material. If they do, drill the top skin and the core oversize and dig out as much core from the cavity as possible.

1

Scrape away all old sealant. Sand if necessary.

2

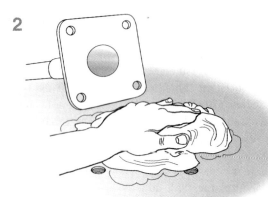

Wipe both clean surfaces with toluene or acetone.

3

Apply sealant liberally to one surface and around fasteners.

4

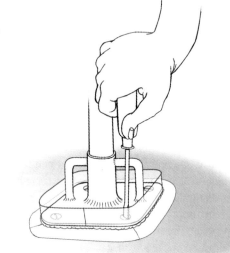

Snug fasteners until sealant squeezes out on all sides.

5

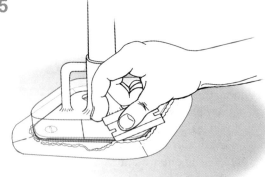

Trim away cured sealant.

6

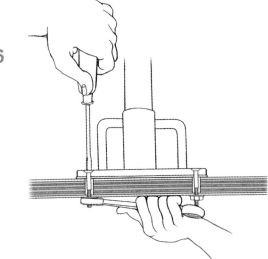

Tighten nuts slightly to put "gasket" under pressure.

Good bedding technique.

Seal the bottom and fill the cavity with epoxy. Redrill for your fasteners.

Rule 3. Apply the sealant liberally. If it does not squeeze out all the way around the joint, you will have to do it again. There is no reason to be miserly. The sealant you save is almost certain to harden in the tube or cartridge before you use it anyway. If you are using silicone, allow any excess sealant that squeezes out of the joint to cure fully, then slice it free with a razor blade. For the more tenacious poly sisters, put tape around both sides of the joint before bedding, then smooth the ooze with your finger and peel the tape promptly, leaving a neat edge. Remember to seal around the fasteners.

Rule 4. Learn to "snug," not tighten, the mounting screws after applying sealant. You want to pull both parts together sufficiently so that both surfaces are bedded in the sealant and the excess begins to squeeze out on all sides. Then leave the part undisturbed until the sealant cures. The lower flexibility and higher adhesion of polyurethane suggests a thinner seal. To make a reusable silicone gasket, wax the surfaces of both parts lightly or cover them with waxed paper.

Rule 5. Put the seal under compression. After the sealant has cured, tighten the nuts of the mounting screws (turning the screws will break the seal around them). This will ensure a watertight seal even if the sealant does lose its grip.

Rule 6. If you suspect a fitting is leaking, don't even think about a sloppy repair job. Remove the fitting, clean the surfaces, and bed it right. Your diligence will ultimately save you time and money and probably a great deal of aggravation.

Many other plastics have found their way aboard. You are not likely to have occasion to fabricate or repair most of them: ABS housings, Teflon bushings, Delrin sheaves, nylon impellers, polyethylene containers, and PVC ventilators. You will be cutting and fitting PVC hose and servicing Marelon seacocks in Chapter 12, and perhaps working with PVC-coated cloth in Chapter 15. Dacron dominates the chapter on sail construction and repair (Chapter 16), and you will also get some hands-on experience with plastic foams when we examine iceboxes and refrigeration in Chapter 13. But for now let's desert the Space Age in favor of the Bronze Age.

CHAPTER EIGHT

Forks, Eyes, and Studs

"Facts do not cease to exist because they are ignored."
—ALDOUS HUXLEY

A couple of days ago as I surfed the cable channels with some fancy thumb work on the remote control, I paused at an old black-and-white series. The bad guy had just been identified and his photograph televised. To make the point that everyone would now recognize this rat, the director did a split-screen shot—the television broadcast on one side, the roofs of a Southern California residential community on the other. The roof shot was a forest of masts and guy wires supporting spiky TV antennae.

Cable and satellite TV have changed the residential skyline forever but don't miss the point. If you are 40-something or beyond, you probably have some rigging experience. If a broken support wire for your TV antenna led you to call someone, it was because you didn't like heights, not because you didn't think you could handle the complexity of measuring and attaching a new guy wire. Any reluctance you have toward attempting to replace the rigging on your boat should be for the same reason. Major re-rigging suggests lowering the mast anyway.

This chapter is about being your own rigger. It is mostly about the mast and the wires and fittings that hold it up, but you will find a smattering of information about the lines you pull to hoist, trim, and furl.

THE RIG

I'm sure that I will be scalded for this heresy, but the type of rig that is popular at any given time is more a matter of fashion than of performance. I don't mean to suggest that the well-appointed skipper this year is sporting a Bermudan cutter—at least that isn't *exactly* what I mean. It also has to do with the *type of sailing* that is fashionable.

Schooners enjoyed immense popularity when yachting was the sport of the wealthy and owners had ample paid crew aboard to pull all the strings. With the entry of the less prosperous into recreational sailing, the economy of the sloop rig endeared it to a generation of sailors. John Hanna's Tahiti ketch design inspired a decade of interest in the ketch rig. Carleton Mitchell shook up the racing community with an incredibly successful yawl, and for the next 10 years you could buy a dozen different yawl-rigged production boats. Rule changes put the sloop back on top. The phenomenal growth of cruising regenerated interest in the ketch. Then someone coined the phrase "performance cruising" and the sloop reemerged. But as boats got larger, sails got so large that a split rig was obligatory. The ketch was still "out" because it reputedly won't go to weather, so "cutting edge" skippers flocked to the cutter rig. Then along came red-socked Peter Blake to win the Whitbread Round the World race in the ketch-rigged *Steinlager 2*. Four years later another big ketch won, calling into question (again) some of the common beliefs about the ketch rig.

So which is the fastest rig? The safest rig? The best rig? To quote Bob Dylan, "The answer, my friend, is blowing in the wind." Quite literally.

If you can resolve the design and engineering issues that are likely to arise, particularly in the case of mast relocation, you can change the way your old boat is rigged. You might decide to convert from a yawl to a sloop, from a sloop to a cutter, or from a cutter to a ketch. You might even install an unstayed mast or convert to a junk rig. But don't make the change because you have heard that the junk rig is clearly superior. It isn't—not in every circumstance and not in all conditions. Nor is the cat rig, the ketch, the cutter, or the sloop.

The decision to radically alter a boat's designed rig should be based on dissatisfaction with specific

Steinlager 2 *challenged conventional "wisdom" about the ketch rig by winning every leg of the 1989–1990 Whitbread. (Courtesy big-red.org)*

aspects of the boat's performance, not some general sense that a different rig is better. And you need a high degree of confidence that the new rig will correct the performance problems without introducing new ones. This suggests a level of experience that most casual sailors never reach.

If you want to experiment, go ahead. Sailing is, after all, about going your own way. But what follows is not about type; it is about condition. With the exception of a short segment on adding an inner stay, we will be concentrating on evaluating, strengthening, and renewing the *existing rig* on your old boat.

THE MAST

Unless your old fiberglass boat was built in the Far East, it almost certainly has an aluminum mast. Relatively few fiberglass boats have been delivered with wooden masts. Unlike wood, anodized aluminum requires very little maintenance—a coat of wax every year and a thorough inspection about every third year.

You can and should make regular trips to the masthead to check wire terminals, spreaders, and

tangs, but these inspections do not reveal what might be occurring on the underside of hardware fastened to the mast. If your rig is more than 10 years old, you should put a complete inspection on your priority list. This cannot be done with the mast erect. It has to come down.

If you will also be replacing rigging, be sure you tune the rig, then wrap electrical tape around the turnbuckle threads and against the turnbuckle body both above and below to mark the correct adjustment *before* you slacken and release the stays. Label each shroud (e.g., port aft lower). Let the boatyard lower the mast. I once dropped and restepped a 34-foot stick at the dock but I don't recommend it.

With the mast supported on sawhorses and lying on its side, sight down the sail track. There will be some downward sag in the unsupported middle, but don't worry about that. You are trying to ascertain that the mast is straight fore and aft. If you start to hyperventilate trying to decide if it is or it isn't, sit down and breathe into a paper bag. You aren't looking for anything that subtle. Straight is best, but a gentle, regular curvature, preferably *aft*, is no cause for alarm. If the bend is excessive or irregular, seek a professional opinion.

Now turn the mast with the sail track up. Nail or clamp wooden supports to one of the horses to hold the mast in this position. Sight down the track again. The mast should be straight—period. If there is some sideways curvature, go to the far end of the mast and move it to make sure the curve is not being induced by the way the mast sits on the horses. Check again. Straight this time? Good, because any significant sideways curvature is bad, very bad. But I knew all along your mast was going to be straight. They almost always are.

Next you want to check for corrosion. You can give the stick a visual once-over, but damaging corrosion is most likely where the aluminum is in contact with a dissimilar metal. That means you need to check the mast beneath any fitting attached with stainless steel screws. But before you start unscrewing things, you need to do a little preparation.

First, using a felt-tip marker, mark the top (toward the masthead) of each fitting you will be removing. On tandem fittings (e.g., spreader bases, shroud tangs) also indicate port or starboard. Make any other notations that will help you to avoid confusion when you replace the removed items.

Next, put a drop or two of penetrating oil around every screw that you will be removing. Some of the screws are going to be frozen and the penetrant will help. Let the oil do its job while you make a trip to Sears.

Frozen fasteners will usually yield to the caress of an impact driver.

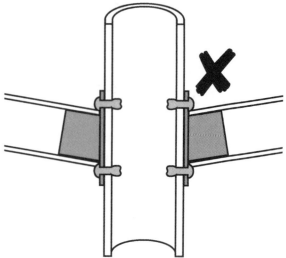

Spreaders attached just to the mast wall are a bad idea.

You are after a Craftsman impact driver. This is an ingenious device that translates a hammer blow into torque. Looking like a beefy, steel-handled screwdriver, it comes with interchangeable tips so it can be used either with sockets or for slot-head or Phillips-head screws. Expect to spend about $25. A 3- or 4-pound sledgehammer is a good companion tool.

SPREADER BASES

Corrosion beneath the spreader bases is particularly serious, so that is a good place to start your examination. Far too often on older boats, spreader fittings are riveted or screwed to the mast. Both are poor methods of attachment. The considerable leverage exerted by any unfair pressure on the outboard end of the spreader, such as the pressure the genoa exerts when it backwinds against the spreaders in tacking or that the mainsail exerts in running downwind, tends to loosen these fasteners, often cracking the thin wall of the mast in the process. And since spreader bases attached in this way are held apart only by the thin walls of the spar, the tightened shrouds try to crush the mast.

If aluminum bases are riveted with aluminum rivets and you do not want to change the way the spreaders are mounted, you may want to check for signs of serious corrosion elsewhere before you decide to remove the spreader bases. If they are attached to the mast with machine screws, remove the screws and the fittings and examine the fastener holes carefully for cracks. Don't even try a regular screwdriver on the screws; at least one will be frozen and you will strip the slot trying to free it. Use your new impact driver. Seat the blade carefully in the slot and turn the grip as far as it will go in a counter-clockwise direction. Now give the top of the driver a whack with your hammer. The blow will twist the screwdriver blade with considerable force and at the same time keep the blade from slipping out of the slot. Don't get overzealous with the hammer; you don't want to dimple the mast.

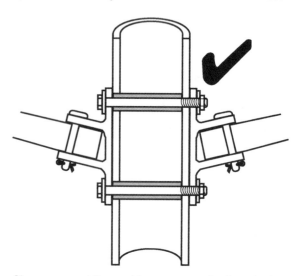

Sleeves prevent the mast from compressing from rigging loads.

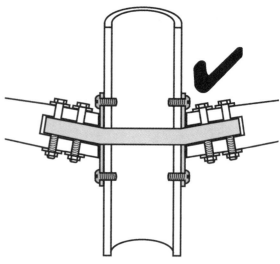

Spigot mounting also eliminates mast compression at the spreaders.

Properly mounted spreader bases will be at least through-bolted. They may also be welded or attached to opposite ends of a fitting that passes all the way through the mast, sometimes called a spigot. When you release the nuts on through-bolted bases, remove one of the fittings before extracting the bolts. The bolts should pass through compression sleeves—thick-wall aluminum tubing as long as the mast is wide—and you don't want the sleeve to fall inside the mast. Without the sleeves, tightening the mounting bolts would tend to pull the opposite sides of the mast together—not good.

If your spreader fittings are not mounted in such a way that the fitting rather than the mast wall absorbs the compressive loads, consider altering them to at least incorporate compression sleeves. You may be able to use the original fittings, or you may have to have new spreader bases manufactured. Make the baseplates as large as possible to spread the load. If you have difficulty locating bolts that are long enough, get a machine shop to thread the ends of stainless steel rods. A tubing supply house can help you with the stock for the compression tubes.

The holes have to be large enough, at least on one side, to admit the compression tubes, so keep the bolt size modest. Be sure the tubes, not the mast wall, take all the compression. A four-bolt pattern works well, but two bolts are adequate if the base is broad and the bolts a size larger than those originally fitted. Holes in the mast weaken it, particularly when they are in a line, so try to use the existing holes, enlarging them as necessary to accommodate the bolts and sleeves. If that is not possible, move the spreader bases up the mast slightly so the new holes will not be among the old ones. This will alter the geometry of the rigging slightly but the implications are far less serious than drilling additional holes in line with the existing ones.

If your spreader bases were screwed to the mast and the holes are not cracked, there is only minor pitting, the spreader fittings have given no trouble in 30 years, you're not headed around the world, you don't see any reason to change the way the spreaders are mounted, and . . . *Take it easy!* Fine. You're right. Don't change them. But if they are loose or if the holes are stressed, don't just put in bigger screws. Fix them right.

CORROSION

We were looking for corrosion anyway, and another likely spot is around the mast step. Typically the mast extrusion slips over a cast heel fitting and is held in place with three or four machine screws. Free the screws with the impact driver and remove them.

With a punch or a screwdriver, tap the heel free. Check inside the mast for corrosion.

Some pitting is tolerable, but if the bottom of the mast is badly corroded, you cannot ignore this. All of the compressive loads on the mast are concentrated at its base. You might cut off the bad section, but shortening the mast will require shortening all the rigging and may be detrimental to the fit of the sails and even to sailing performance. An alternative that maintains rigging geometry is to fabricate a high-compression spacer the same height as the mast cutoff and install it under the heel fitting.

If you can afford it, replacing the mast can be the best alternative to serious corrosion and not just because it restores full integrity. Aluminum mast extrusions have improved since their early days and you might save several hundred pounds of weight aloft with a more modern extrusion. The result can be a stiffer boat with a more seakindly motion. For a new extrusion you will also need new cap and heel fittings and probably spreader roots. Beyond that, mast replacement can be as simple as taking the fittings from the old extrusion and installing them on the new one. Being your own rigger can make mast replacement an excellent value.

Fortunately the corrosion you find is not likely to be serious enough to compromise the mast's integrity. With a soft wire brush, buff away all of the powdery oxide. Paint the inside of the mast as far in as you can reach with an etching primer, one specifically formulated for aluminum. Follow this with a coat or two of corrosion-inhibiting paint. Give the heel fitting the same treatment.

The mast cap will be similar to the heel fitting. Remove it and treat any corrosion. Now is also a good time to service the masthead sheaves (see illustration below). You may be disappointed to find that they are little more than phenolic or aluminum disks rotating on a bolt through the mast. Don't be. Bearings are unnecessary in this instance.

Nothing complicated here.

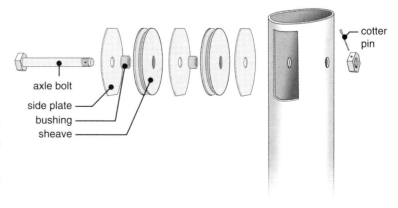

axle bolt
side plate
bushing
sheave
cotter pin

Remove the bolt and extract the sheaves and their side plates. With bronze wool (or a soft wire wheel), polish the sides of both the sheaves and the plates. Insert the bolt through the center bushings to check for wear. Replacements can be obtained from a bearing supplier. Coat the bushings and the sides of the sheaves and plates with a thin layer of Teflon grease.

INSPECTING FOR FATIGUE

Mast tangs—which are the fittings the stays and shrouds attach to—will be through-bolted or incorporated into the cap fitting. First examine the clevis-pin holes. A bit of an elliptical shape due to wear is tolerable, but if the hole is elongated due to stretch, you must replace the tang. Remove the tangs to check for hidden corrosion in the mast and examine the tangs for signs of fatigue.

Metal ages, losing some of its resilience (don't we all?). Under stress, tiny cracks begin to form. Called *propagating defects*, these cracks will continue to grow and weaken the part until it fails. When that happens with a mast tang, it often results in the loss of the mast. Any nick, bend, or hole in the metal concentrates stresses, hastening the process. That's bad news. It's also good news because it means that weakening cracks generally begin on the surface of the part where they can be detected before they become dangerous.

With good light, examine every square millimeter of the tangs. For less than $10 your nearest camera shop will sell you an 8-power loupe that will reveal the texture of the surface in great detail. If your magnified examination does not turn up any flaws, the tangs are probably sound.

Probably? Well, the cracks start out microscopic and may not be visible even with magnification. But if you do not find a visible crack in any of the fittings (later you are going to examine the chainplates with the same thoroughness), your visual check should be sufficient. Only if you find a crack or if the fittings are

more than 20 years old and/or you are headed over the horizon will you want to take your checking one step further.

The only way to assess the absolute strength of the fitting is to put it on a hydraulic ram and crank up the tension until the part breaks, but if you do that with all of your tangs and chainplates, then where will you be? Fortunately the designer specified fittings of adequate strength and the manufacturer fabricated them as specified (we hope), so you are only concerned with weakening defects.

Three types of nondestructive testing may be employed. The parts can be subjected to X-ray but unless the crack is parallel to the radiation, it will not show up on the exposure. In any case, given the expense of X-rays, it will probably be less costly to replace the suspect parts.

Magnetic particle inspection, often referred to by the trade name Magnaflux, is used extensively in industry. The principle involves passing a current through the part. Any discontinuity caused by a surface crack will set up an electromagnetic field. When the surface is coated with a fine metallic powder, the particles are attracted to the field, forming a line that corresponds to the crack. Sadly, magnetic particle inspection can only be performed on ferrous metals and ferrous metal is an anathema in modern rigging.

That leaves us with dye penetrant inspection. The part is thoroughly cleaned, then painted with a very thin liquid mixture of dye and penetrating oil. The oil is allowed to "soak in" for a prescribed time before the surface is wiped clean. Finally a "developer," which is a fine powder, is applied to the surface. It draws out any oil that has remained in a crack, resulting in a dark line. A more sensitive version uses a fluorescent dye and the part is examined under ultraviolet light.

Dye penetrant testing is just as easy to perform as it sounds and can be done right on the boat, sometimes without even removing the suspect item. Dye penetrant kits (Spotcheck) are not cheap, but if the testing results in early identification of a flaw that might have caused the loss of the entire rig or even if it only assures you that the rig is sound, it will be money well spent.

Whether you remove cleats, winches, and any other remaining fittings from the mast may be determined by what you have already found. If corrosion does not seem to be a problem beneath the fittings already removed, the only reason to remove the remaining items is to be thorough. Use your own judgment.

A photographer's loupe can reveal cracks invisible to the naked eye.

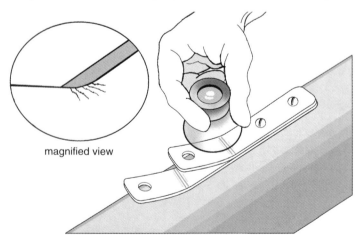

magnified view

THE BOOM

Give the boom the same treatment as the mast. Remove fittings to check for corrosion. Check the gooseneck for cracks, using dye penetrant. Also check the bails for the mainsheet blocks. Be sure that all of the fasteners are appropriate and sound.

For a couple of decades many sailboats were delivered with roller-reefing booms. It was an aberration, and slab reefing has since returned to favor. Roller reefing does work, so unless you reef often, you may not feel any pressing need to get rid of it. I lived with roller reefing on my own old boat for more than two decades, not because I liked it, but because changing it was always in the low-priority column of my plan. But had I realized earlier the full benefits of a fixed boom and a slab-reefing main, I would have made the change much sooner. Roller reefing is cumbersome, the shape of the reefed sail is laughable compared to a tied-in reef, and the rolling boom adds complications to the rig. Most of the loading on a boom is upward, so a fixed boom will have a vertical section that is deeper than its width. A roller-reefing boom is usually round or nearly round, so either it has an insufficient vertical dimension, which allows the boom to flex and destroys the shape of even the full mainsail, or it is far wider than it needs to be, adding undesirable weight. Roller-reefing booms must also be free of hardware so the sail can roll around them smoothly. Consequently sheeting is at the end of the boom, and a proper vang attachment is not possible.

Unlike replacing the mast, replacing a roller-reefing boom involves more than removing the hardware from the old boom and attaching it to the new one. You do not want the new boom to be configured like the old one. That is the reason you're replacing it. A fixed boom provides unlimited sheeting and vanging possibilities, including mid-boom sheeting and the possibility of fitting a rigid vang. There are too many variables to provide specific directions here, but if you are replacing your roller-reefing boom, you should give ample thought to three considerations—sheeting, vanging, and reefing—before you attach any hardware to the new boom.

INTERNAL WIRING

If your mast is rigged with internal halyards, you can replace them now if you like, but having the mast horizontal does not make the job any easier. However, now *is* the time to deal with the electrical wiring inside the mast.

When wires hang loosely down the hollow center of an aluminum mast, the slightest cross-chop sets up an incessant clanging that would easily qualify as a human rights violation under the provisions of the Geneva convention. One common solution is to seize butterfly-shaped pieces of soft polyurethane foam to the wire every 3 to 4 feet before it is inserted into the mast. The foam keeps the wire away from the walls of the mast. This solution has obvious drawbacks when there are internal halyards. Also, I don't like the idea of damp foam (of course it will be damp) lying against the inside of my aluminum mast. A better alternative is to tightly zip three wire-ties to the wire every meter, orienting them at 120-degree intervals. This three-legged spider holds the wire away from the mast wall.

The best solution is a wire conduit inside the mast. New mast extrusions often incorporate a wire conduit, but it is easy enough to retrofit one in your old mast. While the mast is on horses is the time to do it. *Thin-wall PVC water pipe (Schedule 20)* is ideal for this purpose. Select a diameter that will allow the easy passage of all the wires you anticipate running from the masthead and the spreaders—lights, antennae, and instruments. For spreader lights and a tricolor at the masthead, a 1-inch conduit will be adequate, but if you are running coaxial cable to the masthead for an antenna connection, make the internal diameter (ID) at least $1^1/_4$ inches. You will be even more pleased with a $1^1/_2$-inch conduit when you eventually need to add a new wire.

To install the conduit you need a handful of $^3/_{16}$-inch *aluminum* pop rivets and the installation tool. The rivet length will depend on the thickness of the mast and conduit walls. Borrow the tool if you like, but this is a good item to add to any onboard tool chest.

Plastic water pipe is available in 20-foot lengths. Two sections will handle a mast up to about 45 feet. First determine where the conduit will lie. Typically it will interfere with the tang or spreader mounting if it runs down either side. A bow light may preclude mounting against the front of the mast, and the mainsail track has the same effect aft. Often the best place is in the corner formed by the inside wall of the track and the side of the mast. Be sure the conduit can run the length of the mast without interfering with anything. Do not overlook any fittings that you may have temporarily removed.

You want to install the conduit in two separated sections to allow the easy exit of wires that run only to the spreaders. Position the conduit alongside the *outside* of the mast to determine the location and the length of the two pieces. The space between the two should be a couple of inches and should be located where the midheight wires exit the mast. The top section should reach to within a foot or so of the cap and should be cut accordingly. The bottom piece should stop several inches above where the wires exit the mast. Mark the appropriate locations of the ends of the two sections on the outside of the mast.

With a felt-tip marker, draw a straight line from end to end on the outside surface of both sections of conduit. Rotate the mast so that the conduit will lie on the "bottom," and insert the top section of conduit into the mast, leaving a short length sticking out. Rotate the conduit until it sits on the black line and draw a corresponding line on the outside of the mast. Extract the conduit and rotate the mast to make the new line convenient. Extend this line the length of the mast, or simply measure its relationship to some full-length feature— e.g., the edge of the sail track or an extruded seam. This is the rivet line. All the rivets that will hold the two sections of conduit in place will be on this line.

Starting about 2 inches below the mark that represents the top of the top section, mark your first rivet location on the rivet line. Mark a second location about 2 inches from the first, toward the base of the mast. From there, place a mark on the line every 18 inches until you near the end of the top section. The final two marks should be 4 inches and 2 inches from the end of the section. Following the same pattern, mark the rivet locations for the lower section of conduit.

Before drilling the marked holes, hold the sections of conduit against the markings to make sure everything looks right. Carpenters live by the old adage, "measure twice, cut once." The same applies to drilling holes in your mast. If everything looks right, place the tip of a center punch on each mark and give it an authoritative whack. Now use a sharp $3/16$-inch bit to drill all the holes. If you try to drill the holes without using the punch, your drill bit will dance all over the curved surface of the mast.

Drill the first hole in the conduit 2 inches from the end and centered on the black line. Rotate the mast back down and insert the top section of conduit, lining up the hole in it with the first hole in the mast. With one hand (or a helper) holding the conduit in place, insert a

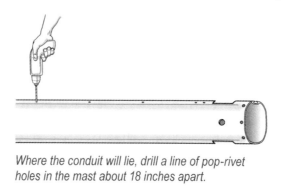

Where the conduit will lie, drill a line of pop-rivet holes in the mast about 18 inches apart.

Draw a straight, bold line the full length of the conduit.

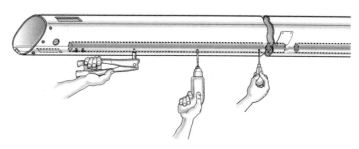

With the mast positioned holes down, insert the conduit. One hole at a time, drill it through the hole in the mast and rivet it in place. Jockey the conduit with an awl as necessary to place the straight line across each mast hole for drilling.

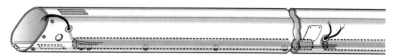

Installing conduit in two sections separated by a short space allows the exit of midmast wiring.

Installing a wiring conduit inside an extruded mast.

rivet into the hole in the mast and through the hole in the conduit; squeeze the tool until the stem "pops." Be sure the rivet is long enough to flare inside the conduit. Line the black line up over the second hole and drill the conduit through the hole in the mast. Install the second rivet. Do the same for the third hole. You are working from beneath the mast so the conduit will lie in place.

After the third hole you will not be able to position the conduit by reaching inside the mast. The black line will probably fall across the next rivet hole in the mast, but when it doesn't, use an awl or an ice pick in the *next* hole to jockey the plastic pipe into position. It is imperative that you line up the black line each time to insure that the rivet grips the two pieces at their point of tangency. The previous rivet will hold the conduit against the wall of the mast but your drill bit must be very sharp and you must apply very little upward pressure to keep from pushing the conduit to one side or the other.

After all the rivets are in, check each one to make sure it's smooth. Occasionally the mandrel breaks above the surface of the rivet. The last thing you want is a sharp little spike sticking out of the mast beside the sail track. In fact, because the mandrels are steel, you would be smart to tap them out with a pin punch. You will need to incline the mast to "pour" them out of the conduit before closing the mast with the heel fitting.

With both sections in place, simply run all of the mast wiring through the conduit. A length of light ($^3/_{32}$- or $^1/_8$-inch) 1×19 wire can serve as an electrician's snake if you do not have access to the real thing. With the mast cap and base both removed, feeding the masthead wiring should present no difficulty. Wiring that exits midmast may be somewhat more troublesome. The exit hole in the mast should be large enough to accept a grommet, but leave the grommet out until after you have fished the wire out through the hole. Take the sharp edges off the drilled hole with sandpaper or a strip of emery cloth to keep the metal from stripping or nicking the insulation. Coating the wiring with beeswax (or soap) will help it slip past other wiring in the conduit more easily.

SPREADERS

If the spreaders are wood, now is the time to check them for rot. Even if they look OK, poke them a few times with your awl. Don't hold the spreader in your hand while you are doing this. I have seen wooden spreaders so rotten that the awl went all the way through. If that happens to you, be glad you have a fiberglass *boat*.

Conventional wisdom is to varnish wooden spreaders rather than paint them so that rot will be visible immediately. The truth is that rot almost invariably

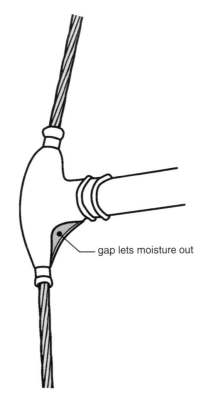

Spreader boot open on the underside is less prone to trapping destructive moisture.

gap lets moisture out

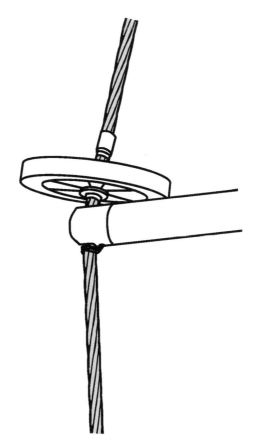

Roller protects sail without fostering corrosion.

begins on the top of the spreader, so looking up from the deck at the still-sound varnished undersides can be disastrously misleading. Another truth is that paint protects the wood better than varnish. If you have aesthetic reasons for choosing varnish, at least add a couple of coats of paint to the *top* of the spreaders. It won't be seen and it will add years to the life of your spreaders.

Aluminum spreaders are not without their own problems, particularly at their outboard ends. Remove all chafe guards and tape to expose the tip. Interaction of the stainless steel shroud with the aluminum tip often results in destructive corrosion. Corrosion is hastened by wrapping the tip with tape because the tape tends to hold water. Boots are preferable. Modify them so they are as watertight as possible above the spreader, but trim the boots below the spreaders to leave a generous gap in the seam so that any rain that does find its way into the boot can escape or evaporate. I have come to prefer leaving spreader tips completely uncovered and installing Delrin rollers on the shrouds just above the spreaders to protect the genoa from the tip.

STAYS AND SHROUDS

Every stay and shroud should be checked from one end to the other for broken strands. When a strand breaks, it tends to curl out, forming what

is descriptively called a "meathook." If G. Gordon Liddy is your hero, locate the broken strands by running your bare hand down the stays, wrapping your lacerated palm with gauze afterward. If you're a wimp, wrap the gauze *around the stay* and run it down the wire. My preference is to do this test with the cotton wadding in Nevr-Dull metal polish, checking, cleaning, and protecting the wire all at the same time.

A single broken strand means it is time to replace the wire—and not just the one that is broken. When one shroud starts to go, all the others that are the same age will not be far behind.

WIRE SIZE

You will probably want to replace the old wire with new wire of the same diameter, but it can be very useful to know if that diameter is adequate. Rigging calculations begin with the righting moment (RM) of your boat. In yacht design books, such as *Skene's*, you will usually find a graph providing the RM at 30 degrees for various waterline lengths. The graph has serious limitations. Imagine a paper cup and a straw as a sailboat and mast. Insert the straw through the lid of the empty cup and tilt the cup with pressure against the top of the straw. No problem. Fill the same cup with sand. Instead of tilting the cup, pressure against the top of the straw just bends the straw. Now empty the cup, glue it to the center of a 6-inch cardboard disk and try to tilt it with the straw. Clearly displacement and beam affect the RM. The only way to know the RM of your boat is by measuring it, a procedure called an *inclining test*.

Did I say *test*? I'm sorry. There are no tests in this book. I meant *measurement*. You have to do this measurement while the boat is rigged and in the water and preferably fully loaded.

Tie a weight—a fishing sinker or a large nut—to a length of string and tape the string to the cabin overhead on the centerline of the boat so the nut is suspended a couple of inches above the cabin sole. Putting the weight in a bucket of water will dampen (aha!) its motion. Rig a yardstick or a strip of wood athwartships next to the string to record the travel of the pendulum.

To perform this measurement you need a couple of heavy (easy) and honest (not so easy) friends. Get their accurate weights and ask them to stand on the centerline of the boat. You will be standing on the centerline too but inside the cabin to record the heel. Mark the spot where the line crosses the board. Now ask your big buddies to stand upright

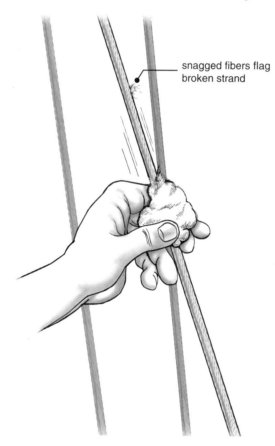

Use a cotton ball or cheesecloth bundle to check rigging wire for broken strands.

snagged fibers flag broken strand

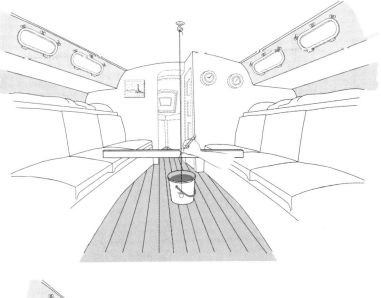

Rig a plumb line inside the cabin on the boat's centerline and position a board athwartship to serve as a scale. Mark where the line crosses the board with the boat upright.

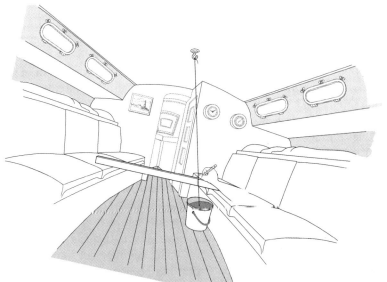

Heel the boat at least 6 degrees with a known weight a known distance from the centerline. Measure or calculate the actual angle of heel. Multiply the weight times the distance and divide by the angle to get RM per degree.

Multiply RM per degree by 30 to derive RM at 30 degrees, then multiply by 1.5 to allow for severe conditions. Divide the result by the distance from the centerline to the chainplate to calculate rigging load (PT).

Measuring righting moment (RM).

on the rail at the main shrouds. You are going to owe them a big meal for this. When the boat has stopped oscillating, mark where the string now crosses the board. If the weight hits the side of the bucket, *move the bucket.*

You want to know the angle of heel. You can derive it trigonometrically by dividing the distance between the two marks by the length of the string from the overhead to the board to obtain the tangent of the angle. Look up that tangent in the trig tables or key it into a fancy calculator to get the angle. If you've never heard of trigonometry, measure the angle with the protractor you keep by the chart table. If the angle is less than 6 or 7 degrees, get some more friends and do it again.

Now multiply the total weight of your assistants by the distance from the centerline to the rail. Divide that number by the degree of heel to get the righting moment per degree. Traditional calculations use the RM at 30 degrees, so multiply your one degree number by 30. Multiply that result by 1.5 to allow for severe conditions that might heel the boat beyond 30 degrees. (Occasionally 2.78 is used rather than 1.5, a good precaution if you are headed for high latitudes, but empirical data suggest that the higher factor is rarely essential under more normal conditions.)

To convert the calculated righting moment (at 30 degrees with a 1.5 safety factor) to the total load on the chainplate, usually called PT, you need only

Total rigging load
(PT) is divided
among the
shrouds.

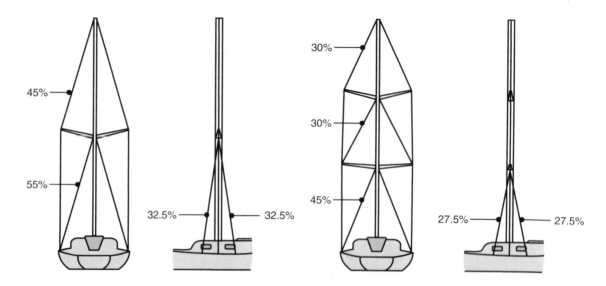

divide by the distance from the centerline of the boat to the chainplate. This assumes that all the shrouds come to a single point on either side. In actuality, the load is divided among multiple shrouds. The distribution varies according to the rig configuration. No single method of calculating shroud loads is universally recognized, but you should get satisfactory results if you assume, for a single-spreader rig, 45% of the load on the upper shroud and 55% on the lower. With twin lowers, each carries about 32.5% of the load. (I know that adds up to more than 100%; I don't make the rules, I just report them!) For a double-spreader rig, the upper shroud and the intermediate both carry 30%, and the lower gets 45% of the load. Twin lowers get 27.5% each.

We are almost finished. The numbers you have calculated are the *theoretical loads* on each shroud, but when the boat rolls off a wave and the mast whips, the load on the shrouds goes up. The situation is made worse if the rigging is loose. A thread that cuts a red line into your fingers when you attempt to break it with a steady pull pops effortlessly if you subject it to a sudden jerk. The headstay and backstay are subjected to similar load escalation from pitching motion or a shuddering impact with a wave.

By how much does the load increase? I don't know. Neither do the experts. But the best and brightest say that even the worst conditions will not triple the load, so if you use a safety factor of 3, the rig will be strong enough to take whatever Mother Nature hails down on you. Actually, unless you are really planning to challenge the Old Girl, a factor of 2.5 should be adequate. If you are wondering why you should even consider the lower factor, it is because weight aloft is detrimental to both the performance

and the comfort of the boat. The stays and shrouds should not be a millimeter larger than *big enough*.

So . . . multiply the calculated shroud loads by 2.5 to get the required strength of the wire. Consult the table to determine the wire size that provides the strength you need. If it agrees with the size of your old rigging, perfect. If you calculate that lighter rigging would be adequate, consider carefully before you re-rig lighter. I know what I just said about the weight aloft, but it is equally true that profit-motivated manufacturers do not incur the extra expense of oversize rigging without a reason. I would not ignore their decision on the sole basis of the preceding calculation.

Even if you calculate that the original rigging is too small, you may not want to change sizes. If the mast has been standing for a couple of decades, if all the sister ships you have seen still have the same-size rigging, and if the sailing you have in mind is not that unusual, the expense of the change and the added weight aloft are probably not justified. Should your future sailing plans develop into something more ambitious, strengthening the rig at that time would be in order.

We have not sized the forestay or the backstay in this exercise. The forestay should be at least as strong as the strongest shroud, and in actual practice the forestay is often one size larger unless the shrouds are oversize. The extra strength is in recognition of the risk to the crew in the cockpit should the headstay fail and to allow for the chafe of jib snaps on the wire. From a load standpoint the (standing) backstay can be a size smaller than the forestay, but since the tension on the forestay depends on backstay tension, it is better for the two to be the same size. An inner stay can be a size smaller.

TYPICAL BREAKING LOADS FOR 1 × 19 STAINLESS STEEL WIRE ROPE

Nominal Diameter		302/304		316		316 compact strand	
Inches	MM	Pounds	Kilograms	Pounds	Kilograms	Pounds	Kilograms
1/16		500	227				
—	2			706	320		
—	2.5			1,103	500		
3/32	—	1,200	544				
1/8	3	2,100	952	1,588	720		
5/32	4	3,300	1,497	2,822	1,280		
3/16	4.76	4,700	2,131	3,969	1,800		
—	5			4,410	2,000	5,380	2,440
7/32	5.56	6,300	2,857	5,447	2,470		
—	6			6,351	2,880	7,828	3,550
1/4	6.35	8,200	3,719	7,100	3,220		
9/32	7	10,300	4,671	7,828	3,550	10,802	4,910
5/16	8	12,500	5,669	10,232	4,640	13,530	6,150
—	9			12,944	5,870		
3/8	9.53	17,500	7,936	14,509	6,580		
—	10			15,987	7,250	21,544	9,770
7/16	11	23,400	10,612	19,338	8,770	26,620	12,072
—	12			22,933	10,400	31,812	14,430
1/2	12.7	29,700	13,469	25,689	11,650		
9/16	14	36,500	16,553	31,268	14,180	42,460	19,256
5/8	16	44,000	19,954	40,926	18,560	56,320	25,541
3/4	19			47,674	21,620	70,100	31,926
7/8	22			64,101	29,070		
1	26			89,526	40,600		

If you do not already know this, 1 × 19 stainless steel wire rope is really your only choice for stays and shrouds. You will also encounter 7 × 19 wire rope, used for running rigging because of its flexibility, and 7 × 7 wire rope, popular for lifelines and luff wires. But for standing rigging aboard a fiberglass boat, 1 × 19 is what you need.

Stainless steel wire rope comes in various types. The most common are Type 302 and Type 304, high-carbon alloys offering high strength at relatively low cost. These alloys give long service in a temperate climate, but in the tropics 302 and 304 stainless demonstrate an unsettling inclination to corrode rapidly. Boats headed for the tropics often choose Type 316 stainless for its considerably higher corrosion resistance but it is as much as 15% weaker than 302 and 304. That can necessitate going to larger-diameter wire, but then you may be faced with mismatched end fittings since the fittings for larger wire typically have larger clevis pins. A path out of this minefield used to be *compact strand* rigging wire, known in America as Dyform (a registered trademark). Constructed of shaped rather than round strands, Type 316 compact strand wire has the corrosion resistance of 316—because that is what it is—but diameter for diameter it is as strong or stronger than regular 302 or 304. The cost has been about 25% more than regular 316 1 × 19 wire on a size-for-size basis but very little more on a strength basis, making it an alternative worth considering. Unfortunately Dyform is now manufactured only in metric sizes so it no longer offers the benefits of a same-size substitution if your existing rigging is fractional, meaning inch sizes.

This raises a related issue worth considering. When you re-rig an old boat, there can be value in changing to metric sizes. This is because the majority of sailboats are now manufactured somewhere other than the United States and virtually all of those are built to metric dimensions, including the rigging. It follows that the majority of rigging components being manufactured today are likewise manufactured to metric dimensions. This fact has even American builders coming around to metric rigging because of the wider range and better availability of metric components. If your sailing dream includes foreign cruising, you are going to find only metric components readily available outside of America. That puts you ahead of the game if your boat already has metric rigging. If your change is to the nearest metric size, the difference in clevis pin size may be modest enough to be accommodated without changing chainplates, tangs, or even turnbuckles and toggles. A change to metric also makes available the possibility of substituting the higher strength compact strand wire to maintain adequate strength without the dramatic change in clevis pin size typically required to move up a full fractional size.

Back to the issue of wire type, a steel alloy that is both stronger and much more corrosion resistant than any of the other types is Type 22-13-5, also called Nitronic 50. Cost is also higher. Nitronic 50 is used in the manufacture of rod rigging. Rod rigging has been around for a long time, but its tendency to succumb to fatigue and part without warning has made cautious sailors regard it with suspicious eyes. After all, when one "strand" of a rod breaks . . . Many of the early problems with rod rigging have been engineered out, and there is little reason for properly installed rod rigging to fail, but it remains a less forgiving material than wire rope. Lower elasticity and less windage make rod rigging very attractive to the racing sailor, but for re-rigging a 20-year-old production boat, the benefits are not likely to justify the cost—or the potential risk.

WIRE TERMINALS

If any of the original rigging is still aboard (God forbid!), it almost certainly has swaged terminals. Even if the rigging has been renewed, swaged terminals are likely. Swaged terminals are attached to the wire by a special machine that literally compresses the barrel of the fitting so that it grips the wire. In the right conditions swaged fittings last a very long time. In the wrong conditions they fail before your insurance agent sends you another tacky calendar.

Swages fail because the machine that installed them was inadequate or the operator did not use it correctly. They fail because compressing the metal weakens it. They fail because the die marks concentrate the stresses. They fail because water runs down the wire into the fitting and the resulting rust expands inside the fitting. They fail because the same water freezes and expands. They fail because any unfair lead or pull tends to pry open the squeezed barrel. They fail.

If you have swaged fittings, check them with dye penetrant. If they fail the test, replace them. When a swage cracks, it is—or soon will be—severely weakened. Even if they pass, don't just forget about them. They should be checked for cracks *every year*.

Every swaged terminal I have ever owned eventually had to be replaced, whereas not a single cone-type swageless terminal of the scores I have been to sea with has ever been replaced or even given me a moment's concern. You can see where my loyalty lies. And swageless terminals have the added benefit of being *intended* for do-it-yourself installation. Swageless terminals are, in my opinion, the *only* terminals to consider. I personally prefer the design of those made by Sta-Lok, but once installed, the equally common Norseman terminals are just as secure. There are also some other swageless terminals that are not as well known.

Each terminal comes with detailed installation instructions, making instructions here redundant, but if you have your palms in the air at the thought of trusting your mast to fittings *you've* installed, let me at least give you a sense of how easy it is. You slide the threaded body of the fitting over the wire, then slightly unlay the outer strands. The small cone has a hole in the center that allows you to slip it over the center strands of the wire. A light twist of the outer strands will cause them to assume their original lay on the outside of the cone. Next you slide the body of the fitting over the caged cone and apply a couple of drops of red Loctite to the male threads—to prevent stainless-to-stainless galling during assembly and to lock the threads after assembly. Screw the end fitting to the body and tighten wrist tight with a wrench to clamp the wire around and inside the cone. In the case of Sta-Loks there is a little metal cap called a former that needs to be dropped into the hollow end fitting before assembly. Now unscrew the fitting to make sure the wires are still evenly spaced around the cone and one has not dropped into the slot in the cone. Put a pea-size blob of 3M 101 polysulfide sealant inside the end fitting then screw it back together. As you tighten, sealant will squeeze out where the wire enters the fitting. I know the instructions that come with the terminals call for silicone, but polysulfide does a better job of waterproofing the terminal. That's it. Inside, the compression of screwing the two parts together forms the wire into a secure cage around the internal cone, giving you a fitting that is stronger than the wire it is attached to. Do not over-tighten—no more force than you can apply with one hand—and do not fail to lubricate the threads with Loctite before the initial assembly. Swageless terminals are reusable indefinitely. All you will need are new cones and maybe new formers.

4

Re-lay outer strands.

1

Slip socket over wire.

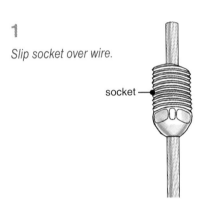

socket

5

Fit former and end fitting.

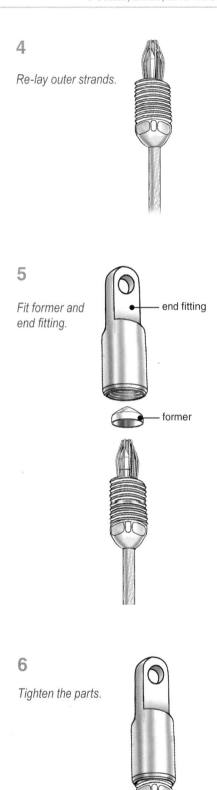

end fitting

former

2

Unlay outer strands.

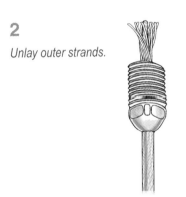

3

Slide cone over core.

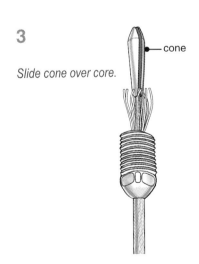

cone

6

Tighten the parts.

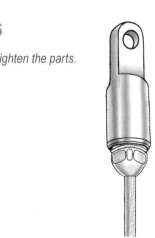

Installing a Sta-Lock eye.

Before you begin re-rigging you need to gather all the parts together. If you are just replacing old wire with new wire of the same diameter, preparation involves little more than buying the appropriate terminals—eyes, forks, or studs—and an adequate length of wire. Determine how much wire you need by measuring each of the stays and shrouds you are replacing. Measure from clevis pin to clevis pin to make sure differences in the end fittings will not leave you short of wire. Add all the measurements together and buy the wire in a single length, ordering a couple of extra feet as cheap insurance.

Matching Components

If you are changing the rig in any way, make sure all of the new parts are compatible. That means you must preassemble each piece with whatever it connects to. If you decide to replace the rigging with wire one size larger, the pin size of the fittings will likewise be larger and will no longer fit the holes in the mast tangs and chainplates. So you just get out your trusty drill and . . . *Hang on, hang on, hang on!* Drilling out the pin hole to a larger size reduces the amount of metal on either side of the hole, weakening the fitting. Heavier wire usually necessitates thicker and wider tangs and often heavier chainplates.

You can calculate the strength of a tang by multiplying its thickness times the *remaining* width of metal at the hole times the tensile strength of 316 stainless steel, which is around 80,000 pounds per square inch. A $^3/_8$-inch hole in a 1-inch-wide tang leaves $^5/_8$ inch of remaining width, so this calculation for a 1-inch-wide tang fabricated from $^3/_{16}$-inch-thick stainless drilled to accept a $^3/_8$-inch clevis pin would be $^3/_{16} \times ^5/_8 \times 80,000$, which yields a strength of 9,375 pounds. This is more than adequate for $^3/_{16}$-inch 304 wire with a breaking strength of 4,700 pounds. Step the wire size up to $^1/_4$ inch and the corresponding clevis pin diameter will be $^1/_2$ inch. Drill out the old tang and the new calculation would be $^3/_{16} \times ^1/_2 \times 80,000$, or 7,500 pounds—inadequate for the 8,200-pound breaking strength of 304 wire. The tang should be wider and probably thicker. In some circumstances the load on the tang can be concentrated on one side of the hole, so it is a good idea to make sure the tangs are at least twice as strong as the wire. If you are replacing tangs and/or chainplates, you should specify Type 316L stainless steel, which is more corrosion resistant but has a lower tensile strength of around 75,000 pounds per square inch. This is the number you use to calculate the appropriate size of the new fitting.

Heavier wire also means heavier turnbuckles. Continuing with our example, $^3/_{16}$-inch rigging will be fitted with $^3/_8$-inch turnbuckles. Even if the pin sizes were not incorrect for $^1/_4$-inch wire (which they are), a $^3/_8$-inch bronze Merriman turnbuckle (Merriman is gone but its excellent bronze hardware lives on aboard a huge number of old boats) has a rated strength of only 6,500 pounds, far less than the 8,200-pound strength of the wire. You need to step up to $^1/_2$-inch turnbuckles, which will have a tensile strength of at least 10,000 pounds.

If your re-rigging does not require replacement of the turnbuckles, inspect them carefully. It is a very good idea to check the body of each turnbuckle with dye penetrant. If the threads of the turnbuckle, particularly one that is stainless steel, have not been kept lubricated, the threads may have galled. If so, replace the turnbuckle. Also be very suspicious of old turnbuckles with an integral toggle. Water invariably finds its way inside the joint where the bottom stud is threaded into the pin of the toggle, leading to dangerous and undetectable corrosion. Newer toggle turnbuckles use a forged T-bolt to correct this flaw, but with the fervor of personal experience, I strongly recommend replacing *every* old turnbuckle that has a threaded T-bolt pin at the bottom end.

Right Length

With all the pieces in hand, the biggest difficulty in replacing your own rigging is in getting it to come

Tang strength calculation.

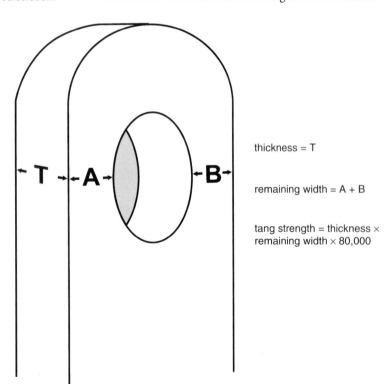

thickness = T

remaining width = A + B

tang strength = thickness × remaining width × 80,000

out to the correct length. If you taped the threads of the turnbuckles while the rig was properly tuned, your job is much easier. Start with your longest piece of rigging so a measurement or terminal installation failure leaves you with a piece of wire usable for a shorter shroud. Adjust the turnbuckle to the tape and lay the old stay or shroud on the ground, pulling it straight. If you are working on a dock, drive two stiff nails through the clevis-pin holes at each end. If you are working on the ground, nail a couple of scraps of plywood to the ground (it sounds odd, but it works), then put nails through the ends of the stretched wire and into the plywood. The two nails mark the pin-to-pin length—from the mast tang to the chainplate—of the shroud you are duplicating.

Now remove the clevis pin that attaches the end fitting of the wire to the turnbuckle, or unscrew it if the end fitting is a stud. The turnbuckle is adjusted to the way it was on the boat but that may not be the way you want it adjusted on the new shroud. Ideally the turnbuckle should be about half-extended, so adjust it to that condition. If you are replacing the turnbuckle, it should be the new one you are adjusting.

Is there a toggle under the turnbuckle? If not, you are going to add one. No turnbuckle should ever be installed without a toggle beneath it. Go ahead and install the correct toggle on the lower end of the turnbuckle now. On the upper end of the turnbuckle, thread in the new wire terminal stud from a disassembled swageless wire terminal (Sta-Lok or Norseman), or pin an eye terminal into the turnbuckle jaws if the wire will attach to the turnbuckle with a clevis pin.

On the end of your coil of rigging wire, install the proper fitting—the one that will attach to the mast tang. Do not neglect to apply red Loctite to the threads before assembling the fitting, then disassemble it after you have snugged it the first time to make sure the wires are formed properly and none are crossed. Add a blob of 3M 101, then retighten, but with no more torque than you can apply with one hand and a normal-length wrench. Wipe off the excess sealant that should be collared around the wire.

Hook the just-installed fitting over one of the two nails. Hook the properly adjusted turnbuckle and toggle assembly over the other nail. Uncoil and stretch the wire until it reaches the end fitting attached to the turnbuckle. When the wire is cut to the proper length, you should be able to insert the wire into the end fitting, just touching the bottom of the hole. Mark the wire to this length and cut it.

If you have a 2-foot-long pair of precision Felco cable cutters or one of those nifty but expensive

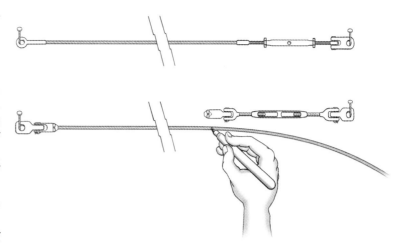

hydraulic jobs handy, cutting the wire rope will hardly be more difficult than trimming a thread end from your sleeve. Cheap cutters tend to crush the wire and cut the strands to different lengths. I have used a hammer-blow cutter for many years with excellent results. The main thing is that for maximum strength from the end fittings, the cut must be straight and regular, which rules out clipping each strand separately. A Dremel rotary tool with a cutoff wheel can make a clean, straight cut. A hacksaw also does the job perfectly if you first make yourself an ad hoc miter box to keep the blade from running all over the cable.

Scrounge up a 4- or 5-inch-long piece of 2 × 4 and drill a hole through it *lengthwise* near one edge and slightly larger than the wire rope you want to cut. With a saber saw, make a perpendicular cut in the edge of the block nearest the hole; it should be deep enough

Getting the new wire the right length.

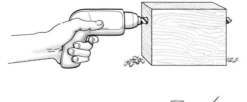

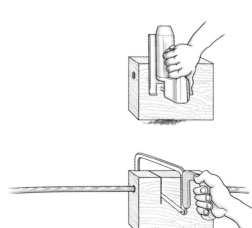

A miter block lets you make perfect rigging wire cuts with a hacksaw.

to cut through the drilled hole. Now feed the wire through the hole until your cut mark lines up with the slot. Use a hacksaw in the slot to cut the wire. If you are working with a long coil of wire, slip the miter block over the wire *before* you install the first terminal.

Perhaps you have heard that the rigging wire stretches when it is placed under a load. That's true. So shouldn't we cut the wire a bit short to allow for this stretch? No. This initial elongation, called "constructional stretch" is typically only about 0.02% in 1×19 stainless steel wire rope. That means a 50-foot stay will stretch about $1/8$ inch, not enough to be of concern.

Don't confuse constructional stretch with elasticity. In a good breeze with the main and genoa sheets two-blocked, the lee shrouds will be slack because the weather shrouds have stretched. Release the sheets and stand the boat up, and all of the shrouds will again be tight. Like very strong rubber bands, the weather shrouds return to their original length. The larger the diameter of the wire, the less it will stretch under a given load, and rod rigging has lower elasticity than wire rope. You do not need to be concerned about this when you are cutting the wire. You made all the accommodations necessary for elasticity when you marked the adjustment of the turnbuckles while the rig was properly tuned.

Back to the matter at hand. Install the second end fitting and thread or pin it to the turnbuckle. The shroud assembly is complete, and if it matches the nail-to-nail length on the ground, you can be confident that it will be the right length when you step the mast. I prefer this method because it requires no calculations, and added toggles or different turnbuckles don't throw you off since they are already in place when you measure the wire.

Some calculations could be necessary if you are replacing chainplates or tangs and the clevis-pin holes of the new ones are not the same distance from the mounting holes. In such a case it will be simpler to move the nail a specific distance than to add to or subtract from the wire. Be sure you move the nail in the right direction. If the tang is shorter, the shroud must be longer and vice versa.

The forestay—and inner stay if your boat has one—should also be toggled at the top. The sideways pressure on headsails will put an unfair load on the end fittings. If the top fitting can articulate in only one direction, the most benign result will be flexing the wire where it enters the fitting, resulting in a shorter life. (I meant the life of the wire, but . . .) If you are adding a toggle to the top of a stay, be sure to assemble it to the end fitting *before* you determine the length of the wire.

HEADSAIL FURLING

There is a good chance that your forestay is enclosed in the foil of a roller-furling system. If not, headsail furling is one of the most popular old-boat upgrades. Early jib furlers were just a wire luff sewn into the sail and attached to a swivel at the top and a rotating drum at the bottom. With the halyard tensioned tight enough to keep the luff kind of straight, the swivels wouldn't spin, but without high halyard tension, the sail bag had better shape. And when the wind really piped up, luff tension went up anyway. Too often in strong winds the only way to get the headsail in was to drop it, no casual task since it was not hanked to the headstay.

Foil systems were a giant leap forward, but even these had growing pains. For a while boatyards were littered with the twisted wreckage of failed furlers. However, the current generation of jib furlers deliver exactly what they promise—easy headsail handling without the need to go forward, plus sail shape even better than hank-on because the luff is fully attached. And they are as dependable as a diesel engine. The only requirements are that the furling unit be large enough for the boat and installed properly. There is also a need for minimal maintenance, which is covered in the next chapter.

Whether your old boat lacks a jib furler and you want to install one or the existing furler is an older unit you want to replace, while you have the mast down is a good time to do it. Conceptually modern furlers are pretty simple. A foil—essentially a long extruded aluminum tube assembled in sections for easier shipping—slips over the headstay and is attached at the bottom to a rotating drum. The sail slides into a slot in the foil, hoisted by a fitting that can rotate with the foil. Tension in the headstay keeps the foil and the leading edge of the sail straight. Halyard tension only straightens the luff in the foil. Pulling a line wrapped around the drum rotates the foil around the headstay, winding in the sail. Unrolling the sail winds the line back around the drum. Equilibrium.

New furling systems all come with a thick installation manual. If you take the time to understand the process first, then follow the instructions exactly, there is absolutely no reason why you cannot successfully install your own system. It takes a professional rigger about 6 hours, so you should anticipate spending the better part of two days on this project. Because of its relative complexity, do not make a jib-furler installation your first enhancement project. If you lack the confidence to tackle this project, you can certainly hire a rigger to do it for you, but don't do that because you think the rigger will do a better job. Follow the manual instructions and your installation will be the equal of a professional's.

Installation specifics depend on the brand and model of furler, but there are some generalizations we can make here that may be helpful. Number one is that you should install a roller furler only over a new headstay. Using the old headstay is false economy, even when the wire seems sound. The stay is not loose inside the foil but passes through "bearings" typically located at each foil section junction, so replacing the wire later is likely to be more complicated than pulling out the old one and snaking in a new one. Typically the furler has to be brought down and at least partially dismantled, a process made more difficult by the use of adhesives and high-strength thread lockers during original assembly. (*Not* using insulating thread lockers, however, guarantees galvanic corrosion that likewise inhibits disassembly *and* may make reassembly impossible.) You don't want to be faced with this prospect any sooner than absolutely necessary, which dictates starting with brand-new wire.

Here is a tip if the above wisdom comes too late and you need to replace the wire. Attach a small-diameter wire messenger to the old stay before you pull it from the foil and you *may* be able to pull the new wire through the internal bearings with this messenger without disassembling the foil. Attach the messenger to the center wire and trim away surrounding wires to make the leading end conical. A molded epoxy "nose cone" can help.

Before you screw anything together, actually attach the toggle-and-eye assembly for the top of the stay to the mast to insure that it is free to articulate in all directions. Similarly, pin the drum to the stemhead to check for clearance and alignment. The integral toggle here must also be unimpeded. The drum can typically be raised with either link plates or an additional toggle.

A couple of additional points worth reinforcing are that the foil must be cut to the correct length and the pull of the halyard must be away from the swivel when every sail is hoisted. The manual will give detailed instructions and usually a chart to tell you exactly how short to cut the top foil section. One caution here is that the pin-to-pin length in the chart is probably not from the tang to the chainplate. Rather, it assumes a toggle at the mast with the stay length being measured from the stemhead chainplate to the pin that joins the stay to the upper toggle. There is the potential for confusion here because there is also a toggle at the bottom but this one *is* included in the

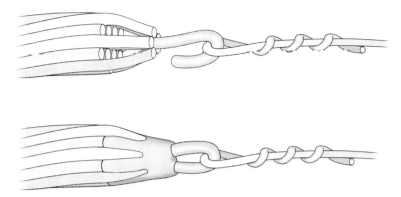

pin-to-pin dimension because it is integral to the lower end of the furler.

As for the angle the halyard makes with the stay, if it is less than about 7 or 8 degrees, you run the risk of the dreaded *halyard wrap*—the halyard winding around the foil when you furl the sail. This will—at a minimum—jam the furler and may damage the foil, the halyard, and even the stay. On an old boat you should anticipate the need to install a halyard restrainer near the top of the mast to force the correct halyard geometry. The halyard swivel should be within 3 or 4 inches of the top of the foil with every sail you hoist on the furler, which requires similar hoist lengths. You achieve this by adding a wire pendant to the top or bottom (or both) of any sail that is too short.

A messenger can allow fitting an assembled furler with a new wire.

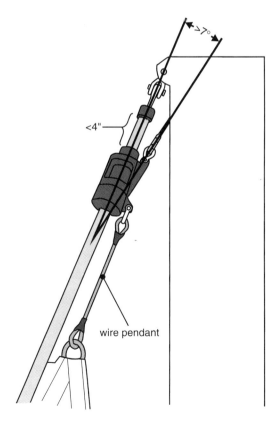

wire pendant

A wire pendant attached to the head (or tack) of a sail with a short luff lengthens the hoist length to place the swivel near the very top of the foil. At full hoist the halyard should lead away from the swivel at least 7 degrees.

Furlers are always assembled on the ground, then hoisted and pinned to the mast for the final adjustments. The length of the assembled unit must still stretch between your two nails, but if the instructions define the headstay length from the toggle rather than the tang, move one of the nails the toggle length (pin-to-pin) toward the other one to avoid having to take this difference into account.

Install the upper eye on the new wire first. In this unique instance, do not assemble the toggle to the eye—you have accommodated the additional length of the toggle by moving the nail—but so you do not forget to attach the upper toggle later, go ahead and pin it to the headstay tang now. Hook the installed eye over the repositioned nail and stretch the wire toward the other nail. The correct cut length of the wire is typically specified as a setback from the full length of the bare stay, so measure from the second nail back up the wire to mark the proper cut location. Slip your 2 × 4 miter box over the wire and cut it squarely at the mark. Follow the manual instructions and you will end up with a new headstay of the right length with a new jib furler installed on it as part of your re-rigging effort.

CHAINPLATES

If the chainplates are attached to the outside of the hull, you can see what is going on with them, but most of the time chainplates penetrate the deck and are attached below to the hull, knees, or a bulkhead. On some boats the below-deck portion of the chainplate is observable. More often they are hidden behind cabinetry and hull liners.

No matter where they are attached or how inaccessible they are, if you have 20-year-old chainplates, they must be removed and carefully examined. Those attached to the hull, because they sit in a fore-and-aft plane while the stresses on them are athwartship, are subject to fatigue, especially where they bend. It is usually not possible to inspect the inside of the bend without removing the chainplate.

For those chainplates that pass through the deck, the critical area is that hidden by the thickness of the deck. Often water is trapped against the chainplate in this area, setting up destructive corrosion that can literally eat the chainplate in half. The only way to inspect this area of the chainplate is to extract it.

Some manufacturers have fabricated chainplates in the shape of a T and fiberglassed them in place. I don't think they chose this method because it is better than bolting. To inspect such chainplates you will have to grind away the capturing fiberglass. If your boat has this type of chainplates, I strongly recommend that you fabricate new chainplates and bolt them in place.

Every chainplate should be inspected visually for surface cracks. If any are noted in *any* of the chainplates (or other related components), you should check *all* of the chainplates with dye penetrant.

Water trapped against the chainplate may induce corrosion hidden from view above and below.

this part where corrosion is most likely can be examined only by removing the chainplate

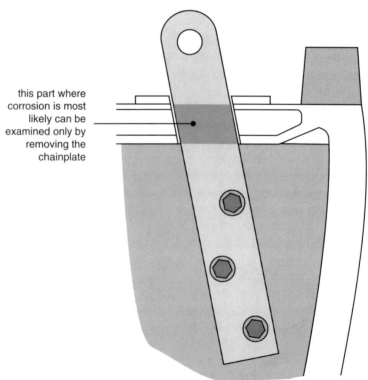

Also inspect the mounting holes in the knees or bulkheads. If they have become elongated, fill them with epoxy putty and redrill them.

After you inspect all the chainplates, reinstall them. There should be a backing plate on the opposite side of every through-bolted chainplate. If they aren't there, now is the time to fabricate and install them. Make sure that chainplate holes through the deck do not expose core material. If they do, dig out the core as deeply as possible and fill the cavity with thickened epoxy. Also be sure all old sealant has been removed, then rebed the chainplates in the deck with polyurethane sealant as you install them. Despite the reality that someday you will have to extract them again and the polyurethane is going to make that more difficult, chainplates test less adhesive sealants. Do not bed deck trim plates with polyurethane. Bedding under the plate adds little if anything to leak prevention, and even the small amount of sealant that squeezes out around the slot when you install the dry trim plate over the wet bedding for the chainplate will make later removal of the trim difficult. If you want to bed under the trim plate, do it with polysulfide in a separate application.

A very worthwhile enhancement is raising the opening for the chainplate above the surface of the deck. A rise sufficient to prevent the chainplate opening from sitting under standing or flowing water limits the demands on the sealant and can dramatically reduce the

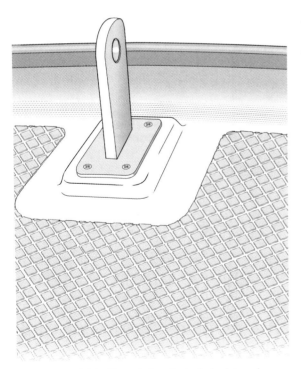

Raising the slot for through-the-deck chainplates above deck level reduces their propensity for leaking.

occurrence of deck leaks at the chainplate. You can raise the opening by bonding a block of solid material to the deck over the chainplate slot but the joint between block and deck is still at deck level. You will do better to grind the surface as for a fiberglass repair, then cast an island from epoxy resin thickened with colloidal silica. Kids' modeling clay can serve as the form, with the resulting structure a permanent feature of the deck. The opening in the deck must continue up through whatever riser you fabricate. A cast riser will require some shaping. Bed the chainplate as before, installing the trim plate on the top of the riser. Protect exposed epoxy with paint.

INNER STAY

The praise heaped on double-headsail rigs in magazine articles and books leads many sailors to consider the possibility of converting their own boats to double headsails. The sloop, the ketch, and the yawl are all candidates for this "enhancement," and the addition of an inner stay does not seem all that complicated. My advice? Not so fast.

Why do you want double headsails? They can allow the headsails to be smaller and correspondingly easier to handle. They do provide sail combination possibilities that are not available with a single headsail. And the staysail is regarded as an outstanding heavy-weather sail that's easier on boat and crew alike.

But a sail suitable for heavy conditions cannot be set on a casually rigged stay. Additional sail combination possibilities do not necessarily translate into better performance. And if handling the headsail is difficult, better furling gear and more powerful winches will likely be a less expensive option than adding an inner stay, installing inboard tracks, mounting a second pair of sheet winches, buying a new sail, and having the existing sail or sails appropriately recut.

I am not advising against double headsails. On the right boat, in the right conditions, with the right sails, they have much to recommend them, but a sloop with an inner stay does not a cutter make. And the conversion requires more than stretching a wire between a tang on the mast and a deck eye.

Because of the mast location, the foretriangle of a sloop is smaller than that of a comparable, legitimate cutter. Moving the mast aft is usually not a practical alternative, but sometimes the overall length of the boat is extended with a bowsprit and the forestay moved to the end of the sprit. This does increase the size of the foretriangle, but it also alters the balance of the boat. The longer the sprit, the more pronounced the effect.

Since the integrity of the rig, not to mention windward ability, depends on a securely anchored forestay, the bowsprit must be held down with its own stay attached to the hull. Adding a sprit and staying it to the hull is not a particularly difficult modification, but because of the potential to adversely affect the balance of the boat and probably because of the way a sprit will alter the lines, most owners contemplating double headsails simply add a second stay inboard of the original forestay.

How far inboard should the inner stay be? Typically the distance between the deck fitting of the two stays will be about a quarter of the J dimension—the distance between the stem fitting and the mast—although there is nothing sacred about this ratio. The foredeck of most fiberglass boats is too flexible for a fitting bolted to the deck to be an adequate anchor for the lower end of the stay. When the wind fills the sail, the load will flex the deck upward, causing the stay to sag to leeward and destroying the shape of the sail. Fortunately most fiberglass boats have a bulkhead between the forward cabin and the chain locker. If this bulkhead sits between 20% and 35% back from the stem, locating the lower end of the stay at the juncture of the bulkhead and the foredeck will simplify the installation. A chainplate of adequate strength is passed through a slot in the deck and bolted to the bulkhead, effectively spreading the load to the full width of the deck (and to the hull if the bulkhead is strongly bonded in place). It is

imperative that the protruding part of the chainplate is properly bent so that the pull of the stay is fair.

If the chain locker bulkhead does not lie in the right spot, a satisfactory installation will oblige you to use a tie rod (or wire) to attach the underside of the deck eye to the hull. The tie rod needs to be a straight-line extension of the stay.

If you intend to fly two headsails at the same time, the inner stay should be parallel to the forestay. This allows the two sails to be trimmed for optimum interaction (slot effect) along the full length of the slot between them. Once you have decided how far inboard to set the new stay, this requirement will determine the location of the hound on the mast.

Before you install the mast hound or the deck fitting, take a look at your spreaders. If you have double spreaders, the size of the staysail will be limited.

Keep in mind that the staysail will be sheeted *inboard* of the shrouds and that the leech of the sail will pass *under* the spreaders. The lower the spreaders, the more they limit the sail size. If you have a genoa staysail in mind, you might decide to open the slot wider by locating the deck fitting farther aft (and the mast hound lower) since the lower spreaders will limit the luff dimension anyway.

The mast hound should be a wishbone-shaped fitting that attaches to the sides of the mast. It must provide a strong attachment point for the stay and a

Mast attachment for inner stay and running backstays.

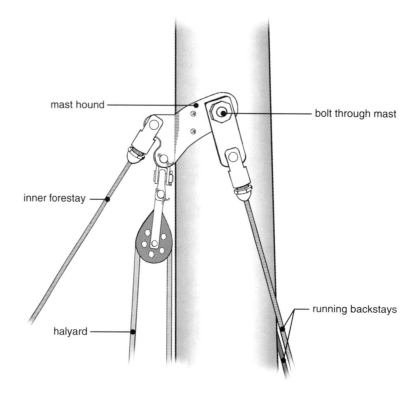

bail for the halyard block that is required. I recommend against attaching the stay with a T-bar fitting through a reinforced slot in the mast because sideways loading on the stay necessitates a toggle at the top. If the hound can be fabricated to be through-bolted to the mast and incorporate integral (or at least mounted to the same bolt) tangs for the running backstays, so much the better.

Running backstays? That's right. What do you think is going to happen to the mast when you tighten that new stay? Or when 40 knots of wind is filling your new "heavy-weather" sail? If your mast has a generous fore-and-aft dimension, you might dispense with the backstays on those lazy days of summer, but if you plan to use the staysail when the wind pipes up, the pressure will pull the mast out of column. Running backstays are part of the package.

You might get adequate support from a second pair of aft lower shrouds attached to the mast at the same height as the new inner stay, but to be effective in resisting the *forward* pull of the stay, the shrouds should form an angle of *at least* 12 degrees with the transverse plane of the mast. Multiply the height of the new tangs above the deck by 0.21 (the tangent of 12 degrees) to find out how far aft of the upper shroud chainplates the new lowers will have to be located. With a 40-foot mast and an inner stay set inboard 25%, the stay will attach 30 feet above the deck. Multiplying 30 by 0.21 yields 6.3, the number of feet aft that a fixed lower will need to attach to the deck. Such a lower is almost certain to interfere with easing the boom adequately for efficient downwind sailing. The solution is running backstays.

If you think of running backstays as no more troublesome than an additional sheet when tacking, you will not mind this aspect of double headsails. You can set up running backstays with tackles, winches, or levers, depending on your preference, what seems appropriate for your boat, and how much you are willing to spend.

In its simplest form the new inner stay is connected to the deck eye with a heavy-duty pelican hook or some other quick-release fitting so it can be released and lashed out of the way when sailing with a single headsail. Otherwise tacking your big genoa with the staysail in the way is going to be a pain. With such an arrangement you might likewise equip the running backstays (rigged at 12 degrees) with quick-release fittings and attach both before hoisting the staysail. From close-hauled through a beam reach on either tack, such backstays require no attention. When the wind gets far enough aft for the boom to

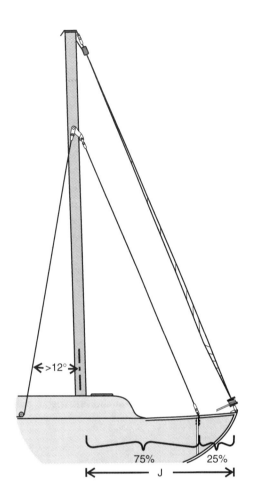

Inner stay and running backstay geometry. (The J dimension is the distance between the stem fitting and the mast.)

chafe the backstay, the staysail is probably blanketing the jib anyway and ought to come down. Running backstays that can be tensioned under load are more versatile, but this system is adequate for most uses of the staysail and has the advantage of being less complicated and less costly.

Even after you have worked out the backstays, you're still not done. There is a litany of deck-mounted hardware—inboard sail track or at least pad eyes, cars, snatch blocks, winches, and cleats. All things considered, unless your boat has a vast foretriangle, this seems like a lot of work and expense for scant performance improvement. On the other hand, twin headsails look awfully nice in silhouette against a red sunset.

SOLENT STAY

There is an inner stay that can make sense as a retrofit for single headsail rigs. A solent stay is mounted just aft of the headstay and is intended to allow flying an *alternative* headsail rather than an *additional* one. Because of its geometry, it is easier to rig. Beyond the wire and fittings to attach it, it does not necessitate much—if any—additional hardware.

At the deck you want the stay as far forward as possible to maximize the foretriangle available for the sail you fly from this stay, but it must be far enough aft not to foul the headstay, which likely has a roller-furled sail on it. At the masthead you want the stay attached as near the backstay attachment as possible to avoid the need for runners. Making the solent parallel to the headstay looks better but is not actually necessary since you will never have both stays in use at the same time, except perhaps when running. So you can stray from the ideal attachment point at the deck to make use of some reinforcing feature. The deck still is not stiff enough to anchor the stay, but a short link to a knee fiberglassed into the bow in the chain locker resolves this issue.

You will need a way to disconnect the stay when it's not in use, but this does not have to be complicated. You simply back off the turnbuckle and pull the clevis pin that attaches it to the wire. The turnbuckle remains attached and lying on the deck, and the wire without the turnbuckle is short enough to attach to an eye at the rail with a pelican

hook–like fitting. If you want to spend the money, quick-disconnect stay fittings are available.

Cruising the eastern Caribbean, where nearly all sailing is on the wind in 20 knots or better, our roller-furled genoa proved ill-suited. Rigging a solent stay allowed us to easily fly a hank-on jib sheeted inboard, both standing the boat up and making us significantly faster. Eventually we put a working jib on the roller furler and acquired a hank-on genoa, thus changing our trips forward from heavy conditions to light.

PROTECTING THE MAST

Meanwhile, back at the boatyard, the disassembled mast still reclines on sawhorses. While it is free of all its hardware is a good time to take protective measures. If the mast is in good shape and the anodized surface is still resisting corrosion for the most part, a good coat of wax is all that is necessary. Use a top-quality automotive wax and apply several layers, buffing between coats. It only takes a few minutes to apply a coat of wax when the mast is waist-high and horizontal, so get plenty of wax on it while you have the opportunity. This is also a good opportunity to lubricate the sail track.

If the mast is covered with fine white powder, the original anodizing has ceased to protect the aluminum. The powdery oxide offers some protection from further corrosion, but it also stains the sails. You might consider having the mast reanodized if you can find a facility with a tank large enough to handle your spar. The cost seems to remain pretty close to $5 per square foot. If, for example, the circumference of your mast is 24 inches, reanodizing would cost around $10 per linear foot, or $400 for a 40-foot stick, with you doing the stripping and prepping. But while new clear anodizing does provide durable surface protection, it does not hide the scars of age, so you could be disappointed with the appearance of the mast. Plus, when you add in the cost to ship the spar to and from the anodizing facility, you could end up spending close to half of what a new stronger and lighter extrusion would cost. The cheapest alternative is wax. Removing the corrosion with a metal cleaner and waxing the mast will protect it even after the original anodizing has given up the battle, but the protection wax alone offers will probably not last beyond about six months. That means a semiannual ride in the bosun's chair, but it is a good idea to check the masthead fittings every six months anyway.

Painting the mast is perhaps the most cost-effective choice. The mast will not have to be sent

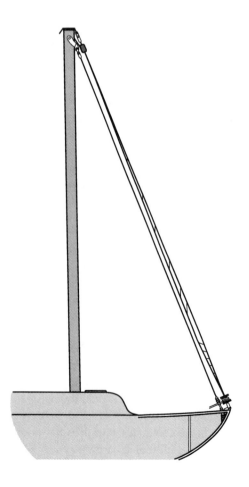

A solent stay allows flying an alternative rather than an additional headsail.

anywhere, the cost of painting will be a fraction of the cost of anodizing, and paint will protect the mast as long or longer. On the negative side, paint can chip and scratch, and it does not adhere readily to aluminum. Forget about just spraying the mast with some type of clear coat. The mast will soon drop the coating onto the deck like so many cellophane leaves. Successfully painting an aluminum mast is a very exacting process. Polyurethane coatings are especially durable, and we will examine this type of coating and how it is applied in Chapter 14.

REASSEMBLY

Before you reattach the hardware to the mast, you should "chase" the threads with a tap. Don't run out and buy a set of taps. You will never use most of them. All of the machine screws you have removed from the mast are likely to be only one or two sizes. Take the screws with you to the hardware store and buy only the taps you need. You will also need to buy a small tap handle if you don't have one already. Now is also the time to replace any of the screws with damaged heads. If you don't, you will be very sorry the next time you try to remove the damaged screw. Be sure the screws you buy are good-quality stainless steel. Clean the threads of the reusable screws with a wire brush or on a soft wire wheel.

I have never seen a sheet metal mast but some builders still persist in using sheet metal screws in the mast. If there are any in your mast, replace them with machine screws. You will have to clean up the hole with a drill, then tap it. The size of the tap will depend on the size of the hole. Coarse

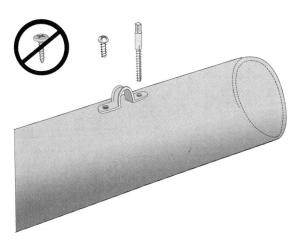

Tap fastener holes in spars and use machine screws.

threads are better than fine because they tolerate the inevitable thread corrosion better. Be sure the machine screws will pass through the fastener holes in the hardware you are attaching. Drilling the holes in the fitting *slightly* larger will usually resolve any problems.

INSULATE

If you take a couple of extra steps when attaching fittings to your mast, you can avoid a lot of future problems. First, if you have not already done this, clean up the fitting. Remove all old sealant, then wipe the fitting with acetone or toluene to remove oils. Insulating fittings with gasket material—Mylar tape is a good choice—will prevent galvanic corrosion, but the problem with a gasket is that it can trap moisture against the mast. Moisture, especially moisture containing salts, will set up simple electrochemical or single-metal corrosion so that even though the hardware is insulated, corrosion can occur beneath the gasket. Bedding in silicone sealant is often recommended and can work well, but silicone tends to lose its grip eventually, becoming simply a gasket and taking us back to the problem of moisture getting into the crevice between the gasket and the mast.

The better solution is to seal out moisture with some type of adhesive shield. One option is to lightly sand the mast where the hardware will be mounted and paint it with at least three coats of epoxy or an epoxy primer to create a moisture barrier. Now install the hardware on some type of insulating gasket, and corrosion should be limited to the fastener holes.

A second alternative, especially for small hardware items, is to bed the item on an unbroken seal of adhesive polyurethane sealant but not 3M 5200. Choose a reduced-adhesive polyurethane such as 3M 4200 or Sikaflex 291 to make future removal easier. For plastic fittings, you will have to use a silicone that does not contain acetic acid (vinegar smell). Mask around where the fitting mounts, then give the entire mounting surface of the fitting a generous application of sealant. Mount the fitting and snug the screws. Sealant should ooze out around the full perimeter of the fitting.

If you are riveting the fitting to the mast, it is worth the effort to fit a thin O-ring around each rivet between the fitting and mast to prevent the compression of the rivets from squeezing out all of the sealant. Also coat the rivets with a corrosion inhibitor such as Duralac.

Allow the sealant to cure overnight or longer, then remove threaded fasteners one at a time and coat the threads with Loctite or a similar thread sealant. Reinstall the screws and tighten them evenly. Take it easy when you are tightening screws in the mast. If you put your shoulder into it, you will easily strip the threads in the thin aluminum. Trim the sealant free of the fitting and remove the masking tape.

If your double lower shrouds attach to a single tang, it is essential that the tang remain free to rotate on the mounting bolt to prevent fore-and-aft movement of the mast from transferring all the load to a single shroud. This is a good place to insulate with Mylar tape. Cover the mast-side surface of the tang with two layers of tape. Apply a little Teflon grease to the mast around the mounting bolt holes before installing the tangs. Do not overtighten the nut. These tangs must rotate freely.

All nuts on the mast should either be castle nuts or drilled so that they may be secured with a cotter pin. There is nothing quite so disconcerting on a black, blustery night as the sound of a nut falling on the deck, let me tell you.

Before you install *any* cotter pin, round the ends with a file. After the cotter pin is in place, spread the legs about 20 degrees. Unless the pin represents a genuine risk to a sail, do not tape it. Taping encourages corrosion. In the event of an unanticipated encounter, the rounded ends will be easier on flesh and sailcloth alike.

Check *every* clevis pin for fit and straightness as you attach the rigging. Any pins that are worn or bent need to be replaced. If the problem is an elongated hole in the tang, replace the tang. Be sure that every clevis pin is locked in place with a cotter pin. Check twice.

The threads of all the turnbuckles should be well lubricated. Old salts around the world recommend anhydrous lanolin for this purpose. More modern salts use Teflon grease. Make sure *all* the turnbuckles are turned the same way, preferably with the right-hand threads downward. Also lubricate the toggles so they can do what they were designed to do. In fact, you should also lubricate all the clevis pins.

If you have eliminated any of the fittings, moved them, or changed the way they are mounted, don't leave the old mounting holes open. Put a screw in each one, coating the threads of the screws with thread sealant.

There should be a drain hole at the base of the mast, usually drilled through both the mast and the heel fitting. Be sure that the hole is clear; if you found significant corrosion inside the mast, enlarge the hole.

SPREADER ANGLE

After all these years I am still amazed at all the spreaders I see that are horizontal. Spreaders are designed to withstand compression loading, not leverage. Unless the spreaders bisect the angle between the lower half and the upper half of the shroud, you are inviting spreader failure with catastrophic implications. Precise adjustment is not critical, but if the spreaders on your mast are not canted upward (above horizontal) by about half the angle the shroud forms with the mast—typically making spreader inclination around 7 or 8 degrees—you may need to modify the base fittings. Seize the upper shrouds temporarily to the tip, but wait to do the final adjustment until after the mast has been restepped.

With the mast in place and the upper shrouds set up loosely, get yourself hoisted to the spreaders. A bevel gauge will help you to position the spreader tip, but if you don't have one, a square of cardboard and a pair of scissors will do the job. Lay one edge of the cardboard along the centerline of the back of the spreader and trim the adjoining edge to match the lower half of the shroud. Now flip the cardboard over as though it were hinged to the spreader. The upper half of the shroud should also parallel the cut edge. If it doesn't, slide the tip up or down to take out *half* the difference.

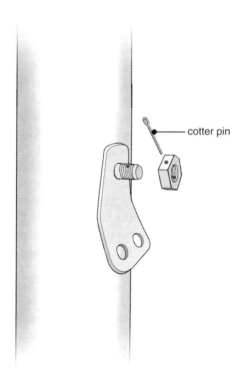

All nuts on the mast must be secured with cotter pins.

cotter pin

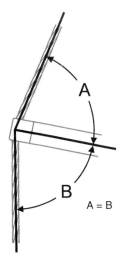

The angle between spreader and shroud should be the same above and below the spreader.

Retrim the cardboard to take out the other half and check again to confirm that both angles are the same. Tighten the tip clamp or seize the shroud *securely* to the spreader tip with Monel seizing wire. If more than one shroud passes over the tip of a spreader, tightly seize only the upper shroud. Use your cardboard template to position the opposite spreader.

If your mast is keel stepped, don't forget to slip the boot over the mast *before* it is stepped. A section of tire inner tube will work just as well as a special molded boot. Turn the boot up on the mast inside out and clamp it to the mast with a giant hose clamp (mast boot clamp). Turn the boot over the clamp, as if you were turning down the top of a sweat sock, hiding the clamp. With a second clamp, attach the boot to the deck flange. Protect the boot from the sun with a fabric skirt (see Chapter 15).

LIFELINES

Before we desert our discussion of wire rigging, let's talk about lifelines. Most old boats have been delivered with lifelines rigged with coated wire. Coated wire is an astonishingly bad idea. Not only does the coating promote corrosion by depriving the stainless steel of essential oxygen, but by design the inevitable corrosion of the wire is hidden from view. The true strength of aging coated lifeline wire is a bad-odds gamble, with the ante being someone's life. That is why they are called *life*lines. Just for the record, the Offshore Racing Congress (ORC) bans coated lifelines.

Examine coated lifelines closely. As they age, the vinyl coating hardens and cracks, and soon enough rust appears at the cracks in the vinyl. This instantly condemns the wire—no ifs, ands, or buts. Likewise any kind of bump or lump in the vinyl covering means a tumor of corrosion inside. If you see rust stains anywhere on coated lifelines, even at the ends of the coating, put lifeline replacement on your S1 list. Falling overboard is far and away the most serious risk boaters face, and weak lifelines greatly increase your exposure. You are safer without lifelines.

I urge you not to replace old coated lifelines with new coated lifelines. The best wire for lifelines is Type 316 1 × 19 rigging wire. The same outside diameter will deliver more than three times the strength of coated wire, the 316 alloy will resist corrosion for a long time, and if any does occur, it will be immediately visible for evaluation. Given that safety at sea is surely more important than convenience at the dock, I also advocate abandoning gates in favor of a continuous lifeline from bow to stern. In my experience gates are rarely in the right place anyway. They are like an open manhole in the dark if accidentally left

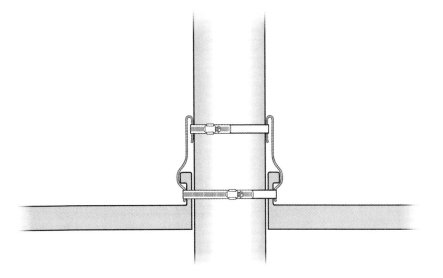

Clamp boot inside-out to mast, then turn the boot down over the clamp. Attach to deck flange with second ring clamp.

open. They at least double the number of end fittings, thus doubling to the possibility of fitting failure, not to mention doubling the fitting cost. (If safety is your concern, you are paying more to get less.) And as an added benefit, a pair of boat-length runs of rigging wire can be a priceless onboard resource in the event of a rigging failure. On our boat, a ketch, the upper lifelines are the same wire as our main shrouds, and the lower lines are the same as the mizzen shrouds.

You have three options for end fittings. There are do-it-yourself hand-crimp terminals available that claim to deliver about 70% of the wire strength, but that is on 7 × 7 wire. I fear that the grip of these crimp fittings will have significantly less strength on the smoother surface of 1 × 19 wire. I have only anecdotal data to support this concern, but if you decide on the greater safety of uncoated wire, you should pair this with the greater strength of either machine-swaged or swageless terminals. You will need a rigging shop to install swaged terminals. Several manufacturers offer complete lines of swaged lifeline fittings, including integral pelican hooks, gate eyes, turnbuckles, and threaded adjusters. These make for very attractive lifeline installations, and because the swages live their lives horizontal, internal corrosion is less prevalent.

A do-it-yourself alternative is to terminate the lifelines with swageless terminals, typically fork or toggle jaws at the bow and studs or eyes at the stern joined to turnbuckles. You can lower the cost without much compromise of strength by eliminating the turnbuckles and substituting a multipurchase lashing of high-modulus, small-diameter line to tension the lifeline and attach it to the stern rail. However, I prefer a turnbuckle because it allows tension to be eased and the clevis pin removed to drop the entire lifeline to deck level between any pair of stanchions, effectively giving you a wide and ideally located boarding or loading gate.

High-modulus (or hi-mod) lashings inevitably lead to the question, why not just replace the wire altogether with high-modulus rope? A $1/4$-inch double-braid line with a polyester cover for abrasion and UV protection and a high-modulus (Dyneema) core can have a breaking strength exceeding 4,000 pounds, about twice as strong as coated lifeline wire of the same outside diameter. The rope is more expensive than the wire but only modestly so, and it has the advantage of being much lighter and more comfortable. A thimbled eye splice at each end would be all the "terminals" required, with one end tensioned with a multipurchase lashing. Hi-mod rope lifelines

Uncoated 1 × 19 wire with mechanical end fittings delivers the most trustworthy lifelines.

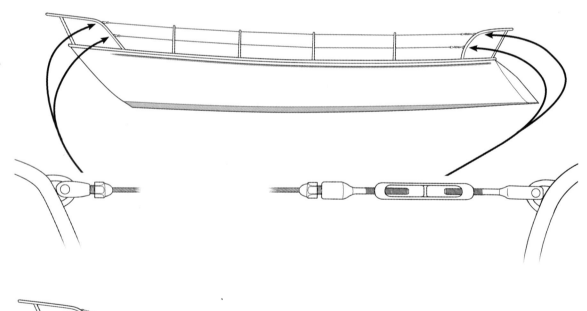

Releasing one end of the lifeline effectively creates an open gate located wherever it is needed.

would require you to learn to do a core-to-core splice. Beyond this intellectual demand, the other drawback is that there is no way to tell when or if the strength of the line has been degraded by exposure. I would caution against trusting rope lifelines more than five years old based on the life of polyester halyards that have the longevity advantage of being vertical rather than horizontally exposed to the sun's rays 24/7. By contrast, Type 316 lifelines should last two decades or more.

Crimp Nicopress-style sleeves in two places.

WIRE PENDANTS

The single legitimate use for coated lifeline wire is to make up tack or head pendants for your sails. A tack pendant is just a length of rope—wire being used here because of its very low stretch—with eyes formed around thimbles at both ends. One eye encloses the tack grommet of the sail, and the other attaches to the fitting that the grommet would otherwise have attached to. The effect is to lift the foot of the hoisted sail farther above the deck the equivalent of the length of the pendant. A tack pendant can solve a lifeline/sail chafe problem, can make a sail less susceptible to catching green water, and can improve safety by letting the helmsman see forward under the sail.

A head pendant is identical to a tack pendant except that it attaches to the head grommet. It is used primarily on roller-furling sails to adjust the total hoist length of the sail so the upper swivel reaches all the way to the top. Otherwise sails with a shorter hoist will create a condition that is likely to result in halyard wrap, mentioned earlier in this chapter.

To make up wire pendants, you need a length of coated wire of an appropriate size—typically either $^1/_8$ or $^3/_{16}$ inch—two thimbles, two crimp (Nicopress) sleeves, and a swaging tool. The tool is two stiff metal bars with a series of crimping dies machined into the joint between them and a pair of bolts to allow you to close this space. The cost is about $50, and you will likely find that having onboard swaging ability can be quite handy.

Determine the desired finished length of the pendant and cut the wire, allowing sufficient additional length to form the eyes. Strip the coating from both ends of the wire. The part of the wire that passes through the crimp sleeve, around the thimble, and back through the crimp sleeve should be bare. Put the two bolts through the adjacent holes on either side of the appropriate die in your swaging tool. Position a sleeve inside the die opening with the longer dimension of the sleeve perpendicular to the space between the bars and with the die located near one

end of the sleeve, not in the middle. Tighten the two bolts enough to securely grip the sleeve but not to compress it. Feed the bare wire through the sleeve, bend it around the thimble, and feed it back through the sleeve. Work the wire to get it tight around the thimble with the sleeve as close to the thimble as possible and the cut end of the wire just peeking out of the sleeve. Holding everything tight—yet one more example of two hands being less than the optimal number—tighten the bolts evenly until the two bars come together. This compresses the metal of the sleeve into the texture of the wire. Release the bolts, move the compression die to the opposite end of the same sleeve, and crimp it again. Compression sleeves are intended to have dual crimps.

The dual advantages of coated wire are flexibility—the core is 7 × 7 lanyard wire—and the fact that the coating prevents the pendant from leaving rust stains on the sail when it is stowed. Toward that end, it is a good idea to tightly wrap all of the exposed pendant, including the crimped sleeve and the thimble, with plastic tape.

RUNNING RIGGING

For the most part, replacing running rigging is no more complicated than buying the right size of braid-on-braid polyester line, heat-sealing the ends, splicing an eye or tying a bowline in one end, and running the other end through the appropriate blocks. You don't need my help, but indulge me anyway.

REEVING INTERNAL HALYARDS

Replacing internal halyards is usually just a matter of pulling a light line messenger with the old halyard, then pulling the new halyard with the messenger. But sometimes halyards and/or messengers get lost. Then what?

The coolest trick I know for reeving internal halyards requires 2 feet of steel window-sash chain tied to a mast length–plus of light cord. Take the chain end of this messenger to the masthead. While you

A ferrous chain messenger can be "fished" with a magnet.

hold the chain centered at the top of the masthead sheave, an assistant on deck should hold the cord against the mast and mark it where it reaches the exit box. Now feed the chain the rest of the way over the sheave and let it drop inside the mast, controlling its descent with tension on the messenger cord. The chain will follow a straight path down from the sheave. When the mark on the cord reaches the top center of the sheave, the bottom of the chain will be at the exit box. Your assistant can retrieve it with a magnetic pickup tool—essentially a magnet on a telescoping wand. These are available from tool suppliers and automotive stores (and are great for retrieving dropped wrenches in the bilge). With the chain outside the exit box, sew the new halyard to the other end of the messenger and feed it through the mast.

LINE SELECTION
What rope should you use for new halyards and sheets? As I write this, the current West Marine catalog offers sailors no fewer than 33 different sail-handling lines. Let's deal with *that* new reality

first. Unless you are a top-tier racer—unlikely with an old boat—30 of the 33 have no application for you. For sheets, buy double-braid polyester. Period. For rope halyards, especially for hank-on sails, you might want to spend a few cents more per foot for parallel-core polyester. Parallel-core line feels stiff and is a pain to splice, but if you are seeing scallops in your sails at the luff when the wind pipes up, you need the lower stretch of parallel-core. The only high-tech line that has any sail-control application on a cruising boat is double-braid with a polyester cover and a core of high-modulus polyethylene (Spectra or Dyneema) or Vectran. The high-modulus core creates a line with almost no stretch. Club racers and big-boat cruisers can get better sail shape in strong winds with halyards of this kind. Smaller cruisers can accomplish the same thing for much less money by just increasing the diameter of the halyard. All other high-tech ropes are intended to deliver low stretch and light weight for racing applications, where subtle changes in sail shape and extra ounces aloft can make the difference between winning and losing.

As a general rule, high-modulus ropes should not be used in any application that requires a knot. Knotting high-modulus rope can reduce its strength by as much as 80%. No, that is not a typo. The current generation of hi-mod ropes do not like being bent sharply, which is exactly what a knot does. In addition, many high-strength, high-tech fibers are extremely slick, so they tend not to hold a knot very well. Some will not even hold a splice. These characteristics can make a plain-Jane polyester line the safer choice for sail control and going to the top of the mast despite the higher-rated strength of the high-tech line. If you want to experiment with high-tech line for some use aboard your boat, be sure you ascertain how to attach it safely.

Ironically, the lowest-stretch halyard material remains wire despite the movement away from wire halyards in favor of low-stretch rope. Part of the reason for this is that wire can be less than gentle on a mast. It also cannot be handled by hand, so either a reel winch or a rope tail is required. Reel winches have a horrible safety reputation, although I happen to believe they are exacting rather than inherently dangerous. But reel winches have all but disappeared, which puts a rope tail on most wire halyards. In light of the realities of low-stretch ropes, wire halyards still have much to recommend them. It is, I think, the necessity of splicing a rope tail to the wire that makes sailors seek an alternative. Yet the tail splice is strikingly similar to a long splice between two pieces of ordinary three-strand rope.

Sure it is.

I swear. So here is your graduate-level rigging project, not because it is difficult, but because everyone thinks it is difficult. Skip the game on Monday and give this a try. You will be finished in plenty of time to see the second half.

SPLICING WIRE TO ROPE

Start with a length of 7 × 19 wire in the diameter you need and an equal length of braid-on-braid polyester rope *twice* the diameter of the wire. (If you are practicing, you need about 8 feet of each. Practice is a good idea.)

Start the splice by tapering the wire. Unlay the six outside strands one at a time, cutting off each one

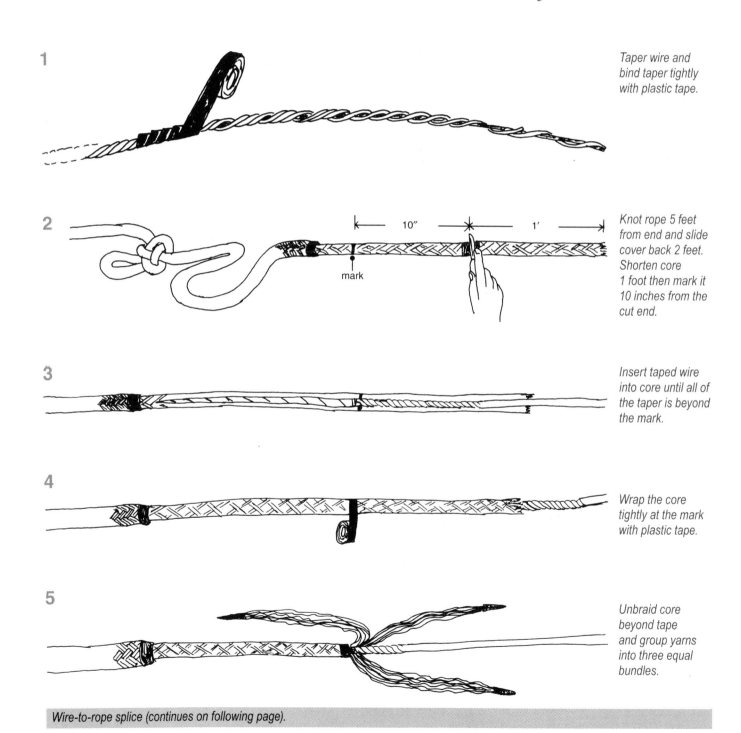

1 Taper wire and bind taper tightly with plastic tape.

2 Knot rope 5 feet from end and slide cover back 2 feet. Shorten core 1 foot then mark it 10 inches from the cut end.

mark

10″   1′

3 Insert taped wire into core until all of the taper is beyond the mark.

4 Wrap the core tightly at the mark with plastic tape.

5 Unbraid core beyond tape and group yarns into three equal bundles.

Wire-to-rope splice (continues on following page).

Lift two strands of the wire and tuck one bundle through.

6

Lift the next two strands and tuck the second bundle. Make six tucks with each bundle, thinning bundles by $1/3$ on each of the last three tucks.

7

Milk cover back over spliced core. Tape cover tightly where core splice ends, unbraid cover beyond tape, and divide yarns into three equal bundles. Tuck full bundles four times, then reduce the bundles by two yarns for each subsequent tuck until just a few yarns remain.

8

Cut off the remaining yarns and serve the last inch of the splice with waxed twine. Wax the entire cover splice and roll it between your palms to smooth.

9

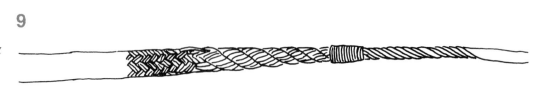

(Continued from previous) Wire-to-rope splice.

progressively farther up the wire. The length of the taper is not particularly important, but making each strand about 2 inches shorter than the previous one works well. Bind the taper tightly with two thicknesses of electrical tape.

Tie a knot in the rope about 5 feet from the end. Wrap the end with tape—not too tight—and cut off the heat-fused end. Slide the cover back at least a couple of feet. Cut a foot off the core, then mark the core about 10 inches from the cut end. Insert the tapered wire into the core until all of the taper is beyond the mark on the core. Wrap the core very tightly at the mark with electrical tape to hold the wire in place.

Unbraid the core below the tape and group the straightened strands into three equal bundles. Tightly tape the ends. Using a metal fid, *carefully* lift two strands of the wire where it enters the core. Tuck one of the bundles of rope beneath the two strands. The tuck should be with the lay; i.e., parallel to the next strands of the wire, not perpendicular, and the bundle of rope should be smooth and pulled snug. Lift the next two strands and tuck the second bundle. Lift the last pair of strands and tuck the third bundle. Adjust the bundles until they all exit the wire at the same level. Now take two more tucks with all three bundles, being careful to make each smooth and even.

Is this starting to sound familiar? You thought I was lying to you about the long splice, didn't you?

After the third tuck, cut $1/_3$ of the yarns from each of the bundles and tuck them again. Thin the bundles again by $1/_3$ and tuck. Thin one more time and tuck. Cut the remaining yarns, allowing them to protrude about $1/_8$ inch.

Slide the cover back over the core, burying the core splice. Milk the cover vigorously to be sure all the slack is out of it. Where the core splice terminates, wrap the cover tightly with tape. Remove the piece of tape on the end of the cover and unbraid the cover, gathering the straightened strands into three bundles, just as before.

This time do four complete tucks, taking even greater care to have each tuck snug and smooth. Now cut *two yarns* from each bundle and take another tuck. Remove two more yarns and take another tuck. Continue tapering the bundles and tucking until you have only six or so yarns left. Trim the remaining yarns and serve the last inch of the splice tightly with waxed twine. Remove the tape and smear the splice lightly with beeswax, rolling it between your palms to compact it.

Now go watch the game. You don't need to know anything else about rigging.

CHAPTER NINE

Nuts and Bolts

"Think you can or think you can't, either way you will be right."
—HENRY FORD

Archimedes pushed a pencil or a reed or whatever it was they wrote with in ancient Greece, but his desk job notwithstanding, he no doubt could have made all necessary mechanical repairs on boats of the time. And despite twenty-three centuries of "progress," I am absolutely certain (without much fear of being proved wrong) that he could likewise repair the mechanical systems of today's boats—of your boat.

The justification of such an assertion is that Archimedes understood the *five simple machines* that were the basis of all mechanical devices then and now. To understand the principles of the lever, the wheel and axle, the pulley, the wedge, and the screw is to understand the workings of every mechanical device likely to be found aboard a boat, including those occupying the toolbox.

Maintenance—the dismantling and reassembly of a device to clean or lubricate it—requires little more than care and audacity. Pay attention to how the device comes apart and you should be able to put it back together. Repair, on the other hand, is not a by-the-numbers process. The insight to repairing a mechanical device comes from understanding how it works. By the end of this chapter you should be able to make a creditable effort at repairing any mechanical item on your boat, including the engine, but getting to that level of competence requires a sound understanding of the basics.

Perhaps the explanation of mechanical principles by your high-school physics teacher was so spellbinding that it echoes in your ears even today. If your recall is less distinct, it will serve you well in this noble endeavor to become reacquainted.

THE SIMPLE MACHINES
LEVER

The lever is the oldest of the machines, and understanding it is the key to understanding all five. You probably learned about levers on the seesaws in kindergarten. When you sat farther from the pivot—the fulcrum—you could lift a bigger kid. The relationship between the two ends of a lever can be defined in simple mathematical terms: the effort arm is equal to the resistance arm. The *arm* is the force (effort or resistance) multiplied by its distance from the fulcrum. On the seesaw, what you lacked in effort (your weight) you made up in distance.

Perhaps this would be clearer if we put some numbers with it. A lever with the fulcrum in the middle does not develop any *mechanical advantage*. To lift an 80-pound weight on one end requires an 80-pound effort on the other. Move the effort twice as far from the fulcrum as the resistance is, and you need apply only half the force; four times the distance, a quarter the force. In other words, if the weight is 1 foot from the fulcrum and the effort 4 feet from the fulcrum, 20 pounds of effort will lift an 80-pound weight (20 × 4 = 80 × 1). This principle is the same even if the effort and resistance are on the same side of the fulcrum. A pelican hook comes to mind; a 20-pound effort 4 inches from the pivot translates into 80 pounds of force 1 inch from the pivot. Of course, this multiplication of force has a price—the additional distance through which the effort must move.

An astonishing number of the mechanical devices aboard a boat are nothing more complicated than applications of the lever principle: the tiller, winch handles, manual windlass, shift control,

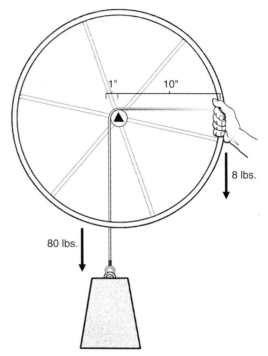

Wheel and axle.

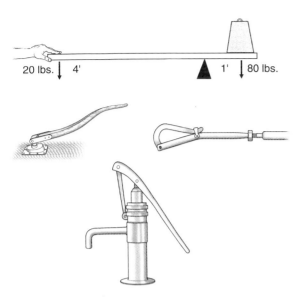

Simple machines: lever.

snapshackles, pelican hooks, cabinet latches, and oars, to name a few. The lever has an essential function in the operation of hand or foot pumps, toilets, and seacocks; in the control of the mainsail; and in the opening and closing of engine valves. It is found among your tools as a pry bar, wrenches, socket handles, pliers, scissors, and cable cutters. The relationship between mast and keel is that of a lever.

WHEEL AND AXLE

The wheel and axle is nothing more than a lever that can rotate a full 360 degrees. Mechanical advantage is computed exactly as before, with the radii of the wheel and the axle equivalent to distances from the lever's fulcrum. A 10-inch wheel on a 1-inch axle magnifies force by 10. As with the lever, this magnification of force requires the effort to move through additional distance, and it is this additional distance that is often the main consideration in the design of wheel-based mechanical devices. In this example, a point on the surface of the wheel will travel 10 times as far in a single revolution as a point on the axle. Because both parts complete a revolution in the same amount of time, to make the longer journey the surface of the wheel must be moving 10 times as fast as the surface of the axle.

All three functions find their way aboard. The purpose of the steering wheel is to reduce the amount of effort required to turn the shaft (axle); the larger the steering wheel, the less effort required to steer the boat. Each blade of the propeller (wheel) scribes a circle of thrust with every revolution of the shaft (axle); the larger the prop, the more water it pushes against. The

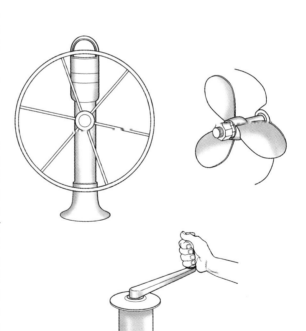

drive-belt pulley (wheel) attached to the engine crankshaft (axle) multiplies the speed of the belt; the larger the pulley, the faster the belt travels. The principles of the wheel and axle are also visible in winches, capstans, roller reefing, roller furling, gears, sprockets, logs, faucets, valves, tap handles, and screwdrivers.

PULLEY

Pulley, as it refers to a simple machine, does not mean a drive-belt pulley like those found on your engine, alternator, or water pump. A drive-belt pulley is actually a wheel and axle, a toothless gear. A pulley—the machine—is what a sailor calls a block.

The pulley has no mechanical advantage when it is fixed. Lifting an 80-pound weight requires 80 pounds of pull. Its usefulness is in changing the *direction* of the effort; you pull down on the main halyard to raise the sail. But a *movable* pulley does provide mechanical advantage. Pass a line around the pulley, anchoring one end, and 40 pounds of effort applied to the other end will lift 80 pounds attached to the pulley. The same trade-off with distance applies. You will have to pull the free end 2 feet to lift the weight 1 foot.

To determine the mechanical advantage of a system of pulleys—the mainsheet tackle, for example—you need only count the number of times the line runs *to and from* the movable block. In the previous example the mechanical advantage is 2, but if the standing part of the line is anchored to a becket on the movable block, the advantage becomes 3. A double block provides the opportunity for a mechanical advantage of 4 or, if the standing part is attached to the movable block, 5. In this last instance it only takes 16 pounds of effort on the hauling part, ignoring friction, to exert 80 pounds of pull on the boom, but you will have to pull the hauling part 5 feet for every foot the movable block travels. An understanding of pulleys is most useful in solving problems with the running rigging.

WEDGE

The fourth of the simple machines is the wedge. Every anchor you have aboard is a wedge. Every knife is a wedge. So are the cutting edges of chisels, planes, and hatchets. Punches, awls, fids, needles, and nails are all wedges. The stem of a pop rivet is a wedge. The lobes of the camshaft are wedges. The boat itself is a wedge, splitting the water rather than pushing it.

Pulley.

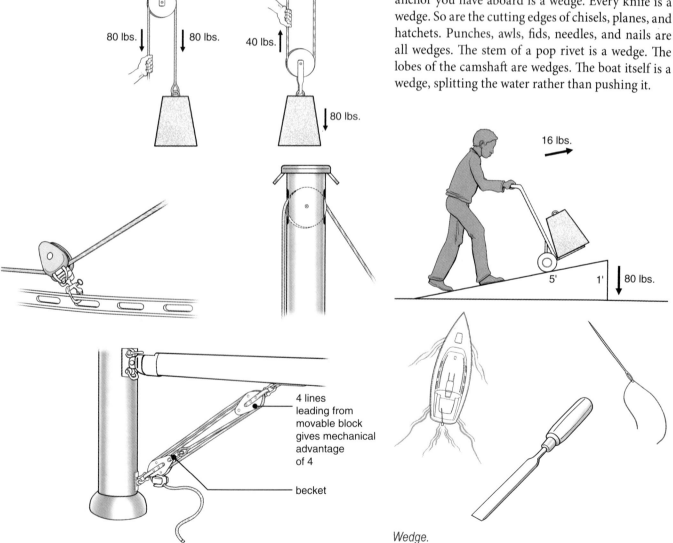

4 lines leading from movable block gives mechanical advantage of 4

becket

Wedge.

If you lay a wedge on one of its surfaces, it becomes an inclined plane—a ramp—and the mechanical advantage is easier to fathom. The ratio of the length of the ramp to its height defines the advantage. A ramp 5 feet long and 1 foot high has a mechanical advantage of 5. Again ignoring friction, to lift our 80-pound weight by rolling it up the ramp requires only 16 pounds of effort, but of course we have to push the weight 5 feet to lift it 1 foot.

SCREW

Cut a piece of paper diagonally, forming an inclined plane. Starting with the wide end, wrap the paper around a pencil. You have just demonstrated the principle behind the screw. The mechanical advantage of a screw depends on the *pitch* (the incline of the threads) and the lever arm of the effort applied. Turn a screw with threads $^1/_8$ inch apart by applying effort to the end of a 10-inch wrench and you magnify your effort by a factor of 80. With a small pitch (fine threads) and a long lever arm, a screw can provide a tremendous mechanical advantage.

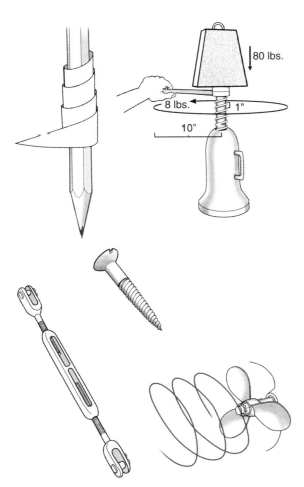

Screw.

In use, the screw almost always depends on another machine for its operation—either a lever (such as a wrench) or a wheel and axle (such as a screwdriver). A lot of other onboard items are based on the principle of the screw. The propeller is a screw, threading its way through the water. The tension of the standing rigging is adjusted by the matching screws of turnbuckles. A worm gear (steering) is actually a screw. A screw converts the rotary motion of the handle to the straight-line motion of gate valves and stove burner valves. Screws compress opening portholes against their sealing gaskets. The pressure of a vise or a clamp is applied by a screw. Pipe wrenches and other adjustable wrenches are adjusted with a screw. A drill bit is a sharp screw, as are taps and dies. But by far the most common use of a screw is as a fastener, holding pieces of wood or metal together and assembling all things mechanical.

TOOLS

Most (but certainly not all) mechanical tools exist for the single purpose of tightening and loosening screws. Their function is no more exotic than the twist knob on a lamp switch, the T-bar on a corkscrew, or the handle on a decorator faucet, yet some people wilt at the thought of using a screwdriver or a wrench. Look around. If you felt the same abhorrence for the handles on your shower, your social standing would surely suffer.

The only "trick" to being successful with tools is to be certain that you have the right tool for the job. For the moment we are talking about turning tools, the levers that allow us to turn screws. The lever could be an integral part of the screw, but it is not hard to see the problems and limitations such a design would present. Instead, screws are usually manufactured for removable levers. This should present few problems if you think of the screw and the lever as a matched set, like a lock and key. You must have the right key to turn the lock.

Four types of "drives" dominate in all screw applications. A hexagonal (six-sided) head is most often associated with the word *bolt*. *Bolt* most appropriately refers to a screw that does not thread into the parts being fastened but passes through them and is held in place by a threaded nut. The head of a bolt is not necessarily hexagonal, but the nut almost always is. Instead of hexagonal, the head of a screw may be round, with a slot machined across the center. This is called standard or slot drive. The screw may also be machined with what appears to be a crossed slot but is actually a special beveled socket. This is

The four most common drive types.

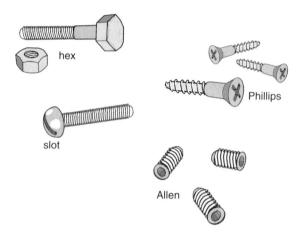

hex

Phillips

slot

Allen

called Phillips drive. The fourth type of drive is also a machined socket in the screw, but in this case the socket is hexagonal. This is Allen drive and is most often used on headless screws such as setscrews.

You may run across other types of screws aboard. For example, the deck-fill caps for fuel and water are screws, and they probably open with a special wrench that fits into two drilled holes in the cap. This is called face-pin or spanner drive. Whenever you encounter a screw with a special drive, you will have to obtain the appropriate tool to turn it.

If the type of drive were the only consideration, you would only need about a dozen hand tools to turn every screw aboard. Hex-head bolts and nuts come in sizes from microscopic to titanic, but those aboard will rarely be smaller than $1/4$ inch and rarely larger than 1 inch. Actually the installation of mostly foreign-built diesel engines in sailboats since the early 1970s means that you are likely to need wrenches in metric rather than inch sizes. Metric wrenches come in millimeter increments, with 6 mm the smallest you are likely to need and 19 mm the largest. One quarter to 1 inch in $1/16$-inch increments comes out to 14 different sizes. Coincidentally so does 6 mm to 19 mm in millimeter increments. But a single wrench typically has a socket on both ends, so seven inch-size wrenches and/or seven metric-size wrenches should handle all the possibilities. With fit as the only consideration, the choice of type of wrenches is easy; the shape of the wrench should be identical to the shape of the bolt head—hexagonal. Such a wrench is called a 6-point box-end wrench.

For all the screws with slotted heads, you need standard screwdrivers in about three different blade sizes. For the Phillips-head screws, you need Phillips-head screwdrivers in three sizes—conveniently called #1, #2, and #3. And for the Allen or hex key screws, you need a set of Allen wrenches, which are available individually or as a single tool resembling a Swiss Army knife.

Time out. If *hex key* and *Phillips head* and *box-end* and *six-point* and *face pin* seem like a foreign language, don't let that put you off. After all, you have mastered *bow* and *stern* and *port* and *starboard* and *chine* and *sheer* and *sheet* and *halyard* and *helm*. The terminology of mechanics is far less obscure than that of boating. Phillips head and Allen wrench and a few others are named after the person or company that developed them, like Stetson, Thermos, or Levis. Otherwise, with rare exceptions—monkey wrench being one—the names of tools and mechanical devices are descriptive. A 6-point box-end wrench encloses the hex nut (as opposed to an open-end wrench, which has an open end) and the interior of the box has six points. A combination wrench has a box end on one end combined with an open end on the other. An offset wrench is a wrench that is bent. When an offset wrench is flat against the surface beneath the nut being turned, the handle of the wrench is clear of the surface. Whatever a tool sounds like, that's probably what it is.

Back to the issue of tool requirements. The type of drive is unfortunately not the only consideration. The location of the screw—its accessibility—often determines the type of tool that is required. In a tight space a screwdriver with a very short shank, a "stubby," may be required. Conversely, a screw may only be accessible with an extra-long shank. Occasionally space is so restricted that the only tool that will work is the offset screwdriver, one with the blades perpendicular to the shaft and operating like a wrench.

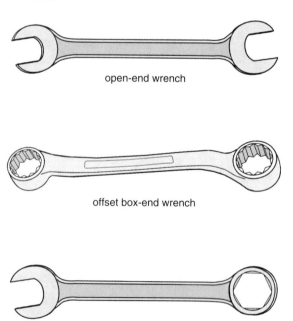

open-end wrench

offset box-end wrench

6-point combination wrench

Put a wrench on a hex nut and you often discover that you can rotate the wrench only a short distance before another screw or some other feature interferes. To accommodate this limited rotation, you remove the wrench and reposition it on the nut, swinging the small arc available to you each time until the nut is tight (or loose). But if the arc is less than 60 degrees, you have a problem with your six-point wrenches. Each possible position of the wrench is 60 degrees from the previous one (360 degrees divided by six sides), so if you have less than 60 degrees of swing, you cannot reposition the wrench.

You might assume the same limitation would exist with an open-end wrench, since repositioning it means sliding it onto the next set of *flats*—the parallel sides of the nut. That is still a rotation of 60 degrees. You would usually be wrong because the jaws of most open-end wrenches are at an angle of about 15 degrees to the handle. When interference is encountered, the wrench is removed, inverted, and slipped back onto the same flats, allowing an additional 30 degrees of swing. If you continue to invert the wrench, you can rotate the nut 30 degrees at a time.

Open-end wrenches are popular because of this versatility, the ease with which they are slipped onto the nut, and the fact that they can be tilted somewhat to accommodate an awkward reach. But they are second only to the adjustable wrench in their propensity to damage nuts and knuckles. The problem is that all the force is concentrated on two corners of the nut, which is trying mightily to spread the jaws of the wrench. A weak corner or a weak jaw and the result is a rounded nut, bloody knuckles, and blue air. If at all possible, do not use an open-end wrench to do final tightening or initial loosening.

A better choice for limited swing is a 12-point box-end wrench. A 12-point wrench can be repositioned on the nut in 30-degree intervals, just like the open-end wrench, but it distributes the force to all six corners of the nut. The circular (box) construction of the wrench makes distortion unlikely.

When a nut or bolt is accessible only from the top, a socket wrench is indicated. A socket wrench actually has two parts, a socket and a handle. One end of the socket has an opening identical to that of a box-end wrench and may be either 6-point or 12-point. Six-point sockets are better because they grip the nut more securely. The other end of a socket has a square hole for the handle. Depending on the size of this hole, the socket is designated as $1/4$-, $3/8$-, or $1/2$-inch square drive.

The simplest socket handle is the hinged handle, or break-over bar. The hinged lug allows the handle to be at right angles to the socket for maximum leverage for tightening and loosening, then moved to a vertical position where it acts much like a screwdriver for quick removal. For screwdriver-like use only, the socket may be fitted to a nut-driver handle, particularly useful for small nuts and bolts. But by far the most common socket handle is the *ratchet*, and for good reason: it eliminates the need to remove the socket from the nut when swing room is limited, and it allows for very rapid turning of the nut. Turning the handle in one direction turns the attached socket, but the handle is free to move in the opposite direction without turning the socket. A reversing lever allows the same handle to tighten and loosen.

When access is difficult, extension bars can allow you to move the handle clear of interference. If straight access is not possible, a universal joint allows the socket to be driven from an angle. When the item you are working on designates specific torque settings, a torque wrench is required and is used with your sockets. A socket set is one of the most versatile tools you will encounter, potentially useful in assembling and dismantling any mechanical device and essential for significant engine repair.

You should be at least acquainted with a few other turning tools. One that is unfortunately included in almost every toolbox is the adjustable (Crescent) wrench. Adjustable to fit nuts of various sizes, including the occasional odd size, it seems like a great idea. And used properly, the adjustable wrench is a wonderful tool, but it is often misused. Its nickname of "knucklebuster" is well deserved.

The knuckles heal, but the damage done to a nut when the wrench slips can add *hours* to a simple repair. Never think of the adjustable wrench as taking the place of a set of box-end or open-end wrenches. It is

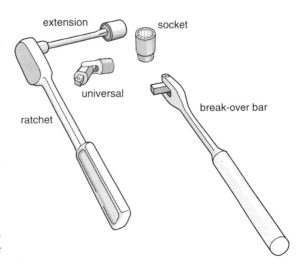

not rigid enough to grip the nut securely when heavy force is applied. If you use an adjustable wrench for any purpose, great care must be taken to insure that the wrench is adjusted for a tight fit. If there is any play in the wrench in either direction, it is not tight enough. Until you consider yourself accomplished in handling tools, you will save yourself a great deal of grief by shunning adjustable wrenches.

This advice does not apply to adjustable pipe wrenches (Stillson wrenches). The pipe wrench has a pivoting action that causes it to grip tighter as more force is applied to the handle. The force must always be applied in the direction of the jaw opening. While not particularly designed for gripping nuts, a pipe wrench serves well for tightening the large nuts found on through-hull fittings and stuffing boxes. The wrench always marks the work being gripped, so never use a pipe wrench on a threaded piece or a polished shaft.

Pliers do not belong in a discussion of *turning* tools, but the frequency with which they are misused as turning tools leads me to include them. Pliers are a *gripping* tool, period. Are you paying attention? Pliers have hundreds of legitimate uses—bending wire, crimping sheet metal, holding parts for machining, removing cotter pins, pulling nails, extending reach, the list is endless—but turning nuts and bolts is not among them. For appropriate uses, your tool selection should include tongue-and-groove, needle-nose, and probably locking pliers. Tongue-and-groove pliers, also called water-pump pliers, or Channellock pliers after the most popular brand, are much more versatile than standard slip-joint pliers. Needle-nose pliers are ideal for electrical work, for reaching into confined areas, and for installing and removing cotter pins. Vise-Grips, the brand name most of us use to refer to locking pliers, are useful as both a clamp and a portable vise.

I have never understood those who insist on trying to make do with a tool kit consisting of an adjustable wrench, a pair of pliers, and a couple of crooked screwdrivers. Nor is it necessary to fill a seven-drawer cabinet with tools. You should have a modest set of six-point sockets with a ratchet handle and extensions, a set of combination wrenches (six-point box on one end, open on the other), a set of hex keys (Allen wrenches), five or six standard screwdrivers in a variety of blade sizes and shank lengths, a comparable complement of Phillips screwdrivers, a pair of tongue-and-groove pliers, and a pair of needle-nose pliers. These are the tools you will use again and again, and their total cost is less than the typical mechanic's bill for a single simple repair.

Don't be misled into thinking that these are the only tools you will need. They aren't, but they are the ones you are *sure* to need. Eventually you will also need a hammer, a center punch, a chisel, metal snips, a file, a hacksaw, and a drill and bits. You might include these in your initial selection, but beyond these I strongly recommend that you purchase tools *as you need them.*

Never hesitate to buy a tool you need. Tools are one of the very few things you can acquire today that will last a lifetime. But if you don't use them, they are just worthless for a lifetime. In the previous chapter I suggested adding an impact driver, a pop-rivet tool, and a couple of taps to your kit. In the projects that follow, special tool requirements will be noted, but unless these projects have application for your boat, you don't need the tools. Save your money for the tools you do need.

MEASUREMENTS

Once you have the principles of the five basic machines in hand and have defeated any sense that the operation of a screwdriver is somehow beyond your genetic capabilities, you need one more qualification before you dismantle the genset. You need a sense of measurement.

A good mechanic can look at the head of a bolt and know instantly whether the wrench he needs is $1/2$ inch or $9/16$ inch. That ability saves a lot of time and frustration, especially when you have to stand on your head in the bilge to get your wrench on the bolt. A good mechanic can likewise look at a socket and tell if it is $1/2$ inch or $9/16$ inch without consulting the engraving on the side. He can look at a threaded hole and know that it will require a $1/4$-inch screw or look at the thickness of a bracket and ascertain that a 1-inch-long mounting screw will be too short.

Sure you can measure. I have always thought that it would have been very useful to have a 3-inch ruler tattooed on the palm of my left hand between the little finger and the wrist, but after I had the snake done, there just wasn't room. So measuring involves climbing out of the bilge, finding the scale, climbing back in, holding the flashlight in your mouth, contorting your arm painfully to get the scale exactly right, squinting, and then guessing. Wouldn't knowing be easier?

There is no trick to this. Go to the hardware store and buy one each of the following hex-head bolts: #5, #6, #8, #10, #12, $1/4$ inch, $5/16$ inch, and $3/8$ inch. These are the sizes you are most likely to encounter. The length doesn't matter. Now spend an hour with these bolts and the wrenches that fit them until you can identify each by sight.

You should also be able to make a reasonably accurate guess at larger measurements. Is a through-hull fitting $1^1/2$ inches or 2 inches? Are 6 inches of aluminum sheeting wide enough to cover an opening? Will it take more than 2 feet of hose to reach from the water pump to the heat exchanger?

All it takes is practice. It can be helpful to know the length of your forearm and the width of your hand as a reference. My hand, for example, measures 3 inches across the knuckles, but I've got hands like a concert pianist—if you overlook the snake.

MOUNTING HARDWARE

High noon, Pardner. Time to strap on your tool belt and see if you've got what it takes. (Just kidding about the belt, but you are going to make canvas rolls for your tools when we get to Chapter 15.) If you consider yourself to be either an infant or an idiot when it comes to anything requiring a wrench or screwdriver, begin with something simple. For example, do you have a sufficient number of fire extinguishers? Are they located where they should be, or are they going to be on the other side of the fire when you need them? Perhaps you want to mount an additional extinguisher to the engine compartment bulkhead.

This is a two-screw job. Attach the extinguisher to its bracket, position the unit as you want it—making certain that you have adequate clearance to release it—and outline the bracket on the bulkhead with a pencil. Separate the bracket from the extinguisher. Position the bracket inside the outline and mark the location of the two mounting holes on the bulkhead.

Unless the mounting screws supplied are stainless steel—very doubtful—take them to the hardware store and buy stainless screws just like them. Back at the boat, deep-six the plated screws. If you keep them, you will one day be tempted to use them. Now select a drill bit smaller than the screw for drilling the pilot holes. In wood, a pilot hole should be approximately half the diameter of the screw. But wood screws come in number sizes, not fractional sizes, so without a handy table, how do you select the pilot drill? The simplest way is to hold the shank of the drill bit behind the threaded portion of the screw. If the bit is visible on both sides of the screw, the bit is too large. The right bit will be the same size as the screw's *root diameter*—the diameter of the screw if the threads were ground away.

Before you drill any hole on a boat, *know what is behind where you are drilling*. If there is a tank or a wire or an ocean on the other side, you are in for a most unpleasant surprise. Drill into the ocean with an electric drill and it could be your last surprise. In this case check the opposite side of the engine compartment bulkhead, then drill the two pilot holes. Hold the bracket in place and insert the two screws. Be sure you hold the screwdriver perpendicular to the screw head as you tighten.

How do you know which way to turn the screwdriver? Just remember "righty-tighty." Almost all screws have right-hand threads. That means you turn the top

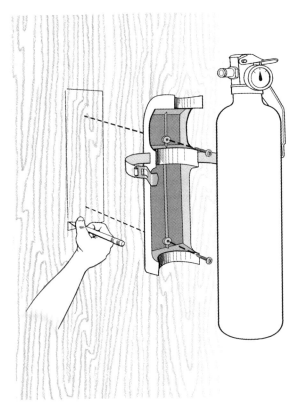

Practice your tool handling on simple things first.

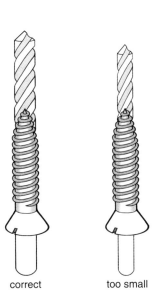
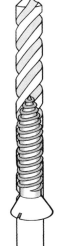

Choosing a pilot drill size.

correct   too small   too large

Righty-tighty.

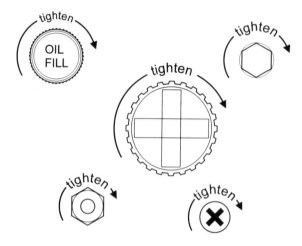

of the screw or nut to the right—clockwise—to tighten it. One of the two screws in a turnbuckle has left-hand threads, so the screws move in opposite directions when the body of the turnbuckle is turned. The threaded fitting that attaches the supply hose to your propane tank may also have reverse threads. These are probably the only left-hand threads you will find aboard. Turn that screwdriver clockwise.

Whenever you have a choice, *select Phillips-head screws.* The screwdriver will hold the screw more securely, you can fit the screwdriver into the screw even when you can't see it, and you will know immediately what size screwdriver you need. Slot screwdrivers are less secure and more difficult to fit, and the proper size is less clear. When you are using a slot screwdriver, the blade should be a snug fit in the slot and as wide as the screw head but not wider. If you use a screwdriver that does not fit the slot, the screwdriver is likely to slip, rounding the slot and making removal of the screw very difficult.

Proper slot screwdriver fit.

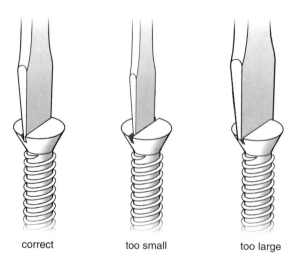

correct   too small   too large

CLEATS

Mounting a cleat can present a bit more of a challenge. Stock cleats are almost always too small, and you may decide to replace them with something more substantial. Don't assume that the original placement was well considered. Often it wasn't. Most cleats are designed for a load in line with the horns. Cleats should be angled about 15 degrees from the lead of the line that will be attached—far enough to prevent the line from jamming but not far enough to result in unfair loading.

Cleats generally come in two- and four-bolt varieties. Two-bolt cleats of adequate size will work well in any application where the load will always be fair; e.g., cleats intended to secure a halyard or a sheet. But mooring cleats—any cleat primarily intended to secure the boat to an anchor or the dock—will eventually be subjected to severe side loading. Mooring cleats require the added strength and better load distribution of four-bolt cleats.

The mounting holes in the cleat will be countersunk, and the stainless steel flathead mounting bolts should be the largest diameter that will pass through the mounting holes. They should fit flush with or below the surface of the cleat.

When replacing a cleat, remove the old cleat and run a slightly oversize drill bit through the mounting holes in the deck to remove all traces of bedding compound. Run a countersink on both sides of the holes to chamfer the edges. Seal the bottoms of the holes with tape and fill them with epoxy putty. The chamfer gives the epoxy plugs a rivet shape, making them more secure. Place the new cleat in position and outline the mounting holes with a sharp pencil. Drill a small pilot hole in the center of each mounting hole location. Select a drill bit the same diameter as the mounting bolts and drill the new mounting holes through the deck, using the pilot holes as guides. If you are drilling through a cored deck, remember to drill the holes oversize, excavate as much core as possible, and refill the cavities with epoxy (see Chapter 6). If you have difficulty drilling a straight hole, you can buy an inexpensive drill guide that will keep the drill perpendicular to the surface you are drilling.

Cleats *must* be through-bolted, and a strong backing plate larger than the base of the cleat is required. Builders often use scraps of the deck laminate. Plywood can be used, but when it is, the through-bolts must be fitted with large-diameter washers under the nuts. Aluminum is a better choice. Light and strong, the aluminum doesn't require washers and will spread the load evenly. The fact that the backing plate is dissimilar to the bolts is actually beneficial in this case, since powdery corrosion will immediately "flag" the location of any leaks that may develop.

The most professional installation uses a backing plate of polished stainless steel threaded to accept the mounting screws. The extra effort this approach requires is probably not justified if the backing plate is out of sight, but when it will be seen, a threaded plate looks better. If you elect this route, you should have the plates cut to size wherever you purchase the stainless steel. You will wear out blades and ears cutting stainless steel, but a good metal salvage yard will have a shear that will slice ¼-inch stainless like kindergarten construction paper.

Round all the corners with a file or a grinder. Center the cleat on the plate and mark the mounting holes. Check the plate against the underside of the deck to be sure it will fit. Place the point of a center punch in the center of *one* of the marked locations and give it a solid whack with a hammer.

Now you need a taper hand tap the size of your mounting bolts (e.g., ¼-20: ¼-inch diameter, 20 threads per inch), a tap handle, and the correct drill bit. It is imperative that you drill the right size hole. Too small and the tap will bind and break; too large

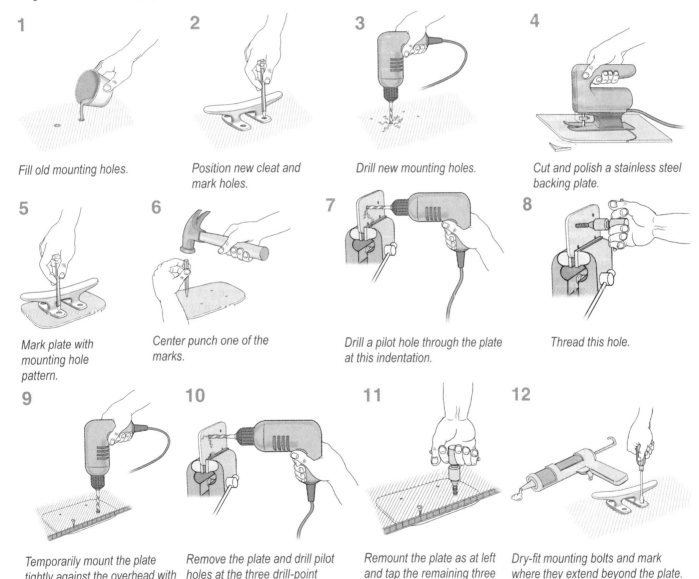

1 Fill old mounting holes.

2 Position new cleat and mark holes.

3 Drill new mounting holes.

4 Cut and polish a stainless steel backing plate.

5 Mark plate with mounting hole pattern.

6 Center punch one of the marks.

7 Drill a pilot hole through the plate at this indentation.

8 Thread this hole.

9 Temporarily mount the plate tightly against the overhead with the one screw through the deck. Lightly feed the drill bit through the other three holes in the deck to mark the plate with the proper location of the remaining holes.

10 Remove the plate and drill pilot holes at the three drill-point indentions.

11 Remount the plate as at left and tap the remaining three holes through the deck to assure proper alignment.

12 Dry-fit mounting bolts and mark where they extend beyond the plate. Cut the bolts to the marked length, then bed and install cleat.

Installing a cleat with a threaded backing plate yields a strong mount that is also handsome below.

and the threads will strip when you tighten the screw. The tap will probably indicate the correct bit. If not, pick up a tap/drill chart. A $^1/_4$-20 tap requires a $^{13}/_{64}$-inch drill bit.

Drilling will be much easier if you grip the backing plate in a vise. On this subject, a momentary digression is in order. You cannot have a more useful tool aboard than a solidly mounted bench vise. Once relatively expensive, vises are now regularly available from discount building suppliers at less than $20 for a 4-inch model, which is ample for almost all onboard uses. The "workshop" aboard most boats, particularly sailboats, is the cockpit, and that is where an onboard vise should be mounted. But no one wants a vise permanently mounted in the cockpit, standing proud and rusting. So . . .

Pick a spot over a cockpit locker—not on the locker hatch—and preferably toward the rear of the cockpit, where you will encounter less interference when working on long items. Position the vise and mark the mounting holes. Now open the locker hatch and hold the vise upside down against the underside of the deck in the same place to make sure it can be mounted against the underside with the same bolts. When you are satisfied, drill the mounting holes. Carriage bolts and wing nuts will make solid mounting of the vise a snap. When not in use, fit the carriage bolts with rubber washers (to make them watertight), push them through the deck, and mount the vise *inside* the locker with the wing nuts.

Mounting and storing an onboard vise.

Back to the backing plate. Drill a small pilot hole in the center-punched hole; the exact size is not important. You will need first-quality carbide bits to drill stainless steel. And you will need patience. Do not try to run the drill too fast or apply too much pressure. The pilot hole will make it much easier for the correct bit to penetrate and give you a cleaner and more accurate final hole. Drill this first hole to the correct size.

Now thread the hole. Using a tap is not difficult, but because the tap is brittle, it does require care, particularly in a hard metal like stainless steel. Chuck the tap securely into the tap handle and put a drop of engine oil on the cutting threads. Insert the tapered end of the tap into the drilled hole. Exerting inward pressure on the tap and taking care to keep it perpendicular to the plate, turn the tap clockwise. When it begins to feel tight, back it up $^1/_4$ turn. Turn the tap clockwise again another $^1/_2$ turn, then back it up $^1/_4$ turn. After about two full turns, it will no longer be necessary to keep inward pressure on the tap. Continue the "$^1/_2$ turn forward, $^1/_4$ turn back" sequence. If the tap gets very hard to turn, back it out completely and clean the chips from the tap and the hole. Put a fresh drop of oil on the tap and try again. When the tap turns freely, the hole is threaded. Back the tap out carefully and check the hole with one of your mounting bolts.

If the plate is to be mounted to the cleat, you could bolt the two together with the first hole and use the cleat as a drill guide for the other three holes. But there is $^1/_2$ inch or more of deck between the cleat and the plate. Any curvature in the deck or inaccuracy in your drilling will alter the relationship of the holes. For this step, you need a helper. With your helper holding the backing plate in place, insert one of the mounting screws through the deck and into the threaded hole. Tighten. While your helper watches the plate to make certain it doesn't move, chuck the bit you used to drill mounting holes through the deck. Use those holes as a template and mark the plate with the exact location of the other three holes with your drill. You do not want to drill through the plate, just cut a slight indentation.

Remove the plate and use the drill indentations like center-punch marks to first drill pilot holes, then the tap hole. To minimize alignment problems, bolt the plate in place again and tap the other holes from on deck. When the plate is finished, screw the cleat in place. Mark the screws where they extend through the plate. Remove the screws and cut them at the mark. You can do this with a hacksaw, but a rotary tool (Dremel) with a cutoff wheel is wonderful for shortening bolts. Because the thickness of the deck may not be uniform, it is a good idea to code each

screw with one to four dots on the head so you can insert them into the appropriate hole. Dress the cut threads with a grinder or a file. Polish the plate to a mirror shine with metal polish.

Bed the cleat generously with polysulfide sealant and bolt it to the deck, tightening the machine screws into the backing plate only enough to squeeze sealant out evenly all around the perimeter of the cleat base. *Never bed a backing plate.* If a fastener leaks, you want the leak to announce itself with a drip below, not become trapped overhead. Also because you do not have nuts to tighten but will have to turn the screws, do not put sealant on them initially. Allow the sealant to firm up (usually overnight), then remove the screws one at a time and give them a collar of sealant. Tighten them evenly to put the "gasket" under compression.

This same procedure is used for attaching any item of deck hardware, from a pad eye to an anchor windlass. Deck gear should *always* be through-bolted, *always* reinforced with a backing plate. You can never mount hardware too securely, only not strongly enough. When hardware under tension rips free, it becomes a deadly missile. I watched an unbacked cleat from a grounded boat miss a small girl by mere inches on its way to burying a horn in the cabin side of a Good Samaritan's boat, whipped by the tension of a nylon towline. You don't ever want to be part of such a scenario.

OPENING PORTHOLES

Early fiberglass boats were fitted with the same bronze opening portholes that had been installed in wooden yachts for more than half a century, but soon enough manufacturers were tempted by the low cost of all-plastic portholes. There is nothing wrong conceptually with plastic portholes—what could be more natural in a plastic boat?—but the execution has been less than laudable. Most plastic opening portlights are simply not robust enough for the realities of boats. Dogging down plastic portlights to stop a drip quickly exposed a fatal flaw—the metal screw could apply more force than the plastic ears could withstand. Charter fleet operators found themselves ordering replacement portlights with the same frequency as oil filters. If your old boat has plastic portlights, at least some are likely to have broken dogs or hinges. Plastic ports are a lower-cost alternative that can do the job in protected waters provided they are treated gently, but no boat headed offshore should entrust the safety of the crew to plastic-framed opening ports.

In sharp contrast, bronze portlights are nearly indestructible. The chromed bronze portlights on my own old boat function today exactly as they did when they were installed in 1969. There are bronze portholes in service today that were manufactured in the *19th century.* More recently portlight frames have been cast, machined, or extruded from both stainless steel and aluminum. These materials do not have the long maritime history of bronze, but I see thousands of aluminum opening portlights that are more than 20 years old and show no signs of failure or weakness.

Maintenance of opening portlights involves little more than rinsing the frames regularly and applying an occasional coat of wax to retard surface corrosion. Lightly lubricate the screw dogs. Barring broken glass, the only problem you are likely to experience with bronze or aluminum portholes is leaking.

If the leak is around the frame, the porthole will have to be removed from the cabin side (or hull) and rebedded. This involves removing the mounting bolts that hold the two halves of the porthole together. The part that extends through the cabin side is called the spigot, and the flared end of the spigot is called the flange. The frame that slips over the opposite end of the spigot is called the finish ring. Old-style portlights tend to have the spigot inserted from the inside with the finish ring outside, while modern designs have the reverse. From an engineering standpoint, an outside flange (and inside finishing ring) makes the portlight easier to bed.

Whichever style you are rebedding, you should anticipate recalcitrance from mounting screws that have not been turned in 20 years—it is habit. Start applying penetrating oil to the nuts as soon as you decide on rebedding, even if the job is weeks or months in the future. The effect of penetrants increases with time.

When you eventually do attempt to loosen the fasteners, don't be overly concerned if some of the bolts break rather than release. Unless they turn freely, you should replace them anyway. Frozen bolts are only a problem when they are threaded into either the flange or the ring. In such cases, you should drill out the threaded holes and reassemble the porthole using cap nuts. This process was detailed more fully in Chapter 7.

Be sure that all traces of the old bedding are removed from the cabin side, flange, spigot, and ring before seating the parts in fresh polysulfide sealant. As a rule you only bed exterior contact surfaces. This

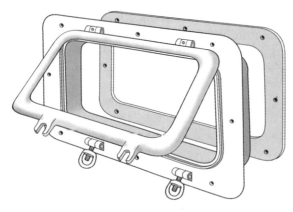

When the finish ring is outside, the sealant must also seal the space between the spigot and the ring.

is straightforward if the flange is outside. However, if the finish ring is outside, the sealant must also prevent water from penetrating between the inside perimeter of the ring and the outside surface of the spigot. The best assurance is filling the space between the spigot and the cabin side with a generous application of sealant, carrying the sealant out onto the spigot beyond where the finish ring will lie. Also coat the back side and inside perimeter of the ring. Because the sealant can be compressed farther into the cutout, it will not squeeze out around the inside perimeter of the ring, so you must be sure there is sufficient sealant on the ring and the spigot to form a watertight seal between the two components.

If it is the portlight that leaks, the first step is to replace the rubber gasket. Remove the old gasket and clean the corrosion and/or old adhesive from the channel with bronze wool or a *soft* wire wheel chucked in your drill. Measure the channel and buy new gasket material (sold by the foot). Be sure that you get the right size. Cut one end of the rubber on a 45-degree diagonal and place the thin "edge" of the diagonal in the bottom of the channel at the center of the top of the porthole. Press the gasket into the channel all around, taking care not to stretch the length of the rubber. When you arrive back at the top of the porthole, cut the other end at a matching diagonal so the two ends mate in a 45-degree overlap that closing the portlight will compress together. If the channel does not "grip" the gasket material sufficiently to hold it in place, you will need to glue it

Overlapping gasket ends with a diagonal joint improves the seal.

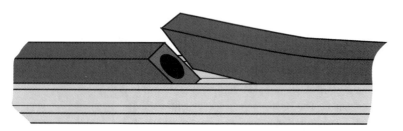

with weatherstrip adhesive or Pliobond applied to the channel with an acid brush. With the new gasket in place, close the portlight and dog it down *gently*. Flood it outside with a hose. If it doesn't leak, you are done. If it does, you need to make an adjustment.

You should find a setscrew on each of the hinges. By adjusting these screws in or out, you can adjust how tightly the *top* of the portlight seals against the gasket. For a proper seal, the portlight should seat against the gasket evenly when the screw dogs at the bottom are snugged.

The first step to making an adjustment is to determine if the setscrews will turn freely. Select the correct Allen wrench (the screws may also be slotted) and try to turn the screw using finger pressure. Do not force it. If a screw is frozen, apply penetrating oil to both ends and try again in a day or two. Be patient and you should be able to free the screw. You do not want to strip the Allen socket or break one side of the slot. If all else fails, you can apply heat, but caution is required.

Metal (and most other material) expands when it is heated and contracts when it is cooled. You can use this physical property to help you free frozen nuts. If you play the flame of a propane torch on the nut, the nut will expand, often loosening its grip on the screw sufficiently to allow you to turn it. Do not heat the screw. If you do, the screw will expand inside the hole, becoming tighter, not looser.

Be very careful with any open flame on a boat. If I have to tell you not to use a torch around a gasoline engine, you should find another interest. In the case of the porthole, if you heat the part that frames the light, you will probably crack the glass. Unscrew the hinge pins and remove the portlight. (If the hinge pins are also frozen, your problem is more complicated.) If the rubber gasket is in the fixed part and not in the frame of the light you just removed, you will also need to remove the gasket. Adjust the torch for a small blue flame and play the blue tip on the hinge around the setscrew. Keep the flame moving and try the screw every few seconds. If the hinge begins to discolor, take away the flame. You want to expand the metal, not melt it. If the hinge pins were also frozen, preventing removal of the portlight, you can still heat the hinge, but hold your fingers on the portlight frame near the hinge and stop if it gets hot. Be careful not to let the flame near the glass.

With the setscrews free, adjustment is a breeze. Loosen the screws until the closed portlight just makes contact with the gasket, then tighten them one turn. Coat the rubber gasket with talcum powder, then close

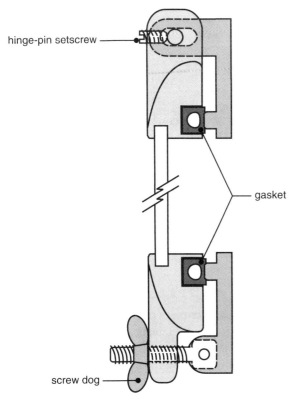

hinge-pin setscrew

gasket

screw dog

Adjust the hinge-pin setscrews to get the portlight to sit flat against the gasket when dogged lightly.

and dog the portlight. Flood the porthole outside with a hose, spraying all around the seal. Wipe up the standing water and reopen the portlight. The talc will show where the leaks occurred. If one side leaked, tighten the setscrew on that side. If the leak was all around, tighten both. Repowder the gasket and check it again. When it is properly adjusted, an easy turn or two on the screw dogs will make the porthole watertight.

BLOCK REPAIR

To gain a bit of experience in dismantling and reassembly, take a closer look at the various blocks you have aboard. When schooners were king, they carried dozens of blocks—sometimes more than a hundred. On modern yachts, gaffs are gone and winches have replaced the block and tackle for most tensioning applications. Consequently the number of blocks aboard has diminished but their importance hasn't.

There is an interesting problem with blocks: how do you know if they are working the way they should? A block that turns freely in your hand may not be turning at all under load. And if it isn't, how do you know? If the sheet runs to a winch, there is undoubtedly ample power in the winch to pull the line through the block whether the sheave turns

or not. Deck-mounted blocks can be observed but observation is more difficult for those above the deck. Most of us pay very little attention to the blocks aboard, rarely giving them a second thought.

You can extend the life of the block, the life of the line that runs through it, and probably the life of the person who winches the line by giving blocks just a few minutes of TLC. Care of blocks that are riveted together is limited to flushing them regularly with fresh water to remove salt deposits and occasionally giving them a water-and-soap bath to also remove dirt and grease. Soak badly corroded blocks in white vinegar, then rinse them in *hot* water. As a general rule, dry lube (dry Teflon or dry silicone) is better for blocks than grease or oil because it does not attract or hold damaging grit. Spray the lube onto the axle pin and around the swivel if it is a swivel block.

Blocks that are screwed together should also get regular freshwater rinses, but they can be serviced more thoroughly. I strongly recommend that you dismantle any block for the first time over a towel-covered table. If the block has bearings, they are probably "caged" (held together as an assembly), but if they are not, the towel will keep them from making a break for it. Pay attention as you dismantle the block. Is one cheek different from the other? On which side is the nut? How is the head positioned? Which way do the reinforcing straps go? If you have two blocks alike, service one at a time, keeping the other on hand as a reference.

Digital cameras have become a great tool for the amateur mechanic. Take pictures of the block (or other mechanical item) before you start disassembling it. Take additional photos if the disassembly reveals interior components not visible in the initial photos. Now you have one or more photographs that will show you the proper orientation for reassembly.

The component parts of a typical standard block.

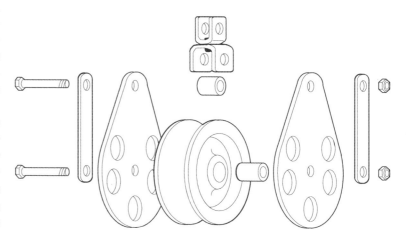

A roller/ball bearing block has a few more pieces.

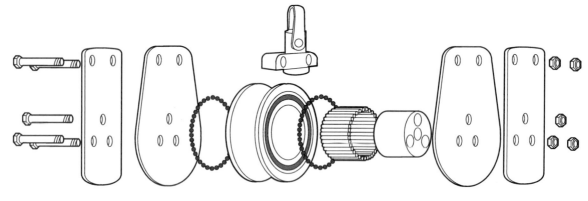

A single screw fastens the parts of a snatch block together, whereas a conventional block is typically held together with two or more screws. The screws may thread into the reinforcing strap, or they may be secured with nuts. A single wrench, a screwdriver, or possibly both will be the only tools required. (The center screw of some snatch blocks is face-pin drive.) Remove the screws and the block separates into pieces. Clean everything with soapy water, using bronze wool to polish away corrosion, especially on the insides of the cheeks and the sides of the sheave where roughness will prevent the block from turning freely under load.

What you are most interested in is the bushing or bearings found in the center of the sheave. A bushing looks like a short length of metal, phenolic, or plastic tubing. It fits inside the sheave, and the axle pin (the center bolt) passes through it. The bushing should be pushed out of the sheave and, along with the sheave and the pin, cleaned with kerosene. When all old lubricant has been removed and the parts are dry, coat them with a film of dry lubricant, such as McLube Sailkote or CRC Marine Dry Lube.

Instead of a bushing, the sheaves of higher-quality blocks turn on roller or ball bearings. Remove the bearing assembly and soak it in kerosene to dissolve old grease and oil. Wash away the residue with water and detergent, flush, and allow the bearings to dry. If the bearings are steel, apply a drop or two—no more—of light oil (3-in-1) to the bearing race. *Never, never oil plastic bearings.* Plastic bearings—Torlon or Delrin—do not require any lubricant, but a shot of dry lubricant won't do them any harm. If they have been left loaded when not in use, the bearings can become distorted and require replacement. Press the bearing assembly back into the sheave. Reassemble the block, being sure to use insulating washers and gaskets (Mylar is best) between stainless steel and aluminum components. Coat the threads of the screws with a thread sealant (Loctite) before threading them into the strap or installing the nuts. Check the sheave to make sure it turns easily and smoothly.

CARS

Traveler and batten cars should be maintained according to the manufacturer's recommendations, but when they are part of the equipment that came on your old boat, you may not know what the manufacturer recommended or even who the manufacturer is. In the absence of specific guidance, maintain cars exactly like bearing blocks. Flush them often, wash them with a soap solution once or twice a year, and lubricate metal bearings with light oil. As a rule, it is not a good idea to use dry lube on car bearings—metal or plastic—because it may cause them to skid rather than roll.

JIB FURLING

The bearings in roller-furling systems require similar care to block bearings. Unless the bearings in the drum unit are sealed, they should be given a freshwater rinse at every opportunity and washed with soap and water a couple of times a year. Plastic bearings should be given a spritz of dry lube after they have been allowed to dry fully. Exposed metal bearings need to be degreased with either kerosene or WD-40, washed a second time to flush out the grit the degreaser releases, then recoated with fresh grease specified for the particular furler. You may have to partially dismantle the drum assembly to gain full access to service the bearing, but failure to clean and appropriately lubricate exposed bearings will result in hard furling and short bearing life.

Because the halyard swivel spends its life above spray, it can usually tolerate longer servicing intervals, but don't just forget about it. At least once a year, lower the sail and the halyard swivel with it, and thoroughly wash the bearing with soap and water. Lubricate the bearing as appropriate—dry lube for plastic bearings and oil or grease for metal bearings.

It is also a good idea to spray the foil grooves as high as you can reach with dry lube to promote easier hoisting. To lube the entire groove, stitch a foot length of soft cotton fabric tightly around a light line to imitate luff tape, spray the fabric heavily with dry lube, attach one end to the halyard swivel and the other to a downhaul, then hoist it so that it wipes and lubricates the full length of the groove.

WINCHES

There is a perception that winches found aboard boats are somehow complicated pieces of equipment. That perception is wrong. A single-speed winch is a simple wheel and axle, the drum of the winch being the axle, the handle being the wheel (or a 360-degree lever). The mechanical advantage accrues solely from the difference between the two and is calculated by dividing the diameter of the wheel (twice the length of the handle) by the diameter of the axle (the drum). A winch with a 4-inch drum and a 10-inch handle will have a mechanical advantage of 5. Twenty-five pounds of pull on the handle will become 125 pounds of pull on the clew.

The only added complexity is ratchet drive. *Pull* a stick along a picket fence and you get a kid-pleasing click-click-click. Try to *push* the stick and you come to an abrupt halt. The ratchet works exactly the same way. Spring-loaded pawls are pulled over a notched

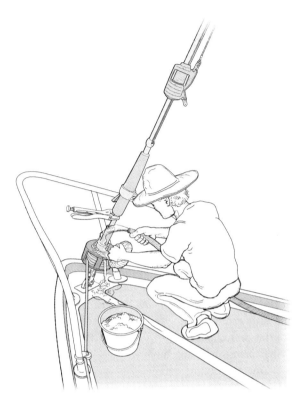

Furlers operate longer and easier when the bearings are kept clean.

Both the drum and the upper swivel should be regularly lubricated unless the bearings are sealed.

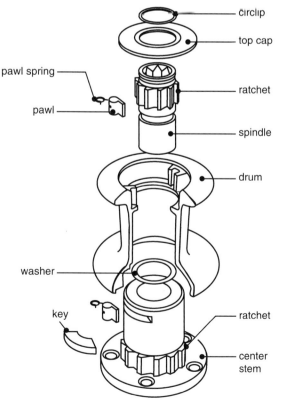

Uncomplicated innards of a single-speed winch.

ring as the drum is turned. When the pull of the line tries to turn the drum in the opposite direction, the pawls engage the notches and prevent the drum from turning in that direction. A second notched ring and set of pawls allow the handle to turn the drum in one direction and spin freely in the other. To minimize friction, the drum rotates on a caged roller bearing. The bearing, the drum, and the pawls are all there is.

More power is obtained from a geared winch. Instead of the handle turning the drum directly, it turns a small gear that engages an idler gear, which engages teeth machined or welded on the inside of the drum. If the small gear has 15 teeth and the drum has 60, the gear ratio (mechanical advantage) is 4. (The idler gear just links the two and has no effect on mechanical advantage.) To get the actual power of the winch, ignoring friction, you have to multiply the advantage gained from gearing by the advantage from the leverage of the handle—in this case 5×4, or 20. Now 25 pounds of pull on the handle becomes 500 pounds of pull on the clew. The cost in complexity? Two small gears.

If your old boat is not *that* old or if the winches have been updated, they may be two-speed. There are no additional parts in a two-speed winch (unless both speeds are geared, in which case you will find a couple more gears inside the drum). The pawls are just configured to allow the handle to turn the drum directly when cranked in one direction and to turn it through the gear drive when cranked in the other.

A regularly maintained winch will be almost totally trouble free. The only common failure is a broken pawl spring. Listen to your winches. Pawls operate in pairs, and when the spring on one fails, the click-click sound of the winch will change to click . . . click. If you don't replace the spring immediately, you are subjecting the remaining pawl to twice its designed load. Not good, not good at all. And don't let their dependability lull you into complacency. Winches should be dismantled, cleaned, and lubricated every year.

Forget what you have heard about winches flying apart when the drum is removed. Jack-in-the-box was a friend of mine, Senator, and a winch is no jack-in-the-box. The only springs are the pawl springs, and only rarely do they release unexpectedly. If you are the cautious type, clip a towel to the lifelines so flying springs will stay aboard.

You can obtain detailed servicing instructions from the manufacturer of your winch but you probably don't need them. The first step is to remove the drum, which (depending on the brand and model) is released by removing machine screws through a top cap, unscrewing a threaded cap, loosening a bolt in the bottom of the handle socket, or *gently* prizing off a snap ring around the top of the shaft. In the latter case, keep your hand over the ring to keep it from flying. If the winch is self-tailing, you will need to remove the tailing arm.

Lift the drum slowly, and as soon as it is above the main shaft, get a hand under it. The bearings can come up with the drum rather than staying on the shaft; if that happens, you do not want them to fall. Stop now and study the exposed viscera of your winch. Pay particular attention to how the pawls are positioned. It is not always necessary to remove them, but if you do, it is sometimes possible to reinstall them in reverse. Get a piece of paper and sketch them the *right* way before you remove them. Better yet, get out your digital camera and take several photos. One additional caution: the springs *will* fly if you don't keep a grip on them when removing the pawls.

Once you have it all figured out, dismantle the rest of the winch. The caged bearings are generally lifted off the main shaft first, but they may be topped or separated by spacers. Taking photos and/or laying out the parts in sequence will help you to get everything back together correctly. A particularly foolproof ploy is to place a tape recorder by the winch

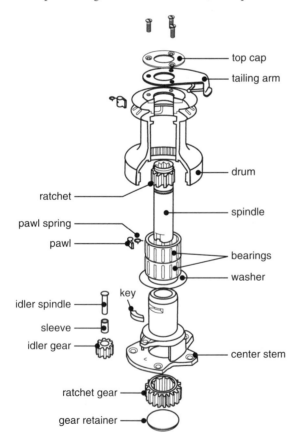

A self-tailing two-speed winch has only a few more parts.

top cap
tailing arm
drum
ratchet
spindle
pawl spring
pawl
bearings
washer
key
idler spindle
sleeve
idler gear
center stem
ratchet gear
gear retainer

and describe what you are doing as you dismantle it: "The Teflon spacer comes off first, chamfered side up. Next is the top bearing. The ID numbers are up. Now I am removing a thin stainless spacer. Next, the second bearing . . ." and so on. You probably will not need to refer to the recording when you put the winch back together, but if you have parts left over, the answer is at hand.

With the winch completely dismantled, pour kerosene or diesel fuel into a small basin and submerge the parts. While the kerosene is dissolving the old grease is a good time to check the mounting bolts. As inconceivable as it may seem, I know of at least one manufacturer that mounted winches to the decks with self-tapping screws. Be sure it is not the yard that built your boat. Through-bolt mounting with a heavy backing plate is the only acceptable way to attach a winch. If you find anything less, fix it now.

Remove the parts from the kerosene and dry them with a lint-free cloth. If they are not completely clean, put them back in the solvent and use a toothbrush to dislodge stubborn guck, then dry them again.

Now go wash your hands. If you are going to use gritty hands to repack the bearings, you might as well have left the old grease in there. Lubriplate Marine Lube "A" was long the standard for lubricating winches, softened by racing crews by mixing in Marvel Mystery Oil and sometimes STP, but such lithium grease has all but been replaced by Teflon-based products. Your best choice for winch lubrication is a proprietary grease from one of the winch manufacturers, which you can also use almost everywhere else aboard that waterproof grease is needed.

Cover all the parts and surfaces—except the pawls and ratchet notches—with a light coat of grease. Pack the bearings with grease, but not excessively. Lightly oil the ratchet mechanism—the pawls and notches—with machine oil. Do *not* use engine oil. The detergents in engine oils will eat into the bronze parts of the winch. Reassemble the winch and give it a spin. I told you it wasn't complicated.

While you are still flushed with success, take your wrenches on a little stroll to the anchor windlass. If it is a capstan type, it should look quite familiar to an old hand at winch maintenance such as yourself. When you remove the drum, it is going to look even more familiar. What about a horizontal windlass, an old Simpson-Lawrence or the like? It wouldn't surprise me at all if you found a couple of gears inside. And a bearing. And a couple of ratchet pawls. Are you getting the hang of this?

STUFFING BOXES

The most difficult aspect of stuffing-box maintenance is usually access. I never adjust my own without wondering if the paramedics would need the jaws of life to extract me if the blood pooling in my head caused me to pass out. Or how many days one of my feet would stick out of the cockpit locker before someone investigated. Or . . . well, you get the picture.

So the first step is to crawl in and figure out how you must lie to reach the stuffing box with *both* hands. You are going to need both hands because there are *two* nuts on the stuffing box—a big, fat adjusting nut and a slender locknut—and you are going to have to have wrenches on both, pulling on one while pushing on the other. Unless you have a world-class muscle in your thumb, that will require two hands.

A stuffing box seals out water where a rudderstock or a propeller shaft passes through the hull, while still allowing the shaft to turn. In principle it is identical to the packing nut on a common faucet. Typically the shaft passes through a hollow tube somewhat larger than the shaft and threaded at the inboard end. This "box" is filled with a packing material—in this case, three or four rings of braided flax heavily impregnated with wax and lubricants. A metal ring, usually slightly wedge-shaped at the bottom and flanged at the top, slides into the box on top of the packing. This is usually called the compression spacer. A hollow nut threads onto the box to push the compression spacer against the packing rings, squeezing the packing against the shaft. A locknut tightened against the adjusting nut maintains the pressure (see next page).

If you open your stuffing box and don't find packing or even much space between the threaded tube and the propeller shaft, look inside the nut. In some designs the adjusting nut is also the stuffing box. The nut is loaded with rings of packing that are compressed against the shaft when the nut is threaded onto the tube around the shaft. You might also encounter a stuffing box that closes with a two-bolt clamp plate. They all function exactly alike inside.

Some stuffing boxes are rigidly attached to the hull, but more often they are connected to the shaft tube by a length of flexible hose. This must not be common water hose, but very durable and very stiff five-ply (or more) exhaust hose. The hose must be double clamped to both the tube and the stuffing box. These clamps are prone to corrosion, especially at the lowest part, which you cannot see without a mirror and a bright light. They should be checked *all the way around* for signs of corrosion every time the stuffing box is serviced. If you cannot get a clear view with a mirror, release the clamps one at a time and rotate them 360 degrees to inspect them. This is an especially good place to use embossed hose clamps rather than the common perforated-band type.

Conventional packing requires some water for lubrication and cooling. The target setting for the stuffing box is for it to drip about 3 drops a minute when the shaft is spinning and not at all when the shaft is stopped. With the boat at rest, get your eyes below the shaft and shine a light on the box. If it is dripping, it probably needs adjustment. If it is not dripping, wait until the next time you are underway and check it then. A steady drip, up to about 10 drops per minute, is OK. More than that requires tightening. If it is not dripping at all, stop the shaft after some run time and put your hand on the stuffing box. It can be warm, but if it is too hot to touch, you need to relax the packing by backing off the adjusting nut. Never forget that a spinning shaft can do unspeakable things if it snags any part of your clothing, so stay well away from it when it is turning.

To adjust the stuffing box you must first release the locknut. You will need open-end wrenches to fit both nuts or two pipe wrenches. Fit the wrenches and maintain counterclockwise pressure on the adjusting nut while you turn the locknut clockwise (looking down the shaft toward the stern). If you are using pipe wrenches, remember to apply force only in the direction of the jaw opening. Never try to turn the locknut without a second wrench on the adjusting nut. You will twist the stuffing box inside the hose, tear the hose, or damage the shaft tube.

With the locknut released a couple of turns, tighten the adjusting nut. Keep the stuffing box from turning by gripping the flange near the flexible hose with your other pipe wrench. Turn the nut a flat ($\frac{1}{6}$ of a revolution) at a time, then give the packing a chance to reshape. Stop adjusting as soon as the drip stops. This may not be the final adjustment, but it will be close. Hold the adjusting nut stationary and tighten the locknut against it. (This is one time when "righty-tighty" will fail you since you are *backing* the locknut against the adjusting nut; turn it counterclockwise.) After you spin the shaft for a while, check the drip rate with the shaft both spinning and stopped. Readjust the box if necessary.

REPACKING

Rudderstock stuffing boxes almost never need repacking, but after you tighten the adjusting nut a few times on a prop shaft gland, the packing becomes so compressed that it loses all resiliency and gets hard enough to actually wear a groove in the shaft. To avoid this, a powerboat that is used regularly should have the prop shaft packing replaced every 2 years. A sailboat may not need to have the shaft packing

Typical stuffing box.

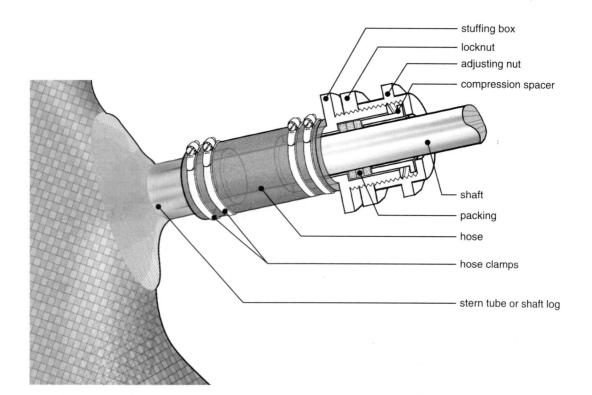

- stuffing box
- locknut
- adjusting nut
- compression spacer
- shaft
- packing
- hose
- hose clamps
- stern tube or shaft log

replaced for 5 years or more, but when the stuffing box begins to feel warm or starts requiring frequent adjustment, it's time.

Release the locknut and unscrew the adjusting nut completely. Slide it and the compression spacer up the shaft to allow access to the interior of the stuffing box. This is a job best done when the boat is out of the water, but if you do it at the dock, wrap the shaft with a towel to direct the incoming water into the bilge, where your pump should have little difficulty keeping up with it. Better still, go over the side with a mask and pack non-hardening plumber's putty around the shaft where it enters the hull. This will stop all flow as long as you do not turn the shaft. Just don't forget to go back under and remove it when you're finished.

With a piece of stiff wire bent at the end, dig out the first ring of the old packing and take it with you to the chandlery to select the right size—but not if you are doing this job with the boat afloat. Do not leave the stuffing box open with the boat in the water. If you know what size packing the box requires, you should have it on hand before you open the box. Typically you will find $1/4$-inch packing around a 1-inch shaft and $3/16$-inch packing around a $1^1/8$-inch shaft (both use the same stuffing box diameter), but there is no real standard, so if you don't know, you will need to measure. With the adjusting nut and the compression spacer out of the way, measure the space between the shaft and the inside of the stuffing box. This is easy to do if you trim a piece of card stock until it is a slip fit, then measure the card. Stuffing boxes typically have three rings of packing and rarely more than four. The straight length of each ring is about 4 times the shaft diameter, so buying a length equal to 16 times the shaft diameter should be sufficient. Close the stuffing box and hand tighten the adjusting nut before leaving the boat for the chandlery.

Traditional waxed flax packing, if your supplier carries it, is the least expensive but also the least durable. You will do better to select a packing lubricated with PTFE (polytetrafluoroethylene, if you really care). PTFE is usually called Teflon, the DuPont brand name. I prefer PTFE-lubricated flax braid because it is softer than a synthetic braid, but the synthetic type may be better for the higher shaft speeds of a powerboat. Either will do the job for the sailor.

Back at the boat, first check that your new packing will slide into the box. Next wrap it around an open area of the shaft in a tight helix. Use a razor knife or a single-edge blade to make a 45-degree cut across each individual wrap, making each cut at the same height to create shaft-diameter rings that close with a

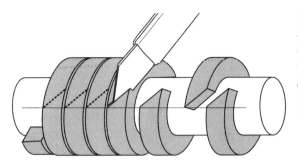

Wrap the packing around the shaft and make diagonal cuts to create packing rings that will seal when compressed.

diagonal joint. Dig *all* the old packing out of the stuffing box, taking care not to scratch the shaft. The best tool for this is probably a corkscrewlike extractor tool, sold in most chandleries, but a bent wire or a large fishhook that's been straightened will usually serve. Be sure your digging tool finds only metal at the bottom of the box before putting in the new packing.

Wrap the first ring around the shaft above the open stuffing box, noting the location of the joint, then push it into the box and all the way to the bottom. A short length of PVC pipe with the same interior diameter as the shaft diameter and split lengthwise into two halves makes the perfect tool for seating the packing. Otherwise use a skinny dowel or a blunt-tipped screwdriver. Wrap the second ring around the shaft, orienting the joint in it about 120 degrees from the first ring's joint, and push this one home. Add a third ring, staggering the joint an additional 120 degrees. Push the compression spacer into the box and hand tighten the adjusting nut. If it threads beyond where it started, you need to reopen the box and add a fourth ring of packing. Screw the adjusting nut back onto the stuffing box. If you are out of the water, you cannot adjust the stuffing box until you are afloat, so just hand tighten the adjusting nut and lock it with the locknut.

If your boat is in the water and you packed plumber's putty around the shaft outside the boat, now is the time to remove it. With the boat afloat, the initial adjustment is to tighten the adjusting nut to *almost* stop all dripping. You want to allow a slight drip initially to make sure the packing has water lubrication when the shaft first spins against it. You cannot fully adjust the stuffing box until the shaft has "worn in" the new packing. After an hour or more of run time, adjust the box as already outlined so that it does not drip when the shaft is not spinning and the stuffing box does not get hot when it is. Check the drip rate again after a couple more hours of use and readjust if necessary.

Dripless Packing
Conventional packing depends on water to lubricate it, and if you have the box well adjusted, it drips only

Shredded Teflon "dripless" packing does not require water lubrication, so the box can be adjusted to stem all dripping.

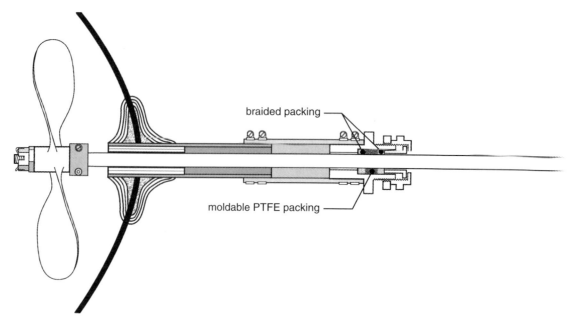

braided packing

moldable PTFE packing

when the shaft is turning. Most boaters find this drip inconsequential, but there is a way for sailors to make a conventional stuffing box essentially drip free. A moldable low-friction PTFE packing has been available for a number of years. This type of packing is self-lubricating. You still need two rings of conventional braided PTFE packing to corral the claylike compound, but the packing nut can be adjusted after launch to stop all drips. This type of packing runs hotter than water-lubricated flax, so to avoid excessive heat, do not tighten the nut any more than necessary to stop the gland from dripping. The box should not run too hot to touch.

Note that I said this option was available to *sailors*. If the surface speed of the shaft exceeds around 1,000 feet per minute, the heat generated will melt the compound. That makes it unsuitable for powerboats turning high shaft speeds.

Installing moldable packing into your stuffing box is about six times more expensive than using flax alone, but I ran dripless packing in my own stuffing box for 5 years without requiring adjustment. For a stuffing box that is difficult to access for service (like mine), the extra cost will be justified.

However, moldable packing may be at this writing in danger of being superseded by a new generation of dripless braid. GFO Packing Fiber, made by Gore, is compression packing braided from expanded PTFE fiber. It does not require a flow of water for lubrication or cooling. It costs around 50% more than regular PTFE packing and is installed in exactly the same manner as conventional packing except that the box should be adjusted to stem all dripping. User feedback suggests that stuffing boxes packed with GFO

packing run cool and should remain drip free for at least 2 years, perhaps longer. One caveat is that GFO packing contains some graphite, which may present a risk of electrolysis, although I have not seen any reports of this actually occurring.

Shaft Seals

Another drip-free option is to replace the stuffing box with a mechanical seal. Shaft seals that do not require packing have become increasingly popular. Face seals operate on the principle of a sealing ring rotating against a machined flange, one turning with the shaft, the other held stationary by clamping it to the stern tube. The two are pressed together by some type of "spring" pressure, usually a rubber bellows but sometimes water pressure. Lip seals are simply an adaptation of a common oil seal. They are installed in a bearing housing that clamps inside the shaft tube hose. The thin rubber lip of the seal runs against the surface of the shaft, usually held in contact with an internal elastic or spring collar.

Shaft seals are not supposed to require any maintenance. Don't you believe it. All of them use hose clamps that need to be checked at least annually for corrosion. Some face seal designs depend on setscrews to secure half of the seal to the shaft. I know personally of a boat that sank at the dock when the seal slipped on the shaft. If you have this type of shaft seal on your old boat and you did not install it, you should remove one of the setscrews and make sure it is not just tightened against the hard, smooth surface of the shaft. The shaft should have been dimpled with a drill when the seal was installed. If it wasn't, buy a new cobalt bit smaller

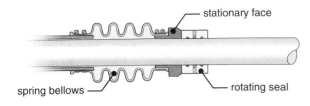

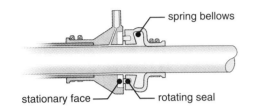

Face seals.

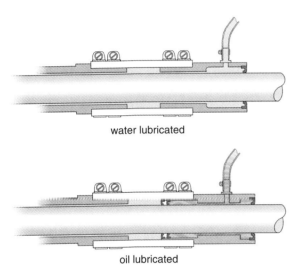

Lip seals.

Mechanical seals promise a drip-free alternative to the common stuffing box.

than the hole, shrink an inch of electrical shrink tubing onto the bit to avoid damaging the threads, and dimple the shaft through the threaded hole. Turn the shaft to roll the hole down, and blow or flush out the drill shavings with an ear syringe. Coat the setscrew with Loctite and reinstall it. Give the remaining setscrews the same treatment, one at a time. For belt-and-suspenders security, tighten a hose clamp or a new zinc collar around the shaft hard against the seal collar.

Lip seals are nearly always plumbed for lubrication by either water injection or gravity-fed oil from a reservoir mounted above the seal. Blockage in the water line or a dry oil tank will cause the seal to fail in short order. Unvented face seals need to be "burped"

after launch by compressing the bellows at the top until water pours out. Otherwise trapped air will cause the seal to run dry, which it is not designed to do. Burping the seal each time you service it is probably not a bad idea. Bellows "set" combined with weakening engine mounts can allow enough forward shaft movement when the prop is engaged to open a gap in a face seal. Poor engine alignment or excessive drivetrain vibration will stress any mechanical shaft seal.

For an old boat with a persistent shaft drip, I tend to prefer dripless packing over retrofitting a shaft seal. Repacking is less complicated, way cheaper, and I believe safer. Stuffing boxes lose their seal gradually and never catastrophically. Shaft seal failure is more likely to be sudden and dramatic. If you are determined to install a shaft seal or your old boat came with one, you will need to learn what care your particular shaft seal requires and see that it gets it.

RUDDERS

The stuffing box on the stock of an inboard rudder should be tightened until it does not drip at all. Some water penetration helps to lubricate a spinning prop shaft, but an oscillating rudderstock doesn't need any additional lubrication.

The constant motion does, however, result in wear, and the exposure of rudders always places them at risk of being damaged. The success of any rudder repairs you undertake will depend on your understanding of the forces at work on your particular rudder. This is an area where your fresh reacquaintance with the principles of the lever will be helpful.

If you have a spade rudder, all of the bending force exerted on it by the water is concentrated on the rudderstock where it enters the hull. Under normal circumstances the bending force is manageable, but when, for example, a boat spills sideways off a steep wave, the bending force increases alarmingly. The higher the aspect ratio of the rudder, the greater the bending force. The designer should have taken sea conditions into account when he or she specified the diameter of the rudderstock. But if the rudder *kisses* something solid, like a rock or a coral head, the stock of most spade rudders will bend like a pipe cleaner.

Straightening a rudderstock requires the services of a machine shop, and the rudder must be removed from the boat. Before you begin, support the rudder to keep it from dropping when released. Now release the clamp bolts on the tiller arm or the steering quadrant, along with any bearings or collars that may be clamped to the stock, and loosen the packing nut on the stuffing box. On a powerboat it is simply a matter of lowering the rudder until the stock comes out of the hull. The length of the rudder assembly on a sailboat makes the problem somewhat more complicated, generally requiring that the boat be lifted. Digging a hole under the rudder can serve in an unpaved yard.

The only preventive measure available—short of redesign—is to increase the size of the rudderstock. Same-material strength increases with the *cube* of the diameter. Double the stock diameter and strength goes up eightfold, but increasing the size of the stock of a spade rudder comes with its own set of problems. It obviously requires the construction of a new rudder, which could be necessary anyway if the old one has been badly damaged. A larger stock also means a new rudder tube, new rudder bearings, a new stuffing box, and a new quadrant or tiller clamp.

The biggest problem, however, goes back to the principle of leverage. If you ground the rudder and the shaft is strong enough not to bend, all the leverage bears on the hull. A bent stock is *infinitely* more desirable than a rip in the hull. Any effort to strengthen a spade rudder must incorporate reinforcing the hull around the rudder tube in combination with adding robust support of the rudderstock as high as possible inside the hull.

If your rudder has a full-length skeg in front of it, the lower end of the rudderstock probably fits into a cast heel fitting at the bottom of the skeg. The skeg protects the rudder, reducing the likelihood of a bent

stock. The procedure for removing a skeg-mounted rudder is the same as that for a spade rudder, with the addition of unbolting the heel fitting from the skeg. The bolts may not be immediately visible under a dozen coats of bottom paint, but scrape the paint away (or lift it with paint remover) and you will find them.

Maybe you are wondering why you would need to remove a skeg-mounted rudder if it is unlikely to suffer a bent stock. Because there is another leverage-related problem common to inboard rudders. A rudder 2 feet wide with a 2-inch-diameter stock is, in effect, a wheel and axle with a 48-inch wheel (twice the width of the rudder) and a 2-inch axle. It has a mechanical advantage of 24. Imagine a 30-foot sailboat making hull speed when a crewmember drops a 3-foot-diameter sea anchor overboard attached to a stern cleat with a $^1/_8$-inch flag halyard. What happens when the boat reaches the end of the line? The line snaps like thread. A 500-pound breaking strength is no match for the drag of the sea anchor against the inertia of a 10,000-pound boat moving at 6 knots.

Same boat, same speed, and the rudder previously described is suddenly put hard over. The load on the rudder is similar to that on the sea anchor. We could calculate the actual load, but that is not what I am trying to get at. The point is that it is not hard to imagine subjecting the outboard edge of the rudder to 500 pounds of pressure. When we do, we generate *6 tons* of force where the rudder blade is attached to the stock. Far too often, this joint fails.

On powerboats the metal blade and the metal stock are welded into a single immensely strong and trouble-free unit. Metal rudders are not often seen on sailboats because sailboat rudders need nearly neutral buoyancy (weighing the same as an equal volume of water). When the boat heels, the aft edge of a metal rudder would tend to sink, causing the bow to pay off. A buoyant rudder would have the opposite effect.

So an inboard sailboat rudder has a metal stock and a wood or composite (fiberglass and wood or fiberglass and foam) blade. The two are joined in various ways, some of which are shameful. Commonly, two or three metal rods or narrow plates are welded to the stock, like long fingers, and sandwiched inside the rudder blade. The force on the rudder is concentrated on these small welds, and they eventually fail, allowing the stock to turn inside the blade.

Check your rudder by jamming the wheel or tiller *rigidly* in place with a couple of lengths of wood, then trying to move the trailing edge of the rudder. If the rudder moves and the stock doesn't, you're in trouble. You will have to remove the rudder and grind away

A bent rudderstock is an infinitely more desirable consequence of grounding or snagging than a ruptured hull. Any "upgrade" to rudderstock strength must be accompanied by hull strengthening and enhanced support.

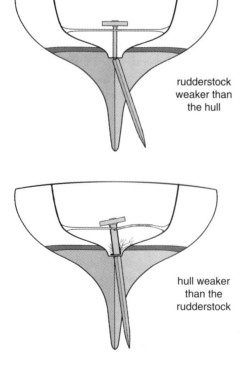

rudderstock weaker than the hull

hull weaker than the rudderstock

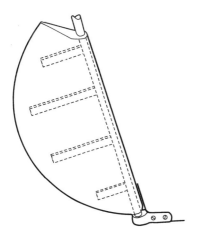

Poor: twisting stress concentrated on four small welds.

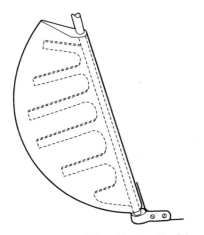

Good: stress is distributed along the length of the stock.

Securing the rudder to the stock.

the fiberglass that encapsulates the stock. When you have new plates welded to the stock, make them several inches wide and closely spaced. A stronger joint is achieved by welding a broad metal plate to the stock the entire length of the joint. If you shape the metal plate like a comb, you spread the attachment to more of the rudder blade without the need for additional welding.

Once you have a strong attachment system, the decision to reuse the old blade or construct a new one will depend on the condition of the old blade. The fiberglass almost always encapsulates a plywood or foam core, and rudders are notorious for delaminating. If the core is saturated, you may be better off using the old rudder as a pattern for the construction of a new one. Use the skills from Chapter 6 to take a pair of molds off the old rudder and lay up a new one in two halves to be foam-filled, bonded over the rudderstock, and laminated together into a *monocoque* construction. Or lay up a new rudder over a shaped foam core.

Either way, be sure the internal metal structure is in direct contact with the laminate, not the foam core.

By comparison, outboard rudders are nearly trouble free. Hanging on the back of the keel like a hinged door, they do not penetrate the hull and have no bendable rudderstock or vulnerable blade-to-stock joint. The turning force is applied through a robust tiller arm through-bolted to the blade itself. The biggest damage risk to an outboard rudder is backing into a solid object.

Of course outboard rudders do develop problems. They are just as subject to delamination as any other rudder. The strength of the tiller arm attachment can be inadequate. And the hinge fittings—the pintles and gudgeons—eventually wear from the constant back-and-forth motion. Don't panic when you discover you can shake your outboard rudder. It is not necessary for the fit between the pintles and gudgeons to be precise—just strong. But if the play has reached a point where it seems excessive to you, it is time to remove the rudder and examine the fittings.

With some outboard rudders, removal is a simple matter of removing the cotter pins through the bottom of the pintles and drafting some help from other sailors in the yard to lift the rudder out of the gudgeons. On others, gudgeons extend into notches in the leading edge of the rudder and small filler blocks are screwed or bonded in place in the notches beneath the gudgeons to prevent the rudder from lifting. An outboard rudder may also extend under the counter and be prevented from lifting by the hull. In this last case, the rudder is removed by unbolting the fittings from either the rudder or the hull. Like the heel fitting mentioned earlier, pintles and gudgeons should be through-bolted. Some paint removal may be required to find the heads of the various fasteners. Gudgeon fasteners are often deep in the keel cavity, installed before the engine, and difficult to access.

STEERING SYSTEMS

Not much can go wrong with a tiller, and for that reason alone it has much to recommend it. It requires almost no maintenance—an occasional application of grease or oil to the pivot and a protective coating on the wood. Tiller heads occasionally fail, especially when they are aluminum. Installing a stainless steel or bronze tiller head is a wise enhancement. If a tiller breaks or rots, removal is simply a matter of releasing a couple of nuts and extracting the mounting bolts.

Worm-gear steering is almost as maintenance free as a tiller. Disassembly is *not* necessary, but the gears should be cleaned thoroughly with cloths soaked in kerosene or diesel fuel to remove old grease

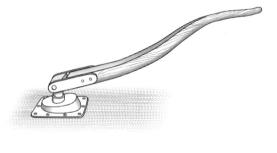

Tiller.

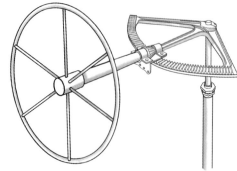

Geared quadrant.

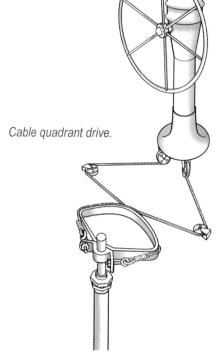

Cable quadrant drive.

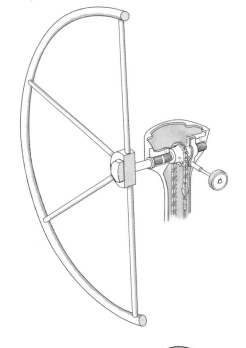

Pedestal/cable.

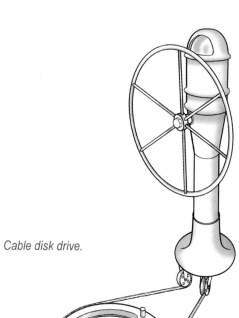

Cable disk drive.

Worm gear.

Steering systems.

and grit. When they are clean and dry, coat them with winch grease or water pump grease. Universal joints in the wheel shaft should be packed with grease. Pivots and bearings should be lubricated with non-detergent 30W motor oil. Pillar bearings are lubricated most thoroughly by removing the cap bolts and sliding the inserts clear of the bearing area.

Maintenance of geared quadrant steering is identical to that of worm gear except that it is the pinion and geared quadrant that require cleaning and coating with grease. A geared quadrant may also be adjusted to remove excess play between the gears. On older units this adjustment is usually made by a screw *beneath* the quadrant where it engages the pinion. A locknut that holds the screw in position is loosened, and the screw is adjusted to force the quadrant tightly enough into the pinion to eliminate the play but not tightly enough to cause the steering to bind or feel tight. Because the quadrant rides on the adjusting screw (or on a plate in later units), the underside of the quadrant should also be coated with grease.

The most common wheel steering on a sailboat is pedestal steering, a system that connects a pedestal-mounted wheel to the rudder with wire cables. In concept, pedestal steering is only slightly more complicated than the simple leverage of a tiller. Imagine a grooved wheel—a pulley—attached to the top of the rudderstock. Now imagine a second wheel mounted horizontally in the cockpit. If we connect the two with a belt, turning the wheel in the cockpit will turn the rudder, which is exactly how pedestal steering works.

Maybe it troubles you that in this example the rudder turns the wrong way. Picky, picky. So cross the belt, like a figure eight, and when the steering wheel turns to the right so does the boat. Don't like the horizontal steering wheel either? You don't hear long-suffering bus drivers complain about that, but suppose we run the belt through a couple of turning blocks fastened to the cockpit sole and orient the steering wheel vertically? Happy now?

Instead of a belt, pedestal steering systems use cable that, with the help of sheaves, can be routed in any direction. And since the rudder turns through less than 90 degrees, or a quarter of a circle, we can substitute a quadrant for the pulley on the rudderstock. To prevent any slippage, we use a sprocket instead of a pulley at the steering wheel and insert a length of drive chain (similar to motorcycle chain but more corrosion resistant) into the middle of the cable to run over the sprocket.

While the other three steering systems will shrug off indifferent maintenance for a long time, pedestal steering will not. If you do not give it the attention it requires, it will fail, often spitefully.

Required maintenance begins with regular lubrication of all the sheaves. If you don't know where they are, it is time to climb down into the sail locker and lazarette to find them. Trace both cables from the base of the pedestal to the quadrant and oil the bearings of each sheave with 30W oil. Manufacturers recommend that you oil the sheaves every month. It really depends on how much you use the boat, but oil them regularly and often.

When you oil the sheaves you should make sure that all the cotter pins securing the axle pins are in place. Also check all mounting bolts for tightness. The sheaves are subjected to heavy loading by the action of the rudder and must be strongly and

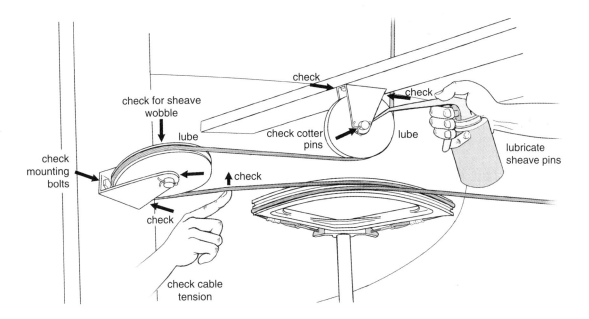

Cable steering maintenance.

securely mounted. Check the rudderstops for wear or any signs of movement. Check also to make certain the cable has not loosened.

Annually (or more often if the boat sees heavy use) more extensive maintenance is required. To gain access to the chain and sprocket in the pedestal, the compass and its housing cylinder have to be removed. Before you unscrew anything, put three vertical strips of tape from the compass dome down across the compass housing and onto the tapered section of the pedestal, spaced unevenly around the binnacle. With a razor knife, slit the tape where the various pedestal components join. The tape simplifies realignment when you reassemble the parts. The compass should be checked, but adjustment will probably not be required.

Slitting continuous strips of tape placed vertically on the binnacle before disassembly will insure perfect compass realignment.

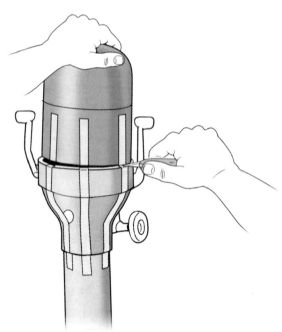

Now remove the screws and lift the compass and its housing from the pedestal. If the engine controls are in the pedestal, the control housing will also need to be removed. To do so, remove the cotter pins and slide the pins out of the clevises that attach the levers to the control cables. Clevis pins have a nasty little habit of binding and then releasing with a jerk, so be careful not to let them drop inside the pedestal.

With the steering mechanism exposed, squirt *winch grease* into the holes on top of the bearing housing while you spin the wheel. Teflon grease may be recommended by the manufacturer. Oil the chain and sprocket with 30W oil, just like you did with your bicycle when you were a kid. Check the chain-to-wire connections for wear or broken strands. Make sure the master links and clevises are properly secured with cotter pins.

Down below, release the locknut, then back off the adjusting nut on one of the take-up eyes on the quadrant, loosening the cable. With slack in the cable, check each of the sheaves. They should rotate easily and smoothly. If they wobble, replace the axle pins.

Fold a paper towel into a pad and squirt oil in the center of it. Now fold the pad around the cable and slide it back and forth all over the wire, oiling it lightly and checking for broken strands at the same time. If a strand snags the toweling, replace the cable immediately.

Check the cable attachment to the take-up eyes. A cable should either attach with a cone-type mechanical fitting (Sta-Lok or Norseman) or loop around a stainless steel thimble and be secured to itself with two compression sleeves (Nicopress). Unfortunately you are just as likely to find the quadrant ends of the cables secured with wire rope clamps. This is an inferior

The snag of a single broken strand condemns a steering cable immediately.

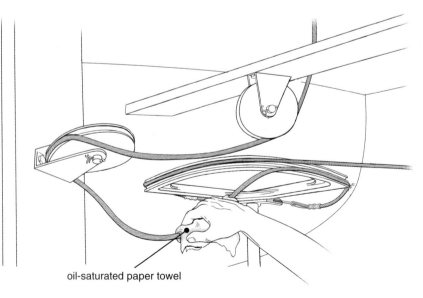

oil-saturated paper towel

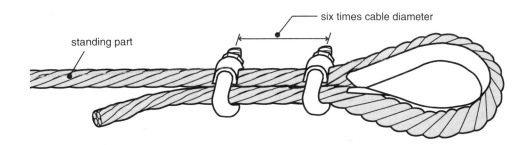

standing part

six times cable diameter

The saddle of a cable clamp always lies against the standing part.

attachment method, but if that is what you have, make certain that the cable loops around a thimble and that each eye is secured with two clamps separated by about six times the cable diameter. Also check that the U-bolts of the clamps bear against the dead end of the cable and the cast portions bear on the standing part. Check both nuts on every clamp for tightness.

With the wheel tied or locked, readjust the tension on the cable by tightening the nut on the take-up eye. Proper tension is reached just when the quadrant cannot be moved by hand—no tighter. Lock the take-up eye with the second nut. Recheck the cable tension with the helm hard over in both directions.

Nearly ever steering failure I learn about can be traced to old cables. If your steering fails at the wrong time—when else?—the consequences can be catastrophic. You can inoculate your boat against this particular breakdown by replacing the cables at least every 5 years, even if your regular maintenance fails to reveal broken strands. Cable replacement is a matter of pinning the new cable to the ends of the chain, feeding it through the sheaves, and attaching it to the take-up eyes on the quadrant. With access to a Nicopress tool (see Chapter 8), there is no reason that you cannot· make up your own steering cables from a length of 7 × 19 stainless wire rope. The cost will be nominal.

Installing wheel steering is a common enhancement to older, tiller-steered boats. If you can handle a wrench and a drill, there is little reason why you cannot handle such a retrofit. Some fiberglassing may also be required to reinforce mounting points against the tremendous forces the steering components are subjected to. In addition to the most common systems detailed previously, you may have the option of hydraulic, solid link, and conduit (push-pull or pull-pull) steering systems. The steering system manufacturer will be able to assist you in selecting the "right" system for your boat and providing detailed instructions for its installation.

ZINCS

Without sacrificial zincs the underwater metal parts of your boat are at risk from galvanic action. To protect against this destruction, every underwater metal part should have an electrically conductive contact with a zinc anode. The most direct way to achieve this is to bolt a zinc button directly to each of the underwater parts. On an old boat, hopefully, the means of attaching zincs to the underwater parts has already been resolved and you will only need to be concerned with replacing the zinc buttons and

GALVANIC SERIES (IN SEAWATER)

← Most active or least noble

← Least active or most noble

Anodic

Magnesium and magnesium alloys
Aluminum sacrificial anodes
Zinc
Aluminum alloys
Cadmium
Mild steel
Iron
Stainless steel type 304 (active)
Stainless steel type 316 (active)
Aluminum bronze
Brass
Muntz metal
Tin
Copper
Aluminum brass
Manganese bronze
Silicon bronze
Bronze
Chromium stainless steel type 401 (passive)
Lead
Copper nickel
Nickel
Stainless steel type 304 (passive)
Monel
Aquamet 17 & 19
Stainless steel type 316 (passive)
Titanium
Hastelloy C
Aquamet 22
Platinum
Graphite

Cathodic

collars every year—a matter of removing the mounting screws, discarding the old zinc, fitting the new one, and retightening the screws.

A zinc on one of the pintle fittings protects the attached gudgeon fitting because the metal-to-metal contact is electrically conductive, but it *does not* protect the other pintle fittings. Each fitting requires a zinc. Do not, however, think that if one zinc button is good, two will be twice as good. Too much zinc will bubble your bottom paint. You need more or larger zincs only if the existing anodes are depleted by more than 50% a year. If additional zincs are indicated, the easiest attachment method is generally to remove one of the through-bolts from the fitting and replace it with a bolt long enough to accommodate the two halves of the zinc button–like washers on either side of the rudder. An alternative is to drill and thread a hole in the fitting to accept a mounting screw. Be sure you clean away all paint and/or corrosion beneath the zinc to insure a good electrical contact. Never paint a zinc anode or you will prevent it from doing its job.

The shaft and the propeller are both protected by the installation and renewal of a zinc collar that clamps around the shaft. If the shaft bolts directly to the output flange on the transmission, your prop is electrically connected to the shaft, the engine, and every other metal item on the boat that is grounded to the engine. A bronze prop is the least noble of the submerged parts of this chain and can be ravaged by corrosion unless protected by a less noble zinc. However, when the shaft is isolated with a flexible coupling, the only electrical interaction is between the shaft and the prop. The corrosion potential depends

Zinc anodes require metal-to-metal contact with the underwater part they are intended to protect.

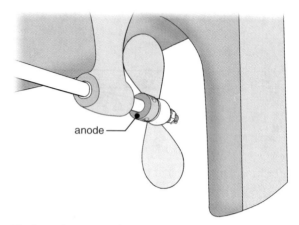

Shaft anodes protect the prop. Be sure the anode does not restrict the flow of lubricating water to the Cutless bearing.

on the type of alloys used for the shaft and the prop and on their relative submerged surface areas. Some sailors leave off the shaft zinc on their isolated shafts, convinced that the slight electrical current that flows from the prop discourages the attachment of barnacles. You should first see how long a shaft zinc lasts on your boat before you give this a try. Rapid depletion of the zinc signals that your prop will suffer from its omission. Replace zincs—all anodes—when they are 50% depleted.

Where direct attachment of a zinc collar or button is not practical—bronze through-hull fittings, for example—protection from galvanic corrosion is effected by electrically connecting the fitting with a heavy electrical cable to a zinc anode, typically some anode-protected underwater fitting. This is called bonding, and while it will indeed afford the through-hull galvanic protection, it opens the door to much more destructive stray-current corrosion. Bonding is a complex and controversial subject, but there is little doubt that bonding underwater metal components that are otherwise electrically isolated is a bad idea. *Don't do it.* A good bronze through-hull plumbed with rubber hose will resist corrosion for decades without anode protection. Marelon through-hulls (fiber-reinforced nylon) eliminate this issue altogether.

PROPELLERS

Bronze propellers are intended to screw their way through water, and as long as you use yours as intended, a zinc-protected bronze prop should outlast the installer. Unfortunately, in a moment of inattention or just plain bad luck, the propeller can have an encounter with something solid. On a sailboat

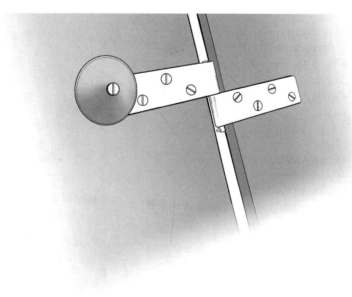

that something is usually rope—the dinghy painter, a trailing sheet, the anchor rode, or a lobster pot warp—or less often floating debris. Powerboat props are more likely to have a hard encounter with sand, rock, and coral. Mangled propellers are so common that prop reconditioning is a legitimate industry.

Prop reconditioners straighten bent blades by heating them white-hot and hammering them into shape against a cast-iron form. Straightening a prop yourself is not a very good idea except in an emergency. An often-overlooked old boat improvement is to have the prop computer measured, trued, and tuned. European props must meet an ISO (International Standards Organization) standard, but no such standard exists in the United States, so *pitch*—the angle of the blade—can vary blade to blade by more than 10%, even on a brand-new prop. Truing and tuning a prop can allow it to deliver higher speeds with lower fuel consumption and make a jaw-dropping difference in drivetrain vibration and noise.

The performance of your old boat, under both power and sail, might also be improved by changing to a different prop. Just because the wheel under the counter has been there for 20 years is no assurance that it is the best choice. Propellers generally bear a two-number designation. The first number is the overall diameter in inches and the second is the pitch, which is specified not in degrees but in inches. Pitch is the distance the prop would move forward through solid material in one revolution conceptually the same as the distance between the threads of a screw. A prop stamped "15 × 12 RH" is 15 inches in diameter and would push the boat 12 inches with every full revolution but for the fact that water is not solid. The RH tells you this is a right-hand propeller, meaning the top of the prop rotates to the right (clockwise) as viewed from the stern.

Prop choice is not very exact. Engine manufacturers make recommendations based on horsepower, shaft rpm, and displacement, but how you load your boat, how you use it, and the sea conditions you normally encounter are also factors. The classic test for a good prop match is to slowly advance the throttle to full forward. Both the prop and the bottom need to be clean for this test, and it is a good idea to have the boat loaded the way you will when you use it. If the tachometer shows the engine running smoothly right up to or just below the engine's maximum continuous rating and the boat achieves hull speed (1.34 times the square root of the waterline length), then the prop is a relatively good match. If you get this same result but feel vibrations or a thumping from beneath,

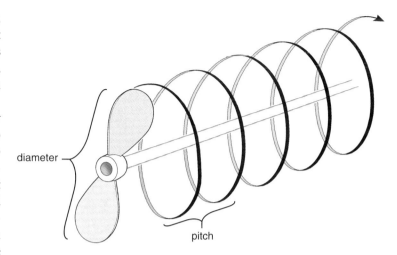

you have inadequate tip clearance between the blades and the hull. You need a smaller prop with additional pitch to make up for the reduction in diameter. If the engine runs past the continuous rating to the maximum no-load rpm, the prop is either too small or has too little pitch. If the engine fails to approach the maximum continuous rating and black smoke pours from the exhaust, you are overpropped and need to reduce the pitch.

All things being equal, a larger-diameter prop turning at a slower speed is more efficient, but you need about 15% of prop diameter in tip clearance—more than 2 inches for a 15-inch prop—or the proximity of the hull will have a negative effect. And you are stuck with the shaft speed your engine/transmission combination delivers unless you plan to repower or at least change the reduction gear. Sailors almost always want to swing the largest-diameter prop that provides adequate clearance. Some prop shops have loaners that can help you "dial in" the correct pitch.

However, maximizing your speed or ability to punch into a head sea under power might not be your only objective. The idle prop on a sailboat, especially a three-blade prop, creates drag that makes the boat slower under sail. If sailing performance is your primary interest, you are going to want to minimize your prop's underwater profile. The cheapest way to do this is to install a fixed two-blade prop that can be locked vertically behind the keel, but on a performance-oriented boat, the keel doesn't extend to the prop. Without a means to hide the prop from the flow of water past the hull, the low-drag choices become folding or feathering props.

Cruisers nearly always find a sailboat's powering ability is much more important than they ever imagined, so how much sailing performance must you give up to take full advantage of your engine?

A 12-pitch prop would move the boat forward 12 inches in one revolution if it were turning in a solid material.

Hidden two-blade fixed.

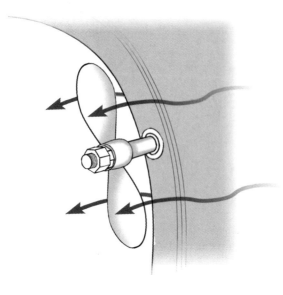

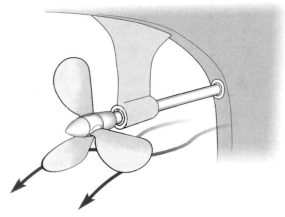

Three blade feathering—some drag results from the downward angle of shaft.

Exposed two-blade fixed.

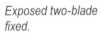

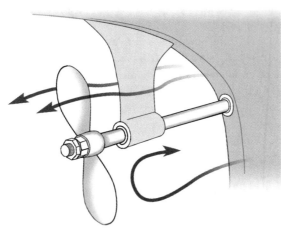

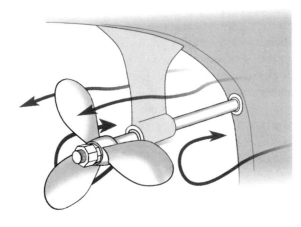

Folding—the least drag.

Not that much. An MIT velocity prediction program suggests that the average impact of a three-blade prop compared to *no* prop is about 5% of boat speed, with the impact being greater in light air and less as sails develop sufficient power to overcome additional drag. Rare is the cruiser who does not hit the start button when boat speed drops to 2 knots. When the wind is blowing at 20 knots, you are probably reducing sail, which suggests that being slowed by the prop is not an issue. So even in light to moderate conditions, dragging a three-blade prop is likely to cost you less than 20 minutes in a 40-mile sail. Punching ability under power might make up every bit of that if you have sagged off under sail and have to motor upwind to reach your harbor.

Exposed three-blade fixed.

As usual, I tend to come down on the side of less complexity. Fixed props are simple and foolproof. Feathering and folding props are neither, so be sure the benefit for *you* will justify the added complexity.

Whether you are having your old prop reconditioned or fitting a different prop—fixed or folding—prop removal is not difficult. Typically the threaded end of the shaft is drilled for a cotter pin. The pin may lock a drilled or castellated nut in position, or it may only prevent a loosened nut from backing completely off the shaft. In either case, remove the cotter pin. Fit wrenches to the two nuts on the shaft, and loosen and remove the aft one. Now grip the prop to prevent the shaft from turning, and release and remove the second nut.

The hole in the prop is tapered to fit tightly against a similar taper at the end of the prop shaft. Sometimes you can pull a prop from the taper by hand, but it usually requires some type of prop puller. *Never* try to remove a prop by hitting it with a hammer. You will succeed only in destroying the balance of the prop, bending the shaft, or damaging the bearings in the transmission.

You can rent or borrow a commercial puller—an octopus-like gizmo with hinged arms that grip the hub or lengths of chain that loop around the blades and a central screw that tightens against the end of the shaft—or you can make a simple puller from a couple of 6-inch squares, triangles, or disks of stiff steel plate. Clamp the two pieces together and drill three evenly spaced $3/_8$-inch holes in a triangular pattern (for a three-blade prop) somewhat larger than the hub of the prop. Cut a notch into one of the plates wide enough and deep enough to allow the plate to slide over the shaft and center against the hub of the prop.

With the notched plate in place, insert $3/_8$-inch bolts through the holes in it and between the blades of the prop. Slide the second plate over the bolts and install the nuts, tightening until the aft plate seats squarely against the end of the shaft. Now tighten the bolts evenly $1/_2$ turn at a time; the compression will pull the prop. Occasionally a prop will literally leap aft when the taper releases, so be careful. If the prop fails to release after a few turns, hit the aft plate in its center with a hammer. Don't haul off and whang it; you are not

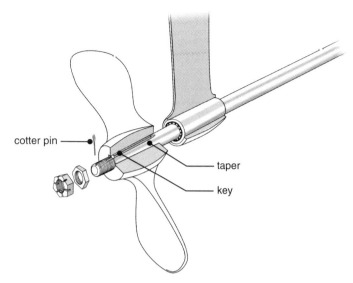

trying to impress the crowds at the fair. A single sharp rap should do the trick. If not, try heating the hub with a torch. Expansion should release it from the taper.

The prop and shaft are locked together rotationally with a key—a square metal bar—that fits into a machined slot in the shaft and a corresponding keyway in the prop. Be careful not to lose the key, particularly if you are pulling the prop in the water. If the key comes off with the prop, remove it by prying it out of the keyway before you send the prop to be reconditioned. If the key stays in the slot in the shaft, there is no real reason to remove it unless it is in danger of falling out and getting lost.

When reinstalling the prop, be sure the key is in place. Grease the taper lightly to insure that the prop seats fully. If the two nuts are different thicknesses, put the thin one on first and tighten it against the hub of the prop. Putting the thicker nut on second gives it more threads to lock against. Insert and spread the cotter pin.

Put the thicker nut on last to give it more thread contact to lock against.

CUTLESS BEARING

A Cutless bearing is nothing more than a short length of naval brass or composite tubing with a splined hard-rubber liner. The rubber supports the propeller shaft where it exits the hull, and the channels allow water into the bearing to serve as a lubricant and to wash out sand and other abrasives. The bearing's inner diameter matches the diameter of the shaft, and the outer diameter is a snug fit for the stern tube or bearing housing in the strut. A Cutless bearing can last 10 years or longer when the shaft is properly aligned. No maintenance can be done on a Cutless bearing; either it is OK or you replace it.

How do you, a mere novice at such matters, know if it needs replacing? A low rumble when motoring is

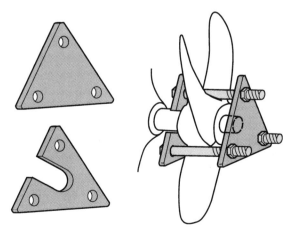

A simple prop puller.

Cutless bearing.

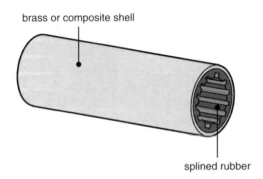

brass or composite shell

splined rubber

the classic indicator. You may feel it more than hear it. Out of the water, grab the prop and shake the shaft. Some play is normal in an older shaft bearing, but if it feels loose when you shake the prop, you need a new bearing. If you can rattle the shaft in the bearing, replacement is overdue. Don't freak; a worn-out Cutless bearing will not sink your boat. However, that rumble is shaft vibration, which isn't doing the shaft packing or transmission bearings and seals any favors. Transmission bearings are expensive and difficult to replace. Cutless bearings are cheap and easy.

Cutless bearings typically slip into the stern tube or strut from outside the hull and are clamped in place with setscrews. They may also be held in place by a flange or an extended housing bolted in place. Replacement varies from dead easy to a pain in the transom.

The first step is to remove the prop as detailed earlier. Locate the setscrews in a strut-mounted bearing and remove them. The bearing can often be pushed out of a strut with the shaft in place using a piece of tubing or an old Cutless bearing halved lengthwise. Use the pair of half tubes to push or tap the bearing from the housing.

If the shaft exits the hull through a housing, this must be removed to gain access to a log-housed bearing. The mounting bolts are likely to be well camouflaged by layers of bottom paint, but when you have located and removed them, the housing will slide aft

An old Cutless bearing or similar diameter tubing split in half makes a good tool for pushing a worn bearing from a skeg.

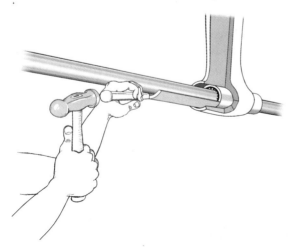

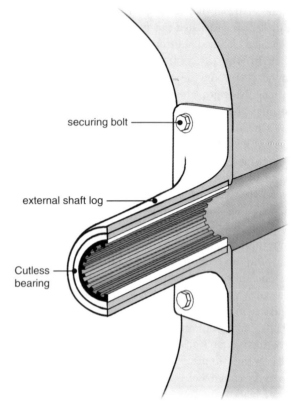

securing bolt

external shaft log

Cutless bearing

A Cutless bearing in an external shaft log can normally be replaced by removing the log.

and off the prop shaft. The Cutless bearing may be contained in the housing. Locate the setscrews in the side of the housing and unscrew them to release the bearing. Tap the old bearing out with a dowel or a pin punch.

Removing an external collar may just reveal the bearing in the stern tube in the hull. If you have the good fortune of part of the bearing shell being exposed, it is usually possible to grip the exposed portion with a band wrench, tongue-and-grove pliers, or a pipe wrench and extract it by twisting it out of the housing and off the shaft.

With the collar out of the way, if all you can see of the Cutless bearing is an end, or if there is no collar and the bearing is held in place with setscrews in the side of an irremovable housing, you will probably have to drive the bearing out of the tube from inside the boat. I have occasionally been able to pull an internal Cutless bearing with the shaft in place by bending the ends of a loop of thin but stiff wire into tight hooks and feeding these through the bearing in two of the water channels on opposite sides of the shaft, hooking onto the inside edge of the bearing shell. If this trick fails, you will have to remove the prop shaft.

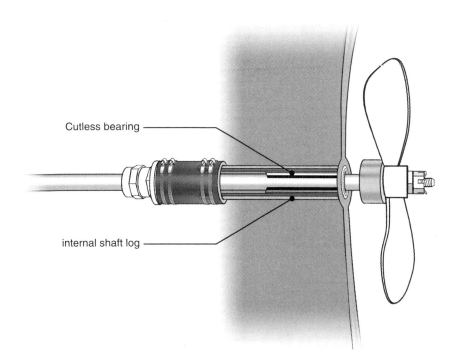

Cutless bearing

internal shaft log

When the bearing is inside the stern tube, you usually have to remove the prop shaft to replace the bearing.

PROP SHAFT REMOVAL

Cutless bearing replacement is not the only reason for removing the prop shaft. The absence of a zinc collar can lead to destructive corrosion, especially of the threads for the prop nuts. An impact or a wrapped line can bend the shaft, causing severe vibration when underway. The rubber hose attaching the stuffing box to the stern tube can split. A new engine can necessitate a shaft of a different length and/or diameter.

The prop shaft in some boats cannot be removed, I am sorry to report, with the rudder in place. If your boat is not one of these but has a more maintenance-friendly design, shaft removal should be straightforward. The inboard end of the shaft is typically pressed into a flange and secured with a clamp bolt, setscrews, or a retaining pin. This flange is bolted to a similar flange on the rear of the engine, forming the coupling. When the shaft is removed from the flange and the compression nut on the stuffing box is eased, the shaft should simply slide out of the boat, providing that the rudder does not interfere. What could be easier?

Unfortunately, getting the coupling off the shaft is usually a bastard. Start by soaking the screws, bolts, and coupling with penetrant at least a week before you plan to remove the shaft. The longer you allow the penetrant to work, the better. Next loosen the clamp bolts, remove the setscrews, and/or tap out the pin retaining the shaft. Mark the shaft so you will know how far in it needs to go when you put it back, then, just for laughs, pull aft on the shaft. If it should

actually come free of the coupling, make a large donation to your church or favorite charity. You owe.

For the less favored, the next step is to separate the two halves of the coupling. First place the point of a sharp center punch on the edge of one of the flanges and tap it *lightly* with your hammer. Make a similar punch mark on the other flange directly across from the first one. These two marks will allow you to reassemble the two halves exactly as they came apart. This is a good practice to follow whenever you disassemble parts that could be reassembled in different ways.

Remove the bolts that hold the coupling together using a six-point box-end wrench or a six-point socket to be sure the wrench will not slip. Back off the compression nut on the stuffing box, then slide the shaft back and note whether the end of the shaft is flush with the face of the flange or recessed. Now find four or five nuts and short bolts of different lengths to use as spacers. Tape the shortest spacer against the end of the shaft and slide the shaft forward, sandwiching the spacer in the middle of the coupling. Insert the coupling bolts and tighten *evenly*. As the coupling bolts pull the shaft flange forward, the spacer prevents the shaft from coming with it, thus pressing the shaft out of the flange. If the shaft doesn't budge, don't crank down on the coupling bolts until you warp or break the flange. Try expanding the flange with heat from a propane torch. Do not heat the half of the coupling that's attached to the engine or you will destroy the rubber oil seal around the driveshaft. Replace the

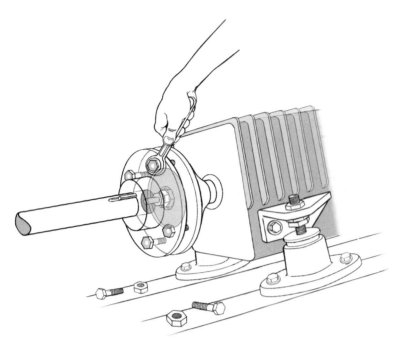

Spacers that prevent the shaft from going forward allow you to press it from the flange by tightening the flange bolts.

initial spacer with progressively longer ones to press the shaft all the way out. Be sure to spread a cloth under the shaft to prevent the shaft key or the spacer from dropping into the bilge. From outside, slide the free shaft completely out of the boat.

Pressing the shaft back into the flange can be even more difficult. With very fine emery cloth, first polish the shaft and the bore in the coupling until they are free of all imperfections. Insert the shaft through the stern tube and fit the key, if there is one, to the shaft. Spray the shaft and the bore with a lubricant such as WD-40 and slip the flange onto the shaft as far as it will go. From the forward side of the flange, measure the depth to the end of the shaft. While a helper holds the shaft, hold a block of wood against the face of the flange and hit the wood with a heavy hammer. The shaft will move aft despite the helper's grip, but hopefully not before the flange slides farther onto the shaft. After three or four blows, measure the depth again to see how you are progressing. If the flange is moving, keep pounding on the block until the shaft reaches its original depth in the flange. Of course, this assumes you have room between the transmission and the stuffing box to swing a hammer, which may not be the case.

Inadequate or cramped space could tempt you to assemble the coupling and hammer the shaft into its bore from outside the boat. Forget about it! The transmission is not designed to be hammered on and is almost certain to suffer damage. But the transmission is designed to handle thrust; after all, it is the prop that pushes the boat. You can build a Rube

Goldberg contraption with a piece of scrap timber (4 × 4, or similar) to allow the shaft to be *pressed* into the coupling. Plant the lower end of the timber in a shallow but straight-sided hole in the ground, and lash the upper end against the transom so the timber stands directly behind the prop shaft and perpendicular to the angle of the shaft. Thread the prop nut onto the shaft to protect the end threads, and wedge a *small* hydraulic "bottle" jack between the end of the shaft and the vertical timber, using wooden blocks as spacers. Be sure the jack remains centered. If the timber is far from the shaft, a rigid support for the jack and spacers will be needed. As you pump the jack, it should press the shaft into the flange. Be sure the timber is lashed to the boat so you are not pushing the boat forward.

If you have difficulty getting the flange to go on the shaft, try packing the shaft in ice for a couple of hours, then heating the flange with a torch just before assembly. The combined effects might just give you the clearance you need. And try not to brand yourself, Pardner.

If you are having your prop reconditioned or trued, take the shaft and flange with you, and get the prop shop to also true the flange and dress the two parts for a slip fit. Then you can ignore all of the preceding text and just slide the shaft in place. All of life should be this easy.

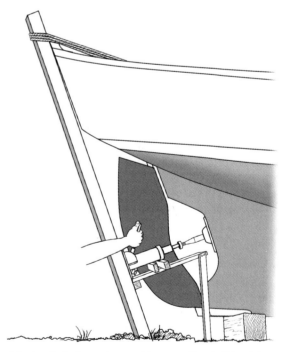

A hydraulic jack can be used to press the shaft back into the flange.

CUTLESS BEARING REDUX

Gaining access to the inboard end of a Cutless bearing housed in the stern tube will require releasing the hose clamps holding the stuffing box hose to the stern tube and removing the stuffing box assembly. A failure of this oft-neglected hose *will* sink your boat, so while the shaft is out is your opportunity to renew it. Be sure you use the right stuff—five-ply or better exhaust hose.

If the inboard end is not hidden by a flange stop, you may be able to tap the bearing out of the stern tube with a hammer and a length of hardwood dowel. If it does not tap out easily, check again for retaining screws hidden beneath the bottom paint. You can cobble together an effective puller with a length of threaded rod, two nuts, a couple of shoulder washers, and a short length of pipe that the bearing can pass through. One of the shoulder washers should be able to pass through the stern tube (or strut), but not through the bearing. The other should be big enough to rest on the end of the pipe. Insert the rod through the bearing and put the smaller washer and one nut on the inboard end. Outboard, slip the pipe and the larger washer over the rod and thread on the second nut. Tightening the outboard nut will pull the bearing from the stern tube into the pipe. If you can't easily locate washers and pipe in the required diameters, you can substitute a hardwood through-hull plug for the inboard washer, and a 2 × 4 bridge for the pipe. Saw off the part of the taper plug that is larger than the stern tube; drill a center hole in the remaining section; and slide it over the rod, fat end against the bearing.

Since the bearing shell is usually brass, an alternative method of removal is to thickly tape one end of a new hacksaw blade and use it like a keyhole saw to slit the bearing longitudinally. This will allow you to collapse the bearing with a punch and pliers, reducing its diameter. If you elect this method, take care not to cut through the bearing and into the stern tube or strut.

Compared to removal, replacement is a piece of cake. First lubricate the new bearing with soap—never grease—and slip it onto the shaft to confirm the fit. It should rotate easily. Lightly coat the outside of the shell, this time with a thin grease, and try to slide the bearing into the housing. A few love taps with the bearing protected from the hammer by a wood block are OK, but if doesn't go easily, don't just hit it harder or you'll distort it. Put it in a freezer or pack it in ice for a few hours, then try again. The cold

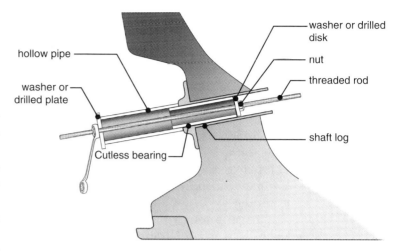

should contract the metal case enough to make the difference.

If the bearing is retained with setscrews, put shrink tubing or a wrap of plastic tape around a drill bit to protect the hole threads and drill dimples in the bearing shell. Coat the setscrews with Loctite and tighten them only enough to seat them in the dimples.

You may also find Cutless bearings around the rudderstock where it exits the hull. These bearings are removed and replaced in the same manner.

ENGINE ALIGNMENT

If you replace a cutless bearing, take a close look at the old one. More wear at the ends than at the center is a sure indicator of poor engine alignment. Misalignment also stresses the output shaft, shortening the life of expensive-to-replace bearings and seals in your reduction gear. Keep in mind that your engine sits on rubber mounts that, like your mattress, compress with time. As the engine settles lower, alignment with the shaft is inexorably altered. Engine alignment should be checked annually. Compressed mounts also lose their ability to isolate the hull from engine vibrations. The time to replace worn-out or broken mounts is before you align the engine, not after, so check the mounts first.

Replacing a Cutless bearing will not alter engine alignment, but having the coupling apart affords an opportunity to check it, even if it's an imperfect one because your boat is probably out of the water. I know you don't want to hear this, but the hull of your old boat distorts when deprived of the full support of floating. That distortion can cause temporary misalignment between the engine and the

With access to the inboard end, you can pull a Cutless bearing with a length of threaded rod.

shaft. Any alignment done in the yard will need to be rechecked at least a week after launch to let the hull assume its normal shape. Rigging tension also affects hull shape, so stays and shrouds should be under normal tension.

Alignment necessitates keeping track of the relative orientation of the two halves of the coupling when they are apart, so if you have not already punched alignment marks into both flanges as described in the earlier Prop Shaft Removal section, do that now. Also loosen the packing nut to allow the shaft to slide aft more easily.

The only tools you will need other than wrenches and perhaps pliers (to release the safety wire) are a straightedge and a *feeler gauge*, which is an inexpensive tool that looks like a pocket knife with 15 or 20 blades. Each blade is etched with its thickness.

FLANGE RUN-OUT

Unbolt and separate the two halves of the coupling, then push them back together, realigning the two dimples. Use the thinnest feeler gauge to check for a gap between the two flanges anywhere around their circumference. If you find one, hold the coupling halves together tightly and find the thickest feeler blade that will slip into the gap. This is the gap width. With the transmission in gear to lock the output flange, rotate the prop shaft 180 degrees. The gap should neither move nor change in width. If it does, the flange is crooked on the shaft. This flaw is called flange run-out and must be

corrected before you attempt to align the engine. You will need the assistance of a prop shop to true the flange.

BORE ALIGNMENT

If we imagine the output shaft as hollow and look through it from the engine, the end of the prop shaft should completely block our view. If we see light above the shaft, the engine is sitting too high; light below, the engine is sitting low; light to port, the engine is to port; and so on.

Of course we can't actually sight through the shaft, so we make do by laying a straightedge across the two halves of the coupling. This is called *bore alignment*. However, the weight of the propeller shaft causes its forward end to sag if unsupported. Move the shaft up and down against a scale to find the middle position—where it should be in perfect alignment with the Cutless bearing—then rig a loose loop of line to support the shaft in this position. Be sure your

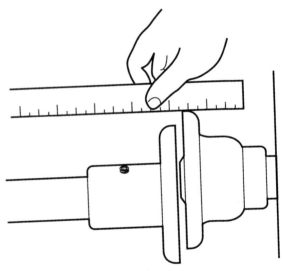

Check with a straightedge across the top, bottom, and both sides of the uncoupled coupling.

Rotating the shaft moves the gap. The flange will have to be machined or replaced.

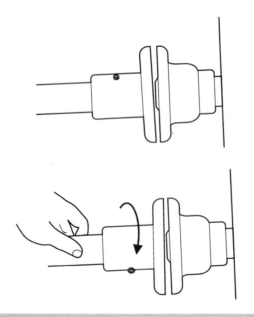

Flange run-out.

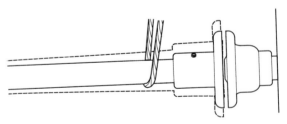

Prevent a long shaft from "drooping" by supporting it midway between maximum up and down travel.

Bore alignment.

support doesn't alter the side-to-side alignment of the shaft. Spin the shaft to be sure nothing is binding.

Place the two coupling halves as close together as possible without engaging them, then check the flange alignment with a straightedge. If the engine flange is lower than the shaft flange (a likely result), adjust this by raising the engine equally on all mounts. Mounts typically sport three nuts, one above the bracket attached to the engine and two below it. Release the top and bottom nuts, keeping in mind that they loosen in opposite directions. Once these two locknuts are loose, adjustment is merely a matter of turning the middle nut, called a jacknut. The jacknut raises that corner of the engine when you turn it *counterclockwise* as you're looking down on the mount.

Raise the engine on all the mounts equally. Make small adjustments—not more than ¼ turn—then check the flanges with your straightedge. Keep lifting (or lowering) the engine until the tops of the coupling halves are at the same height. Correct lateral misalignment by loosening the bolts that secure the mounts to the engine beds and shifting the mounts toward the appropriate side. Making the same lateral adjustment to all mounts is more difficult since the usual method of shifting the mounts is to smack them with a heavy hammer. To provide a visual reference, trace around the mounts before you loosen them. A small bottle jack used horizontally is better than a hammer for shifting the engine laterally (with the added benefit of having lots of other onboard uses). Always push or hammer the mount, never the engine.

FACE ALIGNMENT

If both shafts were hollow and the bore alignment correct, looking through the output shaft would let you look into the prop shaft, but if the two shafts fail to match up in a straight line, instead of seeing straight through the propeller shaft, you would see only a portion of the opening at the far end or none at all. You determine the magnitude of this angle between output shaft and propeller shaft by measuring the imperfection of the face-to-face mating of the two flanges, which is why it is called face alignment.

To check face alignment, align the dimples and mate the two flanges of the coupling. Install the bolts and hand tighten to snug it. Check all around the coupling for a gap between the flange faces. The traditional standard is no more 0.001 inch of misalignment per inch of flange diameter. If your coupling

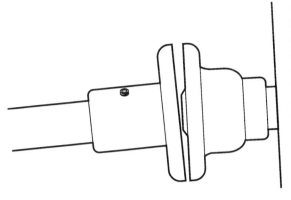

Gap exaggerated for clarity. With flanges touching, the maximum allowable gap is 0.001 inch per inch of coupling diameter.

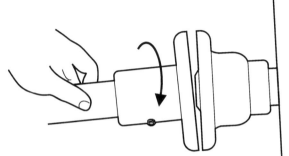

Rotating the shaft should not change the location or size of the gap. Correct by raising, lowering, or shifting the forward engine mounts.

Face alignment.

uses 4-inch flanges, you want the maximum gap between the two measured at the edge to be no more than 0.004 inch—the thickness of a single sheet of copy paper. Softer mounts have led some engine manufacturers to relax this standard to 0.002 inch per inch of flange diameter but the 0.001 standard remains twice as good for your bearings and seals. Check all around the (4-inch) coupling with a 0.004 feeler gauge. If it fails to slide between the flanges anywhere, the alignment is fine. Tighten the bolts, pick up your tools, and head for the light.

You should be so lucky. More likely the flange is going to swallow your skinny gauge and a number of its fatter companions. Face alignment adjustment takes place primarily at the forward mounts because rear-mount adjustment has a greater effect on bore alignment. To reduce the gap, you are going to need to tilt or swing the front of the engine in the direction of the gap. You would lift the front of the engine with the front-mount jack screws to reduce a gap at the top of the flange or shift the front of the engine to port to close a gap on the port side. Unfortunately the maximum gap is not likely to be so conveniently located. Rather it will be at, say, the 10 o'clock position, requiring both tilting and swinging the engine.

The only special skill required to align your engine is patience. Release any tension on the flange nuts, then make single, small adjustments and check the gap after each. Adjusting the front mounts does cause the part of the engine behind the rear mounts to move in the opposite direction, so it is common for face-alignment adjustments to throw the bore alignment slightly out. When you have the face alignment within tolerance, separate the coupling slightly and recheck bore alignment. After you correct this, expect the face alignment to need a bit of fine-tuning. Check the coupling yet again *after* you tighten all the engine mount nuts and bolts, as this often throws the alignment out again. Releasing the top nuts and rechecking the alignment one mount at a time usually reveals which mount needs a little tweaking to make it come in right when it is retightened. See what I mean by patience?

You might wonder how effective even perfect static alignment will be once the engine begins to jump around on the soft mounts. The motion is nearly all rotational around the crankshaft, so if the output shaft is in line with the crankshaft, it will be rock steady. Typically, however, a reduction gear offsets the output shaft, and the greater the offset from the crankshaft centerline, the more side loading there will be on bearings and seals when the engine rocks on its mounts. Fortunately diesels are jumpiest at idle, when the prop is turning slowly or not at all. Once up to "cruising" speed, inertia takes over and the output shaft will tend to spin in one place.

Typical "soft" engine mount.

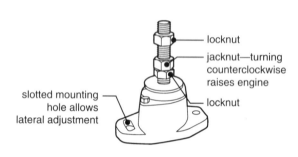

Raising front mounts (or lowering rear mounts) moves top of flange aft to correct face misalignment.

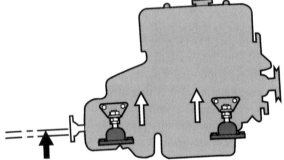

Raising all mounts raises the flange to correct bore misalignment.

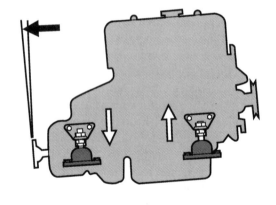

Lowering front mounts (or raising rear mounts) moves top of flange forward to correct face misalignment.

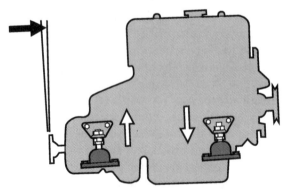

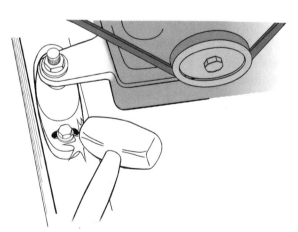

Lateral adjustment for both bore and face alignment is accomplished by shifting engine mounts with a hammer or a bottle jack used horizontally.

Adjusting engine alignment.

Don't forget to safety-wire the coupling bolts if the heads are drilled. If they are not, use a thread locker on them. Also retighten the packing nut. You are going to do this again in a year, so coating both the coupling and the stuffing box with an anticorrosion spray will make it easier.

ENGINE MAINTENANCE

"Old boat" usually means "old engine." "Old engine" suggests more frequent breakdowns or at least heightened concern about breakdown, but with an adequate maintenance program this need not be the case. How much of your own engine work you elect to do is up to you, but ordinary maintenance and common repairs are no more difficult than servicing the sheet winches.

The objective of this chapter has *not* been to detail every mechanical repair that an old boat may require, but rather to expose you to a sampling of such repairs, illustrating their similarity and the limited number of skills necessary to effect them and innumerable others. Likewise, the objective of this section is to expose you to a sampling of engine-servicing procedures requiring little more than a degree of proficiency with hand tools.

KEEP IT CLEAN

Engine maintenance starts with a box of rags. Since all the important stuff is going on inside the engine, maybe your attitude is, what's the big deal about a little grease and grime on the outside? I only have space here for the short list: some of that engine room dirt is being ingested by the engine; a coat of grime hides developing problems that would be obvious on a clean engine; it is human nature to prefer the "clean" jobs, so a dirty engine gets less attention; and whenever you do service or repair the engine, some dirt is going to get inside as surely as it gets on your hands. From a diesel engine's point of view, nothing says "I love you" like a clean engine room.

Heavy encrustation requires a degreaser, such as Grez-Off, but you can spritz away less serious neglect with Fantastik and a sponge. Avoid petroleum-based degreasers. Don't forget to clean all the interior surfaces of the engine compartment.

Deposits on the engine offer useful clues to conditions that may need your attention. Pendulous oil drops on the bottom or the flange of the oil pan along its forward edge may suggest that the front main seal is leaking. If the drops are at the rear of the pan or on the flywheel housing, suspect the rear seal. Any wetness beneath the transfer (lift) pump suggests that it needs servicing. Black fluff on the forward part of the engine or in streaks on compartment surfaces indicates belt wear—belts are loose or out of alignment, or corrosion has roughened the surface of a pulley. Rust streaks, depending on their location, can suggest various conditions, including a failing water pump, a blown head gasket, or a perforated freeze plug. You should watch for these clues as you clean, recognizing, of course, that if you are cleaning away a decade of deposits, some might stem from conditions long since corrected.

Where your cleaning efforts uncover flaking or bare spots, hit these with a wire brush to remove rust and loose paint. Treat bare metal with a rust converter or primer, followed by a coat or two of touch-up paint to close the door on corrosion.

OIL CHANGE

The most basic engine maintenance procedure is the oil change, and it is no less essential when an engine is older. Most engine manuals say to change the oil every 100*, 125*, or 150* hours. When you use your engine a lot, the hours are the thing, but if your engine gets light use, pay attention to that asterisk. It invariably means "but no less than once a year." Because clean oil wards off breakdowns and can extend engine life by thousands of hours, you will never spend a better $20 than changing your oil twice a year or every 100 hours.

You change the oil in your car by removing a plug at the bottom of the oil pan and letting the old oil drain out. The drain plug on most marine engines is either inaccessible or nonexistent, so you have to suck the oil out through the dipstick tube. Aboard most old boats the standard tool for this is a small brass piston pump with a reedlike polyethylene or brass tube that inserts into the dipstick opening. The agonizing inefficiency of this system has sent many a skipper in search of a better way. Chandleries offer as many as a dozen electric, vacuum, or drill-powered alternatives, some costing more than $150.

Save your money. There is nothing wrong with the piston pump. The real problem is that you are trying to suck molasses through a soda straw. You need a bigger probe. Hardware and hobby stores sell thin-wall brass tubing. Buy a tube long enough to reach the bottom of the oil pan and the largest diameter that will slip into the dipstick hole (typically $^{11}/_{32}$ or $^3/_8$ inch). Mate this to your pump with a short length

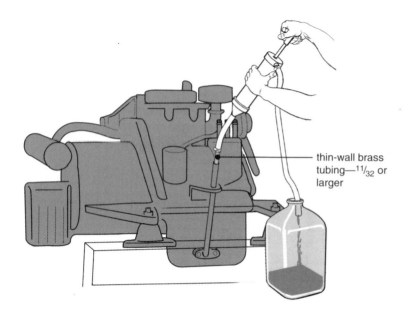

thin-wall brass
tubing—$^{11}/_{32}$ or
larger

freezer bag to contain leakage

The oil filter for older engines may be a cartridge type inside a metal canister. The canister will leak oil as soon as you loosen the center bolt.

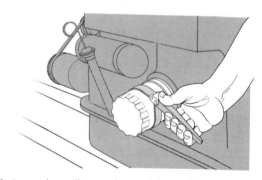

Later engines all use spin-on oil filters. Turn counterclockwise with a strap wrench to loosen.

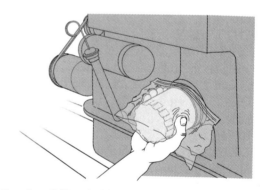

Opening oil filters inside a freezer bag prevents oil from running into the bilge and ultimately into the water.

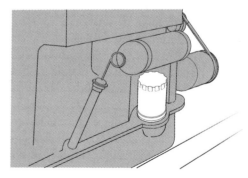

Before unscrewing a filter mounted this way, puncture the shell near the bottom and where you can catch the oil that runs out.

To make oil changes quick and easy, fit your oil-change pump with the largest diameter thin-wall brass tube that will slip easily into the dipstick tube. The oil should be hot.

of rubber hose. Stick the discharge hose into a plastic milk jug, and a dozen strokes on the pump will empty the engine. Price: $2.

The engine should be hot before you begin an oil change. Hot oil is much easier to suck through your brass straw, but the reason for running the engine first is more basic than that. You're changing the oil because it's dirty. Some of the harbored impurities will be abrasive, causing wear to piston rings, bearings, and other internal parts. You periodically remove the dirty oil and put in clean to get rid of these abrasives. Except that the dirt in oil is just like dirt in water; leave it undisturbed and it will settle to the bottom. Suck out the oil cold and most of the contaminants stay behind, corrupting the fresh oil as soon as you run the engine. Run the engine *before* you change the oil to get the contaminants into suspension so they come out with the oil. Wear cloth gloves or wrap a thick towel around the pump before you suck hot oil through it, unless your past would make the loss of your fingerprints a desirable consequence.

OIL FILTERS

Engine manufacturers often specify a filter change with every other oil change, and a good filter is no doubt good for 200 to 300 hours. The problem is that on some engines the filter harbors a significant amount of oil. Not changing the filter strikes me as pouring this morning's coffee over $^1/_2$ inch of yesterday's dregs in the cup. The next time you change filters, empty the old one into a glass container. Then you can decide for yourself whether skipping the filter change is a good idea for your particular engine.

Older engines may be equipped with cartridge-type oil filters. These are typically held in place with a single center bolt. Release the bolt to remove the canister, but be careful that oil does not leak out around the loosened bolt. Pour the oil out of the canister and discard the old filter cartridge. Clean the housing with diesel fuel (or kerosene) and insert the new cartridge. If a separate sealing ring is included with the cartridge, carefully pry the old seal out of its seat by pricking it with a straight pin. Coat the new seal with oil, and push it into position. Reinstall the canister.

Later-model engines all have spin-on oil filters that are simply unscrewed and thrown away. Removing them requires a filter wrench or strap wrench that grips the canister when pressure is applied to the handle. Strap wrenches work in only one direction, so if the wrench slips, take it off the filter and reverse it. Virtually every other kind of filter you will encounter sits vertically so the fluid it contains does not spill when the filter is opened, but for some reason that totally eludes me, engine designers mount oil filters at odd angles, horizontally, and even upside down. You can guess what happens when you open them. For all but the upside-down variety, you can contain the spilling oil by slipping a freezer bag over the filter and its fitting before you break the seal, then unscrew the filter inside the bag. The trick for the upside-down filter is to puncture the metal canister close to the mount to drain it into some container before you unscrew it.

Smear a light coat of oil on the gasket of a new spin-on filter with your finger before screwing the filter in place. Hand tighten until the gasket makes full contact, then tighten another $^3/_4$ turn. Don't forget to pour fresh oil into the engine through the oil-fill opening on top of the valve cover. Using a funnel avoids a lot of mess.

COOL RUNNINGS

The heat generated when internal combustion engines burn their fuel would soon evaporate the lubricating oil if the cylinders were not cooled. In a marine engine, cooling is normally accomplished by circulating water through drilled and cast passages inside the engine. The water absorbs the heat and carries it out of the engine.

Many older engines are (were!) raw-water cooled. Raw-water cooling (also called direct cooling) seems like a good idea. After all, the boat *is* floating in water. What could be easier than drawing in some of the ocean and pumping it through the engine and back over the side? Not a darn thing, which is exactly why the manufacturer did it that way—not because it was best.

Raw-water cooling has three serious problems. The most obvious is that the water we do our boating in is not always crystal clear, and whatever extraneous particles are in the water flow through the engine. Some of them are left behind. Intake filters screen out the big stuff, but not the particles in suspension. Too much mud, sand, and bits of weed will block the cooling passages and lead to overheating and damage.

The second problem applies to boats used in salt water. Corrosive by nature, seawater attacks the engine, causing corrosion inside passages and chambers. The insulation effect of $^1/_{16}$ inch of rust exceeds that of 4 inches of iron, so the engine runs hotter, even as the temperature gauge shows cooler.

The least obvious and most serious drawback to raw-water cooling, especially in a diesel engine, is the inability to regulate and optimize engine temperature. Clearly the temperature of the lake or ocean may vary widely, but it is the absence of a thermostat that most limits regulation. The thermostat is a valve that remains closed, restricting most of the coolant flow until the coolant reaches a certain temperature, then the valve opens and remains open unless the temperature of the coolant drops below the specified number. The straight-through nature of raw-water cooling generally prohibits the use of a thermostat, and even when the system is configured to allow its inclusion, it is prone to failure from contaminants.

When a raw-water system does include a thermostat, it *must* be one that opens at around 135°F, because the formation of passage-blocking scale increases markedly as the cooling water temperature approaches 160°F. Avoiding this problem, however, creates two others in a diesel engine. Running a modern diesel cooler than 185°F virtually insures incomplete combustion—the engine smokes, power declines, and carbon deposits build up on pistons and valves. Even more serious, the lower operating temperatures cause condensation to form inside the cylinders, washing the oil from the cylinder walls, contaminating the oil, and forming corrosive acids that attack the bearings and other internal parts. Engine life suffers.

This catch-22 is largely academic since most raw-water-cooled diesels have long since succumbed to the corrosive effects of hot salt water. Gasoline engines in new powerboats are still delivered standard with raw-water cooling (which remains a bad idea for engines used in salt water), but virtually all diesel installations in pleasure boats are configured for freshwater cooling, circulating noncorrosive coolant through the engine in a closed loop. The heat absorbed by the coolant is transferred through a radiator-like heat exchanger to a flow of raw water in the same way that the hot contents of a pot may be cooled by running tap water over its exterior. This is called *indirect cooling*, and not surprisingly, the raw-water side is still at the root of most overheating problems. When the engine alarm sounds or the temperature gauge needle climbs into the red, that is where to look first.

Easy Things First

You can significantly reduce the incidence of overheating by simply checking the exhaust every time you start the engine. A dry exhaust signals imminent overheating well in advance of the heat-gauge needle. Even when the problem materializes underway, recognizing a change in the sound of the exhaust gives early warning. Raw-water flow might be interrupted by airlock in boisterous sea conditions but the more usual causes of diminished flow are blockage or a pump failure.

Equating the intake fitting to a bathtub drain might help you visualize its susceptibility to sucking in weeds, jellyfish, and the now-ubiquitous plastic shopping bags. A blocked intake can stop the flow of raw water as positively as a closed seacock (an embarrassingly common oversight). The cure might be as simple as turning off the engine, allowing blockage sucked against the intake grate to "fall" free—provided you have a grate over the intake

fitting. Otherwise blowing or poking through the connected hose or even diving over the side may be required. Be sure your intake is fitted with a grating.

A raw-water strainer after the seacock prevents most intake debris from reaching the pump, but you need to clean the strainer regularly or the flow of raw water can drop below the rate necessary to carry away as much heat as the engine generates. The line between normal operation and overheating is quite sharp—the proverbial straw that breaks the camel's back. My preference is for above-the-waterline plastic strainers because they are immune to corrosion and easy to clean. Simply unscrew the lid, lift out the strainer basket, empty it, give it a quick scrub with a brush (and detergent if needed), drop it back into the housing, grease the seal, and reinstall the lid. Modern bronze strainers are nearly as easy to service, but old-style strainers without removable lids must be disassembled for cleaning. Leak-free reassembly depends on carefully seating the canister on the rubber gaskets and tightening the screws evenly. To open any strainer mounted below the waterline, you must first close the seacock. Don't forget to reopen it.

A kinked or collapsed hose is another cause of raw-water blockage. All hoses on the suction side of the pump must be wire-reinforced (a good choice for all engine hoses). If a hose between the pump and the intake is not reinforced, it can collapse like a straw in a shake. This can be the cause of intermittent

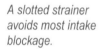

The absence of a strainer allows plastic litter and other flotsam to become lodged in the intake plumbing.

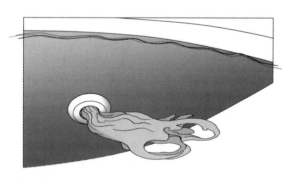

A slotted strainer avoids most intake blockage.

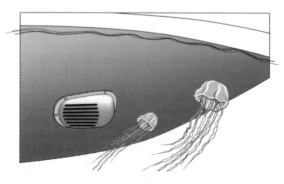

A generous intake strainer keeps water—and only water—flowing to the raw-water pump.

overheating, with the hose collapsing only with the increased suction of higher engine speeds or when rising compartment temperatures soften the rubber. Hoses that seem fine from the outside can still be crumbling inside, packing water passages with bits of rubber. If I bought an old boat and did not know the age of the hoses, I would replace them all. Waiting does not avoid the expenditure, it only delays it—and at considerable risk. Hose replacement is detailed fully in Chapter 12.

V-Belts

Belt failure disables belt-driven pumps. Periodically run your fingers along the underside of V-belts to make sure they are not cracked, gummy, or glazed. Visually inspect notched belts. V-belts are designed to ride on the sides of the pulley—the reason for the V shape. If the belt is sitting on the bottom of the pulley or the back of the belt is not flush with or higher than the shoulders of the drive pulleys, replace it. Do I need to point out that the engine *cannot* be running when you are messing with V-belts?

Too much belt tension causes premature bearing failure, but paradoxically so does too little tension—due to heat generated by the slipping belt. The traditional gauge of correct tension is $1/_2$ inch of deflection from firm thumb pressure in the middle of the longest span. A more reliable setting for small engines is to tighten the belt just until turning the alternator pulley by hand also turns the crankshaft pulley. Because tensioning the belt that drives the coolant pump is nearly always accomplished by repositioning the alternator, I need to point out here that belts are sized for their intended load. That means if your engine was delivered with a 35- to 55-amp alternator, the standard belt is probably $3/_8$ inch. The largest alternator you should try to drive with a $3/_8$-inch belt is about 75 amps, so if you upgrade to an 80-amp alternator, you also need to increase the belt (and pulley) size to $1/_2$ inch. Alternators putting

out more than 100 amps require tandem belts. That means tandem pulleys on the crankshaft and on the coolant pump unless you alter the configuration. When you have tandem belts, they must always be replaced together as a set. Otherwise they are at different depths on the pulleys and consequently run at different speeds. Slippage and heat are the inevitable results.

Alternators are typically hinged to the engine with a single bolt and held away from the engine with a second bolt through a slotted bracket. Belt replacement and/or tensioning is accomplished by loosening (not removing) the pivot bolt, the adjusting bolt, *and* the bolt that attaches the slotted bracket to the engine. With all three loose, the alternator will collapse against the engine, allowing the old belt to be removed and a new one put in its place. If the belt size or number is not visible on the old belt, take it with you to the parts supply store and match it. While the belt is off, spin the coolant pump by hand to check the bearings for roughness. Try to move the pulley in and out and from side to side. If you find "slop," replace the pump.

Belt tensioning is simply a matter of pulling the alternator away from the engine until the belt is tight, then tightening the adjusting bolt. This is easy when the adjusting bolt threads into the

Belt tensioning tool.

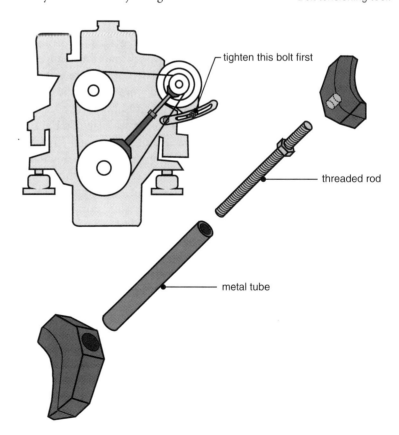

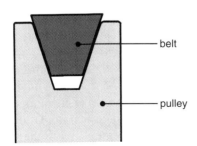

A proper V-belt will be flush with or above the sides of the pulley. When it isn't, you need a new belt.

alternator, but sometimes it threads into a nut. In this case you need one hand for the wrench on the bolt, one for the wrench on the nut, and one to keep tension on the alternator. Unless your last employer was Barnum & Bailey, that's a tall order. The tool illustrated, constructed from threaded rod, metal tubing and some shaped bits of wood, solves this problem. The same tool can also make it easy to achieve adequate belt tension when access is awkward. If you lever the alternator out, be absolutely certain your lever—whatever it is—rests against the engine block and not on a fuel line, wiring, or a freeze plug. Always tighten the adjusting bolt first, then the other two. Recheck the belt tension after all three bolts are tightened. If you have installed a new belt, check the tension again after the first few hours of engine time.

Pump Maintenance

Raw-water pumps are universally flexible-impeller pumps because these can pass pebbles, plants, and pilchards. Stop the flow of water to this type of pump, however, and the impeller sheds vanes like leaves in an October storm. An open seacock, submerged intake, clean strainers, and clear hoses will keep water available to the pump, but the pump will fail anyway if you neglect it. It takes only minimal attention to limit pump failure to a rare manifestation of bad luck.

Cultivate the habit of regularly touching the bottom of the pump body with your finger after running the engine. There is a weep hole there; if it is dry, the seals are sound. A wet pump needs to be checked visually with the engine running. An occasional drip is normal, but a steady leak signals the need for seal replacement. Do not ignore water streaming from the weep hole. Pump-stopping bearing failure is just in the offing. Worse still, where the pump is gear driven, a leaking seal can let seawater inside the engine, turning the oil into something that looks like—and probably lubricates like—chocolate milk. New pump-shaft bearings and seals and three back-to-back-to-back oil changes can save the day, but not without nagging worry about future implications. To preclude a recurrence, many sailors eventually abandon the gear-driven pumps in favor of one that is belt driven. Engine manufacturers have taken the same precaution.

Actually replacing a water pump impeller is usually easier than describing the procedure. With the seacock closed, remove the screws that secure the pump's cover plate. Removing this plate exposes the impeller. If it is too small to grip with your fingers, adjust the parallel jaw width of tongue-and-groove pliers slightly wider than the hub, then grip the hub with the pliers. The impeller should slide out without too much coaxing.

The shaft may be splined, have a flat surface (or two), or have a center slot for a drive pin. My old engine had a half-round notch in the impeller hub that slipped over a round pin sitting loosely on a flat on the shaft. This pin dove for the bilge every time I pulled an impeller until I learned to spread a towel under the pump first.

A missing vane condemns the impeller. It also sends you on a search-and-retrieve mission for the stripped vane(s). Representing actual or potential blockage, missing vanes or pieces of vanes must not be dismissed. They normally fetch up on the inlet side of the heat exchanger. Flex the vanes for signs of aging. If they show cracks or feel stiff in comparison to a new impeller, replace the impeller. Also replace it if the vane tips are nicked or worn.

Like automobile tires, rubber impellers have a predictable life. A vane typically flexes in excess of 150,000 times per engine hour. A tired impeller can look fine, but ignore that. Replace the impeller every 500 hours or at least every other year. Do this and impeller failure will be as rare as a new-tire blowout. For an additional measure of protection, install elastomer impellers like those manufactured by Globe Composite Solutions, which tolerate running dry for some minutes.

While the impeller is out, check the cover plate and pump chamber for wear. Excessive scoring will reduce the flow through the pump. If you are replacing leaking seals, replace the bearings at the same time. Failure to fit new bearings while the pump is dismantled is penny-wise and pound-foolish. For the specifics of dismantling your specific pump, consult a service manual.

Use a nylon cable-tie to bend and secure the vanes of a new impeller in the right direction and to reduce the impeller's diameter for easier insertion. When the tie hits the housing, clip it to remove it. If you are reinstalling a used impeller, always put it back the way it came out; never reverse it. Lubricate the chamber and end plates. If you are going to run the engine immediately, a bit of dishwashing liquid will do. Otherwise use Teflon or silicone grease. Replace the O-ring or gasket under the cover and screw the cover in place. *Open the seacock.*

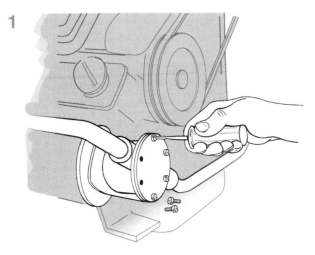

Remove the cover plate to expose the impeller.

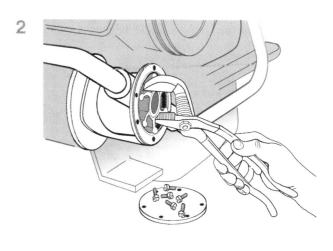

When fingers aren't sufficient, grip the hub of the impeller with tongue-and-groove pliers to extract it.

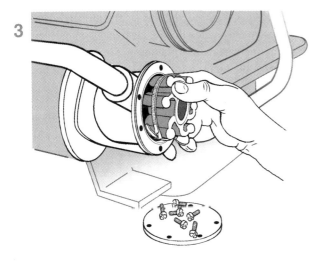

Use a zip tie to collapse the vanes for easier insertion of new impeller into the pump body.

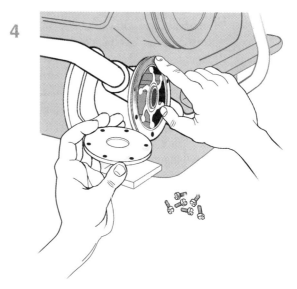

Grease and fit a new O-ring or replace the paper gasket before closing the cover.

Replacing the flexible impeller in a raw-water pump.

Heat Exchanger Maintenance

Blockage downstream of the pump is not limited to errant pump vanes. Mineral deposits form inside the raw-water tubes in the heat exchanger. Raw water passing through the exchanger does not get hot enough to precipitate significant scaling, but when the engine is shut down, the temperature of the stagnant seawater in the exchanger rises and scale forms inside the tubes. To avoid this, never shut the engine off immediately after motoring. Allow it to run at idle for a few minutes to let the engine cool and extend the life of your heat exchanger.

Water flow through the heat exchanger is also restricted by the buildup of silt and debris, but the more sinister consequence of silt lying in the bottom of the tubes is that corrosion may be occurring beneath it. Even cupronickel is susceptible to damage from sulfide concentrations caused by stagnant water and sulfate-reducing bacteria in sediment. Engines that get infrequent use are at the greatest risk of this. Run your engine every week to disrupt this corrosive brew.

Heat exchangers with removable end covers should be opened and pressure flushed annually unless a consistently clean interior suggests less

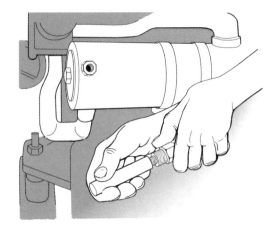

Replace the threaded zinc "pencil" in the heat exchanger when it is depleted by about half.

frequent servicing. Remove constricting scale from the tubes by "rodding" them with a slim wooden dowel or a brass rod with the ends dulled, or let a radiator shop boil out the core in a noncaustic solution. Acid cleaning is a dice roll. Immersion in a 25% solution of muriatic acid will certainly dissolve mineral deposits, but it also attacks the metal. Some heat exchangers will stand up to acid cleaning while others will not. Attempt this method only with full knowledge that it can leave you with a pristine but perforated heat exchanger.

Heat exchangers often employ a zinc "pencil" to protect the tubing from galvanic corrosion. You will find this anode under a hex plug somewhere on the exchanger shell. Check it annually—more often if it shows significant deterioration. Tap off flaky oxides and replace the pencil when its size is reduced by half.

Exhaust Plumbing

The raw water's last hurrah is the mixing elbow, where high temperatures cause scale to form. No matter how efficient the pump is and how clear all the other passages are, if the exit is restricted, the flow of raw water is reduced. The usual symptom is overheating under load, but not at reduced rpm. Typically a blocked elbow will also prevent an engine from reaching its continuous rating rpm.

Coolant

There are fewer uncertainties on the recirculating side of the cooling system. A centrifugal pump, the same type of pump that cools your Beemer, is probably what circulates the coolant. Centrifugal pumps rarely fail, and when one does—signaled by water dripping from a hole in the bottom of the pump—you simply replace it. The primary maintenance requirement is to replace coolant that is (or might be) 2 years old.

Antifreeze doesn't wear out, but the corrosion inhibitors in it do. If your engine does not have draincocks, disconnect the lowest hose connection and

open the pressure cap. The coolant you drain out will reflect the condition of the internal passages. If it looks new, so does the inside of your engine. If it looks brown, which it will if you wait much beyond 2 years to change it, the cooling passages have an insulating coat of rust. You might remove the worst of this rust with a chemical radiator cleaner, but only with the knowledge that these acid-based products could finish off an already weak heat exchanger. If you do use an acid-based cleaner, follow the instructions to the letter, particularly regarding the neutralizing procedure.

Refill the engine with nontoxic (propylene glycol) antifreeze not only because it is "greener," but because a seal or gasket failure that allows as little as 1% of the other kind (ethylene glycol) into the engine's oil can cause rapid bearing failure. If you are not using premixed coolant, premix antifreeze 50-50 with water before pouring it into the engine. Wash your hands with soap before combining the antifreeze with water—not so you will have clean hands, but to determine the hardness of the tap water. Hard water will form scale deposits inside the engine, so if the soap doesn't lather abundantly, use distilled water.

Be sure you fill the system completely. Where the header tank and the heat exchanger are combined, keeping the tubes completely immersed contributes to their longevity. Do not check coolant level just by looking at the recovery tank. If the siphon between the recovery tank and header tank breaks, the recovery tank can be full of coolant while the engine is decidedly not. Remove the pressure cap on a cold engine and look inside or dip your finger to determine the level.

On the subject of pressure caps, their function is to raise the boiling point of the coolant to allow the engine to operate safely at higher temperatures, but you need to make certain that the one installed on your old engine has the pound rating specified by the manufacturer. Too much pressure stresses gaskets, hoses, and seals. Too little allows the coolant to steam destructively in local hot spots. It is a good precaution to test the cap at a radiator shop every couple of years.

Thermostat

The thermostat is typically contained in a housing on the top or front of the engine, and you can safely ignore it unless the normal operating temperature of your engine changes.

A thermostat that fails to open will cause overheating, but when the alarm sounds or the needle climbs toward the red, some other cause is more likely. Check the exhaust first. If it isn't spraying water, the problem is on the raw-water side. Shut the

You can determine whether a thermostat opens and closes at the temperatures stamped on the body by suspending it and a thermometer in a pan of water you heat on a stove.

engine down. If water is spraying normally, reduce the load on the engine by reducing the throttle setting and shifting to neutral. If the temperature declines, overloading—a line around the prop, a foul bottom, etc.—is at least the catalyst and perhaps even the full cause of the overheating. If the rising temperature does not retreat, the pump belt is broken, the coolant level is low, or something—perhaps a closed thermostat—is blocking circulation.

In contrast, when an engine begins to run cool or take longer to reach operating temperature, the thermostat is nearly always the cause. The potential for engine damage is not as immediate with an open thermostat as with a closed one, but it is just as sure. I have already pointed out that low engine operating temperatures result in increased formation of ring- and bearing-damaging acids. Acid in the oil is already the main reason for frequent oil changes in diesel engines, and low engine temperatures mean more acid. If your engine begins to run cooler, replace the thermostat. And should you remove a defective thermostat to solve an overheating problem, replace it. Operating a marine diesel without a properly functioning thermostat shortens the life of the engine, guaranteed.

FUEL

The biggest story this decade was the report in the *Journal of the American Medical Association* that a substance found in nearly all fresh water has been implicated in an astonishing number of diseases. According to health experts, the simple expedient of passing all drinking water through a pair of special filters that block this substance will essentially inoculate an individual from 90% of all human illness. If you missed this story, it could be because I just made it up, but an exact parallel of this fiction is fact when it comes to the health of a diesel engine. Make sure that only unadulterated fuel reaches the engine and you eliminate 90% of potential ailments. *Ninety percent!* This I am not making up.

While a fuel filter on a gasoline engine has much to recommend it, it is a discretionary accessory. Fuel filters—plural—are not optional when the engine is a diesel. Gasoline is sprayed into the intake manifold with about the pressure of a cologne atomizer, but diesel is injected directly into the cylinder at the moment the compression forces in the cylinder are the highest. The tolerances of the pump that puts the fuel under such high pressure are incredibly small, as close as 0.00004 inch, and the holes in injector nozzles are barely larger than a human hair. Any fuel impurities that reach the pump or the injectors are almost certain to cause problems.

Diesel engines almost always come with an attached fuel filter. It is located between the diaphragm lift pump (fuel pump) and the high-precision injection pump. The filter's purpose is to arrest the finest-particle impurities before they reach the injection system. Despite the fact that it is the only filter supplied by most manufacturers, it is universally referred to as a *secondary* filter. That label begs a question.

The answer is that before the fuel ever reaches the engine, it should pass through a remotely mounted *primary* filter. The primary filter prevents most particle contaminants from ever reaching the secondary filter, and perhaps most important, it removes moisture from the fuel. Not only will water in the fuel deprive your expensive injection pump of essential lubrication, but if a droplet of water reaches the tip of an injector, the superheated air of the cylinder will instantly convert it to steam, blowing the tip off like a tiny boiler explosion. Then the tip plays ping-pong inside the cylinder. Oh boy.

To keep this from happening, be sure you have a primary filter, be sure it also acts as a water separator (or install a separate water separator in the line), and regularly drain out the water that accumulates in the bowl. The filter will have a plug or a petcock in the bottom. Open it and drain the filter into a container until only fuel runs out, then close the petcock.

Your engine manual will specify filter element replacement in terms of engine hours, but you will save money in the long run if you install a vacuum gauge in the fuel system. As the filter element clogs, the fuel pump has to suck harder, which registers as vacuum on the gauge. Think of drinking a Coke versus a shake through a straw. There is no need to replace the filter element until the needle on the gauge climbs at least into the yellow, which it may never do if you prefilter the fuel going into your tank.

Prefilter? Right. For about $30 you can buy a fuel funnel with a screen that will pass diesel but not water. The decreased fill rate might be unacceptable for pumping several hundred gallons of diesel into a power yacht, but sailors taking on modest amounts of fuel should filter *every gallon* before it goes into the tank. Why? Because it is the stuff in the tank that clogs fuel filters and stops engines, perhaps putting both boat and crew at risk. Keeping stuff out of the tank avoids this drama. Sailors almost never wear out a diesel engine. They murder it. To avoid this fate for your engine, make "clean fuel, clean fuel, clean fuel" your mantra.

Unfortunately an old boat is likely to already have sediment and perhaps water in the tank. It can be enlightening and sometimes shocking to draw a sample of what is at the very bottom of your tank. Don't be lured into complacency by clean fuel in the filter bowl. The fuel pickup is an inch or so above the bottom of the tank. Dead engines due to in-tank debris stirred up when the sea roughens are so common that such an occurrence qualifies as a cliché.

Representative diesel fuel flow path. Three filters between the fuel provider and the injectors are the minimum.

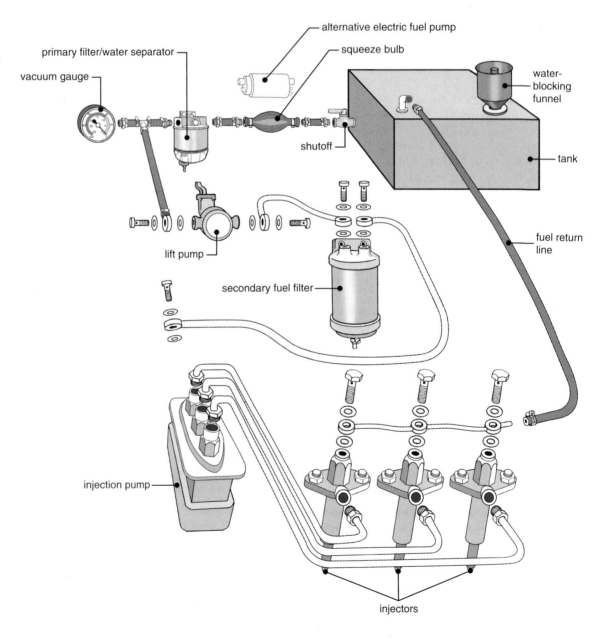

To find out what is below the pickup, you need a tube that reaches the bottom of the tank at its lowest spot. Attach it to a manual pump and extract the sample into a clear container. If your container exhibits something other than light-amber fuel, you need to remove it from the tank. A neat trick is to heel the boat a few degrees with a line from the mast. This creates something of a sump on the low side of the tank. Put your probe into the corner of the tank and keep pumping until only clean fuel comes out. If the tank has an access hole, brush the interior surface first to break loose the debris film, then allow it to settle overnight before pumping.

Water is the most prevalent contaminant. Most comes aboard with the fuel, which prefiltering will stop. A second source is a poor seal around the deck-fill cap. Fill the thread gap around your fuel fill with water, then wait a few minutes. If the water drains away, guess where it went? At a minimum you need a new O-ring on the cap.

Also check the location of the tank vent fitting to be sure it is never immersed when the boat heels or is overtaken by a following sea. Every vent admits moist *air* and some of that moisture condenses into droplets inside the tank. Warm return fuel from your engine fosters this. The inevitability of condensation is one reason to take periodic bottom samples even if you prefilter all your fuel.

Water sinks below the fuel to the bottom of the tank. There it promotes corrosion, especially when it is seawater and the tank is aluminum. Mineral-free fresh water "distilled" from moist air is equally troublesome, providing a habitat for a particularly fecund microorganism capable of fully reproducing itself in as little as 20 minutes. These so-called "fuel bugs" live in the water and feed on the fuel. (Biocide treatments do kill these organisms, but their little dead bodies remain in the tank unless you pump them out.) As long as the layer of water and its associated organisms is shallow, all seems fine—until the boat rolls. If the pickup tube sucks up enough water to overwhelm the separator, I have already mentioned the dire consequences of water reaching the injector pump and injectors. By comparison the mat of organic matter poses less risk of damage—assuming your engine is naturally aspirated—but it will plug a filter in short order, starving the engine into silence no matter how badly you need it at the moment. A turbocharged engine is at greater risk, depending on plenty of fuel to keep cylinder pressures and temperatures below destructive levels.

Changing Fuel Filters

A generous primary filter is essential to the long-term health of a marine diesel. Always on duty, it faithfully guards the gate, free of the human failings of oblivion and sloth. It is not, however, free of the effects of those traits. You must monitor and service fuel filters to insure their continuing protection.

Replacing a fuel filter should be as easy as replacing an oil filter. If the primary filter in your old boat is a canister style, borrow the money if you have to, but replace it with a spin-on filter. Canister filters, particularly those with a center bolt, lack the visual convenience of a clear bowl, inevitably spill fuel when changed, and require tedious cleaning before fitting the new cartridge. By contrast, to replace a spin-on filter, you simply close the fuel supply (if you do not have a shutoff valve in the fuel line between the filter

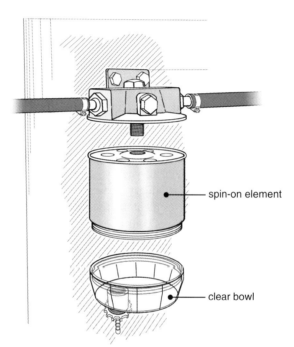

Spin-on filters are easier to change and less likely to spill fuel than center-bolt canister types.

spin-on element

clear bowl

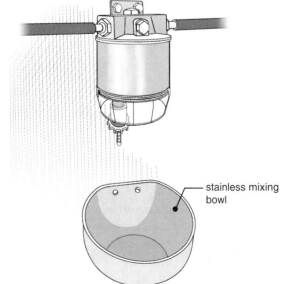

A catch basin beneath the fuel filter keeps drips and spills out of the bilge.

stainless mixing bowl

and the tank, install one), then unscrew the filter element—with the aid of a strap wrench if necessary. Fuel filters are always vertical, so you should be able to remove the full element without spilling fuel. On the subject of spilling fuel, a fine enhancement to your old boat is a basin beneath the primary filter, adapted from anything from a milk jug bottom to a stainless steel mixing bowl.

Pour the fuel out of the removed filter, then unscrew the bowl from the filter element. Wipe everything clean, lubricate the new gaskets with clean fuel, then screw the bowl to the element and the assembly to the filter head. Reopen the fuel shutoff and prime the new filter.

Some filters have a prime pump under a screw knob on top of the filter head. By far the least expensive and least complicated method of priming the fuel filter is to install an outboard motor primer bulb in the fuel line between the fuel shutoff and the primary filter. A few squeezes on this bulb fills the filter with fuel. Crack the bleed screw on top of the filter head to allow trapped air to escape.

The primary filter element should not be as fine as the secondary element when you have a choice. For example, if the secondary element is 2 microns, install a 10-micron element in the primary filter. This effectively increases your filter capacity by putting both filters in play. If the primary filter has a short life, you need a bigger filter, not a coarser one. Whenever you change the primary filter, you should also change the secondary. Specific instructions will be in your engine manual. Also, some engines have an often-overlooked screen or paper filter in the lift pump. If your pump has this, it should be cleaned or replaced each time you change the secondary filter element.

Look inside the removed primary element. If it is coated with black "mayonnaise," you need to take corrective measures, but what they are depends on whether this foul substance is bug or tar. Smell it first. If it smells like varnish, your fuel is old and "flat." Next, subject a smear to a few drops of bleach; if it whitens, it is organic. If the bleach has no effect, see if a spray of WD-40 disperses a second smear, confirming tar. If the slime is organic, treat the fuel with a biocide, then pump out the bottom layer. Varnish-smelling diesel must be discarded—period. The varnish is coating the interior of your injector pump. If the tar still smells like diesel, you can safely use the fuel, but draw the tank down to near empty before refilling. And if the fuel in question is not old by your reckoning, find yourself another source of diesel fuel. By the way, less-refined fuels can actually be better for the engine, so don't shy away from a fuel simply because it is thicker or darker than you may be used to.

Bleeding

Changing filters inevitably introduces air into the fuel system. Air also gets into the system when you run out of fuel, when deep heeling or heavy rolling uncovers the bottom of the pickup tube, or when a fuel line or connection develops a leak. It is interesting to note that when gasoline is the fuel, sound lines and tight connections are essential to keep the fuel *in*, gasoline leaking inside a boat being a very serious matter. However, when diesel is the fuel, keeping the fuel in is secondary to keeping air *out*. The slightest leak in the fuel system will stop the engine, and it will not start again until the fuel system is airtight.

Why does air in the fuel lines prevent a diesel engine from running? Because the injection pump essentially hammers a column of "solid" fuel against a check valve in the injector that "pops" open when the pressure reaches a preset level. But if you put an air bubble in the line, the bubble acts like a spring between the pump and the injector. It compresses, and the pressure at the injector never rises to the level needed to pop the valve. No fuel reaches the cylinder. This doesn't self-correct because the pump terminates injection by "spilling" pressure near the end of each stroke.

Modern high-speed diesels are often self-bleeding (sounds masochistic to me), which means they have a fuel return line from the injection pump to the tank to allow a continuous flow of fuel through the pump. This allows air to pass through the pump rather than becoming trapped in the injector lines. The air vents inside the tank. Self-bleeding engines have the admirable ability to handle a small amount of air in the fuel and keep running, but few will handle a large amount of air with the same aplomb. After running out of fuel, for example, getting the system to self-bleed can require spinning the engine with the starter for a very long time. You must never run the starter for more than 30 seconds or you will overheat it, so purging the lines can take several tries. And if the engine is going to fail to start, you may not know this until the battery goes flat. It pays to make every effort to minimize the amount of air introduced into the fuel system.

When a diesel engine cranks but fails to start, runs irregularly, or dies, bleed the fuel system. Even in the rare instance when bleeding alone fails to correct these troubles, the effort is still rewarded with the diagnostic value of making sure fuel is flowing freely from tank to injector. If your engine is self-bleeding, cranking the engine with the throttle wide open (see your operator's manual) may do the job. The rest of us have to purge the system manually.

Bleeding is nothing more than opening the system at various high spots to let the air escape. The two essential "tools" are a six-point box-end wrench to fit the bleed screws and an absorbent towel. When the bleed screw stops bubbling air, fuel will flow out. Diesel fuel will severely shorten the life of flexible engine mounts; it will soften wiring insulation; and if it trickles into the bilge, the smell will linger inside your boat for months. All of these are easy enough to avoid by strategically placing an absorbent towel before opening a bleed screw.

A word of caution is in order about the bleed screw on the primary filter. If the filter is below the fuel tank, just cracking the screw should bleed the filter once the flow to the filter from the tank is established. But if the filter is mounted higher than the tank or just higher than the current fuel level in the tank, it must only be opened when you are pumping fuel via the integral pump or a primer bulb (or electric fuel pump) upstream of the filter. Otherwise opening this screw lets air into the system rather than out.

The first bleed screw on the engine is typically on top of the secondary filter housing. You do not remove bleed screws; just loosen them about ¼ turn. Crack this first one and operate the lift pump, either by moving the lever (manual) or turning on the key (electric). When bubble-free fuel pumps out around the screw, close it. Note that the manual priming lever will not operate the fuel pump if the pump's rocker arm is in contact with the actuating cam lobe inside the engine. If the lever feels "dead," manually rotate the crankshaft pulley on the front of the engine one full revolution. Because the camshaft where the actuating lobe is located turns at half the speed of the crankshaft, this moves the actuating lobe to the opposite side, freeing the pump diaphragm for manual actuation.

After bleeding the filter housing, open the bleed screw(s) on the injection pump and again operate the lift pump until only clear fuel emerges. Once you have air-free fuel from the tank to the injection pump, see if the engine will start normally. If it doesn't fire immediately, set the throttle wide open and try again. If the engine doesn't light off with 30 seconds of cranking, stop. Loosen the nut that connects one of the delivery pipes to its injector. Turn the engine with the starter until you see regular pulses of fuel spurt out from the loose connection. If that doesn't happen in a few seconds, you failed to get all the air out of the low-pressure side and will need to

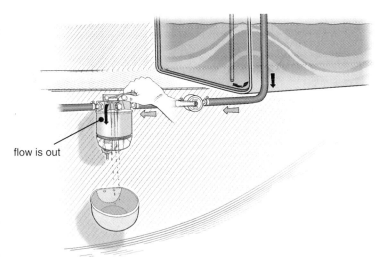

When the primary filter is below the level of fuel in the tank, fuel flows naturally toward the filter once flow has been established, purging air through the open bleed screw.

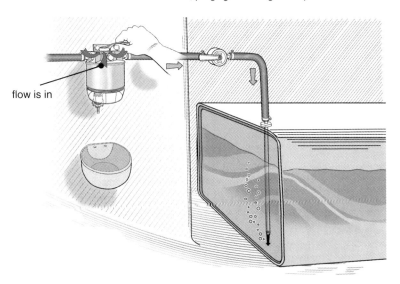

When the primary filter is above the level of fuel in the tank, opening the bleed screw will allow fuel in the line to flow back toward the tank, causing air to enter the fuel system through the bleed screw.

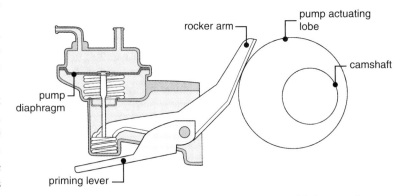

If the engine is stopped with the actuating lobe in contact with the pump's rocker arm, the manual lever will not pump fuel. Rotate the engine one revolution to place the rocker arm on the round portion of the cam.

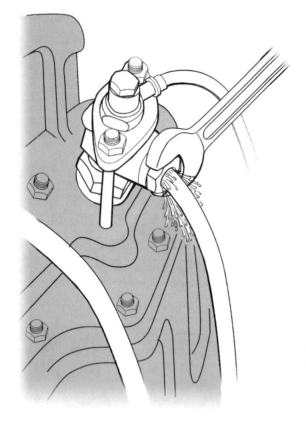

Bleed the system beyond the injection pump by loosening a delivery pipe nut at the injector and spinning the engine, allowing trapped air to escape with the spray of fuel.

go through the entire bleed sequence again. This is a not-uncommon result, so do not hesitate to rebleed.

If your second bleeding attempt is also a failure, disconnect the line from the lift pump to the secondary filter at the filter and submerge it in clean fuel. Operate the pump. If bubbles appear and fail to clear up, you have an air leak that you will have to locate. Check the primary filter gasket first, then all connections upstream of the lift pump.

Smoke Signals

Besides fuel, diesel engines need air, lots of air—the equivalent of about *nine dump-truck loads for every gallon of fuel consumed*—so clean or change the air filter element at regular intervals. Be sure none of your modification efforts restrict the free flow of fresh, cool air to the engine. If you repower for more horsepower, you may need to improve engine compartment ventilation to allow the new engine to breathe completely. The classic sign of air starvation is black smoke from the exhaust at high engine speeds.

When the fuel system is healthy, a marine diesel should emit little or no smoke from the exhaust outlet. We can draw some inferences about the fuel system—and other engine components—by paying attention to exhaust smoke. Black smoke indicates incomplete combustion, just what happens when the engine is starving for air. Black smoke can also result from other conditions—a dirty bottom, a dirty prop, the wrong prop, or too much auxiliary load—all bad for the health of your engine.

If the engine isn't overloaded and opening the engine compartment and/or cleaning the air filter fails to clear up the smoke, the problem is likely a defective injector or a restricted exhaust. If the exhaust elbow has not been cleaned in a year or more, checking this first might save pulling the injectors. Running the engine for long periods under light load—charging batteries, for example—quickly builds up restrictive deposits in both the exhaust manifold and the elbow. When exhaust gases cannot get out of the cylinders, fresh air cannot get in, hence the black smoke. Defective injectors will need to be professionally serviced or replaced.

White smoke is unburned fuel. White smoke can be normal at start-up, but it should clear quickly. Persistent white smoke usually signals a cylinder failing to fire. This can be due to low compression, but if the engine has not logged a lot of hours, defective injectors are again the likely culprit. Water in the fuel—either entrained or leaking from the water jacket—will also cause white smoke. To check for water in the fuel, wet a small strip of paper with fuel purged from a bleed screw, then burn the paper (safely!). If it pops, the fuel contains water.

Don't confuse white smoke with steam. Steam will rise and dissipate quickly, while smoke tends to hang around longer and stay closer to the water. Steam is normal in cold weather. Otherwise it is a sign that raw-water flow is inadequate.

So-called blue smoke is really white (or gray) smoke with a subtle blue tint. If you see a hint of blue, it means lubricating oil is finding its way into the combustion chamber. The normal cause is worn valve guides or worn cylinder walls and piston rings, but check the oil level before drawing that conclusion. Pressure from an overfilled crankcase can force oil up past the rings. A defective turbocharger seal will also spray oil into the cylinders.

TUNE-UP

There are still a significant number of old Atomic 4s (and a few Grays) competently pushing old boats in and out of creeks and channels or back home when the wind dies. If you are vigilant, a gasoline auxiliary can be a good shipmate, running more smoothly and quietly than a diesel. Unfortunately gas engines have two characteristics that make them less suitable. They depend on an electrical spark to run, and in the damp environment of a boat, this can lead to starting problems. However, the most serious defect is the risk of gasoline leaking into the bilge, where the fumes represent a real risk of explosion. Powerboaters still prefer gasoline to diesel by a wide margin, but their total dependence on the engine(s) tends to make them pay more attention to it (them). Sailors are notorious for ignoring the "beast" in the bilge. Ignore a diesel engine and it sulks in silence. Ignore a gasoline engine and it explodes.

That said, if you buy a 30- or 40-year-old boat with a sweet-running gasoline engine, you have to ask yourself if the previous owners, who all managed to keep from blowing themselves into the next life, were all smarter and/or more disciplined than you. If you think not, then there should be no reason why you cannot also learn the required measures to avoid disaster. If you are not so sure, repower with diesel.

Gasoline engines require periodic tune-ups to continue to perform well. Typically a tune-up comprises installing new spark plugs, replacing the ignition points and adjusting the gap, checking the ignition timing, and adjusting the carburetor.

Plugs

To remove and replace spark plugs you need a plug socket for your ratchet handle. A plug socket is a deep socket with a rubber insert to protect the porcelain part of the plug. Sockets come in more than one size, so take a new spark plug with you when you go to buy the socket. You probably need the traditional $1^3/_{16}$-inch.

Replace spark plugs one at a time to keep you from getting the wires confused. Pull the wire off the end of the plug. Unscrew the old plug, using an extension if it helps. Never assume the gap setting for the

Correct plug gap for an Atomic 4 and small Gray Marine engines is 0.035 inch.

new plug is correct out of the box. Consult the engine manual for the specified gap (0.035 for A4s and Grays) and check the new plug with a feeler gauge or a special gap gauge. Put a couple of drops of oil or—better still—antiseizing compound on the threads and install the new plug with your fingers. It should screw in easily. Tighten it, but not too much. You definitely don't want to strip the threads from the hole.

Points

Slip a screwdriver blade between the distributor cap and the mounting clips, and gently twist the screwdriver to release the clips. Lift off the cap and turn it upside down. If the copper terminals inside are not shiny, polish them with a small file. If they are badly pitted, replace the cap. At this writing, Atomic 4 parts remain available from Moyer Marine (www.moyermarine.com).

Pull the rotor from its shaft; polish its tip with a file or, if it is badly burned, replace it. Pull the point wire from its terminal, loosen the screw holding the breaker points, and lift them out of the distributor. Inserting the screw into the new points before you put them in place will make it easier to reinstall the screw. Snug this screw. Now rotate the engine and you will see the cam-shaped distributor shaft opening the points. This is made easier with a long break-over bar and a socket that fits the large nut in the center of the crankshaft. In the absence of such a nut, it is possible to rotate the engine—with the plugs removed so there is no compression—with a socket on the generator/alternator pulley nut or by rotating the prop shaft with the transmission in reverse. Stop the engine with the points resting on the apex of one of the high spots; this represents the widest opening of the points. Loosen the mounting screw just enough to allow the points to move. Locate the notch in the base of the points and the two metal bumps on the distributor plate, and use a slot screwdriver here to adjust the point gap. The bumps act as fulcrum points, allowing you to move the point base in either direction by twisting the screwdriver.

The point gap for newer Atomic 4s fitted with a Delco distributor is 0.025. The point gap for Prestolite distributors installed prior to around 1970 is 0.018 to 0.020. As an aside, a very worthwhile upgrade to newer Atomic 4s fitted with Delco distributors is a solid-state breakerless ignition system.

Check your manual for the specified gap for your engine. Using the corresponding feeler gauge, move the point base until you can just slide the feeler gauge between the points without moving the movable arm.

Tighten the screw, then check again, because turning the screw often alters the setting. Smear the cam lightly with Vaseline or the grease that came with the points. Put a single drop of oil inside the rotor and seat it on the shaft. Reinstall the distributor cap and snap the spring clamps in place.

Timing

Ignition timing is when the spark plug fires relative to the rotation of the engine. If it fires too soon, the combustion will take place while the piston is still on its way up, actually opposing that motion. If it fires too late, the opportunity to get the maximum power from the combustion is missed. Timing is adjusted by slackening a bolt or nut at the base of the distributor and rotating the distributor. The distributor shaft is unaffected by this movement, but you are moving the points, which are screwed to the distributor body. It is easy to see that if you move the points in the same direction the shaft rotates, the high point on the cam will reach the points later, causing ignition to be later. This is called retarding the timing. Turning the distributor in the other direction—opposite to the rotation of the distributor shaft—advances the timing.

A rough adjustment is accomplished by lining up the timing mark on the flywheel or the crankshaft pulley (depending on the engine) with a pointer in the engine. Universal, the Atomic 4 manufacturer, never put a timing mark on these engines, but when the flywheel roll pin is perfectly vertical and the number one cylinder—the one closest to the flywheel—is

on the compression stroke, the engine is at *top dead center* (TDC). This is the static setting for the timing of this engine, the point in the engine rotation when the breaker points should be just opening. The best way to determine if they are is with a 12-volt test light connected across the coil terminals and the ignition on. If you rotate the engine slowly, when the points break, the light will go off. If the roll pin is perfectly vertical, this is the correct static timing. You later "dial in" the timing of an Atomic 4 by loosening the clamp bolt and rotating the distributor slightly in both directions with the engine running at your usual cruising rpm, positioning the distributor for maximum rpm with the throttle setting unchanged.

If you don't have a test light, you can get the static setting close enough by inserting a single thickness of gift-wrap tissue paper between the breaker points. Pull gently on the tissue as you slowly rotate the engine. When the points release their grip on the tissue, stop rotating. Here again, if the timing is correct, the roll pin will be vertical, or on a different engine the pointer and the mark will be in line.

A more accurate way of adjusting the timing requires the use of a strobe timing light, a device that connects to the ignition wiring in such a way that the pulse of current that fires the spark plug in the number one cylinder flashes the light at the same instant.

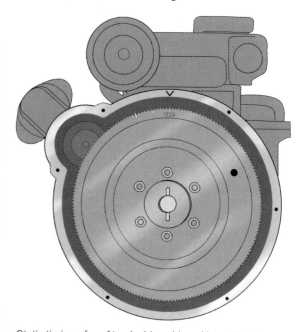

Static timing of an Atomic 4 is achieved by putting the number one cylinder at TDC, determined by positioning the roll pin at the center of the flywheel perfectly vertical. Owner-applied timing marks at the flywheel edge and a pointer on the engine allow for setting the timing with a strobe timing light.

From your disco days you can probably see the reason for this. When focused on the timing arrow the bright flash "freezes" the rotating timing mark. By turning the distributor while the engine is running at a specified speed, you can move the frozen mark until it lines up with the pointer, then tighten the clamp bolt to lock in the setting. In the case of the Atomic 4, you have to put your own pointer and mark. Keep in mind that the faster the engine is running, the earlier you need a spark to get the combustion to take place at precisely the right time. A mark at about 17 degrees before TDC will be about right for timing the Atomic 4 at 1600 rpm. A second mark at around 8.5 degrees should correspond to idle speed. This engine is so docile, however, that just adjusting the distributor for maximum rpm should deliver the same result without the need for a strobe.

Carburetors

The complexities of a common four-barrel carburetor with its jets, linkages, pumps, and valves are likely to seem incomprehensible to the novice mechanic. If you have a powerboat with a naturally aspirated MerCruiser, for example, you might educate yourself on tuning a four-barrel Weber, but there is no discredit in leaving this particular job to a mechanic. Sailors, however, do not face this issue. The carburetor on an old Atomic 4 is short on sophistication and even shorter on complexity. You are faced with only two adjustments—fuel mixture and idle speed. (In the interest of full disclosure, the main jet on some carburetors is also adjustable rather than fixed.)

The needle valve to adjust fuel mixture is a brass screw angled into the side of the carburetor. With the engine at normal operating temperature, set the throttle stop to fast idle—about 800 rpm—and turn the needle screw counterclockwise about $1/4$ turn. Turning the screw to the left opens the fuel jet and makes the mixture richer. Wait about 15 seconds to allow the adjustment to affect the engine. If the engine speeds up, give the screw another $1/4$ turn to the left. If it slows or becomes erratic, turn the screw clockwise back to the original setting and $1/4$ turn beyond. Continue to turn the screw every 15 seconds until further adjustments fail to increase engine speed, returning to the setting that yields the highest steady engine speed. Now turn the screw counterclockwise $1/8$ turn to offset the tendency of the setting to be too lean at slow speeds.

The throttle-stop screw is on the linkage and restricts the travel of the throttle. It is screwed against the stop to raise idle speed and backed off to lower it.

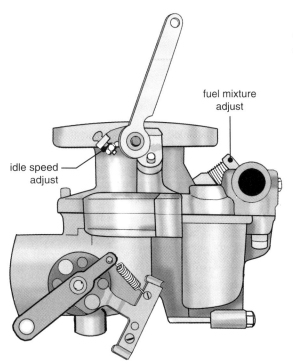

idle speed adjust

fuel mixture adjust

The Atomic 4 carburetor is short on complexity.

After you have adjusted the mixture, set the idle to about 600 rpm.

Carburetors should be dismantled and cleaned every couple of years. Disconnect the fuel line, release the control cables, remove the mounting nuts, and pull the carburetor from the manifold. Don't worry about damaging the mounting gasket; the rebuild kit you are going to buy will include a new one along with all the other gaskets and washers you need. Take a series of digital photos if you have a camera handy, then disassemble the carburetor, laying out the parts in order. You can also photograph each component removal to keep you straight. Soak all the parts that are not plastic in a powerful carburetor cleaner, using a brush on stubborn deposits. Use gasoline to clean the plastic parts. Make sure all old gasket material has been removed (including any left on the intake manifold). Dry the parts and, if you have compressed air available, blow out all the passages. Reassemble and reinstall, then adjust the mixture and the idle.

INJECTORS

There is no such thing as a diesel "tune-up." The only thing that might resemble it is servicing the fuel injectors and that is not something the owner can do properly. What you can do is remove the injectors and take them to an injection shop for cleaning and adjustment.

Before you remove them, clean all around the injector for reasons you already know. Disconnect the high-pressure fuel line. You may have to release it from the injection pump as well to get it out of the way. Also disconnect the return line. Do not lose any of the copper washers that seal these lines. Put plastic tape over the open connections.

The injector is probably held in place by a metal yoke clamped to the engine by nuts threaded onto a pair of studs threaded into the engine. (Some injectors screw directly into the engine.) Remove the nuts and you should be able to withdraw the injector assembly. If it does not come out easily, run penetrating oil around the outside and try again in an hour or two. Modest prying of the yoke near the body of the injector can do the trick but do not apply excessive force here. You may need to extract the studs so you can apply a twisting motion with a wrench on the flat sides of the injector while gently prying the injector up at the same time. You can also enlist the power of cylinder compression by spinning the engine with the starter, but reinstall the retaining nuts loosely before you do this to prevent the injector from blowing completely out of the engine.

The injector seats on a copper washer. Be sure you get this washer out of the hole.

Once the injector is out, do not disassemble it. Take the entire assembly to the injector shop. While the injectors are out of the engine, keep the openings covered. Get new copper seat washers when you pick up the serviced injectors. When you reinstall the injectors, torque the hold-down bolts evenly, using a torque wrench. Consult your manual for the correct torque. If your book does not provide this number, torque the bolts to 15 foot-pounds. When you reconnect the feed and return lines, they must

You can safely remove and install injectors, but except in an emergency, leave their servicing to an injector shop.

fit without any forcing. Thread both ends hand tight before finally tightening either.

VALVE ADJUSTMENT

Adjusting valve clearances is no more difficult than changing oil or replacing a pump impeller, but it feels different. This is the guts of the expensive engine you're mucking with. Opening the valve cover has the feel of surgery—disconcerting if you only feel qualified to dispense Band-Aids. Fortunately doing this job just once will get you past such misgivings.

Valves in internal combustion engines function exactly like the pop-up drain plug in a bathroom sink. When seated, the valve forms a gastight seal, but when it is lifted off the seat—by the press of the rocker arm on the valve's stem—gas can enter or exit the opening the valve plugs. The intake valves in carbureted engines admit a mixture of air and gas into the cylinder, but in fuel-injected engines—including all four-stroke diesels—intake valves let only air into the cylinder prior to ignition. After combustion, the open exhaust valve provides an exit for the hot gases.

When you remove the valve cover, you are going to find what looks like a row of little oilfield pumps. These are the *rocker arms,* and there will be two for every cylinder, one for the intake valve and one for the exhaust valve. One side of the rocker arm sits directly on the valve stem, and the other side has a screw through it that seats in a cup at the top of the *pushrod.* Valve clearance is adjusted by turning this screw. The bottom of the pushrod, which you cannot see, sits on a cylindrical *lifter* that rides on the camshaft. A lobe on the camshaft lifts the lifter with every revolution of the camshaft, which lifts the pushrod, which rocks the rocker arm, which forces the spring-loaded valve open. Big gasoline engines typically have "hydraulic" lifters, but diesels and small gasoline auxiliaries nearly all use solid lifters. That makes the connection between the valve and the cam rigid, which would be fine if temperature weren't a factor. But when these valve train components get hot they expand. We introduce clearance—sometimes called *lash*—to prevent this expansion from holding the valve open when it should be closed.

What happens when a valve fails to fully close? The obvious result is a loss of compression. If the valve leaks when the engine is cold, the engine will be reluctant to start. A leaking valve in a running engine robs the engine of power. Less obvious but more insidious, a valve depends on sitting fully and firmly on its seat to transfer heat to the water-cooled head. This is the valve's primary means of ridding

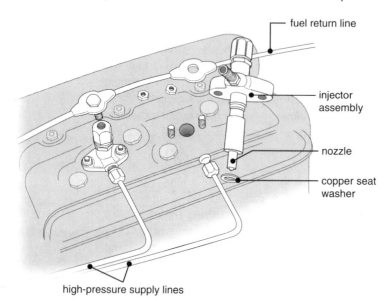

fuel return line

injector assembly

nozzle

copper seat washer

high-pressure supply lines

itself of the extreme heat of combustion. If it does not make solid contact with the seat, a burned valve is the inevitable and costly result.

Too much clearance has its own ill effects. The valve does not open fully, leaving the cylinder unable to "inhale" a full charge of air or to void all combustion gases—or both. The asthmatic engine will not deliver its rated power. Excess lash also causes a rocker arm to hammer the valve, subjecting it to repeated shock loading that can lead to a broken valve. The head of a valve dropping into a cylinder can destroy an engine in an instant.

It can take 500 or more hours of running time for valve clearances in a modern marine diesel to fall out of tolerance, but such expectations overlook Murphy's Law. Check valve clearances every 250 engine hours. If you think the valves "probably" don't need adjusting as long as they are quiet, *snap out of it!* The louder "ticking" of too much valve clearance does signal a need for attention, but valve and seat wear do not increase clearance; they decrease it. The engine may actually run quieter while expensive damage is occurring.

Getting Started

Start this job by looking in your engine manual to see what the valve settings are and if they are set *hot* or *cold*. Hope for cold! If under the heading of "Valve Adjustment," your owner's manual instructs you to "see your dealer"—which for an engine intended for a far-reaching boat strikes me as both unacceptable and mildly insulting—you will need to consult a service manual or other reliable source.

Usually the same clearance is specified for all valves, but the exhaust valves on some engines require more clearance. If this is the case with your engine, you will need to differentiate between intake and exhaust valves. If your manual does not provide a chart, you will be able to make this determination quite easily when you rotate the engine. We will come to that momentarily.

Before you open the valve cover, make sure the top of your engine is squeaky clean—like scrubbing before surgery. The cover is typically secured by two or more cap nuts. Remove these and carefully lift the valve cover straight up from the head. If it resists, do not pry it free or you will damage the mating surfaces. Operating the compression release levers, if your engine has them, will usually lift the cover. Otherwise give the corners of the cover—not the flat sides—a few short, upward smacks with a rubber mallet. If the cover sits on a cork gasket,

have a replacement at hand. If the gasket is rubber and you take care not to damage it, you can probably reuse it.

Finding TDC

You want to measure clearance when the associated lifter is riding on the circular part of the cam, not the lobe. Too often engine manuals unnecessarily complicate valve adjusting instructions by basing them on the TDC mark on the crankshaft pulley or the flywheel. You can do it that way, but if you understand the straightforward relationship between the valves and the piston, you can set the valves on any marine diesel without a manual at hand—as long as you know the correct clearance.

All you need to know is that at the end of the exhaust stroke, when the piston is moving toward the top of the cylinder, the intake valve begins to open before the exhaust valve fully closes. This is called valve overlap, and when it occurs, the piston is very near top dead center *for that cylinder,* but on the exhaust stroke. To check valve clearance, you need the piston at TDC on the compression stroke. You get there by simply rotating the crankshaft one full turn. This works on any cylinder without regard for its relationship to the other cylinders.

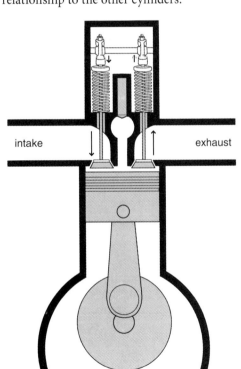

When the intake valve rocker is starting down before the exhaust valve rocker has reached the top of its upward motion, the two valves overlap. Rotating the crankshaft pulley one full revolution puts that cylinder at TDC on the compression stroke.

intake   exhaust

Rotate the Engine

You are going to rotate the engine by hand to position the camshaft appropriately, so to make sure the engine cannot start, leave the ignition switch off and secure the kill knob in the out position. It is imperative to rotate a diesel engine only in the correct direction, which in every marine diesel I know means turning the crankshaft pulley clockwise as you look at the front of the engine. Rotate the engine with a socket wrench and a long handle on the nut securing the crankshaft pulley. If the crankshaft pulley doesn't have a center nut, use the one on the alternator pulley. You may have to apply pressure to the belt to prevent slippage.

Rotate the engine slowly while you watch one pair of rocker arms. For one crankshaft rotation, they will be inactive. On the next rotation, the first arm to move depresses the exhaust valve. Before it "rocks" back completely, the second arm also rocks, pushing the intake valve open. If you overshoot—easy to do—do not try to back up. Rotate the crankshaft pulley shy of two complete revolutions to put you in front of the overlap again. Knowing what is coming should allow you to detect when the intake valve begins to open. Note that if you need to identify the exhaust valve because intake and exhaust clearances differ on your engine, in overlap *the valve closing is always the exhaust valve.* The one opening is the intake valve, in preparation for the downward intake stroke.

With the valves in overlap, put a positioning mark on the crankshaft pulley. Now rotate the pulley one full revolution to return to this mark and you will have the engine correctly positioned to check both valves on this cylinder. Rotate slowly because the engine will suddenly "release" as you pass beyond TDC.

Go, No-Go

Leave your wrenches in the toolbox and simply check the valve clearances first. If the specification is for 0.008-inch clearance, the 0.008 blade in your feeler gauge should slip though the gap while the 0.009 blade should not. Always use this go, no-go tactic for determining the valve clearance. Clearance is measured by the thickest blade to pass easily through the gap. Be careful to use the correct feeler gauge when intake and exhaust clearances differ.

Resetting valve lash is another job where three hands would be helpful. Put a six-point box-end wrench on the locknut and insert a screwdriver in the adjusting screw. Holding the screw in position, release the locknut. Now turn the adjusting screw while you slide the feeler gauge back and forth between the rocker arm and the valve stem. When the rocker arm begins to "pinch" the gauge, hold the screw in position and tighten the locknut wrist tight. Annoyingly, tightening the locknut nearly always alters the clearance setting. Measure the resulting clearance with the go, no-go method. If it is not correct, take the amount of change into account when you reset the valve. For example, if you set the clearance at 0.008 inch, but it ends up at 0.011 when you check it after tightening the locknut, try an initial setting of 0.005. Remember that too much gap will make the engine noisy and inefficient, whereas too little risks burned valves. Keep readjusting until you get it right.

Lash is correct when feeler of the specified thickness will just slip through the gap between the valve stem and the rocker arm.

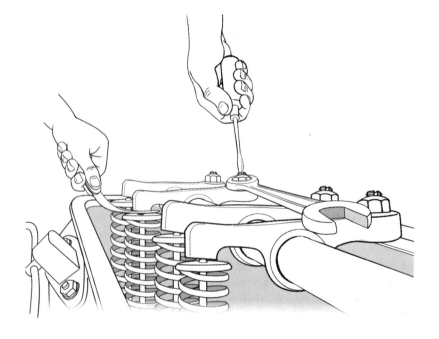

With both valves for this cylinder correctly set, rotate the engine to put the next cylinder into overlap, then around again to TDC on the compression stroke for that cylinder. Set this pair of valves, then move on until all valve pairs have been checked and, if necessary, adjusted.

Replace the valve cover, note the date and the engine hours in your maintenance log, and this job is complete.

COMPRESSION TESTING

When rotating your engine by hand, pay attention to how much force is required to rotate each cylinder through the compression stroke. It should be similar for all cylinders. A noticeable difference suggests a compression problem.

Diesel engines are entirely dependent on high compression in the cylinders. Gasoline engines use a spark to ignite the fuel, but it is the heat generated by compression that ignites diesel fuel. If cylinder compression falls below some critical level, ignition will not occur and the engine will not run.

If your engine has become difficult to start or seems to have less power, lost compression is one possible cause. Checking cylinder compression in a diesel engine requires a pressure gauge—at least 600 psi—and an adapter for your engine. The process is simple enough—replace the injector in one cylinder with the adapter, decompress the other cylinders, and give the engine half a dozen revolutions with the starter.

A mechanic familiar with what his or her gauge normally reads on a particular engine can draw some conclusions about engine condition from individual pressure readings, but for the rest of us, unless the needle is nearly at the bottom of the scale, the amount of pressure shown on the gauge has little significance. This is because it is affected by the volume of the gauge and adapter and by the speed of the piston. What you and I are interested in is comparative values. A healthy engine will give similar readings for all cylinders. Variations of as little as 20% will cause the engine to run noticeably rougher.

Relatively low compression in one or more cylinders suggests a problem in that cylinder—ring wear, a burned valve, a blown gasket, or a cracked head. You can determine whether the engine needs to be rebuilt or the head serviced by squirting a small amount of engine oil into the cylinder and testing it again. If the pressure increases dramatically, compression is being lost to ring and/or cylinder wear. If the reading is unchanged, the problems are in the head.

Warning: Although this method is used regularly by mechanics around the world, it is possible for the increased compression to cause the cylinder to fire, with terminal consequences for the pressure gauge. Stay well clear of the gauge when testing a cylinder "wet."

A more prudent course of action is to have a leakdown test performed on the engine. The mechanic will pressurize the suspect cylinder with compressed air, then determine if the air is escaping into the crankcase (rings and/or cylinder wall), the coolant passages (head gasket or cracked head), the intake manifold (intake valve), the exhaust system (exhaust valve), or an adjacent cylinder (head gasket).

Incorrect valve settings can also be the source of compression variations between cylinders, so always set the valves *before* administering a compression test.

MAJOR REPAIRS

When it comes to engine repairs, it is time to wake up and smell the coffee. No one *fixes* anything anymore. The offending part is *replaced* or *sent out*. You can do that.

If you are afraid you might screw up the repair, forget about it. Think about the last time you took your car to a "factory-trained" mechanic. You were charged a fair price, every problem was corrected, and you never had to take your car back to have the repair repaired. Yeah, right! Did you ever wonder how a well-known automaker expected to enhance its sales by spending millions to tell us what terrific mechanics its dealers have to fix the product when it breaks down? Would you buy a television from a company that touted the experience of its repair technicians? How about a pacemaker from a company that featured a scrub-wearing and wire-lead-gripping Mr. Goodknife?

I'm sorry, where were we? Engine repair, right? The number of different engines makes detailing specific repairs impossible, and I am not trying to make an engine mechanic out of you anyway. I am only trying to show you that if you want to repair your own engine, regardless of how extensive the repair, the process of dismantling and reassembly will be largely the same as what I have already detailed.

The starter fails. A mechanic will check the battery and the switch (which you should have done before calling a mechanic), then remove the three nuts that hold the wires to the solenoid and the two screws that fasten the starter to the engine, and pull the starter out of the engine. He will take it to a starter repair shop and pick it up when the repair is finished. Back on board, he slides it back in place, secures it with the two mounting screws, and reconnects the wires. Is there any part of this repair that requires special training?

Despite a tune-up, your gas engine runs poorly. With the help of a knowledgeable friend, you check the compression and discover it is low in two cylinders. You squirt motor oil into the cylinders, test them again, and find they still have low compression. Three components seal the cylinder—the head gasket, the piston rings, and the valves. The squirt of oil will momentarily seal worn rings, raising compression. If it did not, your problem is either the head gasket or valves. Either way, the head needs to come off. Admittedly this is more complicated than removing a starter, but most requirements are pretty straightforward. Everything attached to the head has to be removed, including intake and exhaust manifolds, and all the head bolts, most of them located under the valve cover, have to be loosened and extracted. Some requirements are more subtle. Coolant must be drained at least below the level of the head, and the head bolts should be released in a specific sequence. Reassembly, after you have the reconditioned head back from the machine shop, requires that each part is returned to its original position. You should not, for example, switch around pushrods even though they seem identical. And you must tighten the head bolts to a specific torque in a specific sequence. As long as you learn what to do to do the job right, you are likely to find the process is not that difficult.

Maybe you are wondering why you shouldn't just hire a mechanic. Despite a youth wasted making old cars dangerously fast, the truth is that if money were not a factor, today my pianist hands would never be soiled by engine grease. But money is a factor. There is also a second consideration. My boating often takes me far offshore, hundreds of miles from the nearest trained mechanic. It is a comforting feeling to know that if the engine quits, I can almost certainly get it going again.

There is more to being a competent engine mechanic than just skill with tools. You must be able to diagnose the problem. If you don't know what's wrong, you can spend a lot of time and money on unnecessary repairs. You would have been better off seeking professional assistance. With experience, engines and other mechanical devices will hold fewer mysteries. When you understand the problem, you can almost certainly make the repair.

If you do decide to be your own mechanic, the tool that will help you the most is a service manual—not the little owner's brochure that came with the engine, but the detailed manual supplied to service representatives. If there was not one aboard when you bought the boat, contact the engine manufacturer. Don't bitch about the cost; it will be worth every penny.

REPOWERING

Old boats have old engines. There comes a time when you have to either completely rebuild your old engine or replace it. Rebuilding has become so expensive that buying a new engine often makes better economic sense. When you consider that every part on a new engine is new—not just rings and bearings and such—a new engine is always the better choice for a boat you plan to cruise or keep. Even in a boat you expect to sell, a new diesel can raise the value of the boat more than the cost of the engine, particularly if you do the installation.

It would be great if you could just yank out the old engine, lower the new one onto the same mounts, and couple it to the existing shaft flange, but it rarely works that way. Different engines have different mount configurations, so besides relocating the new mounts, you may have to modify the engine bed and replace or shorten the propeller shaft. You also need to know that the new engine will fit into your engine compartment in a way that allows easy access for maintenance.

Selecting an engine that you have seen installed in a boat like your own can allay concerns about fit, and the engine supplier can provide you with all the engineering data. Still, modifying or replacing the engine bed and locating the new mounts so that when you set the engine in place it lines up perfectly with the prop shaft is not a task to be taken lightly. Expect the job to require at least 50 man-hours and be prepared for it to take twice that. The payback, besides personal satisfaction, is that doing it yourself reduces the cost by about half over having it done.

Is a new engine installation something you can do yourself? If by now you have discovered that you are reasonably handy, the answer is yes. The safety net here is that if you eventually decide you have been overly optimistic about your abilities or your commitment, you can always bail out and pay to have the installation completed. More likely you will encounter far fewer problems than you might have imagined and learn more than you might have expected. And, of course, there is the benefit of a new engine.

PLANNING

The detailed guidance for repowering that follows will certainly help you through the process, but you will have to resolve issues unique to your engine/boat combination for yourself. There is but one hard and fast rule for installing a new engine in an old boat: *the engine and shaft must be in precise alignment.* Everything else you make up as you go along.

Planning begins with determining how much horsepower you need. For planing boats the sky is the limit, but displacement hulls restrict the amount of power that will be useful. There are formulas for estimating power requirements based on displacement and waterline length, but I can save sailors a migraine. The answer is about 2 horsepower per 1,000 pounds of displacement. I know this because the only variable in these formulas is the speed-length ratio, which at least theoretically is about 1.3 for virtually all displacement sailboats. This is for smooth-water motoring, so you may want additional power for punching through waves, motoring against a breeze, or overcoming the drag of a foul bottom. Also be sure to use "real" displacement, meaning with full tanks and all gear, supplies, and crew aboard.

Since you are *re*powering, you can also deduce your power requirement empirically. How satisfactory was the old engine? If, for example, your old Atomic 4 was anemic against a breeze, you need more than 30 horsepower. On the other hand, if you never saw the tachometer above 2,000 rpm, a look at the Atomic's output curve will show that you have been getting along on about 15 horsepower.

It is common practice to factor in additional horsepower for engine-driven accessories, such as a high-output alternator, a refrigeration compressor, or a watermaker, but I think this is unnecessary and even undesirable except for engines under 10 horsepower. At less than full throttle, the propeller absorbs considerably less horsepower than the engine can produce, so plenty of extra power is available. If your old engine is a diesel, estimate the horsepower you actually use underway by multiplying your average fuel consumption in gallons per hour by 16; 1 gallon of diesel fuel will produce around 16 horsepower for 1 hour. If, for example, your usual consumption is 0.5 gallon per hour, you are only using about 8 horsepower. The difference between this number and the continuous horsepower rating of the engine is unused capacity. It just makes sense to use this excess before adding dedicated capacity. Loading the engine more heavily more of the time also extends its life. On those rare occasions when you want all the engine's power available to the prop, it is a simple matter to turn off the auxiliary loads.

After you arrive at your target horsepower, the next choice is whose engine to buy. Today's engines are nearly all physically smaller than older engines of similar or slightly less horsepower, so the primary issue is likely to be fit rather than size. With your only imperative being getting the engine and shaft in precise alignment, the critical fit issue is the location of the output flange.

With battens, a tape measure, and a few body contortions, you should be able to determine the height of the shaft relative to the engine bed. While you are bent like that, also measure the length, individual width, and center-to-center width of the bed stringers. Wait, don't straighten up yet. How far below the stringers can the engine extend? How much room do you have above the stringers? Now get all these dimensions on paper, and you are ready to qualify or rule out any engine you may be considering.

Access is another concern. Will you be able to service the starter without removing the engine? Will there be room above the valve cover for an upturned oil container? If your engine compartment has primary access on one side, it would be good to have filters, pumps, and dipsticks on that side.

When you begin to zero in on a particular engine, try to ascertain its reputation for reliability. You may also want to investigate the availability of parts, especially if you envision either a distant cruise or a long relationship with this engine.

Surely by now I don't need to deflect you from contemplating a seawater-cooled engine. In fact, let me caution you about allowing economy in any form to have any significant influence on your decision. If the best engine costs $2,000 more than the cheaper alternative, that works out to $100 a year amortized over a 20-year engine life, insufficient to support a compromise. This should not, however, discourage you from negotiating for the best price on the engine you want.

BUY THE BOOK

After you determine what engine you intend to install, but before you place your order, get the dealer to sell you an installation manual for that engine. Not only will the manual's illustrated, step-by-step instructions provide reassurance now and guidance later for the actual installation, it will also be a treasure trove of helpful information—shaft and prop recommendations, detailed engine specifications, and complete wiring diagrams. With a yellow highlighter in hand, read this manual from cover to cover. It will save you the discomfort of uncertainty and maybe the misery of error.

Next, go to a home supply store and buy a sheet of the cheapest foam insulation board available and a roll of duct tape. The installation manual will provide all essential engine dimensions, but you are likely to find these hard to reconcile in three dimensions. The solution to this is a three-dimensional model of the

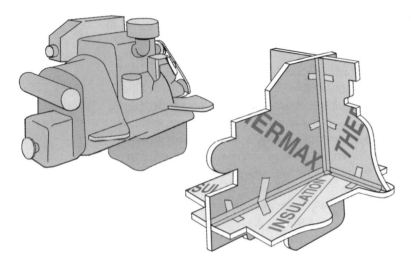

Construct a three-dimensional model of your engine from foam insulation board.

of the engine moves aft if you bolt it to the existing shaft. It is almost always better to move the weight toward the center of the boat by positioning the engine as far forward as possible, but this requires a new, longer shaft. A larger-diameter shaft may also be indicated if the new engine is more powerful than the old one. Having the boat in the water makes it more likely that you will resist shaft replacement.

Even if the new engine mates perfectly with the old shaft, you should still pull the shaft and inspect it for wear and corrosion. And while the shaft is out, it is a good time to replace the Cutless bearing and service the stuffing box. You may also want to replace the hose that connects the stuffing box to the stern tube. You won't do any of these tasks if the boat is in the water.

OUT WITH THE OLD

Take a few digital photos of the existing engine installation, and mark the old shaft where it exits the hull to help you position it later or determine the length of your new shaft. Now follow earlier instructions to remove the prop and extract the shaft from the coupling flange. Slide the shaft out completely and set it aside. If the rudder prevents you from removing the prop shaft, this will be your first individual problem to resolve. You may be able to extract the shaft from inside the boat once the engine has been removed.

Even if you do not intend to replace the stuffing box, release the aft pair of clamps and twist the hose free of the stern tube. You need unfettered access to the stern tube for the alignment process.

The web of cables, wires, and hoses connected to the old engine looks complicated, but take heart. Getting the engine free and out is far easier than you imagine and very satisfying. To avoid unwanted drama, unclamp the positive battery cable(s) first and remove it (them) from the battery post(s).

You are almost certain to have to reroute the exhaust plumbing, so removing the exhaust system in its entirety will give you better access, make cleaning and painting the engine space easier, and give you a clean slate for routing the exhaust from your new engine.

If your boat has a heat-exchange water heater, disconnect the two hoses that lead to it from the engine and connect them together with a nipple. You will separate this connection later and completely drain the engine circuit of the heater before you connect it to your new engine to avoid mixing old and new coolant, but leaving coolant in the exchanger for now reduces the potential for corrosion. The only remaining hose connection to the engine is probably to the inlet side of the raw-water pump. If you have an old-style raw-water filter, here is your opportunity to

engine, which you are going to construct by cutting side, front, and rear profiles from the insulation board and assembling them egg-crate style with the duct tape. The model need not be pretty, only a reasonably accurate rendering of length, width, height, the locations of the engine mounts, and the center of the drive flange. Set your model aside for the moment.

If time is a concern, you can order your engine before you start, having it ready to install as soon as the old one is out of the way, but if you have time available, it is better to postpone consummating the purchase until the old engine is gone and you have had the opportunity to discover overlooked fit issues with your new model. With forewarning your dealer can probably deliver an engine to you in a week or less after you finalize the order—which means sending money. You can use this time to clean and paint the engine compartment and perhaps to reconstruct the engine bed.

HAULOUT

If you are rebuilding rather than repowering, removing and reinstalling the engine can be done with the boat in the water. This can even be the "easy" way, since having the deck and dock essentially level reduces the lifting required. But if you are installing a new engine, do it with the boat out of the water. There are two compelling reasons for this.

First is our mantra for this job: *The engine and shaft must be in precise alignment.* The process of aligning the engine is easier and infinitely more accurate if you can use a centering line that passes through the stern tube. I am going to explain this technique in detail, but it virtually insures a near-perfect alignment right out of the box, saving hours of tedious adjustment.

A second reason to have the boat out of the water is to thwart human nature. Engineering advances have resulted in shorter transmissions, so the weight

replace it with something better. Disconnect the inlet plumbing from both the engine and the seacock, and toss the whole mess.

Close the fuel shutoff, *then* remove the fuel line from the inlet side of the fuel pump, sticking it into a jug to catch the inevitable dribble. If you are going to upgrade your primary filter, remove the old one now.

Detach the throttle, shift, and kill cables next. If your existing controls will not be compatible with the new engine, go ahead and remove them, along with their associated clamps, supports, and mechanisms.

What do you do with all those wires connected to the engine? Here is the reality. Your new engine is going to come with a plug-together harness and a new instrument panel. The only existing wires that will be reconnected to the new engine are the battery cables. The exception to this is a smart regulator or add-on meters, which you will need to disconnect and reinstall on the new engine. Otherwise you can simply clip your engine free. All of the cut wires will lead one way or another to either the old instrument panel or the ignition switch. When you remove these, your engine space should end up free of all wiring.

Unbolt the mounts from the engine bed, and the old engine should be free. Before you move it, however, empty the oil from the engine and transmission and drain out the coolant to minimize spillage if you tilt the engine while lifting it out of the cabin. You may also need to remove the alternator and other bolt-ons to allow the engine to pass through the engine hatch or companionway.

One do-it-yourself way of getting the engine out of the engine compartment is to slide it out on a long 2 × 12. Wedge the board under the engine, then lift and support the forward end to lift the mounts clear of the beds. This allows the engine to be pushed with a jack or pulled with a come-along out into the main cabin, sliding on its pan. There it can be lifted up through the companionway, either with a crane or using a block and tackle attached to the main boom.

MEASURE TWICE

Now is the time to make sure you have not overlooked any fit issues. This is where your foam engine model repays the effort. Start by lowering it through the companionway. Is there plenty of clearance, or do you need to tilt it to get it through the opening? What about through the engine hatch? Do the mounts sit on the engine bed or at least where you anticipated them? Is there going to be enough space between the flywheel housing and the hull, between the top of the engine and the cockpit sole, between the alternator and a cockpit drain hose? Will the new engine

sit farther forward than the old one? If you need to modify the engine bed, your featherweight "engine" will prove invaluable. Mark connection points on it, and it will also help you visualize the configuration of the new exhaust system and the routing of fuel lines and control cables.

When you are satisfied that the real engine will hold no surprises, it is time to call your dealer and finalize your order.

FUEL TANK ISSUES

Don't overlook the fuel tank. If you are replacing a gasoline engine, the existing fuel tank might be galvanized. A galvanized tank must *never* be used to hold diesel fuel. It will flake particles of zinc into the fuel that will block filters and injectors. You must replace a galvanized tank.

If the tank isn't galvanized but you will have to remove the engine to replace it, now is the time for a critical assessment. Replacing it now might be a case of "a stitch in time." At the very least, pressure-test the existing tank. If your deck fill is similar to the one on my boat, a 1¼-inch threaded PVC plumbing plug will thread into it. Drill a hole in the plug and install a standard tire valve. Clamp short lengths of fuel hose to the outlet and vent fittings, then squeeze these hoses airtight with a clamp or Vise-Grip pliers. Half a dozen pumps from a bicycle pump should put the tank under light pressure. *Never* put more than about 3 pounds of pressure in the tank. If the tank holds pressure overnight, it is leak free (at the moment).

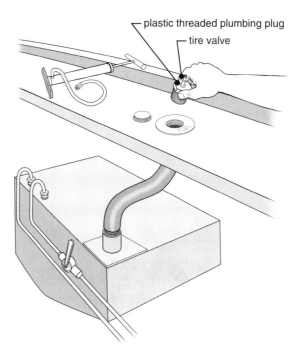

plastic threaded plumbing plug
tire valve

A tire valve mounted in a threaded PVC plumbing pipe plug will allow you to pressure-test your fuel tank.

The next issue is what kind of sludge is lying at the bottom of the tank. You do not want to feed this to your brand-new engine. If the tank has good access, you can scrub the tank clean with lint-free rags stapled to a length of wooden dowel, although you will find this to be a tedious process. If professional tank cleaning is available, that will be a better option.

Converting a gas tank necessitates an additional fitting for the return of excess fuel. This is easily accommodated with a T-fitting at the vent line connection. Return fuel is hot and should not go directly back to the engine, so do not add the return line connection to the pickup fitting.

FINDING THE PROP LINE

If you will be modifying the engine bed, it is essential for the mounting surface to be at the correct height relative to the prop shaft. This is accomplished by stretching a string through the stern tube and across the engine space. Outside, create a toggle by threading the string through a hole drilled through the center of a short stick and tying a stopper knot. Inside, tie the string to a heavy weight and hang it over a notched board clamped across the engine hatch opening. By moving the notched board up and down and side to side and making finer adjustments to the toggle, you can position the string in the exact center of the stern tube at both ends. This is the centerline of the prop shaft, and it must also be the centerline of the engine's driveshaft.

Assuming all the engine mounts on your new engine are the same distance above or below the driveshaft centerline, this string also marks the correct incline for the engine stringers. If your boat is sitting level side to side, you can project this incline onto the existing stringers with a bubble level. Adding or subtracting the specified mount distance above or below the driveshaft centerline will give you both the correct incline and the correct height. If the existing rails are too narrow or too far apart, you will have to trim, supplement, or replace as required, maintaining the height and incline projected from your centerline string.

Engine mounts are routinely attached to the bed with lag screws into the wood core of the stringers, but the preferred method is to through-bolt a steel angle

A taut string centered at both ends of the stern tube projects the centerline of the prop shaft.

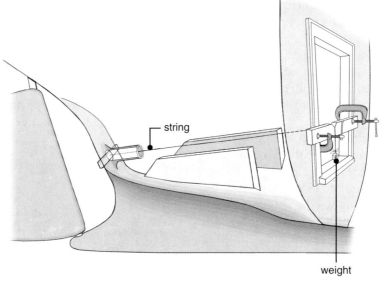

Engine mounts should be through-bolted to the engine bed rather than lag-screwed to the top.

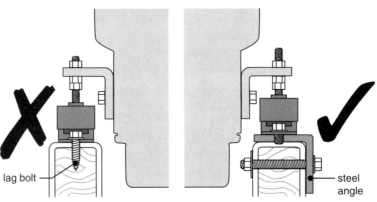

to the rails, then tap or through-bolt the mounts to the horizontal leg of the angle. If you plan to mount your new engine this way, take the additional height of the angle into account when configuring the rails.

ALIGNING THE ENGINE

To eliminate any need to move the heavy engine onto the bed until you are ready to bolt it in place, cut a flat piece of ¹/₂-inch plywood the specified length and width of the engine to create a simple jig. Mark a fore-to-aft centerline, then, letting the aft edge of the jig represent the mating surface of the drive flange, measure along the centerline, then perpendicular to it to locate *exactly* the four holes for the flexible mounts. Drill these to the same diameter as the holes in the engine brackets they represent.

Complete the jig by attaching perpendicular pieces on the centerline at both ends. These will be attached to the bottom or the top, according to whether the bottoms of the engine-mount brackets are above or below the driveshaft. Drill a ¹/₄-inch hole in both projecting pieces on the centerline and below or above the *bottom of the jig* at the distance between the shaft line plane and the bottom of the engine mount brackets as specified in the engine drawing. These are alignment holes and the centering string will run through them. Saw a horizontal cut into both holes so you can fit and remove the jig without dismantling the string.

When the engine arrives, bolt the supplied mounts to your plywood jig and set this assembly on the engine bed. Re-rig the string, centering it in both ends of the stern tube and guiding it through the saw cuts into the jig's ¹/₄-inch alignment holes. Slide the jig fore and aft and side to side to position the mounts where you want them. Keeping the mounts parallel to the centerline and the jig level side to side, turn the engine mount adjusting nuts—the ones underneath—to raise (or lower) the jig until the centering string is in the center of both holes. Trace the mount holes onto the stringer. Lift the jig out of the way and carefully drill the holes. Tap them if you are attaching the mounts with machine screws.

Remove the mounts from the jig and—without turning the adjusting nut—bolt them to the corresponding mount bracket on the engine. A word of caution here: even though the mounts look identical, there may be a difference in the elasticity between front and rear, so make sure you position them correctly on the jig to start.

Once you have the engine in the main cabin, getting it back over the engine beds is the reverse of

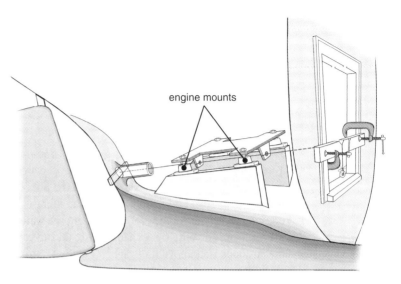
engine mounts

Use a plywood alignment jig to position the engine mounts in advance.

dragging it out, except that you should build a skid of plywood and cleat stock on which to sit the pan so you will not damage the paint. When the mounts line up with the drilled holes, install the screws and snug them down.

NEW SHAFT?

The installation manual will recommend shaft diameter, but the rule of thumb is ¹/₁₄ of prop diameter. This assumes bronze or stainless steel. An Aquamet shaft can be up to 20% smaller. Before you order a larger shaft, be sure you can buy a cutless bearing to fit it, but with the shell diameter of your existing bearing. Otherwise you will have to replace the stern tube, a bigger job than you might want to take on. A larger shaft will also necessitate a new stuffing box, which your prop shop can supply, complete with new hose.

If it is a longer shaft you need, determine the correct length by temporarily bolting the shaft half of the new coupling to the drive flange. Insert the old shaft into the stern tube to the mark you made before extracting it. Now measure from the interior face of the flange to the end of the old shaft to determine how much additional length you need. If you plan to insert a flexible coupling in the drivetrain, take that into account when determining the length. Prop shops often designate shaft length to the small end of the taper (SET), so be careful that you tell them exactly how you arrived at your measurements. A drawing is a good idea. Unbolt the shaft coupling and take it to the prop shop with you to have it "fit and faced." If you are reusing your old prop, have it reconditioned—and rebored if you have increased the shaft size.

With all the drive parts in hand, install the new Cutless bearing, quad-clamp the new stuffing box in place, insert the new shaft, and install the new flange. Now you can test your alignment. If the couplings mate with a satisfying thunk, you have done everything right. All that remains is to dial in the alignment as detailed earlier. It won't hurt to get it as close as possible now, but you are going to need to recheck it after the boat is back in the water.

LOOSE ENDS

From here on you won't need any guidance from me. You will install the instrument panel in a dry location, install a shift and throttle control if the old one is not compatible, and install the coolant subtank if one came with the engine. You will mount the water-lift muffler and route the exhaust hose, taking care that it loops well above the waterline before exiting the hull and includes an antisiphon valve or a vent. You will connect the raw-water line; attach the fuel supply; and hook up the shift, throttle, and kill cables. You will plug together the instrument panel harness and finally attach the battery cables.

After you fill the engine and transmission with the specified oils, the header tank and the subtank with a 50-50 coolant mix, and the fuel tank with fresh diesel, all you will need to run the engine is a flow of raw water. My tool kit includes a short length of hose that is loose slip fit into my intake through-hull for just this purpose. It has a female hose connection at one end and a shutoff valve in the middle. This method is infinitely easier than submerging the disconnected pickup in a bucket and keeping the bucket full with a garden hose, but you must take care not to force water past the raw-water pump, risking filling the exhaust and eventually the cylinders. With a helper adjusting the shutoff to provide just enough flow for some water to trickle back out the intake through-hull, this will not be a risk.

Get some oil to the bearing surfaces before putting them under load by spinning the starter for about 5 seconds with the kill knob pulled out. Shove the knob in and the engine should fire off. As long as you are confident that your helper is opening the water supply valve enough to maintain a slightly positive pressure in the intake line, don't get too nervous

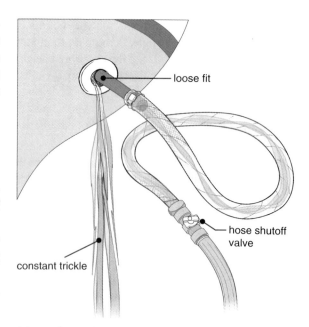

A loose-fit supply hose can make water available to the raw-water pump for running the engine with the boat out of the water. Fill the inlet hose but do not pressurize it. A helper must adjust the flow to maintain just a modest trickle from the through-hull.

if no water comes out of the exhaust immediately. It can take a minute or two to fill the empty muffler enough to submerge the outlet. After the engine clatters for a moment, it will settle into a satisfying purr. A sweeter sound it is hard to imagine.

WORTH THE EFFORT?

Lower levels of irritation and worry are intrinsic benefits of a new engine, and installing it yourself offers some bonuses. There is, of course, the pocketful of money you will have saved. Doing it yourself lets you determine the level of workmanship. You can also expect a satisfying sense of accomplishment. But perhaps the biggest advantage is an immediate intimacy with your new engine. The knowledge of how all the components work together and what they need from you to keep working provides a matchless basis for a long and happy symbiosis.

CHAPTER TEN

Chips and Shavings

*"People love chopping wood.
In this activity, one immediately sees results."*
—ALBERT EINSTEIN

The emergence of fiberglass as the dominant material in pleasure-boat construction has not eliminated the need for woodworking skills. On the decks of fiberglass boats you can find wooden handrails, hatch frames, coamings, toe rails, and tillers. Indeed, the surface of the deck may be wood overlay. Below, many interior fittings—bulkheads, sole, furniture, shelves, ceiling, and trim—will be constructed of wood.

This chapter *is* about working with wood, but it is *not* about repairing ribs or replacing planking. It does not contain a comparison of steam-bent versus laminated frames nor any other explanation of structural components. To me, carlings is a beer, knees are troublesome leg joints, and breasthooks are some sort of frightful medieval torture implement. The prevalent uses of wood in the construction and reconstruction of fiberglass boats (aside from as a core material, which we dealt with back in Chapter 6) are interior accommodations and exterior trim. We will focus on these two areas.

PLYWOOD

If asked to name the principal wood found on your boat, you would probably say teak or mahogany. Few of us would say pine, yet there is almost certainly 20, 50, or 100 times more pine aboard your boat than teak or mahogany. Bulkheads, bunks, settees, counters, cabinets, tables, and cabin soles are constructed of thin plies of pine glued together—plywood.

Why plywood? The builder was saving money at your expense again, right? Not this time. Plywood is just as common in multimillion-dollar yachts whose owners can easily afford to pay for the best. It is widely used because it has advantages over solid wood.

One advantage is strength. Wood cells are long, tubular structures that run vertically in the tree. Since the foliage at the top of a tree depends on moisture and nutrients gathered by the root system, it is not hard to imagine wood cells as bundles of microscopic soda straws. The cells themselves are very tough, but they are held together by a natural adhesive substance called lignin, which is comparatively weak. As a result, wood is much stronger with the grain than across it.

You can confirm this by clamping 3 inches of a 6-inch length of 1 × 6 in a bench vise. If you orient the grain vertically, all smacking the extended half with a hammer will do is aggravate your tennis elbow. But rotate the board 90 degrees and a hammer blow will split it like a potato chip. In the manufacture of plywood this inherent weakness of wood is counteracted by orienting the grain of each ply perpendicular to that of the previous ply, yielding a wood product that is rigid and strong in both directions and virtually splitproof.

A second advantage of plywood is its stability. Wood is *hydroscopic*, meaning it readily takes on and gives up moisture. When the cells absorb moisture, they expand, causing the wood to swell. As the wood dries, it contracts, often checking, cracking, and warping. The marine environment can subject wood to large and repeated changes in moisture content.

Moisture content affects the diameter of the wood cells but has little effect on their length, meaning that wood tends to swell in width but not in length. Because of this, the crossed-grain configuration of plywood tends to oppose any swelling or shrinkage that a single wood ply might undergo. This "balanced" construction makes plywood much less likely to warp, check, or crack than solid wood.

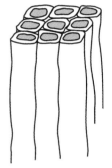

Wood cells.

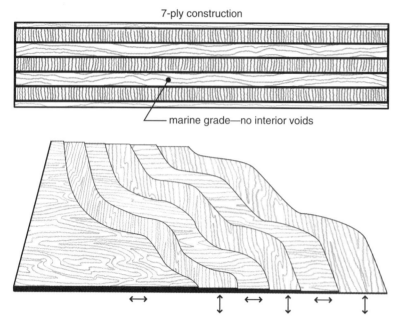

7-ply construction

marine grade—no interior voids

The grain of each ply is perpendicular to those on either side. This makes plywood warp resistant and strong in both directions.

any major changes to the accommodations in your old boat. You will also find plywood well suited for a vast array of smaller enhancements.

Besides being strong and stable, plywood has the additional advantage of being wide, a characteristic that makes it ideal for large surfaces such as counters, cabinets, and bunks. Plywood has another characteristic that endears it to boatowners: it's cheap. You might disagree with this characterization if you buy a sheet of teak plywood, but cost is relative and the plywood will be far less expensive than an equivalent amount of solid teak.

SELECTING THE CORRECT GRADE

Choosing the right plywood for the job can help to hold the cost down. As previously alluded to, regular plywood is usually made from pine, commonly Douglas fir, which is not really a fir. Pine or fir, conifer trees are known as softwoods. Softwood plywood is graded and given a letter designation of A through D, with A signifying the best quality and D the poorest. (Actually there is a grade N that is superior to A but you are unlikely to encounter it.) The grade, however, pertains to the surface veneer *only*. Grade A-A plywood is surfaced on both sides with the best-quality veneer, but the inner plies may be pieced and patched grade C. Consequently, the difference in grade A-A plywood and grade A-C, which also has inner plies of grade C, may only be in the appearance of one side. If that side is not exposed, there is little point in paying extra for the more attractive surface ply.

Plywood is also classified as interior or exterior, the latter including marine grade. Exterior plywood is bonded together with waterproof adhesives and

Plywood is nothing new. The ancient Chinese (no surprise) used the plywood principle in furniture construction. Likewise, early Egyptian furniture reveals plywood construction. Perhaps more interesting, Egyptian mummy cases were fabricated of plywood and veneer. However, it was not until the 1870s with the French invention of the rotary veneering lathe, a machine that *peeled* logs like unrolling a spool of paper, that mass-produced plywood became a possibility.

Use in marine applications had to wait another 60 years for the development of a waterproof glue. Today plywood is the dominant wood product in boat construction. It is the material you will use in

Regular exterior-grade plywood will have voids and butted end-grain joints in interior plies. Neither are allowed in plywood carrying a marine rating.

7-ply construction

interior ply

surface veneer or face ply

exterior grade—inner ply voids

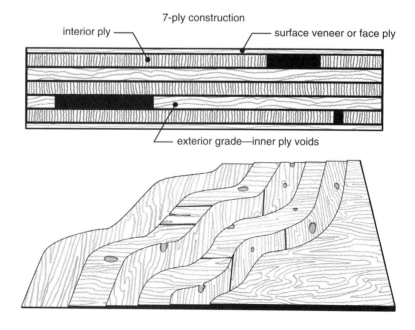

is well suited for the marine environment. Interior plywood is not waterproof and should *never* be used for any purpose aboard a boat. Do not think you can protect the wood by sealing it, painting it, or even sheathing it with fiberglass. The cost of such treatment will be greater than the savings on the plywood, and moisture will eventually penetrate anyway. When it does, interior plywood will flake apart.

To understand the difference between regular exterior plywood and what is known as marine grade, you need to understand that unlike the surface plies, inner plies of standard plywood are not necessarily solid. Smaller pieces are butted together to form the inner plies, and there is often space between the pieces, causing small voids in the plywood. For most uses such voids are of no consequence, but for the original purpose of marine plywood—hull construction—voids are intolerable. Marine plywood is free of voids and permits no butted end-grain joints; all plies are grade B or better. Inner plies are solid in hull-grade marine plywood.

Should you pay the extra money for marine plywood? It depends on how you are using it, but in most cases the answer is no. For shelves, dividers, counters, and bunks, marine plywood offers no advantages over regular exterior plywood. Buy grade A-A exterior plywood if you need to finish both sides, A-B or A-C if only one side will be finished.

HARDWOOD PLYWOOD

For bulkheads and interior furniture you may want to consider hardwood plywood. Similar in construction to standard Douglas fir plywood, hardwood plywood is veneered on one or both sides with a variety of decorative hardwoods. Mahogany and teak are the "classic" boat woods, but they are by no means the only possibilities. Lighter (in color) woods like oak and ash can brighten and expand a small cabin. I recently went aboard a Beneteau with a chestnut interior that was quite striking.

Properly finished, hardwood plywood has the look of fine furniture—not surprising since much of today's furniture is manufactured from this material. It comes in various types, but the only one appropriate for marine use is Type I, which is laminated with waterproof adhesive. The other types are for interior applications.

Hardwood plywood is also manufactured in several grades. Premium Grade #1 is the best, with no defects in the surface ply, matched veneer, and no contrasts of color. Good Grade #1 also avoids surface contrasts. Sound Grade #2 is still defect free but color and grain may not match. The remaining grades have surface defects and are probably not of interest.

OTHER SHEET MATERIALS
PANELING

"Wood" paneling is the thin wood-grain sheets you nail over the wallpaper in the spare bedroom to convert it to a den. Paneling is manufactured in a broad range of qualities. The least expensive are little more than contact paper over cardboard, whereas the best are exquisite wood veneer over thin plywood. All are intended for interior use, but since they are decorative and not structural in nature, they may have uses aboard—such as ceiling or liner panels, for example.

FIBERBOARD

Also known as hardboard and Masonite, fiberboard is available in exterior grades with a tough melamine surface. It is not a very attractive material but it can be used for drawer bottoms and locker dividers.

DOORSKINS

Essentially single-ply plywood, doorskins are another sheet material that can find good uses aboard. These thin (typically $3/32$- or $1/8$-inch) panels are inexpensive and available at almost any lumberyard. Commonly cedar or lauan, doorskins can be *cold-molded*—laminated in place with epoxy adhesive—to form strong curved surfaces.

PARTICLEBOARD

Particleboard, or chipboard, is used extensively in home cabinet work because it is cheap and has very little tendency to warp. Covered with decorative laminate, it serves admirably—as long as you keep it dry. But when it gets wet, particleboard literally disintegrates. *There are no legitimate uses for particleboard aboard a boat with less than 10 feet of freeboard.*

SOLID WOOD

Solid wood is also graded, but in most cases you can simply pick out the pieces that suit you from among those in the bin at the lumberyard. You should be looking for straight, flat boards with fine grain. Similar coloration will allow you to edge-glue boards into wider panels without the joint being obvious.

Look at the end of the board. If the growth rings are short, almost vertical curves from the top to the bottom, the board was quartersawn. If the ring lines form sweeping arches from edge to edge, the board was plain-sawn. Boards that are quartersawn shrink about half as much as plain-sawn boards, and they have less tendency to "cup."

Moisture content is another consideration. Green lumber is about half water so drying is required. When

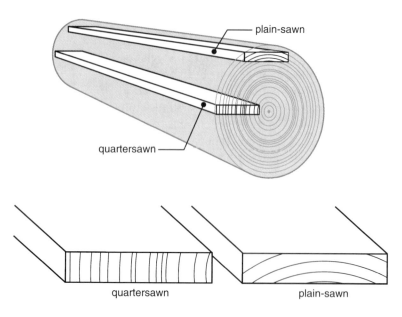

Quartersawn boards cup and twist less than plain-sawn.

the moisture content drops below 30%, the wood begins to shrink. Air-drying is preferable, but most wood is kiln-dried because it gets the wood from the mill to the MasterCard more quickly. If you were building furniture for your home, the ideal moisture content would be between 6 1/2% and 8%, but that may be too dry for boat furniture. If the wood is too dry, it will absorb moisture from the air and swell, causing surfaces to buckle, doors and drawers to jam, and joints to split. Too much moisture in the wood means that it will continue to shrink, cracking, warping, and pulling seams apart.

As long as the wood has been dried, you do not need to be especially concerned about the precise moisture content if you are using solid wood for trim, handrails, or other stand-alone items only. But if your plans are for extensive joinery, moisture content is extremely important.

Determining moisture content is not difficult if you have a sensitive kitchen or postage scale. Buy a single board and cut a small section from the center (the wood will be drier near the ends). Weigh the piece carefully to the nearest fraction of an ounce. Now place it in an oven at about 200°F. Periodically remove the wood from the oven and weigh it. When it stops losing weight, it is completely dry. To determine the initial moisture content percentage, divide the weight lost (the initial weight minus the dry weight) by the dry weight and multiply by 100.

An initial moisture content of about 8% for interior joinery and about twice that for exterior trim will probably minimize swelling and shrinking problems, but climate, heating, and whether your boat is "wet" or "dry" might alter this. If you are doing extensive reconstruction, cut a piece from the wood being removed, which

is presumably in equilibrium with the environment aboard your boat, and determine its moisture content. That will be the correct content for the new wood. If the difference is large, you may want to store the new wood aboard for a few months before you use it.

The type of wood you need will hinge on its intended use. Teak has the reputation, not undeserved, of being the best choice for boat trim. It is a beautiful wood but it is its resistance to rot that makes it so popular aboard boats. Mahogany's popularity stems from its strength, durability, and beauty, but it must be protected with varnish or polyurethane. When similarly protected, scores of other, perhaps nontraditional, woods are equally suitable for use aboard boats, particularly as interior trim.

For framing and cleat stock, do not buy the cheapest wood you can find. That will be *construction-grade* lumber, and aboard a boat it will warp and rot to beat the band. Clear fir is an excellent choice for a framing material and is especially compatible with fir plywood. It is commonly available and not expensive.

TOOLS

Like quality mechanic's tools, quality woodworker's tools should eventually become part of your estate, passed on to the next generation. Cheap tools just add to the landfill crisis. But you already know to buy good tools. The question is *what* tools?

Almost every woodworking project can be broken down into seven distinct steps—design, mark, cut, shape, drill, assemble, and finish. Design is primarily a mental process, but the remaining six steps represent specific activities that we can use to conveniently categorize the tools required. In each step there will be tools that are essential, tools that are helpful, and tools that offer significant time savings. In this section I will try to help you sort out which are which.

MARKING

A sharp pencil is *the* essential marking tool. For more accurate marking, a knife is hard to beat.

Knowing where to mark almost always requires some means of taking measurements. Choose a 10- or 12-foot metal tape. Select one wide enough to remain rigid when extended a couple of feet.

A 12-inch sliding combination square is indispensable for marking perpendicular cut lines and for squaring during assembly. A combination square can also be used to lay out 45-degree angles, but for the odd angles encountered on a boat, you might make good use of an adjustable bevel gauge. A framing square is useful only on large plywood projects, and a level isn't much use at all.

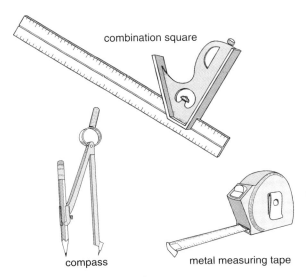

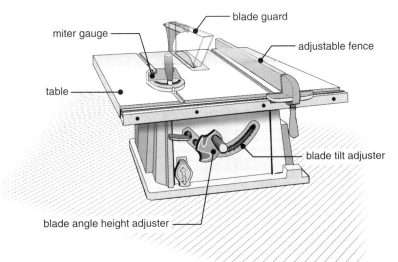

The essential marking tools.

A piece of string and a pencil can be used for marking circles and curved cuts, but a compass is more convenient. You will also use the compass to transfer the curvature of the hull onto a new bulkhead, shelf, or divider.

CUTTING

Cutting is the step that often determines how the rest of a woodwork project goes. Back in Chapter 4, I mentioned that all of my early projects were accomplished without shop tools. Not until I actually owned a table saw did I fully appreciate the indispensability of this one shop tool. Why did it take me so long to make this discovery? Two reasons: size and expense. Until a decade or so ago, table saws were big, heavy, and expensive. Living either in an apartment or on a 30-foot boat, I had no place to put a table saw, nor could I justify the considerable expense just to make a dozen or two cuts per year.

That has all changed. Small, lightweight table saws are now readily available. Catch the right sale at Lowe's or Home Depot, and a perfectly adequate little table saw will cost less than a leaf blower—a win-win if ever I saw one. So while it remains true that you can make every cut you are likely to need for your old-boat improvements with a circular saw and a saber saw, if your woodworking plans rise above a few pieces of trim, spring for a table saw. It will shorten the time for all of your projects, and with a little practice it will turn out satisfyingly precise cuts.

Real shop tools, the kind that are stationary, have a significant drawback for do-it-yourself boat renovation. They are usually one place and the boat is someplace else. That leads either to lots of trips just to fit

and check, or to winging it and hoping for the best. One course kindles frustration and the other, waste. Portable tools that you can use aboard the boat do not suffer from this limitation. A table saw sufficiently portable to use on or near your boat may eliminate any need for a circular saw, but you will still need a saber saw for the curved cuts that are an unavoidable feature of boat woodwork. Buy one that has variable speeds and a heavy-duty, strongly mounted, adjustable bevel plate. Skip the other bells and whistles. The basic saw will do everything more expensive models will.

If you are going to do a lot of trim work, you have an additional reason to invest in a table saw, which will include a miter gauge that makes the creation of perfectly mitered corners a snap. A backsaw and miter box might work for a finish carpenter, but it promises way more than it delivers for the rest of us. In fact, the only handsaw (for woodwork) you are ever likely to need on board is a coping saw.

In the spirit of full disclosure, I need to tell you that the blade that comes with your cheap table saw will be, well, cheap. Throw it away and buy a carbide-tipped combination blade to fit the saw. Don't whine about the additional cost; you would have to do this for a circular saw too. A carbide blade is the only kind that will cut teak without scorching it. Tungsten carbide teeth will stay sharp about 50 times longer than steel, which means one blade should last through your entire project and the next one too.

SHAPING

Once the part has been cut, some trimming and shaping is almost always required. For straight cuts made with a table saw, a sheet of sandpaper and a small wood block

An inexpensive table saw improves the quality of nearly all woodwork projects and reduces the time required.

may be the only shaping tool necessary, but boat carpentry involves a plethora of odd shapes and angles. The usual hedge is to cut slightly oversize, then trim to fit.

For trimming straight edges, nothing is better than a *sharp* plane. A woodworking craftsman will own several planes of different lengths, each of which excels in a particular situation, but a single plane is all that is required for our purposes. The best choice is a 6-inch block plane. The small size makes it convenient and allows you to use it with one hand, holding the material with the other (larger planes require two hands to be used accurately, which means the work must be held by a helper or in a vise). The biggest advantage of the block plane, however, is not the size, but the angle of the blade. Typically about 14 degrees—less than half the angle of most other planes—the low angle of the block plane makes it excellent for trimming the edges of plywood and allows it to make exceptionally fine cuts, even across the grain. The blade bevel should be *up* on a block plane, by the way.

An alternative to the block plane is the Stanley Surform, which looks like a cross between a plane and a cheese grater. Despite its questionable pedigree, it is easy to use for many shaping jobs, but it is not as versatile as a plane.

For putting a radius on corners and trimming curved edges, a belt sander can get the job done in a hurry. If you cut out a simple jig to hold the belt sander on its side, it becomes a bench sander and can be used to shape almost any wooden part, no matter how small. Because the belt is exposed on the front roller, the sander can also shape inside curves. However, beyond radiusing or shaping wood pieces before they are installed, a belt sander is a bad boat tool, flattening surfaces that should have curvature. Because of this I

have come to prefer a high-speed disk sander for sand shaping, because it is a tool that has many other uses aboard. Clamping it (gently) in a vise creates a makeshift bench sander, minus the table.

Often you need to secure the wood rather than the tool, which makes some kind of vise essential to the shaping process. If you installed a machinist's vise as suggested in the previous chapter, all that is necessary to allow it to do double duty for woodwork is a pair of plywood inserts to spread the grip and protect the wood from the jaws. Clamps can be substituted for the vise if you have a rigid surface to clamp to.

A chisel is another essential shaping tool. Instead of buying a set of five or six, spend the same amount on two chisels of top quality. One with a 1-inch-wide blade will get the most use, but you should also have a $1/4$-inch chisel for tight work. Also buy a leather or wooden mallet to use with the chisels, which are precision tools and should be treated with care. Keep a cheap chisel on hand for those inevitable instances when you need to trim something besides wood—such as fiberglass or epoxy.

The incredible versatility of a router earns it an "essential" designation in all but the most modest alterations. The router opens up a whole new realm of possibilities in working with wood. Spinning a wide variety of razor-sharp blades at 25,000 rpm, it allows you to do complex and ornate shaping that is simply not feasible with any other tool. It will create fancy moldings or put a simple-but-uniform finished radius on sharp edges. It will trim wood and plastic veneer perfectly every time. It will also bevel, rabbet, groove, dado, mortise, and make interior cutouts. With the aid of an inexpensive fixture, it will even do perfect dovetail joints. And it is no more difficult to use than a circular saw.

Shaping requires very few tools.

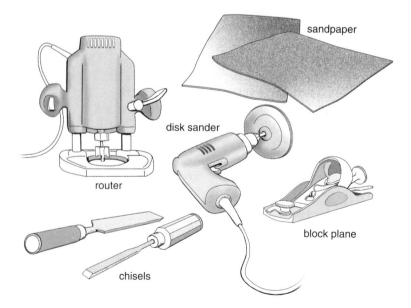

sandpaper

disk sander

router

chisels

block plane

As with saw blades, select only carbide-tipped bits. Initially purchase a $^3/_8$-inch double-flute straight bit and a $^3/_8$-inch round-over bit with a ball-bearing pilot. If you are installing plastic laminate, add a straight laminate trimmer bit to your selection. And if you anticipate doing any cabinet work, a $^3/_8$-inch rabbet bit may prove useful, although you are likely to cut simple rabbet joints on the table saw. Buy other bits only if the need arises, which is unlikely unless you get into fancy carving with the tool.

DRILLING

A hand-powered drill is a good tool to have on board, a potential day saver in an emergency, but hand drills are definitely not the tool of choice for renovation. If you limit yourself to a single electric drill, it should be a plug-in $^3/_8$-inch variable-speed reversible (VSR) model with a keyless chuck. The reversing feature allows backing out a bit when it binds, a situation more likely to occur when drilling metal than wood, but if you have a single drill, it will see both uses.

It is true that a fixed-speed $^1/_4$-inch drill will drill holes just as well at half the cost. But the $^1/_4$-inch model will not handle large bits, will not have the power to drive a spade bit or a holesaw, is unsatisfactory for grinding, and cannot double as a screw gun. The limitations of a small drill make it a false economy.

A cordless drill seems like a natural on a boat, and it does have some safety advantages, but an 18-volt drill will not develop the torque of one with 110 volts. You need dual battery packs so running out of juice doesn't stop you mid project, which means you probably have the charger plugged in anyway, so why not cut out the middle man and just plug in the drill? A cordless is hard to beat as a second drill, but potential cruisers beware. A plug-in drill can lie dormant in your tool locker for years without ill effect, but the battery packs for cordless tools demand regular exercise or they will be beyond redemption when a need for the tool eventually arises. Inverters have made plug-in drills fully functional away from the dock, robbing cordless drills of their primary appeal.

A modest set of bits is a good initial choice. Ten or 12 bits will cover most needs. Buy only commercial-quality bits; cheap ones quickly lose their sharpness. High-speed twist drill bits have the point ground at an angle of about 40 degrees, ideal for metal but less so for drilling wood. A sharper angle, about 60 degrees, is better for woodworking, but this makes the bit almost useless for drilling metal. If you will be doing a lot of woodwork, having a separate set of bits reground for

wood is not a bad idea, but it is by no means essential. For combined use leave the bits alone.

When you buy the bits, also pick up a countersink. You will need it to seat flathead screws. Another worthwhile accessory is an inexpensive drill stand, which will allow you to use your power drill with the precision of a drill press. Other drill accessories such as spade bits and holesaws should be purchased as needed. The same goes for grinding, buffing, and wire wheels. If you will be doing a lot of "finish" work, buying a plug cutter for your drill could enable better-matched plugs at a lower cost compared to buying precut teak or mahogany plugs. For other woods, cutting your own plugs is likely to be your only choice.

One hand drill that will get a lot of use at the dock is a push drill. Sometimes called a Yankee drill, it resembles a screwdriver but the handle is spring-loaded and spins the bit as you push it. It is an ideal tool for drilling pilot holes, particularly when the space is confined. A selection of bits comes with the drill, stored inside the handle.

ASSEMBLY

Most woodworking projects will involve more than a single piece of wood. Nails, screws, and glue—alone or combined—are used to assemble the parts.

The essential tool for nailing parts together is a hammer and almost any hammer will do. Only after a loan turned larcenous and I needed to buy a new hammer did I give any real thought to what might be the best one to have aboard. At the hardware store I was confronted with a *wall* of hammers of different weights, shapes, sizes, and construction. A 20-ounce carpenter's hammer is too heavy for cabinet work, and a 12-ounce cabinetmaker's hammer is too light for general-purpose use. A 16-ounce hammer with a curved claw (better for removing nails) is about right for home use, but it's heavier than needed for driving wire brads—the only nails you are likely to use in boat carpentry—and aboard a boat, the claw represents more menace than merit. For a hammer you leave on the boat, choose a 12-ounce ball-peen hammer. Not only will you find it nearly perfect for driving brads and finishing nails, but it is intended for hitting metal harder than a nail head, making it equally useful as a mechanic's tool.

You will drive finishing nails below the surface of the wood and fill the indention. This "setting" requires a nail set, a punchlike tool with a small tip. A $^1/_{32}$ nail set is the most useful for cabinet work, but sets are cheap enough to buy two or three different sizes.

In the last chapter we covered the need for three or four standard screwdrivers and a similar complement of Phillips screwdrivers. And in this chapter I have pointed out the need for a drill, bits, and a countersink. Assembly with screws requires no additional tools. However, if your plans call for a lot of screws, there are a couple of other tools that you will find quite useful. The first is a special drill bit that drills the pilot hole, the shank hole, the countersink, and the counterbore in a single operation. These combination bits come in various sizes, and selecting one for the screws you are using can save a tremendous amount of time.

Driving half a dozen screws with a screwdriver leaves you with a sense of satisfaction; driving a hundred screws leaves you with bandages on your hand. Instead of spending money on gauze and surgical tape, buy screwdriver bits for your variable-speed drill. Better yet, buy a cordless power screwdriver (screw gun). It will avoid the need to remove the drill bit from your drill every time you want to install a screw, and the screw gun's built-in clutch will keep you from stripping or twisting off screws. If you already have a cordless drill, you are probably all set because most have an adjustable clutch that allows them to function as screwdrivers.

Today's glues are typically stronger than wood fibers, meaning that the wood itself will pull apart before a properly glued joint fails. With glue that holds that tenaciously, there is little need for nails and screws in permanent joints except to hold the glue-coated parts together initially. A great deal of nailing and screwing can be avoided if you have the right clamps. C-clamps are the most useful. They come in sizes from tiny to humongous. The absolute

minimum complement of clamps is four 4-inch C-clamps. If you can afford an equal number of 6-inch clamps, so much the better. A couple of 2-inch clamps will likely also earn their way. I never met a woodworker with *too many* C-clamps.

Cabinetmakers often prefer wooden hand-screw clamps because they grip a broader area, do not mark the surface of the clamped item, and can be adjusted so their jaws are not parallel (for clamping odd-shaped items). Their bulk is their biggest drawback for boat use; they are awkward or unserviceable in a confined area, and they occupy considerable stowage space. Faced with the choice, choose C-clamps.

For edge-gluing planks, assembling cabinets, or building drawers, clamps with feet rather than inches between the jaws are useful. Bar clamps in widths up to 8 feet or more are available with various jaw depths. As clamp width increases the pipe clamp can be a more economical alternative. Virtually identical in operation to a bar clamp, a pipe clamp consists of one jaw that screws onto the threaded end of common $^3/_4$-inch steel pipe ($^1/_2$-inch sizes are also available) and a second jaw that slides up and down the pipe. With different lengths of pipe, the same clamp can be used to clamp 6 inches or 6 feet. Find a building or house being demolished, and the contractor will likely let you carry away all the $^3/_4$-inch water pipe you want. Three pipe clamps should be adequate for most uses.

You should also be aware of spring clamps (good for quickly positioning small parts), edging clamps (for gluing wooden banding to the edge of plywood), and miter clamps (for accurate gluing of miter joints). The usefulness of these will depend on the type of woodworking you attempt.

Most onboard clamping can be handled with C-clamps and a couple of 2-foot bar clamps.

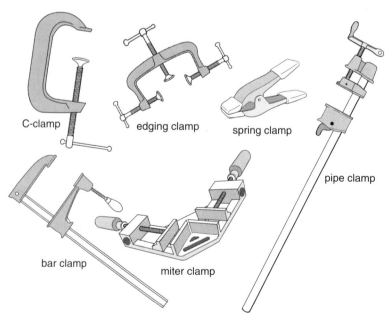

C-clamp   edging clamp   spring clamp   pipe clamp

bar clamp   miter clamp

FINISH

In this chapter we are going to limit our examination of finishing to the process of preparation. The actual application of paint, varnish, or some other coating is detailed extensively in Chapter 14.

Finish preparation essentially means sanding. Once again, a rubber or wood block and a few sheets of sandpaper are the only essentials, but a finishing sander can do the job better and faster. The most versatile is a palm sander with a 4-inch pad to take $1/4$ sheet of sandpaper. Making about 14,000 orbits per minute, these lightweight (about 2 pounds) sanders can make short work of almost any sanding project, including minor shaping.

An alternative is the random orbit sander, which reputedly cuts more quickly and leaves no scratch or swirl marks. True, but the downside is that you have to buy specific disks to fit your random orbit sander, whereas a quarter-sheet palm sander can be loaded—four times— with a regular sheet of any type or grit of paper. In the end, both are equally capable, but the palm sander is lighter and less expensive to supply with fresh paper.

Having outlasted a number of palm sanders, I have come to the conclusion that the most important design consideration is the paper clamp. Clamps with teeth are too quickly rendered toothless by their contact with the business side of the paper. I have had the best luck with the spring-bar type of clamp such as the one used by Black & Decker.

All palm sanders come with a dust bag or canister, and amazingly enough these actually work. Punched holes in the sandpaper vent to a high-speed fan that vacuums up the dust and blows it into the bag or canister. The sander is infinitely more efficient when it is not riding on a layer of sawdust, so develop the habit of using the supplied punch plate.

The problem of sawdust is not limited to clogging sandpaper. If dust is on the surface, it will seriously weaken any glue joints. If it is in the air, it will roughen or ruin paint and varnish. For anything more than minor interior modifications, some type of vacuum cleaner is essential. You might press a home vacuum cleaner with attachments into service, but a shop vac is generally far more satisfactory. Small shop vacs, ideal for onboard use, are available at low cost.

A ONE-PIECE START

Almost any locker on a boat can benefit from a shelf. Dividing the lockers in the galley will allow you to get to the stockpot without removing every other pan and skillet. A shelf in the head cabinet will keep paper products away from the potential dampness of the hull. A shelf in the cockpit locker will provide a flat surface for storage boxes and jerry jugs. A shelf on one side of the lazarette will provide convenient stowage for small cans of paint, oil, polish, and other items.

Even the hanging locker can benefit from shelves. If you live aboard you may need a place to hang your Brooks Brothers suits, but for most boating the value of the hanging locker is suspect. It wastes space; hanging clothes are not compactly stowed, and there is generally a large amount of unused space in the top and bottom of the locker. It is hard on your clothes; hanging clothes in a boat crashing to windward or rolling downwind is not unlike storing them in a tumble dryer. And if you are hanging your clothes to keep them from wrinkling, take a look inside the locker the next time the boat is heeled; they pile themselves on the hull or the locker door and wrinkle anyway.

The best use for a hanging locker is to convert it to a bureau. Your clothes will do better folded or rolled and stowed in a drawer, and drawers allow for efficient onboard stowage of hundreds of other items as well. Unfortunately the design of most old boats will not allow for such a conversion; there is insufficient room to open drawers because the space in front of the locker is narrower than the locker's depth. The next best thing is to build shelves in the locker.

THE DESIGN PROCESS

Whether the shelf will be in the galley, the lazarette, or the hanging locker, there is very little difference in construction and installation, but there will be some variation in design. We barely touched on design earlier, yet regardless of how exquisite your craftsmanship, poor design will doom the project.

Come on, you say. How much design can a shelf require? Let's consider that question for a shelf in a galley locker. Obviously you need to know the size of the shelf, and you can get that by measuring the locker. But have you given adequate thought to what will be kept in the locker? With the new shelf in place,

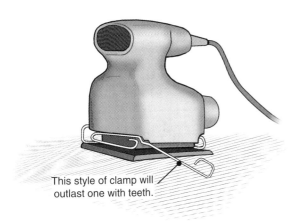

This style of clamp will outlast one with teeth.

Palm sander.

will the space between it and the bottom of the cabinet opening be wide enough to admit the stockpot? Can you remove the saucepan stowed inside the stockpot without removing the pot? That requires at least the *combined* height of both between the bottom of the locker and the underside of the shelf. With the shelf in place, will you be able to see what is in the locker? Will you be able to actually reach to the back of the shelf? Try holding a board across the center of the opening to see how far you can reach. Does anyone aboard have shorter arms? If you open the cabinet on the wrong tack, is everything on the shelf going to end up on the cabin sole? How heavy are the items you will store on the shelf? Would ventilation be beneficial? Does the shelf need to be removable for access to plumbing, wiring, or hardware? We could go on and on.

The basic premise is to determine *exactly* how the shelf will be used and then decide on its design, not the other way around. In this case I am going to assume that you have discovered that a "generic" shelf will make storing the large pots more difficult and retrieving small items that migrate to the rear of the shelf nearly impossible. Mounting the shelf higher resolves the first problem but makes the second one even worse. A shelf that extends from the back of the locker only halfway to the front solves both problems, but if you think about it a little more, you realize that the first time this locker is on the weather side in a decent breeze or the boat rolls off a steep wave, the half shelf will dump its contents into the bottom of the locker. What will you do?

The obvious solution is a fiddle rail across the front of the shelf, but that has its own problems. First, if the fiddle is high enough to be effective, it will make seeing the contents of the shelf difficult. Second, narrowing the access to the shelf may limit what can be stored on it. But the most serious, at least from my perspective, is that an attached fiddle adds complexity to this first project. The one-piece solution is to mount the shelf with about a 20-degree downward slant toward the rear. With such a slant, even a 30-degree heel is not likely to spill the contents of the shelf.

The materials list is not very extensive—a piece of plywood and a length of cleat stock. But even here there are some design considerations. If you are only adding a shelf or two, you do not need to concern yourself with weight, but if you are adding a dozen shelves or reconstructing interior fixtures, weight becomes a major consideration. When weight is a concern, $^3/_8$-inch plywood will be adequate for shelves, but the better stability and greater rigidity provided by the five-ply construction of $^1/_2$-inch plywood make

it a better choice most of the time. Additional thickness beyond $^1/_2$ inch offers no advantages. You want exterior grade A-B or A-C plywood.

Cleat stock, if you don't already know, has nothing whatsoever to do with the things the docklines are attached to. Cleat stock is nothing more than a length of wood with a small, square cross section—ideally $^3/_4$ inch $\times$ $^3/_4$ inch. You can buy square molding for this use, but a less expensive route is to rip $^3/_4$-inch strips off a length of clear fir "1-by" (1 $\times$ 4, 1 $\times$ 6, etc.). Forget about "truth in advertising"; 1-by lumber is actually $^3/_4$ inch thick. The lumberyard may be willing to rip a board for you if you ask.

Measuring begins with drawing a line on one side of the locker to approximate the location of one edge of the shelf. To get us on the same wavelength, the locker I am describing opens athwartship. In other words, the rear of the locker is the hull. Somehow you have to cut the shelf to the curvature of the hull, but because this shelf does not reach the front of the locker, you can just cut it square and then trim it to fit. So you need two measurements for the shelf.

First you measure between the sides of the locker. Measure across where the front of the shelf will be and where the rear will be to insure that the sides are parallel. If they aren't, use your square to determine which side is square with the front of the cabinet and make that the square side of your shelf. It can be helpful to sketch the shelf and note the different measurements on the drawing.

You also need a depth dimension. Measure from the point where you want the front of the shelf to the hull along the line you have drawn. If the hull has a pronounced curvature, be sure you measure on the

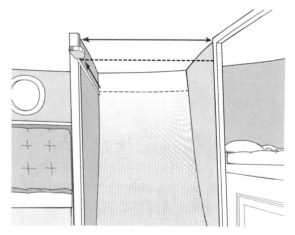

Measure maximum depth and width. When front and rear widths differ, determine which side is square with the cabinet face.

deepest side of the locker or the finished shelf will be slightly shorter than you expect. With your two measurements, you are ready to cut the shelf.

SAW CHOICE

The original edition of this book, written before lightweight and affordable table saws became widely available, was circular-saw-centric. Although a table saw makes nearly every cut easier and probably more accurate, you do not have to buy one to cut a shelf or to do any of the other wood projects in this book. Nor do I think that every old-boat owner is going to add a table saw to his or her inventory of tools, no matter how good the idea.

Besides, making wide cuts in plywood on a small table saw has its own challenges. Without additional support surfaces and/or a helper, a circular saw can be easier for an amateur to handle. So for this first project, I have opted to stick with circular saw instructions. That does not mean you cannot make these cuts on a table saw, but as you will see later, to make a straight cut with a table saw we generally set up a *fence* and run one edge (or end) of the wood against it. The smaller the table, the shorter the possible distance between the blade and the fence. This is usually not a problem with a circular saw because the wood itself is our work surface.

SAWING PLYWOOD

Sawhorses are very convenient for making cuts with a circular saw and for other woodworking processes. Inexpensive clamp-on legs allow you to convert a single 8-foot stud (2 × 4) into a pair of 4-foot horses. For onboard cutting, span the coamings with a couple of 2 × 4s.

First Make a Fence

Making straight cuts with a circular saw also requires a fence, but in this case it guides the sole plate of the saw rather than the edge of the material. A new sheet of ½-inch plywood provides a good opportunity to make yourself a fence long enough to span the length of a plywood sheet. Select the best long edge of the plywood and get your lumberyard to accurately rip a 4-inch-wide strip from it. *Rip* means to cut with the grain; *crosscut* means to cut across the grain. In the case of plywood, rip means a lengthwise cut.

If the yard can't do it, it won't be particularly difficult for you to make the fence yourself using your circular saw's edge guide. Start by adjusting your saw. Make absolutely sure that it is unplugged, then push the sole plate all the way up, adjusting for the maximum depth of cut. Place a square against the bottom of the sole plate and the side of the blade to make sure the blade is perfectly perpendicular, adjusting as required. Do not trust

the bevel gauge stamped on the plate. Now put the saw on the plywood with the fully extended blade against an edge. Reduce the cut depth until the blade extends beyond the bottom of the wood by just half the depth of a tooth. This is always the correct depth setting for a circular saw blade—penetrating the material by half a tooth—and you will need to readjust the depth of cut every time the thickness of the material you are cutting changes. This same rule applies to a table saw.

Turn the best face of the plywood *down*. The circular saw cuts with an upward motion and has a tendency to splinter the top surface of plywood, so always mark and cut plywood with the best face

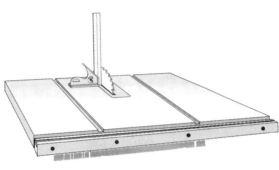

The initial saw adjustment for all square cuts is to make sure the blade is perpendicular to the sole plate or the saw table.

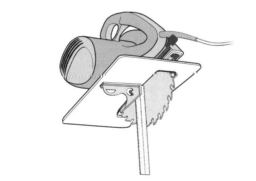

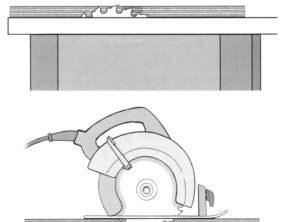

The second adjustment is to set the cut depth so that the blade will penetrate the stock by about half the length of a tooth.

down. (An additional advantage of a table saw is that you cut with the best face up.) Install the edge guide on your circular saw and adjust it so that the distance between the face of the guide and the face of the blade is 4 inches, then tighten the lock securely. Place the forward part of the sole plate on the plywood with the blade of the saw in the air and the guide against the plywood edge. You always start a circular saw with the blade in the air, never in contact with the wood. Squeeze the trigger on the saw and, keeping the guide flush against the edge of the plywood, run your saw the length of the sheet. Pressing against the edge guide with your free hand will help you to keep it in contact with the edge. Feed the saw slowly, and do not worry about cutting the top of the horses.

If you've made the cut, the straightest edge is likely to be the original edge of the plywood. Mark this edge with something indelible so you will always make this the contact side of your fence. Also, if there are any voids in the edge, plan on filling them with something to prevent them from giving all your cut lines a wiggle when the edge of the sole plate drops into the void.

You are likely to find an 8-foot fence inconvenient for shorter cuts, so you may want to rip a second 4-inch strip from the other edge and crosscut it into a 5-foot and a 3-foot length. You will use these guides for virtually every circular saw cut, so do not begrudge the loss of 8 inches of your plywood sheet to them.

To use your new fence, all you need are a couple of C-clamps to hold it in position. You can typically run either side of the saw's sole plate against the fence, depending on which suits the circumstances better. A worthwhile preparatory step is to clamp your fence across a wood scrap and run your saw against it from both directions just far enough to start to cut. Now measure accurately from the fence to the inside edge of both cuts. These two measurements, one for the wide side of the sole plate and one for the narrow side, are the offsets for positioning your fence to place the cut line where you want it. Write these offsets on all of your fences so they will always be handy. Keep in mind that when you clamp the fence on the outside of the cut line, meaning off the part, the cut line will need to be along the outside edge of the saw blade relative to the fence, so you will have to add the cut (blade) width to these offsets when positioning the fence.

Cut the Shelf

If you are still with me after that last sentence, the shelf itself is going to be a piece of cake. Measuring from the end of the plywood sheet along its left-hand edge (so my instructions match up), mark the width of the locker, less about $1/_8$ inch to give the shelf ample clearance. Measure in perpendicular from the edge at this mark the approximate depth of the shelf, and make a second mark on the plywood. Measure back along the edge from your first mark the smaller of your two offset numbers and align your fence at this mark, squaring it with the edge of the plywood. Clamp the fence to the plywood with C-clamps on both ends. Put the blade side of the sole plate against the fence, start your saw, and just nick the edge of the plywood. Does the nick correspond exactly with your original shelf-width mark? If it does, crosscut the plywood from the edge to your second mark, keeping the blade side of the sole plate in contact with the fence. Stop when your cut just reaches the mark. Remove the fence.

Keep the sole plate of the saw against the cutting guide to make straight cuts.

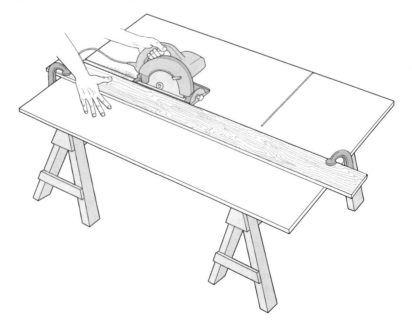

Measure along the end of the plywood the depth of the shelf, plus the shorter of your two offsets, *plus* the width of the saw blade; put a mark on the plywood. You need to add the saw-blade width because the fence is going to be on the outside of the cut line. Put the inside edge of your fence at this mark and square the fence with the end of the plywood, again clamping the fence at both ends. Start your saw and again just nick the plywood. Measure from the edge of the plywood to the inside edge of the nick to make sure this is the width you are after. Carpenters live by the adage "measure twice, cut once," and you would do well to cultivate this habit for your own woodwork. If your fence is in the right place, run the saw against it until you just reach your other cut. Use a saber saw to complete the two cuts and release the shelf from the sheet. The reason you use a saber saw here is to avoid cutting into the unused plywood, thus conserving it for other uses.

Cleats

Cut two pieces of the cleat stock about an inch shorter than the depth of the shelf to make sure

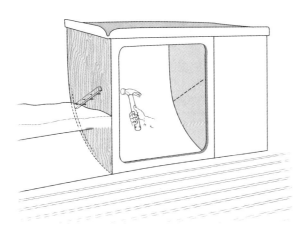

Temporarily install one supporting cleat.

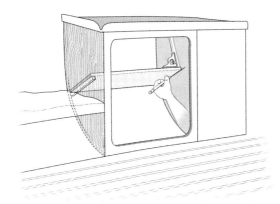

Set the shelf on the cleat, square it with the side of the locker, and trace the bottom to mark the location of the other cleat.

the cleats will not reach the radius of any tabbing that might affix the locker side to the hull. With a pair of finishing nails, tack one cleat in place against the line you previously drew on the side of the locker. Do not drive the nails flush; you are going to remove this cleat later. Place the shelf on the cleat and "level" it by using a square to position it perpendicular to the locker side. Hold it in this position and trace its underside on the opposite locker wall. Remove the shelf and temporarily tack the second cleat in place using this new line as a guide. Put the shelf in place to make sure it sits flat on both cleats. This is also the time to actually try the pots and pans for fit to confirm that the shelf is exactly where you want it.

Contour

With the shelf in place, mark the contour of the hull on its back edge. This is most easily done with a compass adjusted slightly wider than the widest gap between the shelf and the hull. Always keeping the line between the point and the pencil approximately perpendicular to the front of the shelf, drag the point against the hull and allow the pencil to trace the contour onto the *bottom* of the shelf.

Remove the shelf and cut along the contour line with your saber saw. You mark the contour line on the bottom of the shelf because the saber saw, like the circular saw, cuts on the upward motion, putting the cleanest cut on the underside of what you are sawing—the underside in this case being the top of the shelf. There is no depth adjustment on a saber saw, but the angle of the cut is adjustable. You might be tempted to set the saw for a 20-degree bevel to correspond with the upward cant of the shelf, but that overlooks the vertical curvature of the hull. To achieve a fairly accurate fit requires measuring the

Use a compass to copy the hull contour to the back edge of the shelf, marking the bottom if possible.

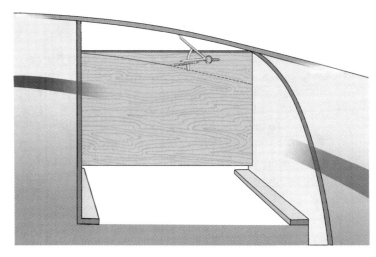

actual angle between the shelf and the hull with a bevel gauge and setting the saw to that angle. It is a good exercise if you want to do it, but for the back of a shelf such accuracy is superfluous.

A saber saw cannot be counted on to make an absolutely accurate cut anyway, because the unsupported blade can be deflected by the wood. Checking the blade against the sole plate initially to make sure it is vertical and feeding the saw slowly will give the best results.

All that is left to finish your shelf installation is to permanently install the cleats and secure the shelf in place. You might drill and screw the cleats in place, but gluing them will be much stronger—if you use the correct adhesive.

ADHESIVES 101
There are half a dozen adhesives you should be familiar with. Everyone has used Elmer's Glue-All, the ubiquitous white glue that most of us assume is somehow a dairy by-product but we *really* don't want to know how it is made. Good news, animal lovers; the only dead cattle in this *polyvinyl resin* glue died a couple of million years ago. It says it's "for wood" right on the package, but it has a very low tolerance for moisture and should never be used aboard a boat.

On the same shelf at the hardware store you will find yellow carpenter's glue, an *aliphatic resin* adhesive. Aliphatic resin is an excellent adhesive—easy to use, fast setting, long lasting—and it will form a strong bond even when the two parts do not mate well. It is less moisture sensitive than its white cousin, but if the joint gets soaked, it will fail. Most interior joints will never get that wet, and I have had to use a chisel to remove shelf cleats that I attached with carpenter's glue more than a decade earlier. Still, for boat woodwork it should be used selectively. While I might depend on carpenter's glue to hold a shelf containing pots or clothes, I would not trust it with a television or a loaded wine rack.

A more reliable yellow glue is the so-called weatherproof variety. A good example is Titebond III. Slightly more expensive than regular carpenter's glue, it is worth the extra cost for boat carpentry.

I have always liked the way the word *resorcinol*, like the name Spiro Agnew, exercises all the muscles around the mouth. It is also an elitist word; everyone knows about epoxy, but knowledge of resorcinol sets you apart. Totally waterproof, resorcinol is an excellent adhesive (better than epoxy by some reliable accounts for boat construction), but it depends on a very thin (0.005-inch) glue line for a strong bond. If the parts being joined do not mate perfectly (which generally lets me out) so that a thin glue line can be achieved without excessive clamp pressure, the bond will be weak. The joint must be clamped for at least 8 hours. Resorcinol is a two-part adhesive and must be mixed before use.

Plastic resin (actually urea-formaldehyde resin) is another moisture-resistant glue with excellent bonding properties. Many boat carpenters swear by Weldwood Plastic Resin Glue. It is not quite as impervious to water as resorcinol is, but it's certainly up to any challenges it might face on a fiberglass boat. The major drawback to plastic resin is that it must be under heavy pressure to bond, always necessitating closely spaced clamps. It sets quickly, which is not always a disadvantage, and it comes in a powder form that must be mixed with water before use. The low cost of the adhesive is a definite plus.

In the last few years *polyurethane* glues have begun to dominate hardware store shelves. The best known of these is Gorilla Glue. Polyurethane glue is an excellent product for boat use. It is similar in strength to yellow glue. It is waterproof according to manufacturers, water resistant according to government tests, but certainly up to the task of boat bonding that will not be submerged. It is relatively easy to use and has some gap-filling capacity, although the wider the gap, the weaker the bond. The downside is that it is more expensive than yellow glue and has a relatively short shelf life—about 1 year—after the glue package is open.

No glue, however, has proven to be more versatile than *epoxy*. Epoxy is completely waterproof, at least for all uses it is likely to see on an old fiberglass boat. It will readily fill virtually any size gap and requires no clamping other than what may be necessary to hold the two parts in contact. Epoxy is the clear favorite among amateur woodworkers. Available in various viscosities, epoxy adhesive is essentially thickened epoxy resin. In fact, many boat carpenters mix their own from resin by adding fiber filler, silica, graphite powder, or simply dry sawdust. The chief disadvantage of epoxy is its relatively high cost.

INSTALLING THE SHELF
Check the contoured shelf for fit, noting whether the cleats protrude beyond the front of the shelf. If they do, reposition them so they are slightly recessed. Remove the shelf and outline both cleats on the sides of the locker. Also pencil a small arrow on each cleat pointing toward the top so you cannot get confused

when you glue them in place. Now remove both cleats and coat them and the outlined areas on the locker sides with the glue of your choice. If the inside of the locker has been painted, you will need to sand the paint off the area being glued or you will just be gluing the cleats to the paint film. Nail the cleats back in place, this time driving the finishing nails home. Add additional nails as necessary to hold the cleat tightly against the side panel.

If you want to mount the shelf permanently, wait until the glue cures on the cleats, then coat the top of the cleats and the underside of the shelf with glue and tack the shelf in place with finishing nails. You can skip the nails if you can find an alternative way to press the shelf onto the cleats. C-clamps will do the job at the front of the shelf, but there is no way to get a clamp on the back. Measure from the top of the shelf (near the rear) to the top of the locker, and cut a couple of pieces of cleat stock slightly longer than this measurement. Place the lower ends of these pieces on the shelf directly above the cleats, and wedge the upper ends against the top of the locker. Tap the upper ends sideways with your hammer to wedge the struts tighter and increase the pressure on the glue joints.

It is rarely necessary or even desirable to attach a shelf to the hull, but if you need to for some reason, keep in mind that, like a bulkhead, the rigid shelf can cause a hard spot on the hull and should be insulated with a fillet of foam. With the foam in place, tab the shelf-to-hull joint with two or three layers of fiberglass. If you are only after rear support for the shelf, fiberglass a cleat to the hull. A short cleat in the center will generally be adequate. Do not attach the shelf to the cleat.

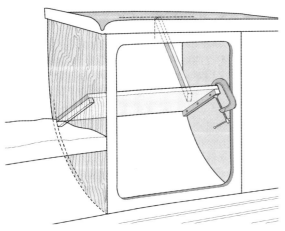

Gluing a shelf permanently in place. Wedged cleat stock applies clamping pressure to the rear of the shelf.

Making It Removable

It is sometimes imperative and almost always a good idea to make shelves removable—you might buy a larger stockpot. The common way is to screw the shelf to the cleats rather than gluing it. Two screws to a side are typically adequate. Select a pilot drill by comparing it to the screws you are using. It should be approximately the same size as the screw's root diameter—the diameter if the threads were ground away. Hold the drill behind the screw to compare. For fastening $^1/_2$-inch plywood to a $^3/_4$-inch or thicker cleat, 1-inch-long #8 flathead screws are a good choice. A #8 screw calls for a #48 pilot drill, but numbered drills will not be included in a modest bit set, so use a $^3/_{32}$-inch bit. With the shelf in place, drill the four pilot holes through the shelf and into the cleats.

You will find these holes impossible to drill vertically because the bulk of the power drill keeps the bit more than $^3/_4$ inch away from the sides. Drilling them at an angle is fine, or use your push drill here if you have one. Remove the shelf and drill the holes in it larger. If you fail to do this, the screws will thread into both parts. You need them to turn freely in the shelf so tightening the screws will clamp the two parts together. Whenever you can, drill the shank hole *from the bottom* when you are enlarging a pilot hole. Few of us can run the second drill right down the center of the first hole with a hand-held drill. The trick is to hold the drill lightly and let the pilot hole dictate the orientation of the drill, but the hole still tends to shift a little. If you drill the shank hole from the top and it shifts, the screw may miss the pilot hole in the cleat, but if you drill from the bottom, the shank hole and the pilot hole will always align. For #8 screws the shank hole should be $^5/_{32}$ inch.

Turn the shelf back over and countersink the shank holes from the top. Make sure the entire head of each screw will be below the surface of the shelf. Ideally you want the top of a flathead screw to be exactly flush with the surface of the wood, and you can normally check the countersink without inserting the screw by touching the head of the inverted screw to the hole. When the diameter of the countersink is the same as the diameter of the head, the countersink is correct. In this case, because the screws are installed at an angle, it will be best to check the depth of the countersinks by inserting the screws. When they are correct, screw the shelf in place.

I prefer an alternative method of holding the shelf in place. Cut two pieces of cleat stock, each $1^1/_4$ inches long, and glue them vertically to the locker sides against the front edge of the shelf and flush with its top. They will prevent the shelf from sliding

WOOD SCREW DRILL SIZES			
Screw Gauge	**Shank Hole**	**Pilot Hole**	
		Softwood	*Hardwood*
0	1/16	1/64	1/32
1	5/64	1/32	1/32
2	3/32	1/32	1/16
3	7/64	3/64	1/16
4	7/64	1/16	5/64
5	1/8	1/16	5/64
6	9/64	5/64	3/32
7	5/32	3/32	7/64
8	5/32	3/32	7/64
9	11/64	7/64	1/8
10	3/16	7/64	1/8
11	13/64	1/8	9/64
12	7/32	1/8	9/64
14	1/4	9/64	5/32
16	9/32	11/64	3/16
18	19/64	3/16	13/64
20	5/16	3/16	7/32
24	3/8	7/32	1/4

(The four sizes highlighted are the most common.)

Removing one top cleat releases a shelf secured in this manner.

forward. Tack or tape them in place while the glue sets, making certain they do not press against the shelf so tightly that they prevent its removal. Next cut two 6- or 8-inch lengths of cleat stock. Center one along the shorter side of the shelf and tack it horizontally about 1/4 inch above the shelf. (You are clamping the shelf between a bottom cleat and a top cleat, but you do not want it clamped tightly or you won't be able to lift the opposite side to slide the shelf free.) Now drill the other piece for a single screw in its center and screw it to the

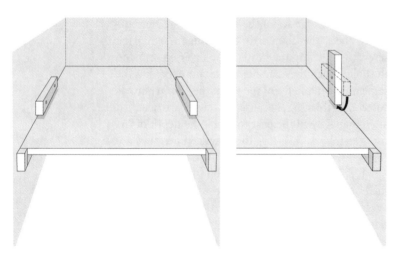

opposite side of the locker, pressing it tightly against the shelf. A shelf installed this way is very secure but can be removed with a single screw.

If you need to remove the shelf often, you might install the last cleat vertically as a long turn button and eliminate the necessity of removing a screw. Or you could attach a door hook or even a "bird" catch to the bottom of the shelf.

You may be tempted to sand your new shelf. Don't. When you sand fir plywood, all you succeed in doing is removing the soft fibers, leaving the surface even rougher. Finishing is another chapter, but plywood should always be given a couple of coats of paint or sealer before you attempt to sand it.

VENTILATED SHELVING

If the shelf you just completed was in the head or a hanging locker rather than in the galley, ventilating it would be a good idea. You could drill the plywood with a pattern of holes with your largest twist drill (probably 3/8 inch), but it will take a lot of holes to be effective. You will get better ventilation with far fewer holes using a spade bit between 1 inch and 1 1/2 inches in diameter. A spade bit, particularly one with edge spurs, cuts a very neat hole—until it exits. To keep the bit from tearing the bottom ply, do not feed the bit all the way through the shelf. When the point breaks through, invert the shelf and finish boring the hole from the opposite side.

Another method of ventilating a shelf involves making a series of parallel cuts. This is especially easy to do on a table saw, but it will not be that difficult with a circular saw either. To minimize the impact on the strength of the shelf, make the cuts parallel to the front and stop them well short of the sides. Draw limit lines about 1 1/2 inches from the sides, and do not extend the cuts beyond these. Clamp a fence across the shelf so that your first cut will be parallel to and about 1 1/2 inches in from the front of the shelf.

You are going to do a *plunge cut*. With the saw in position against the cutting guide, tilt the saw onto the front edge of the sole plate until the blade guard is just above the wood. Pull the guard back with its handle to expose the bottom of the blade. Squeeze the trigger switch and, with the saw running, slowly lower the blade into the wood. When the sole plate sits flush, you can release the blade guard and carefully back the saw until the back edge of the blade touches one of the lines. Now push the saw forward along the cutting guide until the blade touches the other line. Tilt the saw up to extract the blade and release the trigger. Move the cutting guide an inch

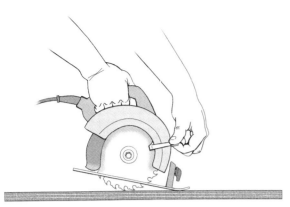

To begin a cut in the middle of the wood, start the saw with the blade in the air, then lower the spinning blade slowly through the wood, making a "plunge cut."

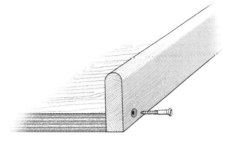

Poor: Neither glue nor screws hold well to end grain.

and make a second cut. Repeat until the entire center of the shelf is vented.

If you are doing this on a table saw, you will be lowering the wood onto the blade rather than the blade into the wood, and your guiding limit lines will need to be drawn farther from the edge since the curvature of the blade means the cut extends forward (and backward) from the edge of the cut visible from the top.

WHAT KIND OF JOINT IS THIS?

In a lot of applications you will want a shelf to have a fiddle rail across the front. The shelf will still be plywood, but if it is exposed—as in an open (no door) hanging locker—or even if it isn't but you want your work to be "yacht" quality, the fiddle will be solid wood.

Before fabricating the fiddle rail you need to decide how it will be attached to the shelf. Why not just butt the inside of the rail against the front edge of the shelf? Because such a joint will be very weak. Glue does not bond well to any end grain, including that exposed in the edge of plywood. Mechanical fasteners—nails and screws—are ineffective when driven into the *edge* of plywood.

You can make the joint substantially stronger by placing the rail on *top* of the shelf. In this case, end grain is not involved, so the glue joint should have greater integrity. Screws driven from the bottom of the shelf into the solid wood of the fiddle will develop their full holding strength. This remains a *butt joint*, the weakest of joints, but in this configuration it is plenty strong enough to withstand the assault of 7 pounds of escape-minded clothing. The real problem with attaching the rail this way is that it leaves the edge of the plywood shelf exposed. You can do nicer work.

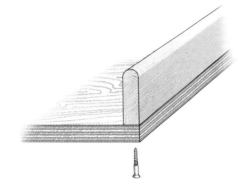

Better: A glue joint will be strong and screws driven into the fiddle will deliver maximum hold but the exposed shelf edge is unattractive.

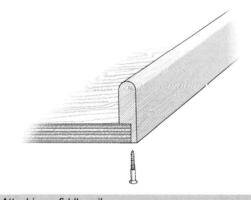

Best: The rabbet joint allows for a strong glue joint and fasteners driven into solid wood, and it hides the raw edge.

Attaching a fiddle rail.

THE RABBET JOINT

Joining the two parts with a *rabbet* is your best option. Don't squirm; there is nothing difficult about a rabbet joint. All that is required is a notch along the bottom edge of the fiddle rail. Assuming that the shelf is $^1/_2$-inch plywood, you want the notch $^1/_2$ inch wide so that the bottom of the rail will be flush with the bottom of the shelf. The deeper the rabbet, the stronger the joint it will be, but you don't want to leave less than about $^1/_4$ inch of wood at the bottom of the rabbet or the remaining piece may break off. With $^3/_4$-inch-thick stock, cut the rabbet to a depth of about $^1/_2$ inch.

Use a fence to establish the width of the rabbet and to make the first cut accurately.

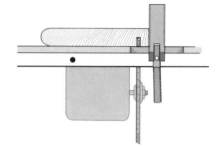

Freehand the second cut at the edge of the board to give the outside of the rabbet a cut edge and avoid chipping.

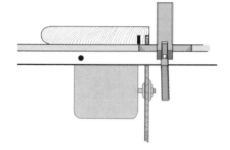

Make additional freehand passes to remove the material between these two initial cuts.

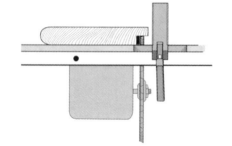

The finished rabbet.

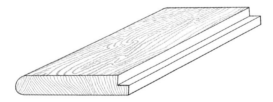

Cutting a rabbet joint with a table saw.

Imagine a saw blade $1/2$ inch wide. If you set the depth of cut to $1/2$ inch and used a rip guide to place the inside edge of the blade $1/2$ inch from the bottom edge of the rail, a single pass with the saw will give you the $1/2$-inch-deep, $1/2$-inch-wide rabbet you want. This is exactly how a dado blade on a table saw works. The regular blade on your table saw is more likely to give you an $1/8$-inch-wide cut, but if you move the guide $1/8$ inch and make a second cut, you now have a $1/4$-inch notch. Two more passes and you have the $1/2$-inch rabbet. Actually, after the first cut, you can freehand

the remaining cuts. It is advisable to make the second cut right along the edge of the rail, then remove the wood between the two cuts with additional passes of the saw. This will minimize the risk of chipping when you remove the last of the material.

Whether Router

You can also cut a rabbet with your router. Most piloted rabbet bits are limited to a $3/8$-inch width, so use a straight bit. If the router has an accessory guide fence, you can use it to limit the width of your cut to $1/2$ inch. You can accomplish the same thing by clamping a straight board or a length of $3/4$-inch aluminum angle to the base of the router. Set the depth of the cut to $1/2$ inch, and check both depth and width by making a practice cut on a scrap of material, adjusting the guide and the depth as required.

Red Alert

A word about safety is essential. You *can* drill a hole in your hand with a power drill, but it is not *likely* to happen unless you hold the material you are drilling from behind. A circular saw is dangerous enough, but the blade guard provides a good deal of protection from momentary lapses of caution. A finishing sander cannot injure you, and if your belt sander runs amok, the consequences will be similar to those of tangling your two left feet on an asphalt tennis court. A router, on the other hand, is about as benign as a cornered bobcat. The razor-sharp bits are totally unprotected and accelerate from stopped to 25,000 rpm in an instant. *Every time* you change bits, disable the tool by unplugging it and never, *never* rest a router on your leg or in your lap. Accidentally hit the trigger switch while any part of your body is in contact with the bit, and you will spend the rest of your life without that part.

Keep Right

Move the router in the direction opposite to the rotation of the cutter. With the router on top of the workpiece, the cutter spins in a clockwise direction, so you should move the router in a counterclockwise direction. That means left to right when the cutter is between you and the board, right to left when the board is between you and the cutter. A router will cut in either direction, but if you feed it in the wrong direction, it will be harder to control because the bit is trying to push the tool away from the stock, and the finish will not be as good. Always start and stop the router with the bit clear of the wood.

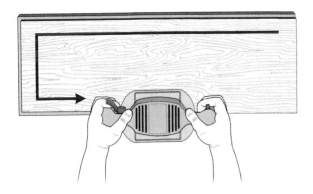

When making an outside cut, move the router counterclockwise.

The only trick to using a router is to avoid overloading the cutter. For a rabbet that means making two or three passes to make the cut. Keep the sole plate flat and run the blade across the wood to cut away about half a cutter width of material. Your guide fence will not be in contact with the edge yet. Pull the blade away from the wood, go back to the other end of your cut, and make a second pass, again taking about half a cutter width of material. If you are using a $^3/_8$-inch bit, this means you will have cut about $^3/_8$ inch in from the edge in two passes, leaving only about $^1/_8$ inch of material to be removed to give you your $^1/_2$-inch rabbet. This is when your fence rides against the remaining edge. Sometimes it is even wise to set the depth slightly shallow, then make a second series of passes with the tool reset to the correct depth to give you a finish cut that will be smooth.

If you are putting sea rails on several shelves, cut the rabbet in the board *before* you cut it into sections. Any problems that you experience in cutting a rabbet with a router are almost certain to occur while your guide is only half engaged—when you start the cut and as you finish it. A single start and finish reduces the opportunity for trouble, and if you screw up anyway, the bad section can be cut away before you divide the board into the lengths you need.

Taking the Edge Off

Unless the ends of the rails are to be contoured, radius the top edge before the rabbeted board is cut into sections. The sharp corners can be removed by block sanding or with a finishing sander, but a more attractive edge is achieved with the router and a $^3/_8$-inch round-over bit. A round-over bit with a ball-bearing pilot is pretty much foolproof. Adjust the depth so the curve of the bit ends just *above* the router sole plate, and run the cutter along the edge

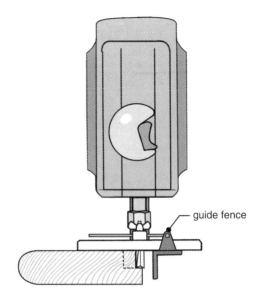

First pass should remove about half a cutter width of material from the edge. It can be advisable to set the initial cutter depth slightly shallow.

— guide fence

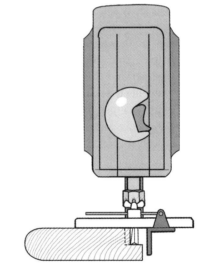

Keep sole plate flat on the material and remove a half cutter width of material on subsequent passes.

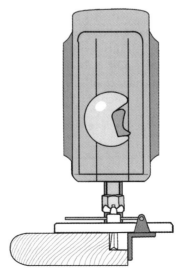

When the fence engages the fiddle it will limit the last pass of the cutter to the intended rabbet width and insure a straight final cut.

Cutting a rabbet with a router.

A ³/₈-inch round-over bit will put a near-perfect radius on the top of a ³/₄-inch-thick fiddle rail.

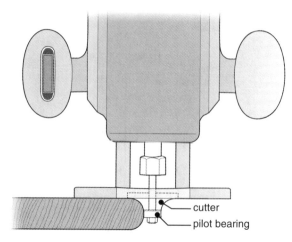

cutter

pilot bearing

with the pilot in contact with the wood. Check it on a scrap of the same material. Turn the wood over and run the router against the same edge. This will give you an almost perfectly rounded top edge.

From the rabbeted and radiused board, cut a rail to the same length as the width of the shelf. The front edge of the shelf fits into the rabbet. Hold the two parts tightly together and drill pilot holes from the bottom of the shelf into the rail. Space screws between 6 and 12 inches apart. Open up the pilot holes in the shelf to shank diameter and countersink them into the bottom of the shelf. If you have the proper combination bit, you can drill the pilot hole, the shank hole, and the countersink all at the same time. Coat both surfaces of the rabbet and the top and edge of the shelf with glue and screw the parts together. The rabbet gives you a strong joint and hides the raw edge of the plywood.

GLUE BLOCK

A quick and easy alternative to the rabbet is the glue-block joint. Screw and/or glue cleat stock along the bottom of the shelf flush with its front edge. Screw and/or glue the fiddle rail to the cleat stock. The wood must be wider than the height you want the fiddle by the combined thickness of the shelf and

the cleat stock. This joint does not exhibit the same level of craftsmanship as the rabbet joint, but it is equally strong and quite adequate in many applications.

REVIEW OF AN INDEPENDENT BOARD

Sometimes a rail that is not permanently attached to the shelf will be a better choice. For example, instead of canting the shelf in the galley, you might have installed a removable rail in front of it. Such a rail would be effective at greater angles of heel or roll than the inclined shelf, yet it would not interfere with access to the contents of the shelf when the boat is not underway.

You can make a simple and elegant sea rail quite easily by running the round-over bit of your router along the top and bottom of both edges of a teak or mahogany board. The size of the board will depend on what the rail is intended to hold in place. For a galley shelf I would use a board ³/₄ inch thick and about 2 inches wide.

If the rail will sit on the shelf, you need only slots at each end that you can create with short parallel lengths of small cleat stock. If you want to locate the rail some distance above the shelf, you will have to add a bottom across your cleat-stock slots, or you can improve the look and probably the durability of the rail mounting by cutting a pair of U-shaped brackets.

These brackets can be cut from almost anything. If they will be exposed, you might elect to fashion them from the same material as the rail, but inside a cabinet ¹/₂-inch plywood is a good choice. The depth of the U should be about the same as the height of the rail. In this example, you would lay out (not cut out) a rectangle 2¹/₄ inches wide and about 3 inches long. Place a mark on the centerline of the rectangle and about 1⁵/₈ inches from one end. Put the point of your compass on that mark and open it until the pencil just touches one of the sides, then swing a half-circle arc to the opposite side. Use a spade bit to drill a ³/₄-inch hole—the width of the rail—at the mark. Note that the radius of the drill (³/₈ inch) added to the dimension from the edge to the mark (1⁵/₈ inches) equals the height of the rail (2 inches). No, that is not a coincidence.

Use your square to draw two lines from the straight end tangent to the drilled hole and parallel to the sides. Cut from the edge to the hole along these two lines with your saber saw, creating the U-shaped cutout. Now cut out the piece by running the saw along one side, around the half-circle arc, and back along the other side, releasing the completed bracket. You can fabricate a pair of identical brackets at the same time by clamping two pieces of material together before you start.

Glue-block joint.

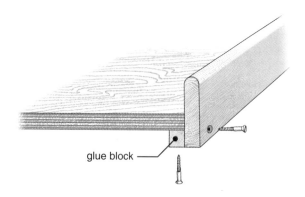

glue block

1

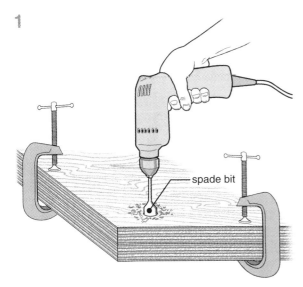

Clamping two boards together to make a pair of matching brackets at the same time, bore a hole the width of the fiddle to create the bottom of the slot.

2

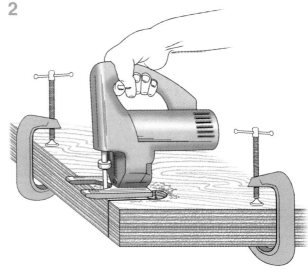

Make parallel cuts from the top edge to the hole perimeter to complete the slot.

3

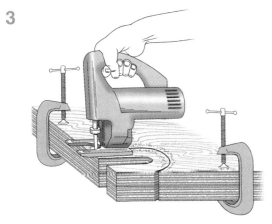

Make a U-shaped cut to complete the bracket.

4

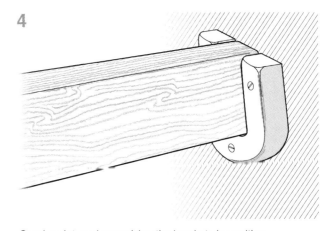

Sand, paint, and screw/glue the brackets in position.

Fabricating brackets for removable fiddle/sea rails.

Round the sharp edges on the front of the bracket with a sander. Using the rail as a guide, tack the brackets in place, making certain the rail does not bind. When you have them positioned, glue them in place.

Rant on Rails

Like shelves, rails have numerous applications. Installed across the shelves typically found above bunks and settees, a removable rail fabricated and mounted in exactly the same way provides secure stowage for tall items such as books and bottles.

A rail installed in the icebox or refrigerator corrals breakable items. Sliding countertop items to the back of the counter and dropping a removable rail in front of them when you are getting underway is easier than finding space for each of the items inside a cabinet.

An effective bunk board is nothing more than a large removable sea rail. A bunk board that drops into U-shaped brackets has the advantage of allowing you to install it on *top* of the cushion so that you can narrow the bunk into a proper sea berth. In port you want bunks to be as wide as possible, but you will be thrown around at sea if the bunk is more than a couple of inches wider than your shoulders. More than one set of brackets allows the width to be adjusted to the individual off watch. You will not have this versatility with a hinged board or a canvas lee cloth.

CEILING

Ceiling strips are little different from fiddle rails. While newer boats usually hide the inside of the hull with some type of inner liner—not necessarily an improvement—the hull is exposed in a lot of older boats, especially in the forward cabin. Sometimes it is painted like the inside of a bass boat (real nice!), and sometimes it is covered with a piece of carpet or vinyl. A wooden ceiling is easy to install and can make a marvelous difference in the appearance of a cabin.

The first step is to get rid of what is there now. This can be easy or nasty, depending on what the covering is. I leave this part to you. You are out to expose the bare interior surface of the hull, or at least enough of it to allow you to bond vertical frames on about 16-inch centers.

LAYING THE FRAMEWORK

Like wall studs, vertical frames give you something to attach the horizontal ceiling slats to. Saw them from a solid plank if the hull sides are nearly straight, or laminate them with strips of ¼-inch plywood if there is lots of vertical curvature where you are installing the ceiling. You want the frames to be about 1½ inches wide and about ¾ inch thick.

Cut solid frames by sawing several ¾-inch strips from a 2 × board. You can do this with a circular saw with an edge guide, but it is far easier on a table saw. Crank the blade all the way up and use a steel square to check that it is perpendicular to the table. Never trust the bevel gauge on the saw, particularly on an inexpensive table saw. With your board lying against the blade, crank it back down until its height exceeds the height of the board by just half the length of a tooth. Install the supplied fence next to the blade; adjust it to make the space between the fence and the tooth of the blade ¾ inch. Start the saw, then feed the board through it, pressing it against the fence. You will need a wood "pusher" to push the cut strip beyond the spinning blade. Keep flesh well away from the blade whenever it is running. You can keep

Ripping strips from a wide board. Use a pusher to complete the cut, keeping your hands well clear of the blade.

feeding the same board through the saw for one cut after another—like shaving deli slices off a Boar's Head Tavern ham—until you have as many pieces as you want or until you have cut it entirely into ¾-inch strips.

These frames will be glassed over, so they can be sliced from a common fir or pine 2 × 4—which will actually measure 1½ by 3½. You can allow a solid wood frame to bend to the curvature of the hull by cutting kerfs in the back side. *Kerf* is just a specialty term for the groove a saw cut makes. Make cuts across the back of the board about every 2 inches to a depth of about half the thickness of the board, and you should be able to press it into the curve of the hull without a lot of force. If the hull has lots of curvature where you are installing the ceiling, you will do better to build the frames from three thicknesses of ¼-inch plywood glued into place one layer at a time. This in effect creates a laminated curved frame.

Glue either the solid frame or the first layer of plywood to the hull with quick-set epoxy. Use tape across the ends to position the frame. Hold it against the hull with a brace wedged across the boat. An adjustable brace is easy to create with two lengths of

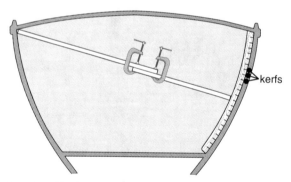

A series of kerfs—half-depth cuts across the board—will let a solid wood frame assume a modest curve.

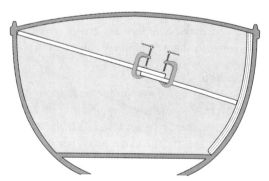

For greater curvature laminate the frames from strips of thin plywood.

Bonding frames for wood ceiling to the hull.

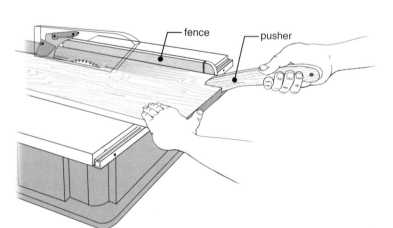

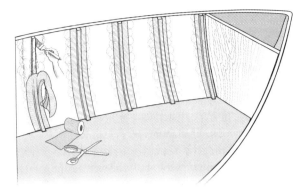

Fiberglass frames in place with a single layer of cloth.

cleat stock clamped together. If you are laminating the frames, apply the second and third plies after the epoxy holding the previous one sets. Because you are going to fiberglass these frames, you will be ahead of the game if you round off the top corners before you install them. After they are glued in place, thicken some epoxy and create a fillet between the hull and the frame on each side to remove the sharp inner corner that the fiberglass would bridge. Glass each frame to the hull as detailed in Chapter 6, but use a single 8-inch-wide strip of 4- or 6-ounce fiberglass cloth. Don't forget to grind away the bass-boat paint! You need a frame near each end of the area to be ceiled and intermediate frames as required to keep the span between frames under 20 inches.

Filling the space between the frames with insulation will make your boat cooler in summer and warmer in winter, and it will reduce or eliminate condensation wherever the insulation is installed. You can use common $3/4$-inch rigid foam wall insulation found at your home supply store. You want the kind with foil on one or both sides. If you put the foil side against the hull, it serves as a radiant heat barrier. The foil also might improve your boat's radar reflection.

Cut the insulation to fit between the glassed frames. Spray the interior surface of the cut pieces with flat black enamel so they will not show if you leave a space between your ceiling slats. You can slit the outboard covering as necessary to allow the rigid board to assume the hull contour. You will not need to attach the insulation; the ceiling will capture it.

RIPPED SLATS

Just to validate the intelligence of the human race, a 2-inch hardwood board will not be 2 inches, and it won't be $1^1/2$ inches either. It will be $1^3/4$ inches thick. Hey, that's okay. An inch and three quarters is a pleasing

ceiling slat size. Buy 2-inch (ha!) planks of the wood of your choice at least as long as the section of hull you are covering and of sufficient total width to rip the number of slats you require. Remember that each cut makes sawdust out of about $1/8$ inch of the board, so cutting $3/8$-inch-thick slats will actually consume $1/2$ inch of your board. A quarter inch is normally thick enough, but you may need to sand the cut slats heavily to remove the saw marks, depending on the quality of your blade, so cut thickness should greater.

Set your blade height to a half tooth more than $1^3/4$ inches and your fence to a rip width of $3/8$ inch (or slightly less if you like). Here is a tip. Clamp the plank upright and rout both edges before running it through the table saw. This will give you a cut slat with the edges already rounded uniformly. Rout before each cut. This might seem kind of herky-jerky,

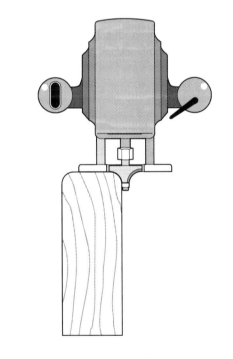

Round over two edges of the plank first.

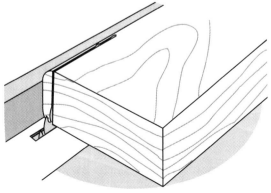

Rip a slat-thickness strip from the rounded edge. Repeat as many times as necessary to cut as many slats as you require.

Turning out shaped ceiling slats.

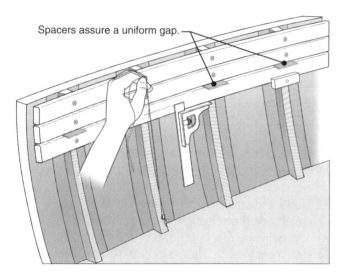

Spacers assure a uniform gap.

A string pulled tight provides alignment guidance for installing the screws in a straight line and in the center of the frame.

with stainless steel. If you want the screws hidden behind plugs, you will need to use shorter flathead screws, and your slats will need to be not less than $^3/_8$ inch thick to allow a counterbore of sufficient depth to hold a wood plug. A combination bit will create a counterbore if you simply feed it farther into the wood, but it can leave a ragged edge in some materials. For holes to be plugged, use a Forstner bit, which bores very cleanly.

To align the screws, mark the slat centerlines with a combination square set to half the slat width. Attach strings to nails centered at the bottom of each frame, and use these to position the screws in vertical alignment and centered on the frame. Assemble the entire ceiling, cutting each slat to the necessary length and angle to provide a slight clearance at the ends, again to avoid creaking. Disassemble the ceiling, numbering and orienting each slat on the back side, and apply whatever finish you choose. When the wood is coated and dry, reinstall the slats; add trim molding to the ends and perhaps above and below to hide any cut edges.

but it will save you a lot of shaping and give you more uniform slats. If you have a planer, by all means use it to finish the top surface of the slats. Otherwise sand them as necessary to remove all saw marks. Making the initial pass with 60-grit paper in your palm sander will reduce the time this takes.

Wooden boats leave space between ceiling slats to allow air to circulate. This is not a bad idea even for a fiberglass boat, plus it looks traditional and avoids a potential source of creaking when the boat is underway. Keep the spacing even with temporary spacers (cut from almost anything hard the thickness of the space you want) between the slats.

Pilot drill the frame, and drill and countersink the slat. This is where a combination bit that does all three at once will save you a lot of time. Use #8 oval-head screws, either $^3/_4$ or 1 inch long, depending on the thickness of your slats. No matter how nice brass screws look when they are new, in a couple of years they will be ugly, so stick

A vast improvement over bass-boat paint.

DIVIDE AND CONQUER

I do not mean to be obsessive about stowage, but I have never seen a boat where everything the owner wanted aboard could be stowed out of sight. I wonder if that's what Water Rat meant when he called it "messing about"? I have also never seen a boat that could not gain *usable* stowage with the addition of a shelf or a divider or a cabinet. But the real reason for this emphasis is because these kinds of projects are, for the most part, out of sight—the perfect location for anyone's first attempts to take a sheet or block of wood and shape it into something else.

Dividers are nothing more than shelves turned on end. Any large storage area used for keeping small items will benefit from a divider. Drawers in particular are more efficient or at least less annoying when they are compartmented.

DRAWER DIVIDERS

Making a drawer divider requires $^1/_8$-inch plywood and some thin cleat stock. Determine the length of the divider by measuring the inside width of the drawer. The height of the divider should be about $^1/_2$ inch *less* than the depth of the drawer. Set your saw fence to this latter dimension and rip the divider from your plywood. To crosscut the divider square, set the saw's miter gauge to 90 degrees and use it to feed just a sliver of the edge of the divider strip through the saw blade. Check this cut with a square. Now measure along the leading edge of the divider the width of the drawer less about $^1/_{16}$ for clearance, and put a pencil mark on the strip. With the

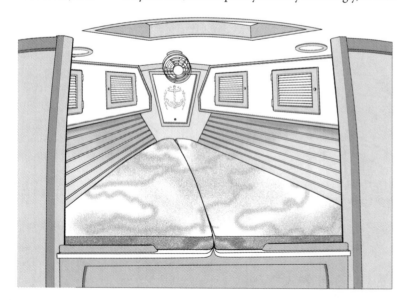

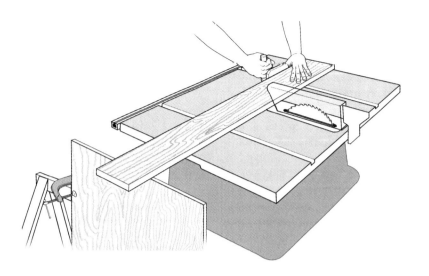

A miter gauge makes it easy to make square crosscuts.

saw stopped, hold the strip against the miter gauge and feed it forward until it touches the saw blade. Slide it left or right to align the tooth edge with the mark, taking care that you will be cutting outside the mark. Back the material away from the blade, start the saw, and make the cut by simply pushing the miter gauge forward in its channel. Tell yourself again how smart you were to buy this table saw.

In addition to the divider, you are going to need to cut four lengths of cleat stock to the divider height. Small square stock or quarter-round molding, $^1/_4$ or $^3/_8$ inch, will be better proportioned for this use than the $^3/_4$-inch cleat stock we used to support shelves.

Mark the drawer sides with the desired location of the divider. Glue and clamp one cleat on each side against that mark. Wrap a piece of waxed paper under the bottom and across each end of the divider and hold the divider against the two cleats. Glue and clamp the second pair of cleats to the drawer sides, locating them against the divider. The waxed paper protects the divider from accidental bonding and provides clearance between the divider and the sandwiching cleats.

To separate the drawer into four compartments requires a second divider inserted perpendicular to the first. Where the two intersect, each will need an $^1/_8$-inch-wide slot cut halfway through the height dimension. Crank your table saw blade up to full height to make these cuts, which will minimize the curvature at the bottom of the slots. Install the first divider with the slot open at the top. The second divider, with the slot open at the bottom, slips slot to slot over the first, the uncut portion of each divider fitting into the slot of the other. If you interlock several dividers in this

quarter-round molding

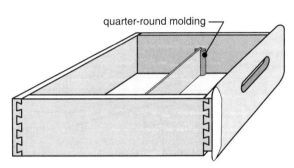

Slots created with cleat stock secure divider ends.

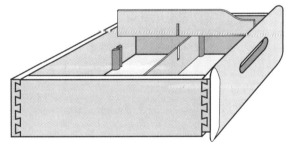

Half-height interlocking slots allow intersecting dividers.

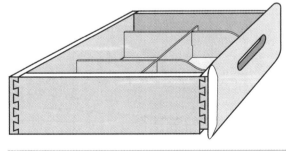

Crate-like divider configurations may not need cleats.

Drawer dividers.

manner, dividing the drawer into additional compartments Coke-case style, you can dispense with the cleats. The interlocked dividers will be sufficiently rigid to stay in place.

LOCKER DIVIDERS

Locker dividers are less likely to be square since most boat lockers are positioned against the hull. As a result, fitting and attaching a locker divider is slightly more complicated. There are a number of methods for transferring the curvature of the hull to a piece of plywood, and you have already seen how to do it by dragging the point of a compass along the hull while the pencil duplicates the contour on the wood. But to use the compass method you have to be able to hold the wood in place near the hull. If the shelf you contoured earlier using this method had extended all the way to the front of the locker, it would not have fit inside the locker until the contour was cut, but you could not have outlined the contour until it went inside the locker.

Smart Stick

The solution to this catch-22 is a sharp stick. A length of screen molding with a point whittled on one end is perfect. You also need a square of cardboard, maybe a flap from the surprisingly small box your new table saw came in—a little extra value from your purchase.

Place the cardboard where you want the divider and tape it there to the top and front of the locker. Two straight sides of the cardboard should correspond with the straight sides of the divider. All you need is the irregular part. That is where the stick comes in. First draw a vertical line on the hull where you want the edge of the finished divider to be. Now place the pointed stick flat on the cardboard with the point extended to touch the hull at the highest point that the divider will touch. Trace a pencil mark onto

Put the point against the contour, trace alongside the stick, then "tick" both line and stick with an alignment cross mark. Number the mark on both stick and trace line.

1
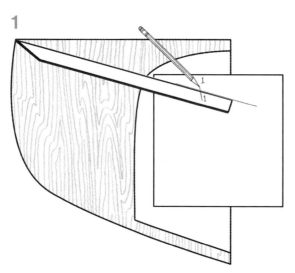

2
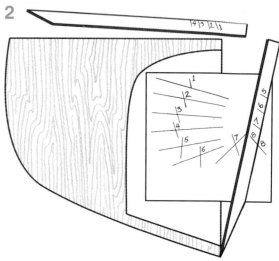

Move the point to a different place on the contour and trace and tick this stick position. Continue following the contour, marking and numbering each stick position.

Affix the tracing to the wood and realign the stick to each trace line and numbered cross mark. Mark the wood at the location of the stick's point. Join the marked points with a smooth curve.

3
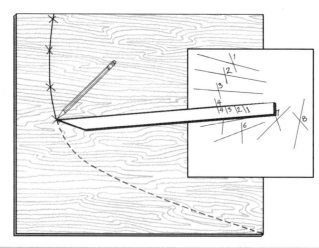

With a pointed stick and a piece of stiff cardboard, you can duplicate any contour on the boat.

the cardboard alongside the stick, then put a cross mark on the cardboard and the stick. Label this cross "1" on both the stick and the cardboard. Reposition the stick to put the point against the hull in a lower spot on your vertical line, and trace a new line on the cardboard to follow the stick's new position. Put matching alignment marks on the cardboard and the stick in this new position and label them both "2." Continue repositioning the point of the stick and tracing it on the cardboard until the point has reached the bottom corner of your divider location. Along the way you may need to change to a shorter stick. The number of measurements you take will depend on how accurate you want the contour to be. A half-dozen evenly spaced measurements will generally be sufficient to freehand a fairly accurate fit for a divider, but for a new bulkhead you might want to "tick" a position at 1-inch intervals.

To transfer the curve to the wood, simply tape the cardboard square to a square corner of the plywood and realign the stick with the traces and numbered alignment marks. Mark the location of the point of the stick onto the plywood. Join this mark with a smooth curve and cut along this curve with your saber saw. The divider should be a perfect fit.

Install the divider by gluing cleats to the front and top of the locker, then screwing or gluing the divider to the cleats—like installing a shelf sideways. The easiest way by far to attach a permanent divider to the hull is to run a bead of polyurethane adhesive sealant along the curved edge of the divider before you install it.

When you do not want the divider to reach either the front or the top of the locker, you can still attach it to the hull with polyurethane sealant, but somehow you must stabilize the front and top. A rail across the front of the divider several inches above the bottom will hold the front rigid and may be desirable anyway to contain the items that will be on either side of it. You can use either solid wood or $\frac{1}{2}$-inch plywood.

Measure the width of the locker and cut the rail to that length. The width of the rail will depend on its function. Hold the cut rail in place against the front edge of the divider and trace both sides of it onto the rail. Now cut an $\frac{1}{8}$-inch-deep dado between those lines.

DADO

Both vowels are long—"day dough." What is a dado? For nonwoodworkers it could be something you shout just before daylight come (and you want to go home). Serious woodworkers use the word *dado* for the same reason sailors use *starboard*—to give the impression of specialized knowledge. A dado is a groove, period.

Well, technically, it's a groove across the grain. I suppose that makes you wonder what they call a groove parallel to the grain. A groove. Pretty impressive stuff, huh? Not every writer is this erudite.

How do you make a dado? Continue the trace lines up the edge of the rail so you can see them. Set the blade height to $\frac{1}{8}$ inch above the table. Put the rail against your table saw's miter gauge and align one of the marks with the tooth edge, with the blade between the two marks. Start the saw and run the rail over the blade. Reposition the rail to make a second cut at the other mark, again taking care that the blade is between the two marks. Now you can remove the material between the two kerfs with additional passes of the saw. Slide the rail along the miter gauge just less than $\frac{1}{8}$ inch between cuts.

Glue the edge of the divider into the dado and attach the ends of the rail to cleats glued to the sides of the lockers. If you need it, you can add a similar brace across the top of the divider(s) as far toward the front as use will permit.

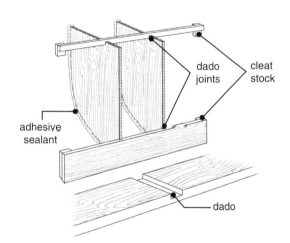

Assembly details.

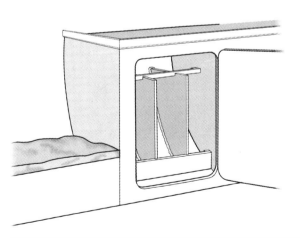

Locker dividers.

BIN THERE

The cavernous nature of cockpit lockers typically results in wasted space, particularly the space high on the hull close to the underside of the side deck. You can gain the use of this space by attaching two or more triangular bulkheads—the inboard side of each triangle vertical (or near vertical), the top matching the underside of the deck, and the outboard side matching the curvature of the hull. Tab these bulkheads to the underside of the deck and to the hull with epoxy and fiberglass strips on each side that turn out onto the laminate at least 2 inches. Don't forget to grind

before you glass (Chapter 6). Rip $1^1/_2$-inch-wide slats from $^1/_4$-inch plywood and screw (and glue) three or four of these across the front of the bulkheads about $1^1/_2$ inches apart. If you really want to impress the marina set, make the slats from solid teak.

I *know* what I said earlier about fastening and gluing to the edge of plywood, but the strength of the bond should be adequate here if you don't stow your storm anchor in the bin. If you remark on my inconsistency, you will tempt me to inquire why you didn't just use a free slat as a spacer instead of measuring between the slats to position them. You can add a cleat stock glue

Tab vertical bulkheads to hull and underside of deck.

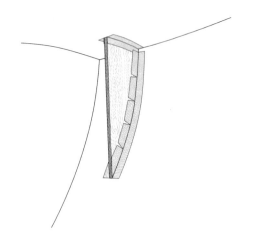

1

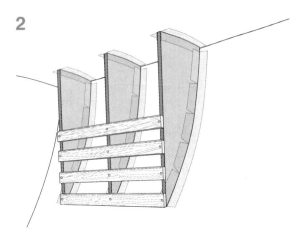

2

Span bulkheads with horizontal slats to create a bin.

Making top slat removable combines wider access with increased security. Secure with end slots, keyholes, or latch hooks.

3

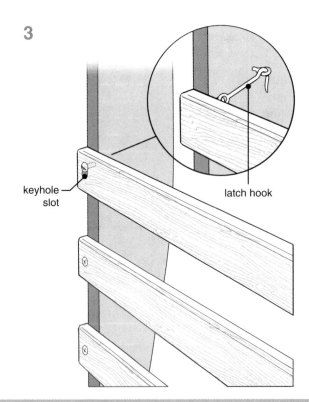

keyhole slot

latch hook

block inside or outside the bulkhead along the inboard edge if you want to pump up the slat-to-side strength.

A removable top slat can improve access and allow for the insertion of larger items. I like hook latches for this, but you can also use a keyhole mount or fabricate a slot.

THE BASIC BOX

In plywood box construction you will again find yourself gluing the edge of the plywood unless you elect to make glue-block joints. And why, exactly, are you building a plywood box? Because the box—sometimes modified to accommodate the curvature of the hull—is the basic structure of most of the interior features of your boat and several items on deck. It is also the basis for an almost limitless number of additions and modifications.

Consider the chain locker. The chain and line stack or coil into the bottom of the locker. As in cockpit lockers, the space high in the forepeak—up against the underside of the deck—is typically wasted. More modern designs might include a box in the top of the chain locker with a hatch on deck for anchor stowage, but you will not find this feature in early fiberglass boats. Personally I prefer the anchors on rollers at the bow ready to do their job in an instant, but I do like the idea of a box in the top of the forepeak for other items. Rather than compromise the integrity of the deck with a hatch, access for this box will be from below through the forepeak bulkhead.

BOXED BIN

The forepeak bulkhead usually has an opening into the chain locker. The area of the bulkhead above the opening will determine the maximum box height that will be practical for your boat. Width will be limited by the width of the chain locker, and depth by the curvature of the bow or the location of the chain pipe.

The intended use of the space will also influence the size and shape of the box. Perhaps you would like his-and-her bins for individual stowage of personal items. Maybe a bookcase appeals to you. The broad and deep but short-height aspect of the available space may be perfect for stowing extra charts, the *World Atlas* (which absolutely, positively will not fit anywhere else on a boat), or the V-berth filler board.

Once you have determined the configuration of the box, construction is a breeze. How you measure the parts will depend on whether available space makes the external dimensions the critical ones or the planned contents make the internal dimensions more critical. Once again, a quick sketch with the dimensions written on it can help you to avoid confusion.

For this example the box sides will be constructed of $1/2$-inch plywood and the back piece of $1/4$-inch plywood, but you can use thinner plywood or other sheet or solid materials as appropriate. Set your fence to the intended depth of the box and rip a strip of $1/2$-inch plywood long enough to provide all four sides of the box. If you are constrained by the external dimensions, cut this strip $1/4$ inch—the thickness of the back piece—narrower than the intended exterior depth dimension.

Working again with the miter guide on the table saw set at 90 degrees, you can cut the sides to the correct length by marking the wood and sawing at your mark or by setting a fence to the side length and running the end of the stock—still in the miter guide—against the fence. The fence method will give you sides of identical length. Cut the longer two side pieces $1/2$ inch shorter than the desired external dimension because these will fit into rabbets you are going to cut into the shorter side pieces.

The design calls for a $1/4$-inch rabbet along both edges of the shorter side pieces, but when cutting a rabbet in plywood, you will have better results if you set the blade to finish the cut at the glue joint between two of the plies. Determine a cut depth that gives a smooth bottom surface by making test cuts on a scrap of the same plywood.

Set your fence $1/2$ inch from the *outside* of the blade. With the wood square against the miter guide and the fence, feed it across the spinning blade to make the first cut. Slide the piece along the miter guide and away from the fence to place the second cut right at the edge of the stock. Make additional cuts to remove the stock between the two initial cuts, sliding the piece along the miter guide about a saw-blade width between passes. After you do this once, you will see that you can actually cut the rabbet more quickly than I can describe it.

Leave the fence in position, turn the side piece around, and cut a rabbet in the other end in exactly the same way. Put rabbets in the ends of the other short side piece.

Hold the two rabbeted sides against one of the side pieces without a rabbet; measure the finished width of the box, which may have changed slightly due to the depth of the rabbets. Use this dimension and the length of the side pieces to cut the back/bottom piece from $1/4$-inch plywood.

If you have bar clamps or pipe clamps, you can simply coat the joint surfaces with glue and assemble the box back/bottom-up on a flat surface. Hold the parts together with the clamps. Before the joint glue sets, coat the up edges of the assembled box with glue and tack the back/bottom piece in place with six or eight finishing nails, squaring the box as necessary. When the glue sets, the box is finished.

If you do not have clamps long enough to reach across the box, dry assemble it with flathead screws, then dismantle and apply the glue, using the screws to provide the needed clamping pressure.

The Opening

After the box is built, it's time to cut the access hole in the bulkhead. If the box will be a utility bin, you will want the hole to be somewhat smaller than the mouth of the box to restrain the contents. As a bookcase, on the other hand, the hole and the mouth of the box should be approximately the same size. Cutting the hole an inch or two shorter in height than the mouth of the box will provide an integral fiddle rail.

Position the box inside the forepeak, allowing room on all four sides for the cleats that you are going to attach it with, and trace the outline. Draw a second outline $1/2$ inch inside the first to represent the mouth of the box. If the opening will be smaller, and perhaps with circular ends, lay this out inside the smaller outline.

Rout the opening if there is room. If you limit the travel of a router with a surrounding frame—essentially a four-sided fence—the router will make a uniform cutout with radiused corners. The size of the cutout is determined by the frame. It is easy enough to tack together a frame for the cutout size you need, then affix it to the forepeak bulkhead with double-sided tape. With the frame in place as a restraint, freehand the initial cutout, keeping the router base just clear of the frame. Normally you want to limit the depth of a plunge cut with a router bit to less than $1/2$ inch, so to rout an opening through a 1-inch plywood bulkhead, plan to make two or three passes with the router, increasing the depth of the cut by about $3/8$ to $1/2$ inch each time. After you have made a cutout and removed the center piece, make a finish pass with the router base against the frame to clean up and square the cutout perimeter.

Unfortunately you will probably not have room for a standard router. (Small size is what makes a less powerful but more nimble laminate router a wonderful boat tool.) You may have room for a saber saw. If you make the cutout with a saw, start by drilling at the corners to create the corner radiuses. If you use a spade bit, remember to drill from the back only until the point penetrates and then finish the hole from the front. When you drill the corners, you only need to make straight cuts between the holes to complete the opening. Aside from being easier and probably resulting in a more accurate cutout, this also allows you to

feed the saw from either direction, which can be important when clearance is restricted.

Saber Saw Candor

Two cautions and a truth about saber saws: they are notoriously inaccurate, they chip plastic laminate, and all that saw behind the blade often prevents completing the entire cut.

If your sideways pressure on a saber saw is a bit uneven, and it will be, the blade will deflect and the cut will be beveled rather than square. This is why routing the opening is preferred.

Wood-cutting blades chip plastic laminate. If the bulkhead is covered with high-pressure laminate, use a laminate blade in your saber saw. This blade has no set to it and cuts on the downward stroke, so it will not cut the plywood quickly, but it will minimize chipping of the cut edge of the laminate.

A saber saw turns corners like an 18-wheeler. The bigger the saw, the worse the problem, so shorter saws are generally better for boat use where much of your cutting will be done in situ. This project is a case in point, with the required cutout near the underside of the deck and probably close to the hull. Cutting from drilled corner to drilled corner avoids turning the saw and allows for making the cut with the back of the saw away from the restriction. With a large holesaw, you can make the ends of a narrow cutout circular, limiting the saw cuts to two straight cuts. Where there is insufficient clearance to allow making the entire cut with your electric saber saw, you will need the manual equivalent—a keyhole saw.

Mounting

Cut four pieces of cleat stock to completely frame the box. To avoid the difficulty of trying to drill straight holes in the cleats after they are attached, predrill and countersink shank-diameter holes 3 to 4 inches apart in the cleats. Glue and clamp the cleats *flush* with the front edge of the box and with the countersinks facing the rear.

Hold the box in place and mark the screw locations on the bulkhead with a prick mark, using a sharpened nail the size of the holes in the cleats. Measure the thickness of the bulkhead and fold a piece of paper tape around your pilot drill at least $1/4$ inch less than that from the point. Press the ends of the tape together into a flap. This is your depth guide, and you will want to stop the drill just before the flap sweeps against the wood. Do not allow the tape to be pushed up the bit or the holes will be deeper than you want, perhaps even penetrating the bulkhead. Drill all the pilot holes, then glue and screw the box to the bulkhead with flathead screws.

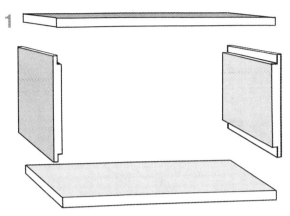

All sides can be cut from a single plank. Rabbet two sides.

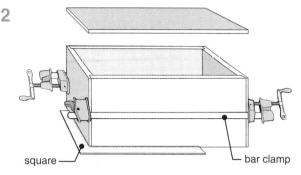

square — — bar clamp

Glue sides together, then glue/nail on back/bottom.

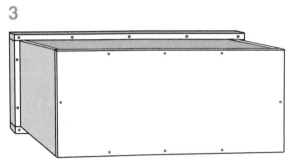

Frame outside of open end with cleat stock for mounting.

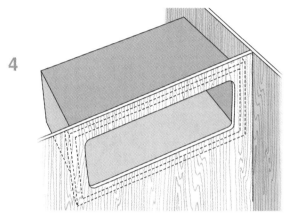

Cut opening in bulkhead and screw box to backside over opening.

Forepeak box.

BOX ENCLOSURE

The outside of the box bin is out of view, with the rabbet joints giving you a smooth interior, but what if you want a box where the exterior will be exposed—a speaker enclosure or perhaps a toiletry cabinet. The first difference is that you will want to use a different material, either solid wood or hardwood plywood. The second difference is that to hide the end grain you will join the sides with rabbet blocks.

The Versatile Rabbet Block

Rabbet blocks are easy to make on a table saw. Start with solid wood, square stock with a cross section of $1^1/_4$ inches or a little more. Set the blade to make a $^1/_2$-inch-deep cut. Set your fence $^1/_2$ inch from the outside of the blade—assuming the box is constructed of $^1/_2$-inch material. Run your stock through the saw against the fence, putting a $^1/_2$-inch kerf the length of the stock.

Now pay attention. Rotate the stock clockwise 90 degrees. In other words, turn it on its right side. Next turn it end for end. If you did this right, the face with the kerf is now against the fence. Run the piece

through the saw again; this second cut intersects the first one, finishing the rabbet.

However, to make a rabbet block you need two rabbets, one diagonal from the other. Rotate the stock 180 degrees, putting the rabbet you just cut at the top and away from the fence. Run the stock through the saw against the fence. Now repeat the earlier sequence of rotating the stock clockwise 90 degrees, then spinning it end for end. One more cut and the second rabbet is complete.

When you rip the stock for the sides of your box, crosscut the rabbet block stock with the same setup to yield four corner blocks of matching length. Rabbet blocks at the four corners of the box serve the dual function of providing a glue block and hiding the end grain of the side pieces. Gluing the box together is also made easier because you don't need bar clamps. You can assemble this box with C-clamps—in two steps—using pads under the clamps to prevent marring the face of the wood. After the box is assembled, the solid corners can be routed with the round-over bit. Another possibility is to make the rabbet slightly deeper than the

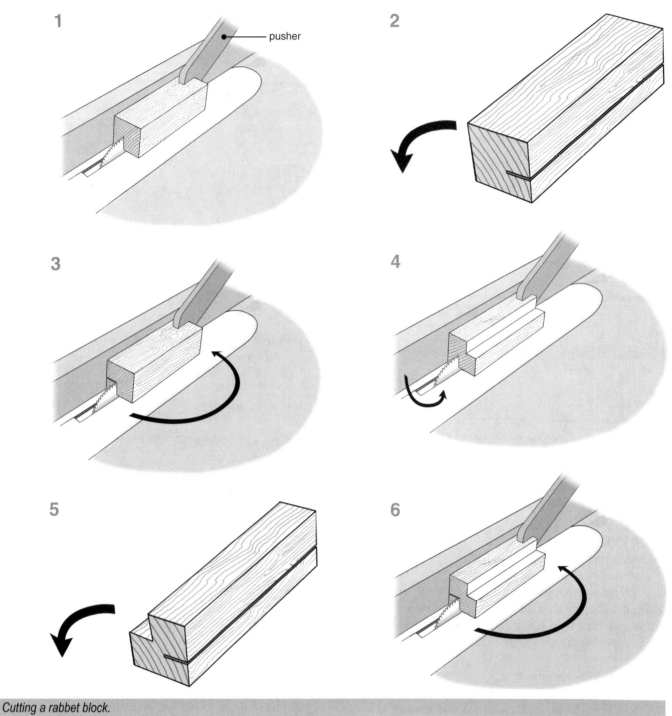

1 — pusher

2

3

4

5

6

Cutting a rabbet block.

thickness of the sides of the box so the corner block stands out like molding.

If this is a speaker enclosure, you will need a plywood front and back with a cutout or cutouts in the front piece of the appropriate size(s). Screw the speaker(s) to the interior of this front piece, then stretch speaker cloth—or any open-weave cloth—across it and staple it in place on the back. Screw the front in place with a pair of stainless steel oval-head screws in finishing washers or attach it with Velcro or plastic cabinet latches.

Mitering

If you want the speaker enclosure to look like fine furniture, frame the front with molding. Both the front and back pieces will need to be cut to fit *inside*

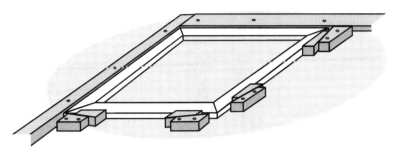

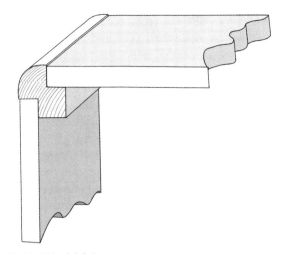

Rabbet block joint.

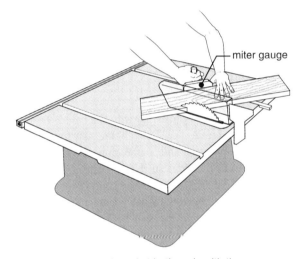

Flat stock can be mitered at both ends with the same miter gauge setting.

the box, held flush with cleats inside. With the front inside the box, the molding can be assembled into a simple mitered frame. A face miter is easy to cut on a table saw with a miter gauge. Set the gauge to 45 degrees and make a test cut on flat stock. If you flip the cutoff piece over top to bottom and mate it to the angle cut on the main piece, it should form a perfect 90-degree angle. Check it with a metal square. If the angle is less than 90 degrees, increase the angle of the miter gauge slightly; if it is greater than 90 degrees, decrease the gauge setting.

While it is modestly wasteful, it can be easier to square cut your frame pieces to the box dimensions, then set the fence and miter guide to trim the ends to 45 degrees with this cut, leaving the piece full length on its outside edge. You can make all of the cuts with the same setup if you use rectangular stock for the frame, but shaped molding must be

Clamping a mitered frame.

mitered with the flat side on the table, so you can only cut the right ends of the frame components with one setup. You will have to reverse it to miter the left ends.

Mitered joints, by the way, are decorative rather than strong because they are glued end grain to end grain. Gluing mitered parts together is easy with special miter clamps or with four bar or pipe clamps. Without these, it requires a little ingenuity. Nail two boards to a flat surface to form a 90-degree corner. Cut four 4-inch pieces of 1 × 2 or 1 × 4 and rip these in half, making the cut at an angle of about 10 degrees so the two halves are slightly wedge-shaped. Assemble the frame with two sides against the two boards and press a pair of wedges near each end of the other two sides. Nail down the outside half of each of the wedge pairs. Now by tapping on the fat ends of the loose halves, you can increase clamping pressure and keep the frame square. So coat the mitered ends with glue and do it.

If your box enclosure is a cabinet, you will want a lid/door on the top/front. Cut a solid lid from whatever stock seems appropriate and rout a simple or fancy edge around the perimeter. Attach it to the box with hinges—and a latch if necessary. Doors can also be solid, but they are more often constructed with a frame around a thinner panel of wood, woven cane, or overlapping louvers. We will get to frame-and-panel door construction shortly.

DORADE

Remaining on the subject of building boxes (and hopefully not to beat a dead horse), but the dorade ventilator is no more than a box with a pair of baffles inside. Most old boats, especially those left closed up for long periods, can benefit from a dorade or two. If you don't object to exposed end grain, you can build the dorade box from solid wood, butting the parts and joining them with screws. Counterbore the shank holes with a $^3/_8$-inch Forstner bit and plug them with matching bungs after the screws have been installed.

Bungs

You can cut bungs with a plug cutter or buy them from your lumber supplier. The closer you can match the color, the less visible they will be. Do not install bungs with epoxy or any other glue. Instead, wet the perimeter of the bung with varnish before you install it. Align the grain of the plug to the grain of the wood and gently tap the bung into the hole as far as it will go. After the varnish is dry, place the point of a chisel—beveled side down—against the plug about ¹⁄₈ inch above the surface of the wood. Tap the chisel with a mallet, and the top of the plug will split away. Note the lowest edge of the plug. Turn the chisel over, and cutting with the grain from the lowest edge, pare away the plug until it is almost flush. Finish the job with sandpaper.

Plugs can be avoided altogether by joining the pieces with glue blocks. Rabbet blocks will allow the sides of the box to be constructed of hardwood plywood, although the top should still be solid wood.

The box may be more attractive if you make the forward face slanted rather than vertical. This is accomplished by cutting the front edge of the sides to the desired angle. To get both sides the same, stack the two pieces and cut them together. The angled front will require the front piece to be somewhat wider than the other three sides and the top and bottom edges to be beveled rather than square. Use one of the sides as a guide to set the angle of the saw blade to cut this bevel. While the blade is set to this angle, you can also bevel the front edge of the top.

Make the two forward rabbet blocks longer than necessary and trim them to size (and angle) on your table saw, or use a saber saw after the four sides have been assembled. Cut a hole at the forward end of the solid top for the cowl ventilator and butt the top to the edges of the sides. You can round three edges of the top with the router, but because of the bevel you will have to round the forward edge with a sander.

Baffles

What makes this box a dorade are the interior baffles. The cowl vent is no longer directly above the opening into the cabin. Rather, it is located near the front of the dorade box and the cabin opening is near the rear. This still allows air entering the cowl to flow into the cabin. Without baffles, water entering the cowl would also pass directly into the cabin. To prevent this, a dorade box has a baffle just forward of the cabin opening. This baffle must be flush with the bottom of the sides so that it forms a watertight seal with the deck when the box is installed. Make it extend slightly more than halfway to the top of the box. Install a second forward baffle just behind the cowl opening. This one sits against the underside of the top and extends slightly more than halfway to the bottom of the box. The overlap of the two baffles allows the free passage of air but traps water forward of the aft baffle.

Scuppers at the bottom of the front compartment let the water out of the box. The easiest way to create effective scuppers is to use your router and straight bit to cut notches about ³⁄₈ inch deep and 1 inch long in the bottom edges. Locate the scupper holes in the sides of the box near all four corners of the area forward of the baffle.

Use a disk or belt sander to shape the bottom of the box to the curvature of the deck. If the sides are plywood, seal the edges with several coats of epoxy. Install the box by screwing cleats to the deck so that the box sits over the cleats. Be sure the cleats do not block the scuppers. Bed the edges—including the aft baffle—with polysulfide sealant and screw the box to the cleats. Install wooden bungs to hide the mounting screws and trim the plugs. Lightly sand the box and finish it to match the other wood on deck.

Tap plug with the edge of a sharp chisel about ¹⁄₈ inch above the wood to split off top.

From lowest edge, pare away the remaining plug, cutting with the grain.

Sand flush.

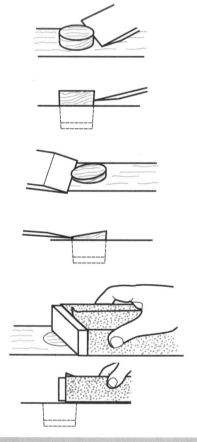

Trimming wood plugs.

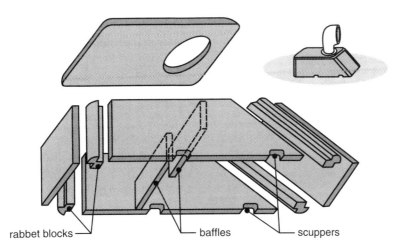

Constructing a dorade box.

rabbet blocks —   — baffles   — scuppers

MOVING THE FURNITURE

Adapting an old boat to your dream may involve changing the accommodations. In an earlier chapter I mentioned a 34-footer with nine bunks. If I possessed such a boat, there is little doubt that I would tear out most of the interior and start all over. Fortunately most of us find ourselves with boats with accommodation plans that *almost* work for us. If we could just . . .

NOT SO FAST

Before you destroy the old accommodations, you should carefully evaluate the changes you're planning. It is not easy to accurately assess changes that only exist in your mind. If you are too hasty, you may end up with accommodations that are less comfortable than the original.

Before you start renovating, buy a few sheets of the cheapest-grade 1/4-inch plywood and a dozen construction-grade 1 × 2s to mock up each cabin and try out your ideas for space and function. If that seems like wasted effort and unwarranted expense, allow me to report that most of the major renovations I have seen aboard boats are *less* functional than the original plan. Invariably the owner apologizes for the most glaring shortcomings with a sentence that begins, "I didn't realize . . ." Besides dismaying you with the discovery that you are personally dissatisfied with the results of your efforts, butchered accommodations will make resale difficult and have an adverse effect on the value of the boat. Not a good way to spend your winter.

None of this is to say that improvements are not possible. Au contraire. I have never been aboard a stock boat that could not benefit from some accommodation changes. Sometimes very small tweaks can make a very big difference in comfort or convenience.

LARGE LIDS

Consider the lockers beneath the bunks and settees. Regardless of the size of the locker, most manufacturers of older boats used a standard template to cut the access hatches. Fill such a locker with canned goods and someone aboard is going to spend hours emptying and repacking it in repeated searches for specific items. There are more enjoyable ways to exhibit great buns.

The solution: locker-size lids. Trace the perimeter of the locker on the surface of the top. Draw a second outline 2 or 3 inches inside the first. This is the size the lid should be. Radius the corners by tracing around a quart paint can. Check for wiring and plumbing by running your hand *inside* the locker beneath the outline. Also be sure there is adequate space under the top for the piercing saber saw blade to clear. If the curvature of the hull causes the locker to be very shallow on one side, move that edge of the lid inboard a few inches.

You don't need a hole to start this cut. You can make a plunge cut with your saber saw. Straddle one of the straight lines of your cutout outline with the front of the sole plate, with the saw tilted forward on this front edge until the blade is almost parallel to the wood you are about to cut. The blade edge should be in line with the cutout line and just above it. Now start the saw and, holding it with two hands, tilt it back until the reciprocating blade begins to scratch the wood. Be sure this scratch is along your cutout line. Continue to apply slight pressure and allow the end of the blade to saw its way through the wood. Moving the saw forward a bit as you lower the blade will help to keep the point from jabbing the bottom of the cut. When the blade penetrates, rotate the saw to the flat position and follow the pencil outline to make the cutout. Support the lid to keep it from tearing free before you complete the cut. Lightly sand the cut edges.

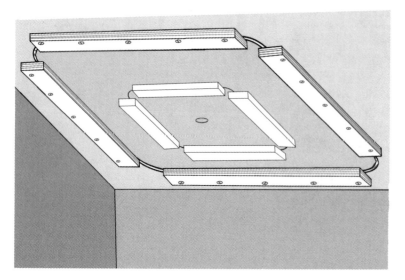

Bigger lids improve locker access.

Where does the sink go? Will there be an ice chest? Can you incorporate a garbage bin into the top? Will you have drawers or lockers or some combination of both? Will the stove be gimballed? Do you need mounting space for foot pumps? How will the cabinet be finished? How will it be trimmed?

Fitting a Bulkhead

In this example the new galley attaches to an existing bulkhead at one end and requires a new partial bulkhead at the other. The first challenge is to cut the new bulkhead to the correct size and contour. Mark the top and front lines on the existing bulkhead; use a straight-edge to transfer them to a square of plywood or hardboard clamped to a frame temporarily rigged where the new bulkhead will go. The frame can be braced between the overhead and the sole with the front and top lines projected onto the plywood square.

Without moving the square, use the pointed-stick method to put a series of numbered alignment marks on the plywood that will let you transfer the hull contour to your new bulkhead. Ticking the hull at 1- to 2-inch intervals will allow you to make a very accurate cut.

Unclamp the pattern square and lay it on your stock—probably ³/₄-inch plywood. Align the top and front lines on the pattern with the intersecting edges at one corner of the plywood. Generally you want the face-ply grain to be vertical when the bulkhead is in place, so the top line would align with the end of the plywood and the front with the side. Clamp the pattern to the stock and use your pointed stick and alignment marks to make a series of dots on the plywood. Connect these dots smoothly. You really should plan to seat the bulkhead on a foam pad (see Chapter 6) to both avoid creating a hard spot and to provide a radius for tabbing. If you will be doing this, measure the thickness of the foam and draw a second contour inside the first by this amount. Sawing the plywood along this second line will release a fully formed bulkhead ready to be tabbed in place.

It can be easier to glue the foam to the edge of the bulkhead ahead of installation. Very carefully position the new bulkhead parallel to the existing one and aligned front and top. Clamp it in this position using the sole-to-overhead brace and any other braces you want to add. Check twice to make sure that fastening the top and front to this bulkhead will not introduce a twist in either. The foam pad makes modest fit adjustment easy. When you are satisfied beyond a reasonable doubt (ladies and gentlemen of the jury), tab the bulkhead to the hull with two or

Rip 1-inch-wide strips from a piece of ¹/₂-inch plywood for seating cleats. Cut the strips into appropriate lengths and glue them in place against the underside of the top of the locker. About ³/₈ inch of the cleats should extend beyond the edge of the opening. If you do not have a sufficient number of clamps, you can use nails or screws driven from inside the locker to hold the cleats while the glue dries.

As for the original lid, you can leave it unaltered, or you can screw or glue it to its cleats. If the new lid is too big to be convenient, cut it in half and install a divider in the locker or support the joint with a piece of 1 × 2 bridging the opening.

Unless you have a specific need for stowage space for longer items, the space beneath a 6-foot-long bunk or settee should be divided into either three or four separate lockers, each with its own full-size lid.

THE HARD STUFF

If you are still with me at this point, you are in possession of adequate woodworking skills to make any repair or bring about any change to the wooden portions of your old fiberglass boat. Let's take on the installation of a new galley and you'll see what I mean.

NEW GALLEY

First, you need to recognize that the top of a cabinet is nothing more than a shelf, the sides no more than dividers. Add a front piece to the shelves and dividers, and you have the basic box. And you thought the box section was long because I was just short on ideas. Aren't you ashamed?

As with any complex project, the best place to start is with a pencil and paper. Sketch out what you have in mind and get the rough measurements down.

three layers of fiberglass tape—on both sides of the bulkhead if the outside attachment will eventually be hidden, or on just the inside if it will be visible.

Face and Top

You only need the front and the top to complete your "box." Fabricate the front first, using ¹/₂-inch plywood and squaring the top edge with the two sides. Install cleat stock on the bulkheads to act as glue blocks for the joints between them and the front. Screw the front into position temporarily.

To support the top, install cleat stock to the inside of the front, flush with its top edge and along the bulkheads toward the hull, using your square to keep all the surfaces square. Do not carry the cleats all the way to the hull to allow for the tabbing between the hull and the top.

The top should be fabricated from ³/₄-inch plywood if you plan to cover it with plastic laminate or from ¹/₂-inch plywood if it will be topped with solid surface material (Corian). In the latter case, be sure to allow for the additional height of the ¹/₂-inch-thick solid surface material in your original layout.

The plywood top will need to be contoured to fit against the hull, so cut it a bit wider than the widest dimension from the front to the hull. Lay the top in place and trace the hull contour with a compass. If you mark the widest front-to-hull dimension on the top and set your compass so the pencil just touches that line, when you cut the contour, the front of the top should be in perfect alignment with the front of the cabinet. If you use a foam pad between the top and the hull (you should), allow for this in your front-to-hull dimension.

Little is new from here on out. For example, you need a cutout for the sink. Outline the cutout and make it with your router and/or your saber saw exactly as you did for the bin opening in the forepeak bulkhead or for enlarging the access hole for the underbunk locker. The same procedure applies to cutouts for bins, lockers, and drawers.

Fitting and installing shelves and dividers for a cabinet you have built is no different than fitting and installing them in existing cabinet work. Install full dividers first, cleating them to the front and the top and tabbing them to the hull. It may make the job easier if you finish all of the interior features of your new cabinet before permanently installing the top. Tab it to the hull and screw and/or glue it to the cleats.

You will probably surface the top—and the sides if they are not hardwood plywood—with plastic laminate, a process we examined back in Chapter 7. Fiddle rails for the counter are fabricated just like those for a shelf.

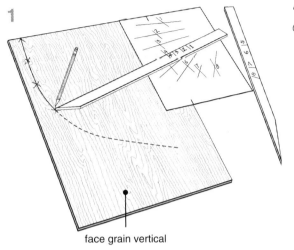

"Tick" the contour of new bulkhead.

face grain vertical

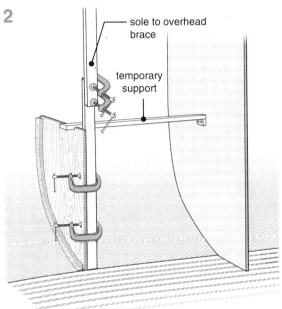

Align and tab bulkhead to hull.

sole to overhead brace

temporary support

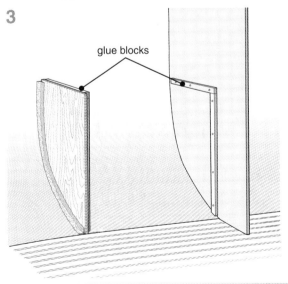

Install cleat stock to serve as glue blocks for face and top.

glue blocks

Building a new galley (continued next page).

(Continued) Building a new galley.

Cut and fit face.   **4**

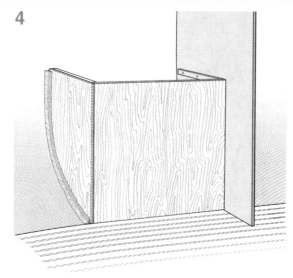

Contour and fit top.   **5**

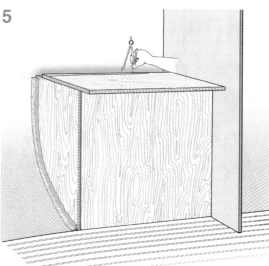

Cut top and face openings.   **6**

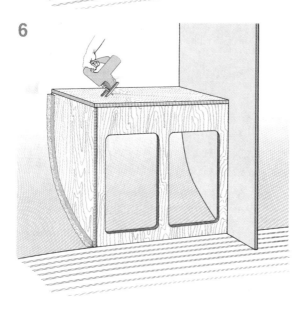

7 Install dividers and shelves.

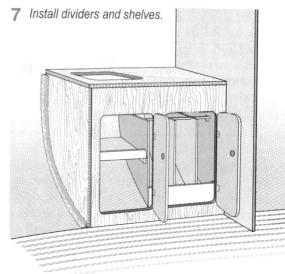

8 Cover with plastic laminate or liquid finish. Install rail, trim, and hardware.

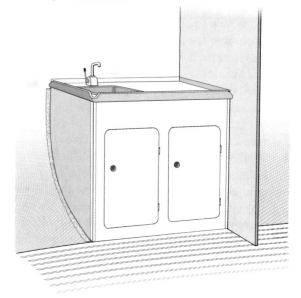

Molding

Wood trim can be purchased, or you can cut your own. For example, put a $1/2$-by-$1/2$-inch rabbet in the edge of a length of $3/4$-inch-thick solid wood, then rip a $3/4$-inch strip from the rabbeted edge; you have a length of $3/4$-inch corner molding. You also have a big pile of sawdust, so purchased molding may not be much more expensive. Some molding should be

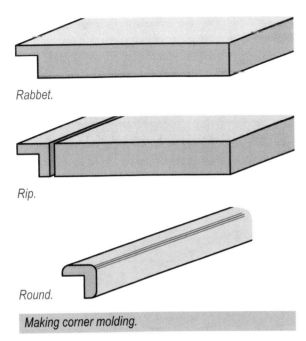

Rabbet.

Rip.

Round.

Making corner molding.

joined with miter cuts, some with butt joints, and sometimes you may need to cut and shape a rounded corner piece.

Drawers

If your cabinet will have drawers, you will need to install guide rails. There are numerous options, but I like the plastic glides that screw to the rear of the drawer and slide on an inverted T-shaped rail *above* the drawer. The glides and the hardwood rails are available from lumber suppliers.

If the drawer is large or will contain heavy items, side rails become the better option. For a single drawer, cleat two lengths of straight 1 × 2 to the inside of the cabinet front, making the 2-inch side flush with (or just slightly recessed from) the sides of the drawer cutout. Half of the 2-inch width of these rails should be above the bottom of the drawer cutout, the other half below. Attach the other ends of these rails to framing in the back of the cabinet installed just for this purpose. The rails must be square (in both directions) with the front and parallel to each other. Glue $^3/_4$-inch cleat stock to the inside face of each rail about $^1/_8$ inch below the level of the bottom of the cutout. This creates a pair of L-shaped rails that will support the drawer and align it. With a table saw, you can avoid the glue step by cutting a length of 2 × 2 into L-shaped railing.

The reason the top surface of the cleat stock—the bottom of the L—is $^1/_8$ inch lower than the cutout is that the sides of boat drawers should be notched at the front so they have to be lifted to open. This prevents

them from sliding out when the boat heels. Attach a wooden turn button to the inside of the drawer at its rear to keep you from accidentally pulling it all the way out. You will also need "tip" rails above the drawer to keep the front from tipping downward when it is fully opened. If you have a tier of drawers, the support rails of each drawer can serve this function for the next drawer down. For a tier of drawers, you can substitute plywood dividers for individual 1 × 2 side rails.

The drawers themselves are nothing more than boxes. Cut the ends and sides from $^3/_8$-inch plywood. Cut the ends square and give each side a rabbet about $^1/_4$ inch deep. Rabbeted corners will be strong enough for normal use, but if you are so inclined, you can buy a dovetail jig for your router and dovetail the drawer joints. A dovetail joint will last forever.

The bottoms should be $^1/_8$-inch hardboard or plywood. Drawers are stronger when the bottom panel is captured in a groove. Before you assemble the sides, or even while they are all still a single strip, put a kerf that is $^1/_8$ inch deep by $^1/_8$ inch wide down one side about

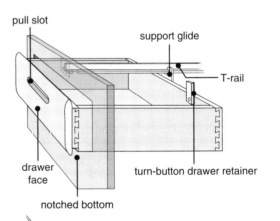

pull slot
support glide
T-rail
drawer face
turn-button drawer retainer
notched bottom

Drawer construction details.

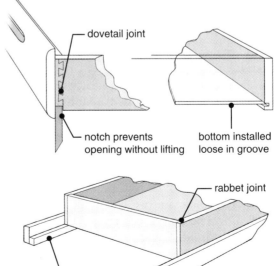

dovetail joint
notch prevents opening without lifting
bottom installed loose in groove
rabbet joint
side rails

¹/₄ inch from the edge. Cut the bottom piece just a little less than ¹/₄ inch larger than the inside dimension of the drawer. When you assemble the drawer, do it with the bottom piece in the groove. Do not glue the bottom panel into the groove. It should be able to expand and contract without affecting the corner joints.

With the drawer assembled, set the blade height on your table saw to slightly more than the thickness of the cabinet front. Stand the drawer on its front face and set your fence to make a blade-width (¹/₈-inch) cut across the drawer at the bottom edge of the front. You are creating an ¹/₈-inch-deep notch that will hold the drawer closed until you want it open.

Faces. The simplest drawer face is a piece of solid wood that is an inch or so larger all around than the cutout. You can combine the forward end of the drawer and the face into a single piece of wood, but this requires a lot of additional layout. It is easier to build a plywood box and attach a separate face to it. Round the front edges of the face piece with a router and glue it to the front of the drawer. Protruding knobs and handles are dangerous on a boat, so make a slot instead. In the center of the face, a couple of inches from the top, bore a pair of 1-inch holes about 4 inches apart. Make two parallel cuts between the holes with your saber saw, creating an inch-wide slot with radiused ends for gripping the drawer to open it. Round the edges of the slot with your router, and the face is finished.

Laminate-covered plywood with contrasting wood edging also makes a simple and attractive drawer face. With seating cleats at the top and bottom of the cutout, flush drawer faces are possible. However, a close-fitting flush face will prevent the drawer from being lifted, so an alternative to the notched bottom must be used to hold the drawer closed. You can buy push-button latches that lock the drawer when it is pushed in and both unlock it and serve as a drawer pull when "toggled" out. Unfortunately these ingenious latches are not cheap. A lower-cost alternative is a simple "bird" or elbow cabinet latch that releases through the pull slot. Because the flush drawer will not have a notch, the support rails must be flush with the bottom of the cutout, not ¹/₈ inch below.

Doors

Cabinet doors also present you with numerous choices, but there are two basic types—solid and paneled. A solid door is constructed exactly like a solid drawer front. A paneled door is composed of a frame—like a picture frame—surrounding a panel of some other material. The centers of paneled cabinet doors on a boat are typically thin plywood—either

hardwood plywood or laminate covered—or they are louvers. Woven wood and cane are also possibilities because they provide much-needed ventilation.

Earlier we constructed a mitered frame, but to withstand the rigors a cabinet door is prey to, the substantially stronger *end-lap joint* is a better choice. This is formed by giving all of the frame-piece ends a half-thickness rabbet the width of the adjoining piece. You

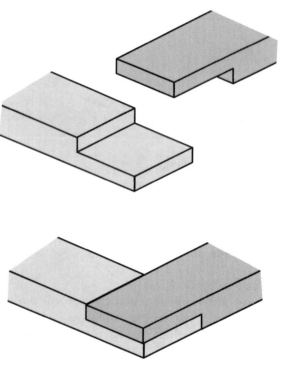

End-lap joint.

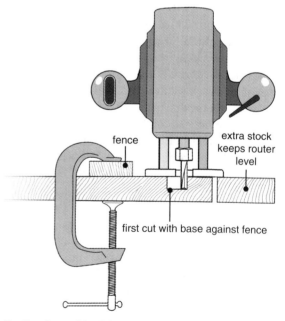

Routing the end-lap joint.

can cut this rabbet on the table saw, but because of its size, it is likely to be either easier or more accurate to mill with a router. All four pieces can be rabbeted at the same time if they are clamped edge to edge with their ends flush. The setup for these rabbets is no more than a fence across all four pieces positioned to guide the cutter a rail width from the ends. The rest of the material can be removed freehand. Place a fifth piece of the same stock in front of the ends to support the router base to keep the router level. A second setup is required to mill the opposite ends.

Paneled. A cabinetmaker would install the center panel loose in a groove around the inside perimeter of the frame (exactly like a drawer bottom), but cutting this groove can be a challenge with just a table saw. You cannot groove the full length of the frame pieces or the cut will create a void in the outside perimeter. If the frame pieces are wide enough, you can stop the cut short of the end and have it full depth for the inside length. Otherwise you will have to finish ends of the groove with an $\frac{1}{8}$-inch chisel or a rotary tool (Dremel).

A good alternative is to route a rabbet on the inside perimeter of the finished frame, then capture the center panel with a molding nailed in place—much the way window glass is mounted in a wooden window frame. The width and depth of the rabbet will depend on the center panel. You will still have to square the corners of the rabbet with your chisel, but this is less exacting than chiseling grooves. Do not try to cut this rabbet in end-lapped frame pieces before the frame is assembled.

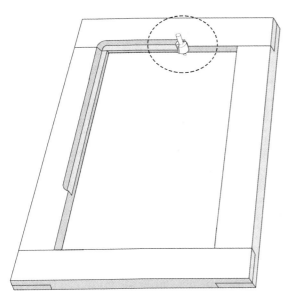

Cut the rabbet for the center panel after the frame is assembled.

When you assemble the frame, clamp it to a flat surface until the glue dries. This will insure that the frame does not warp. If you are installing the panel in a groove, don't forget to fit it before you glue the frame together.

Caned. If you want to use cane, a $\frac{3}{8}$-by-$\frac{3}{8}$-inch rabbet will be about right. Cut the cane about 2 inches oversize and soak it in warm water for a couple of hours. Stretch it evenly—watch the alignment of the pattern—and tack it in place with brass brads through quarter-round molding pressed into the corner of the rabbet. While it is still soft, trim the excess with a razor knife. An alternative method is to rout a $\frac{1}{4}$-inch groove around the frame and secure the cane by stretching it over the groove and pounding *caning bead* into it. Either way, when the cane dries, it will be drum-tight.

Louvered. Louvered doors are great for boats because they hide what is behind them while allowing almost unrestricted ventilation—and they look beautiful. For louvered doors, you will need to buy the prefabricated components and then just assemble doors of the size you require. The *stiles*—the vertical parts of the frame—are always purchased in pairs because they are

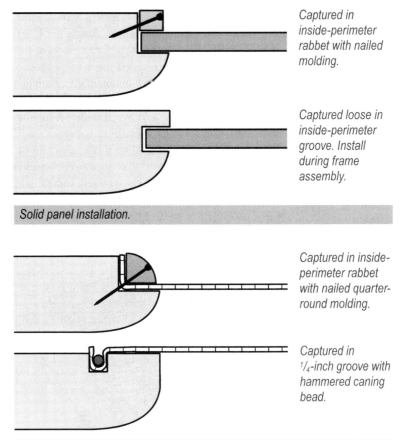

Captured in inside-perimeter rabbet with nailed molding.

Captured loose in inside-perimeter groove. Install during frame assembly.

Solid panel installation.

Captured in inside-perimeter rabbet with nailed quarter-round molding.

Captured in $\frac{1}{4}$-inch groove with hammered caning bead.

Cane inserts.

already mortised to capture the ends of the slats, and the angle of the mortise is reversed on opposite sides. The top and bottom *rails*—the horizontal pieces of the frame—can be cut from the same piece of rail stock, which will be identical to the stile stock, except without the milled slots. The louver slats typically come in 4- or 8-foot lengths. When buying louvered door components, pay attention to color and grain.

You can join louvered door rails and stiles with end-lap joints, but you may be disconcerted by the open mortises when you rabbet the stiles. These will ultimately be hidden inside the joint, so they are of no real concern.

An alternative way to assemble the rails and stiles is with glue dowels. This requires matching holes in the side of the stile and the end of the rail. There are commercial doweling jigs, but for a few joints you should be able to create your own jig that will allow you to drill aligned holes in both pieces. Typically, you want two $1/4$-inch or $3/8$-inch dowels in each joint—eight dowels per frame. Be sure you do not put the outermost dowels too close to the top or bottom edge of the stiles. If you do, you will cut into them if you rout a perimeter step in the back side of the door to allow half of its thickness to fit inside the opening. For dowel joints the precut mortises will interfere with drilling dowel holes. The solution to this problem is to fill the milled slots that fall in the joint area with pieces of slat glued in place and then trimmed flush. (You can do this before creating end-lap joints also.)

It is, by the way, a very good idea to prefinish all of the components of a louvered door before you assemble it—at the very least finish the slats and inside edges of the stiles and rails. A word of caution, however: Sometimes the slots and slats do not slip together as easily as they should, and this is likely to be made worse by a coat of varnish. Always assemble the entire door, slats and all, to reveal fit problems before gluing the frame together.

Louvered doors of almost any size can be constructed from pre-milled stiles, rails, and slats.

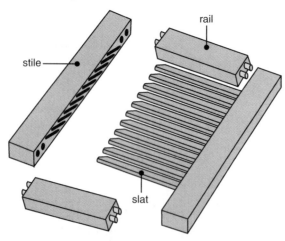

When gluing, hold the stiles tight against the ends of the rails with bar clamps, but also clamp the frame against a flat surface to prevent twist. You do not need to glue the slats.

ON DECK

The original brightwork of your old boat is almost certain to be mahogany or teak. If it is mahogany and has been neglected for a long time, it is likely to be split, checked, or even rotten. If it is unvarnished teak, on the other hand, you should *hope* that it has been neglected. Every time a previous owner lovingly scrubbed or sanded the teak in preparation for a treatment of oil or sealer, another layer of the wood departed through the scuppers. After a couple of decades of scrubbing, handrails are too thin to be safe, not enough wood remains in toe rails to hold bungs, and the mounting screws through wood coamings are on islands standing proud above the eroded surface.

Replacing the wood on deck is typically a matter of removing the old piece and using it as a pattern to cut a new one. While much of the work below involves plywood, solid wood is the dominant material on deck. You will need to pay attention to the direction of the grain, and you may need to join short or narrow pieces to make longer or wider ones.

TOE RAIL

Fabricating and replacing a wooden toe rail is not very difficult. Determine the height and width that you want, and buy your lumber as close to those dimensions as possible. Getting the length required will necessitate joining more than one board. These pieces must be joined with scarfs.

Scarf Joints

If the glue line between two pieces of wood is perpendicular, you are looking at a butt joint. If that line is at 89 degrees, I suppose that is technically a scarf, but the angle of a true scarf—one that forms a strong joint—is more *likely* to be between 5 and 10 degrees. Scarfs are not described by their angles but by a ratio of the length of the joint to the thickness of the material. For example, the joint of a 12-to-1 scarf between two lengths of 2-inch-thick lumber would be 24 inches long. For a toe rail, 8-to-1 is ample.

A scarf is especially easy to cut with a table saw. Simply set the miter gauge to the shallow angle necessary—about 7 degrees for an 8-to-1 scarf—and cut the ends of both boards to this angle top to bottom (not side to side). The strength of a scarf depends on the accurate fitting together of the parts, so be sure your saw blade is both sharp and absolutely perpendicular.

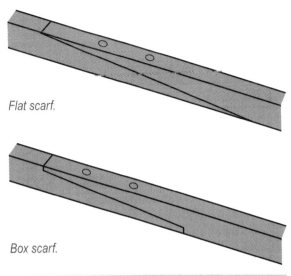

Flat scarf.

Box scarf.

Scarf joints.

Coat the cut surfaces with glue, align the two pieces, and clamp them together. You may need a screw or a nail through the joint to prevent the pieces from sliding while the glue sets. Bonded with epoxy or resorcinol, this joint should be as strong as the wood. However, be careful about making up a single piece the length of your boat or the wood may snap of its own weight when you are handling it. Where the joint falls in a relatively straight area of the rail, you can glue it together in place, putting at least two mounting screws through the joint. If the rail has a lot of curvature at the joint location, you will have to make the joint in the air, let it cure completely, then worry the lengthened rail into shape.

High rails are often laminated, eliminating the need for scarf joints. Instead, the joints in each laminate are staggered to fabricate a long section. If the toe rail is higher than it is wide and it is not laminated, a box scarf is preferable. The difference is that the scarf does not run all the way from top to bottom, but begins with a notch in the top and ends with a matching square end at the bottom. Assembled, the joint looks like a long, skinny Z.

All that remains is to shape the toe rail and attach it. Shaping is accomplished by inclining the saw blade and running the wood against the rip fence. Radius the top edges with a sander or router. Unless the rail is through-bolted, do not try to reinstall the mounting screws in the same holes. Carefully fill the old screw holes in the deck with resin putty and drill new ones through the rail as you bend it into place. Start at one end and drill and install one screw at a time, bedding as you go. Be sure you get a solid layer of sealant under the rail, without gaps. Use polysulfide sealant, or polyurethane if the rail will be varnished. (Remember that teak cleaners can soften polyurethane, so do not use it to bed teak that will be left raw.) Both polys take a long time to cure, so you have plenty of time to bed in sections unless you must wait on a scarf joint to cure. In this case, stop the bedding between fasteners so that you can restart it without the sealant joint being critical.

Coat bungs with varnish and tap them into place, taking care to align the grain. Trim the bungs, sand the rails, and finish them as you prefer.

COAMINGS

Cut to size. Shape. Screw in place. If you cut a replacement coaming from a single plank, these are the only instructions required, but if the coaming is high, it can be difficult to find teak or mahogany of sufficient

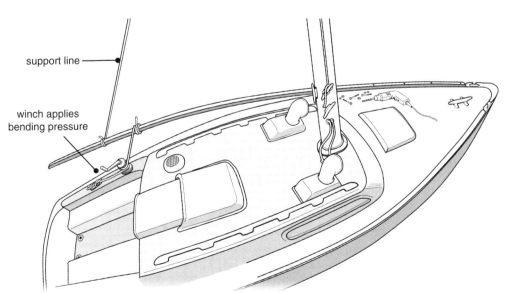

support line

winch applies bending pressure

Coaxing the curvature into a wood toe rail. Go slow and install the screws in sequence.

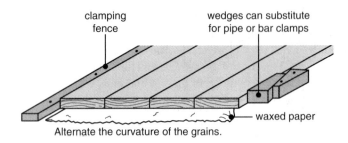

clamping fence

wedges can substitute for pipe or bar clamps

waxed paper

Alternate the curvature of the grains.

Edge gluing.

width. The solution is to edge-glue more than one piece of wood. Rather than being less desirable, this alternative has a distinct advantage. A single board can be prone to warping and splitting, but a coaming made up of several pieces properly assembled is not likely to exhibit either tendency.

Choose boards less than 4 inches wide, with straight, smooth edges. If the edges are not perfect, run the board through your saw carefully to straighten them. Now look at the end of each piece to determine whether the grain curves up or down, and reverse every board to offset any warping tendency. Coat the edges with epoxy glue and clamp them together, taking care to keep the boards flat and flush. Traditionally dowels were often used when edge-gluing, but the strength of modern adhesives makes dowels unnecessary.

If you do not have sufficient pipe or bar clamps to apply even pressure, assemble the boards against a straight board nailed to a flat surface and apply clamping pressure with a number of wedge clamps as described earlier for the construction of a mitered frame. If you edge-glue the boards in this manner, be sure to put waxed paper between them and the flat surface. Do not wipe the excess glue; slice it away with an old chisel after it dries.

When the glue dries, sand both surfaces. This is when a belt sander can be useful. If you are using one, be sure you keep it moving to prevent dishing the surface. With the panel assembled and surfaced, you already know the rest.

Cut to size. Shape. Screw in place.

HANDRAILS

I am particularly fond of handrails because they look so complicated and are so easy to make. Begin with a solid plank about $1\frac{1}{4}$ inch thick and with a width equal to twice the height of the old handrail, or not less than $5\frac{1}{2}$ inches. This method turns out two identical handrails at the same time, so you need a single board for the pair.

Draw a line down the center of the board. If you are replacing handrails, lay one of the old ones on your board with the standoffs against the line and mark the location (both sides) of each standoff on the centerline. If you are adding and not replacing, divide the length of the handrail equally to determine the centers of the standoff locations. The span between standoffs for $1\frac{1}{4}$-inch-diameter rails (what we are constructing here) should probably not exceed 18 inches. Mark standoff locations on the board's centerline with a pair of marks. The width of handrail standoffs, and thus the distance between these pairs of marks, should generally be around 3 inches. Measure $1\frac{1}{2}$ inches away from each standoff mark, including the inside one for the end standoffs, along the board's centerline and put an $\times$ on the centerline at each of these locations. Use a push drill or an awl to dimple the wood at each $\times$ to help in positioning your holesaw. Chuck a 3-inch holesaw in your drill and carefully center the pilot drill on the first $\times$. Bore this hole from the marked side until the drill penetrates the bottom, then turn the piece over and finish the hole from the opposite side. Repeat this at every $\times$. It is no coincidence that the perimeter of these holes should just touch the marks you made for standoff locations.

Use a saber saw to make parallel cuts between pairs of holes—exactly as you cut the slots for drawer pulls. Don't get confused and cut between the wrong holes. Where the holes are close together is a standoff and you do not want to cut there. If you have done

Mark the standoff locations on the centerline, evenly spaced, then put an X on the centerline $1\frac{1}{2}$ inches (half the holesaw diameter) away from both sides of each standoff mark.

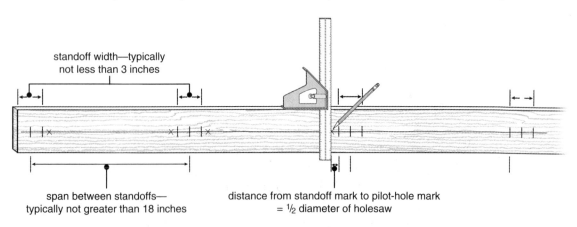

standoff width—typically not less than 3 inches

span between standoffs— typically not greater than 18 inches

distance from standoff mark to pilot-hole mark = $\frac{1}{2}$ diameter of holesaw

1

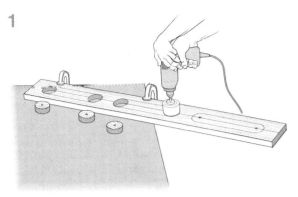

Bore a 3-inch hole centered on every X mark.

2

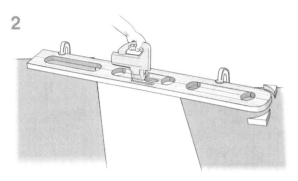

Saw between the widely separated pairs of holes and cut the end radius.

3

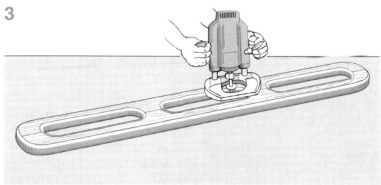

Round all the edges with a ¹/₂-inch round-over bit.

4

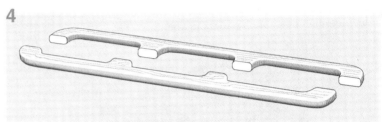

Ripping the board down the centerline releases two identical handrails.

this correctly, you have a board with one or more long centerline slots—the number depends on the length of the handrail—with radiused ends and 3 or more inches of solid wood between the slots and at the ends of the board.

Using the old handrail as a pattern for selecting a radius you find pleasing, saw identical contours on each corner of the board. Now round all the edges, including the slots, with a router and a ¹/₂-inch round-over bit. Finally, set the rip guide on your table saw to align the center of the blade with the centerline on the board and rip it exactly in half. *Shazam!* Two finished handrails.

Young and Rockless

There is one more small step. To keep the handrails from rocking after they are mounted, the base of each standoff should be *slightly* hollow. This is accomplished most easily by setting the saw blade about ¹/₁₆ inch above the table. Place a straight board diagonally across the table in front of the blade; a 30-degree angle between the board and the blade is good. Slide the board toward the blade until the distance to the highest tooth on the blade measured perpendicularly from the board is half the thickness of the rails you are about to shave. Clamp the board in this position.

Start the saw and run a scrap of material *slowly* along the fence and diagonally across the blade. The rotation of the blade toward the fence will help hold the stock against the fence. Adjust the blade up or down to leave about ¹/₈ inch of material on either side of the hollow untouched by the saw. When the setting is right, run the bottom of the handrail over the blade.

Handrails should always be through-bolted. A matching handrail inside the cabin attached to the overhead with the same bolts makes a yachtlike and functional installation. Fabricating the handrails in pairs insures perfect alignment.

Give the bottom of the standoffs a slight hollow by running them diagonally over the table saw blade. This will make the handrail less prone to rock and the fasteners less prone to leak.

GRATINGS

The big problem with gratings is the cost. After you price the necessary teak, you may decide to skip this enhancement. But cost is the only thing that should keep a determined owner from fabricating a cockpit grating.

A table saw and a dado blade greatly simplify the process, but it can be done with a router. Begin with the widest $^3/_4$-inch-thick stock you can obtain. You are going to cut $^3/_4$-inch dadoes across the board, $^3/_8$ inch deep and $^3/_4$ inch apart. After all the dadoes have been cut, rip the board into $^3/_4$-inch-wide strips. Turn half the strips over and place them perpendicular to the other half; they will interlock to form a grating. All that is left to do is put a drop of glue at each intersection, build a frame the size of the cockpit, and cut and rabbet the grating to fit the frame.

The difficulty comes in getting all these cuts precise. I strongly suggest that you make a grating for the wet locker or the refrigerator before taking on one for the cockpit.

With a Saw

If you will be cutting the dadoes on the table saw, you will need a straight 1 × 2 more or less the width of your table to function as an extension to your miter guide. Run this extension—edge down—over the $^3/_4$-inch dado blade to cut your first dado (again, $^3/_4$ inch by $^3/_8$ inch). Now very accurately make a second dado

1

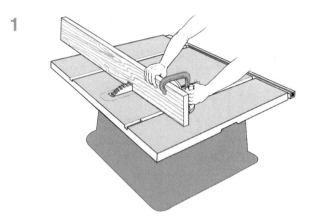

Saw a dado in straight plank to serve as an extension of your miter gauge.

2

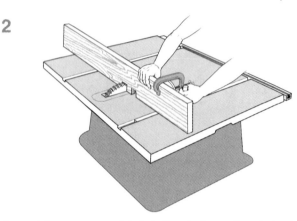

Accurately saw a second dado in the plank exactly a dado width from the first one.

3

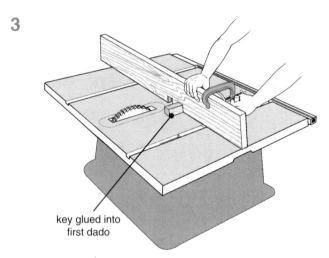

key glued into first dado

Shape a block to exactly fit into the first dado and glue it in place extending forward at least $^3/_4$ inch to create a key. Position the second dado exactly over the blade and clamp the extension/jig securely to the miter gauge.

4

Single strip width shown for clarity but it is normally quicker to dado a wide plank, then rip it into strips.

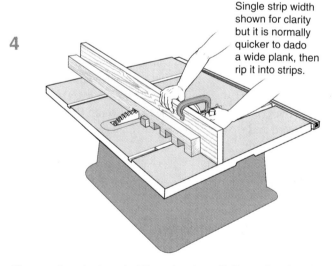

Place grating stock against the extension with the end against the key and feed the stock across the blade and back. Reposition the stock to put this first dado over the key and again feed the stock across the blade and back. Continue moving each new dado over the key until the stock is notched to the far end.

Cutting dadoes for grating construction on a table saw.

in the edge of the 1 × 2 exactly ³/₄ inch from the first. Shape a small wooden block to fit into the first of these notches and glue it into the notch, extending out at least ³/₄ inch. This will serve as a key. Realign the second notch over your dado blade and clamp or screw this fence to the miter gauge.

The first step is to square the end of the board. Next put the board against the miter gauge extension with the end against the key, and slide the gauge forward to cut the first dado in your stock. Reposition the stock to place this dado over the wood key and cut a second dado. Fit this one over the key and cut the third, and so on. The result will be a series of perfectly spaced dadoes—if your key is accurate. It would be a very good idea to dado some scrap 1 × 4 first, rip it into ³/₄-inch strips, and make sure these fit together accurately before making sawdust out of your expensive teak.

With a Router

If you are going to cut the dadoes with a router, use a ³/₄-inch straight bit and set it to a ³/₈-inch depth. Use contact cement to glue a foot-long batten ³/₄ inch wide and ¹/₄ inch thick to the base of your router. The batten must be exactly ³/₄ inch from the closest edge of the cutter. With the batten flush against the end of the board, make the first dado across the board. Now put the batten in the groove you just cut and make a second dado. If you positioned the guide correctly, the two dadoes will be exactly ³/₄ inch apart. Move the guide to the next dado and continue making cuts until you reach the end of the board.

Whether you cut the dadoes with a saw or with a router, you must take the time necessary to get the setup exactly right. If you do, the rest will go easily.

Once you have all the dadoes cut into your plank(s), set the rip guide on your saw table to exactly ³/₄ inch and rip the board into strips. It is essential that the cuts have the correct width and depth and that the strips are a snug fit in the dadoes, so try out each new cut before continuing.

Frame to Finish

Assemble the grating with glue at every joint. Construct a frame from wood the same thickness as that used in the grating and at least 2 inches wide. Connect the frame pieces with end-lap joints. It will be easier to make the frame straight on all sides and trim it to fit after it is assembled. Put a ³/₄-inch-wide and ³/₈-inch-deep rabbet on the bottom of the frame around the perimeter of the inside—just as in making a panel door.

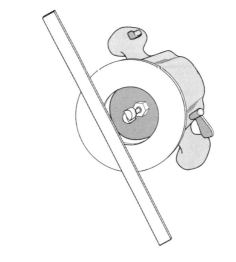

Using contact cement, glue a dado-width guide to the sole plate exactly a dado width from the cutting edge of the bit.

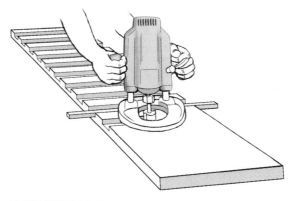

Make the first dado with the guide against the end of the stock, subsequent dadoes with the guide in the previous dado.

Cutting dadoes for grating construction with a router.

Cut a scrap of plywood or doorskin to tightly fit the rabbeted cutout. Using this as a pattern, trim the grating to size. Clamp a straight board to the router (to bridge the ends of the grating) and route a ³/₄-inch-wide by ³/₈-inch-deep rabbet in the top of the grating around the perimeter (see next page). Check it in the frame for fit, then glue the two together. What else is there to say? Grate.

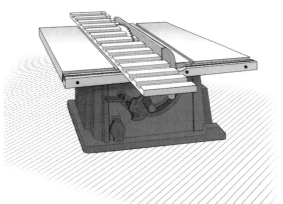

Rip the dadoed plank into strips.

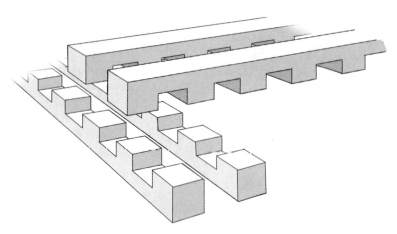

Assemble the grate by interlocking the dadoed strips, applying glue at every joint.

TEAK DECKS

I don't approve of teak decks on an old fiberglass boat. It isn't that I don't like the way they look; I do. And it isn't the maintenance they require; it's not that bad. What it is is all the screws through the deck. The decks of most old boats have plywood sandwiched between layers of fiberglass. It is hard enough to keep water from finding its way to the plywood and destroying it without drilling a thousand holes through the top laminate. So I pass.

Not that I expect you to care. If teak decks get your juices flowing, the risk of a spongy foredeck some years hence probably won't be much of a deterrent. So if you want to install a teak deck, can you do it? Yes.

Build a frame using end-lap joints to join the sides. Rabbet the inside perimeter on the bottom side of the frame

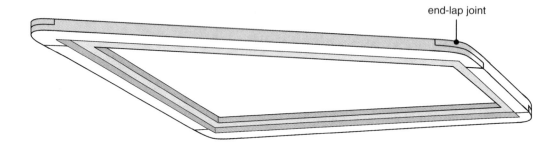

end-lap joint

Cut the assembled grating to the fit into the frame rabbet. Cut a matching rabbet around the perimeter of the grating on the top.

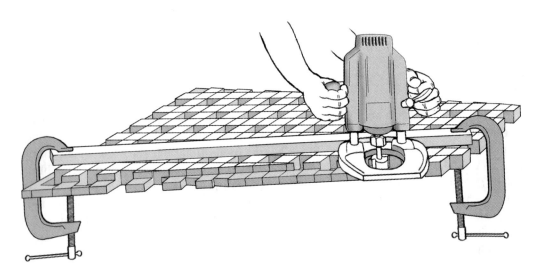

Set the frame over the grating and glue the two together at the rabbet joint.

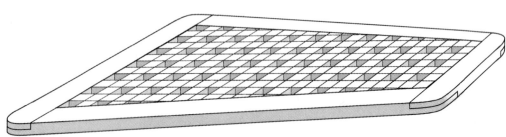

Assembling the grating.

The covering board—the wide plank nearest the rail—is cut to the curvature of the hull, not unlike the grating frame you just built. To accommodate a lot of curve, short pieces are joined with a box scarf, a joint you are familiar with.

The planks are straight lengths of $^3/_4$-inch-thick teak no more than 2 inches wide. Along the top of one edge is a $^1/_4$-inch-wide, $^1/_4$-inch-deep rabbet that provides the caulk groove when the planks are laid edge to edge. Nothing new here.

To get the planks to assume the contour of the covering board requires a great deal of clamping pressure, but what do you clamp to? Remember those wedge clamps we ripped out of scrap and used to clamp door frames and edge-glued planks? That's right. Screw half to the deck (what's a few more holes?) and drive the wedges in place to force each board against the previous one. You will need a couple of friends to hold the boards down while you are doing this or the boards will spring loose and slap you cross-eyed.

The king plank—the zigzag piece in the middle of the deck that the ends of all the other planks butt against—is cut to shape with a saber saw. How do you determine the shape? Parallel pencil lines on either side of the centerline of the deck define the maximum width of the king plank. Where those lines intersect the outboard edge of each plank, use a square to draw a perpendicular line across the plank. This is where each plank will be cut, and the staggered ends provide the outline for the king plank.

Drill and counterbore every hole, then screw the sprung planks to the deck. Wooden bungs hide the screws, and you already know to line up the grain, cut the bung off well above the surface, and pare them smooth from the lowest edge.

I am not trying to suggest that laying a teak deck is easy. It most emphatically is not. There is a great deal more involved than the half-dozen steps outlined here—things like setting the deck in a generous bed of polysulfide, dealing with narrowing side decks, trimming around deck features, and of course caulking. A teak deck may be the most difficult woodworking project anyone is likely to take on in renovating an old fiberglass boat. And therein lies the point of the last few paragraphs. Screwed down teak decks nearly guarantee eventual core damage, so as boat enhancements go, I would provide you more valuable guidance if I went back to Chapter 6 and detailed factory teak deck removal. I'm not really trying to show you how to lay a teak deck. I just want you to recognize that you could.

CHAPTER ELEVEN

Amps and Volts

"Electricity is really just organized lightning."
—GEORGE CARLIN

There is something wonderfully romantic about the golden light of kerosene lamps spilling out into the harbor through bronze portholes. The soft glow speaks of the independence of the crew aboard—free from noisy generators or yellow umbilical cords. It was just this kind of independence—leaving behind the excesses of modern life ashore—that first attracted me to boating.

My first boat had electric cabin lights, but away from the dock there was no way to charge the battery that powered them. Rather than add some kind of charging equipment, I chose to install kerosene lamps—lovely fixtures of polished brass with smoke bells on gracefully arched supports. When I lit those lamps, I was transported to Tonga or Tahiti even though the boat was still tied securely in her slip.

Then I took the boat on a cruise through the Bahamas. I nearly went blind trying to read by the reflected yellow light from those beautiful lamps. It was impossible to sit near them because of the heat they generated. When I turned them up to give off a reasonable amount of light, they heated the cabin so much that it was uninhabitable. On more than one warm, tropical night I risked becoming a late-night shark snack in a desperate effort to cool off.

I saw the light, so to speak. Kerosene cabin lamps, even the pressure kind that do generate enough light to read by, make poor shipmates south of Mason-Dixon. An electrical system capable of *brightly* illuminating the cabin became my top priority. If your boating dream features a wardrobe limited to bathing suits, an adequate electrical system will also be one of *your* priorities.

Of course the same power source that lights the cabin can also start the engine, pump the bilge, pressurize the water system, lift the anchor, cool the refrigerator, illuminate channel markers, gauge the depth, transmit your voice tens or hundreds of miles, let you "see" through fog, make you visible at night, bring you Beethoven, and tell you exactly where you are. You will no doubt find at least some of these other uses appealing.

THE SHOCKING TRUTH

Mention electricity to a lot of people and they will tell you about their Uncle Elbert, who was up in the attic repairing a wire when Aunt Minnie came home early from bingo and flipped on a switch, sending poor Elbert into the next life. The point of their lamentable tale is that messing around with electricity is just asking for it.

Where the electrical system of a boat is concerned, nothing could be further from the truth. Adding and repairing electrical circuits on your boat exposes you to the same shock risk as replacing the batteries in a portable lantern—none. Here I am talking about the battery-powered 12-volt system on your boat, not circuits that are connected to shore power or alternating current (AC) circuits powered by an onboard generator. AC power—110- or 220-volt—is dangerous whether the circuit is in an attic, on the dock, or in the galley, but except for a short segment on shore power, this chapter is about 12-volt direct current (DC) electrical systems. Twelve volts is simply inadequate to give you a dangerous shock, so let Uncle Elbert rest in peace.

The absence of shock risk does not relieve you of the need for caution. Current overloads can generate enough heat to start a fire. An electrical spark in combination with propane or gasoline fumes inside the boat can have you bunking with Elbert. Rapidly charging batteries give off hydrogen—the same gas that filled the Hindenburg. Sulfuric acid inside the batteries can cause blindness if you get it in your eyes.

Just being aware of these dangers should be sufficient to prevent them, like knowing that dropping a 100-pound battery can smash the hell out of your foot, that you can cut yourself stripping insulation off a piece of wire, and that touching the tip of a hot soldering iron will lead to a painful burn. I don't mean to be flippant, but working on a 12-volt electrical system is no more dangerous than crossing the street. Your mom gave you the key to being safe: look both ways.

ELECTRICAL UPGRADES

Old boats are almost a blank canvas for electrical upgrades. These can range from simply replacing subpar wiring or dated lighting fixtures to the redesign and installation of the total distribution system and/or the commissioning of a considerable array of networking electronics. The skill set required to perform virtually any of these upgrades is surprisingly small. The bigger challenge is likely to be developing a basic understanding of electricity so you will not only be capable of sound upgrades but you will also be comfortable with the process. Much of this chapter focuses on conveying the basic precepts that will defuse (sorry) any apprehension you may feel. Along the way we will also practice the needed skills.

THE BASIC CIRCUIT

Wiring an electrical appliance such as a cabin fan to a battery is a matter of connecting one wire to the positive terminal and one to the negative terminal. When the circuit is completed in this way, the fan runs.

Why is it called a circuit? Because it creates a path for free electrons to flow between the positive and negative plates in the battery. Think of a battery as a high-school gymnasium packed with teenagers, boys at one end, girls at the other, separated by a partition. Hormones are pumping; the battery is fully charged. The circuit is an outside corridor that connects the two ends of the gym. Someone opens the door to the corridor and the guys, being more aggressive, race out of the gym, through the corridor, and back into the gym at the girls' end. This "flow" will continue until the boys and girls have all paired off. When the gym is full of happy couples, our battery is dead.

To carry this sophomoric analogy a step further, if there is a turnstile in the corridor, as each boy passes through it, it spins—much like our fan. The turnstile stops when we interrupt the flow by closing the door or when we run out of randy boys. The same

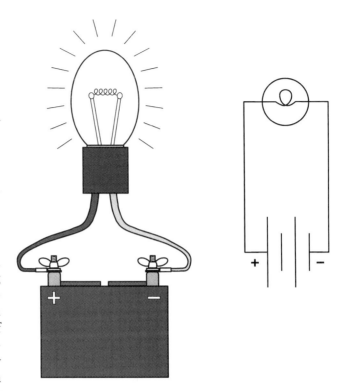

is true for the fan; it will continue to run until we disconnect it or until the battery loses its charge.

Connecting to the positive and negative battery terminals creates the basic circuit.

TERMINOLOGY

A case can be made for crediting an unknown Italian frog with the discovery of electric current. George Washington still had almost 3 years to go in his first term as president of the United States when Luigi Galvani, untroubled by animal rights concerns, hung the hapless croaker on an iron hook and stuck in a copper probe, noting that the frog's muscles contracted convulsively. Galvani did not understand the discovery, although it is likely the frog did—briefly. Yet to this day the flow of electric current between dissimilar metals immersed in a conductive liquid (ugh!) is called *galvanic action*. Go figure.

It would be another 10 years before fellow Italian, Alessandro Volta, finally deduced what the frog knew intuitively. As unfair as it may seem, the martyred frog was quickly forgotten, but not Volta, whose name now appears on virtually every item of electrical equipment.

After Volta came a whole gallery of scientists, inventors, and engineers who expanded on the frog's discovery, each carrying it a step further. For their contributions, most were honored by having some unit of measurement named after them. Besides the volt, you need to be familiar with the ampere (named after a man named Marie!), the ohm, and the watt.

The *ampere*, commonly shortened to amp, is a measurement of the *rate* of the flow of electric current. It indicates the number of electrons that pass a point in a given time. Back to our analogy: If we counted the number of boys passing through the turnstile in 1 minute, we would come up with a rate. If we counted 120, we might say that the "current" was 120 boys per minute. But if we had a term that signified 100 boys per minute—let's call it a frog—we would then rate the current at 1.2 frogs. Big deal, right? Except that when we are counting electrons, we are dealing with much larger numbers. How big? One ampere is equal to a flow of 6,280,000,000,000,000,000 electrons per second. Would you rather say, "5 amps" or "31.4 billion billion electrons per second"? Amps it is.

The *volt* is a measurement of force. It is what causes the current to flow. Voltage is a measurement of what is called *potential,* a term easily understood from our analogy. For example, if both sides of the gymnasium were filled with boys, there would be no flow through the corridor; the flow occurs because the boys are attracted to the girls. Potential. We could raise the potential by filling one end of the gym with sailors who have been at sea for a year and putting their wives and girlfriends at the other end. If you suspect that this increase in potential would also increase the rate of the flow of men through the corridor, you would be right.

The *ohm* is a measurement of resistance. If the corridor is nice and wide, the flow of boys from one end to the other is uninhibited. But if the corridor is narrow, only so many boys can pass through at a time. Smaller wire inhibits the flow of electrons in a similar manner. A small corridor may not be a problem for the lower potential of high schoolers, but the sailors are going to push and shove trying to get through the small hall. More will get through, but things are likely to heat up. So will a wire that's too small for the job.

The last of the essential terms is the *watt,* which is a measurement of power. The only reason we are interested in electricity is to get it to do work for us. The watt is the rate of doing work. We could tap the power of our gymnasium battery by wrapping a few turns of line around the turnstile and connecting the loose end to a weight, converting the turnstile into a windlass. Every time someone passed through the turnstile, he would move the weight. The more guys passing through the turnstile in a given time, the higher the rate of work. We can see that the rate of work is directly related to how many guys are moving through the corridor—current—and how motivated they are to get through the turnstile—potential.

TWO ESSENTIAL EQUATIONS

If a beer costs $2 and you have $4, how many can you buy? How much money do you need to treat yourself and three friends? If at happy hour your $4 bought four beers, what was the price of one beer? While you are saying, "Duh," suppose I call this three-part relationship Bud's law: namely that the number of beers you can buy (N) is directly proportional to the total cash you have (T) and inversely proportional to the price of a beer (P). Even if I express it in an algebraic equation as $T = P \times N$, that won't make the math involved any more difficult. To answer the happy hour question, we can reconstitute the equation as $P = T \div N$.

If you are going to successfully conceive and/ or troubleshoot your old boat's electrical system, it is essential to understand the relationship between voltage, current, and resistance. This relationship is called Ohm's law: current is directly proportional to voltage and inversely proportional to resistance. The equation that expresses this is $V = I \times R$. Sound familiar? Duh, indeed. Sorry about the "I" in this equation, but it is the traditional abbreviation for current, stemming from the concept that currents are *induced* to flow. And current is usually our unknown, making the reorganized equation $I = V \div R$. Remember this. Unlike the algebra you were taught in high school, you are actually going to use this equation—and soon.

But first there is a second equation you are going to need to know (Bud's law doesn't count). It is called the *power equation.* Power is the rate of doing work. You are probably more familiar with horsepower than watts, but the concept is the same. Fifty horsepower pushes a boat faster than 25. Likewise, a 50-watt bulb provides more illumination than one with only 25 watts. Multiplying voltage in volts by current in amps gives us electrical power in watts. The equation for this relationship is $P = V \times I$.

You are likely to use the power equation most often to determine current. In this case, the equation becomes $I = P \div V$. It tells us that our 25-watt lamp operating at 12 volts draws a little more than 2 amps ($25 \div 12$) in use, that the brighter illumination of a 50-watt bulb draws an additional 2 amps ($50 \div 12$), and that a 150-watt SSB transmission draws 12.5 amps ($150 \div 12$). This knowledge will be important for some electrical system issues we will get to later, such as sizing wire and fusing circuits, but our interest in current magnitude is more immediate than that.

CON ED 'R' US

If you decide that a room in your home is too dark, the solution is simple. You either install higher-wattage bulbs or add additional lights. It probably would not occur to you to wonder if there is enough electricity available to power brighter illumination. The only nod you are likely to give to power consumption ashore is for large appliances like air conditioners and refrigerators, and even then your concern will be about the cost of the electricity rather than the availability. For all practical purposes electricity is unlimited ashore. This is not the case with the electrical system on your old boat. You are not just the consumer. You are also the electric company. You must generate every amp that is consumed by the appliances you decide to put aboard.

Thinking of yourself as the electric company can be, well, illuminating. You should be familiar with *kilowatt-hours,* the unit power companies use to calculate your electric bill. A kilowatt is 1,000 watts of electrical power and a kilowatt-hour represents 1,000 watts of power consumption for a period of 1 hour. It might also be 500 watts for 2 hours or 100 watts for 10 hours. My electric company charges me slightly more than 11 cents for every kilowatt-hour I use.

What will a kilowatt-hour that you generate onboard cost? We can use the power equation to convert from watts to amps. When we are solving for current, the equation is $I = P \div V$. $P = 1,000$ watts, and because we are talking about 12-volt power here, $V = 12$ volts. Thus $I = 83.3$ amps $(1,000 \div 12)$, except that in this case we are actually converting kilowatt-hours, so the answer is in amp-hours. *Amp-hour* (Ah) is a common term in any discussion of 12-volt electrical systems. One amp-hour simply represents a current of 1 amp flowing for 1 hour.

The cost to generate 83.3 amp-hours depends on your generating equipment. A standard engine-mounted alternator might have an output of 35 or 40 amps. With this type of alternator, it would take more than 2 hours of engine time to generate a kilowatt-hour of power. Just the fuel cost to run your engine for 2 hours would currently exceed $10, making the electricity on your boat more than 90 times more costly than what a kilowatt-hour costs ashore.

Of course, when you are running your engine for propulsion, the electricity the alternator provides is almost free. In any case, cost is not generally the controlling issue. The real issue is capacity. How much power can you generate? How much are you *willing* to generate—i.e., how many hours each day do you want to run the engine? And how much power can you store? When the load exceeds the capacity of your generating or storage equipment, the cost to increase capacity can be substantial. So before you place additional demands on your old boat's electrical system, you need to do a few load calculations.

CALCULATING LOADS

A few years back I shared an anchorage with a small cruising catamaran whose electrical system defined simplicity and low cost. From the broken taillight of a junk car, the skipper had stripped a single light socket and mounted it inside a discarded plastic Rolaids jar. The 10-watt bulb lit the tiny cabin admirably.

Using our trusty power equation, we can determine that the *current draw* of this minimalist cabin light was 0.8 amp $(10 \div 12)$. The load this lamp (or any appliance) places on a battery is determined by both the draw and the time the fixture is in use. Multiply the draw in amps by the time in hours to arrive at the load in amp-hours. In this case, the cabin light was used about 4 hours per day, so the daily load of the light was 3.2 Ah (0.8×4).

Since the one light was the only electric appliance aboard the cat, 3.2 Ah was also the total daily load. *Total daily load* is the sum of the daily loads of all the electric appliances aboard. You should have in hand an estimate of the total daily load aboard your old boat before you contemplate adding a single new electrical item. A daily load calculation is also the best place to start when your existing electrical system falls short of your expectations.

Don't just nod in agreement. Get a pencil and make a list of every electrical appliance presently aboard your boat. Beside each appliance, note its current rating in amps. If it is a light, the bulb will show the watt rating, which you now know to convert to amps by dividing by 12 $(I = P \div V)$. Appliances with motors—such as pumps, fans, and refrigerators—typically have a specification plate that indicates either watt rating or draw in amps. Convert all ratings in watts to amps. Electronics will have a similar plate or the specifications will be listed in the owner's manual. If you cannot find any indication of the power requirements of a specific item, check the manufacturer's website for technical data. Or use the current draw specified in catalog listings of similar equipment, which will be close enough for this exercise.

Next to the current rating, estimate the number of hours the item is or could be in use each day. Your estimates should be liberal. Like your electric company, you want to be able to handle even the highest-demand day.

Finally, multiply the amp ratings by the hours to get the estimated daily load in amp-hours of each item. Add all of the individual loads together to get the total daily load.

Continue your list by writing down every additional electrical item you are considering. Obtain amp ratings from the Internet or catalog listings, and estimate daily hours of usage. Calculate the daily loads and add them to the previous total to estimate the total daily load of all the equipment you plan to have aboard your boat. You should end up with something similar to the table shown.

Without some frame of reference, these calculations have little significance. Recalling that 83.3 Ah at 12 volts is equivalent to 1 kilowatt-hour, you might be led to conclude that a couple of hundred amp-hours—less than 3 kilowatt-hours—is no big deal, especially when you compare it to home consumption. For example, my electric company informs me that my average daily home use of power is about 27 kilowatt-hours. But home consumption is irrelevant. The electric company isn't supplying the power used onboard, you are. And 200 Ah may be a very big deal.

The typical power source aboard an old boat is a single engine-driven alternator. Under the most ideal conditions a 40 amp alternator will take 5 hours to supply 200 Ah of power, but for reasons that we will see shortly, a more realistic estimate is 10 hours of engine time. However, regardless of the size of the alternator, it is usually the batteries that supply the power. The function of the generating equipment is

DAILY POWER USAGE				
Device	*Amps*	×	*Hours of Use*	=	*Daily Amp-Hours*
Cabin light—incandescent (4)	2.1		16		33.6
Pump—freshwater	6.0		0.08		0.5
Pump—bilge	15.0		0		0
Starter—diesel (1,800 W)	150.0		0.02		3.0
Anchor windlass	150.0		0.2		30.0
Depthsounder	0.2		8		1.6
VHF—standby	0.5		4		2.0
VHF—transmit	5.0		0.2		1.0
GPS	0.5		8		4.0
Gas detector	0.3		24		7.2
Anchor light	0.8		12		9.6
Running lights (3)	0.8		0		0*
Running lights—tricolor	0.8		0		0*
Current Total Daily Load in Amp-Hours					92.5
Cabin light—fluorescent (3)	0.7		12		8.4
Cabin fan (2 add)	0.2		24		4.8
Reading light—fluorescent (2)	0.8		4		3.2
Autopilot (above deck)	0.7		8		5.6
Chart plotter	2.0		8		16.0
Refrigerator	6.0		12		72.0**
Radar	4.0		4		16
SSB—receive	2.5		1		2.5
SSB—transmit	30.0		0.2		6.0
Inverter—standby	0.2		6		1.2
Television (13-inch)	3.5		2		7.0
DVD player	2.5		2		5.0
Projected Total Daily Load in Amp-Hours					240.2

*Running light usage is partially or wholly offset by decreased use of cabin and anchor lights.

**Cycling 12-volt refrigeration typically draws power about half of every hour of operation.

to recharge the depleted batteries. So the batteries must have sufficient capacity to supply your electrical demands between chargings. Let's take a look at what that means.

BATTERY LIES AND HALF-TRUTHS

When two dissimilar metals are immersed in an *electrolyte* (a conductive liquid), a voltage develops. Devices that supply electric energy from a chemical reaction are known as *voltaic cells*. Combining two or more voltaic cells creates a battery.

The voltage of a cell depends on the metals and the electrolyte. Stick a strip of zinc and a strip of copper into an olive, and you will probably measure a potential of about half a volt. A *dry cell* has a voltage of about 1.5 volts. Four dry cells are combined in a 6-volt lantern battery. There are six inside a 9-volt radio battery. *Wet cells* have a peak voltage of around 2.11 volts. When six wet cells are combined inside a plastic case, they become a 12-volt battery (a somewhat misleading designation since the actual fully charged voltage is about 12.65 volts).

CAPACITY

Determining the capacity of a battery is not as easy as determining the voltage. Even defining capacity presents some problems. For example, if a manufacturer specifies that a particular battery has a capacity of 100 Ah, it is probably safe to assume that it can handle a 1 amp load for 100 hours, but can the same battery supply 100 amps for 1 hour? It looks like the answer should be yes, but it is emphatically *no*. The maximum load this battery can sustain for 1 hour will be closer to 50 amps. So is this a 50 Ah battery or a 100 Ah battery?

Most batteries manufactured in the United States specify the amp-hour capacity based on a constant discharge over a period of 20 hours that reduces the cell voltage to 1.75 volts. This is known as a C20 rating, and by this standard a battery capable of supplying 5 amps for 20 hours is rated at 100 Ah. But the same battery will not supply 20 amps for 5 hours. Why not?

While a full water tank with a 30-gallon capacity yields 30 gallons regardless of how quickly you pump it out, battery capacity is more complicated because the energy is being produced by a chemical reaction going on inside the battery. The more rapidly the energy is removed, the less efficient the process. Subject the 20-hour-rated battery I just described to a 10 amp load, and the true capacity of the battery will be about 80% of the rated capacity. A 20 amp load

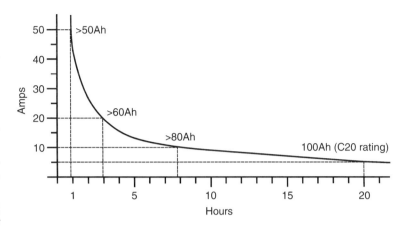

Typical discharge performance for a battery rated at 100 Ah.

will discharge the battery in about 3 hours—around 60% of the advertised capacity. A 50 amp load will flatten a 100 Ah battery in less than an hour, meaning that the battery delivers less than half of its rated capacity at this discharge rate.

Adding to the bad news, batteries are normally rated at 80°F (27°C), but true capacity declines with the temperature. As the temperature approaches freezing, you should expect all of these capacities to be reduced by about a third.

Boaters find the waters muddied further by the absence of Ah capacity ratings on many batteries in favor of *cold cranking amps* (CCA). The CCA is the number of amps that the rated battery can deliver for 30 seconds at 0°F before battery voltage drops to 7.2 volts. No battery manufacturer would actually encourage you to discharge its 12-volt battery down to 7.2 volts, so this rating is essentially dishonest—but for starting your car throughout a Michigan winter, the higher the CCA rating, the better.

Some marketing whiz noted that if the temperature is 0°C rather than 0°F, the number of cranking amps increases by about 25%. Hey, boaters don't go out when it is 0°F, and 500 amps is better than 400, isn't it? So let's put a boat on the label, up the cold cranking amp rating by about 25%, and call this—uh, let's see, how about *marine* cranking amps (MCA)? The truth is that neither CCA nor MCA provides any useful information for batteries used aboard a boat unless the battery will be used *exclusively* to start the engine. Even then, the primary value is to compare batteries for purchase.

Yet another rating you are likely to encounter is *reserve minutes*. This is another form of amp-hour rating, but it is based on a constant discharge rather than a fixed time. Reserve minutes are the number of minutes that the battery will supply a constant 25 amps. This rating tells you nothing about a battery that you won't already know from the amp-hour rating. Here is the rule: for batteries intended to power lights and appliances aboard your boat, you are *only* interested in the amp-hour rating. Give any battery that does not specify its capacity in amp-hours a pass.

Since you're after ample battery capacity to handle your daily electrical demands, the 20-hour rate is especially relevant—although perhaps not as apt as you might think. If your projected daily consumption is 100 Ah, you may have the silly notion that you need a 100 Ah battery. Snap out of it! If you draw 100 Ah from a 100 Ah battery, what do you suppose is going to happen when you hit the starter button? Is that your answer or the sound you expect the starter to make?

Even if you have a dedicated battery for starting the engine, a house battery with a capacity equal to the projected load is still inadequate. For one thing, the C20 rating is based on a terminal cell voltage of 1.75 volts. That is a battery voltage of 10.5 volts for a 12-volt battery, but in use a 12-volt battery is effectively dead at around 11.8 volts. So while a 100 Ah battery is rated to deliver 5 amps for 20 hours, by hour 17 of the test, the battery voltage will have declined to 11.8 volts, making the real-world capacity 85 Ah—15% less than you thought you purchased. Hmmm.

But hold on! You don't actually have even 85 Ah available, because fully discharging a battery damages it. Doing so repeatedly will *severely* shorten its life. Imagine donating a gallon of blood instead of a pint and you get the idea. As a rule, wet-cell batteries should not be discharged much beyond 50% of rated capacity. As we will see later, you may want to bend this rule in real-world conditions, but you should base all of your capacity calculations on a maximum discharge of 50%.

So does this mean a 200 Ah battery bank will support a 100 Ah load? The answer might finally be yes, except that if you are charging your batteries with an alternator, you are almost certain to discontinue the charge before the batteries reach full charge. This is because batteries accept a charge at a decreasing rate as they approach full charge, and by the time your battery nears 90% of rated capacity, the input from your high-powered alternator will be down to a trickle. We will examine this reality in more detail later, but because recharging beyond about 90% requires hours and hours of engine time, you can anticipate normally operating your batteries between a maximum charge of 90% and a maximum discharge of 50%. This reduces the usable capacity to 40% of the rated capacity, which gives us just 40 usable amp-hours from 100 Ah of battery capacity. The rule we can derive is that battery capacity needs to be at least $2\frac{1}{2}$ times consumption in amp-hours between charges. This translates into a 250 Ah battery bank to support a 100 Ah load.

Applying this rule to the 240 Ah from our load calculation illustration suggests a battery capacity of around 600 Ah. At this writing, top-quality, deep-cycle marine batteries cost around $2 per amp-hour of capacity. Spending $1,200 on batteries is something to think about. So is their weight. Deep-cycle batteries weigh around $2/_3$ pound per amp-hour, so 600 Ah of battery capacity will weigh in at close to 400 pounds. What does your engine weigh?

This is the reality of supplying all of your electrical needs from storage batteries. Reducing the load may be a more palatable alternative. The prudent boatowner will make load projections in advance.

BATTERY BANKS

Suppose you trim back your projected consumption to 100 Ah per day. That suggests you need around 250 Ah of battery capacity if you are going to recharge the batteries every day. If you want to be able to leave the boat for a day—to take an inland tour, for example—you need 500 Ah of capacity. The reality for a cruising boat is that the house bank is going to be defined by space, weight, and perhaps cost, and you will ultimately have to make changes either to your consumption patterns or to your charging equipment to balance the discharge/charge equation. We will examine both options momentarily, but first let's pose the question of where exactly you would find a 500 Ah battery.

The answer, of course, is that you won't. To get 500 Ah of battery capacity, you are going to combine two or more batteries of lesser capacity (and lesser weight!).

Parallel

To combine 12-volt batteries into a bank that combines their capacities, you wire them together *in parallel*. If you sketch a parallel circuit, it looks like a ladder. All the positive posts are connected and all the negative posts are connected. Joining like batteries in parallel has no effect on voltage but it combines their amperages. Wire two 100 Ah, 12-volt batteries in parallel and you create a 200 Ah, 12-volt bank. Wire five of these batteries together and you have a 500 Ah, 12-volt bank.

The rotary battery switch that was probably a component of the original wiring of your old boat, when turned to the "Both" setting, parallels the two batteries or battery banks. This is useful for charging both banks from the same source and sometimes for accessing the combined power of both banks for cranking the engine, but for delivering more than instantaneous power, batteries wired in parallel should be of the same type, size, and age. Otherwise there is a current flow between the batteries, which is undesirable.

Series

Components combined in series are linked together like railroad cars. Connecting two batteries in series—the negative post of one to the positive post of

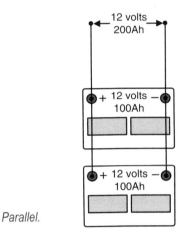

Parallel.

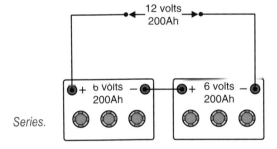

Series.

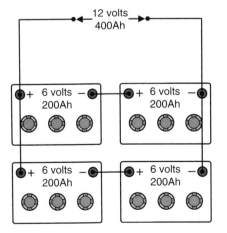

Series and parallel.

Combining batteries.

the other—combines their voltages. Why would you want to do that? Large boats often have 24-volt, or even 36-volt, electrical systems. The reason has to do with the transmission of the power—the higher the voltage, the lower the amperage to deliver the same amount of power (recall that $P = V \times I$), so the long wire runs necessary on a big boat can be made with smaller wire. To get a 24-volt bank, you would wire two 12-volt batteries (or banks) in series. Or four 6-volt batteries. Or 12 2-volt cells.

For the rest of us, connecting batteries in series is likely to be limited to connecting a pair of 6-volt batteries to deliver 12 volts. We will see the reasons for this in the next section. Connecting cells or batteries in series does not increase their amperage rating.

A battery bank might contain both series and parallel connections. For example, a very common house configuration is to series wire a pair of 225 Ah, 6-volt batteries into a 225 Ah, 12-volt battery. Two such "batteries" are then combined in parallel to create a 12-volt bank with 450 Ah of capacity.

Batteries wired in series must be identical—same make, model, capacity, and age. If one battery in a series pair fails, you must replace both.

One Bank or Two?

Production boats often come with two identical battery banks. The idea is that one serves as the house bank with the other reserved for engine starting, but both can do either job. Somehow from this a dogma evolved that the best battery configuration was two battery banks used on a rotating basis. *This is dead wrong!* You do need a separate battery for starting the engine, but whatever batteries you intend to use to supply your house power should be combined into a single bank. The logic for this is dead simple. The larger the bank, the shallower the discharge for a given time between charging. Shallower discharges extend battery life. Alternatively a larger bank allows you to extend the time between recharging, reducing wear and tear and operating costs. A larger bank will also accept charge at a higher rate, allowing your charging equipment to operate more efficiently and reducing the recharge time.

Polarity

Most DC appliances will have one wire labeled with a plus sign (+) and perhaps the other with a minus (–). The plus wire is often—but sadly not always—red. It is essential that the positive wire from the appliance ultimately connect to the positive post of the battery, also labeled with a +. I mention this here because if you inadvertently reverse the battery connections, you reverse the polarity to every electrical item on the boat. Your incandescent cabin lights will tolerate this gaffe, but it is almost certain to instantly damage your alternator and/or regulator, and any electronics you turn on while the polarity is reversed will also suffer damage. You must pay close attention to the correct polarity of both the battery bank and the batteries that comprise it. Note that one battery may configure the positive and negative posts in the opposite way to another battery. Sometimes you have a choice. Be sure of your battery connections before you make them.

BATTERY SELECTION

All 12-volt batteries (suitable for our purposes) are *lead-acid batteries*, meaning that they are composed of lead plates and lead dioxide plates submerged in a sulfuric acid solution. Lead-acid batteries are called storage batteries because they appear to store electricity. Actually the electricity is produced by an internal chemical process—as in every other battery. What distinguishes a storage battery is that you can reverse the chemical process by passing a current back through the battery, restoring it to its fully charged state. Recalling the gymnasium full of couples, if a chaperone shows up and forces all the boys back through the corridor to their end of the gym, the potential will be reestablished. Same idea.

Among lead-acid batteries, there are three types that you should be aware of.

Automotive

Automotive batteries have been the most common type since Charles Kettering installed the first electric starter in the 1912 Cadillac. Starting the engine is still the primary function of an automotive battery. This requires the delivery of 100 or more amps for a few seconds. High currents mean the chemical reaction inside the battery must take place rapidly, dictating the need for thin plates. This concept may be easier to grasp if you think of dissolving ice in water; 5 pounds of shaved ice will dissolve much more rapidly than a 5-pound block. But even if you grind away on the starter for a minute or two—an eternity when you are trying to start an engine—the total discharge will be less than 5 amp-hours. Then the battery is *immediately* recharged. Automotive batteries live in a fully charged environment. The demands of headlights and other electrical equipment are simultaneously offset by input from an alternator that operates when the car is in use.

Automotive batteries are fine aboard boats to start the engine, but if this type of battery is connected to your house bank with a paralleling switch and by either design or accident you use it for your house loads, the deep discharge will damage it. Deeply discharged automotive batteries can fail in as few as 20 discharge cycles, making this type of battery unsuitable for even occasional house duty.

One type of automotive battery you should avoid like the plague is the so-called maintenance-free battery. Although these batteries enjoy a more or less normal battery life in cars, the higher-charge voltage that is typically a feature of a boat electrical system will cause these "sealed" batteries to gas and vent. This results in lost water, and because the batteries have no fill caps, you cannot replace it. Short battery life is assured.

Deep-Cycle

The deep-cycle battery is different in concept. It is designed to be deeply discharged over a period of time before requiring a recharge. The thicker plates reduce the amount of time that a deep-cycle battery can supply very high currents (relative to automotive batteries), but they allow the battery to be deeply discharged without damaging it. If a first-quality deep-cycle battery is not discharged below about 50% of its rated capacity, it may be discharged and recharged as many as several *thousand* times. Deep-cycle batteries are often called "marine" batteries in recognition of their suitability for the typical demands of onboard use.

Six-volt deep-cycle batteries intended for golf carts and industrial electric vehicles merit special mention because of their economy. These batteries are designed to be discharged all day, then recharged so they can do it all again the next day—pretty darn close to how sailors use house batteries. There are way more golfers than sailors, and 6-volt golf cart batteries are manufactured by the millions. That necessarily drives the price down. No battery that I know delivers more power for less money than golf cart batteries, and given basic care—which means keeping the water topped off and not allowing the battery to sit in a discharged state—good-quality golf cart batteries should deliver 4 to 5 years of dependable service. They also have the comforting quality of lowering the price tag should some killing misfortune befall your batteries.

Sealed Valve Regulated

The third type of lead-acid battery that you can consider for your old boat is the sealed valve regulated (SVR) battery, a collective term for a technology that includes both gel-cell and absorbed glass mat (AGM) batteries. Gel-cell batteries derive their name from the form of the electrolyte used, which has the consistency of butter rather than water. Absorbed glass mat batteries are a more recent offshoot of the same idea, but an AGM battery captures liquid electrolyte in microporous separators between the metal plates. Both gel cells and AGMs come in sealed cases. They cannot spill acid, never need water, can be mounted in almost any position, and give off no gas during normal charging. All these qualities are advantages aboard a boat, to be sure, but it is the way SVR batteries combine automotive and deep-cycle battery characteristics that merits examination. Design and chemistry differences allow good-quality gel-cell and AGM batteries to be deeply discharged repeatedly like a deep-cycle battery and to accept a fast charge like an automotive battery. Some sealed batteries will accept a charge so quickly that they can be fully charged in 30 minutes (although a charging current of about five times the battery capacity would be needed—i.e., 500 amps for a 100 Ah SVR battery).

The idea of a battery that can be discharged deeply and recharged rapidly has instant appeal. But wait. Before you run out and replace your aging deep-cycle batteries with either gel cells or AGMs, take a closer look. While their internal chemistries—primarily the substitution of calcium for antimony in the lead alloy—allow these batteries to delivery 10 times more deep cycles, their thin and closely spaced plates make them essentially automotive-type batteries. In deep-cycle use, these are fragile batteries operating close to the edge, and they require exacting charging regimens. Gel cells in particular will not tolerate the charging voltage delivered by a standard marine alternator/regulator. You must have specialized charging equipment to operate gel-cell batteries successfully, and you cannot mix gel-cell batteries with flooded or AGM batteries aboard unless you have a means of separately regulating the charging voltages. It is telling that gel-cell technology, with all of its promise, has garnered only a minor following in a quarter of a century of availability.

AGM batteries are somewhat less finicky and can be charged at the same voltage as flooded batteries, but taking advantage of the primary benefit of an AGM—rapid charge acceptance—necessitates specialized charging equipment. This must include temperature compensation. All batteries heat up during the charging process, and the faster you charge, the more heat you generate. This leads to gassing, which a sealed battery must not do to any extent or it will vent, permanently damaging the battery.

Gel-cell batteries have an amazing tolerance for idleness, and AGM batteries are capable of providing very high currents. These and other unique qualities make both batteries ideal for specific uses or for specific battery owners. However, you should have an explicit reason for choosing one of these technologies. If that is rapid charging, be aware that in yet another battery half-truth, the rated number of cycles of gel-cell and AGM batteries is based on standard charging practices. Neither battery will deliver its rating if subjected to repeated high current charges. Gotcha.

Most boatowners will be best served by *flooded batteries*—an automotive-type or so-called "dual-purpose" battery for starting duty and a bank of deep-cycle batteries to supply house loads. Flooded batteries require no additional expenditure for special charging or regulating equipment (although you may want to eventually add such gear for better charge performance). They are more tolerant of chronic overcharging, a typical consequence of long engine hours. For the same expenditure, you can expect flooded batteries to last four times as long as gel cells or AGMs. Alternatively, you can spend half as much on golf cart batteries and still expect twice the battery life. In use, the contrast is likely to be even greater because perhaps half of all SVR batteries taken aboard die an early death due to some charging impropriety.

By the Pound

Relative battery weight is a good comparative indicator of the number of cycles a battery will deliver. This is because the lead in a battery is porous. The more spongelike the lead, the more surface area exposed to contact with the electrolyte and the greater the current the battery can deliver. However, spongelike lead is more fragile, and there is less active material, so the battery will have a shorter life. Plates constructed of denser material will deliver more cycles and generally tolerate more abuse. Denser material weighs more, so the heavier the battery relative to other batteries with the same capacity rating, the more life cycles you should anticipate.

MONITORING

Since I keep prattling on about a 50% discharge level, you might be wondering how you know the state of charge of your batteries. Good question.

Voltage

Battery voltage is about the closest you will come to having the equivalent of a gas gauge for the charge level of your house bank. At-rest voltage is a pretty good indicator of charge level, but unfortunately the batteries on a boat in use are rarely at rest. If the battery is being discharged—say the refrigerator is running—it will register lower than true voltage. If it is being charged, the voltage reading will be higher. Even if neither is occurring at the moment, batteries "recover" for several hours after discharge. The voltage also rises for some time after charging stops. For an accurate assessment of charge level based on battery voltage, the batteries should have rested for 24 hours. In practice, you will get a fairly accurate reading of battery condition after a couple of hours of rest. A good time to check battery voltage on a cruising boat is just before sunrise. The cycle time for electric refrigeration will be at its longest, there are likely to be few other loads, and any fixed solar panels will still be dormant.

Between fully charged and 50% discharged, battery voltage declines by less than 0.5 volt, so assessing the charge state of the batteries based on voltage requires a digital voltmeter. A voltage reading above 12.6 suggests that a 12-volt battery is nearly 100% charged. When 25% discharged, battery voltage will have declined to around 12.4 volts. A reading of 12.2 volts corresponds to the 50% discharge (or half-charge, if you like) level. Not allowing battery voltage to decline below this level is generally considered to maximize the total number of lifetime amp-hours a battery will deliver. A reading of 12 volts indicates that the battery (or bank) is around 75% discharged, and the battery is effectively dead when the voltage declines below 11.8.

Specific Gravity

The specific gravity (SG) of a liquid is its density compared to that of pure water. Since water is the standard, it has a specific gravity of 1.000. The specific gravity of sulfuric acid is 1.830. The water-acid mix that is the electrolyte in a flooded battery will have a specific gravity of around 1.265, but the acid gets used up during discharge, so the SG declines toward 1.000. Between fully charged and fully discharged, the decline is around 150 points and is linear, so an SG reading of 1.250 indicates a 10% discharge. The cell is at half-discharge when the SG declines to 1.190. A battery at the 75% discharge level the SG will be around 1.150. Any SG reading below 1.120 tells you that the cell is dead.

Checking specific gravity requires a battery hydrometer. Don't buy one with colored balls inside; you want the kind with a little glass man-overboard pole. With the battery caps open, squeeze the bulb, stick the flexible tip into a cell, and ease your grip slowly to draw enough electrolyte up into the clear tube to float the little overboard pole. Where the fluid crosses the scale on the float tells you the SG of the cell. Note the reading, then squeeze all of the electrolyte back into the cell. Make sure the hydrometer is empty before you move it to the next cell. Keep in mind that you are handling sulfuric acid, so take care not to spray, splash, or drip. As with voltage readings, specific gravity readings will be most accurate if the battery has rested for several hours before you take them.

SG values are for an electrolyte temperature of 80°F. Add 0.004 to the reading for every 10° above 80°F, and subtract the same amount for every 10° below. The hydrometer will contain a thermometer.

Within a lead-acid battery's operating range, the relationship between specific gravity and voltage is linear. Add 0.84 to your SG reading and you will have the voltage of the cell. For example, we have defined an SG of 1.190 as indicating a 50% discharge level. If we add 0.84 to this reading, we get a cell voltage of 2.03. Multiplied by six cells, this gives us a battery

	Battery Voltage	Specific Gravity (8°F)
	12.6	1.265
	12.4	1.225
	12.2	1.190
	12.0	1.155
	11.8	1.120

The relationship between charge level, battery voltage, and specific gravity.

voltage of 12.18—pretty close to the 12.2 voltage that indicates 50% discharge. The primary advantage of assessing battery condition with a hydrometer is that it tells you the condition of each cell. A healthy battery will give consistent cell-to-cell readings. If the readings vary by more than 15 points (0.015), the battery needs to be given a full charge, perhaps even a controlled overcharge—called, appropriately, *equalizing*. If any SG reading varies from the others by 50 points when the battery is fully charged, that cell is failing and the battery should be replaced.

Hardwired Monitors

Nothing is more convenient than a hardwired monitor for keeping track of the condition of your house bank on a day-to-day basis. The ageless Link 10 or some other smart battery monitor will keep you informed of the real-time voltage as well as the current level of load or input. This not only tells you the charge level, it allows you to instantly assess the true draw of a particular appliance, determine how much current your alternator is actually delivering, and maximize the output from solar panel positioning. No boat that stays away from the dock for more than a few days should be without a hardwired battery monitor.

The voltmeter and ammeter functions will prove most valuable. A reading of 13.8 volts tells you your alternator is charging (and switching to the amps function will tell you the rate of charge). A voltage reading of 11.9 tells you that you are overdue for recharging. A daily early-morning check of voltage after the batteries have rested overnight lets you conveniently track charge status. The amp function reassures you that running a fan all night will have little impact on your batteries. It can also warn you of a current leak or a failing appliance.

What you should not put great faith in is the amp-hour function of a battery monitor. We have noted that a 50 amp load will deplete a 100 Ah battery in less than an hour, so keeping track of amp-hours available is not as simple as offsetting amp-hours out against amp-hours in. The rate of discharge needs to be taken into account. Monitors have a microcomputer that tries to do this, but over time the inaccuracy accumulates. If you have the typical discharge/recharge pattern of a boat equipped with solar and wind charging, the depth of discharge in amp-hours will be out of sync with the level of charge the voltmeter suggests within a few days. Believe the voltmeter. After a few days without a resetting charge, the amp-hour reading of a battery meter is pure fiction.

GASSING AND SULFATION

Overcharging causes the electrolyte to percolate, giving off hydrogen and oxygen molecules. SVR batteries must not be allowed to gas, at least not with sufficient vigor to raise the internal pressure enough to cause the battery to vent. In flooded cells, however, *modest* gassing is actually beneficial. The rising gas bubbles improve the charge acceptance of the battery by mixing the electrolyte, which tends to stratify when motionless. Lost molecules are easily replaced by simply adding water to the cell.

During charge, a portion of the energy is converted to heat. Expect battery temperature to rise between 20°F and 40°F during a complete charging cycle. Gassing is directly related to battery voltage and electrolyte temperature. If the battery temperature rises to 120°F, gassing starts at just 13.4 volts, but hold the battery temperature at 100°F, and you delay gassing until the battery voltage rises to 13.8. House batteries given a cool location should experience only beneficial gassing and that only near the end of the charge cycle. They will require the addition of water only occasionally. It also will not hurt to keep the starting battery out of the engine compartment, although if 100 years of automotive experience count for anything, you should be able to mount the starting battery in a well-ventilated engine space without notable ill effect.

Sulfation is the result of undercharging or, more accurately, of leaving the battery in a state of discharge. Sulfates that form on the lead plates during discharge are initially soft and readily recombine with the electrolyte when a charging current is applied. But if the battery is not charged, these soft sulfates crystallize in a matter of hours, becoming a hard coating on the plate and permanently diminishing the capacity of the battery. Daily charging current provided by solar panels or a wind generator can virtually eliminate sulfation.

HERESY . . . AGAIN

We are about finished with the subject of batteries, but before we move on, let's kill a sacred cow, shall we? In cycle-life testing, deep-cycle lead-acid batteries typically deliver the most lifetime amp-hours when discharge is limited to about 50% of capacity, so this is the maximum depth of discharge normally recommended. If maximizing the "value" you derive from your batteries were the controlling issue, the 50% discharge rule would, well, rule, but value isn't *really* what you want from your batteries. What you want is convenience. You want plenty of light, fans when you need them, pumps that don't require muscle, radio communications, movies, and the ability to recharge your laptop battery. And you want to run your engine as infrequently and as little as possible. The best solution to the generating capacity/storage capacity equation is solar and/or wind-generating equipment, which we will come to later, but what can you do to maximize convenience on the storage side?

We have already noted that the decreasing rate of charge acceptance will not allow us to efficiently charge deep-cycle batteries above around 90% of capacity, so restricting discharge to 50% limits usable battery capacity to just 40% of rated capacity—180 Ah from a 450 Ah battery bank made up of four golf cart batteries.

What if you ignored the 50% rule and discharged your batteries to (drumroll here) *80%*? Wouldn't this shorten the life of the batteries? Yes it would, but having a bacon and egg breakfast probably isn't doing *your* life span any favors either.

There is little doubt that discharging your house batteries to 80% rather than 50% reduces the number of cycles the battery will deliver, but that is just half the truth. Discharging the bank more deeply also has the effect of reducing the number of times you cycle the battery. If the deeper discharge reduces the number of cycles your batteries will deliver by 40% but also extends the time between recharges by 40%, guess what? The reality is not quite this good, but probably better than you imagine. Test data from Trojan Battery Company reflects a reduction in total lifetime amp-hours delivered of just 6% when their industrial batteries are discharged to 80% rather than 50%. Much less than you thought, right? For this nearly negligible reduction in battery life, your 450 Ah battery bank now delivers 315 Ah between charges rather than 180. You get this additional 135 Ah of convenience without spending a cent on more batteries and without changing your charging equipment in any way. Even accounting for the reduction in battery life, the net effect on per-amp-hour cost is likely to be positive because batteries accept charge at a higher rate at deeper levels of discharge. This means the alternator operates at the upper end of its output capacity for a greater portion of recharge, which translates into fewer total engine hours, saving fuel and wear and tear. You also run the engine less often. If you have been running it every other day, you can now go almost 4 days between charges.

If you have lots of solar and wind-charging capacity, baby your batteries. However, if you rely on your engine alternator for recharging, you are likely to get better service from them drawing the batteries down more deeply. If you discharge good-quality deep-cycle batteries to an at-rest voltage of around 12 volts (but not below) between charging cycles, the positive effect on your quality of life should far overshadow any negative impact on the batteries.

Have cereal with skim milk for breakfast if you like. I'm going for the bacon.

CIRCUITS

Buy a fan for your house and it will come with a plug at the end of a two-wire cord. Just for a moment forget that the electrical outlets in your house ashore are linked by miles of wire to a power plant somewhere. Imagine each as a battery with slots as terminals. When you insert the plug, the narrow prong connects to the positive "terminal" of your "battery," and the wide prong connects to the negative terminal. This creates a circuit that will power the fan. (Ignore the third opening, the one that looks like a tunnel entrance; this is a safety feature to prevent *you* from becoming part of the circuit when you reach out of your bathtub to flick the switch.)

A fan for your boat likewise comes with two wires, but you don't get a plug. That makes creating the necessary circuit less convenient but otherwise the same. You still only have to connect the positive wire to the positive battery terminal and the negative wire to the negative battery terminal. Circuits on a boat, at least those you are likely to get involved with, are rarely more complicated than this.

TAPPING IN

Of course you don't actually connect appliances directly to the battery. Well, sometimes you do. Connecting an automatic bilge pump directly to the battery insures that it will function even when you have turned off the main battery switch. And connecting radio transmitters directly to the battery can maximize transmitting power and eliminate interference from other electrical appliances. But most of the time you wire a new appliance by tying it into the electrical system somewhere other than at the battery terminals.

If you choose any energized wire on your boat, cut it, and connect the two cut ends to a voltmeter, you will find 12 volts there. One end of the wire eventually leads back to the positive terminal of the battery and the other to the negative terminal. So why can't you just open an existing circuit and pick up the needed 12 volts for your new appliance there?

The answer is that whatever current was on its way to whatever appliance is already on this circuit must now pass through the new appliance also. That's trouble. You'll remember that electrical components connected like railroad cars are wired in series. We have already seen that connecting batteries in series combines their *voltages*. Connecting loads in series combines their *resistances*. Now don't bail out on me, but we need to do a little math to understand the implication of loads in series.

Remember the two equations back at the beginning of this chapter that I warned you would come up again? Now is the time. Back there we used the power equation—P = V × I—reconstituted as I = P ÷ V to calculate that a 25-watt lamp operating on 12 volts draws slightly more than 2 amps (25 ÷ 12). We were working toward calculating daily loads, but it is the same 2 amps that make the lamp function. And if 2 amps must flow through the lamp, they must also

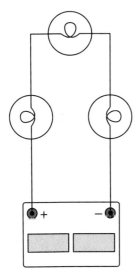

Series—the wrong way to connect multiple loads.

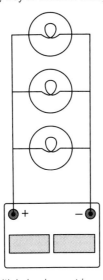

Parallel—how multiple loads must be connected.

flow through the circuit to get to the lamp. So back to our cut wire. If we make it supply a 25-watt cabin lamp, we don't have to do any recalculation.

The second equation was Ohm's law, expressed as V = I × R. We know the voltage (V) is around 12 volts, and we just calculated the current (I) through the lamp at around 2 amps, so the resistance of the cabin light must be around 6 ohms. (The math is R = 12 ÷ 2. Don't try to make this hard!) To keep the arithmetic uncomplicated, let's suppose that the cabin is not bright enough at night, so the appliance you are adding is another 25-watt lamp. What happens?

The second light also has a resistance of 6 ohms, and because wiring loads in series combines their resistances, this circuit has a resistance of 12 ohms. So how much current is going to flow through this circuit now? When solving for current, Ohm's law becomes I = V ÷ R, so 12 ÷ 12 gives us a current of 1 amp, half of what either lamp needs to function. *You must never connect loads in series.*

Since you have only two choices, that leaves parallel. As described earlier, a parallel circuit looks like a ladder, with each component forming a separate rung. You can achieve this in various ways. You could wire your two lamps individually directly to the battery posts, but that means long wire runs and an eventual rat's nest of wires at the battery post. If you are putting the new lamp near the existing one, you already know that the existing wires from that lamp lead back to the battery, so you could tap into that circuit with your positive wire somehow connected to the positive wire of the existing lamp and the negative wire connected to the negative wire in the same way. This is not the same as connecting the new lamp in series. The two lamps are sharing the supply line, but the circuit branches before the current flows through either lamp. However, you should be able to see that when both lamps are on and drawing 2 amps each, 4 amps must be flowing through the wires leading back to the battery. This is probably OK, but suppose you are installing a radio rather than a light, and suppose the radio draws 12 amps when you transmit. Now you have 14 amps passing through the shared supply wire when both appliances are in operation. If the original wire was appropriately sized for the original lamp, you are overloading it, creating a fire hazard if it is not protected by a fuse or breaker. And even if it is protected by a 5 or 10 amp fuse, what happens when you try to pass 14 amps through it?

The third alternative is to terminate your new circuit to some sort of distribution panel. This might be the main breaker panel or a more conveniently located bus or fuse block. In the first case, your circuit would originate directly from an unused or underused breaker terminal. In the second case, several small loads would share a supply line leading back to the main panel, with each individual branch circuit fuse-protected as appropriate.

You have nearly all the tools you need to determine whether a new appliance can be added safely to an existing circuit or you need a new circuit. The part you are missing is the necessary nod to wire size.

WIRE SIZE

If you don't know much about electricity, you might wonder why the wires on your boat are all different sizes, ranging from rope-size battery cables to the hairlike leads for the compass light. Finding out that they all carry the same voltage—12 volts—just makes the variety of sizes more confusing. The simple answer is that the more current you expect to pass through a wire, the larger it needs to be. In principle, it is the same reason firefighters don't arrive with garden hoses.

How far you expect the wire to carry the current is also a factor in determining the appropriate wire size. The longer the run, the greater the total resistance of the wire. This resistance uses up your available voltage. Let's say that a previous owner of your old boat (not you!) wired the automatic bilge pump with a 25-foot length of 18-gauge lamp cord, making the total wire length—from the battery and back—50 feet. Eighteen-gauge copper wire has a resistance of 0.654 ohm per 100 feet, which means 0.327 ohm for our 50-foot run. That doesn't seem like much until you factor in the 10 amp draw of the pump. If we plug these two values—0.327 ohm and 10 amps—into the Ohm's law equation ($V = I \times R$), we get 3.27 volts. But what exactly is this? This is how many volts it takes just to push 10 amps through this level of resistance. We call this *voltage drop*. If this circuit suffers a voltage drop of 3.27 volts and our battery voltage is around 12.6, that leaves us just 9.3 volts at the pump. This voltage might spin the pump when it's dry, but for pumping water, if the pump runs at all, it will be far below capacity. To avoid such detrimental voltage drops, we mitigate the higher resistance of extra wire length by increasing the wire diameter.

I'm sure most readers would prefer that I provide the conductivity of copper—the only material appropriate for boat wiring—so they can compute the resistance of the wire from its length and cross section and then calculate the voltage drop. Sadly someone else has already done the calculations for you and put them into a table. From the load in amps and the wire length in feet *to and from* the device, the table provides the minimum wire size to limit voltage drop to 3%. A higher voltage drop of up to

	ROUND-TRIP LENGTH OF CONDUCTOR (FEET)								
Current (Amps)	10	20	30	40	60	80	100	120	140
	Minimum Wire Size (AWG)								
1	16*	16*	16*	16*	16*	14	14	14	12
2	16*	16*	16*	14	14	12	10	10	8
5	16*	14	12	10	10	8	6	6	6
10	14	10	10	8	6	6	4	4	2
15	12	10	8	6	6	4	2	2	1
20	10	8	6	6	4	2	2	1	0
25	10	6	6	4	2	2	1	0	2/0
30	10	6	4	4	2	1	0	2/0	3/0
40	8	6	4	2	1	0	2/0	3/0	4/0
50	6	4	2	2	0	2/0	3/0	4/0	
60	6	4	2	1	2/0	3/0	4/0		
70	6	2	1	0	3/0	4/0			
80	6	2	1	0	3/0	4/0			
90	4	2	0	2/0	4/0				
100	4	2	0	2/0	4/0				

*18-gauge wire has adequate current capacity but is too fragile for boat use.

10% is "allowed" (according to ABYC standards) for nonessential circuits, but what circuits aboard are really nonessential? And what happens as corrosion introduces additional resistance or when you put bigger bulbs in your light fixtures or replace an appliance with one that is more powerful or has more bells and whistles? Cutting corners on wire size is pound-foolish. Forget about the 10% drop table you may run across in less enlightened texts, and stick with the extra conductivity and more robust nature of the larger-gauge wiring the 3% table specifies.

WIRE TYPE

If you have done house wiring, you know that the wire most often used is solid rather than stranded. Solid wire is an excellent conductor and perfect in the sedentary environment inside a wall or an attic, but the constant motion on a boat will flex solid wire until it hardens and eventually breaks. *Never* use solid wire aboard your boat, not even for AC circuits, no matter how many partial boxes of it are gathering dust in your garage. *All* boat wiring must be done with stranded copper wire, preferably what is designated as Type 3, the most flexible type. Unfortunately copper is quick to corrode when exposed to moisture- and salt-laden air, hardly a remote concern for boat wiring. To dramatically improve corrosion resistance, use *tinned* Type 3, in which every strand is plated with a thin coat of tin.

Another household wire that too often finds its way aboard is lamp cord. Aside from the bare copper conductor, the insulation on lamp cord is inadequate for the rigors of the marine environment. On a boat, lamp cord begins to corrode overnight. Don't use it. Boat wiring requires the protection of insulation designed for wet locations.

The safest course is to do all of your wiring with boat cable. This wire type meets Underwriters Laboratories standard UL 1426, created specifically for the marine environment. It is Type 3 and has a moisture- and heat-resistant jacket. Unfortunately the UL standard does not specify tinning, but nearly all boat cable is tinned. Be sure the one you buy is. Because circuits invariably require both a positive and a negative wire, duplex wire—two insulated wires sheathed together—is the most convenient to use. If you can, buy duplex cable with the two wires red and yellow. Because AC wiring uses black and white conductors, with black being the "hot" wire, a black wire on the DC side could lead to dangerous confusion. Red positive and yellow ground wires avoid this.

If you live in middle America, far from chandleries selling boat cable, and you don't want to order all of your wiring, then the wire you buy from your local wire supplier should still be stranded Type 3, tinned if available, and with an insulation designation of either THWN (*t*hermoplastic, *h*eat resistant, suitable for *w*et locations, *n*ylon jacket for abrasion resistance) or XHHW (cross-linked [*x*] polymer, *h*igh-*h*eat resistant, suitable for *w*et locations).

MAKING CONNECTIONS

Wiring connections ashore are made by clamping—either by shoving the bare end into a spring clamp, gripping it with a screw clamp, looping it under the head of a screw, or twisting together two or more wires inside a wire nut (a plastic-covered metal cone that threads onto the twisted wires to clamp them together). None of these methods should be used aboard a boat. While clamping provides a relatively stable connection for solid wire, it is less trustworthy for stranded wire. Plus, bare stranded wire is at significant risk of corrosion, eventually resulting in, if not total connection failure, at least voltage-robbing resistance.

All wiring aboard a boat should terminate with crimped connectors. The solid connector is then clamped under a terminal screw or inserted into a mating receptacle. For attachments to screw terminals, always use ring connectors unless the screw is captive. Spade connectors will slip free if the screw loosens even slightly. For extending

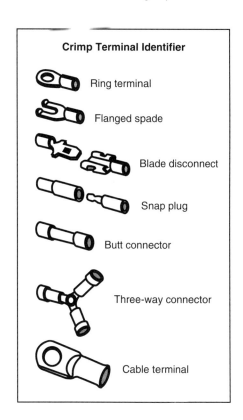

Crimp Terminal Identifier

Ring terminal

Flanged spade

Blade disconnect

Snap plug

Butt connector

Three-way connector

Cable terminal

a wire, there are crimp terminals known as butt connectors that you crimp to the bare end of the too-short wire and the bare end of the extension. Butt connectors should be sealed inside a length of heat-shrink tubing. This is spaghetti-like insulation that you slide over the connection. When you heat it by playing a flame underneath, it shrinks to a skintight fit around the wire and joint, sealing it and adding strain relief.

It is true that we are still clamping the bare wire inside the barrel of a crimp connector, but the difference is that the wire is compressed rather than flattened. This distinction depends on using a crimp tool to attach the terminal. Neither pliers nor a hammer nor any tool other than a crimp tool will deliver a dependable crimp. If you want trouble-free wiring, buy yourself a *ratchet* crimping tool, which requires a specific level of pressure before releasing and delivers uniform and trustworthy crimps every time.

Also buy yourself a wire stripper. You can strip the insulation from the ends of electrical wiring with your rigging knife, but rarely without nicking the wire, which opens the door to corrosion and voltage drop. A wire stripper cuts through the insulation without damaging the wire. Besides being better, a stripper is cheaper than a decent knife, vastly easier to use, and eliminates the risk of thumb amputation.

Coating crimped terminals with liquid insulation lowers their susceptibility to internal corrosion.

If you have used tinned wire and a tinned-copper crimp connector, the terminal is finished when the crimper releases. However, if either component is not tinned, corrosion inside the crimp is a risk, especially if this terminal has any possibility of getting wet. The solution is for *you* to tin the wire and connector by melting solder into the terminal, perfecting the electrical connection as well as permanently excluding moisture from the junction. Even tinned connections can benefit from this extra step. An easier and nearly as effective waterproofing method for tinned connections is to fully encase them, including the exposed end of the wire, in Liquid Tape, a paint-on electrical insulation. Heat-shrink can also be used here for insulation, but a watertight seal is unlikely.

Soldering

Anyone can make perfect solder joints every time. The requirements are good-quality electrical solder, a properly tinned soldering iron or gun, clean wires and terminals, and three hands. Use rosin-cored solder (never acid-cored) that is designated 60/40, meaning it is 60% tin and 40% lead. Some solders seem to flow better than others. I have always had good results with Kester.

Tinning a soldering iron involves nothing more than coating the tip with solder, but if you heat the iron and touch solder to it, the solder will simply roll off in silver drops. First, you must clean the tip thoroughly with a file or a piece of emery cloth. This will be a lot less painful if you do it *before* you heat the tip. Now heat the iron and touch the solder to the tip. If you have cleaned it well, the solder will coat it entirely—as if you

A ratchet crimper attaches wire terminals perfectly every time.

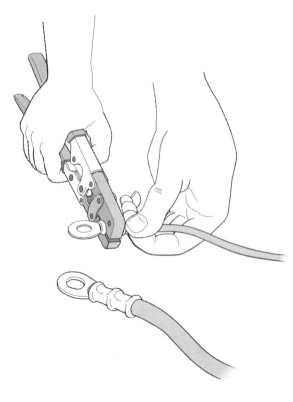

had dipped it into shiny, silver paint. Wipe away any excess with a damp cloth, and the iron is ready to use.

The trick to getting a perfect solder joint is that the *wire* must melt the solder, not the iron. But the heated wire can also melt the insulation near the joint, releasing chemicals that can lead to corrosion. Snip a 2-inch disk from an aluminum can and cut it about $^2/_3$ of the way across. Spread this cut and slide the disk onto the bare wire between the insulation and the barrel of the connector. The disk will act as a heat sink to protect the insulation and prevent solder from wicking down the wire to create a potential hard spot that could fracture from vibration.

Hold the hot, tinned iron against the barrel of the crimp connector and touch the end of the solder to the exposed end of the wire. When the solder begins to melt, flow in just enough to fill the barrel. Withdraw the solder, then the iron, and let the terminal cool undisturbed. The solder should be smooth and shiny. Shininess is essential. If the solder turns dull or lumpy, you have what is known as a cold joint, and you must reheat the joint until the solder is shiny and flows smoothly.

Solder, by the way, is not appropriate for retaining a wire. Soldered wires *must* be mechanically fastened first, because resistance at the connection could cause it to heat sufficiently to melt the solder. If it is the solder that is retaining the wire, the bare wire simply falls out of the terminal. A loose bare wire is capable of all kinds of mischief. A crimper in your toolbox eliminates the temptation to solder on connectors, except for battery cable terminals, which are too large for the tool. The high currents passing through battery cables make them particularly liable to generate enough heat to melt solder, and a loose battery cable is singularly dangerous. *Never attach cable lugs with solder.* Either buy ready-made battery cables, have end fittings crimped on by a cable fabricator, or buy yourself a hammer-blow crimper capable of securing cable lugs.

PLUGGING IN

Hardwiring is the best way of supplying power to most boat appliances, but for a few items—such as spotlights, vacuum cleaners, and chargers for electronic equipment—plug connectors are appropriate. Unfortunately the plug standard that has evolved is the automotive cigarette lighter socket. A more unsuitable plug and socket design is hard to imagine, but a couple of electrical component manufacturers have done a good job of creating lighter-style sockets and plugs that work reasonably well. Simple, polarized, two-prong plugs—like those attached to most AC appliances—would be infinitely better, but every portable 12-volt appliance you buy is going to come with a cigarette lighter plug. Besides, using two-prong AC plugs and outlets for 12-volt power is not a good idea because of the risk of confusion with real AC outlets on the boat. Stick with cigarette lighter–style outlets in the cabin. The center contact of a cigarette lighter plug is always positive, the perimeter contact negative.

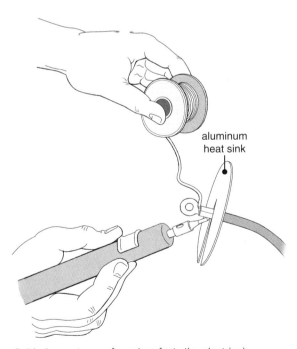

Soldering waterproofs and perfects the electrical connection. The aluminum disk absorbs heat that could otherwise melt the insulation.

aluminum heat sink

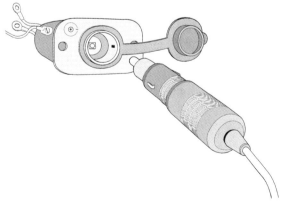

The center contact in cigarette lighter–style sockets and plugs is always positive.

For supplying power to appliances used on deck, you will need something better. I have gotten excellent service from Dri-plugs, a socket and plug pair manufactured in England that uses an O-ring to seal moisture out quite effectively. There are other waterproof plug designs, but look closely before you buy; some so-called waterproof plugs most assuredly are not. For boats with a dry cabin, a simple expedient is to simply equip deck items with cords long enough to allow them to be plugged in below.

DISTRIBUTION

By now you know how to determine the amp draw of any old or new appliance, how to determine the correct wire gauge for connecting the appliance, and how to attach terminals to the wire ends. Now all we need to resolve is what to attach the terminals to and how this appliance relates to the rest of the boat's electrical system.

ADDING A CIRCUIT

Replacing a circuit is simply a matter of disconnecting existing positive and negative wires from the old appliance, perhaps crimping on new connectors, and connecting these to the new appliance, being sure that the wire and fuse or breaker are of sufficient size if the new current draw will be greater. There is no risk of shock, but there is a risk of a short when you are working with loose wire connections, so turn off the circuit breaker, remove the fuse, or disconnect the battery before you start disconnecting or reconnecting wires.

If you are adding a circuit, I noted three viable possibilities earlier. If the current requirement is modest, you might pick up the necessary power from the positive and negative terminals of an existing appliance. You might tap into or install a conveniently located distribution bus. Or you might connect your new appliance with a dedicated wire run directly to the main breaker panel. Except for the length of the wire, the mechanics are essentially the same. Connect the positive wire lead to the positive terminal at your power source and the negative lead to the negative terminal at the source. If the provided leads are too short or if the appliance has terminals rather than leads, then you have to extend or create leads by attaching the required terminals to an appropriate length of duplex wire.

It is always wise to route the wire for your circuit before attaching the terminals. This insures that the wire length is correct, and the absence of terminals makes it easier to feed or pull the wire. Original wiring in old boats often runs across the top of a molded headliner, between the headliner and the deck, out of sight but inaccessible. You will have to find a different route for new (or even replacement) wiring. Finding a suitable route can sometimes prove challenging. To keep the wire out of sight, it typically runs through lockers, but do not let it lie in the bottom where sharp or heavy items can damage it. Wiring should run across the top, either through PVC conduit attached to the underside of the top of the locker or supported by cable clamps spaced at intervals of less than 18 inches.

If you are fortunate enough to have an unused breaker in the distribution panel (fat chance), all that is required is to connect the red wire of your new circuit to the open terminal on the breaker and the yellow wire to the panel's ground bus. Old-style fuse panels may have soldering lugs rather than screw terminals.

Breaker or Fuse?

Only older boats are likely to have fuses in the main distribution panel. New boats have been delivered with breakers rather than fuses for at least three decades. Twelve-volt breakers work like their AC cousins in the breaker panel in your kitchen or garage. They perform the same function as fuses, opening the circuit when it becomes overloaded for any reason. The advantage of a breaker is that once the problem that caused the overload has been corrected, reestablishing the circuit is merely a matter of flipping a switch.

There is a tendency to think of fuses as old-fashioned and somewhat inferior to breakers. Actually, in the marine environment, the fuse has a number of advantages. With no mechanical component, it cannot corrode and fail to trip. If it fails, it always fails open, protecting the circuit. A fuse panel can be custom-configured by simply changing the sizes of the fuses in the various holders. And the cost of fuses and panels is about a third of the price of breakers. If your old boat is equipped with fuses, there is no reason to change. And if you add an auxiliary panel, buy a fuse panel and spend the money you save on something else.

Back to your new circuit. Since it is unlikely you'll have an open breaker in the main panel, what about sharing a breaker that's already in use? You know how to answer this question. Whatever amperage your new circuit requires will be added to the amp draw already flowing through this breaker when all appliances are functioning. So you cannot connect a 12 amp radio to a 15 amp breaker already protecting a couple of 2 amp lights, but you could add another light or two to this breaker.

If you want to add the radio to this circuit, how about just replacing the 15 amp breaker with a 20 or 25 amp breaker? You can do that, provided that all of the wiring to all of the appliances on this circuit can safely carry 25 amps. Since the radio costs $1,500 and the wire $15, a lot of boaters are astonished to learn that breakers and fuses not components of the appliance are not there to protect the appliance. They are there to protect the *wire*. That is not as bizarre as it seems at first. Overloaded wires can and regularly do get hot enough to start a fire, risking not just the wire but the entire boat. So if you increase the size of the breaker, you must know that no wire anywhere in the circuit will be overloaded with a current of up to 25 amps. Never mind that a wire is supplying just a fraction of an amp to an LED. Consider Ohm's law yet again. If $I = V \div R$, as R decreases, I increases. A short can create an R value approaching zero, which sends the I value toward infinity. Heat—lots of heat—is the inevitable result unless the breaker disconnects the power, which it will not do in this case until the current flow exceeds 25 amps. A 20 amp short would continue to overheat the wire until it melted, hopefully without igniting anything. Small wires are unprotected by big breakers.

You have several choices here. Radios in particular should have a dedicated circuit to reduce the risk of electrical interference, so in this instance you might move the light circuits to share a different breaker where there is still some available capacity, freeing up a breaker for your new radio. If you are going to be adding a number of appliances, you might consider replacing the original distribution panel with one that has more breakers. Or you can accomplish the same thing by adding fused terminal blocks, allowing individual circuits to be protected by individual fuses of the appropriate value, with the main breakers essentially protecting just the wire between the breaker and the fuse block. You can also incorporate an in-line fuse holder to protect a particular branch of a circuit. If you do this, be sure the fuse holder is in the positive side of the circuit and locate it near the distribution panel rather than near the appliance so that all the wiring will be protected.

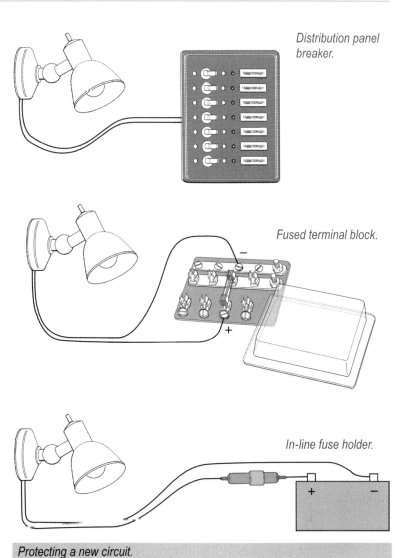

Distribution panel breaker.

Fused terminal block.

In-line fuse holder.

Protecting a new circuit.

SWITCHES

Most equipment you install will have its own switch, but occasionally you may need to install a separate switch in the circuit. Let's use a switch for an electric bilge pump as an example.

Switches, like fuses and breakers, are always installed in series with the device they control, and they are always installed on the positive side of the circuit. We install a switch in series by cutting the positive wire of the circuit and connecting the cut ends to the two terminals on the switch. When the switch is open (off), the entire circuit is open and no power reaches the pump. When the switch is closed (on), current passes through it to the bilge pump, causing it to run.

For our bilge pump, however, a manual switch is probably inadequate. We want the pump to run automatically, even when we are not aboard. This is easily accomplished by substituting a float switch for a manual switch, wired in exactly the same manner—in series on the positive side of the pump circuit. This might be satisfactory . . . until the first time you come aboard your boat after it has been unattended for a while and find water over the floorboards. What the—?!

Float switches stick. They also fail, which is when you will wish you still had that manual switch. The time to make that wish come true is when you first wire the pump. All it requires is a three-position switch—what is known as a single-pole double-throw (SPDT) switch—which has three terminals. Flipping the switch lever to the right connects the center terminal to the terminal on the right. Flipping the switch lever to the left connects the center terminal to the left terminal. The middle position disconnects all the terminals. The wiring here will be easier to understand if for the moment we forget about the float switch and revert back to just a positive wire from the pump to our power source—in this case, probably the positive battery terminal. To insert a switch, we cut this wire, but now we have just two wire ends and three terminals on our switch. How is that going to work?

Easier than you might imagine. Connect the end that is coming from the battery to the switch's center terminal, and connect the other end to either of the other terminals. When you flip the switch to that side, the pump will run. However, we really want to energize the pump with the switch in either of the on positions. We could splice a second wire to the one running to the pump and connect that to the open screw terminal. Now flipping the switch either way connects the battery to the pump. But rather than splice wires, suppose we just put ring terminals on a short length of wire and connect this "jumper" to the left and right terminals. That means one of these terminals will have two connectors under the screw, one on the end of the jumper and the other on the wire leading to the pump. Again, flipping the switch either way runs the pump.

Still with me? Now instead of a wire jumper, suppose we crimp ring terminals onto the two leads from the float switch and connect these to the right and left terminals on the switch. If we flip the switch one way, the current must run through the float switch to reach the pump, so the pump will not run until the float switch closes. This would be the normal setting for the switch. Flipping the switch the other way bypasses the float switch to deliver power directly to the pump, giving us a way to run the pump manually. The middle position turns everything off. If you understand this, you are unlikely to encounter any circuit issues aboard your old boat that you won't be able to figure out.

SCHEMATICS

It is often helpful to draw out a circuit before you work on it. Electricians call such drawings *schematics,* but don't let the term put you off; it is just a map of the wiring. Solid lines represent wires, dots are junctions, a zigzag is a resistor, a curlicue is a light, a wave

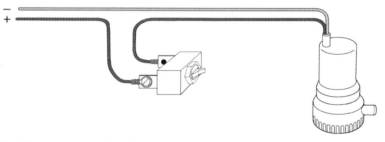

Switches are always wired in series on the positive side of the circuit. Current flowing to the appliance may be interrupted by opening the switch.

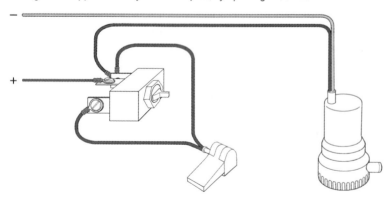

A three-position switch (SPDT) allows current to be directed to the right or left terminals. "Jumping" these terminals with a float switch puts the float switch in the circuit and in control with one switch setting while the other setting bypasses the float switch for manual pump operation. The middle position is off.

Switch wiring.

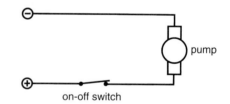

Manually operated electric pump.

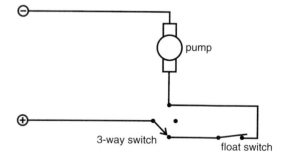

Automatic pump with manual override.

Planning and recording circuits—the schematic.

is a fuse, and a little doorway is a switch. Almost all the standard symbols will be clear to you if you look at them for a few minutes, but use whatever symbols you want for your own drawings. Circles or boxes with the name of the item written in are as good as zigzags and curlicues any day of the week.

A diagram of your boat's entire electrical system would be very useful, but creating one might be a time-consuming exercise. At the very least, every time you work on an electrical circuit, you should sketch what you learn on paper. For circuits you modify or add, always diagram the wiring first, then make this drawing a permanent part of your project notebook. Such drawings will save you a lot of effort in tracing circuits if you have problems or make additional changes at some future date.

The American Boat & Yacht Council (ABYC) long ago established a recommended color code for various applications. If the manufacturer followed those recommendations during the construction of your boat, identifying and tracing existing circuits will be infinitely easier, but don't get too excited over this possibility. Few manufacturers were so conscientious. Color-coded wires are rarely practical for add-on wiring. What is helpful is labeling both ends of every wire. Home supply stores and electrical suppliers sell books of adhesive wire markers that make it easy to give each wire a unique code, which you should also write on the schematic. Coating the markers with clear vinyl rope dip (for sealing the ends of line) makes the labels permanent.

DIGITAL MULTIMETER: THE ESSENTIAL TOOL

Here is a simple truth. Your fancy-schmancy chart plotter is just a blank screen if your electrical system fails and you cannot figure out what happened. So before you buy *any* other electronics, get yourself a digital multimeter and keep it aboard. You cannot troubleshoot electrical problems effectively without one.

Whatever you spend above around $50 is purely for status. All you need is an auto-ranging meter that accurately measures volts, ohms, and up to 10 amps. *Auto-ranging* means you just set the meter to the function you want and it does the rest. A rugged case is a plus.

Do not try to make do with a needle-type meter. No matter how fine an instrument it was when you bought it, analog meters are inherently far less accurate than even the cheapest digital meter. Give your old multimeter to a school, claim a generous tax deduction, and buy yourself a digital meter.

Don't imagine that multimeters are complicated. Checking the voltage in a circuit is no different from checking your speed on the turnpike except that the meter reads 12.6 volts instead of 65 mph. A new meter will come with a manual, but I still need to provide some meter basics here, so the test procedures that follow will make sense to those of you who only read the manual as a last resort.

VOLTS

Of the three values you are going to use the meter to measure—voltage, resistance, and current—voltage is the easiest. If the leads are separate on the meter you bought, plug the black one into the common socket, probably marked—COM, and the red lead into the socket probably marked +VΩmA. (The third socket, the one marked 10A, is for measuring current only.) Now simply set the function selector to DCV (DC volts) and touch the probes to any two points in the circuit. If there is a difference in potential between the two points, the meter will display it in volts. For example, if you touch one probe to the positive battery post and the other to the negative post, the meter displays battery voltage *at that moment*. If the battery is fully charged, the reading will be around 12.6 volts.

Warning: We are only measuring 12-volt DC circuits. The meter, set properly, will also measure AC voltage, but you must be extremely careful when you are working around 110-volt AC circuits.

Another shortcoming of analog meters—besides inferior accuracy—is that if the polarity is reversed, the needle tries to deflect the wrong way with meter-damaging consequences. Digital meters have automatic polarity, indicating with a minus sign in the display when the red probe is reading a negative value relative to the black probe. It is a good habit to always decide which leg of a circuit you expect to be positive, then touch the red probe to that leg so that a negative value will get your attention.

A voltmeter is a most useful tool for locating problems with the wiring of your old boat. If you touch the probes to the positive and negative sides of any circuit, the meter will measure the voltage of the circuit *at that point*. Try it with a 12-volt outlet somewhere on the boat. Ideally you would like the meter to display the same voltage measured at the battery terminals, but if the outlet is some distance from the battery, the reading will be lower due to voltage drop caused by the resistance of the wire. Since the maximum acceptable drop is 3%, any voltage reading below 12.2 volts when the battery voltage is 12.6 tells you that either your wires are too small or you have a poor connection somewhere in the circuit.

Anytime an electrical item fails to work, check the voltage at its terminals. If there are no exposed terminals or connections, you can push the pointed probes through the insulation of the wiring. (It is

COLOR	USE
Red	General DC positive conductor
Yellow	Preferred DC negative conductor
Black	Alternative DC negative conductor
Green or green w/yellow stripe	General DC grounding conductor
Dark blue	Cabin and instrument lights
Dark gray	Navigation lights, tachometer
Brown	Pumps, alternator charge light
Brown w/yellow stripe	Bilge blower
Orange	Accessory feed
Purple	Ignition, instrument feed
Yellow w/red stripe	Starting circuit
Light blue	Oil pressure
Tan	Water temperature
Pink	Fuel gauge

The wiring in your old boat might follow these ABYC recommended wiring colors.

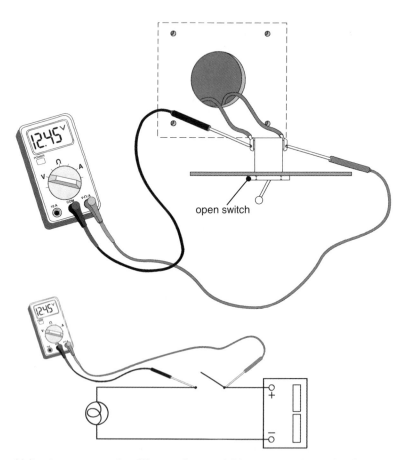

open switch

Voltmeters measure the difference in potential between any two points in a circuit. Reverse the probes and a digital meter will still display the correct voltage but with a minus sign to alert you to reversed polarity. Close the switch here and the meter should measure 0 volts.

advisable afterward to seal probe punctures with a dab of silicone.) A good reading tells you the problem is with the item; an absence of voltage tells you the problem is with the circuit.

No voltage in a circuit should send you immediately to the main electrical panel. If it is a breaker panel, operate the breaker for this circuit. If it is a fuse panel, check the fuse. If these actions fail to solve the problem, there is a break in the circuit and you will have to locate it.

Begin by opening the panel and checking the voltage between the *output* terminal of the breaker or fuse for the defective circuit and the *negative bus*— the terminal strip in the panel with all the yellow or black wires connected to it. If you read 12 volts, the break must be between the panel and the not-working appliance. If the meter reads 0 or some small voltage, the breaker or the fuse holder is bad. Keep the black probe in contact with the negative bus and move the red probe to the output terminal for a different breaker or fuse to make sure there is voltage in the panel. It is embarrassing to discover that the whole problem is that you failed to turn on the battery switch.

Output voltage at the breaker means the problem is in the wiring or the appliance. Check the hot wire to the appliance by leaving the negative probe attached to the negative bus in the distribution panel (you may need to extend the meter lead with a piece of wire) and moving the red probe to the appliance end of the wire attached to the breaker output terminal. No voltage there indicates a break in the wire or an open connector. If you find voltage between the positive terminal at the appliance and the negative bus, move the black probe again to the negative terminal of the appliance to reconfirm your initial reading of no voltage. This tells you that the problem is an open circuit on the negative side. You can confirm this by leaving the black probe attached and touching the red probe to any hot terminal—the output terminal in the breaker panel or even the positive battery post. If the negative side of the circuit were sound, you would read 12+ volts.

Trace the ground wire to its next terminal or connector and move your black probe to that location. When the meter displays voltage, the break is in the wiring you just bypassed. This is all simple logic— voltage here, no voltage there; the problem must be between here and there.

Another regular use for a voltmeter is to determine polarity prior to attaching a new appliance. Polarity does not matter to some items, such as lights, but you still want to connect the wire marked + to the positive side of the circuit to put the switch on the hot side. For DC motors—fans, pumps, etc.—and all electronics, correct polarity is essential. Touch the wire you believe is the positive one to your red probe and the other wire to the black probe. If the meter display does not indicate a negative reading, the polarity is confirmed.

OHMS

Switch the multimeter to the function usually marked Ω, and it becomes an ohmmeter to measure resistance. Unlike voltmeter tests, there must *never* be *any* voltage in a circuit being checked by an ohmmeter (other than a small voltage delivered by the meter). If there is, the meter will be damaged or at the very least a protective fuse inside the meter case will be blown, so the circuit being tested must be disconnected from any power source. Individual devices should be removed from the circuit entirely to insure that the meter is measuring just the device and not the circuit.

You will most often use your ohmmeter as a continuity tester, so you are actually checking for conductivity—the opposite of resistance. You will want to see low readings on the display to confirm unbroken continuity and good conductivity. Before checking circuits, first touch the probes of the meter to each other. The meter will not read 0, but probably 0.1 or 0.2 ohm (Ω) due to the internal resistance of the meter and the resistance of the leads.

Use the ohm function to check a wire, a fuse, or a switch. To test a wire run, disconnect it at one end, then touch your ohmmeter probes to both ends. The meter will tell you immediately if the wire is continuous, if it is introducing significant resistance, or if it is broken. Test a fuse by holding the probes against the fuse's contacts. A reading near 0 confirms that the fuse is good. To test a switch, connect the probes to the two terminals of the switch. The meter will either read near 0, telling you the two terminals are connected, or it will read infinite ohms—usually displayed as O.L (overload, really meaning overrange)—telling you the terminals are not connected. Flip the switch; if the switch is working, the meter should display the opposite reading—O.L if it was 0, and 0 if it was O.L. If the switch has more than two terminals, connecting the meter probes to any pair allows you to determine which terminals are connected for any switch setting.

You can check other electrical components—lightbulbs and motor windings, for example—but expect the meter reading to be significantly greater than 0 due to the resistance of the component. Comparing the reading with one taken from a similar component you know to be good is the best way to derive the most information from the test. An O.L reading still tells you that the circuit is open, meaning the filament or the winding or some internal connection is broken.

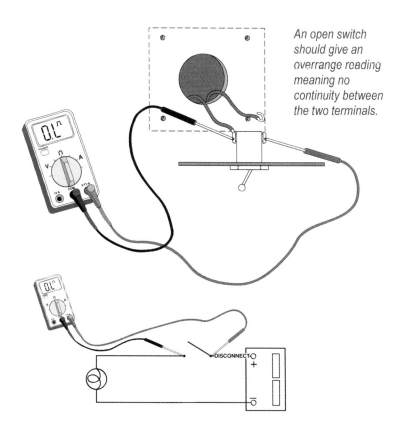

An open switch should give an overrange reading meaning no continuity between the two terminals.

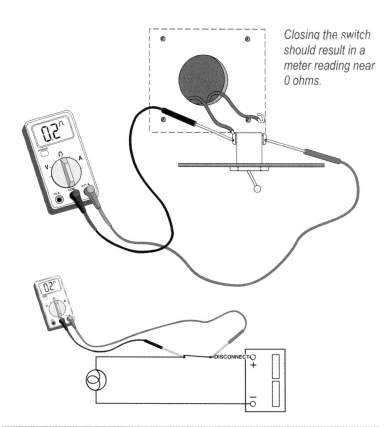

Closing the switch should result in a meter reading near 0 ohms.

Whatever you test with an ohmmeter must be disconnected from its circuit.

Diodes are also tested with the ohmmeter, although most digital multimeters have a special diode function, usually labeled ➤⊢. This setting simply changes the display to read forward voltage rather than ohms, but the test is what you should anticipate for a component that is supposed to exhibit continuity in only one direction. The meter should register a small forward voltage (or low resistance) with the probes connected one way, O.L (or very high resistance) when you reverse them. If the diode registers O.L both ways, it is open. If it registers near 0 both ways, it is shorted. When testing a diode, the flow direction is from the red probe to the black probe.

AMPS

Amperage measurements also require breaking the circuit, but in this case you must insert the meter into

Ammeters are connected in series by breaking the circuit and connecting the meter across the break.

the circuit. That means the meter is connected across the break, not across the component. If, for example, you want to know how much current a specific appliance uses, you disconnect the supply (hot) wire to the appliance and connect the meter between this wire and the now-open terminal. If the switch is off, the meter should read 0, but when you switch the appliance on, the meter will register the actual current draw.

A word of caution is in order here. Meters that do not show a 10 amp (or higher) range will be capable of handling only small currents—measured in milliamps. Higher currents will ruin the meter or at least blow the internal fuse. Be sure your meter is 10 amp capable, that you have the function selector set to 10 amps, and that you have the red probe plugged into the socket labeled 10A. Because of the risk of meter damage, you need a good idea of the magnitude of the current you plan to measure before you make an ammeter connection. You might deduce this from the rating of the appliance. For example, we determined earlier that a 25-watt light draws about 2 amps. When you do not know what to expect, it is prudent to find out. You accomplish this by first setting the meter to measure ohms. With the circuit broken and all related breakers and switches on, connect the red probe to the appliance side of the break and the black probe to the ground bus for this circuit. The ohmmeter will display the combined resistance of the entire circuit. (You must not connect the black probe to the other side of the break because this will include the battery in the circuit.) If the meter reads O.L, a switch is off. Once you have a resistance measurement, you can estimate the current. Remembering that $I = V \div R$, divide the circuit resistance (in ohms) *into* battery voltage—say 12.6 volts—to estimate circuit current. If it is less than 10 amps, you can safely connect your 10 amp ammeter across the break.

The truth is that you are likely to use the ammeter function only rarely. You might use it to measure the actual draw of some or all of your appliances to help you understand your daily power consumption, but if you have a good battery monitor, you can accomplish the same thing more easily by just observing the amp reading as you turn on each appliance. Beyond draw measurements, the primary use of an ammeter is to trace ground faults—typically tiny currents that "leak" out of a circuit via a short, dampness, or some other electrical path. If such a current leak reaches the water, it becomes a *stray current,* which can corrode underwater metal components at an astonishing rate. The sensitivity of an ammeter makes it the tool of choice for locating these tiny and potentially destructive leaks.

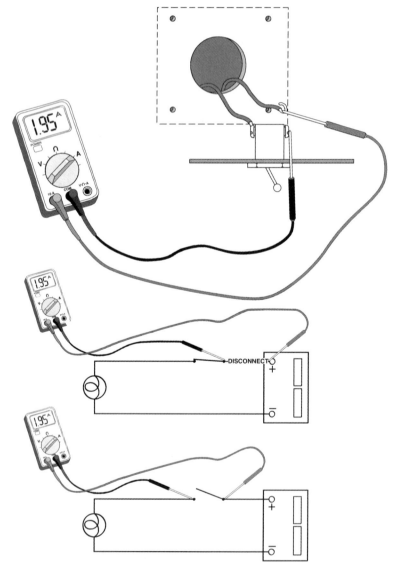

Measuring across an open switch achieves the same thing.

YOUR "GRAY METER"

Even before you get out your multimeter, if you switch your brain to the *observe* setting, you can often detect a problem and sometimes its solution at the same time. How many chagrined captains have watched an observant mechanic cure an engine problem by reconnecting a loose wire? Small diesel engines are notorious for vibrating electrical connections loose, especially those attached to the alternator. Look! However, be cautious about jumping to a conclusion if you discover an unattached terminal. Engine wiring harnesses often serve more than one engine configuration, so extra wires are not uncommon. It will be worth your time now to identify unused wires in the engine compartment and encase their terminals in heat-shrink tubing or electrical tape so they don't confuse matters at a later date.

Hot wiring has a distinctive odor. If you smell this, it means the wiring is overloaded, either due to a short or excessive resistance. Sometimes you can literally sniff out trouble.

Flickering lights can warn of a poor connection or a broken wire. So can a dimming light, but if all the lights dim, check the battery voltage.

Wires and terminals that have been sized correctly generate little heat during normal use. The "gray meter" is analog, but it has wonderful "digital" probes that are heat sensitive. Get in the habit of touching bare 12-volt terminals. A terminal that feels hot is almost certainly making poor electrical contact. A wire that feels hot is too small for the job, or some appliance downstream is drawing more current than it should be.

When an alarm sounds in your gray meter, don't ignore it. Get out the digital meter and chase it down.

CHARGING

Before we look at various methods of recharging the batteries aboard your boat, we need to establish the relationship among charging capacity, storage capacity, and consumption. I don't mean the sequential relationship—charge, store, consume, charge, etc.—but how to determine how much charging capacity is enough.

The maximum absorption rate of an automotive (thin-plate) battery is no more than 50% of the rated capacity of the battery; i.e., a 100 Ah automotive battery may accept a charging current of up to 50 amps. However, a battery charged this rapidly will get hot and start to gas (bubble) by the time the battery is 50% charged. If the current is reduced to about 25% of battery capacity, the battery will reach 75% of its charge before the gassing begins. To fully charge the battery, the current must be decreased to 4% or less of battery capacity. In concept this is much like pouring a carbonated drink into a glass. Pour it fast, and when the foam dissipates the glass is only half full. Pour it slowly, and you can fill the glass to the top.

Vigorous gassing, besides filling the battery locker with highly explosive hydrogen gas, depletes the electrolyte in the battery. Excessive heat damages the plates and separators inside the battery. Both conditions will kill a battery in short order.

Deep-cycle batteries have a much slower absorption rate than the thin-plate variety. A deep-cycle battery should never be subjected to a charging current higher than 25% of its capacity, and even this current will cause the battery to begin gassing long before it is fully charged. This means that if your total battery capacity is 100 Ah, a 25 amp alternator is all you need. A 50 amp alternator will provide the *maximum* charging current for a pair of 100 Ah batteries.

This is where SVR batteries hold some advantage. Their natural absorption rate is about the same as standard automotive batteries—about 50% of capacity—but their construction allows them to be charged at an even higher rate without generating hydrogen or overheating. A totally discharged 100 Ah sealed battery might be fully charged in half an hour, but the inefficiencies of such overcharging would require a charging current of about five times the capacity of the battery—not very practical and brutal on the battery. Without abusing it, a gel-cell battery can safely be charged about twice as fast as a deep-cycle battery.

There is a degree of inefficiency in the charging process even if you are not exceeding the absorption level of the battery. Generally speaking, you must replace about 20% more power than you removed to return a battery to a fully charged state. In other words, a 50 Ah discharge will require that you put 60 Ah back into the battery.

ALTERNATORS

Alternators have almost completely replaced generators on marine engines and for good reason. They are more efficient, they are more dependable, they are lighter, and they do not spark. But the main reason is that they can endure higher rpm, which allows them to have a higher engine-speed ratio. Alternators typically develop full rated output at between 5,000 and 6,000 rpm, but if you belt an alternator with a $2\frac{1}{2}$-inch drive pulley to a 5-inch crankshaft pulley, 1,000 engine rpm will turn the alternator at just 2,000 rpm. To increase alternator speed and raise output, you can run the engine faster or increase the pulley ratio. Either increasing the diameter of the crankshaft pulley or reducing the diameter of the alternator pulley raises the alternator speed. To calculate alternator rpm, divide the diameter of the crankshaft pulley by the diameter of the alternator pulley and multiply the result by engine rpm.

When you are cruising or living aboard, if you do not have an alternate power source, you will be doing much of your charging at idle speed. Resist the temptation to try to change the pulley ratio to get full alternator output at this speed. Your alternator also has an upper limit—usually 10,000 rpm—and the pulley ratio must not spin the alternator faster than this at maximum engine output. If it does, alternator damage is likely. A better alternative for this situation may be to select an alternator that maintains its output at lower rpm. At 2,000 rpm, some alternators generate less than 30% of their rated output, while others generate as much as 80%. Get a look at the output profile before buying.

Most boatowners will find that their involvement with their alternators will be limited to adjusting belt tension and removing the unit to take it to a repair shop when it develops a problem. Good move. Alternators do not lend themselves to amateur repair efforts.

The number of terminals on the back of the alternator can be confusing, especially since some of them may not have wires attached. Before you disconnect the wires to the alternator, sketch the features of the back—chart fashion—and locate each of the terminals on the sketch. Note on the sketch which wire—by color and size—is connected to which terminal, and reinstallation will be a breeze. A digital photo will perform the same function but is less convenient than a sketch in your notebook.

If you are replacing your alternator with a larger one or a different type, take the old one and your sketch with you when you buy the new one so a technician can show you how the new one should be connected. This is not all that complicated—there are typically just three, maybe four, wires—but you want to make sure they are on the correct terminals.

Sizing the alternator depends entirely on the battery capacity and how fast you want to charge. The maximum charge rate for deep-cycle batteries is 25%, so if you have 200 Ah of deep-cycle capacity, the maximum charge rate is 50 amps. If the alternator is only charging the batteries, you need a 50 amp alternator. But if you have other equipment on during charging, the alternator should have enough capacity to supply the equipment and still deliver maximum current to the batteries. This could be a few additional amps for cabin or running lights that happen to be on, or it could be 40 or 50 amps for the concurrent operation of an electric holding-plate refrigerator.

If you install a larger alternator to cut charging times, the reduction may fall short of your expectations. Suppose you double the capacity of your house bank to 400 Ah. Given the 25% of capacity rule, you should be able to make good use of a 100 amp alternator, but if you monitor the actual output, you will find that the big alternator will drive up the voltage sufficiently in just a few minutes to begin cutting back the output current. At the end of an hour it will have delivered perhaps 70 amp-hours of charge rather than 100. The original 50 amp alternator, running at its maximum capacity for longer, would have taken only about an additional 25 minutes to reach this charge level. For the remainder of the charge, outputs from both alternators will be essentially the same. Your big alternator takes $3^{1}/_{2}$ hours to reach the 90% charge level, the small one 3 hours and 55 minutes. That is a time reduction of less than 11% from a 100% increase in alternator capacity. The difference is even smaller when the batteries are not deeply discharged—a common scenario when the engine runs daily for mechanical refrigeration. Conversely, discharging house batteries to the 80% level will make better use of a high-capacity alternator. Likewise, the acceptance profiles of gel-cell and AGM batteries can take better advantage of a big alternator.

You should also be aware of the horsepower required to run an alternator under load. In a

Record by photo or drawing what wires attach to what terminals before disconnecting an alternator.

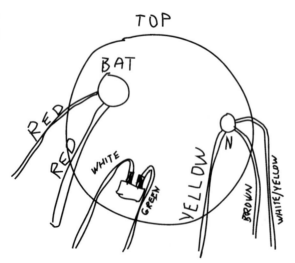

perfect world you could convert 1 horsepower (hp) of mechanical energy into 746 watts of electrical energy. You could also trust your senator with your tax money and your daughter. A closer approximation is achieved by cutting your expectations in half—in both cases. Alternator output voltage will be around 14 volts. Multiplying this by the rated current yields the power in watts—700 watts for a 50 amp alternator. Dividing wattage by 373 ($^1/_2$ of 746) reveals that the alternator will require around 1.9 hp. The belt and pulleys consume an additional 1 hp, so a 50 amp alternator reduces the power to the prop by about 3 hp. A 150 amp alternator will require close to 7 hp under full load. I sure hope you don't have a 10 hp engine.

REGULATORS

When a 50 amp alternator is running at the rated rpm, it puts out 50 amps—period. But we have already noted that if you have a 100 Ah deep-cycle battery, you *never* want to charge it with a current greater than 25 amps. And as it approaches full charge, the charging current should decline to a tenth of that level.

Limiting the output current of the alternator is the job of the voltage regulator. It works much like a thermostat, only instead of sensing room temperature, it senses battery voltage. When the voltage is low, the regulator turns on the spinning alternator by passing current to the field winding. The now-charging alternator raises the voltage in the charging circuit to a preset level—typically 13.8 volts for an automotive regulator and up to 14.4 volts for a marine regulator. When the voltage reaches this level, the regulator cuts the current to the field winding, turning the alternator off. (It continues to spin, of course.) The voltage in the circuit decays. The regulator senses this drop in voltage and turns the alternator back on. In a solid-state regulator this off-and-on switching takes place hundreds of times *per second,* and the output current is an average of the current pulses such switching causes. As the battery voltage rises, it takes progressively less time for the alternator to elevate the voltage in the charging circuit to the cutout voltage. The "on" times become shorter and shorter, lowering the level of current output from the alternator.

The voltage regulator is almost always the weak link in a boat's electrical system, limiting the *available* electrical power to far below the potential of the other components and shortening the life of the batteries in the bargain. Consider how a deep-cycle battery should be charged. Charging current should never exceed 25% of battery capacity—i.e., a 25 amp charging

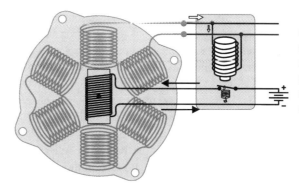

With the switch allowing current to the field winding closed, the alternator begins generating electricity.

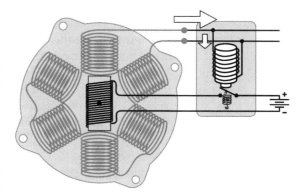

Voltage in the charging circuit is driven up until at some preset level it opens the field current switch, causing the alternator to stop generating.

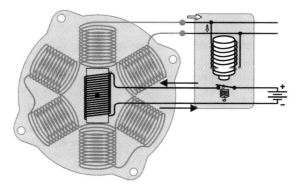

Falling circuit voltage allows the field current switch to close, restarting the cycle.

Modern regulators are solid state, but a mechanical regulator more clearly illustrates regulator function.

current is the maximum desirable for a 100 amp-hour battery—but the battery will accept this maximum until it is about 75% charged. At this time the battery voltage should be around 14.4 volts, and the electrolyte should be gassing lazily. This initial stage is called the *bulk charge* stage. I noted earlier that mild gassing is actually beneficial to flooded batteries.

At this point the charging source should maintain a constant charging voltage of 14.4 volts and allow the charging current to decline according to what the battery can accept. This is called the *absorption* or *acceptance charge* stage.

When the current drops below around 4% of battery capacity, we abandon voltage regulation and feed the battery a constant current at this low level until battery voltage stabilizes at its maximum level—typically around 16 volts. This is called *equalization*. Once the battery is fully charged, we want to go back to a voltage-regulated charge, but now we want the voltage to be held constant at around 13.3 volts. This is called the *float charge* stage—maintaining the battery at full charge without overcharging. In actual practice, the equalization step is usually omitted because it takes several hours to raise the battery charge from 90% to 100%. Heavy-duty, deep-cycle, flooded batteries should, however, be equalized periodically to maximize their performance.

So for your half-discharged 100 Ah battery, you want to have a 25 amp current until you have pumped about 30 amps into the battery—the 25 amps needed to raise the charge level from 50% to 75% plus another 5 amps for the 20% battery inefficiency. This requires about $1^1/_4$ hours of charging time. If you continue the charge, you want to maintain a voltage of 14.4 volts until the charge level reaches 90%, by which time the charging current will have declined to about 2 amps (2% of battery capacity). That makes the mean charge current for this stage around 14 amps. You need 15 total amps plus 20% to raise the charge level from 75% to 90%. That works out to another $1^1/_4$ hours of charging time. You would normally terminate the charge at this point, but if you continue to run the engine—it does, after all, also serve the function of turning the prop—you want the charging voltage to cut back to 13.3 volts.

How does a typical regulator actually perform? Much depends on the cutout voltage. Let's consider a standard automotive regulator with a set voltage of 13.8 volts. Sensing a battery voltage of 12.2 volts—the 50% discharge level—a 13.8-volt regulator would limit current output to about 35% of battery capacity. This exceeds the maximum desirable charge rate by 40%, but this surplus lasts only a few minutes before the regulator begins to reduce the current. After an hour the battery is only 70% charged, and charging current has dropped below 10 amps and is still declining. It takes another $1^1/_2$ hours to reach the 80% level. At 13.8 volts, raising the charge level to 90% will take several hours of additional charging time. When the battery *is* fully charged, a continuous voltage of 13.8 volts results in mild overcharging.

Two and a half hours to reach an 80% charge level and more than 5 hours to reach a 90% charge means that the battery will only get fully charged when you are under power for a long period. The rest of the time the battery will be undercharged, resulting in sulfation—the main cause of battery death.

To avoid this problem, regulators intended for marine use often have the cutout voltage elevated, up to a maximum of 14.4 volts. This cuts charging time dramatically but can damage the batteries in a different way. A 14.4-volt regulator starts with a current of around 40% of battery capacity—40 amps for our 100 Ah battery—and abuses the battery for close to 40 minutes before the steadily declining current drops below the safe 25% rate. The battery reaches an 80% charge level in about 1 hour and 40 minutes, 90% in an additional hour—not much longer than the ideal—but if you continue to run the engine, the 14.4-volt setting will result in serious overcharging, boiling away the electrolyte and corroding the positive plates. Corrosion of the positive plates is the number two cause of battery death.

If voltage regulators do such a lousy job, why does every boat have one? Because boatowners are stupid. Just kidding. Regulators are standard fare because they are simple, *cheap*, dependable, foolproof, and manufactured in the zillions every year for automotive use—where, by the way, they do a darn good job. And if you run your engine a lot, they will do the job for you.

If you don't run your engine a lot, at the very least you need your regulator to be set to 14.4 volts. You can determine the setting by measuring the voltage across the battery terminals while the engine is running at charging speed, but the battery must be *fully* charged (check it with a hydrometer). Some regulators have an adjusting screw, some have a multiposition switch, and some have output terminals for differing voltages, but most are not adjustable. In the latter case, if you need a higher setting than your test reveals, you will have to replace the regulator. If you cannot find a regulator on your boat, it is likely internal, meaning inside the alternator case. In this instance, switching to a higher-output or more sophisticated alternator is likely to require some technical assistance.

High-output regulators are not without problems. Undercharging your batteries is more damaging—not to mention frustrating—than is some overcharging, but continuing to apply 14.4 volts to fully charged batteries will definitely shorten their lives. They will tolerate being charged occasionally for several hours with a 14.4-volt regulator as long as you pay attention to their water level. But if you motor a lot, the high-output regulator will be doing a number on your batteries. A different solution is indicated.

ALTERNATOR CONTROLLERS

One such solution is an alternator controller. Instead of regulating alternator output by pulsing the field current (switching it on and off), it can also be controlled by setting the field current to a specific level.

Manual Controllers

In the bad old days, desperate cruising sailors bypassed the regulator with a variable resistor, typically a rheostat intended to dim the track lights in the den. Like light level, field current level could be raised or lowered by rotating the knob. The idea was to dial in the desired alternator output—around 25% of capacity—and hold it there until the batteries began gassing vigorously, thus bringing the charge level up to around 75% with the shortest engine run time. At this point the vigilant operator either lowered the field current by adjusting the resistor or opened a switch in the bypass, returning output control to the regulator.

It is not hard to see that a few minutes of inattention could spell doom. Cooked alternators, electrical fires, and exploding batteries were not unknown. Adding an automatic switch that disabled the controller when charging voltage reached a preset level helped avoid the worst consequences. Still, since a set field current does not actually regulate alternator output, if engine speed was allowed to fluctuate when the bypass was in control, either output would decline or alternator voltage would rise to damaging levels. Happily, manual controllers have all but disappeared.

"Smart" Controllers

Silicon has replaced cerebrum for the current generation of alternator controllers. A computer chip integral to the controller monitors voltage and increases or reduces alternator output as appropriate to maximize the charge level and minimize the charging time. Beyond some initial program choices when the controller is first installed, no manual intervention is required. Smart controllers generally operate in three distinct steps. Initially the controller induces the alternator to provide a constant current of around 25% of battery capacity, but the level may be adjustable or at least selectable to allow a faster charge for SVR batteries, particularly gel cells. (Keep in mind that your alternator must also be capable of the higher current level.) When battery voltage rises to around 14.4 volts (14.1 volts for gel-cell batteries—also selectable), the controller abandons current regulation in favor of voltage regulation, holding the charging voltage at 14.4. This allows the battery to accept current at its natural rate. The acceptance phase continues until the current declines to around 2% of capacity, or it may be terminated by the controller based on time. Either way, the charge level should be approaching 90%. Then the controller cuts the voltage back to around 13.3 volts and holds it there so the batteries will not be overcharged if the engine continues to run.

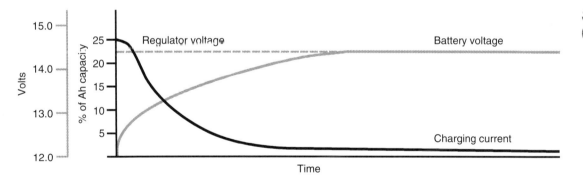

Standard regulator (14.4-volt).

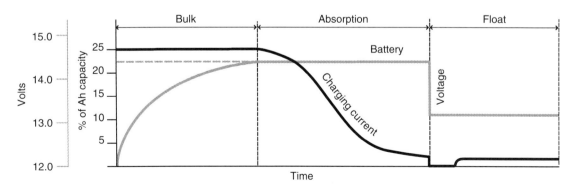

Smart controller (3-step).

Regulator charging profiles.

Many, but not all, smart controllers also have the ability to include the equalization phase, holding the output current fixed at 4% or less of battery capacity until voltage rises to around 16 volts. Equalization is generally on demand and is probably not particularly beneficial more often than every 50 cycles. Equalization is only appropriate for deep-cycle batteries. Neither automotive (starting) nor SVR batteries should ever be equalized.

A smart controller typically reduces charging times by 25% or more if the batteries are discharged to the 50% level. Perhaps more important, the charging profile is gentle on the batteries, helping to give them a long life. However, if you run your engine daily for other reasons—to operate refrigeration or make water—the actual charging profile is not likely to look appreciably different from a standard (read *cheap*) regulator. That is because a controller operating in the acceptance stage functions essentially as a standard regulator. Likewise, if you equip your boat with adequate solar or wind-generating capacity to satisfy most of your power requirements, you could find yourself deriving very little benefit from the considerable amount of money you will spend on a smart controller.

One benefit of a smart controller that accrues regardless of your charging regime is the float stage. Murphy's First Law of Sailing says that a sailboat sailing from point A to point B will encounter winds blowing from point B to point A; this assures that when you add a destination to your sailing, the engine in your boat will run far more hours than you anticipate. Cutting the charging voltage back to 13.3 keeps those long engine hours from overcharging your batteries. However, if this will be your only benefit from installing a smart controller, there are less expensive ways to achieve a similar result.

DUAL REGULATORS
One alternative is two regulators. Solid-state regulators are relatively inexpensive. Connecting two of

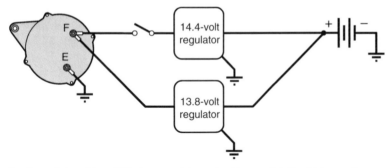

Dual-regulator wiring: With two regulators wired in parallel, the higher-voltage one will be in control until it is disconnected from the alternator, yielding control to the lower-voltage unit.

them in parallel, one with a 14.4-volt setting and the other with a 13.3-volt unit, will allow you to select the charge voltage. This is accomplished with a switch in the field wire from the 14.4-volt regulator. When the switch is closed, the higher alternator output called for by the 14.4-volt alternator exceeds the cutout voltage for the other regulator, essentially turning that regulator off. When the switch is open, the 14.4-volt regulator is off-line and alternator control is taken over by the lower-voltage regulator.

Unfortunately you may have difficulty finding a 13.3-volt regulator, but take heart—a common 13.8-volt unit will probably do a yeoman's job. The reason for this is that almost all regulators are temperature compensated, losing as much as 10 millivolts (0.010 volt) per °C increase in temperature. So if the regulator is mounted in the engine compartment and the temperature there rises by 30°C to 40°C—not unlikely given the long run times we are attempting to accommodate—the charging voltage declines to 13.5 or 13.4, low enough that any overcharging is likely to be inconsequential.

DUAL-VOLTAGE REGULATORS
Another way to skin the same cat is through deception. If we add resistance to the sensing wire of the regulator, we fool it into thinking that the voltage in the charging circuit is lower than it actually is. As a result the regulator compensates by increasing the alternator output.

This ploy is particularly applicable for an alternator with internal regulation, and it can satisfy two objectives. If we size the resistance to cause a 0.6-volt drop in the sensing wire of a 13.8-volt regulator, it will behave like one set to 14.4 volts, the charge voltage we normally want to see from our alternator. However, a simple switch around the resistance takes it out of the sensing circuit, reestablishing 13.8 volts as the cutout voltage. In concert with a hot engine compartment, this reduces or eliminates the risk of overcharging while motoring.

The best way to establish the desired voltage drop is with a diode rather than a resistor, because the level of the drop is unaffected by the magnitude of the current flowing through the wire. Conveniently the typical voltage drop through a silicon diode is around 0.6 volt, just the drop we need. A specific diode that will serve is an IN5400 or the equivalent. Current in the sensing wire flows toward the regulator, so be sure the *cathode* end (the marked end) of the diode is on the regulator side of the circuit.

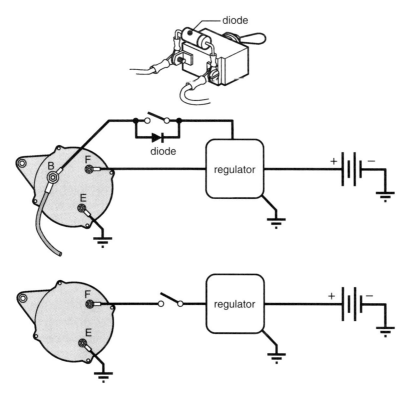

Dual-voltage wiring: Inducing a known voltage drop in the sensing wire raises the cutout voltage by the magnitude of the drop. Bypassing the resistance with a switch returns the regulator to the lower cutout voltage.

Field-disconnect wiring: Opening a switch installed in the field wire disconnects the field and turns off the alternator.

FIELD-DISCONNECT SWITCHES

If all this seems too complicated, just replace your existing regulator with a 14.4-volt unit and protect against overcharging with a simple field-disconnect switch. A switch installed in the field wire (*not* in the sensing wire) interrupts power to the alternator field, turning the alternator off. The 14.4-volt regulator will provide good charging performance—only 20% to 25% off the pace of the best smart controller—and if you find yourself with full batteries and still motoring, just flip the switch. There is a lot to be said for simple and cheap.

BATTERY CHARGERS

The engine-mounted alternator is not the only device for maintaining the charge on batteries. Battery chargers convert AC input from a shore-power connection or a generator into DC power.

Battery chargers ought to be simple. You buy the size you want, connect the red wire to the positive terminal of the battery, the black wire to the negative terminal, the power cord to a convenient outlet, turn the charger on, and forget about it. Bad move, Bunky.

All chargers are not created equal, and it is difficult to ascertain from a retailer the differences in various models. Ignore faceplates that say "50 amp" and "automatic," and advertising copy that claims it "will not overcharge." Pay no attention to anything except the specifications.

Most battery chargers operate on the principle of maintaining a constant voltage—exactly as the voltage regulator on the alternator does—and they suffer from the same drawbacks as the regulator. The usual setting of 13.8 volts results in a very low rate of charge. Before the batteries are even 75% charged, the actual output of a so-called 50 amp charger will be less than 5 amps and declining.

If your charging pattern is to connect the charger on Sunday night and disconnect it a week or two later—the next time you use the boat—perhaps the *rate* of charge is not really a problem, but overcharging definitely is. Leaving a constant-voltage charger operating for weeks at a time will murder your batteries. After such a charger has been on for 24 hours, you can be sure that it is doing more harm than good. Turn it off.

A crude but effective way to safely use a constant-voltage charger unattended is to connect it to a common lamp timer—one of those gizmos that turn the lamps on in your house to make roving burglars think someone is home. Set the timer to turn the charger on for 1 hour a day. For the initial charge of discharged batteries, set the clock so that the on/off cycle is at least 12 hours away, then use the manual switch on the timer to turn on the charger. It will turn off automatically at the end of the cycle. The charging circuit should have a blocking diode to prevent the turned-off charger from draining the battery.

"Automatic" chargers represent another, but not necessarily better, alternative. They sense the battery voltage and turn off the charger when the battery reaches a set level. The automatic feature should prevent overcharging, but knowing what you now know about the way batteries accept a charge, it is easy to see that chargers with an automatic shutoff leave your batteries chronically undercharged. That's bad.

Some chargers provide a constant current rather than a constant voltage. *Trickle* chargers generally fall into this category, providing a current of 1 to 3 amps. Because of the low current levels, they are almost always unregulated, but even a current of just an amp or two can damage your batteries over a long period of time. Used with a lamp timer, an inexpensive trickle charger with a 2 or 3 amp output can satisfy the charging needs of most weekend boaters.

Another constant-current type is the high-output *boost* charger. The output can be set to a specific amperage and turned down manually when the battery begins to gas. Boost chargers require constant attention or they will cook your batteries. Most come equipped with a timer switch to prevent the charger from being inadvertently left on for too long.

The best chargers match output to the requirements of the batteries, charging in steps exactly like a smart alternator controller. The output current is constant until the batteries reach about 14.4 volts, then this voltage is maintained until the current drops below some percentage of capacity—usually around 4%—when the charger reduces output voltage to around 13.3 volts to safely float the batteries. Unfortunately such chargers are also the most expensive, and unless you have a real need for quick charging—maybe you are powering the charger with an onboard AC generator—the only real benefit from your substantial expenditure is likely to be the float stage. If you have limited boat dollars, spend them on something else.

Your choice of a battery charger should be guided by how you will use it. For unattended dockside charging, a constant-current charger connected to a timer is likely to be your best choice. A constant-voltage charger *without* an automatic shutoff feature, also connected to a timer, will do about the same job. The main thing is not to leave either type charging continuously for more than a day.

Discount-store automotive chargers are perfectly adequate, *provided* they are both overload protected and isolated. If the DC output from a battery charger is not isolated from the AC input, *severe* electrolysis of the underwater metals on your boat and boats around yours is very likely, and in the marine environment such a charger presents a serious risk of electric shock. Do not use an automotive charger on your boat without first making sure it is isolated. This is easy to check with your multimeter. Set it to the diode-testing function, then hold one probe across both prongs of the plug and touch the other probe to each output wire or terminal. The meter should read 0.0 volts (or O.L if you are doing this test with the ohm function), meaning there is no continuity—no connection—between the AC input terminal and any of the DC output terminals. Any other reading tags this charger as unsuitable for boat use. Now reverse the probes and do the test again to make sure a diode is not blocking the circuit one way. If the charger is UL approved, it is supposed to have an isolated transformer.

As for capacity, the charger should be capable of replacing your average daily consumption in 24 hours. A 5 amp constant-current charger will handle a 100 amp daily load, including the 20% battery inefficiency, but you need a 15 or 20 amp constant-voltage charger for the same load, because the charger is going to severely reduce its output as the battery reaches higher levels of charge.

For liveaboard use, a constant-voltage charger will be the most convenient. It should have ample capacity to meet the *maximum* average demand. If lights, fans, refrigeration, the stereo, and pressurized water are likely to place a 25 amp drain on the battery, a 25 amp charger will be about right. There is no point in having a charger with an output higher than 25% of your total battery capacity. If you turn off all the appliances, turn off the charger as well.

For use with an AC generator, the best budget-minded choice is a fixed-current charger capable of providing around 25% of your battery capacity. Voltage-regulated chargers waste up to 45% of the energy in heat, whereas fixed-current chargers can be as much as 90% efficient. If you do not want to monitor the charge, then get out your credit card and spring for a smart charger that switches automatically from constant current to constant voltage to float voltage.

BATTERY SWITCHING

Every boat should have a *battery disconnect switch*, and those with more than one battery should be equipped with a *battery selector switch*. The reason for the disconnect is to enable you to turn off all power to the boat's electrical system—advisable anytime the boat is left unattended and essential in the event of an emergency, such as a short circuit or an electrical fire. A selector or isolator switch serves the additional function of isolating two or more batteries or battery banks from each another, allowing them to be discharged independently and charged in tandem.

Battery Selector Switches

Selector switches generally have four positions and three terminals. Heavy cables—typically #4 or larger—independently connect the positive terminals of the two batteries (or banks) to two of the terminals on the switch. The third terminal normally has several wires attached: a heavy cable leading to the starter solenoid to carry the high starting currents, a smaller wire to the ignition switch to energize the solenoid, the output lead from the alternator, and a cable leading to the distribution panel to supply all of the boat's other electrical requirements. The negative cables from both batteries connect to a common grounding lug—normally a bolt somewhere on the engine—either directly or via a grounding bus. A cable from the negative bus in the distribution panel also connects to the grounding bus or lug.

The idea here is that you rotate the switch to the BOTH setting when the engine is running so that both banks receive a charge; when the engine is not running, you set the selector to either 1 or 2 so that only one bank is discharged by house loads, insuring that the charge in the other bank is reserved for starting the engine. This configuration works fine if you are vigilant, but forget to rotate the switch away from the BOTH setting after charging, and you may inadvertently discharge both batteries below the level needed to start the engine. There is also the guarantee of alternator damage if you rotate the switch through the OFF setting while the alternator is charging. This last danger can be avoided by connecting the alternator output directly to one of the battery banks rather than to the common terminal on the selector switch. Rotating the switch to BOTH is still required to charge the other bank.

Isolator Diodes

One way of charging two banks without the necessity of rotating the selector switch is by using diodes in the charging circuit. Current flows in only one direction through a diode. If you split the alternator output and feed it to each bank through a diode, charging current will flow to both banks but be prevented from flowing in the other direction, so the batteries cannot discharge through this route. The easiest way to install isolator diodes is to buy a battery isolator. This is an aluminum heat sink fitted with two or more silicon diodes of appropriate capacity. You connect the output from the alternator to the input terminal

of the isolator and the two (or more) isolator outputs to the positive battery terminals. Usually the easiest way to accomplish this is to simply connect the isolator input to the common terminal on the battery selector switch (assuming the alternator output is also connected to this terminal) and the outputs to the other two switch terminals. This is not only convenient, but it uses the heavy cables already connected to the switch to good advantage. And because the alternator is now connected directly to both batteries, the isolator also protects the alternator from the damage that would otherwise be caused by rotating the selector through the OFF setting.

Adding an isolator, however, introduces a new charging problem. Diodes need a little "push" to get them to conduct in the forward direction, and in a silicon diode this consumes about 0.6 volt. If you fail to account for this, the consequence of your isolator installation will be slower charging times and chronic undercharging of both batteries. The reason is simple. The voltage level sensed at the alternator will be 0.6 volt higher than the voltage at the battery. That makes the regulator prematurely reduce the charge level. If you have a rare adjustable regulator, you may be able to raise the alternator voltage sufficiently to compensate. Otherwise this problem may be partially overcome by taking the regulator sensing wire directly to the positive terminal on one of the batteries; however, this causes the regulator to sense the condition of only that battery (or bank) and may result in the other bank being undercharged. You cannot connect the sensing wire to both batteries or they will no longer be isolated. The most common fix is to install a silicon diode in the sensing wire—exactly as I've already described to fool a 13.8-volt regulator into delivering 14.4 volts. In this case the higher alternator output this diode precipitates approximately offsets the voltage drop through the isolator diode.

If your old boat came with an isolator and you are having trouble keeping your batteries fully charged, the isolator is a prime suspect. Your best course is to remove and discard it, but if neither your vigilance nor your budget is sufficient to support an alternative, then alter the charging circuit to compensate for the voltage drop through the isolator.

Electronic Combiners

Currently the best way to interconnect independent battery banks for common charging is through the use of a relay or solenoid that automatically connects the two banks in parallel. Your old boat may

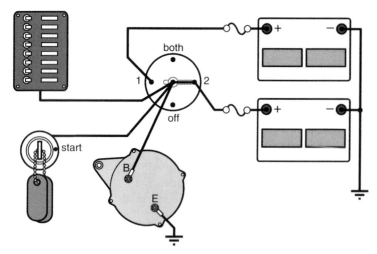

Traditional battery selector switch.

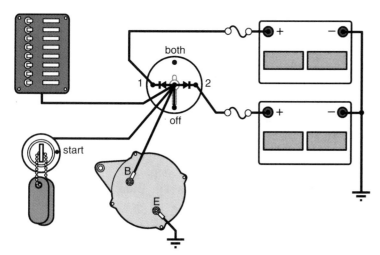

Isolator diodes in the charging circuit.

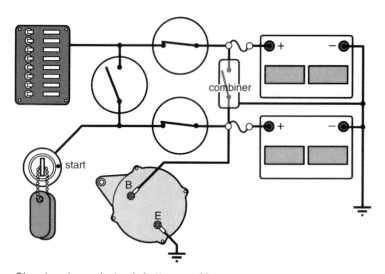

Charging via an electronic battery combiner.

Methods of maintaining dual battery bank isolation.

be fitted with such a relay that is energized by either the ignition switch or the oil pressure switch. If your boat is so equipped and the system is working, leave it alone.

If you want to install a paralleling relay, current technology is for the relay to take its cue from voltage in the charging circuits. The alternator is connected directly to one battery bank. When there is output from the alternator, it drives up the voltage in that charging circuit. The relay is an open switch between the positive battery posts of both banks and is capable of sensing the voltage on either side of the switch. When the voltage rises to some triggering level, typically 13.1 volts, the switch closes, providing a path to the other bank for charging current. (Notably, a combiner will combine whenever it senses charging voltage from *any* source.) When the charging voltage is removed, the voltage in the circuit decays below the trigger level and the relay opens, separating the two banks.

Sometimes called an echo charger or an automatic charging relay, a battery combiner is likely to cost less than an isolator and does not introduce a detrimental voltage drop into the charging circuit. The only precaution is to make sure your combiner is rated to handle the level of current that might pass through it. That means it should be rated for at least the maximum amperage your alternator can provide; however, significant differences in the level of charge of two battery banks when the relay first combines them might result in a short-term current flow from the charged bank to the discharged bank that exceeds the alternator output. When selecting a combiner, err on the side of high capacity.

Combining unequal battery banks by any means results in a charging rate too low for one bank and too high for the other. The result will be slower-than-optimum charging times and perhaps shorter battery life. A derivative of combiner technology is the series regulator. Rather than feeding the charging current directly to the second bank, the series regulator feeds it into a second regulator that charges the second bank according to its current level of charge and its specific acceptance profile. As a practical matter, starting batteries are the usual beneficiaries of series regulation, but they are robust enough and ultimately cheap enough that the benefit may not justify the cost. Series regulation can improve charging times for the house bank, but if the starting battery is relatively small, the effect on sensed voltage and thus on charging profile will likewise be relatively small.

There is the question of which bank the alternator output should connect to. Connecting it to the house bank minimizes the current flow through the combiner, since the house batteries invariably consume the greater part of the charge. However, availing yourself of this "advantage" can turn out to be more complicated than merely moving the alternator output from the starting battery to the house battery, because the wiring harness of a modern diesel often incorporates other connections to the alternator. Fortunately it turns out that this bit of conventional wisdom is probably wrong anyway for the weekend sailor. Brief engine run times in concert with a discharged or tired house bank can prevent battery voltage from rising to the level needed to trigger the relay, leaving the starting battery uncharged. Leaving the alternator connected to the starting battery avoids this problem and simplifies a combiner installation. For a cruising boat with a monster house bank, there are no doubt benefits to connecting the alternator directly to the house bank, but these are mostly imaginary for a boat with a modest house bank.

The best battery switching arrangement for use with a battery combiner is to wire each bank through an independent disconnect switch. In addition, a third on/off switch wired in parallel with the combiner allows manual combining to bypass a failed combiner, which lets you use the house bank in combination or alone for engine starting duty. At least one double-pole battery switch is available to serve as a disconnect to two banks simultaneously but independently, with a third switch position that joins the two banks. This does almost the same thing as three on/off switches, except that it only allows the banks to be used together; one cannot substitute independently for the other.

PASSIVE CHARGING

Keeping batteries charged with alternator output is fine if you run your engine a lot for other reasons. If your boat spends most of its time at a dock, a charger will keep the batteries topped off. But for any boat that spends the bulk of its life at anchor or on a mooring, depending on an alternator to keep the batteries charged is not only inconvenient, it's murder on the engine and usually on the batteries as well. Away from a shore-power connection, idle boats or boats with otherwise idle engines benefit from being equipped with an alternative power source.

SOLAR POWER

The *potential* of solar power is impressive. In just 15 minutes the sun bombards the earth with more energy than all of humanity consumes in a year. In the same 15 minutes about 6,000 watt-hours of energy fall on the deck of a 30-foot boat, enough to fully charge five dead 100 Ah batteries. Unfortunately the best available solar panels (not deployed in space) are only about 12% efficient at converting sunlight to electrical energy. Still, cover the deck with photovoltaic cells, and they will convert enough energy in an hour to fully charge a pair of 100 Ah batteries. We only need a fraction of this area to get the same output in a day, so why aren't solar cells the dominant source of electricity on boats?

Let's look at daily output. Nontracking solar arrays reach their peak output when the sun is directly overhead. Output drops slightly at first, then dramatically as the sun arcs downward toward the horizon. Total daily output varies with latitude, season, and weather, but even in the best circumstances daily output will rarely exceed five times the rated peak output. In other words, we should expect a panel rated at 50 watts to deliver no more than 250 watt-hours of power daily, even during a summer cruise along the Baja, California, coast.

The amount of solar energy available per square meter of surface area is about 1,000 watts. A 12% efficient module 1 square meter in size would yield 120 watt-hours at peak periods, so five times peak gives us a best-possible daily output of not more than 600 watt-hours. We convert this to daily amp-hours with our now-familiar power formula ($I = P \div V$). In this case the voltage is the rated voltage for the panel, normally around 17 volts. So if we divide 600 watt-hours by 17 volts, we find that under perfect conditions daily output per square meter will not exceed around 35 Ah. To replace 100 Ah of consumption plus 20% battery inefficiency will require more than 3 square meters of solar cells, meaning that you will need to find horizontal space for an array larger than a full 4×8 sheet of plywood. Array size is the first problem.

The second problem is cost. Here there is good news and bad news. The good news is that in the 40 years solar panels have been commercially available, the cost per peak watt has fallen from $75 to as low as $4.50. The bad news is that the cost seems to have flattened out in the last decade and may even have crept higher due to increased worldwide demand precipitated by rising oil prices. The current cost of around $6 per peak watt makes the panel cost per daily amp-hour of capacity around $20. The cost of a solar array capable of handling a 100 Ah daily load will exceed $2,000.

Old-boat owners (that hyphen is essential) operating on a budget like my own will be hard-pressed to meet all onboard power requirements with solar energy, but since the original edition of this book, the average size and value of cruising boats has ballooned. That is not necessarily a good thing, but it does reduce the apparent significance of a $2,000 expenditure. Of course, the motivation for bigger, more "comfortable" boats brings with it a similar increase in power appetite, so the cost to make such a boat 100% solar will significantly exceed $2,000. Still, it is not unusual today to see cruising boats sporting huge solar arrays.

In general, stern arches offend my aesthetic sense, spoiling the lines of even the loveliest boats, but for those who are less sensitive, stern arches (and their even uglier and more lubberly cousins, stern davits) do provide an out-of-the-way mounting location for a substantial solar array. Catamarans also seem to have lots of vacant flat space available to accommodate generous solar arrays. Notably even charter operators have taken to equipping their boats with solar panels.

Battery Maintenance

Even small expenditures on solar panels can deliver big benefits. A perfect application for solar power is maintaining the batteries aboard a boat stored on a mooring. A relatively small panel can provide a constant float charge, avoiding harmful self-discharge and prolonging the life of expensive batteries. Surprisingly to some, solar power is also the best way to float the batteries of an idle boat in a marina because it eliminates the risk of stray-current corrosion associated with the constant shore-power connection a battery charger necessitates. You need solar output of around 0.3% of your total battery capacity to float fully charged flooded batteries. That works out to around 5 watts per 100 Ah of battery capacity. Solar charging at a float level is so healthful that it grants the favored battery seeming immortality, in stark contrast to the typically short life untended batteries on a sporadically used boat otherwise suffer. If you take nothing else away from this section, take this: failure to outfit an idle boat with solar charging is just throwing away money.

In sunny climates a panel not much larger can fully recharge the typically modest battery drain of a boat used on weekends. A 40-watt panel, for example,

should be capable of replacing up to 60 Ah over the 5 days between Sunday night and Saturday morning. It would also offset an additional 20 or so amp-hours on the weekend. The cost for a solar panel this size would be similar to or less than the cost of a battery charger, and it has the same advantage already cited for docked boats of potentially saving your underwater metals from corrosion by eliminating the need to plug it in. Solar charging is also environmentally conscientious.

Solar Cell Types

Of the three types of silicon-based solar cells on the market, single-crystal cells produce the most power in optimum conditions, having an efficiency of around 12%. Multicrystal cells, which look like shattered blue glass, are less costly and slightly less efficient, but better performance at low sun angles can make their daily output equal to or better than the single-crystal versions. Amorphous silicon, also called thin-film and likely familiar to you as a featureless blue or gray panel on solar calculators, is the cheapest to produce but only about half as efficient, making the per-watt cost of these panels sometimes higher. Thin-film silicon has the admirable characteristic of not being brittle like crystalline cells, so thin-film panels can be flexible rather than rigid.

Solar panels give maximum output when they are perpendicular to the sun's rays, but since boat movement can make inclining the panel toward the sun less than a sure thing, fixed mounting should normally be horizontal. An articulating mount can improve daily output dramatically if you are willing to reorient the panels every hour or so as the sun and boat both move. It is also essential to mount solar panels where they will be clear of all shadows. This can be a tall order on a sailboat. Even the seemingly inconsequential shadow cast by a line or wire can have a detrimental effect completely out of proportion to the area shaded. This occurs because the cells are connected in series, and when one or two cells feel the effect of shade, they quit producing and resist the flow from other cells in the train, effecting a precipitous decline in output. "Shade protection" diodes found in most thin-film solar panels bypass nonproducing cells, making the output decline more or less consistent with the relative amount of shading. This can make thin-film panels a better choice when shadows cannot be avoided. Thin-film panels also suffer less from shade caused by cloud cover; in overcast conditions they may outperform the more efficient crystalline modules in total daily output. If you do your boating where daily sunshine is by no means a given, a thin-film panel is likely to be the better choice for battery maintenance duty Sailors trying to maximize their solar power output will need sunnier climes and should stick to crystalline panels.

As incongruous as it seems, it is essential to keep solar panels cool. How essential? For every 10°F (6°C) increase in the temperature of the silicon, the cell voltage declines by around 3%. Panel ratings are usually (but not always!) at 77°F (25°C), so in the tropics you should expect the true output voltage to be about 15% less than the rating. You cannot prevent the silicon from heating in direct sunlight, but you can avoid a greater voltage decline from heat buildup by providing plenty of air space beneath the panel. Never mount solar panels flat on the deck or any other solid surface. In another seeming incongruity, it is particularly important for tropical use to select higher-voltage panels (more cells) to compensate for the inevitable higher operating temperature.

On this subject, panels sold for 12-volt use can have from 30 to 36 cells in them. The voltage of an individual cell is just under 0.5 volt, so panel voltage varies from around 14.5 to 17.5 volts. Manufacturers are fond of calling modules with 33 cells or fewer "self-regulating." *Right!* So is my bank account. With the loss of output voltage due to elevated tempera tures, a 33-cell panel on a hot day will have insufficient potential to fully charge your batteries. Count the number of cells, and don't buy a panel that has fewer than 36.

Solar panel connections are basic. If the output of the panel is less than 0.5% of your battery capacity, it can be connected directly to the battery without regulation. This is precisely how you should connect a solar panel sized to provide a float charge. If you are floating more than one bank, separate panels for each bank are preferable to a single panel with its output fed through isolating diodes, because the diodes introduce voltage drop that's particularly unwelcome for expensive solar power. Similarly, solar panel input is often fed through a blocking diode to prevent discharge back through the panel at night, but the loss in daily output this diode causes will likely be greater than any nighttime discharge it avoids. It is usually best to omit it. Better solar regulators disconnect the panels from the batteries when they sense any reversal of current.

On the subject of unwanted voltage drop, be sure you size the wires connecting to solar panels

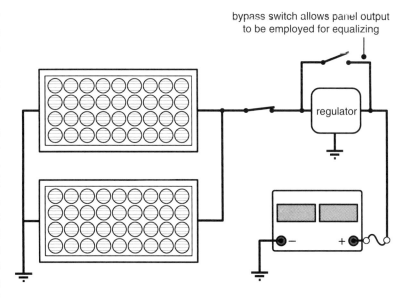

bypass switch allows panel output to be employed for equalizing

regulator

Solar panel wiring: Connect multiple panels in parallel. A regulator is required when output exceeds 0.5% of battery capacity.

generously. Like batteries, the panels should be wired in parallel to increase their capacity. Finally, do not forget to include a fuse in the positive cable as near the battery as possible.

WIND GENERATORS

Another source of passive charging is the wind. Wind-powered generators have become a common cruising boat accessory and for good reason. They are mounted in the air, thus occupying no deck space; they have the potential for much higher output than solar panels; and in the right conditions they deliver a charge 24 hours a day. In cruising areas favored with a relatively constant breeze, wind power can meet all of a boat's electrical requirements.

There are a lot of different wind generators on the market, but it is most instructive to separate them into two categories—small diameter and large diameter. Small-diameter alternators typically have a 3-foot-diameter turbine turning a self-exciting alternator. Large-diameter alternators have a blade-sweep diameter of up to 5 feet and spin a permanent-magnet DC motor converted to a generator. The bigger the generator, the more powerful it will be, but output differences are more a function of physics than of technology.

Blowing Smoke

Wind generator output is related to blade-sweep diameter squared and wind speed cubed. Let's consider wind speed first. If wind speed doubles, output goes up about eightfold (2 × 2 × 2). A more useful view of this relationship is that halving the wind speed reduces output eightfold. Be aware—or maybe *beware*—of rated output at high wind speeds.

A specification of 33.3 amps at 28 mph (I am not making this up!) should suggest $^1/_8$ of that output—4.16 amps—at 14 mph. At 14 knots, output will be 2.74 times the 10-knot output (1.4 × 1.4 × 1.4 = 2.74), so we go the other way and divide by 2.74. That gives this "33 amp" generator a real-world output of just 1.5 amps in 10 knots of wind. That means you should expect no more than 36 Ah of daily output (1.5 amps × 24 hours) from this generator in the average wind conditions found in most harbors and anchorages. It is output at 10 knots that will be most meaningful, both for comparing wind generators and for calculating expected daily output.

Increase blade-sweep diameter by a third—from 3 feet to 4 feet—and generator output should almost double (1.33 × 1.33 = 1.77). Increasing the sweep diameter to 5 feet nearly triples output (1.67 × 1.67 = 2.79). So in a breeze wavering around 10 knots, where a 3-foot generator may be putting out 1 to 2 amps, the output from a 5-foot generator should be between 3 and 6 amps. If you have high current demands, this might be all you need to know, but read on before arriving at any conclusion.

Wind generator output cannot be regulated in the same manner as engine alternator output because the magnetic field is created by permanent magnets, rather than by passing a (variable) current through a field winding. Suppose you have a 400 Ah house bank connected to a large-diameter wind generator capable of putting out, say, 15 amps in 20 knots of wind. When the wind blows at 20 knots, this generator is going to be pumping 15 amps into the batteries, regardless of their charge level. This is good when the batteries are discharged, but bad when they are nearly full. And nearly full is what you expect them to be if you are feeding them a more or less constant charge from solar or wind power. Since you cannot lower the generator's output, by the time the charge level of the battery bank reaches 85%, your choice becomes overcharge or no charge.

The consequences of overcharging are more immediate and pernicious, so you have to stop the charge. Unfortunately even this is complicated. You cannot simply disconnect the charging circuit because that unloads the generator, allowing it to spin freely—like a pinwheel. Burnout is likely as output through the windings climbs beyond capacity, and the long blades are at risk of self-destruction as their tip speed increases to perilous levels. For this reason, charge-circuit-opening solar panel regulators must never be used to regulate a wind generator.

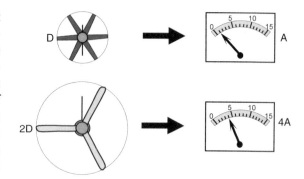

Doubling blade-sweep diameter quadruples potential output.

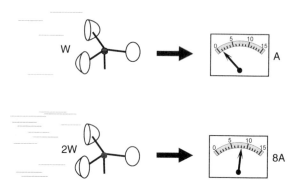

Doubling wind speed increases potential output eightfold.

Wind generator output is related to sweep diameter squared and wind speed cubed.

Good Governance

Strong winds will put a large-diameter wind generator at risk of overspeed destruction, even under load, unless it has some form of speed control. Every sailor I know who has used a large-diameter generator not equipped with some type of automatic brake has at least one horror story to tell. The action dictated by a sudden squall was to rush on deck—if they were fortunate (?) enough to be aboard—and turn the generator away from the wind. Except that by the time they got there, the blades were already screaming like an airplane prop just overhead. The terror this induces must be experienced to be fully appreciated. No one of sound mind leaves a large, unbraked generator running unattended when bad weather threatens or when the crew is sleeping. Such necessarily conservative measures can reduce the daily output of a large-diameter generator by a half or more.

The better response, taken by most manufacturers, is some method of automatic braking. There are three primary methods in use: feathering, centrifugal braking, and electrical braking. Feathering can be a hinged mount that cants the generator away from vertical in stronger wind, or it can simply be flexible blades that stall at higher speeds. Centrifugal braking can be inside the generator housing, or it can be a centrifugal air brake on the blades. Electric braking is typically effected by shorting out the generator windings. All of these methods are effective in ordinary winds, but only the relatively rare tilt-back method can handle really strong winds. As a result, the most powerful wind generators are less in evidence than they once were, and those in use are almost invariably tied off when the boat will be unattended for any significant length of time. It is a consideration to ponder if you want your wind generator to keep your refrigerator cold while you tour inland.

Small-blade alternator-type wind generators, on the other hand, will survive any winds that most sailors are likely to encounter, especially if the stator coils have iron cores (as opposed to "air-filled" cores). This feature makes the alternator self-limiting, meaning that it cannot produce more than the rated output, which virtually eliminates the possibility of the unit's burning out in high winds. Small-blade generators can also be regulated after a fashion with a simple device called a *shunt regulator*. Instead of reducing the output when it senses increasing voltage (like a regular voltage regulator), the shunt regulator diverts—shunts—some of the output into a "dummy" load, where it is dissipated as heat. Shunt regulators do not work well on the more powerful motor-type generators because current levels can rise too high. High-wind capabilities and a means of regulating the charge mean that a small-blade alternator-type wind generator can be mounted permanently and more or less ignored. Average daily output can be estimated at 24 times the rated output.

Of course, if that rated output is 1 amp at 10 knots, such a generator may not satisfy the needs of a boat with high power consumption even if it can be allowed to run 24 hours a day. There are two equally popular responses. One is twin small-diameter generators. The other is a generator with a larger blade-sweep diameter, but not one so large that it challenges overspeed protection. That typically means a diameter of around 4 feet. Either of these options will approximately double wind generator output. It has become more common to see twin 4-foot generators. This option provides output comparable to that of a single large-diameter generator, but the smaller units can be left unattended

with greater confidence. And their smaller individual outputs allow for either shunt regulation or short-circuit regulation—a pulsing kind of short that slows down the alternator and thus reduces its output.

Bad Neighbors

One other factor that is often overlooked is the noise a wind generator can make. Small alternator types are typically powered by a six-blade turbine and should be virtually silent in normal wind conditions. Five-foot generators, particularly those with two blades, can make you think you are on an airboat in the Everglades instead of a sailboat in a previously quiet anchorage. Three blades have mostly replaced two, and these tend to be quieter. Midsize generators also tend to have three blades and should by rights be quieter still, but one particular brand (which shall remain nameless) has single-handedly destroyed the serenity of virtually every anchorage where cruising boats gather. I would never own a wind generator from this manufacturer on principle, but its evolving product *has* become quieter. The number of blades, by the way, has no real impact on output, but all things being equal, more blades will result in quieter operation. In any case, you should endeavor to hear the generator you are considering in operation in high wind before you make your choice. While it seems clear that the owners of obnoxious wind generators apparently become deaf to the howl, I can assure you that the crews on the boats around them never do.

ELECTRONICS

Today's array of available electronic equipment that is intended for boat installation is mind-boggling. Adding electronics is a common enhancement to old boats. Their installation differs from that of a light or a fan by at least one additional connection—from a transducer, a sensor, or an antenna. Even with this added complication, most marine electronics can be installed successfully by the owner. In fact, the manufacturer expects you to install the equipment and includes the necessary instructions with every unit. The equipment is calibrated and aligned at the factory and rarely requires technical adjustments during or after installation. If you follow the manufacturer's instructions carefully, your results should be at least as good as what you can expect from hiring someone to do the job for you.

Power connections present no problems—positive lead to the positive side of the circuit, negative to negative. If the unit has a fuse, either integral or contained in a fuse holder in the positive lead, the purpose of this fuse is to protect the equipment. You must also protect the wiring either by taking your power connection from the output side of the breaker or fuse in the main panel/subpanel or, if you connect the unit directly to the battery, by including a fuse in the positive leg as near the battery connection as possible. Electronic equipment can be very sensitive to insufficient voltage, so make sure the wire size is adequate for the current draw. Using wire a size larger than the 3% chart indicates will insure adequate voltage even when battery voltage is low.

Give appropriate thought to *where* you are going to locate the piece of equipment. I once installed the control portion of an autopilot on the cabin side at the forward end of the cockpit, and it would periodically deviate from the designated heading by 20 or 30 degrees but work perfectly at other times. The problem turned out to be a handheld compass mounted inside the cabin opposite the autopilot control. When the handheld compass was in its bracket, it deflected the compass in the autopilot.

Regardless of a manufacturer's claims about how waterproof or weatherproof a particular unit is, mount it as though a single drop of water could ruin it—because it can. High and dry is the order of the day. Radios should be mounted up against the headliner or under the side deck, not in a cutout in the face of a settee. When you get a little water below and onto the wrong tack, it will immediately become obvious why a low mounting is never a good idea. Do not mount your electronics under the companionway or below an opening port, and make every effort to find a mount location that also keeps the unit out of direct sunlight and far from engine heat and vibration.

TRANSDUCERS

Most electronic equipment has a companion component—a transducer or an antenna—and where and how you install this component is also critical. Depth-sounder transducers, for example, are adversely affected by turbulence and should not be located too far forward or too far aft. Best results are usually obtained when the transducer is mounted slightly aft of amidships. A fairing block is usually required to position the face of the transducer parallel with the seafloor. And despite what you may have heard, installing the transducer *inside* the hull—in a water- or oil-filled box

or bonded directly to the hull in a blob of silicone—is always inferior to a through-hull installation. The sturdier the hull, the greater the loss in sensitivity and range, but even in a lightly built coastal boat you should anticipate that an inboard transducer is likely to reduce the range of the sounder by half.

Speed-log impellers need to be mounted clear of interference, so do not install these components in the flow shadow of some other through-hull fitting or any other hull feature that might create a disturbance. Similarly, wind instrument sensors need to be mounted where they can operate in undisturbed air.

ANTENNAS

Sailors should mount the VHF antenna at the top of the vessel's tallest mast because the higher the antenna, the greater your communication range will be. However, height does not benefit all antennae. There is, for example, no advantage to elevating antennae receiving signals from overhead satellites. To the contrary, the higher you mount a GPS antenna, the less accurate the speed and directional information will be because the antenna will be whipping around due to sea conditions. GPS antennae should be as close to deck level as possible while still maintaining an unrestricted "view" of the sky.

There is also generally little point in mounting an SSB antenna above deck level. Although ground transmissions over a short distance may benefit from additional antenna height, long-distance SSB transmissions are accomplished with sky waves. Antenna length is critical, but the height of the antenna has little effect.

Signal Wires

The various impellers, sensors, and transducers will all incorporate a length of cable to attach them to their associated piece of gear. This connection is typically made simply enough by inserting the plug on the end of the cable into the provided socket in the rear of the equipment. A cable that is longer than required should not be shortened. Simply coil the excess cable in some out-of-sight location and secure it there.

An antenna may have a threaded terminal rather than an attached cable. In this case, you will also need to purchase an appropriate length of the correct cable and install the needed connectors on both ends. The correct cable for a radio installation is RG-213/U. You can also use RG-8U, which is exactly the same size and a little cheaper but has a less durable jacket.

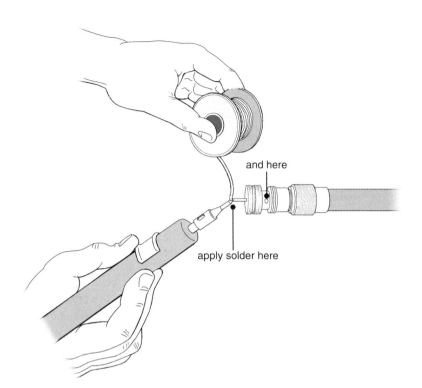

and here

apply solder here

Always install soldered coax connectors, never the solderless type.

A smaller cable will cut your radio's transmitting power at the antenna by about 1% per foot of cable length. You are better off spending less on your radio and more on your cable than vice versa.

Make the cable run as short as possible, but leave yourself enough extra cable to allow for servicing the radio and for cutting off the ends and replacing the connectors later in the event of end corrosion. The radio manufacturer may supply connectors that attach mechanically, but corrosion at the junction between the connector and the cable will almost certainly degrade your radio performance within a couple of years, sometimes less. (If your existing radio installation suffers from poor range, this is where to look first!)

Never use solderless coaxial connectors on a boat. With a soldering pistol and a pair of manicure scissors to trim the braid evenly, almost anyone with determination can solder on a PL-259 coax terminal. You need to melt just a small amount of solder into the hole in the end of the pin and a similar amount into the solder hole in the plug shell. The solder perfects the connection between the conductor and the pin and between the braid and the shell. Corrosion can still take its toll, but degradation will take much longer to occur. After you solder the terminal, use your multimeter on the ohm setting to make sure there is no continuity between the center pin and the shell.

GROUND

Some electronics, notably high-frequency radios—ham and SSB—require special grounding systems. A ground plane of up to 100 square feet of copper or bronze screening located somewhere in the boat may be recommended. At the very least the equipment will have to be grounded to the engine with a heavy copper strap. Hull-mounted porous bronze groundplates marketed for this purpose can prove inadequate, particularly for ham and SSB transmissions. The ground plane is the base from which your signal is launched, and for good transmitter performance, it cannot be too large. Because radio frequency (RF) current travels on the surface of the conductor, the ground for your high-frequency radio needs to be made with 3-inch-wide copper-foil ribbon rather than wire.

All wires and cables to your electronic equipment should be routed carefully to keep them out of wet areas and avoid chafing of the insulation from the motion of the boat. Capture the wiring every foot or two with plastic clips screwed in place or with nylon cable-ties. Using electrical tape for this is a bad idea. Do not bundle antenna or transducer cables with electrical wiring or you risk introducing electrical interference. In fact, keep antenna leads as far from electrical wiring as possible.

INTERFERENCE

Even when the cables are all routed separately, electrical interference can be a big problem with many electronic items. The ignition systems of gasoline engines are especially likely to generate electrical noise, but alternators, fluorescent lights, and even a spinning prop shaft can also be culprits.

You may be able to hunt down the sources of radiated noise with a transistor radio tuned to a blank spot on the band and used like a Geiger counter. Charging equipment, fluorescent lighting, and electric motors are the most common sources. You can turn off the lights—the engine too, I suppose. I regularly hear radio exchanges that include a "Hey, George, turn off your refrigerator." A better solution is to shield the offending wires or replace them with shielded cable. The shielding must be grounded. Some types of noise are best eliminated by installing a filter in the positive lead, or a capacitor (typically 1 μf, 200 volt) between the hot lead and ground. If your electronics appear to be suffering from interference and you don't have the foggiest idea what the hell I'm talking about, get someone to help you who does.

DIESEL ENGINE ELECTRICS
One of the great strengths of the diesel engine for marine use is the absence of an ignition system. Because the heat of compression rather than an electrical spark ignites the fuel charge inside the cylinders, the basic diesel engine requires no electrical connections of any kind. This precludes the myriad problems that inevitably accrue from having ignition wiring in a damp environment.

So what, you might well ask, are all those wires connected to the diesel engine in your boat? Diesel engines are "electrified" primarily for the convenience of electric starting. But an electric starter requires a battery and a switch or two. The battery necessitates a charging source. Then, as long as we have electrical power anyway, some sensors to monitor engine condition seem like a good idea. And then why not preheat the cylinders for cold starting with electricity? Oh, what a tangled web we weave . . .

Engine electrics take on even greater significance when we draft the charging system into supplying the power for our house functions as well. If you also derive mechanical and/or hydraulic power from the engine, the domino consequences of, say, an electric starter failure increase even more.

Fortunately the essential engine electrics are not all that complicated. Learn how to bypass a failed start button and carry a spare starter solenoid, and 90% of the time you will have the solution in hand to any engine-stilling electrical problem. But only half of the time will it be either of these two items.

GROUND RETURN
As with nearly all 12-volt diagnostics, the first thing to check is the integrity of the connections that are part of the circuit. In the case of circuits involving your engine, the engine itself serves as the ground side of the circuit. A circuit will not normally have two wires. If the electrical component is bolted to the engine, the mounting serves as the negative connection. This is a ground return circuit. It turns mounting bolts into electrical connections, and if they are loose or corroded, they cause the same problems as any other loose or corroded connections. Keep this in mind when the starter is sluggish or fails to function. It doesn't take much corrosion to cause starting problems. When a starter motor draws 100 amps—yours may draw more—a resistance of just 0.1 ohm in the circuit results in a voltage drop of 10 volts, meaning only 2 volts reach the starter. Sometimes removing the starter and cleaning the mounting flange and bolts will correct the problem.

You also need to pay attention to the black battery cable bolted to the engine. All engine electrics depend on this cable and its connections to complete the circuit back to the battery. Disconnect this cable and you open all of the engine circuits. If more than one ground cable is bolted to the engine, that typically means the ground from the distribution panel terminates here rather than connecting directly to the negative terminal on the battery. In this case, all of your

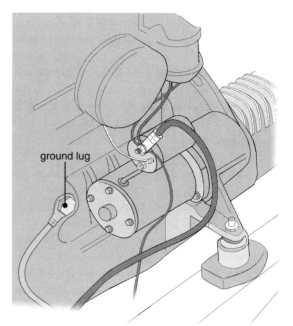

Sound ground connections are equally essential to current flow. Engine starters are typically grounded through their mounting bolts.

ground lug

boat's circuits will depend on the integrity of this connection. Both corrosion and vibration are enemies. Keep this connection bright and tight. Remember to use your multimeter to check for voltage drops on the ground side of circuits as well as the hot side. This can be especially useful on ground return circuits.

ALL THE COMFORTS OF HOME?

Shortly after the publication of the first edition of this tome, considerate sailing guests, astonished at the trivial price of island rum, gave us a 12-volt blender to take better advantage of this "natural resource." The small market and corresponding high price for such an appliance made it quite the luxury. It remains aboard—still turning out piña coladas—but its panache is long gone, because today if you want a blender aboard, $20 and a quick trip to Wal-Mart will satisfy that urge.

The difference is the maturing of inverter technology and the precipitous drop in the price of these electronic marvels. With a modest inverter aboard, you can operate standard kitchen appliances, run drills and saws and sanders, recharge phones and cameras and laptop computers, watch movies and television, and do all of it without going anywhere near a dock or a shore-power connection. Inverters yield only to the GPS in my vote for the most revolutionary electronic addition to any old boat.

Inverters, however, are not magic. They answer to the same physical laws as all other things electrical, and you should understand this fully before you start imagining refrigerated air pouring deliciously from a humming air-conditioning unit in some beautifully isolated but hot and humid cove. *It ain't gonna happen,* at least not for long. Consider the most parsimonious of air conditioners with a mere 5,000-Btu output. The rated current draw for this little unit is 5 amps. So, let's see, if we have a 400 Ah house bank, we should be able to . . . Hold on! Hold on! Hold on!

ELEVEN-FOLD

Every appliance you are running from an inverter is operating at 120 volts, not 12, so the amp rating is likewise at 120 volts. This is where you get to use the power equation yet again. (You can't say I didn't warn you.) We calculate the power in watts by multiplying the voltage by the current draw: $P = V \times I$. In this case, the voltage is 120 and the current 5, so the power rating of our little air conditioner is 600 watts.

Here's the thing. We are operating the unit at 120 volts but supplying the power at 12 volts. How much current is required *at 12 volts* to deliver 600 watts of power? The answer is 50 amps: $I = P \div V = 600 \div 12$. That is why you need husky cables on the battery side of the inverter. It is also why your sweetly humming air conditioner is going to discharge your 400 Ah house bank 50% in 4 hours. Except that a 50 amp discharge rate exceeds the C20 rating of the batteries by 150% and reduces their real capacity to less than 300 Ah. Throw in the fact that the inverter will only be about 90% efficient, so it is going to draw 55 amps from your battery bank to supply the 50 amps needed to deliver 600 watts at the AC outlet. A 55 amp load will discharge a 300 Ah bank below 50% in under 3 hours. Gonna be a hot night.

So a 5 amp inverter load puts a 55 amp load on your battery—11 times the draw listed on the rating plate of the AC appliance. You can use this 11:1 ratio to add AC appliances into your daily load calculation. Clearly you are not going to run an air conditioner for hours, but what about a blender drawing 4 amps? The draw on your battery will be around 44 amps, but you are going to run it for less than 30 seconds to make a pitcher of frozen drinks. Your daily sundowner will add less than 0.4 Ah to your daily load. Even for a party, the blender is likely to run less than 10 minutes in total, extracting perhaps 7 Ah from your battery.

Inverters are wonderfully convenient for powering a vast array of electric tools and appliances that are used for seconds or minutes rather than hours. They are likewise great for very small AC loads, such as topping off rechargeable batteries in cameras, phones, and portable media devices. But to power heavy or even modest AC loads continuously, the demand on your batteries is likely to exceed their capabilities. You should look askance at the 3,000-watt inverters listed in marine catalogs. A 3,000-watt load represents a 250 amp draw at 12 volts (not including losses to inefficiency). I leave it to you to consider what size battery bank would be needed to deliver current at this level for any length of time, never mind that deep-cycle batteries are not very good at supplying high currents. SVR batteries are more compatible with big inverter loads, but you are still discharging them way above their 20-hour rating, slashing their real capacity. And you still have to put all of those amps back somehow. If you are determined to power big AC loads at anchor, a genset will ultimately make more sense.

ALTERNATING CURRENT

That a little learning is a dangerous thing was first observed by 18th-century English poet Alexander Pope. This 300-year-old truism is particularly apt when it comes to 120-volt (or higher) AC power on boats. I would like to advise you to leave the AC wiring on your boat alone, but there is an equal likelihood that total ignorance of the system represents just as great a danger. So let's talk.

Alternating current is as different from direct current as a bear is from a bunny. The most obvious distinction on a boat is that the AC voltage will be 10 times higher than the DC voltage, but the nature of AC is also fundamentally different. Provide a charged battery with an outside circuit, and the excess electrons in one side flow toward the other side—like liquid from a full container into an empty one. Direct current is, by definition, a one-way flow of electrons. With AC, on the other hand, the electrons don't flow, they vacillate. This lack of resolve is not their fault.

In the same way that one magnet will exert a push or tug on another magnet in proximity, passing a magnet near a conductive wire exerts push or tug on electrons in the wire. This is how generators work. Coils of wire surround a spinning magnet, and as a pole of the magnet passes near each coil, it induces electron movement in the wire of that coil—kind of like getting a wave going in a football stadium. However, because electrons have a negative charge, they are attracted to the positive pole of the spinning magnet but are repelled when the negative pole arrives. When you flip the switch to turn on a light ashore, electrons start through the circuit just like DC for an instant, but at the generator the positive pole of the spinning magnet is followed by the negative pole, which induces the electrons to flow in the opposite direction. Just as the current starts to flow in the new direction, along comes the positive pole and reverses the direction again.

The direction of flow of the output current from an AC generator reverses with the polarity of the rotor.

Yet the light comes on! With the electrons just juking in place, how can that be? Consider a lightbulb illuminated by connecting it to a battery. Reverse the connections and the bulb still lights. If you do the reversal quickly, the impact on the bulb will be just a flicker. With AC power the reversal is happening so fast—*120 times per second* with 60-cycle AC (the U.S. standard)—that the bulb's white-hot filament does not have time to cool during the "off" times. The light glows steadily even though current is only flowing through the filament intermittently. This pulsating nature, in concert with higher voltage, also makes AC as dangerous on a boat as a rattlesnake in your sock drawer.

There is an old shaggy-dog story about a train crewmember who was found guilty of murdering his engineer and fireman and condemned to the electric chair. When three attempts to carry out the sentence were unsuccessful—the last with cities and towns darkened to direct every volt of the state's generating power through the body of the murderer—the governor, citing a higher authority, commuted the sentence. Asked by reporters what prevented the electricity from killing him, the railroad man said, "I guess I just never was a very good conductor." Bad joke, good physics.

Hand-to-hand resistance through the human body is usually at least 1,200 ohms. You can check yours by rotating your multimeter's selector to the Ω position and—with wet fingers—holding a probe in each hand. Being by now an Ohm's law expert, you can see instantly that if you grab the two terminals of a 12-volt battery, your body will conduct a current of perhaps 0.01 amp ($I = V \div R = 12 \div 1,200$)—insufficient to pose a serious risk. Ohm's law is equally applicable to AC, and in this case, the voltage will be 120, increasing the potential current flow through your body by a factor of 10. This is enough to make your muscles convulse like Galvani's departed frog. If the current passes near your heart, you may also be departed, because in combination with the pulsating nature of AC, 0.1 amp is about twice the level needed to disrupt electrical impulses that control heart rhythm.

You must remain mindful of this danger if you have or bring AC aboard your boat. With due respect to the verity of Mr. Pope's observation about a little knowledge, ignorance does not diminish the peril. In fact, given the deplorable wiring I have often seen on old boats, blind trust in existing components may represent a greater risk than cautiously reworking the AC system or installing a new one. Apply the

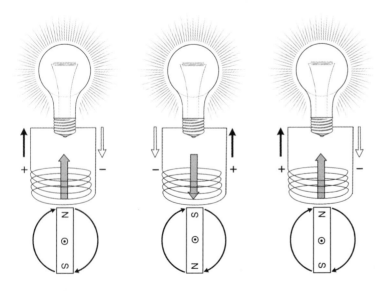

discipline of a snake handler, and you can be your own AC electrician. If you are impatient, reckless, or forgetful, hire someone to do it.

THREE WIRES

Getting AC aboard can be as temporary as draping an extension cord over the lifeline or as permanent as a watertight inlet fitting feeding a dedicated distribution panel. However you bring it aboard, be sure the supply cord has three conductors. For AC circuits, the third wire is the most important one. As with DC circuits, you only need a supply wire and a return wire to complete an AC circuit. In DC we call these positive and negative, but AC is reversing the direction of "flow" every 8.3 milliseconds, so it makes no sense to call one side positive and the other negative. Instead, we call one side hot and the other side neutral. How do we know which is which? Back at the generator, one side of its output is connected to a buried metal plate to hold it at ground potential. Since there will be no voltage on this side of the circuit relative to ground, we call it neutral. The voltage is in the hot side, oscillating from about +170 to –170 volts. Neither your AC voltmeter nor any appliance you plug in cares about the plus and minus polarity, so what we have is an average (called root mean square, or RMS) voltage on the hot side of the circuit of around 120 volts. We measure this voltage between the hot wire and the neutral wire, but we would also measure 120 volts between the hot wire and ground.

By code the hot wire in an AC circuit is black, red, or blue; the neutral wire is always white. It is the black wire, the hot side of the circuit, that should be the most dangerous, but despite what I just said, you cannot be sure which wire is the hot one without testing it. Hello? Here's the problem. A wire reversal anywhere between you and the power source will make the wire you expect to be neutral hot. The consequence of this exceedingly common occurrence is that switches and fuses and breakers will be on the wrong leg of the circuit. A switch still turns off the appliance, but it has disconnected the ground, not the power. That means all of the wiring in the appliance is still hot.

This is where that third wire comes in. It is called the grounding wire, and somewhere back upstream from your boat, it too is connected to a metal rod in the ground. At the other end the grounding wire connects to the metal housings that contain the wiring and the appliances. In the case of plug-in equipment, the grounding wire connection is made via the third socket—the one that in a 15 amp receptacle looks like a tunnel entrance. In a 30 amp receptacle it is the

socket with the crook. The purpose of this wire is to always provide a path to ground with a lower resistance than through you. Suppose, for example, the wire insulation inside an appliance melts or abrades and the wire comes in contact with the metal case. Let's consider this scenario first *without* the grounding wire. The contact goes unnoticed. No fuse blows because no current flows through the case since it does not provide a circuit, and in all likelihood the appliance functions normally. When there is power to the appliance, however, the case is essentially a bare live wire—the snake in the sock drawer. When you touch the case, your body completes the path to ground. If you are lucky, you pick yourself up off the sole and reel off a few swearwords. If you are less lucky . . .

The grounding wire avoids this particular drama. The instant the contact occurs, it is a short to ground, probably blowing a fuse or tripping a breaker. If the short fails to trip the breaker or occurs while you are holding the appliance, the current still follows the path of least resistance, flowing to ground through the grounding wire rather than through your vital organs. Anything that increases the resistance of the grounding circuit—corrosion or small wire size—jeopardizes this protection. An improperly wired outlet, a broken connection, or a missing ground prong (shame on you) leaves you vulnerable.

Ashore the grounding wire is often bare, but in boat wiring it should be insulated and green. We will be coming back to this all-important green wire later.

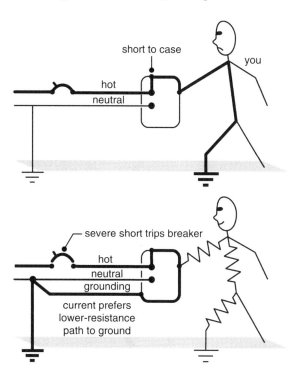

The grounding wire provides a low-resistance path to ground.

Thirty Amp Service

Because the 30 amp locking receptacle has become the norm at most North American and Caribbean marinas, configuring *your* AC system for 30 amps avoids the compatibility problems that will plague you if you arrive with a straight-blade 15 amp cord. The power cord is the first in the train of components necessary to safely power AC appliances aboard. An outdoor extension cord from Home Depot has an additional problem besides plug compatibility. Even with an adapter it is still a 15 amp cord and you are plugging it into a circuit protected with a 30 amp breaker. That makes this cord lying on your boat a fire hazard. I can tell you from personal experience, this is not some hypothetical danger. From the dock to the boat you need a power cord rated for the amperage of the dock outlet (#10 AWG or larger for 30 amp service) and carrying a hard-service rating of SO, ST, or STO to withstand submersion, abrasion, exposure, and strain. The boat end of your cord should attach with a sealing collar to a weatherproof inlet. This generally necessitates a legitimate shore-power cord—expensive, I know, but it should enjoy a very long life.

Hot, neutral, and grounding sockets in 120-volt receptacles.

The weatherproof inlet should be located as high on your boat as is practical and not more than 10 feet (wire distance) from the boat's main AC circuit breaker. This wire, protected only by the 30 amp breaker ashore, must also be at least #10 AWG. Don't be shocked (pun intended) if you don't find an AC breaker in your old boat's existing AC wiring. Builders once reasoned that a boat was just another "appliance" plugged into the marina circuit, which should already have a protective breaker. Reasonable economy, unreasonable risk.

Breakers

If your AC system lacks a breaker, add one. Because of the uncertainty of the polarity at a dock, a single-pole breaker is also risky economy. Protect your AC wiring with a dual-pole breaker. This breaker opens both sides of the circuit, so when you use it as a switch or an overload trips it, none of the wiring beyond the breaker can still be hot, even if the polarity at the dock is reversed. The service limits the *maximum* rating of this breaker, but it is the wire size and outlets downstream that determine the actual rating. If you are installing 15 amp outlets in your boat, they must be protected by a 15 amp breaker. This can be the only breaker, or you could have a 30 amp main breaker feeding more than one branch circuit, each protected by its own 15 amp breaker. Commercial AC distribution panels are often configured with single-pole breakers for the branch circuits—to lower the price per circuit, I suppose—but the reason for a dual-pole main breaker applies equally to branch breakers. A

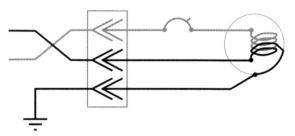

A single-pole breaker leaves the circuit unprotected if the polarity becomes reversed.

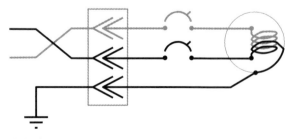

A dual-pole breaker protects without regard to polarity.

reverse-polarity light can warn you (if you see it), but it will not protect you. You need a reverse-polarity indicator even with double-pole breakers, because reversed polarity still puts switches on the neutral side, leaving "off" appliances dangerously energized.

Neutral and Grounding

Before we leave the breaker/distribution panel, there is an essential difference for boat wiring that your brother-in-law the electrician will not know about. In your breaker box at home the neutral wires and grounding wires all connect to the same terminal strip or bus bar. On a boat the neutral (white) conductor and the grounding (green) conductor *must never be directly connected*. Instead, the AC grounding wire should connect to the DC ground, usually at the ground lug on the engine. I will explain the reason for this seeming incoherence momentarily, but with the grounding wire so connected, if you connect the neutral wire to the grounding wire on a boat, underwater hardware becomes a current-carrying path to ground. For anyone in the water nearby, this makes your boat the equivalent of a giant bug zapper. Keep the white and the green wires separated.

WIRE

From the distribution panel to outlets and hardwired appliances, the same rules expounded earlier for DC wiring apply, including where to route it, how to support it, and what wire type and size to use. A prime advantage of the higher voltage of AC is lower amperage for the same amount of work. A 120-watt appliance operating at 12 volts draws 10 amps, but at 120 volts it draws just 1 amp. With the combination of low current levels and short wire runs, we wouldn't expect voltage drop to be much of a concern with AC, but it can be. In particular, modern compressors require start-up current (called inrush) as much as six times the compressor's nominal draw. Voltage drop increases correspondingly. If the wire is too small, supply voltage may actually drop below the level required to start the compressor. So if you expect to run an air conditioner or an AC refrigerator, install wires at least one size larger than the table suggests. A two-size increase is not overkill. If you bundle wires for two or three circuits—not recommended but sometimes nearly unavoidable—their combined potential for heating (think *crowded room*) necessitates wire two sizes larger than normal anyway. Larger wires offer the added benefits of running cooler and giving your system add-on capacity.

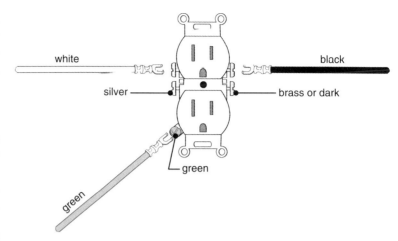

OUTLETS

AC outlets are all polarized, and the Lone Ranger's white horse, Silver, has long provided the association necessary for me to make the correct terminal the hot one. White goes with silver, so the black wire, the hot one, connects to the opposite terminal, usually brass but sometimes dark. The green terminal is for the green grounding wire.

Knowing that the white wire connects to the silver terminal should be sufficient to keep you straight on wiring outlets.

Despite how you may have wired replacement outlets in your kitchen, do not loop the stripped wire end under the terminal screws on boat outlets. Also the spring-clip attachments found on lots of outlets are for solid wire, which you are not using. Commercial-grade outlets with screw-tightened clamps are a good choice, and you can attach stripped wire ends directly to them. Otherwise crimp ring terminals to the wire ends, or locking spade terminals if the terminal screws in the outlet are captive.

GROUND FAULT CIRCUIT INTERRUPTERS

Regular circuit breakers are fire-protection devices. They do not provide any protection from shock because the current flow through your body will be insufficient to trip the breaker. Unfortunately it can be more than sufficient to blow the breaker for your heart. Shock protection requires a ground fault circuit interrupter (GFCI). When a GFCI senses a short to ground, it instantly disconnects the circuit. If you are the short, the $1/40$ second it takes the GFCI to disconnect will be too little time for the current to build to a dangerous level.

In recognition of the increased risk of shock in damp environments, many municipal building codes mandate GFCIs in bathrooms and, increasingly, kitchens. Boats are damp environments, and every outlet on a boat should be protected by a GFCI. GFCI outlets are inexpensive—around $10—and if you

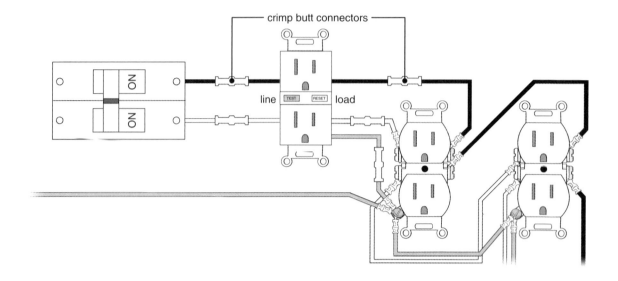

install one as the first outlet on a circuit (counting from the breaker), it provides protection for all of the other outlets on that circuit. The terminals marked "Line" attach to the wires from the breaker and those marked "Load" feed the remainder of the circuit.

You test a GFCI by plugging in a lamp, turning it on, then pushing the Test button. The lamp should go off. Reset the GFCI fixture and perform the same test for every outlet you expect it to protect. Always keep in mind that a GFCI does not defang the rattlesnake; it only senses a short to ground. Get across the hot and neutral, and it won't protect you.

Also be aware that if you plug your power tools into the dockside socket directly or through an extension cord, you will not have ground-fault protection. This puts you at risk on a wet dock. If you have GFCI outlets aboard, power your tools from there.

THAT DAMN GREEN WIRE

The green grounding wire provides a low-resistance path to ground should any AC wiring come in contact with various metal housings. But what if the metal enclosure also contains DC wiring, as it does in a battery charger, an inverter, and a dual-voltage light fixture, or what if the AC and DC wiring are just in close proximity and the unexpected contact is with the DC wiring? AC that leaks into the DC system will seek ground, meaning it will travel through the DC wiring to the ground connection on the engine and down the prop shaft to the water. This is essentially the same as dropping a hot wire into the water. In fresh water this poses a real and immediate danger of electrocution for anyone in the water nearby. The better conductivity of salt water tends to pass the current straight down to ground, reducing

the risk of electrocution, but the current field can still be sufficient to paralyze muscles and cause a swimmer to drown.

This danger is the reason we connect the green wire directly to the grounding terminal on the engine. The green wire provides AC leakage seeking ground through the DC wiring a lower-resistance path than the engine and prop shaft, eliminating the

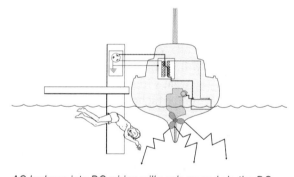

AC leakage into DC wiring will seek ground via the DC ground connection, flowing into the water and putting nearby swimmers at mortal risk.

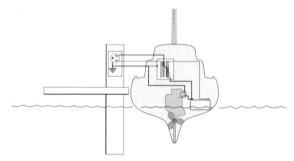

Connecting the AC grounding wire to the DC ground bus provides a path to ground with lower resistance than the water.

The green-wire connection.

risk to swimmers—but only if the grounding wire connection is sound. If there is a fault in the grounding wire anywhere between the boat and the buried groundplate—suppose, for example, that the grounding wire connection inside the dock outlet has corroded open—the prop shaft again becomes the path to ground with its attendant risk to swimmers, but now not just from AC to DC leakage but from all ground-fault current. GFCIs eliminate this risk for the circuits they protect, but something as seemingly innocuous as corrosion on the ground prong of your dock cord can make circuits unprotected by a GFCI lethal. It is essential to test the ground connection at the dock and to maintain cords and plugs in good condition.

Corrosion

When the grounding wire connection is perfect, connecting the green wire to the DC ground lug still has the negative consequence of electrically connecting some or all of the underwater metal fittings on your boat to those on other boats with their own green wires grounded. With seawater as the electrolyte, every grounded fitting essentially becomes part of a big battery. If your fittings are less noble on the galvanic scale than your neighbors, they are anodes and begin to erode. Even if your prop and shaft are similar to those around you and are well protected with zinc, stray DC currents from a nearby boat can seek ground through your green-wire connection, causing electrolysis. A serious stray-current leak can fully consume underwater components in a matter of hours.

Disconnecting the green wire from the ground lug on the engine does avoid both galvanic and stray-current corrosion caused by other boats, but it leaves you horribly exposed to the potential tragedy of electrocuting or drowning someone dear to you who's swimming off your boat. *Do not disconnect the green wire.* The safer strategy for breaking the green-wire connection to other boats is to unplug. If you leave your boat plugged in mostly to power a battery charger, a small solar panel will be easier on your boat and better for your batteries.

Isolate

If you *must* stay plugged in, install a galvanic isolator—essentially a pair of diodes in series connected in parallel to a second pair conducting in the opposite direction. The opposing pairs of diodes let the isolator pass current in both directions, allowing both AC and DC to flow freely, but you might recall from the "Battery Switching" section that diodes need a little "push" to get them to conduct. In a silicon diode this consumes about 0.6 volt, so two in series will block all

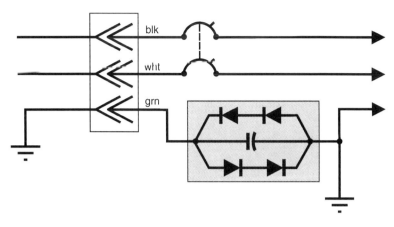

current flow unless the voltage exceeds 1.2 volts. All galvanic voltages between underwater metals are lower than this and so are most stray currents by the time they reach your boat through the water, so this device essentially disconnects the green wire for the currents that cause corrosion but maintains the connection for AC leakage. Since the isolator is inserted into the green wire, any failure opens the grounding circuit with hazardous consequences, so its diodes must be sufficiently hefty to carry short-circuit current—up to 3,000 amps in a 30 amp circuit—long enough for the circuit breaker to trip. A parallel capacitor that would still pass AC in the event of a diode failure is a desirable feature.

A third way to isolate your boat from the potential negative consequences of a shore-power connection is with an isolation transformer. AC from shore flowing through one side of the transformer induces AC power on the other side that energizes the boat's AC circuits, but there is no direct electrical connection between the boat's AC system and shore. The transformer also isolates the DC wiring from shore, eliminating external galvanic and stray-current corrosion as effectively as unplugging. Unfortunately isolation transformers are big, heavy, and expensive, limiting their practicality to relatively large boats.

This is not all there is to know about AC aboard your boat but it is the minimum you need to know. If your AC wiring falls short of the standards outlined

An isolator blocks low-voltage stray currents.

An isolation transformer disconnects your electrical system from shore.

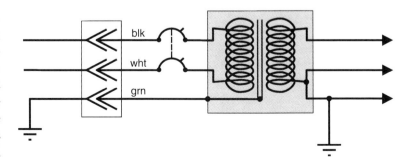

here, take corrective measures. AC wiring is no more complicated than DC, only more dangerous, so with sufficient care you can make the required changes yourself. Even if you decide to take the more prudent course of leaving AC system repairs to a qualified marine electrician, you should still understand the dangers.

Treat AC circuits with respect. You can experiment all you want with 12-volt DC circuits. If you get the wires crossed, the only real risk is to your equipment, and if it is properly fused, even that risk is minimal. But don't mess around with 110-volt circuits. Especially around water, AC kills.

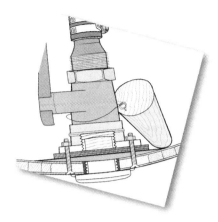

CHAPTER TWELVE

Going with the Flow

*"Oh, a sailor travels to many lands; any place he pleases.
But he always remembers to wash his hands so he won't catch no
diseases."*

—PEEWEE HERMAN

You would likely freak if someone called you and told you there was 2 feet of water inside your hull, but guess what? There is! The ocean is standing 2 feet deep inside the galley drain line, in the cockpit drain hoses, in the cooling water lines, in the head connections, and in every other hose that is connected to an underwater through-hull fitting. If you doubt it, pull one of those hoses off and see for yourself.

So? Did you ever hear the old saying that a chain is only as strong as its weakest link? While you are blissfully content that the extra-thick solid laminate hull of your old boat is a veritable fortress against any breach by the ocean, the truth is that the only thing keeping your old boat off the seafloor is $^1/_{16}$ inch of rubber—the wall thickness of some types of hose. Strong, supple new hoses are invariably up to the task, but old hoses become brittle and split or crumble.

Old boats have old hoses.

HOSES
CHECKING HOSES

How can you tell the difference between a hose that is perfectly good and one that isn't? You *squeeze* it. If you also have a piece of new hose to squeeze, differences will be immediately apparent. But even without a piece of new hose for comparison, you can identify questionable hoses.

Suspect any hose that you *cannot* squeeze, unless that hose is reinforced with helical wire. If it is not obvious whether the hose has wire in it or not, you can check by examining one of the cut ends. When an unreinforced hose is rock-hard, that generally means it is brittle inside. Aside from the risk of rupture, it may be shedding flakes of brittle rubber. If

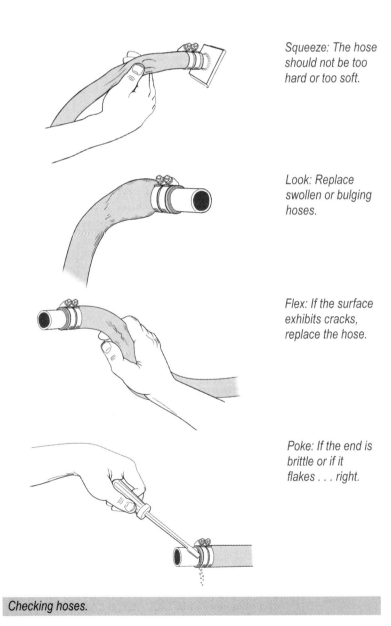

Squeeze: The hose should not be too hard or too soft.

Look: Replace swollen or bulging hoses.

Flex: If the surface exhibits cracks, replace the hose.

Poke: If the end is brittle or if it flakes . . . right.

Checking hoses.

this is the inlet hose for your engine cooling water, those flakes can lodge in the narrow passages of the heat exchanger or inside the engine, resulting in overheating or worse. Replace hard hoses.

At the other end of the spectrum is the spongy hose. If the hose feels like foam rubber, heat or chemicals have attacked the inside. Soft hoses may also appear swollen, especially where they attach to the fitting. Replace spongy hoses.

Always check your hoses in good light. When you squeeze or flex a hose, examine its surface closely. Cracks suggest that the hose is beyond its useful life. Look for flattened, kinked, or collapsed hoses. Check carefully for any signs of chafe where hoses pass over other items or through bulkheads. Use a small screwdriver to "dig" at the end of the hose to determine if it is still supple or has turned brittle. If anything about a piece of hose—particularly one connected to a through-hull fitting—raises the slightest doubt about its integrity, replace it. A split hose is just as potentially calamitous as a split hull and far more likely.

REPLACING HOSES

Hose replacement is conceptually the same as changing socks—pull the old one off, slide the new one on. In ideal conditions it also offers a similar level of difficulty, but you should have sensed by now that when it comes to working on boats, especially old boats, ideal conditions are rarely encountered.

Unlike your socks (one assumes), hoses tend to adhere to the fittings on which they have spent some time. This is an admirable quality, sealing the hose to the fitting and preventing leaks. Admirable, that is, until it comes time to remove the hose. Adding to the difficulty is the fact that flexible hose acts like Chinese handcuffs when you tug on it. You *do* remember those woven pink and yellow tubes you used to have as a kid? You stuck your fingers in the ends and the harder you tried to pull them out, the tighter the tube gripped. When you try to *pull* a hose from its fitting, it tends to grip even more tenaciously.

Perhaps I am getting ahead of myself. The first step in hose removal is to stop the flow to the hose. That means you need to close the seacock if you are working with a through-hull fitting, drain the coolant below the level of the engine hose you are replacing, or shut off the flow from freshwater tanks.

The next step is to release the hose clamps. While your old sweat socks are right there at the end of your legs, hose connections too often are almost inaccessible. Use the largest screwdriver that will fit the clamping screw and the space available, and release

the clamp until you can slide it along the hose out of the way. There should be dual clamps on all through-hull connections. If you cannot turn the clamp screw with a screwdriver, see if the screw has a hexagonal head. If so, use a socket wrench to apply as much force as necessary to release the clamp. Don't worry about breaking it. If it is frozen with corrosion, you are going to replace it anyway. If all else fails, cut the clamp with snips.

With the clamps gone, grip the hose and *twist* it. If it breaks free and turns, you should be able to work it off the nipple by pulling on it as you twist it back and forth. If it fails to break free, don't look for ways to increase your leverage. You don't want to unscrew or damage the nipple. Take a short break and put a kettle of water on the stove. After a soothing cup of oolong tea, pour the rest of the boiling water over the stubborn connection. The heat will soften the bond and expand the hose slightly. Using gloves or a towel to protect your hands, try twisting the hose again. If it still won't budge and you can apply pressure to the end of the hose, try pushing it off the fitting. Alternatively, push the hose farther onto the nipple. The trick to the Chinese handcuffs was to push the ends toward each other, which made the tube expand in diameter. Push and twist.

No? Desperate measures are called for. If the hose is being replaced, the easiest approach is to use a very sharp razor knife to slice it free of the fitting. Wield the knife like a surgeon rather than a butcher, and don't slice all the way through; you don't want to risk cutting a channel into the nipple. Instead, slice the hose twice, on opposite sides, as deeply as feels safe. Twist again. The hose is almost certain to come off. If not, carefully finish one of the cuts and peel the hose free.

A wire-reinforced hose will be very difficult to split, and you will not want to cut a hose that you intend to reuse—perhaps you are replacing what the hose is attached to rather than the hose itself. When the end of a hose is accessible, you may be able to break the grip by working an awl or small flat screwdriver with rounded sides between the hose and the nipple. If not, your only choice will be to cut the hose from the fitting. If the shortened hose is still long enough to be reconnected, this has the advantage of giving you a fresh end.

Getting new hose onto a fitting generally presents fewer problems, as the pushing tends to expand its diameter. If the hose does not go on easily, hold the end in a pan of boiling water for a couple of minutes. Now coat the fitting with a little dishwashing liquid and the hot hose should slip on without difficulty. If it doesn't, suspect that you have the wrong size hose. Push the hose on all the way to the base of the nipple. If the nipple is barbed, center the clamp; if it has a ring, the clamp should grip the hose just beyond that ring. If you slide the clamp onto the hose before you install it, you will not have to open the clamp fully.

In an emergency, any clamp that will fit around the hose can be pressed into service. You can even combine two (or more) small clamps into a large clamp by inserting the end of one into the screw of the other. When fitting new clamps, however, select the clamp specified for the hose diameter, because the radius of the base of the tightening screw varies. Tighten clamps adequately to insure that the hose grips the nipple securely and that the connection is leak free, but be aware that overtightening risks cutting the hose with the clamp band.

Provided the nipple is long enough—and it should be—dual clamps are imperative on both ends of any hose connected to a through-hull fitting. If a hose clamp fails on your car, it lets the water *out*. The worst case is that you will find yourself walking. When the wrong clamp fails aboard your boat, it lets the water *in*, and you could find yourself swimming. How far can you swim? That is the farthest from shore you should sail until you have tandem clamps on all hoses that have the ocean running through them.

Clamps can vary widely in quality, and despite the fact that they are stainless steel, they do corrode. I was mildly surprised once to discover a loose clamp on the short but essential piece of hose between the stern tube and the stuffing box. Surprise changed to shock when each of the other three clamps popped free as I checked them for tightness. From the top all four clamps looked brand-new, but the drip of the stuffing box had caused all of them to corrode through on the bottom where the damage could not be seen. Naturally!

Automotive hose clamps use a plated adjusting screw that soon rusts in a salt-rich environment. The screw assembly also needs to be stainless on any clamp you use on your boat. Such clamps are typically labeled "all stainless" and/or "marine grade," but when you look at them critically, even they turn out to have not a great deal of metal between the notches for the screw and the edge of the clamp. The best clamps are the ones that are not perforated but have the screw tightening against indentions embossed into the band. This type of clamp is far less prone to corrosion failure, and the smooth inner surface and rolled edges eliminate the risk of cutting the hose by

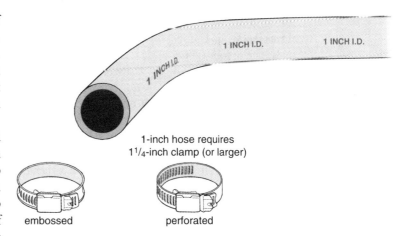

1-inch hose requires
1¼-inch clamp (or larger)

embossed   perforated

overtightening. I like everything about embossed hose clamps except the fact that they cost about three times as much as the perforated types, but for critical hose connections, they justify the expense.

Both the hose and the clamp sizes are specified by ID, but the clamp has to be large enough to go around the *outside* of the hose. In general, buy clamps a size larger; i.e., for 1-inch hose buy 1¼-inch clamps.

Occasionally I still see spring-type hose clamps on boats. It must be because they last so long. Spring clamps are loops of spring wire that are released by squeezing together the turned-out ears of the overlapping ends. They are fine for lightweight bilge blower hoses or for holding the filter element in your air cleaner, but not for *any* water hose connections. Spring clamps are designed to be used in tandem with special fittings. On any other type of connector they exert inadequate compression on the hose for a secure connection. If you find any spring-type clamps aboard your old boat, replace them.

You can hold hoses clear of chafe by clamping them to bulkheads. Pipe straps (plastic strap eyes)—available at any hardware store or plumbing supply—are ideal for this use. When chafe cannot be avoided, protect the hose by cutting a short section of the same size hose, splitting it lengthwise, and fitting it around the hose you want to protect. To hold it in position, run a couple of beads of silicone around the inside of the short section before installing it. Chafe protection is especially critical where a hose lies against a vibrating engine.

HOSE CHOICES

I usually purchase hose (and clamps) from a commercial hose supplier in my city at about half the price charged by marine chandlers (guess where *they* buy their hoses?). I was initially intimidated by the vast array of hoses offered, but soon enough

Embossed hose clamps are less likely to succumb to corrosion and they are easier on the hose. The inside diameter (ID) of a hose clamp must be larger than the outside diameter (OD) of the hose.

discovered that when I described the use of any hose I was replacing, I almost invariably went out the door with one of four types.

Heater Hose

Hoses connected to through-hull fittings need first and foremost to be tough. Where the hose is part of an engine cooling system, heat resistance also will be important. Automotive *heater hose* satisfies both requirements. Tire-like construction with a center ply of woven nylon or rayon makes the hose strong and durable, and the "heater" designation means it is designed for high-temperature use. The rubber compound is usually ethylene propylene diene monomer (EPDM), but a big hose supplier will also have silicone rubber heater hose, which has about four times the heat tolerance and twice the life expectancy. Silicone heater hose is more expensive, but it is your best choice for most raw-water and cooling water hoses, and I like its durability for through-hull connections.

The most common size aboard is $^3/_4$-inch ID. Where flow rate is not compromised, standardizing as many fittings as possible to one size will allow you to limit your emergency spare to a single length of hose (or to borrow a temporary replacement from some less vital application).

Radiator Hose

If you are *sucking* fluid through a hose rather than pushing it through, blockage on the suction side can cause heater hose to collapse like a straw in a thick shake. *Radiator hose* corrects this flaw by constructing the hose around a wire helix—like incorporating a stretched coil spring as the center ply. Just as the inelastic woven ply in heater hose prevents it from expanding when subjected to heat and pressure, the helical wire in radiator hose prevents it from collapsing when subjected to suction. The reinforcing wire will also prevent the hose from kinking when it is

bent. Better radiator hose, also called *wire-reinforced* or *hard-wall hose,* also has a woven ply or two to restrict expansion.

Wire-reinforced hose is your only choice for hoses on the suction side of both the coolant and the raw-water plumbing for your engine or generator. Use hard-wall hose on the suction side of a deck-wash pump or a raw-water pump for refrigeration or air conditioning. Also use only hard-wall hose for any run that requires more than a gentle bend from one end to the other. Here's a tip: if your plumbing requires a sharp bend in a water hose, a trip to an auto parts store with a friendly salesclerk can often turn up a hard-wall hose with a molded bend that can be adapted to your needs by shortening one or both ends.

Standard $1^1/_2$-inch radiator hose is an excellent choice for hoses connecting to $1^1/_2$-inch through-hull fittings—cockpit drains, high-capacity bilge pump hose, even head discharge lines. We will come back to this last one momentarily.

Exhaust Hose

Radiator hose can be found aboard old boats as wet-exhaust hose. Bad choice, Bunky. Like standard heater hose, radiator hose is typically constructed from EPDM, which will endure temperatures of 250°F all day. As long as your exhaust is spitting water, no problem. But as everyone knows, you will eventually strip a raw-water impeller, suck a grocery store plastic bag into the raw-water intake, or just roll the pickup out of the ocean and suffer an airlock. Now your exhaust turns into a blowtorch, melting EPDM like a plastic bowl on the stove, maybe even setting the hose on fire. For exhaust applications, radiator hose will not do. You need exhaust hose.

Exhaust hose is similar in construction to radiator hose. Actually you may find exhaust hose without wire reinforcing—sort of a high-temperature heater hose—but soft-wall hose is a bad idea for exhaust. Hard-wall hose will not collapse in bends or be crushed by shifting contents in a locker it passes through. Exhaust hose is constructed of synthetic rubber and should carry an SAE J2006 designation, which will be stenciled right on the hose. This tells you the hose can withstand a temperature of 1,100°F for at least $2^1/_2$ minutes—hopefully enough time for you to notice the change in exhaust note, or the heat gauge needle climbing toward the red, and shut down the engine. The best exhaust hose, like the best heater and radiator hoses, is constructed of silicone and can carry a continuous temperature rating of up to 500°F, almost insuring that other consequences of no

Use wire-reinforced hose for all suction duty.

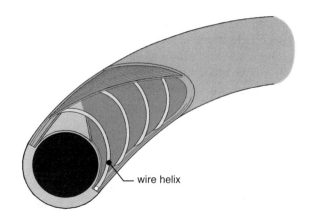

wire helix

cooling water flow will preempt exhaust hose damage. A hose supplier may call all high-temperature-tolerant hoses "steam hose," but be sure that what you buy for exhaust use is also petrochemical resistant.

Another tip: Before you replace exhaust hose, consult the manual for your engine to see what diameter is specified. New engines are too often fitted to old and undersized exhaust plumbing to the detriment of the engine. Exhaust hose can never be too big, only too small. The time to correct this is when you are replacing the hose anyway.

Clear Vinyl (PVC)

If you plumb your freshwater system with hose, use *nontoxic clear vinyl hose*. Be sure it is FDA approved for potable water systems. You can use unreinforced hose for plumbing hand and foot pumps, but for a pressurized water system the hose must be reinforced to prevent it from expanding like a balloon. Any hose that will carry hot water also must be reinforced. Because the cost difference per foot is pennies, I buy only reinforced hose, and I think I am rewarded with longer hose life. Reinforced clear hose is easily identified by the crisscross of braided polyester threads inside the hose wall.

For any line that carries seawater, especially the head inlet or a galley saltwater supply line, clear vinyl hose stinks. This is not a value judgment; it *really* stinks. Aside from consigning the responsibility for keeping your boat afloat to a hose better suited for aquarium plumbing, clear hose has another problem: the light passing through the hose will encourage all manner of marine life to set up housekeeping inside the hose. The colony may go unnoticed as long as the line gets daily use, but if you leave the boat for a few days, much of the marine life dies in the stagnant water. The next time you pump the head or the

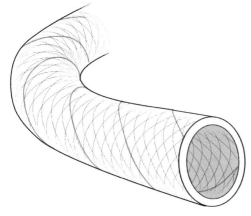

Reinforced clear vinyl hose for potable water plumbing.

saltwater pump in the galley, the low-tide odor will send you scurrying for the companionway. Pray you are not already offshore and a little queasy.

The short-term solution is to go over the side with a squirt bottle of bleach and squirt it into the through-hull fitting while someone aboard operates the offending pump until the smell of bleach is overpowering inside. Give the bleach 20 minutes to do its job then flush the system with some vigorous pumping. The long-term solution is to replace the clear hose with heater hose.

Algae can also become a problem in freshwater hose, especially if the water is stale and stagnant. Boats that see only weekend use are likely to see their clear vinyl hose take on a green tint. Allowing a bleach solution to sit for an hour or so in the hose kills the algae but does not remove it. Clear water hose on weekend boats is likely to need cleaning annually by disconnecting the hose and pushing or pulling a detergent-and-bleach-soaked rag through it, perhaps repeatedly. If after you flush the cleaned hose with a blast of water (from a dock hose) the interior is shiny and/or feels waxy, put the hose back in service. A rough interior surface can harbor bacteria, dictating hose replacement.

Other Hose Options

In the bilge of your old boat, you could find ribbed, thin-wall polyethylene or PVC hose between a large electric bilge pump and its overboard discharge fitting or from a strum box/bilge strainer to an under-deck manual bilge pump. This hose is usually white or sometimes gray. You might be familiar with it as vacuum cleaner hose or (in other colors) as the hose on a swimming pool vacuum. It is so poorly suited for onboard plumbing of any type that it astonishes me that reputable chandlers persist in offering it to unsuspecting boaters. The turbulence caused by the ridged interior decreases the flow rate through this type of hose as much as 30% compared to smooth-bore hose, hardly a responsible choice for a hose that you are counting on to save your boat in the event of a leak. Do not plumb your bilge pump(s) with hose with a corrugated interior, and replace any you find aboard with smooth-bore hose.

Ridged, thin-wall hose is an equally poor choice for head plumbing. It is invariably odor-permeable, and the ridged interior holds an ample supply of odor-generating matter, particularly when used on the discharge side of the toilet. If your head smells like a construction-site outhouse and you see ridged hose in there anywhere, that will be the primary propagator of the obnoxious effluvium. You can easily confirm this by vigorously wiping the surface of the hose with a clean rag dampened with hot water and—I'm sorry—sniffing the rag. This is a good test for any hose connected to your toilet, holding tank, or discharge or pumpout fittings. If the cloth smells, the hose has to go.

Radiator hose generally works fine for toilet discharge plumbing. The thick, multi-ply wall resists odor permeation, and the smooth bore offers less opportunity for solid matter to remain in the hose. The more vertical the hose, the less odor will be a problem, so as long as you avoid flat hose runs—or worse still, a sag—you are likely to find radiator hose perfectly satisfactory. When the installation requires a tight bend in the discharge hose, a preformed radiator hose can often be used to advantage. However, the antifreeze smell that sometimes emanates from a hot car engine attests that not all radiator hoses do such a fine job of containing odor; also, locally purchased radiator hose will be of unknown quality. If yours turns out not to be up to the task or if you just don't want to run the risk, you will find "sanitation hose" at marine chandleries. Such hose will be either specially constructed to provide the necessary odor barrier or selected for its odor resistance. Either way, you have some assurance that it will not smell, but you will pay a premium for that warranty.

All you need to know about fuel hoses is that they bear an A or B rating for fire resistance and a 1 or 2 rating for permeability. An A-rated hose must resist a flame for at least $2\frac{1}{2}$ minutes; B-rated hose doesn't have this requirement. Use only A1 fuel hose on your boat, whether for gasoline or diesel. Because the tank-fill line carries fuel but does not normally contain it, you might use the less permeable A2 hose here, but it is not hard to imagine fuel standing in this hose—the hose has a sag, you leave the tank topped off in the off-season, or you are sailing on one tack for several days. You won't be wrong using A1 hose for all lines carrying fuel. If the A1 (or A2) rating is not printed right on the hose, it is not an approved fuel hose. This type of hose is usually constructed from nitrile-butadiene rubber (NBR), a synthetic that gives the hose excellent flexibility and chemical resistance.

Special hoses are also required for oil or gas lines. Hot oil is especially hard on hoses, and any flexible oil lines should be checked regularly. Replacement hose must be designed for this use. Hydraulic lines must be rated for the pressures of the system they are part of. A high-pressure rating is also essential for thermoplastic propane hose. Refrigeration hose is specially compounded to contain refrigerant, which will pass right through the walls of any other type of hose you might be tempted to substitute. Except for refrigeration hose, which may be connected with special hose clamps, most oil and gas lines will require machine-installed end fittings. The supplier will be able to fabricate the hose to your required length.

RIGID ALTERNATIVES

To avoid the problem of hose deterioration altogether, you might well ask why boats can't use the kind of rigid piping that is used in homes and seems to last for half a century or longer. Good question.

You don't need a great deal of imagination to figure out what would happen if you connected your fidgety engine to the intake through-hull with a rigid pipe. And if you are going to isolate the pipe from the engine with a short length of hose, you may as well connect the hose between the engine and the through-hull.

Vibration is not the only concern. Suppose the sole of the cockpit is 3 feet above the hull, and the connection between the cockpit drains and through-hull fittings is rigid. Now take the boat for a rigorous sail. Any movement of the hull or the cockpit sole will apply significant leverage to the through-hull fittings. Hose simply flexes.

Once you think about a rigid pipe trying to tear your through-hulls loose, we can probably agree that rigid piping to through-hull fittings is ill-advised. But why not in the freshwater system? Wouldn't copper or rigid PVC pipe be better than vinyl hose? Generally speaking, no.

Rigid PVC (or rigid copper) piping is far more difficult to install than hose. Every piece must be cut to a precise length, and every change in direction requires an elbow and two connections—potential leak sources. Even when the run is straight, the restricted spaces on a boat are likely to prevent installing a long length of pipe as a single piece. And unlike houses, the "walls" in a boat are not straight and square, so unless the pipe has considerable flexibility, it will "bridge" the hull rather than lie against it. Given that the pipe is sure to pass through stowage areas, rigid PVC is at greater risk of damage than hose from a shift of the other contents of the locker.

Soft copper tubing is flexible enough to snake through restricted spaces, tough enough to fend for itself in a packed locker, and durable enough to last the life of the boat. A freshwater system plumbed with copper is definitely top-drawer, but copper tubing is relatively expensive and the fittings to join the tubing to other components add additional expense and complications, with both compression fittings and threaded connectors having an annoying tendency to leak. Cold-weather sailors tell me copper also has a propensity to fracture in freezing temperatures.

Yet another problem with rigid piping is that many plumbing components for boats are manufactured with hose fittings. Such fixtures can only be installed in a rigid-pipe system with hose-to-pipe adapters. If you are forced by design to have some hose in the system, why not all hose? Clear vinyl hose may not have the class of copper plumbing but it excels in value and ease of installation. As for life expectancy, I have seen vinyl hoses deliver 30 years of trouble-free service. Even in the least favorable circumstance, vinyl hose should not require replacement in less than 5 years.

POLYETHYLENE TUBING

Lots of old boats built in the late 1970s and 1980s—along with about 10 million American homes—were plumbed with semirigid polybutylene (PB) tubing. This hard, flexible pipe is typically gray, sometimes black, and secures to barbed fittings with aluminum or copper crimp rings. Unfortunately PB is apparently incompatible with chlorine (duh!), and class action suits brought against the various manufacturers have resulted in a settlement of more than a billion dollars to repair and replumb homes that suffer PB tubing failure. Unfortunately boats are specifically excluded from the suits. The good news is that PB has proven fairly reliable in the low-pressure environment of boat plumbing, and when leaks do occur, they are more often annoyances than catastrophes. Still, if your boat is plumbed with PB tubing, it may be flaking inside with who knows what health consequences, so you might want to replace it.

The replacement is semirigid polyethylene (PE) tubing. The PE tubing used in potable water systems is either cross-linked polyethylene (PEX) or linear low-density polyethylene (LLDPE). Unlike PB, PE enjoys an unsullied reputation, having been used for residential plumbing in Europe for more than two decades. Long in use for RV plumbing, it has found its way aboard boats, both as original equipment and as an excellent choice for owner-installed plumbing. With quick-connect fittings, a PE tubing water delivery system assembles with the simplicity of Tinkertoys. The only negative to PE plumbing is the cost of the fittings, which at this writing run $4 to $8 each. The tubing is actually cheaper than reinforced clear PVC hose, and the opaque or at least semitranslucent

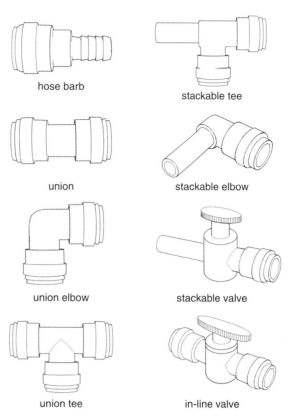

hose barb

stackable tee

union

stackable elbow

union elbow

stackable valve

union tee

in-line valve

A wide variety of available quick-connect fittings allow for unlimited configuration options for freshwater plumbing with PE tubing.

nature of the PE tubing discourages algae growth that can be a problem with clear hose. PE tubing also comes in colors—typically red for hot water and blue for cold—which looks nice and might make plumbing failures easier to trace.

Installing PE plumbing is slightly more demanding than PVC hose because the tubing is less flexible and needs to be cut to the correct length. Also, the semirigid nature of the tubing can be troublesome when the connector you want to attach the tubing to points away from the way the tubing needs to run. Both $5/_8$-inch and 15 mm OD PE tubing can safely be bent as tightly as a 7- or 8-inch radius, which is the preferable way to change direction when the configuration allows, but changing direction of a PE tubing run in a confined space will require an elbow fitting or even two.

First on Paper

The first step in installing PE plumbing is to sketch your freshwater plumbing, including any new fixtures you might want to add. A cockpit shower is probably the most common addition. The sketch will let you visualize and list all of the fittings you'll require, which will allow you to put a price tag on this particular "upgrade." On a larger boat, it can make sense to route all of your water lines from a central manifold rather than in series where each fixture is

A plumbing road map will get you to your destination without wrong turns.

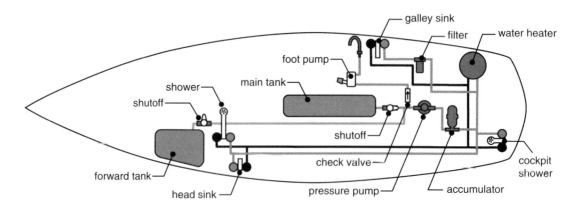

supplied by teeing off of the main line. PE fitting systems all have *stackable tees,* which allow the simple assembly of a manifold with as many outlets as you need. You will also need to measure the approximate lengths of all tubing runs and sum these to determine how much tubing you will need to purchase. If you are plumbing cold- and hot-water delivery, segregate your measurements accordingly so you can purchase the tubing in two colors.

You are going to need to know how the tubing attaches to every fixture—barb or thread, straight or tapered, male or female, metric or inch, $1/2$ inch or $3/4$ inch—so you can purchase all the correct connectors. Get all of this information on your sketch. With your component list in hand, you can buy both the tubing and the fittings. Square ends are absolutely essential for leak-free connections, so include a tubing cutter in your purchases. This is the only tool you will need, but do not try to get by without it, no matter how simple your water delivery system. You can cut hose with a knife or hacksaw, but not PE tubing.

Assembling the Pieces

With all the pieces in hand, the actual plumbing is simply a matter of cutting the tubing to length and inserting the ends into the appropriate quick-connect fittings. Sealing is accomplished with an internal O-ring that is part of the connector, but the tubing *must* be square cut and scratch free, and it must be inserted into the fitting all the way to the internal stop. It is held in the fitting with a spring-loaded grip ring. A release collet allows you to remove the tubing from the fitting for system modification or tubing replacement. The lower-cost alternative to the quick-connect fitting is the equally available compression fitting, which is arguably more secure but takes more effort to assemble. If you use PE tubing for raw-water plumbing—seawater to the galley, for example—opt for compression rather than quick-connect fittings. Where failure can sink your boat, a push-together connection strikes me as less than prudent!

PE tubing expands and contracts with temperature changes, so do not make your tubing runs too tight; allow a little sag. Long, horizontal tubing runs need to be supported about every 2 feet to avoid side loading on the fittings. Keep PE away from heat sources. Water heater connections should be made with metal-braid-covered flexible hose. Pressurize the system and check all fittings for leaks.

Sanitize new plumbing with $1/4$ ounce of bleach per gallon of water, opening faucets one at a time until the water running out smells of chlorine. Close the faucet and let the bleach solution sit in the tubing for an hour, then empty and flush the tank and the water lines. Now fill your tank and forget about freshwater plumbing for a decade or two.

Choose compression fittings for raw-water plumbing.

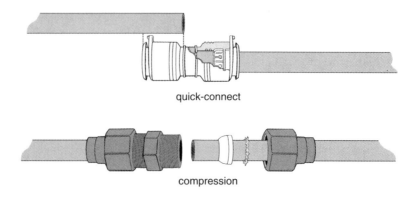

CONFIGURING THE FRESHWATER SYSTEM

Your old boat may or may not be equipped with a pressure water system. There are valid arguments on both sides of this issue. Many boatowners think the convenience (or is it familiarity?) of pressure water outweighs the potential for waste and the modest electrical demands that accompany a pressure system. Others find prematurely empty tanks far more inconvenient than pumping water.

I come down strongly on the side of the latter view. Pressurized delivery wastes an intolerable amount of water. However, hand pumps are not an acceptable alternative in my opinion. While hand pumps *may* save water, I cannot stand the irritation of trying to wash one hand at a time or of washing dishes one-handed. The hand intervention required to turn pressure water on and off when conservation is a concern is only slightly less inconvenient. The hands-down (there's a pun here if you look for it) best water delivery system for a boat with limited water capacity is the foot pump. Having been shipmates with all varieties of freshwater delivery systems for more than 35 years, I would add that for all freshwater use except showering, the foot pump not only makes the best use of available water, but it is actually the most convenient because it leaves both hands free.

To those who contend that pressure water is not necessarily wasteful, I suggest you imagine what your daily consumption ashore might be like if you had to pump every drop used. In light of droughts, unrestrained development, and water shortages all over America, maybe I'm on to something. Environmental considerations aside, the simple fact is that you *will* use more water with a pressure system. This may not be a big issue for weekending, but it can be if cruising is in your future. Of course, this is not necessarily an either/or decision. Pressure water and foot pumps can coexist, allowing both pressure showers and water conservation.

PUMP INSTALLATION

Regardless of the type of pump you select, installation and connection are not difficult. Hand pumps are installed through an appropriate-size hole in the counter and held in place by tightening a nut from the bottom against the underside of the counter. The installation is completed by slipping the supply hose (from the water tank) onto the single hose fitting and clamping it.

Foot pumps can be somewhat more difficult to install, not because of the plumbing but because

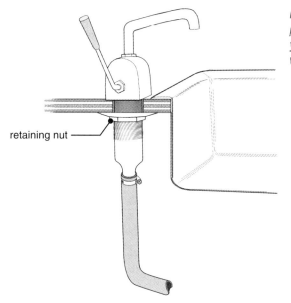

Hand-operated pumps will make you want pressure water.

retaining nut

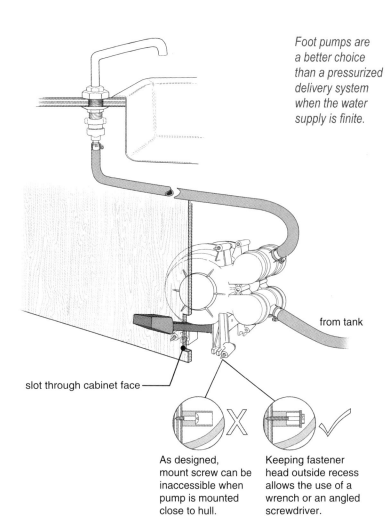

Foot pumps are a better choice than a pressurized delivery system when the water supply is finite.

from tank

slot through cabinet face

As designed, mount screw can be inaccessible when pump is mounted close to hull.

Keeping fastener head outside recess allows the use of a wrench or an angled screwdriver.

of the mounting. Different types of foot pumps are available—some mount through the sole, some mount on the sole, and some mount inside a cabinet and are operated by a lever. The lever type typified by the original (and still the best) Irish-built Whale Gusher is the most versatile, the most popular, the most powerful, and the most difficult to mount. Since these pumps are invariably mounted with the lever protruding through a hole in a cabinet, it remains a mystery to me why they were originally designed with only bottom-mount brackets. Thankfully the current models can be screwed directly to the inside face of the cabinet, but the curvature of the hull can make getting to the bottom-mount screw problematic. The solution to this is a longer screw passing through a washer that prevents the screw from disappearing into the mount-screw recess. With the head of the screw standing proud, you can see it to fit a screwdriver and the screwdriver can be cocked somewhat to clear the ascending hull.

A foot-pump installation also requires a spout mounted over the sink. The spout mounts through a hole in the counter and is held in place by a nut on the underside. The supply hose is clamped to the inlet side of the foot pump. A second length of hose connects the outlet side of the pump to the hose fitting at the bottom of the spout. As alluded to earlier, because of the hose-barb connections, PVC hose is nearly always a more sensible choice than semirigid tubing for foot- and hand-pump plumbing.

ELECTRIC PUMPS

The least expensive pressure system merely substitutes a small electric pump for the foot pump and routes the power to the pump through a switch near the spout. Turn the switch on and you get a fixed flow. Turn the switch off and the flow stops. Sounds simple, but the lack of flow control is particularly wasteful, and the availability of low-cost automatic pumps makes the remote switch an unnecessary and avoidable complication.

An automatic pump necessitates a faucet. The pump incorporates a pressure switch on its outlet side. When output pressure exceeds the switch setting, typically around 40 psi, the switch opens the circuit, turning off the pump. Connect an automatic pump to an open spigot, and the pressure will not rise, causing the pump to run continuously. Conversely, connect a pump without a pressure switch to a closed faucet, and back pressure will either damage the pump or blow the line (centrifugal pumps excepted). However, when you pair an automatic pump with a faucet, opening the faucet causes the pressure to fall and the pump to start. Closing it causes pressure to build, shutting off the pump.

Plumbing is identical to that of the foot pump except that a single pump supplies all outlets. The pump supplies equal pressure to all plumbing downstream, so opening a faucet in the galley, the head, or out in the cockpit causes the pump to run. An automatic pump is typically located somewhere near the freshwater tank, but one advantage is that it can be located virtually anywhere in the boat. Wiring is a matter of connecting the positive and negative leads to a fused circuit in the distribution panel. Electric pumps also tend to have threaded inlet and outlet fittings, allowing them to be plumbed directly into a PE tubing system.

There is a nonelectric method of having pressure water. In this configuration you mount a small tank high in the boat—up against the overhead or on deck. You fill this "day" tank by manually pumping water from the main tank. A hose from the bottom of the day tank to a faucet allows water to flow by gravity whenever the faucet is opened. This system, once popular with spit-to-windward voyagers, is seldom seen today, probably because it combines the worst aspects of both freshwater delivery possibilities. It is as wasteful as a pressure system and as inconvenient as a manual one. If you are going to pump the water anyway, it is better to pump it when you need it and only as much as you need. That said, in sunny climes, a small deck tank painted black can be a good way to have on-demand hot water.

If you want to have a pressurized system for when water is plentiful and foot pumps for when it

A single electric pump normally supplies all of the faucets aboard.

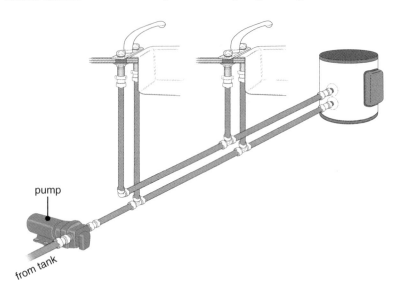

pump

from tank

isn't, simply plumb foot pumps and paired spouts separately and supply them by tapping into the supply line between the tank and the electric pump. An in-line check valve in the line to the foot pump is a good precaution, relieving the foot-pump check valves of the need to resist the pull of the electric pump.

PUMP TYPES

Different pumps operate on different principles, and there may be occasions when understanding *how* a pump works will assist you in selecting the right one for your specific need.

Most hand pumps operate on a piston principle—similar to the operation of a bicycle pump. When the piston inside the hand pump is lifted, the vacuum formed in the cylinder sucks water from the supply line into the cylinder, where it is trapped by a check valve at the inlet. The downward stroke opens a second check valve in the piston, allowing the water in the cylinder to flow from the bottom of the piston to the top. On the next upward stroke, the piston simultaneously forces the water on top of the piston out the spout and sucks a fresh fill of water from the supply line into the cylinder. The downward stroke transfers the water to the top of the piston, and every upward stroke pumps water.

Foot pumps are almost always diaphragm pumps. The principle of operation is similar to that of a piston pump. The manual diaphragm pump is basically a short, squatty cylinder with a rubber lid—the diaphragm. A pivoting lever (like a playground seesaw) is attached to the center of the diaphragm. The cylindrical chamber has two openings, an inlet and an outlet, both fitted with check valves. When you push the lever down, the opposite end pulls up on the diaphragm, increasing the chamber volume and creating a vacuum that sucks water into the chamber just as your lungs suck in air when you expand them. When you release the lever, a spring pushes it up and causes the opposite end to depress the diaphragm, reducing the chamber volume and forcing the contained water through the outlet check valve. Step on the lever again, and the suction of the expanding chamber volume closes the outlet check valve and opens the one on the inlet side, again filling the chamber. And so on.

If the pump is configured with the diaphragm in the middle of the chamber—in effect creating two chambers—and each chamber has its own inlet and outlet, you have a double-action pump. As the diaphragm expands the volume in one of the chambers, it simultaneously decreases the volume in the opposite chamber. Such a pump delivers water with both the downward and the upward motions of the lever. The Whale Gusher and similar lever-action foot pumps work on this principle, although for design reasons the Whale pump actually has two diaphragms operating in tandem from the same lever.

A check valve is typically nothing more than a rubber flap attached on one side or a rubber disk pinned in the middle. The flap is like a door without a knob—going one way, you simply push the door open, but you cannot pass through the door going the other way. The disk is like a leaf over your cockpit drain—it prevents flow one way, but pressure from the opposite side opens the seal. In either form, when the flow is going the correct way, the flap or disk yields and allows the water to pass, but any reverse flow closes the flap or disk and holds it against its seat.

Electric pumps will almost always be one of three types: diaphragm, flexible impeller, or centrifugal. Electric diaphragm pumps operate just like manual diaphragm pumps, except the diaphragm is actuated by a belt or connecting rod from an electric motor or by an internal wobble plate.

Electric flexible impeller pumps are similar to the raw-water pump on your engine. The rubber vanes on the impeller divide the interior of the pump into a half dozen or more pie-slice-shaped chambers. A flat (or at least flatter) spot intruding into the otherwise circular pump interior is located between the outlet and the inlet openings. That flat, called a *cam,* flexes each vane in turn as the pump spins. The flexed blade reduces the space of the chamber behind it, squeezing out any water in that chamber. As the vane passes the flat spot, it springs apart from the one behind, increasing the volume of this chamber and drawing in water from the inlet. This happens with each chamber in turn, as each carries its charge of water around the pump interior until the leading vane again encounters the cam, squeezing the water out through the pump outlet opening.

Centrifugal pumps work like a squirrel-cage blower, moving water instead of air. Water in the center of the vanes is slung out to a chamber around the rigid impeller. This flow builds pressure in the chamber and forces the water to flow out the outlet opening.

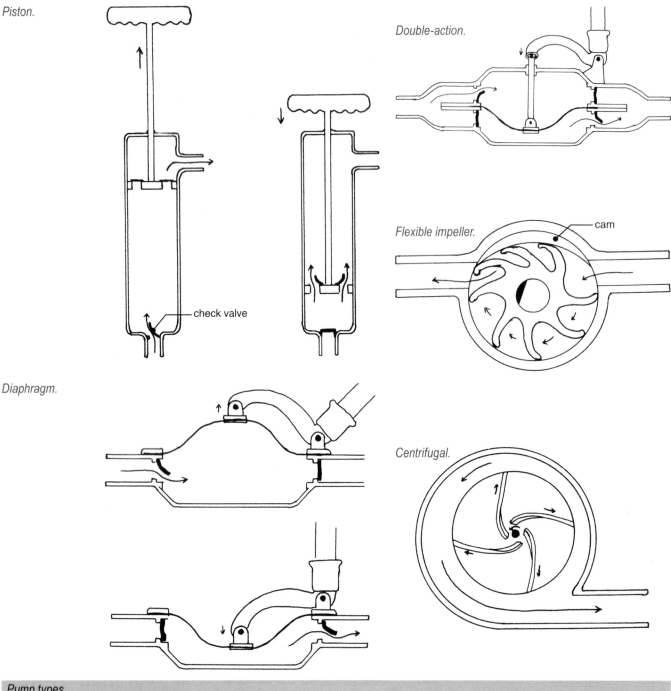

Piston.

Double-action.

Flexible impeller.
cam

check valve

Diaphragm.

Centrifugal.

Pump types.

PUMP PROS AND CONS

Knowing that a hand pump is probably a piston pump or that a foot pump is probably a diaphragm pump may not be very important since you probably have no alternative, but in choosing a pump for a pressurized system, understanding the different types is essential. For example, centrifugal pumps can run with the flow inhibited without damage and without generating excessive output pressure. This characteristic makes it possible to omit the pressure switch, even with the pump connected to a flow-restricting faucet (though an on/off switch is still required). Centrifugal pumps can also run dry without damage. In fact, centrifugal pumps are almost trouble free, and they are the least expensive of the three common types. What keeps them from being the pump of choice in most pressure water systems is that they are *not* self-priming. To work, the pump has to be full of water to start. That means that the pump must be mounted *below* every freshwater tank (so water flows to the pump by gravity), but because water is heavy, we generally want tankage mounted as low in the boat as possible. That makes mounting the delivery pump even lower quite a challenge on most boats.

Both flexible impeller pumps and diaphragm pumps are self-priming and may be mounted in almost any convenient location. Both can also be damaged by excessive flow restriction and thus require a pressure switch to protect the pump by turning it off when output pressure rises to a preset level. What sets these two types apart is that when a flexible impeller pump is allowed to run dry for even a few seconds, it will be damaged—usually shedding the vanes of the impeller. A diaphragm pump can run dry indefinitely without damage.

Why would the pump in a pressure water system run dry? Because the tank is empty, which—take my word for it, Skip—is going to happen a lot more often with a pressure delivery system. When the tank is empty, not only is there no water on the inlet side of the pump, but there will be no pressure on the outlet side. The pressure switch will turn on the pump, and it will continue to run until you manually turn it off at the electrical panel. Meanwhile, a flexible impeller pump is likely to have been damaged. That makes the electric diaphragm pump normally the best choice by default for a pressurized freshwater system.

Electric diaphragm pumps come in two types. One has a separate motor driving a large-diameter, single-chamber diaphragm pump through either a belt drive or a connecting rod. In the other, the pump and motor are essentially a single unit, with the pump head having three or four small chambers and an equal number of diaphragms activated in series by rotation of the shaft. The large-chamber pumps are capable of delivering a greater volume of water, but the multichamber design is more compact, costs less, and should be more than adequate to pressurize the normal onboard freshwater delivery system.

A recent development is the variable speed pump; rather than just turning the pump on and off, it varies the speed of the motor to match water demand. As with most new products, the safer and less costly course is to stick with the tried-and-true pressure switch type until this technology matures and the cost declines.

Electric pumps can be noisy, particularly when rigidly mounted. You can reduce the resonance by attaching the pump with soft mounts. A simple way

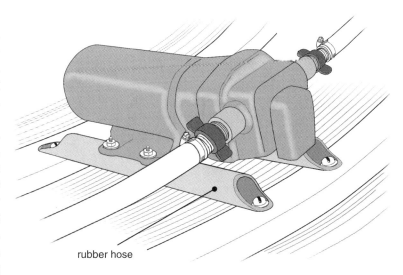

rubber hose

to achieve this is to bolt the pump feet to a pair of short lengths of heater hose—like skids—then screw the heater hose to your mount base.

Soft mounting reduces pump noise.

Leak Detection

If you hear your freshwater pump cycle when no one is drawing water, either you have a leak or the check valves are not sealing completely. While you are sanitizing lines (described earlier) is a good time to check for leaks. With a chlorine mix in the system, run your hand around the body of every pump, electric or manual. If your fingers come away damp and smelling of chlorine, the pump is leaking and needs to be serviced. Also check for leaks at all fittings and connections the same way. Tightening the clamp usually stops a weep at a hose connection. Stop leaks at threaded fittings by dismantling and wrapping the male threads with Teflon plumber's tape.

If you don't detect any leaks, the pump's check valves are probably not maintaining pressure. You can confirm this by turning the pump off and opening a faucet to relieve pressure. Pinch the outlet hose from the pump closed by clamping it between two wood blocks. If your boat is plumbed with PE tubing, disconnect the outlet line and seal the pump's outlet port with a threaded plug. Turn the pump on. Cycling confirms check-valve leakage.

SPOUTS AND FAUCETS

Hand pumps have an integral spout but foot pumps require a spout overhanging the sink. Since galley sinks are usually shallow—this is mostly a consequence of needing to keep the bottom of the sink above the boat's waterline so it drains rather than fills—the spout should loop as high as possible to allow the biggest pot and/or the deepest pitcher to

Pipe-to-hose adapter.

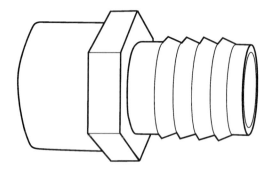

fit easily underneath. Unfortunately all of the commercially available spouts I have seen are shorter than ideal. Buy the tallest spout you can find, but only one made of stainless steel or plated brass. Aluminum spouts have an irritating tendency to clog with corrosion. If you are a metalworker or have a friend who is, a tall custom spout is likely to be an enhancement you will long appreciate. A less attractive alternative is to raise a commercial spout by mounting it on an elevated construction rather than directly on the counter.

Pressurized water requires a faucet, and if you have both hot and cold water, you will need a mixer faucet. Marine catalogs may be your best source for single-knob (cold water only) faucets, but for mixers there is no reason you cannot consider the incredible range of household faucets available. Bar faucets in particular, because of their high spouts and smaller footprint, work well aboard. I prefer a single-lever mixer because it lets me turn on the water with my elbow when my hands are grimy, but dual-knob faucets give better control, especially when you want only cold or only hot. Faucet connections are typically threaded male $1/_2$-inch NPT (National Pipe Thread),

to which PE tubing will readily connect. Hose will require inexpensive pipe-to-hose adapters.

SHOWERS

Adding a shower to a boat that is not equipped with one is more of an accommodation change than a plumbing problem. From the plumbing perspective, pressure water may seem essential, and indeed it is if you want a hot shower. If you do not have hot water aboard, a foot pump can supply water to a showerhead very effectively. In either case, plumbing a shower is a matter of connecting the showerhead to the dedicated pump or to the hot- and cold-water supply lines.

The drain represents the larger challenge. A pan is required to contain and collect the water, and too often the shower pan drain leads directly or through a hose into the bilge. With this system, hair, scum, and unmentionable gra-doo ends up in the bilge. This not only gives the bilge and probably the boat interior a locker-room stench, but the accumulation eventually renders the bilge pump inoperable, placing the boat in peril.

Water from a shower pan should be captured in a separate sump and pumped overboard. The sump can be remotely located (it can even be located in the bilge), but it should either contain its own float-operated electric discharge pump or be large enough to hold the water from the shower, which will be manually pumped or poured overboard afterward. You can construct your own sump by mounting a small automatic bilge pump in some type of water-collecting container, or you can buy a shower sump system that will include box, fittings, pump, and float switch. The cost difference will not be significant, so

A sump with its own pump and float switch is the best solution for waste shower water. A cleanable strainer prevents hair and other debris from reaching the pump.

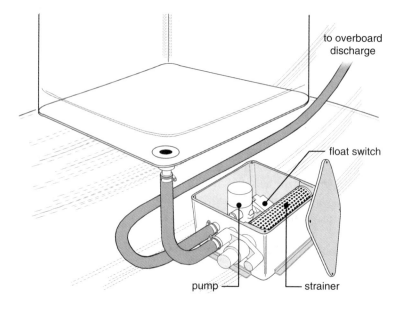

the issue is more likely to be fit. If you buy a commercial sump, give preference to one with an integral strainer. For a shower sump of your own construction or if the commercial sump you select omits this feature, install a strainer in the drain line. A strainer dramatically reduces pump failures.

For tropical cruising, a pressurized garden sprayer with the wand shortened makes a miserly and effective freshwater shower. On chilly evenings, a kettle of boiling water added to the tank provides a satisfying hot shower.

ACCUMULATOR TANKS

The pressure switch in a pressure water system will cause the pump to cycle on and off when a faucet is open. If the faucet is wide open, the pump may run continuously, but if the water is being used more frugally, pressure will build up in the restricted line and shut the pump off momentarily until the pressure drops again. The cycling can be quite rapid, but except for wear on the pressure switch, it really doesn't hurt anything. The pump is going to be subjected to about the same amount of total run time to deliver a full tank of water whether it is in intermittent trickles or a constant flow.

If the rapid cycling bothers you, you can reduce it somewhat with the addition of an accumulator tank. Accumulator tanks are available with and without a rubber bladder inside. The bladder keeps the water and the air inside the tank separate so the tank does not become "saturated," meaning full of water, but if you are willing to drain the accumulator occasionally, one without a bladder will do exactly the same thing at a much lower cost and no risk of failure.

In its simplest form, an accumulator is an empty tank with a single opening in the bottom fitted with a tee connector. It must be mounted vertically. It is plumbed into the system by cutting the hose on the discharge side of the pump and slipping the cut ends over the two exposed barbs of the tee on the bottom of the tank. When the pump runs, it also fills the accumulator tank, but since it is filling the tank from the bottom, the air already in the tank is trapped at the top and compressed. When the pump shuts off, the pressure of the compressed air continues to deliver water until the water pressure drops below the cut-in point for the pump. One feature of an accumulator in the system is that when you draw a small amount of water, the pump may not run at all. Avoiding or at least reducing that middle-of-the-night thumpa-thumpa-thumpa will be much appreciated by a crewmember who sleeps with his or her head next to the pump.

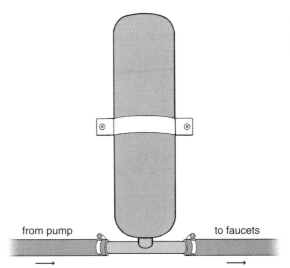

Accumulator plumbing—a study in simplicity.

from pump   to faucets

Accumulator tanks are available for a reasonable price, or you can make your own if you can pick up a foot-long scrap of 5- or 6-inch PVC pipe. (Ask a plumber or try a construction site.) Buy two PVC caps from a plumbing supply store and generously cement the caps to both ends of the pipe to make a tank. Drill a hole in the center of one of the caps and thread or glue a $1/_2$-inch hose connector into the hole. Install a tee connector in the hose connected to the pump outlet, and connect the tank to the tee with a hose.

Over time the air inside an accumulator tank without a bladder mixes a bubble at a time with the water in the tank and gets carried out. No new air enters the tank, so eventually most of the air is lost and the accumulator ceases to store pressure. The solution is to drain the water from the tank so that air again fills the chamber. This is made easier with a vent plug in the top of the tank or with an air valve—a tire stem—that will allow you to reintroduce air without draining the tank by simply pumping it in from the top.

FILTERS

Every time you refill your boat's water tanks, you also take aboard iron, copper, and probably lead from the supply piping and perhaps bits of plastic from the sun-degraded dock hose. And while most municipal water is chemically treated, the amount of chlorine—typically around 1 part per million—is only intended to control the growth of algae and bacteria between the filtration plant and the faucet. In your tanks, the chlorine dissipates, allowing slime and bacteria to flourish. Well water is no better, bringing aboard a multitude of minerals and a plethora of wriggling organisms. Even rainwater carries dust, dirt, and organic and chemical pollutants washed from the sky.

The absence of chemical disinfectant in these "pure" water sources invites microbiological debauchery in your tanks. Fill your freshwater tank(s) often and sediments accumulate; fill them infrequently and organisms proliferate. In both cases, some form of filtration is indicated.

For dealing with organic impurities, chlorine is by far the most common purifying agent. Many boaters routinely add chlorine to their tank water, but ingesting excessive chlorine has been linked to coronary heart disease and arteriosclerosis. The usual ratio of 1 teaspoon of 5.25% chlorine bleach (Clorox) per 5 gallons works out to be about 14 times the concentration typically found in tap water, so it is prudent to remove it before drinking the water. This is easily accomplished with an activated charcoal filter, which also eliminates most objectionable tastes and odors. However, unless a charcoal filter gets frequent use, bacteria soon set up shop inside it. The health risks of a seldom-used charcoal filter are sure to exceed those from a few ounces of overchlorinated water, so if you mainly sail on weekends, a charcoal filter is a bad idea. If you absolutely need a filter—maybe you have fiberglass tanks that make the water unpalatable—then get one labeled "bacteriostatic." Such filters are impregnated with silver, which inhibits the bacteria development *inside* the filter, but this type of element still requires replacement at least annually, no matter how little you use it.

The ideal way to avoid sediment in your tank is to filter the water *before* it comes aboard, but for this you must not use an activated charcoal element. Charcoal removes chlorine and other chemicals put into the water to control bacteria, so prefiltering through charcoal will hasten organic growth in the tanks. Select a filter that removes only particulates. Be cautious about plumbing a fine-particulate filter into your water delivery system. Fine filtration severely restricts the flow of water through the filter, especially as the element becomes clogged by the particles it is removing. In shoreside plumbing, high water pressure continues to force water through the filter, giving the element a reasonable life span, but in the low-pressure environment of a boat, an extremely fine filter element will have to be replaced much more often.

The most sensible plumbed filter is a common threaded canister style that uses activated charcoal elements. This type of filter removes chlorine, tastes, odors, and particulates larger than 2 microns. Do not pay extra for a "boat" filter. Drinking water filters using standardized and inexpensive cartridges are available from home supply, discount, and hardware stores. They have threaded connections, which you will appreciate if you are plumbing with PE tubing. For hose you will need $^3/_8$-inch NPT to $^1/_2$-inch hose adapters. Install the filter downstream of the pump. Since the only water that really needs filtration is what you drink or use in food preparation, locating the filter in the cold-water line to the galley sink can make the most sense, greatly lengthening the life of the filter cartridge and probably extending pump life as well.

For manual water delivery I have come to the conclusion that *no in-line filter should be installed.* A good foot pump is a joy to use, delivering water at a satisfying rate with easy action. An in-line filter makes you pump harder for less water, and as the filter clogs, flow declines to a begrudging trickle. When back pressure becomes stronger than the pump's return spring, pumping is reduced to a single stroke, the depressed pedal rising tediously. A hand pump avoids the contest between spring and filter, but pumping becomes increasingly stiff, and because the filter has to be on the inlet side, many hand pumps simply will not pull water through a partially clogged

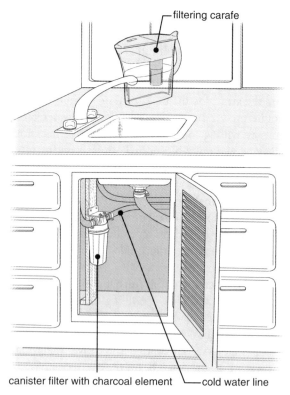

filtering carafe

canister filter with charcoal element   cold water line

For pressurized water a standard under-counter canister charcoal filter installed in the cold water line in the galley will remove chlorine and particulates from all cooking and drinking water. The best filter for water delivered by foot pump is a drip carafe.

filter. All of these problems go away if you eliminate the in-line filter.

The solution for manual delivery systems is a filtering carafe such as those sold by Brita. Water pumped into the top chamber of the carafe drips through the separating filter, filling the bottom chamber with purified water. Having filtered every drop of our drinking and cooking water this way for the last 15 years, I recommend it over in-line filtering without reservation.

WATER HEATERS

When the water heater at home shows signs of cashing in, it sends a chill through the spines of ordinary men. It is big, heavy, awkward, wired to a 220-volt circuit, soldered into the plumbing lines, and has 30 or 40 gallons of water inside it. By comparison, replacing or adding a typical marine water heater is child's play.

A boatowner who lives aboard or cruises from marina to marina might select a large unit (marine water heaters are commonly available up to 20 gallons), but most others will find a 4- to 6-gallon heater more than adequate unless they have an abnormally large freshwater capacity. Regardless of the size of the heater, the connections are basically the same. A pressurized water delivery system is a prerequisite.

The power requirements of a water heater heating element are too high for battery operation. Marine water heaters sold in the United States have a 110- or 220-volt heating element, useful only when a boat is hooked up to shore power or is equipped with an AC generator of adequate capacity to supply the power. To counteract this limitation, most also contain a heat exchanger so that some of the heat generated when the engine is running can be transferred to the water in the tank.

If your boat already has a 110-volt shore-power system, the three-wire electrical connection —hot, neutral, and grounding—to add a 110-volt electric water heater is not difficult. Be sure you include a dedicated circuit breaker and that it is a *double-pole* breaker. If polarity is ever reversed, a tripped single-pole breaker will break the neutral side of the circuit, meaning there would still be power to the heating element—an extremely dangerous situation. The double-pole breaker opens both the hot and the neutral sides of the circuit. You also need a switch in the *hot* side of the circuit to turn the heater off and on. A common household wall switch works fine.

The danger from electricity increases exponentially with the voltage, so get a professional to wire a 220-volt water heater. This is a good course even for 110-volt wiring if you are not absolutely sure what you're doing. The truth is that unless you are living aboard at a dock, you will rarely use an electric water heater, so electrocuting yourself while installing one is a frivolous way to cross the bar. Don't take any chances! And once the water heater is wired, be sure you do not turn it on until it is also plumbed and full of water. Unless the element has overheating protection, energizing it when the tank is empty will burn it out in a matter of minutes.

How you connect the water heater's heat exchanger will depend on the cooling system your engine has. If the engine is raw-water cooled, disconnect the cooling water hose from the injection point on the exhaust pipe and connect it to one side (the inlet side if it is marked) of the heat exchanger. Attach a second length of hose to the other side and connect it back to the exhaust pipe. If your engine is freshwater cooled, disconnect the freshwater (coolant) hose from the inlet side of the engine's heat exchanger and connect it to the inlet side of the heat exchanger in the water heater. Connect a second hose from the outlet side of the water heater exchanger back to the inlet side of the engine's exchanger. If your engine has a high operating temperature (let's say above 180°F), this configuration may overheat the water in the heater and cause the safety valve to vent. In that case, connect the water heater into the cooling system *after* the engine's heat exchanger rather than in front of it. If the water heater connections are smaller than the engine hose or piping, you will have to find an alternative method of making the connection; do not reduce the coolant flow through your engine. Most modern small diesels have integral heat exchangers, and these engines normally provide plugged, threaded ports for water heater connections. Check your manual.

Water heaters must be mounted *lower than the engine* with the connecting hoses rising continuously toward the engine so that air cannot become trapped in the piping, causing circulation problems and possible engine overheating. Because of the weight of the full heater, you want it low in the boat anyway and securely mounted. If it is not possible to position the heater lower than the pressure cap on your engine, your installation will need to incorporate a header tank above the heater.

To make the freshwater connection, install a tee connector in the discharge hose from the pump. The same pump can pressurize both the hot and cold sides of your system. If you have an accumulator in the system, install the tee downstream of it. A hose

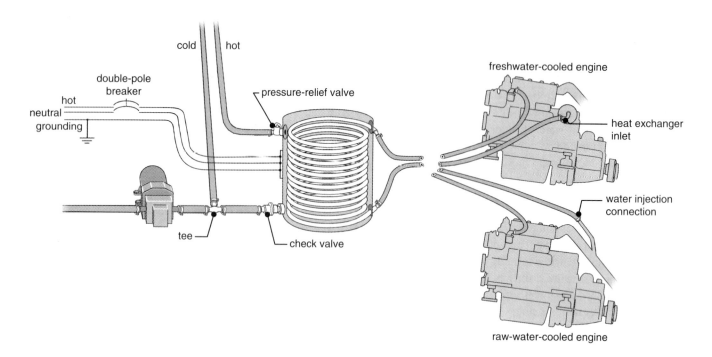

Water heater installation.

from the tee connector leads to the inlet side of the water heater. A hose from the outlet side leads to the hot-water faucet. Be sure the outlet hose can handle the heat. If you install PE piping, you will need special metal-shielded hoses for both of the water heater connections. Multiple faucets may be supplied through a manifold or by tee connections in the outlet hose.

Most water heaters are factory equipped with a check valve on the inlet side to keep the hot water from migrating back toward the pump and with a safety valve on the outlet side in case pressure rises too high. If the water heater you install does not have these features, you will need to install both devices in the respective lines near the inlet and outlet ports.

If water usage is a concern, mount the water heater as close to the galley as you can. The water in the hose will be cool, and if the hose is long, you will waste a lot of water waiting for hot to arrive. Sailboats away from the dock and primarily using wind and solar power will find a water heater useful only after motoring. The least complicated and least costly way to satisfy on-the-hook hot water needs is to heat water in a kettle. This is the only option for boats without pressure water, but it need not be a hardship. A kettle full of boiling water poured into a pump thermos mounted near the galley sink can supply hot water all day long. If you boil water for coffee every morning anyway . . . Aboard a smaller boat you might, as we did, decide to remove the water heater in favor of putting the space it occupies to an alternative use.

TANKS

Hot or cold, water quality at the spout is influenced by water quality in the tank. Keeping tanks clean and fresh insures clear water for washing and reduces the demands on whatever type of filtration you rely on for drinking water.

Cleaning

Cleaning a water tank is easier when the boat is out of the water and you can enlist the aid of gravity to drain the tank. Insert a garden hose into the inspection port and open the faucet for a few seconds (long enough to fill the hose), then unscrew the hose from the faucet. The disconnected hose will siphon the tank empty. While that happens, if you sweep the tank end of the hose over the bottom surface of the tank, it will vacuum out loose accumulated sediment.

For a boat in the water, you can drain a high tank into the bilge, giving the bilge a freshwater wash in the process. (Be sure your bilge is oil free!) Undersole tanks must be pumped empty with a portable pump or by opening a faucet. Before you drain a dirty tank through the boat's plumbing, remove all in-line filter cartridges.

If the water and/or the tank walls are green, add a generous squirt of dishwashing detergent to a bucket of hot water and pour this into the empty tank. Use a sponge and/or a long-handled dishwashing brush to scrub all interior surfaces. If the tank is slimy, it is worth the effort to find a way to wipe as much of the interior surface as possible. Surge holes in baffles may be large enough to pass a cloth stapled to the end of a dowel. Where interior baffles prohibit scrubbing, you will have to soak the tank clean by boosting the detergent and water with a cup of chlorine bleach (not more than $1/4$ cup if this mixture will be pumped overboard). Because chlorine attacks aluminum (stainless steel, too, but more slowly), substitute a pint of white vinegar when cleaning an aluminum water tank. Fill the tank completely and let it sit for a day.

For a particularly foul tank, a rough-water sail is an excellent way to agitate the cleaning solution. (In this case, fill the tank just half-full.) When that is not possible, I drop a small, submersible bilge pump ($15) through the inspection port; fit it with a short hose (after the pump is inside the tank when the port is small); and let it agitate the cleaning solution for a day or two. Professional steam cleaning is another option.

Once the tank is clean, drain it and rinse it well with a high-pressure nozzle. You will need to rinse and drain the tank several times to remove all traces of detergent. When the tank is suds free, pour in a box of baking soda and refill it. Draw water through the boat's plumbing to flush detergent residue from the lines, then let the tank and hoses sit full overnight. The baking soda will deodorize both. Drain the tank one final time, and it is ready to supply clean and taste-free water.

Adding or Replacing

For an old boat being prepared for a cruise, adding water-carrying capacity by adding a tank (or tanks) is a common enhancement. There are six distinct options: integral, flexible, fiberglass, aluminum, stainless steel, and polyethylene.

An integral tank uses the hull as the bottom and sides. When located in the bow—the usual place for a retrofit—all that may be required is a strong aft bulkhead and a top. Internal bulkheads may also be needed because an onboard tank of any construction that is more than 3 feet in any direction should incorporate internal baffles to prevent potentially damaging surge.

Digressing for a moment, putting 300 or 400 pounds of water (at about 8.34 pounds per gallon) in a tank of any type that's high up in the eyes of the boat is a bad idea from a boat performance standpoint. Extra tankage ideally should be located low and near the center of the boat, but if this were an ideal world, the damn boat would have enough water storage to begin with! Besides, if the tank replaces 250 pounds of tools or stores, how much effect is it really going to have? Put extra tankage somewhere else if at all possible, but if under the V-berth is the only choice, strike a compromise by using the water from that tank first. Empty, a tank is the *best* thing to have in the bow,

Integral. An integral tank forward is often praised as also serving as a watertight compartment in the event of holing the bow. Maybe, but if you hit something hard enough to punch a hole in the hull, I wouldn't count too heavily on a tabbed bulkhead to remain attached. To even succeed as a water container, integral tanks located anywhere need to overcome three impediments. Because fiberglass hulls flex, tank "walls" must be strong and robustly attached or eventual leakage is certain, but a rigid bulkhead can create a hard spot that causes the hull to hinge rather than deflect evenly, potentially compromising the hull's integrity. The lighter the hull construction, the lower the potential for integral tankage.

The second problem is taste. A purpose-built fiberglass tank can be (almost) taste free, but the processes involved in hull layup do not anticipate using the interior surface of the hull to contain potable water. Even after it has cured for 20 years, polyester resin gives the water a bad taste. While it can be mitigated with filtration, I suspect that the taste is only symptomatic of an unhealthy level of toxic chemicals that water sloshing around in a fiberglass tank likely contains. Even if such suspicions prove baseless, integral tanks are definitely risky for the health of your boat. The 1988 hull blister study done by the University of Rhode Island concluded that allowing water to stand *inside* the hull will hasten laminate saturation, leading to serious and potentially disastrous blistering.

If you insist on integral tankage, the requirements are a stiff hull without current or past blisters, an epoxy barrier coat on all interior surfaces (including the hull) at least 20 mils thick using an epoxy resin suitable for use in potable water systems, and robust bulkhead and top attachment with care taken to extend and taper tabbing to the hull sufficiently to avoid the creation of hard spots. If plywood is used for bulkheads and/or baffles, it must be at least $1/2$ inch thick, and all exposed edges should be sealed with penetrating epoxy before the plywood is sheathed with fiberglass. The top should be tabbed in place on the inside of the tank, but this is usually not possible. Never attach the top with screws. The alternative is to seat the sealed and sheathed top on a continuous bead of thickened epoxy, then tab the complete circumference of the top on the outside to strengthen the joint. A generous inspection opening into every tank compartment is an essential feature.

Bladders. Flexible tanks have their uses, but because of motion they are always inferior to a rigid tank for internal water storage aboard a boat. They are difficult to restrain, impossible to clean, susceptible to chafe, and difficult to plumb. If you elect to install a flexible tank, separate it from all hard surfaces with carpet or foam, and be sure all hose connections can move with the tank without straining the fittings. Locate a flexible tank only where the eventual failure will not do damage to other components of the boat.

Fiberglass. It is possible to lay up a custom tank with fiberglass. Create a male mold by gluing together sheet Styrofoam into a rigid hollow box. Round all of the edges and wrap the mold in plastic film to give you a smooth surface. Give the plastic about six applications of potable-water-safe epoxy resin, then cover the entire mold with several layers of fiberglass cloth saturated in epoxy resin. The thickness of the layup depends on the size of the tank, but when you think it is thick enough, add two more laminates. This is a labor-intensive process made more complicated by the need to alternate sides during the layup. When the tank has cured fully, cut an access hole in the top and dig out the Styrofoam and plastic film. Install plastic through-hull fittings for vent, fill, and pickup, and a threaded deck plate over the access hole. Shazam—a seamless water tank to your exact specifications.

Most boatowners are likely to prefer that someone else make the tank so all the owner has to do is install it. There is much to recommend this course, but never forget that the very first measurement you must take is the *size of the companionway opening*. It is the height of folly to pay to have a custom tank constructed only to discover that it will not pass through the companionway—or

through some other access restriction. A to-scale Styrofoam mock-up is not overkill to make sure you can get the tank from the dock to its intended location. Removing the sliding hatch and perhaps framing trim can expand the size of the companionway opening, perhaps enough to make the difference.

Metal. Metal water tanks are commonly constructed of aluminum, which is too bad. A typical aluminum tank has a life expectancy of less than a decade, and for more than half of that time the tank will discharge corrosion into the plumbing system. Even a pristine aluminum tank imparts an off taste to stored water. Aluminum would seem to be better suited to fuel stowage because the petroleum coating inside should limit corrosion to primarily an exterior concern, but this ignores the problem of water in the fuel, which sits on the bottom of the tank. Indeed lots of old boats are fitted with aluminum fuel tanks, but because failures are depressingly common, aluminum is a questionable choice here as well.

Aluminum tanks must be mounted in such a way that the metal remains dry. That means the tank cannot sit on wood bearers or be foamed in place, a prohibition too many manufacturers seem to have ignored. The simple expedient of insuring that an aluminum tank sits on bearer pads of Delrin, nylon, or other nonabsorbent material will triple the life of the tank. New tanks should incorporate mounting flanges or tabs that totally eliminate tank-wall contact with bearers or straps. The other requirement is that the aluminum must *never* have direct contact with any type of copper alloy. Copper and aluminum in the presence of just the moisture in the air will result in rampant galvanic corrosion. Unthinkingly

Oh my! Measure the companionway opening and other potential access restrictions before ordering a custom-built tank.

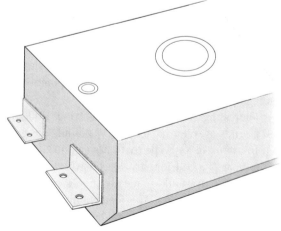

Welded mounting flanges that eliminate all contact of the tank wall with support surfaces will greatly extend the life of a metal tank.

threading a common brass fitting into an aluminum tank is a costly oversight. Use only aluminum or stainless steel fittings, never brass or bronze.

I strongly recommend against aluminum for water tanks. If you decide on an aluminum fuel tank, eschew the 0.090-inch plate the fabricator will suggest in favor of 0.125, which will triple the life expectancy of the tank. If you really want to do this just once, construct the tank from $1/4$-inch 5052, 5083, or 5086 aluminum alloy. Neither the cost nor the additional weight will be that significant, and if you take appropriate precautions with the mounting and connections, such a tank should last as long as the boat or you, whichever expires first.

Stainless steel is a much better choice for a metal water tank, but only if the proper alloy is used. Tanks made from common 304 alloy are no more durable than aluminum. If you are having a stainless steel tank fabricated, specify only 316L or 317L (or something even more corrosion resistant, such as a 6% molybdenum, if you are willing to pay the premium). Pay just as much attention to the reputation of your tank fabricator. Stainless steel tanks fail at the welds, so skill in construction is just as important as the correct alloy. Typical plate thickness is 12 gauge (0.105 inch), and because of the weight and cost, thicker material is usually not practical. As with aluminum, stainless steel tanks should have robust tabs and flanges that avoid tank-wall contact with bearers or straps. Such a tank, skillfully constructed and mounted well above the bilge, should last a very long time.

The original water tank in my old boat is Monel (a nickel alloy). Today Monel is prohibitively expensive but if your boat has a Monel tank, treasure it. Mine has delivered taste-free water for 40 years.

Molded plastic. The ideal tank material would not be subject to corrosion. It would be strong, light, taste free, and low cost. Polyethylene meets all of these requirements, making it the best choice for both water and holding tanks. PE tanks are constructed by putting linear polyethylene resin powder inside a closed mold, then rotating the mold in two directions while heating it to liquefy the resin. Imagine coating the inside of a sealed jar with a spoonful of paint and you get the idea. The result is a seamless tank of uniform wall thickness, determined by the amount of resin loaded into the mold. The great thing about PE tanks is that once the fabricator has a mold, turning out a tank is quite inexpensive. The bad thing is you need the mold, so constructing a PE tank unique to your requirements is not practical. However, PE tank manufacturers such as Kracor, Todd, and Inca have been

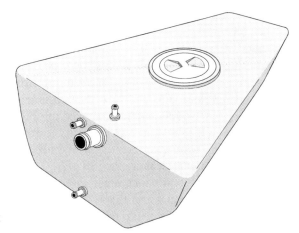

Molded polyethylene tanks are available in hundreds of shapes and sizes. This one is intended for bow installation.

molding PE tanks for boat manufacturers for decades, so they have vast selections of shapes and sizes. Some may actually be designed specifically to fit under the V-berth or beneath the settee of the boat you own. Otherwise you are almost certain to find a tank or tanks that will satisfy your needs (if not your vision) if you bring a modicum of flexibility about location and positioning to your search. Catalogs and websites provide tank dimensions for hundreds of designs.

PE fuel tanks are also available. In this case, the tanks are molded from cross-linked polyethylene, which chemically changes the material into a thermoset resin, meaning it will not soften if reheated. The more important benefit in this case, however, is that PEX is not attacked by petroleum. There is much to like about a PEX fuel tank. One oddity is that a PEX tank will increase in size by about 2% during the first few weeks it holds fuel. That means a 2-foot tank will "grow" about $1/2$ inch. You must either use nylon webbing hold-down straps—which will accommodate this expansion—or otherwise allow for the change. Never foam a PEX tank in place. Once the expansion runs its course, the tank will stabilize at its new size.

The absence of internal baffles is often cited as a drawback to PE tanks. In fact, molded-in baffles of a sort are incorporated into some designs, but if you need a large tank capacity, dividing it into two or more small tanks is nearly always better than a single baffled tank. Small tanks not only shorten the slosh distance, which is easier on the tank, but multiple tanks can make a leak or contamination an inconvenience rather than a catastrophe.

Tank Plumbing

Every tank requires three connections—the fill, the vent, and the outlet. A hose from the fill is usually led to a deck plate, although the fill plate is sometimes installed directly in the top of the tank to simplify the installation and avoid the risk of saltwater contamination. For the same reasons, it is almost always advisable to terminate water tank vent lines inside the boat. Run the line as high as possible (inside the chain locker or up into molded cockpit coamings are both good vent locations) and turn the end down (like a candy cane) to keep anything from falling into the hose. Unless the vent line is higher than the deck fill, it is *likely* to pour water every time you fill the tank, so don't terminate it above the SSB.

A hose from the tank outlet would normally lead to the freshwater pump, but if this is an additional tank the pump is already connected to the original. You could just tee into the hose between the original tank and the pump, but if you do that you give up the benefits of separate tanks. Configure both tanks with shutoff valves in the outlet hose to allow you to isolate one tank from the other and to draw water only from the tank of your choice. For a hose-plumbed system, a cheap and easy way to accomplish this is to connect both tank outlet hoses to a dual-hose adapter—a Y-shaped fitting for connecting two garden hoses to a single faucet. You want a *plastic* one with dual shutoff valves. Install the appropriate hose connectors—the kind you buy to repair a garden hose—onto the ends of the hoses. The hoses from the two tanks connect to the two valved branches, and the hose supplying the pump connects to the tail of the Y. By turning the two valves, you can supply the pump from one tank and isolate the other one from the system. A third tank can be plumbed in with another adapter.

For semirigid plumbing you can tee into the inlet line to the pump, then add shutoff valves between the tee and both tanks. Stackable valves allow the tee and both valves to be incorporated into what is essentially a single unit. If you have more than two tanks, a conveniently located manifold incorporating a labeled valve for each tank will simplify tank management.

MUNICIPAL SUPPLY

If you do not have pressure water aboard, you cannot tie into the municipal system because the water would flow through the pumps and out the spouts continuously, but if your onboard water system is pressurized, there is no reason that you cannot use city water pressure when you are tied to the dock. More than one manufacturer offers special deck fittings (you will find them at RV supply stores also) that contain a regulator that drops the high municipal pressure to a more manageable 40 psi. Regulators are also available that simply screw onto the faucet before the hose is attached, but you still need a threaded inlet fitting plumbed into your water delivery system so you can attach the dock hose.

You connect shore water into your system by connecting a hose or PE tube from the inlet fitting to a tee connector in the outlet line from your pump. In addition to a regulator, you are also going to need at least one separate check valve, which you will install between the tee connector and the pump to make sure the pressurized water cannot flow back through a leaky valve, damaging the pump or overflowing your tanks. If you have an accumulator tank, it is not necessary for it to be in the system when you are on shore pressure, so the tee connector and the check valve should be on the faucet side of the accumulator. If the regulator does not have a built-in check valve, you will need one at the inlet fitting to allow you to disconnect the hose without being sprayed by the pressure in the system.

It is risky to leave your boat unattended when it's connected to a municipal water supply. You can imagine what happens if a hose blows off a fitting. Turning off the dock faucet is all that is required, but doing this repeatedly becomes a chore if you are living aboard. One alternative is to install a water timer at the faucet. Made to turn off sprinklers, this inexpensive gizmo turns off the water after so many gallons (adjustable) have passed through it, limiting the amount of water that will flow into your boat in the event of a hose failure.

A simple way of plumbing multiple water tanks.

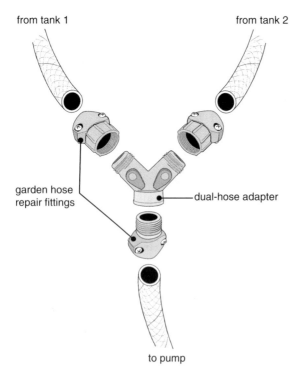

from tank 1

from tank 2

garden hose repair fittings

dual-hose adapter

to pump

SEACOCKS AND THROUGH-HULLS

Seacocks and through-hull fittings have to be considered together. Every through-hull fitting installed below the waterline needs a seacock attached to it. Tens of thousands of boats have been delivered without regard to this most basic tenet of safety, but the guy who made the decision to omit the seacocks from your boat was concerned about his ass, not yours. If a previous owner has not already equipped every through-hull with a seacock, doing so should be one of your top priorities.

Seacock Selection

Tapered-plug and other cylindrical seacock designs have all but disappeared in favor of the ball valve. This is a good thing because, unlike maintenance-intensive tapered-plug seacocks, ball valves require zero maintenance other than monthly exercise and annual lubrication.

Unfortunately gate valves have not yet been relegated to a historical footnote. Gate valves are *not* seacocks and despite being installed by innumerable boat manufacturers because they are cheap, they are patently unsafe for keeping the ocean out of your boat. The dangers are numerous, beginning with the fact that the valve gives no visual indication of whether it is open or closed. Even cranking the handle clockwise (righty-tighty) until it stops does not insure that the valve is closed. It will still be open if a bit of debris has found its way under the gate, so "closing" a gate valve when you leave the boat fails to provide the measure of security you may be expecting. Most gate valves are also brass (sometimes mixed with steel) and quickly corrode in seawater. They may look bright and new, but the corrosion is internal and sinister. When you *need* to close the valve, you are likely to discover that the threaded shaft that raises and lowers the gate has dissolved and the valve is useless. Lastly, gate valves are invariably mounted by simply threading them onto the through-hull fitting. Aside from the lack of a mounting flange—essential to prevent side loading from breaking the not-very-strong through-hull—common gate valves nearly always have tapered threads, whereas through-hulls have straight threads. That means the two will thread together only about three turns before jamming. Just two or three threads standing between your boat and the bottom of the ocean? Jeepers!

A seacock is everything a gate valve isn't. The position of the handle tells you instantly whether the seacock is open or closed. If trash in the valve prevents its closing, you will know immediately because the handle will not move to the closed position. Seacocks are bronze or glass-reinforced plastic (Marelon)—never brass—so corrosion is only a modest concern or none at all. The threads in the bottom of a seacock match those around a through-hull fitting, and seacocks have a flange that allows them to be bolted to the hull, making through-hull failure both unlikely and inconsequential.

The longevity of bronze means a lot of old boats still have tapered-plug seacocks threaded onto their through-hull fittings. As durable as they are, without proper maintenance these valves eventually seize, leaving you no better off than if they weren't there at all. Tapered-plug seacocks should be completely dismantled and serviced at least once a year. If the valve is to seal properly, it must be *lapped* by smearing the plug and the seat with (automotive) valve-grinding compound and turning them against each other until they fit perfectly. Be sure to thoroughly remove all the grinding paste before reassembly.

With age, corrosion takes its toll on the tapered plug, causing it to become wasp-waisted around the hole. When this happens, lapping will not correct it and the valve will no longer completely stem the flow of water in the closed position. Less dramatic imperfections can be accommodated by packing the valve with waterproof grease, but if the seacock is turned often, the grease is displaced and water soon begins to seep between the plug and the body of the seacock. Crank the nut that holds the tapered plug in the valve tight enough to stop the leak and the valve becomes impossible to open and close. Loosen the nut and water trickles down the hull. Even adjusted "just right," opening and closing the valve a few times soon gets it out of adjustment, but if you don't operate it regularly, it seizes and cannot be turned at all when the need arises. As long as tapered plugs on your old boat remain functional and watertight, just maintain them, but when you tire of trickles, green paste on the valves, and soggy backing rings, replace them with ball-valve seacocks.

On an old boat you might also find a type of bronze seacock with the flow controlled by the 90-degree rotation of a cylindrical neoprene plug rather than a tapered bronze one. This type of seacock has a threaded T-bar located opposite the handle. Tightening the T-bar pushes against a metal disk at one end of the rubber cylinder, forcing it to swell in the middle and creating a very effective seal. Before the seacock can be opened or closed, the T-bar must be unscrewed several turns to release pressure on the neoprene plug. I have always found this type of seacock less prone to leaking or weeping, and the only maintenance it requires is cleaning and greasing during haulout and occasionally oiling the threads of the

T-bar. However, rubber-plug seacocks are not recommended for sink or head discharge lines because certain chemicals attack the rubber, causing the plug to swell permanently and making it difficult or impossible to turn the valve.

The best seacocks, by a wide margin, are ball valves. The port, rather than being through a cylindrical rubber or tapered bronze plug, passes through a ball sandwiched between two circular seats. Bronze ball–type seacocks have a ball of hard chrome-plated bronze or stainless steel rotating in Teflon seals. Plastic ball-valve seacocks are manufactured from Marelon, a remarkably tough and durable fiber-reinforced nylon. High-quality ball-valve seacocks are virtually maintenance free, requiring only a light application of Teflon grease to the ball annually to keep them turning easily.

Today the primary question when selecting a seacock is, bronze or plastic? Plastic is better. The supposed advantages of a bronze valve is that it won't melt in a fire and it is stronger. I guess the benefit of a fireproof valve installed in a plastic boat eludes me, and as for strength, I have never seen a report of a single Marelon seacock failure other than broken handles on the smallest valves (which will not happen if you exercise the seacock). The advantage of plastic is that it is immune to corrosion. This is a *real* advantage. Beginning with my very first seacock-equipped boat (a long time ago), I have never seen a 12-month period when all installed bronze seacocks were simultaneously easy to operate, watertight, and corrosion free. All of them needed to be dismantled at every haulout. "Time to replace?" was a perennial question. When I did replace them, I installed Marelon seacocks and the change was dramatic. In more than 20 years these valves have never failed to operate smoothly, are so watertight that I periodically need to dust them, require no maintenance other than a dab of Teflon grease at haulout, and are not dissolving in seawater nor attracting stray currents from marina neighbors. To be fair, the functional differences were due to changing from tapered-plug to ball-valve seacocks, but only the plastic variety will relieve you of all seacock-related concerns.

This is not an indictment of bronze seacocks. If you feel more comfortable with bronze, that is what you should use. Just don't let anyone convince you that Marelon is inferior. Among a long list of boatbuilders installing Marelon seacocks are Hinckley and Morris, whose clients presumably both prefer and can afford the best.

Installation

A tee (or Y) connection to an existing seawater inlet or discharge line is almost always preferable to a new through-hull opening. Most old boats already have far too many holes in the hull. One exception to this is a watermaker inlet, which probably should not share a through-hull, but even here perhaps you

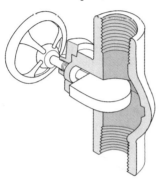

Gate valve—leave this one ashore.

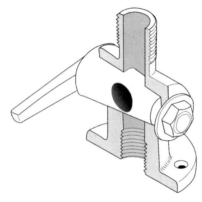

Bronze tapered plug.

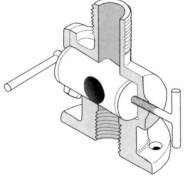

Cylindrical rubber plug.

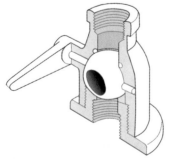

Marelon ball valve.

Seacocks.

can double up some other through-hull to make a dedicated one available for the watermaker. When an additional through-hull is your only practical solution, its installation differs from replacement only in the need to drill a hole in the hull. If the fitting will be below or even near the waterline, the boat must be out of the water.

Position the new through-hull where you will have ready access to the seacock. Consider the location carefully, checking inside that there will be ample room to throw the handle and that the attached hose will not obstruct access to space or equipment. Check outside that the new fitting will not set up turbulence in front of your depth sounder or speed-log impeller.

When you are satisfied with the location, drill a small centered pilot hole from inside the hull and check to confirm that the outside location is where you expect it to be. If the hull has only a small amount of curvature here you can use a plywood ring, detailed later in this section, to give the seacock a flat mounting base and to spread the load, but if there is a lot of curvature, you might want to cast the mounting pad with epoxy putty. This will be easier to do before you saw the hole for the through-hull. Plug the pilot hole with a bit of matchstick, then cut a ring from an empty plastic soda bottle. Trim it to seat on the hull around the pilot hole, then tape or hot-glue the ring in place. Thicken epoxy resin to a peanut-butter consistency with glass fibers or colloidal silica, and fill the inside of the plastic ring at least enough to create a flat surface—thicker if you want the pad to replace the wood ring. After the epoxy cures, remove the plastic ring and block sand the surface flat if necessary. Redrill the pilot hole from outside the hull.

Load your drill with a holesaw of the appropriate size for the through-hull fitting you will be installing and start the hole from outside the hull, but do not try to cut it all the way through the hull from outside. When the pilot drill in the center of the holesaw penetrates the hull, take your drill aboard and finish the hole from the inside. Clean up the edges of the hole with emery cloth.

If the hull is cored rather than solid laminate, you will have to dig out the core around the hole. The bolts that hold the seacock flange must not pass through core, so the hollow you create must be at least as large as the flange of the seacock you are installing. With all the core material removed and both skins scuffed on the inside with coarse sandpaper, wet the exposed core with epoxy resin to seal it, then thicken the remaining epoxy to peanut-butter consistency and completely fill the hollow area. If the core was so

thick that the hollow is large, you will need to do the filling in modest batches to prevent the epoxy from overheating. The epoxy provides a solid base for the through-hull and, in the event of sealant failure, prevents water from reaching the core material. Allow the epoxy to harden fully before proceeding.

If you are replacing an existing fitting, the hole is already there, but emptying it of the old through-hull can be something of a challenge. Start by removing the nuts on the bolts through the mounting flange, and use a hammer and a punch to drive out the bolts. If you are dealing with a gate valve, it will not have a flange, but the through-hull will be secured with a large ring nut. With the aid of a pipe wrench, unscrew the seacock or the gate valve and the ring nut from the through-hull. A through-hull installed with polyurethane sealant probably will not turn with the valve or the nut and is likely to prove just as recalcitrant when you try to push or pound it out of the hull. Don't get a bigger hammer. The solution is to *pull* the through-hull out. Get your hands on a $^3/_8$- or $^1/_2$-inch bolt about 4 inches longer than the through-hull. You will also need a nut to fit this bolt and a pair of washers too big to pass through the fitting. Slide one of the washers onto the bolt, and from inside the boat, pass the bolt through the fitting, seating the washer flat on the fitting. Outside the hull, pass the bolt through a hole drilled in a short length of 2 × 4, and fit the second washer and the nut. Now support the length of wood on both sides of the fitting with a couple of wooden blocks. As you tighten the nut, the bolt will pull the fitting from the hull. If the fitting does pull out immediately, crank down on the nut, then give it some time for the sealant to "tire." When you have the old through-hull out, scrape away all sealant residue with a razor knife. Wipe the area around the hole—both inside

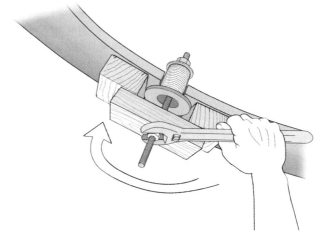

Use a long bolt or threaded rod to pull a through-hull fitting from the hull.

and outside the hull—with toluene or acetone. Make sure the hole does not expose core material.

Once the hole is prepared, the remaining steps are identical for installing a new through-hull or replacing an old one. With a saber saw, cut a circle of $^3/_4$-inch plywood 2 or 3 inches larger than the flange of the seacock, and use your holesaw to cut out the center of this circle. This ring will spread the compression load and provide a flat surface for the seacock flange. Use a rasp or sander to shape the bottom of the ring to sit flat against the hull. Mark it so you will be able to orient it correctly later. If you have already cast a substantial flat mounting pad, you can omit the plywood ring.

Next dry-fit the parts. From outside the hull, insert the new through-hull fitting. Inside, slip the wooden ring in place and thread the seacock onto the through-hull. Bronze and Marelon have differing coefficients of expansion, so it is never a good idea to install a Marelon seacock on a bronze through-hull or vice versa. Also be aware that most of the plastic through-hull fittings you will find displayed at your local chandlery are *not* suitable for below-the-waterline use. Install only Marelon (or bronze) through-hull fittings below the waterline.

Joining through-hull and seacock is a two-person job. Turning the through-hull fitting requires some type of tool that will grip or wedge against the pair of "ears" inside the fitting. Boatyards often have a step wrench—a kind of stepped cone with notches that fits a range of through-hull fittings—they will lend you. Some rely on a slightly wedge-shaped piece of steel that jams against the ears. A short length of hardwood with a width equal to the through-hull diameter can do the job. If you would like to have a through-hull wrench in your toolbox, buy a cheap socket (wrench) that will just slip into the through-hull, and grind notches on opposite sides that the ears can slide into.

With the wooden ring in place (if you are using one), tighten the through-hull into the seacock. If both the seacock and the through-hull get tight against the hull, take them apart again, counting the turns. If they separate in less than five full turns, you will need to make a thinner ring so that at least five full threads of the through-hull are inside the seacock.

Through-hull fittings are nearly always too long rather than too short, so it is more likely that the through-hull will bottom out inside the seacock before either is snug against the hull. While your assistant pushes the seacock and ring tight against the hull, measure the space between the hull and the flange of the through-hull. Disassemble everything and shorten the through-hull by a thread width or so more than this measurement. Put it all back together and confirm that you can now snug both components against the hull.

Rotate the seacock to the position you want, making sure you can throw the lever without risking tetanus. If the seacock has a drain plug, try to orient it on the low side of the valve. If you will be putting in a 90-degree tailpiece, now is the time to install it, at least temporarily, on the seacock. Because the threads are tapered, it can be less than a full turn between loose enough to leak and as tight as it will go, which can leave you with an awkward lead. Finding out now where the tailpiece is going to point relative to the seacock will allow you to strike a compromise by turning the seacock. Once you are satisfied with the position, drill the mounting holes through the hull from inside the boat, using the holes in the mounting flange as a drill guide. A long bit is typically required. If the flange is not predrilled, drill three evenly spaced holes through the flange and the hull. From outside the hull, countersink the three holes and insert the flathead mounting bolts, checking that they are the correct length and that the heads will be flush. For securing a plastic seacock, you can use either stainless steel or bronze bolts, but if the seacock is bronze, the mounting bolts must also be bronze. When you are satisfied with the length and fit of the bolts, remove them and unscrew the through-hull from the seacock.

Despite my own dusty seacocks, I have seen dozens of backer blocks turn to the consistency of damp toilet tissue from the constant weeping of a through-hull fitting. Avoid this by taking the time to give the plywood ring three coats of unthickened epoxy. If you are coating the ring one side at a time, you can give the edges—the place where the plywood is most vulnerable—six coats. You should enlarge the center hole slightly before you start so the epoxy will not reduce the diameter enough to inhibit passage of the through-hull.

Reassemble the seacock and through-hull with the now-sealed ring. Put a bead of polyurethane sealant just below the heads of the mounting bolts and install them, using a washer under each nut on the seacock flange. Snug the nuts. Back the through-hull completely out, and wipe inside and around the hole one more time with acetone. Wrap the threads that will be inside the seacock with Teflon tape or coat them with Teflon thread sealant. Do not use polyurethane here or

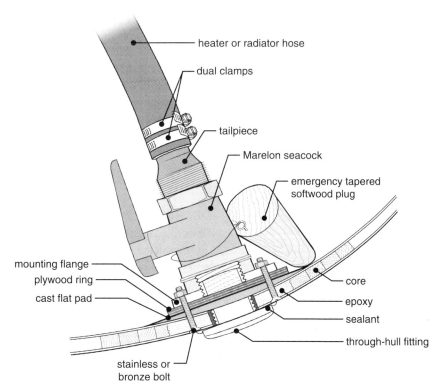

heater or radiator hose

dual clamps

tailpiece

Marelon seacock

emergency tapered
softwood plug

mounting flange

plywood ring

cast flat pad

core

epoxy

sealant

through-hull fitting

stainless or
bronze bolt

you will rue the day if (if you are familiar with Murphy, that means *when*) you have to remove this seacock. You do, however, want a heavy bead of polyurethane sealant on the other end of the through-hull—completely around the shoulder and up a couple of threads. Screw the through-hull back into the seacock and tighten it until it is snug against the hull and sealant squeezes out all around the head of the through-hull. Pick up and fair the squeeze-out around the fitting. Also use some of the excess to fair over the heads of the screws.

All that remains to put your new seacock into service is to wrap the tailpiece threads with Teflon tape and fit (or refit) it to the valve. Slide on the hose and secure it with tandem clamps. There is, by the way, no ABYC requirement for dual-hose clamps, but you should do it anyway if the hose barb is long enough simply because it is prudent.

On the subject of prudence, it is worthy of mention here that ABYC standards no longer require seacocks to be independently bolted to the hull. My home state has also repealed the requirement for motorcycle helmets, but that doesn't make riding without one any less risky or wearing one any less sensible. Allow me to relate my defining experience with a seacock simply threaded onto the through-hull. This was the raw-water inlet for the engine, a $^3/_4$-inch bronze seacock on a bronze through-hull. Impeller failure and a dying breeze mandated an offshore pump repair, but when I tried to close the barely

accessible seacock, it wouldn't budge. Undaunted, I braced my feet and gave the stubborn lever a mighty tug. Instantly I found myself lying on the cabin sole, seacock in hand, looking between my knees at a foot-high column of water spouting through the hull and into the engine room. Unseen corrosion inside the through-hull had severely weakened it. The ABYC standard is predicated on the strength of a new through-hull, but as the whole boat ages, so do the parts. From my reclining vantage point the lowering sun was refracted by the clear water outside the hull, tinting the unstemmed flow a rainbow of colors, but my admiration was fleeting. Diving back into the engine room, I held out the ocean with my bare hand.

Which brings me to the final step. A seacock installation is not complete until you have a tapered softwood plug attached to it with a piece of light twine. Imagine if the little Dutch boy had whipped out a mallet and a wooden plug from his hip pocket and tapped the plug into that hole. It would have ruined a good story but who can doubt that the Dutch boy would have been a lot happier? It's not easy to feel terribly smug when it is your thumb in the dike, particularly when you are responsible for the hole . . . but it's possible. In my situation, tied to the seacock still attached to the intake hose was the appropriate wooden plug. The necessary hammer to tap it into place was close at hand. Hardly enough water came in to activate the automatic bilge pump.

Good outcome notwithstanding, that seacock and all others on my boat are now bolted to the hull, and yours should be too.

SEAWATER GALLEY PUMP

Whether your water delivery is manual or pressurized, a seawater pump at the galley sink can reduce your freshwater consumption dramatically. Such a pump might have limited value when your boat is tied to a dock in the East River, but anywhere the water is pure enough to swim in, it can be used for dishwashing as well. Dishwashing in seawater not only saves the fresh water you would otherwise use, but it allows you to use as much water as you please.

The choice of pumps is up to you. I prefer the foot pump, but you can install an electric pump just as easily as a manual one as long as you select one that specifies that it can be used in a saltwater system. Pressurized seawater delivery has none of the drawbacks of pressurized fresh water since conservation is not a concern. Power consumption could be a consideration if your battery capacity is modest. You will need a separate faucet or spout at the sink.

If you can, avoid installing a new through-hull fitting to supply seawater to the galley. You should be able to share an existing through-hull by teeing into the attached hose. Because of the potential consequences of the engine raw-water pump sucking air, I recommend against sharing the raw-water inlet for the engine. You also should not tee into any discharge line—the sink drain, for example—although this does not absolutely rule out cockpit or deck drain lines if no other source is

available. If you already have or plan to equip your boat with a deck-wash pump, you can draw galley water from the input side of this system. Or you can tee into the outlet hose, letting this pump do double duty.

Whether you share an existing through-hull fitting or install a new one, it should be on the opposite side of the keel or at least well forward of any head discharge fitting. Plumb a strainer into the pump's supply line to prevent grass and other debris from reaching the pump. Use only opaque heater hose, never clear vinyl for seawater plumbing.

DECK-WASH PUMPS

Few old-boat enhancements deliver a better return on investment than a deck-wash pump. Blasting mud out of your anchor chain before it comes aboard is way better than washing down the deck with buckets of water, not to mention easier on your back. The cost of an adequate deck-wash pump is so low—around $100—that I am baffled when I see owners of otherwise well-equipped boats lifting buckets to sluice down the decks.

The main component is either a positive-displacement diaphragm pump or a flexible impeller or rigid vane pump rated for saltwater use. Most marine pump manufacturers offer pumps intended for deck-wash use. Because these pumps are reliable and their function is not critical, the mounting location need not be particularly accessible, allowing installation in an otherwise wasted or at least inconvenient space. They may even be fastened vertically to a bulkhead. Pumps push better than they pull so the closer the pump is to the through-hull, the better.

Plumb galley saltwater and deck-wash pumps to the same through-hull inlet fitting.

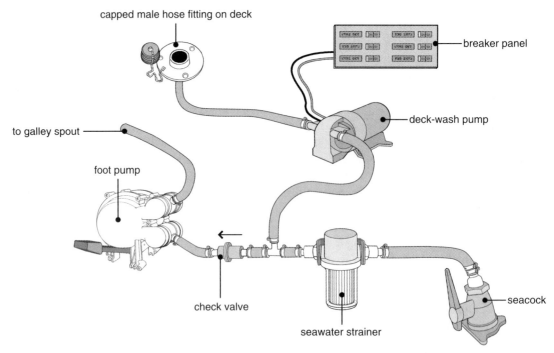

capped male hose fitting on deck

breaker panel

deck-wash pump

to galley spout

foot pump

check valve

seawater strainer

seacock

If it must be remote, mount it below the waterline. If you want your new pump to enjoy a long, fruitful life, you must have a strainer between the pump and the seacock. The strainer will need to be accessible for occasional cleaning. Remember to use wire-reinforced hose on the suction side of the pump.

The deck-wash pump can share a through-hull with the galley pump, the head inlet, or any other inlet except the engine intake. A check valve in the other line sharing the through-hull can avoid prime problems. For around $5, most home supply stores sell small threaded check valves that are adaptable to hose connections with a pair of pipe-to-hose adapters.

The deck fitting at the bow should be a capped male hose connector. There is no need for a line-snagging toe-stubbing spigot at the bow because a short hose is normally left attached with flow controlled by a nozzle. The integral pressure switch controls the pump, but switching it off when it's not in use is a good precaution.

If you are so inclined, there is no reason that you cannot plumb more than one deck fitting from the same pump. A tee connector on the output side, a run of hose, an additional deck fitting, and a few hose clamps are all you require. An outlet aft can be convenient for cockpit showering or fish cleaning.

Electrical connections are straightforward, but resist the temptation to pick up the power for the pump from the nearest pair of wires. A washdown pump can draw 10 amps or more, which can dangerously overload a lighting circuit. The safest course is a dedicated circuit with a new fuse or breaker in the main electrical panel.

A powerful deck-wash pump has added value in that in an emergency it could be pressed into service as a bilge pump. With a little ingenuity, it can even get you home when the raw-water pump on your engine fails.

WATERMAKERS

Watermakers draw in seawater and put out fresh water and brine, so they need a seawater connection and at least two output connections. However, any watermaker you purchase will come with a thick installation manual, so plumbing guidance from me is likely to be superfluous. What I can help you with is sorting out reality from delusion.

Reality number one is that few boats have any difficulty carrying ample drinking water, so the plentiful supply a watermaker promises is to provide more fresh water for washing (as opposed to seawater washing). This is important because it places watermakers squarely in the category of convenient rather than essential for all but the relatively few voyagers cruising far off the beaten path. If you are outfitting your old boat for coastal or Caribbean basin cruising, you do not *need* a watermaker.

Reality number two is that a watermaker aboard is not the same as "running" water. Supply interruptions are likely to be frequent and prolonged. This is because you cannot (or will not, after pricing prefilters) operate a watermaker in many of the most frequented anchorages and harbors. If you spend a storm season somewhere safe, expect your watermaker to be idle the entire time. This will relegate your water management to some combination of collecting, buying, storing, and conserving.

Reality number three is that as convenient as lots of water is, making it is inconvenient. Watermakers should be run daily and *must* be run weekly. That may not sound onerous until your eighth day in a secure harbor when your options become pick up the anchor and go find cleaner water or pickle the membrane—which you will later have to "unpickle." Not install-and-forget systems, watermakers require constant monitoring and regular maintenance. A functioning watermaker is not unlike a pet, making regular and sometimes unexpected demands that can dictate your daily schedule and restrict your flexibility. A nonfunctioning watermaker is wasted money.

Reality number four is that converting seawater to fresh water on a small scale is *really* expensive. If you spend $4,000 for a watermaker and another grand in fuel and engine wear or for solar panels or a wind generator to power it, your water cost for your first year of cruising will be $14 *per day*. That is *every* day, whether you make water or not. Higher-capacity watermakers lower the per-gallon cost but not the daily cost. Spend $7,000 on the watermaker and $2,000 to power it, and your first-year daily water cost is $25. Even after 5 years, when you factor in essential maintenance costs, the cost remains at least $6 per day, and closer to $9 if you have been supplying the power by running your engine. Contrast that with water normally available for free in the States or for pennies in most countries catering to cruisers. Or consider that in a half hour of rainfall in the tropics enough "distilled" water will run off the deck of your boat to fill your tanks to capacity. All you have to do is catch it, which on some boats can be as simple as plugging the scuppers and opening the on-deck fill cap. Watermakers are a wonderful enhancement for boats headed where water supplies are unsafe or water is unavailable, but a budget-minded cruiser with a more modest itinerary should have a difficult time justifying this expenditure.

If these realities do not dissuade you, here are some essentials for watermaker plumbing. So called reverse osmosis (RO) watermakers purify seawater by pushing it through a porous membrane where the microscopic pores are large enough to pass water molecules but too fine to pass most minerals, particularly salt. This membrane material is expensive and easily damaged by chlorine or oil, so a watermaker should never share a through-hull with a sink drain. You can share an intake through-hull, but only one that's not at risk of ingesting sink, head, or engine discharge. A forward location is normally better, with the intake as deep as possible to avoid oil contamination—normally confined to the surface.

On this subject you should be aware that the watermaker is taking in water flowing across the bottom of your boat, probably painted with the most toxic paint the law allows. There can be little doubt that some of this toxin finds its way into the intake (also painted, no doubt), particularly if you are using a soft paint. I know of no science that suggests this is a serious health risk, but the membrane does not remove all chemical contaminants. I mention this here mostly for those who view rain catchment suspiciously because of the possibility of bird droppings contaminating the catchment surface.

Membranes and high-pressure pumps are expensive, filters (relatively) cheap, so your installation should insure complete filtration. This typically requires five stages: a strainer, followed by an oil separator, followed by a cleanable 100-micron "critter" filter, followed by a 25- or 30-micron filter, followed by a 5-micron filter. Pulling the water through all these filters is an

Representative watermaker plumbing.

inefficient and life-shortening use of your expensive high-pressure pump, so include a boost pump—usually located just downstream of the initial strainer—to push the water through the various filters.

On the output side you will need an above-the-waterline through-hull fitting for discharging the brine. The least complicated plumbing of the freshwater side necessitates a two-way valve that allows the initial output to be sent to a spout over a sink for testing and discarding. When the level of total dissolved solids (TDS) in the water flowing from this spout drops below 500 parts per million, measured by a TDS meter, the output is redirected to a storage tank. Be very cautious about sharing your RO water storage with water you take aboard from shore, because if you use this water to flush the watermaker, even very low levels of chlorine will destroy the watermaker's membrane.

Powerboats are most often fitted with chassis-mounted units with all components in a housing, but these sea chest–size units are about as easy to accommodate as a hard suitcase on a typical sailboat. Not surprisingly, most sailors install modular watermakers, allowing the various components to be spread out and tucked into available nooks. However, do not make access too difficult. Watermakers operate at pressures above 800 psi—20 times higher than your galley water—so there is no such thing as a small leak. Also be aware of reality number five, that the thumpa-thumpa-thumpa of a watermaker pump will

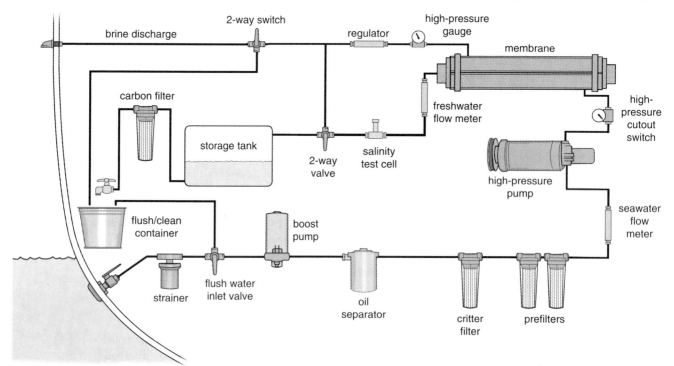

eventually disturb your peace, so try to locate the pump away from your primary living area.

Prefilters need to be easily accessible for frequent changing. Gauges are essential for monitoring the process and should include a pressure gauge to monitor the final prefilter (or a vacuum gauge if you do not have a boost pump), a high-pressure gauge monitoring watermaker pressure, and a freshwater flow meter. You will also need to configure and *clearly label* valve manifolds that will allow water-quality testing, flushing, pickling, etc.

A plentiful water supply aboard can indeed be a joy, but achieving that with an onboard watermaker, at least in the short term, is likely to be expensive. Watermakers also do not enjoy an unsullied reputation for trouble-free operation, but sound plumbing should enhance your experience.

HEADS

If your old boat is old enough, it was originally equipped with a manual head that discharged directly overboard. Plumbing was limited to connecting the toilet's inlet to a $^3/_4$-inch seacock and the outlet to a $1^1/_2$-inch seacock.

THE STRAIGHT POOP

How you plumb your toilet is likely to be a matter of conscience. Federal law has forbidden overboard discharge in coastal waters since 1972, yet many (perhaps most) recreational boats still pump raw sewage overboard. It is our dirty little secret. Given our vested interest in clean water, how can we publicly support clean water while secretly pumping our heads overboard?

Let's put aside political correctness and face the truth. Who honestly believes that storing excrement under your bunk is a good idea? Holding tanks stink, leak, and sometimes blow. Handling a pumpout hose is not just unpleasant, it is a clear and present health hazard. From the perspective of boat and crew, disposing of excrement immediately is simply the most sanitary way of dealing with it.

It seems to me that the fundamental question is, is pooping in the ocean a villainous act? To answer that, we need to understand the impact of human waste on water quality. I believe it is possible to draw a valid parallel with another natural bodily function—breathing. Every time you exhale, you are "polluting" the air with carbon dioxide. Scientists believe that rising temperatures worldwide are due to excessive amounts of carbon dioxide in the atmosphere. It is called global warming, and scientists in increasing numbers warn that the long-term effects will be catastrophic.

Here is the point: when you exhale, *you are contributing to global warming.* Of course, your car puts a million times more carbon dioxide into the air than you do, but it is undeniably true that your breathing contributes to air pollution. Or does it? If we stopped driving internal-combustion cars, stopped burning fossil fuels, stopped slash-and-burn deforestation, would the carbon dioxide we each exhale be pollution or merely a part of the natural equation of life on earth?

W. C. Fields decried drinking water because "fish [procreate] in it." They also [defecate] in it. Pooping in the water may be aesthetically offensive, but it isn't polluting unless it's harmful. There has never been any evidence linking fecal water contamination to overboard discharge except when the boats are densely packed in enclosed waters. The same dynamic is at play with air quality in a crowded room, but step outside and you can breathe in the same spot for 100 years without degrading the air around you.

Am I advocating overboard discharge? Most of the time it is the only reasonable way for the small boat to deal with excrement, and most of the time direct discharge represents the least risk to both crew and environment. If your boat has sufficient electrical power, an onboard treatment system might be better for the environment, but not one that uses formaldehyde or chlorine. The residue of these sanitizing agents is, according to scientific study, more harmful to marine life than the raw sewage.

The real sources of fecal water pollution are municipal sewage systems and agricultural runoff. In a seemingly endless repetition of "accidents," municipalities pump *hundreds of millions of gallons* of raw sewage into the waters every year. The impact of agricultural runoff—including the fertilizer you may use on your lawn—is greater still. Agreeing that flushing your head contributes to the problem is no different than saying that breathing contributes to bad air. You should quit making that concession. Allowing boat toilets to be painted as contributors to water pollution only deflects attention from the real problems. Overboard discharge may be a crime against the state, but it is not a crime against nature. I don't think there is any question that conscientious direct discharge—one flush at a time—is better for the planet than disposing of 30 gallons of concentrate. Conscientious discharge means you never discharge your head in an enclosed basin, into sluggish waters, or when another boat is close enough to hear you flush.

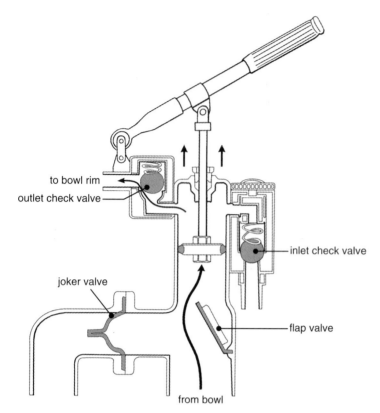

to bowl rim

outlet check valve

inlet check valve

joker valve

flap valve

from bowl

The upstroke of the piston draws sewage from the bowl past the flap valve and into the lower chamber of the pump. Simultaneously clean flush water in the upper chamber is expelled through an outlet check valve and into the bowl via the bowl rim.

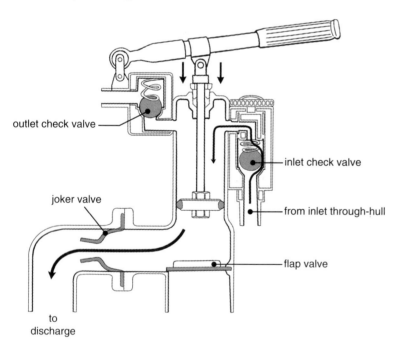

outlet check valve

inlet check valve

joker valve

from inlet through-hull

flap valve

to discharge

The downstroke forces the sewage through the joker valve and into the discharge hose. It also draws a fresh charge of flush water into the upper pump chamber through the inlet check valve.

Typical toilet pump operation.

Fortunately toilet plumbing is not as arbitrary as toilet politics. Most toilets installed aboard American boats use a double-action piston pump operated with a handle or lever attached directly to the pump rod. A manual inlet valve on the toilet allows the operator to stop the inlet flow. With the valve open, the first upward stroke of the pump draws sewage from the bowl through a flap-check valve and into the chamber below the piston. The first downward stroke pushes the sewage out of the lower chamber through a duckbill-style check valve called a joker and into the discharge hose. The same downward stroke draws water from the inlet hose through a flap or ball-check valve and into the chamber above the piston. The next upward stroke expels that charge of water through a second check valve and into the bowl via a pattern of holes under the bowl rim, at the same time again drawing sewage from the bowl. After a sufficient number of strokes to empty and rinse the bowl and the discharge hose, the operator closes the inlet valve. Operating the pump with the valve closed pumps the bowl dry.

INLET

Inlet plumbing is the same for nearly all toilet configurations. Typically manufacturers locate both the inlet and the discharge fittings in or near the head compartment. While this no doubt saves a few bucks on hose cost, you do not need to be a deep thinker to see that when plumbing a toilet where inlet and discharge happen simultaneously, putting the inlet fitting close to the discharge fitting is a bad idea. The inlet through-hull should *at least* be well forward of the discharge through-hull. The configuration I favor is to abandon the original head inlet (meaning remove and close the hole) and plumb the head to the galley sink drain through-hull if it is on the opposite side of the hull. This eliminates one hole in the hull, and by closing the seacock you can regularly flush dishwater or other discarded fresh water through the toilet, which works wonders for keeping the head functioning trouble free. This configuration has another benefit. If you plumb your toilet correctly you will have no odor from effluent but the head will still develop a low-tide smell from the flush water due to the accumulation of dying sea life in the inlet hose. The drain connection makes it easy to fill the inlet hose with white vinegar or mildly chlorinated fresh water, which solves this problem.

Whether the head inlet is plumbed to a drain or an inlet through-hull, an easily serviceable strainer must be plumbed into the line as close to the through-hull as is practical. The absence of a strainer is the primary cause of bad-smelling head compartments.

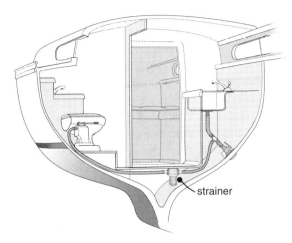

Sharing a seacock with the galley drain allows for frequent convenient freshwater rinses of the toilet with waste water. A strainer prevents vegetation from reaching the bowl rim.

The inlet draws in seaweed and other biological detritus, which eventually becomes foul-smelling muck lodged in the under-rim passage of the bowl. A strainer prevents this.

Heads in sailboats are normally located below the waterline. When the ocean is higher than the head and you connect the two with a hose, guess which way the water flows? Even a loop above the waterline won't stop the flow once it starts unless it has a siphon break—a one-way valve that lets air into the line. Such vented loops work perfectly on discharge hoses, but in an intake hose, the suction of the pump opens the valve, decreasing the volume of water the pump draws with each stroke. While a prudent precaution, a vented loop in the intake line is a pain.

There is less danger of flooding from the inlet side because the toilet has an inlet valve that positively shuts off the flow, but its reliability depends on every user remembering to close that valve after flushing. In heads with ball-style check valves, gravity-fed water may not push hard enough to overcome the spring that holds the ball closed, preventing or at least severely limiting intake leakage. A sometimes easy and always foolproof solution is to raise the toilet to a position that places the rim above the waterline. This will preclude inlet siphoning and contain any siphoning that might occur on the discharge side. If this is not practical, remove the short hose that connects the pump outlet to the bowl and replumb this flow through a vented loop located well above the waterline.

DISCHARGE

To my knowledge, boaters are the only living organism obligated to decide after every evacuation where to route the excrement. As ludicrous as it sounds, there is no single marine toilet discharge path that can satisfy both the laws of the state and the laws of nature. Of the three discharge possibilities—directly overboard, overboard after treatment, or into a holding tank—you will need to plumb your toilet for at least two of these. First, let's consider them independently.

Treatment

Federal law allows for the installation of onboard sewer plants to liquefy and sanitize sewage and discharge the treated effluent overboard. The legalese for this discharge option is Type I MSD (marine sanitation device; the law also specifies a Type II MSD, which is a similar unit with more stringent sanitizing standards for vessels over 65 feet). The best of these units, those *not* using chlorine or formalin, do a better job than municipal sewage treatment plants. The units are expensive and power hungry, but less so than watermakers. For the boater willing to back up green rhetoric with dollars, a first-tier Type I MSD should provide a turnkey solution . . . except for the no-discharge zone (NDZ).

With boaters as an easy and often-willing target, state and local officials have discovered that there is political capital to be made being "tough on pollution" by calling for NDZs in local waters. Unfortunately the NDZ designation does not prohibit pumping raw sewage overboard. A federal law did that nine administrations ago. What the NDZ prohibits is the use of a Type I or Type II MSD. All Rhode Island waters are designated NDZs. The only legal discharge option there is the holding tank. NDZs, despite the hullabaloo, have no effect on water quality locally, but they do have a detrimental effect on the water in crowded harbors elsewhere because such ill-conceived laws discourage both the installation and the continued development of onboard treatment systems.

If you are able and willing to give NDZs a pass—consider it a boycott—and you have the space and electrical capacity for a Type I MSD, plumbing could not be easier. The discharge hose from the toilet connects to the inlet for the MSD. The MSD outlet connects to the seacock—via a vented loop if the treatment unit is located below the waterline.

Holding Tank

If you do not treat your sewage you must legally hold it when your boat is within 3 miles of shore. Compliance requires a holding tank. The only appropriate material for a retrofitted holding tank is linear polyethylene because of its seamless construction and noncorrosive nature. Look for wall thickness of $^1/_2$ inch or more. Thicker is better in this application.

Holding tanks are typically provided with three threaded ports fitted with hose barbs. The discharge from the toilet connects to the $1^1/_2$-inch port on or near the top of the tank. A second $1^1/_2$-inch hose from the bottom of the tank leads to a deck-mounted pumpout fitting. The third port is in the top of the tank and is usually $^5/_8$ inch. This is the vent for the tank that allows potentially explosive gas to escape and lets odor-reducing oxygen enter. The vent port connects to a straight through-hull fitting installed through the topsides or the deck.

The idea is that you flush your head into this tank, then before it is completely full, you vacuum out the contents at a shoreside pumpout station. However, unless your boating never takes you far from a pumpout facility for more than a few days and the one you are counting on is 100% reliable, you are going to need some other way of emptying the tank. The usual response is to install a Y-valve in the tank discharge line with one side of the Y connected to the deck fitting for emptying the tank at a pumpout station and the other side to a manual diaphragm pump for emptying the tank overboard. The outlet hose from this pump connects to the discharge seacock previously connected directly to the head. Electric macerator pumps are available for about the same cost but draw

15 or more amps, and even though they are designed for this particularly hostile environment, failures are common. A hand pump is usually less complicated to install, always less vulnerable to sudden failure, and will empty a 20-gallon tank in less than 2 minutes.

Beyond U.S. coastal waters, emptying the head into a holding tank only to discharge the raw sewage overboard with another pump makes little sense and has the added drawback that a tank full of effluent is less environmentally benign than a single flush. Federal law prohibits your head from being connected *directly* to an overboard discharge fitting, but it can be connected to a Y-valve with one side of the valve leading to the tank and the other side to a through-hull fitting. An oft-overlooked aspect of this proviso is that inside the 3-mile limit, the valve must be *secured* in the holding tank position. Padlocking the handle or securing it with a nylon wire-tie to an eyebolt is acceptable, but wiring or taping it in position is not. If your installation is missing this feature, it can cost you up to $2,000.

If you have been paying attention, it may have occurred to you that the through-hull discharge fitting is already occupied with the overboard discharge line from the holding tank. Another hole in the hull for an additional through-hull fitting is *never* a good idea if it can be avoided. In this case, all that is needed is an inexpensive Y-connector. Or you can simplify the

A Y-valve before the tank allows the individual flush to be discharged overboard.

A Y-valve after the tank allows the tank contents to be discharged overboard.

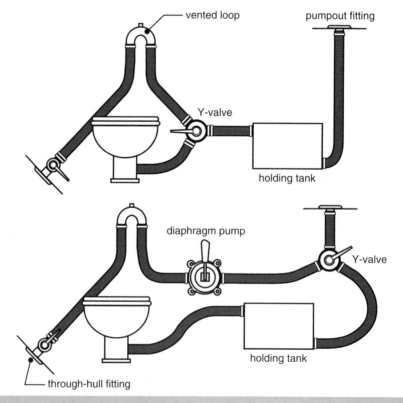

Toilet discharge plumbing.

plumbing by dispensing with the overboard discharge from the tank. The Y-valve between the head and the tank allows the consequence of a full tank to be side-stepped by flushing directly overboard. This configuration can work where pumpout facilities are normally available. It is also appropriate for a tank installation dictated by statute rather than function. The unvarnished truth is that there are thousands of installed holding tanks that have never contained anything but air. They were installed only to comply with the law, not to be used. When the objective of the installation is only compliance, an overboard discharge from the tank is an unwarranted complication and expense.

Newtonian Discharge

There is a holding tank configuration that dispenses with all valves except the seacock, complies with all existing laws, and affords three discharge options. The essential requirements for this configuration are that the bottom of the holding tank must be above the even-keel waterline, the top must always be above the heeled waterline, and the discharge through-hull must be more or less directly below the tank. If you can find a tank-mounting location on your boat that can satisfy this height requirement, there is so much to like about this streamlined composition that it is likely to be worth the effort to close the old discharge through-hull hole and install a new one beneath this location.

The idea is that the holding tank is just a wide section of the overboard discharge path. The toilet discharges into the top of the holding tank, and a hose connecting a bottom opening to a seacock directly below allows the flush to simply pass through the holding tank on its way to being discharged overboard by gravity—provided the seacock is open. Closing the seacock allows sewage to be held in the tank. Accumulated tank contents can be pumped out through the deck fitting via a tee connection in the discharge hose just above the seacock or dumped overboard by simply reopening the discharge through-hull.

Because the two check valves—the joker and the discharge flapper—that are supposed to stop water from flowing back into the bowl of a marine toilet can and do fail to seal completely due to solid debris, an above-the-waterline vented loop is always required between the toilet and the discharge seacock for a toilet located below the waterline. Through-the-tank discharge with the tank above the waterline eliminates the need for this component because the vent at the top of the tank doubles as a siphon break.

One characteristic of this configuration is that when the seacock is closed, sewage will stand inside both the discharge and the pumpout hoses. Odor will likely be the eventual consequence. If you anticipate holding sewage regularly, use only the most odor-proof hose for the discharge and pumpout lines or plumb them with standard schedule 40 PVC pipe connected with short hose runs for flexibility. An alternative is to install a ball valve at the tank drain and close this rather than the seacock to activate the holding tank. This avoids standing sewage in the hoses but does detract from the simplicity of the seacock-only configuration.

Pumping the toilet sufficiently to clear and rinse the hose from the toilet to the tank should keep it odor free, but if the distance is long, incorporating PVC pipe will reduce the risk. Regular use of the toilet should keep the interior of the tank well rinsed.

The tank vent must be at the top of the tank and kept clear to insure its siphon-break function. It should be as large in diameter as is practical. Making the vent fitting outside accessible will allow you to easily rinse the tank after emptying it by simply putting the nozzle of your deck-wash hose against this fitting and pulling the trigger. The tank can also be backflushed to dislodge blockage by closing the through-hull and directing a pressure flow (at some risk of eruption) down the pumpout fitting. That rare clog that fails to yield to either of these treatments can be dislodged with a snake fed into the discharge through-hull. If the bottom of the tank dips below the waterline on one tack, the occasional sail will be all the tank cleaning this system will ever require.

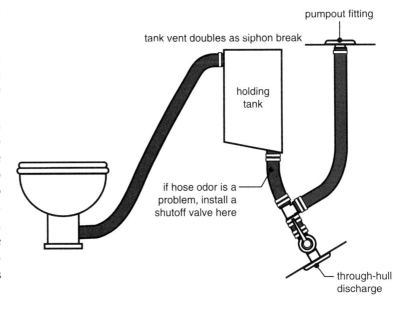

Properly configured, a flow-through holding tank can utilize gravity to eliminate most discharge plumbing.

pumpout fitting

tank vent doubles as siphon break

holding tank

if hose odor is a problem, install a shutoff valve here

through-hull discharge

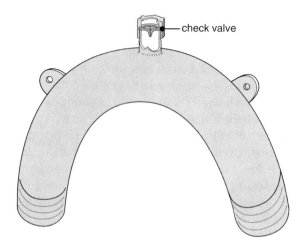

check valve

A typical vented loop. To assure siphon break, make sure the check valve is functional.

Vented Loops

If your discharge from a below-the-waterline toilet bypasses the holding tank or if the holding tank is not located above the waterline, failure to incorporate a vented loop is a blockhead oversight that can sink your boat. The typical vented loop is an inverted U-shaped pipe with a hole at the apex sealed with a small rubber check valve. Pressure through the loop keeps the valve closed, but the suction of water siphoning back through the line pulls the valve open, admitting air and breaking the siphon. The valve will not open if the loop fills with water under pressure, so it must be above the waterline on all points of heel.

Siphon loops have two potential shortcomings. The valve can clog shut, rendering the loop ineffective, or conversely it can sag open, filling the head compartment with noxious fumes. To avoid the first problem, the check valve should be removed from the loop periodically and washed in warm soapy water. In addition, you should remove the loop whenever you service the head and blast it with a high-pressure water flow to dislodge grunge that may be blocking the vent. But before you stick the garden hose nozzle in one end of the loop and pull the trigger, try to remember why it is called a loop. If servicing and/or replacing the check valve does not eliminate foul odors coming from the vent, clamp a hose over it and connect the other end to a deck-mounted vent fitting.

MAINTENANCE

Rebuilding a marine head is more a matter of mechanics than plumbing. The exact procedure for rebuilding your head will depend on the make and model, but manual heads are very simple machines and you are unlikely to encounter many difficulties. Head manufacturers have had a little racket going for nearly half a century, requiring head owners to buy a service kit when a single part may be all that

is required. Ah, well, in the scheme of things this is a very small larceny, and given the potential of a crapped-out toilet (or would that be *not*-crapped-out?) to spoil even the shortest of cruises, having a full complement of spare toilet parts has merit. In any case, the kit includes disassembly instructions.

As with all mechanical items, pay attention to how the parts are assembled and lay them out in order as you take them apart. Digital photos are a good way of solidifying your memory. Once disassembled, the interior of a scale-filled base can be cleaned by "boiling" it out with a 10% solution of muriatic acid—sold by most hardware stores for swimming pool use or concrete cleaning. Protect your eyes and hands if you do this. After the acid loses its fizz, hose the body thoroughly from a safe distance to remove loosened deposits and all traces of the acid.

A few general rules that apply to virtually all manual heads may help you to avoid problems. Weighted flapper valves always have the weight up and always open to give the least restricted flow. That means the flap should be oriented so the widest opening faces the direction of flow. The bill on a joker valve also points in the direction of the flow. The walls of the pump cylinder should be polished clean and lubricated lightly with Teflon grease. Likewise, all O-rings and seals will benefit from a light coating of Teflon grease. Also lubricate the pump rod. If the rod seals with packing rather than an O-ring, wait until you have put the head back into service to adjust this, and tighten the packing nut only enough to stop the rod from leaking.

If you have removed the bowl, you are going to need a new bowl gasket. The old one will have lost its resiliency, making it difficult to get the bowl to seal without risking cracking the porcelain by overtightening the mounting bolts. Tighten these bolts gently and evenly.

BILGE PUMPS

Somehow water always manages to find its way inside a boat. Hopefully the interior configuration of your hull forces such water to collect in the bilge. Every boat *must* have some means of ridding itself of this accumulation. The plumbing of a pump to empty the bilge is pretty basic—a hose from a strainer in the bilge to the pump, a hose from the pump to an overboard discharge. If you select an electric submersible bilge pump, the only plumbing required is a hose from the pump to the overboard discharge. So what's the big deal?

For one thing, you need to know what you expect from a bilge pump before you select and install one. I always thought of the bilge pump primarily as essential safety equipment, there to keep me from becoming shark fodder if the hull suddenly began to leak. Capacity was the only significant consideration; bigger was better. So I installed the largest submersible bilge pump I could shoehorn into my narrow bilge, connected it to a float switch, and except when the float stuck occasionally, forgot about it for about a decade.

The fact that there was always a couple of inches of water in the bilge never concerned me. There was supposed to be water in the bilge, right? Why else is the term *bilge water* in the language? Then along came a study from the University of Rhode Island concluding that the likelihood of destructive blisters in the hull laminate increases dramatically if water is left standing in the bilge. To quote the report, "prolonged stagnation of bilge water is the *surest* method for destroying hull integrity." That is bad news for high-capacity bilge pump installations.

What does the capacity of the pump have to do with how much water stands in the bilge? I'm glad you asked. It gives me a chance to show off my logical bent. The link is not the size of the pump; it's the size of the hose. On my old boat the most direct route from the pump to the overboard discharge requires about 9 feet of hose—probably shorter than the norm. The high-capacity pump necessitates a $1^1/_2$-inch hose. When the pump shuts off, that hose is full—like a 9-foot-tall stein. All that water flows back through a centrifugal pump and back into the bilge. A check valve might initially keep the water from draining back, but deposits of debris from the bilge water would soon prevent the valve from sealing. Besides, a check valve in a bilge pump discharge line is a bad idea because it reduces the output and introduces a real risk of blockage.

The only safe way to minimize the amount of water draining back into the bilge is to keep the run as short as possible and to use the smallest hose you can. Discharging the water through a $1/_2$-inch hose rather than a $1^1/_2$-inch hose reduces the amount of water that drains back by 89%! Unfortunately it also imposes a similar reduction on the amount of water you can pump out. Reduce the $1^1/_2$-inch discharge hose on a 3,700 gallons-per-hour (gph) pump down to $1/_2$ inch, and you cut the output to less than 400 gph. This is woefully inadequate for any serious breach.

If a $1^1/_2$-inch through-hull fitting just 6 inches below the waterline sheds its hose, it will admit the ocean at the rate of about 1,900 gph. To stand a chance against such a leak, the discharge hose of a high-capacity pump must match the pump outlet, but even with a $1^1/_2$-inch discharge hose, a pump rated at 3,700 gph will probably fail to keep up with a 1,900 gph leak. This is because centrifugal bilge pumps are typically rated at their theoretical maximum delivery with *zero lift* and equally inexplicably at *13.6 volts* (for 12-volt pumps). If this is not dishonest, it is certainly misleading. If you could configure your bilge pump for zero lift, a drain plug should serve. With the discharge fitting 5 or 6 feet above the bilge (the minimum lift in even a modest sailboat), a centrifugal pump is unlikely to expel water from your boat at more than half the rated capacity. Output can decline by half again when you factor in real-world battery voltage.

Where does this leave you? You can let your boat either delaminate or sink. What kind of choice is that? The fact is that you cannot accommodate both objectives—dealing with serious flooding *and* keeping the bilge dry of errant rain and stuffing-box drips—with a single pump. Two pumps are required. The good news is that there is almost no additional cost for this dual-pump system. Honest.

TANDEM ELECTRIC PUMPS

The key is the purchase of a small (500 gph or less) pump with an *internal* float switch. Such a pump should cost less than a reliable float switch for the high-capacity pump—a switch you are going to omit. In the event of major water intrusion, you will manually switch on the high-capacity pump with a clearly labeled toggle switch near the companionway. The money you don't spend on the float switch will pay for the small automatic pump.

Shouldn't the high-capacity pump also have a float switch? It clearly doesn't matter when you are aboard, but let's consider what happens if a hose fails while the boat is unattended. The 400 gph automatic pump will have very little effect. With 1,900 gph pouring in, anticipate that a 36-foot sailboat will sink in under 6 hours.

Connect your high-capacity pump to a float switch, and it may be able to keep up with the leak—but for how long? The pump draws more than 15 amps. It will flatten a 100 Ah battery in 6 hours. Then the boat begins to fill.

Won't someone notice? If you mean notice the pump running, probably not. Boats all over the marina are discharging water from generators or air-conditioning units. If you mean notice the boat sinking, someone probably will notice if it happens in the daytime. And if you are really lucky, they will try to stop it. But by the time another sailor notices your boat settling and calls you or breaks in, a float-switch-operated pump has already run for hours and drained the battery. On the other hand, if the high-capacity pump is *not* on a float switch and the batteries are still above water, the emergency pump can be turned on. This can pause or at least slow the immediate threat, providing time to find the leak and stem it. If you insist on installing a second float switch for the high-capacity pump, also connect it to an alarm horn (or connect it only to the horn) to make sure the trouble does get someone's attention.

Install the 400 gph pump in the *lowest* part of the bilge and wire it through a fuse directly to one of the batteries. A pump this size will have a $^3/_4$-inch outlet, but insert a reducer in the line and run $^1/_2$-inch hose as directly as possible to a discharge fitting installed in the hull just below the rail. It is imperative to have the discharge clear of the water on all points of sail or the ocean will siphon in when the pump shuts off. Try not to locate the discharge where you come aboard from the dinghy.

Several inches higher and *not* directly above the small pump, fiberglass a plywood bridge across the bilge. Mount the high-capacity pump to the plywood bridge and wire it to a dedicated breaker in the main panel. The breaker can double as the switch, or you can route the hot wire through a separate toggle switch mounted in some prominent location near the companionway. In a moment of intense stress or when your boat's potential savior is crew or even a good Samaritan, having the bilge pump on/off switch clearly labeled, wherever it is, can make all the difference. Wiring this pump to the panel allows either of the battery banks to supply the power to run it. The wiring should be not smaller than what is recommended in the 3% voltage drop table, but you are likely to find that the wire leads emerging from the pump are undersize—particularly unforgivable given the deceptive 13.6-volt flow rating. On this subject, the cheapest little table lamp will come

with a 6-foot electrical cord, but the wire leads on submersible pumps are often too short to reach out of the bilge. That pump manufacturers have ignored this complaint for decades is the kind of thing that detracts from the boat ownership experience and ultimately hurts the marine industry. If your pump has short leads, you will need to extend them carefully using oversize tinned boat cable; make the connection watertight with adhesive heat-shrink.

Pivoting-arm float switches, the least expensive and most common design, are a study in simplicity but generally less reliable than they should be given their responsibility. A housing over the float can avoid one vulnerability, jamming by solid debris, but the pivot in nearly all pivoting-arm switches eventually sticks, which you discover when bilge water floods the sole. Ergo, forget about a pivoting-arm float switch for a long time and you will be reminded by bilge water where you do not want it. The floating doughnut style of switch with a free float around a central rod inside a perforated tube is mechanically more reliable but also more expensive. Other technologies, such as immersed contacts, have been applied to bilge pump switches, but none has proved superior to float activation. Float switch wiring was detailed in the previous chapter.

Connect the pump outlet to a second discharge fitting with $1^1/_2$-inch hose. The size of the hose is no longer a concern. If the pump is operated, any water that drains back into the bilge will be removed by the smaller pump.

This dual-pump installation will result in a bilge that is bone dry if you maintain the stuffing box. The small pump, because of its size, pumps the water level lower to begin with, and the small discharge hose minimizes the amount of water that drains back. The shallow puddle that does remain soon evaporates,

Dual bilge pump installation.

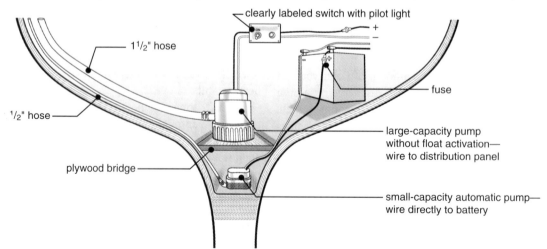

clearly labeled switch with pilot light

$1^1/_2$" hose

$^1/_2$" hose

plywood bridge

fuse

large-capacity pump without float activation— wire to distribution panel

small-capacity automatic pump— wire directly to battery

absorbed by the air instead of the hull. An added advantage of this arrangement is that the expensive high-capacity pump, because it sits high and dry, should never require replacement.

AN ENGINE-DRIVEN ALTERNATIVE

If the $1\frac{1}{2}$-inch through-hull fitting that loses its hose is 3 feet below the waterline rather than 6 inches, the greater pressure increases the flood rate to 4,620 gph. That is more than 19 tons of water coming aboard in an hour. How quickly even a seemingly small leak can overwhelm a boat is frightening. If you are preparing an old boat for bluewater sailing, the inadequacy of even a large electric bilge pump might lead you to consider an engine-driven pump to deal with major water intrusion. Such a pump will operate for as long as you can keep the engine running, and the capacity of large engine-driven pumps puts electric bilge pumps into the "wimpy" class. A commonly seen model from Jabsco is rated at 4,980 gph and will deliver close to that even with 6 feet of lift. When you are there to throw the switch, it might as well be for a pump that has half a chance against a major leak.

If you go this route, make certain that the pump you select is self-priming. I think a manual clutch is a better choice than an electric one because it keeps the pump independent of the electrical system. Unless your main engine is rigidly mounted (no flexible mounts), you will need to mount the pump to the engine rather than to the boat. Otherwise the independent oscillations will subject the bearings in both pump and engine to destructive shock loading. Pumps are standard, but the mounting bracket will be custom-made. Use heavy-gauge steel for the bracket. The mount must be adjustable or incorporate an idler pulley to allow tensioning the appropriate belt. Size the pulleys correctly to get maximum output from the pump.

Engine-driven pumps are usually flexible-impeller types and don't handle solids well, so the pickup hose should lead into a strum box—a strainer. Traditional bronze strum boxes are expensive, but you don't want a strainer with holes just in the bottom anyway. You will be trying to get ahead of a leak with this pump, not *dry* the bilge. (We have already assigned that job to the small electric pump.) You need a strainer that will not restrict the pump's capacity and will be difficult to clog. You can fabricate an excellent strainer from a foot of 3-inch PVC pipe. Cap one end and fit the other end with a threaded adapter and a hose connector to match your pump. Now drill the bejesus out of the pipe with a sharp

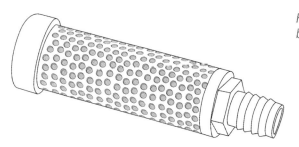

Homemade strum box.

$\frac{3}{8}$-inch bit. Settle in. You are not finished until there are more holes than plastic.

You cannot ignore an engine-driven pump as you can a submersible. Make a habit of rotating the pump by hand every time you check the oil to keep the impeller from taking a set. Run or pour a few gallons of fresh water into the bilge and engage this pump occasionally to exercise it, but do not allow it to run dry. Check the belt tension after you run the pump. Open the pump and inspect the impeller once a year. Replace it if it shows any cracks or signs of hardening. Lubricating the chamber with a little petroleum jelly will reduce the wear and stress on the impeller when the pump is priming.

MANUAL BILGE PUMPS

If you are out for a pleasant sail and rising water gets over your batteries before you realize you are sinking, neither electric nor engine-driven pumps are likely to do you any good. Regardless of how many other pumps you have aboard, the only one that is certain to work when you need it is a manual pump. No boat should be without one.

But don't put all your faith in a manual pump. The biggest ones around (Edson) are rated at 30 gallons per minute. Before you decide that this sounds like 1,800 gph, go down to the spa and see how long you can last on the rowing machine. A sizable crew can keep a manual pump pumping at capacity for a long time, but one or two people are not going to last very long at 30 strokes a minute. And somebody has to be trying to locate the leak and stop it, not to mention controlling the boat. A manual pump is not a substitute for a tireless electric or engine-driven pump, but it is your last line of defense, and you should install the largest and least tiring pump you can find.

Although large manual diaphragm pumps are less likely to choke on trash than either centrifugal or vane pumps, the consequences if it happens are the same. Protect the pickup with a bilge strainer. Here again, a strainer you fabricate from scrap PVC pipe will be cheaper and probably better than the commercially available type with holes only in the bottom.

CYCLE COUNTER

Since buckets gave way to pumps, sailors have counted strokes to monitor the watertightness of the hull. The loss of this vigilance is a fault many sailors find in automatic bilge pumps. Leaks often start small, growing more serious over time but if your pump is keeping your bilge dry, you don't know you have a problem until it is a *big* problem. The solution to this is an electronic counter that keeps track of the number of pump cycles.

Unfortunately the commercial units I see are yacht priced. If you have a more restricted budget, you can adapt a $5 pedometer with a $5 reed relay (RadioShack part number 275-233 or any other 12-volt relay). Electrical contact by a spring-loaded pendulum in the pedometer normally advances the counter. If you open the pedometer case, you should be able to remove the pendulum and delicately solder the switch wires from the relay to the two contact surfaces. Now a 12-volt current across the relay closes the reed switch and advances the counter. Connect

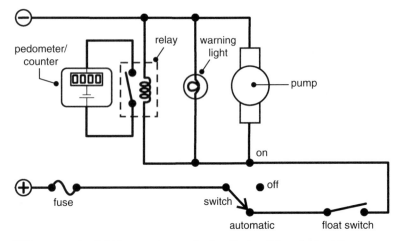

Wiring a warning light/horn and a counter to a float-switch-activated bilge pump.

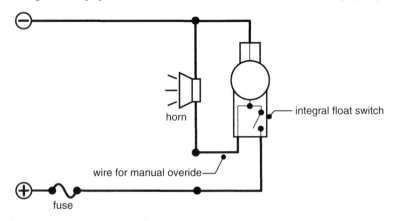

Wiring a warning horn/light to an automatic bilge pump.

Knowing about a leak can be more critical than pumping out the accumulation.

the relay to the pump exactly like you would an alarm or a warning light, by connecting one lead to the positive lead from the pump and the other to ground. When the pump is energized by the float switch, the relay closes and the counter advances. An automatic bilge pump with an integral float switch should have a third wire for manual override, which will be energized when the pump runs. Connect the counter (or warning light) to this wire.

I have already pointed out the value of a *loud* high-water alarm on an unattended boat, assuming others are around to hear it. A buzzer, something that gets your attention but not that of the rest of the anchorage, is better for monitoring "normal" bilge pump activity, but a red warning light in the cockpit will be more crew friendly for a boat underway. You can have both (and a counter, all wired in parallel) with a disabling switch in the buzzer circuit to avoid disturbing the off-watch crew. The light in the cockpit will keep the on-watch crew apprised.

EXHAUST PLUMBING

Early pleasure boat engine installations commonly used a dry exhaust system, aptly named because the exhaust plumbing became red-hot when the engine was running. Dry exhaust systems set many a good boat on fire. Jacketed exhaust systems followed—essentially a pipe inside a pipe, with the inner pipe carrying exhaust gases and the outer one engine cooling water on its way overboard. Aside from being heavy and rigid, the Achilles' heel of a jacketed exhaust is that an internal failure, unnoticeable while the engine runs, allows seawater to leak from the jacket into the exhaust pipe when the engine stops. Where the exhaust pipe is higher than the engine, the water floods the cylinders.

Then somebody asked, "Why cool the exhaust pipe from the outside?" and the wet exhaust was born. Raw water that has passed through the engine or the heat exchanger is discharged by injecting it *inside* the exhaust pipe as close to the exhaust manifold as possible. This cools the exhaust and has the added benefit of muffling combustion noise. The cooling of a wet exhaust is so effective that rubber hose can be used to plumb the exhaust beyond the water injection point. This allows a soft-mounted engine to jump around without stressing the exhaust plumbing.

In powerboats with the engine mounted high enough that the exhaust manifolds are well above the waterline, wet exhaust plumbing is straightforward. The exhaust gases carry away the water when the engine is running. At shutdown, any water still in the pipe drains overboard. Risers may be incorporated at the manifold to raise the exhaust pipe connection and water injection point to increase the exhaust drop and reduce the risk of backflooding.

Sailboat engines are invariably mounted near or below the waterline, placing the discharge outlet above the exhaust manifold. If you plumbed the exhaust directly to the outlet fitting, water in the exhaust hose when the engine is shut down would drain back into the manifold and into the cylinders with disastrous consequences. The solution to this is a canister plumbed into the exhaust and located below the manifold to serve as a sump for water still in the hose. However, if the canister is just a hollow tank with an inlet and an outlet at the top, accumulating cooling water will soon fill it and water draining back from the downstream hose will overflow it back into the engine, so our canister has a simple but ingenious design feature. The outlet pipe extends into the interior of the canister almost to the bottom.

Now the injected water accumulates in the canister only until it covers the bottom of the pipe where it blocks the outlet. When sufficient exhaust pressure builds up in the canister, the water and exhaust gases are literally blown out of the submerged outlet pipe, so the canister remains mostly empty. This canister is known as a waterlift (or waterlock) muffler.

Boats equipped with a waterlift muffler are easily detectable by the bursts of cooling water from their overboard exhaust instead of a continuous water flow. They are also detectable by how quiet they are, a point brought home to me one cold December morning shortly after I had installed a waterlift exhaust on my own old boat. Friends on a sister ship with the identical engine and the original jacketed exhaust had stopped at our dock for the night. As they prepared to leave, I also started our engine. From the back deck of the house 50 feet away, I could hear only the pulsating splash of our own exhaust, but as our friends motored away from us on the river, I could hear their exhaust clearly for almost 20 minutes!

Unlike rigid exhaust systems, a wet exhaust is easy to plumb. The only rigid part is a short section attached to the manifold that incorporates the water injection fitting. This is the mixing elbow and is supplied on most marine engines. For an older engine originally plumbed to a dry or jacketed exhaust, you can fabricate a perfectly satisfactory injection fitting from a galvanized tee you get at a plumbing supply store. Once water has been injected into the system, exhaust plumbing downstream may be rubber exhaust hose.

The standard mixing elbow can be plumbed directly to a waterlift muffler with rubber exhaust hose, as long as the water injection point is at least 6 inches above the waterline and the waterlift muffler can be mounted lower than the exhaust manifold. Unfortunately the location of most sailboat auxiliaries puts the mixing elbow below the waterline. If the muffler can still be located lower than the exhaust manifold, the only real accommodation you have to make is to prevent raw water from continuing to flow into the exhaust system when the engine is stopped by looping the cooling water discharge line well above the waterline and equipping it with a vent at the top. The usual installation uses an antisiphon valve, but these valves are notorious for packing up with minerals and seizing. If the valve seizes in the closed position, it will not break the siphon and the engine could fill with raw water. If it seizes while open, it is like a saltwater sprinkler going off in the engine room. The antisiphon valve should be removed and washed in warm soapy water with every oil change, then its operation checked by blowing through it in both directions. Dispensing with the valve and venting the loop with a $1/4$-inch tube leading to an overboard vent is a less trouble-prone alternative, although the overboard fitting may weep a bit.

On the exhaust side of the waterlift muffler, the hose must be looped at least 12 inches above the waterline. In a very deep boat this can result in an excessively high lift. If the distance from the bottom of the muffler to the top of the exhaust loop is more than about 3 feet, engine performance will suffer due to excessive back pressure. In this case, the muffler must be mounted higher.

If for this reason or any other the muffler must be mounted above the exhaust manifold, you will need to configure the exhaust plumbing to prevent the muffler from draining back into the engine. Riser extensions or a dry stack will be necessary to, in effect, raise the exhaust manifold above the muffler. If this also lifts the water injection point well above the waterline, the need for a vent on the cooling water discharge line will be eliminated. A dry stack is easy to construct with galvanized water pipe and threaded unions. If the stack is short, it can be left bare, but a tall stack should be insulated to prevent it from adding heat to the engine compartment.

Some additional cautions apply. The first is to be certain that your waterlift muffler is firmly attached to the boat. Do not be fooled by the light weight of an empty plastic muffler. (Plastic mufflers work perfectly, by the way, despite the seeming incongruity).

When partially filled with seawater, the muffler will have considerable momentum in a pitching or rolling boat.

The second caution is to avoid mounting the muffler to one side of the engine. This is particularly important for sailboats, because a side-mounted muffler will be elevated relative to the exhaust manifold on one tack. At large angles of heel, residual water in the muffler could flow into the engine. Try to mount the muffler close to the fore-and-aft centerline of the exhaust manifold.

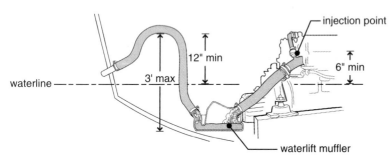

Water injection point at least 6″ above the waterline.

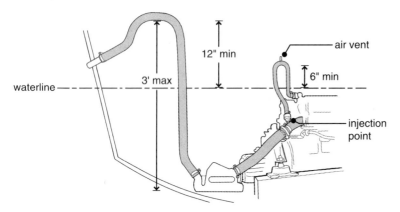

Water injection point below the waterline.

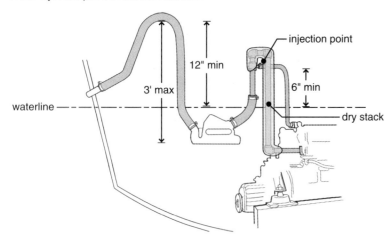

Waterlift muffler above the exhaust manifold.

Exhaust plumbing.

Transom exhaust outlets should be protected from following seas. The high loop is supposed to provide this protection, but more than one skipper has seen the pressure of a following sea push water over the loop and back into the idle engine. A ball valve in the exhaust line is your best protection from this disaster, but you must remember to close it (and open it!). Also, it is usually difficult to make access to this valve convenient. A flap at the exhaust outlet is less trouble but might prove ineffective, depending on the angle at which your discharge outlet exits the hull.

If your engine is difficult to start, you have a special problem. Cooling water continues to fill the muffler as you spin the engine, but without combustion there may not be enough exhaust pressure to blow the water out. The result can be water in the engine. A well-designed muffler will have a drain to allow you to deal with this situation.

Waterlift exhaust systems have become ubiquitous on sailboats and with good reason. Properly installed, they are trouble free. If your old sailboat still has a jacketed exhaust, you will do yourself and your engine a favor by replacing it with a waterlift system.

LPG PLUMBING

Weekend boaters can get along fine with an alcohol stove, and a few hardcase types hang on to pressure kerosene, but most with cruising aspirations will opt for liquefied petroleum gas (LPG) as their galley fuel. From the cook's perspective there are no drawbacks: the burners are instantly hot and nearly as quickly cool, the flame burns clean and hot, and the heat level is easily adjusted with a simple turn of the knob. Unfortunately gas is safer in a kitchen than in a galley. This is because LPG—propane or butane—is heavier than air, so leaks spill like water instead of floating away on air currents. The bowl shape of a boat hull accumulates and concentrates leaking gas in the same way that a cistern holds rainwater. Free propane in the bilge is a bomb waiting to go off.

TANK LOCATION

Available safety features and devices combined with proper safety habits can reduce the danger to near negligible levels, but only if your LPG plumbing is up to par. Safe LPG plumbing begins with putting the tank(s) where a leak at the tank cannot find its way into the interior of the boat. This means a locker containing LPG tanks must be vapor tight, isolated from the rest of the boat, and incorporate a free-flowing overboard drain in the bottom. A gas locker must open above deck, never inside another locker. The locker drain should not vent near any opening into the boat, and it must be located where it cannot become submerged when the boat is underway.

When the gas installation is a retrofit, it is common for the propane tanks to be located on deck. This might not be as safe as it seems, depending on site and deck configuration. Bulwarks and coamings, for example, will keep leaking gas from spilling overboard, perhaps allowing it to find its way below through deck vents or cockpit lockers. When the boat is sailing downwind or lying to current, gas leaking from an on-deck tank at the stern can be blown directly below through the companionway or open hatches. If you have or plan to have on-deck gas tanks, consider them critically.

TANK CONNECTIONS

A pressure gauge is the first thing connected to the gas tank. It can be threaded directly into the valve on top of the cylinder or mounted elsewhere inside the locker and connected to the cylinder with a short high-pressure hose called a pigtail. A pressure gauge does not tell you the level of the gas in the tank. You weigh the tank for that. What the gauge does is provide for easy leak testing of the entire LPG system. If your installation lacks a gauge, install one.

Next in line comes an electric solenoid that shuts off the gas inside the locker with the flip of a switch that's conveniently located in the cabin. Safe propane use means shutting off the gas at the tank after *every* use. You can do that manually by turning the knob on the tank—but you won't. Leaving the gas lines that run through your boat pressurized is risky business. The solenoid makes it easy to avoid this exposure.

The switch should be paired with a bright panel light that warns you that the solenoid valve is open.

From the solenoid, the gas should flow directly into a step-down regulator that reduces the pressure from, say, 150 psi on the tank side (this varies widely with temperature) to less than 0.5 psi in the line that carries the gas to the galley stove or other appliance. This order can be reversed, with the solenoid plumbed after the regulator rather than before, but in my experience low-pressure solenoids tend to be of lesser quality. I also favor a high-pressure solenoid because it shuts off the gas upstream of the regulator and its connections, but as a practical matter either configuration shuts off the gas inside the locker. If you install your solenoid on the high-pressure side, be sure it is rated for high pressure.

GAS DISTRIBUTION

You can use either copper tubing or hose to deliver gas to the stove or other gas appliance. With copper there is the risk of fatigue failure from motion or vibration. Hose is at risk from chafe and sharp edges. I tend to favor hose because the danger is visible.

Copper tubing can be refrigeration or water tubing and must be attached with flare fittings, not compression fittings. Hose must be LPG rated with end fittings permanently attached, which means you need to buy a hose in a standard length with fittings already installed on the ends, or you will have to have the hose fabricated with permanent end fittings. A hose clamp over a barb is not acceptable for this plumbing application.

The line from the regulator or the low-pressure solenoid valve to the appliance must be *continuous*. There can be no connections inside the boat except

LPG plumbing.

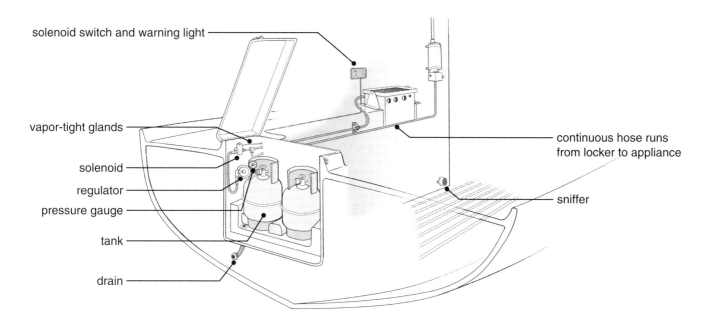

solenoid switch and warning light

vapor-tight glands

solenoid

regulator

pressure gauge

tank

drain

continuous hose runs from locker to appliance

sniffer

the one at the stove. If you plumb your supply lines with copper tubing, there is an exception to this rule for a gimballed stove. In this instance, the rigid tubing connects to a short piece of hose that is connected to the stove to allow the stove to gimbal. This is another reason to choose hose over copper tubing. Continuous hose all the way from the regulator to the stove eliminates the necessity of this extra connection, essentially halving the leak potential inside the boat.

Whether the fuel line is tubing or hose, it must exit the propane locker through a vapor-tight gland near the top of the locker. Likewise, the hole admitting the solenoid wiring must also be high and vapor tight. Gas supply lines should run through the top of lockers in the boat rather than through their bottoms. Check that the fuel line is supported at least every 18 inches and is protected against abrasion, especially where it passes through bulkheads. Be sure it doesn't run close to the exhaust plumbing or any other source of high heat (> 140°F).

No matter how convenient, you must never tee off a gas line inside the boat. If you have more than one gas appliance, the supply line to each must be continuous and originate inside the gas locker. Every hose or pipe must exit through its own vapor-tight gland.

Given that the second gas appliance is often a grill, the plumbing of propane barbecue grills requires some clarification. Rail-mounted gas grills designed for disposable propane canisters have regulators that require propane under high pressure. However, running a high-pressure line outside the gas locker is inherently unsafe and you shouldn't do it. If you want to supply your grill with propane from the ship's supply, purchase a low-pressure control valve from the grill's manufacturer. This allows you to plumb the grill supply hose into the low-pressure side of the regulator. Again, this connection must be made *inside* the propane locker.

Lastly, a bilge blower is an often-omitted requirement for a safe LPG installation. Should LPG find its way below, you are going to have a hell of a time clearing it out of the boat safely without an ignition-protected blower with the pickup deep in the bilge.

VIGILANCE

Safe propane use begins with regular leak testing. Testing requires such a small effort that complacency is the only possible reason for not doing it on a regular basis, and where LPG is concerned, you must guard against complacency.

After you have just used the stove, close all the burner valves but leave the solenoid switch on. Go to the gas locker and read the pressure gauge. Turn off the hand valve on the supplying tank. Read the pressure again after 3 minutes. If it is unchanged, wait 15 minutes and read it a third time. The same reading all three times assures you that the system is leak free. A drop in pressure indicates a leak that must be located (with soapy water) and sealed.

I strongly recommend having at least one electronic gas detector inside the boat. Gas sensors, often called sniffers, constantly monitor the air for the presence of LP gas. They should be mounted where gas is likely to accumulate; i.e., as low as possible and in the vicinity of the galley stove (or other gas appliance). A sensor will shut off the solenoid and activate an alarm anytime it detects gas at about 10% of minimum explosive level. Keep in mind that electronics can fail or gas can accumulate in some other part of the boat, so a sensor is not a substitute for regular leak testing.

The solenoid switch should always be in the Off position, except when the stove is in use. To reduce the possibility of gas leaking from the stove into the interior of the boat, learn the habit of turning off the solenoid before turning off the last burner. When the burner goes out, then close the burner valve. This empties the line of gas so that none will leak into the bilge should a burner valve fail to seal. When you leave the boat unattended for a while, close the hand valve on the tank to eliminate all risk of undetected leakage. With this modest level of vigilance, propane can be as safe for the boat as it is a delight for the cook.

OK, so now that you are a plumber, let's take a look at a specialized application—refrigeration.

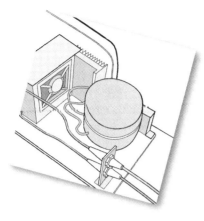

CHAPTER THIRTEEN

Cold Truth

"There's booze in the blender
And soon it will render
That frozen concoction that helps me hang on."
—JIMMY BUFFET

It was August 1974. Nixon was about to resign, but the water that commanded our attention was limpid and radiant, a fantastic pattern of splotches of countless shades of aquamarine—impressionism on the grandest of scales. Our Bahamian courtesy flag hung limply in the sweltering heat. We were one of only two boats anchored off a perfect crescent beach, and we had just shattered the serenity by firing up our diesel engine. Over the clank of reciprocating iron I called below from the shaded cockpit to ask my shipmate to switch on the refrigerator. Two minutes after this unguarded utterance, a dinghy from the other boat rounded to a stop alongside and the lone occupant proposed a symbiotic relationship. If we would cool a six-pack of beer—his beer—he would supply us with all the fresh lobster we could eat.

Refrigeration aboard a sailboat back then was the ultimate luxury. While happy hour on other cruising boats usually consisted of warm rum and Tang, we served iced drinks to our guests. We were very popular.

Those days are gone forever. Today virtually every boat sharing faraway anchorages with us has refrigeration aboard. Even among the weekend fleet, refrigeration is likely to be the rule rather than the exception. Refrigeration now comes as standard equipment on nearly all new boats larger than about 30 feet. Increasingly rare is the old boat without some form of refrigeration aboard. Rarer still is the old-boat owner content without refrigeration.

And why not? Marine refrigeration has made quantum leaps in the last three decades. A typical 12-volt system only draws about 50 Ah per day. With a 100 Ah battery you can go two days before you need

to run the engine, and then your 100 amp alternator will recharge the battery in an hour. With a decent wind generator and 10 knots of breeze, you can forget about running the engine altogether, and if the wind in the anchorage is too light to spin the generator, a couple of solar panels will handle the load.

Get a grip! Not a single statement in the last paragraph is true, not even the part about quantum leaps. Refrigeration mentality has made quantum leaps—we all want refrigeration aboard—but the physics involved has remained unchanged. Systems today are better engineered and more dependable, but only marginally (if at all) more efficient than a Freon-12-based system from 1974. The problem with marine refrigeration back then, besides the cost, was that it consumed a lot of energy. Today the cost is higher and the energy requirements undiminished.

WHAT HAS CHANGED

That 1974 refrigeration system that chilled beer and preserved our fresh lobster (oh come on, it would have been impolite *not* to take it) was assembled mostly from automobile air-conditioning components. A mechanically inclined sailor could spend an hour in a wrecking yard and come away with all the parts needed except a holding plate and a heat exchanger, both of which could be homebuilt or adapted from something intended for some other function. The way we determined which car to scavenge was to crack an air-conditioner hose fitting and listen for the hiss. Escaping gas told us the system remained sealed, suggesting that all the components were still good. That hiss was also contributing to the hole in the ozone.

THE LAW

It is still possible to build a boat refrigeration system from wrecking yard parts, but *you* can't do it unless you are an EPA-certified refrigeration technician. That telltale hiss has been illegal since the early 1990s. The only person allowed to open a refrigeration or air-conditioning system is a certified technician with recovery equipment that allows him or her to vacuum the gas out of the system and save it prior to opening any fittings. You *could* buy the various disassembled components and assemble them into a refrigeration system, but you would need a certified technician to vacuum, charge, and test the system and to empty it again if it did not turn out perfectly on the first try. As a practical matter, a refrigeration system assembled from cobbled-together components is no longer a realistic alternative unless you happen to be a refrigeration mechanic, in which case you don't need my help anyway.

Maybe you are wondering about those cans of refrigerant you see in the automotive department at your local Wal-Mart. If only certified technicians are allowed to work on automotive air conditioners, who are those cans for? They are for you—us. First, those cans contain R-134a, the refrigerant that replaced R-12 in automotive use. R-134a is not without its evils, but it is not a chlorofluorocarbon (CFC) so it does not deplete the ozone. Because of this, it is not as tightly regulated. Currently it is legal for retailers to sell R-134a, it is legal for you to buy it, and it is legal for you to use it.

This loophole—which could close—is of interest to you because R-134a is also the refrigerant most often (but not always) found in marine refrigeration systems. Belt-driven compressors, in particular, seal with a face seal—something like a dripless shaft seal. Over time, small amounts of refrigerant can escape through this seal, so it is not uncommon for a belt-driven system to require topping off. With a small can of refrigerant and a charging hose (also from Wal-Mart), you can do this yourself. The small release of refrigerant to purge the hose is not illegal and probably inconsequential. In any case, the technician would also purge the hose, so you doing it does not add environmental damage.

THE WORLD

The biggest change affecting marine refrigeration, especially for vagabond sailors, is neither mechanical nor legal. It is worldwide development. In the 1970s when setting off for a 6-month cruise through the Bahamas, we put aboard every food item we expected to need for the entire 6 months. The only item we normally bought ashore was bread, and that was usually from the kitchen of an island resident. Island stores, where there were any, typically had a few dusty cans and maybe some frozen chicken parts.

Today well-stocked markets, even supermarkets, are the rule rather than the exception. You will find everything you need and the majority of things you want available as you cruise. You do have to learn to buy when you find, because markets without daily truck deliveries tend to have lots of an item one week and none for the next three. And prices for the items you are familiar with are likely to be higher, though not high enough to offset the cost of keeping the same items frozen aboard your boat for several months. The bargains are on items you are not familiar with. Local products and those from countries with favorable trade relationships with the country you are visiting can be astonishingly cheap. Even where the food isn't particularly cheap, you may still find it appealing. We can arrive in St. Martin, for example, without a single food item aboard because our first errand after clearing is to the French market. Ooh-la-la!

The point of this is that the cavernous refrigerators and freezers of a previous generation of cruising boats are less necessary for the typical cruiser today. A smaller box expands your refrigeration options, probably lowers your original investment, and certainly reduces the operational cost. Our own refrigerator is around 3 cubic feet and that includes the freezer compartment. It is usually full, but that is preferable and more efficient than half-empty. How big your box needs to be will depend on how you use it, perhaps where you are going, how adventurous your tastes are, and how much energy you can provide to keep it cold. We will get to this last point soon enough, but all things considered, you are at greater risk of disappointment with your refrigeration system from making the box too big than from making it too small.

LEARNING THE LANGUAGE

Refrigerators do not create cold. They remove heat. It is an important distinction. To have any kind of frame of reference for matching refrigeration machinery to the space we are trying to "cool," we need to be able to measure this heat transfer. Oddly, the unit in common use in America is Btu (British thermal units). One Btu is the amount of heat required to raise 1 pound of water 1°F. It goes the other way as well. To cool 1 gallon of water, which weighs 8.34 pounds, from 80°F to 33°F requires the removal of 392 Btu (47×8.34) of heat.

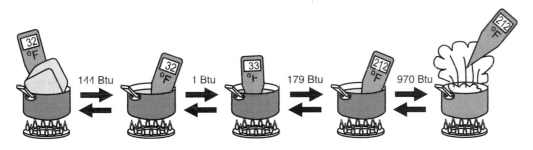

From ice to steam requires a total of 1,294 Btu per pound.

Staying with water for the moment, suppose we want to freeze water rather than just cool it. It takes only 1 Btu per pound (8.34 Btu per gallon) to lower the temperature of water from 33°F to 32°F, but we do not have ice yet, just cold water. Removing 1 more Btu should lower the water temperature to 31°F, but that is not going to happen because the water changes state, from liquid to solid, at 32°F. This change of state requires the removal of more heat, a lot more heat. In the case of 1 pound of water, to change it from 32° water to 32° ice requires the removal of an additional 144 Btu of heat. This is called *latent heat* because it does not result in any change in temperature. So to cool our gallon jug of water from 80°F to 32°F takes just 400 Btu of refrigeration, but to freeze the water will take an additional 1,200 Btu (144 × 8.34). This is a big part of why freezers consume so much more power than refrigerators.

Latent heat plays another role in refrigeration. Water is only water between 32°F and 212°F (0°C and 100°C). Below 32°F it is ice, and above 212°F it is steam. The change of state from liquid to gas or vice versa requires even more Btu, 970 per pound for water. In other words to convert a pound of water to steam, you must add 970 Btu of heat—what the burner on the stove is doing when you boil water. To convert steam to water, you must remove 970 Btu per pound.

The temperatures and latent heat numbers are different for other liquids, but the concept is the same. Refrigerant changing state from liquid to gas inside your box absorbs large amounts of heat. Outside the box the circulating refrigerant releases this heat as it changes back to a liquid. We will come back to exactly how this works, but first let's consider the box.

CART BEFORE THE HORSE

Unless you are tied to a dock, you are going to be supplying all of the energy necessary to run your refrigerator. Because the energy required depends so heavily on the design of the box—how big it is, how it is constructed, and how it is insulated—box realities is where this discussion needs to start. If the existing box aboard your boat is only nominally smaller than

a cockpit locker or separated from the engine room by just half an inch of plywood, get used to the sound of your engine or plan to make some changes.

TEST THE BOX

It is a relatively simple matter to test the efficiency of your box. Heat always transfers from a hotter object to a colder object. What we want to determine is how much heat in the air surrounding the box passes through the walls—and the insulation if there is any—and into the box's interior. The unit of measurement is the one you already know, Btu. You also know that you have to remove 144 Btu of heat to convert 32°F water to ice. Ice *absorbs* the same 144 Btu in melting. It is this simple relationship between melting ice and absorbed Btu that lets us measure the efficiency of the box.

Begin getting the interior of the box cold by loading it with block ice. If you already have refrigeration, you can use it to chill the box, but *not* if it is a holding plate system. Once the box interior temperature is below 40°F, remove the ice (and water) and plug the drain if the box has one. Reload the cold and dry box with around 4 pounds of block ice *per cubic foot of box interior*, weighing the ice just before you put it in. Try to work out a way of keeping the block or blocks above the water that is going to accumulate as the ice melts. Close the lid and note the time. Twenty-four hours later, remove the remaining ice and weigh it to determine how much melted. Multiply the weight loss in pounds by 144 to determine how much heat has passed through the insulation.

Let's assume that your box melts 27 pounds of ice in 24 hours. That is 3,888 Btu per day, or 162 Btu per hour, a number consistent with what we might expect of a medium-size (9-cubic-foot) box indifferently insulated with 2 inches of polystyrene foam. This is the amount of cooling required *just to keep up with heat leak*. Allow me to point out that a number like 3,888 gives a false suggestion of precision, sort of like airline arrival times. This number and the other equally imprecise values we are about to derive from it are very useful, but more in a relative sense than in absolutes.

If you install a 12-volt refrigerator in this box, how much power is it going to require? Without getting into the math and the efficiency assumptions, the current generation of 12-volt refrigerators will consume about 1 amp-hour of power to remove 60 Btu from a refrigerator or 50 Btu from a freezer. For a combined-use box, we won't be too far off using 55 Btu of heat removal per amp-hour of power consumption. Dividing the hourly heat leak of 162 Btu by 55 gives us almost 3 Ah. That makes the daily battery draw to keep up with the heat leak into this box around 71 Ah. That doesn't sound *too* bad. But wait! We haven't actually refrigerated anything yet. Or frozen anything. Or opened the lid. Or given any consideration to ambient temperatures.

Temperature Differential

Suppose the outside temperature during this test is about 80°F and the ice held the box temperature at around 40°F. That makes the temperature difference between inside and outside 40°F. But take your old boat south where the ambient temperature is 100°F and what happens? The relationship between temperature differential and heat leak is direct. A 60°F temperature differential will yield 1.5 times the leak of a 40°F differential—5,832 Btu daily in this case. That raises the daily electrical requirement to offset the heat leak to 106 Ah.

Four of the six sides of the original icebox in our old boat were inside the engine compartment. We used half the original box as a freezer, but for the purpose of illustration let's make the whole box a freezer. Now we are trying to hold the interior of the box near 10°F. An engine room temperature of 120°F would give us a temperature differential of 110°F, raising the leak number to 10,692 Btu (2.75 × 3,888) and the power demand to around 195 Ah daily—probably more because the refrigerant is less efficient at colder temperatures, which is why we normally assume 50 Btu per amp-hour for a freezer. Don't miss the point here. A big freezer takes lots of power. If you are intent on a big freezer, plan on an engine-driven system or an *extremely* robust 12-volt system.

Effect of Insulation

Why does your box leak heat? Some enters through cracks around openings, but most passes through the walls. We insulate the walls to inhibit the transfer of heat from outside to inside; thicker insulation lessens the leak. Assume the test box has 2 inches of foam insulation. What if we increase it to 4 inches (lid included) of the same foam? The effect of more insulation can be estimated by the fractional relationship

of the old insulation to the new, so doubling the insulation halves the leak. Tripling the thickness of the insulation reduces the leak to $\frac{1}{3}$ of the original, and quadrupling it (from 2 to 8 inches in this case) brings it down to $\frac{1}{4}$ of the original. If we apply these fractions to the original leak, we get leak numbers of 1,944 Btu with 4 inches of foam, 1,296 Btu with 6 inches, and 972 Btu with 8 inches. Note that the benefit of more insulation is a decreasing one. The first 2 inches of added insulation reduced the leak by 1,944 Btu, but the last 2 inches reduced it by just 324 Btu.

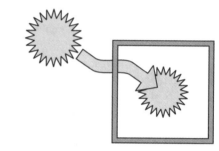

Insulation = 1; Heat leak = 1.

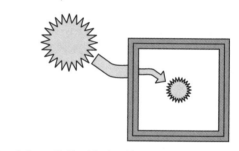

Insulation = 2; Heat leak = $\frac{1}{2}$.

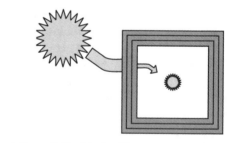

Insulation = 3; Heat leak = $\frac{1}{3}$.

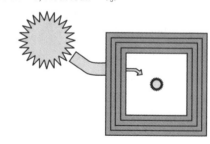

Insulation = 4; Heat leak = $\frac{1}{4}$.

Heat leak has a reciprocal relationship to insulation thickness.

The measurement for heat conductivity is expressed in terms of a K-factor (which tells us the rate at which heat travels through a substance), with the efficiency of insulation expressed as the reciprocal of the material's K-factor, or the R-value. Foam board normally used to insulate iceboxes is likely to have an R-value between 4 and 6.5. The higher the R-value, the better the insulating properties. Replacing lesser-quality insulation with better insulation will also reduce heat leak. As with additional thickness, the effect of a higher R-value is also fractional. Replacing 2 inches of R-4 insulation (total R-value = 8) with 4 inches of R-6 insulation (total R-value = 24) reduces the leak to 1,296 Btu, $^8/_{24}$ of the original.

Suppose you do this—replace the old foam with twice as much of a better foam. Your box should now require only about 54 Btu per hour of refrigeration to keep up with heat leak, which translates into a daily load of around 24 Ah in Connecticut but 36 Ah in hotter St. Thomas. And you still have not actually refrigerated anything and certainly not made ice.

Box Size

Since heat passes through the walls of the box, it can be useful to imagine the walls as uniformly porous—like screen—and the heat like a mist of water. The bigger the area of the screen, the more water is going to pass through. Likewise, the greater the surface area of the box, the more heat will leak through. Heat leak into a closed box relates directly to the box's total surface area, conventionally the outside surface area. Your 9-cubic-foot box will have an outside surface area (insulated) of about 45 square feet. Cutting the interior size by 50%, to 6 cubic feet, reduces the outside surface area to about 37 square feet—a reduction of about 18% with a similar reduction in leak. Smaller boxes are more efficient.

Of course you are not installing refrigeration machinery to cool an empty box. When you actually

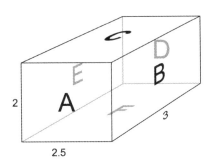

Sum the surface areas of all sides of a box to arrive at total outside surface area. Here the total outside surface area is 37.

chill something, that adds to the load. For example, the six-pack we cooled in exchange for fresh lobster required about 250 Btu. Cooling the lobster required another 300 Btu. About 10 Btu fell out of the box every time we opened our front-opening door. Assuming that you are cooling drinks, putting fresh food in the box, rechilling the pickles after they have been out for lunch, and opening the door or lid normally, you can expect to require another 2,000 Btu of refrigeration daily, probably more. Applying the 55 Btu per amp-hour, you need about 36 Ah to handle the "real" load, so even if we have tripled the R-value of the insulation around our example box, the total daily load is still going to be close to 60 Ah in a temperate climate and 72 Ah in the tropics.

PARTS BEFORE THE WHOLE

You don't really need to know how refrigeration works to outfit your boat with it, but you should know an evaporator from a condenser. So let's quickly follow the refrigerant on its circular path.

I have already mentioned that the change of state from liquid to gas requires a substantial amount of latent heat. If this change of state occurs inside your sealed box, the heat required must come from inside the box. That is exactly what happens. Refrigerant with a low boiling point—minus 15°F in the case of R-134a—enters the box as a liquid and is allowed to vaporize inside, absorbing large amounts of latent heat as it does. That same heat is released outside the box when the refrigerant changes back to a liquid. The circulation functions as a heat conveyor with the evaporator at the loading end and the condenser at the shipping end. The motor that runs the conveyor is the compressor.

Let's start at the compressor. Since R-134a boils at –15°F, its natural state even at freezer temperatures is going to be a gas. You need it to be liquid if you want it to absorb latent heat with a change in state, so how do you keep it from boiling before you want it to? The same way you raise the boiling point for your engine coolant—by putting it under pressure. A 1-psi pressure increase raises the boiling point of water about 3°F, so a 7-pound radiator cap raises the boiling point of water from 212°F to 233°F. To raise the boiling point of refrigerant from −15°F to something above 100°F so it will not boil at ambient temperature requires a lot of pressure. That is where a mechanical compressor comes in. The liquid is not compressible, but the gas is, so the compressor usually compresses the gas to between 125 and 175 psi, depending on the type of system.

Refrigeration cycle.

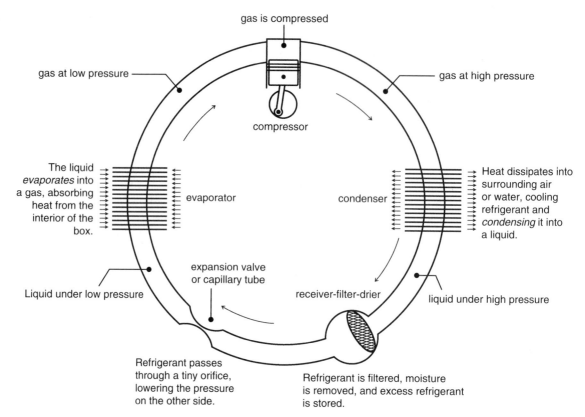

gas is compressed

gas at low pressure

gas at high pressure

compressor

The liquid *evaporates* into a gas, absorbing heat from the interior of the box.

evaporator

condenser

Heat dissipates into surrounding air or water, cooling refrigerant and *condensing* it into a liquid.

expansion valve or capillary tube

Liquid under low pressure

receiver-filter-drier

liquid under high pressure

Refrigerant passes through a tiny orifice, lowering the pressure on the other side.

Refrigerant is filtered, moisture is removed, and excess refrigerant is stored.

Like packing a room, compressing the gas raises its temperature. The hot compressed gas then flows through the tubes of the radiator-like condenser, where it cools to its boiling point at this pressure. As it continues to release latent heat, the gas changes state to a liquid.

From the condenser, the liquid refrigerant typically passes through a canister that has a filter screen and is loaded with a desiccant to absorb any moisture that may have found its way into the refrigerant. Moisture is an anathema because it will freeze into ice inside the system, blocking the flow of the refrigerant. This canister may be called a drier or a receiver or an RFD (receiver-filter-drier). Often the drier incorporates a clear sight glass that allows you to observe the flow of refrigerant.

From the drier, the refrigerant goes into the box where, still under pressure, it is forced through a tiny opening in the form of a very slender tube appropriately called a capillary tube or through a more complicated valve called an expansion valve. Either way, the pressurized liquid sprays out of the tube or the valve into the relatively open space of the tubing loops that comprise the evaporator. The other end of the evaporator tubing is connected by hose or tubing to the suction side of the compressor, so the spraying liquid finds itself in a low-pressure

or even a slight vacuum environment. Once it is not under pressure, the refrigerant boils, absorbing heat. When the evaporator tubes are inside a metal plate—which can be flat, contoured to the box, or most often formed into a closed rectangular bin—they absorb heat directly from the interior of the box. When the tubes are inside a holding plate—a closed tank full of a liquid—the heat is removed from the liquid.

From the evaporator, the heat-bearing *but not hot* refrigerant completes the circle, traveling back to the compressor where it is recompressed, and the cycle repeats itself.

CHOICES

All you need to know to buy a new refrigerator for a house kitchen is the measurements of the space where you want to put it. The choice of marine refrigeration has not yet reached this level of simplicity.

ICE

When you realize the work involved to adequately insulate your existing icebox or to rip it out altogether and start all over, when you learn the cost of installing refrigeration and the cost to run it, and when you consider the mechanical and/or electrical complexity refrigeration inevitably adds, you could decide that refrigeration aboard *your* boat is not a particularly good idea. Any contribution to comfort or convenience that it provides for a boat that sees only weekend use is likely to be more imaginary than real. Ice is cheap and simple and often required anyway to transport supplies between home and the boat. Refrigeration will not preserve your food any better. Here is the rule: when you can load the box just once with ice and keep your food cold for the entire time you are aboard, installing refrigeration has a greater potential to detract than to enhance; stick with ice.

DC PORTABLE

The exception to this rule might be the 12-volt cooler. Technically, portable refrigeration is no more a boat improvement than a cooler with wheels, but because it can serve as well as a built-in system for some boaters, it merits inclusion here. Twelve-volt coolers are more appropriate for short-term use, but I have seen the efficient boxes sold under the Engel and Norcold brands used quite successfully on cruising boats whose cavernous built-in refrigerators turned out to consume more than the boats' owners were able or willing to provide. After you read this chapter you will not make that mistake, but for a boat preparing for a single seasonal cruise, the 12-volt portable can be a sensible alternative to the expense and undertaking of installing built-in refrigeration. Twelve-volt coolers are available in two distinct types.

Thermoelectric

The technology of thermoelectric cooling has been around since 1834, when Frenchman Jean Peltier applied voltage across two dissimilar metals and noted that one of them became cool to the touch while the other heated. Thermoelectric (TE) units have no refrigerant and no moving parts other than a small fan to dissipate heat. They are virtually silent in operation, and module life is about 250,000 hours of running time, so you can will the thing to your children. Unfortunately thermoelectric cooling is not very energy efficient. A typical unit will require about 100 amps per day to cool 1 cubic foot of capacity. That means you can expect a 40-quart thermoelectric cooler—which works out to about 1.35 cubic feet—to require 135 amps daily. And a thermoelectric cooler can reduce inside-the-box temperature only about 40°F below outside-the-box temperature, so if cabin temperatures get above 90°F (a common occurrence in southern waters), the temperature inside the box climbs into the 50s, no longer sufficiently cool to safely preserve meat or dairy products. In cooler climates TE coolers provide more food capacity size-for-size than an ice chest because none of the interior space is occupied with ice. The premium for a TE cooler over the cost of a regular ice chest is typically around $50, making it a true bargain if it provides adequate cooling for your needs and you can supply its voracious power appetite.

It is also possible to buy just the module to install in your own box. This is rarely practical for refrigeration because built-in boxes tend to be too large for efficient TE cooling, but a compact, well-insulated medicine cabinet using the smallest available thermoelectric unit could provide a solution for the sailor who needs to carry a supply of heat-sensitive prescription drugs to the tropics.

It might be worth mentioning that some very interesting things are currently happening in thermoelectric efficiency that show promise for the future. This "chip" technology on a small scale is already more efficient than compressor-powered refrigeration. Viable TE refrigeration could be just around the corner, or it could be like the long-awaited fuel cell. Only time will tell.

Compressor-Driven

Portable compressor-driven refrigerators are as different from thermoelectric coolers as computers are from typewriters—at a similar cost differential. A compact 12-volt compressor in one end of the cabinet is capable of holding the inside temperature as cold as 0°F, allowing the box to serve as a refrigerator or a freezer—but not both at the same time. Typically you can set the inside temperature to anything between 0°F and 45°F with the turn of a knob.

Starting at around $600, these self-contained units are not inexpensive, but they are still less costly than any other true refrigeration you can put aboard—except one with a wall-socket plug. They do not require any modifications to the boat other than a secure location. Given their relatively thin outside walls, the power consumption of these refrigerators can be unexpectedly small. A 40-quart model set to serve as a freezer will draw around 50 amps per day. Dial the in-box temperature up to a refrigerator setting, and the power consumption will decline by $1/3$ or more. Compressor-driven portables have found their way aboard some cruising boats, and this seeming efficiency accounts for that choice over the onboard machinery. Of course the real efficiency is that the box is 1 or 2 cubic feet, not 8 or 9. You can certainly construct a more efficient small box, one with concurrent refrigerator and freezer capability, but not with the ease or for the price of a portable.

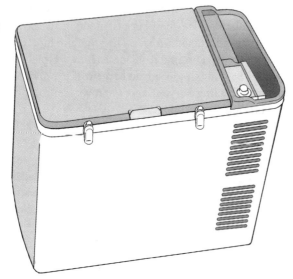

A compressor-driven portable can provide efficient refrigeration.

Portable refrigerators need to be located where the vents are unrestricted, and they need to be restrained. They also release the heat removed from the box into the cabin.

AC

At the other end of the spectrum from the weekend boater is the liveaboard. Refrigeration is a fundamental requirement aboard a boat serving as a home. The question simply becomes what kind you need.

If you plan to live aboard your old boat in a marina slip, even for some interim period while you line up your ducks, the availability of shore power pushes energy consumption from the top concern all the way to the bottom. In fact you can skip this energy-obsessed chapter altogether for now. In less time than it will take you to read the rest of it, you can have refrigeration aboard and already be chilling your shrimp cocktail, because the only sensible choice for you is an off-the-shelf 110-volt unit. Such refrigerators are cheap; they require no complicated installation; they are virtually trouble free (after several hundreds of millions of units, the manufacturers have worked out most of the bugs); and they are available from your local appliance dealer or "superstore" at a fraction of the cost of "marine" refrigeration. AC refrigeration is likewise the sensible choice for any boat that keeps an onboard generator running constantly. Your size choice can range from dorm room to apartment to restaurant, depending on the space available and the size of the companionway.

ABSORPTION

There is yet another type of refrigeration that occasionally finds its way aboard boats, particularly catamarans. The ice cream vendors who once plied their trade in the Tuileries gardens in Paris pushed wheeled carts that were distinctive for a large, black ball atop a pole sticking up from one corner. That ball was part of a refrigeration system that kept the ice cream solid even on relatively sultry summer days, seemingly without any power source. When I first encountered this system many years ago, I immediately thought I had discovered the end-all solution to marine refrigeration. But things that appear too good to be true usually are. The system is called absorption refrigeration, and what I discovered when I investigated further was that at the end of the day the vendors prepared their carts for the next day by heating the ball over a flame for a couple of hours. My enthusiasm waned.

Absorption refrigeration typically uses common ammonia as the refrigerant. Instead of a compressor, a gas-fired flame puts the refrigerant in motion. Often called LPG refrigerators, these models are built by a number of manufacturers for the RV trade. Silent operation, virtually no power drain (safety sensors and perhaps a circulating fan), and no engine-running requirement are all seductive characteristics, but the danger of an unattended flame aboard a boat cannot be ignored. And it isn't—not by insurance underwriters. Most will not insure a boat with LPG refrigeration aboard.

Nor is the danger ignored by absorption refrigeration manufacturers and distributors. None that I've heard of will knowingly sell a flame-powered refrigerator for use aboard a boat. They cite the imperative of proper venting of the burner as one difficulty with marine installations. Like a heater, an unvented refrigerator in a closed boat can be a killer. And to function properly, the refrigerator (or at least the plumbing) must not remain tilted. That necessitates gimballing aboard a monohull sailboat, which accounts for the higher incidence of gas refrigeration aboard catamarans.

In concept, absorption refrigeration has great appeal. Its advantages have been touted over the years by numerous cruising luminaries, including the almost legendary Eric Hiscock. But even Hiscock acknowledged the risk, and aboard his various *Wanderers* the refrigerator was operated only in port, never while underway. I suspect a constant flame aboard is more palatable in the cold dampness of Hiscock's home waters around the United Kingdom than it would be in the already oppressive heat of, say, Baja, California. Besides, an LPG refrigerator is only going to lower the inside-the-box temperature a maximum of about 60°F, so don't count on ice from this baby. Speaking of ice, the flame runs constantly, so propane consumption just for the refrigerator will likely be close to 1 pound a day. Combined with your normal

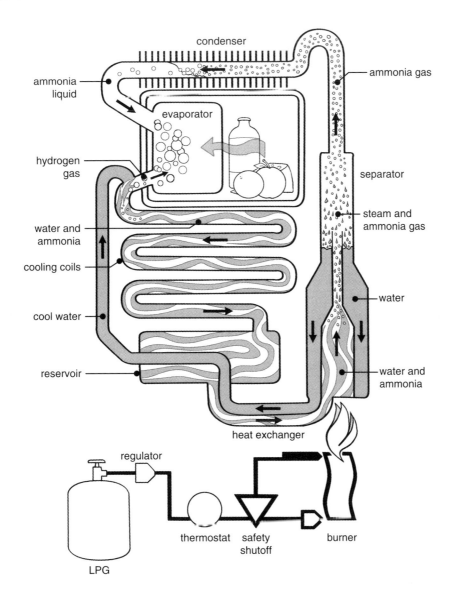

condenser

ammonia liquid

ammonia gas

evaporator

hydrogen gas

separator

water and ammonia

steam and ammonia gas

cooling coils

cool water

water

reservoir

water and ammonia

heat exchanger

regulator

thermostat   safety shutoff   burner

LPG

Absorption refrigeration uses ammonia as the refrigerant and a flame as the "engine."

consumption for cooking, that will have you looking to refill a 20-pound bottle every 10 days to two weeks. This is not quite as often as you might have to chase after ice, but LPG refill stations are often far from the waterfront, requiring some kind of delivery arrangement or the expense of your own transportation. Propane is not as cheap as it once was either.

Cabin heat, punishing fuel demand, and the absence of ice in your sundown G&T aside, the potential for disaster with a gas refrigerator surreptitiously installed, improperly vented, and casually monitored seems to me to be unjustifiably high. Prudence suggests leaving absorption refrigeration to the RVers and off-the-gridders.

HOLDING PLATE

A *holding plate* is nothing more than a liquid-filled metal tank with the evaporator tubes inside. Passing refrigerant through the tubing extracts heat from the fluid, causing it to freeze. The idea here is that you make your own block of ice by running your refrigerator one time, then let the ice keep the box cold until it melts. If we fill the holding plate with something other than water, we can make "ice" that is colder than 32°F and use the same method to chill a freezer. In fact, holding plates intended for refrigerator installation typically freeze at around 26°F, and those for freezer installation freeze at around 5°F. However, before looking more closely at holding plates, we need to go back to our Btu calculations for heat leak.

When we left this discussion, we had replaced the original insulation of our 9-cubic-foot box with 4 inches of R-6 foam, cutting the leak from the (hypothetical) original amount of 162 Btu per hour to a more palatable 54 Btu at 80°F ambient temperature. Let's assume a common configuration of dividing this box in half and putting the holding plates on the freezer side, "spilling" chilled air into the refrigerator side. (Actually we need to spill warm air out of the refrigerator side but this is just semantics.) Presumably half of our leak will come from each side, but on the freezer side the temperature differential is going to be close to double that on the refrigerator side, which will double the leak on that side. We have a 27-Btu leak on the refrigerator side and a 54-Btu leak on the freezer side. Raise the ambient temperature from 80°F to 100°F, and these leak numbers become 40 Btu and 70 Btu for a total of 110 Btu per hour or 2,640 Btu daily.

Keeping the daily refrigeration load at our earlier estimate of 2,000 Btu, let's assume that on most days all you use the freezer for—other than keeping the already-frozen stuff frozen—is to make a couple of trays of ice for cocktail hour. A tray of ice weighs about 1 pound, so 2 pounds of water cooled from 85°F to 32°F requires 106 Btu (2 × 53). Freezing requires another 288 (2 × 144), so your total freezer load is 394 Btu. This puts the total combined load at around 5,000 Btu per day (2,640 + 2,000 + 394).

Plate Size

If your holding plates are part of an engine-driven system and you are hoping to run your engine every other day, you need plates capable of absorbing 10,000 Btu. The solution inside commercial holdover plates varies with manufacturer and with the purpose of the plate (refrigerator or freezer), but we will not be far off if we assume that a gallon of solution will absorb about 1,000 Btu. That means you are going to need 10 gallons. At 231 cubic inches per gallon, you need 1.34 cubic feet of frozen solution inside the box. Unfortunately the tubing inside holdover plates takes up about 30% of the internal space, so for 1.34 cubic feet of solution, the plates will occupy 1.9 cubic feet of the box interior, nearly 40% of the total freezer space. Looking at it another way, a 12-by-18-by-3-inch plate contains about 2 gallons of solution. You need *five* such plates. You are more likely to opt for two or perhaps three plates, settling for a single day of holdover capacity.

Most of the engine-driven systems available are enough alike that parts are interchangeable. Compressors are the same. Fittings, hoses, driers, and controls are standard. Condensers may differ in design but not in function. Assuming ample compressor displacement, how quickly you can freeze the plates depends mostly on the internal structure of the holdover plates. Here there are real differences in design.

Internal compromises. Some manufacturers place the greatest emphasis on the solution inside the plates, insisting on a true eutectic solution. A eutectic solution freezes at a fixed temperature and maintains that temperature until it thaws completely. The other choice is usually a glycol solution—antifreeze. Glycol solutions warm as they thaw, allowing the temperature of the box to warm as well. Water is the eutectic solution of choice, with salts added to lower the freezing temperature. A brine solution is as much as 30% more effective at absorbing heat than a glycol solution, but it is highly corrosive, necessitating that brine-filled plates be constructed entirely of zinc-coated or stainless steel.

However, there is more to holdover-plate efficiency than heat absorption. How quickly the heat can be removed from the plate is equally important to the user. This is a function of the plate's construction. If you compare the construction of holdover plates from two different manufacturers, you may find four times as much tubing inside one compared to another with the same external dimensions from a different manufacturer. The tubing may be in a single serpentine length or several parallel coils. Fins attached to the tubing can also enhance heat transfer. Solution in

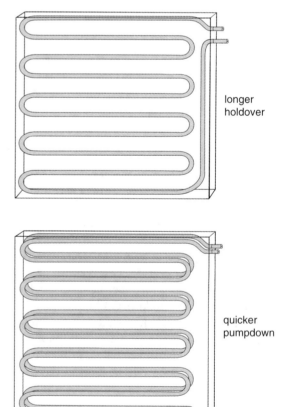

longer holdover

quicker pumpdown

Holding-plate construction is a compromise of material choices and tubing versus solution volume.

contact with the tubing freezes first, but this frozen solution then insulates the rest of the solution from the refrigerant. The more direct the contact, the smaller this effect, so the greater the surface area of the cooling coil, the quicker a plate can be frozen. That would seem to make plates with more tubing better, but more internal structure also reduces the volume of brine and thus the holdover capacity of the plate. Internal tubing length and size will be a compromise between maximum heat transfer and maximum holdover capacity.

Heat transfer is also improved if the tank is constructed of a heat-conductive material such as cast aluminum. Cast-aluminum holding plates can be further enhanced with internal finning, but a brine solution will quickly corrode aluminum, so these plates must be glycol filled, yet another compromise.

Holdover plates of the kind typically used in marine refrigeration have a practical pumpdown limit of around 1,500 Btu per hour. If our example box has a single large plate, we are looking at more than 3 hours of run time (5,000 ÷ 1,500) daily under normal use conditions. Because the capacity of the compressor is nearly always greater than that of the plate, dividing desired volume into two or three plates will be more efficient but not two or three times as efficient. Three properly designed and connected plates might be pumped down at the rate of 2,500 Btu per hour, cutting the run time to around 2 hours. If you don't want to run the compressor for 2 hours a day, you must increase the number of holdover plates (and maybe the compressor size) or reduce the load. After insulation and size, the way you use the box has the most potential for load reduction.

As a practical matter, holding plates are often sized for half the daily load to limit their reduction of the usable capacity of the box. For a DC-driven compressor, this compromise has little effect on power consumption—you are removing the same number of Btu from the box. For an engine-driven system, it requires running the engine at least twice a day.

Engine-Driven Compressor

Freeze the holding plates with a compressor mechanically driven by your main engine and you avoid the whole issue of battery drain. With plenty of available horsepower you can easily run a compressor powerful enough to freeze holding plates at their maximum rate. Matched with the appropriate holding plates, an engine-driven system will have no problem keeping a freezer frigid *and* a generous refrigerator cold. Engine-driven refrigeration is inherently more energy efficient because it avoids the conversion of energy from mechanical to electrical and back to mechanical. Battery inefficiencies are also avoided.

Because of their power, engine-driven systems have long been favored by voyagers and other boaters wanting a large-capacity freezer away from the dock. Power, however, is the only attribute where an engine-driven system will excel. These systems are relatively complicated and thus have more potential for trouble. Belt-driven compressors suffer from the inherent weakness of a leak-prone shaft seal, meaning you can plan on servicing an engine-driven system periodically to top off the refrigerant. The initial cost of this type of refrigeration, while commensurate with its greater capacity, is nevertheless twice to three times that of a constant-cycling DC system. Perhaps the most significant negative is that engine-driven refrigeration is not automatic. It requires your intervention *every single*

Engine-driven holding-plate refrigeration.

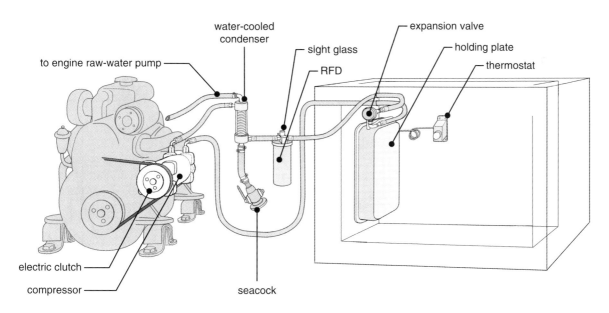

to engine raw-water pump

water-cooled condenser

sight glass

RFD

expansion valve

holding plate

thermostat

electric clutch

compressor

seacock

day in the form of starting and running the engine. Most often the engine will need to run twice a day for between 45 minutes and an hour each time. Aside from the engine hours and the bad-for-the-engine, light-load condition, this short but relentless demand can initially seem inconsequential. However, it can present some unanticipated difficulty if you find you want to see more of a place than you can explore in day trips or if some emergency takes you off the boat for more than 24 hours. If you spend any time in marinas, running the engine twice a day is going to be a vexation—to you and your neighbors.

If your primary source of electrical power is an engine-driven alternator, then an engine-driven compressor can essentially deliver free refrigeration. Or you can turn this around and conclude that if you run your engine daily for refrigeration, you are getting free power for your battery bank. Either way, if you have settled on engine-driven refrigeration as the best system for meeting your needs, your run-time goal is likely to be somewhere around an hour per day in the tropics. The physics that govern your holding plates may make this objective difficult to achieve.

DC Compressor

One alternative to reducing engine hours is to drive your compressor with an electric motor. This is how high-capacity DC refrigerators are often configured, with a belt-driven compressor and a $\frac{1}{2}$ hp motor mounted together on a skid. This type of drive is less efficient in an absolute sense than engine drive, but it's more efficient in terms of energy management. Here's how.

Staying with the same box and holding plate assumptions we've been using, we need 5,000 Btu daily. The minimum freeze time of our holding plates means this is going to take at least 2 hours of compressor time. With an engine-driven system, that also means 2 hours daily of engine time. If you drive the compressor with a DC motor, you have to run it for the same 2 hours, but now the issue becomes power consumption.

A $\frac{1}{2}$ hp DC motor will draw around 40 amps under full load, but as the plate freezes, the load eases.

Belt-driven high-capacity DC holding-plate refrigeration.

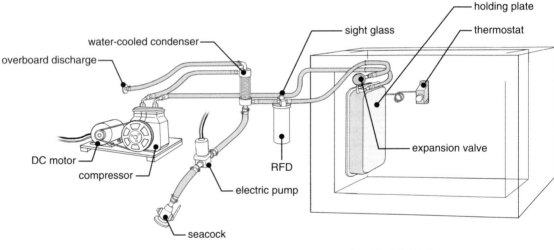

A more trouble-free high-capacity DC holding-plate system powered by a hermetically sealed compressor.

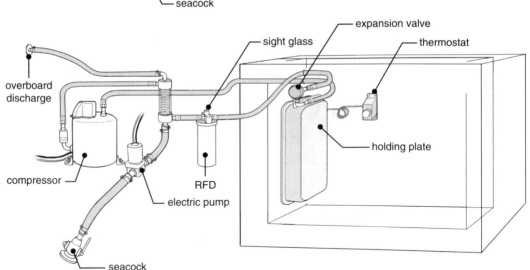

You should expect the average to be closer to 30 amps. If you have a battery bank powerful enough to sustain a 40 amp discharge, at the end of 2 hours the total discharge is around 60 Ah. Even allowing for a 20% loss to charging, you only need to put 72 Ah back into the battery bank. A robust charging system matched with a large battery bank can accomplish this in an hour. So for the same amount of refrigeration, you have cut your engine time in half. There is the added benefit that you can run the compressor twice or even 10 times a day if that is the most efficient way of maintaining a consistent freezer temperature. If you do not have adequate alternative power, you will still have to run the engine every day to keep the batteries charged, but the timing will not be so rigid.

The downside to DC refrigeration is the cost of the equipment to meet these assumptions. A continuous 40 amp draw is twice the C20 rating for a 400 Ah bank. You should plan on 600 or even 800 Ah of battery capacity to run this system, plus whatever capacity you need for the other electrical loads on the boat. (Should I mention that all this lead is going to weigh 400 pounds or more?) You are also going to need an alternator capable of charging a 600 Ah bank. Applying the 25% rule from Chapter 11, you are looking at fitting a 150 amp alternator. Toss in a smart regulator, and you will have spent $2,000 upgrading your electrical system over and above the cost of the refrigeration system.

This type of high-capacity DC refrigeration suffers from the same complexity and attendant breakdown vulnerabilities as an engine-driven system. Switching to a hermetically sealed compressor eliminates most of the failure and maintenance issues. A hermetic compressor, which most often resembles a black ball with slightly squashed sides, is sealed inside the refrigeration system. Hermetic sealing eliminates refrigerant leaks from the compressor, since any leakage that might occur remains sealed inside the system. A number of refrigeration manufacturers pair a hermetic compressor with a holding plate, but in general these smaller-capacity compressors will be stretched to their limits or beyond to keep up with a 5,000-Btu load. Expect such a system powered by the ubiquitous Danfoss BD50 compressor to run almost constantly at full capacity in hot weather with a daily power consumption of well over 100 Ah. At this writing some more powerful 12-volt hermetic compressors are just coming on the market. These are likely to supplant belt-driven compressors in DC holding-plate systems.

DC CONSTANT CYCLE

Constant-cycle 12-volt refrigeration works exactly like the refrigerator in your kitchen. It kicks on automatically when the temperature inside the box rises to some preset level and shuts off when it has cooled the box down to the lower thermostat setting. How often and how long the compressor runs is a function of the size and efficiency of the box. We have already seen this type of refrigeration in compressor-driven portable refrigerators. It is also available in stand-alone and built-in boxes that are seen more often in powerboats (usually allowing both AC and DC operation). Conversion units are also available to convert an existing ice chest into a DC refrigerator. The constant-cycle DC conversion unit is easily the most popular refrigeration system among sailors. It is easy to see why. It uses the box already built into the boat (maybe). It has the lowest initial cost of any

Twelve-volt constant-cycle refrigeration.

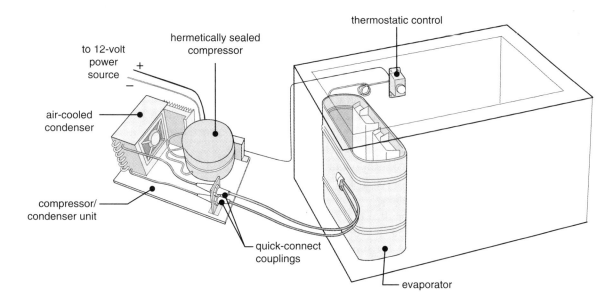

- to 12-volt power source
- +
- −
- hermetically sealed compressor
- air-cooled condenser
- compressor/ condenser unit
- quick-connect couplings
- thermostatic control
- evaporator

built-in refrigeration system. The units are efficient, long-lived, and trouble free. And with just two major components—the evaporator that goes inside the box and the compact compressor/condenser unit that goes outside—installation is simple.

The knock on constant-cycle systems is that the small compressor is only about $2/_3$ as efficient as the higher-capacity compressors normally used in holding-plate systems. This is partially offset by the fact that the direct cooling of an evaporator plate is more efficient than the indirect cooling of a holding plate. The evaporator plate also occupies a lot less space, so you can get the same usable interior space in a smaller box, and a smaller box will improve the efficiency of the refrigerator.

Still, you are pretty much stuck with a limitation of around 55 Btu of heat removal per amp-hour of 12-volt power, assuming some freezer capacity. That means if you bolt the evaporator of a conversion refrigerator to the same 9-cubic-foot box we put the holding plates into and assume the same 5,000-Btu load, you are looking at a daily battery draw of more than 90 Ah. It is worth noting that this type of compressor normally draws around 6 amps when it starts and declines toward 3 amps or less as the evaporator chills. If we peg the draw at a 4.5 amp average, the compressor is going to run 20 out of 24 hours or 50 minutes of every hour. That is not going to leave much extra capacity for market days when you load it with hot cans, bottles, meat, and produce. At 5,000 Btu, you are approaching the maximum capacity for this generation of conversion refrigerators.

You need to grasp the reality of an inflexible 90 Ah daily load before installing this type of refrigeration. Applying the $2^1/_2$ times consumption rule from Chapter 11, a 90 Ah load requires a minimum of 225 Ah of dedicated battery capacity. This is less than that required by a DC holding-plate system, even though the consumption is higher, because the rate of discharge is just 6 amps. But discharge is only half of the equation. You also need to put these amps back. Deep-cycle batteries are going to accept a charge rate no higher than about 25% of their capacity, so your recharge of this bank is going to start at 55 amps and decline. That suggests more than 2 hours of engine time per day; the reality is likely to be closer to 3 hours. Yikes! This is what too many optimistic sailors discover to their profound disappointment only *after* they have installed 12-volt refrigeration.

Doubling the size of the battery bank can cut your engine time to something over an hour if your alternator is up to the task. This is better, but it involves the expense of both more batteries and more alternator power. The level discharge of constant-cycle refrigeration can also be matched to alternative power sources, meaning solar panels and/or wind generation. It is quite possible for a 5-foot wind generator or a pair with smaller blades to supply all or most of the power needed for 12-volt refrigeration. Likewise, a significant solar array can drastically reduce engine time, but both of these options are costly, doubling or tripling the real cost of your refrigeration.

Water Cooling

What about water cooling to reduce power consumption? A water-cooled condenser *is* more efficient than one that is air cooled, but water cooling adds complexity, the real risk of system-destroying corrosion, and an additional power demand for the circulating pump. One of the advantages of constant-cycling refrigeration over a system the runs once or twice a day is that the heat load on the condenser is much smaller. That makes an air-cooled condenser perfectly satisfactory until the ambient temperature is quite high. If you can feed the condenser air that is below 100°F (not that hard to do in a boat floating in 85°F water), an air-cooled unit will draw less power. There are passive condensers that are submerged, either in a through-hull fitting or as a keel cooler. They eliminate the pump draw but require some boat motion to prevent them from sitting in their own heat. Fouling is also an issue. In general I think you are better off locating the air-cooled condenser where it will draw the coolest air aboard. That rules out the engine room.

An air-cooled condenser also allows you to incorporate a smart compressor controller in your system if you choose. Oddly, compressors are more efficient at lower speeds, and this bit of electronic wizardry adjusts the compressor speed to the minimum required to pull box temperature down, with a run time of 50 minutes or more every hour rather than the usual target of 30 minutes or less. The compressor runs longer but at slower speeds, reducing current draw for the same amount of cooling. The gains are modest, typically around 6%, but as Illinois Senator Everett Dirksen famously observed, "A dollar here, a dollar there, and pretty soon you are talking about real money."

Evaporator Size

You will also have a choice of evaporators. Most units are offered with bin-shaped evaporators in a variety of sizes, but you will also find some that are L-shaped or flat. Large flat evaporators can be bent to match the inside dimensions of the box. Similar to the volume of solution in holding plates, it is the surface area of an evaporator plate—both sides if it is on standoffs—that quantifies the evaporator's capacity. Because the compressor normally has more heat-transferring capacity than the evaporator, installing the largest available evaporator that will fit inside your box will result in the quickest heat removal but not necessarily the shortest run times. This is because the space inside a bin-shaped evaporator in a combined refrigerator-freezer installation is typically the freezer, and more freezer volume translates into higher power consumption. If you can use the additional freezer volume, a larger evaporator is the most efficient way to get it. You can increase freezer volume even more by partitioning the box, but this will definitely raise the daily electrical load. Another way to gain a bit of extra freezer capacity is to locate vertical ice trays on the outside wall of the bin. Since they are in contact with the evaporator, they will freeze the same, and their absence from the interior provides freezer space for other items.

The best ways to lower the demand of constant-cycle refrigeration are to reduce the size of the box and/or increase the thickness of the insulation. These refrigerators are a joy in small boxes. They maintain a more consistent box temperature than holding-plate systems. They are automatic, nearly silent, and remarkably reliable. When combined with alternative power, there is something organically satisfying about ice cubes derived from wind or sunlight. But this type of system can just as easily become an expensive boondoggle when installed in a box that is too large and/or poorly insulated. A refrigerator box should have not less than 4 inches of foam insulation on all sides and a freezer should have 6 inches. For a big box, consider partitioning it and installing separate systems for the refrigerator and the freezer.

I shouldn't need to say this, but refrigeration should never be operated from the starting battery. This is especially a risk where charging and discharging is managed by turning a battery selector switch. The unrelenting demand of refrigeration will flatten a starting battery—particularly one that's long in the tooth—in a matter of hours. More than one captain has experienced the start-up failure at a critical moment because the refrigerator has drained the batteries. Do not be misled by the "low voltage cutout" feature you may see mentioned in the documentation. This is for the protection of the compressor. By the time it shuts down the system, the battery will be far too low to start any engine.

Twelve-volt refrigeration can be operated dockside by simply plugging in the battery charger.

SELECTION CRITERIA

How do you know which of these eight refrigeration possibilities (plus some hybrid versions) will represent the best enhancement for your old boat? It may not be as difficult as you expect. As long as ice can satisfy your real refrigeration needs, it is your lowest-cost option and requires no modifications. A compressor-driven portable can be a good alternative for a cruise that's long enough to make chasing ice an irritation but too short to justify the cost and effort of a custom refrigeration installation. If you are dockside, AC is the intelligent choice. Thermoelectric is cheap but still too inefficient for more than limited application. Because the dangers of absorption refrigeration outweigh its appeal, we can remove it from consideration. That leaves just holding-plate refrigeration—engine or battery powered—and 12-volt constant-cycle.

FOOD NEEDS

To choose between the last two, you have to start with your eating habits. I have already mentioned that you are going to find well-stocked markets in most of the places where cruisers gather. This fact essentially eliminates the true need for a lot of freezer volume unless voyaging is in your plans, you plan to cruise remote areas, or your idea of cruising is being mostly alone for weeks at a time. Even if your plans necessitate more cold stores than normal, vacuum packing now allows items that previously required freezing to be stored safely for weeks simply refrigerated.

Foreign markets will not carry a lot of your usual products, so if you like only Oscar Mayer bacon, you will have to freeze a supply. However, aside from the cost and annoyance of keeping your brands frozen, you risk missing out on one of the best aspects of travel. Try *poitrine fumé* on a French island and you will be using your bacon in beans. The point is that eating local foods reduces your refrigeration needs.

You will also be doing most of your shopping on foot or using public transportation. It is the same way locals shop in much of the world and why their domestic refrigerators are tiny by American standards. Small-volume shopping affects your refrigeration needs the same way. It also values freshness over convenience and might change how you view food.

If despite my counsel you are determined to have a cavernous freezer aboard, your refrigeration choice is simple. You need either an engine-driven or a high-capacity DC holding-plate system. If you can get by with a freezer the size of a boot box, the only choice is 12-volt constant-cycling, unless your cruise will be short enough that a compressor-driven portable makes more sense than a custom installation.

BOX SIZE

If your old boat was delivered with an ice chest, part of the interior volume is intended to accommodate ice. Such a box might be compatible with holding-plate refrigeration, with the plates necessitating extra interior volume, but installing DC constant-cycling refrigeration in the same box is unlikely to prove satisfactory.

In a no-compromise world, the existing box size will not be a factor because you will reconfigure it to the size you expect to actually need. How big is that? Try this. Find a cardboard box about 1 foot wide by 2 feet long and cut around it to make it about 1 foot deep. Sit it on the floor in front of your refrigerator at home and load it with items that you expect to have in your onboard refrigerator. Forget about six jellies, nine pickles, or four mustards. Put in one bottle or jar of each unique item, one or two of those with flavor options. Include a few drink cans and a couple of leftover containers. Don't put in eggs; fresh eggs keep perfectly without refrigeration. Don't put in gallon containers of milk; you will be buying UHT milk in quart boxes. Don't put in gallon water jugs; if you need refrigerated water you will use smaller bottles. Do include the stuff in the vegetable crispers and meat drawers. Most people are surprised to discover that everything fits into the box. It doesn't matter that it's packed; the fuller the refrigerator on your boat, the more efficient it is. If everything fits, you will be able to get along quite well with 2 cubic feet of refrigerated space.

Whatever size box this exercise suggests, double it if you like, but be aware that the exterior surface area of a 4-cubic-foot box with 4 inches of insulation will be 38% larger than a similar 2-cubic-foot box, resulting in about the same percentage of increased heat leak. Still, a 4-cubic-foot box is likely to be half

or a third the size of the ice chest. The bottom line here is that the bigger the box, the less happy you are likely to be with 12-volt constant-cycle refrigeration. The reverse is also true. The smaller the box, the happier you are likely to be with 12-volt refrigeration—as long as the box is not so small that it will not hold all the things you ultimately want to refrigerate.

COST TO BUY

A powerful holding-plate system will cost $2,500 to more than $6,000. A 12-volt constant-cycle refrigerator will cost a third to a quarter of that amount. If you install this system in a small, thickly insulated box so the daily battery drain is 35 to 40 Ah, this is a fair comparison. But what if you are trying to cool a 9-cubic-foot box? Now the daily drain is simply going to overwhelm the boat's normal electrical charging and storage capabilities. Between additional battery capacity and more alternator power, it will be hard to spend much less than $1,500 upgrading the electrical system. And while there are other reasons to outfit your boat with alternative power, 12-volt refrigeration is typically both the catalyst and the primary beneficiary. Assigning the cost of the wind generator and/or solar panels will put the total outlay for 12-volt constant-cycle refrigeration on a par with engine-driven refrigeration—when the box size is large.

The big loser in the cost-to-buy comparison is the high-capacity DC holding-plate system. These systems cost substantially more than a nearly identical engine-driven system because of the DC motor and a 12-volt water pump, *and* they require a more expensive electrical system upgrade than a constant-cycle system because of their higher rate of discharge.

COST TO RUN

Here you might rationalize that if you have no alternative power sources and intend to run your engine daily to charge your batteries, the run cost of an engine-driven refrigerator will be zero. Those of us less philosophical will look at the balance sheet. If electric refrigeration allows you to reduce your daily engine run time, that necessarily reduces your fuel expense. Where 12-volt refrigeration leads to alternative power sources aboard—accounted for in the cost-to-buy comparison—and as a result you spend little or nothing on fuel to power the refrigerator, this will be the cost-to-run winner.

EASE OF OPERATION

The ideal refrigerator is the one in your kitchen. It is just *there*. You set the thermostat when the delivery

Find the minimum volume your array of refrigerated items can be consolidated into to determine the size for your refrigerator box.

guys unpacked it and haven't touched it since. Expect this ease of operation only when someone else is supplying the power.

Mechanical refrigeration is the most demanding system to operate. You have to monitor the temperature of the box and be aboard to start the engine when the holding plates need freezing. You have to monitor the plates or time your run time and also be there to shut down the engine. And you usually have to do this twice a day every day. Engine-driven refrigeration gets no ease-of-operation points.

A big 12-volt holding-plate system can be configured to operate automatically, either via a thermostat or a timer, but it is still essential to keep an eye on the box temperature. You also need to keep a close watch on battery voltage. And whenever the engine runs for any reason, it is normal to start the high-draw compressor manually to maximize the benefit of alternator output.

The only truly automatic refrigeration system is constant-cycle. A well-configured 12-volt constant-cycle refrigerator can function as automatically as a domestic refrigerator except for the need to occasionally defrost the evaporator and the need to maintain the batteries. If you do not have alternative power, that puts you right back to the necessity of running the engine daily. Even with alternative power, neither the wind nor the sun are constant, so battery level monitoring and sporadic engine running will be required. Still, on balance, 12-volt constant-cycle refrigeration will require the least attention and intervention.

DEPENDABILITY

Any system with a hermetic compressor is going to be more dependable than one powered by a pulley-drive compressor. Over time the maintenance requirements of a pulley-driven component system seem to grow more onerous as the various components and their connections fail due to age, wear, vibration, or corrosion—like small waves combining to form a big wave. Pulley-driven systems always require maintenance. Hermetic systems typically do not.

CRUISING OR TRAVELING

Maybe this section is overkill because it is almost the same as ease of operation, but if you install a system that requires daily intervention, it prevents you from leaving refrigerated food aboard an unattended boat. This becomes an issue when you want to take an overnight sightseeing tour, when you want to travel inland, or if you want to help a fellow cruiser with a sail or an adventure. It takes away the possibility of spontaneous overnight stays away from the boat and adds complications in the event of a health crisis. Only a 12-volt constant-cycle system matched to alternative power will free you to be away from the boat for days or even weeks at a time. It is one thing to ask a friend to check your battery level once a week and run the engine if necessary. It is quite another to obligate the same friend to go aboard and run your engine for an hour twice every day.

INSTALLATION CONSIDERATIONS

I might have included ease of installation in the selection criteria, but I doubt that this has much influence on selection. However, when you are doing it yourself, a "good" installation will be more difficult to achieve if you have to engineer the drive of the compressor than if the compressor and its drive come as a single unit.

Whatever refrigeration system you buy will come with comprehensive installation instructions and usually with support personnel intimately familiar with the system just a telephone call or an e-mail away. In fact, buying a system from some manufacturers is a lot like joining a club. Solid factory support is a worthy consideration, particularly for sometimes-finicky engine-driven systems. It would be a waste of printer's ink for me to provide generic installation instructions here when the manual provided with each system will detail specifics, but an understanding of the relationship of the various components might be helpful in your decision about whether to tackle the installation alone or enlist assistance.

TWELVE-VOLT

By now you should know that constant-cycle refrigeration is your hands-down best choice unless you need a large freezer space. Guess what? These systems are also the easiest to install. Don't you love it when the planets line up like that? Twelve-volt refrigeration systems typically have only three parts, come precharged, and can be installed by an average boat-owner or an above-average baboon in an afternoon. You mount the evaporator unit to an interior wall of the box with four screws through standoffs. The thermostat typically can be located inside or outside the box. Inside is easier but outside is more convenient. The greatest difficulty is likely to be finding the right location for the compressor/condenser unit. Don't compromise here. The condenser must have a plentiful supply of cool air or you will pay for your error in amp-hours. Ducting can work, but direct flow is better if you can arrange it. Don't be too hesitant to relocate some other item to free up the "ideal" spot.

The efficiency of your refrigerator is likely to make or break your entire electrical system.

Connecting these systems is no more difficult than mounting them. There will be a two-tube coil of soft copper tubing attached to the evaporator that you uncoil and feed through a hole in the box wall before you mount the evaporator. You route the thermostat's wire or sensing tube, depending on whether the thermostat is inside or outside, through the same hole. Clamp the thermostat tube to a special bracket on the evaporator. Route the two refrigerant tubes and the wire from the thermostat to the compressor/condenser unit. Plug the wire into the corresponding socket at the compressor and screw the refrigeration tubes to couplings in a manner similar to the way you attach a hose to a dockside faucet. Tightening the couplings opens internal poppet valves, allowing the charge of refrigerant to circulate. Reinsulate and seal the hole in the box where the wire and/or tubing exits. Make the electrical connections, properly fused and with a switch in the hot side, to the plus and minus terminals on the compressor/condenser unit. Click. Whir.

The installation of a belt-driven system will be more difficult. To start with there are more pieces, with the compressor and condenser separate, the RFD, probably multiple holding plates, pumps and hoses and a strainer for the raw-water plumbing, and several coils of precharged refrigeration hose or tubing to link all the parts into a whole.

COMPRESSOR MOUNTING

For an engine-driven system, finding a way to mount the compressor is likely to be the biggest challenge. It should mount like the alternator—directly to the engine. System manufacturers typically provide a "universal" (would that it really was) mounting

bracket. However, the location envisioned by such brackets does not account for the large-frame alternator you have already mounted or the proximity of the engine compartment bulkhead. If you find a spot that can work, designing and fabricating a bracket mount precise enough to give perfect belt alignment and robust enough to handle the load will bring its own challenges.

If off-the-engine mounting was a *good* idea, car manufacturers wouldn't go to such sometimes heroic lengths to mount the same compressors on their belt-congested engines rather than to the car. However, if you cannot find a way to mount the compressor to the engine—a not-uncommon circumstance—you will have to mount it to the boat. This should always be a second choice, even though the system manufacturer will tell you it is OK. Side loading caused by the independent motion of the engine puts both the compressor and crankshaft bearings at some risk, but less than you might imagine because the engine actually moves *around* the crankshaft. At the crankshaft pulley the engine is essentially motion free, so if the compressor belt leads just from this pulley and not around any other pulley attached to the engine, harmful loading should not occur. Long belt runs may need an idler pulley, which should be mounted to the compressor or the boat rather than the engine.

Rigidly mounting the compressor to the boat does have the benefit of reducing stress on the refrigeration connections to the compressor. The main problem with bolting the compressor to the boat is that it is going to set up vibrations when it is running, particularly if it is a reciprocal type. Reciprocal compressors are the big, square ones that look like lawn mower engines. These are nearly always aluminum Climate Control compressors (the same compressor that used to be sold under the York brand). Swash-plate compressors are the round ones, not much larger than an alternator. Sankyo/Sanden swash-plate compressors have totally replaced reciprocal compressors for auto air conditioning and are likely to be the compressor that comes with your refrigeration system unless you buy a particularly high-capacity system. Because these operate much more smoothly, they are better suited to off-engine mounting.

Smoother, cheaper, lighter, and more compact, but swash-plate compressors also suffer a higher incidence of failure than their reciprocal counterparts. Because they do not have an internal oil supply, swash-plate compressors are entirely dependent on oil circulating with the refrigerant for lubrication. If the refrigerant leaks out of the system and

The belt driving a compressor mounted off the engine should not run around any pulley on the engine other than the crankshaft pulley.

compressor

rigid mount

idler pulley

crankshaft pulley

the compressor runs, damage is likely. In a freezer installation the compressor may pull the system into a deep vacuum, resulting in reduced refrigerant circulation and correspondingly less lubrication. A low-pressure cutout switch can protect the compressor from damage due to lost refrigerant, but for a freezer installation, a reciprocal compressor will be at lower risk.

Whether it's on or off the engine, you must get the compressor pulley to align precisely with the crankshaft pulley. A good tool for evaluating this is a straight $1/2$-inch dowel, which should drop smoothly into the grooves of both pulleys. Once you have the compressor solidly mounted and belted to the engine, everything else should be easier. Mount the other bits and pieces in convenient locations and plumb the water-cooled condenser. Mounting holding plates is not much different from evaporator mounting. There will also be some wiring involved for the various pressure, temperature, and/or time controls; the electric clutch on the front of the compressor; and possibly solenoid valves. With everything in place, connect the precharged hoses to link the components and charge the system.

TOPPING OFF

It might be prudent to get a licensed technician to look over your installation, checking for leaks and for the level of the initial charge. Once the system is operational, *you* cannot legally open the system to service it if doing so will release refrigerant. That applies anywhere in the world on a U.S. vessel. Even if the likelihood of enforcement is remote, the environmental insult is real, so do not blow off a full charge. However, if you are going to have pulley-driven refrigeration aboard and are going to depend on it, you'd better learn how to put refrigerant into the system and how to determine when it contains the right amount.

A set of refrigeration gauges is *not* essential, but for $30 or $40 they can tell you what is happening inside the system if trouble develops. However, all you really need for topping off is a charging hose, a container of refrigerant, and a can tap. There are trigger or push-button taps, but a rotating valve is more secure for storing unused refrigerant. Buy your refrigerant in 12-ounce cans from your local automotive or discount store. You should only need a small amount, and this size will be easier for you to use and store than bulk tanks. The current cost is around $10, less on sale, but the price could escalate or retail refrigerant could go off the market altogether with a change

in the laws. Wipe the top of the can. Open the valve tap completely (counterclockwise) and screw the tap onto the can. Close the valve completely. When the pin pierces the top of the can, some refrigerant may hiss out of the hose port, but it will stop when you have the valve fully closed. Connect the charging hose to the tap, making the end with the metal piece in the center the free end.

Your pulley-driven compressor will have either Schrader or Rotolock service valves, and they will be marked SUCT(ion) and DISCH(arge). The topping-off procedure is similar for a hermetic compressor but the ports may not be labeled. No problem. The larger line is the suction line. Ignore other capped ports your system might have and use the one on or closest to the compressor on the suction side. (Likewise for the high-pressure side if you are using a gauge set.) Schrader valves are easy to identify because they have a single knurled or hex cap, whereas Rotolock valves have two caps—a large one covering a valve stem with a square end and a small one sealing the port. Schrader valves are spring-loaded, exactly like tire valves, so you can remove the cap without losing the refrigerant charge. This is emphatically *not* the case

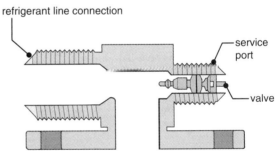

Schrader valve.

refrigerant line connection

service port

valve

Metal center piece in service hose opens the valve.

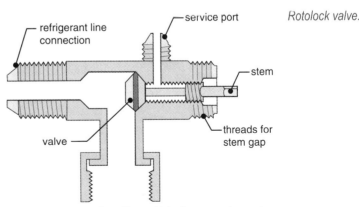

Rotolock valve.

refrigerant line connection

service port

stem

threads for stem gap

valve

Shown in "backseat" position, which closes service port. Turning stem allows both ports to be open (mid-position) or the compressor to be isolated from the line (front seat).

Service valves.

with a Rotolock valve. If you remove the smaller cap without first turning the squared stem fully *counter-clockwise* to close the service port, you will blow the entire refrigerant charge. The valve would normally be in this "backseat" position except during servicing, but some systems tee-connect pressure switches to the service ports, requiring that the valve be open during normal operation.

When topping off a system with Rotolock service valves, start by removing the large cap on the valve marked SUCT to expose the valve's squared stem. Turn this stem fully counterclockwise. Refrigeration suppliers sell a $1/4$-inch square ratchet wrench that makes turning this stem easier and should be among your tools if you have Rotolock valves. Do *not* turn the valve fully clockwise to its "front-seat" position, as this closes the suction line from the evaporator or holding plate. Remember to remove the cap on the service port *only* after you are sure the valve is backseated.

If you have Schrader valves, just remove the cap. Be sure this is the suction port. You are making this connection with the refrigerator and the engine off, but if you mistakenly connect the can to the discharge side, when you start the system the high pressure can actually blow the can apart, probably spoiling your day. Make sure the loose end of the charging hose is the one with the metal center, then attach it to the uncapped port but just loosely—about two turns. You need to purge the hose before you tighten it.

With the can upright, open the valve on the tap and refrigerant will begin to hiss out around the loose connection. This minimal discharge is necessary and

Always purge the service hose with refrigerant before sealing the connection to the service valve.

Refrigerant should escape vigorously before you tighten the service hose connection.

R134a

legal. The refrigerant is nontoxic, so the gas will not hurt you (I do not make the same claim for its effect on coming generations), but it can freeze your skin and cause eye damage, so exercise some caution. Open the valve a couple of turns so the hose is pressurized and the hiss insistent, then tighten the hose-to-port connection to stop the leak. All the air and moisture will have been expelled from the hose. If you have Schrader valves, tightening the connection will have depressed the valve pin and refrigerant will be going into the system. Close the tap valve to stop the flow. Rotolock valves will not admit refrigerant until you turn the stem clockwise a full turn or a turn and a half.

Always keep the can upright. If you invert it, the refrigerant enters the system as a liquid. In a moment you are going to start the refrigerator, and should liquid refrigerant enter the compressor while it is running, the compressor will be damaged.

If you have a gauge set, the red hose from the red gauge goes to the high-pressure port marked DISCH, the blue hose from the blue gauge goes to the low-pressure port marked SUCT (or the larger line to the compressor), and the center yellow hose connects to the refrigerant can. There is no need to connect the red hose to top off the system, but I am detailing the connection here so you will know how to do it for troubleshooting. You must always, *always* purge the manifold and all three hoses before connecting any of them to the open system. Start by attaching the red and blue hoses loosely to their respective ports. Connect the center hose to the tapped can. Close both manifold valves and open the tap valve to charge the manifold. Open the red (high-pressure) manifold valve to let refrigerant blow out of the loose connection at the compressor for a moment, then tighten the connection to stop the leak and immediately close the manifold valve. If this is a Schrader valve, tightening the hose opened the port and the red gauge will now read the pressure on this side of the system. If it is a Rotolock valve, you will need to turn the stem a bit more than a full turn clockwise to open the port.

Purge the blue side the same way. With the hose connections tight, both manifold valves closed, and both compressor valves open, the two gauges should read the pressure on both sides of the system, which on a system that has been idle long enough to equalize should be the same. Notice that the gauges read the system pressures regardless of the position of the manifold valves—open or closed. The function of two valves on the manifold is to connect the center hose to each side.

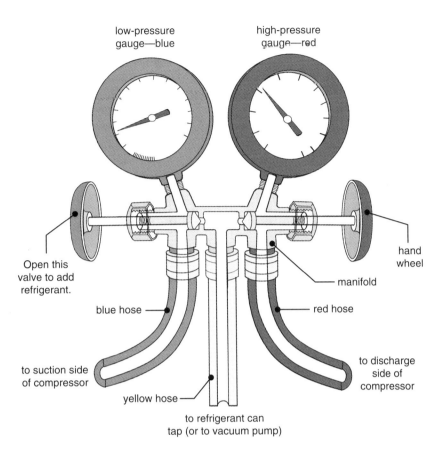

low-pressure
gauge—blue

high-pressure
gauge—red

*Refrigeration
gauge set.*

Open this
valve to add
refrigerant.

hand
wheel

manifold

blue hose

red hose

to suction side
of compressor

to discharge
side of
compressor

yellow hose

to refrigerant can
tap (or to vacuum pump)

That means you *never* turn the red-side valve when the system is running, only the blue-side valve.

To top off, start the refrigeration system, starting the engine if required, and let the compressor run for a minute. If you are using just a charging hose, open the tap valve, count to five, then close it. If you are charging through a gauge set, the tap valve is already open, so open the blue-side valve on the gauge manifold and count to five. Close it. On a hermetic compressor system the gauge of how you are doing will be the evaporator plate. When it only partially frosts, the refrigerant level is probably low. Add refrigerant in 5-second bursts spaced about 10 minutes apart to give the system time to adjust. Keep adding refrigerant until the entire plate frosts, but don't overfill the system—indicated by frosting or sweating of the suction line all the way to the compressor.

If you have a holding-plate system, the gauge of how you are doing will be the sight glass. Watch it right after you start the compressor and you should see a froth of bubbles become a stream of bubbles and then a stream of bubble-free refrigerant when the system is fully charged. If the bubbles continue, you probably need to add refrigerant, but you cannot determine this for sure until the plates are frozen. Let the system run at normal speed for close to your normal

freezing cycle, then recheck the glass. If bubbles are still streaming through, open either the tap valve or the blue-side manifold valve to allow additional refrigerant into the system. Watch the sight glass. The bubbles should decrease. Warming the refrigerant can with your hands will hasten the transfer. (When a venting can is no longer cold, it is empty.) When the bubbles stop streaming altogether—a trapped bubble doesn't count—shut the manifold or tap valve to stop the addition of refrigerant and let the system continue to run. If the bubbles start again, add refrigerant until they stop. You want no bubbles flowing past the sight glass, but here again do not overcharge the system. Stop as soon as the glass runs clear.

System Pressures

What about the gauge readings? They vary with temperature and refrigerant, but assuming R-134a and a box that is already cold, the low-side gauge should read somewhere around 30 to 40 psi after a minute or two of running the compressor. It will slowly decrease from there. If the system runs long enough to get the box very cold, you might see a vacuum reading, but 0 to 10 psi is more likely.

If you have the high-side gauge connected, it may start at over 200 psi, but after a minute or two it should drop below 200 psi if the system is air cooled and quickly down to around 125 psi for a water-cooled system in southern waters. If the high-side pressures do not decline to these levels, the system is probably overcharged. If the high-side reading exceeds 300 psi, shut down the system and make sure there is a water flow through the condenser.

When you are satisfied with the level of the charge, close the manifold or tap valve, backseat (by turning counterclockwise) the Rotolock valve, and remove the service hose. With Schrader valves, just remove the hose. If you also have a service hose on the high-pressure side, shut the system down and wait a few minutes for pressures to equalize before removing it. Cap the service ports and the (Rotolock) valve stems. If the pressure switches are connected through the service ports of your Rotolock valves, turn the valve stems about a turn and a half clockwise before capping them.

Monitoring

The sight glass can also tell you the ongoing status of the charge. Pulley-driven compressors commonly leak a little around the shaft seals, necessitating the occasional addition of refrigerant—like adding water to your batteries. Foaming in the sight glass when the system is first turned on is normal, but after the system has been running for several minutes in an evaporator system—longer for holding-plate refrigeration—the foam should be replaced with a clear stream of liquid refrigerant. A few stationary bubbles are OK, but if you don't see any bubbles at all from the start, the system could be empty instead of full. Be careful. An absence of refrigerant will damage a swash-plate compressor very quickly. If the glass is filled with foam and does not clear up, add refrigerant until it does. Then add a six-pack.

Reading the sight glass.

Stationary bubbles are normal.

Foam indicates low charge.

Clear can indicate full or empty. Look closely to make sure clear liquid refrigerant is flowing past glass.

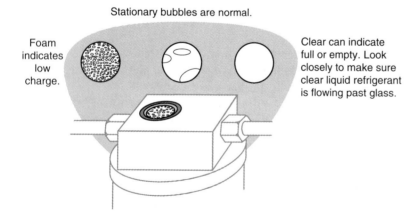

IT'S THE BOX, STUPID

Which brings us full circle to where we started. Marine refrigeration is not really about refrigeration. It's about power consumption. No matter how carefully you evaluate the various systems; no matter how efficient the compressor, how big the evaporator, or how many holding plates; no matter how much money you spend on the machinery—if you install it in a poorly insulated box, satisfactory performance will be limited to temperate climates. In southern waters your expensive upgrade will wear you and your engine out trying to keep up with heat leak or it will fail altogether. Some upgrade.

You avoid this by building yourself a great box before you even contemplate the equipment to cool it. There is a saying among music aficionados about sound equipment: put your money into the speakers. The same applies to refrigeration. It is the box that makes the difference. It is so easy to be seduced by the seamless molded interior of an existing ice chest or refrigerator into believing that it is probably OK. You will be right more often if you assume that behind that pretty liner is . . . nothing, naught, zero, zilch, nil, nada. Lots of old boats had an icebox that was uninsulated, or perhaps an inch or two of fiberglass batting was inserted into the space between the liner and the outer box. Spray-in foam has since replaced batting, but it is often applied thinly and/or inconsistently.

If you can gain access to the exterior of the liner, you can get a rough idea of whether your particular builder really considered the function of the box or was more interested in impressing prospective buyers with its generous size. Don't be surprised if you find no insulation or an amount more appropriate for a drink cozy. Even if the side you can see is insulated, you should not assume too much. Listen to me. It is *always* a mistake to add refrigeration to a factory box without doing the ice-melt test detailed at the start of this chapter. Never mind that it infringes on two days. Never mind that you need a scale. Never mind that you may have to freeze water at home to come up with block ice. How heat-tight the box is determines whether your refrigeration succeeds or fails. Simple as that. And you cannot know the answer to this without testing the box.

At 55 Btu per amp-hour, for every pound of ice that melts (144 Btu) your refrigeration is going to consume around 2.6 Ah just to offset heat leaking into the box. That is over and above the daily 36 Ah we have already predicted for chilling the contents. These combine to more than 100 Ah daily in our hypothetical but real-world-consistent, unimproved 9-cubic-foot box and to more than 140 Ah for the same box in a tropical climate. The only escape from this disheartening reality is a more efficient box.

If you have access to all sides of the original box, and if there is room on all sides to insulate with 4 to 6 inches of rigid foam, *and* if it is top loading and not big enough to echo, you can add insulation and proper lid gaskets and be content with the result. More often access and space are inadequate and interior volume exaggerated. Before you let that discourage you, here is another reality. Building a whole new box from scratch almost always turns out to be the easier course and should always result in a more efficient box.

Despite what wows new-boat buyers, a bigger box is a less efficient box. On the other hand, unless you are planning on rearranging the accommodations, the size of the new box is going to be determined by the space the old box occupies, so the bigger the original box, the more space you are likely to have to work with, which is a good thing. Measure the length, width, and depth of the space available. If the space lies against the curvature of the hull, your measurements should be for the largest cube that will fit into the space.

These measurements are for the outside of the box. Determine the inside measurements by subtracting twice the thickness of the insulation from each of the three dimensions. Multiply the new length, width, and depth dimensions to get the interior space in cubic inches. Dividing this number by 1,728 (12 × 12 × 12) gives you the interior volume in cubic feet.

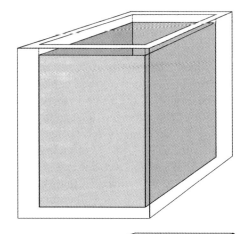

Two inches of insulation inside a 14 cubic foot box reduces interior volume to 9 cubic feet.

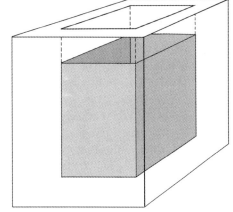

Six inches of insulation inside the same box reduces interior volume to 2.75 cubic feet.

Given a fixed exterior dimension, thicker insulation drastically reduces interior volume.

INCREDIBLE SHRINKING BOX

Let's see how this works. Suppose the existing cabinet housing the ice chest is 34 inches long, 24 inches wide, and 30 inches deep. We have already postulated 2 inches of original insulation for our hypothetical box, so if we subtract 4 inches from each dimension, that gives us interior dimensions of 30 × 20 × 26. It wouldn't surprise *me* if that worked out to 9 cubic feet. Increasing the insulation to 6 inches cuts the heat leak by $2/3$, more if you use an insulation with a higher R-value. Beyond 6 inches the incremental gains are pretty small—just 8% from 2 more inches. That makes 6 inches the accepted practical limit when trying to balance efficiency against "lost" volume. If you build a box in this space with 6 inches of insulation all around, what will the interior volume be? You have to subtract 1 foot from the exterior dimensions. That makes the new box 22 × 12 × 18 inside. Instead of 9 cubic feet, the interior volume becomes 2.75 cubic feet. It is not hard to see why boatbuilders scrimp on insulation. "But Marvin, look how tiny the refrigerator is in this boat . . ."

I suspect most boatowners are shocked at the box size that this exercise exposes. Before this sends you scrambling for some more palatable solution because 2.75 cubic feet—or whatever it turns out to be for your available space—is absolutely, positively too small, let me repeat an intrinsic truth about marine refrigeration: *you are a thousand times more likely to be dissatisfied because your box is too large than because it is too small.* Chilled drinks and cold-preserved foods can add immeasurably to the pleasures of being on the water, but such pleasures are diminished by dead batteries or listening to the clatter of an engine for hours. All other things being equal, the larger the box, the more power and/or engine time is required to keep it cold. If these are concerns, keep the box as small as possible.

This is where that cardboard box in front of the refrigerator comes in. If you discovered in that exercise that all your refrigerated items will fit into 2 cubic feet, you are home free. Putting the evaporator at one end gives you a 0.75-cubic-foot freezer and leaves you 2 cubic feet of refrigerated space. Empty space in the box—interior volume beyond what is required to contain the things that need refrigeration—does not contribute to the convenience of refrigeration, only to inefficiency. By the way, you can put more than 10 six-packs in a single cubic foot of space. Not that that matters to *you*.

If you need more interior space, you have three choices. The easiest of the three is to reduce the thickness of the insulation, but don't go to less than 4 inches. In the same space, decreasing the insulation from 6 inches to 4 inches of foam increases interior volume to 5.3 cubic feet. The cost is giving up the potential 16.7% efficiency gain that the thicker insulation would have provided. The daily load of 46.7 Ah that we might predict for this box in the tropics with 6 inches of foam becomes 70 Ah with just 4 inches of foam (or in a temperate climate, 35 Ah becomes 53 Ah). But you have almost twice the interior volume. If you *need* the box volume, this is a viable trade-off that you can quantify in terms of additional alternator minutes or the cost of additional solar panel area.

Choice two is to expand the available area by some change in the existing galley configuration or by relocating the box altogether. Within the typical main cabin it is not possible for the refrigerator to be as far from the counter as in a typical kitchen configuration, no matter where it is located, so some creativity is possible. You can also gain some interior volume by stepping the interior wall that is closest to the curvature of the hull. Slanting the box wall is never a good idea (it just adds volume to cool without much utility), but a step or even two can create volume-expanding shelves.

The third choice is vacuum panels. This is evolving technology, and the current generation continues to be very expensive with a high potential for failure. Such panels are fragile, difficult to install, and increase the vulnerability to heat leak in the corners. Despite impressive R-number claims, there is little independent research to substantiate equivalent gains for the entire box. I am fairly sure that a box with 6 inches of foam will outperform any current vacuum-panel configuration that does not rely on additional insulation. I suspect it is also likely to be true even for 4 inches of a high-R-value foam. If your budget allows the contemplation of vacuum panels, research them for yourself, but keep in mind that the only current benefit is less total wall thickness—and maybe not that much less if the panels are encapsulated in conventional foam. While a higher R-value is adequate reason to choose one insulation over another when their prices are similar, the cost for vacuum panels is way out of proportion to their value if you have other options. The lose-lose potential is spending the money and having the panels fail—not something you even want to contemplate.

FOAM CHRONICLES

Let's talk about types of foam for a moment. *Pour-in polyurethane foam* can do a yeoman's job of correcting the builder's oversight when you discover nothing but air around the built-in ice chest. It typically has an R-value of around 6 (per inch) but a high potential for voids, and oversize cells can lower this. It begins life innocently enough as a couple of syrupy liquids that you mix together. A color-change flash signals that it is time to pour the foam—right now! Like some creature from an old horror movie, the foam bubbles and fumes, giving off a foul odor and expanding rapidly and with tremendous force. If you pour too much at once, it can easily distort the liner and dismantle the cabinet. Large pours are also prone to voids, particularly in corners. Experiment with very small batches before you pour any around the box. Even after you get the hang of it you will be wise to limit the quantity of each pour to no more than a pint. Horror stories abound, so go slowly. Any framing pieces that support the molded liner will become heat-leak conduits unless you remove them as the foam takes over support.

Spray-in foam handles similar to poured foam but is most appropriate for filling irregularities and spatial voids that rigid foam board cannot. Both poured and sprayed foams can be cut and shaped after they cure.

Rigid Foam

If you follow my advice to build a new box rather than trying to salvage the existing one, rigid foam board will be the only foam you will be concerned with (other than perhaps a bit of filling with a spray can). There are four types that you need to know about.

Molded expanded polystyrene (MEPS or sometimes just EPS) is the ubiquitous white foam you are familiar with as coffee cups, shipping pellets, and cheap picnic coolers. When it is made into sheet insulation, it is called beadboard. This is a closed-cell foam—just what you want to avoid convective heat transfer—but the problem with beadboard is that there is space between the closed cells. That space can absorb moisture, which conducts heat and allows it to transfer through the board around the closed cells rather than through them. The possibility of condensation generated by the cold inside/hot and humid outside nature of a marine refrigerator or freezer makes common white polystyrene board insulation your poorest choice.

Most people call the white stuff "styrofoam," but it isn't. Styrofoam, always with a capital S, is the

Dow Chemical Company brand name for *extruded expanded polystyrene* (XEPS). Today there are other brands from other manufacturers, but Styrofoam was the original XEPS. It is usually given a blue tint; hence it is often called blueboard (although Blueboard is also a trademark of Dow Chemical). Owens Corning tints its XEPS product, Foamular, pink. XEPS is created by heating the polystyrene to a liquid state before extruding it into boards or other products. This process eliminates the space between cells found in MEPS, making XEPS less susceptible to moisture penetration. It also has a somewhat higher R-value—around 5 per inch compared to less than 4 for MEPS. Some people consider XEPS the best choice for cold box insulation. Maybe.

A third type of rigid foam is *polyurethane*, sometimes called uethane board. This is essentially the same as poured foam but formed under controlled conditions. Polyurethane board has more or less disappeared from the market, replaced by *polyisocyanurate* (or polyiso for short). The latter is simply an improved polyurethane, using the same raw materials in more optimized proportions to achieve better dimensional stability and better insulating properties. You will find polyiso insulation board in virtually every home supply store in America. It will be yellowish or cream colored and covered on both sides with foil facers.

Aside from the benefit of availability, polyiso also has an R-value about 30% higher than that of XEPS. Proponents of XEPS cast doubt on this difference because the R-value of polyisocyanurate foam may decline over time, particularly in the first year after manufacture. Fine. It starts out way higher and it still ends up higher. Dow Chemical, which manufactures both types, pegs XEPS (Styrofoam) at an R-value of 5 and polyiso (Tuff-R) at 6.5. That makes the total R-value for 6 inches of XEPS 30 compared to 39 for polyiso. More to the heart of the matter, using polyiso lets you reduce either the insulation thickness or the daily Ah load, whichever better suits your circumstances.

A second knock on polyiso is that it is not as moistureproof as XEPS. There is a difference when you compare just the foam but less difference when you factor in the foil facing on polyiso board. Let's also remember that we are not using this foam on a roof or behind a brick facade. It is probably inside a plywood cabinet, about as susceptible to moisture as the box of crackers in the adjacent locker. Presumably the risk is that a cold-box interior can result in condensation, which permeates the insulation which ruins its insulating properties. Yada, yada, yada. Sometimes you need a BS filter, and mine says that when you laminate six or eight layers of insulation board together with

two thicknesses of impermeable foil between each layer, *if* there is any moisture penetration due to condensation, it will be confined to the initial laminate. In practice, the run times for the polyisocyanurate-insulated refrigerator on our boat have not changed in a decade. That suggests to me that the insulating properties of the polyisocyanurate have not changed either. And that they are unlikely to.

Here is the bottom line. XEPS is a great product and it is hard to argue against a waterproof material used on a boat, but XEPS is not readily available everywhere. Polyisocyanurate is. You will not be shooting yourself in the foot if you use what is available. The result might be better. It will not be worse.

BOX CONSTRUCTION

The easy way to build a box is to start with a box. By this I mean you need to empty out the cavity where your new efficient icebox will be. By now you have already reconciled yourself to a smaller box than you imagined or you have determined how to provide a bigger space. You need the bottom and sides of this space boxed with plywood and the top open. That likely means removing the countertop, which should not present too much difficulty as it is typically installed last. You may have to remove cabinet facings at the back of the countertop to free it. If one side of the space is defined by the hull, box this side with plywood perpendicular to the bottom of the cavity. Resist any temptation to move this side outboard as this would move the outboard corner of the insulated box closer to the hull than your intended insulation thickness allows. Six inches of insulation all around means *all around*. You can step this outboard wall vertical, horizontal, then vertical again, which will not compromise the insulation thickness but will increase interior volume by creating a shelf. Be sure you configure the shelf so it is wide enough to be useful.

Also leave yourself access to the back side of this wall so you can add insulation or at least a radiant heat barrier. Or you can do this before you install the outboard wall by covering its outboard side with a layer of foam board with the shiny side facing the hull. If you are using foam board without a foil facing, glue heavy-duty foil—shiny side out—to the outboard surface. Your box is likely to get significant radiant heat only from the sun-heated hull or the engine. If one or more walls of your box is inside or close to the engine compartment, give those the same treatment—a reflective radiant heat barrier combined with at least $1/_2$ inch of foam. Radiant heat is reflected by the foil, but this only works if there is

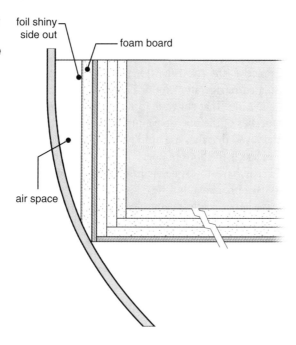

foil shiny side out

foam board

air space

air space for the heat to be reflected into. When your box already has 6 inches of insulation all around, any performance benefit from filling the wedge-shaped space between the outside of the cabinet and the hull will be minimal. While foam here would no doubt provide more insulation, an airspace gives your radiant heat barrier a chance to work and eliminates any possibility of trapping moisture against the hull.

Top Loading

The reason we want the top open is that we are building a top-loading box. I am astonished at the reemergence of front-opening refrigerators. Try this little experiment and you will see why. Fill a sink with warm water and two small glasses with ice-cold tea. Grip a glass in each hand with your palms sealing the tops. Submerge both in the sink, sitting one upright to simulate a top-opening refrigerator and laying the other one on its side to simulate a front-opening one. Draw your hands away slowly. The tea allows you to *see* what is happening. After 15 seconds, lift both glasses out of the sink and compare the color of the liquid in the glasses. If you stick your finger in the one with color, it will still be cold—but cold is not the point. A complete change of air from 35°F to 95°F only increases the refrigeration load by around 11 Btu (pretty insignificant), but warm air holds much more water vapor than cold air. So that load of hot air brings in moisture that necessarily condenses out like the proverbial morning dew as it is cooled by the box. The result is ice on the evaporator or holding plate, which insulates either and reduces the rate

of heat transfer. The inevitable result is more amp-hours or engine hours until you defrost the plate.

If you have power to spare, install any door configuration you like, but if minimizing the load is your primary objective, it just seems dopey to go to great lengths to fit double airtight seals around the lid, then defeat this effort with a front-opening door. You might hear the argument that the easier access of a front-opening box reduces the amount of time the door is open, which actually results in less air exchange than digging around for the horseradish from the top. To that I say, "Horseradish!" There is no appreciable difference in trying to find an item in the *bottom* of the box or in the *back* of it, and when the lid is at the top, the heavier cold air reposes mostly undisturbed by your rummaging.

Moisture is not likely to be much of a problem 4 or more insulated inches from the cold box but you should nevertheless protect the interior walls of the cavity with a coat or two of enamel paint or epoxy resin. I also line the box with polyethylene plastic—6 mil or thicker—less as a moisture barrier than to separate the foam from the plywood. This really isn't necessary, but if you do it, overlap the seams an inch or more and seal them with packing tape. Leave a couple of extra inches at the top to provide overlap when the countertop is screwed into position.

You can use the foam board in whatever thickness is available. The thicker the foam, the fewer pieces you have to cut and assemble, but do not use foam thicker than 2 inches because you want the joints to have at least one stagger. Thinner foam is actually easier to work with. I tend to use $^3/_4$-inch foam because that is the thicker of the two sizes my supplier stocks. You are also going to need epoxy resin to glue and seal the foam.

One layer at a time. Start the box by cutting two pieces of foam to the full length of the cabinet cavity and exactly $^1/_4$ inch less than its depth. The $^1/_4$ inch is an allowance for the thickness of the fiberglass sheathing to come and for seals with a compressed thickness of about $^1/_8$ inch. If you plan to use thicker seals, you will need to increase this allowance accordingly. If you are using foam with a foil facing on only one side, that side should face "out," meaning away from the interior of the box. The best cutting tool for thin foam is a razor knife. Thicker foams may be easer to cut with a saw or knife with teeth or serrations. The more accurate your height cuts, the less adjusting you will have to do later. Widths should be ever so slightly oversize to make the foam panels fit snugly.

If you are using faced polyiso foam, paint the bottom and side edges with catalyzed epoxy and let it cure. This is just to seal the exposed edge and is not necessary with XEPS. You do not need to seal the top edges because these will get sheathed later. Put these pieces in place and seat them firmly in the front and back of the cavity.

Next cut the two side pieces to the remaining width of the cavity and the same height as the front and back. If the ends of these two pieces will butt against the facing of the front and back insulation, epoxy only their bottom edges, but if the ends butt even partially against wood cleats that assemble the cabinet, seal the end edges also. Again, the top edge should not be sealed. When the epoxied edges are dry, fit these pieces into the cabinet, shiny side away from the interior.

Finally, cut a piece of foam to be a snug fit in the bottom of the reduced cavity. The edges of the bottom piece will be sealed by the facings of the perimeter pieces, so sealing with epoxy won't be necessary. Mark the orientation of the two sides and remove them and the bottom piece. Coat the side edges of the side pieces, not the top and bottom edges, with thickened epoxy and reinstall these two pieces. Paint epoxy at the bottom of the perimeter piece facings where the edges of the bottom piece will be, then put the bottom piece in place. Put a weight on the bottom and push the tops of the foam against the cabinet wall by wedging 2-inch-wide strips of foam, cut slightly too long, across the length and width of the box. Carefully wipe up any epoxy smears or squeeze-out at the corners.

Except for sealing the edges, which is not needed except for the outer layer, you are going to follow this

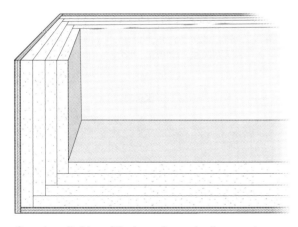

Covering all sides of the box a layer at a time creates staggered joints that offer greater resistance to heat leak at the corners.

same sequence—front and back, sides, then bottom—to add layer after layer of foam until you are one layer shy of achieving the thickness you are after. Do *not* fit 6 inches of sheet foam in the front and back, then 6 inches on the sides. Heat leaks into your box are most likely to occur at the joints in the insulation, so you do not want straight butt joints making it easier. Increasing total insulation thickness evenly creates staggered corner joints that will obstruct heat leak.

Cut and fit each set of five panels, trying to keep their top edges even at $1/4$ inch below the cabinet edge. Install each set as you go, marking their relative positions, removing them, then reinstalling them with thickened epoxy, now not only at the edges but on the back sides of each panel. The intent here is to create a solid structure. Shorten the foam spreaders you used to clamp the previous layer and use them to hold the next set of panels in contact with the set behind. Weight each bottom panel.

Lid thickness. When the penultimate layer of insulation is in place, it is time to think about the lid. In a proper refrigerated box, the entire top opens. Otherwise you need an extra elbow to extract something from the bottom on the side with the solid top. For me that rules out prefabricated refrigerator hatches. (The breathtaking cost might also have an influence.) Not to worry. You can construct a great lid that will seal perfectly for little money and only modest effort. You begin by determining how thick the lid will be.

If you want maximum efficiency, the top will be the same thickness as the other five sides, but a 6-inch-thick lid can be awkward and will half block a 12-inch-wide opening even when open 90 degrees. This will present a problem if you cannot open the lid 180 degrees. I generally recommend a lid thickness of 4 inches. The calculated effect will be to reduce the total efficiency gain by just 2.8%, but the real effect will be smaller because the top of the box is generally the warmest, so the temperature differential is the smallest here. If you have reason to make the lid even thinner, you can, but I would not shave it below 3 inches. Besides making it easier to handle, a thinner lid adds interior volume and interior height.

For our box building, let's settle on a 4-inch-thick lid. However, for the process I am describing, the exact thickness must be determined by stacking blocks of foam board together until their combined thickness is close to the target thickness. A bit more or less makes no difference, but for preparing the box we need to use the thickness of the stack. For example, if you are using $3/4$-inch foam, the closest you can get to 4 inches is $3^3/_4$ inches. And don't trust the specified thickness. Stack the foam and measure. Let's assume our measured thickness turns out to be $3^7/_8$ inches.

Beveled opening. If you cut your installed foam pieces fairly precisely, all the top edges should be even with each other. If they are seriously uneven, spend a little time getting them to form a uniform surface. This can be harder than it looks with faced foam because of the foil. Once you are satisfied that the top surface is pretty even and uniform, measure down from the top edge by the thickness of the lid insulation—$3^7/_8$ inches in this case. Put a mark on the insulation at that location, then measure up to that mark from the bottom of the box. In this example, our original cabinet was 30 inches deep. We are using $^3/_4$-inch foam board and are one board short of 6 inches, so we have raised the bottom $5^1/_4$ inches. We have also ended our panels $^1/_4$ inch short of the cabinet top. That should make the box $24^1/_2$ inches deep at this point. If we measure down from the top $3^7/_8$ inches, that mark will be $20^5/_8$ inches above the bottom. Very precisely draw a line on the insulation $20^5/_8$ inches above the bottom across all four sides. This is where the bottom of the lid will be when it is closed.

Now move your attention to the even top edges of the insulation and measure from the interior edge back by the same amount you just measured down—$3^7/_8$ inches in this example. Precisely draw a perimeter line all around the box this exact distance from the interior surface. If you cut the foam with a straight blade and the blade follows both of these lines at the same time, you will end up with a 45-degree bevel all around the top of the box. How do you do that? Slowly, using a free hacksaw blade. A beveled opening is required to allow the internal lid to hinge open.

A beveled opening is required to allow the lid to hinge open. Draw lines around the perimeter of the box insulation both down and back the exact thickness of the lid insulation. Follow both lines at the same time with a hacksaw blade to bevel the top of the insulation.

The liner. We are ready to fit the final layer of foam board. Cut the perimeter pieces so their top edges will line up exactly with the inside edge of the bevel. In other words, the front and back and side pieces will be $20^5/_8$ inches tall for this box. Their top edges will form the lower lip the lid sits on. Also cut the final bottom piece, but for this piece only, cut it for a very loose fit.

Do not glue this set of five pieces in place yet. Instead, remove them and note their positions and orientation on their back sides. On their front sides we are going to create the refrigerator liner by simply laying up fiberglass on the faces of each of the pieces. Two layers of 9- or 10-ounce cloth laminated with slightly thickened epoxy resin will be sufficient, but I generally add a third laminate for good measure. (If you need layup instructions, go back to Chapter 6.) When the layup has kicked but is still green, you can scissor away any overlap. The slight undersizing of the bottom piece is to accommodate the thickness the fiberglass adds to the four sides.

This is the time to provide for more secure evaporator or holding-plate mounting than the thin liner allows. Temporarily install the fiberglassed pieces

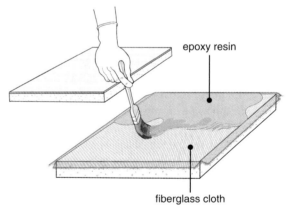

epoxy resin

fiberglass cloth

Sheathe the innermost insulation boards with two or more laminates of fiberglass cloth to fabricate the box liner.

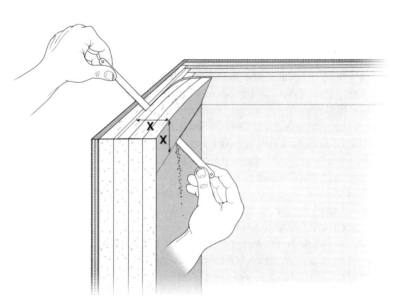

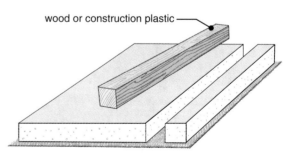

wood or construction plastic

Incorporate mounting blocks for the evaporator or holding plate(s) before installing the final layer of foam board.

into the box and use the actual plate(s) or a pattern of the mounting holes to mark its (their) location(s). Remove the fiberglassed insulation and replace the foam where the mounting screws will penetrate the liner with some material that will hold a screw. For example, to mount the evaporator plate on an end wall in this box, you might slice through and remove two horizontal strips of foam, one centered behind the top two mounting screw locations and the other behind the bottom two. With the fiberglass liner and the front facing still intact, epoxy two pieces of white oak 1 × 2, which is actually $3/4 × 1 1/2$, into these slots. Don't use plywood unless you saturate it with several coats of epoxy to protect it against the potential dampness that might occur directly behind the liner. Construction plastic, if you can manage it, is probably the best material choice. The screw strips can be thinner than the foam, but they must not be thicker or they will interfere with the flush fit of the piece.

Remember that once epoxy passes out of the green stage into final cure, which typically happens at around 2 hours, subsequent epoxy applications will not bond chemically to the cured epoxy. If you do not work out your layup schedule to get the liner pieces installed well under this time limit, you will need to let them cure fully, then scrub the waxy blush from the cured epoxy with water and an abrasive pad (Scotch-Brite) and prepare the dry surface for a mechanical bond by sanding it with 80-grit paper. Or you can scrub and sand at the same time by wet sanding. If you have to wash and sand the liner surfaces, do it while they are out of the box.

Epoxy the five pieces in place, then with thickened epoxy put a large-radius fillet at all of the joints. A tongue depressor gives about the right radius. To make absolutely sure that the liner will never crack at the seams, reinforce these fillets by laying light 3-inch fiberglass tape into all of the corners after the fillets are firm and saturate the tape with fresh epoxy. Except for some finish work, the box is complete. We will come back to it, but first we need to construct the lid.

Generic lid. Measure the width and length of the box opening at the top edges of the bevel. Cut a rectangle of foam to these dimensions and check it by placing it over the opening. It should sit on the top edge of the bevel all around. Cut additional foam rectangles to the same dimensions until you have enough to stack to the thickness of the lid. In this example that would be five pieces of nominally $3/4$-inch foam that we have already determined are actually $37/8$ inches thick when combined as a stack. Apply epoxy to the facings between the pieces and

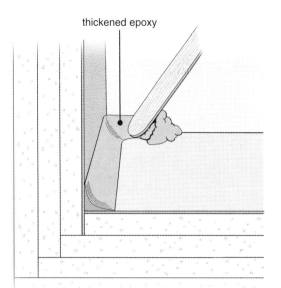

thickened epoxy

Round all interior corners with a fillet of thickened epoxy.

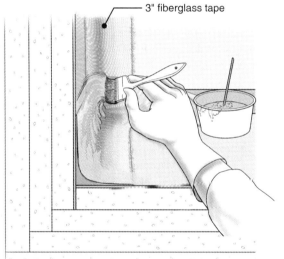

3" fiberglass tape

Finish the corners with a lamination of fiberglass tape to create a seamless liner.

stack them into a block, aligning one side and one end against vertical surfaces to make sure the two edges of the block are vertical. Weight the stack and let the epoxy cure. On one face, draw a rectangle that is back from the edge the thickness of the bonded block—$37/8$ inches in this example. Measure the length and width of the rectangle and compare these to the length and width of the opening at the bottom edge of the bevel. They should be exactly the same. Once again use a free hacksaw blade to cut a 45-degree bevel on the lid foam by cutting along the line marking the rectangle and at the outside perimeter of the opposite face of the block at the same time. This will be easier to do if someone else holds the block securely against the surface of a table or bench with the marked rectangle up and the edge you are

Follow the marked line and the opposite edge to cut a matching bevel on the lid.

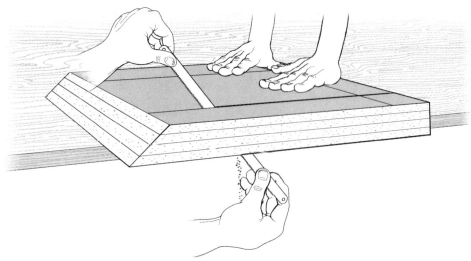

cutting extended beyond the edge of the work surface. Work slowly and carefully to make this bevel as accurate and uniform as you can.

When you have the block trimmed all the way around, drop it into the opening. Ideally you want it to sit on the top edges of the foam that is part of the liner. If the two bevels engage first, try rotating the lid block 180 degrees to see if the fit is better. Trim or rasp the two bevels as necessary to provide adequate clearance between them to let the bottom of the lid block sit on the horizontal lip formed by the final layer of foam.

Remove the lid and place it big-side down on a piece of hardboard (Masonite) or other flat surface that you have protected with plastic kitchen wrap (Saran). Sheathe the exposed surfaces of the block with three laminates of 4-ounce fiberglass cloth, trimming the cloth to overlap at the four corners and turning it out onto the plastic wrap for at least 1 inch. You use 4-ounce cloth here so it will make sharp turns from the bottom of the lid onto the bevel and from the bevel out onto the plastic. When the laminate has cured but is still green, scissor the flange to a uniform $^3/_4$-inch width all around and put the piece back down on the flat surface to let it cure completely.

Creating the lid liner.

Perfecting the fit. If all of your cuts were perfectly accurate, you could just similarly sheathe the box bevel and be done, but stuff happens, so let's not take any chances. When the lid is solid, try it in the opening

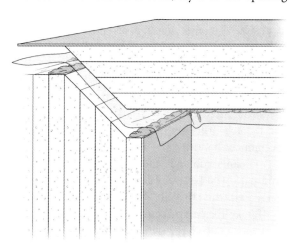

Cover the flat surfaces of the box perimeter with a layer of thickened epoxy. Drape plastic wrap over the wet putty.

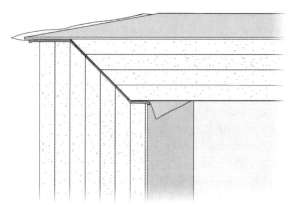

Put the lid in place and weight it lightly. When the now-flattened epoxy has cured, the mating surfaces will be a perfect fit.

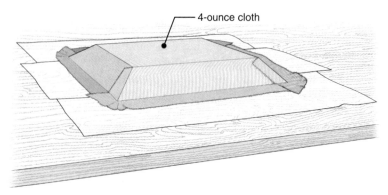

4-ounce cloth

again. If the bevel interferes, trim the one around the opening until it doesn't. You want the bottom of the lid to sit on the bottom lip of the opening and the flange to sit on the top surface of the insulation. Of course the only one of these you can actually see is the flange. Here is how you make sure that the lid and the opening mate the way you want them to. Mix up a batch of epoxy thickened to a consistency a little stiffer than mayonnaise. Quickly spread a thin layer of this epoxy putty on both support surfaces—the top edge of the inner foam panels and from the top edge of the bevel back ³/₄ inch. Lay plastic wrap over the wet putty, overlapping the wrap sufficiently to be sure that the epoxy

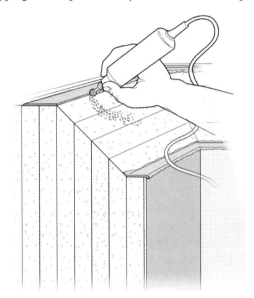

Grind away epoxy squeeze-out and smooth all surfaces.

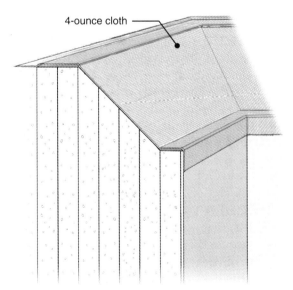

4-ounce cloth

Sheathe the top of the insulation from the plywood box across both flat surfaces and the bevel and down onto the vertical interior.

cannot come in contact with the lid. Now put the lid in place and lightly weight it—a book is perfect (but not one as big as this!). Wait.

When the epoxy paste has had time to kick, remove the lid, peel away the wrap, and you should have two support surfaces that are exact mates to the bottom and flange of the lid. Use a knife and/or a rotary tool to remove epoxy squeeze-out from adjacent surfaces. Now you are ready to sheathe the bevel. First scrub and sand the epoxied mating surfaces and the radiused corners of the box where this sheathing will overlap them. Again using light cloth—4 ounces or lighter—sheathe across all of the top edges of the perimeter insulation, down the bevel, out onto the horizontal edge of the inner layer of foam, then down onto the fiberglass liner.

From here on out, it is essentially finish work. A neat trick I have discovered is to create two or three sets of divider slots by epoxying parallel plastic strips to opposite walls. By moving a divider either closer to the evaporator bin or farther away from it, you can change the relative sizes of the freezer and refrigerator compartments. If you stepped the outside wall of the box to take better advantage of the space next to the hull, you should also fabricate slots on the liner for a fiddle for the shelf that will have created.

When all the features you want are in place, scrub and sand the interior surfaces of the box and fair it with thickened epoxy. When the fairing has cured fully, scrub and sand again, this time with 120-grit paper to prepare the box for painting. Prime with one or two coats of epoxy primer.

I really like two-part urethane for the interior of the box because its superslick surface is wonderfully

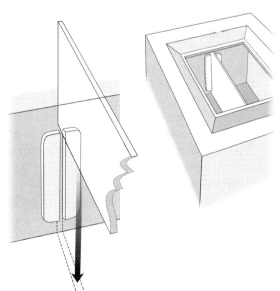

Create slots by gluing cleats to the liner to make dividers or fiddles removable or adjustable.

Dual gaskets are essential.

easy to clean, and it is almost impervious to damage from the contents of the box. The problem is that there cannot be a more unhealthy environment for applying urethane than belowdeck with your head and the paint inside a small box. However, if you wear a respirator with fresh cartridges and play a fan across the top of the box, the surface area is so small that you can hold your discomfort to a minimum. Since you are applying white, it should flow out to a quite pleasing surface if you roll it on without tipping (see Chapter 14). You will have to paint the radiused corners with a brush. Apply two coats 24 hours apart—three if you can stand it. This should give you a lifetime finish. If you do not want to work with a two-part paint, then paint the interior of the box with a top-quality topside enamel such as Brightside or Easypoxy. Do not paint the lid at the same time; you are not quite finished with it.

To do the final fitting of the lid, you first need to install rubber seals on both seating surfaces around the box opening. You will find weatherstrip rubber in shapes and thicknesses that can do a perfectly adequate job of creating an airtight seal. I think solid rubber seals with a hollow center are better than foam seals.

Top options. Constructing the lid separate from its top allows you complete flexibility in giving it whatever kind of top you like. If the box is inside a galley cabinet, the lid normally matches the counter. That might be plywood with a high-pressure laminate finish (Formica) framed with teak, or it might be a solid surface material (Corian) if you can afford the weight. You might also make it a cutting board or do fancy woodwork. You can shim the counter or the lid top as required to get their top surfaces level, then simply epoxy your top of choice to the foam lid.

You also have to decide how you will handle the lid. It can be hinged with surface hinges so the entire lid opens like a chest, but if the box is big, you end up with a lid that is also big, making it both heavy and awkward. Often it is better to cut the lid in half across its long dimension and rejoin the two pieces with a piano hinge. This allows you to open only one side of the box at a time, reducing the air exchange, but you can still tilt the entire lid up for full access or remove it altogether when packing the box after shopping. There is no law that says the "halves" must be equal, so you could have a small freezer-side lid and a larger refrigerator-side lid if that suits you better. If you do cut the lid in half, you have to sheathe the exposed foam.

Wait until you have the lid in its final configuration to fair, prime, and paint it. Paint it outside in open air. A lid hinged in the middle requires thin dual seals that run completely across the joint to make it airtight when both sides are closed. Be sure to install handles or lift rings before you install the lid and after the counter is in place or you could find yourself feeling foolish. A big suction cup might bail you out.

Your box. There is nothing in these instructions that you cannot change to suit your particular needs, skills, or inspiration except the need to provide adequate insulation, the need for a watertight and durable liner, and the need for a solid double seal on the lid. The movable divider (and the fiddle) I mentioned earlier are simply $1/4$-inch sheet plastic—clear or white acrylic is fine—cut to fit reasonably tightly to the contour of the liner and usually a couple of inches shorter than the depth of the box to allow heat exchange between the refrigerator side and the evaporator side. In my experience this works quite well without fans or thermostats or other complications. If you are installing a dual holding-plate system—a refrigerator plate and a freezer plate—then you will need to incorporate an insulated divider or build two separate boxes. A single holding-plate spillover system may need a thermostatically controlled fan to keep the refrigerator cool.

Note that I have not described installing a drain. Drains are for ice chests only. You do not want a drain in a refrigerator. If you need to remove liquid from the box, use a sponge.

Let's see, what's left? Install the machinery. Flip the switch. Chill.

THE COLD TRUTH

When it comes to what really puts the "pleasure" into pleasure boats, you will normally find me solidly on the side of simplicity, but my dedication to this premise wavers when it comes to the inevitable complexity that refrigeration brings aboard. I simply cannot imagine being aboard a boat for more than a few days without refrigeration, because there is no

Configure the lid to suit your needs.

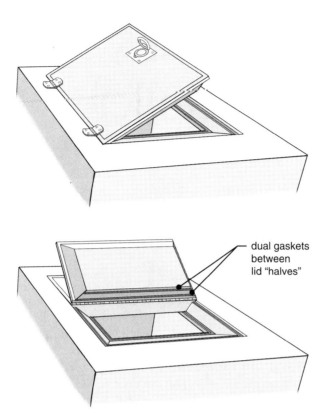

dual gaskets
between
lid "halves"

sweeter symphony to my ear than the susurration of wavelets running along the beach of a deserted cove mixed with the clinking of ice cubes in slender glasses. Our carefully conceived and installed refrigeration system has played that symphony for us over and over. Sadly we encounter less fortunate sailors every year, particularly in southern waters, who have spent thousands of dollars to equip their boats with refrigeration in a quest for the same joys only to be bitterly disappointed.

If you are planning to install refrigeration, you can avoid this fate by testing your box honestly. If the results suggest three-digit current drains or hours of engine time, there is little point in "hoping" that it won't actually be that bad. It will be The solution is insulation and lots of it. If you fail to invest in a perfect box right from the start, you will pay dearly for your recalcitrance, probably by doing it all over again at twice the inconvenience and twice the cost. It's a cold world.

CHAPTER FOURTEEN

Brush and Roller

"If everything seems under control you're just not going fast enough."
—MARIO ANDRETTI

L onger ago now than I like to confess, my boat shared a seawall with an old Pearson with a weathered blue hull. The new-boat gloss was long gone from the hull of my boat, but next to the partly cloudy Pearson it still looked good. Then one weekend I arrived to find the Pearson in a cradle onshore, her owner sanding away on the hull. The next time I saw the boat, the hull looked as though it had been coated with blue mercury. The paint was a new product, something called Awlgrip, and never had I seen such a beautiful finish. In a week, the hull of this old boat had been transformed from blue chalk to blue diamond. I never looked at my own boat through the same eyes again.

Nothing has a more immediate impact on the way a boat looks than putting a mirror finish on the hull. Thanks to space-age technology, doing just that is within the capability of almost any boatowner. But before you take on refinishing the hull, you need to develop, at the very least, a certain rapport with a brush, sandpaper literacy, and an adequate grasp of the essentials of surface preparation.

PAINTING 101

The place to start any painting project is an inconspicuous spot. How about the inside of a locker? Most old boats can benefit from a coat of paint in the lockers. And most boatowners can benefit from a painting project where runs and brush marks will be of little consequence. You are more interested in the locker being clean and perhaps in protecting the raw fiberglass than in a flawless finish.

You could paint the inside of the lockers on your old boat with two-part polyurethane (Awlgrip and similar) if you wanted to, but it's not a very good idea. Aside from the expense, the strong solvents in two-part paints discourage their application in an enclosed space. Besides, these milk-thin paints require meticulous preparation to deliver a flawless finish. Save this effort for surfaces that show.

The paint of choice for lockers and most other interior surface applications is *alkyd enamel*. Alkyd enamel is quite durable, less sensitive to temperature and humidity, does not require strong solvents, goes on easily and has good flow characteristics (i.e., brushstrokes tend to disappear), and requires minimal preparation. Additives such as silicone and acrylic can improve gloss and color retention.

Choosing from among the scores of brands and formulas of alkyd enamel can be intimidating, but it doesn't need to be. Trot down to your favorite local paint store—I'm talking house paint here—and just ask them for their *best* alkyd enamel. House paint? Absolutely. Topside enamels, the alkyd enamels your marine chandlery stocks, are formulated to maximize gloss. Gloss is not a high priority inside a locker. In fact a semigloss or low-luster paint will look better initially and remain attractive longer. Wall enamels also tend to tout toughness and washability—just what you want in the bottom of a locker. Even though this is an interior application, you want the durability of exterior-grade enamel.

There are a couple of additional advantages to using wall paint. House enamel will cost you about a third as much as enamel in a can with a boat on the label, and the house-paint store will tint their best enamel to any color you can imagine. Topside enamels tend to be available in several shades of white, a few shades of blue, a dark green, a strident red, and black.

Painting settee lockers and the spaces inside cabinets white imparts a clean look and makes the

Exterior house enamel in light colors is the ideal coating for boat interior surfaces.

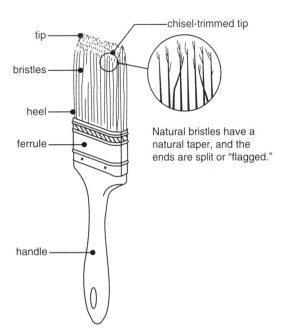

Brush features.

Natural bristles have a natural taper, and the ends are split or "flagged."

space seem larger, but the biggest advantage of white is that it brightens the locker, making dark lockers less so. And if you paint all the lockers bright white, you can do it from a single gallon of paint and still have plenty left over to paint all of the underbunk surfaces (we will come to that).

Despite such astute logic, I never paint locker interiors white. For me a flash of color adds a bit of gaiety every time I open a locker lid or door—not light-robbing colors, but light shades with names like mist green, ice blue, heather pink, and butter yellow. Pastels are almost as effective as white at brightening the locker and more effective at brightening my day, and color is a wonderful memory aid for organizing stores and equipment: meats in the pink locker, vegetables in the green locker, fruits in the yellow one. Painting the lid underside to match is a nice touch.

So you can buy a gallon of white or quarts of a variety of soft colors at the paint store. In addition to the paint, pick up a gallon of mineral spirits—much cheaper by the gallon—and a quart of acetone. You also need some small plastic paint "buckets" and a supply of brushes.

BRUSH BASICS

I have heard the virtues of synthetic bristle brushes extolled, but I have never used a synthetic brush that I liked. Conversely, I have rarely been badly disappointed with the performance of a natural bristle brush, even the cheap, throwaway variety. Most natural bristle brushes are made from hog bristle and are called China (or Chinese) bristle because China is the principle hog-bristle supplier. Ox and camel hair are also used in better-quality brushes. The finest brushes are made of badger bristle.

What makes natural bristle brushes superior is split ends. This splitting or "flagging" on the ends of the bristle works like the split tip of a drawing pen, allowing the bristle—and the brush—to hold more paint and give it up more uniformly. The natural taper of the bristle also serves to give the brush a lighter touch at the tip. Toward this end, better brushes are also trimmed to a point, called a chisel trim. Less expensive brushes are straight at the tip or only slightly rounded.

The best-quality brush is not always the best brush for a given job. For example, a cheap throwaway China brush will be better than ox or badger for painting the inside of a locker because you have to clean an expensive brush when the painting is finished, whereas a throwaway brush you can, well, throw away. Cleaning a brush thoroughly is a time-consuming and messy job and requires quite a bit of solvent. Aside from the cost of the solvent and the volatile organic compounds (VOCs) it releases into the air, there is the question of how to dispose of it responsibly. If you allow the used thinner to sit undisturbed for a couple of days (in a sealed container to retard evaporation), the paint will settle to the bottom and most of the thinner can be poured off carefully to be reused for additional brush-cleaning duty, but unfortunately for the environment few people seem inclined to go to this trouble. Tossing the brush when you are finished is infinitely easier, and since sending a mostly biodegradable wood-and-hair brush to the landfill is almost certainly more environmentally conscientious than dumping a pint of used thinner behind the shed, a disposable brush should always be the brush of choice when it can deliver an adequate finish. This it can surely do in the case of the inside of a locker.

Often called "chip" brushes, disposable bristle brushes are commonly available in widths from $1/2$ inch to 4 inches. I tend to use $1^1/_2$-inch for trim and $2^1/_2$-inch for bigger areas, but you should experiment a bit to find what sizes feel comfortable to you. You may also want to shop around for suppliers because chip-brush prices can vary by a factor of four and there is no discernible correlation between price and quality.

LOOSE BRISTLES

One problem common to all bristle brushes is that they shed bristles. Not surprisingly, cheap brushes shed more than expensive ones, but there can be huge differences among cheap brushes. Loose bristles will spoil any paint job, no matter how dense or well shaped the brush, so when shopping for even cheap brushes, tug on the bristles. If they come out in clumps, find a different source. If *no* bristles pull out, buy all of the size you need that are in the bin. You have stumbled onto a miracle.

Every loose bristle you can get out of a brush before you paint is one less that will end up in the finish. Slapping the bristles across the heel of your hand will eject the loosest, but here is a surer way to a bristle-free finish. Encase your hand with a dozen or more wraps of masking tape with the sticky side *out*. Now "paint" your new brush back and forth across the tape. The tape adhesive will grab individual loose bristles and pull them out of the brush. When the brush quits shedding, clean it with the thinner that is specified for the paint you are using (mineral spirits in the case of wall enamel) to remove any adhesive from the bristles, and this brush is ready to use.

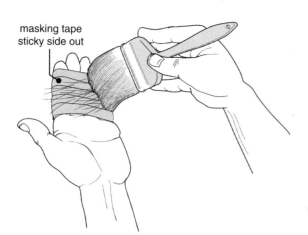

Use a wrap of masking tape, sticky side out, to remove loose bristles that will otherwise end up in the finish.

ROLLER COVERS

One way to avoid bristles in the paint is to not use a brush at all. For large surfaces without compound curvature, a roller can put the paint on quicker and deliver an excellent finish with the right paint. As with brushes, roller covers come in a variety of thicknesses, compositions, and sizes. For boat use, you will nearly always use foam rollers—with two exceptions. You will use short-nap roller covers to apply antifouling bottom paint and to paint uneven surfaces such as molded nonskid or the raw fiberglass of the inside of the molded hull. The latter is what you are likely to find inside lockers, so buy a package of short-nap rollers for this job. The denser the better, but do not spend a lot on nap roller covers. You are going to throw them away after one use. Mostly check to make sure the nap is firmly attached. Any fibers that come loose will end up in the finish. Cheap roller covers come in 9-inch lengths, which is fine.

You do not need foam rollers for this job, but for a smooth surface—the under-the-bunk surface, for example—a foam roller can lay on paint quickly to a uniform thickness. A foam roller is the tool you will use most often for painting the (mostly) flat surfaces

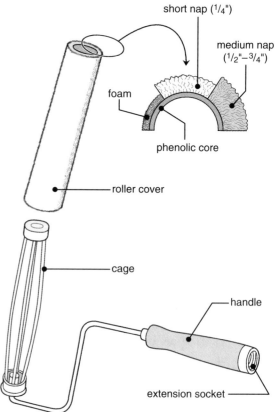

Use foam roller covers for a smooth finish, nap rollers for uneven surfaces.

of your boat. Unlike nap rollers, you will need to buy the best foam rollers you can. In particular you must avoid rollers with cardboard cores. The solvents in many paints, particularly two-part paints, will release the foam from the core. The result is a mess you do not want to experience. Buy only foam rollers with a solvent-resistant phenolic core. These will be available in both 7- and 9-inch widths. I like the better control and the shorter span of a 7-inch roller when painting a curved surface like a hull, so I tend to use 7-inch for everything. Suit yourself.

To accompany whatever roller covers you select, you will also need a handle to match the cover length and a plastic paint tray. Most roller handles today are birdcage style, which is good because they support the cover in the middle as well as at the ends and they tend to make cover removal easier than other styles. You need a good handle but you can buy a cheap paint tray. Or buy one good tray and some throwaway liners. You can also line the tray with heavy-duty aluminum foil, which makes cleanup a snap. Since the paint does not adhere well to the slick surface of the tray, another option that usually works is to let the paint remaining in the tray dry, then worry up one corner and peel the cured paint out of the tray like bikini wax.

SANDPAPER SAVVY

You *always* have to sand before you paint, so plan on acquiring a selection of sandpaper. You may find yourself standing in front of stacks of bins holding half a dozen different sandpapers in a dozen different grits. Exhale. You are interested only in two kinds of paper and three or four grits. The type and grit will be printed on the back of each sheet.

Most of your sanding will be done with dry or "production" paper, and the kind you want is *aluminum oxide*. Aluminum oxide is only slightly less hard than diamond, which makes it a tough, long-lasting abrasive. You will usually need 80-grit, 100-grit, and/or 120-grit for initial preparation and 220-grit for sanding between coats. The grit number will be followed by an A, C, D, or E designation to indicate the weight of the paper backing, with A being the lightest. When you have a choice, select C or D, which will last longer for hand sanding and be durable enough for power sanding. Aluminum oxide paper is tan or brown in color. Avoid lighter-colored *flint* paper or red *garnet* paper. Both are too soft to last on fiberglass.

The other type of sandpaper you are likely to use during a painting project is *silicon carbide*. This is the charcoal-colored paper you may know as *wet-or-dry* or by the brand name Carborundum. Use wet-or-dry sandpaper between coats of paint or varnish when a very fine finish is desired. For this use, select 320- or 400-grit. You might also use coarser grits wet as a substitute for production paper to minimize dust when sanding toxic compounds (bottom paint, for example), but sanding sponges—exactly what they sound like—are better for this use.

SANDPAPER CHOICES			
Type of Paper	*Identifying Color*	*Uses*	*Suggested Grits*
Aluminum oxide	**Tan or brown**	**The most versatile paper for all-around use.**	**60D—rough sanding and paint removal; 100C—surface preparation for painting; 220A—between coat sanding**
Silicon carbide (closed coat)	**Dark gray**	**Waterproof paper usually called *wet-or-dry*. Used wet this paper yields the finest finish.**	**320A—wet sanding between coats of polyurethane; 600A—pre-polish wet sanding**
Silicon carbide (open coat)	**White**	**Fine finishing paper; the best choice for sanding disks.**	**180A—between coat sanding; 400A—pre-polish sanding**
Emery cloth	**Black**	**Except to prepare aluminum for paint, emery cloth has no refinishing uses. Good for polishing metal and sharpening plane irons.**	**None**
Garnet	**Red**	**Hand sanding fine woodwork; expensive and will not stand up to machine sanding.**	**None**
Flint	**Light beige or light gray**	**Dime-store sandpaper; useless—never buy flint paper.**	**None**

You can buy sandpaper for about half the individual sheet price if you buy it by the sleeve—25, 50, or 100 sheets, depending on the grit. Sleeves of a couple of grits—probably 100 and 220—can be a good early investment in a boat refurbishing/upgrading project. You will need a moisture-proof box to store the paper in.

MEANWHILE, BACK AT THE BOAT

With supplies in hand, it is time to paint. Begin by emptying the locker and scrubbing away all the dirt and oils with trisodium phosphate (TSP, available in a box from your hardware store) dissolved in water. TSP once was a principal ingredient in all laundry detergents, but it has long been banned because it was introducing vast amounts of phosphate into the waste water. That is a good thing. Most clothing does not need the extra power of TSP, but for heavy cleaning, two or three spoonfuls in a bucket of water will give you a gallon of cleaner for a few pennies, which contrasts sharply with the niggardly amount of commercial cleaner $10 buys. The active ingredient in said cleaner is just as likely to be TSP, so you are paying about $9.80 for a quart of water. It should at least be Perrier. Apply this mix generously and use a brush to clean the weave of the fiberglass cloth or roving surface. Rinse the locker *thoroughly*. Satisfied? Rinse it again. If you are painting a cockpit locker, use the dock hose to rinse it.

DEWAX

While the locker dries, put on your rubber gloves and saturate a clean cloth with acetone. Now wipe down the locker thoroughly with the acetone, turning the cloth to a clean face frequently. If you recall way back in Chapter 6, the final layer of fiberglass is finishing resin, which contains a wax that floats to the surface or, if it was laminating resin, was coated with a wax to seal it so that it would fully cure. Either way, the surface is coated with wax, old though it may be, and you have to remove that wax for the paint to adhere. Do *not* sand first, because the sandpaper will pack the wax into the sanding scratches and getting it back out will be difficult. Xylene (also xylol), a chief chemical in proprietary wax removers, is more effective but also more dangerous, especially in the confined space of a locker. Stick with acetone assisted by a little extra elbow grease.

If the surface was previously painted, the preparation is the same, with the added step of testing for compatibility. Saturate a cloth with mineral spirits and lay it against the old paint for 10 minutes. As long as the old paint doesn't soften and lift, you can paint right over it. If the old coating is peeling, you will have to remove all the loose paint. If it is peeling badly, stripping will be your only choice.

SAND

After you have dewaxed the surface, sand it. Sanding before painting serves two functions. The first is to smooth the surface, knocking down high spots and fairing low ones. When you are painting the outside of the hull, getting the surface flawlessly smooth is critical. When painting the inside of a locker, the only smoothing you are likely to be interested in is rounding any points or sharp edges.

The second function of sanding is to give the paint or varnish a good surface to grip. Paint will not adhere to a mirror-smooth surface. Sanding removes the gloss and puts tiny scratches—called "tooth"—into the surface that vastly improve adhesion. Improving adhesion is the only reason for sanding the inside of a locker.

However, the inside surface of your hull is probably knobby or lumpy rather than smooth, so sanding is not going to be very effective. The stiff sandpaper will ride across the high spots of the roving or weave, leaving the valleys untouched. If you did a good job of removing all traces of grease and wax from the hull surface, this haphazard sanding will be adequate because the higher surfaces are also going to be the most abused after you paint. If you want to go to the effort, running a soft wire wheel quickly over the entire surface *before* you sand will give the valleys some tooth.

You have three basic choices of *how* to sand the locker surfaces. A disk sander will do the job quickest, but inside a locker it is going to feed you a faceful of fiberglass dust and cut through the resin to the fiber. It will also be the most awkward to use in a confined space, and it doesn't do corners. If you want to try disk sanding, you need a soft foam disk and a light touch.

An orbital sander is a better choice for power sanding in preparation for painting. It is not called a finishing sander for nothing. If the locker surface

Use a soft wire wheel to prepare an uneven surface for painting.

is relatively flat and you load the sander with 80-grit paper, it will prepare the surface very quickly.

Your third choice is sanding by hand, which in the case of a small locker, tight corners, or pronounced curvature of the hull surface, can be the best choice. For hand sanding, fold a quarter-sheet of sandpaper into thirds. This prevents the paper from sanding itself, but it doesn't do your fingertips any favors. Unless you are learning to read Braille or want to work on your safe-cracking skills, wear leather work gloves or dot-studded garden gloves when you will be sanding for more than a few minutes.

As a general rule you should prepare most surfaces for painting or varnishing by sanding them with 120-grit production paper. This grit promotes good adhesion, while the scratches it leaves behind will be completely hidden by the flow of the paint or varnish. Teak presents an exception to this rule, as 100-grit sanding provides better tooth for this oily wood. Most single-part paints can also benefit from the better tooth of 100-grit paper. Paints obscure scratches better than varnish does, and many will hide even 80-grit marks, but finish sanding with 80-grit paper is rarely worth the risk. You can initially sand the surface with 80-grit paper for more rapid smoothing, but you should follow with 100-grit and perhaps 120-grit.

You need not work to such exacting standards when recoating a locker, however. Sand that sucker with 80-grit and stop right there. Sweep up the sanding dust—the only legitimate use I have ever found aboard for a synthetic brush. Better still, buy yourself a small shop vacuum and vacuum away the dust. Wipe the surface one more time with acetone, and you are ready to paint.

PROUD MARY

Time to do a little rollin'. You should have had your paint shaken at the paint store, but if not your first step is to stir it thoroughly with a flat paddle. Use a paint opener (the paint store will give you one or sell it to you for a few cents) not a screwdriver, to pry open the lid. Buy several because they tend to get misplaced. Might have something to do with the beer-bottle opener on the other end. A paint opener lifts the lid while a screwdriver tends to unroll the lip. Work your way around the lid, taking care to not distort it or bend the lip. Stir the paint a little or a lot, depending on how long ago it was in the shaker. Stop when the paint pulled up by the bottom of the stirrer is the same as that at the top.

Line your paint tray if you are going to, then pour some stirred paint into the well of the paint tray. Use your brush to clean out the rim of the can, wiping the brush

against the inner lip to return the paint to the can. Once most of the paint is removed from the lid, wipe away all remaining residue with a piece of paper towel, and reinstall the lid. No matter what the fun guys at the paint store did, *do not* hammer the lid in place. Push it into the groove with your weight over your thumbs, again working all the way around the lid. Closing the lid immediately and keeping it closed will keep the paint fresh.

Slip a new cover onto the cage of the roller handle and dip the bottom surface of the cover into the paint. Lift it out and roll it down the sloped part of the tray several times, dipping it into the paint

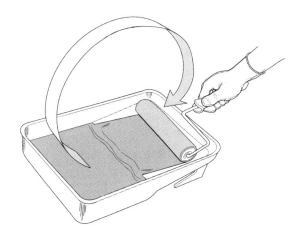

Dip the roller then lift it clear and roll it down the tray slope to distribute the paint and unload excess.

To prevent roller "tracks," tilt the roller and roll one end down with heavy pressure to unload the roller edge.

Unload the opposite edge the same way.

Loading a roller.

again as necessary to get paint evenly on all sides of the cover. After initially loading the roller, the process to reload it is to dip it into the paint once, then lift it and roll it two or three times *down* the slope to even the load and unload the excess. You can prevent the roller from leaving end tracks as you use it by tilting the loaded cover up a few degrees from the horizontal and rolling the end of the roller down the slope with heavy pressure. Unload the opposite end the same way.

Take the loaded roller to the surface you want painted, and roll on the paint in a big M or W pattern. Continue rolling over the same area until the coverage is complete and uniform. The size of the area covered should generally not be more than a 3-foot square. The direction of your strokes does not matter. In this case, because the surface is uneven, rolling in two directions is likely to deliver better coverage. If the roller fails to cover, you may need a roller cover with a longer nap or you might do better with a brush.

Rolling typically delivers a coating with a light stipple. In paints like alkyd enamels with good flow characteristics, particularly light colors, this will smooth out to a slight orange-peel texture. On a surface that already has a texture, this will not detract from the appearance of the finish in any way. When we get to a smoother and more conspicuous surface, you will "erase" the orange-peel texture by *tipping* the rolled-on paint with a brush, but there is no need for that additional step for locker interior surfaces.

Lay on paint in an M or W pattern, then continue rolling over the same area until coverage is uniform.

Brush Application

You will need a brush to apply paint into the corners of the locker and to trim around features. For a small locker or when the surface is exceptionally rugged, you might be better off dispensing with the roller and painting the entire locker with a brush. Never paint right out of the can the paint came in. Aside from exposing the paint to the air, causing it to begin to thicken, you will also contaminate it with bristles, dust, and old paint. Pour as much paint as you need into one of the plastic buckets you bought, then clean the paint can rim and close the lid.

Dip just the bottom third of the bristles.

Unload one side of the brush against a solid edge.

Make the initial stroke with the loaded side down.

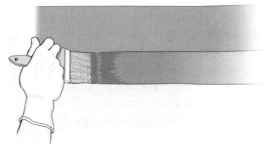

Use as few additional parallel strokes as possible to spread the brushload into a thin uniform coating.

Painting with a brush.

When applying paint with a brush, dip only the bottom third of the bristles into the paint—not half, not three-quarters, just a third. Then you will need to drag one side of the brush across the rim of the container to unload that side. One side of one-third of the brush doesn't seem like a very efficient use of all that bristle, but if you want good results, do it this way.

Make your initial stroke on the surface with the loaded side of the brush down, then use several straight back and forth strokes to spread the paint evenly. Use just the tip of the brush, angling the handle in the direction of travel—like leaning into a strong wind—and bending the bristles only slightly. As a rule, the fewer strokes, the better the finish will be. You want to spread the brushload of paint into a uniform, thin coat, then stop. Skill with a brush comes with practice. When you get it right, you'll know it. If the paint is not covering, don't try to put it on thicker. You are going to need a second coat.

Thinning

Thus far I have failed to mention thinning. As long as the paint is fresh and you have ideal weather conditions (not too hot but not cold, not too much humidity but some, not much wind, no front approaching, and no direct sunlight), you should be able to use the paint as it comes from the can, which is to say you had better learn how to thin. The thinner for alkyd enamel is mineral spirits—sometimes labeled "paint thinner." Same thing. Penetrol, a proprietary mineral spirits mixture that enjoys a dedicated following, is another option for thinning enamel. The same instructions apply.

Nearly everyone initially has trouble thinning paint. Thin it too little and the brush (or roller) drags, the paint fails to flow out, and every brushstroke shows. Thin it too much and it sags or runs and the gloss is destroyed. You don't have to be well schooled or particularly clever to get the proportion of thinner just right. You just have to be *patient.* The trick is to creep up on the correct viscosity by adding thinner in very small, measured portions. Add just a few drops too much thinner, and you will render the paint useless—unless you have some unthinned paint left to save it. This alone is sufficient reason to thin only the paint you are using. You are thinning for the conditions anyway, which are likely to be different the next time you use this paint. Never thin the entire can.

Test First

Test your paint on a smooth vertical surface. A piece of window glass is ideal. If you cannot scrounge up a piece of glass, go to your home supply store and buy a sheet of tempered hardboard paneling (Masonite) with a glossy plastic surface. Shiny plastic laminate will also work, but surfaced hardboard is cheaper and stiffer. Whatever "perfect" surface you test your paint on, if the brushstrokes fail to disappear, add a few drops of thinner, mix thoroughly, and try again. Continue to add thinner a few drops at a time until the paint flows out the way you want it to. If it develops a tendency to run, you have gone too far. You will need to add more paint, but keep in mind that it will take a cupful of paint to offset the effect of a capful of thinner.

By the way, the spout on lots of thinner and solvent cans is offset so you can pour without spilling. To do that, however, you must counterintuitively have the spout at the high side of the can when you tilt it. That means also holding the container you are pouring into at a tilt against the spout, at least until the thinner can is less than full. It is a good practice to add thinner by the capful or less, which lets you use the cap as your receiving container.

Once you have started painting, what do you do when nature calls or you suffer a Big Mac attack? The answer is you wrap the paint roller and/or brush in plastic kitchen wrap. Also pat a layer of plastic onto the surface of the paint in the tray, including the wet paint on the slope. Protect the paint in whatever container you are using for brush application the same

Add thinner in small amounts and test the flow of the thinned paint.

way—by covering the surface of the paint with plastic wrap. When you are ready to start painting again, just peel away the plastic and your roller, brush, and paint will be as fresh as when you left.

A bit of plastic wrap will also preserve paint you are not using. The less paint inside the can, the more air and the more drying that will take place. When storing a half can or less, you can extend its shelf life by covering the paint surface with plastic before sealing the can. Push the plastic down onto the surface of the paint and against the can at the paint level all around. The plastic will protect the paint (varnish too) from the air in the can and keep the top from forming a skin. To use the paint, remove the plastic and pour the amount you need through a paint filter, thinning as required.

Filters

Ah, filters. I haven't mentioned filtering yet because it is generally not necessary when you are opening a new can of paint. It is essential, however, when you are *reopening* a can of paint because over time the paint will skin and/or form gummy or hard bits that will show up as lumps in your painted surface. Pour old paint—new stuff too, if you are after the perfect finish—through a cone-shaped, mesh paint filter, available for pennies from all paint suppliers. For small jobs I stretch a square cut from discarded pantyhose—plentiful in most working households—across the top of a small container and secure it with a rubber band. Pouring the paint through the stretched weave filters it perfectly.

A piece of discarded stocking makes an effective and free paint filter.

MORE THAN SKIN DEEP

Painting the interior of the hull can serve more than a cosmetic function. As I noted in Chapter 12, a study of hull blistering conducted by the University of Rhode Island concluded that "prolonged stagnation of bilge water is the surest method for destroying hull integrity." The bilge pump installation detailed in that chapter should keep most of the water out of the bilge, but not all.

The researchers also found that two coats of alkyd enamel were as effective at protecting the *outside* of the hull from saturation as any other barrier treatment they tested. Presumably such treatment would provide the same protection for the inside of the hull. However, submersion is not recommended for most alkyd paints, and a few decades worth of oil in the bilge is likely to compromise paint adhesion. A better approach for protecting the laminate from the inside is the same as the current protocol for the outside—an epoxy barrier coat. If, however, your bilge is normally cobweb dry, alkyd enamel should provide adequate protection and will be easier to apply, brighter, and probably easier to keep clean.

Put on your rubber gloves and scrub the bilge thoroughly with TSP or some other strong detergent and a stiff brush. Rinse the area, then scrub it a second time. Twenty years of bilge slime will not clean away easily, but the bilge must be squeaky clean for the paint to adhere. Rinse away all of the detergent, using the scrub brush as you rinse to dislodge all the residue from the crevices of the weave. After the fiberglass is completely dry, wipe it down thoroughly with a clean rag soaked in acetone. Twice. This is a good time to run a fan. Acetone fumes concentrated in the confines of the bilge can dissolve brain cells as readily as acetone dissolves oil and grease.

Wire-brush the surface, then sand it with 80-grit production paper. Wipe it thoroughly again with acetone. You want to seal moisture out, not in, so the laminate should be dry before you paint it. Your best chance of accomplishing that in a northern climate is to prepare the bilge after the boat has been hauled for the winter but wait until just prior to spring launch to coat it. If you boat where there is no winter haulout, select a time when the boat will be out of service for at least a couple of weeks, preferably longer. In both instances a dehumidifier can help the process. For a boat in the water, wrap the shaft and rudderpost stuffing boxes with towels to keep the occasional drip from falling into the bilge. Put a tag on the ignition switch that says "*Wait!* There is a towel around the stuffing box!" If your memory is like mine, it ain't what it used to be. Don't trust it. Make the tag.

After you have let the bilge dry out as long as you can, wipe it down one more time with acetone, then paint it. Do not use a primer. Apply alkyd enamel exactly as you did inside the lockers, except give the bilge at least three coats. If you decide to use an epoxy barrier coat instead, take a look at the "Barrier Coat" section in Chapter 6 for detailed instructions. However, the recommended foam roller will not give you good coverage on the textured inside surface of the hull, so put the epoxy on with a chip brush, changing to a new brush with each mixed batch of epoxy. Brush out the epoxy so it's as thin as possible to reduce the number of trapped bubbles. Recoat time is critical with epoxy. If you wait too long—usually any more than 2 hours— you will have to wash and sand the surface completely before applying the next coat. Unless you just enjoy sanding while standing on your head, get each successive coat on within the recoat time specified for the epoxy you are using. The dry film thickness (DFT) of the epoxy needs to be close to 20 mils, which will require not less than six coats. Put on each coat as soon as the previous coat is no longer tacky. Plan on this job taking the better part of a full day.

By the way, whatever you are painting with while your head is down in the bilge, keep that fan running. A few specks of dust in the paint is a small price to pay to avoid the loss of 10 or 20 points on your IQ. If you're thinking "What?" it's already too late.

OUT OF THE CLOSET

Now that you have the driest bilge and the whitest or pinkest lockers in the marina, it is time to test your painting skill on a more visible surface. Unless the "furniture" in your old boat is part of a molded pan, the tops of the settees and bunks—that area beneath the cushions—is plywood, and they are invariably painted. With age the old paint gets a bit dingy, so now is a good time to freshen it. Scrub the surface,

then wipe it lightly with an acetone-soaked rag. Check the old paint for compatibility by putting a mineral spirits–soaked rag on it for a few minutes. Use your orbital palm sander loaded with 100-grit production paper to prepare the surface for painting. Vacuum and wipe the surface one more time with acetone.

You do not want to use a nap roller for smooth surfaces. Instead you will use a foam cover. Let me repeat that except for uneven surfaces like locker interiors and applying bottom paints, the only roller covers you should ever buy are foam covers. Use a foam roller exactly the same way you do a nap roller, including unloading the ends of the roller to avoid roller tracks. If you have the paint thinned perfectly, it will exhibit a multitude of tiny bubbles behind the roller that will deflate into pits and then flow out into barely discernible dimples. You should paint at least one underbunk surface by rolling only and allow the paint to dry fully so you can see the kind of finish rolling with a foam roller delivers.

Roll and Tip

For a smoother finish you will need to tip the rolled-on paint with a brush. To derive much benefit from this, you need a better brush than a chip brush. The better the brush, the better the finish. For a surface hidden by bunk cushions you don't need a $40 brush, but if you don't use a reasonably good chisel-point brush, you will not learn the possibilities that the roll-and-tip technique offers.

Tipping should always happen immediately after the paint has been applied to take maximum advantage of the paint's subsequent flow-out. Apply a roller load of paint, rolling it out to uniform coverage. Lightly drag the tip of a dry brush—meaning one that has not been dipped in paint—in long, uniform strokes across the painted surface. Ideally you want the bristles to sweep across the surface with the weight of butterfly eyelashes and you want to tip the entire surface in single, parallel passes. When

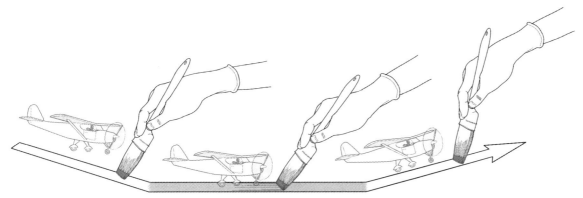

Land the brush lightly just behind the latest paint application and drag it beyond the wet edge.

you have tipped all of the area just rolled, roll paint onto the next area and tip it. Avoid marks where your brushstrokes start and end by starting each tipping stroke in the air and "landing" the brush on the paint just inside the previously tipped area. Drag the brush in a light, continuous stroke across the fresh application and lift it again as it passes onto the unpainted surface. Keep making these parallel touch-and-go landings with your brush until the new application has been tipped. Rolling and tipping combines the uniform film thickness that a roller delivers with the flawless surface a brush can create.

Where there are removable hatches, remove them and paint them separately. If you leave them in place, their edges will work just like the ridges on the paint tray slope or the rim of the paint bucket, unloading the roller or brush into the crack. Removing the hatches eliminates this problem and provides access so you can paint the edges of the hatch and the opening. Anytime you are painting to an edge with a roller or a brush, stroke off the surface, not onto it.

STUFF YOU'VE BUILT

What about shelves and dividers and new furniture you've built? Painting is the same except that, as a rule, you want to paint raw plywood *before* you sand it. I know that sounds bizarre, but the woods used in most plywoods are soft, and sanding will just make the surface fuzzy. Coat the plywood with sealer or primer if you have it, or just apply the first coat of alkyd enamel. House paints, in particular, are generally self-priming, so the only advantage to using a real primer is likely to be its lower cost but the total cost will be more if you buy primer and end up with extra paint.

After you have a coat of something on the plywood, sand the surface with 100-grit paper. It is, by the way, an excellent practice to seal all cut edges of plywood components with two or three coats of epoxy. It is the edges where plywood is the most vulnerable. With the edges sealed, one or two topcoats of enamel should give you an attractive finish that is also durable enough to shrug off even the unthinkable, which in a boat is generally water where it shouldn't be.

A NEW DECOR

Before high-pressure plastic laminates came along, bulkheads were either varnished or oiled wood or they were painted. Plastic laminates were both a blessing and a curse. When they were used as a substitute for paint, they offered definite advantages. As a substitute for teak or mahogany they were a bad joke.

The best way to refinish a laminate-covered bulkhead is to glue a new layer of laminate over the old one, but doing this properly requires the careful removal of all molding as detailed in Chapter 7. An easier alternative is to paint the bulkhead, and if done with care, there is no reason why a painted bulkhead should not look as good as or better than one covered with laminate.

Plastic laminate presents a stable and nonporous surface, an ideal base for paint; however, paint will not adhere well to the melamine surface of plastic laminate. The solution is to thoroughly sand the surface. Load your palm sander with 80-grit sandpaper and sand the surface you intend to paint until it is uniformly dull. The 80-grit paper will cut the tough surface of the laminate more quickly than a finer paper will. After the hard gloss of the laminate has been removed, load your sander with 100-grit paper and sand the surface again to remove the 80-grit marks and prepare the surface for painting. You will make the job easier and the result better by protecting all adjacent trim with masking tape.

Priming

Primer is normally a good idea on any surface that has not been previously painted. While not as essential for good adhesion on a synthetic (resin) surface such as fiberglass or plastic as it is for metal and wood surfaces, it will cover some surface imperfections and is especially helpful when you are painting a light color over a dark one. This is a good place to gain some experience with primer.

I have mostly omitted priming up to now either because the surfaces were already coated, which serves as the primer, or because it just adds an unnecessary step for painting unseen surfaces like the insides of lockers. Priming raw fiberglass might yield marginal benefits to adhesion and/or coverage, but when you omit the undercoat, the first coat of enamel serves as the primer. Unpainted wood, however, even inside a locker, *should* be primed before it is coated with enamel.

Use the primer recommended by the paint manufacturer. It will be specified on the label of the paint you are using. Treat the primer just like the enamel, stirring it thoroughly and pouring it into the paint tray. Apply it with a foam roller to the sanded and acetone-wiped bulkhead surface. You can often get by without tipping primer because you are going to sand it to a smooth surface before overcoating.

Dust

Primers are typically fast drying. After allowing the drying time specified on the can, sand the primer evenly with 120-grit production paper. Brush or vacuum the surface to remove the sanding dust, then wipe the surface with a clean, damp cloth. You can use a tack cloth, available from your paint supplier, but I am always concerned about the tack cloth leaving something behind that will interfere with the adhesion of the paint. I know the damp cloth will not do that as long as I give the surface a few minutes to dry before painting. If you use a tack cloth, use it with a light touch.

No tack cloth eliminates or even reduces airborne dust, so remove dust generators such as cushions and curtains from the cabin and vacuum the entire cabin before you start applying the top coats. I use a trigger-spray bottle filled with water to mist the surfaces near where I am painting to hold the dust down. I also mist my clothes, but this particular fanaticism has its drawbacks for winter painting. It should go without saying that all fans must be turned off and hatches that face the wind should be closed.

Before you paint the bulkhead between the cabins, the one everyone sees when they first come below, experiment on the engine room bulkhead or some other less conspicuous laminated surface. If you examine plastic laminates closely, you will find that many have a texture not unlike what results from a roller application of enamel. You could find that you prefer the uniformly textured surface of a roller application over the more reflective surface tipping creates. If you decide to tip the surface, this is where you are going to need a soft, well-flagged, and chisel-trimmed China, ox, or badger brush. As a rule I recommend

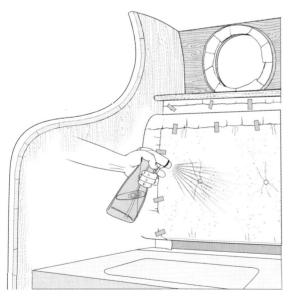

To hold down dust, wet fabrics that cannot be removed easily.

tipping horizontally, but because the wood-grain texture of a bulkhead is normally vertical, any brushstrokes that might be visible when the paint dries are less likely to draw attention if they too are vertical. Where the eye expects vertical grain, horizontal grain will be jarring. Tip full bulkheads vertically.

Paint Choices

If you want a gloss finish, use a single-part polyurethane or silicone topside paint rather than house paint. Topside paints are optimized for maximum flow-out, so you are likely to see fewer or no brushstrokes when they are applied carefully. Even if you do not want a glossy finish, you could still be wiser using a topside paint with a flattening agent added over house paint. That said, thin the house paint perfectly and you are likely to get nearly indistinguishable results for a third the cost. I personally think that a brushstroke or two on a bulkhead can actually add character to the typically too-sterile look of a fiberglass boat.

The reason for satin finish or semigloss over glossy is that the less-reflective finish will not highlight imperfections, will be easier on the eyes, and will give the cabin a softer, warmer atmosphere. White is traditional. Trimmed with teak or mahogany—the so-called Herreshoff look—it is no wonder that it remains popular. Some people find off-white or beige more pleasant, and there is really no reason why color cannot be introduced into the cabin with paint rather than cushion covers. The only rule is that lighter colors will make the cabin appear larger, while darker ones will make it close in.

Once the paint on your test surface is dry and you are satisfied with the results, damp-wipe the remaining surfaces and apply the paint. If you apply the second coat within the recoat time specified, you will not need to sand the surface between coats. The "green" surface of the previous coat will be softened by the solvent in the fresh paint, forming a chemical bond between the two coats. If you are unable to get a subsequent coat on within the time specified, you must sand the surface with 120-grit production paper or the second coat will not adhere to the first one. You may want to wait and lightly sand anyway to perfect the surface for the final coat.

Don't Go Back

If, after the paint has started to set, you notice an error—a run, a sag, or obvious brushstrokes—do not attempt to correct it with your brush or roller. It can be hard to resist the temptation to try to "fix" it, but you will only make it worse. You can trust me on this. Allow the paint to dry thoroughly (normally at least 24 hours), then remove the blemish with

120-grit sandpaper and repaint. For best results, sand and recoat the entire bulkhead.

The ease with which the surface may be recoated is one of the major advantages of painted bulkheads. If the color that looked so great in your mind's eye assaults your sensibilities when you actually get it on the bulkheads, a few minutes of preparatory sanding and a coat of a different color will make things right. Sticking to some shade of white generally avoids this kind of problem.

THE PAPER CASE

There is little reason why paper and fabric wall coverings cannot be used as successfully on a boat as they are in fine homes. The conditions in the main cabin of most boats will be easier on wallpaper than, say, the steamy environs of most bathrooms, yet paper of all types is a common bathroom wall covering. This is a commentary on the tenacity of modern wallpaper glues.

The concept of wallpaper on boats is not a revolutionary one. Luxury yachts have been using fabric and vinyl coverings on bulkheads for years, to good effect. The same coverings can similarly enhance the interior of your old boat.

The array of wall coverings that you will encounter in any large wallpaper outlet is mind-boggling. Many you can probably eliminate immediately as unsuitable. Untreated paper, flocks, foils, murals, and florals all seem to belong to this group. Vinyls are the most durable. Some fabric coverings are strikingly elegant. On the small (by wall-size standards) spaces of a bulkhead, solid colors are almost always preferable to patterns. As with paint, light colors will make the cabin appear larger.

For the most secure adhesion, you should prepare the laminate just as if you were going to paint it. Sand it first with 80-grit, followed by 100-grit paper, then prime the surface with an alkyd undercoater. After the primer is dry, sand it with 120-grit paper, then brush or roll on a coat of *resin sealer*. Resin sealer provides a surface the paper will "glide" onto in the hanging process and at the same time provides the tooth needed by the adhesive. Resin sealer is available from the wallpaper supplier and it is superior to the more commonly used wallpaper size. A quality resin sealer will adhere to most plastic laminates without the need to sand and prime, but preparing the surface removes any doubt. Allow the sealer to dry.

Aside from the wall covering and the resin sealer, you need a mildew-resistant paste of the type recommended for the covering you have chosen, a 6- or 8-inch flexible nylon scraper (usually superior to the old-fashioned smoothing brush), a trimming knife (the type that uses a single-edge razor blade), a 10-inch drywall knife (also for trimming), and perhaps a seam roller.

Since the concept of "level" is dubious aboard a boat, align the covering with a vertical feature of the bulkhead, such as a passageway, by measuring away from that feature 1 inch less than the width of the paper and, with a pencil, drawing a parallel vertical line from the top to the bottom of the bulkhead. The edge of the first strip of covering will lie on this line.

Prepare the first piece of covering by cutting a piece from the roll long enough to extend a couple of inches beyond the top and bottom of the bulkhead. Lay the covering facedown on a protected flat surface. Coat the back of the strip with paste, then fold each end of the strip to the middle—paste to paste—and set the strip aside for several minutes. This is called *booking* the paper. If your paper is prepasted, activate the paste by submerging the loosely rolled piece in water for the time specified, then pull it out of the water tray by one end and book it. Normally you would coat or soak the next strip while the first one cures, but if this is your initial experience with wallpaper, don't get fancy.

After the strip sits for about 10 minutes, unfold it and apply it to the bulkhead, aligning it with the line you drew. It should overlap the top, the bottom, and the vertical feature you measured from initially. By

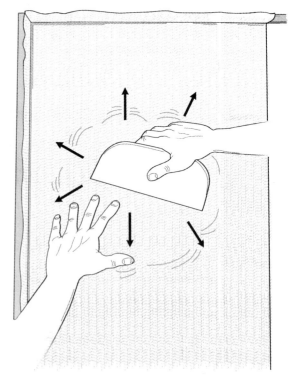

Smooth the covering against the bulkhead with a nylon scraper or a smoothing brush but do not expel the paste and do not stretch the paper.

putting your palms flat on the strip, you will be able to slide it around on the bulkhead until you are satisfied with the alignment. If you are hanging a vinyl, use the nylon scraper to work out all the bubbles by stroking the paper in a starburst pattern from the center. Do not apply much pressure. You are trying to expel the bubbles, not the paste. If you are hanging a cloth covering, you may have better success smoothing it with a clean paint roller. Try to avoid stretching the covering, or it will contract as it dries, opening the seam with the next piece.

Once this strip is in place, load a new razor blade into your trimming knife and trim off the overlap. Trimming against a straight corner or a straight piece of molding is not difficult. Use the drywall knife to pin the paper tightly into the corner between the bulkhead and the molding and draw the blade of the trim knife along the edge of the drywall knife. The trick is a new blade and as low a blade angle as possible. Reposition the drywall knife and extend the cut, repeating this sequence until the trim is complete.

Trimming around curved molding is more difficult. On an outside curve you may be able to use the trim knife with the edge of a putty knife to follow the contour. On an inside curve, force the covering against the molding with something blunt but hard enough to leave a crease. Lift the paper and trim along the crease with scissors. Smooth the trimmed covering back into place.

Measure and cut the next strip from the roll. On the assumption that you have not chosen a printed paper, there are no concerns about matching patterns. Paste and book the strip, and while the glue cures, use a damp sponge to remove the paste from all the surfaces where you trimmed away the overlap. Keep rinsing your sponge and scrubbing until all the paste is gone. If you fail to remove the paste while it is still wet, it will be a bear to get off later. If you wisely taped the trim before priming the bulkhead, you can avoid most of this mess by leaving the tape on until you are finished hanging the wall covering. Don't get your sponge so wet that it injects water under the edge of the paper, which will dilute the paste and interfere with adhesion.

Butt the second strip against the edge of the first one. Because the covering will shrink a bit, the joint between the two strips should be just slightly buckled. Smooth and trim the second piece. Continue the process until the bulkhead is covered. After a strip has been in place for about 20 minutes, go back to it and run a seam roller over the seam between that strip and the prior one to press the two edges together and against the bulkhead. If the roller marks

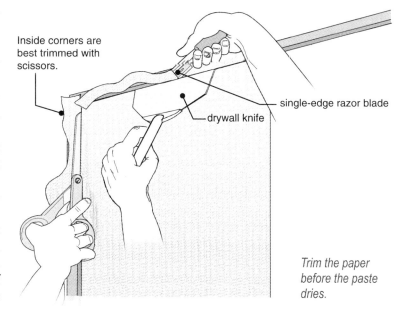

Inside corners are best trimmed with scissors.

single-edge razor blade

drywall knife

Trim the paper before the paste dries.

Buckle seams slightly to allow for shrinkage.

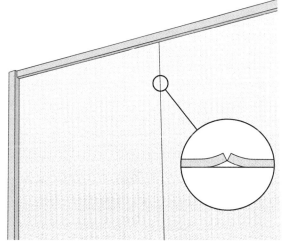

the covering you have selected, use a damp (not wet) sponge instead to compress the seam. Wash off any paste that gets onto the surface of the covering, again taking care not to dilute the paste beneath.

INTERIOR WOOD

If you are lucky enough to have bulkheads covered with honest wood veneer, your interest is not in covering them but in uncovering them. The cure for dull, drab interior woodwork—whether full bulkheads or molding and trim—depends on whether the wood is oiled or varnished and whether you want it to be oiled or varnished.

The first step in resurfacing brightwork is the same as the first step in painting—you need to get the surface squeaky-clean. Interior woodwork tends to harbor mildew in the pores and is subject to a greasy buildup from the galley. You can remove both at the same time by mixing a cup of liquid laundry detergent and a cup of household bleach into a gallon of water and washing the wood with this solution. Wear rubber gloves and use a towel rather than a sponge, taking care not to get the bleach solution on nearby fabrics. You want to wet the surface of the wood enough to soften the grime and emulsify oils, but not so much that you raise the grain unnecessarily. Wring out the towel so it is not dripping wet each time you reload it with the cleaning solution. Wet all of the wood surfaces and allow the solution to stand for 30 minutes. Use a fresh towel wrung out in fresh water to thoroughly rinse the wood. When you are satisfied that you have removed all of the detergent, allow the wood to dry completely. It should be really clean, but it will also seem rather dull and lifeless. That's good.

If you want a *natural* finish, all you need to do is wipe the wood with lemon oil. Do not confuse this with lemon polish or lemon wax, which are lemon only in scent. You want pure lemon oil—not always easy to find locally, but long available from Amazon Lumber & Trading (not the book vendor) and obtainable online. Lemon oil will not stand up to the rigors of exterior exposure, but it is the ideal treatment for natural interior wood. It feeds the wood, replacing lost natural oils and highlighting the beauty; it is

poison to mildew; it doesn't dry sticky; subsequent applications will absorb surface grease; and it smells good. Apply it with a cloth, rubbing it into the grain of the wood. Do a second application in a week. After that, wipe down the interior wood with lemon oil about once a month, depending on how much use your boat sees. Keep in mind that the interior wood is like fine furniture. If you want it to look good, you have to give it *some* care.

You can also finish interior woods the same way you might protect exterior wood. That includes other types of oils and sealers for teak and varnish for any kind of wood. All provide a more durable finish, but each is further removed from natural wood. We will come back to the interior woodwork when we get to the subject of varnishing, but first let's look at exterior oils and sealers.

EXTERIOR TEAK

The only woods that do well naturally in exterior applications are oily woods. Aboard a boat that is likely to be teak. Other woods require a hard, protective finish or they will split and crack. Lemon oil can be used to feed and enhance virtually any wood that might be found in your old boat's cabin, but when we talk about oiling exterior wood, we are talking only about teak. Success on any level at giving exterior teak a natural finish requires a different and exacting regimen. Let's outline the process.

CLEAN

Here again you need to start with cleaning. Most of the time exterior teak is not going to be restored to its virgin golden color by a damp application of chlorine bleach and laundry detergent, but the harsher the cleaning process, the less wood that will remain after you finish. Always use the mildest cleaner that will do the job. If your teak is black from neglect, you can join in when I start singing your tune.

For cared-for teak, the gentlest cleaner will be a 3:1 mix of liquid laundry detergent and chlorine bleach, undiluted by water. Boost this mix with TSP crystals, the same TSP you used to clean the bottom of the lockers. Apply this mixture by *lightly* scrubbing it on with an abrasive pad and let it sit for 5 minutes. The bleach will kill mildew and the detergent-TSP combination will lift dirt. Don't leave it on too long because it will also lift the grain of the wood. Rinse with a strong flow of water, and use a soft scrub brush to dislodge softened dirt and rub away the detergent. Don't be too reluctant to try a second application before resorting to harsher treatment.

BLEACH

Despite being a bleach, chlorine is not very good at lightening the color of wood. For this you need a different type of bleach. You need oxalic acid. You can get it as the active ingredient in nearly all single-part teak cleaners, whether powder or liquid. It is also the principal ingredient in Bar Keepers Friend, sold at your local supermarket for scouring pots, sinks, and counters. Or, as with TSP, you can buy plain oxalic acid crystals that you simply add to warm water. It is this latter form that woodworkers use to create a bleach mixture for lightening wood prior to finishing. Not surprisingly, the crystals are also the most economical.

Dissolving 4 tablespoons of oxalic acid in ¹/₂ gallon of warm water will give you an effective but relatively mild wood bleach that you can simply paint onto clean wood—teak or others—to lighten, brighten, and homogenize the color. Oxalic acid will also dull paint and gelcoat, and it is not good for anodized aluminum either, so wet all adjacent surfaces before you apply the solution to reduce the risk of collateral damage. Let the acid solution dry completely on the wood, then vacuum up the powder that remains. Rinse the bleached wood thoroughly, scrubbing to dislodge all remaining acid residue.

Powdered teak cleaners and Bar Keepers Friend contain cleaners and/or abrasives in addition to the oxalic acid and may do a better job on wood that is weathered or rough. Yes, two-part cleaners are better still at cleaning weathered wood and with less scrubbing, but there is a significant cost to your wood. Besides, exercise is good for you, Bunky. Why pay to go to the gym when you can do your reps for free on your boat and double the payoff?

A lot of boaters scrub teak with a brush but I have never been satisfied with any brush I've tried. For cleaning rather than just bleaching, a synthetic scrubber is better. In the days I worked in an office, I got the janitorial service to save me the center piece from floor buffer pads that they otherwise punched out and discarded. Even if you don't know anyone who uses a floor buffer, buying a new pad (the densest you can) and cutting it into a supply of scrubbers can be more economical than buying Scotch-Brite pads. Bronze wool is also excellent if you have already

1

Dissolve 4 tablespoons of oxalic acid into ¹/₂ gallon of warm water.

2

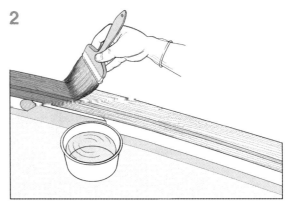

Wet wood with this solution.

3

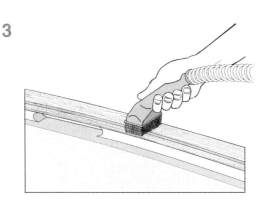

Allow bleach to dry then vacuum the powder residue.

4

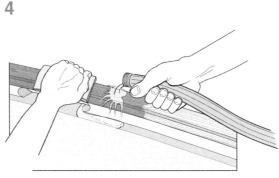

Scrub and rinse with lots of water.

Bleaching wood.

come into your trust fund. Steel wool should never come anywhere near your boat. The particles it leaves behind will become permanent rust freckles on fiberglass and wood alike.

TEAK EATER

Only after the milder methods have failed should you contemplate using a two-part teak cleaner. While these products are dramatically effective, the fact that they must be "neutralized" sounds like what happens to a secret agent run amok. Indeed, the Part A is an assassin with your wood in the crosshairs. The active ingredient is probably hydrochloric acid, which simply eats away the top surface of the wood, especially the soft cellulose, leaving behind just the hard binder called lignin. Wood repeatedly cleaned with a two-part cleaner begins to resemble a plowed field. The only way to make it attractive again is to sand off the hard ridges, so with your help, the acid essentially reduces the thickness of the wood. Do this a few times and your caprails dissolve to veneer with fastener holes too shallow to bung and rail-mounted hardware sitting on wood islands. Handrails shrink to pencil diameter. The acid also attacks sealants and etches gelcoat and paint. This is chemotherapy for your teak, something you do once to restore it to good health.

By the way, you will need to use a synthetic brush to apply two-part cleaners because they dissolve natural bristles. Wear chemical gloves and eye protection while you scrub with the Part A application, then be sure you paint on sufficient Part B to get a uniform color change. Scrub again lightly, then rinse like you are washing off itching powder. When the wood dries, the color will be beautiful but the surface (probably) rough. Plan on sanding—perhaps heavily—before you apply whatever protective coating you have in mind. Use a finishing sander and 100-grit production paper to restore a smooth surface to the wood. Brush or vacuum away all the sanding dust, and wipe the wood with a rag saturated with mineral spirits to remove any embedded dust. Dust you leave behind will darken the color of the wood if you oil it.

OIL

Oiling teak—or any wood, for that matter—is good for the health of the wood, restoring some of the natural oils and resins. Unfortunately oiling is like a workout; the beneficial effects are lost unless you do it regularly.

Basically two types of oil are suitable for exposed teak, and one or the other is found in virtually every teak oil on the market. The less expensive of the two is linseed oil (which ought to be called flaxseed oil). Linseed oil is an excellent preservative but tends to turn the wood dark, a problem that is exacerbated by the resins that are usually also present in most teak oils to make them more durable.

The second type is tung oil, derived from the fruit of the Chinese tung tree. (Don't you wonder exactly what a tung fruit looks like?) Tung oil does not darken the wood, and it is more water resistant than linseed oil, a significant advantage aboard a boat. If a teak oil is tung-oil based, it will say so in big letters because tung oil is significantly more expensive than linseed oil. If the teak oil does not state the ingredients, assume that it contains linseed oil.

The unfortunate truth is that neither oil will last more than a few weeks on a horizontal surface. Both carbonize in sunlight and turn black. To regain the gold, you must scrub off the blackened oil and the dirt it will harbor and apply a fresh coat. To reduce the frequency of reapplication, most teak oils contain one or several synthetic and natural resins. They also contain driers to hasten drying, UV filters, and mildew retardants. These high-tech additives often benefit the label more than the oil.

The best way to select a teak oil is to ignore advertising claims and the "independent" tests. Simply find a boat in your marina that has teak that looks the way you want yours to look and ask the owner what product he or she uses. Teak oils that are widely praised in some regions are just as widely maligned in others. Climate is a major factor. Also ask your marina neighbor how often he or she applies it. Your own teak will not look as good unless you follow a similar schedule.

You can apply oil with a cloth, but it is easier and less messy with a brush. To encourage the oil to penetrate the wood as deeply as possible, thin the first coat about 20% with mineral spirits or turpentine, and apply the oil in the sun. Teak can initially exhibit a thirst that might have impressed Dean Martin, but after three or four coats the oil will begin to stand on the surface. Do not give excess oil the opportunity to dry. Wipe it off immediately with an absorbent cloth. Continue to oil the wood until it refuses to accept any more. The wood should have a matte finish with no sign of gloss anywhere.

Do not be lulled into complacency by the clear, watery nature of the oil. The resins in most teak oils will stain your gelcoat or paint. Apply teak oil with the same care you would show if you were painting the wood. Oil runs are invisible unless you look for them, so you must be vigilant in checking behind you. Drips or runs must be wiped up immediately with mineral spirits. Watch for runs under the sprit or down the hull that may not be visible without leaning over the rail and craning your neck. On day one a run can look as benign as a snail track, but it will soon darken into a Macbethian stain. Once the resins dry, the damned spot will be almost impossible to out.

SEALER

Another approach to the "natural" finish is the application of a sealer. Sealers do not feed the wood, but as the name suggests, they seal the surface to keep natural oils and resins in and moisture and dirt out. An effective sealer can be concocted by thinning varnish 50% with turpentine or mineral spirits.

Sealer alone is not an effective treatment for old teak. Because the natural oils and resins have already been lost, sealing is like closing the corral gate after the horses have escaped. You will be unable to oil teak after it has been sealed, so you need to oil the wood first to restore it. Give the oil a couple of weeks to dry. Wash the oiled wood and let it dry, then wipe it vigorously with an acetone-saturated rag to remove surface oils and give the sealer a better surface to grip. You can apply sealer like oil, without any concern for the quality of the brush or the direction of the brushstrokes.

Sealers and oils have sometimes been blended in an effort to combine the durability of the former with the rejuvenating effect of the latter. Such products are likely to be called dressings or treatments. Their popularity has typically been fleeting as promise gives way to experience. At best these products extend the time between refresher coats by a few weeks.

PAINT

At the other end of the spectrum is paint. Paint the exterior wood and it will be protected from the elements, exempt from the damage of cleaners, and you will not have to recoat it except every few years. Paint it gray and you do away with the whole question of exterior wood. Paint it brown and it will just be brown up close, but from a distance it will still imitate wood. The depressing truth is that the masses won't notice the difference.

Reduce the pigment to a level where the paint becomes semitransparent, and you can fool more people at closer range. When you coat your exterior teak with this "weak" paint, the eye sees the grain behind and notices the pigment even less. This is the sleight of hand those so-called varnish alternatives such as Cetol and Armada perform. The trade-off, of course, is that less pigment means less UV protection, so these products are not as long-lived as paint, but they will outlast a pigment-free varnish coating.

VARNISH

If you want the beauty of varnish, there is no shortcut. Nor is there any liberation. The secret to having beautifully varnished brightwork is not the brand of varnish, although some are undoubtedly better than others. It is not the brush; anyone can buy a good brush. It is not the number of coats. It is not keeping the varnish bubble free. It is not the grit of the sandpaper selected for the final sanding. It is not wrist action or the way you hold your mouth. All of those things (except maybe the one about the mouth) are important, even essential, but the secret to having beautiful varnish is *vigilance*. You must touch up every nick and scratch immediately, and you must recoat the varnish regularly and at the first sign of deterioration. If you fail to notice or fail to act, even for a week or two, the consequence can be stripping the surface back to bare wood. Good varnish, good brush, good preparation, and good technique will not count for a thing.

Why am I telling you this? Take a stroll down the dock and look at the varnished brightwork. When it is maintained, it adds an air of elegance, even opulence, to the most humble boat. But when the varnish has been neglected, even sweet lines are disgraced by the peeling and blackened wood. Which effect will varnishing have on your boat? Deciding to varnish—particularly exterior brightwork—is not a one-time decision; it's a long-term commitment. Exterior surfaces will have to be sanded and a fresh layer of varnish applied at least twice a year—three times a year on horizontal surfaces. Unless you are both able and willing to accept this responsibility, save yourself a lot of grief and just oil or paint the wood. Stripping varnish is a job you only want to do once.

Stripping

If the varnish on your old boat is in bad shape, there is good news and bad news. The good news is that most of the original wood thickness is probably still there, since the wood has not been scrubbed every 8 weeks for 20 years. (That alone is a good reason to elect to varnish.) The bad news is that all the old varnish has to come off.

Cabinet scraper. Stripping old varnish with a scraper is the cleanest, the safest, and (for some)

In skilled hands a cabinet scraper can remove old varnish quickly and cleanly.

the easiest method. If you have never used a scraper, buy one and give it a try before resorting to one of the other methods of varnish removal. You need a 4- or 5-inch cabinet scraper, sometimes called a card scraper, which is nothing more than a rectangular piece of hard sheet steel. An old handsaw blade is the right kind of steel if you want to make your own scraper. You can buy a handle, but cabinet scrapers are usually easier to use without one. The edge of the scraper has a microscopic burr, which acts as a cutting edge. Hold the scraper at an angle of about 75 degrees to the wood surface and pull it toward you. The tiny edge, in effect, planes the old varnish from the wood. In skilled hands, a scraper can put a remarkably smooth finish on wood.

The edge lasts quite a while against varnish, but it eventually dulls. Renewing the cutting edge of a cabinet scraper is simple once you master it. You must always

1

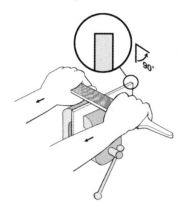

Draw a mill file over the edges to square them.

2

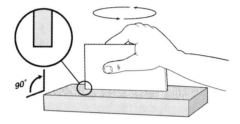

Whet each edge on an oilstone.

3

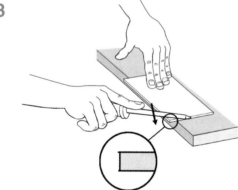

Burnish all sides to deform the corners into microscopic overhangs.

4

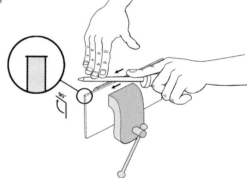

Burnish the edges to turn the overhangs out.

5

Tilt the burnishing tool 10 degrees to give the out-turned burr a slight hook.

Sharpening a cabinet scraper.

start with a square edge. A two-fisted horizontal draw of a mill file across the edge of a scraper clamped in a vise will work, but some craftsmen create a jig of some sort to hold either the file or the scraper. After you file every edge square, whet each on an oilstone, always holding the scraper perpendicular and using a circular motion. You may also need to whet the sides if filing created any burrs there. Now lay the blade flat just back from the edge of your work surface and use the round shank of a Phillips screwdriver to burnish the front edges of the face. You do this by placing the shank almost flat on the blade and stroking it with heavy pressure along the edge and slightly out. What you are trying to do here is deform the corner of the metal out into a microscopic overhang. Turning and flipping the scraper as necessary, burnish it across all four edges on both faces.

Now reclamp the scraper vertically in a vise and use the screwdriver shank with heavy pressure to burnish the up-edge square. Here the objective is to turn out the two extensions you created with your first burnishing. The scraper should be T-shaped in cross section after you burnish this first edge, although the arms of the T may be too small to see. After half a dozen or more heavy horizontal passes, tilt the shank of the burnishing tool up about 10 degrees and burnish one side of the edge with two or three passes to turn the burr down into a bit of a hook. Tilt the tool 10 degrees the other way and shape the opposite cutting edge. When you have done all the edges, you will have eight fresh cutting edges. You should be able to resharpen the scraper perhaps a dozen times by simply burnishing, depending on the metal, before filing and whetting will be needed again.

Heat gun. If a cabinet scraper in your hands is like one of those slicer-dicer-julienne gizmos on late-night TV—not gonna work as advertised—hey, it happens. You can still scrape off the varnish, but you are going to need the assistance of heat. A heat gun is not expensive, and it's a nice tool to own. It is, however, modestly dangerous for you and for your boat. You will surely burn yourself at least once to fully appreciate that you must never allow the business end to point toward flesh. You will also scorch the wood if you are the least bit inattentive when you have the trigger depressed. Fortunately superficial scorch marks sand away easily enough. The biggest risk may be to your fiberglass. Think of setting a Tupperware container on a hot burner. Do not overheat fiberglass or you will scar it at the very least.

Stripping varnish with heat is one of those Tom Sawyer jobs you might sell as fun to crew, relatives, or friends. The idea is that you play heat over the varnish until it begins to bubble. It will be soft and

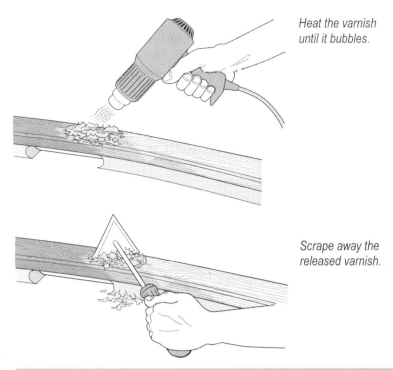

Heat the varnish until it bubbles.

Scrape away the released varnish.

Stripping with a heat gun.

gummy and will yield easily to the tug of a scraper. There are special scrapers available for heat stripping that simply provide a sharp edge. You don't need the burr of a cabinet scraper here. Do not use a hook scraper or a putty knife or other push tool on wood; they will gouge the wood. Stripping with heat can go very quickly. When you have the bulk of the old varnish off, you may want to use a chemical stripper to clean up the residue and lift varnish from the grain.

Chemical stripper. Chemical strippers work like magic, converting most finishes into a toxic gelatin that you could just hose off with a blast of water if you didn't need to worry about where it went. Unfortunately most strippers will happily feed on any resin, meaning in this case, your topside paint and even your gelcoat. So not only can you not hose off the goo, you must mask all surrounding surfaces to make sure the stripper doesn't steal off on its own and wreak havoc. Strippers also attack skin. And internal organs. Hardware-store strippers, in particular, contain methylene chloride, a bad boy among chemicals. No one will find chemical stripping fun.

Aside from the health risks, and they are myriad, common strippers dissolve polyester resin as readily as paint and should not be used for boat-stripping projects. Stripping varnish is the single exception. As long as you are stripping exterior wood in the open air and you take extra care to prevent the stripper from coming into contact with other surfaces, the type of strippers not sold for boat use will do the job quicker. Buy the thickest stripper you can find.

Pour a little into a can, not onto the wood. Dip your brush, but *do not* wipe it. Apply the stripper with a single stroke, probably no more than 4 inches. Dip and apply the next 4 inches, and so on. It is the vapors from the stripper that do the work, and if you brush back and forth, you release them into the air, reducing the effectiveness of the stripper by as much as 80%! To give the stripper longer to work before it dries, try to avoid working in strong sunlight.

After the stripper has been on the surface about 30 minutes, you should be able to scrape off the softened varnish. You will need to use a wide putty knife

1

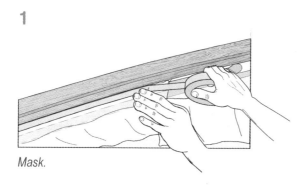

Mask.

2

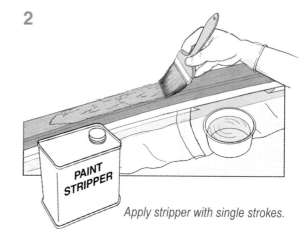

Apply stripper with single strokes.

3

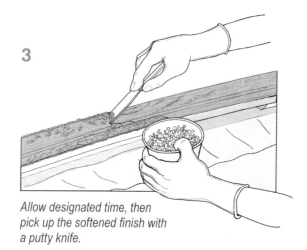

Allow designated time, then pick up the softened finish with a putty knife.

4

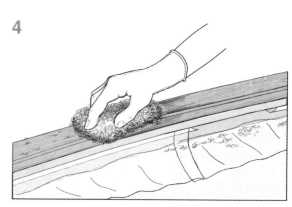

Clear the grain with bronze wool.

5

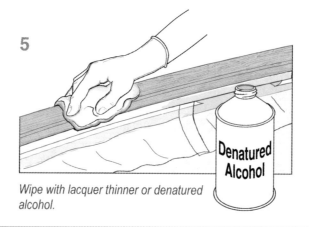

Wipe with lacquer thinner or denatured alcohol.

Chemical stripping.

and push it forward, the reason being that you are carefully picking up this caustic mess and depositing it into a container you have at hand. Once you have scraped away the stripper and varnish, scrub the wood with bronze wool to clear the grain. If you are just cleaning up after heat stripping, you are finished, but if you are removing all of the varnish with chemical stripping, you may have to give the wood a second treatment. Once all the varnish has been removed, wipe the wood with clean cloths saturated with denatured alcohol or lacquer thinner (toluene) to remove stripper and varnish residue.

Sanding. Sanding is the hardest way to strip old varnish. Rather than lifting the varnish in shavings or sheets, sanding grinds it to dust, and to grind the bottom layer, you must have ground through the layers above. If you don't want this to take forever, you need a high-speed sander. A belt sander can work, but it is a particularly awkward tool that's suitable only for flat surfaces (which are in short supply on a boat), and you cannot really see what is going on underneath. A disk sander is easier to keep track of, but it sands in circular swirls, which is necessarily going to be across the grain when the paper reaches the wood. Both of these can do irreparable damage to the wood before you can say, "Oh, fudge."

An orbital sander is safer but slower. Loaded with 50- or 60-grit paper, it will cut through old coatings fairly quickly. The problem with an orbital sander is that the motion of the grit is small and fast, so it tends to heat the varnish, softening it to a gum that clogs the paper. You need to keep the sander moving in big sweeps to counter this, which may not be possible depending on where and what you are stripping. If you strip varnish by sanding, you are likely to be doing a good portion by hand.

Final prep. Whatever stripping method you adopt, after the old varnish has been removed and the wood scrubbed, you should plan to lighten and homogenize the surface color by bleaching the wood with oxalic acid. Let the acid treatment dry completely and vacuum off the powder that remains. Hosing combined with brushing is generally adequate for removing all traces of acid from the wood, but prior to a first coat of varnish it would not be a bad idea to mix a cup of the soda ash or borax into a bucket of water and wet all of the bleached wood generously with this solution to neutralize the acid. Then vigorously hose and brush the wood and all surrounding surfaces.

When everything is dry, sand the bare wood thoroughly with 100-grit paper. When sanding for varnish, always sand *with* the grain. Scratches across the grain will show through the varnish. If the wood has just been bleached, this initial sanding dust might still harbor

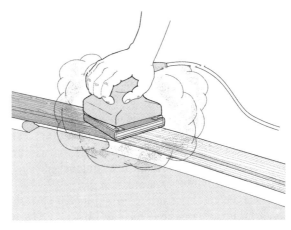

Where you have access, use a palm sander loaded with 100-grit paper to sand the wood to the smoothness of ivory.

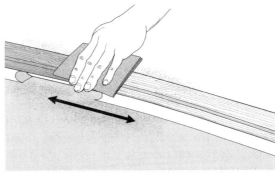

For hand sanding, fold a quarter sheet of 100-grit paper into thirds. Always sand with *the grain.*

Preparing bare wood.

some acid, so rinse it away thoroughly. Of course, the rinsing may again raise the grain, so one more application of sandpaper is called for. For teak, stick with 100-grit paper to provide better tooth for the varnish. If you are preparing mahogany, 150-grit will contribute to a better finish. Somewhat finer paper should be used on interior furniture. Use 120-grit for interior teak and up to 220-grit for interior mahogany and other hardwoods. Wipe the sanded wood down with a rag dampened with mineral spirits, and you are ready to varnish.

Laying It On

Ah, the promise a new quart of varnish offers. Under the lid you find a clear, thick liquid emitting amber light. When perfectly applied, it transforms sunlight into dazzle. When perfectly applied, it transforms wood into jewelry. When perfectly applied, it transforms scow into yacht.

When perfectly applied . . . Therein lies the rub. A less-than-perfect varnish application has an inordinate potential to disappoint, and initial efforts at applying varnish often meet with less-than-perfect results. You can only learn to lay on a flawless coat of varnish with a brush in your hand, but there are some near-universal rights and wrongs that can be assimilated from the printed word.

The right attitude. Let's start with realistic expectations. Varnish is simply paint without pigment. Its primary function is to protect the wood. Only the thickness of the film matters, not the perfection of the top surface. So even if your first attempts at varnishing look like first attempts, apply the requisite number of coats and the wood derives the full benefit. Wood sealed with varnish will not dry out and split, will not absorb moisture and rot, will be unaffected by pollution, and will be untouched—and thus unstained—by oily or greasy spills.

Here is another truth: even indifferent varnish looks infinitely better than bare wood. Most observers see the gloss, not the flaws. And because varnish is applied in coats, each new coat provides a fresh opportunity to achieve whatever level of perfection you seek.

The right varnish. Oil-based spar varnish is traditionally a relatively soft varnish, delivering better flexibility to eliminate or reduce splitting and cracking. Marine spar varnishes also tend to be loaded with UV inhibitors since the thing that matters most to boatowners about a varnish is how long it will last, and the primary reason for varnish failure is UV degradation. However, just because a product is labeled spar varnish or marine varnish there is no real assurance that it will deliver either flexibility or long life. The best approach remains to find a local boat sporting the finish you are after and ask the owner what kind of varnish was used.

Modern alkyd spar varnishes, because they are relatively soft, may not be the best choice for interior furniture. Less subject to the killing effects of the weather, interior finishes are murdered by abrasion. It is against abrasion that polyurethane varnish shines—so to speak. Actually the choice of gloss or satin finish is a matter of taste, but take my point. Polyurethane varnish is harder and often the better choice for interior brightwork. It also provides better wet footing, making it the *only* choice for a varnished sole. UV inhibitors are still required for varnishes used belowdeck.

I distrust polyurethane varnishes for exterior application because of their plastic-film nature. Urethane varnishes exposed to the elements have a well-earned reputation for releasing their grip on the wood and peeling off in sheets. The clear urethanes commonly sold in paint and hardware stores usually contain no UV inhibitors and are patently unsuitable for use on a boat. There are some polyurethane blends on the market formulated for exterior application, but none have the history of user satisfaction that comes with marine or spar varnish. Unless you have

reliable information—not advertising copy—about a particular polyurethane, stick with alkyd varnish.

Polyurethane varnish should not be confused with clear, two-component, aliphatic linear polyurethane (LPU, also called ALP). Clear two-part linear polyurethane is the same product, without a color-adding pigment, that has revolutionized boat painting. Handled properly, LPU has the *potential,* and I emphasize "potential," to put a finish on exterior brightwork that will last for 4 or 5 years without attention. This is, however, an exacting and relatively expensive process fraught with equal potential for problems. Even if your application is perfect, the instability of the wood can and usually does reduce the life of the finish to that of plain varnish. And it is virtually inevitable, sooner or later, that the finish will have to be renewed. When that happens, the incredible toughness of two-part polyurethane will switch from blessing to curse, and you may come to regret your choice. We will come back to this.

The right brush. Varnish will forgive some flaws in technique, but it will not forgive the wrong brush. You need a brush that absolutely will not shed bristles, which rules out chip brushes and most midprice China brushes, even for buildup coats. A bristle brush for applying varnish must be dense with a light-touch chisel point. Plan on spending $20 or more for a first-quality badger-hair brush.

There is ample evidence that a badger-hair brush can deliver an unexcelled finish in the right hands, but that does not necessarily make it the best brush choice for *your* hands. Having encapsulated too many errant bristles in otherwise perfect varnish applications, I have become a fan of foam brushes for applying varnish. *Foam brushes do not shed!*

That is not their only virtue. Foam brushes also hold less varnish per brush load. Almost everyone tends to lay on varnish too thickly, and in hot or sunny weather this results in alligatoring. Foam

Foam brushes have significant advantages for applying varnish.

brushes tend to limit this. They are also cheap enough to toss, while expensive bristle brushes require meticulous care after every use. However, throwing away foam brushes between coats is an unnecessary waste. Squeeze a foam brush nearly dry and store it in a folded foil pouch with a capful of thinner. When you are ready to apply the next coat, all the brush needs is another good squeeze.

As for finish quality, the flow characteristics of modern marine varnishes are such that in my hands the bristleless tip of a foam brush delivers the better finish. If you want to try a badger-hair brush, by all means do it. If it gives you superior results, that is the brush for you. But if you are new to varnishing, you will reduce both your expense and your irritation level by starting out with a foam brush.

Know your enemies. Things that will spoil your varnish are inadequate preparation, unfiltered varnish, loose bristles, dust, insects, bubbles, moisture, and unstable weather. Take appropriate preventive measures for each of these, and you reduce the perfection equation to just your skill with a brush.

Adequate preparation means the surface of the wood is ivory smooth. Decant *all* varnish through a fine-mesh filter before you use it. A foam brush takes bristles out of the mix. Wiping the wood with a spirits-dampened cloth or a tack rag right before varnishing will remove surface dust. Wash the dust from all surrounding surfaces if you can do so without wetting the wood; otherwise wipe them with a wet towel. Mist dust generators you cannot remove. Don't varnish on windy days. Never varnish at dusk, under lights, or at any other time when insects are swarming. The amount of airborne contamination finding its way into your varnish is directly related to your boat's proximity to land, so don't do your varnishing in a boatyard. In the marina is better; on a mooring, better still. Anchoring out to do your exterior varnishing can effectively eliminate both dust and insect contamination.

Varnish is sensitive to both moisture and temperature, especially in the first 2 hours after application. Do not start varnishing until after the morning dew evaporates, and plan to finish well before the moisture settles again in the evening. Temperatures between 50°F and 85°F are varnish friendly. Don't varnish when the humidity is above 80%, if rain is possible (or occurring!), or if conditions are right for fog. A sudden temperature change during the critical 2 hours will cloud the varnish, so check the weather map for approaching fronts before you start. *Red sky in the morning, varnisher take warning.* Too much

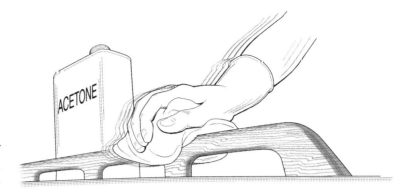

Wipe teak vigorously with an acetone-saturated rag to remove surface oils before you apply the initial coat of varnish.

sun is also undesirable. If you need shade, so does the varnish.

The high oil content that makes teak so durable in the marine environment also taxes the grip of varnish. It is essential to remove as much oil as possible from the surface of teak to be varnished. Just before varnishing, wipe bare teak vigorously with an acetone-saturated rag. This has no effect on the oil content of the wood but provides a relatively oil-free surface for your first seal coat of varnish. Omitting this step will severely shorten the life of varnish on teak.

The varnish *is* the enemy when it comes to the remainder of your boat. Almost-invisible varnish that runs onto gelcoat or painted surfaces will become ugly stains. Don't even think about applying varnish without masking adjacent surfaces. No matter how steady your hand, masking delivers a sharper border with less effort. Masking also allows you to apply the varnish more quickly, which pays dividends in the quality of the finish. Use long-life tape and you will need to mask only once.

Thin initial coats. Never apply varnish directly from the can. Filter just what you need into a clean container. If you do not pour the varnish through a filter, you risk ruining the finish with jellyfish-like blobs even fresh varnish can harbor. Decant varnish in small amounts to avoid exposing it to the air any longer than necessary before it is actually on the wood. Cat food cans make perfect varnish containers. You don't have a cat? So mix the stuff with a little celery, onion, and mayo and make sandwiches for a dock party. Who will know? Tuna cans are good too, so maybe tuna sandwiches are a better idea.

Never clean the rim of the open varnish can with your brush. That potentially defeats filtering the varnish and invests the brush with bubbles. Clean the rim with a rag or paper towel and reseal the can immediately.

Varnish achieves a mirrorlike finish by filling the grain of the wood, which requires the varnish to be relatively viscous. Viscous is how it is delivered in the can, but we want the early coats of varnish to penetrate. Otherwise it bridges the pores of the wood, trapping air and finish-lifting moisture under the coating. On raw wood, thin the first coat of varnish 50% by volume. That is $1/2$ ounce of thinner to every ounce of varnish. This is where we talk about bubbles, which are generated when you disturb the varnish. This is why the can should never be shaken or even handled roughly. The label on oil-based varnishes will even say "Do Not Stir," but stir you must to mix the thinner into the varnish. However, if you stir with slow deliberation—not faster than one revolution every 4 seconds—you will avoid creating bubbles. Stir long enough to fully introduce the thinner. You can thin spar varnish with mineral spirits or turpentine, but use the specified thinner for polyurethane varnish.

Thinning the first coat 50% allows the varnish to fully penetrate the wood, effectively converting it into a sealer. Applying a sealer other than thinned varnish as a base coat is not a good idea since these products often give the varnish an off color. Professionals sometimes use fast-drying varnish for buildup coats, which may speed the job but does not improve the quality of the finish. You should use the same varnish for all coats. The one notable exception to this applies when you are after a satin finish. In that case, use gloss varnish, not satin, for all the buildup coats. Switch to rubbed-effect varnish only for the last coat or two. This method will yield a noticeably deeper satin finish.

Brushing technique for early coats is much the same as I described earlier, except that you always want to use the fewest strokes possible when applying varnish. Also, when loading the brush—still dipping not more than a third of the bristles or head—you need to give the brush a moment to become saturated or it will lay on bubbles rather than varnish. Unload one side of the brush by drawing it slowly and nearly horizontally across the rim of your container, then lay on this first coat quickly and without fuss. The wood will change color, but most of the varnish will be absorbed.

As soon as the initial coat is dry to the touch, decant enough fresh varnish for a second coat. Thin this application about 25% by volume ($1/4$ ounce thinner to 1 ounce varnish) and apply it with the same speed as the first. Let this coat dry overnight.

On the second day, apply the third coat, thinned 10% by volume. As long as you are within the recoat time specified on the can, you can safely apply this coat without sanding. Otherwise scuff the previous application with 180-grit sandpaper.

Wait 48 hours. It is possible to add additional coats without sanding, but when you take that expedient, each successive coat accentuates the flaws of the previous coat and adds its own. Sand between coats and the top surface gets progressively smoother. Fail to sand and it gets progressively rougher. If you want a five-star finish, sand between coats.

Varnish labels typically say the finish can be sanded after 24 hours. *Don't you believe it.* After 24 hours, everywhere your coating was a bit too thick, your sandpaper is going to roll off gummy varnish. Wait at least two days between coats, longer if it suits your schedule. You will be rewarded with a dry surface that sands easily without clogging the paper. Before you sand, wipe the varnish surface with a thinner-soaked rag to remove any pollutants that may have settled on it. After sanding, wipe the surface thoroughly with a damp cloth or a tack rag. You can make an excellent tack cloth for varnish work by wringing out a clean cotton cloth soaked in warm water and sprinkling it with turpentine, followed by a spoonful of your varnish. Wring the cloth again to distribute the varnish and store it in a plastic zipper bag between uses. Toss it when the job is finished.

On day five (or later), you are going to wipe, sand, wipe, and apply the fourth coat. This is the first one you apply full strength, and it is the last so-called buildup coat. You should consider all coats after the fourth as finish coats and take greater care in their application.

Brushing technique. Applying finish coats of varnish should be more like writing than painting. Worrying the varnish with a lot of brushstrokes just introduces bubbles. Handle your brush like an old-fashioned ink pen. When you apply the nib to the paper, if you move it too slowly, the ink stains the paper in ugly blobs. Move it too fast and the line thins and skips. With just the right speed and pressure, the pen lays down a crisp, perfect line. Similarly, a varnish brush correctly drawn lays down a flawless, glassy finish.

For the fifth and subsequent coats, dip the tip of the brush in fresh, unthinned varnish and unload one side. Artisans unload the brush on a piece of stiff (coat hanger) wire inserted through holes punched in opposite sides of the container rim with the wire ends bent to hold it in place. Unloading the brush on this straight wire fosters fewer bubbles than the curved rim and does a better job of keeping all the varnish inside the can. Apply the varnish with a single,

Unload one side of the brush.

Apply loaded side like a pen stroke.

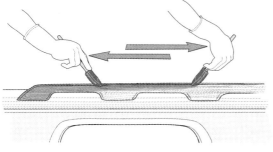

Brush out frugally.

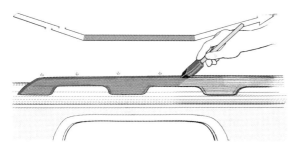

Tip to finish with a light forward stroke "landed" behind previous wet edge and drawn out just beyond the new one.

Applying varnish.

deliberate stroke of the loaded side of the brush. Distribute the varnish with just another stroke or two, touching the surface lightly and drawing the brush slowly. Finish by tipping the fresh varnish with a single long stroke or parallel strokes in the same direction if the coated area is wider than your brush. Begin this final stroke just inside the old "wet edge," which is where the previous brush load of varnish ended, and draw evenly beyond the new wet edge where the

varnish you just applied ends. If you brush *back,* the technique usually recommended, you push excess varnish back into the previous application, causing a ridge or a wave in the finish. Landing the brush in motion, as described earlier, and stroking out of the previous application moves excess varnish forward. Once the varnish has been tipped, leave it alone. You will sand out any flaws.

Six coats are the minimum required to achieve full protection of the wood. Eight or nine coats may be needed to get the foot-deep look. Your skill and your speed will improve with each coat. If you are not as pleased with your "final" coat as you had hoped, stop anyway. One good thing about exterior brightwork is that you never have to look at your mistakes for longer than a few months. No, wait. That's *not* a good thing, but you get my point. If it is an interior surface you are unhappy with, go ahead and correct it now. Interior varnish should last decades before recoating, too long to look at a curtain on the main bulkhead.

Brush care. You preserve a foam brush between coats in a capful of spirits, but you must never leave a good bristle brush soaking in thinner. The thinner removes the natural oils from the bristles, and before long your expensive brush will be no better at laying on varnish than a 50-cent throwaway. Between coats you can safely leave your brush soaking in kerosene, but do not leave it standing on the bristles or the delicate chisel tip will become deformed. Sandwiching the handle with a pair of pencils or dowels held in place with a rubber band creates a simple stop that will allow you to suspend the brush with the ferrule just below the surface of the kerosene. Rinse the brush twice in mineral spirits before you use it. When the job is finished, rinse the brush at least three times in thinner (clean thinner each time, not three times in the same thinner), spreading the bristles gently to make sure all the varnish has been removed. Comb the brush into shape, then dip it into a container of clean motor oil (30W seems to be the favorite) and let it soak for a few minutes. Wrap the bristles in stiff paper and hang the brush or store it flat for future varnish work only. If you ever use it for paint, you will spoil it forever for varnish use. A brush treated this way will last until you wear away the bristles with a few million strokes. Rinse it twice in thinner before you use it again.

Protect the film. About my own varnish, I'm fond of saying, "It's not a Steinway." It is a boat, and in my case at least, that means a machine that sees a lot of use, some not so gentle. Not surprisingly the varnish is sometimes the recipient of abuse. Damaged

Maintain a foam brush between coats in foil pouch containing a capful or so of thinner.

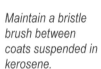

Maintain a bristle brush between coats suspended in kerosene.

Oil the bristles of a clean bristle brush and wrap it in stiff paper to store.

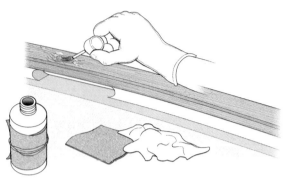

First-aid kit.

varnish is easy to repair—just sand the damage and coat it with fresh varnish. What prevents that from happening when it needs to is the hassle of getting out all the needed materials—sandpaper, varnish, a brush. If you want to add years to the life of your varnish, before you put the varnish can away, empty and rinse (with thinner) a nail polish or paste bottle—the kind with a brush in the lid—and funnel it full of

varnish. Rubber-band a few squares of 220-grit paper around the bottle. This gives you a complete first-aid kit for immediate nick and scratch repair. Put it where it will be handy and use it. If you are vigilant in touching up and follow a schedule of regular recoating, exterior varnish can look as beautiful a decade later as the day the first application was completed. If you neglect the finish, you will be repeating this whole process next year or opting for the weathered teak look.

THE CLEAR POLYURETHANE ALTERNATIVE

The failure of varnish, invariably from neglect, has led some boatowners to seek a system of coating wood that doesn't demand regular maintenance. Properly applied, clear LPU will withstand neglect for a number of years.

A characteristic of varnish that is both an advantage and a disadvantage is that it is semipermeable. While the varnish may not seal out moisture as well as other coatings, it allows the wood to "breathe." Polyurethane, on the other hand, seals the wood. Seal a cruising guide inside a plastic zipper bag and lay it out in the cockpit on a sunny day; moisture will condense on the inside of the plastic. A similar thing happens when you seal moisture-containing wood with clear plastic. In this case, the moisture tends to cause the polyurethane to lose its grip on the wood, a problem that is exacerbated by the natural oils in the wood. Clear two-part polyurethane finishes should *never* be applied directly to bare wood.

Penetrating Epoxy

There are, however, ways to use clear LPU on brightwork with a better likelihood of success. The most common is to "prime" the wood with two to four seal coats of penetrating epoxy. Epoxy is a much better glue than the polyurethane and will be less affected by moisture, but on teak in particular, the oils in the wood will interfere with adhesion. You must remove all surface oils from teak before applying the epoxy or it will lose its grip far sooner than desired. Surface oils can be removed by wiping the wood vigorously with acetone, but bleaching the wood with oxalic acid is more effective. Two applications of neutralizer and final sanding are required before coating with the epoxy. The oil inside the wood begins migrating to the surface immediately, so be prepared to coat the deoiled wood with epoxy as soon as it is completely dry.

Unless you can heat the wood to around 120°F, regular solvent-free epoxy will sit on top of the wood rather than penetrating, limiting its effectiveness as a primer. You can thin regular epoxy resin for priming with a solvent—acetone, toluene, or xylene will all work—but thinning weakens epoxy in about the same proportion as the thinner. Still, a 2:1 mix of solvent and epoxy—66% solvent and 33% mixed epoxy—will create a water-thin penetrating epoxy not much different in strength or handling characteristics from prepackaged penetrating epoxies. You need the watery consistency of a penetrating epoxy to percolate into the surface structure of the wood to seal it and form a complex bond. If you reverse the ratio for the second coat and eliminate the solvent altogether for the third, you should end up with a strong and deeply infiltrated base for the LPU. The alternative with regular epoxy is to warm the epoxy and heat the wood with a heat gun just prior to coating it. This method will thin the viscosity of the epoxy and significantly improve penetration, but it is labor-intensive. Removable brightwork can be primed with epoxy in a superheated workshop to good effect.

All epoxies are sensitive to the mixing ratio. If you do not combine the two parts in the correct proportions, the epoxy will fail to harden and become a mess. Also, subsequent coats will not bond chemically, and the mechanical bond will be weak if you allow the epoxy to reach or even approach full cure before overcoating. Scrubbing and sanding cured epoxy will confer a better mechanical bond, but considering what you are after here and the consequences of failure, you want the strength of a chemical bond between coats. That makes it essential to limit the epoxy application to only as much wood as can be coated within the recoat time so that subsequent coats may be applied without sanding. This is less of a problem with penetrating epoxies—commercial or home-brewed—because the solvent retards the cure time, but it will be an issue if you are heating the wood, which will accelerate curing.

Some epoxy coatings are especially sensitive to humidity, turning cloudy, which is a disaster in this application. Select an epoxy that is tolerant of moisture if you're working in a humid climate. Epoxies generally will not cure fully in cold temperatures. Warmth is also beneficial for penetration. Epoxy tends to change the color and sometimes the clarity of the wood, so it is a good idea to do a test panel before you coat all of your wood with something that turns it orange. There are penetrating epoxies formulated specifically for priming teak for a gloss topcoat of either LPU or varnish, specifically Clear Penetrating Epoxy Sealer (CPES) marketed by Smith & Company. This formulation has been around for nearly four decades and has a loyal following.

Use a foam brush to lay on the epoxy just as you did prime coats of varnish. Tip out any bubbles that you see. You should use a respirator when applying any solvent-rich coating. CPES, in particular, contains a cocktail of powerful solvents that you should avoid breathing. After three coats, allow the epoxy to cure for at least a day. Wash the cured surface with a scrub pad (Scotch-Brite), then sand it ivory smooth with 180-grit production paper, but do not cut through the epoxy.

Top Coat

The chemicals and solvents in two-part polyurethanes are highly toxic and must be handled with great care. In the section on refinishing the hull that follows, I will describe the health risks and the process of working with polyurethane paint in greater detail, but the general procedure for applying a clear polyurethane coating over epoxy-sealed wood is first to wipe the prepared surface with the solvent recommended by the manufacturer of the polyurethane you are using. Be sure you have adequate ventilation and protect your skin from the solvent. Here again, a respirator is a prudent precaution. Mix the LPU according to the manufacturer's instructions. Lay it on with a foam brush, tipping the surface with the same brush. Roll and tip large areas using a foam roller and a "dry" foam or badger-hair brush. Tip the surface immediately and only once, stroking from behind the previous wet edge to beyond the new one. Not all brands of foam brushes will stand up to the solvents here, so test a brush before you use it and before you buy a supply. If you cannot find durable foam brushes, substitute a badger-hair brush. Because the LPU cures quickly, you will need to periodically give your tipping brush a cursory cleaning. After coating is completed, you should throw away a foam brush, but you will need to clean a badger-hair brush immediately and thoroughly in solvent.

Allow the first coat of polyurethane to dry overnight, then wet sand the entire surface with 320-grit wet-or-dry sandpaper. Wet sanding is exactly what it sounds like. The simplest way is to keep a trickle of water from a hose on the surface as you sand, but you can also simply dip the paper in a bucket of water often enough to keep both the paper and the surface wet. You can use a rubber block or just the pressure of your fingers.

Wet sanding polyurethane produces a scum that must be removed. When all the surfaces have been sanded, wash them thoroughly with fresh water and a clean cloth or sponge. You can hasten drying by toweling the surfaces, but be sure all joints and cracks are moisture free before proceeding. Wipe the surfaces with the recommended solvent and apply the second and final coat of polyurethane with a foam roller or brush, tipping it out to a perfect finish.

Polyurethane over an epoxy base *can* last 5 years or longer, but epoxy is extremely UV sensitive, so if the clear LPU lacks UV inhibitors to shield the epoxy, the life of this multicomponent system will be much shorter. Epoxy also tends to darken with age.

Different Strokes

Other combinations are possible. The most common is to apply varnish rather than LPU over the epoxy undercoat. The advantage is that marine varnishes tend to be loaded with UV inhibitors that provide greater protection to the sun-sensitive epoxy undercoat. Application of the varnish is also less exacting, and reapplication is easier. Because the base is plastic—epoxy—rather than wood, a polyurethane formulated for exterior use can perform well in this application.

Another possibility is to apply LPU over a base coat of seasoned varnish. The advantage of this method is that the varnish undercoat has its own UV inhibitors that protect the wood and stabilize the color of the finish, while the clear polyurethane provides a long-lasting and abrasion-resistant top coating. Apply six coats of spar varnish as outlined earlier, and allow the varnish to age for at least 3 months. The aggressive solvents in the LPU will attack young varnish. (Be aware that different chemical compositions open the possibility that the LPU could also attack aged varnish.) Prepare the varnish by sanding with 180-grit paper and wiping with solvent. Apply two coats of polyurethane as detailed previously.

Whether you apply LPU over epoxy, polyurethane varnish over epoxy, or LPU over spar varnish, eventually the coating will fail. When that happens, you are in for a very difficult job to get back to bare wood. For this reason, varnish alone is still the brightwork finish of choice for most boatowners.

REFINISHING THE EXTERIOR

While clear LPU has not displaced varnish, two-component aliphatic polyurethane paint is today the only sensible choice for restoring the gloss to an old fiberglass hull. Remember the old Pearson I mentioned? On the day I saw her owner sanding the hull, in my ignorance of the finish he was about to apply, I motored out the channel feeling sorry for him. I *knew* that once you gave up on the gelcoat and painted a boat, even if you used the very best topside enamel available, you were doomed to repaint it every other year. Linear polyurethane changed all that.

Two coats of properly applied two-part polyurethane should still have most of its gloss after 5 years and may last twice that long. And as with varnish, if the first application has been done with care, when the time finally does arrive to repaint, it is basically a matter of sanding the surface and laying on a fresh coat.

Perhaps you have heard that polyurethane is expensive, dangerous, and finicky. All true, but don't be put off. Take the expense, for example. Polyurethane costs two to three times the price of the most expensive enamels and requires special primers and pricey solvents. But cost is relative. LPU will also last two to three times longer, making it cheaper when you factor in labor. A dazzling shine on the hull adds at least 10% to the value of virtually any boat, so the superior shine of LPU represents a sound investment. Even viewed strictly as a cash outlay, the $300 to $500 you will spend on all the necessary materials, paint included, to refinish a 30-something-foot hull is hardly significant compared to what you likely paid for the boat. For dramatic transformation, no other similarly modest expenditure even comes close.

The reputation for danger is not exaggerated. The reactor in LPU paints contains an isocyanate similar to the one that caused the deaths of more than 16,000 in the 1984 Union Carbide gas-release accident in Bhopal, India. Atomizing any paint hugely elevates the inhalation risk, and when you add a cyanide derivative to the mix, you are courting catastrophe. The solution is simple: *never* spray polyurethane. (Professional refinishers who do spray polyurethane wear protective suits and use positive-pressure respirators.) No paint application is really to die for. Putting LPU on your hull with a roller is hardly more dangerous than applying house paint. Do protect your eyes and your hands from the strong solvent.

What about finickiness? Most of the condition requirements for LPU are the same as for other paints or varnish—temperature between 50°F and 85°F, no direct sunlight, not much wind. What LPU is much less tolerant of is moisture. The chemical reaction is accelerated by atmospheric humidity. That's bad. This paint solidifies in minutes, but if it happens too soon, the surface will not level out. Brushstrokes are the result. The rule is if you sweat while preparing the surface, it is too humid to paint. That can make painting a seasonal proposition in some places. When mild, dry days are possible, you must wait out uncooperative weather no matter how ready or anxious you are or how many extra yard days are added. You can do most of the preparation in any weather, but if you try to apply this paint with the roll-and-tip method when the humidity is much above 50%, I can guarantee that you will get a less than stellar finish.

That begs the question, is it really possible to get a great-looking finish from paint applied by the roll-and-tip method? Here is a true story. In the aftermath of Hurricane Andrew, I found myself in a Florida boatyard repairing some abrasions to the hull of our tough old Seawind, which necessitated repainting the hull. There was a lot of other repainting going on around me, most of it funded by insurance payments. The pros were spraying. I rolled and tipped. Three times before I splashed, other boatowners dragged the yard manager over to our boat to ask why their hull didn't look as good as ours. What they were seeing was not superior skill but higher gloss. Spraying polyurethane requires a more aggressive solvent that flashes off quickly, taking gloss with it. The slower solvent for roller application doesn't have this effect. These other boaters saw only the gloss. None suspected that the paint had been applied by a roller. Commit yourself to waiting until you have two mild, dry days to apply LPU, and I will defy you to tell the difference between a sprayed coating and one applied skillfully with a roller and tipped with a brush.

The question of *who* does the job may be academic anyway. Having your hull professionally refinished starts at around $100 per foot and goes up from there. Deck refinishing is about twice as expensive. Not every old-boat owner can afford those prices. And even if you can afford it, you may find yourself less than enthusiastic about paying $10,000 for a job that you can do yourself for a few hundred dollars.

IF PETER PIPER PICKED A PACK OF POLYURETHANE PAINT . . .

The first step is to select the brand of paint you are going to use. Optimum results are only certain if you follow the instructions of the specific manufacturers, including using the proprietary preparatory products (say that fast three times!) they recommend. Differences in chemical composition may make one manufacturer's primer less compatible with a different manufacturer's finish coat. There is really no way of knowing if a different brand is compatible, so play it safe and buy fillers, primers, paint, and reducer (thinner) from the same maker.

I don't presume to tell you what color to paint your boat, but there are some consequences of that choice that merit your attention. The first is that the temperature of a white hull under the assault of a tropical or semitropical sun might reach 110°F, while the same hull painted navy blue will approach 180°F. This inevitably reduces below-deck comfort by elevating the cabin temperature, and it is a double whammy for refrigeration, increasing both the air temperature for the condenser and the temperature differential for the box (see Chapter 13). Higher power consumption is assured. The paint itself suffers from the greater expansion and contraction resulting from the much higher daytime temperature, shortening paint life by not less than 25%. Believe it or not, your hull can also be punished by the greater expansion on the sunny side compared to the shady side. There is also a safety issue if you boat at night, with a white hull being much more visible than a dark one. Finally, of immediate pertinence to the subject at hand, dark colors, because of their greater pigment content, do not flow out as well as light colors. This makes it more difficult to achieve a stroke-free finish when painting with a dark-colored paint.

PREPARATION

You should start every paint project by washing the surface, and this one is no exception. Mix or employ your favorite surface cleaner. As described earlier, mine is 1 cup of liquid laundry detergent, 1 cup of chlorine bleach, and 3 heaping spoonfuls of TSP in a gallon of water. Sponge the entire hull and rinse thoroughly.

You must, I repeat, *must* dewax the surface. Why would the hull have wax on it? The obvious reason is that you or some previous owner waxed it. Less obvious is that the mold was waxed and that wax transferred to the hull during the original layup. Virtually all bare fiberglass hulls retain traces of the mold-release wax. Acetone will remove mold wax, but the slower evaporating methyl ethyl ketone (MEK) is better. Wiping the hull with MEK is a good idea anyway to remove oils and grease the detergent failed to lift, but MEK (as well as acetone and detergent) will not clean the surface of silicone. Silicone is especially tenacious, which is why it has long been a popular wax additive. Even the tiniest traces of silicone on the hull will ruin your paint job, so you must dewax the surface with a solvent that will remove silicone. You

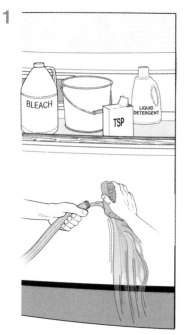

Wash.

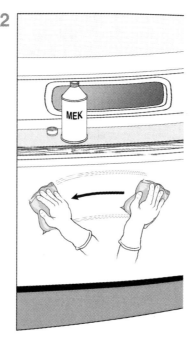

Degrease.

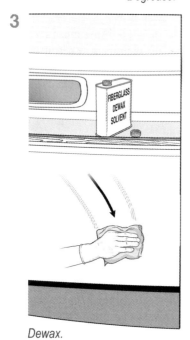

Dewax.

Preparing fiberglass for painting.

as all sides have been used. Always dewax the hull before you sand it. Otherwise the sandpaper drags the wax into the scratches, making it that much more difficult to remove.

Previously Painted

Painted surfaces require a couple of additional steps after cleaning to determine their suitability as a base for the fresh paint. The adhesion of the old paint can be the weak link, so you want to make sure it is well adhered. Crosshatch the old paint with a razor

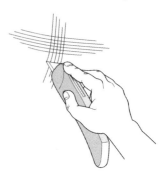

Crosshatch the paint with a razor knife in an inconspicuous spot.

Burnish cellophane tape over the crosshatching.

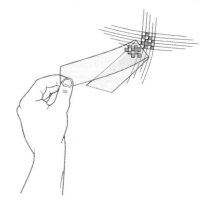

Rip the tape away with a jerk.

Testing adhesion.

need either the dewax solvent specified by the LPU manufacturer or its cheaper sister, xylene.

Do not dewax with a scrubbing motion. Slowly sweep the folded, solvent-saturated rag in one direction, typically in an arc starting at the rail and ending at the waterline. Boxed wipes are especially good for dewaxing. Fold the wipe to a clean side every two or three passes, and change to a fresh wipe as soon

blade in an inconspicuous spot, making half a dozen 1-inch-long cuts about ¹/₈ inch apart in both directions. Place cellophane tape over the crosshatching and burnish the tape down. Now rip it off with a jerk. If the paint comes away with the tape, the adhesion has failed and the old paint has to come off.

The second step is a test for compatibility. Saturate a small rag with the thinner specified for your LPU and tape this rag against the old paint—again, in an inconspicuous location. Wait 10 minutes, then remove the rag and examine the paint. If the solvent has softened or lifted the old paint, the same thing will happen when you paint the surface with LPU. The old paint will need to be removed or separated from the LPU with a conversion coating. Allow the conversion coat at least three days to cure before proceeding.

Chemical vinyl and decal removers are available to remove lettering and graphics; 3M makes one. Vinyl graphics will also yield to a hair dryer or a heat gun, but you must be careful to not overheat the fiberglass. If it is too hot to touch, it is too hot. Remove a painted-on name with a gelcoat-friendly chemical stripper. Be sure you chemically remove adhesive residue and wash away all cleaner and/or stripper residue before you start any sanding.

Perfect the Surface

With apologies to Thomas Edison, brilliance is 1% application and 99% preparation. This paint in particular is not like the enamels you are (now) familiar with. LPU goes on skim milk–thin and will not hide any flaws—none. To make matters worse, the extreme gloss of the finish will actually highlight imperfections. If you want a flawless finish, you have to be painting a flawless surface.

If your boat has an indented cove stripe and you intend to paint it, now is the time to sand it. Tear a quarter sheet of 120-grit sandpaper into thirds, then fold these small pieces twice to give you a "fingertip" sanding pad. Wear cloth gloves to protect your fingers and hand sand the stripe.

When you are finished with the cove stripe and any other areas requiring hand sanding, load your palm or random orbit sander with 120-grit paper and sand the hull stem to stern, waterline to deck. Not long ago, when I stopped to talk with a couple refinishing their hull, I was astonished that they *both* had finishing sanders. The best ideas always seem to be so obvious! If you will be sanding away the existing bootstripe, use a flexible straightedge and a scratch awl to score its location into the gelcoat before you start. *Do not* run your sander over any edges, such as

Use a palm or a random orbit sander loaded with 120-grit paper to prepare gelcoat for painting. Wear earplugs!

solvent-saturated cloth

Testing compatibility.

where the quarter meets the transom. If you do, the sander will cut right through the gelcoat.

If I have not mentioned this before, buy yourself a box of foam earplugs at your nearby pharmacy and use them religiously when operating an orbital sander. They will save you from hearing damage caused by the scream of the sander, *and* they transform the sanding process from teeth-gritting to serene. The difference made by reducing the sensory assault is astonishing. You might want to just leave them in all the time.

It is essential to remove all the gloss (probably not an issue or why are you painting the hull?) and give the surface a uniform anchor pattern for the paint. While you are sanding, you should be "looking" for flaws with both your eyes and your fingertips. Anything you can feel will show in the finish coat. Flush the surface to wash away dust and grit.

Remember how we checked for cracks in tangs and terminals with a penetrating dye (see Chapter 8)? You can flag imperfections in the fiberglass surface the same way. Automotive paint suppliers carry a water-thin dye just for this purpose. It is called guide coat and a common brand is Steel Blue Dye. Wipe it on, let it dry, sand it off. Nicks and scratches you might have otherwise missed will still be blue.

You are going to need to fill all gouges and dings. I typically use epoxy thickened with a low-density filler (West System 407), but you can use prepackaged putty if you prefer. Do not use a polyurethane product here. You want the better adhesion and stability of an epoxy putty such as Marine-Tex. Work your way methodically around the hull, filling every flaw. Epoxy doesn't shrink as it cures, so don't give the repair a bulge. If you do, when you sand it flush, the difference in the hardness of the filler and the gelcoat can result in uneven

sanding and a visible "moat" around the patch. Use a flexible plastic spreader to make the patch as flush as possible (refer to Chapter 6).

When the filler has cured fully, scrub epoxy repairs with water and a scrubber pad, then sand them smooth with the palm sander loaded with 120-grit paper. You should not be able to detect the repair by feel. Expect some of your repairs to require a second application of filler. Minor voids can be taken care of with glazing putty. When you think the hull surface is perfect, do a "sheeting test" by simply spraying the hull with water and observing. If the water flows off in an unbroken sheet and the reflection is undistorted, let the hull dry completely. Mask the waterline, the cove stripe, and other adjacent areas at risk from your flying roller, and your hull is ready to paint.

PRIMER

A hull in need of paint should almost always be primed. In theory you can apply LPU directly to perfect gelcoat, but gelcoat becomes porous with age. Check for porosity by brushing a thin coat of regular enamel—bootstripe paint is perfect—onto a test area. Examine it closely. If it shows even a single pinhole, the gelcoat is porous and must be primed. The test patch might also develop "fish eyes"—you will know one when you see it. These are caused by wax residue remaining on the hull. *Shame on you.* You need to dewax the entire hull again, using plenty of solvent and lots of clean rags this time.

Use the primer specified by the paint manufacturer, which will invariably be a high-build epoxy primer. A good epoxy primer will also permanently repair surface crazing—a random pattern of superficial cracks in the gelcoat resembling a cracked eggshell—provided the cause is not flexibility of

A dye guide coat will make subtle surface flaws obvious.

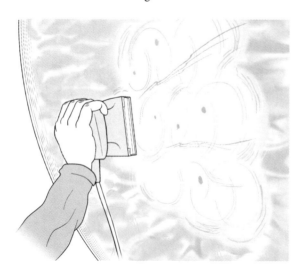

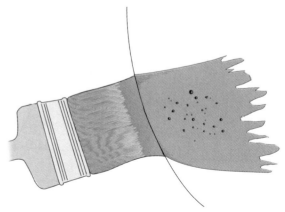

Test for porosity with thin enamel. The cure is primer.

the underlying laminate (see Chapter 6). Apply the primer with a foam roller. Tipping may not be called for, but in my experience it will reduce the amount of sanding required to prepare the primer for painting. If the primer mix does not flow out smoothly, add thinner, a small amount at a time, until it does.

One coat of primer is usually sufficient to cure porosity, but a second coat will be needed to completely hide crazing. You will also need a second prime coat if you are painting a light color over a dark one. Between prime coats is the time to use glazing putty to fill small blemishes the primer failed to cover. Allow the initial primer coat to cure fully, then sand it with 120-grit paper and apply a second coat. If two primer coats are not required, at least reprime over any glazing that you do and resand these spots.

You will need to remove any masking before you sand the primer or you will end up with ridges at the tape lines, but you can get away with peeling the tape only for the sanding of the final prime coat. Remove tape by peeling it back onto itself, not by pulling it straight out. Making your pull slightly away from the paint application so that the stuck and peeled tape form a flat, narrow V minimizes the risk of lifting the edge of the primer—or any fresh paint.

Remember that the LPU is not going to hide anything—nada—so invest time in sanding the primer until it is baby-butt smooth. Scrub and rinse away all scum or dust. Remask the waterline and other adjacent surfaces. You need 3M Fine Line tape to prevent thin LPU from wicking under it, and you need to burnish down the edge with the bowl of a plastic spoon. Just prior to painting, quickly wipe the surface you plan to coat with a clean rag dampened with the reducer for the LPU. This is a safer method of picking up dust than using a sticky tack rag.

PRACTICE

There is nothing particularly difficult about applying LPU, but your chances of getting a perfect result improve greatly with just a little practice. Paint your hard dinghy first if you have one. Otherwise start this project by painting just the transom. This will allow you to get a feel for how the paint goes on and to develop an application technique that is comfortable and gives a good result. If things go badly, a few minutes of sanding the next day gets you back to zero.

Coverage is typically not less than 4 square feet per ounce, so pour up a couple more ounces of paint than you calculate you need for your learning surface. Follow the manufacturer's instructions for mixing and thinning, using cups or spoons for accurate measurement. If you have waited for a dry, mild day, the only thing standing between you and a perfect finish is the perfect amount of thinner. Unfortunately the manufacturer's instructions will be inexact because the ratio varies with temperature, humidity, and wind. Relax. The trick is to sneak up on the perfect mix. For this you need a smooth test surface. A propped-up piece of clean window glass is perfect because any flaws that appear will be in the paint. Plastic-surfaced hardboard will also serve.

Add a little less thinner than the manufacturer recommends to your cup of mixed paint and stir it in completely. Use a "good" chip brush to paint a small test patch on the glass. If the paint runs or sags, you already have too much thinner, but you are more likely to have too little at this point, exhibited by lingering

Test your paint mix on a smooth surface, adding thinner a little at a time until brushstrokes just disappear.

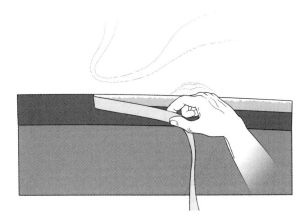

Peel tape back, not away.

brush marks in the paint. If these fail to disappear entirely in a couple of minutes, add a little thinner and try again. Don't get impatient and overshoot. Add the thinner in small amounts and keep testing until the stroke marks just disappear. If the gloss begins to disappear instead, you have added too much thinner and it is either too humid or too hot to paint.

When the test patch is smooth and glossy, pour this mixture into your paint tray and use your foam roller for one final test application on the glass, tipping it with your badger-hair brush. Give it several minutes. The paint should level out as smooth as the glass beneath it. If it does, you should be able to get the same result on the dinghy or the transom. You might also try a test patch without tipping. White LPU applied with only a foam roller can deliver a finish equivalent to a just-less-than-perfect spray application. If you like the look, it makes the job easier.

Use your test brush to cut in any part of your practice surface that your roller will not reach—under a turned-out hull-to-deck joint, for example—then roll on one load of paint, always from rail to waterline to have a single wet edge. Drag your tipping brush horizontally across each new roller application, landing it just behind the old wet edge and lifting it just beyond the new one. When you tip the paint horizontally, gravity is your friend, drawing the highs into the lows, but some excellent painters believe they get a better result tipping vertically, pushing excess paint onto the masking. If you have the mix correct, there is no excess paint, and for me, vertical tipping always leaves a mark at the top where the brushstroke starts. Also, vertical stroke marks that fail to flow out will be more visible because reflected light from the water tends to mask horizontal stroke marks. If you want to

Roll and tip to a flawless finish.

try vertical tipping for yourself, however, now is the time. Whatever your pattern, work as fast as you can, with no delay between rolling and tipping, and never go back. You will sand out flaws.

If you end up with curtains (sags) or obvious brush marks, run a second practice session, adding more or less thinner, depending on the result. You may have to wait a day to do this so you can sand your learning surface. If you are stunned at the finish you just applied, you are ready to paint the hull.

Use a razor blade scraper to clean off your glass test panel. Calculate how much paint you will need to paint one side of the hull and give yourself a little extra; running short is an intolerable error. As a rule you will not continue right around to the other side of the boat because you do not want to paint in direct sunlight. Sunlight hastens the set time, preventing the paint from achieving maximum leveling. This typically means painting one side in the morning, the other in the afternoon.

I should repeat here my earlier caution about foam roller covers. Be absolutely sure the ones you are using are not going to come off the core or start flocking the hull halfway through your application. This is also *the* job you bought your expensive badger brush for, so be sure you clean it thoroughly after every use to keep it eyelash soft for the next area/coat. You will also get better results if you clean the brush after every five or six roller loads of paint. An open cup of thinner and a lint-free cloth tacked to a board make this easier. Simply dip the tip of the brush in the thinner, unload it on the rim, and quickly paint out what remains onto a clean section of the stretched cloth.

Back to the decanted paint. Mix in the reactor, then thin and test this batch on the glass until it flows out exactly as your initial batch did. Load your roller handle with a fresh foam cover and pour the paint into a paint tray. Test your paint one more time on the glass, rolling it on and tipping it with your clean brush. While you give it time to reach its terminal leveling, wet down the ground around your boat to hold down the dust.

PAYOFF

As with the transom, you should start by cutting in any part of the hull your roller will not reach. Even if you used a chip brush to test the paint, use a small foam brush for cutting in. Brush the paint out to a thin film with several quick strokes to make sure it doesn't run, or leave a proud edge that will show when you roll on the main application. Cut in only the periphery ahead of time, not around skin fittings or other topside features.

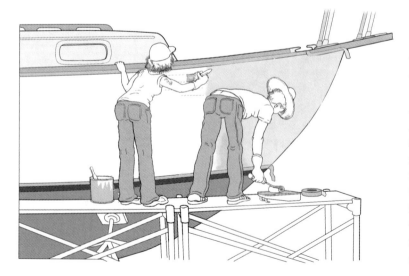

Rolling and tipping a big expanse like the side of the hull is ideally a two-person process. Beginning at one end of the hull, one person rolls on a uniform, thin coat of paint from the waterline to the deck. The width of the hull section coated—typically 18 to 24 inches—is not critical and is determined by how much surface a roller load of paint covers. A thin coat is essential, so unload excess paint on the ramp of the paint tray before putting the roller to the hull. The person rolling should work quickly but not hastily. Do not spin the roller so fast that it stipples and sprays the paint. Strokes should be deliberate, and you should use no more of them than necessary to spread the roller load uniformly.

While the "roller" reloads (and unloads) his or her roller with paint, the "tipper" makes quick but deliberate horizontal, parallel strokes through the paint, gently landing the brush in the previously tipped paint just behind the fresh roller application and drawing the brush evenly beyond the wet paint onto the dry hull. The tipper must work rapidly, without fuss and with the lightest of touches. The roller immediately coats the next section of hull, overlapping the tipped area by an inch or two.

Continue this process—roll, tip/load, roll, tip/load—without pause or hesitation until you reach the other end of the hull. While the next roller application is going on, the tipper should examine the just-tipped section for sags or holidays that an extra stroke or two can correct. Once you start tipping a new section, you must never go back to a previous section to "repair" a flaw. You will only make it worse. All flaws are corrected with the following coat. The tipper should also clean the brush every six to eight roller loads as detailed earlier. Trim around skin fittings or other obstacles as the roller reaches them, using the small foam brush, never the tipping brush.

Painting with two-part polyurethane is a sprint. With two people painting, the job should take *less than a minute per linear foot*. If it is taking you longer than that, your pace is too slow.

"Gang" painting is easier and reduces the opportunity for disaster, but on boats up to around 30 feet in length, you will be able to get equally good results doing both rolling and tipping yourself. You must not pause, even for a minute, so forethought is required to have plenty of paint in the tray and both thinner and rags at hand for quickly cleaning the brush. I find I tend to lose momentum when painting solo, so I have learned to keep urging myself on to keep up the pace. "Go faster" is my mantra. You cannot go too fast, only too slow.

DO IT AGAIN

LPU will not deliver its maximum gloss without at least two coats. The second coat is going to bond chemically with the first if you get it on within 48 hours, but you still need to wet sand between coats with 320-grit wet-or-dry paper. Since you are not trying to give the surface tooth, you do not want to sand any more than is necessary to remove flaws in the first coat and to perfect the base for the second coat. It can be very difficult to see where your sandpaper has been when you sand lightly with such a fine grit. The high gloss also tends to make your eyes lose focus. The solution is to mist the paint with contrasting spray lacquer—black on white, white on

A light mist of contrasting lacquer will let you see where you have sanded.

Wet sand with 320-grit paper.

Wash away all sanding scum.

Sand between coats of LPU.

Like magic.

black or blue. Spray lacquer—do not use enamel—dries immediately and sands away easily, indicating clearly where you have sanded and giving your eyes a feature to focus on.

Sanding polyurethane produces a tenacious scum that you must wash off with the aid of a hose and a sponge. When the hull is completely dry and just before you are ready to apply the top coat, wipe the surface one final time with the thinner for the LPU.

You have the significant advantage of experience when you apply the second coat. With the first coat results and the now-dry test panels from the previous day as a guide, thin your paint and test it carefully on a fresh test surface. When it is *exactly* right, lay it onto the hull in as close to one continuous flow as you can manage. When you finish, look at your reflection in the hull with that stupid grin on your face. Try not to be too smug. Anybody can paint the flat expanse of a hull. When you can put the same flawless finish on the multifaceted surface of a deck, then you are entitled to brag.

RESTORING THE DECK

Painting the hull is easy. Painting the deck is hard. Decks present a variety of faces, not a smooth expanse. They are interrupted at every turn with openings and hardware. And they are a mosaic of two types of surfaces that require at least differing painting techniques, usually different paints, and sometimes different mediums entirely.

A common compromise is to paint the deck with a single-part polyurethane or silicone topside enamel. Longer open times allow the paint to be brushed out around obstacles at a civil pace. It is *easier* to get a nearly stroke-free finish on the restricted areas of the deck with a single-part paint, but I think this is usually a poorly considered trade-off. To start with, the majority of the deck will be nonskid, where brushstrokes are not an issue and the thinner consistency of LPU will have less tendency to smooth out the texture. The mostly horizontal surfaces particularly lend themselves to getting a stroke-free finish from LPU on smooth areas and nearly all of the shorter open-time problems are easily resolved with forethought and perhaps a bit of extra preparation. The result is usually a better finish over the whole of the deck. Most compelling, painting the deck is not something you will want to do again any sooner than you have to and using LPU doubles or triples the life of the paint job.

Preparation is essentially the same as for the hull—scrub, dewax, sand, patch, and prime—but there are three additional requirements to putting a superior finish on the deck. The first of these is to remove as much of the deck hardware as you can. By the time most of us get around to repainting the deck, the hardware is long overdue for rebedding anyway. And even if it isn't, when the paint extends under an item rather just up to it, the paint edge is protected by the bedding of the reinstalled hardware and a potential spot of paint failure is eliminated. And, of course, there is the benefit that every piece of hardware you remove is one you don't have to mask or paint around.

The second requirement is that you have to decide how you are going to deal with the "nonskid" portions of the deck. While some molded-in patterns provide admirable traction, the best thing you can say about the so-called nonskid texture on many older boats is that it is less slick than the untextured surfaces. Even that may not be true after you paint it. Without some kind of help, two coats of any high-gloss paint added to two decades of wear will yield a surface more suitable for ice skates than deck shoes. You may also want the nonskid to be a different color from the rest of the deck.

The third requirement is painting the deck in sections. If you are painting the nonskid a different color or adding grit to the paint, you will obviously paint these areas separately from the smooth areas, but this is not the separation I am mostly talking about. You are also going to need to paint the smooth surfaces in segments. To keep a single wet edge, you have to tape off all smooth surfaces that branch from the one you are painting.

Think of a parade route with all of the side streets barricaded. This is not as onerous as it sounds. You can normally paint all of the fore-and-aft strips with one paint mix, moving from one lengthwise section to the next until all are coated. On the second day you move your tape "barricades" onto the painted sections and paint all of the athwartship segments. You end up with all of the smooth areas coated in two days rather than

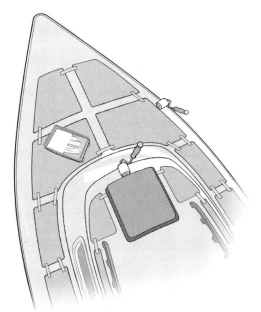

The rule is always a single wet edge. Mask all branching surfaces.

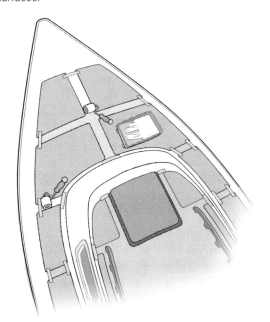

When the paint is dry, move the masking onto the painted surfaces and paint the unpainted branch surfaces.

Painting the deck.

one and only a tiny straight tape line between segments. Two more days gives you the required second coat on all smooth surfaces. Sectional painting will also let you cut the job down to match your available time. There is nothing to prevent you from doing the foredeck this month, the cabin top next month, and the cockpit two months after that.

Often you can cut foam roller covers to slightly less than the width of the smooth strips, fit them onto a trim roller handle, and roll these areas in less time than it takes to describe. On a horizontal surface, a roller application should smooth out to a nearly perfect gloss, with any slight texture having the benefit of reducing glare.

Smooth First

Paint the smooth areas first for two reasons. First, the smooth areas are invariably white or at least a lighter color than the nonskid. Dark covers light better than the other way around. The second reason is that if the final masking is done on the nonskid rather than the smooth surface, a sharp line between the two will be difficult to achieve. Actually you do not need to mask the nonskid at all when painting the smooth surfaces. Allowing the white to extend a bit onto the nonskid will give the two coatings a beneficial overlap when you do mask off the painted smooth area and paint the nonskid panels. To reduce the length and the visual effect of the barricade masking, locate it back far enough from the intersection to cross from straight nonskid edge to straight nonskid edge.

In general you can prepare the entire deck without segregation, but sanding the textured nonskid panels harkens back to how you prepared the uneven surfaces inside cabin lockers. You will need to heavily dewax the texture, this time using xylene or a proprietary dewaxing solvent. Sandpaper will not reach into the texture, so scrub the nonskid with bronze wool or run a soft wire brush over it before sanding the top surface *lightly* with 120-grit paper. You will probably need to prime the smooth surfaces, but do not prime the nonskid areas unless you are using the primer to adhere grit or it is necessary for a color change. Otherwise it just has the undesirable effect of filling the texture. You also will not sand the nonskid areas between coats, but be sure you recoat within the time specified.

When you have all of the smooth surfaces painted, you will need to mask around the nonskid panels. Exactly how you paint them will depend on if and how you want to enhance their nonskid properties. If the texture is adequate, you can simply roll on two coats of LPU and you're finished. There is no reason to tip nonskid, but you could have better success applying the paint to the uneven texture with a brush rather than a roller.

Better Grip

To improve footing you can mix a nonskid additive—typically polymer beads—into the paint. This is one paint system component where there are no compatibility issues, so if you want to use a more (or less) aggressive nonskid additive from a different LPU manufacturer, feel free. This method is effective, but because the beads tend to settle almost immediately to the bottom of the paint tray, the resulting texture is usually irregular. Use the additive only in the top coat of LPU.

Shaking grit onto a painted surface while the paint is wet generally delivers a more uniform and more attractive grit pattern. Foundry sand (#36 grit) is cheap and delivers an aggressive texture, but the plastic spheres and beads of nonskid additives can also be applied this way. Prime the surface with epoxy primer, and while it is still wet, cover the surface *entirely* with grit sifted from your fingers or distributed with a big shaker. This is the only circumstance in which you will prime nonskid surfaces. Otherwise the primer simply degrades the footing by filling the texture. When the epoxy kicks, use a soft brush to gently sweep up the grit that did not adhere. It can be reused on the next nonskid area. Roll on your two coats of polyurethane to encapsulate the grit.

More secure footing is possible by painting the nonskid areas with a rubberized deck paint such as Durabak 18. This is the type of surface you see on ferry decks and military vessels. Generally it is bits of rubber suspended in a polyurethane paint. The rubber particles provide extreme UV protection, giving these products a very long life expectancy, and the footing they provide is excellent. Preparation is the same as for applying LPU, and these products are normally applied in two coats in a crisscross pattern using special roller covers. A wide array of colors is available.

For the most secure footing, nothing beats a rubberized overlay. This treatment is expensive and adds undesirable weight to the deck, but you will stick like a tree frog to the surface it provides. Offshore, any aggressive rubberized overlay—in particular Treadmaster Original (long called Treadmaster M)—provides a degree of security unmatched by any other deck surface option.

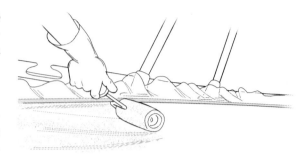

Roll on paint with the nonskid additive mixed in.

Sift sand or other grit onto wet epoxy primer. Paint over the adhered grit.

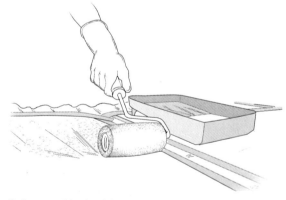

Roll on a rubberized deck coating.

Painted on nonskid coatings.

Nonskid Overlay

To properly install a sheet overlay, you are going to need to get rid of the molded-in texture. It may already be mostly gone by the time you get to this choice. What remains can be ground away in a trice with a disk sander loaded with a 36-grit disk. You should do this before you paint the smooth surfaces so the overlay can slightly overlap and seal the paint. Be careful not to let the sander get outside the textured area. It is not necessary and usually not desirable to sand away all of the texture. Rather, fill the remaining depressions with epoxy putty and fair the surface when the epoxy cures.

Cut a paper pattern of each of the nonskid panels from heavy (kraft) paper. Panel sizes will be limited by the sheet size of the overlay, usually 3 feet by 4 feet, so you may have to cover an existing single nonskid area with two or more panels. Do not butt them together. Leave at least a 1-inch gap between panels and 2 inches between the nonskid and any vertical surfaces (cabin sides, rails, coamings, etc.). This not only looks better and avoids mismatch and the dirt harbor of a butt joint, but it provides for better drainage. Cut the paper oversize, place it on the deck, and use a pencil to draw the exact outline. A flexible wooden batten will help you to parallel the curvature of the rail and other features. Use a lid or a can to put a uniform radius on the corners of the panels.

Take your time getting the patterns right, then cut them to size and tape them temporarily in place. Write "Top" on each pattern, and draw a line on it parallel to the centerline of the boat with an arrowhead toward the bow. When all the paper patterns are in place, look at the overall effect to be certain you are satisfied. Do not feel restrained by the original nonskid pattern. For example, if the area outboard of cabin-top handrails is wide enough to step on, you should give it a nonskid surface no matter what the builder did originally. Also, do not cut patterns for only one side with the intention of reversing them for the opposite side. Boats are almost never symmetrical, and hardware is certain to be in different locations.

Trace each pattern lightly on the deck with a pencil, then remove them all. Now paint the smooth areas of the deck, including any new ones your layout may have created. Carry the paint $^{1}/_{2}$ inch or so inside the penciled outlines.

Transfer the fore-and-aft alignment line on each pattern to the bottom side of the paper, then put the patterns with this side up (i.e., the side marked "Top" facing down) on the *back* side of the sheets of overlay. Align the line with the long side of the sheet to insure the correct orientation of the nonskid's design. Arrange the patterns to make the most effective use of each sheet. Trace each pattern onto the overlay, then cut out each piece with shears, snips, or heavy scissors.

Take all of the cut pieces back to the deck and put them in place. Give each a number and orientation marks on the back side, and make corresponding notations underneath on the deck. Measure gap widths and adjust panel locations until they are exactly how you want them installed. Take one more look at the overall

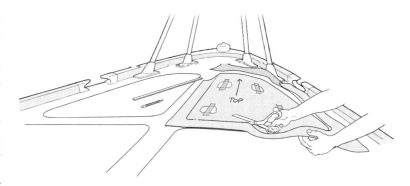

Make a paper pattern of each overlay piece.

effect, then lightly trace around each panel with a pencil. This will be the outside perimeter of the adhesive. Masking the deck outside of the pencil line will keep the adhesive off your freshly painted deck.

If the overlay manufacturer does not specify a different adhesive, glue the nonskid to the deck with slightly thickened epoxy. Use a serrated trowel to spread the epoxy on both the back of the covering and the deck area inside the pencil outline. Carefully position the section of overlay and press it to the deck. A rubber roller normally used for installing

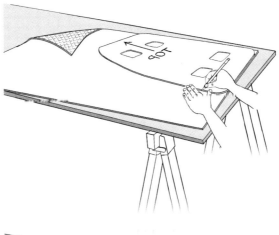

Align the fore-and-aft arrow on the pattern with long side of sheet.

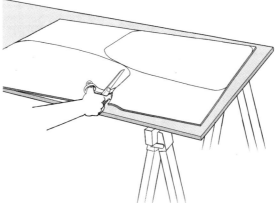

Trace around the pattern and cut the overlay with shears.

Cutting the overlay.

plastic laminate can be used to good effect here to flatten the overlay against the deck, but don't lean on it too hard. Use a plastic scraper to pick up the bulk of the epoxy that squeezes out. Pour a couple of ounces of acetone into an open container, dip bits of fresh paper towel into it, and wipe up the epoxy residue in single sweeps of the saturated towel along the perimeter. Have a second container at hand for discarding the toweling. Be careful not to get the toweling so wet that acetone squeezes out and runs under the overlay, as this will compromise the bond at the edge.

Use a serrated trowel to coat contact surfaces with thickened epoxy.

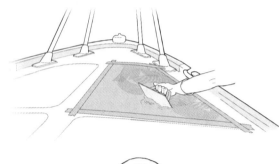

Press the overlay flat against the deck.

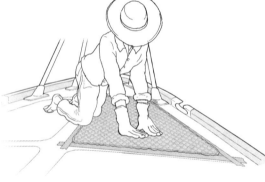

Pick up excess adhesive at the perimeter with a plastic scraper.

Use small pieces of acetone-saturated paper towel to clean the smooth perimeter and the vertical edge of the overlay.

Installing the panels.

Peel away the masking tape and make one final wipe around the perimeter to pick up adhesive residue hiding at the tape edge.

Apply each section in turn. By the time you get the perimeter wiped, the epoxy will have solidified. When the epoxy cures under the final panel, your tread is good for 50,000 miles. At least.

GRAPHICS

If you have just given the hull a drop-dead gorgeous shine and the deck a two-tone or at least two-texture treatment, you may find it hard to imagine your old boat looking any better. If so, you need more imagination. Computer-generated vinyl graphics let you give your boat just the individual touch required to set it apart from every other sister ship, whether that is nothing more than the name of the vessel on the transom or stylized dolphins leaping at the bow. This is the fun part.

If you are into tattoos, you are going to love computer-generated graphics. Any design you can scan into a computer can be delivered to you as a vinyl appliqué in virtually any size you can conceive. If you are just after a boat name and hailing port, lots of sources can supply just what you want at a remarkably low price. Typically all you have to do is decide how big you want the graphic and pick the font, the color or colors, and perhaps a special effect like outlining or shadow. The supplier will also require some specific measurements to define the curvature of the hull so your graphic doesn't end up exhibiting an arch you do not expect. You can do all of this on the Internet with a graphics company thousands of miles away and see an exact rendering of what you will be ordering right on your computer screen. The completed graphic will arrive in a mailing tube.

The typical appliqué comes as a single sheet. Actually it is two sheets—a wide *application tape* stuck to peelable *backing paper*—with the vinyl graphic sandwiched in between. The transparent tape will have both a baseline and a centerline marked on it.

Prepare the surface by washing it and, if this is not a surface you just painted, dewaxing it conscientiously with xylene. Start the application by positioning the entire graphic assembly on the hull. If, for example, this is a name you want centered on the stern, find the center of the transom and pencil a centerline long enough to extend beyond the appliqué at both the top and the bottom. Aligning this line with the centerline on the graphic, slide the appliqué up or down as needed to get it to the correct height. Tape the graphic in place, then back away to evaluate its position. When the boat is on the hard, you may not be able to properly assess this from the ground, even

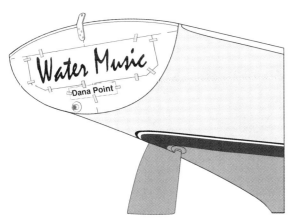

Position the graphic and put alignment marks on the hull.

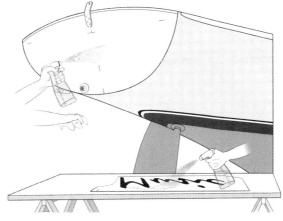

Wet both the hull and the exposed appliqué with application fluid.

from a distance. Use a stepladder or other means to raise your eye level above the deck to get a better on-the-water perspective.

If there is a second component—a hailing port for example—tape it in place at the same time so you can evaluate the combination. When you are satisfied with the position(s), extend the baseline(s) on the tape out onto the hull. Take down the graphic and connect the baseline marks with a light pencil line, using a flexible straightedge. Measure up from the waterline (or down from the rail) at both ends of this line to confirm that it is relatively level.

Once you have alignment marks on the hull, there is no reason that you cannot actually install the graphic in smaller pieces if it is made up of disconnected components, as a name is almost certain to be. Scissor the decal into more manageable pieces, making the cut or cuts between the disconnected components. Make these cuts with a gentle S-curve rather than straight so that the separate pieces will fit together only one way when you put them on the hull.

NO WIND, NO EXCEPTIONS

You are ready to apply the graphic, but *only* if it is a calm day. You must never even contemplate applying graphics with *any* wind blowing. When you peel away the backing paper, you have, in effect, a giant piece of cellophane tape. Even a tiny gust can flip it over onto itself, ruining the graphic—and your day—in an instant. You need a still day. A second pair of hands can lower the stress level for the short time the graphic is vulnerable to this potential catastrophe.

To keep the tape from sticking to the hull initially so you can jockey the decal into position, you are going to wet the hull and the tape with a slippery solution. You can brew your own with a half teaspoon of dishwashing liquid (not one with lanolin or cream or moisturizer) in a quart of water, but you will be better off to buy real application fluid such as Rapid Tac. It works better, goes away faster, and comes in a spritzer bottle.

You are going to need a flat surface at least as big as the largest piece of the appliqué. Lay the graphic tape-side down and carefully peel the paper backing. If the decal starts to come away with the backing, gently separate the two with a knife edge and smooth the vinyl back onto the application tape. Wet a clean finger with the application fluid and hold the graphic against the tape while you continue peeling the backing. If you have cut your graphic into sections, start your application with the section that has the centerline.

When you have removed the backing, the upper side of the graphic is adhesive, just aching to stick to itself or leaves or bugs or dirt. Spritz it immediately with the application fluid. Also spritz the fluid onto the hull where the graphic or this section is going. Use your (clean) hand to spread the fluid on the hull to make sure the entire surface is wet. Take care not to wash off your alignment marks.

Pick up the wet decal by the top corners and press the wet side onto the hull. If it is large, draft a helper so you can pick it up by all four corners to keep it flat. The slippery application fluid will let you slide the decal to get it perfectly aligned, but try to hit the target when you put it in place. Slide it until the centerlines and baselines on the hull and the decal are aligned.

Holding the graphic with a flat palm to make sure it does not move, smooth it down and squeeze out most of the fluid under it using a plastic squeegee. If the graphic supplier did not supply this, the soft yellow spreaders sold for spreading epoxy resin work well. Start at the center and squeegee in a starburst pattern to push the moisture to the edges. Once you have smoothed the entire decal, rub down the graphic through the tape with additional passes of the squeegee to burnish the vinyl against the hull.

Position decal according to the alignment marks.

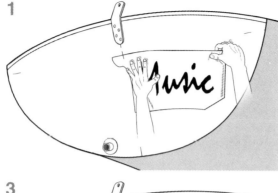

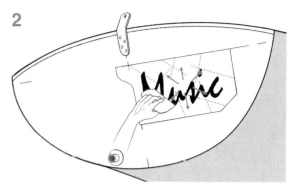

Using a soft, flexible squeegee, rub down the decal from the center to the edges to press it against the hull and to squeeze out most of the application fluid. Burnish the actual graphic.

Wet the tape with application fluid and burnish the graphic again heavily.

Peel the tape—back, not out—to complete installation.

If the decal is in pieces, peel and wet the piece that adjoins the one you just applied, wet the hull, and put that section in place. Squeegee it. Continue applying the pieces in turn until you have the entire graphic in place and burnished against the hull. Now take a 15-minute break to give the adhesive time to set. You will have to wait longer in cool or humid conditions, or if you are using a soap solution rather than application fluid.

After 15 minutes, wet the surface of the application tape by spritzing it liberally with the application fluid. Burnish the graphic one more time with heavy pressure from your squeegee against the wet application tape. Now starting with the section you applied first, peel up one corner of the application tape and double it back on itself. *Slowly* pull on that corner—not out and away, but sliding against itself, like turning back a bedsheet. When the moving fold reaches the graphic, watch closely for any signs of the vinyl lifting with the tape rather than remaining attached to the hull. If the vinyl comes up with the tape, smooth the tape back down, rerub the lifted section of decal, and wait another 15 minutes. When the graphic exhibits no tendency to lift, continue pulling the application tape back on itself until you have peeled it away completely. Peel the tape from each section in turn, always making sure the graphic does not lift with the tape.

When the entire graphic is exposed, burnish it with a folded cloth to expel trapped air. You will have to prick larger bubbles in the center of the graphic to allow the air to escape. Burnish these bubbles flat.

Small bubbles you can ignore. They will disappear on their own in a few days. Leave the graphic undisturbed for a day before you wash off the alignment marks and the glue residue with soapy water.

An owner-applied graphic is identical to one put on by a pro, and I cannot think of another job this easy that can have such a dramatic effect. Imagine.

SPRUCED SPARS
Unlike wooden masts that used to come out of the boat every year for a fresh coat of varnish and a careful heel-to-truck examination for splits or rot, aluminum masts tend to remain stubbornly vertical until the rigging requires replacing or something bad happens. Inspection and maintenance—if there is any—happens from a bosun's chair. The aluminum masts in older boats will

have been anodized originally to protect the aluminum from the elements. Anodizing is extraordinarily durable, but age *always* triumphs in the end (don't we know it?), and an old anodized mast is likely to be streaked with the white powder of oxidation and crosshatched with halyard scars. Reanodizing requires removing every bit of hardware and every fastener—you cannot leave a single rivet in the tube—and while it will renew the protection, it will not hide the scars. Besides, unless you have an anodizing facility nearby with a tank longer than your mast and you have access to a mast trailer, the combined cost of anodizing and shipping (see Chapter 8) is likely to make this alternative unattractive. Newer boats often sport painted masts, which likewise yield to age, but the most obvious finish damage can be hidden with a touch-up.

An admirable characteristic of aluminum is that the oxide that forms on the surface actually protects the aluminum from further corrosion, so you can get away with doing absolutely nothing to an aluminum spar for decades. A dull, streaked mast, however, is going to detract from the appearance of your just-painted boat, and the white oxide oddly puts black streaks on sails. Cleaning is effective for only a short time. A good coat of wax can hold the oxidation at bay for a season. Forget about protecting your mast by giving it some kind of clear coat. By fall you will be clearing cellophane leaves from the deck scuppers. The only real choice for sprucing up an unsightly mast is to paint it, or repaint it, with LPU.

You need the spar you are refinishing out of the boat. The more hardware you remove, the more continuous the coating and the longer you can expect it to last. Support the unstepped mast on sawhorses and wipe it with a cloth soaked in acetone or xylene. If this is a painted mast, the old paint will be LPU. Simply wet sand it with 220-grit paper, then 320-grit to prepare the old paint for a fresh coat. Prepare damaged areas as detailed here for bare aluminum.

Bare aluminum only needs to be etched, but your spar is not bare aluminum. Much of it may still have the hard surface coating created by anodizing. Sand the entire mast with medium-grit emery cloth to abrade the surface and remove heavy oxidation. Flush the sanded mast with water and scrub it with a brush to remove all loose particles. Do not wipe the mast with a rag after you sand it because the microscopically rugged metal will snag tiny fibers from the cloth, causing adhesion problems.

After you sand, the "secret" to a long-lived coating on aluminum is correctly preparing the bare metal with an acid etching solution. This treatment both cleans the metal and creates tooth to foster adhesion. To allow the uninterrupted etching and painting of the full circumference of the mast, suspend it above the horses with supports in the ends of the tube and a dowel or rod through a midmast hole. Position the track up.

Typical treatment is to dilute the etching solution—probably Alumiprep 33—according to directions, normally 1 part etching solution to 2 to 5 parts water, according to the amount of oxidation on the spar. Be aware that this is moderately nasty stuff, so protect all body parts, especially your eyes. In general you brush on a quick coating of the acid solution, leave it in contact with the metal for not more than 5 minutes, usually less, then wash it off by flooding the surface with water. Because oxidation on the now-clean aluminum will start immediately, the normal protocol is to follow the rinse with a conversion-coating wash, usually clear Alodine, which is also rinsed immediately to wash off any excess. Once the treated area dries, it is ready for priming and painting. This process is done commercially by dipping the entire spar for both the treatment and the rinse. You will need treat the mast in sections you can coat within the time allotted for the solution to be in contact with the metal.

After this there is nothing particularly new. Rather than the high-build epoxy primer you used on your hull, you are going to prime the prepared mast with an anticorrosive epoxy primer thinned to flow out smoothly. You will have to cut in the track with a brush, taking care to minimize film thickness here, then you can roll the primer onto the spar with a foam roller, running the roller around the spar. Again, take care that you do not unload the roller into the sail track.

When the primer has cured fully, you can wet sand it with 120-grit paper to remove any roller tracks or other obvious flaws. If you are using an acid primer, do not sand. Acid primers are applied as a single thin coat and should never be sanded. Note that if the instructions from the manufacturer of your LPU of choice recommends a different preparation protocol for painting an aluminum spar, you should follow those directions.

You can paint your spars any color you like, but you will not make a mistake choosing white or buff. Thin and test the paint until it flows out nicely from a roller-only application. Tipping out is normally not needed. Cut in the track with a brush, keeping the film thickness to a minimum, then start your roller application at the top of the mast. By the time you get down to deck level, you will have perfected your technique. Trim around any hardware still on the

Cut in the track with a thin coat.

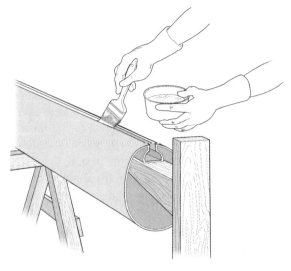

Roll primer and paint around the mast with a foam roller.

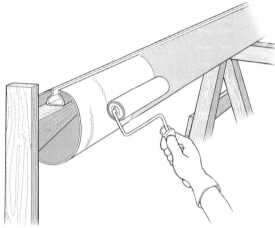

Painting an aluminum spar.

mast with a foam brush as you reach the spot with your roller.

Let the first coat dry overnight, wet sand it lightly with 320-grit paper, and apply the perfect top coat.

PAINTING THE BOTTOM

After you have put a mirror finish on the topsides and painted all your spars, how much of a challenge can painting the bottom be? Not much. Sand the old coating smooth and roll on a couple of new coats. But if you have never done a bottom job before, a bit more exposition might help your confidence and improve your results.

RAKE AND SCRAPE

Preparation for painting begins as soon as the keel clears the surface of the water. While the bottom is still wet, the slime and growth will be relatively easy to remove. If you let the stuff dry, it will take a chisel to get it off. I am not making this up. Scrape and

scrub the bottom growth free the instant it comes out of the water.

Fortunately most boatyards have a pressure washer at the lift (or ramp) that will blast all the little sea critters off your hull while it hangs from the slings. A few passes with a long-handled scraper takes care of the mussel colony on the bottom of the keel. If bits of bottom paint flake off under the pressure of the washer nozzle, have the yard worker make another pass to remove as much of the loose paint as possible. Unless you have been scrubbing the bottom in the water or paying someone to keep it clean, this is not the place to try to reduce the total cost of your haulout. By the time the workers set your boat down in the yard, the bottom should be completely clean.

STRIP?

No! Not unless you absolutely have to. An incontrovertible truth about painting anything is that the adhesion of the new paint is only as good as that of any coating beneath it. You do need to check the old paint ruthlessly for any signs of adhesion failure. Anywhere you find the old paint flaking or lifting, worry the exposed edges with a knife or small chisel. If the paint zips off, the bottom needs to be stripped.

What if your old boat is hauling around 20 annual applications of epoxy bottom paint? This question will answer itself. Another incontrovertible truth is that one or more of those aging coats is eventually going to lose its grip. When that happens, the bottom paint will start to peel off in big patches and you will have to strip. Until that happens, don't go looking for trouble. Here's why.

Stripping all the paint from the bottom of your boat is nearly always an awful job. The only exception is when the oldest coat or one close to the oldest has failed completely. When that happens, a determined owner can peel the bottom completely in less than a day using a 1-inch hook scraper—like peeling a giant potato. This is unfortunately a rare reality, and all other methods of stripping are, well, horrible.

Heat is *not* an option. While you can *hopefully* avoid overheating the polyester (gelcoat) when lifting an old graphic, trying to soften bottom paint this way is a guaranteed disaster.

Never, ever let a boatyard staff convince you to sandblast, sodablast, or shotblast with any medium to remove paint from your hull—unless the hull is steel. Sandblasting a fiberglass boat *always* damages the gelcoat, compromising its impermeability and almost certainly leading to hull blisters. Even if you are planning on sealing the gelcoat after stripping, sandblasting is still a bad idea. Any operator incompetence or inattention will cause damage to the underlying laminate. Yards like sandblasting because it is fast, not because it is smart.

With the arms of a weight lifter and the stamina of a marathoner, you could use a disk sander to quickly convert multiple layers of bottom paint into a colorful cloud of toxic dust—with you in the middle. It will make a cloud out of your gelcoat just as quickly if you lose concentration (or consciousness). Even if the health hazards—for you and for your boat—do not deter you, the yard management is almost certainly going to pull the plug. Most American yards allow only "dustless" sanding, meaning the sander must have some type of vacuum attachment to contain the bulk of the dust. That rules out the flying disk in favor of some flavor of orbital sander. Even a random orbit sander is going to wear you out before it wears through more than a couple of layers of paint.

That leaves chemical strippers as your only real choice for multilayer stripping, and a poor choice it is. This is not like stripping the top of Grandma's antique oak dining table—not unless the table has a dozen layers of thick, poisonous paint and you hang it upside down outside to strip it. Even this fails to capture the full reality unless you can imagine a table big enough to seat 200. You cannot use regular fast-acting paint strippers because they can't distinguish between paint resin and gelcoat resin. So-called safe strippers are really just *slow* strippers, counting on the chemicals to run out of potency or you to run out of patience before the stripper does any real damage. If you don't leave the stripper on long enough, you have to do it all again, and if you leave it on too long, it dries concrete-hard and/or attacks the gelcoat. And no matter how "eco-friendly" the stripper, the goo that results is toxic and messy and has to be scraped off, much of it over your head.

There is simply no nastier boat job than stripping the bottom, so avoid it if you can. When it cannot be avoided, use a chemical stripper to remove most of the paint, but not all. You must sand the bottom after chemical stripping in all cases anyway. Whether the sander is just cleaning up residue or taking off the final layer or two of paint will make little difference to the sanding process but a very big difference to your gelcoat. Do not believe assurances that the stripper will not damage gelcoat. It will. Don't give it a chance.

SAND

When the old paint is sound, you need only sand it, wash it, tape the waterline, and roll on a fresh coating. Power sanding is one option, but expect your yard to

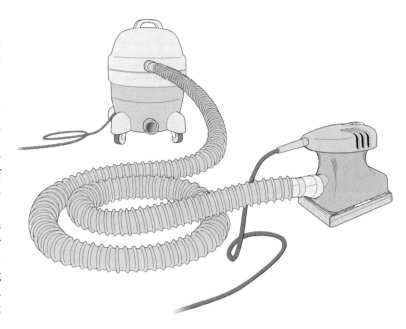

"Dustless" sanding may be dictated by the boatyard.

require you to contain the dust. Almost any random orbit or finishing sander can be made dustless by fitting a shop-vac hose over the dust-bag mount on the sander, but this is boatyard dustless—something of an oxymoron. You will still need a tight-fitting respirator, the rubber kind with replaceable filters. Paper masks are as useless as paper condoms. If you don't believe me, blow your nose after sanding for an hour in a paper mask. The blue tissue tells you that you have just barnacle-proofed your nasal passages. This stuff can turn you into a rutabaga, so buy yourself a comfortable respirator and use the thing. Your skin is also a vital organ, so wear long pants and long sleeves to shield it. Goodwill and other thrift stores are good sources of loose-fitting clothes that can be discarded at the end of the day. If you also wear earplugs to shut out the din of the sander and the shop vac, you'll save your hearing and find the work much less tiring.

The best way to avoid toxic dust is to not create any. Wet sanding the bottom by hand with a medium-grit sanding sponge can prepare the bottom just as quickly. However, the loaded runoff is also likely to be frowned on by your yard. Tarps may satisfy the yard, although it seems to me that they mostly pay lip service to the real issue. In any case, you will have to comply with whatever sanding restrictions your yard imposes.

To avoid paint buildup, it is a good practice to sand away all of the prior application. Take off a couple of extra layers at each haulout, and you might work yourself out of a thickening coat without ever having to endure the unpleasantness of stripping.

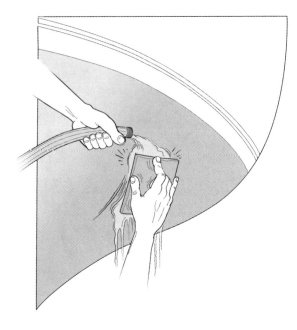

Another dustless method. Sanding sponges are perfect for bottom-paint sanding.

BARE BOTTOM

You may never see bare fiberglass on the bottom of an old boat unless it develops blisters and/or you decide to apply a barrier coat (see Chapter 6). Bare or not, wash the bottom with TSP after stripping or sanding, and blast it with a vigorous stream from a hose to flush away all chemical and particle residue. If the gelcoat is exposed, take the opportunity to clean it with xylene or some other dewaxing solvent. If the old paint has lost its grip, failure to properly dewax was a contributing factor.

When you are starting from bare gelcoat or a new barrier coat, make the first coat of paint you apply a different color from the top coats. This is called a flag coat, and it will give you a visual indication when your "real" bottom paint is gone. A flag coat is useful for two reasons: to tell you that it is time to paint because the current coating has eroded or been scrubbed away, and to warn you against thinning the barrier coat or the gelcoat by additional sanding.

PAINT CHOICES

All bottom paints are either soft or hard. Choose a soft paint if your boating is seasonal; choose a hard paint if it is endless. Despite the paralyzing number of bottom paints out there, it really isn't much more complicated than that.

Copper

Except for a 20-year illicit affair with tin—now banned worldwide—all mariners have depended on copper to forestall reef building on the bottoms of their boats for more than two centuries. Copper sheathing has morphed into copper paints, with resin replacing nails, but painted-on copper is necessarily thin with a correspondingly short life. The active ingredient in virtually all antifouling paints is either metallic copper or copper oxide, so it must be something else that accounts for performance differences. That something else is the paint.

Soft. Soft paints are called *ablatives.* They function like a bar of soap, wearing away in use. Ablatives come in two types, sloughing and copolymer. In a *sloughing* paint the copper is simply mixed in, like nuts in a chocolate bar. As the water nibbles away the paint, it exposes fresh copper. The copper in a *copolymer* is more like the chocolate. The paint and the copper are combined chemically. In the water this difference is immaterial, but out of the water the exposed copper in sloughing paints oxidizes like a new penny, losing potency in a few days. Copolymer paints simply become dormant in air, ready to go back to work when you relaunch.

If you haul every winter and paint every spring, apply the cheapest sloughing paint you can find. It will likely ward off fouling as well as a paint costing three times as much, and it has the added convenience of being mostly washed away by fall, minimizing the prep for next season's application. Or you can spend the extra money for a copolymer to avoid the sanding and repainting next spring and maybe—just maybe—the spring after that.

Where antifouling is needed, dry-stored boats will get better performance from copolymer bottom paint. A copolymer can also be a good choice for a boat that remains in the water year-round. Haulout costs are avoided by a multiseason copolymer. The paint's ablative characteristic means the bottom remains cleaner without the need for scrubbing (scrubbing soft paints is rarely a good idea), and it is not accumulating a paint buildup that will eventually require stripping (nooo!). There is, however, one major caveat regarding the life of a copolymer in year-round use. The paint dissolves more quickly on a boat underway than on one at rest. If you put a lot of miles on your boat, a copolymer may not last as long as you expect. Cruising sailors, particularly those on the move, are less likely to be disappointed with a hard paint. The life of a copolymer is also shortened by speed, so hard paints are a better match for planing boats as well.

Hard. The stronger binder in hard paints allows the coating to carry more copper. That typically translates into longer antifouling action, but because the paint does not wash away, expect to have to scrub a hard paint with an abrasive pad occasionally to maximize paint life. Also, most hard paints suffer the same potency loss in air as a sloughing paint, so they are not the usual choice for boats that are dry-stored either after use or annually.

South of the Mason-Dixon line, where boats stay in the water year-round and barnacles are particularly virulent, hard paints reign. A top-quality epoxy-based paint should keep the bottom clean for more than a year. Many warm-water sailors go 2 years or longer between haulouts, extending the life of the paint by abrasive scrubbing after around 18 months.

How do you tell soft from hard? If the label says "ablative," "sloughing," "copolymer," "self-polishing," or "multiseason," it is a soft paint. Everything else is hard. Nearly all hard paints are modified epoxies, with a few remaining vinyls just to keep you off balance. Hard vinyls should say "not compatible with nonvinyl paints," or something to that effect, on the label.

Slick Finish

Vinyl bottom paints are more appropriately grouped under the slick finish category. Vinyl paints can be burnished to a smooth (translation: *fast*) finish. Antifouling properties are secondary. So-called thin-film paints, typically incorporating Teflon, are similarly formulated for boat speed. Teflon paints can also be a better choice for the low-fouling environment of fresh water. If your boating is competitive or exclusively in fresh water, slick coatings will be of interest. For everyone else, they are a poor choice.

Compatibility

If the existing bottom paint is hard, you can apply hard or soft. If the existing paint is soft, vigorous sanding is required to overcoat with hard paint. Removing the soft paint entirely is a more prudent course when changing from soft to hard. Vinyl paints contain strong solvents that will soften both hard and soft paints, so they cannot be applied over anything except another vinyl. Thin-film paints are intended for application directly to the gelcoat.

Environmental Issues and the Future

There is a good chance that during the life of this book all of the preceding paint-choice guidance will be rendered obsolete. The astounding environmental damage that tin-based bottom paints caused in a relatively short time has lots of government entities viewing copper paints with a jaundiced eye. Leaching copper is clearly less of an environmental insult, but anyone who has ever scrubbed a boat in the water knows in their heart of hearts that the resulting blue cloud can't be doing marine life any good. Any way you cut it, most of every gallon of bottom paint manufactured—especially ablative paints—ends up in the water as surely as if we simply emptied the paint cans over the rail. Except for the solvents, of course, which evaporate into the air.

You don't need to be a tree hugger to see that less-poisonous bottom paints are a good idea. Unfortunately coatings that do not release chemicals or toxins into the water remain less effective at keeping the bottom clean. Until some manufacturer sweeps the competition with an affordable, nonpolluting coating that repels both barnacles and grass, boaters have few options.

The Wild Card

The *type* of paint you should use depends almost entirely on *how* you use your boat. What *brand* you should use often depends on *where* you use your boat. Different waters foster different types of fouling. A paint that works well against the fouling conditions in one body of water can give disappointing results in another. The surest way of selecting an effective brand is to ask other boaters in your area who have boats like yours (meaning sail or power, planing or displacement) what paint they like, then buy the one you hear praised most often.

How much paint do you need? A rough estimate of wetted area can be calculated by multiplying the length overall (LOA) by the beam by 0.90. The paint label will specify the coverage per gallon.

PAINTING

Typically the only masking required will be the bootstripe. Use Fine Line tape and rub down the bottom edge to prevent the paint from "fingering" under it.

On the shelf, the copper in hard and sloughing bottom paints settles into a solid lump at the bottom of the can. If the boatyard has a paint shaker, run it for at least 5 minutes to get the copper and the pigment evenly distributed throughout the paint. In the absence of a shaker, use a drill-powered mixer or stir the paint with a flat paddle stirrer until your arm falls off. You can slosh $50 worth of paint out on the ground while you stir, or you can pour half the paint into another container—your choice. Keep digging and stirring with the paddle until the bottom is clean and all the copper is distributed through the half remaining in the can. If the other half is in another container, pour it back into the original can slowly while you continue to stir. If it is in the dirt, just leave it there.

Roll on bottom paint with the aid of a long handle.

The thicker the coating, the longer the life of the paint, so do not add any thinner to bottom paint unless the manufacturer specifies otherwise. You may need to break this rule on hot or windy days to get the paint to flow out satisfactorily.

Roll the paint onto the hull using a short-nap roller cover. Wear sleeves and gloves to shield your skin from flying droplets. Put an extension on the roller handle and you should be able to paint the hull in a white linen suit (although it's *not* recommended). Work fast; many bottom paints dry quickly. Each time you refill the paint tray, first stir the paint in the can to keep the copper in suspension.

A second coat lengthens the life of any bottom paint. Copolymers benefit from three or four coats. The second coat can usually be applied in a continuous operation; i.e., by the time you have finished painting the hull, the paint on the area where you started will be dry enough to recoat. Check for the specified recoat time on the paint you are using. No between-coat sanding is needed.

Even if you apply only one coat, roll on all the paint you have left at the waterline, where the scrubbing action of the water tends to remove the paint more quickly. Save just enough to paint the areas under the stand or cradle pads and maybe the bottom of the keel.

Get the yard staff to move the stands as soon as the rest of the hull is dry. Don't even consider backing off a screw. Never mind that your boat is likely to do a little pirouette and fall over, squashing you like a roach. *My* boat could be sitting next to yours in the yard. Be sure the yard worker protects your fresh

paint by putting plastic sheeting on the repositioned pads. Prep the bare spots and apply the appropriate number of coats. You can paint the bottom of the keel on launch day, but it won't do any good unless you can arrange for your boat to remain suspended long enough to allow the paint to dry.

Metal Keels

If your boat has an exposed metal keel or centerboard, do not paint it directly with a copper-based paint. The iron or steel will react galvanically with the copper unless the two are electrically separated. A coat of primer will not be up to the task submerged in seawater. If you want bottom paint to stay on iron or steel, even lead for that matter, you need to seal the metal with an epoxy barrier coat.

A barrier coat needs to be applied to bare metal. That means you will need to strip all previous coatings. Sand blasting is the quickest way but you can do it yourself with a grinder and a few 36-grit disks. You are likely faced with grinding anyway because the barrier coat needs to go on while the metal is still bright so the epoxy bonds to the metal and not to surface oxidation. To accomplish this you must start with metal that you have just sanded. Solvent wash it to remove chemical contaminants, then without delay, mix your epoxy—only as much as you can apply well within the open time. Roll it on quickly with a foam roller, then wire-brush the metal through the wet epoxy. This scratches away all flash oxidation and gives the epoxy direct contact with the bare metal. To remove bubbles the brushing generates and to force the epoxy into the grain of the metal, squeegee with a 120-degree segment of a foam roller. The resin coating will inhibit further oxidation.

When this initial seal coat has fully cured, scrub it with water and a Scotch-Brite pad to remove the amine blush, then fair all irregularities in the surface of the keel with epoxy filler. Once the entire keel has been coated and faired, scrub it again, sand it lightly, and roll on six more coats of epoxy, applying subsequent coats as soon as the previous one is firm. You need a dry film thickness (DFT) of close to 20 mils to insure long-term impermeability. Squeegee each coat. Get all coats on the same day and you avoid sanding between them. To add abrasion resistance, work a couple of layers of 4-ounce fiberglass cloth into this schedule or add the cloth layup later as a separate step, at least to the bottom of the keel.

Avoid adhesion problems between the epoxy and the bottom paint by giving the barrier coat at least a week to cure before painting. Scrub the surface again with flowing water and a Scotch-Brite pad to remove the waxy blush, then wet-sand it with 100-grit paper. You should be all set to apply the same paint you have selected for the rest of the bottom.

Prop and Shaft

Over four decades of boating I have seen every effort to prevent prop fouling fail. Methods have ranged from rubbing the prop with diaper rash cream (really!) to gold plating. That is not to say that some new product won't eventually solve this problem, but as long as you see only bare props in a walk through any boatyard, you can bet that the hoped-for breakthrough has not yet happened. Paint your prop if you like, but not with copper-based paint. It won't stay on a bronze prop. Use only a coating intended for props, and if you find one that actually works, tell your friends. Or simply polish and heavily wax the screw. That doesn't work for long either, but it costs a lot less.

Never paint the shaft, and be sure you leave all zinc anodes unpainted. If you are installing new zincs (which is easier while the boat is in the yard), make certain you don't paint over their mounting locations. Good electrical contact is essential for zincs to do their job.

Let bottom paint dry at least overnight before you put masking tape on it to paint the bootstripe. Get hard bottom paint into the water within the time specified on the label.

BOOTSTRIPE

The bootstripe is a narrow strip of black or contrasting color that caps the bottom paint and gives it a finished look. Bootstripe tape is the easiest way to create a bootstripe. Vinyl tapes intended for bootstripe use are amazingly durable and available in a variety of widths, colors, and multistripe effects. The problem with bootstripe tape, particularly for use on a sailboat, is that it is a uniform width. The curvature of a hull near the waterline will make a uniform-width stripe appear to narrow. To easily get a visual understanding of this effect, stretch a foot of masking tape between your hands with the width vertical, then twist one end toward horizontal.

Because we want the stripe to appear the same width from bow to stern, we need to make it wider as it becomes less vertical. That dictates a painted bootstripe. The *width* will vary along the length of the stripe, but the top of the stripe will always be a fixed distance *higher* than its bottom.

MARKING THE WATERLINE

Regardless of how you intend to apply the bootstripe, the first step is to establish the waterline of your boat. The existing stripe, if there is one, should mark it. If you removed the stripe for painting the topsides, you should have scored its location into the gelcoat. Some newer boats have a molded-in reference line or even two lines to position the bootstripe. If your hull is without a waterline reference of any kind or if you do not trust the one it does have, you will need to establish the waterline some other way.

The surest easy way to locate the true waterline is to do it while the boat is afloat. Pick a mirror-calm morning, and check the trim of your boat with a borrowed carpenter's level. Use the cabin sole to check fore-and-aft trim, and span the cockpit seats with the level to check for list. Redistribute equipment and supplies until the boat sits level in both directions. Old-timers used to pour a little dirty oil on the water, and the resulting deposit on the hull marked the waterline perfectly. You risk a substantial fine doing it that way today, so get in the water with a scratch awl and mark both sides of the hull at the bow and the stern and both sides of the transom. A midship mark on each side might also prove useful.

Once in the yard, you need to have the yard workers level the hull. Again use the carpenter's level on the sole and across the cockpit seats. With the boat level, marking the waterline is easy. The high-tech way is with a laser transit. The cheap high-tech way is with a laser pointer. You will need to devise some way of supporting the pointer at the same height as your waterline and of rotating it in a flat, horizontal plane. A tall camera tripod can serve. So can a planted or braced vertical PVC pipe with a smaller or larger piece configured to rotate at the top. The idea here is simple. You locate the laser midships and as

A laser transit can make short work of marking the bootstripe.

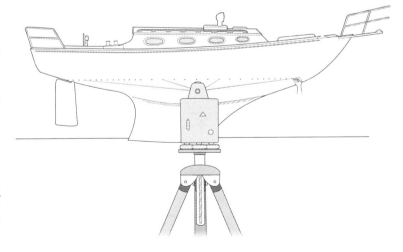

much as a boat length away. Once you get it leveled so that the dot is on the waterline mark at the bow, and when you rotate the pointer the dot is also on the mark at the stern, any position in between the laser dots will also be at the waterline. Move the dot across the hull 6 inches at a time, 1 foot at a time on the flatter sections, and score the hull at each dot. You can mark the location of the opposite side of a boot-stripe by simply raising the laser whatever you want the apparent width of the line to be and marking a second set of dots.

There are a couple of potential problems with this method. The first is that the beam from lots of cheap laser pointers will be indistinct or not visible at all on a white hull in sunlight at 30 feet. The second is that the dot is going to elongate as the hull turns hor-izontal at the stern. A smaller dot limits this problem, but you may have to estimate the center of the dot.

If laser beams are too Buck Rogers for you, you can do the same thing with a water level. You need a relatively rigid garden hose half again as long as your boat; 3 feet of clear ³/₄-inch vinyl hose; and a couple of garden hose replacement fittings, one male and one female. Put the fittings on either end of the clear hose, then cut the hose in half. Now screw the two pieces to the garden hose to provide each end with about 18 inches of clear hose.

Punch a hole through the wall of one of the clear pieces of hose near its cut end and rig a long piece of stiff wire through it. Use the wire to hang this end of the hose from the rail so that your reference waterline or bootstripe mark crosses the clear hose approxi-mately in the middle. Hold the other clear end verti-cal above your other reference mark and fill the hose completely with water from a bucket or another hose. Once the hose is full, lower the free end until it is level with the waterline mark, spilling out some of

the water. Raise the hose again, and you will notice that the water level in both clear sections is exactly at the waterline. If it isn't, add or spill a little water until it is. If it is above or below one mark when even with the other, either the boat is not level or your reference marks are off.

Since water seeks its own level, you can walk around the boat with the loose end and hold it against the hull to mark as many points as you like that are level with the control point. Because the hose is flex-ible, the internal volume could vary as you move it around the boat. Put a second person at the hanging hose to monitor the level, and add or spill water as required to put the water level exactly at the reference level before you mark each new spot. Some oscilla-tion will also occur as you move the hose. Allow the water to settle before marking the hull. Mark the hull at least every foot, closer where the hull is changing shape quickly such as under the counter.

KEEP IT CLEAN

If you locate the bottom of the bootstripe exactly at the waterline, immediate fouling will occur if the boat is slightly out of trim. Even wave action can keep an enamel (or vinyl) stripe wet enough to foul. My preferred solution to this is to paint the boot-stripe with antifouling paint. This effectively raises the bottom paint by the full width of the bootstripe. Wave action normally keeps the stripe wet, providing enough gloss that an antifouling bootstripe is usu-ally indistinguishable from one painted with shiny enamel. If you are unconvinced or want some effect that cannot be achieved with the limited palette of bottom paint colors, your bootstripe should be at least an inch above your boat's usual load waterline, with the bottom paint carried up to the bottom of the stripe. You may want more bottom paint showing on a cruising boat. The load waterline moves up the hull as you add fuel, water, gear, supplies, and people. You can estimate the amount of movement by calculat-ing the pounds per inch (PPI) immersion factor for your boat. The PPI can be determined precisely by multiplying the water plane area by 5.33, but for this purpose an approximation calculated by multiply-ing the waterline length by the waterline beam by 3.4 is adequate. My old Seawind, with a 24-foot water-line and a 9-foot beam, has a PPI of approximately 735 pounds (24 × 9 × 3.4). Ninety gallons of water will sink my waterline approximately an inch. So will a crew of four.

Once you have marked the bottom of the stripe, you can mark the top the same way with either the

A garden hose level is the low-tech way of marking the bootstripe.

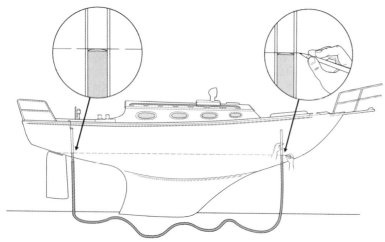

laser or the water level. Both will result in a boot-stripe of uniform height rather than width. You can scribe both lines into gelcoat to permanently mark the location. The best tool for this is a scoring tool for plastic laminate used against a flexible batten. You should not score a painted surface.

Connect the series of marks with masking tape, always working with a couple of feet or more of tape stretched horizontally with one hand while you press the tape to the hull with the other. Place the tape above the lower series of marks first and apply the bottom paint before the bootstripe. Sight along the edge of the tape to keep it straight and touch the tape to the hull only lightly. The wider the tape, the straighter your tape line is likely to be. When you finish, check the fairness of the line from the side, from the bow, and from the quarter, and correct any hills or valleys. Once you are satisfied, run your thumb along the edge of the tape to seal it and insure a clean line.

Give the bottom paint a day to dry or the tape is likely to lift some paint when you remove it. Before you remove this masking for the bottom paint, put the masking for the bootstripe edge to edge against it. This delivers perfect alignment with the least effort.

Now peel the tape above, pulling it back on itself and slightly away from the painted edge. Mask the top-sides above the second series of marks.

Lightly sand the area between the tape, taking care not to damage the tape. Clean the sanded surface with a thinner-dampened cloth. If you are using bottom paint—try it, you'll like it—apply it with a foam roller cut to a narrow width and loaded onto a trim roller handle. If you are using bootstripe paint (usually alkyd enamel), you can also apply it with a roller, tipping for a better finish, or you can put the paint on with a brush. As soon as the first coat dries, give the stripe a second coat. When the top coat is dry or only slightly tacky, immediately remove the masking tape, always pulling it back on itself and slightly away from the painted edge. Be careful to keep the paint-covered tape away from the hull.

With her wood glowing, her topsides blinding, and her name freshly applied to both quarters, your old boat should be looking pretty sharp by now. Nothing has a more immediate impact on the look of a boat than paint and varnish, making even a tired old dowager suddenly seem young and fresh. But don't stop with cosmetics. It is time to give the old girl a new wardrobe.

CHAPTER FIFTEEN

Material Things

*"Clay is molded to make a vessel,
but the utility of the vessel
lies in the space where there is nothing."*
—LAO TZU

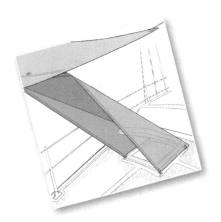

The enhancement possibilities for your old boat represented by a few yards of canvas or other fabric and some basic sewing skills are virtually limitless. There are the obvious improvements like new upholstery on the cushions and a bright new sail cover on the boom. There are features you admire on other boats, like a sun-deflecting bimini or bum-cradling cockpit cushions. There are cruising essentials like windscoops and harbor awnings. And there are unexplored ideas like storage pockets and canvas tool rolls.

The skills required to accomplish all of these things are amazingly few. A machine does all the hard work. All you have to do is cut the fabric to the appropriate dimensions and guide the pieces through the machine. A reasonable analogy can be drawn between running a piece of canvas through a sewing machine and a piece of plywood through a band saw. The big difference is that if you get off your line with the sewing machine, the material is not ruined. You can simply remove the errant stitches and do it again.

Of all the traditional marine crafts, canvaswork is my personal favorite. I *love* to sew and I make no excuses for that sentiment. It is a creative, artistic, and therapeutic activity. It provides a sense of satisfaction similar to the one you get fashioning a lump of wood into a thing of beauty or utility, but without risk to your fingers and eyes. Like painting and varnishing, it yields the gratification of immediate visual enhancement without dust and fumes. A missed stitch is not going to let the mast go over the side or the ocean flow into the cabin. Canvaswork doesn't leave you itching, like working with fiberglass, or grimy, like mechanical repairs. Weather is not a factor. Projects can be done at a single sitting or as time permits over

a period of weeks or months. But the main reason I enjoy it is that it's just plain fun.

THE SEWING MACHINE

Many years ago—back when the Japanese were making cheap imitations of American products instead of the other way around—I traded an old black-and-white television for a Japanese sewing machine. The other party to the trade could hardly control her glee as the deal was consummated, but I got the last laugh. For the next decade while, according to the Nielsens, *The Dukes of Hazzard* was the number-one show on television, I coaxed a hundred yards of upholstery material and canvas through that sorry machine, saving hundreds of dollars outright and adding thousands of dollars of the value to the old boat I owned at the time.

I eventually replaced that machine with a much better one, a commercial-quality tailor's machine, and if I tried to claim that the old machine did as good a job, I would be lying. The tailor's machine—which was also Japanese, by the way—did most things better and everything easier. If it hadn't, what would have been the point in buying it? But with that old machine I did manage to sew awnings and sail covers and settee cushions and every other fabric project I attempted. The point is that almost any domestic sewing machine, even one of doubtful virtue, can do the job if you will help it along. A *good* domestic machine should not need much help.

If you do not have a machine and are going to buy one, there are a few features that you should look for. You want a machine that sews a lockstitch. Because you will be sewing bulky fabrics, more underarm space is always better than less. For canvas, particularly acrylic

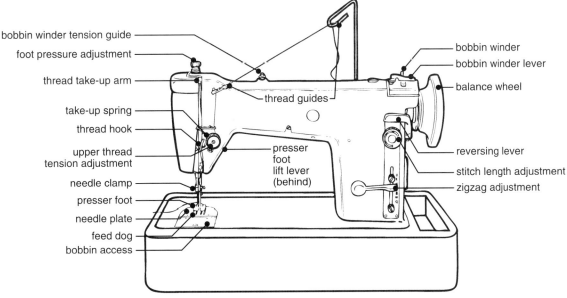

The various knobs and levers.

bobbin winder tension guide
foot pressure adjustment
thread take-up arm
take-up spring
thread hook
upper thread tension adjustment
needle clamp
presser foot
needle plate
feed dog
bobbin access

thread guides
presser foot lift lever (behind)

bobbin winder
bobbin winder lever
balance wheel
reversing lever
stitch length adjustment
zigzag adjustment

canvas, the longer the stitch, the better. Four millimeters is the minimum, and you will get better results with a 6-millimeter stitch—about four stitches to an inch. A zigzag stitch is useful (but not essential) for sail repair, but you will never need a zigzag stitch for canvaswork. If the only sail sewing you expect to do is an emergency repair, buy a straight-stitch machine, which will be more robust and cost a lot less. Only if you want to make or repair your own sails should you opt for a zigzag machine, but before you say, "No way," you might want to read the next chapter. If you are considering a zigzag machine, be sure the stitch width is at least 6 millimeters.

Adjustable foot pressure is mandatory, and a wide feed dog—the toothed claw that drags the fabric through the machine—will make some jobs easier. Some machines have interchangeable feed dogs and matching needle plates—the polished plate around the dog. A fairly recent development is the availability of small machines with a walking foot. A walking foot steps forward on the fabric with each stitch and moves back with the feed dog, effectively gripping the fabric and pulling it through the machine. A walking-foot machine handles difficult sewing jobs better and delivers more uniform stitches. If you are choosing between walking-foot and zigzag, go

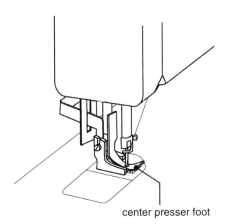

center presser foot

Both feet are down while the machine stitches.

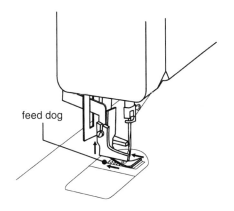

feed dog

The outer foot lifts and the center foot travels back with the feed dog, drawing the fabric through the machine.

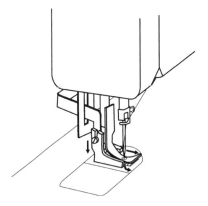

The outer foot drops to clamp the material in the new position. The center foot lifts and steps forward, a mirror image of the feed dog motion down and forward. With both feet down, the machine sews the next stitch.

A walking foot makes every sewing job easier.

with the walking-foot. You will use the zigzag only occasionally (if at all), but the walking-foot model will improve the quality of every one of your sewing projects. If your budget allows, you can buy a walking-foot zigzag machine.

What you don't need is a machine that does 20 different decorative stitches. In heavy fabric you want the machine to drive the needle straight down, so bypass machines with slant needles. Heavy fabric also necessitates a stronger needle, so be sure the machine can be fitted with #20 needles. When you start looking around, don't consult a blue-haired lady in a sewing center at the mall. Find a commercial outlet or a reputable repair shop and tell the salesperson you want a cheap, sturdy machine without any bells and whistles. Emphasize *cheap*. They often take trade-ins or have unclaimed repairs. Old heavy-duty, straight-stitch machines can sometimes be purchased for a pittance. When garment and textile businesses close or purchase new machines, the abandoned machines are often offered in classified ads. For domestic machines, thrift shops, garage sales, and sometimes flea markets can be good sources. The Internet is a possibility if you are trying to find a particular model, but if you are just looking for a suitable machine, you should sew with it before you buy. Carry a piece of acrylic canvas with you, and do not buy a machine that has difficulty sewing through six layers. As you will see, hems can be nine layers thick in the corners, but a machine that easily sews six layers can usually be coaxed through these short areas. As a matter of reference, my tailor's machine will sew through more than a dozen layers of acrylic canvas.

Size might also be an issue. While we had a home ashore I did all canvaswork in expansive, climate-controlled comfort with the machine mounted in a power table, an industrial version of a sewing cabinet. With all stitching in good order when we left, we were unlikely to have a real need for a sewing machine during cruises that lasted just weeks or months, so we chose not to carry the weight, occupy the space, or expose the machine to the marine environment. That changed when our only real estate became rental storage and our cruise had no sunset clause. The sewing machine I took aboard was a new straight-stitch, walking-foot machine (the LS-1 from Sailrite) in a portable case. Small (but not light), this machine has proven to be an excellent choice, stowing compactly on a purpose-built shelf in a cockpit locker. If you are looking for a machine to carry aboard, you may have to give up arm length for case size. As an aside,

the positive feed of a walking-foot machine will be especially appreciated in the confined space sewing on a boat imposes.

If you expect to be messing about in boats for decades to come, I strongly recommend that you do your homework, then spend the extra dollars for a quality sewing machine. Like any good tool, it can return the investment many times over—but only if you use it. So first use the machine you have, one you borrow, or one you obtain inexpensively to do a few of the projects that follow to determine your interest and aptitude.

OTHER TOOLS

A pair of sharp scissors is a pleasure to use. Don't dig out the old rusty pair you use for paper and gasket material. Treat yourself to a new pair just for canvaswork. The new generation of lightweight, vanadium steel scissors with bright plastic handles (Japanese made, of course) are generally excellent, and 9-inch scissors—a convenient size—still cost less than $10.

While you are buying scissors, pick up a seam ripper. This is a little gizmo that resembles an undersized fountain pen when the lid is in place. Under the lid is a metal shank that ends in what looks like a thumb and a pointing index finger. The metal "skin" between these two digits is razor sharp. Slip the finger under a stitch, push the ripper forward, and it slices right through the thread.

A measuring tape and a straight yardstick are essential for the initial layout, and a carpenter's square can be useful. Use a lead pencil or chalk to mark the material. The ink from a marker or pen will bleed through fabric.

Grommets are a common feature of many marine canvas items, and a special die set is required to install them. Washer grommets are sold in hardware stores and chandleries and are commonly used in amateur canvaswork. These are adequate for light duty, but spur grommets—which have a heavy rolled edge and half a dozen spurs that lock the grommet to the cloth—are infinitely superior. The installation of spur grommets is identical to that of washer grommets, and the cost difference between the two

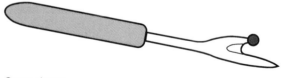

Seam ripper.

is pennies. So why would anyone use washer grommets? Beats me. Probably because washer grommets are more readily available and often sold in a kit that includes a setting tool and a hole cutter. A spur grommet die set should cost $35 to $50, depending on the size. That is about twice what a washer grommet kit costs, but at the risk of sounding like a broken record, a good tool will last a lifetime. As for the cost of the grommets, buy them by the gross and they are inexpensive. They won't spoil.

The most common sizes (measured as the diameter of the hole through the grommet) are $^3/_8$ inch, $^7/_{16}$ inch, and $^1/_2$ inch. For washer grommets these sizes are designated as #2, #3, and #4, respectively. For some obscure reason, equivalent rolled-rim spur grommet sizes are #1, #2, and #3, and the #1 grommet is $^1/_{32}$ more than $^3/_8$ inch while the #3 is $^1/_{32}$ *less* than $^1/_2$ inch. There are undoubtedly logical explanations for these numbering and size disparities but you are unlikely to care. Unless exceptional stress is likely or you need the larger diameter, #1 spur grommets will serve most purposes.

Mechanical fasteners are also commonly used in boat canvas. As we will detail later, twist fasteners are installed with a heated knife and a pair of pliers, but snap fasteners require a special tool for correct installation. The tool most widely available is a contoured die used in concert with a special punch, but if you already own a pair of Vise-Grip pliers, for about the same price as the punch-and-die set you can buy an easier-to-use installation tool that snaps over the jaws of the pliers. Squeezing the plier grips gives you a perfect snap installation every time.

One final item you may find very helpful, especially if you are new to sewing, is a roll of transfer tape. Transfer tape looks a bit like a narrow roll of brown packing tape. You apply it to the cloth like any tape, then carefully lift the paper and peel it away, leaving only the adhesive behind. Transfer tape allows you to assemble two pieces of fabric or form a hem before you take the fabric to the sewing machine. The parts may be peeled apart and repositioned as necessary—kind of like a Post-It note. It is used mostly to assemble the slick Dacron or nylon panels of sails, but it is equally effective on acrylic canvas and other marine fabrics. Basting seams with transfer tape before you attempt to stitch them can make the difference between frustration and disdain.

When you baste seams with transfer tape, you will need to clean adhesive from the needle periodically. Rubbing alcohol will work, but Goo Gone is better.

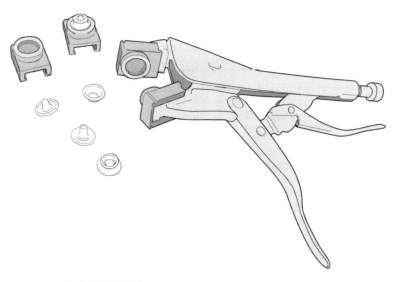

Die set for installing snap fasteners.

GETTING STARTED

The first step in canvaswork is a familiarity with your sewing machine. If you have a manual, read it carefully and locate every guide and screw and lever. If you don't have a manual, try to get one. It not only details the major components, but it will show you how to thread your particular machine and where to oil it—both essential for good results.

OIL OFTEN

Oiling is a good place to start. Don't think a couple of drops of oil in holes in the top of the machine is all that is required. The manual for my tailor's machine

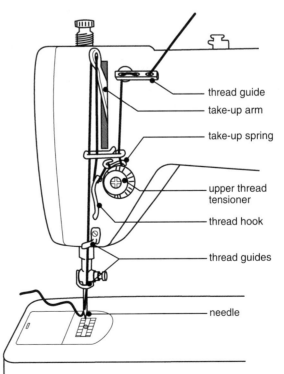

Typical threading sequence. Find out how to thread your machine.

- thread guide
- take-up arm
- take-up spring
- upper thread tensioner
- thread hook
- thread guides
- needle

shows 42 specific oil points, and there are 29 for the machine on the boat. If you don't have a manual, put two drops of sewing machine oil in every hole in the top, sides, and base of the machine. Open the hinged cover on the presser foot end, and put two drops in every hole you see in any moving part and on every round shaft or bushing you see. Tilt the machine on its back; apply two drops to every hole, to both ends of every bushing, and to any exposed gears. With no thread and the presser foot up, run the machine to distribute the oil, then wipe the exterior of the machine. Always oil the machine before you start a project.

It is important to thread the machine correctly. If you do not have a manual, get someone to show you how to thread your machine, and draw a sketch so you do it the same way every time. Virtually all machines pass the top thread halfway around the tension knob and up through the take-up arm before it goes through a guide on the needle clamp and through the eye of the needle, but there can be various fixed and spring guides that the thread must pass through in the proper direction and sequence. Even the orientation of the eye of the needle can vary, with the thread passing through the needle from front to back on some machines and from left to right on others.

NEEDLE SIZE

Needle size will depend on the weight of the fabric you are attempting to sew. As a general rule, the heavier the fabric, the larger the needle. Machine needle designations are logical; i.e., the larger the number designation, the larger the needle. For very light fabric such as spinnaker cloth, a #11 or #12 needle should work well. For medium-weight or loosely woven fabrics such as corduroy, chintz, or oxford cloth, try a #14 or #16 needle. Heavy, tightly woven fabrics such as canvas—both natural and synthetic—and sailcloth require a #18 or #20 needle.

You want ballpoint needles, which tend to shoulder the weave aside rather than pierce the yarns. Buy plenty of needles. They will bend, break, and dull regularly, which is perfectly normal. In fact, anytime you begin to have problems with your machine, the *first* thing you should do is *change the needle.* When a new needle doesn't help, try a larger needle.

THREAD SELECTION

For canvas and upholstery work you are going to need heavy-duty polyester *fiber* thread, not the brightly colored spools of spun polyester found in variety stores and fabric shops. Fabric shops usually do carry some heavier, cotton-wrapped polyester, which is reasonably strong and has the advantage of sewing easily because the cotton surface pulls through the tension devices more consistently. However, polyester fiber thread is much stronger, more durable, and better suited to outdoor applications. Unfortunately the relatively "slick" surface of polyester can lead to tensioning problems, especially with cheaper thread. It is difficult to tell whether a thread will sew well or not just by looking at it. If you can find it, buy bonded Dabond polyester thread. This used to be sold under the brand name Heminway and Bartlett but now it is Coats. If your fabric supplier carries a different brand, I strongly suggest you buy a small cone (1 ounce, or about 1,000 yards) and try the thread before purchasing a large amount. A 1-ounce cone will cost $3 or $4. If you like the way the thread handles and you have several fabric projects in your upgrade plan, you may want to invest in a 16-ounce cone ($25 to $35), which will last you a very long time.

The pigment in black thread protects it (like a coat of paint) from UV damage, making black thread your best choice for stitching that will see lots of sun. You will quickly get accustomed to black stitching, especially when you consider the longer seam life it affords. I have abandoned white thread almost altogether for boat use.

I have also evolved to using only V-92 thread rather than the lighter and weaker V-69 weight. You might find V-69 a tad more forgiving of tension settings, but once you get your machine "dialed-in" to sew with V-92, you will be rewarded with more durable and longer-lived seams. A reasonable alternative is to use black V-92 for your exterior canvas projects and white V-69 for upholstery.

You want "bonded" polyester, not a "soft" finish. You also need left-lay, also called Z-twist, which is more or less standard. Right-lay is called S-twist and will not sew well on your machine. Do not buy thread that is not twisted. Do not buy monofilament thread. Do not buy any thread except bonded polyester Z-twist V-92 or V-69. Getting in tune with your machine can be trying enough without the contribution of the wrong thread.

Unlike spools of dress thread that sit over a pin on the back of the machine and spin as the machine pulls thread from them, cones of industrial thread do not spin. The thread is pulled from the top of the cone, necessitating some kind of guide directly above the cone. One fabricated from coat hanger wire can perform this function perfectly, or for about $6 you can buy a real thread stand with a spindle and a thread guide that sits on your work surface behind

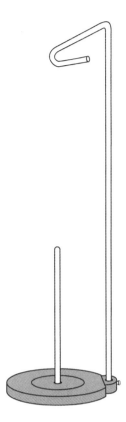

Thread stand.

the machine. Pulling the thread from the top introduces some additional twist that keeps the filaments tight as the thread passes through the machine.

FABRIC

There are tens of thousands of fabrics available in various weights, colors, patterns, weaves, and compositions, hundreds of which are suitable for marine use. Almost any fabric that would be suitable for upholstering a heavily used sofa in the family room could also be used for cabin upholstery, provided it is mildew and stain resistant. Textures, colors, and patterns are more a matter of taste than suitability.

Outdoor fabrics are more limited. Among the materials that you are likely to use are nylon, polyester, reinforced vinyl, clear vinyl, vinyl-coated mesh, and both natural and synthetic canvas. Reinforced vinyl is universal for small-boat upholstery exposed to the weather, but it is not a particularly good fabric for other applications, with the possible exception of bimini tops. Among the sailing set, synthetic canvas—Sunbrella and similar materials—is the dominant exterior cloth. Most of the projects that follow are constructed of either synthetic or treated natural canvas.

Natural canvas is a wonderful material. Even though it is tightly woven, it "breathes," preventing the condensation underneath that breeds rust, rot, and mildew. Yet when the natural fiber—usually cotton—gets wet, it swells, making the cloth completely waterproof. This last part sounds a lot like the way traditional wooden hulls seal. Like these hulls, natural canvas requires special care. It is highly susceptible to mildew and rot, particularly in the marine environment. Other fabrics are almost invariably a better choice.

One alternative is treated canvas, natural cotton duck treated to resist rot and mildew. Treated canvas has most of the best attributes of natural canvas without the worst deficiencies. The best-known treated canvas is boat-shrunk Sunforger (formerly Vivatex), but it is not the only one. Sunforger is available in "natural" colors: colorless (off-white), pearl gray (looks green to me), and khaki. Some other brands offer a wider variety of colors, but these will not have the lasting quality of colored synthetics.

Synthetic canvas is similar in weave and weight to natural canvas, but instead of cotton, the fiber is a synthetic. Nylon is used to make some strong, lightweight, canvaslike materials—Cordura and oxford cloth come to mind—but nylon has a very short life in the sun. Polyester (Dacron) is also subject to UV damage, although deterioration can be delayed with a UV coating. The biggest problem with polyester canvas is that it does not accept dye readily and tends to fade quickly in sunlight.

The best fiber by far for maintaining its strength and color despite constant exposure to the sun and other elements is acrylic. The fade resistance and long life of acrylic canvas has revolutionized the marine canvas industry. My old ketch has spent 38 years under the assault of the tropical or subtropical sun, yet she is wearing only her third set of sail covers. In temperate climes, acrylic canvas displays near immortality. It once seemed to come in only one color—the ubiquitous sail-cover blue—but today is available in dozens of colors and patterns. The original acrylic canvas fabrics were Sunbrella and Yachtcrylic—identical fabrics except that Sunbrella came in a 30-inch width, while Yachtcrylic was 40 or 46 inches wide. Today Yachtcrylic is gone, and Sunbrella comes in 46- and 60-inch widths. The same company, Glen Raven, also makes a slightly lighter-weight woven acrylic under the Dickson brand.

There is a tendency to think that when canvas is the fabric of choice, acrylic canvas is always superior.

That is not necessarily true. Treated canvas has three noteworthy advantages over synthetic. It is water-*proof*, whereas synthetic canvas is water-*repellent*—a major distinction when you are sitting under the drip. Natural fibers are less susceptible to chafe damage than acrylic fibers. And the cost of treated canvas is about half that of acrylic. As for life expectancy, I used the same Vivatex harbor awning for two decades before retiring it in favor of a different design. I am still using the cloth from that awning for other canvas projects.

It is instructive, however, to mention that my satisfaction with a treated canvas harbor awning led me to construct a full boat cover from boat-shrunk Sunforger, which turned out to be a disaster. An awning in the air dries soon after the rain stops, but a cover on deck remains damp. Add a few bird droppings, and the fiber under the treatment reverts to its natural susceptibility to mildew and mold. This cover lasted less than a year. I replaced it with a cover sewn from acrylic canvas that is still sound after a decade of use. The point is that the longevity of treated natural canvas is entirely dependent on the canvas being kept in free air so it can dry and never being stowed damp.

For the initial canvaswork project here I recommend using 10-ounce treated canvas—and not just because treated canvas is a relatively inexpensive material to learn on. It also happens to be the best material for this particular project. You will need from 1 to 3 yards of 31-inch (the most common width) material, depending on the dimensions you choose, but if the price is good, buy a couple of extra yards to make the boat bags described later. If your supplier carries wider material, that will be OK. Also ask about end rolls and remnants. When these are available they can save you quite a few dollars.

A REAL TENSION HEADACHE

Before you start a project, you need to get your sewing machine adjusted for the material and thread you are using. That is generally not very complicated (I did not say "easy"), since you will normally be concerned with only four adjustments.

The first is the dial that adjusts the length of the stitch. Set it to the highest number and forget about it. Shorter stitches are for sissy stuff like taffeta and chiffon, not the two-fisted fabrics you will be sewing. Acrylic canvas tends to pucker from the penetration of the needle and especially benefits from long stitches.

The second adjustment is presser-foot pressure. It is adjusted by pushing a button or turning a knob on top of the machine directly above the presser foot. You won't need to adjust it unless you are having feed problems. Light materials require light pressure or the feed dog will pucker the material rather than feed it. But if the foot pressure is too light, heavy materials will feed unevenly—causing irregular stitches—or stop feeding altogether. Domestic machines often will not feed heavy fabrics regularly without some help from the operator, no matter what adjustments are made, but increasing presser-foot pressure can help. If your machine allows you to set the height of the feed dog, raising it will also improve the machine's ability to feed heavy fabric.

Another problem that might relate to improper presser-foot pressure is skipped stitches in heavy material. A lockstitch sewing machine operates by forming a loop in the thread at the end of the needle, which is picked up by a hook on the rotating shuttle. The loop is formed as the needle lifts, leaving the thread behind. In heavy, tightly woven fabrics, the needle may jam in the fabric and cause it to lift with the needle. When this happens, no loop is formed and the stitch is skipped. Increasing foot pressure prevents the material from lifting.

Bobbin tension is the third adjustment. First be sure you have the bobbin in the bobbin case correctly. On most machines the loaded bobbin winds clockwise (as you look into the open case), but on some it winds counterclockwise. You adjust bobbin tension by turning the tiny screw in the flat spring on the bobbin case. With the wound bobbin in the case and the thread leading out from under the bobbin tension spring, pull on the thread. It should pull out smoothly but with some resistance. If the thread has little or no resistance, tighten the adjusting screw $1/8$ turn. If the thread is hard to pull or feeds in jerks,

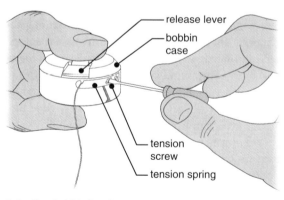

Adjusting bobbin tension.

loosen the screw ¹/₈ turn. Either way, pull the thread again and keep making tiny adjustments until it pulls with smooth resistance. This is an initial setting, and you may have to readjust the bobbin tension after you see how the machine sews.

The last adjustment is the upper thread tension, which after the initial adjustment of the other three, is usually the only adjustment that will be necessary each time you change materials unless the change is drastic. Upper tension is adjusted by looking at the way the machine stitches. So . . .

TIME TO STITCH

If you have never run a sewing machine before, getting someone to show you the basics will be easier than following my instructions. For those of you in isolation, after you have the machine threaded, a loaded bobbin in the case, and the case installed, the first thing is to pick up the bobbin. You do this by holding onto the end of the upper thread and rotating the machine by hand (the top of the balance wheel turns away from you) through one stitch. When the needle is back at its highest point, pull on the thread and it will bring up the bobbin thread. Both threads should always trail behind the presser foot about 3 inches before you start to sew.

You normally use scrap material to adjust the thread tension, but since you don't have any scrap yet, cut a 6-inch square from one corner of your piece of canvas fabric. Fold the square into thirds so you will be sewing through three layers. Slip the short edge of this test panel under the raised needle and lower the presser foot onto the material with the lever on the back of the machine. Be sure the loose end of the thread passing through the eye of the needle leads down through the hole or slot in the presser foot and under the foot, not over the top. Now step on it, dude. If the machine just hums, either sing along or give the balance wheel a little help with your hand to get the needle started. Most machines operate with a foot pedal, but some domestic machines use a knee bar. You will quickly adapt to either.

It is not necessary to sew as fast as the machine will go. You will have better control if you sew slowly. After you sew 4 or 5 inches, stop. Rotate the top of the balance wheel away from you by hand to lift the needle to its highest position or just beyond, then raise the presser foot. Remove the fabric to the left, pulling about 3 inches of thread from both the needle and the bobbin. Snip both threads close to the fabric. Brush the thread ends toward the back of the machine and you are again ready to sew.

Check the stitching to see how to adjust the thread tension. When the tension is correct, the stitching on the top and bottom of the fabric will look exactly the same. If the bottom thread just looks straight, like a piece of wire, with the top thread looped around it, you need more upper thread tension. Turn the tensioning knob clockwise. If it is the top thread that is straight, with the bottom thread looping over it, the upper tension is too tight. Make a small adjustment and sew another line of stitches. Keep testing and adjusting until the interlock between the two threads is buried in the center of the material. There is no other way to adjust thread tension, so just take your time and get it right.

A lot of sewing problems that seem to relate to thread tension are actually caused by using too

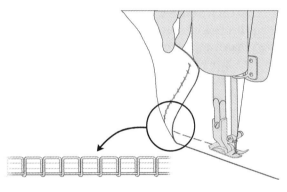

Not enough upper thread tension (or too much bobbin tension).

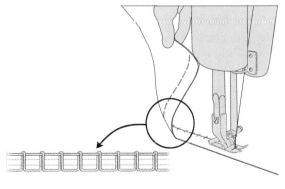

Too much upper thread tension (or not enough bobbin tension).

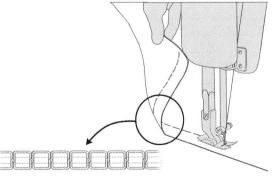

Just right.

Adjusting thread tension.

small a needle. With cotton-wrapped polyester or V-69 polyester thread, start with a #16 needle. If you are using V-92 thread, you should have a #18 needle in the machine. If you seem to be unable to get both threads to pull into the material, try a larger needle.

If the thread starts breaking or the material puckers before you get enough upper tension to pull the lower thread inside the fabric, your bobbin tension is too tight. Loosen it and start all over. On the other hand, if the bottom thread forms a "bird's nest" or you can pull the layers apart and expose the stitching, the bobbin is too loose. Again, adjust and start all over. Not until you have a tight, regular stitch with the interlock buried are you ready to make something.

THE FLAT SHEET

A bunch of useful canvas items for your boat are little more than flat sheets of cloth with the edges hemmed. This is where we are going to start, beginning with a fender skirt. No, I am not talking about a car part found on low riders in East L.A. The kind of fender skirt I have in mind I saw on a 60-foot gold-plater tied up at Pier 66 in Fort Lauderdale. If it is good enough for the idle rich, it ought to be good enough for you. And after all the work you just put into that great finish on the hull, you are going to appreciate my observant nature.

The fender I am referring to is the kind that keeps your hull off the pilings, but fenders have a bad habit of scuffing the hull. Colorful fleece covers have become popular, and coordinated with sail covers and canvas tops, they do look spiffy. But against an oiled piling, a fleece cover works exactly like a fleece paint roller, painting your previously pristine hull black. At low tide the cloth picks up bits of barnacles and other crustaceans, and as the fender rotates, the sharp bits of shell grind into your hull. Bad. Very bad.

The solution is a fender skirt—a flat piece of canvas that hangs from the rail between the fender and the hull. No matter what the fender gets into, the hull is always protected. The gold-plater had a single piece about 30 feet long that protected one entire side of the hull from all of the fenders, but if you only have two fenders aboard, 60 feet of canvas skirt seems like a bit of overkill. The skirts were also acrylic canvas, matching the sail covers, the dodger, and the Jet-Ski cover. If your social standing will be unaffected, treated canvas is a better choice. Aside from the savings, the natural fiber will sustain the chafe of the fender better and will be easier on the hull.

The size of the skirt is up to you, but to protect the hull from a single fender, a skirt 3 or 4 feet long and somewhat less than the distance between the rail and the water in width should be adequate. Add about 4 inches to both dimensions to allow for a $1^1/_2$-inch hem on all sides. If my math troubles you, relax. You need a 4-inch allowance for a pair of $1^1/_2$-inch hems because you are going to turn under an additional $^1/_2$ inch to hide the raw edge completely.

HEMMING

A hem is nothing more than turned-under edge. It strengthens the edge of the finished item and hides the raw edge of the fabric. If we make the hem wide enough, it gives us a double thickness of fabric where we install grommets and fasteners.

To put a $1^1/_2$-inch hem in the canvas, fold over 2 inches of the material and rub the fold firmly with the back of your scissors to crease the canvas. Take the fabric to your machine and run a row of stitching about $^1/_4$ inch inside the fold to hold the hem in place. It is not necessary to draw a line on the cloth to keep the row of stitching straight. Use a reference on the machine. For example, the edge of the presser foot may be about $^1/_4$ inch from the needle, so if you just keep the fold flush with the edge of the foot, the stitches will be where you want them. Many needle plates have reference lines engraved into them that you can use the same way. Or mark the plate with a pencil or a piece of masking tape as a reference.

When your row of stitching is 3 or 4 inches long, stop the machine with the needle buried in the fabric and turn the hem behind the foot over to check the stitching. You adjusted the tension for three layers of fabric, but you are only sewing two. If a tension adjustment is necessary, make it and continue sewing. It is a good habit to check the stitching every time the thickness of what you are sewing changes.

It is also always a good idea to lock the stitches by taking a few stitches in reverse when you start and finish sewing. Start the hem by locating the needle about an inch from the edge of the material. Depress the reverse lever and start the sewing machine, stitching back to the edge. Stop sewing, release the reverse lever, then sew forward to the opposite edge. Depress the reverse lever and backstitch about an inch. If your machine has no reverse lever, you can accomplish the same thing by stitching in from the edge an inch or so, then lifting the needle and the foot, and without cutting the thread, repositioning the fabric to place the needle back at the edge and stitching over the first few stitches. Finish the same way, backing up the fabric and overstitching the last inch.

As long as the feed dog pulls the material through the machine, all you need to do is guide the fabric. I find it easiest with my right hand actually holding the hem just in front of the foot and my left hand palm-down on the fabric to the side of the needle. This allows me to both direct the material and slide it forward.

When the material is heavy and the piece large, it can overpower the feed dog. In that case, the place for your left hand is behind the needle, pulling the material while you feed it from the front with your right hand. You do not want to pull hard enough to slide the material, only hard enough to help the dog move it. It is a skill acquired with practice.

Another such skill is keeping the top and bottom of the hem (or any seam) feeding at the same rate. While the feed dog is clawing the bottom layer of fabric forward, the presser foot is rubbing heavily against the top layer, impeding its movement through the machine. Thus the top layer tends to "crawl," resulting in a wrinkled hem (or an uneven seam). Experienced machine operators learn to counter this tendency, but the easiest solution for the amateur is basting the hem with transfer tape before you sew it. An alternative is to pin the hem with straight pins every 6 or 8 inches, removing them as they reach the front of the foot.

It is here that the extra cost of a walking-foot machine returns the investment. The walking foot moves with the feed dog, pulling both the top and bottom layers through the machine evenly. Aside from uniform stitch length, smoother hems, and even seams, a walking foot can save hours of basting on a complicated project. For fixed-foot machines, there are presser feet that roll over the cloth rather than slide over it. If you can locate one of these to fit your machine, it should improve the feed.

Back to the skirt. After the first row of stitching is in the hem, you want to turn $1/2$ inch of the raw edge under and crease it by rubbing the edge. A hem that is folded twice is called a *double-rubbed hem* or just a *double hem*. Baste or pin this fold if it helps you, and run a second row of stitches $1/4$ inch inside the fold to complete the hem. You are now sewing through three layers, so check the stitching to make sure the thread tension is correct. You might try sewing this second row of stitches with the fold underneath. If the feed dog of your machine is sufficiently wide, it will engage both the bottom layer and the underside of the top layer, feeding both evenly.

You are going to hem the other three edges the same way. Hem the opposite edge first, then the

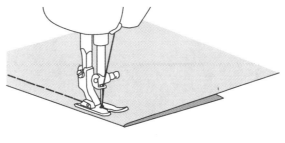

Fold and stitch.

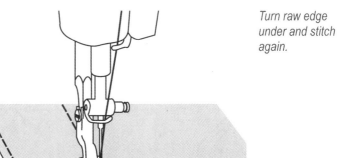

Turn raw edge under and stitch again.

Double-rubbed hem.

two ends. When you do the end hems, it may surprise you to discover that where the inner edge of the end hem crosses the inner edge of the side hem, you have *nine layers* of material to sew through. Fortunately this is a very short section—only three or four stitches—so it should not present any serious problems, although you may have to help your machine across this ridge by turning the balance wheel by hand.

MITERED CORNERS

If your machine struggles here, you can reduce the bulk of hemmed corners in the future (or now if you want to pull out some of your stitching) by mitering them. To create a mitered corner, you need to put the initial fold in both edges that meet at that corner and rub them to crease the material (see next page). Unfold them and cut the corner off diagonally $1/2$ inch beyond the intersection of the creases. Fold this diagonal edge over $1/4$ inch, then over again to create a $1/4$-inch double-rubbed hem with its edge at the two creases. A single row of stitching completes the diagonal hem. Now put your regular double-rubbed hem in the sides. They will not overlap but meet diagonally on the underside of the fabric. This reduces the number of layers of cloth you need to sew through from nine to six, and it gives a flatter corner.

1
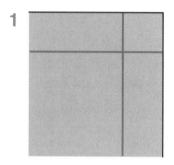
Crease hems to mark them.

2
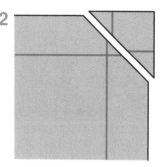
Cut corner diagonally ¹/₂ inch beyond crease intersection.

3
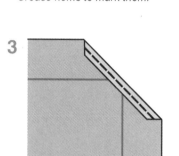
Fold over diagonal edge ¹/₄ inch twice and stitch to form double hem.

4
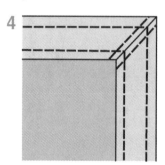
Put normal double hem in sides.

Sewing a mitered corner.

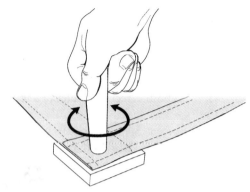
Twist the cutter against the cloth with a wooden block beneath.

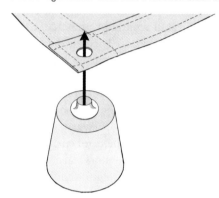
Seat the male grommet in the die and work the hole over it.

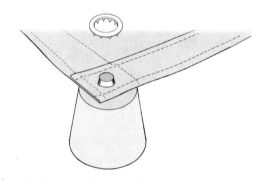
Seat the ring over the protruding grommet.

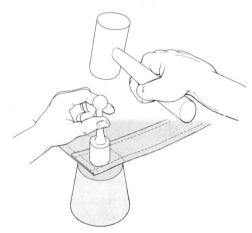
Use the setter and a mallet to set the grommet.

Installing grommets.

INSTALLING GROMMETS

All that remains is to install grommets in the two top corners. In the center of the square formed by the overlapping hems, make a hole with the cutter that accompanied your die set. Note that overlapping hems provide four layers of cloth, which will reinforce the grommet installation. If you made mitered corners, placing the grommet in the center of the miter gives you only a single thickness of cloth completely around the grommet; the other cloth under the grommet only half encircles it. You will get a stronger installation if you offset the grommet to one side of the miter.

The usual instructions are to place the material on a piece of wood and hit the cutter with a hammer, but you will greatly extend the cutter life if you simply twist it back and forth on the material rather than pounding on it. A sharp cutter will slice through several layers of cloth with only a slight twisting action. Never let the edge of the cutter touch anything but fabric or wood. If you're a wimp, you will want to protect the palm of your hand with several layers of folded cloth—uh, so I've heard.

Seat the male half of a grommet on the die and work the hole in the cloth down over the protruding grommet. Put the ring portion of the grommet on top of the cloth over the male half and press it down. Insert the cone of the grommet setter. Making sure the grommet is still seated in the die and the setter is vertical, *lightly* tap the setter with a hammer to roll the edge of the grommet and compress the two halves together. Finally, hit the setter a little harder to set the grommet. If you are using a ring grommet, set it firmly enough so that it will not twist in the cloth, then go back and read the section on spur grommets.

With the two grommets installed, the skirt is ready to use. Hang it with lengths of line stopped in the grommets with figure-eight knots. If you decide to make a long skirt, additional grommets spaced along the top hem will be necessary to support the middle of the skirt.

The treated canvas will protect your hull from stains and scratches, but you can make the skirt even easier on the hull by lining one side with terry cloth. Hem a piece of terry cloth to the size of the skirt, then hold the two pieces together and stitch them along both ends and across the top. Leaving the two pieces open at the bottom will make washing the skirt easier and more effective. It is not necessary to turn under the raw edge of the hem in the terry cloth, except at the bottom, since the other three edges will be hidden when you sew the terry cloth to the canvas. Also leave the terry unstitched above the grommets, running a U-shaped row of stitches around the bottom

of the grommets instead. This will allow you access to the grommets to attach the mounting lines, and the terry will protect the hull from the grommets.

LEE CLOTHS

I remain devoted to the leeboard for staying securely in my bunk at sea, but leeboards tall enough to be secure are not easy to install on all bunks. And for a boat that is only occasionally underway overnight, lee cloths have the advantage of stowing completely out of the way when not in use—which is most of the time.

There are only subtle construction differences between the fender skirt we just finished and a traditional lee cloth. However, the often-damp environment of underbunk stowage rules out treated canvas in favor of something less susceptible to mildew. Phifertex—the vinyl-covered screenlike material that dominates outdoor furniture upholstery—is a popular choice for boats headed toward the tropics because it does not inhibit air circulation, but vinyl in any form feels clammy against bare skin. Sailcloth is another option, but I prefer the feel and mildew resistance of acrylic canvas.

Typically a lee cloth should be a couple of feet shorter than the bunk and stand about 18 inches high in use. That means for a $6^{1}/_{2}$-foot bunk with a 5-inch-thick cushion, you need a piece of canvas $4^{1}/_{2}$ feet long and 23 inches wide, plus hem allowances. Actually you probably need a couple of inches more width to allow for the cloth to be screwed down to the bunk.

REINFORCED HEMS

Hem the canvas just as you did the fender skirt but with one change. To make the attachment points to the bunk very strong, enclose nylon webbing inside the hems of the long sides. Nylon webbing in $1^{1}/_{2}$-inch widths is readily available, but if all you can easily locate is 1-inch webbing, just reduce the width of the

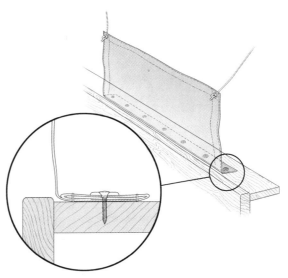

Traditional lee cloth. Enclosing webbing inside the hem provides a very strong attachment point.

Fender skirt in use.

hems to 1 inch. To seal the webbing and prevent it from raveling, cut it with a soldering pistol or a hot knife, or pass the scissored edge through a flame.

Install grommets through the hem and the webbing in the two corners of one long side. Lines from these (a good place to use Spectra) to strong overhead attachment points will suspend the top of the cloth. The opposite edge should be fastened to the wood base under the bunk cushion with oval-head screws and finishing washers spaced about 8 inches apart. Heat the tip of an awl or an ice pick to punch the mounting holes through the hem and enclosed webbing, and to cauterize the perimeter of the holes.

The lee cloth should be installed with the fastened edge away from the edge of the bunk so the cloth sweeps smoothly from beneath the cushion and the pull on the screws is mostly shear, but mounted this way the cloth folds over itself in the stowed position. If this raises the edge of the bunk noticeably, an alternative is to install a boltrope track at the front edge of the bunk and sew a boltrope rather than webbing into the bottom hem. Boltrope attachment makes lee cloth removal for remote stowage easy and practical.

Cut away most of the excess fabric at the corners before stitching.

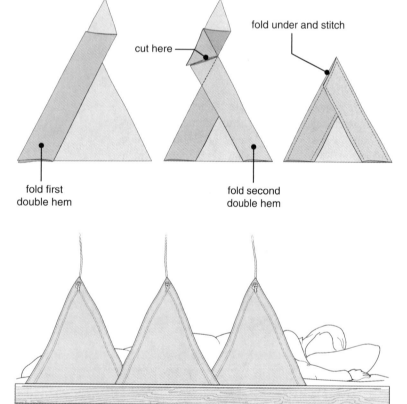

fold under and stitch

cut here

fold first double hem

fold second double hem

Mount the center panel outside the end panels to serve as a gate.

Triple triangle lee cloth.

A BETTER MOUSETRAP

If you expect to give your lee cloths regular rather than rare use, consider a "tri-tri" configuration. Instead of a single rectangle per bunk, you are going to cut and hem three equilateral triangular panels with a cut size of about 37 inches per side, which should give you a finished size of around 30 inches. You can enclose webbing in one hem of each triangle, but I prefer equal double-rubbed hems all around—meaning that instead of folding 2 inches over, then $1/2$ inch under, you fold 2 inches over, then 1 inch under. This gives you triple thickness around the full perimeter. You will find that the 60-degree corners get kind of messy, with lots of extra cloth beyond the hem. In general you will need to just cut off the extra cloth, leaving enough to turn under and stitch down. Do this trimming when you rub down the second hem, not after you sew it.

You are going to attach one edge of each triangle under the bunk cushion. Because woven cloth is stable with the grain of the fabric (i.e., parallel to the threads) but stretches and distorts when pulled on the bias (diagonal to the threads), the attached edge must be the one parallel to the weave of the cloth. (If you are reinforcing an edge, this is also the one you must reinforce.) Install a grommet in the corner opposite the edge that will be attached. This type of lee cloth is installed as a set of three, with the middle one overlapping the other two in such a way that it is outside the end panels when the cloths are in use to allow the middle panel to serve as a kind of gate. Whether that means the middle panel is screwed down first or last depends on whether you elect to put the fastened edges toward the front of the bunk or away from it. The amount of overlap is determined by the length of the bunk but should not be less than 6 inches. Triple triangle lee cloths provide better ventilation, easier bunk access, and generally better support than the traditional rectangle.

WEATHER CLOTHS

Enclosing a cockpit with weather cloths can provide its occupants considerable protection from wind and spray. Weather cloths also provide a good deal of additional privacy. And a lot of sailors just like their salty look.

Acrylic canvas is the best fabric for weather cloths. To determine the size you need, measure the distance between stanchions and from the caprail to the top lifeline (or the underside of the handrail). A single cloth may pass around several stanchions if you choose. If the stanchions are not vertical—where the lifelines attach to the stern pulpit, for example—measure the horizontal distance at the top and bottom.

Cut the canvas exactly to the dimensions you measured, with no allowances for a hem. Following

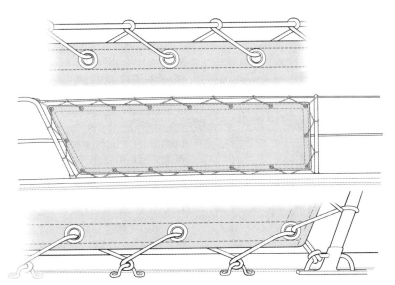

Lace weather cloths to lifelines and strap eyes with half hitches.

this method the completed cloth will have 2 inches of space all the way around it, allowing the canvas to be stretched tightly when it is laced in place. If you want less space, add to the dimensions of the cloth accordingly before you cut it to size.

Hem the four edges of the weather cloths with double-rubbed hems exactly like those on the fender skirt. Even if one end of the cloth attaches to a curved railing, you will be wise to keep the hem of the cloth straight, accommodating the curve with the lacing. Because of the stiffness of canvas, curved edges are difficult to hem attractively.

CURVED HEMS

A convex curve can be hemmed by making evenly spaced darts—small, triangular pleats—in the hem to take up the extra material that accrues when the curved material is folded back on itself. With a curved hem the sequence of stitching also changes. First fold the raw edge over ¹/₂ inch and sew it down, putting darts in the folded edge as necessary to get it to lie flat. Then fold the 1¹/₂-inch hem and stitch it ¹/₄ inch from the edge, spacing the darts that form evenly. Finally, sew a third row of stitches along the inside edge of the hem to close it, completing and sewing down the darts that were started when you stitched the outside edge.

A concave curve is more difficult to hem because the problem becomes a shortage of material, not an excess. The solution is a second piece of material. Using the curve of the cloth as a pattern, cut a matching strip of material 2 inches wide. Along the convex side of this strip, fold the raw edge over ¹/₂ inch and stitch it down, putting in darts as necessary. Now with the stitched fold on top, lay the curved strip on top of the weather cloth so the raw curved edges match exactly and stitch the two pieces together ¹/₂ inch from the edge.

Starting anywhere along this curved edge, use your scissors to make a perpendicular cut to within about ¹/₈ inch of the row of stitches you just made. Make a similar

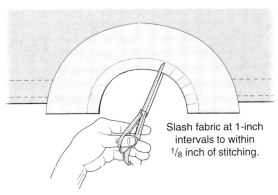

Cut a hem strip to match the cutout and stitch the two together ¹/₂ inch from the raw edge.

Slash fabric at 1-inch intervals to within ¹/₈ inch of stitching.

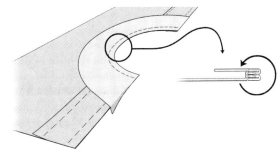

Fold the hem strip to the opposite side to put the slashed raw edge inside.

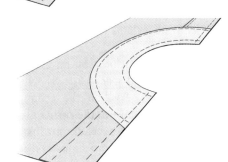

Fold under the raw edges of the hem strip and sew down to complete hem.

Hemming a concave cutout.

Putting a single hem on a curved edge.

Slash a concave curve to allow the raw edge to lengthen when the fold is made.

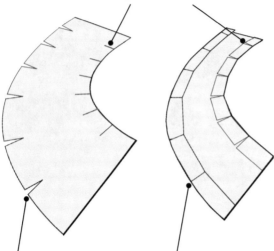

Notch a convex curve to allow the folded raw edge to shorten without bunching excess fabric.

cut every inch along the curve. These slashes allow the edge of the cloth to expand when you fold it and make the seam lie smooth. Be very careful not to cut any closer to the stitching than $1/8$ inch. If part of the edge is straight, slashing is not necessary in the straight portion.

Now fold the strip over to the other side of the cloth. If you have done it correctly, the seam between the two pieces now forms the curved edge, which appears finished from both sides, with the raw edges inside. Stitch the inner edge of the strip down to finish the hem. Hemming the piece in this manner reduces the hem allowance from 2 inches to $1/2$ inch—the amount of weather cloth that is actually turned under.

Darts don't work very well on stiff fabric, so you should use this same method to put a neater hem on a convex edge. The difference is that you will need to slash the inner edge of the strip to hem it rather than sewing darts into it, and after the strip has been sewn to the cloth, you will make a series of 90-degree V-cuts in the edge rather than slashes. The V-cuts remove excess fabric that would otherwise bunch up inside the hem. The best approach is to stick with straight hems on all sides of weather cloths and you won't have to get into this at all.

Finish the weather cloths by installing grommets in the corners and spaced 6 to 8 inches apart along all four edges. Position the grommets by dividing the distance between the corner grommets into equal spaces. The weather cloths are installed by simply lacing them to the stanchions and lifelines. Strap eyes screwed to the deck or the inside of the caprail provide the attachment point for the lower lacing. The eyes should be positioned between the grommets.

FLAGS

Flags probably do not qualify as boat enhancements, but they do illustrate another flat-sheet canvas project and can give you an opportunity to tune your sewing skills productively.

Flags can be made from almost any fabric. Commercially produced flags are usually made from nylon because it is light, strong, and accepts dye well. Four-ounce oxford cloth is a good choice for signal flags or pennants. Yellow is the color for your first flag.

Aside from the material, a single-color flag differs from a fender skirt or a weather cloth mostly in the size of the hems. There is no standard size for flags, but a common size aboard pleasure boats is 18 inches on the hoist by 24 inches on the fly. The hems on three sides need not be any larger than $1/2$ inch, but on the hoist where the grommets will be installed, you will need at least a 1-inch hem. Taking into account the additional $1/2$ inch that will be turned under to hide the raw edges, you need to cut the cloth 20 inches by $26^{1}/_2$ inches to end up with an 18-by-24-inch flag.

Begin by hemming one of the long sides. Fold $1/2$ inch of the cloth over, then fold it $1/2$ inch again to put the raw edge inside. Sew the hem down by stitching as close to both edges of the hem as you can. If slippery cloth gives you trouble, this is a good place to try transfer tape. Hem the opposite side in the same manner, then put a $1/2$-inch double hem on one end of the flag. When you hem the end, you can make the corners neater by putting a diagonal fold on the ends of the hem. Make the first $1/2$-inch fold for the hem, then fold the two corners at a 45-degree angle. Now make the second fold to complete the hem. Stitch down both sides and the diagonal ends of the hem. Note that this is not the same as the mitered corner described earlier; this corner will be stronger—a good thing on a flag whipping in the wind.

This is a good place to learn to change directions while you are sewing. Stitch along one side of the hem until you are near the end, then make the last two or three stitches by turning the balance wheel by hand. When the needle reaches the stitch line you want to sew—usually $1/4$ inch from the edge of the material, but less in this case—stop the machine with the needle buried in the cloth. Lift the presser foot and turn the material, using the needle as an axis, until the new stitch line lines up with the needle. Lower the presser foot and continue to sew. With this project, since the distance along the diagonal edge of the hem is just two or three stitches, continue to operate the machine by turning the balance wheel with your hand. When you reach the stitch line on the opposite side of the hem, stop with the needle down, raise the foot, rotate the cloth, lower the foot, and sew along the edge of the

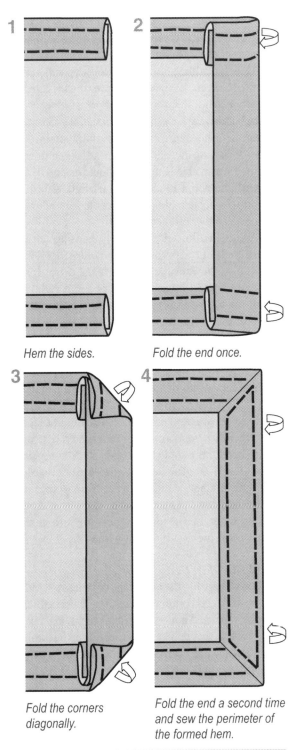

Hem the sides.

Fold the end once.

Fold the corners diagonally.

Fold the end a second time and sew the perimeter of the formed hem.

Sewing a diagonal corner.

1-inch webbing inside the seam, just as you did for the bottom hem in the lee cloth. Try installing the webbing by placing it so that $1/2$ inch of it is lying on top of the raw edge of the flag and stitching down the center of this overlap. Now flip the webbing over onto the cloth, then flip it again. The webbing should be enclosed inside the cloth. Stitch around the perimeter of the hem, about $1/4$ inch in from the edges. All that remains to finish the flag is to install grommets about an inch from either end of the hoist hem.

There may be a minor shortcoming in these instructions. Of the 40 flags and pennants in a set of international flags, only one is a single color. Fortunately it is the solid yellow Q (quarantine) flag, which will serve you well if you are going foreign . . . until it is time to hoist the flag of your host nation. Want to guess how many countries have single-color flags?

Intricate designs are usually embroidered or appliquéd onto a flag of the basic color. Appliqué is not terribly difficult, involving cutting out the design (twice) and stitching it to both sides of the flag, usually with a zigzag stitch to finish the raw edges. Fortunately lots of courtesy flags have simpler designs—two or three colors combined in stripes, blocks, and/or triangles—and these are best made by stitching together the material into the appropriate pattern, then hemming the patterned piece into a flag.

SEAMING

The easiest way to join two pieces of fabric is to overlap their edges and stitch them together. This is called, logically enough, an overlap seam, but it leaves the raw edges exposed and they will ravel—unless they happen to be the ravel-resistant factory edges called *selvages*. Cut edges should be joined with

hem until you reach the other end. Make the turn to sew the diagonal edge at this end, then turn to put the machine back in line with the original stitch line. Sew forward an inch or so onto the initial stitching, then backstitch a few stitches to finish.

Your flag will last much longer if you reinforce the hoist seam with webbing. Enclose a length of

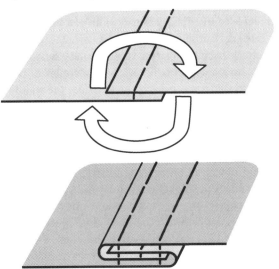

Overlap fabric edges the desired width of the seam and stitch together.

Fold the top piece under, the bottom piece over. Stitch along both folds.

The flat-felled seam.

a *flat-felled* seam, especially where both sides of the material being joined will be visible. Curl your fingers on both hands as tightly as you can at the second knuckle. Now turn your left hand palm-up and your right hand palm-down and interlock your fingertips. This is the way a flat-felled seam interlocks.

To join two pieces of cloth with a flat-felled seam, overlap the two pieces the width you want the seam, typically about $1/2$ inch. Stitch down the center of the overlap. Fold the top piece under at the overlap and the bottom piece over. Finish the seam by stitching along both edges. You may want to turn the fabric over for the last row of stitching so you can see the folded edge. Transfer tape makes perfect flat-felled seams easier.

CURTAINS

Boat curtains are yet another flat-sheet item. Typical boat curtain installations have some type of track above and below the portlight with tabs sewn to the curtain sliding in or on the tracks. Spacing the tabs equally forces the curtain into attractive pleats when they are open. Curtains made longer than the track also have a pleated look when closed.

Fabric choices for curtains are extensive. To ward off confusion we generally go to a department store or two and look at their curtains and drapes, pick something we like, then buy the smallest panel available. For some unknown reason packaged draperies are often cheaper than the price of an equivalent amount of material from a fabric shop. Washable material is a good idea, but because our curtains are also over the galley, we give priority to fireproofing and usually select a fiberglass material.

The dimensions of the material will depend on the length of the tracks, the distance between them, and whether the curtains will comprise a single panel or multiple panels. The horizontal width of a simple slide-pleated curtain should normally be twice the length of the track, but if the material you are using is heavy, such curtains can appear bulky when they are open. With bulky material you may choose to reduce the width to $1^1/2$ times the length of the track or less. Less width also makes sense for curtains that will rarely be closed.

If the portlight (or portlights) will be covered with two panels meeting in the middle, each panel would obviously be half the total length. Curtains for tandem portlights often look nice divided into three panels, one at each end and one that covers the fiberglass between the portlights. Making each panel a third of the total gives the best look when the curtains are open, but do not be surprised that when they are closed, the panels do not meet in the center

of the portlights. If this upsets your sense of symmetry, then make the center panel half the total length and each of the side panels a quarter.

The vertical height of the panels depends on the distance between the upper and lower tracks. Curtains typically extend about an inch above and below the tracks, but this varies with the nature of the fabric. For all of these measurements I am assuming preinstalled tracks. If you do not already have tracks, numerous systems are available. The tracks should extend beyond the portlights about 10% of the total length (20% if the curtain will be a single panel)—enough to allow the curtains to gather off the portlight.

Add hem allowances to the dimensions already determined. Side hems need not be wider than 1 inch, so a 3-inch allowance (don't forget the extra $1/2$ inch that turns under) for each panel is about right. The size of the top and bottom hems will depend on the height of the curtains. Two-inch hems are appropriate for curtains covering portlights. Taller curtains covering or framing large saloon windows will look better with 4-inch hems.

You may want to line the curtains if the material you have chosen is an open weave. If you bought a packaged curtain and it is lined, you can use that lining. Otherwise you can buy lining material at most fabric shops. Lining curtains adds some complexity but not much. Cut the lining to the same dimensions as the curtain fabric, and stitch the two together with a row of stitches $1/4$ inch from the raw edges around the perimeter of the panel. Fabricate the curtain exactly the same as if it were not lined.

INSTEAD OF WHALEBONE

The secret to getting the tops of the curtains to stand up is a size-stiffened cotton or linen material called *buckram* or *crinoline*. Another advantage of buying a packaged drape is that you can often press the buckram it contains flat with a hot iron and reuse it. Otherwise, you will need to purchase a length of this stiffener. It usually comes in 4-inch widths, but you are more likely to need half that. No problem. Cut it to the width you want.

The buckram goes inside the top and bottom hems. For curtains 10 to 20 inches high, a 2-inch stiffened hem is about right. The easiest way to install the stiffener is the same way we installed reinforcing webbing in the flag hoist. Place the curtain fabric and the buckram side by side with the curtain fabric facedown. The top (or bottom) raw edge of the curtain should butt against the buckram. Lift the edge of the buckram and slide it onto the fabric $1/2$ inch; stitch down the center of the overlap. With the fabric

Overlap stiffener ¹/₂ inch onto backside of fabric and stitch.

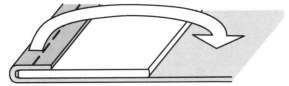

Fold tightly once.

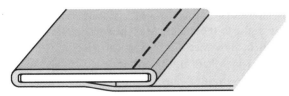

Fold tightly a second time and stitch along the inner fold only.

Sewing in curtain stiffener.

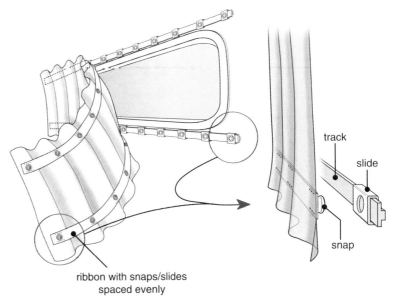

ribbon with snaps/slides
spaced evenly

track
slide
snap

Self-adjusting pleats.

still lying flat, flip the buckram over onto the fabric. Flip it again. You now have a hem, albeit unstitched, with the stiffener inside. Run a row of stitches ¹/₄ inch from the inside edge of this hem. It is not necessary to stitch along the outside edge, and the curtain will have a nicer appearance without the second row of stitches. Turn the panel around and install stiffener in the opposite edge in the same manner. Hem the two sides and the curtain is finished.

All that remains is to attach the slides to the curtain. The end ones should be inboard from the edge an inch or two. Between these two, place a series of equally spaced marks—usually between 3 and 5 inches apart—on the stiffened hems. Determine the exact distance by pleating the panel with your fingers to see what size pleat looks best to you. Be sure the marks are even and the correct distance from the top and bottom of the panel for the slides to fit into the tracks, then sew the slides in place.

SLIDE GEOMETRY

For curtains that will be closed often, you may want to make the pleats self-adjusting. All that is required is a length of ribbon or bias tape. Before you sew the slides to the curtain, cut the bias tape to the length between the end slide locations when the panel is closed; write down that length. Now count the number of *spaces* between the marks for the slides on the curtain. Divide the length of the bias tape by the number of spaces, using the result to mark the tape into the same number of spaces, with the beginning and ending marks at the ends of the tape. Pin the tape to the curtain, matching each of the marks. Now sew the slides in place, sewing the tape to the curtain at the marks at the same time. When the curtain is open, the pleats are always even because the space between the slides is the same—none. The tape holds the slides evenly spaced when the curtain is closed, maintaining even pleats.

Curtains that attach to a single track or a rod and hang free at the bottom are constructed in the same manner with some minor differences. First, the buckram is omitted from the lower hem so the fabric will hang naturally. Second, pleats are often formed by sewing them into the top hem rather than as a result of the location of the slides.

STITCHED PLEATS

Both pinch pleats and box pleats begin in the same manner. On the back side of the curtain, mark the stiffened upper hem into equal divisions of around 2 inches. Starting at one edge, fold the hem so that the first mark is face-to-face with the third one. The second mark will be in the center of the fold. From the top of the hem, stitch straight down through the two marks, joining them permanently. The stitching should extend about ¹/₂ inch beyond the bottom of the hem. Fold the hem to join the fourth and sixth marks and sew in the next pleat. Do the same for marks seven and nine, and so on until the hem is completely pleated.

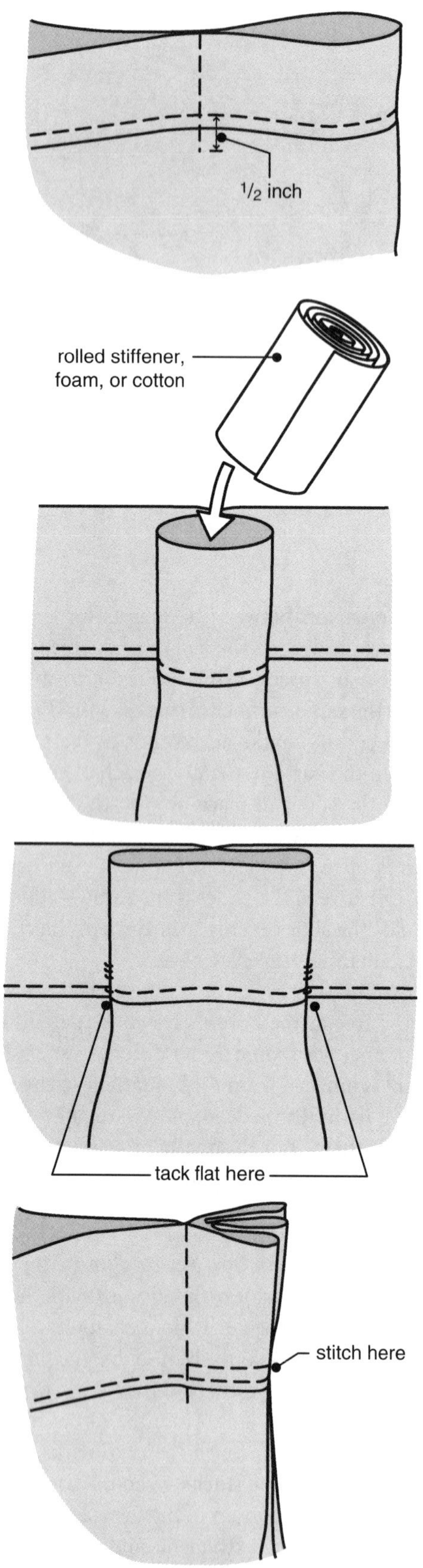

Basic pleat.

1/2 inch

Stuffed or cartridge pleat.

rolled stiffener, foam, or cotton

Box pleat.

tack flat here

Pinch pleat.

stitch here

Stitched pleats.

To make the pleats attractive, they need to be stuffed, boxed, or pinched. *Stuffed* is just what it sounds like. A roll of stiffener or a bit of cotton or foam is inserted into each pleat to give it body. You *box* a pleat by flattening it so that the center—mark #2 on our first pleat—lies against the vertical seam joining #1 and #3. To maintain this flattened shape, you tack the pleat's two edges to the curtain at the hemstitch line with a couple of hand stitches. *Pinch* pleats are made by accordion-folding the single pleat into three smaller pleats and tacking them together by hand, again at the hemstitch line.

Lining free-hanging curtains is also slightly different from lining dual-slide panels. Instead of cutting the lining to the same size as the curtain fabric, omit the hem allowances for the vertical height dimension. Put a 1-inch hem in the bottom edge of the lining. With the unlined curtain already hemmed at the bottom and the buckram stitched and folded into the top hem but the hem not yet stitched down, align the two bottom hems, turned-under side to turned-under side, with the bottom of the lining about 1/2 inch shy of the bottom of the curtain. The side edges of the lining should match the edges of the curtain and the raw top edge should overlap the stiffened and still-unstitched top hem.

Trim the lining as required to reduce this overlap to 1/2 inch. Lift the enclosed buckram and let the raw edge of the lining fall under it, then place the edge of the hem back on top of the lining. Making sure the lining is still aligned with the ends of the curtain and 1/2 inch short of the bottom, sew the hem down, capturing the lining at the same time. Finish installing the lining by stitching both sides 1/4 inch from the edge. The lining is not attached at the bottom, allowing it to hang independently of the curtain. Complete the panel by hemming the sides and pleating in the manner you prefer.

WIND CHUTES

Everyone has a favorite wind chute, and mine happens to be a flat sheet. Besides being easy to make, its advantages are that it is big (funneling in the lightest zephyrs); it is easy to rig and store; and when rain comes unexpectedly, I can close the hatch without involving the chute. The disadvantage is that the boat has to face more or less into the wind, a problem at the docks and in anchorages subject to strong currents. Despite that, this design has done an admirable job of cooling our cabin in the tropics for three decades.

Commercial windscoops are typically made of lightweight nylon—flag cloth or spinnaker cloth. These are strong and light and fill easily, but when there is a crosscurrent in the anchorage or if the boat sails on her anchor, nylon chutes are as noisy as used-car-lot pennants. The chute described here fits over the forward hatch and gets its shape from the way it is rigged, not the wind, so the best material is acrylic canvas. The only noise a canvas chute makes is the rattle of the S-hooks that attach it to the deck, which you can eliminate with lashings if you like.

To adapt this chute to your boat, open the forward hatch to its normal open position, or about 45 degrees if the support is adjustable. Place a piece of stiff paper—about 3 feet wide will probably be about right—on the top of the hatch and slide the paper down until the edge touches the deck behind the hatch. Now fold the paper over the side edges of the hatch and crease it with your fingers where it reaches the deck. Cut the paper along the crease line. What you are after is a three-sided paper lean-to that sits flat on the hatch when the three sides are sitting flat on the deck. This is the pattern for one end of the chute.

If your hatch is square, the width of this chute will be about $2^1/_2$ times the width of the hatch. That makes the chute for a 20-inch hatch about 50 inches wide. If the hatch is not square, you will need to measure the perpendicular distance from the top of the open hatch to the deck just forward of the hatch opening—perpendicular to the *hatch,* not the deck. If the hatch is open to 45 degrees, this measurement will be about 0.7 times the side length of the hatch,

as you would know if you had been listening instead of daydreaming back in trig class. Chute width is twice this distance plus the hatch width. For cut size you will need to add a 4-inch allowance for the side hems. As with horseshoes and hand grenades, close will probably be good enough.

The height of the chute depends on how high above the deck you want it to stand. I used the scientific method for the original design—the cloth I used was 41 inches wide, insufficient for the width or the height and necessitating a seam. If I made that seam horizontal rather than vertical, I could eliminate nearly all waste, provided I made the chute 82 inches high, less whatever was lost in seaming and hemming. There you go: $E = mc^2$.

This doesn't mean that because Sunbrella is 46 inches wide, you have to make the chute 92 inches high. Actually, if you are buying fabric just for this project, you might want to buy 60-inch width and eliminate the seam altogether. As a matter of reference, if the chute is 7 feet (84 inches) "tall," because it tilts forward at about 45 degrees, the actual vertical height is just under 5 feet. It's that 0.7 thing again from trig class. This is the height above the deck the hatch is in, so if you have a trunk cabin, the height above the foredeck might be taller, depending on the sheer of your boat at the bow.

Assuming 46-inch fabric and a 20-inch hatch—60-inch is not always easy to obtain in all colors—you start this chute by seaming two 54-inch-long pieces of cloth together (you can adjust this according to your own width calculations plus seam allowance). Because the edges of the cloth have selvages, an overlap seam is fine. If despite my wise counsel you are using spinnaker cloth, you are going to discover that its slick surface makes it a pain to sew, so you will need to use transfer tape on this seam and all the hems. Overlap the two pieces 1 inch and run a row of stitches near each edge of the seam.

If you have a zigzag machine, an overlap seam is a good place to use that capability. Set the stitch for the widest zigzag and run a row of stitches down the center of the seam to secure it. Now stitch along both edges. The needle should penetrate both pieces of fabric on one side of the stitch and should be just beyond the edge of the seam on the other. This is the same way your sails are assembled.

You now have a piece of material that's approximately 91 × 54. Place the center of the paper pattern on the center of one end of the material and trace

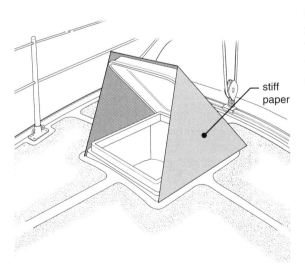

Make a paper pattern for the wind chute's deck end.

stiff paper

Cut one end of fabric blank according to pattern.

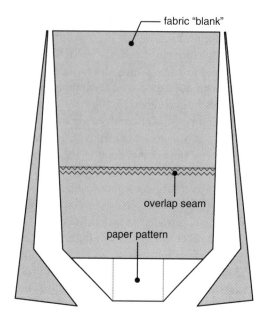

fabric "blank"

overlap seam

paper pattern

Hem all edges except forward end. Install spreader-tie grommets.

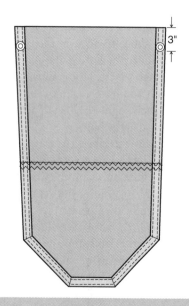

3"

Cutting out and hemming.

the chute in position over the open hatch so you can decide on the final height. You won't go far wrong with 84 inches (plus a 3-inch allowance for the sleeve).

The top of this chute needs a stiff spreader, not a flexible batten. I like $3/4$-inch aluminum conduit for this. You can stitch the spreader inside the spreader sleeve, but a removable spreader lets you easily launder the chute and stow it during off-season. The following instructions are for an open $2^1/_2$-inch sleeve, which is nothing more than a hem with the ends open. But before you sew this sleeve, install grommets in the two side hems, locating the aft/lower edge of the grommets 3 inches back from the raw edge of the chute. When you fold over and rub down 3 inches of the fabric to create the sleeve, you want the edge of these two grommets to be at the fold. Now fold and rub $1/_2$ inch of the raw edge under to create the completed sleeve. Since you have not and will not sew the outside edge of this hem-*cum*-sleeve, you need some way to keep the inside edge straight while you stitch it. You can baste it with transfer tape, pin it, or just put a guiding pencil line on the fabric and keep the edge on the line while you sew. Be sure you backstitch at both ends.

Slip the aluminum tubing in the sleeve, and with the fabric stretched to full width, mark the length of the tube. On the tube, mark the location of the two grommets now in the ends of the sleeve. Remove the tube, cut it to length, and drill $3/_8$-inch holes at the outside edge of the grommet marks. Be sure these two holes are parallel, not out of alignment on the circumference

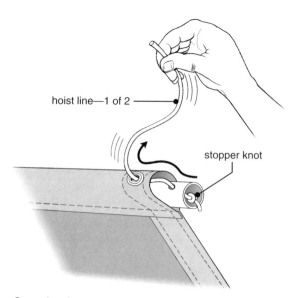

hoist line—1 of 2

stopper knot

Spreader sleeve.

the angled sides of the pattern onto the cloth. With a straightedge, extend these angled lines to the edges of the cloth. If your hatch support is not adjustable, the chute will probably set better if you move these angled lines about 3 degrees toward being perpendicular to the end when you redraw them with your straightedge. Cut the material along the two lines, which will trim off the two corners.

All that is really left is to put a $1^1/_2$-inch hem in the five sides and a hemlike spreader sleeve in the top edge. Hem the five sides first, then get someone to hold

of the tubing. Round their edges with a bit of emery cloth.

At the bottom end of the chute, install grommets in the hem at each of the four corners formed where the angled edges intersect the sides and the bottom. Install brass S-hooks on these four grommets, and close the top of each S enough to secure the hooks to the chute. To mount the chute you need four small strap eyes screwed to the deck at the four corners of the hatch. If my instructions have been adequate, these eyes will correspond with the four grommets at the bottom of the chute. Hook the S-hooks onto the strap eyes.

On my own scoop I recut the hem between the two center grommets into a tall half circle to open up the back of the scoop when the hatch is closed. This allows the wind gusts that probably led to the closing of the hatch to escape out the bottom of the scoop without straining seams and creating too much windage. Whether you need this relief valve depends on how you use your scoop.

Back at the top end, slide the spreader into the sleeve and align the holes with the grommets. Feed a length of $1/4$-inch braided polyester line through the grommet and the hole and out the end of the spreader on each side (a separate line for each side). Tie a figure-eight stopper knot into the spreader end of each line and pull the knot inside the tube. These are the hoist lines. Rigged this way they also tension the chute across the spreader.

Hoist options are numerous. If you have a hank-on headstay, the easy way is to put bowlines in the ends of the two hoist lines and attach them to the jib halyard, snapping the halyard around the forestay at the same time. Hauling the halyard hoists the chute, which, because the bottom folds around the hatch opening, now appears funnel shaped. Rigging the hoist lines to a single snap hook or shackle that is also rigged with a loop for the halyard shackle cleans up and simplifies the hoist. For a roller-furling headsail you will need to make a 4-inch-wide canvas strap with D-rings or grommets in each end for the lines from the chute. A lift ring stitched to the top of the strap in the middle allows it to be hoisted against the furled headsail. The spinnaker halyard may be substituted for the jib halyard.

Adjust the length of the hoist lines until the chute is tight and lays flat on the top of the hatch. In effect, it becomes an extension of the open hatch, but with approximately 10 times the wind-gathering capacity. With this chute flying, you are going to need extra glue for your toupee.

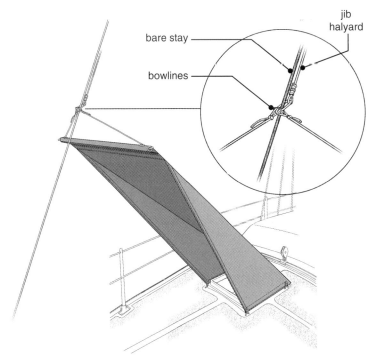

View from forward.

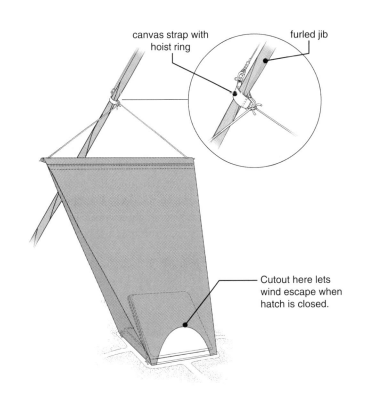

View from aft.

Hoisted chute.

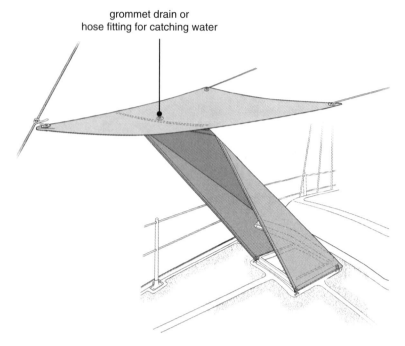

grommet drain or
hose fitting for catching water

*Wind chute
Mark II.*

MARK II

By the time my original chute expired, I had long wanted to eliminate the spreader so the stowed chute could be folded compactly instead of being rolled and needing a long stowage space. The solution turned out to be simple and effective. I simply constructed a triangular awning that spread tightly between the headstay and the forward lowers, then configured the chute so the top edge was sewn to the underside of the awning. This design has a number of advantages. No halyard is involved; the awning is simply rigged to the stays with rolling hitches and to a strap around the headsail with half hitches. The awning in front of the chute provides some additional rain protection for the open hatch, and the awning behind the scoop provides cabin-cooling shade on the deck. The downward pull of the chute draws the tight awning into a pagoda shape, necessitating a grommet just behind the chute

attachment to drain the awning, or you can install a hose fitting here and use the awning to catch water.

MARK III

There are chute designs that will catch the wind from every direction. These typically take the form of a fabric box around the hatch, out of which emerges two vertical panels stitched together vertically in the middle and pulled into an X when seen from above. The lower ends of the panels are attached to the corners of the fabric box, and the upper ends are held in the X shape with crossed spreaders and typically a tentlike fabric top that deflects rain and provides for hoisting. The idea is that no matter which way the wind hits the chute, two sides of the X catch it and send it below. These work fine as long as you can get the lid of your hatch completely out of the way, but they offer a relatively narrow profile to the wind, meaning they are better at redirecting a breeze than they are at gathering it. In contrast, the chute already described presents a generous profile, gathering even the lightest air and concentrating it into a breeze through the cabin.

Still, when the bow faces away from the wind, the sides of a forward-facing chute collapse, not only losing their wind-catching ability, but actually blocking the wind and preventing it from going below. This characteristic leads directly to the Mark III enhancement, which is rather ingenious if I do say so myself. Instead of having a solid side panel, I cut a triangular "window" in both sides of my chute that approximates the triangle defined by the open hatch lid, the hatch coaming, and the forward edge of the side of the chute. I stabilized this window with a couple of vertical and horizontal canvas strips, like dividing the window into panes, but a "screen" of netting or open mesh would work as well. Then I covered each of these windows with a triangular canvas flap slightly larger than the window and stitched that to the inside of

*Mark III: sixteen
compass points
of wind gathering
capability.*

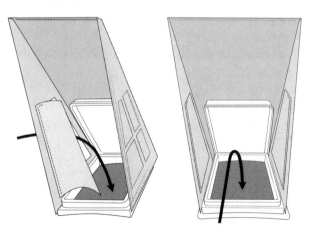

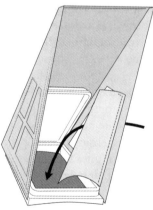

the chute along the forward edge and an inch or two across the top for added support.

When the wind blows from the bow, it holds the flaps closed and the chute works exactly as it did before the flaps, but when the bow faces away from the wind far enough for the wind to get outside of the side panel, it blows the flap on that side open. The one on the opposite side remains closed so the breeze is caught and directed below. This change has no effect when the wind gets behind the beam, but it vastly improves the performance of the chute at anchor. OK, it isn't relativity, but it's pretty good.

AWNINGS

The simplest awning is a flat sheet of canvas, hemmed on all four sides, with grommets on the corners. It is installed by stretching it over the main boom and tying the corners out to the rigging or the lifelines. More complex designs have spreaders, center lifts, and side curtains, but they all begin life as a flat sheet.

WHAT FABRIC?

Despite the proliferation of synthetic fabrics, when it comes to a harbor awning I still remain solidly in the treated canvas camp. Lightweight nylon awnings snap and pop like a flag caught in a gale. Polyester (Dacron) is not much quieter, and neither of these materials offers much protection from the sun's harmful UV rays, which is the whole point of the darn thing in the first place. What good is an awning that acts like a broiler?

Reinforced vinyl "boat top" fabrics such as Weblon Regatta, Stamoid, and lots of others—those usually white on top, blue on the bottom vinyls that are always popular for powerboat tops and are sometimes seen on sailboat biminis—are far more satisfactory on framed tops than as rigged awnings. Vinyls are heavy and bulky, and because the vinyl coating does not breathe, it tends to remain damp, making folding and stowing a problem and mildew a given.

Acrylic canvas is an excellent awning material but with four serious drawbacks. It is usually selected as much for its vivid colors as for its durability, but color is the first liability. Anyone contemplating a sun awning constructed from royal blue, forest green, what-were-they-thinking black, or any other dark-colored canvas has never sat under such an awning in the tropics. The heat under a dark awning is nauseating. Any color absorbs the heat, conducting it to the air below the awning, but the lighter the color, the less heat is absorbed. It is the same reason you wear light-colored clothes in summer.

Why not acrylic canvas in a light color? Good idea. Sunbrella offers oyster, linen, and buttercup.

Or if you want to make a statement, how about the striped sunflower/white fabric? All of these will be way more comfortable to sit under on a hot day. But a relatively modest 12 × 15 awning will require 25 yards or more of 46-inch fabric. If you have a set of curtained awnings to shade the entire boat in mind, expect to need three times that amount. The cost premium of acrylic canvas over treated canvas will be $5 to $6 per yard—drawback number two.

An acrylic canvas awning will be watertight when it is new, but after a couple of years it will leak like Snuffy Smith's roof. It can be reproofed with a spray treatment, but the need is still a demerit. And if you are using the awning to catch water, you won't know the proofing has expired until the heavy rain you have been waiting for arrives and dishearteningly drips right through the fabric instead of flowing into your tanks. Then you need the promise of at least a couple of dry days for reproofing. And there is the question, at least in my mind, about what effect these foul-smelling treatments have on the quality of the otherwise-pure water, particularly when the proofing is fresh.

The fourth problem with acrylic canvas is its susceptibility to chafe damage. Awnings often lay across or against something, and if the contact goes unnoticed or the awning is left unprotected, a patch will be required in short order.

Woven polyester fabrics coated with either urethane (Sur Last) or acrylic (Top Gun, Odyssey III) also make good awnings, but they let UV rays pass through unless they're protected with a dark pigment, a lose-lose choice. These fabrics also become less watertight over time. Woven polyester offers better abrasion resistance than acrylic, but it suffers more from sun exposure.

Treated canvas is chafe resistant, waterproof, relatively inexpensive, and readily available in a heat-reflecting, glare-reducing off-white (colorless) color. It dries quickly for easy stowage. It also provides excellent UV protection, although it pays for this ability by sacrificing itself. And it is strong enough to survive high winds, durable enough to last a decade or more of normal use, and will resist mildew as long as you are vigilant about stowing it dry. The defense rests.

There is one caveat. The fiber in treated canvas is cotton, which lacks the UV resistance of polyester and especially acrylic. This same criticism applies to cotton compared to polyester in clothing, but only a masochist would choose polyester over cotton for tropical wear. Still, if you anticipate sitting for months at a time with the awning rigged, the shorter life of a treated canvas awning will dilute its lower initial cost; all of the other benefits will endure. If longer life is your most important consideration, go with acrylic canvas.

DESIGN CONSIDERATIONS

The first step in building any awning is to settle on a design. Will it be a tent awning supported by the boom and tied to the lifelines? Will external spreaders be used to reduce the pitch of the awning and improve headroom? Will it be flat and held rigid with spreaders inside sleeves or simply by stretching it between main and mizzen rigging? Will it extend from the mast to the backstay, or will it be shorter? Are the aft lower shrouds in the way? What about the topping lift? How will you make it easy to rig? Will it be strictly a harbor awning or used underway? (We logged hundreds of miles between Bahaman anchorages in the shade of the main awning by simply rolling out the genoa—not performance sailing, but effortless and comfortable.) Awning designs are as varied as the boats they shade, and you will need to resolve all of your design considerations before you start.

The next step is to arrive at the dimensions. If the awning will be supported by the boom, measure the length along the top of the boom. Less chafe and more headroom will result from stretching the awning above the boom. To determine the length of such an awning, tie a line between the mast and the backstay (or between the masts on a ketch or yawl) at the height you want the ridge of the awning. Measure along this line from the mast to the topping lift (if your boat has one) or to the backstay or mizzen mast. The maximum length of the awning will be several inches shorter than this dimension to allow for some inevitable stretch.

If the end of a topping lift–supported boom is sufficiently short of the backstay, it may be advantageous to design the awning with a hole for a lift that can be disconnected or a slot for one that is permanently attached, so the awning can extend beyond the lift.

Width dimensions are determined by measuring from the ridge rope to the lifelines. Again, the maximum width will be at least 3 or 4 inches less than the measured dimension to allow for stretch and sag. If the awning will have spreaders, its width will be determined by the length of the spreaders (or vice versa). On our 10-foot-wide boat, we spread a 12-foot awning with external spreaders.

As you measure for your awning and decide how it will be shaped and attached, sketch it on

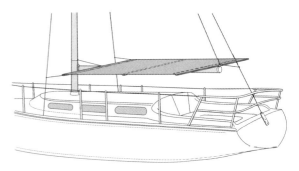

Flat with internal spreaders.

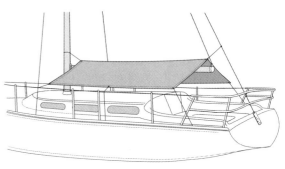

Tent.

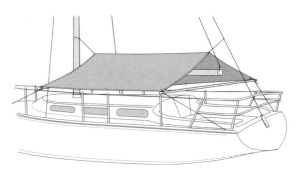

Tent with external spreaders.

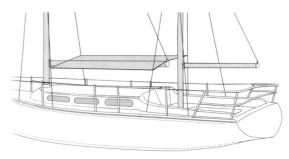

Flat between masts.

Awning possibilities.

paper and note the measurements. I like a 1¹/₂-inch hem turned under 1¹/₂ inches to give the awning triple thickness around the full perimeter. If you rope the awning, a 2-inch hem with ¹/₂ inch turned under will be better. When the ends of the awnings

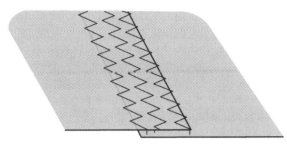

A triple-stitched overlap seam.

have sleeves for internal spreaders, the combination of hem and sleeve will be at least 7 inches wide. Add the appropriate allowances for hems and/or sleeves to your dimensions.

Begin the actual construction by sewing together panels to form a sheet of canvas large enough for your awning, including the hem allowances. Treated canvas (marine-finish boat-shrunk Sunforger) typically comes in 36- or 42-inch widths, acrylic (Sunbrella) in 46- or 60-inch widths. Cut the panels to the width dimension of the awning, including allowances plus 3 inches, which I will explain later. Join the edges in athwartship seams to achieve the needed length. A $1/2$- or $3/4$-inch flat-felled seam here will yield a strong and neat bond, but since the edges have selvages, you can also join the panels in the same manner as the panels of a well-made sail—with a triple-stitched overlap seam. This is a good choice if you have a zigzag machine. The zigzag does not make the seam any stronger, but it does keep the edges from turning up. Overlap the panels 1 inch and stitch down the middle of the overlap with your widest zigzag stitch.

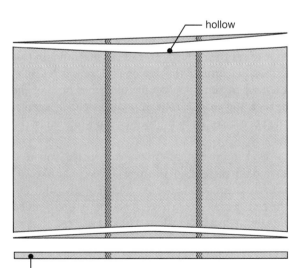

hollow

set aside 3"-wide strip cut from one edge of blank

Hollowing edges will quiet the awning.

Run the second row of stitches along the edge of the top panel, with one side of the stitch penetrating both panels and the other side just beyond the edge of the panel. Turn the material over so the other edge of the overlap is visible, and run a similar row of zig-zag stitches along this edge.

Once the panels are stitched together, cut a 3-inch-wide strip from one side and set it aside, then trim the awning blank to your cut size. It is also a good idea to trim the sides into a slight hollow—like a leech hollow on a sail—to keep the edge from motor-boating in a breeze. About 1 inch of hollow for every 6 feet of side length should be enough. Fold over the hems (and sleeves) on all sides and press the folds to mark them, but do not stitch them.

REINFORCEMENT PATCHES

A well-built awning should be almost bulletproof, which means it needs to be reinforced at every point of stress, specifically at the attachment points. Typically an awning is attached in at least six locations—at the center of both the front and rear edges and at each of the four corners. It may have additional attachment points spaced along the sides, and some awnings have a lift point—sometimes two—in the middle along the centerline. Each of these points will benefit from rein-forcement patches.

Again, let's take a lesson from the sailmaker. Tri-angular patches in the corners and half-circle patches along the edges will avoid stress concentrations and make the awning set better. Two additional layers of material should be adequate. The awning could be sandwiched between matching patches, but it will have a better appearance if you keep the patches on the underside, cutting one an inch or so smaller than the other.

The patches will be less liable to wrinkle if the grain of each patch matches the grain of the fabric where it will be installed. In the case of triangular corner patches, that means the threads run parallel to the two perpendicular sides, not to the diagonal. From extra material cut two 4-inch squares and two 6-inch squares along the weave, then cut the squares diagonally corner to corner to make eight triangu-lar patches in two sizes. Place a smaller patch in one of the corners, aligning the equal sides with the fold lines. The hem will later be stitched on top of the patch. Use transfer tape or pins to hold this patch in place, then put one of the larger patches on top of it, aligning this one with the hem fold lines also. The diagonal edge should lie just less than $1^1/_2$ inches beyond the first patch (that 0.7 thing again!). Turn

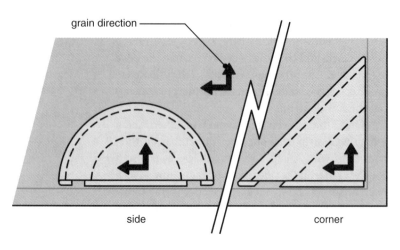

grain direction

side

corner

Reinforcing patches.

$^1/_2$ inch of the diagonal edge under, and $^1/_4$ inch from that edge, run a row of stitches across the patch to attach it to the awning. One inch toward the corner from the first row of stitches, run a parallel line of stitching, sewing both the top patch and the one underneath to the awning. Reinforce the other three corners the same way. There is no reason to sew the other two edges of the patches. They will be sewn in when the hems are.

For each edge patch, cut two half circles, one about 2 inches larger than the other; 4- and 6-inch diameters will be adequate. Be sure the grain of the cloth is parallel to the straight side. As detailed previously, put a series of evenly spaced V-cuts in the circular edge of the larger patch, then turn $^1/_2$ inch of that edge under and sew it down. Notching the edge yields a smoother hem. Center the smaller patch over the attachment point—the eventual location of a grommet—and align the straight edge of the patch with the fold line for the hem. Place the larger patch on top (raw edge turned under), and attach the reinforcement to the awning with a line of stitching $^1/_4$ inch from the circular edge. Run a concentric line of stitching 1 inch from the first row to sew both patches to the awning.

Lift-point patches can be rectangular, but cutting off or rounding the corners will better distribute the stress. As with the corners and edges, use two patches, with the larger one covering the smaller one.

ROPED EDGES

The next step is to stitch the hems down. If you put a triple-thickness hem all around, that will be more than adequate for all but the most severe conditions, but if you want your awning to be absolutely stormproof, rope the perimeter. Sewing rope into the hem represents almost no additional work (the hem

has to be sewn anyway), and it should add less than $30 to the construction cost of a 15-foot awning. Use $^1/_4$- to $^3/_8$-inch low-stretch polyester rope. Nylon rope has too much stretch, allowing high stress to be borne by the canvas. Determine the length of the rope by measuring around the entire perimeter of the awning and adding about 6 inches.

You need a zipper foot to sew the rope inside the hem. Rather than a hole or slot in the center, a zipper foot has a notch in one or both sides for the needle to pass through, allowing the machine to sew right up against a zipper or, in this case, a boltrope. If you have an adjustable foot, adjust it so the needle runs in the notch on the right-hand side of the foot. Beginning a yard or so from one corner on the leading or trailing edge of the awning, fold the hem over the boltrope and stitch right against the rope, capturing it inside the hem. Leave about 1 foot of the rope sticking out where you start. If the rope will fit under the foot, it is a good idea to sew through the rope for a few inches to fix it in place so you can stretch it tight as you sew it into the perimeter. Otherwise make a few stitches with a hand needle to capture the end. Continue stitching right around the awning until the entire perimeter is roped, stopping about 1 foot before you reach your starting point.

Stitching around the corners will present some problems, because the front of the foot encounters the rope before the needle reaches the new stitch line. If your machine has adequate space under the foot to allow it to travel over the boltrope, you can make the corner as usual, pivoting the material around the buried needle. Many domestic machines have insufficient clearance. In fact, when you are finished sewing in the boltrope, you may have to remove the foot to get the material free of the machine. In this case, stitch around the corner as closely as possible, then when you are a couple of inches beyond the corner, tug on the rope enough to pull it against the corner stitching but not enough to pucker the fabric.

When you are back where you started, you need to join the two ends of the rope. The seamanlike way is to cut them with about 6 inches of overlap and join the ends with a short splice. If you have used braided line or are just less zealous, cut and seal the ends so they mate, then hand-stitch them together with a dozen or so long loops of waxed twine. Finish sewing the rope into the hem, then stitch this end of the rope to the canvas the same way you did the other end at the start. With the regular foot back on the

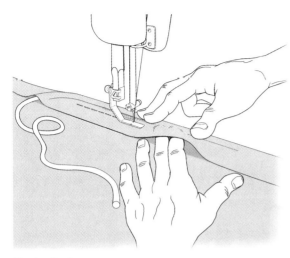

Roping the hem.

machine, turn under the raw edges of the hem and stitch them down.

RIDGE ROPE

If your awning will not be supported by the boom, you will need a ridge rope sewn in to provide support. Here again, you need the low stretch of polyester, and $^3/_8$-inch rope will provide more rigid support than will smaller line. A ridge rope that extends beyond each end of the awning as lanyards doesn't tension the awning, just the rope, and you are certain to be faced with installing a new line when the lanyards wear out. Making the ridge rope entirely internal by looping it around the awning's center grommets is a pain. The best way of installing a ridge rope is to measure the distance between the two centerline grommets (I know they're not actually there yet, but you know where they will be). Now make up your ridge rope by splicing eyes in both ends around nylon thimbles so that the eye-to-eye distance is the same as the grommet-to-grommet distance.

A too-common method of installing a ridge rope is to fold the awning in half (underside to underside), slide the rope into the fold, and run a row of stitches against it. It is a popular method because it is easy. Perhaps it is adequate for a light-duty awning, but all the stresses on an awning with a ridge rope installed in this manner will be concentrated on that row of stitching. To get an idea of what I mean, pull on the sides of a piece of note paper to see if you can pull it apart. Now fold the paper in half lengthwise and run a row of staples $^1/_2$ inch in from the fold. Unfold it and pull on the two sides again. If you're lucky, your expensive awning will fail less dramatically.

To avoid this problem, leave the awning flat and enclose the ridge rope under a separate piece of material. This is where that 3-inch-wide strip of canvas you set aside earlier comes in. If you have been wondering why we cut it from the assembled blank and not just from one edge of the fabric to start with, it is because that would have cut away the selvaged edge and prevented assembling the awning blank with overlap seams.

Start the ridge rope installation by folding the awning exactly in half and running a pencil inside the fold to mark the location of the ridge rope. Open the awning. Turn under $^1/_2$ inch at one end of the strip and sew it to the underside of the awning so the center of the strip will be centered over the pencil line when the strip encloses the ridge rope. This will be easier to do if you temporarily place the rope on the line and position the strip over it tightly. Mark on the strip where the stitch line against the rope will lie and also mark the position of the edge of the strip on the awning. Remove the strip and rope, and lightly extend the mark the full length of the awning parallel to the center line. This is where the raw edge of the strip should be as you place a line of stitching in from that edge the distance of the mark you made on the strip. When you near the end, cut off any excess and turn the end of the strip under $^1/_2$ inch before completing

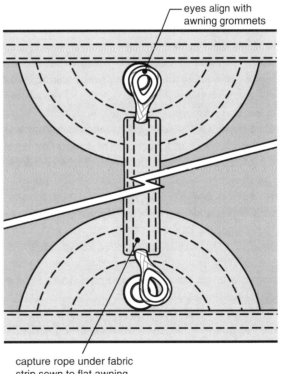

eyes align with awning grommets

capture rope under fabric strip sewn to flat awning

A well-configured ridge rope supports the awning and carries most of the strain.

the seam. Put the ridge rope between the strip and the awning, and use the zipper foot to place a second row of stitches against the rope on the other side of the strip. This should capture the rope exactly over the centerline of the awning. Reinstall the regular foot to fold under and sew down the raw edges of the strip.

All that remains is to install grommets in the reinforcing patches and to rig the lifting point if you are using one. Most awnings can benefit from being hoisted in the center. The traditional method of rigging a lift point is to install grommets on either side of the ridge rope and reeve a strop that passes under the rope, but the grommets are, in effect, holes in the roof when it rains. I prefer a flat triangular tab with a grommet in the apex and sewn to the centerline of the awning at its fore-and-aft center. Cut two canvas triangles about 10 inches on their longest side and 4 inches tall. Stack them and sew them together along their equal sides, then turn the "pouch" you will have created inside out, smoothing the seams. Turn the remaining raw edge of each triangle under—inside the pouch—and sew this edge closed. Continue sewing right around the perimeter of the triangle. Install a grommet in the apex; sew the long side of this triangle to the awning as close to the centerline as the ridge rope allows and centered fore and aft. If the stitching falls on the hem of the fabric capturing the ridge rope, as it should, this will provide all the reinforcement required.

SPREADERS

When spreaders are required, I prefer external ones because they allow the awning to peak, making it less prone to pocketing water. They also subject the awning to less chafe. My first external awning spreaders were $1^5/_8$-inch wooden dowel—closet rod widely available from lumberyards in 12-foot lengths. Later I converted to telescoping tubing to get the stowed poles off the deck. From a tubing supplier I bought aluminum tubing in two sizes that would slide together. A bolt through drilled holes held them extended. To prevent the tubing from cutting the lanyards, I cut off 3 inches of the solid ends of the old spreaders and turned half of each down to fit into the ends of the tubing. Had I been making new ends instead of adapting old ones, I would have made them from aluminum.

There are lots of ways to attach external spreaders, but none simpler than this one. One inch from each end, drill a hole the size of the lanyard line (usually $^1/_4$ inch) completely through the spreader (side to side, not end to end!). The holes must be on the same plane, not twisted in relation to one another. From the end of the spreader, make two saw cuts to

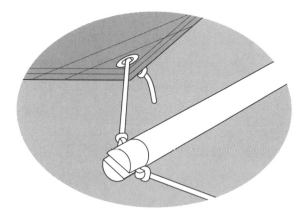

External spreader attachment.

the drilled hole to create a slot the width of the hole diameter. Sand or file the slot to smooth it and to take the sharp edge off the remaining half circle of the drilled hole. Sand the front of the slot into a bit of a flare to facilitate slipping a line into it. A couple of inches from where each lanyard attaches to the awning, tie in a figure-eight knot. When you stretch the lanyard over the end of the spreader and drop it into the slot, the knot holds it in place. Tie off the loose end of the lanyard, usually leading both down and aft or forward, to a stanchion or the rail or whatever. Hoisting the center of the awning will tighten the fit.

Sleeves are required for internal spreaders. The end sleeves present no problem, since they are simply larger hems with the ends left open. Sleeves for spreaders across the middle of the awning are fabricated in a manner similar to the way the boltrope is captured. Stitch a strip of canvas wide enough to accommodate the spreader to the bottom of the awning; turn the raw edges of the strip under before attaching it. To avoid the necessity of sewing across the ridge rope, make center sleeves in two sections,

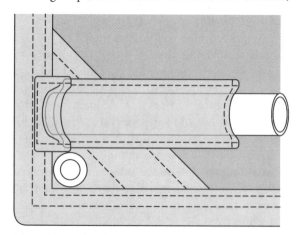

Internal spreader sleeve. A shallow overlapping pocket captures the spreader end.

leaving several inches of the middle of the spreader exposed. Spreaders are most easily captured inside the sleeve with shallow patch pockets at each end that just overlap the sleeve.

A tip to make grommet attachment easier is to allow for both the sleeve and a hem at the ends. If you need a 5-inch sleeve, allow $7\frac{1}{2}$ inches of material. Fold the allowance over and stitch along the fold, then 2 inches from the fold to form the hem. Turn the raw edge under and stitch it down to form the pocket inboard of the hem. Grommets can be installed in the hem.

BELLS AND WHISTLES

If a hole is required for the topping lift, protect the edges of the hole from chafe with a leather binding. *Binding* here simply means folding a strip of material—vinyl, cloth, or leather—over the raw edge and stitching it. The binding will both finish the edge and protect it.

A slot for a permanently attached lift can be closed with snaps, twist fasteners, or a zipper, but if you can still tie your own shoes, the strongest and easiest can be a simple lacing between two rows of grommets. Whatever method you use, a flap with a Velcro edge is required to cover the slot and prevent it from leaking.

Thousands of variations and modifications are possible. Zip-on or snap-on (or lace-on) side panels can keep out the afternoon sun. Screen panels can provide protection from insects. A trapezoid foredeck awning can lower cabin temperatures and allow the forward hatch to remain open even when it is raining. A hose fitting in the lowest spot of an awning can make it as valuable on rainy days as it is when the sun shines. The fact is, your idea of the "perfect" awning is likely to evolve with experience. For example, our current awning is much smaller than earlier versions, exactly filling the modest space between the main and mizzen shrouds. It is normally rigged flat to present only an edge to the wind, allowing it to be left up without concern in any weather that does not induce stripping the boat of other canvas; when rain is possible, we pull the center down rather than up, creating a 100-square-foot catch basin. Zip-on side curtains keep out early-morning and late-afternoon sunlight, but the relatively short life of plastic zippers, even those protected from direct sunlight by a flap, would lead me to choose a rope and track attachment next time. There will be a next time, and that awning will be different from this one. Give your own use ample thought before you start, then make an awning that most satisfies your requirements.

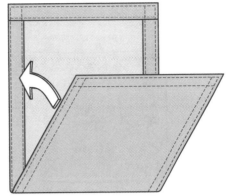

THE ENVELOPE

A number of useful canvas items are nothing more than folded flat sheets with the sides hemmed together—envelopes.

Flat sheet to envelope.

The simple storage pocket typifies the canvas envelope. Dimensions will depend on what the pocket will contain and where it will be mounted, but exact measurements are not necessary to understanding the concept. Put a double-rubbed hem in all four edges of a rectangle of canvas. Now fold the rectangle in half—well, not exactly in half. Instead of bottom edge to top edge, the bottom edge should be about 3 inches below the top. Run a line of stitches on either side to stitch the "halves" together. Put grommets in the top corners and hang the pocket against the hull or inside a locker; it's perfect for pot lids, pill bottles, or personal stereos.

The choice of fabric for a storage pocket depends on its use and location. The most versatile fabric remains treated canvas because of its durability, but the vivid colors and UV resistance of acrylic canvas make it a good choice when the pocket will be visible or outside. Some upholstery materials have the prerequisite stability to make attractive pockets and may make an exposed pocket less obtrusive. For the stowage of light items, 1.5-ounce spinnaker cloth is hard to beat. Linens and clothes will benefit from the unrestricted ventilation afforded by storage pockets sewn from open-weave Phifertex.

BINDING

To cut down on the bulk of the hems where the two sides of the envelope are stitched together and to make the construction quicker and simpler, you may want to bind the edges rather than hem them. Binding involves no more than folding binding tape into a U, with the raw edge of the fabric inside, and stitching it in place. Binding tapes come as flat braid (like soft, thin webbing), double-folded fabric, vinyl, and probably other forms. If you are using Sunbrella you

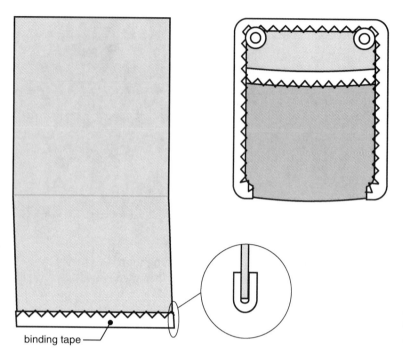

binding tape

Flat blank to envelope. Binding eliminates the need to hem raw edges.

can buy matching cloth or braided binding, but for this application plain black or white braid from your local fabric outlet will usually serve. If your machine will sew a zigzag stitch, that is the better one for attaching the binding.

If you are going to bind the pocket, you don't hem *any* edges. That also means your cut size and finished size are the same—no hem allowance for the outside dimension (you do have to allow for the $1/2$-inch side seams for the inside dimension). Start by binding the edge of the fabric blank that will become the front lip of the pocket. Fold the fabric to place the bound edge the desired distance below the top, then bind the three raw edges of the envelope, stitching the sides together at the same time. The bottom corners will be more secure if you continue the binding around them and an inch are so onto the folded bottom. Or you can bind the entire perimeter of the envelope, including all of the folded bottom. Binding can be easier if you radius the corners. Turn under braided or woven binding tapes where they end or overlap. You can make overlap less noticeable on vinyl tapes by cutting the end on a diagonal before stitching it down.

TOOL ROLLS

The best way to stow hand tools on a boat—better than boxes, racks, or drawers—is in canvas tool rolls. Rolls are easy on the tools (and the boat), keep them quiet, provide instant accounting, and can be stowed almost anywhere. The only fabric choice is treated canvas. Specifically I like a heavy canvas such as #10 (14.73-ounce) or even #8 (18-ounce) vat-dyed, olive

drab shade 7, cotton duck. Besides wearing like iron, the cotton fiber in treated canvas is absorbent, so if you wipe the tools lightly with oil before holstering them, the fabric will absorb the oil, providing a measure of long-term rust protection. Acrylic is not absorbent, but what makes acrylic canvas especially unsuitable is that the sharp edges of tools soon chafe through it.

The tool roll is just a basic envelope with vertical dividing seams to separate the tools, but there are some modifications to the standard pattern that will make the envelope better suited for tools. Let's make a roll for a set of wrenches.

Lay the wrenches out side by side; use a cloth measuring tape or a strip of fabric measured against a ruler to determine the distance from the supporting surface over the widest part of the wrench and back to the surface for each wrench. Add $1/2$ inch to each of these measurements to provide some extra room in each pocket and write down the measurements in order. Add all of them together and add 3 inches to the sum—1 inch for the side seams and an extra 2 inches you will need to align the short side with the diagonal flap that works best on a set of tools of decreasing length. Your final sum will be the cut width. The cut length should be about 3 inches longer than twice the length of the longest wrench.

Fold the material into a pocket deep enough to contain the largest wrench but with the jaws at the open end exposed. Crease the canvas to mark this fold, then put the rest of the wrenches—big end down—side by side in the pocket in size order. Seat them all in the fold, then fold back the top edge of the front of the pocket diagonally to expose the top ends of all of the wrenches; you should be able to easily identify the sizes and to grip each wrench to extract it from the pouch. Rub down this fold to crease it, then cut the fabric on the crease. Bind this edge.

Refold the pocket and place all of the wrenches in it in order, with the largest wrench close to one edge. Fold over the top of the back of the pocket to form a closing flap. When a tool roll holds tools of similar length, this flap is square, but for a wrench set, you need a diagonal flap that will contain both the long and the short wrenches. The fold of the flap should lie just above the top edges of the wrenches. You can fold it and mark it, or mark it and fold it—your choice. Trim the flap parallel to the fold to have a more or less even 3-inch overlap of the front of the pocket.

Once you have the flap creased and trimmed, remove the wrenches and lay the roll flat, with the pocket and flap folded. Draw a straight line parallel to the short side and 2 inches in from it across the exposed pocket and the diagonal flap. Cut the pocket

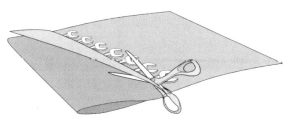

Cut the front edge to match the lengths of the tools the pocket will contain.

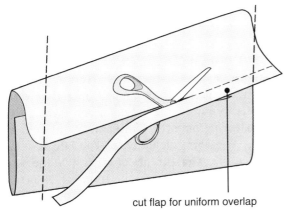

cut flap for uniform overlap

Trim the short side of the pocket to align the side of the flap. Trim the flap only on the long side.

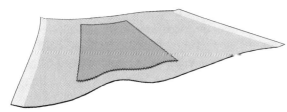

Stitch a leather chafe strip into the pocket centered on the bottom fold to add years to the life of the roll.

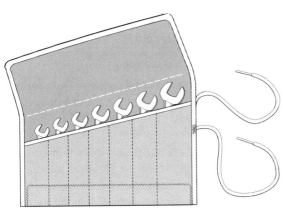

Add vertical stitching between tools and stitch a sneaker lace to the long side seam to complete the roll.

Constructing a tool roll.

and flap straight on this line. This should align all or most of the flap at this side. Trim the *flap only* on the opposite side to straighten it with the pocket edge.

Lining the bottom of the pocket with leather will add years of life to a roll for heavy tools. Before the final folding and stitching, center a 3-inch-wide strip of soft leather over the fold crease and sew it down all the way around with long stitches close to the edge.

The leather bottom is optional. With or without it, refold the pocket and bind all the raw edges, seaming the pocket sides at the same time. Do not continue the binding onto the bottom fold of the tool roll. Stop at the bottom and backstitch each end to reinforce the seam there. Across the bottom of the pocket, just above the fold, place a series of marks corresponding to the series of measurements you wrote down earlier for the individual pocket widths. Make a light pencil line perpendicular to the bottom through each mark and extending to the front lip of the pocket. Sew along each of these lines, backstitching to start and finish.

All that's left is to stitch a sneaker shoelace to the longer side seam. Lay the shoelace perpendicular across the hem on the back side of the roll and a bit above the center from bottom to top; sew across it (inside the seam) three or four times. This is the tie for the roll. I also like to close the flap and stitch as close to the fold as possible to "train" it to close. Insert the wrenches, fold the flap over them, roll them tightly, and tie the roll closed with the lacing.

If you find the result as satisfying as I have, rolls for other wrench sets, as well as for pliers and screwdrivers and chisels and punches, make great winter projects for keeping the dream alive. I even stow my socket set in a canvas roll.

SHEET BAGS

The basic envelope made from acrylic canvas can also be a useful pouch to keep sheets contained and out of the way. A slightly altered envelope makes for a somewhat neater installation on flat surfaces. Instead of folding the canvas and stitching two sides to form the envelope, you are going to cut the front and back separately and seam them together on three sides.

The dimensions will depend on the bulk of the sheets you want the bag to hold and the mounting space available, but for this description I have settled on a 17-inch-wide by 9-inch-deep bag, a size that will fit beneath the lockers in most cockpits. Modify the dimensions to any size that better suits your requirements. It is worth noting that chandleries don't blink at pricing such bags above $50. Your custom-fit bag should not cost a quarter of that.

Because common (translation: *cheap*) braided binding tends to look ugly after a while in outdoor applications, we are going to hem this bag a little differently by putting the hems on top. (This necessitates fabric that is the same on both sides.) For the back piece of a 17 × 9 (or any size) sheet bag, we want about 3 inches of extra *height* to provide a flange for mounting the bag. To determine the cut size, allow for a $\frac{1}{2}$-inch double-rubbed hem on the sides and bottom and a 2-inch hem at the top. If you are getting the hang of this by now, you came up with a cut dimension of 19 × 15$\frac{1}{2}$.

For the front piece, it is extra *width* that we need to give the pouch volume. Four inches should be adequate. We are going to capture the front piece under the hem of the back piece, so we do not need seam allowances. That makes the cut width the finished width—17 inches—plus the 4 extra inches. The same logic applies for height. The front piece would be 9 inches high except that we need a 2-inch casing for elastic. A casing is just a double-rubbed hem with the stitching omitted at the edge. Let's see, 9 + 2$\frac{1}{2}$, carry the 1 . . . How does 21 × 11$\frac{1}{2}$ sound?

Fold and crease the hems on the back—1 inch on the sides and bottom and 2$\frac{1}{2}$ inches at the top. Fold the edges of these hems under $\frac{1}{2}$ inch to create a $\frac{1}{2}$-inch double-rubbed hem on three edges and a 2-inch hem at the top. Rub the hems down with your scissors but do not stitch them. Put this piece aside for a moment.

Fold over $\frac{1}{4}$ inch of one of the 21-inch sides of the front piece and rub this down. We are making the turned-under half the normal amount to try to avoid stiffening the casing with extra thickness because we want the fabric to bunch under the pressure of the elastic—which *new* acrylic canvas does not like to do. Now fold the fabric again 2 inches from the first fold and rub in a crease. If it bothers you that this is going to make the pocket $\frac{1}{4}$ inch deeper than specified, make this fold at 2$\frac{1}{4}$ inches. Close the casing by sewing through the $\frac{1}{4}$-inch fold but do not put the second row of stitches near the edge as you usually do for hems.

You can use waistband elastic for the next step, but unless you are one of those kinky types, you know how quickly the snap goes out of your drawers. If your machine will stitch over it, use $\frac{1}{4}$-inch bungee cord, maybe doubled. Otherwise buy 1$\frac{1}{2}$-inch elastic and use it doubled (two thicknesses, not half width). Mark the cord or elastic to the intended width of your bag—in this case, 17 inches. Tape the cord (or elastic) to a piece of straight wire and thread it through the casing. With the bungee tight against the fold, line up one of the marks with the outside edge of the casing and capture the

bungee cord here with several passes of your machine close to the edge. Turn the part around and pull on the bungee until the other mark comes out of the opposite end of the casing. You have 4 extra inches of fabric, which will be bunched over the bungee. Keep the mark aligned with the casing and again with the bungee tight against the fold, capture this end of the bungee with several stitching passes. Pull on the ends of the casing to straighten the fabric and make sure the bungee is solidly captured, then snip the excess cord off both sides.

The elastic top is not going to keep out rain and spray, so drain holes are essential. It is much easier to insert them before you assemble the bag. All that is required is a pair of grommets in the front piece as close to the bottom seam as possible without any part of the grommets interfering with your ability to sew the bottom seam. Placing the edge of each grommet 1$\frac{1}{2}$ inches from the bottom edge of the fabric should serve. You also have to pleat out the extra 4 inches of material at the bottom, so although you want the grommets near the bottom corners of the bag, you do not want them to interfere with the pleats. Locating the edge of the grommets 3$\frac{1}{2}$ inches from the fabric edge should handle that. An alternative to grommets is to make the front of the bag from Phifertex, a vinyl-coated mesh that will not hold water.

Position the perimeter of the elasticized and grommeted pocket front on the back piece with the side and bottom edges of the front aligned with the side and bottom hem creases of the back. Starting on one side at the top, with the top hem unfolded, stitch down the $\frac{1}{2}$-inch hem on this side, across the bottom, and up the other side, capturing the raw edge of the front piece inside the hem. When you are sewing the bottom hem, take out half the excess material with a 1-inch pleat located $\frac{3}{4}$ inch from the edge you have just sewn; take out the other half with a matching pleat at the opposite side. Refold the 2-inch hem at the top and stitch it on all four edges.

The finished bag *can* be mounted with screws, but snap fasteners allow it to be removed when not in use, extending its life. Install snap buttons (and sockets) in every corner of the finished sheet bag and a fifth centered between those in the top corners. Snap installation is similar to grommet installation (described earlier). Use a heated punch to melt a small hole in the canvas for the barrel of the button. Place the button in the die, and place the material over the barrel of the button. Be sure the button is on the correct side of the fabric. Slip the socket over the protruding barrel, then position the setting tool on the

1

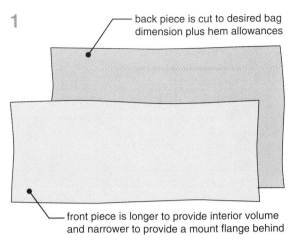

back piece is cut to desired bag dimension plus hem allowances

front piece is longer to provide interior volume and narrower to provide a mount flange behind

This "envelope" is created from two pieces of fabric rather than one.

2

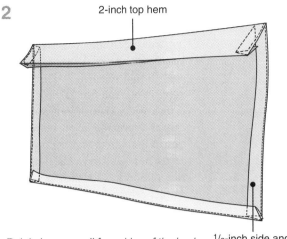

2-inch top hem

1/2-inch side and bottom hems

Rub in hems on all four sides of the back but do not stitch.

3

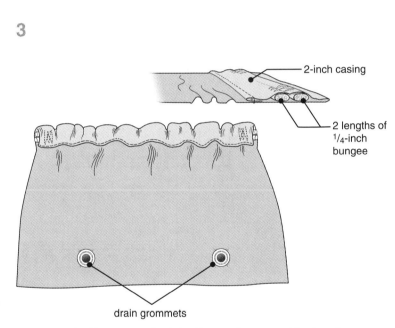

2-inch casing

2 lengths of 1/4-inch bungee

drain grommets

Stitch stretched bungee or elastic inside a casing sewn at the top of the front piece.

4

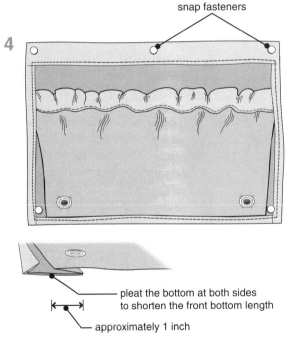

snap fasteners

pleat the bottom at both sides to shorten the front bottom length

approximately 1 inch

Capture the front piece under the hems of the back piece and stitch. Install snaps in the corners to mount.

Sheet bag.

barrel and tap the tool lightly with a hammer to set the snap. A set of snap-setting dies that fit the jaws of Vise-Grip pliers let you clinch the button rather than hammering, giving better installation consistency.

Screw matching studs into the surface where you want to mount the bag. Here is one more idea thrown in for free. Find a spot inside the cockpit locker to install a second row of snaps and you can neatly stow sheets by unsnapping the bag and resnapping it inside the locker.

SMALL-PARTS STOWAGE BAG

One final envelope before we move on. I saw this one mounted on the inside of the door of a mechanical contractor's van and it is too good not to pass on.

As an example, let's make a bag for small-item stowage with nine compartments—three wide and three high. In practice you can make as few or as many compartments as you need. Arbitrarily this particular bag has a finished size of 15 inches wide by 20 inches high, and the back is made from acrylic canvas.

For the front of the bag you will need 0.020 clear vinyl, the material in dodger windows. The type sold from a roll will be cheaper and is fine for this application. You need a piece big enough to cut three 6-inch-wide, 27-inch-long strips. Allowing 1 inch of canvas above and below the pockets for the installation of grommets or other mounting hardware leaves 18 inches, which yields the pocket height dimension of 6 inches for three equal rows of pockets. The 27-inch length is similarly determined by the size of the backing and the number of pockets across. Three equal pockets across 15 inches of canvas means each pocket is 5 inches wide. As with the sheet pocket, we add 4 inches of material to the front to give the pocket fullness, so each pocket requires 9 inches of material. That's 27 inches for the three. A wonderful feature of clear vinyl is that it does not require hemming or hem allowances. Cut pieces are ready to use.

On the front of the canvas (hems on the back), draw two light lines dividing the width into three 5-inch sections. Draw two similar lines on the vinyl strips, but divide the longer vinyl into 9-inch sections. Always start with the top strip when creating the pockets so the next strip does not interfere with sewing the bottom edge. Place the first vinyl strip 1 inch from the top; align the end with one side of the back and stitch down this end. Your presser foot has a tendency to stick to the vinyl. There are two solutions to this. One is to dust the top surface of the vinyl with talcum powder that you will wash off later. The other is to lay tissue—the gift-packing kind, not Kleenex—over the vinyl and sew through the tissue. If your machine has a walking foot, you should not have this problem at all.

Sew the opposite end of the top strip to the opposite side of the back. Place the pencil lines on the vinyl on top of the pencil lines on the canvas and join the pieces here with a row of stitching. Do the same on the second pair of lines, creating three vinyl "loops." Make these into three accordion-fold pockets by pleating the strips in the same manner that you pleated the bottom of the sheet bag. Each pocket will have a 1-inch-wide pleat on either side. The top fold of each pleat will line up with the edge of the bag or the row of stitching between pockets, depending on the location of the pleat. Hold the pleats in position or make them as you go, and run a line of stitches across the bottom of the vinyl. The result will be three clear, wide-mouth pockets. Attach and pleat the other two strips in exactly the same way to create a matrix of nine pockets.

Install grommets or snap fasteners in the four corners for mounting the bag. You can follow this

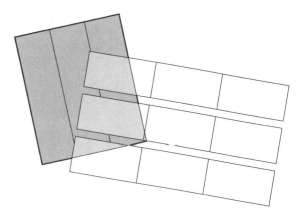

Canvas back, clear vinyl front.

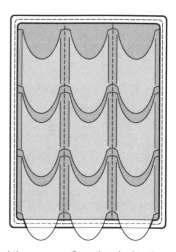

Hem or bind the canvas. Sew the vinyl to the canvas in equal "loops."

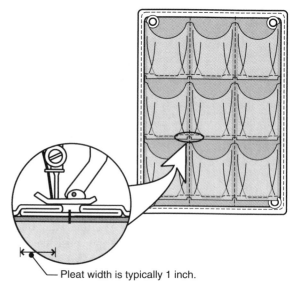

Pleat width is typically 1 inch.

Pleat the bottoms of the loops to create wide-mouth bins. Mount with snaps or grommets.

Clear vinyl bins.

same procedure to make smaller or larger pockets, more or fewer pockets, depending on your stowage requirements.

THE ONE-PIECE BAG

The next level of complexity is the one-piece bag. There are several ways to fold and stitch a piece of canvas into a bag, and we are going to look at three of them. It may be easier to think of this as making an open box out of canvas and putting handles on it.

BOAT BAG I

I was going to call this section Ice Bag I, but with your new refrigeration system, who needs an ice bag? However, a few sturdy canvas bags can greatly simplify getting equipment and supplies to and from the boat. When you're off cruising the boat bag is essential, since the nearest market is never right next to the dinghy dock. If you are wondering what a canvas tote bag has to do with refurbishing your old boat, don't be so narrow-minded. We are on a quest for refurbishing skill and the by-products of that quest might as well be useful. If you need a direct connection, use your bag to haul your tools and brushes to the boatyard.

For clarity let's do a cubic-foot bag. The fabric of choice is 10-ounce treated canvas. The length of the fabric needs to be the width of the bottom (the shorter bottom dimension when the bag is not square), plus twice the depth of the bag, plus a 4-inch allowance to accommodate the hem around the top of the bag. The width of the fabric blank is the length plus the width of the bottom plus a 1-inch seam allowance. That works out to be 40 inches by 25 inches for a cubic-foot bag.

Fold the material in half across the long dimension and stitch the two halves together on both sides with a row of stitches $1/2$ inch from the edge, forming an envelope. Bind the raw edges with binding tape. If you use a zigzag stitch, do not let it extend beyond the seam stitching.

Measure in along the fold $5^1/_2$ inches from the *stitch line* (not the edge) and draw a line on the fabric parallel to the stitching and about 6 inches long. Now measure along the stitched edge $5^1/_2$ inches from the fold and draw a line from the stitched edge to the first line; this one is parallel to the fold. Cut from the side and from the fold along these lines to the point where they intersect, making a square notch in the corner. Measure and cut an identical notch at the other end of the fold. The notch size for a bag of different dimensions is determined by the bag's width—the shorter of the bottom dimensions. The notches are half the bag width less $1/2$ inch to leave fabric for the stitching.

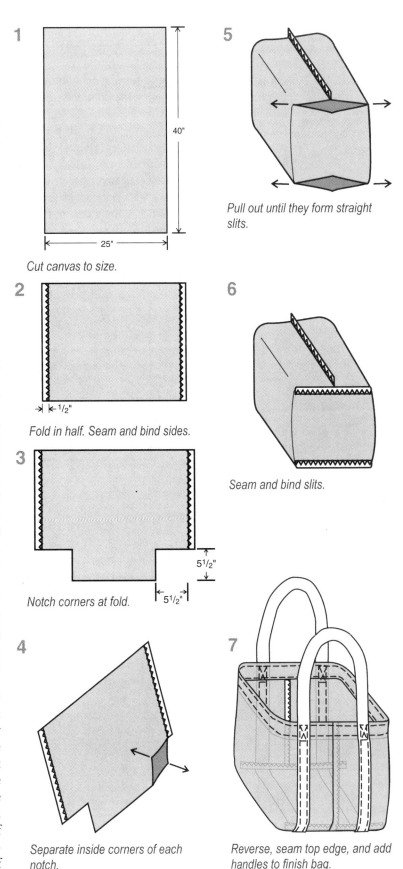

1 Cut canvas to size. 40" 25"

2 Fold in half. Seam and bind sides. $1/2$"

3 Notch corners at fold. $5^1/2$" $5^1/2$"

4 Separate inside corners of each notch.

5 Pull out until they form straight slits.

6 Seam and bind slits.

7 Reverse, seam top edge, and add handles to finish bag.

Boat bag I.

Gripping the two layers of fabric separately at the inside corner of one of the notches, pull the layers apart. The four edges of the hole in the fabric resulting from the notch should form a diamond shape. Continue pulling, narrowing the diamond until the hole closes and you only have two edges, one above the other. Sew these edges together with a row of stitching, then bind the raw edges. Handle the second notch in the same manner.

That you suddenly have a canvas bag gives this technique a satisfying "gee whiz" character. Turn the bag right-side out and put a 1½-inch double-rubbed hem around the top of the bag. All you need are handles. Short ones can be attached to the top hem, but for carrying heavy items the handles should go completely under the bag. I like 1½-inch webbing for handles, and it takes about 10 feet of webbing for a cubic-foot bag. Draw two parallel lines 5 or 6 inches apart from one lip down the side, across the bottom, and back up the other side. Sew the webbing over the lines, allowing about 2 feet on each side—a foot-high loop—for the actual handles. Sew down both edges of the webbing.

BOAT BAG II

An alternative method of constructing the same bag requires a piece of canvas 4 feet by 1½ feet plus allowances. Add 1 inch to the 4-foot dimension for a bound seam. To the 18-inch dimension, add

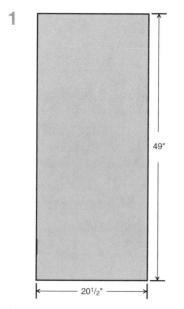

1

49"

20½"

Cut canvas with allowances.

2

Dots mark corner locations.

Fold and bind one side and end. Put reference dots equidistant from fold and stitch lines.

3

Shape envelope bottom square with dots at four corners. Stitch between dots across triangular "ears".

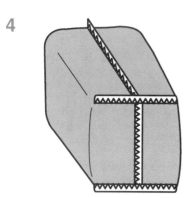

4

Cut away ears beyond stitch line and bind cut edge.

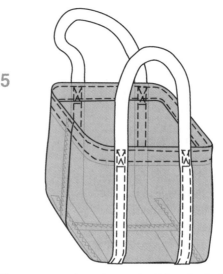

5

Reverse, seam top edge, and add handles to finish.

Boat bag II.

$2\frac{1}{2}$ inches for a $1\frac{1}{2}$-inch top hem and a $\frac{1}{2}$-inch bound seam across the bottom.

Fold the fabric in half across the long dimension and stitch the layers together on *one* side and across the edge opposite the fold. Bind the raw edges.

The transition from envelope to bag will be easier with reference marks. Put a dot on the fabric 6 inches from the stitch lines of the two seams. Put a second dot 6 inches from the fold and an equal distance from the stitching of the adjacent seam. Stick pins straight through these two dots and turn the fabric over, marking a second pair of dots where the pins protrude. Remove the pins.

Stand the envelope up and open the unstitched side. Flatten the bottom and shape it into a square with the reference dots at each corner. You should end up with triangular ears sticking out on two sides of the bag, the bottom seam running from apex to apex. Sew a straight line of stitches across each of the triangles from reference dot to reference dot. Half an inch beyond the stitching, cut off the triangles and bind the raw edges. Turn the bag right-side out, put a $1\frac{1}{2}$-inch hem around the top, and sew on the handles. Another bag in the bag.

BOAT BAG III: HATCH CAP

The third one-piece bag is best illustrated with a cover for a hatch that stands proudly above the deck. Acrylic canvas is the material of choice. Determine the fabric dimensions by measuring the length and width of the hatch. Add twice the height of the hatch to both dimensions, plus an additional 3 inches for 1-inch double-rubbed hems on all sides. A 20-inch hatch $2\frac{1}{2}$ inches high requires a 28-inch square of canvas.

Center the canvas on the hatch, letting the excess drape equally over all four edges. Crease or mark the fabric around the edges of the hatch, making certain that corner locations are clear. At

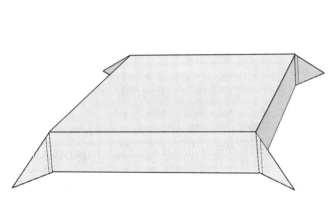

Pinch corners and stitch to shape bag/cap.

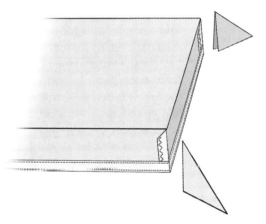

Bind corners. Hem edge.

Boat bag III: hatch cap.

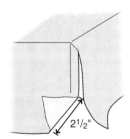

Pinch and trim corners but do not stitch. Fold back fabric corners.

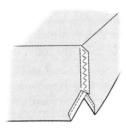

Stitch along fold, and trim away excess fabric. Stitch and bind pinched corner.

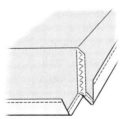

Fold edges $\frac{1}{2}$ inch, then 1 inch and sew through $\frac{1}{2}$-inch fold to create 1-inch casing.

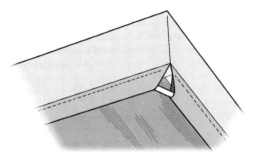

Thread cord or bungee through the four casings and pull tight at one corner to turn the casing under and secure the cap.

Creating a drawstring casing.

the sewing machine, fold each corner diagonally on a line from the corner of the hatch (as indicated by creases or markings) to the corner of the fabric. With the raw edges of the material perpendicular to your line of stitching, sew a straight row of stitches from the raw edge to the fold, crossing the fold about $1/4$ inch wide of the mark for the hatch corner. This boxes one corner and pinches the excess material into a triangle—something like the corners of a tablecloth.

Check the cap for fit before proceeding. It should be snug, but not so tight that it will be difficult to install. Adjust the location of the corner seams if necessary, then cut off the excess material and bind the raw edges. Put a 1-inch double-rubbed hem all around the cover, and one-piece bag III is finished.

A common way to hold the hatch cap in place is with snaps in the hem. One snap in each side is adequate for small hatches but larger covers may need two to a side.

An alternative that eliminates screws into the side of the hatch is the drawstring. Cut the original material 2 inches longer and wider to drop the hem below the bottom of the hatch. Mark the location of the corner seams, but before you sew them, cut off the excess material $1/2$ inch beyond your mark. Now fold up the corners this cut has created, making the straight sides of these folds $2^1/2$ inches. Sew down the corners with a row of stitches close to the fold, then trim off the excess triangle of fabric. When you have two stitched diagonals at every corner, fold the edges $1/2$ inch, then 1 inch. Sew down the center of the $1/2$-inch fold, but not at the edge fold, to create a 1-inch casing. Note that the diagonal seams have given the ends of the casing a finished edge. Now seam and bind the corners.

With a piece of stiff wire, thread a continuous length of $1/8$-inch flag halyard through all four casings with both loose ends exiting at the same corner. Turn the cap right-side out and slip it over the hatch. Pulling on the drawstring will fold the extended cover under the bottom of the hatch. Tie the drawstring ends or fit them with a push-button cord lock to secure the cap. If you don't want to adjust the drawstring each time, you can substitute small bungee cord, but the cap will not be quite as secure.

THE TWO-PIECE BAG

For bag shapes other than square or rectangular, the bag bottom is going to be a separate piece of cloth. I will talk about two such bags, but as you will quickly see, they are almost identical.

THE OBLIGATORY DITTY BAG

What kind of canvaswork instructions would these be without a ditty bag? I could have my license revoked. We have only two true ditty bags aboard—one holding our clothespins and getting daily use, the other containing thread, zippers, Velcro, binding tape, and other sewing supplies. But we have several sailbags that we use when we strip our boat for hurricane season and several in-between bags that hold such things as dive gear, stowed awnings, and "skuzzer" towels and rags. The construction of all of these is essentially the same.

Any sturdy fabric can be sewn into a ditty bag, but smaller bags shape and draw better if they are made of a soft material like nylon oxford cloth (sometimes called pack cloth). Stowage sailbags can also be sewn from oxford cloth or the similar but heavier Cordura. Sailbags that live on deck should be made from acrylic canvas.

The bottom piece of a round-bottom bag will be a circle of material 1 inch larger in diameter than the finished size of the bag. The fabric blank for the rest of the bag will be a rectangular piece with a length that is 3.14 times the finished diameter of the bottom plus 1 inch, and a width 2 inches greater than the finished height of the bag. For those of you who also daydreamed your way through geometry class, 3.14 is pi (π), the ratio of the circumference of a circle to its diameter. The allowances are for bound seams and a 1-inch hem around the top of the bag. For a clothespin bag 6 inches in diameter and 8 inches deep, cut a 7-inch circle and a 10-by-20-inch (rounding 19.84) rectangle.

A grade-school compass will enable you to draw small circles, but what about a large circle? You need a pin, a piece of thread, and a pencil. Put two loops in the thread, separated by the radius of the circle you want to draw. Stick the pin through one of the loops and into the material. This will be the center of the circle. Stick the point of the pencil into the other loop and stretch the thread taut with it. Holding the pin with your other hand and keeping the thread taut, circle the pin with the pencil, drawing a perfect circle.

Round is the usual shape for a ditty bag, but you could just as easily fabricate one with a square bottom. The circular shape is not just a tradition, however. The curved seam of a round bottom distributes the load evenly, whereas a square bottom concentrates most of the stress in the corners. If you make a two-piece bag with a square bottom, put a generous radius on the corners to better distribute the stress on the seam. No matter what the bottom shape, the length of the fabric rectangle should be an inch more than the bottom circumference.

Back to the project at hand, fold the rectangle in half (across the long dimension) and sew together the edges opposite the fold with a ¹/₂-inch-wide seam. Bind the raw edges. Open this fabric "tube" and fit the circle into one end, mating the edge of the tube to the edge of the circle. Pin or baste the two pieces together. Run a row of straight stitches ¹/₂ inch inside these flush edges to join the two pieces. Bind the raw edges. Turn the bag right-side out.

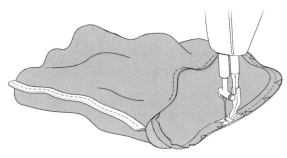

Hem and bind rectangle into tube and sew round bottom inside one end. Notch hem allowance of circle if the fabric is stiff. Bind.

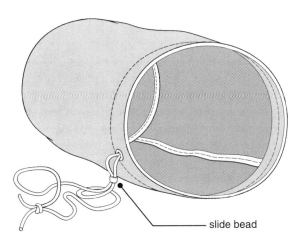

— slide bead

Install grommet below fold line for casing in open end, then sew casing with drawstring inside and exiting through grommet.

Large bags close easier with dual drawstrings exiting through opposite side grommets.

Ditty bag.

If you are sewing stiff material, it may be easier to get the round piece to turn out smoothly if you make a series of evenly spaced V-cuts in the hem allowance of the circle with your scissors. Limit the cuts to about ¹/₄ inch deep. Staples in the hem allowance may be easier than pinning and more secure than basting with transfer tape, but be sure to remove them before you bind the edges.

A drawstring completes the bag. Rub the 1-inch casing down to mark it, then install a single grommet on the outside of the bag just below the crease. It is easier to sew the drawstring into the casing than to thread it in later, so make a bag-sized loop with a piece of ¹/₈-inch flag halyard and feed both ends through the grommet from inside the bag. Knot the ends together so the string doesn't pull back through. Push one side of the drawstring inside the open casing; keep it against the fold as you sew down the turned-under edge of the casing, taking care not to accidentally stitch the line.

Larger bags, such as sailbags, will close much more easily with two drawstrings exiting the hem on opposite sides of the bag. Pulling on the opposing drawstrings in effect chokes the bag. Two grommets (or four if the drawstring is large) and two separate lengths of line are required for this arrangement.

WINCH COVER

Make a ditty bag with the drawstring around the waist of the bag instead of the mouth and you have a winch cover. Or omit the drawstring altogether and tack a tie to the outside of the bag for drawing in the waist. Too crude? Then try this one.

Add 1 inch to the diameter of the winch to determine the cut size of the top. Don't forget to take into account any self-tailing mechanism fitted to your winch. Measure the overall height of the winch and add a 1¹/₂-inch seam allowance for the width of the rectangle. The length will be 3.14 times the diameter of the winch, plus a 1-inch seam allowance. For this fancy cover, you need a second rectangle of cloth the same length as the first one and half as wide. The two bag pieces should be acrylic canvas, but the smaller rectangle needs to be a softer fabric such as nylon oxford cloth.

We want a hem rather than a casing in this "bag," which is easier to do while the fabric is flat. Put a ¹/₂-inch double hem along one edge of the large rectangle, then fold the rectangle in half with the hem outside and seam the ends together. Bind this seam. V-cut and staple the circle into the raw end

Winch cover.

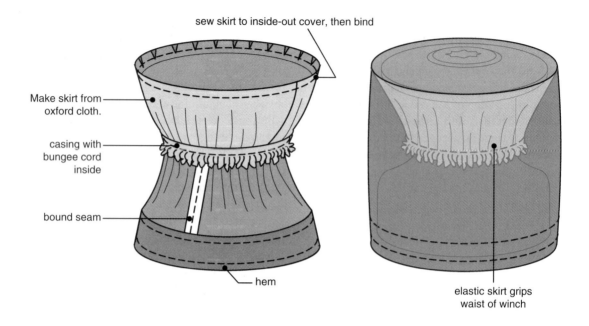

sew skirt to inside-out cover, then bind

Make skirt from oxford cloth.

casing with bungee cord inside

bound seam

hem

elastic skirt grips waist of winch

and sew it in place. Remove the staples, but do not bind this seam yet.

Put a 1-inch casing in one long side of the smaller rectangle. Thread a length of small bungee cord or heavy waistband elastic through the hem. Fold the rectangle in half and sew the ends together; start stitching from the unhemmed edge. Stop the machine with the needle buried when the front of the presser foot reaches the casing. Pull on both ends of the bungee cord, helping the fabric to gather with your other hand, until the diameter of the loop is reduced to about half. The bungee should not be stretched; the fabric should be bunched on it as around a drawstring. Holding the bungee, complete the seam, sewing back and forth across the cord (inside the hem) several times to secure the ends. Snip off the excess cord and bind the seam.

Stretch the elastic mouth over the inside-out acrylic cover, aligning the raw edges. Sew a second row of stitches around the circle to attach the elastic skirt to the cover. Now you can bind the circular seam. Turn the cover right-side out. Reach inside and spread the inner skirt over the winch when you install the cover. The elastic around the waist of the winch holds the cover in position.

THE BOX

The box is the last of the five basic configurations that make up the majority of canvas items found aboard boats. The box is nothing more than a three-piece bag—a two-piece bag with a top. Sew a circle or a square in both ends of the ditty bag and you have a box. You also have a problem. There is no way to turn the box right-side out. Anytime a fabric is sewn together with hidden seams, there must be some opening in the box to allow it to be turned inside out. It is fabricating the opening that represents the only significant difference—other than the third piece—between a two-piece bag and a box. Read on.

COCKPIT CUSHIONS

The most common application of the fabric box is as a cushion cover. Let's start in the cockpit. My original experience with cockpit cushions was a typical set constructed of polyurethane foam covered with reinforced vinyl (Naugahyde) and closed with a metal zipper. A more worthless combination I cannot imagine. While the vinyl was ineffective at keeping the water out, it was great at keeping it in. With the first rain the foam was full of water, never to be dry again. The saturated cushions were as heavy as lead and only slightly softer. The always-clammy vinyl was uncomfortable to sit on, impossible to sleep on, and a ready source of second-degree burns in summertime. It tended to adhere to the deck with such tenacity that whenever the cushions were peeled up, bits of gelcoat came with them. The zippers quickly dissolved into green powder that was two shades lighter than the mildew rioting inside the covers on the cloth backing of the vinyl. I pitched the cushions and swore never to have cockpit cushions again.

Then came closed-cell foam. I coated my first closed-cell cushions with liquid vinyl—like a ski belt—eliminating zippers and fabric, but the vinyl was still clammy and sticky, and these smooth cushions were downright treacherous when wet. Covers were needed.

Our terrace furniture, like all outdoor furniture at the time, had vinyl mesh cushions that did not hold water and were less uncomfortable than solid vinyl. We decided to give this fabric a try on the boat. It is not a bad choice. Combined with closed-cell foam, the vinyl-coated mesh (Phifertex) gave us cushions so waterproof that we also used them as floats when swimming. They don't dry fast, but they do dry completely. The fabric is not slippery when you step on it. The biggest problems were that the vinyl was uncomfortable against bare skin and the white fabric aged to a particularly grungy shade of yellow.

Meanwhile we had re-covered our terrace furniture cushions with acrylic canvas. The canvas turned out to be more comfortable, more attractive, and astonishingly disdainful of UV exposure. We re-covered our cockpit cushions with acrylic canvas and have never looked back. The acrylic is water-repellent and resists staining and mildew. While dark colors dry more quickly (even as you watch), dark-colored cushions are intolerable in the tropics. Light colors still dry quickly. We accent light cushions with a richer-colored welt around the perimeter of the cover.

Closed-Cell Foam

If your old boat is without cockpit cushions, the first step is to cut the foam. Use heavy paper to make a pattern for each cushion to get the angles and relationships correct. Closed-cell foam comes in sheets of varying sizes, so the number and shape of the cushions may be influenced by how you can use the sheet most efficiently. It also comes in a variety of thicknesses. Two-inch foam makes very luxurious cockpit cushions.

Closed-cell foam cuts easily with a sharp knife. Put a razor edge on your fillet knife and draw it across the foam in one direction several times without a great deal of pressure to get the cleanest cut. Closed-cell foam is made up of millions of tiny air-filled balloons, and over time they lose air—not like last month's party balloons, but enough to make the foam shrink in size about 2% per decade. That doesn't sound like much, but the foam we originally cut to 60 inches is today about 4 inches shorter. I'm not whining—that foam has been cradling my bony butt for 30 years—but the shrinkage of closed-cell foam does have implications for the fit of the covers. You can postpone the inevitable by cutting the foam 1% oversize.

It is nearly always wise to cut the circumference piece for a boxed cushion cover before cutting the top and bottom pieces. This strip of fabric, appropriately called boxing, joins the top to the bottom. The width of the boxing should be about $\frac{1}{4}$ inch less than the thickness of the foam, to improve the cover's fit, plus a 1-inch seam allowance. In an ideal world the length would be an inch more than the circumference of the cushion—twice the length plus twice the width if the cushion is rectangular. However, that overlooks the opening the cover needs, which you are going to put in the boxing on the back side of the cushion. This forces you to make up the boxing in two sections, one incorporating a closable opening.

Zippers

I have seen cushions fabricated with snaps and occasionally Velcro to close the opening, but the only closure that will give the cover a tight, consistent fit is a zipper, and the only zipper that you should use is a YKK #10 Vislon zipper. These Delrin zippers are the industry standard, providing extraordinary strength and immunity to corrosion. UV-resistant YKK zippers (and Riri zippers) have recently come on the market and are likely to be worth the additional cost for use in exterior canvas.

You can buy separating #10 zippers (jacket zippers) in a wide selection of lengths up to 12 feet, or if you can find a supplier, you can buy zipper chain—one side of a zipper—and make up zippers of any length (2 feet of chain per foot of zipper). For boat use, buy zippers with plastic sliders only. Metal sliders will corrode and seize. This also applies to the sliders you have to buy for use with zipper chain. (To free existing metal sliders, pack a cotton ball around the corroded slider and keep it wet with vinegar for several hours or longer until the corrosion dissolves and frees it.)

You are more likely to find zippers than zipper chain, and generally the zipper should be the longest available that is not longer than the length of the cushion. The more of the back that does not open, the more difficult it will be to get the foam into the cover. This problem is magnified with smaller cushions.

The zippered section of the boxing will need to be the same width as the rest of the boxing with the zipper closed. Generally that necessitates two strips of fabric a bit longer than the zipper and $1\frac{1}{8}$ inches wider than half the thickness of the foam. If you subtract the zipper length from the circumference, that gives you the length of the rest of the boxing, except that you need to add an allowance of around 4 inches for hem and overlap. So if, for example, you are covering a 2-inch cushion that's 64 inches long and 16 inches wide, you would need two fabric strips $2\frac{1}{8}$ inches wide and 62 inches long to sew to each side of a 5-foot zipper. The remaining boxing would be $2\frac{3}{4}$ inches wide and

104 inches long. If you do the calculations and arrive at the same lengths and widths, you've got this nailed.

Piping

You still may not be finished with cutting strips, which you need to do while the fabric provides the maximum length because you are going to pipe the seams between the boxing and the top and bottom. Piping is a round welt that is sewn into the edge seams to hide the stitching. You can use extruded vinyl piping, purchased by the yard. This is a vinyl tube with a flange on it. It requires no preassembly and sews easily, but it is more appropriate for use with reinforced vinyl or vinyl mesh fabrics. For canvas covers, you will sew a foam or braided cord—$1/8$-inch flag halyard works well—inside a strip of matching or contrasting canvas. The width of

the strip will vary with the size of the cord. Piping with a $1/8$-inch cord requires a fabric width of about $1^3/_8$ inches.

As for length, each side of the cushion requires a continuous strip a tad longer than the circumference of the cushion. However, you can piece piping fabric, and if you do it properly, the splice will hardly show. The trick is to sew the two pieces together on a 45-degree diagonal, but if you stack the two strips and make the seam 45 degrees, the strip makes a 90-degree turn when you unfold them. You have to lay the ends perpendicular, then make the seam diagonal across the outside corner. Now when you unfold, the 90-degree change in direction straightens the strip. Trim the seam to about $1/4$ inch wide and butterfly it, meaning the two sides should lay in opposite directions. I calculate the total length of all

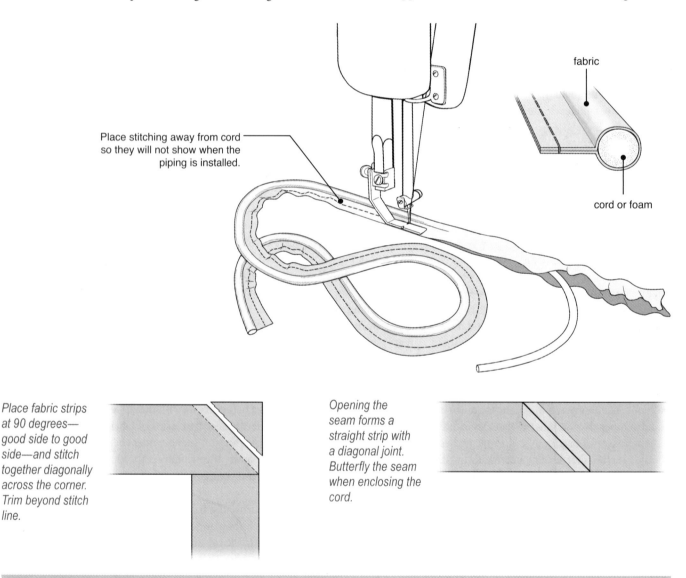

fabric

Place stitching away from cord so they will not show when the piping is installed.

cord or foam

Place fabric strips at 90 degrees— good side to good side—and stitch together diagonally across the corner. Trim beyond stitch line.

Opening the seam forms a straight strip with a diagonal joint. Butterfly the seam when enclosing the cord.

Make piping in long lengths.

the piping for all the cushions, then cut the longest strips I can and sew them all together into a continuous strip, taking care that the raw edges of the seams are all on the same side of the strip. I then sew the cord inside to fabricate a continuous length of piping. Do not put the stitches too close to the cord so they will not be visible when the welt is installed. You do not need to cut the piping to size for each cushion. You just sew in the continuous length until you complete the circle, then cut the piping to allow an inch of overlap. We will come back to this momentarily.

Once you have the boxing and piping strips cut, or at least the fabric for them reserved, you are ready to cut tops and bottoms. If you cut paper patterns, use them to mark the fabric for cutting, adding an allowance for $1/2$-inch seams on all sides. You can also place the cut foam on the fabric and trace the outline, then add a hem allowance. If you cut the foam slightly oversize, be sure you reduce the seam allowance by that amount. If the cushion is not square on all sides, align any stripe or other pattern in the fabric with the edge that is square.

We have already determined that the box requires a bottom *and* a top, and unless the cushion has a beveled side (which we will consider later), both pieces are the same size. If the material has a right and a wrong side—reinforced vinyl, for example—the two pieces need to have wrong sides facing, but this is not a concern with acrylic canvas (or Phifertex).

While the two pieces are stacked, cut a series of notches in the seam allowances. Notch both pieces at the same time every 6 to 8 inches around the entire perimeter. If corners are radiused, cut three evenly spaced notches in each corner. The biggest problem with boxed cushions is getting the orientation of the top and bottom twisted; these notches will help you to avoid that.

Assembly

To assemble the opening section of the boxing, place the zipper with the pull tab down on the good side of one of the strips you cut for this purpose. Position the end of the zipper tape just short of the end of the fabric, and align one fabric edge of the zipper with the raw edge of the strip. Sew the two together with a straight row of stitches near the flush edges. Turn the assembly over and fold the fabric back like a hem, putting this fold at the center of the zipper (or with the teeth just peeking out if you have the zipper separated or are using zipper chain). Run a row of stitching about $1/2$ inch from the fold, sewing through two layers of fabric and the zipper tape. You will need your zipper foot for

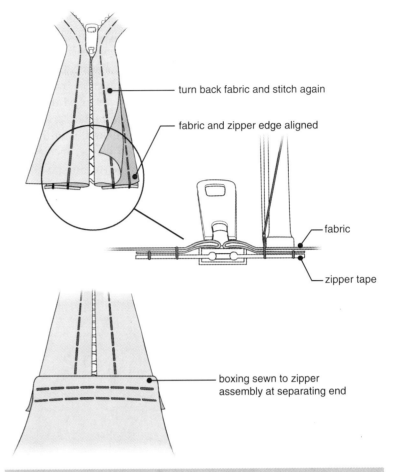

turn back fabric and stitch again

fabric and zipper edge aligned

fabric

zipper tape

boxing sewn to zipper assembly at separating end

Zipper assembly.

this. (Duh!) Sew the other strip to the opposite side the same way. Check the finished width and trim it to the same size as the other boxing if it differs.

To join the rest of the boxing to the zipper assembly, put the zipper assembly on top of the boxing, good side to good side and align the ends. This should be the separating end of the zipper, the end opposite where the slide is with the zipper closed. Sew the ends together. Put a second row of stitching above the end of the zipper to prevent it from separating. When you sew across the zipper, run the machine by hand and move the assembly as necessary to allow the needle to penetrate between teeth. Turn everything over and fold the boxing back short of the line of stitches. Topstitch the fold across the boxing and zipper assembly. You now have a single strip long enough to box the cushion.

Put the zipper assembly, good side down, on top of one of the cover pieces (good side up) with the edge of the assembly flush with the fabric edge that will be at the rear of the cushion. Center the zipper end to end on the back edge. Slip the fabricated piping between the two parts with the welt on the cover fabric and the raw edges of all three components flush. Using the zipper foot, position the needle a couple of inches from the unattached end of the zipper assembly and sew the three parts together, placing the stitches as near the welt as possible. You may find it easier to get the boxing and piping to follow the contour of the fabric around corners if you make a few shallow slits in the seam allowances. Sew right around the perimeter of the cover until you return to your starting point. Stop sewing short of the end of the zipper assembly. Cut the end of the boxing to overlap the zipper assembly by about 3 inches. Cut the piping for a 1-inch overlap with its other end. Unstitch this end of the piping (i.e., open it) a bit more than 1 inch and cut off 1 inch of the cord. Fold the unstitched and now-hollow end under $^1/_2$ inch. Also fold the 3-inch boxing overlap back $1^1/_2$ inches and position it under the zipper assembly.

Now holding everything in alignment, complete the seam, wrapping the folded, hollow end of the piping over the starting end. Binding the raw edges will not be necessary since they will be inside the cover.

The next step is to take precautions to prevent the top of the cushion from being twisted in relation to the bottom. Remember the matching notches you put in the two pieces? Go all the way around the stitched-on boxing, notching the raw edge of the boxing *exactly* opposite the notches in the cover piece it is already sewn to. You can use a business card as a handy square to transfer the locations straight across the boxing.

Make sure the second cover piece is oriented to match the notches in the first piece—not turned around or with the wrong side up—and align the notches in the boxing with the notches around the fabric. Insert the piping between the fabric and the boxing, making sure all edges are flush. Because

1

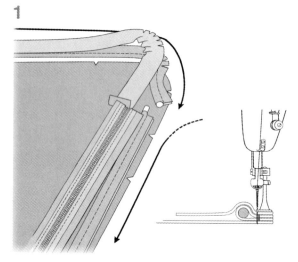

Align all raw edges and sew boxing and piping to one cover piece, good side to good side.

2

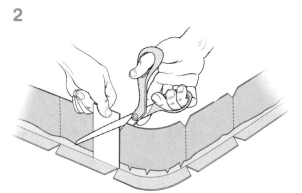

Transfer alignment notches across the boxing with a square-cut card.

3

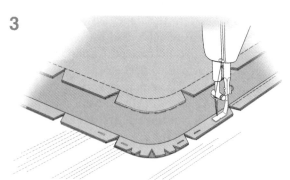

Match notches in cover piece to notches in boxing. Stapling the second cover piece to the boxing can help maintain alignment.

4

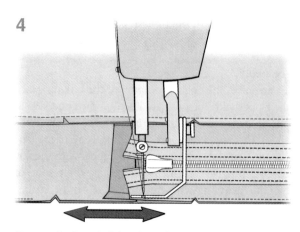

Some adjustment of the circumference is possible when closing the circle.

Sewing the pieces together.

the assembly is turned over, you will be sewing the second seam in the opposite direction to the first, which contributes to the cover's tendency to twist. Start the seam off the zipper assembly and a couple of inches from the folded edge of the boxing to allow some circumference adjustment as you finish this seam.

Pay attention to the notches as you stitch around the cover. If they start to get out of alignment, stretch the bottom fabric slightly as you sew to recover. If the alignment goes out more than $1/8$ inch, stop and pull out some of the stitching you've just done, then resew to get it right. Corners will be particularly troublesome until you have gained a little experience. I still sometimes staple this second seam all the way around before sewing, but the material will still shift if you are not vigilant. If you do use staples, don't forget to remove them.

When you arrive back at your starting point, stop stitching before you reach the folded boxing. Trim the piping for overlap like you did on the first seam. Adjust the boxing fold to be square with the sides and complete the seam. It isn't necessary to stitch this fold down across the zipper unless the slide might go under it too far.

Unzip the finished cover and turn it inside out. Push your fingers inside the cover to shape the corners, taking care not to cut yourself if the piping is extruded. Insert the foam. Sometimes it is easier to insert the foam folded in half and unfold it inside the cover. Work the foam into all the corners with your hand, then zip the cover closed. Place the cushion in the cockpit. Turn around. Sit down. Ahhh.

INTERIOR CUSHIONS

Interior cushions often differ little from those in the cockpit, the differences being mainly related to the materials you use. Foam is an example. As great as closed-cell foam is for cockpit cushions, it is not a good choice for settees and bunks because it compresses deliberately. In the middle of the night you will feel as if you are packed for shipping instead of trying to sleep. The bottom of the depression where you are now chocked will be stone hard because the foam is compressed, and even if you claw your way back to the surface and change positions, the depression remains for some time.

Materials

Interior cushions should be constructed of polyurethane foam, which has better resilience and less memory. Polyfoam is graded by density and compression. The density number is the weight in pounds of 1 cubic foot of foam. The heavier the foam, the longer it will last. However, it is the compression number you will be most interested in. This is the amount of weight required to compress 50 square inches of 4-inch foam down to 3 inches. The higher this number is, the firmer the foam will be. Anything under 30 pounds and your elbows will hit the plywood when you roll over. You will usually be offered foam in the 35- to 45-pound range for mattresses. I prefer the firmer support of 50-pound foam, but I also recline gently to avoid knocking myself unconscious. The best test is to put the foam on the floor and lie on it before you buy. Backrests, if they do not double as bunks, can be softer, around 30 pounds. Be sure to buy only good-quality foam. Bargain foam will not be a bargain in the long run.

As with closed-cell foam you should cut polyfoam cushions 1% to 2% oversize, but for a different reason. The foam does not shrink, but forcing the cover to compress it slightly will give you tighter, more attractive upholstery. If you spray the foam heavily with Lysol before you cover it and periodically afterward, mildew—which seems to like polyurethane foam—will not be a problem.

Fabric choices are virtually unlimited. Fortunately, demon vinyl, which boat manufacturers once thought the only suitable fabric for cushion covers, is no longer common. Herculon, a demon in its own right, replaced vinyl. Common Herculons have poor shape retention and tend to be hot. The name Herculon actually refers to the fiber, and I have to admit to encountering some very nice Herculon (and other olefin) fabrics. The problem is that both vinyl and Herculon are popular mostly because they are waterproof and stain resistant. Maybe I'm just a wild and crazy guy, but what about comfort?

As I indicated earlier, a fabric that you might select for your sofa at home is also a candidate for interior cushions. Most natural fibers are not very compatible with the marine environment, with cotton being the possible exception. Suitable synthetics, either pure or blended, include acrylic, polyester, nylon, and even olefin (polyolefin). These might take the form of canvas, velvet, twill, corduroy, even imitation suede. All upholstery fabrics are a compromise between stain resistance and feel, between low absorbency and breathability, between weight and sewability, between cost and utility, and too often between comfort and durability. Carmakers have done an admirable job of developing fabrics that resist wear and staining but are still comfortable to sit on. These fabrics, not often found in an upholstery fabric store, are equally well suited to the demands of boat upholstery.

In recent years there has been a lot of justifiable buzz about microfiber fabrics. Rather than a specific material, microfiber is a technology applied to various synthetics, particularly acrylic, polyester, and nylon. The tightly woven ultrafine yarns can be engineered to produce some astonishingly comfortable and durable fabrics, among them imitation suede (Ultrasuede). Some automotive fabrics are microfibers. You will also find microfiber upholstery fabrics in most big fabric outlets.

Color and pattern are also important. You are going to pick what you like, but if you are headed to the tropics, you will do well to shy away from "hot" colors like reds and browns in favor of blues, greens, and grays. Also keep in mind that dark colors make a space seem smaller—or cozier if your cabin is expansive. Busy patterns can contribute to seasickness. If you are attracted to a fabric with a bold pattern, keep in mind that you will have to match the pattern from cushion to cushion. While matching patterns is not particularly difficult, it does result in quite a bit of wasted material. If you don't match the pattern or you do it badly, you will wish you had selected a different material.

Whatever fabric you decide on, buy a couple of yards first and take it aboard to see how it looks in natural light, under cabin light, and against interior woods in either light. Sit on this trial piece, sleep on it, and spill on it. Fold it in half to simultaneously cut two identical squares, then wash one of them. Compare it to the unwashed one for shrinkage and color change. If the fabric passes these tests and you still like it after looking at it every day for a couple of weeks, you'll have much more confidence in your selection.

It is just as important to use plastic zippers on interior cushions as it is for those in the cockpit. Despite the "inside" location, do not use metal sliders. You can save a few dollars by using the smaller YKK #5 Vislon zippers if you like.

Piping is the same inside and out, but you can achieve different looks with different-size welts. If a bunk is made up of more than one cushion, the hard ridge of tandem piping will be an irritant for anyone sleeping in the bunk. You can simply omit the piping or opt for a cover design other than the three-piece box.

Beveled Edge

Bunk cushions often lie against the hull, requiring a bevel on the back edge of the cushion. Use a bevel gauge to duplicate the angle when you are cutting your foam. To make the boxing come out right, the boxing on the beveled side—normally the zipper assembly—will have to be a separate piece and run the full length of the beveled side. Note that this section of boxing will also be wider. Determine the actual width by measuring the foam after you cut it. Join the regular width boxing and the wider zipper assembly section with angled seams on the narrower piece, located at the intersection of the beveled side and the square ones. You will achieve the smoothest transition if you make these seams as you are sewing the boxing to the top and bottom pieces.

When the cushion is beveled, the top and bottom pieces will be two different sizes. You can mark them by tracing both sides of the foam. To cut the alignment notches, align the front and sides

Beveled cushion.

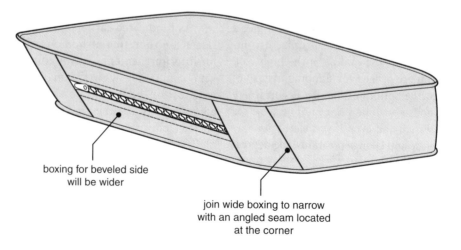

boxing for beveled side
will be wider

join wide boxing to narrow
with an angled seam located
at the corner

of the two pieces and notch the seam allowances. Then slide the smaller piece back, aligning the rear edges and the two sides. Cut matching notches in the rear edge.

Unless you have chosen canvas, the upholstery fabric you are using probably has a right side and a wrong side. Be sure that the pieces are right side to right side when you notch them. When you are seaming pieces together, they should always have the right sides facing.

Bull Nose

Instead of boxed cushions, you might prefer the softer look of bull-nose cushions. The shape of the foam determines the shape of the cushion. In this case, you will need to round the front of the foam. You can do this with shears or by shaving the foam with a very sharp knife (or an electric knife).

As for the cover, there is nothing new here. It is just our old two-piece bag but with both ends closed. Measure the front-to-back circumference of the cushion, plus a $1^1/_2$-inch seam allowance, to arrive at the cut length of the fabric. The cut width is equal to the side-to-side dimension of the cushion plus a 1-inch seam allowance. Note that this is the width of the cushion as you look at the front of it, so be sure you orient any pattern the fabric has accordingly.

Instead of folding the fabric in half and stitching the ends together as you did for a two-piece bag, you are going to sew the two ends to a zipper in the same manner that you sewed the boxing strips to the zipper (i.e., edge to edge), then fold the material to expose the teeth and topstitch the resulting hem. You will need to separate the two halves of the zipper to do this. Also notch the hem allowance at the fold to locate the center of the front edge.

Trace the outline of the end of the cushion onto the fabric, using a compass to make the rounded front uniform, then add $^3/_8$ inch all around for seam allowances. You are actually going to make $^1/_2$-inch seams, so the short allowance will tighten the fit of the cover. Cut out two pieces. Fit one end piece into an open end of the cover, matching the center notch on the main piece to the center of the radius and centering the zipper line on the square ends of the end pieces. Sew the two parts together with a row of stitching $^1/_2$ inch from the flush edges. It is usually a good idea to stitch from the center of the radius to the zipper center, then remove the cover and flip it to put the bulk under the machine arm rather than outside; this way you can sew the other edge of this side from the radius center to the

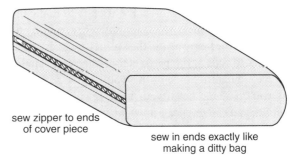

Bull-nose cushion.

sew zipper to ends of cover piece

sew in ends exactly like making a ditty bag

zipper center also. Sew in the other side the same way. This normally results in the least twist from side to side, but you can make sure by cutting matching alignment notches in the two sides before you start, then transferring their location on one side to the other side of the main piece before sewing in the second end. Unzip the cover, turn it inside out, and it is finished.

If you want to pipe the cushion around the ends and across the back, make the back edge a separate piece of fabric. Build a zipper assembly just as with any boxed cushion, and cut the main piece only wide enough to reach from the rear edge at the top, around the front of the cushion, and to the rear edge at the bottom; add a $^3/_4$-inch (cover-tightening) seam allowance. Cut the side pieces an inch or two longer so they will overlap the zipper assembly. Stitch the pieces together with piping between the cover and the boxing. Alignment notches will help you keep the ends from twisting.

Center Welt

A center-welt cushion is yet another look. Remember the one-piece hatch cap? Instead of one big corner dart with the excess cut away, if you use a softer fabric and put a bunch of little pleats in the perimeter at the corner, you still end up with a cap, only with puffy corners. Sew two such caps together with a (usually thick) piping between the layers, substituting a zipper at the back, and you have a center-welt cushion. This design can yield a comfortable, overstuffed look,

zipper in one long side

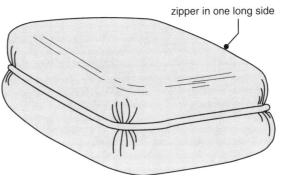

Center-welt cushion.

but it requires a soft fabric. The trick is to make up the welt cord to the correct circumference, round the corners of the fabric blank, then pleat the edges at the corners to reduce the perimeter to the same length as the welt cord. Some of this you have to make up as you go along, but if your basic sewing skills are sound, you can duplicate any look you see.

Solid Back

Backrests are not always loose cushions. They may have plywood backs. In this case you will need to cut a single piece of boxing long enough to go around the cushion—a zipper won't be needed—and wide enough to allow at least an inch of material to turn over the back. Marking the boxing where it should fold over the wood will make it easier to get the tension even. Sew up the cover, then install it by folding the boxing over the plywood and securing it there with closely spaced staples. Use only Monel staples or they will rust, releasing the cover and damaging some fabrics.

Covers for plywood-backed backrests may not be boxed at all. A flat piece of material can simply be folded around the foam and plywood and stapled down. Again, a traced line marking the desired location of the folds will help you get the piece on straight. You will have to work each of the corners with patience to fold the excess material over smoothly and evenly.

Buttons are another common feature in boat upholstery. They help to stabilize a cushion, especially by keeping the fabric in a backrest from sagging. The biggest drawback is that they have to be removed anytime you want to remove the cover. You can buy button "blanks" that you cover yourself, or you can have them done by an upholsterer who will have a machine that does them quickly and easily. If you do your own, try to find blanks with the ring or eye attached to the button rather than to the back.

Buttons on either side of a loose cushion are tied together with waxed sail twine. Put the doubled twine through the ring of the button, then spread the bight of the twine and pass it over the top of the button to put a bale sling on the ring. Thread both ends of the twine into a needle and push it through the cushion. Remove the needle and pass both ends through the ring of the second button. Pull the thread to obtain the tuck you desire, then wrap the ends twice in opposite directions around the shaft or throat of the ring—where the ring attaches—and finish with a couple of square knots. Buttoning a plywood-backed backrest is the same except that the thread must pass through a predrilled hole in the wood, and the two ends are threaded through two holes of a backing button and knotted together.

If you are re-covering cushions that are a different design from any mentioned in this chapter, take the old cover apart to see how it was cut and assembled. If you are trying to duplicate something you came across on a friend's boat, see if they will let you unzip a cover and take a peek inside. Special shapes often are no more than extra batting glued to the foam, but you may also find special flaps or ties inside the cushion that achieve a certain look.

One final comment on interior canvaswork. When you are finished, if there is a small pucker in the corner or a few ripples in the boxing, you are the only one who will notice them. The most effective treatment for these little flaws (professionally made cushions have them too, I assure you) is a couple of stitches—between your upper and lower lips.

CUSTOM CANVAS

Some canvas items found on boats do not fall into any of the categories I have listed. Such items require custom canvaswork, but even here assembly and finishing will not differ from the techniques we have already considered. Custom work is generally facilitated by fabricating the item from stiff paper, then trimming and adjusting and taping the parts together until the desired fit is achieved. You then disassemble or cut the paper apart and use the pieces as patterns for cutting the fabric. More complicated items may first be constructed from inexpensive pattern cloth, fitted, adjusted, then duplicated in canvas.

SAIL COVER

A cover for the furled sail is an essential item for any sailboat that stows its mainsail (and/or mizzen) on the boom. Otherwise the life of the sail will be

Covering a backrest.

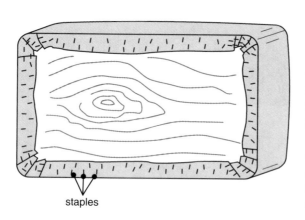

staples

severely and unnecessarily shortened by damage from the UV rays of the sun. A sail cover also serves to "dress" the boat, so most are constructed from brightly colored acrylic canvas.

Little about a sail cover is complicated. It may be helpful to think of it as two wedge-shaped pieces of cloth—wide at the mast and narrow at the end of the boom—seamed together along the top, and buttoned or laced together at the bottom and along the forward edge. Except for the fact that the top edge normally has an upward curve at the fat end, this description pretty well defines a sail cover.

To determine the length of the cover, measure from the center of the forward side of the mast around the bulk of the furled sail and to the end of the boom. The maximum height of the cover can be determined by measuring from the bottom of the boom to a point on the mast about 6 inches above the reposed headboard. Joining these two measurements with straight lines will give you a triangle that is roughly the size of one side of the cover, but you need to dial in the actual measurements a bit more closely.

Lay out the exact shape of the curved spine of the cover by measuring from the bottom center of the boom to the top center of the furled sail every 3 to 6 inches near the mast and every foot or two once the slope of the furled sail becomes regular. Write down these measurements and their stations—their locations relative to the mast. Add 3 inches to each measurement for a $1^1/_2$ inch (both folds) double rubbed seam at the bottom. You also need a $^1/_2$-inch seam allowance on the curved edge, but adding an additional $^1/_2$ inch to the vertical dimension will not give you what you need because the curve turns vertically. Instead, with the end of the fabric cut square to the edges, plot the curve on the fabric, moving all of the stations back from the end an additional 4 inches to provide a hem allowance forward of the mast. Also account for the depth of the mast if you located your series of height measurements from the back of the mast. In other words, if your first height measurement was at the sail track—where it should be—the station on the cloth will be your mast depth, plus half the mast width, plus 4 inches from the end of the fabric. Now move every dot $^1/_2$ inch *perpendicular to the curve* at that dot. You can actually connect all of the dots first, then draw a second line that will be $^1/_2$ inch from the first, or you can just visualize the first curve to move your dots perpendicular, connecting only the second set of dots into a smooth curve.

Except for the smallest sail covers, the curved line of the spine is going to run off the opposite edge of the fabric as it approaches the mast end of the cover. You will have to add fabric here to get the necessary width, but because this is easier to do after the main piece has been cut out, we will come back to it.

Laying out the piece for the opposite side in the opposite direction and from the opposite edge so the narrow ends overlap as far as their widths allow will usually result in the most efficient use of the fabric. However, note that laid out this way the second piece is identical rather than a mirror image. That does not matter when both sides of the fabric are the same, but it matters a lot if the fabric has a "bad" side. Cut out the two halves of the cover.

Now cut a pair of rectangles long enough to add the width you need to complete your curve plus a 4-inch hem allowance and the same width as that of the short selvaged edge of the cover half you've already cut. Orient these rectangles on your fabric to put the weave the same way as with the rest of the cover, i.e., with the edge to be seamed along the edge of the fabric. If cutting the add-on pieces as rectangles wastes a lot of material because the spine curve is not yet approaching vertical where the extension attaches, then cut paper patterns of the extension and lay them out on the fabric to minimize waste. Align the extension piece with the front and top edges of the main cover piece and seam the two together $^1/_2$ inch from the top edge. Match selvaged edges if possible; otherwise bind this seam. Fold the seam flat against the main piece and sew it down with two parallel rows of stitching about $^1/_4$ inch apart. Add the extension piece to the other side in exactly the same way, taking great care to put the hem on the correct side to create a mirror-image piece. Now finish plotting the curve of the spine on both halves, add the $^1/_2$-inch hem allowance (now mostly more width than height), and trim away the excess canvas.

Once the two sides are cut to size, the next step is to seam them together along the spine. A flat-felled seam is the normal choice for joining two raw edges, but a flat-felled seam will be hard to make in the curve of the spine. You will get the same seam quality without the headache if you make the spine seam exactly the way you just added the extension pieces. Put the two halves together good side to good side, determined by the extension seam, and align the spine edges. Stitch the length of the spine about $^1/_2$ inch from the edge and bind this seam. Butterfly the cover, and starting at the small end, fold the seam to one side and sew it down with two parallel rows of stitching about $^1/_4$ inch apart.

Check the cover blank for fit by spreading it over the sail. If mast-mounted winches interfere with the

Measure around
the furled sail.

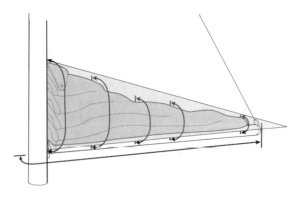

Transfer
measurements
to fabric, adding
allowances.
Normally an
additional piece of
fabric is needed
to meet the cover
height.

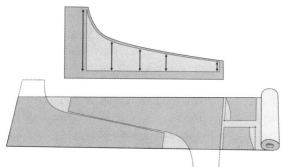

Seam the top piece
to the main piece
for each side, then
join the two cover
halves with a seam
at the spine. Bind
this seam, then
sew it down to
one side with two
parallel rows of
stitching.

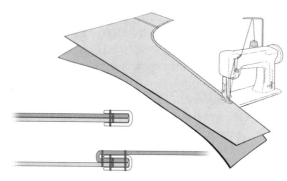

flap behind

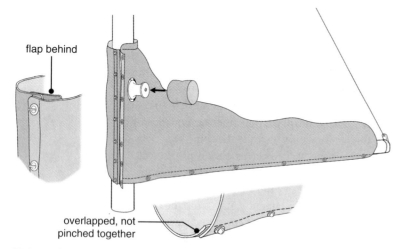

overlapped, not
pinched together

Finish by fitting winch pockets as required and installing closures.

Making a sail cover.

fit, cut holes to allow the winches to protrude, taking great care to get the holes in the right positions. The vertical height of the hole can be transferred directly to the cover blank, provided you have the cover positioned correctly height-wise, but you cannot transfer the fore-and-aft position of the winch directly to the fabric as easily. You must measure the distance from the *center of the base of the winch at the mast* to the spine seam to locate the center of the hole for the winch. Measure twice for the first hole, cut it, and position the cover over the winch. Only after the cover is over the first winch and correctly positioned should you move on to a second winch. Here again, take the fore-and-aft measurement from the base of the winch to the cover spine. Later you will add boots over these holes, but for now we just want to be able to fit the cover.

When you have the cover in place, determine where you want it to end on the mast and at the end of the boom. Allow yourself 3 additional inches of fabric and trim the top and end as appropriate. The bottom and front hem allowances are for triple thickness hems that overlap $1\frac{1}{2}$ inches to accommodate turn-button closure—what I think is the best method for securing a sail cover. However, if you want a hook-and-lace fastening, the finished hems should be a couple of inches short of meeting when hemmed. For a zippered closure the hems should just touch. Make any necessary adjustments.

Closures

Once you are satisfied with the fit, hem all the raw edges. Install fasteners in the front and bottom. You know how to install a zipper, but in this case the hems are already in place, so simply align the fold with the center of the teeth and sew a #10 separating zipper to the hems. You need to hand-stitch or rivet the hooks for a hook-and-lace closure. The opposite side is a pair of grommets. Install turn-button fasteners by melting slits in the fabric for the bend tabs with a heated knife. The turn button has two tabs that simply clinch over an oblong backing plate. The matching eyelet requires four slits for four tabs that clinch over a flat eyelet. Cut the cloth from the center of the eyelet with a hot blade *after* the eyelet is installed and clinched. Always install turn-button fasteners with the fabric overlapping, as with shirt buttons, never with the fabric pinched together edge to edge. Place turn buttons or lace hooks every 6 inches on the front of the mast and every 18 inches along the boom.

If you want a rain collar, you can sew one on that overlaps and fit the end with snaps placed to

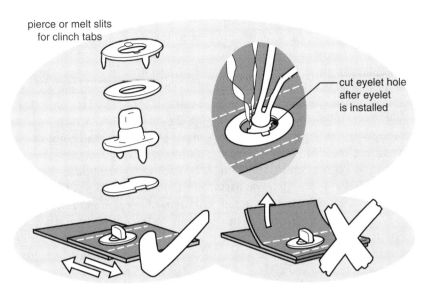

pierce or melt slits
for clinch tabs

cut eyelet hole
after eyelet
is installed

pull should be sideways, not up

*Installing turn
buttons.*

pull the collar tight. Or you can simply eliminate the overlap at the top hem and install two pairs of grommets to allow the top of the cover to be laced tight. However, if you have any external halyards, a collar will not seal, and if you have several external halyards and you tie them off to keep them quiet, it probably won't even close.

All that remains is to sew boots over the winches. Be sure the holes in the cover are plenty large enough to pass the winch easily, then measure the diameter of the hole, add 1 inch, and multiply that by 3.14. Add a couple of inches to the result for a seam allowance and to give you some adjustment flexibility. This is the length of the piece of fabric you need for the boot. The width should be the distance from the mast to the top of the winch plus 1 inch. Cut this piece of fabric.

On the inside of the cover, mark a stitch line $^1/_2$ inch back from the edge of the hole. With the tip of your scissors, make $^1/_4$-inch slits about every inch right around the perimeter of the hole. Put the cover with the marked side up on top of the boot fabric and align the edge of the hole with the long edge of the fabric. Starting 1 inch from the end of the fabric, stitch the cover on the circular pencil line around the hole, keeping the edge of the hole flush with the fabric beneath. If you can manage to start this at what will be the bottom of the hole when the cover is in place, that will put the seam of the finished boot at the bottom.

When you have sewn nearly all the way around the hole, stop and remove the work from the sewing machine. Push the boot through the hole to turn it inside out, then pinch together the ends where they are going to meet when you complete the circumference. Seam them together, keeping them parallel (but probably not flush). Trim the seam to leave $^1/_2$ inch or less of fabric and bind the raw edges. Push the closed tube back through the hole. Finish the perimeter seam and bind it. Turn the canvas tube inside out again. Cut a canvas circle the diameter of the tube plus 1 inch, and sew it into the open end of the tube exactly like you sewed in the bottom of a two-piece bag. You can pipe this seam if you want to get fancy. Bind the seam, push the closed tube back through the hole, and you have a winch boot.

If I've left anything out, do what seems right. And if some step doesn't work for you, change it. It's your sail cover.

LAZY PACK

The integral mainsail cover has been around for more than 25 years, but not until the growth in popularity of multihulls sparked wider interest in the fully battened mainsail did this type of cover receive an enthusiastic reception. Also the trend toward ever-bigger boats has led to mains so big and booms so high that furling is difficult, dangerous, or (above a center cockpit bimini) impossible. Unwieldy mainsails have also sparked the renaissance of a very old technology, lazyjacks, which has contributed to increasing interest in the integral sail cover because lazyjacks tend to interfere with the installation of a boom coat.

The idea behind an integral cover is admirable. Open the zipper on its spine and the cover opens like a peapod, allowing the enclosed sail to be hoisted right out. At the end of the day, drop the sail—corralled by lazyjacks—and it falls back between the open sides of the pod. Zip. Done.

Except that things rarely go quite that easily. The cover is fabric, not a stiff peapod, so unless you hold the top edges up somehow, it is just two crumpled strips of canvas between the jacklines and the boom (or hanging straight down if you don't have lazyjacks). Even if you support the upper edges of the cover halves by stretching them between the mast and the topping lift, the sail is not going to fall into the resulting slot unless the cover is an integral part of the lazyjack system. When you're lucky, the sail collapses in a loose flake, but more often it is just a tall pile of stiff cloth that you will have to crush down some if you don't want the lazy pack to be the approximate size of a storm trysail. And at the end of it all you have to get to that zipper, dead center on the highest point of the furled sail, and pinch the halves together while you draw the zipper slide from the end of the boom all the way up the slope to the mast. This often turns out to be a two-person job. Most of the lazy packs I see are unzipped, which defeats the purpose of a sail cover.

What follows are generic instructions for constructing a lazy pack. You will have to make a number of design decisions, most of which are compromises, and do not be surprised if the finished product is not as easy to use as advertised.

Essentially the lazy pack is composed of two triangular pieces of cloth with their narrow ends cut

A lazy pack is typically closed at the bottom and front, closes with a zipper at the top, and is open at the back.

off. The front and bottom sides attach to each other or to the sides of the spars at the mast and boom. The top edges are normally battened and join with the zipper and the aft edges are left open.

The length dimension is determined from the length of the foot of the sail plus an allowance to let the forward end attach to or wrap around the mast. Determine the height or depth of the panels by measuring from the attachment location of the pack along the boom—we're coming to this—around and to the top of the dropped sail at several stations along the boom. Transfer these measurements to the fabric, then draw a *straight* line that approximately follows the series of marks you have made; be sure this line does not pass below any of your marks. You do not want the cover to be shorter than your measurements suggest. Add hem allowances to the width.

Sewn to the Sail

The original StackPack, an innovation of Doyle Sailmakers, is sewn to the foot of the sail. This is probably the best way to secure a lazy pack at the boom. The halves can also be joined at the bottom with snaps or Velcro straps that pass under a loose or slug-attached foot. They can be sewn to boltrope fed into the empty boom track when the sail is loose footed, or attached at and to slugs that you alternate with the sail slugs. If the foot of your main attaches with a boltrope, you can put slots or grommets in the sail to allow the two sides of the cover to be connected (which I recommend against), you can attach boltrope track to either side of the boom, or you can reconfigure the sail to attach with slugs.

The Doyle StackPack has another feature that makes it more satisfactory than most other designs: the top of the cover is also sewn to the sail. Actually the top of the cover is sewn to a second piece of light fabric—light sailcloth is fine and the least obtrusive—that is the same shape as the cover but about 75% the width (depth) of the canvas piece. The bottom of the canvas is sewn to the foot of the sail. The sail is laid out flat with the light piece of fabric, what Doyle calls a "membrane," extending up the sail from the top of the canvas where it has already been sewn. With the sail, the cover, and the fully extended membrane all laying smooth, the top edge of the membrane is stitched to the sail. When the sail is hoisted, this pulls the top edge of the pack flat against it. When the sail is lowered, it releases the tension on the membrane and the pack falls open as normal. All other designs suffer from a billowing

turn buttons

jacklines

topping lift

grommets

strap eye

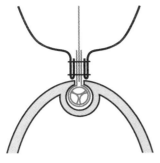

Sewn to foot of sail.

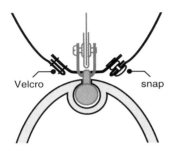

Joined beneath the slug-attached or loose-footed sail with snap or Velcro straps.

Velcro   snap

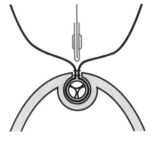

Attached to boltrope in boom track beneath loose-footed sail.

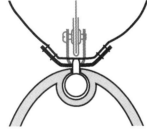

Attached to slugs alternating with sail slugs or beneath loose-footed sail.

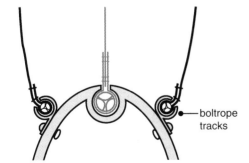

boltrope tracks

Attached to boltrope tracks installed on either side of boom.

Lazy pack bottom closure possibilities.

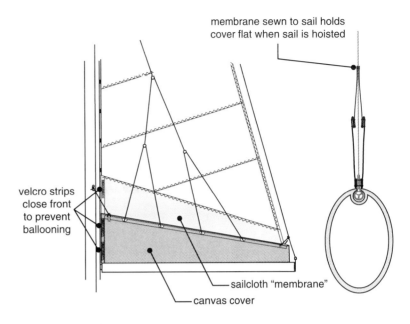

membrane sewn to sail holds cover flat when sail is hoisted

velcro strips close front to prevent ballooning

sailcloth "membrane"

canvas cover

Using a "membrane" to support the top edge.

cover when the wind pipes up, unless you manually reef the cover sides. Even the StackPack design can get air blowing inside the hollow. Self-peeling Velcro strips are used at the ends to hold them closed and prevent this.

At the forward end, you can fasten the two halves of the cover together forward of the mast, fasten them to the mast if the cover is not attached to the sail, or support them with single lines from the forward top corner of each panel leading diagonally upward and forward to an strap eye on the mast. Similar to the latter attachment, the aft ends are normally supported with a line tied to the topping lift. If the topping is not fixed to the end of the boom but passes through a block there, the cover must be attached with a rolling hitch to prevent topping-lift adjustment from putting a strain on the cover. Where the mast is supported by a rigid vang and you don't have and don't want a topping lift, you will have to buy or fabricate a crane to install at the end of the boom to provide the needed attachment point for the cover.

The jacklines must attach to the lazy pack. This can be done in a number of ways, but two are most common. One is to terminate the jacklines to webbing loops sewn to the top edges of the cover halves. The other is to run the lines into, then back outside of each cover half through two grommets positioned one above the other at the top edge, terminating the ends of the jacklines at the bottom of the boom. The grommet method allows a lazy pack released at its forward end to be furled alongside the boom.

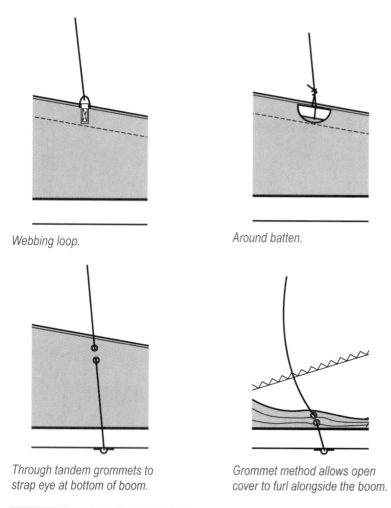

Webbing loop.   Around batten.

Through tandem grommets to strap eye at bottom of boom.   Grommet method allows open cover to furl alongside the boom.

Jackline attachment methods.

Top Battens

One reality of a 12- or 15-foot ribbon of cloth restrained only every 5 feet is that, in a breeze, it will flap like a flag. The usual solution for this assault on the tranquillity of sailing is a full-length batten sewn into the top edge of each side. You can use small-diameter PVC water pipe, but protect the ends or the acrylic canvas will quickly chafe through. You may also want to incorporate a stiff flap over the zipper to protect it from UV damage.

That is about it. Size, cut, and hem the two panels, including a batten pocket at the top edges. Join the panels at the top with a full-length separating zipper that closes toward the mast. Join the bottom edges under the foot of the sail, attach them to the boom, or sew them to the sail. Install the necessary webbing loops to support the ends of the pack, the grommets or loops for the jacklines, and the appropriate fastener or fasteners for closing the front of the cover. It bears mentioning that Doyle closes the front

of its sewn-to-the-sail StackPack with a separate piece of fabric that wraps around the front of the mast and zips to the forward edges of both sides of the cover.

Despite what you have heard, a lazy pack is not automatic. Even if your sail stacks neatly between the halves of the cover when you drop it, the cradled sail remains as exposed to the sun as a tourist on the beach. You have to get the sail stuffed down enough for the cover to close, and you have to zip it closed every time for your sail to benefit.

SUN STRIPS

A roller-furled sail also needs sun protection, but a zip-over or button-on cover is not practical. Most roller-furling sails come with built-in sun protection in the form of a strip of protective fabric sewn to the luff and foot on one side. When the sail is fully furled, only this sacrificial strip is exposed.

Sun strips wear out—or at least die of exposure. Usually it is the thread that fails first, releasing the fabric to beat itself to death as it whips in the accelerated air of the sail leech. When times were particularly lean, I once removed an acrylic sun strip that needed restitching and reversed it to restore the bright color and get 2 or 3 more years of service from this incredibly durable fabric. Replacement fabric would have cost $100 I did not have. Sun strips are deceptive in how much fabric they require.

I recently replaced the sun cover on a sail I bought used. The cover on the sail was still in good shape, but it was not a match for our other canvas, which the mate found offensive. Just for reference, I priced having the strip installed by a sailmaker. It was about three times what I had paid for the sail. Ouch!

Ninety-five percent of sun-strip replacement is dead easy. It helps to have a big space available so the sail can spread out. If the sail is heavy, putting your sewing machine on the floor can also help. Sit in the lotus position and operate the foot pedal with the side of your knee.

Always install solar strips in 46-inch lengths. This is the width of acrylic canvas, and if you cut the panels across the fabric, each strip will have a selvage on both ends. This lets you join the strips with a simple overlap seam, which is both easier and smoother. Short strips also follow the hollow of the leech without the necessity of shaping the fabric.

The location of the strips is determined by the sun strip you are removing. If you are putting a strip on a sail that has not had one, close observation should reveal how much of the leech and foot has been exposed to the sun. If this is not apparent, use a pencil to trace the edge of the foot and the edge of the leech as high as you can reach on the furled sail. Extrapolate the strip width for the portion of the leech you cannot mark. Typically it narrows only slightly.

The inside edge of the strip should be folded under $1/4$ inch and sewn down with a straight stitch in the middle of the overlap or with a zigzag stitch just overlapping the folded edge. The small fold is to minimize weight and bulk. I tend to move the edge slightly inboard of the old stitch line to avoid additional needle perforations in the same line.

The outside edge can be attached in at least three different ways. It can be folded under and stitched just like the inside edge, the fold flush with

or slightly beyond the leech of the sail. Or you can fold the sun strip around the leech, fold under the edge of the canvas on the back side, and stitch it down like the other edge; this adds the most bulk but provides the most protection. The third method is to cut the outside of the strip to match the leech and sew it beneath the leech tape. This is the best method when the sail has a lot of curvature in the leech. It is also the lightest and least bulky solution, but it makes the leech tape sacrificial and gives the furled sail a white spiral. A "cure" for these two concerns is to capture the edge with a matching acrylic binding or *facing* (binding with one side larger) rather than the leech tape.

Begin this project by removing the old sun strip with the assistance of your seam ripper. Be sure you cut only the stitches that secure the strip and not any that hold the sail panels together. A small sewing machine will not stitch through the bulk of head, tack, and clew sail patches, so you may have to

Where reinforced corners are too heavy for your sewing machine, a prefabricated pocket slipped onto the corner like a sock and stitched to the sail beyond the thickest part can serve.

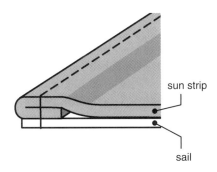

Turned under on top of sail.

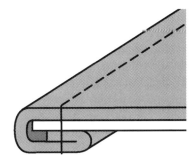

Folded around leech and turned under on bottom of sail.

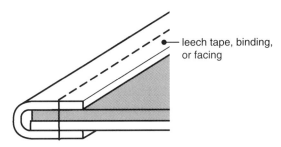

Cut flush and secured with leech tape or matching binding or facing.

Sun-strip leech edge.

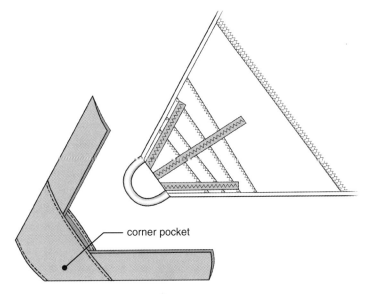

corner pocket

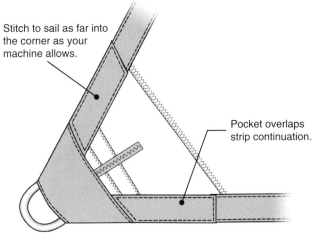

Stitch to sail as far into the corner as your machine allows.

Pocket overlaps strip continuation.

make a choice here. One option is to leave the existing protective canvas in place at the corners of the sail. You do this by cutting the old strip beyond the bulkiest part of the corner. If the corner canvas is in bad shape, you can fabricate a triangular pocket—a kind of sock—that slips over the corner with the ring or grommet exposed. The pocket needs to be long enough to extend onto a part of the sail your machine can penetrate. When you pull the fitted pocket over the corner tightly, stitching across the end will secure it. Your third option is to have a sailmaker do just the corners for you.

You can trace the edge of the old sun cover before removing it, but the old stitch holes will normally outline it adequately. Pay attention to whether the old cover completely protects the sail. I see many rolled sails with a bit of sailcloth showing. If you have this problem, increase the width of the new strip sufficiently to cover the exposed areas. Also be sure you put the new strip on the same side as the old one unless you are also changing the direction the furling gear turns.

However you elect to finish the outboard edge, cut and install the strips one at a time. This is not the fastest way, but it will prove to be the least confusing and is certain to yield the best result. The process is to determine the width of the first strip, beginning at either the head or the tack, then cut that strip and sew it to the sail. The dimensions of the next strip are determined by the strip width on the sail at the end of the strip you just installed and at a point 45 inches from that strip—allowing a 1-inch overlap of your 46-inch fabric. Cut the second strip and attach it. And so on. When you have sewn on the last strip, your sun cover is complete.

Install strip in panels the length of the fabric width, typically 46 inches. Cut and install one at a time to assure the correct width at every location on the sail.

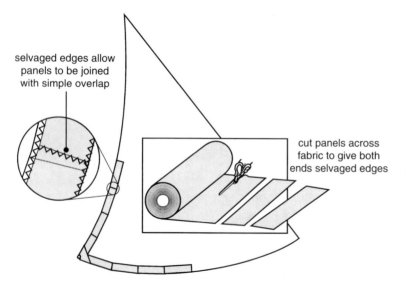

selvaged edges allow panels to be joined with simple overlap

cut panels across fabric to give both ends selvaged edges

BIMINI

The bimini top takes us back to where we started—with the flat sheet. A bimini is nothing more than a flat sheet of canvas or reinforced vinyl hemmed on the sides and cut on either end to the contour of the supporting bows. A strip of fabric cut to the same contour is seamed, right side to right side, to each end and then folded over on the seam line and hemmed underneath to form a contoured sleeve at each end. This is the same as putting a curved hem on a flat sheet, described back in the section on weather cloths.

You install a bimini by slipping the sleeves over the bows before they are assembled into the framework. If the top has more than two bows, you fabricate sleeves for them in the appropriate location by sewing hemmed strips onto the underside of the fabric—exactly like spreader sleeves in an awning. The top can be made readily removable by attaching one side of each of the pockets with a zipper instead of stitches. If the top is pitched slightly by the center bow to improve its water-shedding qualities, it will need darts in the sides to shorten the edges.

It may be necessary for the straps that hold the frame in its unfolded position to attach to the top of the frame. You accommodate this with half-circle cutouts in the outer edges of the fabric strips that form the front and rear sleeves. When you sew the strips to the top, the cutouts end up on the underside of the bow, providing an exit for the tie-down straps.

Where the top is wider than the fabric, the necessary seam should run fore and aft. A single center seam might serve, but the top will look better with a full-width panel in the middle joined with parallel seams to two equal side panels. Tandem seams strengthen the canvas against the pull of the tie-down straps. Configure the double-rubbed seams to put the center panel on top at both sides to make the seams less likely to hold water.

Any bimini top that you make will have a more professional look if you sew "visors" into the front and rear of the top. Visors are simply folded strips of fabric that are stitched between the top and bottom of the end sleeves in exactly the same manner as piping and for the same reasons. Cut a strip of material 3 inches wide and 2 inches longer than the edge of the top. Fold the ends in 1 inch, then fold the strip in half lengthwise and run a line of stitching across each end. When you stitch the contoured sleeve to the edge of the top, put the visor between both pieces so that all raw edges are flush. When you complete the sleeve by sewing the loose edge to the underside of the top, the visor forms an attractive skirt across

1

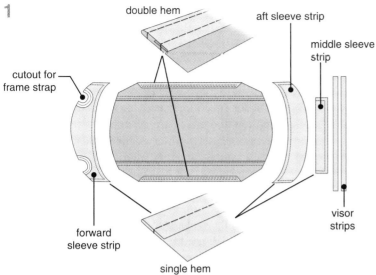

double hem
aft sleeve strip
middle sleeve strip
cutout for frame strap
forward sleeve strip
single hem
visor strips

The needed components.

2

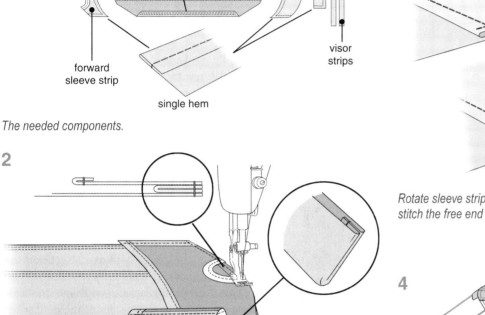

Sew the folded visor strip into the sleeve seam exactly like piping.

3

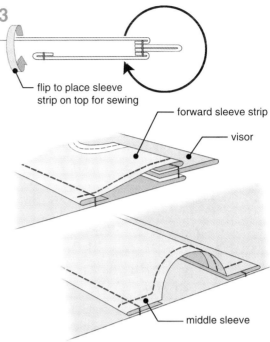

flip to place sleeve strip on top for sewing
forward sleeve strip
visor
middle sleeve

Rotate sleeve strip 180 degrees to underside of top and stitch the free end to close it.

4

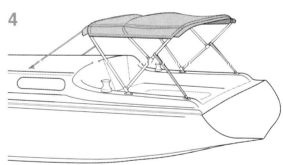

The finished top.

Bimini top.

the front (and rear) of the bimini, hiding the bow sleeve and giving the top a finished look.

ABOUT THE FRAME

This is a treatise of canvaswork, but the relationship between the bimini (or dodger) and the support frame makes some comments on frame construction in order. You can sail around in the bay with any kind of frame you like, but do not go offshore with a frame constructed of anything less rigid than $7/_8$-inch *stainless steel* tubing. There is an unavoidable tendency to grab the frame for support. Aluminum tubing, if it

doesn't pitch you over the side, will be knocked hopelessly out of shape. Don't try to save a few bucks using inferior frame hardware either. Plastic fittings are for runabouts, and pot metal fittings lack the requisite strength and corrosion resistance. High-quality stainless steel fittings are readily available and can make custom frame configurations a snap.

The sticking point is bending the tubing. For my first dodger project, I priced a frame from a local top fabricator and was shocked at the quote, but my visit wasn't wasted when I saw the homemade plywood bender they used to bend the tubing. I found a

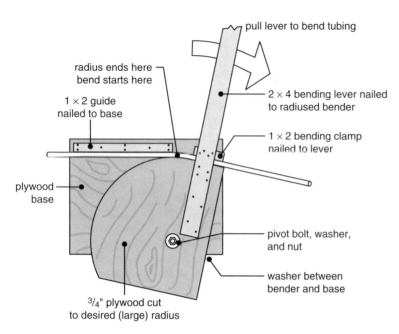

pull lever to bend tubing

radius ends here
bend starts here

1 × 2 guide
nailed to base

2 × 4 bending lever nailed
to radiused bender

1 × 2 bending clamp
nailed to lever

plywood
base

pivot bolt, washer,
and nut

washer between
bender and base

³/₄" plywood cut
to desired (large) radius

*Homemade tubing
bender.*

supplier of stainless steel tubing, nailed together the bender in the sketch, and built the frame myself in a couple of hours for less than $100.

If you design and fabricate your own framework, you will need to make sure that it does not hamper the operation of the boat. Will the boom clear the top in all circumstances? Will the top hamper sail trim? Does it interfere with the mainsheet? Can you comfortably and powerfully crank the sheet winches? Can you get out of the cockpit to go forward without being a contortionist? Have you given adequate thought to where it goes when you want to fold it down? Making up a trial frame from inexpensive plastic water pipe, elbow fittings, and duct tape can show up problems that would otherwise appear only after the actual frame is completed. Covering it with kraft paper and sailing with it in place is an even better test.

Speaking of kraft paper, if you are replacing a bimini top, you can dismantle the old one and use it as a pattern, but if you are making a top to fit a frame you just fabricated, the way to a drum-tight fit is to make a paper top. (Don't do this on a windy day!) Tweak and pull and take apart and retape until you have a smooth, tight, brown-paper top. Mark the paper with lines centered on the tubing at the very front and the very back. Also carefully mark the side height. Trim the sides with scissors, then carefully cut the front and back lines with a razor knife or blade. This will release the paper top and create a perfect pattern. Don't forget to add hem allowances.

DODGER

I would like to say that a dodger is nothing more than a bimini top with a windshield, and in some respects that is an accurate description. But because

the dodger also has panels that enclose the side of the supporting framework and because it must be attached to the deck, it can be somewhat more complicated than a bimini.

Replacing a dodger is easier than constructing one from scratch because the design work has been done for you. Simply take the old dodger apart, noting how the pieces are assembled, and use the old pieces as patterns for new canvas and clear vinyl.

If you are starting from scratch, the project is more involved, but it is not beyond the capabilities of anyone with modest skill on the sewing machine. Perseverance can even make up for a skill deficit, so if you really want a new dodger, read on.

You will need to start by answering most of the questions in the preceding section concerning bimini top frames, plus one or two related to access to the companionway. Crawling in and out over the bridge deck wears more than your knees thin. Additionally, you have to engineer the attachment of the front of the dodger to the deck and across the main hatch. A plastic pipe mock-up is again a good place to start. Angular connections can be made with duct tape. Fold the frame to see where it goes. Guy the bows to hold them in position, and tape paper or fabric over them to get an idea of how the dodger will look. Go below and come on deck to see if you lose any teeth or crush your skull. Reeve the headsail sheets and crank the winches; remember that the sides of the dodger will extend somewhat aft of the rear bow. Hoist the mainsail and slacken the topping lift to check the clearance. Stand at the helm to be sure you can see *over* the dodger, which will be impossible to see *through* when it is coated with salt or spray. Now get off the boat and look at the dodger from every direction. How does it look? Would it look better shorter? Wider? Is the windshield too near vertical? Answer all these questions with your paper-and-plastic-pipe model.

Build the frame and install it. If at all possible put some curvature in the center of the bows to prevent the flat expanse of the top from "puddling" in the rain at anchor. A single curve from deck to deck results in a dodger that sheds water like an umbrella, and although it can be very attractive on some boats, such a dodger tends to restrict the crew's ability to wedge themselves into the forward corners of the cockpit. Be sure you can sit comfortably under the dodger.

PAPER PATTERN

Open the frame and use duct tape straps to position the bows in relation to each other. Rig guys fore and aft to hold the open frame in position. Lay something long, straight, and rigid across the bows to make sure they are the same height—or raked properly if you want some rake. Once again, cover the frame with paper, this time taking care to get the paper over the frame smoothly. With tape and kraft paper, create a paper dodger that looks *exactly* how you want the finished item to look. Tape the front piece to the deck and extend the side "wings" back along the coaming to the point where they will be anchored. Work out any fit problems, such as where the cockpit coaming attaches to the deckhouse, by cutting and fitting until you find a way that will work.

Outline on the front of the dodger what portion will be clear. Draw in the location of the zippers that will allow you to open the front panel. If the sides will have windows, decide on their positions and sketch them in.

Decide how the front of the dodger will attach to the deck. The most watertight, and generally the strongest, attachment is a boltrope inserted into an extrusion screwed to the deck. When this is not practical, turn-button fasteners can be used. Attaching these to the front of a coaming or coamings mounted to the cabin top not only makes the dodger more watertight, it makes the stress on the turn buttons shear, which they will resist with greater strength. Snaps are not a good idea at the front of a dodger because lifting stress will just unsnap them. Snaps are often used to secure the sides, but turn buttons will be more secure here as well. If the side wings extend high enough on the aft bow, the dodger can be fully tensioned with lacings through grommets in the wings' aft corners

A dodger headed south must have an opening windshield. This is easily accomplished with a couple of vertical zippers if the front attaches with turn buttons. For a boltrope-secured dodger you will need to incorporate a windshield that opens with a continuous zipper that scribes a wide U. There are other windshield options; look around at other dodgers before you decide on the design you want.

If your main hatch does not slide into a hood, attaching the front edge across the hatch can present a challenge. Sometimes a mainsheet traveler is providentially located in the right place. If not, blocks on either side of the hatch may be needed to position the edge to allow the hatch to slide through a flapped slot.

Once you have the attachment and the windshield opening worked out, mark the paper mock-up with the dodger's front edge—where it touches the cabin top. Continue this line to define the side edges of the dodger. Mark the seam line on the forward bow by splitting the angle the top makes with the front and continuing this line down both sides of

the forward bow. Mark the aft seam for the aft bow pocket by drawing a line at the aft-most position across the bow, again continuing this line down both sides of the aft bow. This should divide your paper dodger into the four basic pieces common to nearly all dodger designs—a football-shaped top panel, a similarly shaped front panel, and two triangular side wings. Some additional pieces may be necessary to get the dodger to conform to the requirements of your particular installation. Everywhere you are going to need a seam, mark those lines on the paper. Also mark zipper locations. Label each section and draw short lines across the seam lines to show how the pieces should mate after you cut them apart.

Take one more stroll on the docks or a spin in the dinghy to make sure you are pleased with the effect. If so, cut the pattern apart along the seam lines. This should yield flat paper patterns that you can use to lay out the canvas, making adequate seam allowances. Transfer your alignment marks to the hem allowance of the cut canvas to assist in the assembly.

CLEAR VIEW

If the front panel is mostly clear vinyl, fabricate the assembly by framing the vinyl panels with hemmed strips of canvas. Use your longest stitch when sewing vinyl. Fold the canvas strips lengthwise, fold both edges inside, slip the vinyl between the folded edges, and stitch. This gives a finished edge both inside and outside the window. Hem the ends of the strips. Complete the front panel by installing the zipper or zippers.

For the best visibility buy 0.020 clear vinyl in sheet form. The optical qualities of press-polished vinyl sheets are superior to vinyl sold by the yard from a roll. The additional strength of a heavier weight is

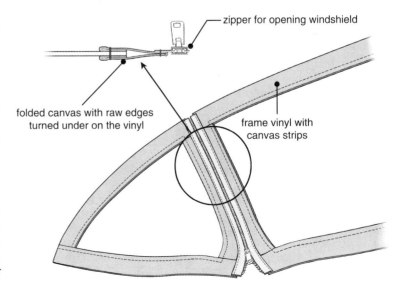

Dodger windshield assembly.

zipper for opening windshield

folded canvas with raw edges turned under on the vinyl

frame vinyl with canvas strips

rarely a real benefit, and because heavier sheet vinyls are often laminated from thinner materials, they tend to darken or cloud sooner, contrary to expectation.

Using the top piece as a pattern, cut two contoured 4-inch-wide canvas strips to form the sleeves for the frame bows. The front one should extend only across the relatively straight length of the bow, stopping short of the side bends. The back one should generally extend around the side bends and slightly beyond where the wings attach. Hem the ends and the inside edge of these two strips, and if you want to be able to remove the dodger easily, sew one side of a #10 separating zipper to the hemmed edge of each strip with the zipper tab on the good side of the fabric.

Cut four triangular reinforcement patches and capture them in the bottom and aft hems of the side panels—just like corner reinforcement for an awning. The diagonal edge of the topmost patch will need to be hemmed. The forward edge of the wing piece is not hemmed. It will be seamed to the dodger assembly.

You should also cut a 3-inch-wide strip of leather or reinforced vinyl about the length of the straight(est) section of the aft bow. The aft bow of your new dodger will instantly become your most-used handhold, so it will soon be soiled, later worn out, if you do not protect it with a chafe strip.

Side windows—round, triangular, or shaped like Mickey Mouse—are not difficult to include in your dodger, provided you follow the correct sequence. Cut the clear vinyl to the shape you want, but add 1¼ inches

The primary dodger components.

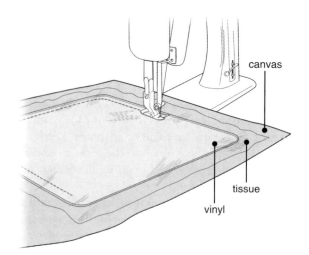

Sandwich vinyl between canvas and tissue paper and sew around the perimeter.

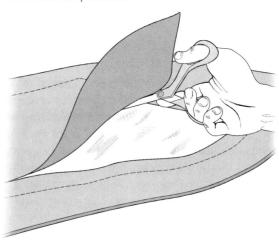

Cut canvas 1 inch inside the stitch line only after the vinyl is sewn in place.

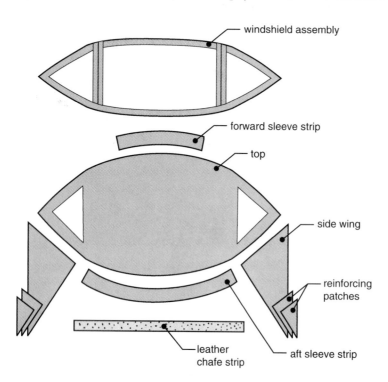

windshield assembly

forward sleeve strip

top

side wing

reinforcing patches

leather chafe strip

aft sleeve strip

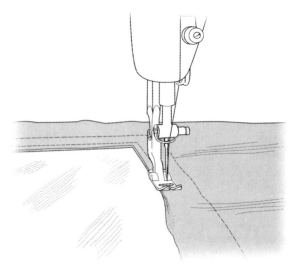

Fold under cut edge and stitch at fold to create hem.

Sewn-in-place vinyl windows.

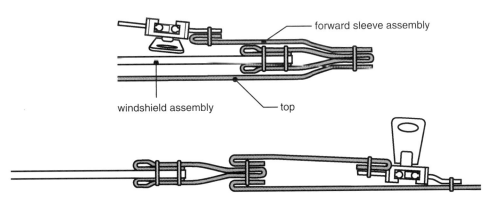

forward sleeve assembly

windshield assembly — top

Fold both sleeve assembly and top 180 degrees and stitch together.

Forward seam detail.

all around. Place the vinyl on the inside surface of the top section of canvas where you want the window located. Pin it in place to hold it, and cover it with a sheet of tissue paper to prevent the presser foot from sticking. Now sew the vinyl to the canvas around the perimeter and about $1/4$ inch in from the edge of the vinyl. *Do not cut the hole in the canvas first.* After the window is sewn to the canvas, tear away the tissue, turn the assembly over, and draw a matching outline 1 inch inside the stitch line. Use scissors to carefully cut the canvas along this line, taking care not to cut or scratch the vinyl. Tuck $1/2$ inch of this raw edge under—between the canvas and the vinyl. Relieving slits in the edge of the canvas will be necessary for curved edges and corners. Sew this hem edge down with a row of stitches $1/4$ inch from the fold. This method does leave a raw edge visible through the vinyl from inside the dodger. An alternative that delivers a better inside finish is to cut the fabric $1/2$ inch from the stitch line, then bind the raw edge with color-matched binding tape. Miter the binding in corners.

You should be about ready to sew the pieces together. Put centerline marks on all the parts by folding them in half. Position the windshield assembly on top of the dodger top panel, outside to outside, and align the raw edge of the windshield assembly with the forward raw edge of the top. Put the forward sleeve strip on top of these two pieces and align the centerline marks. Baste or staple the parts together to hold all the raw edges flush. Position your needle at the centerline mark and sew the three parts together with a straight line of stitches $1/2$ inch from the edges. Turn the assembly around or flip it over, and sew the other side of this seam, starting an inch or two before the center to overstitch the first stitching. The reason you are sewing from the center in both directions is to minimize misalignment by balancing the tendency of the parts to crawl.

Turn the sleeve under and press the seam flat. Mark where the sleeve hem or the other half of the

separating zipper should lie on the bottom of the top fabric. Maintaining this alignment, sew the sleeve edge or zipper to the underside of the top, backstitching at both ends.

Align the sleeve strip and the wing strips along the back edge and staple them to the top. Where this seam is three layers, be sure the wing piece is in the middle. Sew this seam, again starting from the middle on both sides. Turn the aft sleeve under, press it flat, and mark the location of the sleeve hem or zipper, but do not sew it just yet.

Instead, open the seam flat and place the leather or vinyl chafe strip on top of the butterflied fabric. Center the strip side to side and position it so that $2/3$ of the strip width will be on the top, $1/3$ on the sleeve. Sew the strip around its perimeter in this position. If you have a zigzag stitch, use it here, placing one side of the stitch just off the edge of the chafe patch. If you want chafing protection that extends around the bend of the bow, then instead of this topstitched straight strip, you will need two contoured chafing strips that you capture in the seam between the sleeve and the top. When you open the sleeve, you will need to topstitch the ends

Aft seam detail.

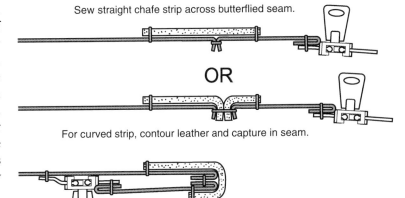

Sew straight chafe strip across butterflied seam.

OR

For curved strip, contour leather and capture in seam.

Fold sleeve under and stitch to underside of dodger.

and forward edges of these strips to the canvas. The strip that stitches to the top should be about twice as "wide" as the one that stitches to the sleeve.

With the chafe strip in place, realign the forward edge of the sleeve with the line you drew earlier and sew the hem or the zipper to the top. Bind any visible raw edges on the underside of the dodger.

Three finished dodger renderings. The possibilities are infinite.

Install the assembled dodger on the bows and mark the locations for the fasteners on the deck. Remove the dodger and install the fasteners on the boat at the marked locations. Reinstall the dodger, and starting at the center forward, smooth and tension the dodger as you install and fasten the fasteners one at a time, working out from the center in both directions. If you are using a boltrope, this is also the time to position it. The boltrope should not be sewn into the bottom hem of the dodger. It should be contained in a strip of fabric sewn to the inside of the hem.

Put grommets into the aft corners of the wings. Tie lanyards to each of these grommets and reeve them through strap eyes screwed to the boat. The entire dodger is tensioned with these two lines, the reason for the reinforcing patches. If the wings do not extend high enough to tension the assembly, you will need to incorporate tie-down straps from the aft bow, similar to the way a bimini is rigged. Work the dodger with your hand as you tension it to get a smooth fit.

Not everyone should attempt to build a dodger, although the cost to have one built may lead you to give it a go no matter what misgivings you have. However, most other canvas items aboard are not so complicated or so exacting. Learning to hem a flat sheet and fold it into an envelope opens a number of possibilities. Manipulating the fabric into a one-piece bag or joining it with another piece to form a two-piece enclosure broadens those possibilities. Sewing a top on the two-piece bag gives you a fairly complete complement of canvaswork skills, allowing you to duplicate virtually any item you see that falls into one of these five categories—which includes about 95% of all fabric items found aboard boats. Whether you go on to designing custom canvas items for your boat will have more to do with desire than skill.

A Lofty Project

"Do or do not. There is no try."
—YODA

Early in the annals of "yachting," the hallmark of the small-boat sailor was self-sufficiency. He often built his own boat, rigged her himself, and even made his own sails. Sails of that era were made of cotton and the shape of the sail was as much a product of how you broke it in and took care of it as of how it was cut.

The hallmark of the cruising sailor today is still self-sufficiency. Some still build their own boats; many rebuild them. Mechanical terminal fittings, as we have already seen, have again made do-it-yourself rigging viable for any sailor who is so inclined. But it is exceedingly rare today for a sailor to attempt the construction of a sail. Sailors may still haunt the woods looking for trees with just the right crook to use as ribs for a boat a-building, cast their own lead keels, graft sugar scoops to conventional fiberglass transoms, and do intricate (and often beautiful) cabinetwork. But nearly all of them leave sailmaking to the professionals.

For competitive sailing you *need* the expertise of a professional. Finely tuned sails that deliver that extra tenth of a knot may well make the difference between winning or losing. But how important is this for a sail down the bay with good friends and a good wine? How essential is sail perfection to the cruising boat with a full keel, a three-blade prop, and towing a net bag of dirty diapers? And how perfect will that high-tech sail be 3 years from now? Six years from now?

Some years ago, after thinking at length along these lines, I decided that I could see three good reasons to give sailmaking a try. The first was that sail years are like dog years, and shocking though it was at the time, our 14-year-old genoa had rightfully expired. Reason number two was that despite two decades of sailing, I was not certain at that time that I fully understood the nuances of sail shape—exactly what made a sail tick—and I figured that to make an efficient sail I would have to learn what made a sail efficient. The deal closer, however, was the third reason—I hoped to save money.

Once I had *almost* decided on this course of action, I made the rounds at the next boat show, going to seven different sailmakers' booths. This proved to be an enlightening enterprise. I described the sail I needed and how I would use it in exactly the same terms at each one, yet no two sailmakers came up with the same concept for my sail. Some said they would build it from 5-ounce cloth, some said 6.5-ounce. Some said they would use soft cloth for the roller furling, some said hard for shape. Some would cut the sail flat, others recommended fullness. There were sails with horizontal panels, sails with vertical panels, and even a radial-cut genoa.

Like the sails, prices seemed to run the gamut. The cheapest price I encountered was around $800, the most expensive was just shy of $2,000. These were quotes for sails that were identical in dimension, similar in weight (depending on the sailmaker's recommendation), all "computer designed," UV protected, hand finished, and triple stitched. The average price among all seven sailmakers was right in the middle of the two extremes—around $1,300.

I left the boat show determined to give sail construction a try. Instead of seven different designs, I figured there were eight. I was satisfied that mine would not be as good as some. Still, if it was not the worst, then it might actually be better than the choice I would have made since I didn't have a clue how to select among the other seven. I selected my sailmaker—me.

Am I really suggesting that you make your own sails? Yes. And no. What I am suggesting is that you consider it. If the projects in the previous chapter seemed (or seamed) to go fairly well, you may be pleasantly surprised to discover that you are perfectly capable of building a very acceptable sail and saving yourself hundreds, even thousands of dollars in the process.

You will recall that the most basic canvas project from the previous chapter was the flat sheet hemmed along all the edges and with grommets in the corners. With a change in shape and/or dimensions, a change in the location of the grommets, a few reinforcement patches, and maybe a boltrope in the hem, the flat sheet was a weather cloth, a windscoop, or an awning. Here comes the essential point of this chapter, so don't miss it. A sail is a flat sheet hemmed along all edges with grommets in the corners. The fact that this particular sheet of cloth is triangular is, well, immaterial.

"Wait a minute!" you protest. "Sails aren't flat." True. But the method of putting "shape" into a sail is so simple it is almost ludicrous. Knowing *how much* shape to put in is not so simple, but the truth is that shape is always a guess.

The ideal shape for 10 knots of wind is not so good in 20 knots. The ideal shape for sailing on the wind is less than ideal when the sheets are eased. Even for identical boats, differences in the way each one is normally loaded, the skill (or attention) of the crew, the usual sail combinations, the number of different sails, the tension on the rigging, and the variety of wind and sea conditions can suggest sails with entirely different shapes. The sailmaker is going to guess at these factors, looking for a shape that gives you—*on average*—good performance. But the person who knows your boat, your skills, and your habits best is you. Borrow a few calculations from sailmakers who have gone before, and you are likely to be quite satisfied with the shape of your own sails.

PRELIMINARIES

This chapter differs somewhat from previous chapters in that it examines a single project—making a sail. No special skills are required beyond the basic ability to operate a sewing machine. Marvelous sails can be made with a straight-stitch machine, but a zigzag stitch does a nicer job on overlap seams and will generally give the finished sail a better look. Use the same V-92 (or V-69 for lighter fabric) bonded polyester thread that you use on canvas. Voyagers may want to use black thread for its UV resistance, but for the rest of us, because the sail is vertical in use and covered when not in use, white thread will give long

service. The neatness of your sewing (or the lack of it) will be less apparent with white thread.

Transfer tape is not optional for sewing slick polyester sailcloth. For consistent results it is essential that you baste *every* seam with transfer tape before sewing. Another essential is a hot knife. If you "cut" sailcloth by searing the fabric along cut lines rather than scissoring them, the synthetic fibers fuse at the edges and prevent the fabric from raveling. You can buy a special hot knife, but if you have a soldering *pistol,* it will have a blade-shaped plastic cutting tip that can do a fine job cutting polyester fabric. You will need a long electrical cord for making 40-foot cuts. Slip a scrap of hardboard (Masonite) or high-pressure laminate (Formica) under the fabric, moving it as you cut, to keep from burning the outline of the sail permanently into the floor. Speaking of the floor, you are going to spend a considerable amount of time there and your knees will turn vindictive if you do not provide them with some type of padding.

In this project as in the previous canvas projects, the emphasis will be on cutting the various pieces to the right size and stitching them together for a good fit. It is not my intent to instruct you in sail theory, although you will almost certainly understand sails much better after you go through the process of making one. Nor will we consider alternative sail designs and construction techniques. That would be to miss the point, which is that for most of the sailing most of us do, a basic design and standard construction techniques will produce a sail that will satisfy our needs.

If you understand and execute the steps that follow, the result will be a sail. And if you use a quality cloth and triple-stitch the panels together with commercial polyester thread, you can expect the same life from a sail you make as from one made professionally. How the performance of your sail might compare to that of the professionally built one will depend less on some special knowledge of the unfathomable mysteries of sail theory and more on how well you assess your particular requirements and how accurately you sew the panels together. I trust it won't come as a surprise to you that the sail loft employee who actually sews your sailmaker sail together may not have a doctorate in fluid dynamics. It is also conceivable, however remotely, that said person might actually be thinking about something else while stitching *your* sail. You won't be.

FABRIC

Except for spinnakers and very light drifters, the fabric you are going to choose is woven polyester, commonly called Dacron. Leave aramid (Kevlar,

Technora) or polycthylene (Spectra, Dyneema) fabrics to the racers with deep pockets. Laminated fabrics have found their way into "standard" sails for sailors willing to give up longer life—and in the case of hoist sails, easier handling—in exchange for better shape-holding qualities and more dollars. A laminated fabric might make sense for a roller-furled sail, but laminates are more difficult to sew, which is likely to result in poorer sail shape for a do-it-yourself sail. For your first sailmaking effort, stick with plain vanilla Dacron.

Choosing the weight of the cloth is the first of your educated guesses. As a starting point, divide the waterline length of your old boat by four. The result is a base cloth weight for the working sails. For a 24-foot waterline, you need a main and working jib of 6-ounce cloth. If all your sailing is done in Long Island Sound in the summer, lighter cloth will make more sense. If you and your boat are off to Patagonia on Tuesday, you won't regret selecting heavier material.

A medium-air genoa can be lighter cloth. A rule of thumb is to make the genoa 75% of the weight of the main. If you want to keep the genoa up until the turnbuckles start to elongate, make the darn thing the same weight as the main. If light-air performance is the thing, so is light cloth. Are you getting the hang of this?

If your boat sports a second stick, the mizzen *can* be lighter than the other working sails, but I always ask why it should be. In company with a lot of ketch sailors, I tend to give up the mizzen last when the wind pipes up. If the mizzen is the same weight as the main, its smaller size will allow it to handle heavier winds. *No one* thinks of a mizzen as a light-air sail, so what is the benefit of using light cloth? Make the mizzen from the same cloth as the main.

Sailcloth of similar weights are woven and treated differently to give the cloth differing "hands," from soft to very firm. Soft is easy to handle and less prone to wrinkle but does not hold its shape well, especially in light air. Firm sailcloth is like heavy paper—hard to handle and subject to wrinkles and permanent creases—but firm cloth holds its shape the best, and it presents the smoothest surface to the wind when handled carefully. Medium cloth is a good compromise, easy to handle while also holding its shape well. Unless you have a special need, select a stabilized Dacron cloth with a medium finish.

Like longer anchor rode, longer yarns will have more total stretch. Since the loads radiate from the clew, the sail will tend to stretch more near the leech than near the foot. You are building a crosscut sail, so you are going to orient the cloth perpendicular to the leech to align the yarns—in this case, the *fill* yarns—with the longest part of the sail. The yarns running the other way, the length of the cloth, are called *warp* yarns. When these two yarns are the same or nearly the same size, the cloth has a *balanced weave*, sometimes called square construction.

Sailmakers tend to use unbalanced cloth. They may call this *high-modulus* or *high-aspect* cloth. *Modulus* in sailcloth means resistance to stretch, so the implication of a cloth called high-modulus is that it stretches less. But which way? In general a high-modulus cloth has fill yarns twice the size of the warp yarns or even larger. As a result the fill yarns are almost straight, with the warp yarns crimped over and under. This gives the cloth more stretch resistance across the cloth, which would seem to be where you want it in a crosscut sail. A so-called high-aspect cloth has even heavier fill yarns.

If you think about it, however, the load on the cloth will be in line with the fill yarns only right

Balanced weave.

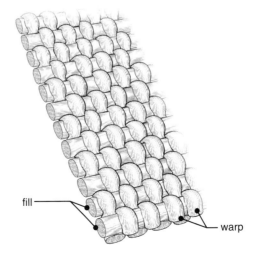

Unbalanced or high-modulus cloth.

fill

warp

at the clew. *Most stretch on the sail will be on the bias*, meaning diagonal to the thread lines, and an unbalanced weave tends to reduce resistance to bias stretch. Cloth manufacturers counter this by saturating the fabric with resin, not unlike fiberglass layup, which "locks" the weave and reduces bias stretch but makes the cloth stiffer. As the resin degrades, so does sail shape.

For most uses other than competition, your best cloth choice is a balanced or nearly balanced weave. If you select a cloth of appropriate weight, it will perform as well as the specialized weaves except under conditions you are likely to avoid. A balanced weave simplifies sail construction by eliminating concerns about which way the fill and warp yarns run. You will be concerned only with the grain of the cloth—the direction of the yarn lines. A tightly woven balanced cloth will have less resin, making it easier to handle and extending its useful life. There are so few amateur sailmakers that you may have some difficulty finding a balanced sailcloth, especially locally. (Whether sailmaker preference for lighter unbalanced cloth is to concentrate the strength where it is needed or to save the cost of strength where it isn't "needed," I leave for you to decide.) If your supplier offers only high-modulus cloth or if that's the cloth you prefer, using it does not alter the instructions that follow except for the need to orient the corner reinforcements to take advantage of the larger fill yarns.

GETTING STARTED

The first step is to cover your dining room table with blank paper. Blank newsprint is perfect and you can get end rolls from your local newspaper for free. On the paper you are going to draw the sail to a scale of 1 inch to 1 foot and make all the lofting calculations. This will allow you to go through the lofting process risk free and make sure you fully understand what you are doing before you start cutting sailcloth. Going through this step first has the added advantage of yielding a scale drawing of the finished sail from which you will be able to take measurements quite easily.

The scale drawing will also allow you to calculate the amount of material you will need for the actual sail. An approximation of the number of square yards of cloth required is 0.15 times the area of the sail in square feet. The construction of a 100-square-foot sail—seam allowances, patches, and all—will require approximately 15 yards of 36-inch-width sailcloth and 10 yards of 54-inch cloth. You

calculate sail area by multiplying the luff length by the perpendicular length from the luff to the clew (LP) and dividing by 2.

It would be redundant to describe the creation of the scale sail drawing and then go through the identical process of laying out the sail to full size. Besides, the function of the scale drawing is to assist you in understanding the actual lofting process. So the description that follows is for lofting the sail full size, but do not omit this first step. It will keep you out of the quicksand.

I should note that you can find open-source software on the Internet that will let you design a sail on your computer. Such programs are intended for use with a plotter, but you can hand plot them from the X-Y coordinates the program will generate. If you are comfortable with CAD software, there is no reason you cannot use it to help you with your sail design. However, the sail-shape concepts written into a CAD program are the same as we will be applying manually, so if the design criteria are consistent between the two methods, you can expect a manually lofted sail to be essentially identical to one lofted on the computer.

THE LOFT

In my experience, the amateur sailmaker encounters only two real problems during the construction of a sail, particularly a large sail. One of those problems is a loft.

To make a sail you need a large, flat surface. On one occasion I used a wooden deck attached to the rear of the house we owned at the time. In a later house, we removed or shoved aside the furniture in the living/dining room and I lofted the sail on the varnished oak floors. Very carefully, I might add. A garage, patio, or driveway can work perfectly if they are clean. Putting a fresh coat of sealer on the scrubbed concrete will reduce the likelihood of soiling the sailcloth, and you were probably meaning to seal the surface anyway. Just another of those intangible benefits of boat ownership.

If you cannot find a large enough space around the house, perhaps the school your children attend would let you use the gym or an empty classroom one weekend. Or maybe your church has a "fellowship hall" you could borrow. Maybe a condo-dwelling friend could reserve the recreation room for you. A real-estate agent friend might be able to arrange access to a vacant warehouse or commercial space. Put your mind to it and you can come up with the needed flat surface.

While I don't particularly recommend it because it adds considerable complexity and introduces additional error potential, it is possible to loft a sail in more than one part. When the wooden deck I planned to use to loft our genoa turned out to be smaller than the sail, I decided to try lofting it in two parts. It was more difficult, but the sail turned out perfectly. The secret to success is overlapping a full panel in the lofting to insure a smooth transition between the upper part of the sail and the lower part. Consider this possibility only as a last resort. The project will go more easily with a sail-size space.

THE BASIC TRIANGLE

Sail lofting is nothing more than drawing the sail to full scale on the floor. You need a 50-foot tape measure, a ball of packaging twine, a roll of $3/4$-inch masking tape, and a pencil. You also need the exact dimensions for the luff, leech, and foot of your sail. If you are replacing a sail, simply take these three dimensions from the old sail. If you are adding a new sail to your inventory, you will have to obtain these dimensions from the sail plan for your boat, by making a scale drawing, or by establishing the position of the clew and measuring to the head and the tack locations.

Begin the lofting process by stretching a length of string longer than the luff of the sail across the floor, taping both ends down to provide a straight line. With two small lengths of tape, mark the length of the luff along this line. A helper will make the measuring process easier.

If the sail will have a headboard, position it next to the string and outline it with tape. While your helper holds the end of the tape measure at the tack end of the luff string, measure away from it by the sail's foot dimension and swing a short arc, marking it on the floor with chalk or tape. Move the end of the measuring tape to the other end of the luff, positioning it at the mark or, if you have outlined a headboard, at the top corner on the leech side of the headboard. Measure toward the arc by the leech dimension of the sail and strike a second arc. The two arcs intersect at the location of the clew. Tape two additional lengths of string to the floor to connect this point to the mark at the tack end of the luff line and to the mark at the head end or the leech-side corner of the headboard. You now have a triangle the approximate size of your planned sail with three perfectly straight sides. To avoid any confusion, label the luff and the leech.

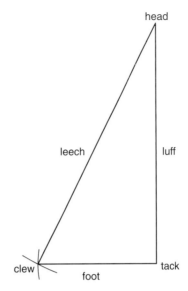

The basic triangle.

HOLLOW LEECH

Headsails rarely have battens anymore, thank God, but as a result the leech wants to flutter. One method of dealing with this is with a *leech line*, a light piece of line inside the leech hem, anchored at the head of the sail and cleated near the clew. Tightening the line puts a hook in the sail, quieting the leech.

The leech line often can be dispensed with if you cut the leech of the sail slightly hollow. How hollow? In normal sailing conditions you should get satisfactory results from a maximum hollow of 2% of the leech length or slightly less. If the headsail will be used only in light air, a light genoa for example, reduce the hollow to about 1%.

The curve of the hollow is not particularly critical but it is still advisable to make it regular. Divide the leech line into quarters and mark these three stations with short strips of tape on the floor inside of the string. The maximum hollow will be in the center or the $1/2$ station. On a 20-foot leech, for example, a 1.9% hollow will be about $4^1/_2$ inches. Calculate the maximum

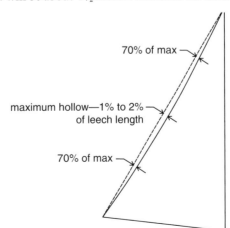

Leech hollow.

70% of max

maximum hollow—1% to 2% of leech length

70% of max

hollow for the leech length of your sail and place a mark on the floor that distance inside the leech line at the $\frac{1}{2}$ station. To achieve a "normal" curve, the offsets at the two $\frac{1}{4}$ stations will be 70% of the maximum hollow—about $3\frac{1}{8}$ inches in this example. At the $\frac{1}{4}$ and $\frac{3}{4}$ stations, mark the appropriate distance inside the leech line.

Use $\frac{3}{4}$-inch tape to make a smooth curve on the floor from the intersection of the leech and luff through the three leech-hollow points and to the clew. Place the inside edge of the tape on the five points so the outside will mark the cut edge, automatically providing the hem allowance.

ROACH

Unlike headsail leech, the leech of a mainsail (and of a mizzen) is usually supported by battens. They allow the leech to be rounded rather than hollowed. The excess material is called *roach* and provides racing sailors with "free" sail area, but this extra area is only beneficial when sailing free. On the wind, roach has little effect on performance unless the weight of the battens folds the sail, breaking the airflow and reducing the efficiency of the sail.

Except for racing—where you are forced to play by the rules—I think battens are a bad idea. Most mainsail repair has to do with batten pocket damage. Battened mains have an annoying habit of getting entangled in the rigging, jamming the sail half-up or half-down, and sometimes tearing it. To rid yourself of these problems, you just leave the battens out and cut the leech hollow exactly like that of a headsail. A battenless mainsail is easier to handle and easier to furl, has less weight aloft, and will require far fewer repairs. The reduced sail area is only a loss in light air. When the wind gets up to reefing speed, the roach is

working against you. If you need more light-air sail area, increase the size of the headsail.

This viewpoint is neither new nor radical—nor, it would seem, is it catching on. To the contrary, fully battened mainsails have been all the rage for the last decade and more. On the assumption that I am swimming upstream and that despite their questionable benefit and obvious problems you still want battens in your main, I am including the necessary instructions. However, I draw the line at full-length battens. The complexity, the weight aloft, the chafe, and the cost of a fully battened sail are all way out of proportion to the benefits for most sailors. Besides, they add construction complications that the amateur will have difficulty overcoming.

Batten lengths are often dictated by rating rules, not by sail theory. You are no doubt replacing an existing main, so the best course is to just use the old battens. Their original length may have been determined by a racing rule that limits intermediate battens to 12% of the length of the foot of the sail along the boom plus 12 inches and limits the upper and lower battens to 10% plus 12 inches. In the absence of rule requirements, battens can be any length, but more length is generally just more of a bad thing.

The maximum practical roach is about $\frac{1}{3}$ the batten length. For example, if you have 24-inch battens, limit the roach to 8 inches. To loft the roach, divide the leech line equally by the number of battens and put strips of tape on the floor at each of these stations. This is similar to dividing the line into quarter stations, but this time the tape strips go outside the line. You are rounding the leech, not hollowing it.

If you have two battens, measure out from the leech line the full roach dimension—$\frac{1}{3}$ the length of your battens—and mark the points. With three

Roach.

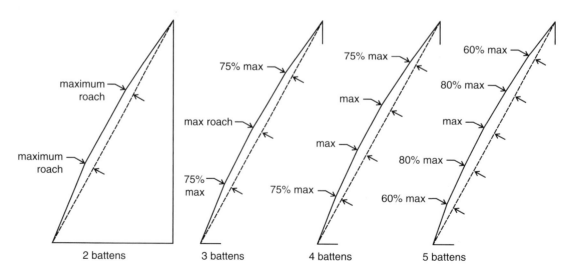

battens, measure out the full distance at the center station and 75% of that distance at the other two stations. A four-batten roach will be at the maximum distance at the middle two stations and 75% at the other two. With five battens, mark the center station with the full roach dimension, 80% at stations two and four, and 60% at stations one and five.

Starting at the head and ending at the clew, connect all these points with masking tape. Unlike what you did for the leech hollow, do not make the roach a smooth curve. Join each pair of points with a straight line. In fact the leech of your sail will be less likely to flutter if you slightly hollow each of the lines between the points. Put the inside edge of the tape on the points so the outside will give you the cut dimension.

LUFF STUFF

One of the ways you introduce fullness or shape to the sail is by rounding the luff. This was the main way when cotton was king. Hoisting the sails straightens the rounded luff, moving excess fabric back into the sail and giving it fullness—called *camber*. The amount of camber depends on the amount of luff round. Camber is expressed as the ratio between the sail depth and the chord. *Chord* is the horizontal distance between luff and leech when the sail is set, and *depth* is the amount of bow in the sail. The appropriate camber for your sails depends on your boat. Fat boat, fat sails. Flat boat, flat sails. The starting point is 10%—1 foot of depth for 10 feet of chord. For an easily driven boat with a fine entry, a camber ratio closer to 5% (1 ÷ 20) might give better performance. A heavy, bluff-bowed cruiser may benefit from the extra power of a 15% camber.

To introduce a camber of 10% to your sail, you are going to add cloth *outside* the luff line the equivalent of 2.7% of the chord of the sail at that point. If you want your sail flatter, reduce this percentage. A luff round of 0.7% will yield a 5% camber—a very flat sail. If you need more powerful sails, increase the percentage, but not beyond about 6%, which yields a very full sail with a camber near 15%. If you are unsure about this

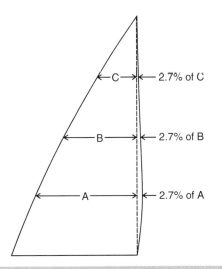

Average draft (10% camber ratio) requires 2.7% extra cloth added to luff. For a flat sail (5% camber ratio) add 0.7%. For a full sail (15% camber ratio) add 6%.

Luff round.

aspect, build your sails with a 10% camber or vary the camber only slightly one way or the other depending on whether you categorize your boat as easily driven, average, or heavy. A camber near 10% will provide good performance over a wide range of conditions.

Divide the luff line into quarters, marking the quarter stations. Measure horizontally (what will be horizontal when the sail is set) across the sail to the leech. Multiply each of these measurements by 2.7%—or an alternate percentage you select—to arrive at the amount of luff round at each of the three stations. Mark these distances on the outside of the luff line and perpendicular to it at each of the stations.

If the sail you are making sets on a mast (a mainsail or a mizzen), you are through with the luff. Using the inside edge of the masking tape, make a new luff line from the head of the sail through the three points and smoothly back into the tack point.

If the sail sets on a wire or an extrusion, you need to compensate for sag before taping the line. A common rule of thumb for a hanked-on sail is to allow 1 inch of sag for every 10 feet of luff, but a roller-furling sail on an extrusion will sag less. And obviously a great deal depends on how tight you have the rigging. I suppose you can tighten or loosen stays to make the rig fit the sail, but the closer the sail shape is to your normal sag, the better.

To determine the sag, go sailing on a 10- to 15-knot day. Tape a ruler *across* the middle of the luff and hoist the old sail. For a roller-furling headsail you will need to drop the sail enough to allow you to tape an L-shaped scale—of your creation—to the sail at midheight and as near the luff as possible without touching the extrusion. Rehoist the sail. Lead the spinnaker halyard to the bow (you can use the main

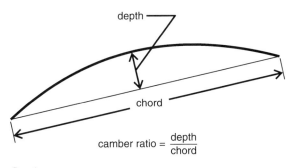

$$\text{camber ratio} = \frac{\text{depth}}{\text{chord}}$$

Camber.

halyard if it is the only other line from the masthead) and set it up tightly to provide a reference. Put the boat close-hauled and note the amount of sag as indicated by the distance the ruler moves across the halyard. Use binoculars to read the ruler if necessary. Be sure to use only the *change* in the distance between the luff and the halyard, not the absolute distance.

The sag allowance is applied in the *opposite direction* as the luff round. (Compensation for a flexible mast is handled in a similar manner but added to the luff round.) At the ¹/₂ station, measure *back toward* the sail the full amount of the measured (or estimated) sag. At the other two stations (¹/₄ and ³/₄), measure back 75% of the sag amount. The new ³/₄ station point is almost certain to be inside the string line and the midstation point may be as well. Not to worry; this is normal. Tape a smooth curve from the head through these three points and to the tack. Typically this curve will have an S shape—hollow in the upper part of the sail, rounded in the lower part.

Measure actual or allow 1 inch for every 10 feet of luff.

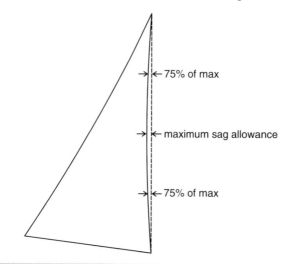

75% of max

maximum sag allowance

75% of max

Sag allowance.

The combined effects of round and sag typically result in an S-shaped luff with the offsets inside the basic triangle at the top of the sail and outside in the lower part.

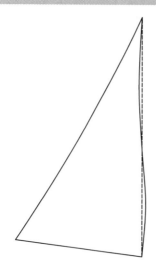

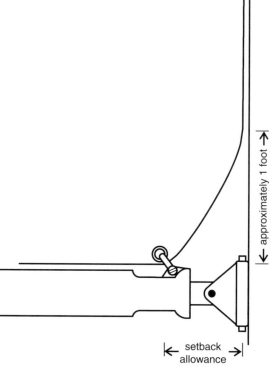

approximately 1 foot

setback allowance

Tack setback.

I lied earlier. Lofting the luff round doesn't quite finish the luff shape for a mainsail (or mizzen). You still need one more small adjustment. Look at the position of the tack attachment on your boom. Typically it will be a few inches from the mast. Measure the normal distance between the mast and the luff, and the distance between the mast and the edge of the sail at the tack; subtract the first from the second. This is the amount of setback your sail should have. Mark this setback distance on the foot of your triangle, measuring from the tack point. Peel up the tape marking the luff round for about 12 inches above the tack and reposition it to form a smooth curve to the new tack point. *Now* the luff is finished. Honest.

FOOT ROACH

The foot of a sail may also be rounded but for different reasons, depending on the sail. Headsails are rounded at the foot to get more sail area and to get the bottom of the sail right down on the deck, reducing the amount of bypass flow at the foot. For maximum sail performance you will usually want to put the maximum roach possible in the foot of a headsail. However, you may want little or no roach in a cruising headsail. A low-cut headsail is dangerous on a cruising boat because it severely restricts the forward view from the helm, and excessive roach puts the sail at greater risk of catching a wave offshore. Roller-furling sails also furl more compactly if roach is kept to a minimum or omitted altogether.

For a sail with the foot attached to a boom, your choices are more limited. You *must* round the foot of the mainsail, but the purpose is not to add sail area. As with luff round, foot round for this sail introduces draft into the sail at the foot.

Despite the differing purposes, the shape of the foot of both types of sails will be similar. For a headsail the maximum practical amount of roach is about 1 inch per foot of foot length. You may not want to put in the maximum roach if the sail will be used in moderate to strong winds. For this type of sail, a roach of about half the maximum will likely prove more satisfactory. Following this recommendation, a 10-foot foot would have a 5-inch roach; the curve of the roach is not critical, but the maximum depth should be slightly forward of the center of the sail, say 45% back from the luff. Use the inside edge of the tape to make a smooth curve from the tack through the point marking the maximum roach and back to the clew.

Because the foot round in a mainsail is for draft, the appropriate amount is determined by the camber of the sail. The exact amount of round will be 40% of the sail depth in the foot—about twice that

percentage for loose-footed or shelf-footed sails. For example, if your sail has a camber of 10% (1 ÷ 10) and is 12 feet wide at the foot, the depth will be 14.4 inches (10% of 144 inches). The amount of foot round should be 40% of that, or 5³/₄ inches.

Like headsail roach, the maximum amount of foot round should be about 45% behind the luff. Connect the tack, the point marking the maximum round, and the clew in a smooth curve with the masking tape. The sail will be less likely to develop radiating creases at the clew if the aft half of this curve is absolutely straight or even *slightly* hollow.

ON A ROLL

Your lofting is finished. The next step is to cover this full-size drawing of your sail with cloth. All of the panels will be *perpendicular* to the straight leech line (the string). It is imperative to make sure the panels are *exactly* perpendicular to this line; otherwise the load on the leech will not be with the thread line but on the bias (diagonally across the thread line), and the shape of the sail will be ruined. It can be helpful to stretch a piece of string from the tack exactly perpendicular to the leech string as a reference.

Start covering the outline at the bottom of the sail. Place the bolt of cloth outside the leech and unroll it across the outline so that it is perpendicular to the leech and the bottom edge of this first panel intersects the tack. The resin-impregnated cloth is slippery and can be slid around easily to position it. Don't cut the panel from the bolt of cloth yet.

If you are making a headsail, measure perpendicular from the bottom edge of the panel to the tape marking the foot. If the maximum distance is no more than 15 inches at any point (24 inches if you are using 54-inch-wide cloth), you can save some fabric by splitting the bottom panel. Reposition this bottom panel, still (always) perpendicular to the leech, by sliding it down until it covers the foot tape by about 3¹/₂ inches. Using scissors—you can make all the rough cuts with scissors—cut the panel from the roll, making certain there is at least 1 inch of cloth beyond the leech and cutting 3 inches beyond the luff. Split this panel down the center, this time using a hot knife. Leave the top half on the outline and set the bottom piece aside.

If the distance to the foot is more than 15 or 24 inches or you are making a mainsail, leave the bottom edge of the initial panel on the perpendicular line from the leech to the tack. Cut the panel from the roll (with scissors), leaving 1 inch beyond the leech and 3 inches beyond the luff.

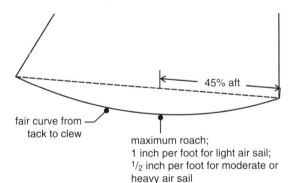

fair curve from tack to clew

45% aft

maximum roach;
1 inch per foot for light air sail;
¹/₂ inch per foot for moderate or heavy air sail

Foot roach *adds sail area.*

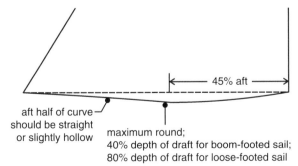

aft half of curve should be straight or slightly hollow

45% aft

maximum round;
40% depth of draft for boom-footed sail;
80% depth of draft for loose-footed sail

Foot round *provides sail draft.*

Lofting the foot.

Covering the plan with cloth.

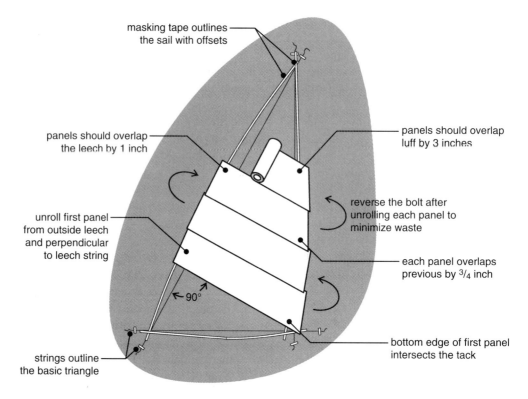

masking tape outlines
the sail with offsets

panels should overlap
luff by 3 inches

panels should overlap
the leech by 1 inch

reverse the bolt after
unrolling each panel to
minimize waste

unroll first panel
from outside leech
and perpendicular
to leech string

each panel overlaps
previous by 3/4 inch

90°

bottom edge of first panel
intersects the tack

strings outline
the basic triangle

Whether your first panel is full or split, turn the bolt of fabric around, and starting from the luff, roll out a second panel above the first. The two panels should overlap by about 3/4 inch. You will notice a faint blue line along both edges of the cloth. This line will help you maintain a consistent overlap. Cut the second panel from the roll, maintaining the same amount of extra cloth at the ends—1 inch at the leech, 3 inches at the luff.

Reversing the bolt each time, continue to roll out and cut overlapping panels until the entire outline except the foot area is covered. By reversing the bolt for each panel, you will notice that you waste very little sailcloth.

If you are going to want numbers or an insignia on the sail, position them on the appropriate panel and glue them to the cloth. Now take that panel to your sewing machine and attach the appliqué by zigzagging around the perimeter. This is much easier to do on a single panel than on the assembled sail. Put the panel back over the outline.

BROADSEAMING

While luff round is sufficient to give canvas sails shape, the paperlike stiffness of resin-impregnated woven polyester cloth tends to prevent the draft from moving back into the middle of the sail. This problem is overcome by *broadseaming.*

Broadseaming would be better named *broadeningseam.* As you seam toward the luff of the sail, you are going to increase the overlap of the panels, broadening

the seam. This has the effect of removing cloth from the edge of the sail, meaning the center of the sail has more cloth than the edge. The exact position of this bagginess—draft in the finished sail—depends on the location and shape of the broadseams.

The position and width of the broadseams are two more of those educated guesses. Measure 2/3 of the way up the luff and mark the point. Measure out from the tack 45% of the sail width along the bottom edge of the bottom panel (or along the top edge if you split this panel) and mark a second point. Mark a third point on the floor halfway between the tack and a point on the leech about 10 inches above the clew. Lay a piece of heavy line on top of the panels from the first mark to the third one, then push it into a smooth curve that connects all three points. Mark every seam where the curved line crosses it; be sure the mark is on both panels. These serve as both panel alignment marks and the initiation points for the broadseams.

This broadseaming pattern will place the draft about 35% behind the luff. This shape is a good compromise for varying wind conditions. For a sail that will be used mostly in light air, moving the draft back by moving this curve aft slightly—not more than 5% of sail width—might give you a better shape. Windward ability in strong air will be improved by moving the curve and the resulting draft forward as much as 10% of the sail width—i.e., placing points two and three at 35% and 40%, respectively.

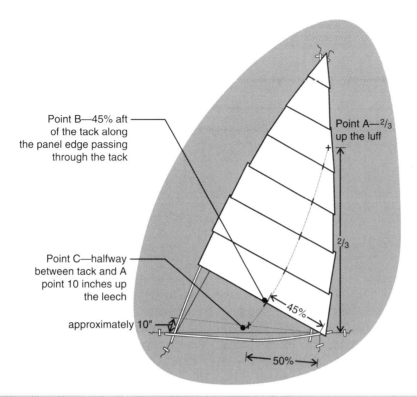

Point B—45% aft of the tack along the panel edge passing through the tack

Point A—²/₃ up the luff

Point C—halfway between tack and A point 10 inches up the leech

²/₃

approximately 10"

45%

50%

A smooth curve through points A, B, and C locates the broadseam starting point on each panel seam. For a light-air sail, move this curve aft about 5%. For a heavy-air sail, move this curve forward about 10%.

Determining broadseam locations.

The amount of broadseaming depends on the hand of the cloth you selected. If you are using a medium Dacron, widen the seam ¹/₄ *inch every 15 inches* of seam length, measuring only the section of the seam you are broadening. Firm cloth requires more broadening—¹/₄ inch per foot. One-quarter inch every 18 inches of seam length is adequate for soft cloth. If you are using wide (54-inch) cloth, you have fewer seams, which means less sewing, but you will need to increase the broadseam width by half—to about ³/₈ inch per instead of ¹/₄—to take out the same amount of fabric at the perimeter with fewer seams.

Measure the distance from the mark on each seam to the tape luff line and write this measurement on the excess cloth. Calculate the amount of broadseaming for each seam by applying the appropriate ratio determined by whether your cloth is firm, medium, or soft, and narrow or wide. Write that also next to the seam on the cloth beyond the luff. Now you are ready to join the panels.

BASTING

You are going to glue all the seams together with transfer tape, including those that get broadened. Start at the head of the sail. Turn the overlapping panel back and stick the transfer tape to the edge of the panel on the floor. Peel away the paper cover, leaving the adhesive behind. Keeping the overlap perfectly even, stick the two panels together.

More than any other single item, how you glue the panels together is going to determine how the sail turns out, so take your time. Use the blue lines to make sure your seams are absolutely straight, and run your thumb over the seams as you put them together to remove any wrinkles or bubbles. The seams must be straight and perfectly flat. If a seam is curved or wrinkled, peel it up and do it again until you get it right.

If you are lofting and sewing in the same location, the sewing will be easier if you stitch each seam as you baste it. Baste the top seam, then take the two joined panels to your sewing machine and sew them together. Return them to the loft, align the next seam, baste it, then take the three panels to your machine and stitch this seam. When you assemble the sail in this manner, you have a single panel under the arm of the machine, you have less cloth to deal with, and you only have one glued seam to keep assembled.

Sailmakers typically glue the entire sail together, and you can do that too if you cannot arrange your work space to allow you to sew where you loft. The transfer tape holds pretty well, but it can be peeled apart, good for adjusting the seams and not so good for holding the sail together. Stronger "super" seam tapes

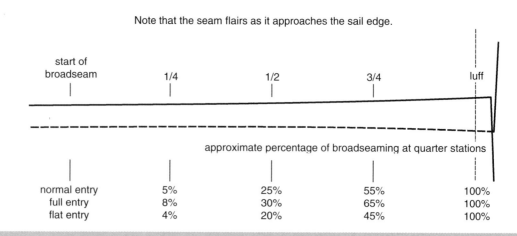

Broadseam detail.

are available, but the adhesives in these can gum up the needle on your sewing machine and make stitching more difficult. To help prevent the seams from coming apart when you are handling the sail, staple each seam a couple of times on either end in the excess material. Put the staples close to the edge and you won't have to remove them; they will get trimmed away.

When you reach the first seam that gets broadseaming, tape it together exactly as you did the higher seams, taking great care to keep the seam perfectly straight from the leech to the point marked on the seam to indicate the starting point of the broadseam. From this point to the luff line, you are going to increase the overlap so that the maximum increase you calculated and noted on the excess cloth by the seam occurs exactly at the luff. Not before. Not after.

The shape of the broadseam is also important. You do not want the seam to have a wedge shape. It needs to be more like a golf tee, flaring near the luff. For a normal entry the seam should only broaden about 5% of the total in the first $^1/_4$ of its length and only about 25% by the halfway point. At $^3/_4$ of the length of the seam, it should be broadened slightly more than 50% with almost half of the broadening occurring in the last $^1/_4$ of the seam. A fuller entry is achieved with slightly lower percentages at the first three stations and more than half of the total in the last $^1/_4$. A flatter entry results from higher percentages early and less than 40% of the total in the last $^1/_4$ of the seam. Get out your calculator and work out the correct broadening for each quarter station for the seam before you start, and use a scale to match the seam widths to your calculations.

Work each of the remaining seams carefully, taking pains to get the straight part of the seams straight and give the broadseams smooth, gradual curves with the appropriate amount of flare. Broadseaming

is going to cause the material in the middle of the sail to wrinkle. No problem. That is just the draft you are going through all of this to achieve. It is a good idea to trace a light pencil line along the edge of each broadseam to insure that you can detect any movement before you sew.

You can prevent a nervous leech while you are broadseaming if you tighten the leech slightly with a couple of broadseams. Pick a couple of seams, one about $^1/_3$ of the way up the leech and a second near the $^2/_3$ point, and peel them apart and back about 2 feet. Now reglue the panels, broadening the seams by about $^1/_8$ inch at the leech—no more. This will cause the leech to be under slightly more pressure than the cloth in front of it and should reduce its tendency to flutter.

SEWING THE PANELS
If you have been sewing the panels together one basted seam at a time, you now have a fully assembled sail and have only had to get a single panel at a time under the arm of the machine. If at this point all the panels are only glued together, you must now confront the other serious problem that making a sail presents to the amateur—how to sew down the center of a room-size sheet of stiff Dacron. The problem is not the sewing machine. It is the bulk of the sail.

The answer is to roll the sail up tightly parallel to the seams, leaving only the topmost seam exposed. After you sew this seam, roll the sail from the top and unroll from the bottom until the next seam is between the two rolls. After each seam, roll the top, unroll the bottom. It will be like sewing down the center of a humongous scroll.

Because the cloth is stiff and slick, the rolls will make every effort to expand to the size of a small culvert as soon as you release your grip on either end. The remedy is four strong spring clamps to clamp the ends of the rolls.

Sail lofts usually have the sewing machines level with the floor, the operator sitting in a well. It is a dynamite arrangement because the sail does not have to be lifted at all to go through the machine. If your machine is a portable, putting it on the floor will accomplish almost the same thing. Sit in the lotus position and operate the foot control with your knee, or kneel on your left knee with your right foot on the pedal. Experiment a bit and you will find a position that works for you.

A table-mounted machine makes sewing the sail more difficult. Somehow you need to get the sail up level with the machine, both in front of the needle and behind it. A couple of long tables will work, or you can construct a pair of 8-foot chutes from a sheet of hardboard with 1 × 4 side rails. Support the chutes with chairs or what have you.

Do not try to sew your sail without a helper. Getting the sail to feed smoothly through the machine is a two-person job. Your helper should keep the unsewn end of the sail free until you near the midpoint of the seam, then move around to the other side of the machine to help the sewn end.

Use a "square" zigzag stitch—$3/16$ inch long and $3/16$ inch wide—or the widest square zigzag your machine will make if it is less than this. Make a few rows of practice stitches on scrap material to get the stitch size and tension adjusted. Unlike canvas, Dacron sailcloth is too hard for the interlock between the top and bottom thread to pull into the cloth. Instead, when the upper tension is adjusted properly, the threads will form a tight knot at each stitch on the bottom of the fabric. This is perfectly normal. You will find the sewing goes better if you use a #18 or larger needle. For Dacron, the needles *must* be ballpoint.

Run the first row of stitches down one edge of the seam with the outside of the stitch right at the edge.

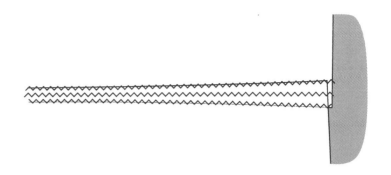

Triple stitch for maximum durability, placing outside of outer rows of stitching at panel edges.

Your sewing machine may feed better if the edge you are stitching is underneath so the feed dog engages both panels. Pay attention to your pencil tracing to make sure the panels have not shifted and your broadseam is stitched with the shape you intend. When one edge is sewn down, turn the "scroll" over so that the two rolls are on the opposite sides of the needle from their previous positions. This puts the bottom side of the seam up. Run a second row of stitches along the unsewn edge of the seam. For maximum durability, run a third row of stitching down the center of the seam between the other two rows.

THE FOOT

With the panels sewn together, it is time to add the foot. Spread the sail back over the taped outline on the floor and align it properly.

If you split the first panel back at the start, cover the foot portion of the sail with the half panel you put aside. Otherwise roll out a new panel to cover the foot. Cut the panel long enough to overlap the leech by 1 inch and the luff by 3 inches. Trim the bottom to the shape of the foot, allowing 3 inches of extra material.

If one panel is not sufficient, reverse the bolt and continue rolling out panels until the foot is covered. Glue these panels together with constant overlaps, then trim them as already described. Take just this section to your machine and sew the seams.

Headsail

If you are building a headsail, split the foot panel vertically into three nearly equal pieces, making the cuts perpendicular to the rounded bottom of the panel. You are going to sew the three pieces back together with broadseams. With the panels positioned on the floor, start the broadseams 3 inches inside the string marking the foot of the original triangle. These seams should achieve their maximum overlap at the tape line for the foot. Widen them $1/4$ inch for every 3 inches of maximum foot roach. Glue the assembled foot panel to the rest of the sail, broadseaming this

Getting the sail through the machine.

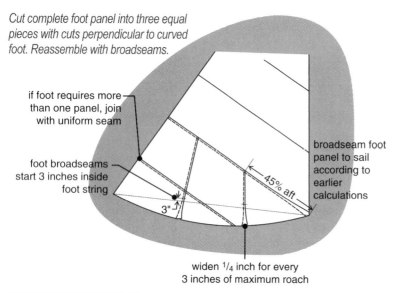

Cut complete foot panel into three equal pieces with cuts perpendicular to curved foot. Reassemble with broadseams.

if foot requires more than one panel, join with uniform seam

foot broadseams start 3 inches inside foot string

3"

broadseam foot panel to sail according to earlier calculations

45% aft

widen ¼ inch for every 3 inches of maximum roach

Headsail foot detail.

seam according to the mark and calculations you made earlier.

Mainsail

The foot for a mainsail gets a different treatment. With a hot knife, cut the foot panel on a straight line from the tack to a point on the leech 10 inches above the clew. Sew the two pieces back together with a broadseam that begins halfway between the tack and the leech (unless you shifted the draft forward or aft) and widens 1½ times the normal amount, meaning ⅜ inch for every 15 inches of seam length for medium cloth (every 12 inches for firm cloth, every 18 inches for soft). Glue the foot

Split complete foot panel from tack to a point about 10 inches above the clew. Reassemble with a broadseam that widens 1½ times the normal amount. Sew foot panel to sail with a broadseam that widens twice the normal amount.

uniform seam

10"

45% aft

50%

broadseam widens twice normal

broadseam widens 1½ times normal

Mainsail foot detail.

panel to the rest of the sail, broadseaming from the 45% location you marked earlier. Broaden this seam twice the normal amount, ½ inch for every 15 inches (or 12 or 18).

Once the foot panel is assembled and glued to the rest of the sail, triple-stitch all the glued seams.

TRIMMING TO SIZE

Position the sail over your outline one final time. Let the center wrinkle but try to get the edges to lie flat. With a pencil, outline the finished size of the sail by tracing the inside edge of the masking tape. Trace the outside edge of the tape along the leech also to provide a hem allowance. Trace the outside edge of the foot tape as well if the foot will be hemmed but not if it will have a boltrope. (Almost all headsails will be hemmed along the foot; mainsails are likely to be roped.) The luff does not require a hem allowance. You can also dispense with the leech and foot hem allowances if you finish these edges by binding with Dacron tape instead of hemming.

With a hot knife, keeping a piece of hardboard or laminate under the sail to protect the floor, cut the sail along the outermost pencil lines.

CORNER PATCHES

The corners of the sail require reinforcement patches. Cut them from the same material as the sail, taking care to align the weave of the patch to the sail weave. If the cloth is unbalanced, you will need to orient the fill and warp to match that of the cloth in the sail in each corner. Three patches in each corner will normally be adequate. Sew them all on one side of the sail with the largest patch on the outside and each of the inner patches an inch or two shorter than the one above.

There is no hard-and-fast rule for sizing patches. A good starting point is to make the largest patch extend along both edges of the sail 1 inch for every foot. In other words, a clew patch on a sail with a 20-foot-long leech and a 10-foot-long foot would reach about 20 inches up the leech and 10 inches along the foot. If a patch looks too tall and narrow, widen it. Make the inside edge of the patch straight or curved as you prefer.

Baste the patches to the sail, aligning them with the edge of the sail or the hemline as appropriate. Sew down the inside edge of the largest patch using a zigzag stitch. You will be able to see the inside edges of the smaller patches through the

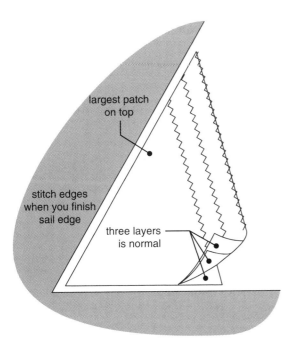

Corner patches should extend about 1 inch for every foot of length of that edge.

Reinforcement patches.

cloth. Run a line of stitching along the inside edges of both smaller patches. Leave the outer edges unstitched for now.

For a sail with reef points, additional patches along the luff and leech are required for the reef cringles. These should be cut and sewn to the sail at this time. Reef patches need to be about twice as strong as the regular corner patches, meaning you may need six or seven layers, all of them matching the orientation of the cloth where they will be installed. Each reef should reduce the height of the sail by 15% to 25%. It is usually a good idea to locate the leech reef cringle about 3 inches higher than the luff cringle to raise the end of the boom in heavier conditions. The grommets across the center of the sail for the bunt ties should each be reinforced with a double-thickness diamond patch. The ties through these grommets are intended just to corral the bunt of the sail, not to carry *any* load, so placing the grommets a couple of inches below the line between the two reef cringles is a good precaution. Three grommets should be sufficient on boats up to about 40 feet.

If you plan to use a D-ring at the clew, now is the time to install it. Fold the corner of the sail and the largest patch out of the way and cut the corner off the inner patches to match the straight side of the D-ring. With your hot knife cut three 1-foot-long lengths of 1-inch webbing. Fold all three pieces of webbing in half around the straight side of the ring, put the ring against the cut clew patches, and sandwich the inner patches between the sides of the webbing. Align one piece of webbing with the leech and one with the foot; position the third in the middle. Sew the webbing and sailcloth together in

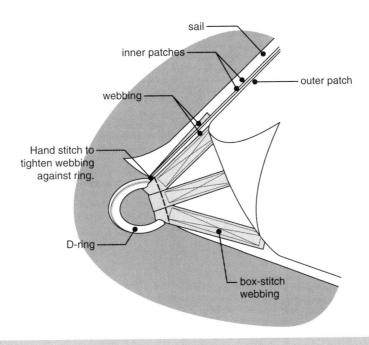

Cut corners of inner patches to match straight side of D-ring, and sandwich ring and inner patches between three lengths of folded webbing.

D-ring installation.

a boxed-X pattern. You can also stitch the webbing on top of the sail if you prefer, but hiding it inside the reinforced corner looks neater and shields the webbing from some UV damage. Hand-stitch the webbing tightly against the flat side of the ring with waxed twine.

HEMMING LEECH AND FOOT

Fold the sail at the pencil line along the leech and the foot (if the foot has one) so the hems fold over the top of the patches. Crease the fold and baste the hems down with transfer tape.

If you want a leech line in your sail, lay a $1/16$- or $1/8$-inch braided Dacron line into the fold of the leech hem before you glue it. A sail with a lot of foot roach can benefit from a similar control line sewn into the foot hem. You can secure the control line to a button sewn to the sail, in which case you also need to install a small grommet in the hem near the clew for the leech line to exit (near the tack for the foot line). Alternatively, use a leech line cleat, which you will rivet to the sail later over a small exit slit in the hem.

Sew the edge of the hems down with a zigzag stitch, being careful not to stitch any control lines you may have installed. Anchor the leech line at the top

Leech and foot lines.

stitch leech line down near head

braided polyester

exit grommet

buttons serve as cleat

stitch foot line down near clew

tack

of the sail by sewing across it several times. Anchor the foot control line at the clew.

BATTEN POCKETS

Now you're going to wish you'd listened to me when I told you to omit the roach in your new mainsail. From the cloth you have left, cut batten pockets 4 inches longer than your battens. Make the pockets $1^{1}/_{4}$ inches wider than the battens, flaring one edge to twice that width beginning about 5 inches from one end. Put a $1/_{2}$-inch hem in the wide end.

You need a few inches of wide waistband elastic, the wider the better. Cut a $3^{1}/_{2}$-inch strip of elastic for each of the pockets. Stitch one end of the elastic to the underside of the pocket (based on the hem you just made) about 5 inches from the narrow end, with the elastic extending toward that end. Fold 2 inches of the narrow end under and crease the fold.

You should be able to identify the proper location of the batten pockets by the change in direction of the leech at each. Battens should be positioned perpendicular to the leech, except for those located below reef points, which should be parallel to the boom. Put the pocket in place on the sail and glue the forward (narrow) end in position with transfer tape between the turned-under portion and the sail. Unfold the pocket and sew down all four sides of the flap. Now sew the other end of the elastic to the sail about an inch aft (toward the leech) of the stitched-down flap. This will form a loop of elastic to keep the batten pressed against the leech end of the pocket.

Position the pocket and glue the edges to the sail with transfer tape. Run a line of zigzag stitches around the entire perimeter of the pocket except the top half of the hemmed end. This is the opening for inserting the batten. If the sail has a leech line, be sure not to sew across it. Double-stitch the lower half of the open end of the pocket to resist the chafe of the battens. To make the battens more secure, stitch in from the leech about $1/_{2}$ inch at the bottom of the pocket opening.

FINISHING THE LUFF

How you finish the luff will depend on whether your sail is a headsail or mainsail; whether it is hanked on, attaches with slides or slugs, or feeds into an extrusion; and whether you want tape, rope, or wire for reinforcement.

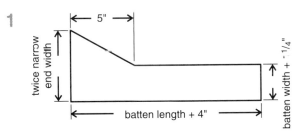

1

twice narrow end width

5"

batten length + 4"

batten width + ⁻ ¹/₄"

Cut out batten pockets.

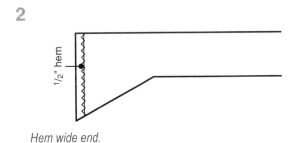

2

¹/₂" hem

Hem wide end.

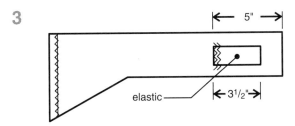

3

5"

elastic

3¹/₂"

Sew elastic strip to inside of pocket.

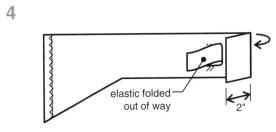

4

elastic folded out of way

2"

Fold narrow end over and crease.

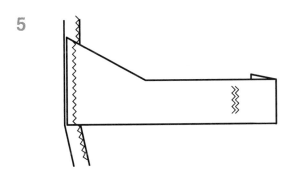

5

Position pocket perpendicular to leech and glue folded narrow end to sail with transfer tape.

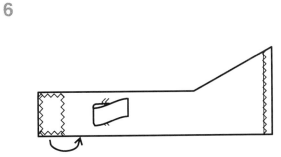

6

Unfold and sew perimeter of glued flap.

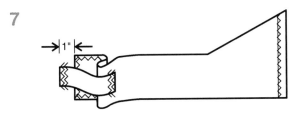

7

1"

Sew free end of elastic to sail.

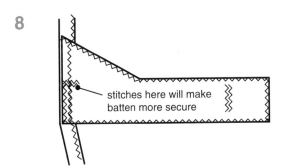

8

stitches here will make batten more secure

Glue pocket to sail with transfer tape and stitch around perimeter, leaving top half of wide end open.

Batten pockets.

Perhaps the easiest of the various possibilities is the continuous support tape required on headsails that feed into an extrusion. These tapes are prefabricated and come in half a dozen different sizes, so be sure to get the correct one for your extrusion. If the tape on your old sail is in good shape, you can reuse it. To install a support tape, position it on the luff, baste the flaps of the tape to both sides of the

Attaching luff tape. Position sail between flaps and sew with two rows of zigzag stitches.

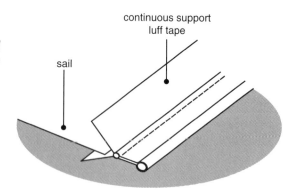

The luff rope will go inside a sleeve sewn to the luff of the sail. The simplest way to make the sleeve is with 5-ounce, 4-inch-wide polyester tape. Crease the tape down the center and sew the sail to one side of

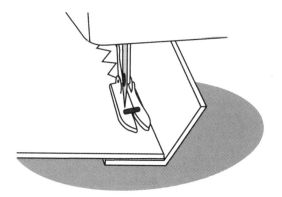

Sew sail luff to one side of a center-creased 4-inch polyester tape.

sail, and sew it to the sail with two rows of zigzag stitching.

Hanked-on headsails can be reinforced just as simply with two or three layers of polyester tape sewn to the luff, but most will have a reinforcing rope or wire. Quarter-inch or $5/16$-inch rope will be adequate unless the sail is quite large. Wire will typically be about half the diameter of rope and should be plastic coated. Whether you use rope or wire is up to you—the method of attachment is virtually identical. Rope is easier to work with but harder to get "right" because of stretch. A sail with a roped luff is easier to stow. High-modulus fiber cordage (Kevlar, PBO, etc.) is finding its way into the luff of sails, combining negligible stretch with easier handling, but for now the cost of these is out of proportion to the benefit for a homebuilt sail.

The critical factor in a rope luff support is to get the rope the correct length so that it, rather than the cloth, takes most of the stress. For all practical purposes wire has no stretch, and you want the finished dimension of a wire luff reinforcement to be the length of the luff of the sail. If you use prestretched or low-stretch polyester braid, it should be about 1 inch shorter than the luff for every 15 feet of luff length. Dialing this in more accurately depends on the stretch of the particular line you use and on your normal halyard tension. You can shorten this line if it turns out to not be short enough, but if you make it too short to begin with, you have to replace it, which is a bigger job. Three-strand polyester and nylon rope both have more stretch than is normally desirable in the luff of a headsail unless the sail is being used competitively. The initial length of a three-strand polyester luff rope should be about 1 inch shorter than the luff for every 6 feet of luff length. Shorten a nylon luff rope 1 inch for every 4 feet. These lengths for a stretchy luff rope should allow the sail to set properly. Cut all luff rope at least a foot too long to allow ample length for spliced eyes at either end.

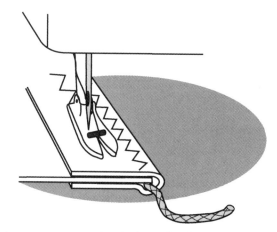

Lay messenger cord under loose flap. With loose side down, sew through all three layers.

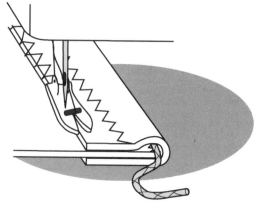

Invert and finish with a third line of stitches along the inside edge of the tape.

Creating a luff-rope sleeve.

the tape with the luff against the crease, placing the zigzag stitches near the edge of the sail. Lay a length of strong twine into the fold to serve as a messenger for pulling the luff rope through the sleeve. Fold the tape over the string and onto the sail and glue the edge down with transfer tape. You will get better results if you turn the sail over and baste the loose edge on the other side as well. Sew the tape down with a row of zigzag stitches 1 inch behind the fold and a second row along the tape's inside edge.

If the reinforcement is rope, splice an eye around a stainless steel thimble at one end. For a wire luff, strip the plastic from the end and put the wire around a thimble, securing it with a Nicopress sleeve. Be sure no raw ends protrude beyond the sleeve and wrap it with plastic tape. Mark the rope or wire to the appropriate length you determined previously.

Attach the messenger string securely to the straight end of the rope or wire and pull it through the sleeve. Slide the sail far enough back, bunching the sleeve as necessary to allow sufficient rope or wire to exit, for you to put a second thimbled eye in at the mark you made. If you are using wire, wrap the crimp sleeve with plastic tape.

With your hot knife, split the fold of the luff sleeve at each end to allow the eyes to recess into the sleeve. The center of each eye should be about where the respective edges of the sail would meet if they were extended. Trim away (with a hot knife) any of the sleeve that covers any part of the eye opening.

Starting an inch or more before the eye, whip the luff rope tightly against the front of the sleeve, using doubled waxed twine and a sail needle. Push the needle through the sleeve and sail just behind the rope, around the front of the sail, and through the sleeve and sail again slightly closer to the eye—and so on. A sewing palm will make pushing the needle through the multiple layers of sailcloth easier. Pliers may also be useful. Pull each loop tight. When you reach the eye, continue whipping up the inside leg of the eye until you reach the leech or the foot. Make a long loop with the loose end and capture it under the whipping, making sure the loop extends far enough to never be fully covered by your stitches. You can tuck the other end through this loop when you finish and pull on the original loose end to bury both ends under the whipstitch. If you are building a headsail, the installation of the luff rope completes the sail except for the handwork, which is detailed in the next section.

A rope is also used to reinforce the luff of a mainsail or mizzen, but with a couple of differences. Because

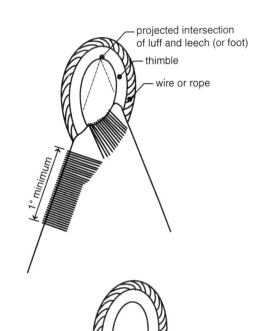

Split sleeve to allow eye to be positioned at the projected intersection of luff and leech (or foot).

Whip the rope and one leg of the eye tightly into the sleeve with waxed twine.

Whip the eye to a sewn ring, or . . .

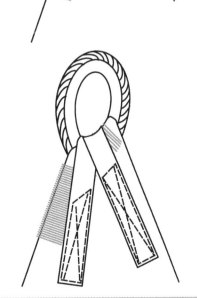

Use two lengths of webbing sewn to the sail to distribute the load.

Finishing the ends of a headsail luff rope.

the sail is normally anchored at the tack with a grommet and hoisted with a hole in the headboard, no eyes are required in the ends of the luff rope. And normally the rope continues around the tack and across the bottom of the sail to reinforce the foot as well.

Three-strand polyester is the usual choice for the boltrope in a mainsail. As already indicated, the polyester rope should be about 1 inch shorter than the luff for every 6 feet of luff length. Use the same factor for the foot if you rope two sides of the sail.

The sleeve for the boltrope is installed exactly as the luff-rope sleeve was, except that if the sail is also reinforced at the foot, the sleeve continues around the tack and along the foot of the sail to the clew. You will need to slit the sides of the sleeve to get it to make the turn at the tack. Be sure you lay the messenger line inside the sleeve before you stitch it closed. Leave a small section of the sleeve open at the tack to make installing the boltrope easier.

Cut the rope to length, leaving several inches at either end to allow for some adjustment after you have had the opportunity to sail with the sail. The different stretch factors of different ropes may require some shortening or lengthening. Mark the calculated lengths on the rope, marking the luff length and the foot length separately and making a third mark where they meet. This last mark you will place at the tack. Use the messenger line to pull the boltrope from the head out the open flap at the tack, then from the tack to the clew.

Securing the luff and foot rope in the sleeve of a mainsail.

Position the tack mark on the rope at the tack and with doubled waxed twine and a sail needle, make a series of ¼-inch-long stitches just inside the rope, forcing the rope tightly into the fold of the sleeve. You may need a sewing palm and pliers. Start

these stitches at the tack and sew about 6 inches up the luff, then whip the boltrope for an additional inch. The whipstitches pass around the outside of the sail and through the sleeve against the inside edge of the rope. Space the loops closely and pull each very tight, finishing by passing the end of the twine under the last two loops.

If only the luff is reinforced, put a second inch of whipping around the rope near the bottom of the sleeve. If the rope continues across the foot, start again at the tack and sew the boltrope into the sleeve the same way you did the luff for 6 inches along the foot, whipping the boltrope for an inch at the end of the stitch line.

Pull on the rope at the head of the sail until the mark on the rope there is at the end of the sleeve. Hand-stitch behind the rope for 6 inches at the head of the sail just as you did at the tack. Whipstitch 1 inch right at the top of the sail and whip the rope a second time at the other end of the stitching, about 6 inches lower. Position the mark for the other end of the rope at the end of the sleeve at the clew and secure the rope tightly the same way.

Take the sail to your sewing machine, and with a zipper foot, run a line of straight stitches—the longest stitches your machine will make—against the inside of the luff/foot rope, forcing it against the front of the sleeve for its entire length. Work the wrinkles out of the sleeve as you sew. Where you whipped and hand-stitched the boltrope, fold a length of Dacron tape over each area to protect it from chafe and sew it to the sail with two rows of zigzag stitches.

THE HARD STUFF

All that remains to be done to your sail is some handwork.

On a headsail you will need to protect the sail at the clew. Pass a butterfly-shaped piece of leather through the D-ring, fold it onto both sides of the sail, and stitch down its inside edges. If your machine will sew through all the layers of various materials now at the clew, by all means machine-stitch this edge. Then use the time you save to write a testimonial letter to the sewing machine manufacturer. The rest of us will have to hand-stitch the edge of the leather. You might even need to burn holes with a heated awl or drill the holes with a tiny twist bit to let you push the needle through if the corners are particularly thick. Join the sides of the leather along the leech and the foot with a baseball stitch—a stitch that looks just like the laces on your sneakers.

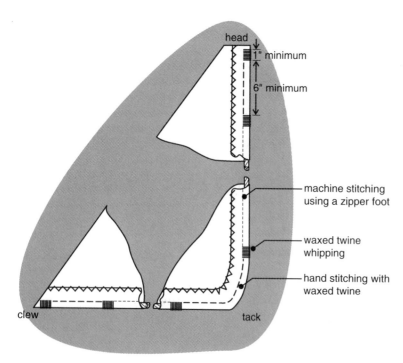

head
1" minimum
6" minimum

machine stitching using a zipper foot

waxed twine whipping

hand stitching with waxed twine

clew

tack

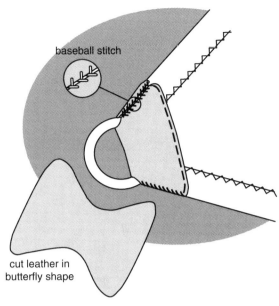

baseball stitch

cut leather in
butterfly shape

Leather clew patch.

If your sail will have a grommet instead of a D-ring at the clew, you have a couple of choices. The easiest is to take the sail to a nearby loft and pay them to install a stainless steel eye with their hydraulic installation machine. Or you can do sewn eyes, which are marginally stronger and a lot more work.

SEWN EYES AND RINGS

A sewn eye is actually made up of a brass ring, which you stitch to the sail, and a brass grommet that is pressed inside the sewn eye to protect the stitching. Installation is time-consuming but not particularly difficult. Position the brass ring on the sail at least $1/4$ inch from any edge and trace around the outside. Cut a hole in the cloth $3/4$ of the diameter of the inside of the ring. With a sail needle and doubled heavy waxed twine, whip the ring to the sail, passing the needle up through the hole and the center of the ring and down through the sail on the penciled circle.

Space the loops about $3/16$ inch apart all the way around the circle, and pull each loop as tight as you can. If you don't pull the stitches tight enough, the sleeve won't fit inside the ring. Wearing a leather glove or wrapping your index finger with several layers of masking tape will minimize nerve damage. Stitch around the ring a second time, placing the second row of stitches between the first ones on the circle. When the stitching is done, you push

the brass sleeve through the ring and flare it like a grommet. This takes a special die that costs around $60, so you still may need to make a trip to your nearest helpful sailmaker. You might be offered a job while you're there.

Sewn eyes are also appropriate for the tack of your mainsail and for the reef cringles. If you are not using a headboard, you can use a sewn ring in the head of the sail also. Use sewn rings at the head and tack of a headsail with a support-tape luff. If you plan to install enough sewn rings, you can justify buying the tool.

Sewn rings can also be used at the tack and clew of a wire- or rope-reinforced headsail for securing the sail to the eyes of the luff reinforcement. For this use, chafe is not a problem and the brass insert is not required. Position these two rings adjacent to the splice or Nicopress sleeve that forms the eye in the luff rope and at least $1/4$ inch from the rope and from the opposite edge of the sail. Once the rings are sewn to the sail, join them to the adjacent eyes with three or four dozen loops of sail twine. Make the loops snug but not tight. Put an equal number of loops of twine around the luff of the sail and through the rings to reinforce the sleeve at the head and tack.

If you do not want to do sewn rings in your headsail, you can accomplish the same objective with webbing. For a tape-reinforced sail, simply attach stainless steel rings to the head and tack with three folded lengths of webbing, one sewn along the leech or foot, one along the luff, and one in the middle of the other two. For a wire- or rope-reinforced sail, you will only need two lengths of webbing, omitting the one that would otherwise lie on top of the reinforcement.

A welded ring captured in doubled webbing and sewn to the cringle patch is also the better way of creating a reef cringle that will attach to a reef hook.

Install a headboard with rivets or stitching, placing it tightly against the boltrope unless the boltrope feeds into a mast track. In that case, set the headboard back about $1/8$ inch. Cut out the hole in the cloth (for the halyard shackle) with your hot knife. Rivet the leech line cleat to the sail, or sew a pair of plastic or leather buttons to the hem near the exit grommet. Sew a small cloth or webbing flap over the cleat or the buttons, leaving it unstitched along the outside edge. This flap will prevent the fitting from snagging on the rigging or lifelines.

1

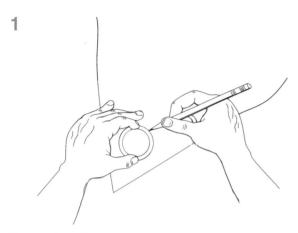

Trace outline of brass ring onto sail.

2

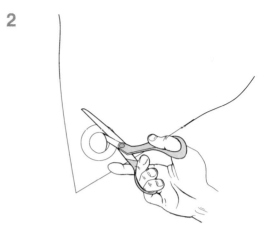

Cut hole ³/₄ of the inside diameter of ring.

3

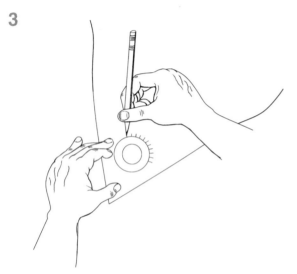

"Tick" the outline every ³/₁₆ inch to aid in getting stitches uniform.

4

leather sewing palm

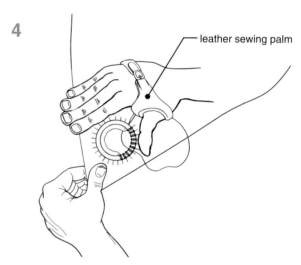

With doubled waxed twine whip ring to sail by passing needle up through hole and down through each tick mark, pulling every loop tight.

5

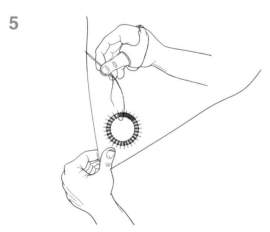

Make a second circle of whippings spaced between the first set.

6

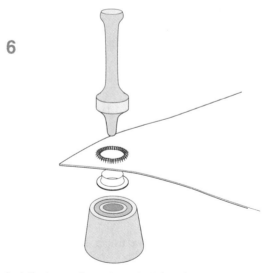

Install a brass sleeve to protect the stitching from chafe.

Installing a sewn ring.

HANKS AND SLIDES

All that remains is to attach hanks or slides. How you attach them will depend on the type of hardware you are using and perhaps on your preference. Slides are often sewn directly to the sail with twine or attached with short lengths of webbing sewn to the sail. Jib hanks and slides attached with cord binding or shackles will require grommets in the luff.

Spur grommets are quite satisfactory for this use. To keep the luff from developing puckers, mount the grommets right against the boltrope. Hanks and slides are typically spaced about 2 feet apart but you can get away with fewer hanks on a light-air sail. It is a good idea to support the headboard with two sail slides.

That's about it. If I left out something, hey, I never claimed to be a sailmaker. Once you have the shape right, you ought to be able to figure out any other problems that crop up. If you need a particular feature, duplicate what was done on your old sail.

How long should all this take? Hard to say, Skip. I spent the better part of five days making my first sail. The next sail I made—a couple of years later—was a mizzen that took less than three days. I don't know if that was because I was "experienced" or simply because the second sail was a lot smaller. Subsequently I also built a main, which also took about three days—do-it-yourself workdays, not the union variety.

Are the sails I built as good as what I might have expected from a professional sailmaker? Maybe not. The professional certainly has the tools to achieve a better finish, but that is at least partially compensated for by the greater care I gave the project. Since I used materials identical to those used by the pros and triple-stitched every seam, I had every reason to believe that my sails would last as long and hold up as well as theirs and that has proven to be true. As for performance, I have now sailed close to 10,000 miles with a suit of sails I built and I remain unconvinced that *in my hands* any differences in the shape of a professionally built sail would have made my boat

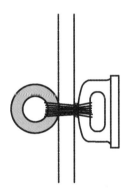

Twine lashing through a grommet.

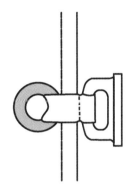

Webbing through a grommet.

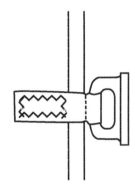

Webbing sewn to the sail.

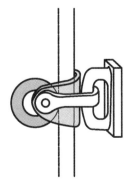

Stainless steel or plastic shackle.

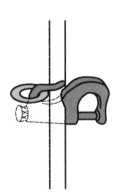

Press-on jib snap.

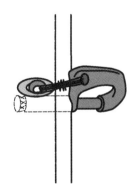

Lash-on jib snap.

Slide and snap attachment.

safer, more fun to sail, or even have gotten me to my destinations significantly quicker. And I saved more than $1,000 on that very first sail alone.

So where does all this leave you? Should you build a sail? I don't know. If you want a sail perfectly cut with a perfect set, the sail you build may not satisfy you. On the other hand, if cost is a big consideration, if you have time available, and if you are reasonably handy, it might be a worthwhile alternative. At the very least you will learn a great deal about what makes your old boat go, and you just may discover that sail perfection is not nearly as elusive as you imagined.

CHAPTER SEVENTEEN

Epilogue

"Just Do It."
—NIKE

Brion Toss, whose knowledge of rigging humbles ordinary sailors, relates in his book, *The Complete Rigger's Apprentice*, a way of tying a bowline that he learned from Paul Newman. OK, so he saw it in a Paul Newman movie; it's almost the same thing. Quit nit-picking and pay attention.

After you pass the line around the bollard or through the clew ring or whatever, hold the standing part of the line in one hand and the end of the line pointed back toward the bollard in the other. Reach over the standing part, then dip your hand under it, forming a loop around your wrist. Now pass the end of the line beneath the standing part, pushing it under with your thumb, then reaching over the standing part to get a new grip on it. Still gripping the end, pull your wrist out of the loop. Draw the knot tight. That's a take.

Why am I telling you this? Because although I first learned to tie a bowline 40 years ago, I still have the rabbit coming out of the hole, running around the tree, and going back into the hole every time I tie this knot. I have progressed to where I no longer have to say it out loud—but I still move my lips. Paul Newman's way is better than mine. It's quicker. It's easier. It has style. But the bowline that results is exactly the same as the one formed by chasing the rabbit around the tree.

Similarly, many of the changes detailed in the preceding pages can be accomplished in various ways. The methods I have elected to illustrate are either the simplest or the best I know—nothing more. In some cases, no doubt, there are quicker ways, easier ways, ways with more style. If you discover a better way to accomplish a particular enhancement, by all means do it that way. I have certainly learned some

new tricks since the first edition that I've shared with you in this one.

The inspiration for the original edition of *This Old Boat* was an unshakable conviction that refurbishing an old boat is a financially sound alternative to the escalating cost of new boats. In that free-spending environment of leveraged acquisitions, obligatory BMWs, and the "art" of making billion-dollar deals, I had some doubts about whether there was anyone left out there who would be interested. As it turned out, a whole generation of boaters embraced the book, spattered it with epoxy, and loaned it to friends.

I have similar misgivings this time around, but the spread between the cost of a new boat and that of an equivalent old boat has only grown in the intervening years. Instead of multiple thousands, new-boat prices are fractions of millions. A production-line builder's least expensive offering might start at a quarter of a million dollars. Mainstream sailing magazines now praise boats costing $400,000 or more as a "good value." Really? What does that say about a boat of equal capability priced at $40,000?

Old boats just make good sense. Aside from the dramatically lower initial cost, they also tend to have lower operating costs than new boats. It's true. It is essential to escape the automobile mentality that makes us think something new is trouble free and something old is "just asking for it." This kind of thinking doesn't apply to boats. While a 5-year-old car may already be well on its way to the crusher, a *good* boat should give 50 years or more of dependable and pleasurable service.

Financial benefits aren't the only attraction. Own any boat for a long time and it becomes an old boat. A long relationship breeds familiarity and trust. Our

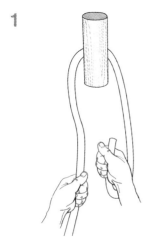

1

Hold the standing part in one hand and the end—pointed back toward the bollard—in the other hand.

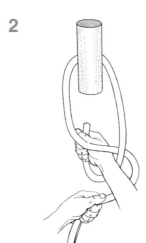

2

Reach over the standing part, then dip your hand under it . . .

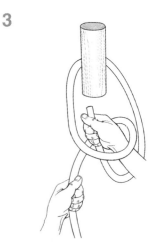

3

forming a loop around your wrist.

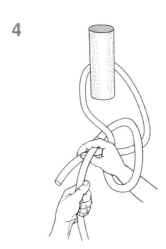

4

Pass the end under the standing part, pushing it under with your thumb, then gripping it again on the other side.

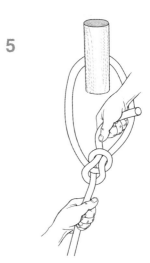

5

Pull your hand—and the gripped end—out of the loop. Draw the knot tight.

The Newman bowline.

old boat welcomes us like a yellow ribbon, embraces us like a sister, soothes us like a favorite slipper, protects us like a cellar, and pleases but never surprises us. (Offshore, surprises I don't need.) She is a trusted partner, an accommodating hostess, a member of our family. I cannot imagine a reason for a new boat.

Putting an old boat back in service rather than purchasing a new one also seems to have ecological implications. Perhaps few large boats end up in landfills, but those that are effectively discarded do end up clogging marinas and waterways. New boats just add to the problem. The sensible alternative is boat recycling.

Nor should we overlook the social benefit of matching unfulfilled dreamers with unused boats and getting them both away from the dock. In truth, it only takes a few dollars to get out on the water, yet how many forgo sailing, fishing, or cruising altogether because the boats featured in the five-color ads in yachting magazines are unaffordable? Old boats being offered for sale today at a fraction of new-boat prices were once featured in similar ads. Today's new boats are tomorrow's old boats.

So I set out originally to call attention to the true value of old boats and create a single volume that would contain all the necessary information a motivated boatowner would need to put an old boat into better-than-new condition. The popularity and longevity of this book has given that effort at least a passing grade. And the gratifying feedback from empowered boatowners has apparently dulled my memory of what a huge undertaking gathering and consolidating such a broad array of information turned out to be, because here I am again. By now you will know better than I the worth of this new effort.

Use this expanded edition of *This Old Boat* as your initial source of information, but not your *only* source. When the information I have provided is inadequate, you may find a more comprehensive explanation in a specialized text on the applicable subject. You might also raise your skill level through educational programs. Local schools often offer courses (credit or noncredit) in carpentry, diesel mechanics, refrigeration, electricity, and even boat repair. An Internet search can turn up product support and firsthand experience. Other boaters, whether on the Internet or at your marina, can be a great resource, provided you can discern between those who know and those who *claim* to know. Magazine articles can be a useful source of information about the latest products and techniques. And don't forget Paul Newman movies; you never know where the clarifying light may come from.

For my part, I have again done the best I can; the rest is up to you. If you have honestly and judiciously evaluated your needs and expectations, if you have taken the time to visualize an unlimited image of your old boat, if you have drawn up a well-considered plan for making the desired modifications, if you have acquired quality tools, and if you have practiced each of the essential skills, you are separated from the boat in your vision only by time.

My parting advice is: don't let newfound boatwright skills cloud your perspective. Boats are to be enjoyed. That's why we call them *pleasure* boats. Working on them should not take precedence over using them. Likewise, writing about them. It is time to close the laptop and retire to the cockpit, padded with cushions, shaded by an awning, and cooled by the constant Caribbean breeze. I'll look for you out here.

Index

"You seek too much information and not enough transformation."
— SAI BABA